Canadian Family Law

SIXTH EDITION

Canadian Family Law

sixth edition

JULIEN D. PAYNE AND MARILYN A. PAYNE

Canadian Family Law, sixth edition
© DANREB, 2015

Published in 2015 by

Irwin Law Inc.
14 Duncan Street
Suite 206
Toronto, ON
M5H 3G8

www.irwinlaw.com

ISBN: 978-1-55221-396-4
E-BOOK ISBN: 978-1-55221-397-1

Library and Archives Canada Cataloguing in Publication

Payne, Julien D., 1934–, author
    Canadian family law / Julien D. Payne and Marilyn A. Payne. — Sixth edition.

Includes bibliographical references.
Issued in print and electronic formats.
ISBN 978-1-55221-396-4 (paperback).—ISBN 978-1-55221-397-1 (pdf)

    1. Domestic relations—Canada. I. Payne, Marilyn A., author II. Title.

KE539.P395 2015   346.7101'5   C2015-905339-0
KF505.ZA2P395 2015   C2015-905340-4

Canadä   Ontario
          Ontario Media Development
          Corporation
          Société de développement
          de l'industrie des médias
          de l'Ontario

Printed and bound in Canada.

1 2 3 4 5   19 18 17 16 15

Summary Table of Contents

Detailed Table of Contents

CHAPTER 8:
SPOUSAL SUPPORT ON OR AFTER DIVORCE   *216*

CHAPTER 9:
CHILD SUPPORT ON OR AFTER DIVORCE *370*

Preface

Family law is a changing and dynamic field. In the twenty-first century, Canadian families will encounter new challenges. Marriage and the family are no longer synonymous. The traditional nuclear family of the 1950s, with its breadwinning husband, homemaking wife, and their two or more children, is a minority group. Two-income families, with or without children, high divorce and remarriage rates, and the increasing incidence of unmarried cohabitation, whether involving opposite- or same-sex couples, have fostered new family structures and radical legal reforms. At the same time, there has been increased recognition of the inherent limitations of the law in regulating marriage and the family.

The public and the legal profession are aware of the devastating impact that family breakdown can have on women and children. The feminization of poverty that results from single parenthood, family breakdown, and divorce continues to be of pressing concern to provincial and federal governments as they seek to enforce spousal and child support payments that have fallen into default, and endeavour to provide a socio-economic safety net for sole parents and children.

Canadian family law is continually in transition as it responds to evolving family structures. Chapter 1 of *Canadian Family Law* identifies the changing character of Canadian families and poses fundamental questions concerning possible future directions of law and social policy in Canada. In addition, it provides a review of the legal consequences of marriage breakdown and divorce since the enactment of the first dominion-wide *Divorce Act* in 1968. The fragmentation of legislative powers between the Parliament of Canada and the provincial and territorial legislatures is also addressed, together with the inefficient fragmentation of jurisdiction between diverse courts that has led to the emergence of specialized Family Courts.

Chapter 2 focuses on the nature of marriage and the legal prerequisites to a valid marriage. Much of the legal analysis in this chapter has a long history that can be traced back to ecclesiastical origins in England. However, Chapter 2 does not ignore contemporary issues that have confronted Canadian courts, such as the validity of same-sex relationships and marriages of convenience that are entered into for the sole purpose of gaining preferred immigration status.

Chapter 3 examines cohabitational relationships between persons of the same or opposite sex in light of the guarantee of equality under section 15 of the *Canadian Charter of Rights and Freedoms*, which has resulted in increasing legal recognition being given to unmarried heterosexual cohabitation and to same-sex relationships for a variety of purposes, including contracts, support rights, and, under some provincial statutes, succession and property rights.

Chapter 4 reviews the statutory regulation of "domestic contracts" as a means of determining the rights and obligations of married persons and of unmarried cohabitants during their relationship and upon its termination. One of the most significant trends in Canadian family law is the degree of contractual autonomy that is now afforded to spouses and unmarried cohabitants to regulate their own affairs, provided that their agreements do not undermine the best interests of any children of the family. Chapter 4 analyzes in-depth the provisions of the Ontario *Family Law Act* that provide a comprehensive legislative framework for marriage contracts, cohabitation agreements, and separation agreements.

Chapter 5 addresses one of society's best-kept secrets: family violence. Some people believe that abuse of the elderly, spousal abuse, and child abuse have reached epidemic proportions. Social and legal responses to these urgent problems are reviewed in Chapter 5.

Chapter 6 deals with the emotional dynamics of marriage breakdown for spouses and their children. This chapter points out the inability of the law to respond to the emotional trauma of family breakdown. Although the *Divorce Act* imposes a duty on lawyers to promote reconciliation, negotiation, and mediation between divorcing partners, the use of innovative processes, such as collaborative family law, mediation, arbitration, med-arb, and parenting coordination, is still evolving in Canadian family dispute resolution.

Chapter 7 reviews the ground rules for determining whether Canadian courts can assume jurisdiction over a divorce petition, the criteria for recognizing foreign divorces, the grounds for divorce in Canada, and bars or impediments to a divorce judgment.

Chapter 8 analyzes the basic principles for determining spousal support rights and obligations under the *Divorce Act*, having special regard to the judgments of the Supreme Court of Canada in *Moge v Moge, Bracklow v Bracklow, Miglin v Miglin, Boston v Boston*, and *Leskun v Leskun*, and the impact of the *Spousal Support Advisory Guidelines*. This chapter reviews the various responses of Canadian courts to the *Spousal Support Advisory Guidelines*.

Chapter 9 provides an overview of the judicial determination of child support under the *Divorce Act* and the *Federal Child Support Guidelines*. A much more detailed analysis may be found in Julien D. Payne and Marilyn A. Payne, *Child Support Guidelines in Canada*, 2012, published by Irwin Law.

Chapter 10 examines issues relating to parenting disputes and their resolution in proceedings instituted pursuant to the *Divorce Act*.

Chapter 11 deals with all aspects of appeals in family law proceedings, including the powers of appellate courts, interim orders, and delays. Chapter 12 briefly reviews spousal support, child support, and custody and access under provincial and territorial statutes in Canada. It complements the analysis of these issues in Chapter 3 (Cohabitational Relationships), Chapter 4 (Domestic Contracts), Chapter 5 (Family Violence), and Chapter 6 (The Crises of Marriage Breakdown and Processes for Dealing with Them).

Chapter 13 analyzes matrimonial property rights on marriage breakdown or death. Because of wide differences among current provincial and territorial statutes, Chapter 13 concentrates on the Ontario *Family Law Act*.

Although *Canadian Family Law* cannot provide an encyclopedic digest of all aspects of Canadian family law, it does provide insights into most of the fundamental legal issues that confront Canadian families today.

This book is current to 31 March 2015.

Julien D. Payne
Marilyn A. Payne

Acknowledgements

The research and word processing costs of this edition of *Canadian Family Law* have been financed by Danreb Inc, a private corporation that engages in legal research and publications and in social policy and management consulting.

The authors thank Jeff Miller for his co-operation in facilitating this publication and arranging for the in-house preparation of a comprehensive case list. The authors much appreciate the efforts of Alisa Posesorski, Tina Dealwis, Aliza Amlani, and Carmen Siu, who discharged editorial responsibilities in their usual efficient manner.

There comes a time in an author's life when he (for those who don't know me, I am a male) should look back and acknowledge with gratitude the contribution that others have made to the development of one's career. Since Google tells me that I have written more than 40 books that it will, free of charge, preserve for posterity on the Internet, this is my time. First and foremost, I want to thank my late parents, Kathleen Mary Payne and Frederick Payne. For the rest of this piece, I shall avoid the word late. If the people I mention continue to influence what I do, then it is unfair to refer to them as late. In any event, I am not always sure whether they are still on the tree of life. Some people have the same thoughts about me. I derive my commitment and dedication from my mother. When my mother was in business with my father, she was the initiator of change. She had an uncanny ability to anticipate changes in market forces. For those who have followed my career, which probably means only me, I always took pride in being the first off the mark. It didn't always work out. In the mid-1980s, I submitted an article entitled "The Mediation of Family Disputes" to the Canadian Bar Review and to the Irish Jurist. They both declined to publish it. I suppose it had nothing to do with law. How times have changed. Not to be defeated, I published the paper in *Payne's Divorce and Family Law Digest* at pages 1861–67 (Richard De Boo Publishers, 1984). My publishers had no choice if they wanted to continue to use my services as a digester of cases. But, looking back beyond that point to the beginning of my writing and law reform careers, I owe it all to Tony Palmer, of Burroughs Company Limited, who invited me to write the second edition of the then-bible in Canadian family law, namely, *Power on Divorce*. After the publication of the second edition in 1964, I was recognized as an authority on Canadian family law by legal practitioners, a remarkable feat for a thirty-year-old academic. What was that: "Those who can't do, teach"? I knew more about evidence, procedure, and costs in family law at that time than any living Canadian — and it was all attributable to that giant in the field, W. Kent Power, who was too ill to write his own second edition. I earned 40 cents per hour rewriting his book but it opened the door to my love affair with Canadian family law and its reform.

In 1966–1967, I submitted a Brief on Marriage and Divorce to The Special Joint Committee of the Senate and House of Commons on Divorce (Canada) (1967) (The Roebuck/Cameron Committee), thereby laying the foundation for my next book on Canadian divorce law, which passed through several editions, ultimately culminating in *Payne on Divorce*, 4th ed (Carswell, 1996). Prior to that edition, I prepared a report for the Department of Justice, *Canada on Spousal and Child Support*, which proposed the appointment of a special committee to consider the desirability of introducing fixed child support schedules. The implementation of the *Federal Child Support Guidelines* in 1996 annihilated my detailed chapter on child support in the fourth edition of *Payne on Divorce*, thus paving the way for diverse editions of *Payne and Payne on Child Support Guidelines in Canada*, which first appeared on Quicklaw as an electronic book in July 1997.

That just about summarizes my rise to fame as a family law author, without identifying many of those who helped me along the way in my career. So let me list them.

First, there is Marilyn, my wife. Not only does she do all the typing/word processing of my publications and our joint publications; she is the only person in the world who can tell me I'm wrong and avoid my paranoic response thereto. Frequent citation in the law reports generates a narcissistic disposition that lends itself to the perception that one is rarely wrong. It's quite amazing how much authority I wield outside of the home, whereas in the home I rank well behind Zoey, our black Labrador.

Let me now turn to some other people who influenced my thinking during my early career. Thank you, Dr Sheila Kessler, for introducing me to the practice of mediation in the 1970s, and to OJ Coogler for his seminal work, *Structured Mediation in Divorce Setlement: A Handbook for Marital Mediators*

(Lexington Books, 1978). You taught me well. Thank you to the Association of Family and Conciliation Courts, particularly Meyer (Mike) Elkin, for keeping me holistic. Thank you, Paul Bohannan, professor of Anthropology at Northwestern University. I never met you, but your chapter entitled "The Six Stations of Divorce," which was published in *Divorce and After* (Doubleday & Company, 1971), laid the foundation for my lifelong involvement in promoting diverse systems of family conflict management and family dispute resolution processes that accommodate the multi-faceted aspects of divorce and family breakdown. It was a short chapter but it has had an immense and ongoing impact on my thinking, my publications, and my frequent involvement with law reform in Canada.

In consequence of my serving as the Director of the Family Law Project undertaken by The Law Reform Commission of Canada from 1972 to 1975, I have sometimes been described as the architect of Unified Family Courts and No-Fault Divorce in Canada. I am prepared to take all of the credit and none of the blame. In fact, it was a team effort, with Professor Terry Wuester of the University of Saskatchewan and Professor Murray Fraser of Dalhousie University being my major co-conspirators, and Drs. Herman (Bobby) Hahlo and Richard (Dick) Gosse, QC providing invaluable input. However, we would have achieved nothing without the vigilant and unqualified support of Justice Patrick Hartt, Chairman of The Law Reform Commission, and of Professor JW (Hans) Mohr, the commissioners assigned to the Family Law Project. We had our battles but we won the war. I also need to express my appreciation to my long-time friend, Justice Claire L'Heureux-Dubé, formerly of the Supreme Court of Canada. She cited my work profusely but we were friends long before that. I always assert that there is no correlation between the two. We just happened to be on the same wavelength. I also want to thank Dave Adamson, Mike Brady, and Carl Leahy, who keep me sane by taking me away from family law for seven days during the first week in November. I venture to think that we consume more liquor during that week than we do during the rest of the year. Maybe that's why we rarely see any deer.

Well, that's it, folks. As for the future, I will continue to write for as long as I have a single reader. And, at my age, I have to repeatedly read what I have written in order to stay on point. So I'll always have at least one reader. It's been a blast and in the words of Yogi Berra: "It ain't over till it's over." In 2014, I celebrated the fiftieth anniversary of the publication of my first book. I can't afford to quit. Marilyn needs the money.

Julien D. Payne, CM, QC, LLD, LSM, FRSC
President, Danreb Inc
(Management and Social Policy Consultants
and Legal Education Specialists

NOTICE

FREQUENTLY CITED LEGISLATION AND GUIDELINES

Canada, Department of Justice, *Spousal Support Advisory Guidelines* by Carol Rogerson & Rollie Thompson (Ottawa: Department of Justice, 2008), online: www.justice.gc.ca/eng/rp-pr/fl-lf/spousal-epoux/spag/pdf/SSAG_eng.pdf

———, *The Spousal Support Advisory Guidelines: A New and Improved User's Guide to the Final Version* (Ottawa: Department of Justice, 2015)

Canadian Charter of Rights and Freedoms, Part I of the *Constitution Act, 1982*, being Schedule B to the Canada Act 1982 (UK), 1982, c 11

Criminal Code, RSC 1985, c C-46

Divorce Act, RSC 1985, c 3 (2d Supp)

Federal Child Support Guidelines, SOR/97-175

CHAPTER 1

Family Structures and Canadian Family Law

A. DEFINITIONS OF "FAMILY"

The term "family" does not have a precise legal definition. Law tends to regulate the rights and obligations of individuals, as distinct from groups, such as families, however they may be constituted. Canadian family law might more properly be called the Law of Persons insofar as it concentrates on the rights of individuals whose family relationships have become dysfunctional. In short, Canadian family law deals primarily with the pathology of family breakdown and its legal consequences.

People often perceive "marriage" and "family" as synonymous, but these words are not interchangeable in law. The term "family" is elusive and defies exact definition. Many, but not all, Canadian families are the products of a marriage. More often than not, the presence of children signifies a family relationship. Children may be born within or outside of marriage. Their parents may or may not live together. The parents may have lived together before or after the birth of the child, but may no longer do so by reason of separation or divorce. Some children are adopted. In relatively rare situations, a child's birth may have resulted from surrogate parenting arrangements or the use of new reproductive technologies. Children are usually family members of the household in which they reside but this is not invariably true. Some children do not live with either of their parents or with aunts, uncles, or grandparents. They may live in foster homes or even with friends or neighbours. A new *de facto* family may co-exist with the family of origin.

Family relationships can exist when there is neither marriage nor a parent-child or ancestral relationship. Unmarried couples of the opposite sex or same sex may be regarded as members of the same family for social or legal purposes.

Whether the indicia of a family relationship involve marriage, parent-hood, a common household, or the sharing of responsibilities, there are many unresolved legal questions concerning the characterization of "families" and the rights and obligations of diverse family members.

Although some will look back with nostalgia to the traditional nuclear family, with its breadwinning husband, its homemaking wife, and their chil-dren, that is a minority group in terms of contemporary family structures in Canada. Today, Canadian families take a wide variety of forms. They include childless marriages, two-parent families, single-parent families in which either the mother or father is the primary caregiver, unmarried cohabit-ants with or without children, and blended or reconstituted families that are the product of sequential cohabitational relationships inside or outside marriage. Family structures may also vary according to ethnic and cultural factors. Customary Inuit adoptions, for example, bear little resemblance to the statute-based systems of adoption that exist in Canadian provinces and territories.

Traditional notions of the family must clearly be re-examined in the search for rational and equitable social and legal policies. In the final analy-sis, it may be impractical for the law to endorse a monolithic definition of "family" that applies for all legal purposes. As in the past, the extent to which the law will recognize a family relationship may turn on the nature of the relationship and the purpose for which such recognition is sought.

B. SOURCES OF FAMILY LAW

The primary sources of family law in Canada are found in provincial, terri-torial, and federal statutes. In some areas, such as nullity proceedings, judge-made principles of law prevail. In Quebec, the *Civil Code* regulates family law other than divorce.

C. EVOLUTION OF FAMILY LAW

Federal, provincial, and territorial legislation regulating the rights and obli-gations of family members has been largely piecemeal in its evolution and no coherent family policy has been articulated, particularly in the context of the relationship between the so-called private system of family law, which regu-lates the personal rights and obligations of spouses, parents, and children as between themselves, and the public system that provides social assistance, tax concessions, pension and medical health schemes, and the like.

The predominant legislative trend has been towards the assertion of in-dividual rights and obligations, rather than the assertion of any family right.

Family law statutes are largely premised on the notion that any form of government intervention is an intrusion upon privacy that can only be justified in the event of a breakdown in the family relationship, a reasonable apprehension of domestic violence, or child abuse and neglect.

Revolutionary changes to family law occurred in Canada with the passage of the first dominion-wide *Divorce Act* in 1968. With this federal legislation serving as a catalyst, Canadians have witnessed radical changes in all aspects of family law. The dimensions of change have been immense. Before 1968, adultery constituted the sole ground for divorce, except in Nova Scotia where matrimonial cruelty constituted an alternative ground for relief. In Quebec and Newfoundland, divorce was only available by private Act of Parliament. With the enactment of the *Divorce Act* in 1968, "no-fault" divorce grounds were introduced in addition to an extended list of "offence" grounds. In addition, formal legal equality of support rights and obligations was established for the first time in Canada between divorcing and divorced men and women. Although the *Divorce Act* of 1986 amended the law relating to the criteria for divorce, spousal and child support, and custody and access in such a way as to shift the focus of the courts from the grounds of divorce to an almost exclusive emphasis on the economic and parenting consequences of divorce, the truly radical breakthroughs occurred with the *Divorce Act* of 1968, which paved the way for future federal, provincial, and territorial statutory changes.

Before 1968, the support of divorcing or divorced spouses was regulated by provincial and territorial statutes that imposed a unilateral obligation on a guilty husband to maintain his innocent wife in the event of a breakdown of their marriage ensuing from his commission of adultery, cruelty, or desertion. The same principles applied to spousal support claims brought independently of divorce proceedings. During the 1970s and 1980s, many provinces and territories enacted legislation that eliminated the offence concept as the foundation of spousal support rights and obligations. In addition, following the precedent established by the federal *Divorce Act* of 1968, the right to spousal support on marriage breakdown in the absence of divorce became no longer confined to wives under provincial and territorial legislation; a financially dependent spouse of either sex might look to his or her marital partner for financial support. The governing consideration was no longer sex-based but turned upon the financial needs of the claimant and the ability of his or her spouse to pay. Each spouse was expected, however, to strive for financial self-sufficiency. Thus, marriage was no longer legally perceived as creating a presumed right to lifelong financial support for a dependent spouse in the event of marriage breakdown.

These changes in the right to divorce and the right to spousal support on divorce or marriage breakdown were accompanied by equally fundamental changes in provincial and territorial statutes governing the division of property on marriage breakdown or divorce. Separated and divorced wives no longer found themselves in the prejudicial position in which Irene Murdoch found herself in 1973 when the Supreme Court of Canada denied her any interest in a ranch registered in her husband's name because her contributions in the home and in the fields were perceived as non-financial contributions ordinarily expected of a rancher's wife.[1] Although three years later the Supreme Court of Canada abandoned *Murdoch* in favour of a more enlightened approach in *Rathwell*,[2] the inequities of the *Murdoch* case triggered provincial and territorial legislation that provided for property sharing on marriage breakdown that was no longer based on ownership or who purchased the property.

Another fundamental change in family law has been the evolution of legal rights and obligations between unmarried cohabitants. Following the pattern established in cases like *Rathwell* from Saskatchewan, which involved married couples before the implementation of statutory property rights in the 1970s and 1980s, unmarried cohabitants have been accorded property rights on the dissolution of their relationships on the basis of the constructive trust and the doctrine of unjust enrichment. Rosie Becker, who did not live to enjoy the fruits of her legal victory in the Supreme Court of Canada in 1980, paved the way for the application of the doctrine of unjust enrichment to unmarried cohabiting couples of the opposite sex,[3] although there is nothing in the Supreme Court of Canada's analysis that precludes the application of similar principles to same-sex couples. Contemporaneously with these judicial developments dealing with property rights, many Canadian provincial statutes provided an extended definition of "spouse" so as to establish spousal support rights and obligations between cohabiting couples of the opposite sex who lived together for a designated period of time or had a child together. A later development in this context has been the extension of similar support rights and obligations between cohabiting couples of the same sex. This was achieved in 1999 by the Supreme Court of Canada's *M v H*[4] judgment applying the equality provisions of section 15 of the *Canadian Charter of Rights and Freedoms*.[5]

---

1   *Murdoch v Murdoch*, [1975] 1 SCR 423.
2   *Rathwell v Rathwell*, [1978] 2 SCR 436.
3   *Pettkus v Becker*, [1980] 2 SCR 834. And see *Sorochan v Sorochan*, [1986] 2 SCR 38; *Peter v Beblow*, [1993] 1 SCR 980; *Nova Scotia (Attorney General) v Walsh*, 2002 SCC 83.
4   [1999] 2 SCR 3.
5   The *Constitution Act, 1982*, being Schedule B to the *Canada Act 1982* (UK), 1982, c 11.

Major statutory reforms in children's rights have also occurred in the last thirty years. Due process changes respecting children were promulgated in the late 1970s and early 1980s in the context of child protection legislation. In the 1960s, no one questioned the practices of residential schools or inter-provincial and international transracial adoptions of children from Aboriginal communities. Contrast this with more recent times when child abuse by institutional personnel has led to criminal convictions in several Canadian provinces as well as to multi-party civil litigation and multi-faceted mediated settlements for victims of abuse. In particular, the mistreatment of Aboriginal children in residential schools and other institutions has been addressed, even if closure is impossible for the victims. Twenty years ago, it was extremely rare for children to sue their parents for damages for emotional, physical, and sexual abuse and recover very substantial compensation. In cases of spousal abuse, few people envisaged domestic violence statutes and specialized domestic violence courts. In the realm of what is somewhat artificially referred to as "private family law," the former legal distinctions between marital and extramarital children have long been abolished, either in consequence of express provincial legislation or because of the judicial application of the equality provisions in section 15 of the *Canadian Charter of Rights and Freedoms*, which were implemented in 1985.

The above substantive changes in the rights and obligations of family members have been accompanied by the evolution of new procedures for resolving family disputes. It is now mandatory for litigating spouses to file financial and property statements to provide data that will expedite the adjudication of support and property disputes. In contested custody disputes, independent expert assessments may be ordered by the court to determine the needs of the children and the respective abilities of the parents to accommodate those needs. It is only a matter of time before parenting plans become mandatory in all contested custody proceedings.

Diverse pre-trial processes are now in place to help reduce or eliminate contentious issues. The discretionary jurisdiction of the court over costs is being exercised aggressively by some courts to promote the consensual resolution of issues, including parenting disputes.[6] The consolidation of disputed issues in a single court proceeding has been facilitated by statutory changes and by amendments to provincial rules of court.

These and other procedural changes have proved their worth but the legal system has remained adversarial. Separating and divorcing parents are still legally perceived as being in conflict with each other. "Fighting it out" is the

---

6   As to a "successful" parent's right to costs in contested custody proceedings, see the compelling analysis of the Alberta Court of Appeal in *Metz v Weisgerber*, 2004 ABCA 151.

legal norm. Significant progress has, nevertheless, been made. In most provinces and territories, parenting education for separating and divorced couples is readily available and voluntary recourse to counselling and mediation is encouraged. In many urban centres across Canada, specialized Family Courts have been established with a comprehensive jurisdiction over family law matters and access to support services that may deflect the need for lengthy and costly litigation. Unfortunately, the support services often face budget cuts in times of economic restraint. Generally speaking, there remains considerable room for improvement in the development of alternative processes to litigation that can facilitate the constructive resolution of family conflict.

Before addressing potential future developments in family law, a few words are appropriate concerning the legal profession. Family law practice has come of age. This is not to say that the family law specialist is held in high regard by the legal profession. Corporate and commercial practitioners and civil litigation lawyers still enjoy prestigious reputations that are not shared by dedicated family law practitioners. The acrimony of the traditional adversarial process in family law matters has been tempered by pre-trial settlement processes and, to a lesser extent, by the evolution of divorce mediation. Lawyers are no longer trained in law school or bar admission courses to be champions who ride into battle on behalf of their clients. Their role is that of the problem solver, albeit from a legal perspective. A new type of family law practitioner is slowly emerging in Canada. Following developments that have occurred in California, Minnesota, and elsewhere in the United States, some Canadian family law practitioners have opted into collaborative family law.[7] This approach differs from the traditional practice of family law in that its practitioners focus on settlement to the exclusion of litigation. Outside experts will often be brought into the process to assist the parties with particular aspects of the negotiation and settlement process.[8] Written agreements are executed to provide full disclosure and to waive discovery and recourse to litigation for a stipulated period of time. During this period, negotiations are undertaken by the clients and their lawyers in an effort to achieve a settlement. If no settlement is reached, the lawyers withdraw from the case and cannot participate in any subsequent litigation.[9] Opportunities exist for made-to-measure individualized Collaborative Family Law

---

7   See Wanda Wiegers & Michaela Keet, "Collaborative Family Law and Gender Inequalities: Balancing Risks and Opportunities" (2008) 46 Osgoode Hall LJ 733; see also Donalee Moulton, "Collaborative Law Reaches Maturity" *The Lawyers Weekly* (6 April 2012). And see *Noble v Arsenault*, 2014 NBCA 39.

8   *Webb v Birkett*, 2011 ABCA 13.

9   *Banerjee v Bisset*, 2009 BCSC 1808. As to the solicitor-client privilege, see *Hogan v Hogan*, 2011 SKQB 479.

Participation Agreements that can reflect the specific interests of the disputants. Collaborative family law practitioners must exercise the same standard
of care as other family law practitioners by insisting on financial disclosure
from their respective clients.[10] The class privilege that attaches to the collaborative family law process does not preclude a subsequent court order for
the disclosure of financial records in the possession of the lawyers who conducted the process where the validity of the marriage contract reached during the process is impugned in contested proceedings for property division,
spousal support, and child support on the basis of the inadequacy and insufficiency of the financial disclosure. There is no class privilege in the collaborative law process for the benefit of the participating lawyers, and where the
spouses have waived any privilege, the lawyers engaged in the collaborative
law process may be required to produce the documents their clients brought
to the table.[11]

For many years, provincial and federal governments have provided book-
lets and pamphlets on family law for the general public. More recently, they
have created relatively sophisticated websites to provide information. In
particular, the federal Department of Justice currently provides a veritable
mine of information on diverse aspects of Canadian family law. Its materials
on the *Federal Child Support Guidelines*[12] are remarkably informative for both
lawyer and lay person alike. Detailed information is also provided online by
provincial departments of the attorney general and on various court sites.[13]
The provinces of Alberta, British Columbia, and Saskatchewan currently include full trial and appellate family law judgments on their websites and the
same is true in Ontario with respect to appellate judgments. Prince Edward
Island identifies relevant provincial family law judgments on its website but
does not provide the contents of those judgments. This website preserves a
high degree of privacy by referring to cases by the initial letters of the names
of the parties. This is one step removed from Quebec's system of referring to
family law cases under the generic heading: *"Droit de la famille, No . . ."* but it is
a step in the right direction. Books, pamphlets, and audio and video cassettes
are now commonplace in various court-connected information centres. Some
far-sighted Canadian family law practitioners are providing wide-ranging information on the web. Information is the primary source of the lawyer's stock

---

10   *Webb v Birkett*, 2011 ABCA 13; application for leave to re-argue the issue of damages and
     costs dismissed: *Webb v Birkett*, 2011 ABCA 170.

11   *Noble v Arsenault*, 2014 NBCA 39.

12   SOR/97-175.

13   See Department of Justice, Canada, *Inventory of Government-Based Family Justice
     Services*, online: www.justice.gc.ca/eng/pi/fcy-fea/lib-bib/tool-util/apps/fjis-rsgjf. See
     also Donalee Moulton, "Power of Information to the People: Nova Scotia Joins Trend of
     Setting up Family Law Websites" *The Lawyers Weekly* (21 September 2012).

in trade, but legal practitioners will have to work harder to communicate information to potential clients if they are to compete with increasing numbers of paralegals, mediators, and facilitators. It is insufficient to have a web page geared to self-promotion. Potential clients need to be informed of their basic substantive rights and of the diverse processes available for the resolution of disputes both within and outside the judicial system. The strategic use of the web, hard copy, disks, and videos will become an integral part of the practice of family dispute resolution. With an increasing number of self-represented litigants, the unbundling of legal services will become widespread within the next few years. "Unbundling" signifies that the lawyer will provide information and input into a client's case, without assuming the responsibility to appear for that client in the courtroom or elsewhere. For the more traditional practitioner, hourly billing may be largely replaced in family law practice by block billings, whereby the lawyer will undertake the carriage of a case through its diverse possible stages, with a maximum global amount being payable at each stage.

The uncontested divorce under the auspices of the judiciary is on its last legs. If the stumbling block of section 96 of the *Constitution Act, 1867* (UK)[14] can be overcome, administrative divorce will replace the desk order divorces that are currently processed on affidavit evidence without any court appearance. In the meantime, paralegals will assume this task with input from court-based information facilities. Adultery and cruelty will disappear as criteria of marriage breakdown under the *Divorce Act*,[15] leaving no-fault separation as the sole criterion. Collusion, connivance, and condonation will disappear from the statute book as bars to divorce, thereby formalizing their present *de facto* status. Spousal support laws will need to be re-assessed with the expanded legal recognition of non-marital domestic partnerships and in light of the aging Canadian population. Mandatory federal and provincial *Child Support Guidelines* were implemented in 1996 and are now complemented by *Spousal Support Advisory Guidelines* that have been developed for use by lawyers and the courts in determining the amount and duration of spousal support obligations.[16]

The obligation of children to support their elderly parents who are not economically self-sufficient has long existed under provincial legislation in Canada but has been relatively rarely invoked.[17] The present legislation is a sleeping giant awaiting arousal. The clock is ticking but the wake-up alarm is

---

14   30 & 31 Vict, c 3, reprinted in RSC 1985, App II, No 5.

15   RSC 1985, c 3 (2d Supp).

16   See Carol Rogerson & Rollie Thompson, *Spousal Support Advisory Guidelines* (Ottawa: Department of Justice, 2008).

17   See *Anderson v Anderson*, 2013 BCSC 129 at para 5, wherein Butler J observes that s 90 of the *Family Relations Act*, RSBC 1996, c 128 was repealed as a result of the operation of ss 258 and 482 of the *Family Law Act*, SBC 2011, c 25.

not yet ringing. But it will. In all likelihood, governmental agencies will more actively pursue liable relatives as the state becomes less capable of absorbing the costs in an aging population with a substantially reduced work force.

With respect to parenting disputes, cultural diversity will attract greater attention than it has in the past. The processing of disputes relating to the treatment of Aboriginal children in residential schools underlines the need to more aggressively recognize cultural heritage in resolving parenting disputes on family breakdown. Children will become more actively involved in the dispute resolution process in cases where their parenting is at stake. The voice of the child will be heard more effectively in the formulation of parenting plans. The proprietary legal terminology of "custody" and "access" will disappear; parenting plans involving extended family members will become common; and mediation may become a preferred alternative to the traditional legal process for the majority of parents. Private arbitration may also become an integral part of family dispute resolution across Canada, and arbitration may ultimately become court-connected with recourse to a panel of screened arbitrators. Courts will, nevertheless, continue to play a major role in the resolution of family disputes. New processes for family dispute resolution are complementary to the legal system. They cannot exist without it. Their efficacy lies in the fact that the legal system is there to fall back on when there are no options available or they have proved wanting. But courts themselves face major changes in an age when 40 to 50 percent of all family litigants, depending on the issue and the province of residence, seek access to the courts without legal representation. As a first step, several provinces are striving to simplify their Family Law Rules so as to make them comprehensible to non-lawyers. The next step will be to develop improved resources to assist self-represented litigants. Videos and computer disks that inform litigants how to fill in the requisite forms and what financial or other material to provide for the court are absolutely vital, if courts are to cope with the increasing number of self-represented litigants. Court lists may need to be divided into cases where one or both of the parties are self-represented and those where both sides are independently legally represented. The assignment of judges may need to be restructured to cope with self-represented litigants. Judges must diversify their roles. They can no longer be confined to an adjudicator's role. They must become case managers in the fullest sense from the time when litigation commences. Court-connected mediation should become the norm.[18]

---

18   Trevor CW Farrow, *Addressing the Needs of Self-Represented Litigants in the Canadian Justice System: A White Paper Prepared for the Association of Canadian Court Administrators*

The private certificate system of legal aid is destined to disappear. It will initially be replaced by a family law clinic system. Ultimately, family legal aid clinics themselves yield pride of place to community-based family dispute resolution centres, with ready access to a network of lawyers, psychologists, social workers, mediators, business valuators, actuaries, and a host of other paid professionals as well as para-professionals and volunteers.

Multidisciplinary private law practices will emerge in the field of family conflict management and family dispute resolution. One can only look back in wonder at the foresight of James (Jim) C MacDonald and Lee Ferrier (subsequently an Honourable Justice of the Superior Court of Ontario), the first lawyers in Canada to establish a specialized family law practice. That was in the 1960s. Now family law boutiques are the rage in Ontario, after brief liaisons with the corporate/commercial law elite proved largely unsuccessful. As long ago as the 1970s, Jim MacDonald and Lee Ferrier introduced a social worker into their practice on an as-needed consultancy basis. They were true pioneers in the practice of family law in Canada. They were also largely responsible for the evolution of family law continuing legal education programs in Ontario in the 1970s and 1980s.

Whether past, present, and future changes should be perceived as good or bad for family stability in Canada is a matter of opinion. Some will view changes in family law and family life in Canada over the last thirty years as undermining the institution of marriage. Others will conclude that the changes already encountered and those yet to be experienced merely reflect the family in transition, rather than the family in crisis. In the absence of sophisticated empirical research, strongly held opinions or convictions on the past, present, or future state of the Canadian family will remain unsubstantiated and unabated.

D. FRAGMENTATION OF LEGISLATIVE POWERS

Exclusive legislative jurisdiction over "marriage and divorce" is conferred on the Parliament of Canada by section 91(26) of the *Constitution Act, 1867*, which was formerly known as the *British North America Act, 1867*. By way of qualification of the above jurisdiction, section 92(12) grants exclusive power to the provincial legislatures to enact laws relating to the "solemnization of marriage." Section 92(13) also confers exclusive authority on the provincial legislatures to make laws in relation to "property and civil rights in the province." Subject to the overriding provisions of section 96, which controls the

---

(Toronto, ON: Association of Canadian Court Administrators, 2012). See also Cristin Schmitz, "'Crisis' Demands Action: Expert" *The Lawyers Weekly* (20 September 2013).

power of appointment and the jurisdictional competence of federally and provincially appointed judges, section 92(14) gives the provinces authority over the "administration of justice in the province, including the constitution, maintenance and organization of provincial courts, both of civil and criminal jurisdiction, and including procedure in civil matters in those courts." This distribution of legislative powers is ratified by the *Canada Act*, 1982.

It is significant that the Parliament of Canada has never seen fit to exercise its potentially broad legislative authority over "marriage." Since the enactment of the first comprehensive federal *Divorce Act* in 1968, a dual system of support and custody has existed in Canada. Where a claim for support or custody arises in divorce proceedings, the dispute is governed by federal divorce legislation, which is currently found in the *Divorce Act*, 1986 as amended. Where, however, such claims arise independently of divorce, they are governed by provincial and territorial legislation.

In federal–provincial consultations on constitutional reform in the late 1970s and early 1980s, the federal government initially proposed that the legislative jurisdiction over "marriage and divorce" be transferred to the provinces. This proposal reflected the opinions expressed in the 1972 report of the Special Joint Committee of the Senate and of the House of Commons on the Constitution of Canada (The Molgat/McGuigan Report).[19] This Committee concluded that such a transfer of legislative jurisdiction would permit "the laws [to] conform more closely to the social and ethical values of the Canadians living in that Province" and "would allow for a more integrated approach to Family Law within provincial jurisdiction." Although a transfer of legislative jurisdiction over "marriage and divorce" from the Parliament of Canada to the provincial and territorial legislatures would facilitate the development of a unified family law regime within a single province or territory, any advantage thereby resulting must be weighed against the disadvantages that would flow from a proliferation of diverse regimes.

It remains to be seen whether the federal government will ultimately transfer legislative jurisdiction over "marriage and divorce" to the provinces and territories. Any decision on this matter must await the outcome of future constitutional negotiations.

---

19   Gildas L Molgat & Mark MacGuigan, *The Special Joint Committee of the Senate and of the House of Commons on the Constitution of Canada: Final Report* (Ottawa: Queen's Printer, 1972).

E. FRAGMENTATION OF JUDICIAL JURISDICTION

The aforementioned distribution of legislative powers contributes to, but is not the sole reason for, fragmentation in the jurisdiction of Canadian courts that adjudicate family disputes.

In most Canadian provinces, two levels of court share the responsibility for resolving family disputes, namely, courts presided over by federally appointed judges and courts presided over by provincially appointed judges. Overlapping and competing jurisdictions exist, especially with respect to spousal and child support and the custody, care, and upbringing of children.

In an effort to redress some of the problems resulting from such fragmentation of judicial jurisdiction, Unified Family Courts or specialized Family Divisions presided over by federally appointed judges have been established in most Canadian provinces. There are two essential features of such courts:

1) The court must exercise an exclusive and comprehensive jurisdiction over legal issues directly arising from the formation or dissolution of the family; and
2) Auxiliary services should be available to the court in the exercise of its judicial functions and also to litigants having recourse to the judicial process. Auxiliary services include information and intake services, counselling and conciliation or mediation services, investigative or assessment services, legal services, and enforcement services.

Pursuant to the recommendations of the Law Reform Commission of Canada and provincial law reform agencies, Unified Family Court projects were first established in the 1970s on a pilot or experimental basis in various urban centres across Canada, including the Richmond, Surrey, and Delta districts in British Columbia; Fredericton, New Brunswick; St John's, Newfoundland; Hamilton, Ontario; and Saskatoon, Saskatchewan. Internal and external evaluations of several of these pilot projects attested to their success in promoting the resolution of spousal and family disputes[20] and they have provided models for more permanent specialized family courts presided over by federally appointed judges. In 1983, Manitoba established a Family Division of the Court of Queen's Bench but its jurisdiction was in-

---

20 See, for example, Bergen Amren & Flora MacLeod, *The British Columbia Unified Family Court Pilot Project, 1974 to 1977: A Description and Evaluation* (British Columbia: Ministry of Attorney General, Spring 1979); Andrea Maurice & John A Byles, *A Report on the Conciliation Services of the Unified Family Court, Judicial District of Hamilton-Wentworth* (Ontario, Ottawa; Ministry of Attorney General, Department of Justice, 1980); *Attempting to Restructure Family Law: Unified Family Court Experiments in Canada, Discussion Draft* (Canada: Department of Justice, August 1983).

itially confined to Winnipeg.[21] Its jurisdiction has since been expanded to additional judicial centres, including Brandon, Selkirk, Morden, Portage la Prairie, Dauphin, Swan River, Flin Flon, The Pas, and Thompson). In New Brunswick, the Family Division of the Court of Queen's Bench serves the entire province from eight judicial centres. The Supreme Court of Prince Edward Island services that province. In Newfoundland, the Unified Family Court originally served St John's but its jurisdiction now includes portions of the Avalon and Bonavista Peninsulas. In Nova Scotia, a Family Division of the Supreme Court of Nova Scotia sits in Halifax, Sydney, and Port Hawkesbury. In Ontario, the Family Court Division of the Ontario Superior Court of Justice sits in seventeen judicial districts. In Saskatchewan, the Court of Queen's Bench has a Family Division with a core of specialized judges. The establishment of such specialized courts, coupled with a shift of judicial emphasis towards case management that can facilitate the resolution of family disputes, promises a more conciliatory climate for families on their breakdown than has been afforded in the past under traditional adversarial legal and judicial processes.[22]

---

21 Freda M Steel, "Recent Family Law Developments in Manitoba" (1983) 13 Man LJ 323 at 324–29.

22 See Department of Justice, Canada, Evaluation Division, Office of Strategic Planning and Performance Management, *The Unified Family Court Summative Evaluation: Final Report* (Ottawa: Department of Justice, 2009).

CHAPTER 2

Marriage

A. ENGAGEMENTS

Engagements are a common prelude to marriage. At the time when the parties agree to marry at some future date, they often exchange gifts as a token of their commitment. The most common gift, of course, is the engagement ring that is traditionally given by the prospective bridegroom to his prospective bride. Not every engagement, however, results in marriage. The parties may mutually agree to abandon their plans to marry. Or either of them may unilaterally break off the engagement. At one time, it was possible for the jilted lover to sue the other party for breach of promise of marriage. These actions have now been abolished in Australia, England, New Zealand, Scotland, and in several American states and Canadian provinces, including British Columbia, Manitoba, and Ontario. Most people would agree that it is better for an engagement to be broken than for a marriage to be entered into after the parties have second thoughts.

B. PROPERTY DISPUTES ON TERMINATION OF ENGAGEMENT

Statutory abolition of actions for breach of promise of marriage does not interfere with the remedies legally available to resolve property or other disputes that arise on the termination of an engagement. For example, an engaged couple may have acquired property for their future married life together, either from their individual or joint efforts. In these circumstances, if the engagement is subsequently broken off, either party may invoke established legal doctrines to determine their interest in the property. If it was a product of their joint financial contributions, whether direct or indirect, the value of the property will be shared between them. If it was acquired solely through the efforts of one of the parties, that person will be exclusively entitled to the property. The reason for terminating the engagement would be irrelevant to any such claims. Different principles apply to gifts made in contemplation of marriage, including the engagement ring. In the absence of express statutory provision to the contrary, the general common law rule is that the engagement ring is forfeited by the party who refused to honour the engagement.[1] If the woman breaks off the engagement, she must return the ring. On the other hand, if the man breaks off the engagement, he cannot demand the return of the engagement ring. In Ontario, the action for breach of promise of marriage was abolished in 1977 but section 33 of the Ontario *Marriage Act*[2] expressly provides for the recovery of gifts made in contemplation of marriage. Pursuant to this statutory provision, where one person makes a gift to another "in contemplation of or conditional upon" their marriage to each other and the marriage fails to take place or is abandoned, the question of whether the failure or abandonment was caused by the fault of the donor is irrelevant to a determination of the right of the donor to recover the gift. Whether a gift has been made in contemplation of or conditional upon marriage is a question of fact to be determined in light of the attendant circumstances. Birthday presents, for example, would not be regarded as conditional gifts. On the other hand, an engagement ring could properly be regarded as a pledge made in contemplation of marriage and should, therefore, be returned under the Ontario statutory provision if the intended marriage did not take place.[3]

Gifts received from third parties in contemplation of marriage, such as wedding presents, are returnable to the donors if the marriage fails to take place for any reason.[4]

C. CHANGE OF NAME

It has been traditional for the bride to take the surname of the bridegroom after their marriage. This tradition is based on convention and is not a legal

---

1   *Seiler v Funk* (1914), 32 OLR 99 (SC (AD)); *Jacobs v Davis*, [1917] 2 KB 532; *McArthur v Zaduk* (2001), 21 RFL (5th) 142 (Ont Sup Ct); *Konopka v O'Meara*, 2011 ONSC 3229; *Cohen v Sellar*, [1926] 1 KB 536; *Robinson v Cumming* (1742), 26 ER 646; see also *Zimmerman v Lazare*, 2007 BCSC 626.

2   RSO 1990, c M.3.

3   See *Mastromatteo v Dayball*, [2011] OJ No 1600 (Sup Ct); *Newell v Allen*, 2012 ONSC 6681. But see *contra: Marcon v Cicchelli* (1993), 47 RFL (3d) 403 (Ont Gen Div); for criticism of this conclusion, see JG McLeod, "*Marcon v Cicchelli*," Case Comment (1993) 47 RFL (3d) 411 at 412.

4   *Jeffreys v Luck* (1922), 153 LTJ 139.

requirement. In the absence of any statutory provision to the contrary, any person may assume the surname of his or her choice, provided that its use is not calculated to deceive or inflict pecuniary loss. A bride is, therefore, free to retain her birth name in preference to adopting her husband's surname or they may agree on some hybrid form of their joint names. When persons marry and give birth to children, however, statutory restrictions are often imposed that restrict their ability to change their surnames at will. In Canada, such legislation is found in provincial and territorial *Change of Name Acts*. These statutes sometimes require applications for a change of family surname to be made through the courts. The current trend of legislation, as exemplified by the Ontario *Change of Name Act*,[5] provides for official changes of name to be made through administrative processes at a modest cost.

D. MARRIAGE: STATUS OR CONTRACT?

Marriage is more than a simple contract between two people who live together as husband and wife. Marriage is a status that is conferred on individuals by the state. Marriage has a public character and, as such, is subject to general laws that dictate and control the rights, obligations, and incidents of marriage, independently of the wishes of those who marry. Although based on a contract between the parties, marriage is a status to which the state attaches its own conditions as to its creation, duration, and consequences.[6] The principle of the contractual autonomy of the parties has, nevertheless, been endorsed in judicial decisions and statutory provisions that expressly confer certain powers on married persons to regulate their own affairs during marriage and on its termination by death or divorce. Marriage contracts and separation agreements are of particular importance in this context; they will be examined later.[7]

E. DEFINITION OF MARRIAGE; MONOGAMOUS AND POLYGAMOUS MARRIAGES

1) Definition of "Marriage"

Between 2003 and 2005, the courts of eight provinces and two territories held that the traditional common law definition of "marriage" as "the voluntary union for life of one man and one woman to the exclusion of all others"[8]

---

5   RSO 1990, c C.7.

6   *Newson v Newson and Davidson*, [1936] OR 117 at 126 (HCJ).

7   See *Miglin v Miglin*, 2003 SCC 24; *Hartshorne v Hartshorne*, 2004 SCC 22.

8   *Hyde v Hyde and Woodmansee* (1866), LR 1 P&D 130 at 133.

contravenes section 15 of the *Canadian Charter of Rights and Freedoms*[9] by precluding same-sex marriage and cannot be saved under section 1 of the *Charter*. Consequently, marriage was judicially redefined to mean the voluntary or lawful union of two persons to the exclusion of all others.[10] Instead of appealing any of these rulings to the Supreme Court of Canada, the Canadian government decided to introduce legislation to reflect the judicial redefinition of marriage to include same-sex marriage.[11] Before doing so, however, it invoked section 53 of the *Supreme Court Act*,[12] pursuant to which the Governor in Council referred the following questions to the Supreme Court of Canada:[13]

1. Is the annexed Proposal for an Act respecting certain aspects of legal capacity for marriage for civil purposes within the exclusive legislative authority of the Parliament of Canada? If not, in what particular or particulars, and to what extent?

2. If the answer to question 1 is yes, is section 1 of the proposal, which extends capacity to marry to persons of the same sex, consistent with the *Canadian Charter of Rights and Freedoms*? If not, in what particular or particulars, and to what extent?

3. Does the freedom of religion guaranteed by paragraph 2(a) of the *Canadian Charter of Rights and Freedoms* protect religious officials from being compelled to perform a marriage between two persons of the same sex that is contrary to their religious beliefs?

4. Is the opposite-sex requirement for marriage for civil purposes, as established by the common law and set out for Quebec in section 5 of the *Federal Law-Civil Law Harmonization Act, No 1*, consistent with the *Canadian Charter of Rights and Freedoms*? If not, in what particular or particulars and to what extent?

The operative sections of the proposed legislation read as follows:

1. Marriage, for civil purposes, is the lawful union of two persons to the exclusion of all others.

---

9   The *Constitution Act, 1982*, being Schedule B to the *Canada Act 1982* (UK), 1982, c 11 [*Charter*].

10 *EGALE Canada Inc v Canada (Attorney General)*, 2003 BCCA 251, supplementary reasons 2003 BCCA 406; *Vogel v Canada (Attorney General)*, [2004] MJ No 418 (QB (Fam Div)); *Harrison v Canada (Attorney General)*, 2005 NBQB 232; *Pottle v Canada (Attorney General)*, [2004] NJ No 470 (SCTD); *Boutilier v Nova Scotia (Attorney General)*, [2004] NSJ No 357 (SC); *Halpern v Canada* (2003), 65 OR (3d) 161 (CA); *Hendricks c Québec (Procureur général)*, [2002] JQ no 3816 (CS), aff'd [2004] JQ no 2593 (CA); *NW v Canada (Attorney General)*, 2004 SKQB 434; *Dunbar v Yukon*, 2004 YKSC 54.

11 See *Civil Marriage Act*, SC 2005, c 33.

12 RSC 1985, c S-26.

13 *Reference re Same-Sex Marriage*, 2004 SCC 79.

2.   Nothing in this Act affects the freedom of officials of religious groups to refuse to perform marriages that are not in accordance with their religious beliefs.

The responses of the Supreme Court of Canada were as follows:

General responses

Question 1 was answered in the affirmative with respect to section 1 of the proposed legislation but in the negative with respect to section 2. Questions 2 and 3 were both answered in the affirmative. The Supreme Court of Canada declined to answer question 4.

Question 1

In ruling that section 1 of the proposed legislation is *intra vires* Parliament, the Supreme Court of Canada held that section 91(26) of the *Constitution Act, 1867* does not entrench the common-law definition of marriage as it stood in 1867, when marriage was perceived as "the voluntary union for life of one man and one woman to the exclusion of all others." Accepting an expansive definition of "marriage" to include same-sex marriage, the Supreme Court of Canada concluded that, while the proposed federal legislative recognition of same-sex marriage would have an impact in the provincial legislative sphere, these effects are incidental and do not relate to the core of the provincial powers relating to the "solemnization of marriage" and "property and civil rights" under sections 92(12) and 92(13) of the *Constitution Act, 1867*. Section 2 of the proposed legislation was found to be *ultra vires* Parliament, however, because it pertains to the solemnization of marriage which falls within the provincial legislative domain under section 92(12) of the *Constitution Act, 1867*.

Question 2

Section 1 of the proposed legislation, which reflects the government's policy stance towards equality rights under section 15(1) of the *Canadian Charter of Rights and Freedoms*, was perceived by the Supreme Court of Canada as flowing from the *Charter* and was, therefore, consistent with the values protected by section 15(1), notwithstanding any potential conflicts that might arise between the right to same-sex marriage and the right to freedom of religion, which conflicts should be resolved within the ambit of the *Charter* itself by way of internal balancing and delineation.

Question 3

The Supreme Court of Canada held that, absent unique circumstances about which the Court would not speculate, the guarantee of religious freedom in section 2(a) of the *Charter* is broad enough to protect religious officials from being compelled by the state to perform civil or religious same-sex marriages that are contrary to their religious beliefs.

Question 4
The Supreme Court of Canada declined to answer question 4 for the following reasons:

(i)   The federal government had announced its intention to address the issue of same-sex marriage, regardless of the Court's opinion on this question.

(ii) Same-sex couples have relied upon the finality of previous appellate and trial court rulings that have recognized same-sex marriage and these acquired rights are entitled to protection.

(iii) While a negative answer to question 4 would promote uniformity with respect to civil marriage across Canada, an affirmative answer would throw the law into confusion because previous judicial decisions that have upheld the validity of same-sex marriages would be cast in doubt, though they would not be technically overruled by an advisory opinion of the Supreme Court of Canada on question 4.

Having received these responses, section 2 of the *Civil Marriage Act*[14] currently provides that "marriage, for civil purposes, is the lawful union of two persons to the exclusion of all others." Notwithstanding the response of the Supreme Court of Canada to question 1, section 3 of the *Civil Marriage Act* invades the provincial domain of legislative authority by providing that officials of religious groups are free to refuse to perform services that are not in accordance with their religious beliefs. In *Re Marriage Commissioners Appointed Under The Marriage Act*,[15] the Saskatchewan Lieutenant Governor in Council requested an opinion on the constitutional validity of two possible amendments to *The Marriage Act, 1995*.[16] The first amendment would have changed the Act so as to allow a marriage commissioner appointed on or before 5 November 2004 — the date on which the Court of Queen's Bench in *NW v Canada (Attorney General)*[17] struck down the prohibition against same-sex marriage in Saskatchewan — to decline to solemnize a marriage if performing the ceremony would be contrary to his or her religious beliefs. The second amendment (an alternative to the first) would have allowed every commissioner, regardless of his or her date of appointment, to decline to solemnize a marriage if doing so would be contrary to his or her religious beliefs. The Saskatchewan

---

14   SC 2005, c 33.
15   2011 SKCA 3.
16   SS 1995, c M-4.1.
17   2004 SKQB 434.

Court of Appeal held that both of the possible amendments would offend section 15(1) of the *Canadian Charter of Rights and Freedoms* because they violated the equality rights of gay and lesbian individuals, and such violation would not be reasonable and justifiable within the meaning of section 1 of the *Charter*. As a result, if put in place, either option would be unconstitutional and of no force or effect. As pointed out by Richards JA, the judgment of the Supreme Court of Canada in *Reference re Same-Sex Marriage*[18] recognizes that the guarantee of religious freedom in section 2(a) of the *Charter* is broad enough to protect "religious officials" from being compelled by the state to perform civil or religious same-sex marriages that are contrary to their religious beliefs. However, "[it] is entirely clear that the Court's use of the words 'religious officials' in this context was a reference to those individuals, such as priests or rabbis, who hold formal positions in faiths or religious organizations. It was not a reference to *civil* officials who happen to have religious beliefs which do not embrace same-sex marriage."[19]

2) Monogamous and Polygamous Marriages

It is generally, but not universally, accepted that the characterization of a marriage as monogamous or polygamous is to be determined by reference to the law of the country where the marriage was celebrated.[20] It has, nevertheless, been held that a husband's acquisition of a domicile of choice in a monogamous jurisdiction is sufficient to convert his potentially polygamous marriage into a monogamous marriage.[21]

Polygamous marriages validly solemnized in a foreign country may be recognized for some, but not all, purposes of Canadian federal, provincial, or territorial laws. For example, parties to a polygamous marriage that was validly solemnized abroad are prohibited from entering into a subsequent monogamous marriage in Canada, and they may also be denied access to Canadian courts for the purpose of obtaining a divorce.[22] They may, nevertheless, be entitled to pursue claims for spousal and child support or for custody or access under provincial or territorial legislation in Canada.[23] A polygamous

---

18   2004 SCC 79 at paras 58–60.

19   *Re Marriage Commissioners Appointed Under The Marriage Act*, 2011 SKCA 3 at para 49 [emphasis in original].

20   *Chetti v Chetti*, [1909] P 67; *Srinivassan v Srinivassan*, [1946] P 67; *Cheni (otherwise Rodriguez) v Cheni*, [1965] P 85.

21   *Ali v Ali*, [1968] P 564; *Nafie v Badawy*, 2015 ABCA 36; *Re Hassan and Hassan* (1976), 12 OR (2d) 432 (HCJ).

22   See *Hyde v Hyde and Woodmansee*, (1866), LR 1 P&D 130. Compare *Azam v Jan*, 2012 ABCA 197.

23   *Lim v Lim*, [1948] 2 DLR 353 (BCSC).

marriage may also be recognized as valid in Canada for the purpose of determining the succession rights of surviving spouses.[24] As Bielby JA, of the Alberta Court of Appeal, observed in *Azam v Jan*, "[s]ome provincial legislation now extends aspects of relief to parties to an actively polygamous marriage."[25] By way of example, subsection 1(2) of the Ontario *Family Law Act*,[26] defines "spouse" to include a party to "a marriage that is actually or potentially polygamous, if it was celebrated in a jurisdiction whose system of law recognizes it as valid." Accordingly, polygamous spouses in Ontario are entitled to pursue claims for an equalization of net family property between the spouses on separation or death, although it has not yet been resolved how the process of equalization will be applied in cases where two or more marriages that are actually polygamous have been celebrated in a jurisdiction whose system of law recognizes them as valid. Polygamous spouses may also pursue claims under the Ontario *Family Law Act* for spousal and child support and may enter into marriage contracts and separation agreements. In addition, they can sue a third party for damages where that third party kills or injures their polygamous spouse. For almost all practical purposes under the law of Ontario, a spouse who contracted a valid polygamous marriage abroad has the same legal rights and obligations as a spouse who is party to a traditional monogamous marriage. Legislative changes such as these broadly reflect the changing nature of family relationships in a multicultural society such as currently exists in Canada.

Pursuant to federal legislation, one aspect of marriage that continues to be denied to members of actively polygamous marriages is the right to immigrate to Canada.[27] And although foreign polygamous marriages have been recognized for many purposes of Canadian law, the practice of polygamy is an indictable criminal offence under section 293 of the *Criminal Code of Canada*.[28]

---

24   *Yew v British Columbia (Attorney General)* (1924), 33 BCR 109 (CA).

25   *Azam v Jan*, 2012 ABCA 197 at para 19.

26   RSO 1990, c F.3.

27   *Ali v Canada (Minister of Citizenship and Immigration)* (1998), 154 FTR 285; *Awwad v Canada (Minister of Citizenship and Immigration)* (1999), 162 FTR 209.

28   RSC 1985, c C-46. See *Reference re: Section 293 of the Criminal Code of Canada*, 2011 BCSC 1588; see also Angela Campbell, *Polygamy in Canada: Legal and Social Implications for Women and Children: A Collection of Policy Research Reports* (Ottawa: Status of Women Canada, 2005).

F. FORMAL AND ESSENTIAL VALIDITY

1) Validity of Marriage; Applicable Laws

The formal validity of marriage is determined by the application of the *lex loci celebrationis*, that is, the law of the place where the marriage was contracted.[29] A party who asserts that a marriage is void because of lack of compliance with the requirements of the law of the country in which it was celebrated has the burden of proving the foreign law by means of an expert witness.[30] Absent such proof, the foreign law will be presumed to be the same as the law of the forum wherein the marriage is impugned.[31]

Matters pertaining to the essential validity of a marriage, which include the capacity to marry and consent to marriage, are governed by the law of the domicile of the parties at the time of their marriage, or possibly the law of their intended matrimonial domicile.[32]

2) Formal Validity

In Canada, the formal requirements of marriage are governed by provincial and territorial legislation. For example, the Ontario *Marriage Act*[33] regulates the solemnization of marriage in that province. It stipulates that no marriage may be solemnized in Ontario except under the authority of a licence or the publication of banns. It also defines specific requirements concerning waiting periods, parental consents, the attendance of the parties and witnesses, and penalties for false declarations. Non-compliance with statutorily presented formalities, though subject to penalties, does not render the marriage void unless the statute expressly or by necessary implication invalidates the marriage.[34] Section 31 of the Ontario *Marriage Act* expressly provides that

> [if] the parties to a marriage solemnized in good faith and intended to be in
> compliance with this Act are not under a legal disqualification to contract

---

29 *Hassan v Hassan*, 2006 ABQB 544; *Nafie v Badawy*, 2015 ABCA 36; *Davison v Sweeney*, 2005 BCSC 757; *Sahibalzubaidi v Bahjat*, 2011 ONSC 4075; *Berthiaume v Dastou*, [1930] 1 DLR 849 (PC).

30 *Ali v Ahmad*, [2002] OJ No 397 (Sup Ct); *Sahibalzubaidi v Bahjat*, 2011 ONSC 4075.

31 *Davison v Sweeney*, 2005 BCSC 757; *Ali v Ahmad*, [2002] OJ No 397 (Sup Ct).

32 *Nafie v Badawy*, 2015 ABCA 36; *Davison v Sweeney*, 2005 BCSC 757; *Sarmiento v Villarico*, 2014 BCSC 455; *Brook v Brook* (1861), 9 HL Cas 193; *De Reneville v De Reneville*, [1948] P 100 at 114 (CA). For an exception applicable to same-sex marriages celebrated in Canada between foreign domiciliaries, see *Civil Marriage of Non-residents Act*, SC 2013, c 30. And see Brenda Cossman, "Exporting Same-Sex Marriage, Importing Same-Sex Divorce (Or How Canada's Marriage and Divorce Laws Unleashed a Private International Law Nightmare and What to Do About It)" (2013) 32:1 Can Fam LQ 1.

33 RSO 1990, c M.3.

34 *Clause v Clause*, [1956] OWN 449 (HCJ).

such marriage and after such solemnization have lived together and co-habited as man and wife, such marriage shall be deemed a valid marriage, notwithstanding that the person who solemnized the marriage was not authorized to solemnize marriage, and notwithstanding the absence of or any irregularity or insufficiency in the publication of banns or the issue of a licence.[35]

There are four elements required for the deeming provision in section 31 to apply, namely:

1) the marriage must have been solemnized in good faith;
2) the marriage must have been intended to be in compliance with the *Marriage Act*;
3) neither party can be under a legal disqualification to contract marriage; and
4) the parties must have lived together and cohabited as a married couple after solemnization.

Applying these requirements in *Isse v Said*,[36] wherein there was an Islamic wedding ceremony that took place according to Sharia law without a marriage licence having been issued and the marriage not having been registered under the law of Ontario, Broad J, of the Ontario Superior Court of Justice, held the marriage to be valid under the Ontario *Marriage Act*. The burden falls on the applicant to prove, on a balance of probabilities, that he or she intended the marriage to comply with the laws of Ontario at the time of the wedding ceremony.[37] The good faith of one of the parties will be sufficient to satisfy the statutory validation clause.[38] Failure to comply with a curative provision, such as section 31 of the Ontario *Marriage Act*, may imply invalidity.[39]

3) Essential Validity

A valid marriage requires the voluntary consent of both parties and the absence of any legal incapacity to marry.[40] These prerequisites to a valid marriage can be traced back to the jurisprudence of the ecclesiastical courts in England prior to 1857.

---

35 See *Upadyhaha v Sehgal* (2000), 11 RFL (5th) 210 (Ont Sup Ct); *Smith v Waghorn*, 2012 ONSC 496.

36 2012 ONSC 1829; see also *Matthews v Mutiso*, 2014 ONSC 4010.

37 *Chhokar v Bains*, 2012 ONSC 6602.

38 *Alspector v Alspector*, [1957] OR 454 (CA).

39 See *Gilham v Steele*, [1953] 2 DLR 89 (BCCA); see also HR Hahlo, *Nullity of Marriage in Canada* (Toronto: Butterworths, 1979) at 19.

40 *Moss v Moss*, [1897] P 263 at 268.

G. JURISDICTION

Canadian courts may assume jurisdiction in nullity proceedings, whether the marriage is void or voidable, if either party is domiciled within the territorial jurisdiction of the court at the commencement of the proceedings, or if the respondent is *bona fide* resident within the jurisdiction of the court, or when the marriage has been solemnized within the territorial jurisdiction of the court.[41]

H. VOID AND VOIDABLE MARRIAGES[42]

Marriages may be valid, void, or voidable according to law. A void marriage is one that is null and void from its inception. It is regarded as though it had never taken place. A voidable marriage, on the other hand, is treated in law as a valid and subsisting marriage unless and until it is annulled by a court of competent jurisdiction.[43] A voidable marriage can only be annulled on the petition of one of the spouses and the annulment must occur during the lifetime of both spouses.[44] Third parties cannot seek to annul a voidable marriage entered into by other people. The parties to a voidable marriage may elect to treat it as valid. A voidable marriage can only be terminated by the judgment of a court of competent jurisdiction at the request of one of the parties to that marriage. A void marriage, however, is impeachable by third parties who "have an interest of some kind; for the object of the suit must be to procure the marriage to be voided on the ground that its validity may affect some right, or interest of the party promoting the suit."[45] A "slight interest" will suffice.[46] A void marriage may also be impugned collaterally after

---

41 See JD Payne, "Jurisdiction in Nullity Proceedings" (1961) 26 Sask Bar Rev 20; *Sarmiento v Villarico*, 2014 BCSC 455, citing *Savelieff v Glouchkoff (or Savelieff)* (1964), 45 DLR (2d) 520 (BCCA); *Ward v Ward* (1985), 66 NBR (2d) 44 (QB (Fam Div)).

42 For a detailed analysis of the differing consequences of void and voidable marriages, including their effect on marriage settlements, separation agreements, gifts, intestate succession rights, the revocation of wills, dependants' maintenance claims against the estate of a deceased person, changes of name, the legitimacy of children, support and property rights, tax consequences, and the like, see HR Hahlo, *Nullity of Marriage in Canada* (Toronto: Butterworths, 1979) at 41–57.

43 *Meunier v Meunier*, 1997 CanLII 3551 (BCSC) (void marriage); *Davison v Sweeney*, 2005 BCSC 757; *De Reneville v De Reneville*, [1948] P 100 at 110 (CA) (voidable marriage).

44 *A v B* (1868), 1 P&D 559; *Cowell v Prince* (1866), LR 1 Ex 246; *Brown v Brown* (1907), 13 BCR 73 (SC); *Fleming v Fleming*, [1934] OR 588 (HCJ).

45 *Sherwood v Ray* (1837), 12 ER 848, Parke B.

46 *Faremouth v Watson* (1811), 161 ER 1009.

the death of one or both spouses.[47] Where the marriage is void, either party is entitled to institute nullity proceedings and a decree may be granted to the party under the disability.[48] If the marriage is voidable, only the party under the disability may be barred from securing an annulment of the marriage.[49] The doctrine of insincerity may bar the annulment of a voidable marriage but is, in principle, inapplicable to a void marriage.[50]

I. ABSENCE OF CONSENT

As stated previously, marriage is "a voluntary union for life." It is not a status that can be imposed on a person without his or her consent. In principle, the absence of consent should render a marriage null and void, regardless of the factor that precluded consent. Judicial decisions have differed, however, on whether factors such as insanity, duress, or mistake render a marriage void or only voidable at the option of the non-disabled or innocent party.[51]

1) Unsoundness of Mind; Alcohol and Drug Intoxication

Freedom of consent to marry may be negated by unsoundness of mind or the effects of excessive alcohol or drug consumption.[52] The degree of impairment must be such that the afflicted person was incapable of understanding the ceremony of marriage and the duties and responsibilities that flow from marriage.[53] The assessment of a person's capacity to understand the nature of the marriage commitment is informed, in part, by an ability to manage themselves and their affairs. Delusional thinking or reduced cognitive abilities alone may not destroy an individual's capacity to form an intention to

---

47 *Fenton v Livingstone* (1859), 3 Macq 497; *Spier v Bergen*, [1947] WN 46; *Ross-Scott v Groves Estate*, 2014 BCSC 435.

48 *Miles v Chilton (falsely calling himself Miles)* (1849), 163 ER 1178; *Andrews v Ross* (1884), 14 PD 15; *Pugh v Pugh*, [1951] P 482.

49 *Harthan v Harthan*, [1948] 2 All ER 639 (CA).

50 See Section L(3), below in this chapter.

51 See, generally, HR Hahlo, *Nullity of Marriage in Canada* (Toronto: Butterworths, 1979) especially at 43–44.

52 *Sullivan v Sullivan* (1818), 2 Hag Con 238, aff'd *Sullivan v Oldacre* (1819), 3 Phill 45; *Meilen v Andersson* (1977), 6 AR 427 (SC (TD)) (drugs); *Barrett Estate v Dexter*, 2000 ABQB 530 (senility); *Davison v Sweeney*, 2005 BCSC 757 (drunkenness); *Ward v Ward* (1985), 66 NBR (2d) 44 (QB (Fam Div)) (intoxication); *Feng v Sung Estate* (2004), 9 RFL (6th) 229 (Ont CA) (mental and physical incapacity).

53 *Brosseau v Belland*, [1932] 2 WWR 632 (Alta SC); *Barrett Estate v Dexter*, 2000 ABQB 530; *Davison v Sweeney*, 2005 BCSC 757; *Ross-Scott v Groves Estate*, 2014 BCSC 435 (mental capacity); *Feng v Sung Estate* (2004) 9 RFL (6th) 229 (Ont CA); *Reynolds v Reynolds* (1966), 58 WWR 87 (BCSC); compare *Milson v Hough*, [1951] 3 DLR 725 (Ont HC).

marry as long as the person is capable of managing his or her own affairs.[54] The affliction must have existed at the time when the marriage was solemnized.[55] The burden of proof falls on the person who seeks to impugn the marriage.[56]

2) Duress

Where improper pressure undermines a person's ability to consent, the marriage is voidable at the option of the coerced party.[57] Duress implies the exertion of pressure that induces fear but it does not require the use of physical force. Although fear is a necessary ingredient, it is unnecessary for the person coerced to feel a threat to his or her personal life, limb, or liberty. It is sufficient if fear for some other person is induced.[58] Coercion sufficient to undermine the consent to marry may arise from external sources, as, for example, where a person marries for the purpose of escaping political oppression in his or her homeland.[59]

In *RH v RT*,[60] Maisonville J, of the British Columbia Supreme Court, accepted the subjective test set out in *Scott v Sebright*[61] whereby proof is required that a "party is actually in a state of mental incompetence to resist pressure improperly brought to bear."[62] She observed that "the duress must be of such a nature that the free will to consent to the marriage is overborne"[63] and identified the following considerations as pertinent to the requisite judicial inquiry:

- the party's emotional state at the time of the marriage ceremony,
- the party's vulnerability,
- the time between the alleged coercive conduct and the marriage ceremony,
- whether the marriage was consummated,
- the residence of the parties during the marriage, and
- the amount of time until the start of annulment proceedings.[64]

---

54   *Ross-Scott v Groves Estate*, 2014 BCSC 435 at para 177, Armstrong J, citing *AB v CD*, 2009 BCCA 200 at paras 21 and 22.

55   *Durham v Durham* (1885), 10 PD 80.

56   *Chertkow v Feinstein*, [1930] SCR 335; *Davison v Sweeney*, 2005 BCSC 757; *Ross-Scott v Groves Estate*, 2014 BCSC 435; *Deal v Deal* (1966), 60 DLR (2d) 411 (NSSC).

57   *AS v AS* (1988), 65 OR (2d) 720 (UFC); *Kawaluk v Kawaluk*, [1927] 3 DLR 493 (Sask KB); *Thompson v Thompson* (1971), 19 DLR (3d) 608 (Sask QB).

58   *Pascuzzi v Pascuzzi* (1955), 1 RFL (Rep) 262 (HCJ).

59   *H v H*, [1953] 2 All ER 1229.

60   2011 BCSC 678; see also *Ross-Scott v Groves Estate*, 2014 BCSC 435.

61   (1886), 12 PD 21 at 23–24.

62   *RH v RT*, 2011 BCSC 678 at para 17.

63   *Ibid* at para 21.

64   *Ibid* at para 28.

She then added that "[t]he most important consideration for the court when considering an annulment on the basis of duress is the parties' emotional state *at the time of the marriage ceremony*. If the parties are mentally competent to give consent even if they may be reluctant and feel pressured, this is not sufficient ground to grant an annulment on the basis of duress. The emotional state must completely overbear the will to consent, however reluctant or hesitant the party may be."[65]

3) Fraud

Misrepresentations as to the character or personality traits of a spouse do not constitute fraud in proceedings to annul a marriage.[66] Fraudulent misrepresentations that induce a person to marry will not undermine consent except where the misrepresentations lead to an operative mistake.[67] As a Saskatchewan judge has observed, "No degree of deception can avail to set aside a contract of marriage duly celebrated by consenting parties with the capacity to enter into the marriage."[68]

4) Mistake

There are only two kinds of mistake that can render a marriage void for lack of consent. They are (1) mistake as to the identity of the person with whom the marriage is entered into, and (2) mistake as to the nature of the ceremony.[69]

A mistake of identity presupposes that A intended to marry B but in fact married C.[70] Mistakes as to the attributes of a person with whom marriage is contracted, for example, his or her age, health, virginity, or wealth, do not amount to mistaken identity and do not negate the consent to marry. Thus, a woman's wilful concealment of her pregnancy by another man at the time

---

65 *Ibid* at para 29 [emphasis in original].

66 *Sahibalzubaidi v Bahjat*, 2011 ONSC 4075.

67 *Smith v Waghorn*, 2012 ONSC 496.

68 *Kokkalas v Kokkalas* (1965), 50 DLR (2d) 193 at 194 (Sask QB). See also *Swift v Kelly* (1835), 12 ER 648 (HL), wherein it was stated:

> No marriage shall be held void merely upon proof that it had been contracted upon false representations, and that but for such contrivances, consent never would have been obtained. Unless the party imposed upon has been deceived as to the person, and thus has given no consent at all, there is no degree of deception which can avail to set aside a contract of marriage knowingly made.

Compare to *Lim v Teav*, 2008 BCSC 1534.

69 See *Iantsis (falsely called Papatheodorou) v Papatheodorou* (1971), 3 RFL 158 (Ont CA); *Sidhu v Chahal*, 2010 ONSC 72; *Smith v Waghorn*, 2012 ONSC 496.

70 *C v C*, [1942] NZLR 356 at 359.

of the marriage has been found insufficient to undermine her husband's consent to the marriage.[71]

Consent will be negated, however, where a person was unaware that the ceremony to which he or she was a party was one of marriage.[72] In determining whether a person was acting under a misapprehension with respect to the nature of the ceremony, credibility becomes a critical factor. In an Ontario case,[73] the trial judge took account of the following circumstances: the parties had recently arrived from Greece where marriage ceremonies take a different form; the parties never cohabited or consummated the marriage; and the petitioner only spoke Greek, whereas the language of the marriage ceremony was English. Custom, language, cohabitation, and consummation are, therefore, important considerations in determining credibility. Where the nature of the ceremony is understood, however, a mistake as to the consequences of the marriage is not sufficient to negate the consent to marry. A mistaken belief that the marriage is polygamous,[74] or that the other spouse would be free to leave her Russian homeland,[75] or that a religious ceremony is required in addition to the civil ceremony,[76] have all been deemed insufficient to render the marriage void.

5) Intention and Motive; Marriages of Convenience

From the legal standpoint, the intention of the parties to contract marriage is all-important; their motive for doing so is irrelevant.[77] In the words of a Manitoba judge,

> In English law, while the purely sham marriage is of no effect, e.g., a masquerade, theatre performance, party entertainment, things of that kind, generally the mental reservations or motive of the parties, or one of them, will not serve to destroy the validity of the ceremony. So, the parties were held to their mutual promises in *Brooks-Bischoffberger v. Brooks-Bischoffberger* (1930), 149 A. 606 at 607, 129 Me. 52, where a marriage performed through the dare of a third party was held to be valid, Dunn J. observing that marriage is "a status wherein public policy rises superior to mere sympathy"; or to win a bet, *Parker v. Parker* (1757), 2 Lee, 382, 161 E.R. 377; to obtain

---

71   *Moss v Moss*, [1897] P 263.

72   *Jiwani v Samji* (1979), 11 RFL (2d) 188 (BCSC); *Vamvakidis v Kirkoff*, [1930] 2 DLR 877 (Ont CA); *Sidhu v Chahal*, 2010 ONSC 72; *Sobush v Sobush*, [1931] 2 WWR 900 (Sask KB).

73   *Nane (Sykiotis) v Sykiotis*, (1966), 57 DLR (2d) 118 (Ont HCJ).

74   *Kassim v Kassim*, [1962] P 224.

75   *Kenward v Kenward*, [1951] P 124 (CA).

76   *Caro v Cebryk* (1965), 54 WWR 447 (Alta SC).

77   *KJW v MDWW*, 2003 BCCA 292.

employment open only to married persons, *Crouch v. Wartenberg* (1920), 104 S.E. 117, 11 A.L.R. 212, 91 W. Va. 91 (West Virginia C.A.); to comply with the terms of a settlement conferring gifts subject to the beneficiary's marriage, *Coppo v. Coppo* (1937), 297 N.Y.S. 744, 163 Misc 249; to avoid a court martial, *Dumoulin v. Druitt* (1860), 13 Ir. C.L. 212 (Q.B.).

In all those cases the protests of the petitioner that the marriage was no more than a sham, an event which one or both of the parties regarded as fictitious or simulated, went unheard, English law considering it irrelevant to consider the motives which prompt a party to enter into the union; and see *Nash v. Nash*, [1940] P. 60, [1940] 1 All E.R. 206.[78]

The relevance of motive has most frequently arisen when marriages have been contracted solely for the purpose of immigration. In a leading case in the United States, the judge stated:

> Mutual consent is necessary to every contract; and no matter what forms or ceremonies the party may go through indicating the contrary, they do not contract if they do not in fact assent, which must always be proved . . . . Marriage is no exception to this rule: a marriage in jest is not a marriage at all . . . . It is quite true that a marriage without subsequent consummation will be valid; but if the spouses agree to a marriage only for the sake of representing it as such to the outside world and with the understanding that they will put an end to it as soon as it has served its purpose to deceive, they have never really agreed to be married at all. They must assent to enter into the relation as it is ordinarily understood, and it is not ordinarily understood as merely a pretence, or cover, to deceive others.[79]

The preponderance of authority in England and Canada, however, has rejected this opinion and concluded that a marriage is not invalidated by reason only that it was entered into solely as a device to evade immigration regulations.[80] It may be otherwise where the marriage was induced by coercion,[81] or the petitioner was deceived by the respondent into believing that he meant to take her as his wife, whereas he went through the marriage ceremony solely

---

78   *Fernandez (Alarcio) v Fernandez* (1983), 34 RFL (2d) 249 at 253–54 (Man QB), Wilson J.

79   *US v Rubenstein*, 151 F 2d 915 at 918 (1945), Learned Hand J.

80   *Silver v Silver*, [1955] 2 All ER 614; *Iantsis (falsely called Papatheodorou) v Papatheodorou* (1971), 3 RFL 158 (Ont CA), overruling *Johnson (falsely called Smith) v Smith* (1968), 70 DLR (2d) 374 (Ont HCJ); *Leonotion v Leonotion* (1977), 4 RFL (2d) 94 (Ont CA); *Kaur v Brar* (2003), 35 RFL (5th) 380 (Ont Sup Ct); *Grewal v Kaur* (2009), 75 RFL (6th) 443 (Ont Sup Ct). See also *Merchant v Dossani*, 2007 ABQB 487; *Peters v Murray*, 2006 CanLII 40977 (Ont CA); *Said v Said* (1986), 33 DLR (4th) 382 (BCCA); compare *Grewal v Sohal*, 2004 BCSC 1549; *Lim v Teav*, 2008 BCSC 1534.

81   *H v H*, [1953] 2 All ER 1229.

as a means of establishing permanent residence in Canada,[82] or where the marriage does not comply with the formal requirements of the place of celebration.[83] Where both parties voluntarily enter into an "immigration" marriage of convenience, the marriage is valid and cannot be annulled by reason of non-consummation, but a divorce may be available under paragraph 8(2)(a) of the *Divorce Act*, which empowers a court to grant a divorce on the basis of a breakdown of the marriage when the spouses have lived separate and apart for at least one year.[84] A finding of collusion, however, would bar the granting of a divorce.[85]

J. LEGAL CAPACITY

A valid marriage presupposes that both parties have the capacity to marry and intermarry. Legal incapacity may have arisen historically because the parties were of the same sex and may arise by reason of age, prior marriage, or under prohibited degrees of consanguinity or adoption.

1) Same-Sex Marriages

As stated previously, marriage for civil purposes has been legislatively redefined as the lawful union of two persons. Consequently, members of the same sex can now intermarry.[86]

2) Age

Pursuant to principles upheld by the ecclesiastical courts in England more than 150 years ago, any marriage involving a person under the age of seven years is null and void. Marriages of males between the ages of seven and fourteen years and of females between the ages of seven and twelve years are voidable at the option of the underage party but may be ratified by continued

---

82   *Kalyan v Lal* (1976), 28 RFL 229 (BCSC); *Torfehnejad v Salimi* (2006), 276 DLR (4th) 733 (Ont Sup Ct); compare *Ali v Ahmad*, [2002] OJ No 397 (Sup Ct). As to liability for damages in the tort of deceit for fraudulently inducing marriage, see *Raju v Kumar*, 2006 BCSC 439.

83   *McKenzie v Singh* (1972), 29 DLR (3d) 380 (BCSC); *Torfehnejad v Salimi* (2006), 276 DLR (4th) 733 (Ont Sup Ct) (fraudulent deception by wife rendering marriage void under Iranian law); *Grewal v Kaur*, (2009), 75 RFL (6th) 443 (Ont Sup Ct).

84   *Ciresi (Ahmad) v Ahmad* (1983), 31 RFL (2d) 326 (Alta QB); *Tefera v Yergu*, 2002 ABQB 215; *Fernandez (Alarcio) v Fernandez* (1983), 34 RFL (2d) 249 (Man QB).

85   See *Johnson v Ahmad* (1981), 22 RFL (2d) 141 (Alta QB); *Kaur v Brar* (2003), 35 RFL (5th) 380 (Ont Sup Ct); compare *Ciresi (Ahmad) v Ahmad* (1983), 31 RFL (2d) 326 (Alta QB).

86   See Section E(1), above in this chapter. As to the treatment of foreign civil law partnerships as marriages for the purpose of applying Canadian legislation, see *Hincks v Gallardo*, 2014 ONCA 494.

cohabitation after the upper age limit has been reached.[87] Provincial and territorial Marriage Acts in Canada also regulate the age of marriage by licensing and other requirements, including parental consent for children under the age of majority, which is eighteen or nineteen years of age depending on which province or territory the child lives in.

3) Prior Marriage

Marriage presupposes exclusivity between the spouses.[88] Accordingly, a valid and subsisting marriage bars any subsequent marriage by either spouse. Any purported second marriage is null and void, regardless of whether it will ground a charge of bigamy or polygamy under the Canadian *Criminal Code*.[89] An order may be made pursuant to section 9 of the Ontario *Marriage Act*,[90] which presumes the death of a missing spouse and permits the applicant to remarry under the authority of a licence or the publication of banns. An order of presumed death has limited effect; it does not validate the remarriage in the event that the missing spouse reappears.[91] The more appropriate course of action, therefore, for a spouse whose consort has disappeared without trace is the institution of divorce proceedings to terminate his or her marital status. Any subsequent remarriage with a third party will then be valid. But divorcees must not jump the gun. Pursuant to section 12 of the *Divorce Act*,[92] a divorce judgment in Canada does not usually become effective until the thirty-first day after the day on which the judgment granting the divorce was rendered. The Ontario Superior Court of Justice has jurisdiction to declare a foreign marriage a nullity where the defendant was already party to a subsisting marriage that had not been terminated at the time of his second marriage.[93]

4) Prohibited Degrees

Marriages between certain persons who are closely related are prohibited by federal legislation. The *Marriage (Prohibited Degrees) Act*,[94] as amended,

---

87   *R v Bell* (1857), 15 UCQB 287.

88   *Hyde v Hyde and Woodmansee* (1866), LR 1 P&D 130. As to the annulment of a polygamous marriage by a Canadian court, see *Azam v Jan*, 2013 ABQB 301.

89   *Sarmiento v Villarico*, 2014 BCSC 455; *Bolentiru v Radulescu* (2004), 10 RFL (6th) 258 (Ont Sup Ct); *Peters v Murray*, 2006 CanLII 40977 (Ont CA).

90   RSO 1990, c M.3.

91   *McCullough v Ralph*, [1942] OJ No 78 (HCJ); *Tomberg v Tomberg (Gilbert)*, [1942] 2 WWR 319 (Alta CA); see also *Tomberg (Gilbert), Re*, [1942] 3 WWR 542 (Alta CA).

92   RSC 1985 (2d Supp), c 3.

93   *Bolentiru v Radulescu*, (2004), 10 RFL (6th) 258 (Ont Sup Ct).

94   SC 1990, c 46, as amended by SC 2005, c 33.

currently provides a codification and amendment of the former law governing the prohibited degrees of consanguinity, affinity, and adoption. Consanguinity involves blood relationships whereas affinity involves relationships arising from marriage. Subsection 3(1) of the *Marriage (Prohibited Degrees) Act* stipulates that "a marriage between persons related by consanguinity, affinity or adoption is not invalid by reason only of their relationship" except where it contravenes the express prohibitions set out under subsection 2(2) of the Act.[95] Subsection 3(2) provides that "a marriage between persons who are related in the manner described in subsection 2(2) is void." Subsection 2(2) of the *Marriage (Prohibited Degrees) Act* provides as follows:

> 2(2) No person shall marry another person if they are related lineally, or as brother or sister or half-brother or half-sister, including by adoption.

Former prohibited degrees based on affinity have been abolished. It is now possible, for example, for a man to marry his divorced wife's sister or niece or for a woman to marry her divorced husband's brother or nephew. Prior to the *Marriage (Prohibited Degrees) Act*, there was some doubt on this issue.

K. NON-CONSUMMATION OF MARRIAGE

Impotence, which is the inability to consummate the marriage, renders a marriage voidable. Canadian law draws a distinction between the inability to consummate a marriage and wilful refusal to do so. It is impotence, not wilful refusal, that constitutes a ground for annulment of marriage in Canada.[96] A continuing and persistent refusal to consummate the marriage may, nevertheless, be indicative of impotence.[97]

Either or both parties to a marriage that has not been consummated may petition the courts for annulment of the marriage. Even the impotent spouse can seek the annulment provided that he or she did not knowingly deceive the other spouse.[98]

---

95   See *PA v CG* (2002), 219 DLR (4th) 446 (Qc CA) (foreign marriage between husband and divorced wife's sister subsequently validated by enactment of the *Marriage (Prohibited Degrees) Act*, SC 1990, c 46).

96   *Heil v Heil*, [1942] SCR 160; *Jomha v Jomaa*, 2010 ABQB 135; *KHL v GQL*, 2003 BCCA 313; *RKS v RS*, 2014 BCSC 1626.

97   *KHL v GQL*, 2003 BCCA 313; *HLC v MAL*, 2003 BCSC 1461; *LeBlanc v LeBlanc*, [1955] 1 DLR 676 (NSSC).

98   *Harthan v Harthan*, [1948] 2 All ER 639 (CA); *Sallam v Sallam* (1988), 73 Nfld & PEIR 136 (Nfld SCTD).

Impotence is not to be confused with the inability to have children. Impotence signifies an incapacity in one or both spouses to engage in normal sexual intercourse with each other.[99] As was stated in an old English case,

> The only question is whether the [spouse] is or is not capable of sexual intercourse, or, if at present incapable, whether that incapacity can be removed. . . . If there be a reasonable probability that the lady can be made capable of a *vera copula* — of the natural sort of *coitus*, though without power of conception — I cannot pronounce this marriage void. If, on the contrary, she is not and cannot be made capable of more than incipient, imperfect, and unnatural *coitus*, I would pronounce the marriage void.[100]

With respect to same-sex married couples, section 4 of the *Civil Marriage Act*[101] provides that "for greater certainty, a marriage is not void or voidable by reason only that the spouses are of the same sex."

The use of contraceptives or the practice of *coitus interruptus* does not preclude consummation of the marriage.[102] Conversely, the impregnation of the wife by artificial insemination does not constitute consummation of the marriage even if the husband's semen is used.[103]

The inability to consummate the marriage may arise from a physical incapacity or from an invincible repugnance or aversion to sexual intercourse.[104] The sexual incapacity may be general in character or it may exist only as between the spouses themselves.[105]

A marriage is consummated on the first occasion when the spouses engage in postmarital sexual intercourse. Once consummated, always consummated, is the criterion.[106] Premarital intercourse cannot constitute consummation of a subsequent marriage between the parties, although it may be presumptive evidence of the capacity of the spouses to engage in sexual intercourse.[107]

---

99 *Baxter v Baxter*, [1948] AC 274 (HL); *KHL v GQL*, 2003 BCCA 313.

100 *D v A* (1845), 1 Robb Ecc 279 at 296 and 299 (Dr Lushington).

101 SC 2005, c 33.

102 *Baxter v Baxter*, [1948] AC 274 (HL); *Wilkinson v Wilkinson*, [1950] 3 DLR 236 (BCCA) (but see dissenting judgment of O'Halloran JA).

103 *REL v EL*, [1949] P 211.

104 *G v G*, [1924] AC 349 (HL); *Heil v Heil*, [1942] SCR 160; *Jomha v Jomaa*, 2010 ABQB 135; *Juretic v Ruiz*, 1999 BCCA 417; *Sangha v Aujla*, 2002 BCSC 1472; *KHL v GQL*, 2003 BCCA 313; *HLC v MAL*, 2003 BCSC 1461; *Grewal v Sohal*, 2004 BCSC 1549; *Lim v Teav*, 2008 BCSC 1534.

105 *C v C*, [1921] P 399; *Sallam v Sallam* (1988), 73 Nfld & PEIR 136 (Nfld SCTD); *HLC v MAL*, 2003 BCSC 1461; *Greenlees v Greenlees*, [1959] OR 419 (HCJ); *Hardick v Fox* (1970), 3 RFL 153 (Ont HCJ).

106 *Goodman v Goodman* (1973), 9 RFL 261 (Ont HCJ).

107 *Ibid.*

The sexual incapacity must exist at the time of the marriage and through-out the marriage,[108] although courts have frequently recognized psychological impotence manifested after the marriage has been solemnized.[109] It must also be incurable but will be regarded as incurable when the condition can only be remedied by an operation attended by danger or when the spouse under the disability persistently refuses to undergo treatment that carries no significant risk.[110]

L. BARS TO ANNULMENT

There are three potential bars to a person obtaining a decree of nullity or other relief from a court of competent jurisdiction. They are (1) collusion; (2) estoppel; and (3) insincerity.

1) Collusion

Collusion constitutes a bar to relief in any matrimonial proceeding, includ-ing nullity proceedings.[111] Collusion signifies an agreement or conspiracy be-tween the spouses to subvert the administration of justice, as, for example, by fabricating or suppressing evidence.

2) Estoppel

A spouse who has obtained a decree of nullity from a foreign court that was incompetent to assume jurisdiction, is precluded from attacking the valid-ity of the foreign decree for the purpose of securing a pecuniary advantage against his or her spouse or the estate of that spouse.[112] Assume, for example, that a wife obtained a decree of nullity of marriage from a foreign court that was not entitled to deal with the issue. The foreign decree would not be recognized as valid by Canadian courts; the marriage would still be valid in Canada. But, if the husband were to die, his wife would be estopped from as-serting succession rights in his estate under a provincial or territorial statute in Canada.

---

108 *Greenstreet v Cumyns* (1812), 2 Hag Con 332 (postmarital defect); *S v S*, [1956] P 1 (cure ef-fected after institution of nullity proceedings); *KHL v GQL*, 2003 BCCA 313; *C v C*, [1949] 1 WWR 911 (Man KB).

109 *HLC v MAL*, 2003 BCSC 1461; *Gupta v Garg*, 2014 ONCA 217; see also cases cited in note 98 above.

110 *S v S*, [1956] P 1; *C v C*, [1949] 1 WWR 911 (Man KB); *Deo v Kumzer*, [1993] BCJ No 2051 (SC); *HLC v MAL*, 2003 BCSC 1461; *Ryan v Ryan* (1985), 74 NSR (2d) 49 (SC (TD)).

111 *Synge v Synge*, [1900] P 180; *Menzies v Farnon* (1909), 18 OLR 174 (Div Ct).

112 *Downton v Downton Estate*, [1973] SCR 437.

3) Insincerity

The doctrine of "insincerity" may constitute a bar to the judicial annulment of a voidable marriage. A spouse may be precluded from impugning a voidable marriage if it has been previously approbated by the conduct of the parties. In an old English case, the doctrine of insincerity was explained in the following terms:

> I think I can perceive that the real basis of reasoning which underlines that phraseology is this, and nothing more than this, that there may be conduct on the part of the person seeking this remedy, which ought to estop that person from having it; as, for instance, any act from which the inference ought to be drawn that during the antecedent time the party has, with a knowledge of the facts and of the law, approbated the marriage which he or she seeks to get rid of, or has taken advantages and derived benefits from the matrimonial relation which it would be unfair and inequitable to permit him or her, after having received them, to treat as if no such relation had ever existed. Well now, that explanation can be referred to known principles of equitable, and, I may say, general jurisprudence. The circumstances which may justify it are various, and in cases of this kind many sorts of conduct might exist, taking pecuniary benefits, for example, living for a long time together in the same house, or family with the status and character of husband and wife, after knowledge of everything which it is material to know. I do not at all mean to say that there may not be other circumstances which would produce the same effect.[113]

An indirect or improper motive is not an adequate test of insincerity. Approbation of the marriage presupposes a knowledge of the facts that render the marriage defective and an awareness of the availability of a legal remedy.[114] There may be cases in which approbation may be found even in the absence of actual knowledge, if there has been the means of procuring knowledge.[115] Delay in the institution of nullity proceedings is not, of itself, a bar to relief,[116] but a culpable delay, with knowledge of the facts and law, is a significant factor in considering the insincerity of the petitioner.[117] The fact that each party continues to share, while under the same matrimonial roof, the

---

113 *G v M* (1885), 10 App Cas 171 (HL), Earl of Selbourne (LC), quoted in *J v J*, [1940] OR 284 at para 14 (HCJ), aff'd [1940] 4 DLR 807 (Ont CA); see also *Aisaican v Khanapace* (1996), 24 RFL (4th) 143 (Sask QB (Fam Div)).

114 *Hill v Hill*, [1959] 3 All ER 754; *B v B*, [1935] SCR 231.

115 *Pettit v Pettit*, [1962] 3 All ER 37 (CA).

116 *J v J*, [1940] OR 284 (HCJ), aff'd [1940] 4 DLR 807 (Ont CA).

117 *W v W*, [1952] 1 All ER 858 (CA); *B v B*, [1935] SCR 231.

normal domestic services derivable from a joint establishment, does not inevitably constitute the bar of insincerity,[118] but if such conduct is accompanied by a premarital agreement whereby the parties undertake not to engage in sexual intercourse after their marriage, the court may properly refuse to annul the marriage on the ground of non-consummation by reason of the petitioner's insincerity.[119] The annulment of a voidable marriage on the ground of non-consummation may also be barred by the petitioner's knowledge of his own or his spouse's impotence at the time of the marriage.[120]

Judicial opinion is divided on the question whether insincerity constitutes an absolute or only a discretionary bar to relief.[121] In an English case wherein the wife was granted an annulment of the marriage by reason of her husband's impotence, notwithstanding that she had given birth to a child after her artificial insemination with the husband's semen, the trial judge stated:

> If I am right the question of discretion does not arise, and it is irrelevant to weigh the public and private advantages of granting or refusing a decree. If I am wrong, I should, in the exercise of my discretion, grant a decree [because] I see no hope of happiness by keeping these two people married . . . . If I grant a decree it seems quite possible that the wife, who seems affectionate and likely to be a good wife, may marry again, and even the husband might marry again and conquer his inhibitions and enjoy normal married happiness. The future holds better augury for the child, I think, if I grant the decree than if he is brought up by an embittered mother who may be tied for life to a marriage that has never been a real marriage and which, only through the unnatural aid of science, has produced the fruit of a real marriage.[122]

The proper approach would seem to be for the court to initially determine whether the conduct of the parties constitutes approbation of the marriage and, if so, to then determine whether it is in the public interest and that of the parties and their children, if any, to grant or refuse a decree of nullity. In considering the public interest, the court should weigh the sanctity

---

118   *Scott v Scott*, [1959] 1 All ER 531, Sachs J.

119   *Norman v Norman* (1979), 9 RFL (2d) 345 (Ont U Fam Ct); *Aisaican v Khanapace* (1996), 24 RFL (4th) 143 (Sask QB (Fam Div)); see also *Scott v Scott*, [1959] 1 All ER 531; compare *Morgan v Morgan*, [1959] 1 All ER 539.

120   *Harthan v Harthan*, [1948] 2 All ER 639 (CA).

121   See *Clifford v Clifford*, [1948] 1 All ER 394 (CA); *REL v EL*, [1949] P 211; *Scott v Scott*, [1959] 1 All ER 531; *G v G*, [1960] 3 All ER 56.

122   *REL v EL*, [1949] P 211 at 218.

of marriage against the legal futility of preserving a marriage that has irretrievably broken down.

The doctrine of insincerity is confined to voidable marriages and has no application to void marriages, at least where the invalidity arises because of lack of capacity to marry.[123]

M. RELIGIOUS ANNULMENTS AND DIVORCE

Some religious faiths, such as the Roman Catholic, Jewish, and Muslim faiths, provide for religious annulment or divorce. A religious annulment or divorce is valid only for the purpose of religious practices. It does not terminate a marriage according to Canadian law. If spouses wish to terminate their marriage in law, they must petition the state courts for annulment or divorce. It is insufficient to obtain a religious annulment or divorce.

---

123 *Hayward v Hayward*, [1961] 1 All ER 236; *Saari v Nykanen*, [1944] OR 582 (HCJ); *Dejardin v Dejardin*, [1932] 2 WWR 237 (Man KB).

CHAPTER 3

Cohabitational Relationships[1]

A. INTRODUCTION

Cohabitational relationships involve two people who share their lives together but are not married to each other. Cohabitational relationships may involve members of the opposite sex or members of the same sex. Unmarried heterosexual cohabitation is sometimes referred to as a common law relationship. Unmarried cohabitants go under a variety of names, including common law spouse, co-vivant, significant other, mate, life partner, cohabitee, and cohabitant.

There are various reasons why some members of the opposite sex enter into unmarried cohabitational relationships instead of marriage. They include the following:

1) There may be a legal impediment to marriage — as, for example, where one of the parties has been previously married but is not divorced.
2) There may be some religious obstacle to marriage.
3) Marriage may be perceived by one or both of the parties as a patriarchal straitjacket that involves traditional homemaking and breadwinning roles that fail to recognize equality between the sexes.

---

1   For excellent sources dealing with the legal implications of unmarried cohabitation in Canada, see Alberta Law Reform Institute, *Towards Reform of the Law Relating to Cohabitation Outside Marriage*, Report No 53 (Edmonton: The Institute, 1989); Ontario Law Reform Commission, *Report on The Rights and Responsibilities of Cohabitants under the Family Law Act* (Toronto: The Commission, 1993); Winifred H Holland & Barbro E Stalbecker-Pountney, *Cohabitation: The Law in Canada*, loose-leaf (Toronto: Carswell, 1990–). As to the possibility of extending legal rights and obligations to a broader range of personal relationships, see Law Commission of Canada, Discussion Paper, "Recognizing and Supporting Close Personal Relationships Between Adults," online: www.lcc.gc.ca.

4) Marriage imposes certain legal rights and obligations that one or both parties might wish to avoid. They may have been involved in a previous marriage breakdown that carries emotional and economic scars and may assume that history cannot repeat itself if they avoid the marriage "trap." Any such assumption is misplaced, however, because the emotional trauma of the breakdown of a relationship is not conditioned on whether the parties are married. Furthermore, unmarried cohabitation may carry significant economic consequences that are legally enforceable on the breakdown of the relationship.

5) Changing social mores and the weakening of religious influences have largely removed the stigma that formerly attached to unmarried cohabitants of the opposite sex.

6) Many young couples enter into unmarried cohabitation as a "trial marriage" that can be informally terminated or legally formalized at some time in the future. Conversion to marital status is often triggered by the anticipated birth of a child.

7) Unmarried cohabitation may enable one or both of the parties to preserve their entitlement to certain benefits, such as support payments or pension payments, which would be lost in the event of remarriage.

8) Many couples who begin sleeping over at each other's houses slip into a cohabitational relationship as a matter of convenience rather than as a consequence of carefully weighing the pros and cons of married and unmarried cohabitation.

On 12 September 2007, Statistics Canada released data from the 2006 Census on the subject of marital status, common law unions, and families. Included in that report is the following:

> The census enumerated 6,105,910 married-couple families, an increase of only 3.5% from 2001. In contrast, the number of common-law-couple families surged 18.9% to 1,376,865, while the number of lone-parent families increased 7.8% to 1,414,060.
>
> Consequently, married-couple families accounted for 68.6% of all census families in 2006, down from 70.5% five years earlier. The proportion of common-law-couple families rose from 13.8% to 15.5%, while the share of lone-parent families increased slightly from 15.7% to 15.9%.
>
> Two decades ago, common-law-couple families accounted for only 7.2% of all census families. Married-couple families represented 80.2%, and lone-parent families, 12.7%.
>
> In Quebec, where the prevalence of common-law-couple families has been one of the defining family patterns for years, the number of common-law-couple families increased 20.3% between 2001 and 2006 to 611,855. They

accounted for 44.4% of the national total. Close to one-quarter (23.4%) of all common-law-couple families in Canada lived in the two census metropolitan areas of Montréal and Québec.[2]

What the above data fail to reveal is that common-law relationships may be less enduring than marital relationships and the risk of children under the age of ten encountering family breakdown is much greater when they are children of unmarried cohabitants than when they are children of married couples. Based on a longitudinal study of approximately 23,000 children in Canada, a report entitled *Growing Up With Mom and Dad: The Intricate Family Life of Canadian Children*[3] concludes that only 13.6 percent of the children under ten experienced family breakdown when they were born after their parents' marriage, whereas more than 63 percent of the children whose parents cohabited but never married encountered family breakdown before the age of ten.

B. LEGAL CONSEQUENCES OF UNMARRIED COHABITATION AS COMPARED TO MARRIAGE

In previous generations, unmarried cohabitants were disentitled to the protection of the law. By the 1980s, social attitudes and the law had undergone radical changes, at least with respect to unmarried cohabitants of the opposite sex. The social stigma that formerly attached to unmarried heterosexual cohabitation has now largely disappeared. The law has, nevertheless, been cautious in its response to unmarried cohabitation. The law does not assimilate the consequences of marriage and unmarried cohabitation, although legal recognition has been extended to unmarried cohabitation in various contexts in light of the judgments of the Supreme Court of Canada in *Miron v Trudel*[4] and *M v H*.[5] In consequence of *M v H*, federal, provincial, and territorial statutes have established diverse rights and obligations as between unmarried cohabitants of the opposite sex and unmarried cohabitants of the same sex.

2   Statistics Canada, *The Daily* (12 September 2007). See also *Quebec (Attorney General) v A*, 2013 SCC 5, rev'g 2010 QCCA 1978.

3   Statistics Canada, by Nicole Marcil-Gratton (Ottawa: Ministry of Industry, 1998) Catalogue No 89-566-XIE.

4   [1995] 2 SCR 18 (spouse judicially redefined pursuant to s 15 of the *Canadian Charter of Rights and Freedoms* to include unmarried heterosexual cohabitants of three years' standing under automobile insurance policy).

5   [1999] 2 SCR 3 (assimilation of statutory support rights of cohabitants of the same sex with those of cohabitants of opposite sex); and see Section D, below in this chapter. With respect to former unmarried cohabitants of the opposite sex, compare *Quebec (Attorney General) v A*, 2013 SCC 5, in Section B, below in this chapter.

In July 2000, the federal government passed omnibus legislation, entitled the *Modernization of Obligations and Benefits Act*, which amended sixty statutes for the purpose of assimilating the rights and obligations of same-sex couples and opposite-sex couples. In 1999, Ontario enacted the *Amendments Because of the Supreme Court of Canada Decision in M v H Act*,[6] which amended the *Family Law Act* so that its support provisions apply to same-sex couples as well as opposite-sex couples. The provisions of the *Family Law Act* with respect to cohabitation agreements, separation agreements, and claims for damages by family dependents were also amended to include same-sex cohabitants. Various other rights and obligations under Ontario statutes were also extended to same-sex couples, namely the *Change of Name Act*,[7] the *Child and Family Services Act*,[8] the *Children's Law Reform Act*,[9] the *Courts of Justice Act*,[10] the *Family Responsibility and Support Orders Arrears Enforcement Act, 1996*,[11] the *Pension Benefits Act*,[12] and the *Succession Law Reform Act*.[13] It is noteworthy, however, that spousal property rights and intestate succession rights in Ontario have not been extended to either same-sex or opposite-sex unmarried cohabitants.[14] Other provinces and territories have introduced amendments to their legislation to bring them in line with the ruling of the Supreme Court of Canada in *M v H*.[15]

The *Canadian Charter of Rights and Freedoms*[16] and federal and provincial human rights codes have generated claims by unmarried cohabitants of the same sex to benefits that have in the past been confined to married couples and to unmarried couples of the opposite sex. These include pension benefits; welfare assistance; workers' compensation; life, health, and disability insurance; and tax advantages. These benefits may be regulated by federal,

---

6 SO 1999, c 6.

7 RSO 1990, c C.7.

8 RSO 1990, c C.11.

9 RSO 1990, c C.12.

10 SO 1994, c 12.

11 SO 1996, c 31.

12 RSO 1990, c P.8.

13 RSO 1990, c S.26.

14 See Lorne H Wolfson & Carol A Dalgado, "Some Thoughts on Family and Estates Matters After *M v H* (Part I)" (February 2000) 15:2 Money & Family Law at 9–12; Lorne H Wolfson & Carol A Dalgado, "Some Thoughts on Family and Estates Matters After *M v H* (Part II)"; "Testate and Intestate Succession and Dependants Relief Post *M. v H.*" (March 2000) 15:3 Money & Family Law at 17–19.

15 See, for example, *Adult Interdependent Relationships Act*, SA 2002, c A-4.5; *Common Law Partners' Property and Related Amendments Act*, SM 2002, c 48; *Law Reform (2000) Act*, SNS 2000, c 9; *An Act instituting civil unions and establishing new rules of filiation*, SQ 2002, c 6.

16 *The Constitution Act, 1982*, being Schedule B to the *Canada Act 1982 (UK)*, 1982, c 11 [*Charter*].

provincial, or territorial legislation but the restrictive application of such legislation to married persons or unmarried heterosexual cohabitants has been successfully challenged for the most part. In the context of private family law, however, the Supreme Court of Canada, in *Quebec (Attorney General) v A*,[17] has rejected a *Charter* challenge of several articles in the *Civil Code of Québec* that deny interspousal property and support rights to so-called *de facto* spouses, that is, couples who are neither married nor parties to a civil union in Quebec.

C. COHABITATION AGREEMENTS

In the distant past, courts refused to recognize or enforce agreements entered into by unmarried cohabitants. Such agreements were regarded as illegal and contrary to public policy on the basis of immorality. In view of fundamental changes in social attitudes in the latter part of the twentieth century, courts have abandoned their original stance by upholding the validity and enforceability of contracts entered into by unmarried cohabitants. In *Chrispen v Topham*,[18] for example, where unmarried heterosexual cohabitants entered into a written agreement respecting the sharing of household expenses and a collateral oral agreement respecting the performance of domestic chores, both agreements were found to be in default and were held enforceable by way of damages or monetary compensation. Recognition has also been granted to contractual arrangements entered into by unmarried cohabitants of the same sex. In *Anderson v Luoma*,[19] a British Columbia court acknowledged the right of a lesbian to pursue contractual and property claims against her mate. The contractual claim was dismissed, however, on the ground that the evidence did not support a finding that a contract had been entered into. The alternative claim to share in property on the basis of the doctrine of unjust enrichment was upheld. Accordingly, the claimant was entitled to a 20 percent interest in certain property that had been acquired by her mate during their relationship. These judicial developments occurred in the absence of any express statutory authority.

Although provincial and territorial legislation in Canada throughout the twentieth century remained silent on the question of whether same-sex cohabitants could enter into legally binding contracts, several provinces and one territory enacted legislation that expressly permitted unmarried cohabitants of the opposite sex to enter into "cohabitation agreements." The

---

17   2013 SCC 5.

18   (1986), 3 RFL (3d) 149 (Sask QB), aff'd (1987), 9 RFL (3d) 131 (Sask CA).

19   (1986), 50 RFL (2d) 127 (BCSC).

relevant statutory provisions in New Brunswick, Newfoundland, Ontario, Prince Edward Island, and the Yukon are broad in scope. In general, they empower unmarried cohabitants of the opposite sex to enter into "cohabitation agreements" for the purpose of regulating ownership in or the division of property, spousal and child support rights and obligations, and other matters in the settlement of their affairs. Except in British Columbia and the Yukon, matters relating to custody of and access to children fall outside the scope of cohabitation agreements, although such agreements may regulate the religious or secular education of children. In Ontario, a cohabitation agreement may be entered into before the commencement of cohabitation or during cohabitation. In New Brunswick, Newfoundland, Prince Edward Island, and the Yukon, the parties must be cohabiting at the time when they enter into a cohabitation agreement. However, these jurisdictions, together with Ontario, also entitle former unmarried cohabitants to enter into "separation agreements" after cohabitation has ceased. Separation agreements may regulate custody of and access to children in addition to the same matters that can be regulated by cohabitation agreements. The provisions of a cohabitation agreement may anticipate a future separation. Indeed, a cohabitation agreement may regulate the rights and obligations of the parties during cohabitation, on separation, or on the death of either party. It may be wise, however, for cohabitants to substitute a new separation agreement for the old cohabitation agreement in the event of a termination of their relationship. This is especially important if children are involved and arrangements for their support and for custody and access must be determined.

All domestic contracts that are governed by provincial or territorial statutes must be in writing, signed by the parties, and witnessed.[20] Independent legal representation or advice is not legally required, although a court is more likely to set aside a domestic contract on the ground of duress, undue influence, or unconscionability if a party was not legally represented. Relevant provincial or territorial legislation empowers a court to set aside any provisions of a domestic contract that are contrary to the best interests of children. In addition, the courts are statutorily empowered to override the support provisions of a cohabitation agreement or any other domestic contract in specified circumstances.[21]

Although the aforementioned provincial and territorial legislation specifically extended a qualified contractual autonomy only to unmarried co-

---

20   Compare *Chrispen v Topham*, (1986), 3 RFL (3d) 149 (Sask QB), aff'd (1987), 3 RFL (3d) 131 (Sask CA).

21   *Family Services Act*, SNB 1980, c F-2.2, s 115(5); *Family Law Act*, RSN 1990, c F-2, s 39(5); *Family Law Act*, RSO 1990, c F.3, s 33(4); *Family Law Act*, SPEI 1995, c 12, s 18(4); *Family Property and Support Act*, RSY 1986, c 63, s 34(4).

habitants of the opposite sex, the decision of the Supreme Court of Canada in *M v H*, which assimilates the rights of unmarried cohabitants of the same sex with those of unmarried cohabitants of the opposite sex pursuant to section 15 of the *Canadian Charter of Rights and Freedoms*, has caused provincial and territorial legislatures to revisit and amend current provincial and territorial statutes so as to assimilate the legal rights and obligations of unmarried cohabitants of either sex.

In *Doe v Alberta*,[22] the Alberta Court of Appeal held that cohabiting partners cannot contractually oust the jurisdiction of the court to grant future orders determining their parental rights and obligations under the *Family Law Act*[23] with respect to a child born to the mother as a result of her artificial insemination by an unknown sperm donor. In upholding the trial judgment, the Alberta Court of Appeal observed that an express declaration in a written agreement that the mother's male cohabitant does not intend to assume a parental role or the legal obligations of a parent will not preclude a finding that the cohabitant's subsequent conduct has demonstrated a settled intention to treat the child as his own within the meaning of section 48(2) of the *Family Law Act*, thus triggering a child support obligation. The Alberta Court of Appeal further concluded that sections 53, 85, and 86 of the *Family Law Act*, which provide qualified recognition of parental agreements subject to the court's supervisory jurisdiction, do not contravene section 7 of the *Charter of Rights and Freedoms*.

D. SUPPORT RIGHTS AND OBLIGATIONS BETWEEN UNMARRIED COHABITANTS

In the common law provinces and territories, statutes confer mutual support rights and obligations on unmarried cohabitants, whether of the opposite sex or the same sex, provided that the prescribed statutory conditions are satisfied. Some statutes require that the parties cohabit or live together in a conjugal relationship for a minimum period, which usually ranges from one year to three years according to the particular province where the parties reside. Several provinces also impose support obligations upon unmarried cohabitants who have lived in a relationship of some permanence and are the natural or adoptive parents of a child.[24]

---

22 2007 ABCA 50.

23 SA 2003, c F-4.5.

24 For a succinct review of the statutory criteria that determine whether parties are interdependent partners who are subject to support rights and obligations under the *Adult Interdependent Relationships Act*, SA 2002, c A-4.5 and s 56 of the *Family Law Act*, SA 2003, c F-4.5, see *EVF v WM*, 2010 ABQB 451. As to the denial of spousal support rights to *de*

In the context of provincial and territorial statutory support rights and obligations, cohabitation signifies a marriage-like relationship. Not all arrangements whereby a man and a woman live together and engage in sexual activity will suffice to trigger statutory support rights and obligations.[25] As was observed by Morrison JA, of the Nova Scotia Court of Appeal,

> I think it would be fair to say that to establish a common-law relationship there must be some sort of stable relationship which involves not only sexual activity but a commitment between the parties. It would normally necessitate living under the same roof with shared household duties and responsibilities as well as financial support.[26]

More specific judicial guidance as to what constitutes cohabitation or a conjugal or marriage-like relationship is found in a judgment of the Ontario District Court,[27] wherein Kurisko DCJ identified the following issues as relevant:

1. Shelter:
    (a) Did the parties live under the same roof?
    (b) What were the sleeping arrangements?
    (c) Did anyone else occupy or share the available accommodation?

2. Sexual and Personal Behaviour:
    (a) Did the parties have sexual relations? If not, why not?
    (b) Did they maintain an attitude of fidelity to each other?
    (c) What were their feelings toward each other?
    (d) Did they communicate on a personal level?
    (e) Did they eat their meals together?
    (f) What, if anything, did they do to assist each other with problems or during illness?
    (g) Did they buy gifts for each other on special occasions?

---

facto spouses in Quebec who are neither married nor parties to a civil union, see *Quebec (Attorney General) v A*, 2013 SCC 5.

25 See *Jansen v Montgomery* (1982), 30 RFL (2d) 332 (NS Co Ct).

26 *Soper v Soper* (1985), 67 NSR (2d) 49 at 53 (CA).

27 *Molodowich v Penttinen* (1980), 17 RFL (2d) 376 at 381–82 (Ont Dist Ct); see also *Sporring v Collins*, 2009 ABQB 141; *Gostlin v Kergin* (1986), 3 BCLR (2d) 264 at 267–68 (CA); *Austin v Goerz*, 2007 BCCA 586; *Roach v Dutra*, 2010 BCCA 264; *Field v McLaren*, [2009] MJ No 155 (QB); *Kelly v Rockwell*, 2010 NBQB 168; *Evely v Evely*, [2003] NJ No 85 (SC); *Bakes v Bakes*, [2003] NSJ No 202 (SC); *Rosseter v Rosseter*, 2013 ONSC 7779 (application under the *Family Law Act*); *Romanchuk v Robin*, 2003 SKCA 50; *Wionzek v Magyar*, 2013 SKQB 194 (application under *The Family Property Act*). For endorsement of *Molodowich v Penttinen* by the Supreme Court of Canada, see *M v H*, [1999] 2 SCR 3 at paras 56–60. And see *Milot v Canada*, [1995] TCJ No 412; *Perron c Canada*, 2010 TCC 547.

3. Services:
    What was the conduct and habit of the parties in relation to:
    (a) preparation of meals;
    (b) washing and mending clothes;
    (c) shopping;
    (d) household maintenance; and
    (e) any other domestic services?

4. Social:
    (a) Did they participate together or separately in neighbourhood and community activities?
    (b) What was the relationship and conduct of each of them towards members of their respective families and how did such families behave towards the parties?

5. Societal:
    What was the attitude and conduct of the community towards each of them and as a couple?

6. Support (economic):
    (a) What were the financial arrangements between the parties regarding the provision of or contribution towards the necessaries of life (food, clothing, shelter, recreation, etc.)?
    (b) What were the arrangements concerning the acquisition and ownership of property?
    (c) Was there any special financial arrangement between them which both agreed would be determinant of their overall relationship?

7. Children:
    What was the attitude and conduct of the parties concerning children?

These seven elements may be present in varying degrees and not all of them need exist in order for the relationship to be regarded as "spousal" or conjugal.[28] Similar factors were identified by Hunter J, of the Saskatchewan Court of Queen's Bench, in *Tanouye v Tanouy*,[29] who observed:

> The authorities seem to indicate that a common-law relationship or marriage requires perhaps not all but at least a majority of the following characteristics: economic interdependence including an intention to support;

---

28 *Molodowich v Penttinen* (1980), 17 RFL (2d) 376 (Ont Dist Ct); *Broadbear v Prothero*, 2011 ONSC 3656.

29 (1973), 117 Sask R 196 at para 36 (QB), var'd on other grounds (1995), 134 Sask R 159 (CA); see also *Martin v Riley*, 2014 ABQB 725.

a commitment to the relationship, express or implied, for at least an extended period of time; sharing of a common principal residence; a common desire to make a home together and to share responsibilities in and towards that home; where applicable, shared responsibilities of child rearing; and a sexual relationship. As well, it appears that, superimposed on the relationship, there should be the general recognition of family, friends, and perhaps to some extent the larger community, that the particular man and woman appear as a "couple", i.e. a family unit.

Additional factors that may be relevant include the following:

1. Provisions made in the event of illness or death. For example, were they named as beneficiaries in each other's wills, RRSPs, pensions, life insurance or health plans? Did they give each other powers of attorney or decision-making authority on health care?

2. Are documents available that identify their relationship as spousal, such as income tax returns and elections under pension or health plans?

3. Did their future plans include each other? For example, were there plans to marry, have children, or for a joint retirement?

4. What is the motivation for the relationship, i.e. why are they together?[30]

Because of the wide variety of interpersonal relationships, no single factor is determinative of whether a spousal relationship exists. All relevant factors must be weighed to reach a judicial determination, although some may be given more weight than others. After considering sixteen factors relating to the interpersonal relationship between the parties in *Yakichuk v Oaks*,[31] Ryan-Froslie J, (as she then was) of the Saskatchewan Court of Queen's Bench, had no hesitation in concluding that a spousal relationship had existed for more than two years within the meaning of section 2(1) of the *Family Property Act* (Saskatchewan).

A flexible objective approach to the relevant factors, rather than a focus on the subjective intentions of either party, is preferable if society and its laws are to respond to the diversity of interpersonal relationships that generate dependence such as justifies the existence of support rights and obligations on the breakdown of intimate relationships.[32]

In summary, the court must examine the relationship as a whole in light of the objective factors identified in relevant caselaw. The presence or absence

---

30 *Yakichuk v Oaks*, [2003] SJ No 216 (QB); see also *Munday v Moore*, 2011 SKQB 122.

31 *Yakichuk v Oaks*, [2003] SJ No 216 (QB).

32 *Spracklin v Kichton*, [2000] AJ No 1329 (QB); *MacMillan-Dekker v Dekker*, [2000] OJ No 2957 (Sup Ct).

of one particular factor will not be determinative. The court must recognize that each relationship is unique and, in applying a flexible approach within the context of the particular relationship, make a determination as to whether the parties intended to and were living in a marriage-like relationship.[33] As Frankel JA, of the British Columbia Court of Appeal, observed in *Austin v Goerz*,[34] "there is no checklist of characteristics that will invariably be found in all marriages." These cases are invariably fact-driven.[35] In *Roach v Dutra*,[36] for example, a marriage-like relationship was found to exist even though the parties had been residing in separate dwellings.

With respect to what constitutes a termination of the relationship, the key factors include the absence of sexual relations, a clear statement by one of the parties of his or her intention to terminate the relationship, the physical separation of the parties into different rooms of the same house or different residences, and the cessation of the presentation to the outside world that they are a couple.[37] As was stated by the Ontario Court of Appeal in *Sanderson v Russell*,

> Without in any way attempting to be detailed or comprehensive, it could be said that such a relationship has come to an end when either party regards it as being at an end, and, by his or her conduct, has demonstrated in a convincing manner that this particular state of mind is a settled one.[38]

Sexual infidelities do not preclude a finding that the parties cohabited continuously for more than three years and accordingly are spouses for the purpose of support rights and obligations under Part III of the Ontario *Family Law Act*.[39]

When support rights and obligations arise pursuant to provincial or territorial legislation, the needs of the applicant and the ability of the other party to pay are critical factors, but the court should also consider legislatively stipulated objectives of support orders that encompass both compensatory and non-compensatory support principles.[40] In addressing the common law wife's claims to lump sum and ongoing periodic spousal support in *Johnstone v Wright*,[41] the British Columbia Court of Appeal had no hesitation in

---

33   *MacKechnie v Schubert*, 2012 BCSC 509; *Broadbear v Prothero*, 2011 ONSC 3656.

34   2007 BCCA 586 at para 58.

35   *Stace-Smith v Lecompte*, 2011 BCCA 129 at para 14, Prowse JA.

36   2010 BCCA 264; see also *Campbell v Campbell*, 2011 BCSC 1491.

37   *Eisener v Baker*, 2007 BCSC 83; *JJG v KMA*, 2009 BCSC 1056.

38   (1979), 24 OR (2d) 429 at 432 (CA).

39   *Conde v Ripley*, 2009 ONCA 480.

40   *Freake v Riley*, 2010 ABQB 562; *Brick v Cross*, 2014 ABQB 35; *McGee v Ranson*, [2003] MJ No 304 (QB); *Halliday v Halliday* (1997), 37 RFL (4th) 192 (Ont CA).

41   2005 BCCA 254.

declaring that these claims could not be advanced on either a contractual or a compensatory basis. With respect to non-compensatory support, the British Columbia Court of Appeal stated that the common law wife's enjoyment of an affluent lifestyle during cohabitation did not imply that the law should turn her emotional need to continue that lifestyle into a legal obligation on the part of her former common law husband. While accepting that some transitional spousal support was appropriate to cushion the common law wife's difficulty in adjusting to her pre-cohabitation lifestyle, the British Columbia Court of Appeal concluded that her receipt of interim support for three and a half years after the breakdown of the relationship had already provided a generous period of adjustment, and to allow any additional support would defeat the statutory goal of encouraging spouses to strive for economic self-sufficiency to the extent that this is reasonable and practicable on the breakdown of their relationship.

E. PROPERTY RIGHTS

Every Canadian province and territory has enacted legislation to provide for the sharing of property between spouses on marriage breakdown or divorce. Unmarried cohabitants are not always covered by this legislation and cannot invoke section 15 of the *Canadian Charter of Rights and Freedoms* to claim statutory property rights.[42]

Although British Columbia,[43] Manitoba,[44] Nova Scotia, Nunavut, the Northwest Territories, Quebec, Saskatchewan,[45] and the Yukon Territory currently confer statutory rights on unmarried cohabitants under prescribed conditions, Alberta, New Brunswick, and Newfoundland and Labrador continue to exclude all unmarried cohabitants from their matrimonial property regimes. Consequently, there is a patchwork quilt of diverse provincial and territorial regimes in Canada, which will continue to generate litigation that may become relatively complex in light of the inter-provincial mobility of Canadians and the implications of private international law rules.

Unmarried cohabitants receive some measure of protection across Canada under the judge-made doctrine of unjust enrichment, but this doctrine, unlike statutory matrimonial support regimes, does not trigger any presumption of equal sharing on the breakdown of the relationship. In order for

---

42 *Quebec (Attorney General) v A*, 2013 SCC 5; see also *Nova Scotia (Attorney General) v Walsh*, 2002 SCC 83; *Jackson v Zaruba*, 2013 BCCA 81.

43 *Family Law Act*, SBC 2011, c 25, effective 18 March 2013.

44 *Jensen v Schevelik*, 2010 MBQB 144; *Stuart v Toth*, 2011 MBCA 42.

45 *Thurlow v Shedden*, [2009] SJ No 59 (QB); *Busse v Gadd*, [2009] SJ No 151 (QB); *Munday v Moore*, 2011 SKQB 122.

the doctrine of unjust enrichment to apply, three conditions must be satisfied; there must be

1)   a benefit or enrichment of one party;
2)   a corresponding deprivation of the other party; and
3)   the absence of any juristic reason or legal justification for the enrichment, such as a contract or gift.

As Handrigan J, of the Newfoundland and Labrador Supreme Court, remarked in *Fewer v Smith*,[46] Huddart JA's "basic outline" in the judgment of the British Columbia Court of Appeal in *Wilson v Fotsch*[47] is rapidly emerging as a template for analyzing claims in family cases based on unjust enrichment. Huddart JA's outline for the requisite analysis is summarized as follows:

1.   Benefit/Enrichment
2.   Detriment
3.   Absence of a juristic reason for the enrichment
     a.   Established categories
          i.   Contract
          ii.   Disposition of law
          iii. Donative intent
          iv.   Other valid common law, equitable, or statutory obligations
     b.   Reason to deny recovery
          i.   Public policy considerations
          ii.   Legitimate expectations
          iii. Potential new category

Defences
     Change of position; estoppel; statutory defences; laches and acquiescence; limitation periods;[48] counter-restitution not possible

Choice of Remedy
     a.   Is a monetary remedy sufficient?
     b.   Is a constructive trust required (or equitable damages for the value of the trust interest)?

Quantification of the Remedy
     a.   Value received (quantum meruit basis)
     b.   Value survived (proportionate share basis)

Set-Off (equitable and legal)

Pre-judgment interest

---

46   2014 NLTD(F) 18 at para 6.
47   2010 BCCA 226 at para 11. See also *Stewart v Stewart*, 2014 BCSC 766; *Wood v Davis*, 2014 BCSC 1513.
48   See *Martin v Sansome*, 2014 ONCA 14.

Remedies for unjust enrichment are restitutionary in nature. A successful claimant may be entitled to a monetary or a proprietary remedy. Only in cases where a monetary award is inappropriate or insufficient will a proprietary remedy be required by way of a remedial constructive trust. Imposed without reference to intention to create a trust, the constructive trust is a broad and flexible equitable tool used to determine beneficial entitlement to property. Where the claimant can demonstrate a link or causal connection between his or her contributions and the acquisition, preservation, maintenance, or improvement of the disputed property, a share of the property proportionate to the unjust enrichment can be impressed with a constructive trust in his or her favour. As to the nature of the link required between the contribution and the property, the plaintiff must demonstrate a "sufficiently substantial and direct" link, a "causal connection," or a "nexus" between the plaintiff's contributions and the property that is the subject matter of the trust. A minor or indirect contribution will not suffice. The primary focus is on whether the contributions have a "clear proprietary relationship." Indirect contributions of money and direct contributions of labour may suffice, provided that a connection is established between the plaintiff's deprivation and the acquisition, preservation, maintenance, or improvement of the property. In this regard, the court may take into account the probability of recovery, as well as whether there is a reason to grant the plaintiff the additional rights that flow from recognition of property rights. The extent of the constructive trust interest should be proportionate to the claimant's contributions. Where the contributions are unequal, the shares will be unequal. The court will assess the contributions made by each domestic partner and make a fair, equitable distribution having regard to their respective contributions. In most cases, a monetary award will be sufficient to remedy the unjust enrichment. However, calculation of such an award is far from straightforward. Two issues have given rise to disagreement and difficulty in domestic unjust enrichment claims. First, the fact that many domestic claims of unjust enrichment arise out of relationships in which there has been a mutual conferral of benefits gives rise to difficulties in determining what will constitute adequate compensation. A second difficulty arises from the fact that some courts have concluded that when a monetary award is appropriate, it must invariably be calculated on the basis of the monetary value of the unpaid services. This is often referred to as the *quantum meruit*, or "value received," or "fee-for-services" approach. These issues were addressed by the Supreme Court of Canada in *Kerr v Baranow* and *Vanasse v Seguin*,[49] wherein Cromwell J,

---

49   2011 SCC 10; see also *Brick v Cross*, 2014 ABQB 35; *JJS v MSW*, 2013 BCSC 287; *Cork v Cork*, 2014 ONSC 2488. Compare *Rubin v Gendemann*, 2012 ABCA 38. See, generally, Berend

who delivered the unanimous judgment of the Court, pointed out that some courts have taken the view that, if a claimant's contribution cannot be linked to specific property, a monetary remedy must always be assessed on a "value received" or fee-for-services basis, whereas other courts have taken a more flexible approach by adopting a "value survived" approach based on the overall increase in the couple's wealth during their relationship. While asserting that it is not the purpose of the law of unjust enrichment to replicate for unmarried partners the legislative presumption that married partners are engaged in a joint family venture, Cromwell J concluded that the common law of unjust enrichment can and should recognize and respond to the reality that there are unmarried domestic arrangements that are partnerships and the remedy in such cases should address the disproportionate retention of assets acquired through joint efforts. In the words of Cromwell J:

> [W]here both parties have worked together for the common good, with each making extensive, but different, contributions to the welfare of the other and, as a result, have accumulated assets, the money remedy for unjust enrichment should reflect that reality. The money remedy in those circumstances should not be based on a minute totting up of the give and take of daily domestic life, but rather should treat the claimant as a co-venturer, not as the hired help.[50]

Justice Cromwell reasoned that

> restricting the money remedy to a fee-for-services calculation is inappropriate for four reasons. First, it fails to reflect the reality of the lives of many domestic partners. Second, it is inconsistent with the inherent flexibility of unjust enrichment. Third, it ignores the historical basis of *quantum meruit* claims. Finally, it is not mandated by the Court's judgment in *Peter [v Beblow*, [1993] 1 SCR 980].[51]

He further noted that "the law relating to when a proprietary remedy should be granted is well established and remains unchanged."[52] Developing the theme that not all unjust enrichments arising between domestic partners fit comfortably into either a "fee-for-services" or a "share of specific property" mold, Cromwell J stated:[53]

Hovius, "Property Disputes between Common-Law Partners: The Supreme Court of Canada's Decisions in *Vanasse v Seguin* and *Kerr v Baranow*" (2011) 30 Can Fam LQ 129. As to the applicability of statutory limitation periods to applications based on unjust enrichment and constructive trust, see *McConnell v Huxtable*, 2014 ONCA 86.

50   *Kerr v Baranow* and *Vanasse v Seguin*, 2011 SCC 10 at para 7.
51   *Ibid* at para 58.
52   *Ibid*.
53   *Ibid* at paras 80–81.

Where the unjust enrichment is best characterized as an unjust retention of a disproportionate share of assets accumulated during the course of what McLachlin J. referred to in *Peter* (at p. 1001) as a "joint family venture" to which both partners have contributed, the monetary remedy should reflect that fact.

In such cases, the basis of the unjust enrichment is the retention of an inappropriately disproportionate amount of wealth by one party when the parties have been engaged in a joint family venture and there is a clear link between the claimant's contributions to the joint venture and the accumulation of wealth. Irrespective of the status of legal title to particular assets, the parties in those circumstances are realistically viewed as "creating wealth in a common enterprise that will assist in sustaining their relationship, their well-being and their family life" . . . . The wealth created during the period of cohabitation will be treated as the fruit of their domestic and financial relationship, though not necessarily by the parties in equal measure. Since the spouses are domestic and financial partners, there is no need for "duelling *quantum meruits*". In such cases, the unjust enrichment is understood to arise because the party who leaves the relationship with a disproportionate share of the wealth is denying to the claimant a reasonable share of the wealth accumulated in the course of the relationship through their joint efforts. The monetary award for unjust enrichment should be assessed by determining the proportionate contribution of the claimant to the accumulation of the wealth.

A joint family venture is characterized by a relationship in which the contributions of both parties have resulted in an accumulation of wealth.[54] The concept of a "joint family venture" can apply to a single asset; there is nothing in *Kerr* that precludes a joint family venture over part of a couple's assets.[55] Justice Cromwell observed that there are no closed lists of relevant factors to consider in determining whether the parties have engaged in a joint family venture, but suggests that courts will find it helpful to evaluate the evidence under the following four main headings:[56] first, mutual effort, which involves the parties working collaboratively towards common goals; second, the degree of economic interdependence and integration that characterized their relationship; third, the actual intentions of the parties as expressed or manifested by their conduct; and fourth, the extent to which the parties have given priority to the family in their decision making, the focus being on their respective contributions to the domestic and financial

---

54   *Symmons v Symmons*, 2012 ONCA 747; *Glasco v Bilz*, 2014 ONSC 7202.

55   *Ibbotson v Fung*, 2013 BCCA 171.

56   *Kerr v Baranow* and *Vanasse v Seguin*, 2011 SCC 10 at para 89.

partnership and on sacrifices made for the benefit of the family unit.[57] Addressing the question of how and at which point in the unjust enrichment analysis the mutual conferral of benefits should be taken into account, the Supreme Court of Canada endorsed the mutual benefit analysis mapped out by Huddart JA in *Wilson v Fotsch*[58] in concluding that

> . . . mutual benefit conferral can be taken into account at the juristic reason stage of the analysis, but only to the extent that it provides relevant evidence of the existence of a juristic reason for the enrichment. Otherwise, the mutual exchange of benefits should be taken into account at the defence and/or remedy stage. It is important to note that this can, and should, take place whether or not the defendant has made a formal counterclaim or pleaded set-off.[59]

Addressing the question of what role the parties' reasonable and legitimate expectations play in determining whether there is a juristic reason for the enrichment in light of the two-step approach to a juristic reason analysis that is mandated by *Garland v Consumers Gas Co*,[60] Cromwell J summarized the conclusions of the Supreme Court of Canada in these words:

1. The parties' reasonable or legitimate expectations have little role to play in deciding whether the services were provided for a juristic reason within the existing categories.

2. In some cases, the facts that mutual benefits were conferred or that the benefits were provided pursuant to the parties' reasonable expectations may be relevant evidence of whether one of the existing categories of juristic reasons is present. An example might be whether there was a contract for the provision of the benefits. However, generally the existence of mutual benefits flowing from the defendant to the claimant will not be considered at the juristic reason stage of the analysis.

3. The parties' reasonable or legitimate expectations have a role to play at the second step of the juristic reason analysis, that is, where the

---

57   See *Rubin v Gendemann*, 2012 ABCA 38; *Montgomery v Schlender*, 2012 ABQB 332; *Macgregor v Hosack*, 2012 ABQB 647; *KLK v KTW*, 2011 BCSC 411; *McNaught v Friedman*, 2011 BCSC 524; *JJS v MSW*, 2013 BCSC 287; *Bartlett v Murphy*, 2011 NBQB 139; *Dunn v Murphy*, 2013 NSSC 444; *Geertsma v Smith*, 2011 ONSC 5521; *Toquero v Ramirez*, 2011 YKSC 81. Compare *Broadbear v Prothero*, 2011 ONSC 3656; *Jackson v McNee*, 2011 ONSC 4651. See also Justice Jennifer Mackinnon & Cheryl Wood, "*Kerr v Baranow*: Initial Judicial Responses to Unanswered Questions" (paper delivered at the County of Carleton Law Association, 21st Annual Family Law Institute, Ottawa, 13 April 2012).

58   2010 BCCA 226.

59   *Kerr v Baranow* and *Vanasse v Seguin*, 2011 SCC 10 at para 109.

60   2004 SCC 25.

defendant bears the burden of establishing that there is a juristic reason for retaining the benefit which does not fall within the existing
categories. It is the mutual or legitimate expectations of both parties
that must be considered, and not simply the expectations of either the
claimant or the defendant. The question is whether the parties' expectations show that retention of the benefits is just.[61]

Applying the aforementioned criteria, the Supreme Court of Canada held
that the Court of Appeal in *Vanasse v Seguin* erred by ruling that the trial
judge ought to have performed a *quantum meruit* calculation in which the
value that each party received from the other should have been assessed and
set off. Acting on its ruling that monetary compensation for unjust enrichment need not always be calculated on a *quantum meruit* basis, the Supreme
Court of Canada reinstated the judgment of the trial judge on the basis that,
though not labelled as such, the trial judge found that there was a joint
family venture and a link between Ms Vanasse's contribution to it and the
substantial accumulation of wealth that the family achieved. With respect
to the *Kerr v Baranow* appeal, the Supreme Court of Canada held that the
British Columbia Court of Appeal was right in setting aside the trial judge's
findings of resulting trust and unjust enrichment in favour of Ms Kerr and
in directing that Mr Baranow's counterclaim for unjust enrichment be remitted for trial. However, the Supreme Court of Canada was unable to say from
the record whether Ms Kerr's unjust enrichment claim would inevitably fail
if analyzed under the legal framework that it had articulated. Accordingly,
it allowed the appeal in part by ordering a new trial respecting the unjust
enrichment claims of both parties.[62] Although the demise of the "common
intention resulting trust" is welcome, trial judges are unlikely to find it easy
to quantify monetary relief in cases of unjust enrichment in light of Cromwell J's statement that the wealth created during the period of cohabitation
will not necessarily be shared by the parties in equal measure and the appropriate monetary award for unjust enrichment should be assessed by determining the proportionate contribution of the claimant to the accumulation
of the wealth.[63] Furthermore, although a joint family venture can form the
basis of an unjust enrichment claim, it cannot do so where there is no evidence of an enrichment and a corresponding deprivation.[64]

---

61 *Kerr v Baranow* and *Vanasse v Seguin*, 2011 SCC 10 at para 124.
62 For the outcome of the new trial ordered by the Supreme Court of Canada, see *Kerr v Baranow*, 2012 BCSC 1222.
63 *Kerr v Baranow* and *Vanasse v Seguin*, 2011 SCC 10 at para 81; see also *Mitchell v Misener*, 2011 ONSC 6600 at para 78.
64 *Depatie v Squires*, 2011 ONSC 1758; see also *Rubin v Gendemann*, 2012 ABCA 38.

Unmarried cohabitants who work together for many years on a farm or in a family business are usually entitled to share equally in the fruits of their joint enterprise.[65] In long-term cohabitational relationships, the requisite causal connection will usually be found, and an equal sharing of specified property may be found appropriate. Although the doctrine of unjust enrichment has most frequently been applied to unmarried cohabitants who have claimed a share of the value of the family home on the breakdown of the cohabitational relationship, it has also been applied to enable a "common-law wife" to share her "husband's" pension.[66] The *Pension Benefits Division Act*[67] provides mechanisms for the division of pensions between spouses and between common law partners when the marriage or partnership breaks down, but it does not itself establish any pension entitlement for marital or common law partners. There must be a court order or a written agreement signed by both partners that provides for the sharing of the member's pension benefits.[68]

F.   DEBTS AND LIABILITIES; FINANCIAL PLANNING

Unmarried cohabitants, whether of the same or opposite sex, often share household expenses. They may purchase a home, cottage, furniture, household appliances, or car, and finance these transactions through a bank, credit union, or finance company. They may also share the use of the same credit card. Questions may subsequently arise as to who is responsible for any outstanding loan or debt after the cohabitants separate.

When loans are obtained from financial institutions, they are reduced to writing and signed by the party or parties legally responsible for the loan. For example, if unmarried cohabitants co-sign a promissory note to finance the purchase of a car, either or both of them can be called upon to discharge the obligation to the creditor. Not surprisingly, financial institutions are likely to look to the person who is better able to pay, even though they can sue either or both of the parties who signed the note. Liability on a mortgage will also be determined by the signature or signatures on the mortgage document.

---

65   *Peter v Beblow*, [1993] 1 SCR 980.

66   *Maloney v Maloney* (1993), 109 DLR (4th) 161 (Ont Gen Div); see also *Bigelow v Bigelow* (1995), 15 RFL (4th) 12 (Ont Div Ct); *Toquero v* Ramirez, 2011 YKSC 81; compare *AY v SDY*, 2011 BCSC 1567; *MacPhee v Russel* (2000), 6 RFL (5th) 340 (NBCA); *Brownie v Hoganson*, [2005] NSJ No 470 (SC).

67   SC 1992, c 46, Sch II.

68   *Harrington v Coombs*, 2011 NSSC 34; see also *Johnsen v Johnsen*, 2012 ONSC 3079 (separated spouses). As to the rights of a common-law partner to death benefits under the *Pension Benefits Act* (Ont), see *Carrigan v Quinn*, 2011 ONSC 585.

When property or services are paid for by credit card, the owner of the card is liable to pay for the goods or services rendered. If an unmarried cohabitant applies for an additional card for his or her partner, the applicant is liable to pay all charges against that card. The important factor is not who uses the credit card but whose name is on the account. The same principle applies to unmarried cohabitants and to married couples. If they separate, the person whose name is on the credit card should cancel the privileges formerly provided to his or her partner by notifying the bank or financial institution that issued the card. Otherwise, the card owner may be responsible for debts incurred by the other party even after their separation.

Unmarried cohabitants of the same or opposite sex should also review other documents, such as wills, insurance policies, pension plans, and bank accounts in order to determine changes that might be appropriate. They are well-advised to enter into agreements to regulate their debts and liabilities as well as their rights. Although such an agreement cannot be relied upon as a defence to any third-party claim against either cohabitant, the agreement can provide for remedies between the cohabitants themselves. For example, it might provide for either cohabitant to be indemnified for any third-party debt or liability incurred on behalf of the other cohabitant.

G. CUSTODY AND ACCESS

Custody and access disputes on family breakdown are legally resolved by reference to the elusive criterion of the "best interests of the child." If the parents lived together in a stable relationship after the birth of the child, it is immaterial whether they were married to each other.

CHAPTER 4

Domestic Contracts

A. TYPES OF DOMESTIC CONTRACTS

The following analysis will focus on "domestic contracts" insofar as they have been statutorily defined in Ontario. Even in the absence of statutory provisions, however, married and unmarried cohabitants[1] are legally entitled to enter into binding and enforceable contracts. In some circumstances, the law restricts the extent to which spouses or unmarried cohabitants can contractually waive rights that would otherwise vest in them pursuant to statute. For example, the splitting of credits under the Canada Pension Plan between divorced spouses cannot be circumvented by a spousal contract or separation agreement, except where provincial legislation specifically permits such contracting out.[2] In addition, courts are entitled to override the terms of spousal contracts that purport to waive child support rights and obligations.[3]

Domestic contracts, as defined under provincial and territorial statutes in Canada, are formal written contracts signed by the parties and witnessed, whereby married couples and unmarried cohabitants may regulate their rights and obligations during their relationship or on its termination. In Ontario, there are five different kinds of domestic contracts: (1) marriage contracts; (2) cohabitation agreements; (3) separation agreements; (4) paternity agreements; and (5) family arbitration agreements.[4]

---

1   See *Chrispen v Topham* (1986), 3 RFL (3d) 149 (Sask QB), aff'd (1987), 9 RFL (3d) 131 (Sask CA). See also *Anderson v Luoma* (1986), 50 RFL (2d) 127 (BCSC).

2   *An Act to Amend the Canada Pension Plan and the Federal Court Act*, RSC 1985 (2d Supp), c 30, s 23; see *also An Act to Amend the Canada Pension Plan (Spousal Agreement)*, SC 1991, c 14. See *Giesbrecht v Giesbrecht*, 2013 SKQB 16.

3   *Richardson v Richardson* (1987), 7 RFL (3d) 304 (SCC).

4   See *Family Law Act*, RSO 1990, c F.3, s 51. And see text accompanying note 5, below.

The right of men and women to enter into agreements or domestic contracts to regulate their affairs is expressly recognized by statute in several provinces and territories[5] but the legislation is not uniform throughout Canada. Because space does not permit a detailed description of the different provincial and territorial statutes, the following analysis will examine the Ontario legislation, which has provided the precedent for similar legislation in several other provinces. Before doing so, however, it is pertinent to review the judgments of the Supreme Court of Canada in *Hartshorne v Hartshorne*[6] and *Rick v Brandsema*.[7] Although both of these cases focused on the British Columbia *Family Relations Act* and that statute has now been superseded by the *Family Law Act*,[8] which came into force on 18 March 2013, the reasons for judgment in both cases will continue to strongly influence courts across Canada, including those in British Columbia, with respect to the effect of prenuptial and postnuptial agreements on matrimonial property rights. The former case dealt with the impact of a marriage contract on an application for spousal property division. While the judgment specifically addresses that particular topic, it also provides insight into how such contracts might be interpreted and applied under statutory property regimes in other provinces and territories. In *Hartshorne v Hartshorne*, the parties cohabited for twelve and one-half years and were married for nine of those years. It was a second marriage for both of them. They had two children. After the birth of their first child, the wife, a lawyer, withdrew from the practice of law to assume a full-time homemaking and child caregiving role. The husband, also a lawyer, made it clear to her prior to their marriage that he would never again allow his property to be divided by reason of a marriage breakdown. The husband brought assets of $1.6 million into the marriage, which included his law practice, whereas the wife had no assets and was heavily in debt at the time of the marriage. At the husband's insistence, the spouses executed a marriage agreement declaring the

---

5   See *Matrimonial Property Act*, RSA 2000, c M-8, ss 37–38; *Family Law* Act, SBC 2011, c 25, ss 92–93; *Marital Property Act*, SNB 1980, c M-1.1, ss 33–41 (marriage contracts, cohabitation agreements, separation agreements); *Family Law Act*, RSNL 1990, c F-2, ss 61–71 (marriage contracts, cohabitation agreements, separation agreements); *Matrimonial Property Act*, RSNS 1989, c 275, ss 23–29 (marriage contracts, separation agreements); *Family Law Act*, SNWT 1997, c 18, ss 2–13 (marriage contracts, cohabitation agreements, separation agreements); *Family Law Act*, RSO 1990, c F.3, ss 51–60 (marriage contracts, cohabitation agreements, separation agreements); *Family Law Act*, SPEI 1995, c 12, ss 50–58 (marriage contracts, cohabitation agreements, separation agreements); *Matrimonial Property Act, 1997*, SS 1997, c M-6.11, ss 38–42 (interspousal contracts); *Family Property and Support Act*, RSY 1986, c 63, ss 58–64 (marriage contracts, cohabitation agreements, separation agreements).

6   [2004] 1 SCR 550.

7   2009 SCC 10.

8   SBC 2011, c 25.

parties separate as to property, subject to the wife being entitled to a 3 percent interest in the matrimonial home for each year of marriage up to a maximum of 49 percent. The wife received independent legal advice that the agreement was grossly unfair but signed it with a few amendments, including her right to spousal support. Pursuant to the agreement, the wife was entitled to property valued at $280,000 on the spousal separation and the husband's entitlement was to property worth $1.2 million. In subsequent divorce proceedings, the husband sought to rely on the agreement to avoid the operation of the statutory property regime in British Columbia while the wife contended that the agreement should be set aside on common law principles or that the distribution of assets should be reapportioned under section 65(1) of the *Family Relations Act* (BC) because the agreement was unfair. The trial judge concluded that the agreement was unfair and ordered a 60:40 reapportionment of most of the assets, including the husband's law practice, in favour of the husband. Each spouse was held entitled to a one-half interest in the matrimonial home and contents. This judgment was upheld by a majority judgment (2–1) of the British Columbia Court of Appeal. On further appeal to the Supreme Court of Canada, the husband's appeal was allowed by a majority of 6–3. In the majority judgment, Bastarache J, with whom McLachlin CJ and Iaccobucci, Major, Arbour, and Fish JJ concurred, formulated the following principles:

1) The primary policy objective underlying the statutory property regime in British Columbia is to achieve fairness.

2) Marriage agreements are expressly recognized by the *Family Relations Act* (BC) as providing an appropriate means of regulating the division of property upon the breakdown or dissolution of marriage. As a prerequisite to enforceability, however, any such agreement must operate fairly at the time of the property division. Otherwise, judicial reapportionment of the property pursuant to section 65(1) of the *Family Relations Act* will be available to achieve fairness.

3) To implement the legislative intention, courts must encourage parties to enter into marriage agreements that are fair and to respond to changing circumstances by revisiting and revising their agreements from time to time to ensure continued fairness. Parties should also be encouraged to take personal control over their own financial well-being upon the dissolution of marriage and courts should be reluctant to second-guess the arrangement upon which both spouses reasonably expected to rely. Spouses may choose to structure their financial affairs in a number of ways and it is their prerogative to do so, provided that the legal boundaries of fairness are observed.

4) The outcome of matrimonial proceedings should reconcile respect for the intentions of the spouses and the assurance of an equitable result.

5) There is no hard and fast rule regarding the judicial deference to be accorded to marriage agreements as compared to separation agreements. In some cases, for example, where a marriage agreement is intended to protect premarital assets or an anticipated inheritance for the children of a prior marriage, marriage agreements may be accorded a higher degree of deference than separation agreements. In other cases, marriage agreements may be accorded less deference than separation agreements because the former type of agreement may be anticipatory and fail to take account of the financial means, needs, or other circumstances of the parties as they exist at the time of the marriage breakdown.

6) In addressing the issue of judicial deference to spousal agreements in the context of property division on marriage breakdown, the court may apply *Miglin v Miglin*[9] to support the general legal proposition that some weight should be given to marriage agreements. *Miglin v Miglin* is also helpful for its general propositions that "a court should be loathe to interfere with a pre-existing agreement unless it is convinced that the agreement does not comply substantially with the overall objectives" of the governing legislation and that the court "must look at the agreement or arrangement in its totality, bearing in mind that all aspects of the agreement are inextricably linked and that the parties have a large discretion in establishing priorities and goals for themselves." Beyond these parameters, however, the *Miglin* judgment, which deals with the effect of a separation agreement on an application for a support order under the *Divorce Act*, cannot be directly applied to regulate property distribution on the dissolution of marriage because this would distort the analytical structure provided by the *Family Relations Act* (BC).

7) In determining whether a marriage agreement is unfair so as to entitle the court to reapportion property pursuant to section 65(1) of the *Family Relations Act*, the court must determine whether the agreement is substantively fair when the application for reapportionment is made. The essence of this inquiry is whether the circumstances of the parties on their separation were within their reasonable contemplation when the agreement was entered into and, if so, whether at that time the parties made adequate arrangements in response to their anticipated circumstances. In determining whether a marriage agreement operates unfairly, the court must first apply the agreement. In particular, the court must assess and award the financial entitlements of each spouse under

---

9   [2003] 1 SCR 303.

the agreement and their entitlements from all other sources, including spousal and child support. The court must then review the list of factors set out in section 65(1) of the *Family Relations Act* for the purpose of determining whether the agreement operates unfairly. At the second stage of the inquiry, consideration must be given to the personal and financial circumstances of both parties and in particular to the manner in which these circumstances evolved.

Because the financial and domestic arrangements of the parties unfolded as expected, and they remained completely independent with respect to their real and personal property during their relationship, the economic impact of the wife's assumption of homemaking and child caregiving responsibilities during the twelve and one-half year spousal relationship, though relevant under sections 65(1)(a) and (e) of the *Family Relations Act* (BC), was found to be offset by her right to spousal support and the fact that the bulk of the property existing at the time of the spousal separation was property that the husband had acquired prior to their spousal relationship, the latter being a relevant factor to consider under section 65(1)(c) of the *Family Relations Act* (BC). Given the availability of spousal support to accommodate any economic disadvantage resulting to the wife from her assumption of homemaking and child caregiving responsibilities during the spousal relationship, coupled with the express preservation of her right to spousal support by the terms of the marriage agreement and the wife's post-separation return to employment as a lawyer, the majority judgment of the Supreme Court of Canada in *Hartshorne v Hartshorne* concluded that the judicial reapportionment of property ordered by the trial judge and affirmed on appeal to the British Columbia Court of Appeal was unjustified and the marriage contract should be upheld.[10] It is noteworthy that Bastarache J, at paragraph 14 of the majority judgment, observed that the *Family Relations Act* of British Columbia sets a lower threshold for judicial intervention than do the statutory schemes in other provinces. He stated:

> Most of the provinces provide for judicial oversight of marriage agreements. For example, s. 56(4) of the Ontario's *Family Law Act*, R.S.O. 1990, c. F.3, permits a court to set aside a domestic contract or a provision thereof if a party failed to disclose significant assets or liabilities, if a party did not understand the nature or consequences of the contract, or otherwise, in accordance with the law of contract. See also *Family Law Act*, R.S.N.L. 1990, c. F-2, s. 66(4); *Family Law Act*, S.P.E.I. 1995, c. 12, s. 55(4), for this language.

---

10   For subsequent proceedings wherein the wife was awarded retroactive lump sum spousal support, see *Hartshorne v Hartshorne*, 2010 BCCA 327.

The threshold in Nova Scotia is a finding that any term is "unconscionable, unduly harsh on one party or fraudulent": see *Matrimonial Property Act*, R.S.N.S. 1989, c. 275, s. 29. Saskatchewan allows a court to redistribute property where an interspousal contract was unconscionable or grossly unfair at the time it was entered into: see *Family Property Act*, S.S. 1997, c. F-6.3, s. 24(2). New Brunswick permits a court to disregard a provision of a domestic contract where a spouse did not receive independent legal advice and application of the provision would be inequitable: see *Marital Property Act*, S.N.B. 1980, c. M-1.1, s. 41. By contrast, in British Columbia, as earlier noted, a court may reapportion assets upon finding that to divide the property as provided for in the agreement or the FRA would be "unfair". Clearly, the statutory scheme in British Columbia sets a lower threshold for judicial intervention than do the schemes in other provinces.[11]

In *Rick v Brandsema*,[12] the spouses separated in 2000 on the breakdown of their twenty-seven year marriage. During their years together, the wife was primarily a homemaker but she also contributed to the operation of a dairy farm in which they were equal shareholders; they also owned additional real property, vehicles, and RRSPs. Before their divorce in 2002, the spouses negotiated a separation agreement with the sequential assistance of two mediators and intermittent legal advice. Approximately a year after their divorce, the wife sought to set aside the agreement on the grounds of unconscionability or, in the alternative, a reapportionment order under section 65 of British Columbia's *Family Relations Act*. The trial judge found that the agreement was unconscionable because the husband had exploited the wife's mental instability during negotiations and had deliberately concealed or under-valued assets. This resulted in the wife receiving significantly less than her entitlement under the *Family Relations Act* despite the fact that the spouses had initially expressed the intention of dividing their assets equally. In light of these findings, the trial judge made an order awarding the wife an amount representing the difference between the agreed payment and the property equalization payment to which she was statutorily entitled. The Court of Appeal disagreed with the trial judge's conclusions about the extent of the wife's vulnerabilities and concluded that, in any event, they were effectively compensated for by the availability of counsel. Accordingly, the British Columbia Court of Appeal upheld the separation agreement. The wife appealed to the Supreme Court of Canada. The unanimous judgment of that

---

11   See now *Family Law Act*, SBC 2011, c 25, s 95.

12   [2009] 1 SCR 295. For an insightful analysis, see Robert Leckey, "A Common Law of the Family? Reflections on *Rick v Brandsema*" (2009) 25 Can J Fam L 257, abstract online: http://ssrn.com/abstract=1448908.

Court was delivered by Abella J, who observed at the outset of her judgment that negotiations on the breakdown of marriage take place in an emotionally charged environment that requires special care to be taken to ensure that the spousal assets are distributed through "negotiations that are free from informational and psychological exploitation." After noting that findings of fact and factual inferences made by the trial judge are not to be reversed on appeal unless there has been a palpable and overriding error or a fundamental misapprehension of the evidence, Abella J observed that the trial judge had concluded that the husband, by accepting a settlement offer he knew was based on misleading financial information, knowingly exploited his wife's mental instability at the time the agreement was negotiated and executed. Reviewing the British Columbia Court of Appeal's rejection of the factual underpinnings for the trial judge's analysis, Abella J concluded that the appellate court's own findings were based on a theory of events that had been squarely rejected by the trial judge. Being of the opinion that the trial judge's findings were fully supported by the record, Abella J proceeded to examine the legal issues in the case. Given the trial judge's finding that the agreement was unconscionable, Abella J stated that it was unnecessary for the trial judge to review section 65 of the *Family Relations Act*, which presupposes the existence of a valid contract. Endorsing the trial judge's application of *Miglin v Miglin*,[13] Abella J stated that, while *Miglin* deals with spousal support in the context of the *Divorce Act*, it also offers guidance for negotiations relating to the division of matrimonial assets.[14] Having regard to the unique character of the negotiation environment for spouses on marriage breakdown, *Miglin* accepts that

> [t]here may be persuasive evidence brought before the court that one party took advantage of the vulnerability of the other party in separation or divorce negotiations that would fall short of evidence of the power imbalance necessary to demonstrate unconscionability in a commercial context between, say, a consumer and a large financial institution.[15]

After acknowledging that *Miglin* also affirms the principle that "[spouses] should generally be free to decide for themselves what bargain they are prepared to make," Abella J further stated:[16]

> This contractual autonomy, however, depends on the integrity of the bargaining process. Decisions about what constitutes an acceptable bargain

---

13   2003 SCC 24.

14   See also *Baker v Baker*, 2012 NSCA 24.

15   *Miglin v Miglin*, 2003 SCC 24 at para 82; see also *Green v Green*, 2013 ONSC 7265.

16   *Miglin v Miglin*, 2003 SCC 24 at paras 46–49.

can only authoritatively be made if both parties come to the negotiating table with the information needed to consider what concessions to accept or offer. Informational asymmetry compromises a spouse's ability to do so. . . .

In my view, it flows from the observations and principles set out in *Miglin* that a duty to make full and honest disclosure of all relevant financial information is required to protect the integrity of the result of negotiations undertaken in these uniquely vulnerable circumstances. The deliberate failure to make such disclosure may render the agreement vulnerable to judicial intervention where the result is a negotiated settlement that is substantially at variance from the objectives of the governing legislation.

Such a duty in matrimonial negotiations anchors the ability of separating spouses to genuinely decide for themselves what constitutes an acceptable bargain. It also helps protect the possibility of finality in agreements. An agreement based on full and honest disclosure is an agreement that, *prima facie*, is based on the informed consent of both parties. It is, as a result, an agreement that courts are more likely to respect. Where, on the other hand, an agreement is based on misinformation, it cannot be said to be a true bargain which is entitled to judicial deference.

Whether a court will, in fact, intervene will clearly depend on the circumstances of each case, including the extent of the defective disclosure and the degree to which it is found to have been deliberately generated. It will also depend on the extent to which the resulting negotiated terms are at variance from the goals of the relevant legislation. As *Miglin* confirmed, the more an agreement complies with the statutory objectives, the less the risk that it will be interfered with. Imposing a duty on separating spouses to provide full and honest disclosure of all assets, therefore, helps ensure that each spouse is able to assess the extent to which his or her bargain is consistent with the equitable goals in modern matrimonial legislation, as well as the extent to which he or she may be genuinely prepared to deviate from them.

Abella J next referred to section 56 of the *Family Relations Act*, which establishes a presumption in favour of an equal distribution of family assets, subject to the court's power to deviate from that presumption in specifically defined circumstances under section 65 of the *Family Relations Act*. Abella J then observed that the trial judge found the separation agreement to be unconscionable for a number of reasons. In particular, the husband failed to make full and fair financial disclosure, he exploited his wife's mental instability, and the financial provisions of the separation agreement constituted a significant departure from the prescribed objectives of the *Family*

Relations Act and the expressed intention of the spouses to equally divide the assets. In the result, the wife received $649,680 less than her presumptive statutory entitlement. Looking to the British Columbia Court of Appeal's overturning of the trial judge's findings, Abella J noted its reliance on *Miglin v Miglin*, which confirms that the vulnerabilities of a spouse may be cured by access to professional advice and assistance. However, Abella J pointed out that *Miglin* does not assert that the presence of professional advice and assistance automatically neutralizes a spouse's vulnerabilities and negates exploitation. Whether a spouse's vulnerabilities and susceptibility to exploitation are cured by access to professional advice and assistance is a question of fact to be determined according to the particular circumstances of each case. In this case, the trial judge found that the wife's vulnerabilities and susceptibility to exploitation were not compensated for. On the contrary, her emotional and mental condition left her unable to make use of the professional assistance available to her. Furthermore, her mental instability was well known to the husband. In the words of Abella J:[17]

> The combination in this case, therefore, of misleading informational deficits and psychologically exploitative conduct, led the trial judge to conclude that the resulting, significant deviation from the wife's statutory entitlement rendered the agreement unconscionable and therefore unenforceable. This conclusion is amply supported by the evidence.

The trial judgment was accordingly reinstated by the Supreme Court of Canada, thereby entitling the wife to receive damages of $649,680 as equitable compensation for the differential between the amount payable under the separation agreement and the wife's statutory property entitlement.

Although it is doubtful whether the judgment of the Supreme Court of Canada in *Rick v Brandsema* breaks new ground, it underscores the vital importance of honest and fair financial disclosure in the negotiation of separation agreements that purport to govern spousal rights on the breakdown or dissolution of marriage. In some provinces, courts are statutorily empowered to override domestic contracts by reason of the absence of effective financial disclosure.[18] In other provinces, financial non-disclosure is addressed by the application of common law principles.[19] The judgment in *Rick v Brandsema* is

---

17   *Ibid* at para 63.

18   See, for example, *Family Law Act* (Ontario), s 56(4)(a) and *LeVan v LeVan*, 2008 ONCA 388; *Green v Green*, 2013 ONSC 7265; see also *Family Law Act*, SBC 2011, c 25, s 93(3)(a) and s 164(3)(a).

19   See *Akkor v Roulston*, 2009 BCSC 258 wherein financial non-disclosure led to a marriage agreement being set aside on the alternative bases of misrepresentation and unconscionability; see also *Green v Green*, 2013 ONSC 7265.

also important in that it reiterates the opinion expressed in *Miglin v Miglin* that there may be persuasive evidence of unconscionability arising from the vulnerability of a spouse in the negotiation of a settlement on marriage breakdown that will not be found in typical commercial negotiations. That is not to say that a spousal settlement on marriage breakdown should be presumed to be unconscionable. Emotional distress typically accompanies marriage breakdown; such distress is not, of itself, sufficient to trigger a finding of unconscionability so as to vitiate a spousal settlement. The emotional distress must be of such a degree as to undermine the effected spouse's ability to negotiate a fair settlement. By way of a final comment on *Rick v Brandsema*, it is apparent that recourse to independent legal advice does not necessarily preclude a finding of unconscionability. The nature and quality of the advice tendered and the ability of the recipient spouse to comprehend the implications of accepting the advice are pertinent factors to be taken into account.

It should be noted that while *Hartshorne v Hartshorne*[20] and *Rick v Brandsema*[21] were both dealing with the *Family Relations Act* of British Columbia, which has since been superseded by the *Family Law Act*,[22] many of the fundamental principles set out in these cases continue to apply not only in British Columbia but also throughout the rest of Canada.

According to Muslim tradition, a prenuptial agreement may be entered into between the bride and groom whereby he will pay her a designated amount in the event of marriage breakdown. Such an agreement is known as a *Mahr*. Canadian courts of first instance have divided on the question of the enforceability of a *Mahr*. In *Nathoo v Nathoo*,[23] *Amlani v Hirani*,[24] and *NMM v NSM*,[25] the British Columbia Supreme Court recognized the validity of a written *Mahr*. In contrast, in *Kaddoura v Hammoud*,[26] Rutherford J, of the Ontario Superior Court of Justice, held that the court should not enter into a "religious thicket" by determining the rights and obligations of the parties under a *Mahr*. Since that judgment, the Supreme Court of Canada in *Bruker v Marcovitz*[27] has ruled that the fact that a dispute has a religious aspect does not render it non-justiciable. Moral and religious obligations can be transformed into legally binding obligations if the relevant requirements imposed by provincial laws are satisfied. Since that ruling, courts in Ontario have

---

20   2004 SCC 22.

21   2009 SCC 10.

22   SBC 2011, c 25.

23   [1996] BCJ No 2720 (SC).

24   2000 BCSC 1653.

25   2004 BCSC 346.

26   [1998] OJ No 5054 (Sup Ct).

27   [2007] SCJ No 54.

upheld the validity and enforceability of a *Mahr*.[28] In *Nasin v Nasin*,[29] Moen J, of the Alberta Court of Queen's Bench, found that the *Mahr*, though not in writing, constituted a contract because it was an exchange of promises that the parties intended to be binding. However, for the purposes of the application under the *Matrimonial Property Act* (Alberta), the *Mahr* was an unenforceable prenuptial contract because it was not in writing and there was no certificate of acknowledgment as required by section 38 of that Act. Accordingly, the substantive rights of the parties with respect to the division of property fell subject to Part I of the *Matrimonial Property Act* (Alberta). In New Brunswick, in the context of the husband's application to enforce a *Mahr* executed by the parties prior to their marriage in Kuwait and the wife's applications for property division and spousal support, Baird J in *MAK v EIB*[30] held that she was entitled to disregard the *Mahr* in light of section 41 of the *Marital Property Act* (New Brunswick) and the failure of the *Mahr* to satisfy the *Miglin* test[31] with respect to spousal support.

B. DOMESTIC CONTRACTS UNDER THE ONTARIO *FAMILY LAW ACT*

1) General Observations

Ontario was the first province to introduce comprehensive statutory provisions regulating domestic contracts. This was achieved by the *Family Law Reform Act, 1978*,[32] which was superseded in 1986 by the *Family Law Act*,[33] Part IV of which is specifically entitled "Domestic Contracts."

Part IV of the *Family Law Act* endorses contractual autonomy by enabling persons to contract out of rights and obligations that would otherwise arise pursuant to the *Family Law Act*. Subsection 2(10) of the *Family Law Act* specifically provides that "[a] domestic contract dealing with a matter that is also dealt with in this Act prevails unless this Act provides otherwise." A significant

---

28   *Khanis [Khamis] v Noormohamed*, 2011 ONCA 127; *Ghaznavi v Kashif-Ul-Haque*, 2011 ONSC 4062; see also *Yar v Yar*, 2015 ONSC 151 (*Mahr* set aside).

29   2008 ABQB 219, [2008] AJ No 390 (QB); see also *Khanis [Khamis] v Noormohamed*, 2011 ONCA 127.

30   2008 NBQB 249.

31   See Chapter 8, Section N.

32   SO 1978, c 2.

33   SO 1986, c 4, now RSO 1990, c F.3. For proposed changes, see Ontario Law Reform Commission, *Report on Family Property Law* (including Executive Summary) (Toronto: The Commission, 1993); Ontario Law Reform Commission, *Report on the Rights and Responsibilities of Cohabitants under the* Family Law Act (including Executive Summary) (Toronto: The Commission, 1993).

qualification to the paramountcy of a domestic contract is found in subsection 33(4) of the *Family Law Act*. This subsection empowers a court to set aside a provision for support or a waiver of the right to support in a domestic contract if the terms of the agreement (1) result in unconscionable circumstances, (2) shift the prospective burden of supporting family dependants to the public purse, or (3) the domestic contract is in default at the time of an application for support under Part III of the *Family Law Act*.[34] Somewhat limited powers are also conferred on the court to vary all or part of a domestic contract under section 56 of the *Family Law Act*, although it is always open to the court to set aside any provision of a domestic contract that undermines the best interests of a child.[35]

Section 51 of the *Family Law Act* defines a domestic contract to mean "a marriage contract, separation agreement, cohabitation agreement, paternity agreement or family arbitration agreement." This definition applies for all purposes of the *Family Law Act* pursuant to the supplementary definition of "domestic contract" in subsection 1(1) of the Act.

Except insofar as the *Family Law Act* expressly provides to the contrary, the general principles of the law of contract apply to "domestic contracts" within the meaning of the *Family Law Act*, 1986. Non-compliance with the explicit requirements of the *Family Law Act* does not necessarily preclude an action on the agreement at common law.

2) Marriage Contracts[36]

Section 51 of the *Family Law Act* empowers persons to enter into marriage contracts before or during their marriage, provided that in the latter circumstance they are still cohabiting at the time of the execution of the agreement.[37] Marriage contracts cannot be entered into by unmarried cohabitants, whether of the same sex or of the opposite sex.[38] In light of subsections 1(1) and (2) of the *Family Law Act*, marriage contracts may be entered into by same-sex married couples, parties to a void or voidable marriage celebrated in good faith, or by parties to a valid foreign polygamous marriage.

Pursuant to subsection 52(1) of the *Family Law Act*, the parties to a marriage contract may regulate their respective legal rights and obligations

---

34 *Stevens v Stevens*, 2012 ONSC 706; *CMM v DGC*, 2015 ONSC 1815 (application by child under *Family Law Act*); see also Section B(14), below in this chapter.

35 See Sections B(7) and B(9), below in this chapter.

36 See Lorne Wolfson & Tami D Pascoe, "Pre-Nups: How to Make 'Em and How to Break 'Em" (2007) 26 Fam LQ 179.

37 See also Section B(4), below in this chapter.

38 See Section B(3), below in this chapter.

during the marriage, on separation, on annulment or dissolution of the marriage, or on death. A valid marriage contract that regulates "the ownership" and "division of property" takes precedence over the statutory equalization entitlements conferred by Part I of the *Family Law Act*.[39] Specific property may also be excluded from the equalization process pursuant to paragraph 4(2)6 of the Act.[40] A marriage contract may also preclude an order for support being granted under Part III of the Act, subject to the court's discretionary jurisdiction to override the contract under the conditions specified in subsection 33(4) of the *Family Law Act* or under section 56 of the Act.

If spouses wish to predetermine their property rights on marriage breakdown or death, declarations of ownership may be insufficient to exclude an equalization claim under section 5 of the *Family Law Act* because such claims are not dependent on ownership.[41]

A marriage contract, unlike a separation agreement, cannot limit the rights conferred on a spouse by Part II of the *Family Law Act*.[42] Pursuant to section 19 of the Act, both spouses have an equal right to possession of the matrimonial home in the absence of a separation agreement or court order to the contrary. Furthermore, neither spouse can unilaterally dispose of or encumber an interest in the matrimonial home in the absence of authority conferred by a separation agreement or court order. However, subsection 52(2) of the *Family Law Act* does not preclude a marriage contract from determining rights of ownership in the home or excluding the home or its value from any spousal equalization claim based on section 5 of the Act. Paragraph 52(1)(c) of the *Family Law Act* precludes the parties to a marriage contract from determining prospective rights to the custody of or access to their children. A marriage contract may, nevertheless, define the right to direct the education and moral upbringing of the children. Any such provision is subject to the court's discretionary jurisdiction under section 56 of the *Family Law Act* to disregard the provision where the best interests of the child are not thereby served.

3) Cohabitation Agreements

Section 53 of the *Family Law Act* provides that cohabitation agreements may be entered into by persons of the opposite sex or of the same sex who are cohabiting or intend to cohabit but who are not married and have no present intention to marry. The fact that two people are sharing accommodation

---

39   *Family Law Act*, RSO 1990, c F.3, s 2(10).

40   *Nurmi v Nurmi* (1988), 16 RFL (3d) 201 (Ont UFC).

41   *Bosch v Bosch* (1991), 36 RFL (3d) 302 (Ont CA); *Webster v Webster Estate*, [2006] OJ No 2749 (Sup Ct); *Borutski v Borutski*, 2011 ONSC 7099.

42   *Family Law Act*, RSO 1990, c F.3, s 52(2).

does not necessarily constitute cohabitation. Subsection 1(1) of the *Family Law Act* defines "cohabit" as meaning "to live together in a conjugal relationship, whether within or outside marriage." Same-sex cohabitants fall within the scope of section 53 of the *Family Law Act* pursuant to statutory amendments[43] that were implemented in Ontario in consequence of the judgment of the Supreme Court of Canada in *M v H*.[44]

Cohabitation agreements, as defined by section 51 of the *Family Law Act*, may regulate the rights and obligations of the respective parties during cohabitation, on the cessation of cohabitation, or on death. Such agreements, like marriage contracts, may predetermine the ownership or division of property, support rights and obligations, the right to direct the education or moral upbringing of children, and any other matter in the settlement of the cohabitants' affairs.[45]

If the parties to a cohabitation agreement subsequently marry each other, the agreement is deemed to be a marriage contract pursuant to subsection 53(2) of the Act.

4) Separation Agreements

Section 54 of the *Family Law Act* provides that a separation agreement may be entered into by persons of the opposite sex or of the same sex who have cohabited and are living separate and apart. The term "cohabit" is defined in subsection 1(1) of the *Family Law Act* as meaning "to live together in a conjugal relationship, whether within or outside marriage." The words "living separate and apart" in section 54 of the Act bear the same meaning as paragraph 4(1)(e) of the *Divorce Act*.[46] Accordingly, the fact of separation and an intention to separate must co-exist before spouses or other persons can be found to be living separate and apart.[47] Continued residence under the same roof does not preclude a finding that the parties are living separate and apart, provided that they are living independent lives while sharing common accommodation.[48] Furthermore, isolated or casual acts of post-separation

---

43 *Amendments Because of the Supreme Court of Canada Decision in M v H Act*, 1999, SO 1999, c 6.

44 [1999] 2 SCR 3.

45 See Section B(2), above in this chapter.

46 RSC 1985 (2d Supp), c 3.

47 Compare *Herman v Herman* (1969), 3 DLR (3d) 551 (NSSC).

48 Compare *Cooper v Cooper* (1972), 10 RFL 184 (Ont HCJ); *Dupere v Dupere* (1974), 19 RFL 270 (NBSC), aff'd (1975), 10 NBR (2d) 148 (CA).

sexual intercourse do not preclude a finding that the parties are living separate and apart.[49]

At common law, married couples could enter into valid separation agreements before withdrawing from cohabitation, provided that a cessation of cohabitation was imminent. The language of sections 52 and 54 of the *Family Law Act* imply that pre-separation agreements are now characterized as marriage contracts. The difference between marriage contracts and separation agreements is not merely a matter of form. Paragraph 52(1)(c) and subsection 52(2) of the *Family Law Act* preclude a marriage contract from regulating custody and access rights and render unenforceable any provision thereof relating to the limitation of possessory or disposition rights in the matrimonial home arising under Part II of the *Family Law Act*. No corresponding qualifications apply to separation agreements.[50] Where separation is imminent, therefore, the execution, as distinct from the drafting of an agreement, should be deferred until the parties have ceased cohabitation. Otherwise, there may be serious impediments to a complete and final settlement of all outstanding issues.

Where a valid and enforceable separation agreement has been executed, its terms prevail over family property and matrimonial home rights that might otherwise have arisen under Parts I *and* II of the *Family Law Act*.[51] Spousal support claims under Part III of the *Family Law Act* may also be barred by the provisions of a separation agreement, subject to the possible application of subsection 33(4) of the *Family Law Act*.[52]

Although a separation agreement, unlike a marriage contract or cohabitation agreement, may regulate the right to custody of and access to children,[53] it is subject to the overriding provisions of subsection 56(1) of the *Family Law Act*, whereby the court may disregard any custody or access provision in a domestic contract where such a course of action is in the best interests of a child.

Pursuant to paragraph 54(e) of the *Family Law Act*, parties to a separation agreement may agree on their respective rights and obligations including any other matter in the settlement of their affairs. This allows spouses to determine responsibility for outstanding debts.

---

49 Compare *Deslippe v Deslippe* (1974), 16 RFL 38 (Ont CA); *Leaderhouse v Leaderhouse* (1971), 4 RFL 174 (Sask QB).

50 See ss 54(d), 19(2)(b), and 21(1)(b) of the *Family Law Act*, RSO 1990, c F.3.

51 See *Puopolo v Puopolo* (1986), 2 RFL (3d) 73 (Ont SC); *Cipens v Cipens* (1987), 8 RFL (3d) 325 (Ont UFC), Steinberg UFCJ; compare Section B(2), above in this chapter.

52 See Section B(14), below in this chapter.

53 *Family Law Act*, RSO 1990, c F.3, s 54(d).

5) Formal Requirements of Domestic Contracts

Subsection 55(1) of the *Family Law Act* provides that a domestic contract and an agreement to amend or rescind a domestic contract are unenforceable unless made in writing, signed by the parties, and witnessed. As was stated in *Sagl v Sagl*, "the policy of the Act is to discourage 'kitchen table' agreements."[54] Subsection 55(1) of the *Family Law Act* is the successor to subsection 54(1) of the *Family Law Reform Act, 1978*.[55] There is, however, one marked difference between these two provisions. Non-compliance with the formal requirements of subsection 54(1) of the *Family Law Reform Act, 1978* rendered the domestic contract void. Pursuant to subsection 55(1) of the *Family Law Act*, non-compliance with the formal requirements of domestic contracts does not invalidate the contract but merely renders it unenforceable.[56]

An agreement to amend a separation agreement, negotiated by letters between the parties' lawyers, will not be enforceable unless it has met the formal requirements of subsection 55(1).[57] The provisions of subsection 55(1) of the *Family Law Act* are inapplicable, however, to authorized settlements entered into by the lawyers for the respective parties after the institution of legal proceedings.[58]

The relevant statutory provisions "do not require that the signature of each party be expressly witnessed but only that the agreement be witnessed."[59] It has also been held that, despite the fact that the witness was not present when the wife signed the agreement, the formalities of subsection 55(1) were satisfied because the wife did not dispute the authenticity of her signature in the presence of the witness.[60] As the Ontario Court of Appeal concluded in *Gallacher v Friesen*,[61] "[there is] a substantial body of case law in Ontario, and in other provinces with similar legislation, holding that the strict requirements of s. 55(1) may be relaxed where the court is satisfied that the contract was in fact executed by the parties, where the terms are reasonable and where there was no oppression or unfairness in the circumstances surrounding the negotiation and execution of the contract."

---

54   [1997] OJ No 2837 at para 16 (Gen Div); see also *Zheng v Jiang*, 2012 ONSC 6043.

55   SO 1978, c 2.

56   See *Zheng v Jiang*, 2012 ONSC 6043.

57   *Miller v Bozzi* (1991), 34 RFL (3d) 371 (Ont Div Ct).

58   *Geropoulos v Geropoulos* (1982), 26 RFL (2d) 225 (Ont CA); *Petruzziello v Albert*, 2014 ONCA 393.

59   *Campbell v Campbell* (1991), 33 RFL (3d) 99 (Ont Gen Div), Steele J; see also *Lemieux v Mercer*, 2012 ONSC 7033.

60   *Hyldtoft v Hyldtoft* (1991), 33 RFL (3d) 99 (Ont Gen Div), Haines J; *Lemieux v Mercer*, 2012 ONSC 7033.

61   2014 ONCA 399; *see also Virc v Blair*, 2014 ONCA 392.

6) Capacity to Enter into Domestic Contracts

In Ontario, a person attains the age of majority and ceases to be a minor on reaching the age of eighteen years.[62] Subsection 55(2) of the *Family Law Act* confers a qualified capacity on minors to enter into a marriage contract, cohabitation agreement, or separation agreement, in that any such contract or agreement is subject to the approval of the court, either before or after the minor enters into the contract.

The guardian of property of a mentally incapable person other than his or her spouse is empowered to enter into a domestic contract on behalf of the person under such incapacity and may also give any waiver or consent required by the *Family Law Act*. In all cases, however, the domestic contract, waiver, or consent is subject to the prior approval of the court.[63] The aforementioned powers cannot be exercised by the spouse of the mentally incapable person, even if that spouse is the guardian of the property of the mentally incapable person. In such a case or where no guardian has been appointed, the Public Guardian and Trustee may act on behalf of the mentally incapable person.

7) Contracts Subject to Best Interests of Child

Subsection 56(1) of the *Family Law Act* confers a broad discretionary jurisdiction on the court to disregard the provisions of a domestic contract relating to the education, moral training, or custody of or access to a child, where the best interests of the child are not thereby served. It is generally acknowledged that parents cannot contract out of their obligations to provide child support.[64] Furthermore, a parent cannot avoid obligations to pay child support under a separation agreement simply because of an inability to exercise a right of reasonable access.[65]

The power of a court to override the provisions of a spousal agreement respecting custody or access has long been established. No spousal agreement can deprive the court of its traditional responsibility for the custody and guardianship of children.[66] In matters of custody and access, the courts are clearly entitled to override the terms of a spousal agreement if the terms of the agreement do not harmonize with the welfare or best interests of the

---

62   *Age of Majority and Accountability Act*, RSO 1990, c A.7, s 1.

63   *Family Law Act*, RSO 1990, c F.3, s 55(3).

64   See Section B(14), below in this chapter.

65   *Wright v Wright* (1974), 12 RFL 200 (Ont CA).

66   *Voegelin v Voegelin* (1980), 15 RFL (2d) 1 (Ont Co Ct); *Statia v Statia* (1981), 29 Nfld & PEIR 464 (PEISC).

child.[67] Opinions may differ, however, as to how a child's welfare or best interests will be served in controversial situations, and the wishes of the parents may be given considerable weight.[68]

In the determination of a matter respecting the support of a child, the court may disregard any provision of a domestic contract pertaining to the matter where the provision is unreasonable having regard to the child support guidelines, as well as to any other provision relating to support of the child in the contract.[69]

8) *Dum Casta* Clauses

The rights and obligations of the parties to a domestic contract cannot be made contingent upon the chastity of either party following separation. Any provision to such effect is unenforceable pursuant to subsection 56(2) of the *Family Law Act*. It is permissible, however, for the terms of a domestic contract to take account of any subsequent marriage or cohabitational relationship. A domestic contract does not offend subsection 56(2) of the *Family Law Act* if, for example, periodic "spousal" support is payable only until the payee's marriage or remarriage or non-marital cohabitation with another person.

It is no longer the practice of the courts to incorporate a *dum casta* clause in an order for periodic support.[70] It is not unusual, however, for a court to order periodic spousal support to be payable until the payee's marriage, remarriage, or non-marital cohabitation in circumstances similar to marriage.

9) Setting Aside Domestic Contracts

Section 56(4) of the *Family Law Act* provides as follows:

A court may, on application, set aside a domestic contract or a provision in it,

(a) if a party failed to disclose to the other significant assets, or significant debts or other liabilities, existing when the domestic contract was made;

(b) if a party did not understand the nature or consequences of the domestic contract; or

(c) otherwise in accordance with the law of contract.[71]

---

67 *Liang v Liang* (1979), 5 RFL (2d) 103 (Ont SC).

68 *Ibid.*

69 *Family Law Act*, RSO 1990, c F.3, s 56.1.

70 *Seeman v Seeman* (1976), 28 RFL 275 (Ont SC); *Sleigh v Sleigh* (1979), 23 OR (2d) 336 (SC).

71 For an incisive analysis of theses statutory provisions, see the judgment of Gordon J in *Dillon v Dillon*, 2014 ONSC 2236.

Section 56(4) of the *Family Law Act* involves a two-stage inquiry: (i) can the party seeking to set aside the agreement demonstrate that one or more of the section 56(4) circumstances is engaged?; and (ii) if so, is it appropriate for the court to exercise its discretion to set aside the agreement?[72] The onus is on a party seeking to set aside a domestic contract to prove his or her case on the balance of probabilities.[73]

Judicial opinion has been divided in the past concerning the effect of non-disclosure on a domestic contract.[74] Section 56(4)(a) of the *Family Law Act* empowers a court to set aside a domestic contract, or a provision thereof, if a party failed to disclose significant assets, debts, or other liabilities in existence when the domestic contract was made. The court should first determine whether a failure to disclose within the meaning of paragraph 56(4)(a) is proven. Only where such non-disclosure is established can the court be called upon to exercise its statutory discretion. The fact of non-disclosure does not compel the court to set aside all or part of the domestic contract. In *Demchuk v Demchuk*,[75] an application to rescind or amend a separation agreement executed prior to the commencement of the *Family Law Act* on 1 March 1986 was coupled with a claim for lump sum and periodic spousal support under subsection 11(1) of the *Divorce Act* of 1968.[76] In denying relief to the claimant, Clarke J reached the following conclusions. Non-disclosure, whether consensual or innocent, falls within the ambit of paragraph 56(4)(a) and waiver of full disclosure is not permissible by virtue of subsection 56(7).[77] Full disclosure presupposes the identification of all significant assets and their value. The trial judge, nevertheless, refused to exercise the statutory discretion to re-open the agreement having regard to the attendant circumstances of the case, including the absence of concealment of the husband's pension and deferred profit-sharing plan; the absence of material misrepresentation, duress, or unconscionable circumstances in the making of the agreement; the neglect of the wife to pursue full legal disclosure and her subsequent failure to expeditiously seek a variation; the absence of

---

72   *Virc v Blair*, 2014 ONCA 392, citing *LeVan v LeVan*, 2008 ONCA 388; *Stergiopoulos v Von Biehler*, 2014 ONSC 6391.

73   *Andrade v Andrade*, 2012 ONSC 2777.

74   See *Farquar v Farquar* (1984), 35 RFL (2d) 287 at 299 (Ont CA), Zuber JA; and compare dissenting judgment of Matas JA in *Tutiah v Tutiah* (1986), 48 RFL (2d) 337 at 356–59 (Man CA).

75   (1986), 1 RFL (3d) 176 (Ont HCJ). For a detailed review of relevant caselaw on s 56 of the Ontario *Family Law Act*, see *Loy v Loy*, [2007] OJ No 4274 (Sup Ct); see also *Ward v Ward*, 2011 ONCA 178; *Petre v Petre*, 2014 ONSC 7033; *Toscano v Toscano*, 2015 ONSC 487.

76   SC 1967–68, c 24.

77   See also *Dayal v Dayal*, 2011 ONSC 1304; *Petruzziello v Albert*, 2011 ONSC 4182, aff'd 2014 ONCA 393.

any catastrophic change in the wife's situation that would compel judicial intervention; the substantial benefits received by the wife pursuant to the agreement; the social desirability of a clean break following the discharge of the obligations imposed by the agreement; the wife's attainment of financial self-sufficiency; and the husband's willingness to assume continuing responsibility for the cost of the children's post-secondary education. The trial judge further concluded that interference with the terms of the separation agreement was also unwarranted because the pension and deferred profit-sharing plan was not a "significant asset" within the meaning of paragraph 56(4)(a) of the *Family Law Act* at the time when the agreement was entered into. Accordingly, the court upheld the separation agreement and refused to order spousal support pursuant to subsection 11(1) of the *Divorce Act*, 1968, notwithstanding the judicial discretion to order such support even when the validity of a separation agreement has not been successfully impugned. The trial judge also concluded that paragraph 56(4)(a) of the *Family Law Act* does not impose a reverse onus. Although each party is now under a positive and absolute duty to disclose, the party who seeks to rescind the separation agreement in whole or in part must demonstrate that the other party has failed to discharge that duty.

In *LeVan v LeVan*,[78] the trial judge set aside a prenuptial agreement in which the wife waived substantial rights to spousal support and her statutory right to an equal share in the increased value of assets that her husband brought into the marriage. The husband was ordered to pay a property equalization payment of $5.3 million, substantial prospective and retroactive spousal and child support based on an imputed annual income of $370,000, and fixed costs of $646,602. The Ontario Court of Appeal was asked to consider whether the trial judge erred in setting aside the marriage contract. The trial judge found that the husband had breached section 56(4)(a) of the *Family Law Act* by failing to reveal certain assets in which he had a beneficial interest and by failing to reveal the value of other assets in which he held a significant interest when the marriage contract was entered into. Addressing this finding, counsel for the husband contended that the trial judge erred by importing the word "value" into section 56(4)(a) of the *Family Law Act*. After noting that the trial judge relied on *Demchuk v Demchuk*[79] in support of her conclusion that the financial disclosure requirements of section 56(4)(a) encompass an obligation to disclose the value of assets, the Ontario Court of Appeal observed that there is no caselaw to support the contention that the requirements of section 56(4)(a) can be satisfied by providing only a list of

---

78   2008 ONCA 388; see also *Virc v Blair*, 2014 ONCA 392.

79   (1986), 1 RFL (3d) 176 (Ont HCJ).

significant assets without some indication of value being attributed to them. However, like the trial judge, the Ontario Court of Appeal declined to engage in a detailed analysis of the significance, if any, to be attached to the absence of the term "value" from section 56(4)(a). The Ontario Court of Appeal reasoned that such an analysis was rendered unnecessary by additional findings of fact made by the trial judge, which clearly demonstrated that the financial information provided by the husband was insufficient to enable the wife to determine his net worth or realize what rights she was surrendering by entering into the marriage contract. In the opinion of the Ontario Court of Appeal, there was an abundance of evidence indicating that the husband had failed to comply with his disclosure obligation apart from his failure to disclose the value of designated assets. In particular, the Ontario Court of Appeal observed that the trial judge had found that (1) the husband interfered with the wife's legal representation; (2) the wife's lawyers were unable to appreciate the consequences of the contract drafted by the husband's lawyer due to misrepresentations and a lack of financial disclosure; (3) the wife had not received effective and sound independent legal advice; and (4) she did not understand the nature and consequences of the contract that she signed. Given that these findings of fact were supported by the evidence presented at trial, the Ontario Court of Appeal saw no reason to interfere with the trial judge's decision to set aside the marriage contract.

Courts should be hesitant to assume that section 56(4)(a) of the *Family Law Act* unconditionally requires the title-holding spouse to disclose the value of significant assets that have been revealed. In some cases, the value of the disclosed assets will be readily discernible by both spouses or discoverable with a minimum of time, effort, and expense. At the other extreme, complex business holdings may not lend themselves to a readily available and inexpensive assessment of their value. Furthermore, experts representing the two spouses may disagree about the value of specific assets or even the manner in which they should be valued. If section 56(4)(a) of the *Family Law Act* is to be interpreted as requiring the disclosure of the value of significant assets and not merely their existence, this duty must be realistically applied by the courts. Accordingly, it is submitted that section 56(4)(a) of the *Family Law Act* will be satisfied if the court concludes that the valuation of an asset was not inherently misleading and constituted a realistic estimate in light of established valuation practices.[80]

While paragraph 56(4)(a) restricts the court's jurisdiction to set aside domestic contracts to instances of lack of financial disclosure, a court may set

---

80 See *Greenwood v Greenwood* (1988), 18 RFL (3d) 273 (Ont HCJ); *Dearing v Dearing* (1991), 37 RFL (3d) 102 (Ont Gen Div); *Lemieux v Mercer*, 2012 ONSC 7033.

aside a separation agreement, at least in part, where there has been a failure to disclose personal information material to the contract, as, for example, where the wife withholds information concerning the paternity of one of the children from her husband.[81] If the offending covenant does not constitute the only consideration for the contract, a separation agreement may be enforced without the offending covenant.[82] More recently, however, Sachs J, of the Ontario Superior Court of Justice, held in *D'Andrade v Schrage*[83] that, when negotiating a marriage contract, couples have an absolute obligation to disclose anything that would be relevant to the purpose of the contract. Since the purpose of the contract is financial, that obligation demands the utmost good faith and fair dealing in disclosing their financial positions, but the obligation does not extend to disclosing the existence of an extramarital affair or an intention to separate.

Paragraph 56(4)(b) of the *Family Law Act* indicates that a court may set aside a domestic contract or a provision in it if a party did not understand the nature or consequences of the domestic contract.[84] Paragraph 56(4)(b) underlines the importance of independent legal advice. A separation agreement signed by a spouse without independent legal advice may be ignored by the court,[85] although the absence of independent legal advice does not inevitably undermine an agreement.[86] Conversely, a court is not prevented from overriding a separation agreement merely because the partners to it have received independent legal advice.[87]

The jurisdiction of a court to set aside a domestic contract or any provision thereof pursuant to the application of established principles of the law of contract is expressly recognized by paragraph 56(4)(c) of the *Family Law Act*.[88] In *Montreuil v Montreuil*,[89] Aitken J, of the Ontario Superior Court of Justice, reviewed several common law grounds in section 56(4)(c) for setting

---

81 *Kristoff v Kristoff* (1987), 7 RFL (3d) 284 (Ont Dist Ct).

82 *Tuxford v Tuxford* (1913), 6 Sask LR 96 (SC); and see *Lotton v Lotton* (1979), 11 RFL (2d) 112 (Ont CA).

83 2011 ONSC 1174, citing *Saul v Himel* (1994), 9 RFL (4th) 419 (Ont Gen Div), aff'd (1996), 22 RFL (4th) 226 (Ont CA); see also *Stevens v Stevens*, 2012 ONSC 706.

84 *Ward v Ward*, 2011 ONCA 178; *DiLeonardo v DiLeonardo*, 2013 ONSC 7064; *Martin v Sansome*, 2014 ONCA 14.

85 *Grossmann v Grossmann* (1982), 29 RFL (2d) 300 (Ont SC).

86 *Loy v Loy*, [2007] OJ No 4274 (Sup Ct); *Demaine v Racine*, 2013 ONSC 2940.

87 *Woods v Woods* (1976), 22 RFL 370 (Ont HCJ).

88 *Ward v Ward*, 2011 ONCA 178; *Lemieux v Mercer*, 2012 ONSC 7033; *DiLeonardo v DiLeonardo*, 2013 ONSC 7064.

89 [1999] OJ No 4450 (Sup Ct); see also *Demaine v Racine*, 2013 ONSC 2940; *Hyatt v Ralph*, 2015 ONSC 580.

aside a domestic contract, including the absence of independent legal advice,[90] a material misrepresentation, undue influence, unconscionability, duress, and breach of a fiduciary duty. A separation agreement secured through the exertion of undue influence may be set aside pursuant to paragraph 56(4)(c) of the *Family Law Act* at the instance of the spouse influenced even though the agreement appears to be fair and reasonable on its face. Cases are divided on the issue of whether the defence of undue influence will succeed if the spouses have had the benefit of independent legal advice. In *Hyldtoft v Hyldtoft*,[91] Haines J observed that there is no presumption of undue influence between spouses. In refusing, however, to give effect to an amendment to a marriage contract that gave the husband significantly more than originally provided, Haines J found specific evidence of undue influence because the husband's repeated threats to leave the wife and force her to manage the business alone amounted to the improper use of unequal bargaining power, notwithstanding that the wife's lawyer had drafted the amendment. Undue influence may be defined as "the unconscientious use by one person of power possessed by [that person] over another in order to induce the other to do something."[92]

Where one party takes advantage of inequality in spousal bargaining power and this brings about an improvident bargain, the spousal agreement will be set aside by the court at the instance of the injured party but a spouse's failure to make a good bargain will not itself satisfy the legal requirements of unconscionability.[93]

Rescission of a separation agreement for duress requires proof of coercion by the use of or threat of the use of physical force or mental pressure. There is no need to establish a pre-existing relationship of dependence as in undue influence.[94]

Subsection 56(5) of the *Family Law Act* empowers the court to set aside all or part of a separation agreement in circumstances where one party has brought pressure to bear on the other by means of the former party's control over the latter's freedom to remarry within his or her religious faith. It is open to question how far, if at all, this subsection qualifies the doctrine

---

90   See *Parent v Morrissette*, 2013 NBQB 408.
91   (1991), 33 RFL (3d) 99 (Ont Gen Div).
92   *Berdette v Berdette* (1991), 33 RFL (3d) 113 at 125 (Ont CA), citing *Brooks v Alker* (1975), 22 RFL 260 at 266 (Ont SC), Henry J.
93   *Rosen v Rosen* (1994), 18 OR (3d) 641 (CA); *Loy v Loy*, [2007] OJ No 4274 (Sup Ct); *Connell v Connell*, 2011 ONSC 4868.
94   *Mundinger v Mundinger*, [1969] 1 OR 606 (CA), aff'd (1970), 14 DLR (3d) 256n (SCC).

of unconscionability previously established by judicial decisions.[95] An issue could arise as to the constitutional validity of subsection 56(5) in light of section 15 of the *Canadian Charter of Rights and Freedoms*. It has been suggested that any constitutional challenge of subsection 56(5) is likely to prove unsuccessful[96] but this opinion has been questioned.[97]

10) Rights of Donors of Gifts

Section 57 of the *Family Law Act* qualifies the common law doctrine of privity of contract by providing a means of protecting the rights of a donor who has imposed conditions on specific gifts made to one or both parties, whereby any subsequent disposition or encumbrance of the property requires the donor's consent. Where a domestic contract prohibits the alienation of third-party gifts without the donor's consent, the parties to the domestic contract cannot subsequently circumvent the donor's interest. Should they attempt to do so, the donor has *locus standi* to enforce the terms of the gift or amend the provisions of the domestic contract.

11) Contracts Made outside Ontario

When parties negotiate a contract, they may expressly choose the "proper law of the contract," which is the system of law that will determine their rights and liabilities under the contract. In the absence of a *bona fide* choice of law clause in the domestic contract, "the proper law of the contract" will be the system of law that has the most real and substantial connection with the contract.[98]

The "proper law of a contract" ordinarily governs its essential validity and effect. Pursuant to the provisions of paragraph 58(a) of the *Family Law Act*, however, the validity and enforceability of a domestic contract will be upheld, notwithstanding non-compliance with a foreign proper law, if the contract is valid and enforceable according to the laws applicable in Ontario. Pursuant to paragraph 58(b) of the Act, domestic contracts that are governed by a foreign proper law cannot circumvent the application of subsection 33(4) or of section 56 of the *Family Law Act*, which empower a court to set aside all

---

95   See, generally, Michel G Picher, "The Separation Agreement As an Unconscionable Transaction: A Study in Equitable Fraud" (1972) 7 RFL 257.

96   See John T Syrtash, "Removing Barriers to Religious Remarriage in Ontario: Rights and Remedies" with "Memorandum of Law" by J Whyte (1987) 1 Can Fam LQ 309.

97   Edwin A Flak, "'Get' Law May Promote Invalid Marriages" *The Lawyers Weekly* (7 May 1993) 5.

98   See *Vien v Vien Estate* (1988), 12 RFL (3d) 94 (Ont CA).

or part of a domestic contract in designated circumstances.[99] Such contracts are also subject to limitation under paragraph 56(c) of the Act, whereby a provision in a marriage contract or cohabitation agreement that purports to regulate custody and access rights is unenforceable in Ontario.

12) Paternity Agreements

Section 59 of the *Family Law Act* regulates paternity agreements. It provides as follows:

Paternity agreements

59. (1) If a man and a woman who are not spouses enter into an agreement for,

(a)   the payment of the expenses of a child's prenatal care and birth;

(b)   support of a child; or

(c)   funeral expenses of the child or mother,

on the application of a party, or a children's aid society, to the Ontario Court of Justice or the Family Court of the Superior Court of Justice, the court may incorporate the agreement in an order, and Part III (Support Obligations) applies to the order in the same manner as if it were an order made under that Part.

Child support guidelines

(1.1) A court shall not incorporate an agreement for the support of a child in an order under subsection (1) unless the court is satisfied that the agreement is reasonable having regard to the child support guidelines, as well as to any other provision relating to support of the child in the agreement.

Absconding respondent

(2) If an application is made under subsection (1) and a judge of the court is satisfied that the respondent is about to leave Ontario and that there are reasonable grounds to believe that the respondent intends to evade his or her responsibilities under the agreement, the judge may issue a warrant in the form prescribed by the rules of the court for the respondent's arrest.

Bail

(3) Section 150 (interim release by justice of the peace) of the *Provincial Offences Act* applies with necessary modifications to an arrest under the warrant.

---

99   See Sections B(1), B(7), and B(9), above in this chapter; and Section B(14), below in this chapter.

Capacity of minor

(4) A minor has capacity to enter into an agreement under subsection (1) that is approved by the court, whether the approval is given before or after the minor enters into the agreement.

Application to existing agreements

(5) This section applies to paternity agreements that were made before the 1st day of March, 1986.

Transitional provision

(6) A paternity agreement that is made before the day section 4 of the *Family Statute Law Amendment Act, 2006* comes into force is not invalid for the reason only that it does not comply with subsection 55 (1).

13) Application of Act to Pre-existing Contracts

Pursuant to subsection 60(1) of the *Family Law Act*, a marriage contract, cohabitation agreement, or separation agreement that was validly made before the *Family Law Act* came into force on 1 March 1986 is deemed to be a domestic contract for the purposes of the Act. Such a contract or agreement accordingly prevails over the rights conferred by the *Family Law Act*, except insofar as the Act provides otherwise.[100] Having regard to the fundamental differences between the *Family Law Act*[101] and its predecessor, the *Family Law Reform Act, 1978*,[102] subsection 70(3) of the *Family Law Act* expressly provides as follows:

Interpretation of Existing Contracts

70. (3) A separation agreement or marriage contract that is validly made before the 1st day of March, 1986 and that excludes a spouse's property from the application of sections 4 and 8 of the *Family Law Reform Act*,

(a) shall be deemed to exclude that property from the application of section 5 of this Act; and

(b) shall be read with necessary modifications.

Subsection 60(2) of the *Family Law Act* upholds the validity of prior domestic contracts entered into in contemplation of the Act, provided that such contracts would have been valid if entered into after the commencement of the *Family Law Act* on 1 March 1986.

---

100 SO 1986, c 4, now RSO 1990, c F.3, s 2(10).
101 *Ibid.*
102 SO 1978, c 2.

Subsection 60(3) of the *Family Law Act* validates transfers of property that occurred before the commencement of the *Family Law Reform Act, 1978*.[103]

14) Setting Aside Provisions of Domestic Contracts Respecting Spousal and Child Support

Subsection 33(4) of the *Family Law Act* confers a discretionary jurisdiction on the court to set aside a provision for support in a domestic contract *and* to determine the right to and amount of support, if any, in an application under Part III of the Act, notwithstanding that the contract or agreement purports to exclude any such right. The discretionary jurisdiction of the court is exercisable pursuant to the subsection: (a) if the provision for support or the waiver of support results in unconscionable circumstances; (b) where the provision for support, if any, is in favour of a dependant who qualifies for public assistance; or (c) if there is default in the payment of support under the contract or agreement at the time when an application is made pursuant to section 33 of the *Family Law Act*. It is submitted that paragraph 33(4)(a) of the Act may be invoked by either spouse, where the contract or agreement is unconscionable.[104] A distinction is to be drawn between the doctrine of unconscionability applicable under the general law of contract and section 56(4) of the *Family Law Act*, and the notion of "unconscionable results" of a domestic contract under section 33(4) of the *Family Law Act*. The former doctrine addresses whether the separation agreement was unconscionable at the time of its execution. Section 33(4) is directed at whether the agreement is unconscionable at the time when an order for spousal support is sought under section 33 of the *Family Law Act*.[105] A wife who seeks to set aside a marriage contract on the ground that her waiver of support rights results in unconscionability within the meaning of subsection 33(4) of the *Family Law Act* is not prevented from examining the husband's financial status by a covenant in the marriage contract whereby she undertook not to compel disclosure for the purpose of pursuing any legal proceeding against the husband.[106]

Subsection 33(4) of the *Family Law Act* is supplemented by subsection 56(1.1) of the Act, which empowers the court to disregard any provision respecting child support in a domestic contract where the provision is unreason-

---

103   See *Cushman v Cushman* (1979), 10 RFL (2d) 305 (Ont SC).

104   Compare *Bruni v Bruni*, 2010 ONSC 6568 and *Gergely v Gergely* (1979), 11 RFL (2d) 221 at 230 (Ont SC).

105   *Scheel v Henkelman* (2001), 11 RFL (5th) 376 (Ont CA); *Desramaux v Desramaux*, [2002] OJ No 3251 (CA); *Harper v Harper*, 2010 ONSC 4845; *DiLeonardo v DiLeonardo*, 2013 ONSC 7064.

106   *Lipson v Lipson* (30 June 1986), Doc 11969/86 (Ont SC Master).

able having regard to the child support guidelines, as well as to any other provision relating to support of the child in the contract.

The provisions of the *Family Law Act* have no direct application to corollary claims for spousal or child support in divorce proceedings.[107]

15) Incorporation of Provisions of Domestic Contracts in Orders under *Family Law Act*

Subsection 2(9) of the *Family Law Act* expressly provides that a provision of a domestic contract respecting a matter that is dealt with by the Act may be incorporated in an order made pursuant to the Act.[108] Insofar as the domestic contract regulates matters pertaining to property rights or entitlements under Part I or possessory or dispositional rights in the matrimonial home under Part II of the *Family Law Act*, such incorporation may only be ordered by the Unified Family Court or the Ontario Court (General Division).[109] The provisions of a domestic contract respecting spousal or child support may, however, be incorporated in a judgment of the Ontario Court (Provincial Division).[110]

A litigant may not, however, bring an action to incorporate the terms of a domestic contract into a court order pursuant to subsection 2(a) of the *Family Law Act* in the absence of judicial jurisdiction to deal with the subject matter sought to be incorporated.[111]

16) Incorporation of Provisions of Domestic Contracts in Divorce Judgments

The current *Divorce Act*, like its predecessor, the *Divorce Act, 1968*,[112] is silent on matters relating to property rights or entitlements and perhaps necessarily so by virtue of section 92(13) of the *Constitution Act, 1867*, which confers exclusive legislative jurisdiction over "Property and Civil Rights" on the provinces. The jurisdiction of a court to incorporate the provisions of a domestic contract in a divorce judgment is accordingly fettered. The court has a discretionary jurisdiction to incorporate the terms of a separation agreement, with or without amendment, in the divorce judgment, but this jurisdiction

---

107 *McMeekin v McMeekin* (1978), 21 OR (2d) 72 (SC).

108 *Cipens v Cipens* (1987), 8 RFL (3d) 325 (Ont UFC).

109 See definitions of "court" in ss 4(1) and 17 of *Family Law Act*, RSO 1990, c F.3; compare s 34(2); see also *Reference re S 6 of Family Relations Act*, [1982] 1 SCR 62; *Lamb v Lamb* (1985), 46 RFL (2d) 1 (SCC).

110 See definition of "court" in s 1(1) of *Family Law Act*, RSO 1990, c F.3.

111 *Cipens v Cipens* (1987), 8 RFL (3d) 325 (Ont UFC).

112 SC 1967–68, c 24.

is limited to those corollary relief matters that fall within the ambit of the *Divorce Act*. The court may, therefore, incorporate in the divorce judgment the provisions of a separation agreement insofar as they relate to spousal and child support or custody and access, but there is no jurisdiction to include covenants respecting the ownership or distribution of real or personal property.[113] Where the provisions of a separation agreement are properly incorporated in a divorce judgment, the spouses must look to the judgment, which supersedes the separation agreement. The agreement continues to be operative and enforceable, however, insofar as its provisions cannot be legitimately incorporated in the divorce judgment, being matters falling outside the jurisdiction of the court under the *Divorce Act*.[114]

17) Filing, Enforcement, and Variation of Support Provisions of Domestic Contracts

Subsection 35(1) of the *Family Law Act* empowers a party to a domestic contract to file the contract with the clerk of the Ontario Court of Justice or of the Family Court with an accompanying affidavit stating that the contract is still in effect and has not been set aside or varied by court order or agreement. Upon such filing, any provision for spousal or child support in the domestic contract may be enforced in the same manner as a support order. The enforcement power conferred by paragraph 35(2)(a) is expressly confined to support rights and obligations and has no application to any provision of the domestic contract relating to such matters as property entitlements or possessory or dispositional rights in the matrimonial home. Subsection 35(1) and paragraph 35(2)(a), being discretionary, do not preclude a party to a domestic contract from pursuing a contractual remedy in the event of noncompliance with support provisions of a domestic contract. Any action arising from default under the domestic contract may fall subject, however, to the two-year limitation period imposed by subsection 50(2), as qualified by subsection 2(8), of the *Family Law Act*.

Pursuant to paragraph 35(2)(b) of the Act, the support provisions of a duly filed domestic contract may be varied under section 37 of the Act.[115] Such variation may be ordered, notwithstanding that the parties agreed to

---

113   *Spooner v Spooner* (1979), 89 DLR (3d) 685 (Sask CA).

114   See *Oeming v Oeming* (1985), 43 RFL (2d) 175 (Alta QB); *Finnie v Rae* (1977), 16 OR (2d) 54 (SC); *Campbell v Campbell* (1976), 27 RFL 40 (Sask QB); compare *Horne v Roberts* (1971), 5 RFL 15 (BCSC); see also *McLeod v McLeod*, [2006] AJ No 1663 (QB).

115   As to the jurisdiction to grant an interim variation order or to stay execution of an order, see *Hayes v Hayes*, 2010 ONSC 3650. As for foreign domestic contracts, see *Jasen v Karassik*, [2008] OJ No 3031 (Sup Ct) wherein the wife was required to comply with the *Interjurisdictional Support Orders Act, 2002*, SO 2002, c 13.

submit any future dispute to arbitration.[116] The spousal support provisions of a domestic contract entered into and filed with the Ontario Court of Justice prior to the parties' divorce may be varied pursuant to sections 35(2)(b) and 37 of the *Family Law Act* after the divorce, if the divorce judgment is silent on the issue of spousal support.[117] Where a support order has been disregarded and followed by a subsequent agreement signed by the parties, the court's jurisdiction to vary the original order is exhausted. If under the agreement itself no right to support exists, the agreement cannot then be filed, enforced, or varied under section 35 of the Act.[118] The onus is on the party seeking to amend the agreement to show clear and compelling reasons to justify change.[119] An application under section 37 of the *Family Law Act* may be made by either party and the court may discharge, vary, or suspend the support provisions of the domestic contract, either prospectively or retroactively, with consequential remission of all or part of any arrears or interest thereon.

Paragraph 35(2)(c) also provides for an annual increase in the amount of spousal support provided under a duly filed domestic contract by means of a court-ordered indexation of the amount based on the Consumer Price Index. The jurisdiction of the court to index support payments and the definition of the indexing factor to be used are specifically defined in subsections 34(5) and 34(6) and in section 38 of the *Family Law Act*.[120]

The provisions of subsection 33(4) of the Act, which fetter the jurisdiction of a court to interfere with the support provisions of a domestic contract or paternity agreement, continue to apply where the contract or agreement is filed with the Ontario Court of Justice or the Family Court.[121]

The statutory rights respecting the filing, enforcement, and variation of domestic contracts under section 35 of the *Family Law Act* cannot be ousted by the terms of any domestic contract.[122] The overall provisions of the domestic contract will, nevertheless, remain significant in the exercise of the court's discretionary jurisdiction. The onus is on the party seeking to avoid a domestic contract to show why the court ought not to attach to it the weight ordinarily given any binding contract.

116　*Grosman v Cookson*, 2011 ONSC 7032.

117　*Abernethy v Peacock*, [2009] OJ No 2066 (Sup Ct).

118　See *Cipens v Cipens* (1987), 8 RFL (3d) 325 (Ont UFC).

119　*Ditullio v Ditullio* (1974), 16 RFL 148 (Ont SC); *Woods v Woods* (1976), 22 RFL 370 (Ont HCJ); *Nador v Nador* (1977), 19 OR (2d) 728 (SC), aff'd (1978), 22 OR (2d) 685 (CA).

120　See *Davidson v Davidson* (1987), 62 OR (2d) 145 (Div Ct).

121　*Family Law Act*, RSO 1990, c F.3, s 35(3).

122　*Ibid*, s 35(4).

Domestic contracts entered into before 1 March 1986 fall subject to the aforementioned statutory provisions, as do arrears that accrued before that date.[123]

18) Remedies for Breach of Domestic Contracts

Traditional contractual remedies such as damages, rectification, rescission, specific performance, and injunctions provide means of enforcing the terms of a domestic contract.[124] Declaratory relief is also available and the appropriate remedy may be specified in the domestic contract.[125]

In the absence of express provision to the contrary, the paragraphs of a separation agreement are deemed to be independent of each other. Therefore, a breach of one or more does not automatically entitle the aggrieved party to refuse to perform his or her own covenants and he or she may be limited to damages for the breach.[126] Only a major breach of the agreement will permit the innocent party to treat the separation agreement as repudiated and so refuse his or her own performance.[127] There is no reason, however, why certain covenants cannot be made the essence of the separation agreement.[128]

19) Termination of Domestic Contracts

A domestic contract does not automatically terminate any more than any ordinary contract does. As it is always a matter of intent and construction, obligations that are to terminate on the happening of one or more events should be clearly indicated.

The effect that any reconciliation or resumption of cohabitation is to have on a separation agreement should be agreed on between the parties. In the absence of such a paragraph, the separation agreement will ordinarily terminate as of the date of reconciliation but the reconciliation does not affect rights that have already accrued or parts of the agreement that have already been executed.[129]

---

123 *Ibid*, ss 35(5) & 35(6).

124 *Spencer v Spencer*, 2013 SKQB 321, citing *Williamson v Williamson*, 2004 SKCA 65.

125 *Griffith v Griffith*, [2001] SJ No 411 (QB); see also *Carwick v Carwick* (1972), 6 RFL 286 (Ont CA).

126 *Graves v Legg* (1854), 156 ER 304; *Quinn v Quinn*, [1949] OWN 614 (HCJ); *Marshall v Marshall*, [1923] 4 DLR 175 (Sask CA); *Griffith v Griffith*, [2001] SJ No 411 (QB).

127 *T v T* (1966), 55 DLR (2d) 183 (Man QB); *Balcombe v Balcombe*, [1908] P 176; *Shoot v Shoot*, [1957] OWN 22 (CA).

128 *Marshall v Marshall*, [1923] 4 DLR 175 (Sask CA).

129 *Christofferson v Christofferson* (1924), 21 Alta LR 13 (CA); *Berman v Berman* (1980), 12 RFL (2d) 165 (Man QB); *Livermore v Livermore* (1992), 43 RFL (3d) 163 (Ont Gen Div).

In the absence of a provision to the contrary, a separation agreement is not automatically terminated by divorce. Courts are usually more willing to imply a termination of the separation agreement upon remarriage of the dependent spouse than upon divorce.[130] However, this is not the case where there is a specific term in the separation agreement that defines its duration.[131]

Unless the domestic contract provides to the contrary, the death of either spouse will normally terminate the obligation to pay spousal support. An unconditional promise to pay, however, raises the implication that a deceased spouse's estate is bound by the agreement even though not expressly mentioned.[132]

---

130 *Murdoch v Ransom*, [1963] 2 OR 484 (SC); compare *Rust v Rust*, [1972] 1 WWR 491 (Alta CA).
131 *Richards v Richards* (1972), 6 RFL 99 (Ont HCJ), aff'd (1972), 7 RFL 101 (Ont CA).
132 *Baker, Re* (1923), 24 OWN 44 (HC).

CHAPTER 5

Family Violence[1]

A. INTRODUCTION

One of the best kept secrets of the twentieth century was the incidence of domestic violence in supposedly intact families. It is only in the last twenty years that family violence has been recognized as a serious social problem that encompasses the abuse of elderly parents or grandparents as well as spousal and child abuse.

In the words of MacDonald J, of the Nova Scotia Supreme Court, in *MAB v LAB*:

> Domestic violence most commonly refers to a situation where an adult intimate or former intimate partner attempts by psychological, physical, financial or sexual means to coerce, dominate or control the other. This violence reveals a pattern of conduct that may be verbal, physical or sexual. The conduct targets another person's self-esteem and emotional well-being. It can include humiliating, belittling, denigrating, intimidating, controlling or isolating behaviour. It can include physical assaults, sexual assaults, sexual humiliation, sleep deprivation, extortion, economic coercion, threats to harm or kill, destruction of property, threatened or attempted suicide, litigation harassment and litigation tactics, manipulation of children, of relatives, of investigation agencies and helping personnel, surveillance, monitoring, and stalking. The abuse and violence in intimate partnerships has a complex reciprocal dynamic not found in violence that occurs between strangers.[2]

---

1 See, generally, Canada, Department of Justice, Family Violence Initiative, online: www. phac-aspc.gc.ca/ncfv-cnivf/familyviolence/initiative_e.html.

2 2013 NSSC 89 at para 20.

B. ABUSE OF THE ELDERLY

A sadly neglected aspect of abuse that has come to the forefront since the 1990s is abuse of the elderly.[3] Although such abuse has been found in situations involving institutional care, it more frequently involves younger family members, often children or grandchildren.

The most common abuse of the elderly is financial abuse, which is often accompanied by emotional abuse. The retirement savings of an elderly parent or grandparent may be squandered by children or grandchildren. Monthly pension or disability cheques may be withheld. Children and grandchildren may "jump the gun" on prospective inheritances without any thought for the impact of such conduct on the elderly parent or grandparent. Theft of money or possessions represents more than 60 percent of all cases of abuse of the elderly. In some instances, resistance by the elderly person may result in physical abuse.

It has been estimated that at least 4 percent and perhaps as many as 15 percent of the elderly in Canada are abused financially, emotionally, or physically by their children, grandchildren, spouses, or caregivers. Health and Welfare Canada has estimated that more than 315,000 Canadians over sixty-five years of age are victims of abuse. However, the incidence of abuse is likely to be much higher because of the ease with which it can be concealed by family members.

The characteristics of the abused victim are similar to those identified with respect to the "battered wife syndrome." Victims of elder abuse feel helpless and sense that they have no place to go in order to avoid the abuse. They often have low self-esteem, are dependent on the abuser, and lack the physical, emotional, and often financial ability to withdraw from the abusive environment. They are fearful of being abandoned or sent to an institution; they are ignorant of their legal rights; and they are often isolated or unable to communicate.

Abuse of the elderly is not a new social problem but its incidence is increasing with the aging of the Canadian population. In 1991, 11.6 percent of the population of Canada was over sixty-five years of age. By 2031, it will be more than 22 percent. Although federal and provincial governments, universities, and social agencies are beginning to show some interest in defining the boundaries and potential solutions to the societal problem of abuse of the elderly, no concerted effort has yet been undertaken to come to grips with it. There is evidence, however, of increased awareness of the need for change.

---

3   See, generally, P Lynn McDonald, Joseph P Hornick, *et al*, *Elder Abuse and Neglect in Canada* (Toronto: Butterworths, 1991); see also Manitoba Law Reform Commission, Report No 103, *Adult Protection and Elder Abuse* (Winnipeg: The Commission, December 1999).

A parliamentary study on abuse of the elderly in 1993[4] recommended that federal funding should be available to provide shelters for elderly victims of abuse.[5] It also recommended that the federal government should work with organizations responsible for professional standards and for the education of physicians, nurses, social workers, bankers, and lawyers so that abuse of the elderly could be identified and dealt with. It further recommended that a large-scale federal study should be undertaken to ascertain the scope of the problem and the means of dealing with it.[6]

C. NATURE OF SPOUSAL ABUSE

Although the expression "spousal abuse" has been traditionally confined to persons who are married, it is also frequently used to refer to conduct between divorced spouses or persons living in a cohabitational relationship. "Spousal abuse" takes various forms but all involve domination or the improper exercise of power or control over a spouse, divorced spouse, or quasi-marital partner. Spousal abuse may involve physical, sexual, psychological, or economic oppression.

Physical abuse involves the application of force. It includes beating, slapping, punching, kicking, choking, stabbing, shooting, and throwing objects at the victim. Even when physical assaults are intermittent or isolated, they may have a long-term impact because the threat of repetition is never far from the victim's mind. Domination established through a single act of violence can produce long-term emotional abuse that is reinforced by subsequent threats, isolation, degradation, or economic control.[7]

Spousal homicide accounts for 15 percent of all homicide deaths in Canada. Four times as many women as men are killed by their spouses or partners.

---

4   House of Commons Standing Committee on Health and Welfare, Social Affairs, Seniors and the Status of Women, *Breaking the Silence on the Abuse of Older Canadians: Everyone's Concern* (Ottawa: The Committee, June 1993).

5   The first seniors' shelter in Canada was opened in east-end Montreal in 1992: *Ottawa Citizen* (12 August 1994) B7.

6   See Canadian Network for the Prevention of Elder Abuse, "A Draft Framework for a National Strategy for the Prevention of Abuse and Neglect of Older Adults in Canada: A Proposal" (7 November 2007), online: www.cnpea.ca/Strategy%20Framework%202007.pdf; and "Outlook 2007: Promising Approaches in the Prevention of Abuse and Neglect of Older Adults in Community Settings in Canada," online: www.cnpea.ca/Promising%20 Approaches%20Final%20%202007.pdf. See, generally, The Canadian Centre for Elder Law, online: www.bcli.org/ccel.

7   For insight into five basic types of inter-parental violence and corresponding patterns in parent-child relationships, see Janet R Johnston & Linda EG Campbell, "Parent-Child Relationships in Domestic Violence Families Disputing Custody" (July 1993) 31:3 Family and Conciliation Courts Review 282.

Sexual abuse is usually an aspect of physical abuse that involves the perpetration of sexual acts against the will of a spouse and may include marital rape. The fact that a couple is married or living together does not entitle either of them to insist that their partner engage in any form of sexual activity. Marital rape or any other forced sexual activity is an offence under the *Criminal Code*[8] of Canada. In 1983, the criminal offence of "rape" was replaced by the offence of sexual assault, which can be committed by a spouse or partner as well as by a stranger.

Emotional or psychological abuse most frequently arises from verbal assaults, such as threats or disparaging comments directed towards a spouse. Emotional abuse often accompanies physical or sexual abuse, but can exist in the absence of physical or sexual abuse. Emotional abuse signifies that one party demeans, belittles, degrades, or threatens the other party to such a degree that the victim's psychological well-being is in jeopardy.

Economic abuse arises from an improper exercise of control over personal or household finances by one spouse to the exclusion and deprivation of the other.

Spousal abuse is not confined to any age group or socio-economic class. Many victims of spousal abuse suffer in silence. Consequently, statistics on spousal abuse are notoriously speculative. A frequently cited statistic is that one in ten Canadian women are victims of abuse by their spouse or male partner. In a national survey of 12,300 women, released by Statistics Canada in November 1993, it was found that 51 percent of women had been victims of at least one incident of physical or sexual assault since the age of sixteen. The survey further indicated that 25 percent of these women had been victimized by their marital partner. More recent national surveys suggest that men are just as likely as women to be the victims of spousal abuse. In a random telephone survey of 26,000 Canadians conducted by Statistics Canada in 1999, 8 percent of women and 7 percent of men claimed to have been victims of violence from their spouses or partners at least once in the preceding five years. Sixty percent of those reporting violence had been victimized more than once. The survey revealed that women living in violent relationships were five times more likely than men to have feared for their life and the same ratio was found with respect to the need for subsequent medical attention. However, the survey also found that men are more likely than women to be slapped, kicked, or have something thrown at them. Rates of domestic violence against women ranged from 12 percent in Prince Edward Island to 4 percent in Newfoundland; rates for men ranged from 9 percent in Alberta

---

8   RSC 1985, c C-46.

to 5 percent in Newfoundland and Labrador and Ontario.[9] In 2005, Statistics Canada reported that 7 percent of women and 6 percent of men encountered spousal violence during the five years up to and including 2004.[10] In 2011, Statistics Canada reported that 6.4 percent of women reported physical or sexual abuse during the preceding five years; 6 percent of men reported spousal violence. In a ground-breaking decision, the Alberta Human Rights Commission in June 2000 ruled that family violence brochures published by an Edmonton counselling centre discriminated against men by perpetuating the myth that only men are abusive in relationships.[11]

Opinions differ on whether spousal abuse is increasing or whether there is simply an increase in the number of reported incidents. Opinions also differ on the causes and appropriate steps to be taken to deter such behaviour.

D. SOCIAL AND LEGAL RESPONSES TO SPOUSAL ABUSE

Domestic violence, and especially spousal abuse, has triggered various social and legal responses during the past twenty years. Although community agencies and resources are limited, they provide services and facilities that were virtually non-existent twenty years ago. Spousal assault "hotlines" and shelters for battered wives are now common in Canadian urban centres. The medical and legal professions, as well as the police, are more responsive to problems engendered by spousal abuse than they were hitherto.

1) Shelters and Transition Houses

In 2008, there were 569 shelters across Canada providing residential services to women and children escaping abusive situations. Transition homes, which provide short- to moderate-term housing, were the most common type of shelter. In 2008, they represented 47 percent of all shelters, while emergency-type facilities accounted for 26 percent.[12] There were about 4,300 women and their 3,400 dependent children in emergency shelters or transition houses

---

9   See Statistics Canada, *Family Violence in Canada: A Statistical Profile*, 2000, online: www.statcan.gc.ca/pub/85-224-x/85-224-x2000000-eng.pdf. And see Statistics Canada, "Violence against Women: Statistical Trends" *The Daily* (2 October 2006).

10   Statistics Canada, "Family Violence in Canada: A Statistical Profile" *The Daily* (14 July 2005); see also Donald G Dutton, *Rethinking Domestic Violence* (Vancouver: UBC Press, 2006).

11   Chris Cobb, "Violence Brochures Discriminate Against Men, Rights Body Rules" *National Post* (19 June 2000).

12   Statistics Canada, "Family Violence and Shelters for Abused Women" *The Daily* (15 October 2009). See, further, Statistics Canada, *Family Violence in Canada: A Statistical Profile*, online: www.statcan.gc.ca/pub/85-224-x/85-224-x2010000-eng.pdf.

on 16 April 2008. Approximately 75 percent of the women were escaping abuse; the remainder were there for other reasons such as housing, addiction, or mental health problems. Between 1 April 2007 and 31 March 2008, admissions to shelters reached just over 101,000 people: 62,000 women and 38,000 children.[13] The various types of facilities providing shelter to abused women include transition homes, women's emergency centres and emergency shelters, second-stage housing, and safe-home networks. They differ in terms of the length of stay and the array of services offered.[14] They are run by a combination of full-time and part-time staff together with volunteers. Their location is closely guarded for the purpose of ensuring the safety of the residents, but relevant telephone numbers are listed in the front of the telephone directory.

For the minority of men who are victims of spousal abuse, there are few comparable resources.

2) Counselling Services

Victims of spousal abuse use a variety of counselling services in urban communities. Family service agencies provide counselling services for dysfunctional families but specialized counselling services are also available to abused women. Governmental funding of specialized services, such as sexual assault centres, distress centres, alcohol and drug abuse treatment facilities, transition houses, and information services for abused women, is often short-term and subject to budgetary cutbacks. Furthermore, few facilities exist in rural communities or to serve special ethnic or cultural groups or recent immigrants.

Counselling for abused women is not confined to dealing with their emotional needs. Housing and financial needs as well as medical and legal needs must also be met. Above all, the future safety of victims of abuse must be assured to the fullest extent possible.

Counselling services are not always limited to the victims of abuse. Where domestic violence is linked to alcohol or drug abuse, some agencies offer counselling for the abuser. In addition, there are a few men's self-help groups for the perpetrators of domestic violence. These groups engage in counselling or therapy under the guidance of a professionally qualified group leader. Their objective is to enable abusers to take responsibility for their misconduct and develop alternatives to violence in dealing with interpersonal relationships. Although there has been some success with individual and

---

13   *Ibid.*
14   *Ibid.*

group therapy for abusers, there are probably no more than thirty-five self-help groups for abusers in all of Canada.

3) Legal Responses to Spousal Abuse

The law provides a veritable arsenal of weapons to deal with problems generated by spousal abuse. How effective they are is open to question. The following are some reasons the Ontario Women's Directorate gives as explanations for the reluctance of abused women to use the legal system:

1) fear of retaliation or revenge instilled in the victim by threats made over an extended period of time;
2) fear that the police and the courts will not believe that the abuse has occurred, will blame the victim for the abuse, or will take no action to protect the victim and her children;
3) desire to keep the family together;
4) fear of living in poverty on social assistance after a family breakdown;
5) lack of information regarding community services such as counselling, shelters, the Children's Aid Society, victim crisis units, and legal rights after marriage breakdown; and
6) for immigrant women, a fear that they or their partners will be deported, and mistrust of the police.

Battered women have traditionally encountered two primary obstacles to invoking legal remedies. First, they often have no money to hire a lawyer and must obtain a legal aid certificate in order to pursue civil proceedings, including matrimonial relief. Even when it is available, legal aid pays low hourly rates and therefore attracts junior lawyers in an area where substantial professional experience judgment is vital. Second, criminal prosecutions necessitate the intervention of the police, some of whom still perceive domestic violence as a private affair that should be resolved by the spouses rather than as a crime in which the public has an overriding interest. Although the police have traditionally been disinclined to use criminal prosecutions as a means of controlling or deterring spousal assaults except in cases of severe bodily injury or death, the Solicitor General of Ontario chartered a new course of action for police in that province by issuing policy directives to provincial police forces stipulating that, in the absence of exceptional circumstances, charges should be laid and prosecutions pursued regardless of the wishes of the victim. At the same time, the training of police has been improved by their introduction to new techniques of intervention in domestic disputes. Improving the response of the criminal justice system for abused women requires changes that include the following:

1) continuing training for everyone involved;
2) women's advocacy services;
3) a legal clinic for women;
4) beefed-up victim crisis units in the police service, and victim/witness assistance programs in the courts;
5) emphasis on front-end police investigation to reduce court costs by providing more guilty pleas and by shifting resources from police court activity to police investigations;
6) specialized prosecutors and courts;
7) making the court process more accessible to and supportive of complainants;
8) preventing defence lawyers from intimidating victims/witnesses;
9) maintaining a zero-tolerance policy for breach of restraining orders, conditions of bail, or probation;
10) insisting on mandatory counselling services for men who batter; and
11) all sectors of the criminal justice system working together to send a clear message to abusers that violence against women is a crime and will not be tolerated.

4) Criminal Law[15]

a) *Criminal Code* Offences

A person who commits a spousal assault may be charged with one or more of several offences under the *Criminal Code*[16] of Canada. The specific offences vary according to the type of conduct and the gravity of the injuries sustained.

Any person who intentionally applies force to another person, or attempts or threatens to do so, commits an "assault" under section 265 of the *Criminal Code* of Canada. This section applies to all forms of assault, including sexual assault. It carries a maximum penalty of five years' imprisonment. If the person committing an assault uses a weapon or causes bodily injury to the victim that is not transient in nature, this constitutes the separate offence of "assault with a weapon or assault causing bodily harm" under section 267 of the *Criminal Code*, which carries a maximum penalty of ten years' imprisonment. An even heavier penalty is imposed by section 268 of the *Criminal Code* for "aggravated assault." This offence is committed by any person

---

15 As to the negative impact of an overzealous response of the criminal justice system to alleged domestic violence on family members and its potential interference with a more nuanced response from family law and its processes, see *Shaw v Shaw*, 2008 ONCJ 130, Pugsley J.

16 RSC 1985, c C-46, as amended.

who "wounds, maims, disfigures or endangers the life of the complainant." It carries a maximum penalty of fourteen years' imprisonment. Sexual assaults are regulated by additional provisions of the *Criminal Code*. Section 271 imposes a maximum penalty of ten years' imprisonment for sexual assault. Section 272 regulates sexual assaults with a weapon, sexual assaults induced by threats to a third party, and sexual assaults causing bodily harm. These offences carry a maximum penalty of fourteen years' imprisonment. Section 273 defines the offence of "aggravated sexual assault," which involves wounding, maiming, disfiguring, or endangering the life of the victim. This offence is punishable by a maximum term of imprisonment for life. With respect to the evidence required to sustain a conviction for physical or sexual assault, corroboration is not required. Section 278 of the *Criminal Code* specifically provides that a husband or wife may be charged with an offence under sections 271, 272, or 273 of the *Criminal Code*, whether or not the spouses were living together at the time of the conduct complained of. The former notion that marriage necessarily implied consent to sexual intercourse between the spouses has been abandoned. Spouses may, of course, be charged with other offences under the *Criminal Code*, including murder.

Section 264 of the *Criminal Code* imposes a maximum penalty of five years' imprisonment on any person who knowingly or recklessly harasses another person by engaging in conduct causing that person to reasonably fear for his or her own safety or the safety of anyone known to that person.[17] The section identifies four kinds of conduct that will sustain a conviction, namely,

1) repeatedly following, from place to place, the other person or anyone known to him or her;
2) repeatedly communicating with, either directly or indirectly, the other person or anyone known to him or her;
3) besetting or watching the dwelling-house or place where the other person, or anyone known to him or her, resides, works, carries on business, or happens to be; or
4) engaging in threatening conduct directed at the other person or any member of his or her family.

There are three elements to the crime of criminal harassment:

1) The accused must be found to have engaged in one or more of the types of conduct prescribed.

---

17   See *R v MH*, 2014 ONSC 36.

2) It must be established that, while engaging in one of the types of prohibited conduct, the accused either intended to harass the complainant, or was reckless as to whether his conduct would harass the complainant. The court may infer intent to recklessness if it finds that the accused had no legitimate purpose for engaging in the conduct complained of.

3) It must be established that the complainant had reasonable fears for her safety or the safety of anyone known to her. This includes both physical and psychological safety.

The court must apply an objective standard when determining whether the complainant reasonably feared for his or her safety or the safety of another person. In making this objective determination, the court must look at all of the circumstances, including the gender of the complainant and the history of the circumstances surrounding the relationship with the accused.

The aforementioned provisions of the *Criminal Code* are triggered by the commission of an offence. Preventative justice is also available, however, under section 810 of the *Criminal Code*. This section empowers a Provincial Court judge or a justice of the peace to require a person to enter into a recognizance or financial bond to keep the peace where there is a reasonable apprehension that he or she will cause personal injury to a spouse or child or damage their property. The recognizance can be required for any period not exceeding twelve months. It may contain such conditions as the court considers desirable for securing good behaviour. Typical conditions preclude access to the complainant's residence, place of employment, or to any school attended by the children, and restrictions or prohibitions concerning telephone or written communications. A person who refuses to enter in a recognizance or who breaches a recognizance is guilty of an offence under sections 810 and 811 of the *Criminal Code*.

The threat of criminal prosecution has not been an unqualified success in deterring spousal assaults. Convictions are difficult to secure when wives refuse to testify against their husbands, against whom charges have been laid. Some wives fear further violence or feel financially threatened by the prospect that criminal prosecution may result in a conviction. Other victims wish to put the past behind them rather than relive it in the witness box. Still others have reconciled with the abuser, notwithstanding that the cycle of abuse may be indicative of future risk. Ironically, wives who refuse to testify against their husbands may themselves be charged with the offence of obstructing justice under section 139 of the *Criminal Code*. In addition to the difficulties encountered in securing convictions for spousal assaults, whether physical or sexual, the sentencing practices of some courts evoke strong criticism. Some judges are inclined to extol the virtues of preserving the marriage by imposing a lenient sentence. Absolute and conditional discharges are too frequently the outcome of criminal prosecutions for spousal assault. Although opinions may differ on whether imprisonment is an appropriate sanction, one alternative that has been effective in less heinous offences is treatment as a condition of probation. This joint application of a carrot-and-stick approach to spousal abusers may offer a constructive response to the complex dynamics of spousal assault. There is, however, a public interest that must also be considered in criminal prosecutions for spousal abuse. The Alberta Court of Appeal has emphasized the significance of criminal sanctions as a general and individual deterrent to spousal abuse. Pleas by the abused victim that a lengthy sentence of imprisonment will produce further victimization, whether economically or otherwise, may have to yield to the pressing need for an effective deterrent.[18] In a sentencing study released in 2004, it was found that family members convicted of violent crimes against spouses, children, and seniors are less likely to receive a prison sentence than other violent offenders. According to police and court records from 1997 to 2002, judges handed down prison sentences in 19 percent of convictions for spousal violence. The comparable figure for non-spousal violence convictions was 29 percent. The only exception occurred with respect to the offence of criminal harassment, where one-third of the spouses received a prison term compared with one-quarter of non-spousal offenders.[19] Family members convicted of physical violence against their children also received less harsh sentences than non-family members, except with respect to convictions for sexual abuse, where the converse was true.

Many people find it incomprehensible that victims of spousal abuse do not withdraw from the threatening environment. Why do they stay? This issue attracted the attention of the Supreme Court of Canada in a celebrated case where a victim of abuse had been charged with murdering her abusive common law husband. In acquitting the accused on the ground of self-defence, the Supreme Court of Canada acknowledged the need for expert evidence to negate popular myths surrounding spousal abuse. Madam Justice Wilson summarized the principles upon which expert evidence is properly admitted in the following observations:

1. Expert testimony is admissible to assist the fact-finder in drawing inferences in areas where the expert has relevant knowledge or experience beyond that of the lay person.

---

18 *R v Brown* (1992), 13 CR (4th) 346 (Alta CA); *R v Bell*, [1992] AJ No 495 (CA), discussed in *The Lawyers Weekly* (3 July 1992) 17.

19 Statistics Canada, "Family Violence in Canada: A Statistical Profile" *The Daily* (6 July 2004), online: www.statcan.gc.ca/pub/85-224-x/85-224-x2004000-eng.pdf.

2. It is difficult for the lay person to comprehend the battered wife syndrome. It is commonly thought that battered women are not really beaten as badly as they claim, otherwise they would have left the relationship. Alternatively, some believe that women enjoy being beaten, that they have a masochistic strain in them. Each of these stereotypes may adversely affect consideration of a battered woman's claim to have acted in self-defence in killing her mate.

3. Expert evidence can assist the jury in dispelling these myths.

4. Expert testimony relating to the ability of an accused to perceive danger from her mate may go to the issue of whether she "reasonably apprehended" death or grievous bodily harm on a particular occasion.

5. Expert testimony pertaining to why an accused remained in the battering relationship may be relevant in assessing the nature and extent of the alleged abuse.

6. By providing an explanation as to why an accused did not flee when she perceived her life to be in danger, expert testimony may also assist the jury in assessing the reasonableness of her belief that killing her batterer was the only way to save her own life.

Quite apart from Dr. Shane's testimony there was ample evidence on which the trial judge could conclude that the appellant was battered repeatedly and brutally by Kevin Rust over the course of their relationship. The fact that she may have exhibited aggressive behaviour on occasion or tried (unsuccessfully) to leave does not detract from a finding of systematic and relentless abuse. In my view, the trial judge did not err in admitting Dr. Shane's expert testimony in order to assist the jury in determining whether the appellant had a reasonable apprehension of death or grievous bodily harm and believed on reasonable grounds that she had no alternative but to shoot Kevin Rust on the night in question.

Obviously the fact that the appellant was a battered woman does not entitle her to an acquittal. Battered women may well kill their partners other than in self-defence. The focus is not on who the woman is, but on what she did . . . .

Ultimately, it is up to the jury to decide whether, in fact, the accused's perceptions and actions were reasonable. Expert evidence does not and cannot usurp that function of the jury. The jury is not compelled to accept the opinions proffered by the expert about the effects of battering on the mental state of victims generally or on the mental state of the accused in particular. But fairness and the integrity of the trial process demand that the jury have the opportunity to hear them.[20]

---

20   *R v Lavallee*, [1990] 1 SCR 852 at 889–91.

The expert evidence adduced before the Supreme Court of Canada on the "battered wife syndrome" demonstrated that a woman who lives in a battering relationship is paralyzed by the tyranny of the abuser. She is psychologically incapable of withdrawing from the abusive relationship regardless of her economic ability to do so. She loses her sense of self-worth and becomes helpless. Some wives find the strength to leave. Others may strike back in self-defence, but few can hope to resist the more powerful aggressor.

b)   Specialized Criminal Courts[21]

In Winnipeg, Manitoba, a provincial criminal court has been established since 1990 to deal exclusively with family violence, which encompasses elder, spousal, and child abuse. Specialized Crown Attorneys prosecute these cases. There is a victim assistance service called the Women's Advocacy Program. There is also a Family Violence Unit within the probation services that provides individual assessments, counselling, and long-term treatment for offenders.

Independent evaluation of this project suggests that it provides a more efficient legal process and a more sensitive legal service for victims of family violence. It has resulted in an increase in the number of criminal charges laid and an increase in the conviction rates.

Since 1997, Ontario has established new domestic violence courts in Hamilton, London, North Bay, North York, Oshawa, and Ottawa.

c)   Provincial Statutory Developments

Several provinces have enacted legislation to protect victims of family violence. For example, in 1994, the *Victims of Domestic Violence Act*[22] was enacted in Saskatchewan. It confers broad powers on justices of the peace, police officers, and social workers to intervene in cases of domestic violence. Justices of the peace are empowered to grant emergency orders at any time during the day or night and such orders may be granted over the telephone. These intervention orders can grant exclusive possession of the family home to alleged victims, can direct the police to remove the alleged abuser from the home, and can restrain the alleged abuser from contacting the victim. Police officers can also obtain entry warrants to allow them to enter a home and assist a suspected victim even when no complaint has been laid. The Act also empowers judges of the Court of Queen's Bench to issue assistance orders to compel abusers to pay compensation to their victims and to give victims temporary possession of personal property.

---

21   See E Jane Ursel, "The Family Violence Court of Winnipeg" (1992) 21 Man LJ 100.
22   SS 1994, c V-6.02.

Provincial legislation regulating domestic violence has withstood constitutional challenge. Thus, in *Baril v Obelnicki*,[23] it was held that the pith and substance of the *Domestic Violence and Stalking Prevention, Protection and Compensation Act*[24] is in the nature of crime prevention and thus falls within the provincial legislative domain. Protection orders granted pursuant to the Act are in the nature of preventive justice, similar to orders historically granted by magistrates and justices of the peace, and therefore do not violate section 96 of the *Constitution Act, 1867*.[25] Although the provincial statute infringes the respondent's freedom of expression in contravention of section 2(b) of the *Canadian Charter of Rights and Freedoms*,[26] such infringement is justified under section 1 of the *Charter*. An order limiting the respondent's freedom of movement in relation to the applicant so as to prevent contact and end stalking behaviour constitutes an infringement of the respondent's liberty under section 7 of the *Charter*. However, such infringement accords with the principles of fundamental justice so long as the respondent is provided a fair trial with fair procedures, the nature of those procedures being determined within the context of the Act's purpose and objectives. The statutory provisions allowing for a protection order to be granted without notice, and for the transcribed evidence from the without notice hearing to be used at the review hearing, are in accord with the principles of fundamental justice. However, section 12(2) of the Act is problematic in that it places the burden of proof on the respondent rather than on the applicant by requiring the respondent "to demonstrate, on the balance of probabilities, that the protection order should be set aside." Rather than strike it down as the motion court judge had done, the Manitoba Court of Appeal read the provision down to constitute an evidentiary burden. Instead of being required to show that the without notice order was granted in error, the respondent need only show, on a balance of probabilities, that there is an issue arising from the without notice hearing that warrants the order being set aside on the basis of an absence of full disclosure or based on the weight of all the evidence adduced at both the without notice and review hearings. This would accord with the principles of fundamental justice.

5) Matrimonial Proceedings

With the exception of divorce proceedings, which may include corollary issues relating to support and custody, matrimonial relief available to abused

---

23   2007 MBCA 40.
24   CCSM c D93.
25   Schedule B to the *Canada Act 1982* (UK), 1982, c 11.
26   The *Constitution Act, 1982*, Schedule B to the *Canada Act 1982* (UK), 1982, c 11.

spouses is regulated by provincial laws. Issues of spousal and child support and of custody and access are governed by the federal *Divorce Act*[27] if they arise on divorce. If they arise independently of divorce, they are governed by provincial statute.

a)   Divorce Act

Spousal abuse, whether physical, sexual, psychological, or economic, may constitute mental or physical cruelty of such a kind as to render matrimonial cohabitation intolerable. In that event, the victim of abuse may petition the courts for divorce on the basis that such conduct manifests a permanent breakdown of the marriage. A husband's violent attack on his wife on a single occasion may justify a finding of physical cruelty that will warrant the granting of a divorce.[28] In the ordinary course of events, however, cruelty involves a course of conduct over a period of time. The cumulative effect of such conduct on the petitioner is the critical test of cruelty.[29] Verbal abuse may constitute "mental cruelty" for the purpose of divorce,[30] as may also a husband's domineering, unloving, and inconsiderate attitude to his wife in the home and his belittling her in public.[31] Excessive or improper sexual demands on a spouse,[32] or the withholding of necessary financial support,[33] may also constitute "mental cruelty" within the meaning of federal divorce legislation. The following quotation aptly summarizes the law:

> When the acts of cruelty relied upon take the form of abuse, quarrels, nagging, selfishness, etc. there is a greater danger of their being categorized as examples of incompatibility rather than of cruelty. However, where one spouse insists on totally dominating the other or deprives the other of his company or ridicules and belittles his spouse or is selfish and ignores his obligations of support he or she may be found guilty of cruelty. Similarly, threats of physical violence towards the petitioner, her children or towards the respondent himself, false accusations of theft, of non-support or of

---

27   RSC 1985, c 3 (2d Supp).

28   *Aucoin v Aucoin* (1976), 28 RFL 43 (NSCA).

29   *Pongor v Pongor* (1976), 27 RFL 109 (Ont CA).

30   *Greggain v Hunter* (1984), 31 Sask R 311 (UFC).

31   *Ratcliffe v Ratcliffe* (1977), 27 RFL 227 (BCSC); *Nichols v Nichols* (1968), 1 NSR (1965–69) 503 (TD).

32   *Rankin v Rankin* (1970), 13 DLR (3d) 630 (BCSC); *M v M* (1971), 3 RFL 350 (Ont CA); *M v M* (1975), 16 RFL 291 (NBCA).

33   *Brewer v Brewer* (1978), 21 NBR (2d) 154 (QB); *Gollins v Gollins*, [1963] 2 All ER 966 (HL).

infidelity, vulgar abuse, constant nagging, and unseemly "scenes" before others, can amount to cruelty.[34]

In the final analysis, each case of alleged cruelty must be decided on its own facts.

b) Spousal and Child Support

An abused spouse who has separated from the abuser may institute legal proceedings for spousal and child support. These claims can be brought as part of a divorce petition, or independently under provincial or territorial legislation. If an abused wife is unable to meet her own financial needs, and those of any children, she may seek a court order for spousal and child support. Entitlement to spousal support under provincial or territorial legislation will depend on whether she satisfies the statutory definition of "spouse." Married people do. Some common law spouses may do so; other common law spouses may not. It depends on the express provisions of the statute in the particular province or territory wherein the legal proceedings are instituted. If the statutory definition of "spouse" is met, spousal support orders will usually be granted or denied on the basis of the applicant's needs and the ability of the other spouse to pay. In divorce proceedings, only married persons or already divorced spouses are eligible to bring claims for "spousal" support.

Although claims for spousal and child support may be triggered by spousal abuse that brings matrimonial cohabitation to an end, courts cannot punish the abusing spouse by increasing the amount of support payable to a dependent spouse or child. Subsection 15.2(5) of the *Divorce Act* expressly stipulates that "the court shall not take into consideration any misconduct of a spouse in relation to the marriage" in making an order for spousal or child support. Similar, though not identical provisions, can be found in many provincial and territorial statutes that regulate spousal and child support proceedings arising independently of divorce. Spousal and child support are usually based on need and are not intended to punish spousal misconduct. If, however, spousal abuse impairs the ability of a dependent spouse to achieve financial self-sufficiency, the need thereby arising can be met by an order for a reasonable level of spousal support.[35]

---

34 *Brewer v Brewer* (1978), 21 NBR (2d) 154 (QB), Stevenson J, citing W Kent Power & Christine Davies, *Power on Divorce*, 3d ed (Toronto: Carswell, 1976) at 64–65.

35 *Anderson v Anderson* (1990), 27 RFL (3d) 358 (Man QB); see also *Jones v Jones*, [1975] 2 All ER 12 (CA), wherein the right to and amount of spousal support were affected by the husband's physical assault of his wife that prevented her from pursuing her nursing career and rendered her prospects of alternative employment somewhat doubtful.

c)   Custody and Access[36]

Federal divorce legislation and many provincial and territorial statutes stipu-late that spousal misconduct is irrelevant to issues of custody of and access to the children unless such conduct reflects on that person's ability to parent. Subsection 24(4) of the Ontario *Children's Law Reform Act*[37] specifically iden-tifies domestic violence as of special significance to custody and access dis-putes. Some judges fail to appreciate that spousal abuse to which children are witnesses may be just as detrimental to a child's development as abuse where the child is the primary victim. Other judges show enlightenment by recog-nizing that, even in the absence of physical or sexual abuse, psychological spousal abuse may constitute a compelling reason for denying custody of the children to the abusive parent.[38]

If an abused wife leaves home to secure her own safety, she may take the children with her. If the children do not accompany her but she wishes to obtain sole legal custody, she should institute legal proceedings as soon as possible. Substantial delay can be fatal to a claim for custody. Courts do not normally grant custody to an abusive spouse. They may, however, grant ac-cess privileges that enable an abusive spouse to preserve meaningful contact with the children. The abusive parent is not free to see or contact the child whenever he wants to. The terms of access will be spelled out in the court order. If the children would be at risk sexually, physically, or emotionally, access may be denied. Alternatively, the court may order that an abusive par-ent exercise access privileges under the supervision of a neutral third party. The Attorney General of Ontario has provided funding for supervised access from time to time but there has been no permanently guaranteed funding.

d)   Orders for Exclusive Possession of Matrimonial Home

Matters relating to property rights, including rights to exclusive possession of the matrimonial home, are regulated by provincial legislation in Canada. Federal divorce legislation is silent on these issues. In Ontario, section 24 of the *Family Law Act*[39] expressly empowers a court to grant exclusive posses-sion of the matrimonial home and its contents to either spouse regardless of ownership rights. Similar legislation exists in other provinces and territories. Subsection 24(3) of the Ontario *Family Law Act* identifies the following six

---

36   See Nicholas Bala, Peter G Jaffe, & Claire V Crooks, "Spousal Violence and Child Related Cases: Challenging Cases Requiring Differentiated Responses" (2007) 27 Fam LQ 1; Pe-ter G Jaffe *et al*, "Custody Disputes Involving Allegations of Domestic Violence: Toward a Differentiated Approach to Parenting" (2008) 46 Fam Ct Rev 500.

37   RSO 1990, c C.12, s 24, as amended by SO 2006, c 1, s 3(1).

38   See *MAB v LAB*, 2013 NSSC 89.

39   RSO 1990, c F.3. See, generally, Chapter 13, Section A(18)(d).

factors that must be considered on an application to the court for exclusive possession of the matrimonial home:

a) the best interests of the children affected;
b) any existing court orders;
c) the financial position of both spouses;
d) any written agreement between the parties;
e) the availability of other suitable and affordable accommodation; and
f) any violence committed by a spouse against the other spouse or children.

"Violence" within the meaning of paragraph 24(3)(f) of the Ontario *Family Law Act* includes psychological violence.[40] Orders for exclusive possession of the matrimonial home may also be granted pursuant to section 34 of the Ontario *Family Law Act* in proceedings for spousal support. In this latter context, section 29 of the Ontario *Family Law Act* defines "spouse" to include unmarried persons who have cohabited continuously for not less than three years or who have cohabited "in a relationship of some permanence" and are the natural or adoptive parents of a child. Judicial opinion is, nevertheless, divided on the question whether unmarried cohabitants are entitled to claim exclusive possession rights in a "matrimonial" home under the Ontario *Family Law Act*.[41]

e) Restraining Orders

In addition to or instead of granting an exclusive possession order of the matrimonial home, a court may grant a restraining order. Section 46 of the Ontario *Family Law Act*[42] provides as follows:

> *Restraining order*
>
> 46. (1) On application, the court may make an interim or final restraining order against a person described in subsection (2) if the applicant has reasonable grounds to fear for his or her own safety or for the safety of any child in his or her lawful custody.
>
> (2) A restraining order under subsection (1) may be made against,
>
> (a) a spouse or former spouse of the applicant; or
>
> (b) a person other than a spouse or former spouse of the applicant, if the person is cohabiting with the applicant or has cohabited with the applicant for any period of time.

---

40 *Hill v Hill* (1987), 10 RFL (3d) 225 (Ont Dist Ct).

41 See *Czora v Lonergan* (1987), 7 RFL (3d) 458 (Ont Dist Ct); *Akman v Burshtein*, [2009] OJ No 1499 (Sup Ct).

42 RSO 1990, c F.3, as amended by SO 2009, c 11, s 35.

Provisions of order

(3) A restraining order made under subsection (1) shall be in the form prescribed by the rules of court and may contain one or more of the following provisions, as the court considers appropriate:

1. Restraining the respondent, in whole or in part, from directly or indirectly contacting or communicating with the applicant or any child in the applicant's lawful custody.

2. Restraining the respondent from coming within a specified distance of one or more locations.

3. Specifying one or more exceptions to the provisions described in paragraphs 1 and 2.

4. Any other provision that the court considers appropriate.

. . .

Order regarding conduct

47.1 In making any order under this Part, other than an order under section 46, the court may also make an interim order prohibiting, in whole or in part, a party from directly or indirectly contacting or communicating with another party, if the court determines that the order is necessary to ensure that an application under this Part is dealt with justly.[43]

The most significant legislative change is that breach of a restraining order now constitutes a criminal offence under section 127 of the *Criminal Code* that is punishable by a term of imprisonment not exceeding two years.

6) Actions for Damages

In *Costantini v Costantini*,[44] Pazaratz J, of the Ontario Superior Court of Justice, made the following observations:

21   Tort actions for spousal violence have become more commonplace in Canada during the past 30 years, at least in part because of increased public awareness and universal condemnation of such behaviour.

22   But given the continuing prevalence of domestic violence in the community, only a tiny fraction of potential tort claims are ever advanced:

a. Many litigants may be unaware the tort option exists.

b. Family law lawyers tend to be more attuned to dealing with claims based on statute rather than tort.

---

43   Restraining orders may also be granted pursuant to section 35 of the *Children's Law Reform Act*, RSO 1990, c C.12, as repealed and re-enacted in section 15 of the *Family Statute Law Amendment Act, 2009*, SO 2009, c 11.

44   2013 ONSC 1626 at paras 21–28 [emphasis in original].

c.   Some lawyers and clients may be reluctant to pursue such a claim fearing it will aggravate an already difficult situation.

d.   Family finances are often so limited, there's little point in adding yet another potential monetary claim to the mix.

e.   There may even be systemic discouragement. Over the years our family court system has worked hard to get away from blame and recrimination — by discouraging "inflammatory" affidavits in favour of case management; by telling conflicted parents to focus more on the future than the past; by promoting conciliation and collaborative dispute resolution; by granting "no fault" divorces. We may have promoted a misconception: that *fault never matters.*

23   During family law proceedings spouses may claim for damages for tortious behaviour that took place during the relationship. *Booth v. Booth* (1995) 80 O.A.C. 399 (Ont. C.A.).

24   Indeed, it is preferable that all potential claims arising from the breakdown of a relationship — including tort claims — be dealt with at the same time. A consolidated action has the advantage of saving litigation costs and court time; ensuring consistency in the outcomes; and allowing a tort judgment to be factored into the overall financial result. *A.(I.) v. S.(R.H.)* (2000) 5 R.F.L. (5th) 1 (Ont. S.C.J.); *Cunningham v. Cunningham* 2013 ONSC 282 (Ont. S.C.J.).

25   The conduct in question must rise to the level of tort and may not simply be evidence of a dysfunctional relationship. *Hill v. Kilbrei* [2005] 11 W.W.R. 1.

26   Tort claims based on physical violence perpetrated by a spouse will almost invariably include a mental health or "emotional impact" component. Claims based solely on "intentional infliction of mental suffering" have been less prevalent — and less successful — perhaps a reflection that mental suffering is hardly a unique circumstance among separating spouses.

27   Behaviours that are conducted in "humiliating or undignified circumstances" may attract an award of aggravated damages (on top of general damages). *Hill v. Kilbrei* (supra) at paragraph 38, citing *Norberg v. Wynrib,* [1992] 2 S.C.R. 226 (S.C.C.) at paragraph 263.

28   A number of recent decisions have reviewed the essential elements of a tort claim, and in some cases significant damages have been awarded.

If a person causes bodily injury to any other person, including a spouse or common law spouse, monetary compensation is available in a civil action for damages.[45] Assault and battery constitute actionable torts in every Canadian

---

45   As to the quantum of damages, see *Dekany v Parenteau*, 2014 ONSC 49 (Div Ct).

province and territory. Unlawful restraints on the freedom of movement of another person may constitute the tort of false imprisonment and the intentional infliction of mental suffering may also ground an action for damages in tort. Most successful claims for damages in Canadian courts have been confined, however, to damages for physical assaults that caused bodily injury. This is, nevertheless, an evolving field of liability, particularly with respect to such matters as the transmission of diseases, such as genital herpes and AIDS. In an Ontario case, a wife sued her husband for substantial damages on the basis of breach of fiduciary duty, negligent or intentional infliction of emotional distress, negligent or fraudulent misrepresentations, and battery. She alleged that her husband was a practising bisexual who had failed to disclose his premarital and extramarital affairs with the consequence that she was fearful of contracting AIDS. The husband brought a preliminary application to strike out the wife's action because it disclosed no foundation for the imposition of legal liability and constituted an abuse of the judicial process. This application was dismissed, thus allowing the merits of the wife's alternative claims to go to trial.[46]

In an Alberta case, harassing telephone calls have been characterized as an actionable tort that entitled the wife to damages in addition to an injunction prohibiting future calls. Remedies in tort law do not stand in the place of criminal prosecution. They provide a financial remedy for the victim as distinct from the *Criminal Code*, which imposes financial or other penalties on the perpetrator.

As an alternative to suing an abuser, who may be incapable of paying damages, a victim of a crime of violence may seek compensation from the appropriate provincial or territorial Criminal Injuries Compensation Board. The criteria for such compensation are prescribed by provincial legislation. Recovery of compensation is not dependent upon the prior criminal conviction of the abuser. In 1994, three women were granted $15,000 each by the Ontario Criminal Injuries Compensation Board because they contracted the AIDS virus after engaging in sexual intercourse with a man who died from AIDS some months before the Board's ruling. The criminality of the man's conduct arose not simply from his transmission of the virus, but from his wanton and reckless disregard for the women's lives that he placed at risk by lying about his health and engaging in unprotected sex when he was aware that he had tested positive for the AIDS virus.[47]

---

46   *Bell-Ginsburg v Ginsburg* (1993), 48 RFL (3d) 208 (Ont Gen Div).

47   *Ottawa Citizen* (8 February 1994) A3.

E. THE VICTIM'S RESPONSE TO SPOUSAL ABUSE

Abused spouses must develop a plan of action to accommodate their basic needs for the following:

- safety;
- medical assistance;
- housing;
- financial assistance;
- legal assistance; and
- emotional support.

The minimum amount of information needed by an abused spouse involves awareness of the wide variety of support services available in the community. As a starting point, an abused spouse should have the local and emergency telephone numbers for the following:

- the police;
- the hospital;
- women's shelters;
- general welfare assistance;
- legal aid services;
- family service agencies; and
- community hotlines.

Police are on call twenty-four hours every day to provide emergency intervention for any person whose personal safety is threatened, but police cannot be at a home all day and every day in order to guarantee protection. As stated previously, there are legal means whereby an abuser may be ordered by a court to leave the victim alone. A recognizance or peace bond can be obtained under the *Criminal Code* of Canada. An order can also be obtained in civil proceedings whereby the abuser is ordered to refrain from molesting or harassing the victim or her children. An order for exclusive possession of the matrimonial home may also be obtainable in civil proceedings. These orders provide some measure of protection to an abused spouse. If they are unlikely to be respected by the abuser, however, the victim must have a fall-back position. Safety must be the paramount concern. Where can an abused spouse go to ensure her safety? Relatives or friends may be available to provide or find a safe place for her. She should also contact a women's shelter. The advantage of this last course of action is that she will then be provided with information concerning other agencies and services that may accommodate her longer-term needs.

An abused spouse should be ready to leave home at any time when she foresees that violence will erupt. She should keep clothes handy for herself and the children so as to be prepared for a quick departure. She should remember to take any necessary documents with her, such as her marriage certificate, birth certificates for herself and the children, passports, medical insurance cards, social insurance cards, and court orders. Keys, a telephone list, and a favourite toy for each child should not be forgotten. If she leaves home and needs to return for something she has forgotten, she should be accompanied by the police or some third person. If there is time to plan, she should put away an emergency fund.

Abused spouses have great difficulty in disclosing what has happened to them. If a lawyer is to give sound advice, full disclosure is essential. Details of specific incidents, rather than bald assertions of violence, must be provided to the lawyer and, ultimately, the court. Visits to a doctor or hospital should be noted so that medical and hospital records may be obtained as evidence of the violence.

Many spouses fear that as soon as any legal documents are served on the abuser, this will itself trigger further violence. If this is a real danger, a lawyer can institute *ex parte* civil proceedings to obtain a restraining order against the abusing spouse before any legal documents are served. The order is then served on the abusing spouse who is given the opportunity to challenge it on the basis that the allegations were improper.

Court orders do not provide any guarantee that violence will not occur. A court order may be contravened. The benefits of an order are, nevertheless, worthwhile. Court orders underline for the community at large the gravity of the behaviour complained of. They are also helpful if the police are called. The police will know that they are dealing with an abusing spouse and they are less likely to regard the matter as one to be resolved by the spouses themselves. Contravention of court orders also carries certain penalties, such as fines or imprisonment.

F. PROPOSALS FOR REFORM

In 1991, the federal government established the Canadian Panel on Violence against Women to examine the incidence of spousal violence and the measures necessary to combat it. The panel presented its report on 29 July 1993. It contains 494 recommendations. Many of the panel members were familiar with spousal abuse by virtue of their involvement with women's shelters, the courts, or public health. They were, nevertheless, shocked by the evidence presented to them at public hearings in 139 Canadian communities. Among the statistics compiled, the following figures paint an alarming picture:

1) Interviews with a random sample of 420 women between the ages of 18 and 64 revealed that 51 percent of them had been the victims of rape or attempted rape and 43 percent reported at least one experience of incest and/or extrafamilial sexual abuse before the age of 16.
2) More than 78,000 people were admitted to protective shelters in 1992.
3) In 1991, 270 women were murdered. Of the 225 cases that were solved, all but 15 women were killed by men — more than half by husbands or lovers.

Using what is termed a "feminist lens," the report characterizes violence against women as inextricably linked to women's social and economic inequality. In consequence, the recommendations in the report are extremely ambitious and far-reaching, so much so that some early critics regarded them as utopian, while others contend that the $10 million cost of the report would have been far better spent on funding women's shelters, sexual assault centres, and advocacy groups, all of which are chronically underfunded.

The following summary highlights the wide range and multiplicity of the recommendations:

1) *Equality Rights*: Make sexual orientation a prohibited ground for discrimination; strengthen human rights laws to address systemic discrimination; recognize persecution on the basis of gender as an explicit ground for granting refugee status; reinstate and expand the Court Challenges Program to enable women to fight for equality rights in the courts.
2) *Services*: Provide core funding for women's shelters, sexual assault and rape crisis centres; establish national standards for the provision of adequate services, such as a crisis toll-free telephone number in each community in remote communities and an emergency shelter or services within one hour commuting distance from each community; set up a committee in every community to co-ordinate services to survivors of violence against women.
3) *Legal System*: Develop mandatory training programs on violence against women for judges and parole board members; support the development of specialized courts to deal with crimes of violence; identify ways to reduce acquittals based on "legal" technicalities; train legal aid lawyers to deal with spousal abuse; initiate programs to remove the abuser rather than the victim from the home whenever possible and use technology such as electronic monitoring devices to safeguard potential victims.
4) *Criminal Code*: Repeal soliciting law, change obscenity provisions to prohibit sexually violent and degrading material; collect DNA evidence from all those accused of sex offences and create a DNA data bank to identify serial offenders.

5) *Family*: Implement a national child care program and encourage work-place child care services through funding or tax relief; implement educational programs for men, women, and young boys and girls to create greater awareness of shared obligations within the family.

6) *Taxes*: Analyze all proposed tax system changes for bias or adverse effects based on gender; address the taxation and collection problems associated with child support obligations; acknowledge through the tax system the costs of raising children and the reduced capacity of families with children to pay taxes.

7) *Police*: Create and enforce the implementation of policies to ensure that initial police response and decisions on arrest, detention, and terms of any release support the safety of the victim and prevent revictimization; establish a women's safety advisory board locally and nationally in the RCMP that includes representation from Aboriginal and Inuit women.

8) *Workplace*: Develop a written code of conduct based on zero tolerance for violence that promotes equality and guarantees safety for all workers and clients.

9) *Military*: Counterbalance combat readiness training, which can make men very aggressive and domineering, with human relations training that emphasizes the inappropriateness and danger of aggression in interpersonal relationships.

10) *Education*: Make violence prevention a part of all school curricula; implement effective policies against sexual and racial violence; train staff to recognize the linkages between inequality and violence and to incorporate this knowledge in their work; make awareness of such linkages a formal rating factor in staff performance appraisals; hold all staff and students accountable for sexist and racist behaviour.

11) *Media*: Broadcasters should develop significantly more women's programming; print media should dedicate space as frequently as possible to issues of violence, women's safety, and equality; advertisers should commit support to non-violent productions and should create anti-violence advertising.

12) *Churches*: Religious institutions must work to revise teachings that promote inequality of women and support violence against women and adopt democratic structures to balance power between religious leaders and followers.

13) *Government*: Adopt and implement a zero-tolerance policy against violence and an equality action plan; require organizations that receive contracts for more than $100,000 to do the same; enact a Status of Women Act to identify the specific obligations and responsibilities of the federal government to ensure that the rights to equality and safety of all Canadian women are supported and advanced.

Many of the above recommendations signify that violence against women will not be checked until we live in an egalitarian society.

G. NATURE OF CHILD ABUSE

Child abuse may involve physical, sexual, or emotional oppression of children. Some definitions include economic deprivation, such as failure to provide adequate food, clothing, housing, or medical care for a child. Other definitions identify these situations as "child neglect" as distinct from "child abuse."

Physical abuse typically signifies an improper application of force that results in bruises, cuts, burns, broken bones, internal injuries and, in its most extreme form, death.

Sexual abuse is conduct that involves the sexual molestation or exploitation of children. Examples include incest, rape, sodomy, carnal knowledge, sexual touching, or procuring a child's involvement in prostitution or pornography.

Emotional abuse refers to conduct that produces psychological harm to the child. Emotional abuse undermines a child's sense of well-being and impairs the child's development and ability to reach his or her full potential. It often produces lifelong difficulties for the emotionally abused victim.

H. SOCIAL AND LEGAL RESPONSES TO CHILD ABUSE

Child abuse is found in all societies. It has often been hidden or ignored. "Spare the rod and spoil the child" has only recently been displaced by the realization that "violence breeds violence." Research studies demonstrate that child abuse must be prevented not only to save this generation of children but also to save the next generation. Far too often, an abused child in turn becomes the abusing parent of his or her own child.

Statistics indicate that sexual abuse of children is predominantly a male offence, although there are a significant number of cases where mothers have been involved. Mothers are just as likely as fathers to physically or emotionally abuse their children.[48] Many instances of child abuse involve preschool children and single-parent households.[49] These factors may partially explain the statistics concerning female perpetrators in that many mothers are left to carry the responsibility of parenthood with little or no help from the fathers.

---

48   See Honourable Senator Anne C Cools, *Senate Debates* (21 March 1996) at 113, citing a study of the Toronto Institute for the Prevention of Child Abuse entitled *The Ontario Incidence of Reported Child Abuse and Neglect 1994.*

49   *Ibid.*

Canada, like many other countries, historically offered greater protection to animals than to children. Canadian legislation prohibiting cruelty to animals can be traced back to 1824. The first statute to prohibit cruelty to children was enacted in 1893 when the Ontario legislature passed an *Act for the Prevention of Cruelty to and Better Protection of Children*.[50] Manitoba enacted similar legislation in 1898 and the other provinces followed these precedents in the early-twentieth century.

Today, every province and territory in Canada has relatively sophisticated legislation that is aimed at providing protection to abused and neglected children. These statutes call for the mandatory reporting of child abuse to provincial child welfare authorities by any professional or other person who reasonably suspects that child abuse has occurred. In addition to provincial child welfare legislation, the *Criminal Code* of Canada may be invoked to punish conduct that constitutes physical or sexual child abuse. It is also possible for the victim of child abuse to claim damages for assault and battery from the perpetrator of the abuse.

1) Criminal Sanctions

The criminal offences relating to physical and sexual assaults, which were previously identified as potentially applicable to spousal abuse, may also be invoked in cases of child abuse. Sexual abuse of a child that involves carnal knowledge may also constitute incest, which is punishable by a maximum term of fourteen years' imprisonment under section 155 of the *Criminal Code*. In the event that child abuse results in the death of the victim, murder or manslaughter charges may ensue. The *Criminal Code* of Canada includes many additional offences that are specifically directed at the protection of children. Sections 151, 152, and 153 of the *Criminal Code* prohibit sexual interference with children, invitations for sexual touching, and sexual exploitation of children. "Sexual touching" includes touching a child for a sexual purpose or having the child touch himself or herself or touch other persons for a sexual purpose. Section 170 prohibits a parent or guardian from procuring his or her child to engage in sexual activities with third parties. Section 215 imposes a duty on parents and guardians to provide necessaries of life to children under the age of sixteen years. Section 223 prohibits the killing of a child once it has proceeded in a living state from the mother. Section 237 prohibits infanticide and section 238 prohibits killing an unborn child during the act of birth.

---

50   SO 1893, c 45.

A parent's infliction of corporal punishment on a child for disciplinary reasons does not constitute a criminal assault unless the force used was excessive. Section 43 of the *Criminal Code* of Canada provides as follows:

Correction of Child by Force

43. Every schoolteacher, parent or person standing in the place of a parent is justified in using force by way of correction toward a pupil or child, as the case may be, who is under his care, if the force does not exceed what is reasonable under the circumstances.[51]

In *Canadian Foundation for Children, Youth and the Law v Canada (Attorney General)*,[52] the majority judgment of the Supreme Court of Canada rejected the appellant's contention that section 43 of the *Criminal Code* contravenes sections 7, 12, and 15 of the *Canadian Charter of Rights and Freedoms*. The dividing line between corporal punishment and physical abuse is not always clear. There are many people, including experts, who regard any degree of corporal punishment as bordering on child abuse. Criminal assault charges are, however, rarely brought against parents. If the police consider that state intervention is appropriate, they will usually refer the matter to the local child protection agency.

The multiplicity of criminal offences that can be committed against children does not guarantee adequate protection for victims of parental child abuse. Indeed, a child may be re-victimized as a witness against an accused parent in a criminal prosecution. The child faces the terror of revisiting the abuse and is subject to cross-examination by the lawyer representing the alleged offender.

In 1988, federal legislation was enacted to reduce the tension and anxiety faced by children who are called as witnesses in sexual molestation and sexual abuse prosecutions against parents or any other persons.[53] The court, on application of the Crown prosecutor, will prohibit the publication or broadcasting of any information that could disclose the identity of the child. In addition, any interviewing of the child by the police or a child protection agency may be videotaped. The videotape can then be admitted as evidence at the trial, although its contents must be confirmed by the child at the trial. A child's testimony may also be presented by closed-circuit television to avoid the need to have the child present in court. Alternatively, a screen

---

51   As to what constitutes reasonable force, see *Canadian Foundation for Children, Youth and the Law v Canada (Attorney General)*, [2004] 1 SCR 76; see also *R v MH*, 2014 ONSC 36.

52   [2004] 1 SCR 76.

53   RSC 1985 (3d Supp), c 19. See House of Commons, *Four-Year Review of the Child Sexual Abuse Provisions of the Criminal Code and the Canada Evidence Act* by Chair, Dr Bob Horner, MP (June 1993).

may be used in the courtroom so that the child does not have to face the accused while giving evidence. Irrespective of how the child gives his or her evidence, the lawyer for the accused has the right to cross-examine the child. Corroboration of a child's evidence is not required in order to obtain conviction of the accused. The judge must decide what weight should be given to the evidence and will direct a jury accordingly. In two recent decisions of the Supreme Court of Canada, it was held that the use of videotaped evidence[54] and the practice of allowing witnesses below the age of eighteen to testify behind screens[55] in sexual abuse prosecutions do not violate the accused's right to a fair trial under the *Canadian Charter of Rights and Freedoms*. No similar statutory concessions apply to child protection proceedings instituted pursuant to provincial legislation, although a judge of the Ontario Court (Provincial Division) has allowed a fifteen-year-old child to give videotaped evidence of sexual abuse allegations against her stepfather in child protection proceedings,[56] and the Ontario Law Reform Commission has advocated changes that go even further than the federal legislation.[57]

Criminal prosecution of a parent, without the availability of support services for the family, may generate additional problems. For example, the child accuser may face hostility from other members of the family, or economic deprivation may be suffered by all family members, including the abused child, as a result of the conviction of an abusing parent. A fine or imprisonment may impair or undermine the abusing parent's ability to provide financial support for his or her family dependants. Punishment of an abusive parent does not always coincide, therefore, with the best interests of the family or those of the abused child. Of course, abuse cannot go unchecked. It must be terminated. But whether this is better accomplished by invoking the *Criminal Code* or by resort to provincial child protection legislation is a matter that necessitates careful evaluation by the police and child protection agencies.

---

54 *R v L(DO)* (1993), 161 NR 1 (SCC).
55 *R v Levogiannis*, [1993] 4 SCR 475.
56 *Children's Aid Society of Brant v R(E)*, [1993] OJ No 2382 (Prov Div), digested in *The Lawyers Weekly* (3 December 1993) 8.
57 Ontario Law Reform Commission, *Report on Child Witnesses* (including Executive Summary) (Toronto: The Commission, 1991).

2) Child Protection Proceedings[58]

Child protection legislation exists in every Canadian province and territory.[59] Although the statutes vary in content, their fundamental character is consistent. Child protection statutes in Canada usually include declarations of the basic philosophy underlying the detailed statutory provisions. Some provinces, such as Alberta, British Columbia, Manitoba, New Brunswick, Ontario, and Quebec, have relatively detailed declarations that stress such matters as (1) family autonomy and the vital importance of parents assuming the responsibility for child rearing; (2) the adoption of the least restrictive and disruptive alternative when state intervention is necessary; (3) the importance of continuity and stability for children; and (4) cultural and religious differences. In Ontario, the statutory "declaration of principles" in section 1 of the *Child and Family Services Act*[60] also includes a specific reference to Indian and native families by providing as follows:

> *Paramount purpose*
>
> 1. (1) The paramount purpose of this Act is to promote the best interests, protection and well being of children.
>
> (2) The additional purposes of this Act, so long as they are consistent with the best interests, protection and well being of children, are:
>
> . . .
>
> 5. To recognize that Indian and native people should be entitled to provide, wherever possible, their own child and family services, and that all services to Indian and native children and families should be provided in a manner that recognizes their culture, heritage and traditions and the concept of the extended family. 1999, c. 2, s. 1; 2006, c. 5, s. 1.

The dominant theme of declarations of purpose in child protection legislation reflects a distinct preference for children to be raised by their parents

---

58 See, generally, Nicholas Bala, Joseph P Hornick, & Robin Vogl, *Canadian Child Welfare Law: Children, Families and the State* (Toronto: Thompson Educational, 1990); see also Nicholas Bala, "Reforming the *Children and Family Services Act*: Is the Pendulum Swinging Back Too Far?" (Quicklaw: SFLRP/2000-007).

59 *Child Welfare Act*, RSA 2000, c C-12; *Child, Family and Community Services Act*, RSBC 1996, c 46; *Child and Family Services Act*, RSM 1987, c C80; *Family Services Act*, SNB 1980, c F-2.2; *Child, Youth and Family Services Act*, SNL 1998, c C-12.1; *Children and Family Services Act*, SNS 1990, c 5; *Child and Family Services Act*, RSO 1990, c C.11; *Family and Child Services Act*, RSPEI 1988, c F-2; *Youth Protection Act*, RSQ 1977, c P-34.1; *Child and Family Services Act*, SS 1989, c C-7.2; *Child and Family Services Act*, SNWT 1997, c 13; *Children's Act*, RSY 1986, c 22, Part 4.

60 RSO 1990, c C.11.

in their own home, except in those circumstances where there is no practical alternative to removing the children and placing them elsewhere.

Child protection agencies, which are often called Children's Aid Societies or Child and Family Services, are responsible for investigating allegations of child abuse or neglect and bringing any necessary application before the courts. They may remove a child from his or her home with or without a warrant but must bring the child before a judge within a stipulated time.

In child protection proceedings, there are two key issues. First, is the child a "child in need of protection," as defined in the applicable provincial or territorial statute? Second, if so, what judicial disposition will satisfy the best interests of the child?

The child protection agency has the legal burden of proving that state intervention is justified because the parents do not meet even minimal standards in discharging their obligations to their children. In the words of one Ontario judge,

> [s]ociety's interference in the natural family is only justified when the level of care of the children falls below that which no child in this country should be subjected to.[61]

Central to provincial and territorial child protection legislation is the definition of "child in need of protection." Circumstances that justify a finding that a child is in need of protection include the actuality or substantial risk of the following:

1) physical harm;
2) sexual molestation or exploitation;
3) emotional harm;
4) abandonment; and
5) parental inability to care for the child.

These factors are spelled out in detail in Alberta[62] and Ontario,[63] where the legislation is more precise than that found in some other provinces or territories. In most statutes, the definition of a child in need of protection includes such vague terms as "a child without adequate care, supervision or control," "a child living in unfit or improper circumstances," or a child beyond the control of the parent or guardian.[64]

---

61   *Re Brown* (1975), 9 OR (2d) 185 at 189 (Co Ct).

62   *Child, Youth and Family Enhancement Act*, RSA 2000, c C-12, s 2.

63   *Child and Family Services Act*, RSO 1990, c C.11, s 37(2).

64   See, for example, *Family Services Act*, SNB 1980, c F-2.2, s 31(1).

If a child is found to be in need of protection, the judge must determine the most appropriate placement for the child. In this context, the judge is required to have regard to the best interests of the child. Many provincial and territorial statutes identify specific factors that are relevant to a determination of a child's best interests. In Ontario, twelve factors have been singled out for consideration. Subsection 37(3) of the Ontario *Child and Family Services Act*[65] provides as follows:

> *Best interests of child*
>
> 37(3) Where a person is directed in this Part to make an order or determination in the best interests of a child, the person shall take into consideration those of the following circumstances of the case that he or she considers relevant:
>
> 1. The child's physical, mental and emotional needs, and the appropriate care or treatment to meet those needs.
> 2. The child's physical, mental and emotional level of development.
> 3. The child's cultural background.
> 4. The religious faith, if any, in which the child is being raised.
> 5. The importance for the child's development of a positive relationship with a parent and a secure place as a member of a family.
> 6. The child's relationship by blood or through an adoption order.
> 7. The importance of continuity in the child's care and the possible effect on the child of disruption of that continuity.
> 8. The merits of a plan for the child's care proposed by a society, including a proposal that the child be placed for adoption or adopted, compared with the merits of the child remaining with or returning to the parent.
> 9. The child's views and wishes, if they can be reasonably ascertained.
> 10. The effects on the child of delay in the disposition of the case.
> 11. The risk that the child may suffer harm through being removed from, kept away from, returned to or allowed to remain in the care of a parent.
> 12. The degree of risk, if any, that justified the finding that the child is in need of protection.

Section 53 of the Ontario *Child and Family Services Act* further provides that a court shall not make an order removing a child from the care of a parent unless the court is satisfied that less restrictive alternatives would be unsuccessful or inadequate to protect the child.

---

65   RSO 1990, c C.11.

A judge may make any one of three different types of order in respect of a child who is found to be in need of protection: (1) a supervision order; (2) a temporary wardship order; or (3) a permanent wardship order.

Under a supervision order, the child is placed in the care of his or her parents and resides at home. However, the child protection agency assumes supervisory responsibilities and periodically visits the child's home.

A temporary wardship order places the child in the custody of the child protection agency for a specified period of time. Temporary wards are placed in foster homes or group homes. Temporary wardship orders envisage that a positive parent-child relationship can be established in due course. To promote this goal, parents are granted reasonable access to the child.

A permanent wardship order, sometimes called Crown wardship, is the most intrusive type of order. It terminates all parental rights of guardianship over the child. Children, who have been made permanent wards may be placed for adoption without parental consent. The parent-child relationship is severed in the hope of finding a new permanent home for the child. Several statutes, including those in British Columbia, Ontario, and the Yukon, expressly prohibit or severely circumscribe rights of access by natural parents whose child has been made a permanent ward. In Ontario, for example, subsection 59(2) of the *Child and Family Services Act* provides as follows:

Access: Crown ward

59(2) The court shall not make or vary an access order with respect to a Crown ward under section 58 (access) or section 65 (status review) unless the court is satisfied that,

(a) the relationship between the person and the child is beneficial and meaningful to the child; and

(b) the ordered access will not impair the child's future opportunities for a permanent or stable placement.[66]

Dispositive orders that have been made in child protection proceedings are subject to review. Review hearings are conducted for the purpose of extending, terminating, or varying the prior order. In some provinces, such as Alberta and British Columbia, parents may only seek a review of orders for supervision or temporary wardship. In Ontario, parents may seek a review of a permanent wardship order but a status review hearing cannot be commenced after a Crown ward has been placed for adoption.

---

66   *Ibid*, as amended by SO 1999, c 2, s 16.

3) Family Law Proceedings

When child abuse is accompanied by spousal separation or divorce, the non-abusing parent may seek matrimonial relief by way of spousal support, child support, custody of the child, or exclusive possession of the family home. These remedies have been previously analyzed in the context of spousal abuse. Suffice it to say, therefore, that it is the parent, rather than the child, who seeks such relief. Although there have been isolated cases where children have personally instituted proceedings for child support against one or both parents, such actions are extremely rare. Almost invariably, claims on behalf of a child are brought by the parent. Indeed, in divorce proceedings, the child has no legal standing to pursue remedies on his or her own behalf.

Allegations of child abuse are of crucial significance in contested custody and access disputes. Where allegations of child abuse are substantiated, the abusive parent has virtually no chance of obtaining an order for custody of the child. Access privileges are not necessarily denied, however, to an abusing parent, although a court is likely to impose conditions whereby the access arrangements will be under the supervision of a neutral third party.

Concern has been expressed from time to time that spouses may seek to affect the outcome of disputed custody and access proceedings by making false allegations of child abuse. Allegations of sexual abuse, in particular, are often difficult to either substantiate or refute. Where a spouse or parent is faced with what he or she claims to be false allegations of child abuse, the appropriate course of action is to seek the assistance of a lawyer and of the local child protection agency that has a statutory responsibility to investigate all allegations of child abuse.

Research studies indicate that children are usually telling the truth when they relate incidents of abuse without prompting or coaching by a parent or any other person. Different considerations may apply when allegations of child abuse are made by a hostile spouse or parent who is caught up in the emotional trauma of marriage breakdown or divorce. Even in these circumstances, however, there is a reasonable probability that there was some foundation for the allegations made, although they were ultimately shown to lack substance. False allegations of abuse are rarely vindictive. They are far more likely to result from a misunderstanding of the circumstances or a misrepresentation of a particular event.

4) Damages for Child Abuse

There are no legal impediments to an action for damages being brought by a child against his or her parent for harm inflicted on the child. A physically or sexually abused child may sue an abusing parent, step-parent, foster parent, or sibling for damages in the torts of assault, battery, and intentional infliction of mental harm. Alternatively, the child victim may sue a parent for breach of his or her fiduciary obligation to protect the child.[67]

Children rarely sue for damages while living in the same home as the abuser. There have been several cases, however, where women have obtained substantial damages for incest committed against them during their childhood. In Manitoba, a twenty-three-year-old woman, who during childhood had been persistently sexually abused by her father, was held entitled to damages of $170,000, which comprised $100,000 for psychological trauma, $50,000 for aggravated general damages, and $20,000 for future therapy.[68] In Ontario, a father has been ordered to pay to his adult daughter, who had been sexually abused by him for more than twelve years of her childhood, the following amounts: $100,000 for general damages, $75,000 for aggravated damages, $50,000 for punitive damages, $50,000 for future therapy, and $9,037.50 for special damages for unpaid expenses for psychotherapy. The father was also ordered to pay interest on all the damages except the $50,000 for future therapy, the interest being declared retroactive to a point midway through the period during which the sexual assaults occurred.[69]

Although actions for damages arising from childhood sexual abuse are most frequently instituted by female victims against male perpetrators, a few instances involve claims by male victims against either male or female perpetrators. In British Columbia, a man has been granted damages of $350,000 for childhood sexual assaults perpetrated upon him by his uncle, these damages representing $80,000 for aggravated general damages, $70,000 for pre-trial loss of wages, and $200,000 for loss of future career opportunities attributable to the traumatization resulting from the frequent sexual assaults.[70] In a subsequent British Columbia case, a man received $260,000 in a successful action against both of his parents who had subjected him to frequent verbal and physical abuse during his childhood.[71]

---

67   See Bruce Feldthusen, "The Civil Action for Sexual Battery: Therapeutic Jurisprudence" (1993) 25 Ottawa L Rev 203; James WW Neeb & Shelly J Harper, *Civil Action for Childhood Sexual Abuse* (Toronto: Butterworths, 1994); Elizabeth KP Grace & Susan M Vella, *Civil Liability for Sexual Abuse and Violence in Canada* (Markham, ON: Butterworths Canada, 2000).

68   *B(KL) v B(KE)* (1991), 71 Man R (2d) 265 (QB); see also *L(B) v B(AR)* (1994), 91 Man R (2d) 1 (QB).

69   *B(P) v B(W)* (1992), 11 OR (3d) 161 (Gen Div).

70   *DS v DAM*, [1993] BCJ No 315 (SC), digested in *The Lawyers Weekly* (19 March 1993) 7.

71   *Y(AD) v Y(MY)*, [1994] BCJ No 375 (SC), digested in *The Lawyers Weekly* (25 March 1994) 1.

Courts have overcome procedural hurdles that ordinarily require the commencement of judicial proceedings within a limited period of time after the commission of any tort. The Supreme Court of Canada has decided that a victim of incest can sue an abusing parent for the torts of assault and battery and also for breach of the fiduciary obligation owed by the parent to the child.[72] With respect to the applicability of statutory limitation periods on the right of a victim of childhood incest to sue the abuser, the Supreme Court of Canada concluded that time begins to run only when the victim appreciates the harmful effect that the childhood incest has had on his or her psychological and emotional well-being as an adult. Several of the judges observed that the victim's appreciation of the harmful effects of the incestuous abuse will not usually occur until the child victim seeks therapy as an adult. Some provincial legislatures have amended their legislation so as to provide a statutory extension of time for the institution of civil proceedings by victims of child abuse. Substantial delay in the institution of proceedings for abuse perpetrated during childhood may, nevertheless, present difficulties of proof.

In two British Columbia cases wherein damages were sought against the provincial government by former foster children who had been abused by foster parents, the following principles were endorsed by the Supreme Court of Canada.[73] The provincial government has a duty under the *Protection of Children Act*[74] (British Columbia) to place children in adequate foster care and to monitor such placements. Liability in damages for the tort of negligence may arise where the provincial government has breached its duty by failing to follow proper placement and supervision procedures to prevent the abuse of children in their foster home. Although the provincial government may be liable on the basis of its own direct negligence, no vicarious liability can be imposed on the provincial government for the activities of foster parents. There are two prerequisites to a successful claim for vicarious liability. The relationship between the tortfeasor and the person against whom liability is sought must be sufficiently close to make a claim of vicarious liability appropriate. In addition, the tort must be sufficiently connected to the tortfeasor's assigned tasks that the tort can be regarded as a materialization of the risks created by the enterprise. In determining whether the tortfeasor was acting "on his or her own account" or acting on behalf of the employer, the level of control the employer has over the tortfeasor's activities will always be a factor. Other relevant factors include whether the worker provides his

---

72   *M(K) v M(H)* (1992), 142 NR 321 (SCC).
73   *KLB v British Columbia*, [2003] 2 SCR 403; *MB v British Columbia*, [2003] 2 SCR 477.
74   RSBC 1960, c 303.

or her own equipment, whether the worker hires his or her own helpers, and whether the worker has managerial responsibilities. These factors suggest that the government is not vicariously liable for wrongs committed by foster parents against children entrusted to them. It is inherent in the nature of family-based care for children that foster parents are independent in important respects and the government cannot exercise sufficient control over their activities for them to be seen as acting "on account" of the government. Foster parents do not hold themselves out as government agents in their daily activities with their children, nor are they reasonably perceived as such. Foster families serve a public goal — the goal of giving children the experience of a family, so that they may develop into confident and responsible members of society. However, they discharge this public goal in a highly independent manner, free from close government control. The *Protection of Children Act* (British Columbia) offers no basis for imposing on the Superintendent of Child Welfare a non-delegable duty to ensure that no harm comes to children through the abuse or negligence of foster parents. Nor can liability be grounded in an alleged breach of the provincial government's fiduciary obligation to children where there is no evidence that the government put its own interests ahead of those of the children or committed acts that harmed the children in a way that amounted to a betrayal of trust or loyalty. In *KLB v British Columbia*, the Supreme Court of Canada concluded that the provincial government's liability to four siblings who had suffered abuse in two foster homes could only arise in consequence of the provincial government's direct negligence. Vicarious liability was deemed untenable and the provincial government did not breach any non-delegable duty or any fiduciary duty owed to the children. In the context of negligence liability, the Supreme Court of Canada addressed the issue of whether the action was statute barred. The *Limitation Act*[75] (British Columbia) imposes a two-year limitation period for actions based on personal injuries resulting from torts (section 3(2)), with the two-year period commencing when a child attains the age of majority (section 7(1)(a)(i)). Having regard to the fact that the youngest of the children reached the age of majority in 1980 and the actions by the four siblings were not commenced until the mid-1990s, the Supreme Court of Canada concluded that the negligence action was statute barred because the children, as adults, had acquired sufficient awareness of the relevant facts to start the limitation period running and they had established no disability that would override the two-year limitation period. In *MB v British Columbia*, the trial judge and the British Columbia Court of Appeal had imposed vicarious liability on the provincial government for the sexual assault of a foster child by her foster

---

75   RSBC 1996, c 267.

father. Alternative liability was also found on the basis of the provincial government's breach of a non-delegable duty. In the absence of any finding that the sexual abuse of the foster child was attributable to negligence on the part of the provincial government and in light of the aforementioned legal analysis, the Supreme Court of Canada concluded that no liability could be imposed on the provincial government and the appeal to the Supreme Court of Canada was allowed.

In an Ontario case, a child, who had been sexually assaulted by her mother's "common law spouse," pursued concurrent claims for damages in tort and for breach of fiduciary duty. She was held entitled to recover general damages and future-care expenses in the amount of $90,700 against the sexually abusing *de facto* parent and the mother. In addition, she recovered punitive damages of $45,000 against the mother who had negligently failed to prevent the abuse and was in breach of the fiduciary obligation to protect her daughter against known sexual abuse.[76]

In a tort action for assault, damages have been awarded to a child who suffered emotional abuse at the hands of his father, which included witnessing the serious consequences of a violent physical assault perpetrated against the child's mother.[77] Claims for damages may not be feasible, however, if the abuser has no ability to pay the damages to which the victim is entitled. In that event, it should first be determined whether there is any household insurance policy that might cover the claim for damages. Although such policies do not insure against intentional wrongdoing, they may leave the door open to claims for damages arising from negligence or breach of fiduciary duty. If there is no insurance coverage and the abuser is "judgment-proof," the victim of abuse may look for monetary compensation from the appropriate provincial or territorial Criminal Injuries Compensation Board, although the amount of compensation available will not match that available through the courts.

A victim of sexual assault may be entitled to a publication ban and to the use of initials in court documents to prevent the disclosure of his or her identity in an action for damages against the alleged perpetrator.[78]

Actions for damages that focus on allegations of sexual abuse are not exclusively brought by the victims of abuse. In an Ontario case, a Children's Aid Society was ordered to pay $120,000 damages to a father who sued the

---

76 *J(LA) v J(H)* (1993), 13 OR (3d) 306 (Gen Div). See also *DM v JAW Estate*, 2014 BCSC 1061.

77 *Valenti v Valenti*, [1996] OJ No 522 (Gen Div), aff'd [1998] OJ No 2242 (CA).

78 *CW v LGM*, [2004] BCJ No 2435 (SC).

agency for its mishandling of unsubstantiated sexual abuse allegations made against the father during a custody battle between the parents.[79]

5) Institutional Child Abuse

There have been a series of instances where childhood victims of physical and sexual abuse have successfully pursued claims for compensation and other relief against institutions, such as churches, hospitals, school boards, children's aid societies, and provincial and federal governments. These cases involved multiple claimants and several have led to innovative consensual resolution. In several instances, a "healing package" was negotiated that went beyond monetary compensation by including psychological counselling, remedial education, the right to remain on social assistance despite the monetary compensation, a healing centre, and a twenty-four-hour crisis hotline. The most notable settlement is the Indian Residential Schools Settlement reached in May 2006, in which the federal government set aside 1.9 billion dollars for the direct benefit of former students. The settlement also provided for a Truth and Reconciliation Commission to promote public education about residential schools. Former students, their families, and their communities have been given the opportunity to share their experiences in a safe and culturally appropriate environment.

The use of non-adversarial dispute resolution processes in preference to litigation has attracted both supporters and critics. Non-adversarial processes, such as facilitation and mediation, can provide more flexibility than litigation, even when class actions in the courts are permissible. Non-adversarial processes can also shield abuse victims from the glare of publicity, whereas adversarial legal processes and attendant media publicity aggravate the risk of abuse victims being re-victimized. Non-adversarial processes may, however, result in abuse victims receiving less financial compensation than would be likely if they had pursued their rights in the courts.[80]

---

79   *DB (Litigation guardian of) v Children's Aid Society of Durham Region*, [1994] OJ No 643 (Gen Div), digested in *The Lawyers Weekly* (29 April 1994) 1.

80   For a settlement wherein New Brunswick approved a multimillion-dollar compensation package for victims of molestation and rape at provincial reform schools, see *Globe and Mail* (9 June 1995) A5. For a similar settlement in Nova Scotia, see *Ottawa Citizen* (4 May 1996) A9. For a multimillion-dollar settlement in Ontario, see *Ottawa Citizen* (16 March 1996) C7. On 10 May 2006, the Canadian government announced a $2.2 billion compensation package for the cultural, emotional, physical, and sexual abuse of Aboriginal children who had attended church-run native residential schools, online: www.residentialschoolsettlement.ca/English.html.

In *FH v McDougall*,[81] wherein damages were sought for childhood sexual abuse that occurred in a residential school, the Supreme Court of Canada held that there is only one standard of proof in a civil case and that is proof on a balance of probabilities. Although there has been some suggestion in the caselaw that the criminal burden applies or that there is a shifting standard of proof where criminal or morally blameworthy conduct is alleged in civil proceedings, there are no degrees of probability within the civil standard and there is no requirement that a sexual assault victim must provide independent corroborating evidence in cases that turn on the contradictory sworn testimony of the parties.

---

81 2008 SCC 53.

CHAPTER 6

The Crises of Marriage Breakdown and Processes for Dealing with Them

A. THE CRISES OF MARRIAGE BREAKDOWN

For most families, marriage breakdown provokes three crises: an emotional crisis; an economic crisis; and a parenting crisis. Both of the spouses and their children suffer severe emotional upheaval when the unity of the family disintegrates. Failure in the most basic of life's commitments is not lightly shrugged off by its victims. Marriage breakdown, whether or not accompanied by divorce, is a painful experience. Furthermore, relatively few families encounter separation or divorce without encountering financial setbacks. The emotional and economic crises resulting from marriage breakdown are compounded by the co-parental divorce when there are dependent children. Bonding between children and their absent parent is inevitably threatened by spousal separation and divorce.

Paul Bohannan identified six "stations" in the highly complex human process of marriage breakdown:

- the emotional divorce;
- the legal divorce;
- the economic divorce;
- the co-parental divorce;
- the community divorce; and
- the psychic divorce.[1]

---

1   Paul Bohannan, "The Six Stations of Divorce" in *Divorce and After* (New York: Doubleday & Co, 1971) c 2.

Each of these stations of divorce involves an evolutionary process and there is substantial interaction among them. The dynamics of marriage breakdown, which are multifaceted, cannot be addressed in isolation.

History demonstrates a predisposition to seek the solution to the crises of marriage breakdown in external systems. During the past 150 years, the Church, law, and medicine have each been called upon to deal with the crises of marriage breakdown. Understandably, each system has been found wanting in its search for solutions. People are averse to losing control over their own lives. Decrees and "expert" rulings that exclude affected parties from the decision-making process do not pass unchallenged. Omniscience is not the prerogative of any profession. Nor should the family's right to self-determination be lightly ignored.

B. THE EMOTIONAL DIVORCE

For many people, there are two criteria of self-fulfilment. One is satisfaction on the job. The second, and more important one, is satisfaction with one's marriage or family. When marriage breakdown occurs, the spouses and their children experience a grieving process. The devastating effect of marriage breakdown is particularly evident with the displaced long-term home-making spouse whose united family has crumbled and who is ill-equipped, psychologically and otherwise, to convert homemaking skills into gainful employment.

Most legal divorces in Canada are uncontested. Issues relating to the economic and parenting consequences of marriage breakdown are usually resolved by negotiation between the spouses, who are often represented by independent lawyers. Because the overwhelming majority of all divorces are uncontested, it might be assumed that the legal system works well in resolving the economic and parenting consequences of marriage breakdown. That assumption cannot pass unchallenged.

In the typical legal divorce scenario, spouses negotiate a settlement at a time when one or both are undergoing the emotional trauma of marriage breakdown. Psychiatrists and psychologists agree that this "emotional divorce" passes through a variety of states, including denial, hostility, and depression, to the ultimate acceptance of the death of the marriage. Working through the spousal emotional divorce rarely takes less than two years. In the interim, permanent and legally binding decisions are often made to regulate the economic and parenting consequences of the marriage breakdown. From a legal perspective, the economic and parenting consequences of the marriage breakdown are interdependent. Decisions respecting any continued occupation of the matrimonial home, the amount of child support, and the amount of spousal support, if any, are conditioned on the arrangements made for the future upbringing of the children. The perceived legal interdependence of property rights, support rights, and parental rights after divorce naturally affords opportunities for abuse by lawyers and their clients. The lawyer who has been imbued with the "will to win" from the outset of his or her career, coupled with the client who negotiates a settlement when his or her emotional divorce is unresolved, can wreak future havoc on the spouses and on their children. Far too often, when settlements are negotiated, children become pawns or weapons in the hands of game-playing or warring adults and the battles do not cease with the judicial divorce.

The interplay between the emotional dynamics of marriage breakdown and regulation of the economic consequences of marriage breakdown may be demonstrated by the following examples. A needy spouse who insists that no claim for spousal support should be pursued may be manifesting a hope for reconciliation or a state of depression. A spouse who makes excessive demands is often manifesting hostility. A spouse who proffers an unduly generous financial settlement may be expiating guilt. Denial, depression, hostility, and guilt are all typical manifestations of the emotional divorce that elicit inappropriate responses to dealing with the practical economic and parenting consequences of marriage breakdown. Furthermore, like most emotional states, they change with the passage of time. Separated spouses, lawyers, and mediators should be aware of the dangers of premature settlements when one or both of the spouses are still going through emotional turmoil. Indeed, the notion of a "cooling-off" period, though unsuccessful as a means of divorce avoidance, might have significant advantages with respect to negotiated spousal settlements upon marriage breakdown. Certainly, spouses and their lawyers should more frequently assess the strategic potential of interim agreements as a stage in a longer-term divorce adjustment and negotiation process.

The legal divorce and the emotional divorce usually involve different time frames. Furthermore, the emotional divorce is rarely contemporaneous for both spouses. Lawyers frequently encounter situations where one spouse regards the marriage as over but the other spouse is unable or unwilling to accept that reality. In circumstances where one of the spouses is adamantly opposed to cutting the marital umbilical cord, embittered negotiations or contested litigation over support, property division, or custody or access often reflect an unresolved emotional divorce. Spouses who have not worked their way through the emotional divorce displace what is essentially a non-litigable issue relating to the preservation or dissolution of the marriage by fighting over the litigable issues of support, property sharing, custody, and access. In such cases, the judicial disposition often fails to terminate spousal hostilities. Even when the legal battles over support and property have been finally adjudicated by the courts, spousal conflict can continue to rage over the children.

The multifaceted aspects of marriage breakdown require more than the typical adversarial legal response. In the words of Paul Bohannan,

> A "successful" divorce begins with the realization by two people that they do not have any constructive future together. That decision itself is a recognition of the emotional divorce. It proceeds through the legal channels of undoing the wedding, through the economic division of property and arrangements for alimony and support. The successful divorce involves determining ways in which children can be informed, educated in their new roles, loved and provided for. It involves finding a new community. Finally, it involves finding your own autonomy as a person and as a personality.[2]

The emotional trauma experienced by the spouses on the breakdown of their marriage is mirrored in the experience of the children of divorcing parents. The manifestation of these traumas takes a variety of forms that are largely conditioned upon the child's stage of development.[3]

Although divorce is rarely painless, especially when children are involved, the trauma of divorce can be eased with the help of therapy or counselling and even by access to informational and educational programs. In some jurisdictions, divorcing parents are required to attend courses that examine the impact of their conduct on the children and offer advice to parents that may reduce potentially harmful conduct, such as using children as weapons or pawns in the spousal conflict, fighting over the children, criticizing the other spouse in the presence of the children, or competing for the children's affection. Time may also be spent in dealing with practical matters, such as household budgets, reaching fair child support arrangements, and providing guidelines or structures for parenting arrangements. Several jurisdictions also provide separate courses for the children of divorcing parents that are designed to help the children deal with the feelings of loss, guilt, fear, and grief.

---

2   *Ibid* at 62.

3   For an excellent overview of the impact of separation and divorce on children, see Canada, Ministry of Health and Welfare, *Because Life Goes On: Helping Children and Youth Live with Separation and Divorce: A Guide for Parents* (Ottawa: Santé Canada, 1994). For a guide to constructive parenting after divorce, see Julien D Payne & Kenneth L Kallish, "A Behavioural Science and Legal Analysis of Access to the Child in the Post-Separation/Divorce Family," Appendix, Proposed Visiting Code in *Payne's Digest on Divorce in Canada, 1968–1980*, loose-leaf (Don Mills, ON: R De Boo, 1982) at 775–77.

C. RECENT TRENDS IN FAMILY DISPUTE RESOLUTION

Many lawyers and judges have now joined their critics from other disciplines by acknowledging the inefficacy of the law in resolving parenting disputes between separated and divorced spouses. The limitations of the law in resolving the economic consequences of marriage breakdown have been more cautiously acknowledged by the legal profession. However, the emergence of statutory provisions, regulations, and rules of court governing such matters as mandatory financial disclosure, case management, mediation, independent expert assessments, pre-trials, and formal offers to settle manifest a growing realization that litigation should be regarded as a last resort in the resolution of all family disputes. These and other developments signal a need for family law to focus much more on processes for dispute resolution. Sections 9 and 10 of the *Divorce Act*[4] pay lip service to the potential benefits of counselling, negotiation, and mediation as processes for resolving disputes arising on divorce but do little to foster the use of these processes. More far-reaching statutory provisions are found in provincial legislation, such as section 3 of the Ontario *Family Law Act*,[5] which endorses voluntary mediation as a process for resolving any matter falling within the ambit of that Act, including spousal support, child support, and property entitlements on marriage breakdown.

To assert the truism that law and lawyers, like all other systems and professions, can lay no claim to omniscience in the resolution of family conflict is not the same as saying that law and lawyers have no contribution to make. We should not overlook the fact that the viability of dispute resolution processes, including negotiation, mediation, and arbitration, cannot be divorced from the legal process as the ultimate means of resolving intractable disputes. Nor should we forget that lawyers, in practice, on the bench, in federal and provincial legislatures, and in academe, have been at the forefront of welcome reforms in promoting dispute resolution processes. To take only one example, the Alberta Court of Queen's Bench has engaged in various judicial dispute resolution processes as an alternative to the conventional trial for more than ten years. These judicial dispute resolution processes include judicial mediation, mini-trials, summary trials, case management, and pre-trial conferences.[6]

British Columbia has always been at the forefront in promoting recourse to extra-judicial forms of family dispute resolution. As long ago as 1984, the British Columbia Professional Conduct Handbook, Rule G12, authorized the

---

4   RSC 1985, c 3 (2d Supp). See Section D(1), below in this chapter.

5   SO 1986, c 4, now RSO 1990, c F.3.

6   *Botros v Botros*, [2002] AJ No 1500 (QB); *Yeoman v Luhtala*, [2002] AJ No 1504 (QB).

practice of family mediation by British Columbia's legal practitioners.[7] More recently, collaborative family law has evolved as a settlement-oriented approach to family law disputes.[8] Additionally, even in the absence of statutory authority, parenting coordination has been frequently judicially endorsed as a means of resolving disputes arising with respect to the implementation of a parenting agreement or a custody/access order.[9] These and other forms of alternative dispute resolution processes, including the use of family justice professionals for informational purposes, agreements to arbitrate, and court-ordered counselling or mandated recourse to other family dispute resolution processes, are the subject of express provisions in the *Family Law Act*,[10] which came into force on 18 March 2013. While many of the substantive law proposals in the *Family Law Act* reflect changes that have already been implemented in one or more Canadian provinces or territories, the broad legislative endorsement of diverse non-court dispute resolution options is innovative and should engage the attention of judges, lawyers, and legislatures across Canada.

D. DUTY OF LEGAL PROFESSION TO PROMOTE RECONCILIATION, NEGOTIATION, AND MEDIATION

1) Duty of Legal Adviser

Section 7 of the *Divorce Act*, 1968[11] imposed a duty on lawyers representing a divorce petitioner or respondent to discuss the possibility of spousal reconciliation and to inform the client of marriage counselling or guidance facilities that might assist the spouses in achieving reconciliation. This duty is restated in subsection 9(1) of the current *Divorce Act* and is now complemented by additional duties under subsection 9(2) that are designed to promote negotiated settlements and the mediation of support and custody disputes arising on divorce.[12]

The experience under section 7 of the *Divorce Act*, 1968 suggests that the duty to promote reconciliation is regarded as a *pro forma* requirement by the legal profession. Once divorce proceedings are instituted, thereby triggering

---

7   See, now, Jeremy Hainsworth, "Change Aim Is to Unclog Courts: Lawyers to Act as Family Law Mediators, Parenting-co-ordinators" *The Lawyers Weekly* (21 September 2012).

8   See Chapter 1, Section C.

9   See *Odgers v Odgers*, 2014 BCSC 717.

10 SBC 2011, c 25.

11 SC 1967–68, c 24.

12 As to certification by the lawyer that the aforementioned duties have been discharged, see *Divorce Act*, RSC 1985, c 3 (2d Supp), s 9(3). As to the impact of s 9 on the finality of separation agreements dealing with spousal support, see *Miglin v Miglin*, [2003] 1 SCR 303.

the statutory duty, few lawyers view spousal reconciliation as a viable option. The institution of the divorce proceeding is perceived as an extremely strong, if not conclusive, indication that at least one of the spouses is adamantly of the opinion that the marriage has irretrievably broken down and that any attempts to reconcile will prove futile. Most lawyers will, therefore, discharge their statutory duty by a brief discussion to ensure that their client is "a serious client" and by handing out a list of available marriage counselling services in the community.

Lawyers are effective, however, in promoting the negotiation of settlements. This is amply demonstrated by the fact that 86 percent of all divorce cases are uncontested from the outset and less than 4 percent involve a trial. Lawyers acting within the scope of their actual or apparent authority may bind their clients to a settlement negotiated on their behalf. If a lawyer negotiates a settlement without actual authority to do so, the client is still bound by the settlement so long as the other party was not aware of any limitation placed on the lawyer's authority.[13] Subsection 9(2) of the current *Divorce Act* may be perceived as promoting third party mediation as an alternative process to litigation in those cases where no agreement can be reached by the lawyers on behalf of their clients. Several provincial law societies have endorsed the practice of lawyers themselves engaging in mediation.[14]

2) Duty of Court: Reconciliation

Subsections 10(1), (2), and (3) of the current *Divorce Act* substantially correspond to section 8 of the *Divorce Act, 1968*.[15] Subsection 10(1) of the *Divorce Act* imposes a duty on the court, before considering the evidence in a divorce proceeding, to satisfy itself that there is no possibility of the reconciliation of the spouses, unless the circumstances are of such a nature that it would clearly not be appropriate to do so. Subsection 10(2) further provides that, where at any stage of a divorce proceeding, the court sees a possibility of reconciliation, the court shall adjourn the proceeding to afford the spouses an opportunity to achieve a reconciliation. With the consent of the spouses or in its own discretion, the court may nominate a duly qualified person or agency to assist the spouses to achieve a reconciliation. Pursuant to subsection 10(3) of the *Divorce Act*, when fourteen days have elapsed from the date

---

13   *Correia v Danyluk*, [2001] AJ No 799 (CA); *Cosper v Cosper* (1995), 14 RFL (4th) 152 (NSCA); *Landry v Landry* (1981), 48 NSR (2d) 136 (SCAD); *Rother v Rother*, [2005] NSJ No 138 (CA).

14   See, for example, *Ontario Rules of Professional Conduct*, Rule 4.07 "Lawyers As Mediators."

15   SC 1967–68, c 24.

of any adjournment, the court must resume the proceeding on the application of either or both spouses.

The duty of the court under section 10 is confined to examining the prospects of reconciliation. By its nature, reconciliation implies a bilateral intention to re-establish the marital relationship. Where the court is faced with a complete denial of any prospect of reconciliation by the petitioner, the court should find against the possibility of reconciliation, notwithstanding a fervent desire for reconciliation on the part of the respondent.[16]

3) Confidentiality

Subsections 10(4) and 10(5) of the current *Divorce Act* correspond to section 21 of the *Divorce Act, 1968*.[17] They provide as follows:

> *Nominee not competent or compellable*
>
> 10.(4) No person nominated by a court under this section to assist spouses to achieve a reconciliation is competent or compellable in any legal proceedings to disclose any admission or communication made to that person in his or her capacity as a nominee of the court for that purpose.
>
> *Evidence not admissible*
>
> (5) Evidence of anything said or of any admission or communication made in the course of assisting spouses to achieve a reconciliation is not admissible in any legal proceedings.

Pursuant to these provisions, the confidentiality of the reconciliation process is guaranteed by a statutory prohibition against the admissibility of evidence which, unlike a common law privilege, cannot be waived.[18] Statements made during marriage counselling aimed at promoting a spousal reconciliation are inadmissible in subsequent divorce proceedings, even though the statements might themselves have been tantamount to cruelty. But a draft domestic contract presented to the wife by the husband is admissible as

---

16 *Pires v Pires*, [2006] BCJ No 698 (CA); *Winstanley v Winstanley*, 2009 MBQB 41; *Gordon v Keyes* (1985), 45 RFL (2d) 177 at 185 (NSCA), citing *Payne's Digest on Divorce in Canada, 1968–1980*, loose-leaf (Don Mills, ON: R De Boo, 1982) at 130, leave to appeal to SCC refused (1985), 69 NSR (2d) 358n, 163 APR 358n (SCC); *McDermid v McDermid* (1989), 21 RFL (3d) 47 (Sask CA); compare *Sheriff v Sheriff* (1982), 31 RFL (2d) 434 at 436 (Ont HCJ); see also *Acchione v Acchione* (1987), 9 RFL (3d) 215 (Ont SC); and see *Perchaluk v Perchaluk* (1988), 56 Man R (2d) 46 (QB).

17 SC 1967–68, c 24.

18 *Piercy v Piercy* (1990), 29 RFL (3d) 18 (BCSC).

indicative of the husband's cruelty where no prior settlement negotiations had been entered into by the spouses.[19]

Judicial opinions have divided on the question whether the statutory prohibition is confined to reconciliation attempts undertaken by a court-appointed conciliator. In *Robson v Robson*[20] and in *Cronkwright v Cronkwright*,[21] Wright J of the Ontario Supreme Court endorsed a restrictive interpretation of subsection 21(2) of the *Divorce Act, 1968*[22] so as to confine its application to admissions or communications made to a court-nominated counsellor. In *Shakotko v Shakotko*,[23] however, Grant J of the Ontario Supreme Court concluded that the statutory evidential prohibition applied to all reconciliation attempts and not merely to those conducted by a court-appointed person. It is submitted that the latter broad interpretation is to be preferred as implementing the social policy underlying the applicable statutory provisions, which is to promote reconciliation between the spouses wherever possible.

Although subsection 10(5) of the current *Divorce Act* prohibits the admission "in any legal proceedings" of any evidence as to what occurred during an endeavour to assist spouses to reconcile, the legislative authority of the federal government does not extend to prohibit the admission of evidence in a proceeding concerning property rights under provincial statute. Furthermore, if a party to such a proceeding seeks to obtain the protection of the common law privilege that attaches to settlement negotiations, there must be some evidence to support the inference that the parties considered the occasions to be confidential and without prejudice, that matrimonial proceedings were being contemplated, and that the focus was on the settlement of a litigious issue.[24]

In *LMB v IJB*,[25] the appellant sought to refute allegations of spousal and child abuse by seeking the production of third-party records relating to marriage counselling and the personal counselling of his oldest child, who had behavioural problems. The Alberta Court of Appeal unanimously refused to order production of either of the records on the ground that they were protected by common law privilege, having regard to the four principles set out in the "Wigmore test," which was endorsed by the Supreme Court of Canada in *M(A) v Ryan*.[26] The Alberta Court of Appeal was divided, however, on the

---

19   *de Araujo v de Araujo* (1986), 11 CPC (2d) 272 (Ont SC); see also *Osmond v Osmond* (1989), 89 NSR (2d) 333 (SC).

20   [1969] 2 OR 857 (SC).

21   (1970), 2 RFL 214 (Ont SC).

22   SC 1967–68, c 24.

23   (1976), 27 RFL 1 (Ont SC).

24   *Piercy v Piercy* (1990), 29 RFL (3d) 18 (BCSC).

25   [2005] AJ No 214 (CA).

26   [1997] 1 SCR 157.

question of whether admissibility of the marriage-counselling records was prohibited by subsection 10(5) of the *Divorce Act*, which provides that "[e]vidence of anything said or of any admission or communication made in the course of assisting spouses to achieve a reconciliation is not admissible in any legal proceeding." While conceding that this prohibition might well apply only to divorce proceedings, the majority judgment of Berger JA, which was concurred in by Wittman JA, concluded that the legislative jurisdictional authority of Parliament over divorce "extends to the enactment of a provision that renders all communications made in the course of assisting spouses to reconcile inadmissible whenever they occurred." In their opinion, the object and purpose of subsection 10(5) of the *Divorce Act* is to promote reconciliation attempts, regardless of whether they occur before or after the institution of divorce proceedings. In a dissenting opinion on this aspect of the appeal, McFadyen JA concluded that, when viewed in the context of section 10 as a whole, subsection 10(5) refers only to court-sanctioned reconciliation attempts after divorce proceedings have been instituted.

In *Duits v Duits*,[27] the mother alleged emotional and verbal abuse in contested custody proceedings, and she brought a motion to call a marriage counsellor as a witness. The motion was judicially dismissed on the bases of the inherent unreliability of the evidence and common law privilege. As Turnbull J observed, the common law views communications made during marriage counselling as privileged, provided that the following four criteria in *Wigmore on Evidence*[28] are satisfied:

1) The communications must originate in a confidence that they will not be disclosed.

2) The element of confidentiality must be essential to the full and satisfactory maintenance of the relation between the parties.

3) The relation must be one which in the opinion of the community ought to be sedulously fostered.

4) The injury that would inure to the relation by the disclosure of the communications must be greater than the benefit thereby gained for the correct disposal of litigation.

As Turnbull J further observed, however, in *M(A) v Ryan*, in which the mother alleged emotional and verbal abuse, the Supreme Court of Canada has effectively ruled that privilege should not be a bar to justice. Thus, the

---

27 [2006] OJ No 1762 (Sup Ct). See also *Children's Aid Society of London v CDB*, 2011 ONSC 5853; *Johnstone v Locke*, 2011 ONSC 7138.

28 JH Wigmore, *Evidence in Trials at Common Law*, vol 8, McNaughton revision (Toronto: Little Brown, 1961), s 2285.

court must determine if the evidence must be produced to get at the truth and prevent an unjust verdict. After conducting a *voir dire* with respect to the evidence of the marriage counsellor, Turnbull J concluded that there was arguably some relevant evidence that might be considered if it met the tests of reliability and necessity. In this case, the test of reliability was not satisfied because both parties had, *inter alia*, violated the trust essential to marriage counselling by tape recording sessions for an ulterior motive, and the marriage counsellor's observations and opinions might be attributable to planning and manipulation to "push the button" of one of the parties to create an adverse inference against that party. In addition to finding that the evidence of the marriage counsellor was inadmissible because it was inherently unreliable, Turnbull J concluded that the public interest in maintaining the confidentiality of marriage counselling would have taken precedence over the immediate relevance of any evidence proffered in the custody litigation (the fourth step in the Wigmore test). Having regard to the evolution of diverse processes aimed at promoting the consensual resolution of family disputes, Turnbull J expressed the opinion that the sanctity of these community-based and court-connected processes should be recognized in most cases. While there may be exceptional cases where the common law recognition of the paramountcy of confidentiality must be abrogated, such cases should be relatively rare.

Subsections 10(4) and 10(5) of the *Divorce Act* are expressly confined to attempts at reconciliation. They have no application to a mediation process where the focus of the negotiations is not on reconciliation, but on the resolution of the economic and parenting consequences of divorce.[29] The confidentiality of the mediation process is, nevertheless, protected by common law principles governing privileged communications, subject to waiver of the privilege by both spouses.[30] When the safety of children is at risk, however, the confidentiality of the mediation process must yield to the overriding welfare of the children.[31]

Provincial laws of evidence apply in divorce proceedings.[32] In several provinces, specific legislation regulates the confidentiality of the mediation process, but there is some doubt respecting the applicability of these provisions

---

29   See *McDonald v McDonald* (1987), 6 RFL (3d) 17 (BCSC).

30   *Porter v Porter* (1983), 32 RFL (2d) 413 (Ont UFC); *Keizars v Keizars* (1982), 29 RFL (2d) 223 (Ont UFC); see also *Sinclair v Roy* (1985), 47 RFL (2d) 15 (BCSC) and compare *McDonald v McDonald* (1987), 6 RFL (3d) 17 (BCSC). See also *AH v JTH*, [2004] BCJ No 321 (SC) and compare *Rudd v Trossacs Investments Inc* (2004), 244 DLR (4th) 758 (Ont Sup Ct).

31   *Pearson v Pearson*, digested in *The Lawyers Weekly* (3 July 1992) (Yukon SC).

32   *Divorce Act*, s 23(1).

to disputes arising in divorce proceedings.[33] Their questionable applicability to spousal and child support or to custody and access disputes arising in divorce proceedings is of limited significance because of the aforementioned applicability of common law principles respecting privileged communications.

Whether the confidentiality of reconciliation or mediation processes is compatible with the *Canadian Charter of Rights and Freedoms* is a question that will, no doubt, engage the attention of the courts. In *M v K*,[34] it was held that, in proceedings where the custody of a child is in issue, a statutory privilege respecting spousal communications to a marriage counsellor constitutes a violation of the child's right to due process under the United States and New Jersey Constitutions.

In *PEC v CEG*,[35] it was held that, in very exceptional circumstances, the common law privilege that attaches to a "without prejudice" report in a contested custody proceeding may be judicially overridden in the exercise of the court's *parens patriae* jurisdiction in order to ensure the protection and best interests of the children. In this case, the parents attended a settlement conference to address issues of custody and access. At the conference, the father raised concerns about the mother's alleged erratic and bizarre behaviour. To address these concerns, counsel for both parents agreed that the mother's mental state would be assessed by a psychiatrist whose report would be "without prejudice." In the report, the mother was diagnosed as having a borderline personality disorder that placed the children at risk. In consequence of this report, *ex parte* orders were granted that transferred the primary residential care of the children from the mother to the father and severely limited the mother's contact with the children. The psychiatrist's report was trenchantly criticized and was inconsistent with expert opinions presented on behalf of the mother, one of which involved a psychological assessment with psychometric testing. Being of the opinion that the mother could not properly reply to the damaging opinion expressed in the psychiatrist's report unless she were permitted access to the psychiatrist's background notes, Guerette J, of the New Brunswick Court of Queen's Bench, issued an order for the production of these notes and for the attendance of the psychiatrist on discovery, if requested. A similar direction was issued with respect to the experts who had presented reports on behalf of the mother.

---

33 See Julien D Payne, "New Approaches to the Resolution of Custody Disputes on Marriage Breakdown or Divorce" in *Payne's Divorce and Family Law Digest*, loose-leaf (Don Mills, ON: R De Boo, 1982) 1983 tab at 83-1255 *et seq*; and see *Sinclair v Roy* (1985), 47 RFL (2d) 15 (BCSC).

34 186 NJ Super 363, 452 A 2d 704 (Ch Div 1982).

35 [2003] NBJ No 193 (QB).

E. MARRIAGE AND FAMILY COUNSELLING

In decades past, families would take their problems to the doctor, priest, or rabbi. These days, family crises are more likely to attract the attention of the police, lawyers, and the courts. Counselling is, nevertheless, available to families in crisis. In urban centres, professionals in private practice who have expertise in social work, psychology, or psychiatry offer marriage, family, and individual counselling on a fee-paying basis. They can be found in the Yellow Pages of any telephone directory together with listings for community services such as Family Service Agencies and Children's Aid Societies. Community agencies may provide counselling services free of charge or assess a fee based on a sliding scale to reflect the ability to pay.

Counselling may deal with an ongoing problem within an intact family or it may involve a family threatened by separation or divorce. In previous generations, marriage counselling existed to promote reconciliation. A couple heading for divorce was urged to reconcile. Today, reconciliation is regarded as only one of the options. Much of the effort of family counsellors is now directed towards helping families understand how they will be affected by separation or divorce and how they can deal with the emotional, economic, and parenting consequences of marriage breakdown.

Of course, not everybody who lives together goes through a ceremony of marriage. People who live in common-law relationships encounter similar types of problems to married couples whose relationship is threatened or terminated. They may need family counselling. Family Service Agencies and private practitioners also provide counselling services for people after separation or divorce. Of particular significance in this regard are blended or reconstituted families arising when divorced people remarry. Although step-parents are not inevitably related to the "wicked witch of the west," notwithstanding fairy tales to the contrary, the blending of children into new family structures is not always a smooth transition and may require insightful family counselling.

Marriage and family counselling has traditionally placed emphasis on the emotional dynamics of dysfunctional families and is regarded as therapeutic in nature, even if it falls short of being a sustained program of family therapy. The day-to-day consequences of marriage breakdown are also important aspects of family counselling. For example, families may be offered advice and assistance on such matters as child care and budgetary planning in light of separation or divorce.

Family Service Agencies are familiar with other support services available in the community, such as safe havens for battered women, alcohol and drug addiction treatment centres, vocational retraining programs, social assistance benefits, and housing services to which needy family members can be referred. In recent years, community agencies have moved into the field of mediation or conciliation, which is aimed at promoting a settlement of disputed issues between separated or divorcing adults. For the most part, however, Family Service Agencies confine their attention to dealing with the parenting consequences of separation or divorce. They do not get involved in issues of property sharing or spousal support.

F. NEGOTIATION[36]

Less than 4 percent of divorces involve a trial of contested issues in open court. People normally settle their differences by negotiation. If each spouse is represented by an independent lawyer, the husband instructs his lawyer, the wife instructs her lawyer, and the lawyers engage in negotiation on behalf of their respective clients. Although information may become distorted in its transmission through the lawyers, the emotional divorce usually presents obstacles to divorcing spouses negotiating directly with each other without the benefit of legal representation. Couples caught up in the emotional dynamics of marriage breakdown often have great difficulty in communicating with each other because their emotions cloud their judgment. Fair and reasonable settlements in the emotionally charged atmosphere of marriage breakdown or divorce may, therefore, necessitate the intervention of lawyers or other third parties, such as mediators, who can bring objectivity to the bargaining table.

1) The Importance of Negotiation

Negotiation is the most effective way of resolving disputes. It leaves the decision-making authority with the disputants and is cost-efficient and timesaving when compared to other means of dispute resolution. Some people have the erroneous impression that lawyers spend most of their time in court. In reality, most lawyers spend the bulk of their time consulting with their clients and engaging in negotiations that will lead to settlements. Good negotiation skills are a prerequisite to the constructive resolution of family disputes.

2) Negotiation Techniques

There are three basic approaches to negotiation:

---

36 With respect to the practice of collaborative family law, see Chapter 1, Section C.

1)   hard bargaining;
2)   soft bargaining; and
3)   principled negotiation.

These approaches are reviewed in detail by Roger Fisher and William Ury in their bestselling book, *Getting to Yes*.[37] At the risk of oversimplification, the following summary may shed some light on their differences.

Hard bargaining reflects a competitive or adversarial approach to negotiation. The hard bargainer takes a position and is difficult to shift from that position. He or she makes concessions reluctantly but demands liberal concessions from the other side. Hard bargaining does not necessarily involve unethical or improper conduct but does imply that the dispute involves a contest of wills that the hard bargainer is seeking to win.

Soft bargaining implies an excessive degree of co-operation and the avoidance of confrontation. Soft bargainers are inclined to make too many concessions without demanding a fair return. Soft bargainers are particularly vulnerable when negotiating with hard bargainers, although soft bargainers may reach a point when they say "enough is enough."

So-called principled negotiators, unlike hard and soft bargainers, strive to avoid positional bargaining. They perceive themselves as joint problem solvers. Fisher and Ury have identified the following four characteristics of principled negotiation:

1)   Separate the people from the problem.
2)   Focus on interests, not positions.
3)   Generate options that will be advantageous to both parties.
4)   Insist that the result be based on objective standards.

In separating the people from the issues in family disputes, it is imperative that settlement negotiations avoid blaming one spouse over the other. Issues of "who is to blame" lead to guilt and hostility, neither of which is helpful in the search for equitable solutions to the financial and parenting consequences of marriage breakdown. The focus of discussions should not be on why things have happened but on how they are to be dealt with. Successful negotiations normally require the parties to re-establish some measure of trust and mutual respect, at least when there will be ongoing parental responsibilities.

Fisher and Ury's insistence that negotiations focus on interests, not positions, signifies that behind any position there is a need, desire, or concern

---

37   Roger Fisher & William Ury, *Getting to Yes: Negotiating Agreement Without Giving In*, 3d ed (New York: Penguin, 2011).

that should be identified. Interests may be material, such as money or property, or they may be psychological, such as the need for recognition or security.

Generating options for mutual gain is acknowledged to be a vital feature of effective negotiations. For example, it may be better for both of the parents to share the responsibility for raising the children rather than leaving the responsibility to one parent and relegating the other parent to the status of a passive bystander. Sharing the responsibility will encourage both parents to contribute to the growth and development of their children and also enables them to have time for themselves when they can enjoy the freedom of not being tied to the children. Options that are advantageous to both sides increase the prospect of reaching a mutually acceptable solution.

The use of objective standards to evaluate possible solutions promotes reasonable and fair settlements that can survive the test of time. Objective criteria that are relied on by family law practitioners include relevant statutory provisions and judgments from cases involving comparable facts.

The notion that principled negotiation will substitute win-win solutions for the win-lose philosophy of adversarial bargaining is not without its critics. It may, nevertheless, prove attractive to separated, divorcing, and divorced spouses who can ill-afford to engage in hostile legal negotiations or protracted litigation.

3) Aspects of Successful Negotiation on Family Breakdown

Successful negotiations are dependent on timing, preparation, and effective use of leverage.

Timing is especially crucial in family disputes. Both parties must be ready and willing to abandon their personal hostilities. They must be capable of controlling emotions that can slow down or prevent reasonable settlements. They must have confidence in their lawyers but should not place the ultimate responsibility for a settlement in the hands of their lawyers. They are the persons who must live with the outcome. They should not lightly ignore legal advice but must make their own decisions.

Many people see no need to prepare for negotiation. After all, they can always "play it by ear." They are mistaken. Successful negotiations require careful planning. Just as good musicians do not "play it by ear," neither do good negotiators. Preparation for negotiation requires a knowledge of the relevant facts, an awareness of your own strengths and weaknesses and those of the other side, and a sense of those factors that can be used as leverage or bargaining chips. It can be useful for the disputants and their lawyers to prepare a written negotiation plan itemizing such matters as the following:

- issues to be resolved;
- your needs and interests, both financial and psychological;
- the needs and interests of the other side;
- the needs and interests of any third parties, such as children or grand-parents;
- those matters that are of paramount importance to you and those where you would be willing to make concessions;
- the strengths and weaknesses of your case;
- the strengths and weaknesses of the other side's case;
- your best alternative to a negotiated agreement ("BATNA"); and
- options for resolution of the issues.

An agenda should be established for the negotiations in order to keep issues on track and to accommodate the anticipated time frame for completion of the negotiations. Be aware that deadlines can be used to force concessions. Family dependants who are in financial need cannot withstand a long negotiation process. It is, nevertheless, possible to negotiate issues in stages. For example, issues of spousal and child support and temporary occupation of the matrimonial home may take on a much greater urgency than the sharing of property acquired by the spouses during their marriage. Lawyers frequently draft "interim settlements" that are intended to apply until they are replaced by a permanent and comprehensive settlement.

Knowledge is power. Experienced lawyers can predict the legal outcome of some of the issues arising between spouses on the breakdown of their relationship. In the ordinary course of events, for example, the value of property acquired by either or both of the spouses during their marriage will be equally shared. The amount and duration of child support is reasonably predictable by family law specialists. But spousal support is not nearly so predictable even though it may be vital to the economic security of a custodial parent and the children. There are, of course, no guarantees that an experienced lawyer's predictions on any of the issues will be borne out if the matter goes to trial. Judges are not always predictable — the human factor can get in the way. In any event, litigation is expensive. It costs money to litigate, even for the so-called winner. And in family law, there are rarely any clear winners. Even clients with a relatively weak legal case have something to bargain with, namely, the financial cost and uncertainty of litigation and the emotional wear and tear of protracted negotiations or litigation.

Knowledge of the relevant facts is an obvious necessity for successful negotiation. Negotiators must know what they are talking about. In family disputes, there is often a significant difference between relevant facts from a legal point of view and relevant facts in the minds of the disputants. Here again, emotions tend to get in the way. For example, many provincial statutes, as well as the federal *Divorce Act*, stipulate that matrimonial misconduct must be disregarded in any legal determination of the right to, amount of, and duration of spousal support. Spousal misconduct is also irrelevant to claims for property division on marriage breakdown. Yet, for many separated and divorcing spouses, the misconduct of their partner is foremost in their minds. The dichotomy between *legal* and *personal* perceptions of relevant facts tends to become blurred in negotiations as compared to litigation, because psychological factors come into play.

Insofar as relevant legal facts are regulated by provincial legislation, as distinct from federal divorce legislation, they will not be uniform throughout Canada. For example, different provinces have different statutory criteria that regulate property sharing on marriage breakdown. Consequently, property rights for separated and divorcing spouses may vary according to whether the spouses live in British Columbia, Ontario, Quebec, or Saskatchewan.

Negotiators must always keep in mind their BATNA — their best alternative to a negotiated agreement. It operates as a tripwire against making too many unreciprocated concessions. It also empowers a person to walk away from a bad deal. Unconscionable settlements in family disputes are to be avoided like the plague. They undermine ongoing relationships involving the children. In addition, they are an open invitation to re-open issues by way of litigation or for a party to abandon his or her commitment by taking the law into his or her own hands.

G. MEDIATION

1) Nature of Mediation

The essence of mediation is that the family members are themselves responsible for determining the consequences of their divorce. Self-determination with the aid of an impartial third party is the cornerstone of mediation. Divorce mediation is a process aimed at facilitating the consensual resolution of the economic and parenting consequences of marriage breakdown.

The mediator must defuse family conflict to a level where the parties can communicate with each other. They can then look at their options and apply objective standards with a view to negotiating a fair settlement. Mediation is neither medication nor meditation. Mediation is not to be confused with family therapy. Mediation aims to resolve the practical economic and parenting consequences of marriage breakdown. It is a time-limited process that is intended to produce a formal written settlement. Mediation looks to the future rather than the past. Mediators are usually unconcerned with the reasons for family dysfunction or the search for possible cures. They are not marriage counsellors or therapists. They deal with the practical consequences, not the causes, of marriage breakdown.

Mediation must also be distinguished from arbitration. In mediation, disputants seek a mutually acceptable solution. In arbitration, they agree to be bound by the decision of a third party.

2) Approaches to Mediation

Mediators come in diverse shapes and sizes. They may be engaged in private practice. They may be connected with courts. They may work in community-based services, such as Family Service Agencies.

Most mediators who deal with support and property disputes between separated and divorced spouses are practising lawyers. Lawyer-mediators usually adopt a pragmatic approach to the resolution of economic and parenting consequences of marriage breakdown by focusing on legal rights and obligations. Parenting dispute mediators are more likely to come from the fields of social work or psychology.

Some mediators have no direct link with the established professions and are self-made, and in some cases self-proclaimed. For many professionals, mediation is still a sideline generated by clientele demands. Some mediation models favour a team approach where a social worker or psychologist and a lawyer jointly or sequentially engage in the mediation process, but there is no one single or preferred model.

Mediation is not a monolithic process. Systems and processes vary even though the goal of consensual resolution is constant.

3) Reasons for Mediation

The most common responses to conflict are "fight or flight." Often neither is the right response. Mediation provides an alternative to conflict when spouses or former spouses are unable to negotiate directly with each other but wish to avoid the adversarial postures of the legal process.

- Negotiated settlements achieved through mediation may be more likely to be respected by the disputants than court-imposed orders.
- The privacy of mediation is less threatening than open conflict in a public courtroom.

Mediation can provide more personal or "tailor-made" solutions than traditional legal procedures.

Successful mediation is much cheaper than protracted litigation. However, comparing the costs of successful mediation and litigation is misleading. The vast majority of divorces involve the negotiation of settlements by lawyers. Very few divorces involve a trial. Negotiation through a mediation process is not necessarily cheaper than negotiation through the traditional legal process. Indeed, many mediators insist that any mediated settlement must be reviewed by independent lawyers hired by each spouse.

Although mediation is not always cheaper, it appears to have several advantages not enjoyed by the legal process. Family members are often intimidated by the formal complexity and adversarial nature of the legal process. When the trial date looms, they would rather surrender than engage in warfare through the courts. For many divorcing couples, mediation offers opportunities for them to retain control over their own lives. In parenting disputes, in particular, mediation can establish a framework for future communication and an ongoing exchange of information and ideas respecting the upbringing of the children.

4) Goals of Mediation

As already noted, mediation is goal-oriented. It aims at an end product — namely, a negotiated settlement. First and foremost, mediation is a process by which people attempt to resolve their disputes by agreement. Important secondary goals may include improving communication and reducing tension between the disputants.

A mediated agreement should be reduced to writing and executed in accordance with established legal requirements. Mediators without legal expertise tread on dangerous ground if they assume the responsibility for drafting a formal settlement. They may even be accused of engaging in the unauthorized practice of law. The law of contract that regulates the validity and enforceability of agreements, and the statutes and family law doctrines that have an impact on contractual autonomy, are relatively complex. Although spousal agreements do not normally oust the jurisdiction of the courts over custody and access disputes, different considerations may apply to spousal support and property agreements. Consequently, many non-legally trained mediators prepare only a memorandum of understanding for submission to the lawyers for each party. This memorandum identifies the areas of consensus reached by the disputants and may be expressly declared as not legally binding on the parties until a formal contract has been executed.

5) Arriving at a Fair Settlement

When parties talk about "a fair settlement," they usually mean a workable agreement that meets their subjective needs. Of course, the parties' own sense of what is fair may not be consistent with standards applied by third parties called in to assist them. When mediators talk about the fairness of the final settlement, they may mean any one or more of the following:

- "not unconscionable" (i.e., no undue influence or duress);
- "not disproportionate";
- "workable," "legally fair" (i.e., in line with decided cases and applicable statute law);
- "objectively fair" (i.e., meets actual as opposed to perceived needs); or
- "meets each party's sense of what is fair."

An American commentator has concluded that the mediator's duty is to facilitate an agreement "that (1) meets the participants' own senses of fairness; (2) does not violate minimal societal notions of fairness between persons who make agreements; and (3) does not violate minimal standards of fairness towards unrepresented third parties."[38]

6) Circumstances in which Mediation is Inappropriate

Various techniques exist to enable mediators to effectively redress imbalances of power. Screening for domestic abuse is usually a prelude to mediation.[39] If an imbalance of power cannot be redressed and an uninformed or intimidated party may be induced to agree to an unrealistic or unfair settlement, the mediator should consider terminating the negotiations. Where an imbalance of power will lead to an improvident result, mediation is inappropriate. In some disputes, inequalities of bargaining power between spouses may be more satisfactorily handled by the legal process.

Clearly, mediation is not suitable for all persons.[40] Many mediators contend that mediation is inappropriate when either of the parties is physically violent, addicted to alcohol or drugs, or cannot face the reality of the death of the marriage. People with a "winner-take-all" mentality are not likely to benefit from mediation, which requires an attitude of "give and take" and compromise.

7) Full Disclosure and Confidentiality

Full disclosure is a prerequisite to effective mediation. A frank exchange of information concerning income and assets is essential to the mediation of support and property disputes on marriage breakdown.

---

38 L Riskin, "Towards New Standards in the Neutral Lawyer in Mediation" (1984) 26 Ariz L Rev 329 at 354.

39 See *Wainwright v Wainwright*, 2012 ONSC 913.

40 *Ibid.*

Mediators stress the advisability of predetermining what can or cannot be disclosed to third parties, including lawyers and the courts, during or following an ongoing mediation process. The parties are free to select "open" or "closed" mediation. Open mediation signifies that the parties waive their rights to confidentiality. Closed mediation implies that confidentiality is critical and that neither the parties nor the mediator will be permitted to give evidence in any subsequent litigation as to what transpired during mediation.

8) Involvement of Third Parties

There is a difference between using third parties, such as lawyers and accountants, for information purposes and involving third parties, such as live-ins or in-laws, as active participants in the mediation process. At an early stage, it is important for the mediator and the disputants to define the direct or indirect involvement of other parties. These decisions will partly depend on the preferences of the negotiating parties and partly on the approach taken by the mediator. For example, a "family systems" mediator may adopt a holistic approach that directly involves third parties, such as grandparents or new common law spouses. A lawyer/mediator would be more inclined to see only the disputants themselves.

9) Involvement of Children

There are differences of opinion respecting the role of the children and, indeed, of the mediator, when the mediation process concerns the resolution of parenting disputes. Ignoring the children's perceptions, wishes, and preferences raises a significant risk of the children undermining the settlement. When children are involved in the process, however, the parents must not delegate the decision making to the children.

A distinction needs to be drawn between involving the children in the mediation process on a continuing basis and consulting them on an *ad hoc* basis in order to ascertain their views or preferences. Whether or not the children are consulted, it is important that their anxieties be allayed, that loyalty conflicts be avoided, that they be kept informed of progress, and that they understand the consequences of any mediated settlement.

10) Involvement of Lawyers

Access to independent legal advice must be assured once the dispute has been resolved. The injection of legal expertise into the mediation process itself, whether directly or indirectly, may also be of vital importance before specific decisions are taken. For example, lawyers for the respective parties might be called upon to provide information about the legal and tax implications of particular types of property division or to advise about the probable disposition that would be reached in the event of contested litigation. In the latter case, the legal input provides criteria against which the fairness of a prospective settlement can be measured.

A mediated settlement of financial and property issues on marriage breakdown should always be reviewed by independent lawyers for each of the disputants. Because review of any proposed settlement opens the door to one or both of the independent lawyers sabotaging the agreement, family disputants are wise to select and consult their respective lawyers at an early stage in the mediation process. Early involvement of the lawyers in the mediation process enables the disputants to evaluate the opportunities for, and the potential obstacles to, a mediated settlement.

11) Issues to Be Mediated

At an early stage, the mediator and the parties must define the issues to be examined. They should also agree that new issues are not to be unilaterally sprung on a party at a later stage. The parties should be discouraged from predetermining what is not negotiable when the parameters of the dispute are being set. Rather, the presumption should be that everything to be discussed is negotiable; otherwise, parties become entrenched and immovable.

The mediator's attitudes and expertise may have as much bearing on the subject matter to be mediated as the views of the parties themselves. For example, many mediators shy away from comprehensive divorce mediation, which includes parenting, support, and property disputes; they prefer to confine their practice to parenting disputes. The inclination of non-legally trained mediators to restrict their roles to parenting disputes may be explicable in part by the readiness of lawyers to opt out of such disputes and confine their attention to the economic consequences of marriage breakdown, such as support arrangements and property division. It is questionable, however, how far parenting disputes can be viewed as separate from the economic reorganization of the fractured family. The potential relationship between parenting arrangements and continued occupation of the family residence and child support is self-evident. Parenting arrangements may also be relevant to spousal support for a custodial parent. Mothers worried about economic security may be prepared to make reasonable concessions in parenting areas in order to obtain appropriate financial benefits. Conversely, fathers who place a high value on maintaining a close relationship with their children are usually more open to discussion of issues such as the amount of support payable or continued occupation of the family residence by the custodial parent and children. The mediator must ensure that neither parent takes undue advantage of his or her position as the primary parent or the primary breadwinner.

12) Neutrality of Mediators

Mediators must not only preserve a neutral stance; they must also be perceived as neutral by the disputants. The term "neutral" does not mean a mediator will be passive. Mediators can take active roles to facilitate settlement and their training and personal value systems will clearly affect their overall approach to the mediation process. Intervention, though quite legitimate for the purpose of restructuring the lines of communication or identifying new options, has to stop short of taking the decision-making authority away from the parties. If a mediator is perceived as taking sides, his or her credibility is destroyed and the parties will lose confidence in the process.

13) Common Impediments to Settlement

a)   Emotional Barriers

Marriage breakdown spawns emotional crises that may totally frustrate any attempt at mediation. Realization by both parties that the marriage is over is usually a necessary prerequisite to a satisfactory and lasting settlement. If one spouse is committed to terminating the marital relationship but the other spouse is unwilling to cut the marital tie, then disputes over property, support, and parenting arrangements may be projections of the unresolved emotional divorce, which, if unaddressed, can present a serious stumbling block to any mediated settlement. Spouses who arrive at the divorce mediator's door are often emotionally distraught. They may be angry and resentful; they usually lack respect for and are deeply mistrustful of each other; they may feel rejected and desolate; they may lack self-confidence; or they may be full of grief or guilt. Such manifestations of an unresolved emotional divorce may demonstrate a need for counselling or therapy either before or during the mediation process.

b)   "Stuck Spots"

At times, the parties may reach impasses on specific issues that are not symptomatic of irreconcilable conflict but are simply temporary failures to find a workable compromise. DT Saposnek aptly calls these "stuck spots." They must be overcome but rarely undermine the success of the mediation process in reaching a final comprehensive settlement.

c)   Imbalances of Power

Imbalances of power between the parties may hinder a fair settlement. They may be so severe that the mediator will find it impossible to redress them without being perceived as favouring one spouse over the other.

d)   War Games

Mediators are in agreement that war games must be suppressed if mediation is to succeed. There should be no clearing out the bank account, no removal of the children without consent, no poisoning the minds of the children, and no acrimonious litigation. The first step of any mediator or lawyer should be to establish a truce between the parties and the cessation of hostile activities.

14) Mediation Strategies to Circumvent or Remove Impediments to Settlement

Mediators have developed techniques for avoiding or removing impediments to settlement. Not all mediators use the same techniques; the strategies are numerous and have many variations.

a)   Dealing with Anger and Hostility

The mediator's main task is to divert the emotional energy generated by anger and hostility into a constructive mediation process. One technique widely used by mediators is to neutralize highly emotional outbursts such as accusations by reframing what was said in such a way as to focus on the issues — not the personalities. Another way to defuse tension and also to clarify feelings is to allow what mediators commonly refer to as "controlled venting." There is general agreement that this should be attempted only if the venting will reduce the emotional charge. Mediators may have to adopt an assertive interventionist role when emotional outbreaks threaten the lines of communication. If a session becomes hostile and unproductive, the mediator may temporarily withdraw and resume discussion after tempers have cooled. Alternatively, the mediator may adjourn the whole session to allow the intensity of feeling to abate.

Hostilities that are manifested in parenting disputes can often be controlled or diverted if the mediator reframes issues so as to place emphasis on the child's need to preserve positive relationships with both parents and the psychological damage that the children may suffer as a consequence of continued friction. Many separated and divorced parents can be brought to reason by asking them to address their child's welfare rather than their personal gratification. Spouses, who may be disinclined to be financially generous to their marriage partners, may loosen their purse strings when the emphasis is placed on the economic and emotional well-being of their children, even though the custodial parent will indirectly benefit from any generosity extended to the children. In the childless marriage, where spouses project their hostility in support and property disputes, the mediator will often encounter much more difficulty appealing to the "better judgment" of the spouses. Much greater emphasis may be placed on the legal rights and obligations of the parties, the degree of uncertainty inherent in the substantive law and the legal process, and the relative ability of each spouse to absorb the risk of uncertain litigation and the financial and emotional consequences of contested legal proceedings.

b) Circumventing "Stuck Spots"

Spacing the sessions and strategic use of an adjournment can be particularly effective to resolve deadlock when an impasse has been caused by lack of information. Disputants may, for example, be given assigned tasks of gathering or supplying additional information or seeking input from third parties. The late OJ Coogler, a pioneer of family mediation in the United States, endorsed arbitration as a means of resolving an impasse, but this should only be used as a last resort to avoid litigation.[41] The better route may be to seek an expert opinion on the matter. If legal norms are applicable, a written opinion may be sought from an independent senior counsel when the facts are not in dispute. This obviates the expense, inconvenience, or apprehension of a personal appearance by the disputants at an arbitration hearing. Information or an independent expert opinion may also be sought from accountants, appraisers, and estate planners. The use of expert custody assessments prepared by psychologists or psychiatrists is, however, more problematic. Proper testing and evaluation necessitates the direct participation of all affected family members and tends to shift decision-making authority from the disputants to the assessor. The use of counselling or therapy to complement the mediation process may, on the other hand, be advantageous and can sometimes eliminate emotional roadblocks to a mediated settlement.

Adjournment is only one of many strategies available to the mediator when discussions reach an impasse. Deadlocks may also be broken by broadening the terms of reference beyond those of the spouses, by reformulating or reframing the issue, or by asking the disputants to generate options to resolve the "stuck spot." The objective is to change adversarial perspectives into co-operative perspectives. With some disputants, it is useful to emphasize the emotional and financial cost of not resolving the impasse. A number

---

41 See OJ Coogler, *Structured Mediation in Divorce Settlement* (Lexington, MA: Lexington Books, 1978) c 8.

of mediators stress the value of temporary agreements as a way of preserving the status quo during mediation or of consolidating progress made. Short-term experimental agreements may provide an effective means of testing the viability of options that have been identified. Temporary or limited-issue agreements have the advantage of emphasizing the positive and relegating an impasse to the status of a negotiable obstacle en route to comprehensive resolution of the dispute.

c) Private Caucusing

Opinions differ on whether private caucusing is an appropriate means of breaking an impasse between disputants. Private caucusing involves the mediator meeting with each of the disputants separately. Some mediators consider that private caucusing can reduce or eliminate logjams when either party is extremely sensitive or hostile. Other mediators are uncomfortable with private caucusing. At the very outset of the mediation process, the parties and the mediator should resolve whether private caucusing will be used.

d) Restoring Trust and Respect

Setting the right tone for settlement is critically important. The mediator must foster co-operative solutions by re-establishing trust and respect between the disputants. In order to establish a positive ambience, mediators adopt a number of useful strategies, such as setting joint budgetary assignments, or encouraging trial parenting arrangements. The rationale is clear: joint tasks promote the search for mutually acceptable solutions and shift attention away from recriminations and fault finding. Mediators and disputants cannot expect to resolve chronic emotional problems, but more limited success may be within their grasp if they focus their attention on workable solutions to practical pressing problems.

Co-operation is harder to achieve in some circumstances than in others. In "zero-sum negotiation," for example, where the interests of the two parties are diametrically opposed and any gain to one spouse represents a loss to the other, co-operation may not be possible. In contrast, in "mixed motive negotiation," where the interests of the parties are partially opposed and partially coincidental, parties may be convinced of the value of co-operating in order to maximize their respective interests.

e) Redressing Power Imbalances

Mediation can be an empowering process insofar as it fosters respect and co-operation, but its success depends on active participation by both parties and requires a relatively balanced capacity to negotiate. True equality in the balance of power may be impossible to achieve, but mediators must prevent an abuse of power by either party. Mediators can use a variety of techniques to redress an imbalance of power between the parties.[42] For example, if inequality of bargaining power stems from lack of knowledge, information can be provided. Unequal negotiating skills can sometimes be balanced by insightful intervention and restructuring by the mediator or by the allocation of joint assignments to the parties. Intimidating negotiation patterns can be interrupted and reframed in order to provide support to the disadvantaged party. However, where the imbalance of power is considered to be so great that the mediator cannot intervene without endangering his or her neutrality, the mediator should refuse to sanction the process and suggest other means of dispute resolution.

15) Steps in the Mediation Process

Sheila Kessler, in workshop materials entitled *Creative Conflict Resolution*,[43] identified four basic steps in the mediation process, namely,

1) setting the stage;
2) defining the issues;
3) processing the issues; and
4) resolving the issues.

a) Setting the Stage

Even when people consider the possibility of mediation as a means of resolving their family disputes, they usually have very little awareness of the mediation process. After the couple meets with the mediator and exchanges preliminary information concerning the couple's needs and the qualifications and experience of the mediator, the stage is set for the mediator to explain the process and the ground rules that will be applied. The mediator explains his or her approach to mediation, how the meetings will be conducted, and how issues will be dealt with. The mediator emphasizes that mediation is voluntary and may compare mediation to alternative methods of conflict resolution. Most mediators insist that the process be confidential so that the mediator cannot be called as a witness in any subsequent litigation between the parties. The mediator will explain his or her role as that of an impartial facilitator who will assist the parties in their endeavours to find a solution to the problems with which they are faced. The mediator will impress on the parties that, while the mediator controls the process, the parties themselves control the substantive outcome of their dispute.

---

42   As to screening for power imbalances, see *Wainwright v Wainwright*, 2012 ONSC 913.
43   Atlanta National Institute for Professional Training, 1978.

b) Defining the Issues

In divorce mediation, the fundamental issues relate to one or more of the following matters:

1) property sharing;
2) spousal support;
3) child support; and
4) parenting arrangements ("custody" and "access").

The parties may have dramatically opposite views on all or any of these matters. At the outset, the areas of agreement and disagreement must be identified. The mediator will then assist the parties in segregating their feelings from the substantive issues. Relationship issues may warrant counselling but mediation must focus on dealing with the practical consequences of the breakdown of the relationship.

In assisting the parties to define the specific issues, the mediator tends to move them from positional bargaining to an identification of their needs and interests.

c) Processing the Issues

Processing the issues involves an examination of the options. The mediator will encourage the parties to "brainstorm," which signifies generating a wide variety of options without evaluating them. After the listing of options has been exhausted, the parties can then evaluate their respective strengths and weaknesses. This presupposes effective communication between the parties. Mutual trust, self-confidence, and the ability to exchange opinions without rancour may need to be re-established between the spouses by the mediator's use of diverse techniques that can promote a climate for meaningful dialogue between the parties. A co-operative search for options that will maximize the advantages to both parties goes a long way towards providing the basis for a fair and reasonable settlement. Mutually advantageous options may be easier to discover when issues relating to the children are the focal point or an integral part of the mediation process. Even in property and support disputes, however, it is usually advantageous to both parties to avoid expensive and emotionally wearing litigation.

d) Resolving the Issues

Resolving the issues involves sifting through all the options until a comprehensive settlement is reached. Although the parties may have temporarily resolved specific issues at different times in the mediation process, it is generally understood that these arrangements are tentative until such time as all issues have been resolved. At that point, the mediator will prepare a draft memorandum of understanding that can be subsequently converted into a formal legal contract.

16) Pros and Cons of Mediation

Mediation can facilitate tailor-made solutions to individual problems. It is usually less threatening than the legal process and its self-determined agreements may prove more durable and adaptable than court-ordered settlements. However, mediation is not appropriate for everybody, nor is it appropriate in all circumstances. And not all self-styled mediators are qualified. Successful mediation presupposes high professional standards because of the control a mediator exercises over the process, and because the clients are frequently psychologically disadvantaged by the trauma of family breakdown. Mediation may "belong" to the parties, but a successful outcome is crucially dependent on the expertise of the mediator. Family members who look to private mediation as a means of conflict resolution must, therefore, undertake careful inquiries to ensure that they have recourse to a qualified and experienced mediator.

17) Professional and Community Responses to Mediation

The future of mediation largely depends on its receptivity by existing professional groups and by the lay community — its potential consumers. There is a need for broadly based ongoing sources of information, whether provided through the mass media, schools, and community agencies, or under professional auspices, such as the Church, medicine, and the law. The professions must themselves become educated.

Information is required to dispel the myths of mediation. Members of the legal community who view their vested interests as being threatened by the emerging process of mediation have to be reassured. Mediation must be better understood by lawyers, among who are to be found both its strongest supporters and its strongest opponents. The legal system is not undermined by mediation. Indeed, the legal system and mediation are complementary, rather than competing or contradictory, processes. Both seek to provide a solution to disputes. Each has its place. Neither is self-sufficient: no profession has a monopoly or omniscience in the resolution of human conflict.

Court-connected mediation services are beginning to play a more substantial role in the resolution of family disputes as governments seek to reduce the costs of access to justice.[44] However, budgetary restraints continue to

---

44   See *Fraizinger v Mensher*, 2012 ONSC 7363 at paras 36–43, citing *Wainwright v Wainwright*, 2012 ONSC 2686 at paras 130 & 131.

limit the resources available to promote the consensual resolution of family disputes with the aid of court-connected mediation services. Consequently, there is an ongoing need for community-based and private services.

18) The Future of Family Mediation

In *Pulkinen v Munden*,[45] Graesser J, of the Alberta Court of Queen's Bench, stated:

> I recognize that the Court has an inherent jurisdiction to ignore contractual provisions relating to dispute resolution. Mandatory arbitration provisions have sometimes yielded to court processes. That is the exception and not the rule. There must be a compelling reason to fail to require the parties to adhere to their agreement.
>
> With respect to mediation agreements between parents, these should generally be enforced. Parents should not be encouraged to abdicate their roles as parents by being able to rush off to court, often self-represented, to have a person who is a total stranger to the child make important decisions regarding the child's health care, education, religion or otherwise. The parents are in the best position to make such decisions in their child's best interests, and if they are unable to do so, they are generally better served by working with a family counsellor or family mediator rather than using the adversarial court system.
>
> There may be exceptions, such as with financial matters or where there is urgency, but when the parents have, with the benefit of counsel, agreed to negotiate and then mediate disputes, they should be held to that agreement, absent strong and compelling reasons to the contrary.

As family mediation continues to develop, there will be increasing recognition that mediation is, first and foremost, a process. Far too many people confuse substance with process. It is this confusion that causes lawyers to assert that, even though parenting disputes arising on marriage breakdown lend themselves to mediation by non-legally trained persons, the economic consequences of marriage breakdown, such as property division or spousal and child support, belong in the hands of lawyers, or legally trained mediators. This thinking shows a lack of understanding of what mediation is. Mediation is the process of bringing about consensus between persons involved in a dispute. The substantive issues must not be confused with the process for resolving the dispute. Though incidental to the process, the dispute in itself does not determine the process. Expertise on substantive issues,

---

45   2013 ABQB 139 at paras 17–19; see also *Vojan v Lauzon*, 2015 ONSC 987.

such as the legal or tax implications of a proposed support or property settlement, can and should be incorporated in the mediation process. Such expertise need not reside in the mediator, provided that all relevant information is brought to the bargaining table before a final settlement is reached. The mediator's role is to promote consensus in light of all relevant data, rather than to personally furnish the necessary expertise on the substantive issues.

The role of the "neutral lawyer" or lawyer-mediator, who will advise the family as a whole in an attempt to reach a negotiated settlement, will emerge to complement the traditional role of lawyers who advise and represent individual family members. Some family law practitioners will discharge both mediation and lawyering functions, but not in relation to the same family. A closer association must be established between lawyers and other professionals engaged in advising and assisting families in crisis. Sequential team mediation involving lawyers and other professionals, such as social workers or psychologists, will likely develop as an effective means of promoting the consensual resolution of family conflict.

Although the day may come when community centres, staffed by lawyers, doctors, psychologists, social workers, and other professionals, as well as volunteers, will provide a multidisciplinary approach to the resolution of the multifaceted crises of marriage breakdown, that development lies in the future. In the meantime, the various professions and, indeed, federal and provincial governmental agencies (including departments as diverse as Employment, Finance, Revenue Canada, Health and Welfare, and Justice), which are directly or indirectly involved in the systemic management of the human process of marriage breakdown, must recognize their own limitations and foster effective lines of communication in the search for constructive and comprehensive solutions to the human and socio-economic problems associated with marriage breakdown.

H. ARBITRATION[46]

The conciliation or mediation of family disputes leaves decision making in the hands of the parties. If they cannot resolve the issues, an independent arbiter must determine their respective rights and obligations. Traditionally, this function has been discharged by courts.

The use of binding arbitration has recently emerged in Canada as a viable alternative to contested litigation as a means of resolving spousal disputes

---

46   See, generally, Julien D Payne, "Family Conflict Resolution: Conciliation and Arbitration as Alternatives to the Adversarial Legal Process" in *Payne's Divorce and Family Law Digest*, loose-leaf (Don Mills, ON: R De Boo, 1982) 1983 tab at 83–1601, especially 1611–1615.

respecting property division, support, and child custody and access on marriage breakdown or divorce. During the last fifteen years, Canadian lawyers have made increasing use of arbitration clauses in drafting separation agreements and minutes of settlement.

1) Advantages of Arbitration

Private arbitration has the following potential advantages over litigation as a dispute resolution process.

a) Selection of Arbitrator(s)

The parties are directly involved in the appointment of the arbitrator(s). An arbitrator can be selected having regard to the nature of the dispute and the arbitrator's qualifications and expertise. A lawyer or accountant might be appointed to resolve a complex financial dispute whereas a psychiatrist or psychologist might be preferred when the dispute focuses on the custody, care, and upbringing of children. More than one arbitrator can be appointed if the parties wish to take advantage of several fields of expertise.

In litigation, the parties have little or no choice. Once proceedings have been instituted in a particular court, the issues will be adjudicated by one of the judges assigned to that court. The parties are not free to select a particular judge. Furthermore, if proceedings are instituted in a court of superior jurisdiction, the judge is not usually a specialist in family law and may have no interest in, or even an aversion to, adjudicating spousal or parental disputes.

b) Type of Hearing

Litigants are often intimidated by the formality and adversarial atmosphere of the court. An arbitration hearing can be as formal or informal as the parties desire. The arbitration process can be tailored to the needs of the parties and the circumstances of the particular case. The parties may favour an adversarial type of proceeding in which pleadings and affidavits are filed, witnesses are examined and cross-examined, and the rules of evidence are strictly observed. Alternatively, they may prefer an informal approach by way of a round-table conference. The role of the arbitrator can be specifically defined by the parties. In custody and access disputes, if the arbitrator is a psychiatrist or psychologist, he or she may be given authority to act as a fact-finder as well as the decision maker. The fact-finding may include authorized access to school records and personnel and to doctors and medical records. It may also involve interviewing members of the immediate or extended family and other persons who may be involved in future arrangements for the care and upbringing of the children. Psychological tests might also be appropriate.

c) Flexibility and Speed

Litigation, at least in courts of superior jurisdiction, necessitates formal pleadings, production of documents, and discoveries. Interlocutory motions are often brought pending a trial of the issues. The parties, their counsel, and any witnesses must accommodate the demands or convenience of the court. There is no guarantee when the case will be heard and time is often wasted in waiting to be reached on the court list. Procedural requirements imposed by provincial Rules of Court must be observed and the judge must have regard to previous decisions in matters of substantive law. It is not difficult for experienced counsel to invoke established procedures to delay a resolution of the issues.

In contrast, arbitration does not normally require formal pleadings, productions, and discoveries. Interlocutory motions are usually unnecessary and the issues can be resolved without delay. The extent to which formal procedural rules shall govern is determined by the parties themselves. The parties and the arbitrator can negotiate a suitable time and location for any hearing: long summer vacations, weekends, and evenings are not precluded, as they would be in the judicial process. The arbitrator has only one case to resolve and can give it undivided attention. Hearings and adjournments can be scheduled to accommodate the parties. Even complex issues can usually be resolved by arbitration within a few weeks. Contested litigation rarely takes less than eighteen months and may take several years, particularly if appeals are taken.

d) Definition of Issues

Parties specifically define the limits of the arbitrator's decision-making power. It can be as broad or as narrow as the parties determine. The jurisdiction and powers of the arbitrator are fixed by the agreement of the parties and cannot be exceeded. An arbitrator may be required to make decisions not only about the present but also the future. For example, an arbitrator may be asked to determine what spousal or child support shall be payable before and after retirement. In contrast, litigants cannot fetter the statute-based discretionary jurisdiction of a court respecting spousal or child support, custody, and access. In addition, courts look to the present and not the future; they cannot, or will not, decide issues that depend on future contingencies.

e) Privacy

Even when the arbitration process selected by the parties has a formal and adversarial character, the hearing is conducted in private. Only the parties, their counsel, and witnesses attend the hearing before the arbitrator. Courts of law are generally open to the public and the press, with the consequential risk of embarrassing publicity.

f) Expense

Whereas judges and courts are provided at the taxpayer's expense, arbitrators in family disputes are paid for their services by the disputants. These additional costs are usually more than offset by the time and expense saved as a result of the arbitration process.

The costs of arbitration are more predictable than those arising from contested litigation. Parties to the arbitration process may predetermine who shall pay the costs. It is not uncommon for each spouse to pay his or her own lawyer and for the costs of the arbitrator to be shared equally between the spouses. In contested litigation, it is often difficult to predict the costs that will be involved in a trial. The time likely to be expended and the results of the dispute are often unpredictable. In addition, after contested litigation, it is the responsibility of the court to determine who shall pay the legal costs. The jurisdiction to order costs falls within the unfettered discretion of the court, and judicial practices vary widely. In some cases, the court will make no order for costs; in others, costs will be ordered on a party-party basis, whereby the recipient will usually recover between one-third and one-half of his or her lawyer's fees; in exceptional circumstances, a court may order costs on a solicitor-client basis, which indemnifies the recipient for all costs reasonably incurred.

2) Disadvantages of Arbitration

Opponents of arbitration argue that the arbitration process denies the protection guaranteed by "due process of law." Any failure to adhere to substantive and procedural laws, including the rules of evidence, creates a vacuum within which the arbitrator's discretion is unfettered and may produce unpredictable results or an unfair process.[47] Arbitrators are sometimes accused of being too inclined to "split the difference." Speaking to limitations of the arbitration process in *Kaplan v Kaplan*, McDermot J, of the Ontario Superior Court of Justice, has stated:

---

47 See *Kainz v Potter*, [2006] OJ No 2441 (Sup Ct). But see text to note 60 below.

Arbitrations, however, depend largely on the goodwill of the parties involved. They are not particularly effective when the litigants are, for lack of a better word, ungovernable. Arbitrators do not have the powers of a court to compel directions through contempt or other means. Awards of an arbitrator, whether temporary or final, are not immediately enforceable; they must be incorporated into a court order through s. 59.8 of the *FLA* which can result in delays in or problems with enforcement.[48]

3) Court-Annexed Arbitration

Some form of court-annexed arbitration might ultimately be endorsed in Canada as an alternative process for the resolution of family disputes. Court-annexed arbitration has been introduced in several jurisdictions in the United States to cope with the flood of civil litigation. Court-annexed arbitration differs from private arbitration in several ways. Court-annexed arbitration is often mandatory rather than voluntary, and the arbitrator is assigned and not chosen by the disputants. Most importantly, court-annexed arbitration is usually advisory rather than binding. If the disputants accept the arbitration award, it is entered as a court judgment and is enforceable as such. If the arbitration award is rejected by either party, the issues go to trial and are adjudicated without reference being made to the arbitration award. Most court-annexed programs impose penalties on a disputant, however, if the trial judgment affords no greater relief than that given under the arbitration award.

4) Judicial and Legislative Responses to Arbitration

It is generally conceded that spousal and parental disputes can be referred to binding arbitration.[49] As long ago as 1917, in *Harrison v Harrison*,[50] it was held that spouses may agree to submit the right to and amount of spousal support to binding arbitration. In *Crawford v Crawford*,[51] however, Berger J of the British Columbia Supreme Court observed that it is still open to either spouse to invoke the jurisdiction of the court conferred by the *Divorce Act*.

---

48   2015 ONSC 1277.

49   *Comeau v Comeau*, 2011 ABQB 69; *Marchese v Marchese*, [2007] OJ No 191 (CA); *Grosman v Cookson*, 2012 ONCA 551; *Dormer v McJannet*, [2006] OJ No 5106 (Sup Ct) (custody and access); *Wainwright v Wainwright*, 2012 ONSC 913; *JAEP v CCP*, 2014 ONSC 7035. See *contra*: *McGrath v Hawketts*, [2009] NBJ No 253 (QB) (arbitration unavailable to resolve parenting dispute).

50   (1917), 41 OLR 195 (SC), aff'd (1918), 42 OLR 43 (CA).

51   (1973), 10 RFL 1 at 3 (BCSC); see also *Merrell v Merrell* (1987), 11 RFL (3d) 18 (BCSC) (arbitration clause in separation agreement no bar to judicial exercise of jurisdiction to vary support order that incorporated financial terms of separation agreement).

The impact of the dispute resolution movement over the last twenty years has tempered this opinion, although some courts have tended to jealously guard their *parens patriae* jurisdiction over custody and access disputes.[52] Different considerations apply to spousal property disputes[53] or to spousal and child support claims arising under provincial statutes that include express provisions dealing with spousal agreements or the arbitration of spousal disputes.[54] For example, many provincial statutes regulating matrimonial property include express provisions that recognize some degree of contractual autonomy that may facilitate a submission to binding arbitration in accordance with the applicable provincial *Arbitration Act*. In Nova Scotia, section 30 of the *Matrimonial Property Act*[55] specifically endorses arbitration as an appropriate means of dispute resolution. Section 30 reads as follows:

Arbitration

   30(1) Parties to a marriage contract or separation agreement may, where both persons consent, refer any question as to their rights under this Act or the contract or agreement for determination by arbitration and the *Arbitration Act* then applies.

Order of court

   (2) A copy of an arbitration award made pursuant to this Section, certified by the arbitrator to be a true copy, may be made an order of the court

---

52   See *McGrath v Hawketts*, [2009] NBJ No 253 (QB); see also *Kaplan v Kaplan*, 2015 ONSC 1277. Compare *Harsant v Portnoi* (1990), 27 RFL (3d) 216 (Ont HCJ) (shared parenting arrangement); *Wentzell v Schumacher*, [2004] OJ No 1892 (Sup Ct) (high-conflict parenting dispute; judicial endorsement of recourse to arbitration); *Fishman v Fishman*, 2012 ONSC 4765.

53   See *Walker v Tymofichuk* (1984), 38 RFL (2d) 330 (Alta QB); compare *Keyes v Gordon* (1985), 45 RFL 177 at 187 (NSCA); see also *Childs v Childs Estate*, [1988] 1 WWR 746 (Sask CA).

54   For recent amendments to the *Commercial Arbitration Act*, RSBC 1996, c 55 (now renamed the *Arbitration Act*), see the *Family Law Act*, SBC 2011, c 25, ss 305–13. For decisions where arbitration awards were upheld or varied in family disputes, see *Willick v Willick* (1994), 118 DLR (4th) 51 (Alta QB) (judicial review of arbitrator's award respecting property and fixed-term spousal support); *Lalonde v Lalonde* (1994), 9 RFL (4th) 27 (Ont Gen Div) (custody, access, costs); *Olmstead v Olmstead*, [1991] OJ No 609 (Gen Div) (registration and variation of arbitral award concerning custody, support, and property); *Nagoda v Nagoda*, [1992] OJ No 136 (CA) (voidability of separation agreements); *Newham v Newham* (10 December 1993) (Ont Gen Div) [unreported] (variation of support provisions of separation agreement); *Ross v Ross*, [1999] OJ No 3971 (Sup Ct) (confirmation of arbitral award respecting property); *Robinson v Robinson*, [2000] OJ No 3299 (Sup Ct) (confirmation of arbitral award respecting property and costs); *Kroupis-Yanovski v Yanovski*, 2012 ONSC 5312 (process of final offer selection used to determine child support, spousal support, and the equalization of property). Compare *Deane v Pawluk*, [2006] SJ No 731 at para 29 (QB).

55   RSNS 1989, c 275.

by filing it with the prothonotary of the court who shall enter the same as a record and it thereupon becomes and is an order of the court and is enforceable as such.

Arbitrations in Ontario are subject to amendments to the *Arbitration Act, 1991*, and the *Family Law Act*, which came into force on 1 February 2006.[56] These amendments were directed towards controlling the arbitration of family disputes based on religious laws that are fundamentally different from Ontario or Canadian family law. The primary changes thereby effectuated are as follows:

- Family arbitration agreements and family arbitration awards are governed by the *Family Law Act* and by the *Arbitration Act, 1991*. In the event of any operational conflict between these statutes, the *Family Law Act* prevails.[57]
- Family arbitration agreements constitute domestic contracts under Part IV of the Family Law Act. They must be in writing and each party must receive independent legal advice before entering into such an agreement.[58] Their enforceability is regulated by the provisions of the *Family Law Act*.
- A family arbitration agreement and any arbitration award made thereunder is unenforceable unless the family arbitration agreement was entered into after the dispute to be arbitrated arose.
- Family arbitrations in Ontario must be resolved exclusively in accordance with the law of Ontario or some other Canadian jurisdiction. Arbitration awards that are not in accordance with the law of Ontario or another Canadian jurisdiction have no legal force in Ontario.
- Regulations passed pursuant to the statutory amendments require all family arbitrators who are not members of the Ontario or another Canadian Bar to complete thirty hours of training in Ontario family law provided by a recognized source of such training. All family arbitrators must have received a training program of fourteen hours in screening parties for power imbalances and domestic violence.[59] They

---

56 See *Family Statute Law Amendment Act*, SO 2006, c 1 and *Family Arbitration*, O Reg 134/07 (effective 30 April 2008); *Kaplan v Kaplan*, 2015 ONSC 1277; see also Anne Marie Predko & John D Gregory, "Overview of the *Family Statute Law Amendment Act, 2006*"; and Philip M Epstein & Sheila R Gibb, "Family Law Arbitrations: Choice and Finality under the *Amended Arbitration Act, 1991* and *Family Law Act*" in The Law Society of Upper Canada, *Special Lectures 2006: Family Law* (Toronto: Irwin Law, 2007) at 1–20 and 21–46 respectively; see also Ann C Wilton & Gary S Joseph, *Family Law Arbitration in Canada* (Toronto: Carswell, 2012).

57 See *Kolupanowicz v Cunnison* (2009), 95 OR (3d) 493 (Sup Ct).

58 *Davies v Davies*, 2011 ONSC 6105; *Starkman v Starkman*, [2011] OJ No 6409 (Sup Ct).

59 See *Wainwright v Wainwright*, 2012 ONSC 913; see also *Kaplan v Kaplan*, 2015 ONSC 1277.

must also keep proper records and submit reports to the Ministry of the Attorney General.

- The current statutory provisions and regulations confining the nature, effect, and enforceability of family arbitration agreements and arbitration awards cannot be waived by the parties.

The wisdom of some aspects of the above statutory amendments and regulations has been seriously questioned by some lawyers who have assumed the role of arbitrators in the past. While screening for power imbalances and domestic violence might be a necessary prelude to the mediation process or the arbitration of parenting disputes, it makes far less sense in arbitrations relating to spousal support, child support, and property division where the parties are legally represented and the arbitration is formally conducted as a "private court" in accordance with Ontario law. Although family law arbitrations are not required to mirror the court process, the parties must be treated equally and fairly, each party must be given an opportunity to present his or her case and to respond to the other party's case, and the arbitrator must apply the law of Ontario or another Canadian jurisdiction and no other law.[60] The purpose of the *Arbitration Act, 1991* is to encourage parties to resolve their disputes through arbitration, and to hold them to that course once they have agreed to do so.[61] Section 6 confers very limited powers on a court to intervene. Judicial intervention is justified, however, "to prevent unequal or unfair treatment of parties to arbitration agreements." As Trimble J observed in *JAEP v CCP*:

> Section 6, exception 3 has been litigated in a family law context, little. The Court has used section 6, exception 3 to intervene when an issue arose as to whether:
>
> 1. Procedures adopted by a rabbinical court in negotiating arbitration agreements were unfair (*Cawthorpe v. Cawthorpe*, 2010 ONSC 1389);
>
> 2. An arbitral award should be set aside because a party to the award lacked capacity to understand what was going on (*Lougheed v. Ponomareva*, 2013 ONSC 4347);
>
> 3. The arbitration proceedings and order were unfair because the arbitrator abandoned the terms of agreement to mediate/arbitrate and relied on unsubstantiated allegations of child abuse in making decisions on access and custody (*Hercus v. Hercus*, [2001] O.J. No. 534; [2001] O.T.C. 108);

---

60   *Kroupis-Yanovski v Yanovski*, 2012 ONSC 5312.

61   *JAEP v CCP*, 2014 ONSC 7035, citing *Puigbonet-Crawford v Crawford*, 2006 CanLII 38881 at para 13.

4. The arbitral award was unfair because of the process adopted and an unanticipated lengthy delay in rendering the decision (*Rosenberg v. Minster*, 2014 ONSC 845);

5. The arbitral award was unfair because the arbitrator continued the proceeding even after receiving a letter from the father's counsel requesting that no further steps be taken because the father was seeking removal of the arbitrator (*McAlister v. Gallant*, 2012 ONCJ 565);

6. The mother's unilateral change to access conditions without mediation or arbitration, contrary to an agreement providing for mandatory mediation/arbitration, amounted to unfair treatment (*E.(E.) v. F.(F.)*, 2007 ONCJ 456);

7. The arbitration award was unfair because the arbitrator was allegedly biased against the mother (*Acimovic v. Acimovic*, [2007] W.D.F.L. 835; 33 R.F.L. (6th) 158).[62]

I. MED-ARB

Mediation and arbitration need not be exclusive of one another. "Med-Arb" is a process that utilizes both approaches. Typically, a fixed time will be set aside for mediation, with the understanding that, if no consensus is reached, the mediator will then act as an arbitrator who will give a final and binding decision.[63] Knowing that the negotiations will proceed to arbitration may help parties to reach a consensus in the final stages of the mediation process.[64]

On an application to confirm or set aside a parenting arbitral award ensuing from a med-arb agreement, a court must ensure that the process reflects the expectations of the parties as set out in their written agreement and that it is conducted not only in accordance with the terms and conditions of the agreement but also the governing legislation.[65] An anomaly is created by agreements that incorporate a med-arb process in that either party is free to withdraw from the mediation process at any time but any such withdrawal triggers the mandatory arbitration process.[66]

---

62 *Ibid* at para 26.

63 *Marchese v Marchese*, [2007] OJ No 191 (CA); see also *Wainwright v Wainwright*, 2012 ONSC 913; *McClintock v Karam*, 2015 ONSC 1024.

64 For a brief analysis of the advantages and disadvantages of med-arb, see Stephen B Goldberg, Frank EA Sander, & Nancy H Rogers, *Dispute Resolution* (Boston: Little, Brown, 1992) at 226–28.

65 *Marchese v Marchese*, [2007] OJ No 191 (CA).

66 *Hercus v Hercus*, [2001] OJ No 534 (Sup Ct) (arbitral award set aside). Compare *Kohut v Kohut*, 2015 ABQB 48; *Marchese v Marchese*, [2007] OJ No 191 (CA); *McClintock v Karam*, 2015 ONSC 1024; see also section 35 of the *Arbitration Act, 1991*, SO 1991, c 17, as amended. As to a finding of an apprehension of reasonable bias in circumstances where the parties

A court is not bound by a parental agreement to accept med-arb to re-solve an access dispute, and a consequential arbitral award may be set aside in the exercise of the court's *parens patriae* jurisdiction.[67] A court may also refuse to sanction med-arb clauses in minutes of settlement where it deter-mines that to do otherwise would risk the best interests of a child.[68]

J. PARENTING COORDINATION

Pursuant to the initiative of an interdisciplinary group of legal and mental health professionals in Denver, Colorado, in the early 1990s, a process known as "parenting coordination" has evolved in several American states and has spread into Canada.[69] Parenting coordination usually involves mental health professionals assisting parents who encounter ongoing conflict after custody and access issues have already been the subject of a parenting agreement or court order. Parenting coordinators usually counsel and advise parents on how to develop a more positive co-parenting relationship that focuses on the children's needs. They may be authorized to mediate disputes arising be-tween the parents and, if the parents cannot settle a dispute, to assume the role of an arbitrator and issue a final decision on the dispute.[70] It is custom-ary for parents to agree to med-arb being used to resolve relatively minor disputes that will not fundamentally change the character of an existing parenting agreement or court order. For example, med-arb may be agreed upon by the parents to resolve issues relating to the children's extracurric-ular activities, vacation plans, preschool and after-school child care, existing communication problems, pick-up and drop-off arrangements, or minor

---

have opted for med-arb to resolve parenting issues, see *McClintock v Karam*, 2015 ONSC 1024, DK Gray J.

67   *Duguay v Thompson-Duguay*, [2000] OJ No 1541 (Sup Ct).

68   *Wainwright v Wainwright*, 2012 ONSC 913.

69   See Linda Chodos, "Parenting Coordination: The Cutting Edge of Conflict Management with Separated and Divorced Families" in The Law Society of Upper Canada, *Special Lectures 2006: Family Law* (Toronto: Irwin Law, 2007) 389–412. For relevant provincial legislation in British Columbia, see *Family Law Act*, SBC 2011, c 25, Part 2, Division 3; see also *Fleetwood v Percival*, 2014 BCCA 502. See Association of Family and Conciliation Courts, "Guidelines for Parenting Coordination," online: www.afccnet.org/Portals/o/ AFCCGuidelinesforParentingcoordinationnew.pdf, cited with approval in *Sehota v Sehota*, 2012 ONSC 848; see also *SLT v AKT*, 2009 ABQB 13; *Rashtian v Baraghoush*, 2013 BCSC 994; *Odgers v Odgers*, 2014 BCSC 717; *JMM v KAM*, [2005] NJ No 27 (SC); *De Melo v Gooding*, 2010 ONSC 2271; *Ricciardelli v Ricciardelli*, 2010 ONSC 4755. Compare *Kaplanis v Kaplanis*, [2005] OJ No 275 (CA); see also *Alberta Court of Queen's Bench Practice Note 7*; *Dahlseide v Dahlseide*, 2011 ABCA 51.

70   *BT v BL*, 2010 BCSC 1813; see also *MH v CS*, 2013 BCSC 2232; *Steels v Butrimas*, 2012 ONSC 5119.

changes to the parenting schedule. Fundamental issues, such as a change of custody, extra-provincial relocation of the children, or substantial changes in the parenting schedule usually fall outside the authority of parenting coordinators.[71] Although parents may delegate such functions as they see fit to parenting coordinators[72] and some Canadian courts may refer consenting parents to a court-appointed parenting coordinator, a court has no jurisdiction to delegate its decision-making authority to a parenting co-ordinator unless there is statutory authority to do so,[73] as is the case under the British Columbia *Family Law Act*.[74] In the absence of explicit statutory authority, a distinction must be drawn between the judicial appointment of a parenting coordinator or assessor as a facilitator and the appointment of a parenting coordinator as a final decision maker who forecloses access to the court. The former appointment would appear to be legally permissible but the latter is not.[75] An order for parenting coordination should be made after a final order has been made establishing a parenting plan. It is not the role of a parenting coordinator to devise a parenting plan, nor to engage in evidence gathering for the court.[76]

K. CONCLUDING OBSERVATIONS

This chapter has focused on counselling, negotiation, mediation, arbitration, and med-arb as processes that can be used as alternatives to, or in conjunction with, litigation as means of resolving the emotional, economic, and

---

71   For examples of the functions of a court-appointed parenting coordinator, see *AML v WLL*, 2008 BCSC 1718 at paras 82–86; *PPW v RSLB*, 2010 BCSC 58 at para 177; *Sukul v Sukul*, 2011 BCSC 507 at para 44; *JMM v KAM*, [2005] NJ No 27 at paras 92–98 (SC); see also *Family Law Act*, SBC 2011, c 25, ss 17–18.

72   As to the variation of child support, see *Kohut v Kohut*, 2015 ABQB 48.

73   *Dostie v Poapst*, 2014 ONSC 6959 at para 46; compare *Clayson-Martin v Martin*, 2014 ONSC 7530 at para 211.

74   See *Family Law Act*, ibid, c 25, Part 2, Division 3; *Rashtian v Baraghoush*, 2013 BCSC 994; *MH v CS*, 2013 BCSC 2232; *SPT v MEB*, 2014 BCSC 1698; *RM v NM*, 2014 BCSC 1755; *JDC v KLMFC*, 2014 BCSC 2182.

75   See *JMM v KAM*, [2005] NJ No 27 at para 92(h), where the responsibilities of a court-appointed parenting coordinator included making changes to access arrangements. As to the incapacity of a court to delegate its decision-making authority, see also *Durocher v Klementovich*, 2013 ABCA 115; *Lake v Lake* (1988), 11 RFL (3d) 234 (NSCA); *Strobridge v Strobridge* (1994), 4 RFL (4th) 169 (Ont CA); *CAM v DM*, [2003] OJ No 3707 (CA); *Antemia v Divito*, 2010 ONSC 578; *Steels v Butrimas*, 2012 ONSC 5119; *SC v JC*, [2009] SJ No 121 (QB). Compare *RL v NL*, 2007 NBQB 394; *Young v Young*, 2010 ONCA 602; *Moreira v Garcia Dominguez*, 2012 ONCJ 128; *GB v SA*, 2013 ONSC 2147 (Div Ct).

76   *SLT v AKT*, 2009 ABQB 13; *MH v CS*, 2013 BCSC 2232; *Sehota v Sehota*, 2012 ONSC 848. See also *Fleetwood v Percival*, 2014 BCCA 502.

parenting consequences of marriage breakdown. It does not canvass or even catalogue all of the processes that can be applied or adapted to family conflict management and dispute resolution, nor does it recommend the outright rejection of traditional legal processes in favour of other processes. Indeed, separated and divorced spouses will usually find it advantageous to avoid locking themselves into a single process in their attempts to resolve the multi-faceted problems generated by their marriage breakdown. A few examples may serve to demonstrate that it is appropriate to utilize more than one process. Negotiations do, and must, continue after legal proceedings have been instituted. Indeed, the very institution of legal proceedings may trigger an early negotiated settlement and, even when matters proceed further, eve-of-trial settlements are common. Divorcing or divorced couples may also use different processes to deal with different aspects of their marriage breakdown. Individual or family counselling and therapy may be appropriate as a prelude to mediation. Arbitration may be used to resolve an impasse that has been reached in mediation. Parenting mediation may co-exist with a motion to a court, perhaps on consent, to determine urgent matters relating to interim possession of the family home or the amount of spousal or child support.

Separated and divorced couples must be made aware of the diversity of processes available to foster family conflict management and dispute resolution. Only then can they examine their options in such a way as to reflect their respective interests and those of any children.

CHAPTER 7

Divorce: Jurisdiction; Judgments; Foreign Divorces; Grounds for Divorce; Bars

A. SEPARATION AGREEMENTS; DIVORCE SETTLEMENTS

Spouses may separate without seeking any order from the courts. If they do so, they usually regulate the consequences of their separation by entering into a separation agreement dealing with such matters as division of property, support rights, and custody of or access to the children.

Rights and obligations under a separation agreement are not automatically terminated by a subsequent spousal reconciliation. For example, if property has already been transferred by one spouse to the other under the terms of a separation agreement, a subsequent reconciliation does not revest the property in the original owner. When lawyers draft a separation agreement, they usually include a provision that specifically deals with the effect of a subsequent reconciliation.

Separation agreements or minutes of settlement can also be entered into by divorcing spouses, but a divorce judgment must be obtained from the court in order to terminate the marriage and render the parties free to remarry a third party. Separated spouses who do not reconcile may subsequently petition for divorce, but may choose not to do so. Some postpone divorce for a few years; others never get a divorce. Separated spouses who never divorce are wise to put their affairs in order by way of a separation agreement. Separated and divorced spouses must also review their wills, insurance policies, pension plans, and other important documents.

Spousal separation is the conventional prelude to a divorce. Separated spouses who wish to obtain spousal or child support, or custody of or access to their children, may apply to the courts pursuant to provincial or territorial legislation. In the alternative, they may immediately institute divorce proceedings and claim spousal and child support or custody of or access to the children as corollary relief in the divorce proceedings. In this event, the relevant legislative provisions will be found in the *Divorce Act*.[1] In most cases, it is immaterial whether a separated spouse or parent seeks support, custody, or access under the federal *Divorce Act* or under provincial or territorial legislation. The outcome of the dispute will not normally be affected. Spousal claims for property division are regulated by provincial or territorial legislation and fall outside the scope of the *Divorce Act*. Spousal property disputes can, nevertheless, be joined with a divorce petition so as to enable all economic and parenting issues between the spouses to be determined by the same court at the time of the divorce. The vast majority of divorces are uncontested, with the spouses settling their differences by a negotiated agreement or settlement. Less than 4 percent of all divorces involve a trial of contested issues where the spouses give evidence in open court.

Before examining provincial and territorial legislation regulating such matters as support, custody, access, and property division, it is appropriate to summarize the basic provisions of the *Divorce Act*. They relate to

- jurisdiction,
- the ground for divorce,
- bars to divorce,
- spousal and child support,
- parenting arrangements, and
- process.

The first three of these are dealt with in this chapter, while spousal support is dealt with in Chapter 8, child support in Chapter 9, parenting arrangements in Chapter 10, and process in Chapter 6.

B. JURISDICTION OVER DIVORCE

1) Introduction

Sections 3 to 7 of the current *Divorce Act* include detailed provisions respecting the exercise of judicial jurisdiction over a "divorce proceeding," "corollary relief proceeding," or "variation proceeding." Each of these terms bears a technical meaning that is defined in section 2(1) of the Act. Once jurisdiction has been established, the doctrine of *forum non conveniens* allows a defendant to contest a court's jurisdiction on the basis that another, more appropriate, forum exists.[2]

---

1   RSC 1985, c 3 (2d Supp).

2   *Wang v Lin*, 2013 ONCA 33; *Karkulowski v Karkulowski*, 2014 ONSC 1222; *Essa v Mekawi*, 2014 ONSC 7409. Compare *Theriault v Theriault*, 2014 SKQB 373 at paras 14–16, citing *Walling v Walling*, 2007 SKQB 43.

2) Definition of "Court"

The definition of "court" in section 2(1) of the *Divorce Act* designates a particular court in each province or territory that has jurisdiction to entertain proceedings under the Act. A designated court must be presided over by federally appointed judges. This reflects the constitutional limitations imposed on both the Parliament of Canada and the provincial legislatures by section 96 of the *Constitution Act, 1867*.[3]

3) Exercise of Jurisdiction by Judge Alone

Section 7 of the *Divorce Act* expressly provides that the jurisdiction to grant a divorce is exercisable only by a judge without a jury.

4) Jurisdiction in Divorce Proceedings

a) Basic Statutory Criteria

Pursuant to section 3(1) of the *Divorce Act*, a court of a province, as defined in section 2(1), has jurisdiction to hear and determine an application for divorce and any accompanying application for corollary relief by way of spousal or child support or custody or access, if either spouse has been ordinarily resident within the province for at least one year immediately preceding the commencement of the proceeding.[4] There is a potential conflict of jurisdiction if the one spouse's ordinary residence has been in one province or territory and the other spouse's ordinary residence has been in another. If, for example, the husband had always lived in Ontario but his wife, after separation, returned to her home province of Saskatchewan, where she has been living for the past year, the Ontario Superior Court of Justice as well as the Saskatchewan Court of Queen's Bench could deal with a divorce petition filed by either spouse. To avoid any such judicial conflict, section 3(2) of the *Divorce Act* provides that, if petitions have been filed in two courts that otherwise would have jurisdiction under section 3(1), the first in time prevails if it is not discontinued within thirty days of its commencement; thus the second proceeding shall be deemed to be discontinued, and the court of the province or territory in which the first petition was filed will assume exclusive jurisdiction over the divorce.[5] If both petitions have been filed on the same

---

3   (UK), 30 & 31 Vict, c 3. See *McEvoy v New Brunswick (AG)*, [1983] 1 SCR 704, (*sub nom Re Court of Unified Criminal Jurisdiction*) 46 NBR (2d) 219.

4   *Nafie v Badawy*, 2015 ABCA 36; *Schlotfeldt v Schlotfeldt*, [2008] BCJ No 984 (SC); *Cantave v Cantave*, 2013 ONSC 4082; *Theriault v Theriault*, 2014 SKQB 373; see also Section B(7), below in this chapter.

5   See *Astle v Walton* (1987), 10 RFL (3d) 199 (Alta QB).

day, the conflict of judicial jurisdiction is resolved by exclusive jurisdiction being vested in the Federal Court.[6] Before granting a divorce, a court has to receive a correctly dated clearance certificate pursuant to the *Central Registry of Divorce Proceedings Regulation*[7] in order to determine that the court has exclusive jurisdiction to deal with the divorce proceeding.[8] Section 3(2) of the *Divorce Act* does not apply when divorce petitions have been filed in two different registries in the same province. In that event, the appropriate course of action may be to consolidate the two proceedings.[9]

There is no constitutional right to a divorce that allows a court to reduce or eliminate the one-year ordinary residence requirement imposed by section 3(1) of the *Divorce Act*.[10] The imposition of a one-year ordinary residence requirement under section 3(1) of the *Divorce Act* does not contravene the mobility right guaranteed to every citizen of Canada by section 6(2) of the *Canadian Charter of Rights and Freedoms*,[11] nor the right to life, liberty, and security of the person that is guaranteed under section 7 of the *Charter*.[12]

Where jurisdiction over a divorce petition arises pursuant to section 3(1) of the *Divorce Act*, a Canadian court may grant orders for spousal support, child custody, and child support even though the applicant and children live abroad. A Canadian court may decline to exercise its jurisdiction where there is another forum that is more appropriate. Factors that a court may take into account in addressing the "forum conveniens" include:

- the location of the majority of the parties;
- the location of key witnesses and evidence;
- contractual provisions that specify applicable law or accord jurisdiction;
- the avoidance of a multiplicity of proceedings;
- the applicable law and its weight in comparison to the factual questions to be decided;
- geographical factors suggesting the natural forum;
- whether declining jurisdiction would deprive the plaintiff of a legitimate juridical advantage available in the domestic court; and
- enforceability.[13]

---

6   *Divorce Act*, RSC 1985 (2d Supp), c 3, s 3(3).

7   SOR/86-600.

8   *Corey v Boucher*, 2012 ONSC 572.

9   *Hiebert v Hiebert*, [2005] BCJ No 1409 (SC).

10   *Garchinski v Garchinski*, [2002] SJ No 465 (QB).

11   The *Constitution Act, 1982*, Schedule B to the *Canada Act 1982* (UK), 1982, c 11 [*Charter*].

12   *Thurber v Thurber*, [2002] AJ No 992 (QB).

13   *Alcaniz v Willoughby*, 2011 ONSC 7045, citing *Muscutt v Courcelles* (2002), 60 OR (3d) 20 (CA) and *Follwell v Holmes*, [2006] OJ No 4387 (Sup Ct); see also *Ogunlesi v Ogunlesi*, 2012 ONSC 2112, aff'd 2012 ONCA 723; *Wang v Lin*, 2013 ONCA 33; *Karkulowski v Karkulowski*,

b) Transfer of Divorce Proceeding to Another Province

A court that is seized of jurisdiction under section 3 of the *Divorce Act* has the discretionary power to transfer the "divorce proceeding" to a competent court in another province, if the divorce proceeding includes a contested application for an interim or permanent custody and access order and the child of the marriage is most substantially connected with the province to which the transfer is contemplated.[14] In determining whether a child is substantially connected with another province and whether the balance of convenience favours a transfer of jurisdiction to a court in that province, the judgment of Warren J in *Chung v Fung*,[15] cites the late Professor James G McLeod,[16] who distilled the following relevant factors from Canadian caselaw:

1) the presence of the child in the jurisdiction;
2) the length of residence in each competing jurisdiction;
3) the strength of the child's bonds to persons and circumstances in each province;
4) whether the removal was wrongful, that is, unilateral;
5) whether the removal was justified in light of abuse directed at the child by the parent remaining in the other province;
6) the behaviour of the parents towards compliance with interim custody orders;
7) the province where evidence of the child's present circumstances is most readily available; and
8) the province where the issue of custody can be most easily and cheaply determined.

The application for transfer must be made to the court in which the divorce proceedings were commenced and not the court to which the transfer

---

    2014 ONSC 1222, citing *Van Breda v Village Resorts Ltd*, 2012 SCC 17. See also *Theriault v Theriault*, 2014 SKQB 373.

14   See *Astle v Walton* (1987), 10 RFL (3d) 199 (Alta QB); *Shields v Shields* (2001), 18 RFL (5th) 357 (Alta CA); *IBP v MSP*, 2012 ABQB 278; *Espinoza v Sutherland*, 2009 BCSC 1225; *Tibbs v Tibbs* (1988), 12 RFL (3d) 169 (Man QB); *Mann v Glidden*, 2011 NBCA 50; *D(TW) v D(YM)* (1989), 20 RFL (3d) 183 (NSTD); *Riehl v Key*, [2007] NWTJ No 66 (SC); *Ruyter v Samson* (1992), 44 RFL (3d) 35 (Ont Gen Div); *Rude v Rude*, [2007] SJ No 398 (QB). For a review of the words "most substantially connected," see *Cormier v Cormier* (1990), 26 RFL (3d) 169 at 171–72 (NBQB). See, generally, Vaughan Black, "Section 6 of the *Divorce Act*: What May Be Transferred?" (1992), 37 RFL (3d) 307; see also *SJH v MEH*, 2011 ONSC 1569 at para 39.

15   *Cousens v Ruddy*, 2009 BCSC 1719 (variation proceeding); *IBP v MSP*, 2012 ABQB 278; *Agnew v Violo*, 2013 ONSC 4430 (variation proceeding).

16   James G McLeod, *Child Custody Law and Practice*, loose-leaf (Scarborough, ON: Carswell, 1992–).

is requested.[17] The primary factor in analyzing the facts of the case is the best interests of the child; a secondary factor is the proper administration of justice.[18] Section 6 empowers but does not compel a transfer to be ordered.[19] The word "may" rather than "shall" in matters affecting custody signifies a judicial discretion that is exercisable having regard to the best interests of the child.[20] A transfer should be denied where the best interests of the child would not be served by a transfer.[21] The transfer jurisdiction conferred by section 6(1) of the *Divorce Act* may be exercised on the application of a spouse or by the court acting on its own motion. Pursuant to section 6(4), where a transfer of the divorce proceeding has been made under the authority of section 6(1), the court to which the divorce proceeding has been transferred has exclusive jurisdiction to hear and determine the proceeding. Although section 6 of the *Divorce Act* enables a court to transfer a petition for divorce instituted in its jurisdiction to another provincial jurisdiction, it does not permit a court to transfer to its jurisdiction a petition commenced in another province.[22]

c) Competing Foreign Proceeding

While conflicts in Canadian provincial divorce jurisdiction are resolved by section 3(2) of the *Divorce Act*, whereby the first to be initiated prevails, this is not the dominant factor when there are contemporaneous proceedings in a Canadian province and in a foreign jurisdiction. The principles applicable to an injunction to restrain foreign proceedings and those applicable to a stay of the Canadian proceedings in favour of a foreign court are not the same. A party should not be enjoined from pursuing foreign proceedings that are not vexatious or oppressive. Since the court is concerned with the ends of justice, account must not only be taken of injustice to the defendant if the plaintiff is allowed to pursue the foreign proceedings, but also of injustice to the plaintiff if he or she is not allowed to do so. Whether the Canadian proceedings should be stayed depends on whether the foreign court provides an alternative forum that is clearly or distinctly more appropriate. In deciding which of two jurisdictions offer the more convenient forum, the court should

17   *Ruyter v Samson* (1992), 44 RFL (3d) 35 (Ont Gen Div).

18   *Mohrbutter v Mohrbutter* (1991), 34 RFL (3d) 357 at 358 (Sask QB), citing *D(TW) v D(YM)* (1989), 20 RFL (3d) 183 (NSTD); see also *SJH v MEH*, 2011 ONSC 1569; *Agnew v Violo*, 2013 ONSC 4430 (variation proceeding).

19   *Palahnuk v Palahnuk* (1991), 33 RFL (3d) 194 (Man CA).

20   *Mann v Glidden*, 2011 NBCA 50.

21   *Newman v Newman* (1993), 89 Man R (2d) 254 (QB); *Ketler v Peacey* (1990), 28 RFL (3d) 266 (NWTSC).

22   *Springer v Springer*, [1994] OJ No 450 (Gen Div).

ordinarily consider which jurisdiction can deal more comprehensively with the issues in dispute. It is not *prima facie* unjust or vexatious to commence two actions about the same issues in different jurisdictions. Furthermore, a court will lean against interference where the plaintiff in one jurisdiction is the defendant in the other.[23]

5) Jurisdiction in Corollary Relief Proceedings

a) Basic Statutory Criteria

Section 2(1) of the *Divorce Act* defines "a corollary relief proceeding" as "a proceeding in a court in which either or both former spouses seek a support order or a custody order or both such orders." Sections 3(1) and 4 of the *Divorce Act* respectively provide that an original application for support or custody may be brought at the time of the divorce or thereafter.[24] A spouse who obtains an uncontested divorce which is silent on the issue of support cannot use the default divorce judgment as a bar to the other spouse's subsequent application for support; such an application should be determined on its merits.[25] And a prior support order granted pursuant to provincial legislation does not preclude a subsequent application for support under the *Divorce Act*.[26]

A court has jurisdiction to hear and determine a corollary relief proceeding if either former spouse is ordinarily resident in the province or both former spouses accept the jurisdiction of the court.[27] Where corollary relief proceedings are pending in two courts of competing jurisdiction, the first to be instituted prevails unless that proceeding is discontinued within thirty days of its commencement;[28] and if the two proceedings are commenced on

---

23 *Kornberg v Kornberg* (1990), 30 RFL (3d) 238 (Man CA), leave to appeal to SCC refused (1991), 32 RFL (3d) 157n (SCC); *Follwell v Holmes*, [2006] OJ No 4387 (Sup Ct). As to the application of the *forum non conveniens* doctrine to a divorce proceeding, see *Bullecer v Mayangat*, 2010 ABQB 680; *Roco v Roco*, 2010 ABQB 683; *Kanwar v Kanwar*, 2010 BCCA 407; see also *Armoyan v Armoyan*, 2013 NSCA 99; *Wang v Lin*, 2013 ONCA 33; *Karkulowski v Karkulowski*, 2014 ONSC 1222.

24 See *Evans v Evans* (1987), 6 RFL (3d) 166 (BCSC); *Currie v Currie* (1987), 6 RFL (3d) 40 (Man QB), aff'd (1987), 10 RFL (3d) 207 (Man CA); *Arsenault v Arsenault*, [2006] NSJ No 114 (CA); *Houle v Trottier*, 2012 ONSC 6661 (Div Ct); *Standing v Standing* (1991), 37 RFL (3d) 90 at 92–93 (Sask QB); see also Section B(4), above in this chapter.

25 *Bull v Bull*, 2013 ABQB 366.

26 *Houle v Trottier*, 2012 ONSC 6661 (Div Ct).

27 *Divorce Act*, RSC 1985 (2d Supp), c 3, s 4, as amended by SC 1993, c 8, s 4(1). See *Arsenault v Arsenault*, [2006] NSJ No 114 (CA); *PMG v JH*, 2009 NBQB 41.

28 *Divorce Act*, RSC 1985 (2d Supp), c 3, s 4, as amended by s 4(2); *Santos v Santos*, 2010 BCSC 331.

the same day, the Federal Court has exclusive jurisdiction to hear and determine the corollary relief proceedings.[29]

The following statement appears in *Payne on Divorce*:

> The amended section 4 of the *Divorce Act*, which became effective 25 March 1993, appears sufficiently broad to enable a foreign divorcee to institute proceedings for support and custody under sections 15 and 16 of the Act, if he or she has established ordinary residence in a Canadian province.[30]

In the opinion of the British Columbia Court of Appeal in *LRV v AAV*,[31] and of the Ontario Court of Appeal in *Rothgiesser v Rothgiesser*,[32] the above statement is untenable. In *LRV v AAV*, the British Columbia Court of Appeal traced the evolution of relevant jurisdictional rules in the *Divorce Act*, 1968 and the *Divorce Act*, 1986, as subsequently amended in 1993, before concluding that there is nothing to lead to the conclusion that Parliament, by section 4, intended to confer jurisdiction on Canadian courts to grant "corollary" relief with respect to foreign divorces. The British Columbia Court of Appeal found it unnecessary to determine whether Parliament has the constitutional authority to enact legislation that would empower Canadian courts to grant orders for support, custody, or access to a foreign divorcee who is ordinarily or habitually resident in a Canadian province or territory, but whose former spouse is ordinarily or habitually resident in a foreign country. However, the British Columbia Court of Appeal did volunteer the statement that "much can be said for the proposition that such an enactment would be invading provincial jurisdiction over 'property and civil rights in the Province': see *Ontario (Attorney-General) v. Scott*, [1956] S.C.R. 137."[33] In *Rothgiesser v Rothgiesser*, the Ontario Court of Appeal had previously concluded that the aforementioned suggestion in *Payne on Divorce* is untenable, being of the firm opinion that Parliament did not intend to give Canadian courts jurisdiction over foreign

---

29 *Divorce Act*, RSC 1985 (2d Supp), c 3, s 4, as amended by s 4(3).

30 Julien D Payne, *Payne on Divorce*, 4th ed (Scarborough, ON: Carswell, 1996).

31 [2006] BCJ No 264 (CA), supplementary reasons, (*sub nom Virani v Virani*) [2006] BCJ No 1610 (CA); compare *Shokohyfard v Sotoodeh*, [2006] BCJ No 1348 (SC) (application for division of immovable property in British Columbia is not precluded by foreign divorce). See also *Armoyan v Armoyan*, 2013 NSCA 99.

32 [2000] OJ No 33 (CA); see also *Ziemann v Ziemann*, [2001] BCJ No 733 (SC); *Leonard v Booker*, 2007 NBCA 71; *Okmyansky v Okmyansky*, 2007 ONCA 427; *Karkulowski v Karkulowski*, 2014 ONSC 1222; *Kadri v Kadri*, 2015 ONSC 321; *Wlodarczyk v Spriggs*, [2000] SJ No 703 (QB). For relevant judgments relating to the jurisdiction of the Quebec Superior Court to provide relief to persons who are ordinarily resident in Quebec after the dissolution of their marriage in a foreign jurisdiction, see *Droit de la famille — 3148*, [2000] RJQ 2339 (Sup Ct) and *GM c MAF*, [2003] JQ no 11325 (CA).

33 *LRV v AAV*, [2006] BCJ No 264 at para 60 (CA).

divorcees. In the opinion of the Ontario Court of Appeal, "[a]ny attempt to deal with [spousal] support obligations in the absence of a Canadian divorce would encroach on provincial jurisdiction [*Constitution Act, 1867*] (s. 92, 'Property and Civil Rights')."[34] It does not follow that relief is unavailable to a foreign divorcee who has established his or her home in Canada. However, in the opinion of the British Columbia and Ontario Courts of Appeal, such relief must be found under provincial or territorial legislative authority. In *LRV v AAV*, the British Columbia Court of Appeal held that the *Family Relations Act*[35] does not empower British Columbia courts to make an original order for child support against a non-resident parent for the simple reason that, by enacting the *Interjurisdictional Support Orders Act*[36] the legislature intended to provide a code that is complementary to legislation existing in jurisdictions with which British Columbia has reciprocal arrangements.[37] Absent reciprocity, however, a foreign divorcee may have no alternative but to seek a remedy against his or her former spouse in the appropriate foreign jurisdiction.[38] The unfairness that can result from this situation has been specifically addressed in England by the *forum conveniens* provisions of the *Matrimonial and Family Proceedings Act 1984*,[39] which were enacted in response to the recommendations of the Law Commission (England).[40]

The fact that the parties have obtained a foreign divorce judgment does not prevent an application being brought for property or contractual entitlements under the Ontario *Family Law Act*.[41]

b) Transfer of Corollary Relief Proceeding to Another Province

Pursuant to section 6(2) of the *Divorce Act*, a court with jurisdiction under section 4 to entertain "a corollary relief proceeding," as defined in section 2(1), may transfer that proceeding to a court in a province with which a child of

---

34   [2000] OJ No 33 at para 59 (CA).

35   See now *Family Law Act*, SBC 2011, c 25, effective 18 March 2013.

36   SBC 2002, c 29.

37   See *DPC v TNC*, [2005] AJ No 1634 (QB) (Florida divorce; child support order registered in Alberta and varied pursuant to *Reciprocal Enforcement of Maintenance Orders Act*).

38   But see now, *RNS v KS*, 2013 BCCA 406 (foreign divorcee entitled to pursue spousal support application under *Family Law Act*, SBC 2011, c 25, which came into force on 18 March 2013).

39   (UK), 1984, c 42.

40   See Solicitors Family Law Association, *International Aspects of Family Law*, 2d ed (Orpington: SFLA, Spring 2004) c 6; and see David Truex, "Matrimonial Financial Applications in England and Wales after Foreign Divorce" (Paper presented to CLT Seminar, London, 1 December 2004), online: www.internationalfamilylaw.com/pub/clt1004.html.

41   *Okmyansky v Okmyansky*, 2007 ONCA 427; *Ghaznavi v Kashif-Ul-Haque*, 2011 ONSC 4062 (enforcement of *Mahr*); *Stefanou v Stefanou*, 2012 ONSC 7265. See also *Armoyan v Armoyan*, 2013 NSCA 99.

the marriage is most substantially connected, if the corollary relief proceeding includes an application for interim custody or access under section 16 and that application is opposed.[42] Pursuant to section 6(4), a court to which a corollary relief proceeding has been transferred under the authority of section 6(2) has exclusive jurisdiction to hear and determine the proceeding.

6)   Jurisdiction in Variation Proceedings

a)   Basic Statutory Criteria

Pursuant to section 5(1) of the current *Divorce Act*, the jurisdiction to vary, rescind, or suspend a permanent order for spousal or child support, custody, or access vests in the court of the province in which either former spouse is ordinarily resident, or in a court whose jurisdiction is accepted by the former spouses, provided that any such court falls within the definition of "court" under section 2(1).[43]

Pursuant to sections 5(2) and 5(3), where variation proceedings are pending in two courts that would have jurisdiction under section 5(1), the first to be instituted prevails unless it is discontinued within thirty days of its commencement,[44] and if the two proceedings are commenced on the same day, the Federal Court has exclusive jurisdiction to hear the variation proceedings.

b)   Transfer of Variation Proceeding to Another Province

Where a variation application in respect of a custody order is opposed in a "variation proceeding" as defined in section 2(1) of the *Divorce Act*, and the child is most substantially connected with another province, a court with jurisdiction over the variation proceeding under section 5 may transfer the variation proceeding to a court in that other province.[45] In exercising its discretion, the court looks to the best interests of the child and whether the

---

42   See Vaughan Black, "Section 6 of the *Divorce Act*: What May Be Transferred?" (1992), 37 RFL (3d) 307. As to whether a court may transfer part of a corollary relief proceeding, see *Godin v Godin*, 2013 NSSC 401.

43   See *Lavoie v Yawrenko* (1992), 44 RFL (3d) 89 (BCCA); *Hiscocks v Marshman* (1991), 34 RFL 12 (Ont Gen Div); *Dixon v Dixon* (1995), 13 RFL (4th) 160 (Alta QB).

44   See *Winram v Cassidy* (1991), 37 RFL (3d) 230 (Man CA); *Droit de la famille — 541*, [1988] RDF 484 (Que CA).

45   See *Ellet v Ellet* (1994), 4 RFL (4th) 358 (Alta QB); *GRB v GMN*, 2008 BCSC 843, [2008] BCJ No 1223; *Staranowicz v Staranowicz* (1990), 30 RFL (3d) 185 (Ont Gen Div); *Agnew v Violo*, 2013 ONSC 4430; *Heselton v Heselton*, 2011 SKQB 234; see also *Kermeen v Kermeen* (1989), 93 NSR (2d) 28 (Fam Ct). Compare *Naylen v Naylen* (1987), 6 RFL (3d) 350 (BCSC); but see Vaughan Black, "Section 6 of the *Divorce Act*: What May Be Transferred?" (1992), 37 RFL (3d) 307.

proposed transfer would impede the proper administration of justice.[46] In the event of a transfer, the court to which the variation proceeding has been transferred has exclusive jurisdiction to hear and determine the proceeding by virtue of section 6(4).[47]

c) Variation of Foreign Orders

Section 5 of the *Divorce Act* confers no jurisdiction on any Canadian court to vary a foreign support order, although such jurisdiction may be exercisable under provincial legislation.[48]

7) Ordinarily Resident

A person is "ordinarily resident" in a Canadian province when that person has his or her customary residence in that province. A spouse will be ordinarily resident in a foreign jurisdiction if that jurisdiction is where he or she regularly, normally, or customarily lives.[49] Ordinary residence signifies that a spouse has taken up residence in the province with the intention of remaining there indefinitely. It is not dependent on citizenship, domicile, or immigration status.[50] Residence in a place on a temporary basis for a specific purpose does not constitute ordinary residence within the meaning of sections 3(1), 4(1), and 5(1) of the *Divorce Act*, which regulate the jurisdiction of Canadian courts over divorce proceedings, corollary relief proceedings, and variation proceedings instituted pursuant to the *Divorce Act*. The test to be applied is "Where is [the spouse's] real home?" It is settled law that a person is ordinarily resident in the place where the person "regularly, normally or customarily" lives.[51] A person may be ordinarily resident although not actually resident in the province.[52] Accordingly, a spouse may retain an ordinary residence in a Canadian province, even though that spouse spends a number of

---

46 *Agnew v Violo*, 2013 ONSC 4430. See also *Crerar v Crerar*, 2013 BCSC 2244; *MacKinnon v MacKinnon*, 2015 NSSC 18.

47 *MacKinnon v MacKinnon*, 2015 NSSC 18.

48 See *Leonard v Booker*, 2007 NBCA 71; *Rothgiesser v Rothgiesser* (2000), 2 RFL (5th) 266 (CA); see also *Kendregan v Kendregan*, 2009 BCSC 23; *Jasen v Karassik*, 2009 ONCA 245; *Stefanou v Stefanou*, 2012 ONSC 7265. See also *Zeng v Fu*, 2014 ONSC 3268 wherein *parens patriae* jurisdiction was assumed with respect to custody/access and child support.

49 *Kadri v Kadri*, 2015 ONSC 321; see also *Nafie v Badawy*, 2014 ABQB 262.

50 *Murphy v Wulkowicz*, [2003] NSJ No 324 (SC); *Kadri v Kadri*, 2015 ONSC 321.

51 *Nafie v Badawy*, 2014 ABQB 262; *Robar v Robar*, 2010 NBQB 8; *Quigley v Willmore*, [2008] NSJ No 144 (CA); *Armoyan v Armoyan*, 2013 NSCA 99; *Ogunlesi v Ogunlesi*, 2012 ONSC 2112, aff'd 2012 ONCA 723; *Cantave v Cantave*, 2013 ONSC 4082; *Droit de la famille — 092181*, [2009] QJ No 9388 (CS).

52 *Alcaniz v Willoughby*, 2011 ONSC 7045, citing *McFadden v Sprague*, [2005] OJ No 4627 (Sup Ct); *Ogunlesi v Ogunlesi*, 2012 ONSC 2112, aff'd 2012 ONCA 723.

years in another jurisdiction to which he or she has been posted by an employer.[53] A voluntary change of a spouse's home and private business may, however, terminate the period of ordinary residence previously established in another province.[54] The arrival of a person in a new province with intention of making a home there for an indefinite period makes that person ordinarily resident in that province. Future intentions unaccompanied by any change of residence will not, however, terminate an existing ordinary residence.[55] A person does not lose his or her place of ordinary residence until he or she has determined to give up that residence and arrives in another province with the intention of remaining there.[56]

A spouse may be ordinarily resident in a province within the meaning of the *Divorce Act*, notwithstanding that the initial entry and continued residence in Canada is illegal. Some degree of volition may be required, however, to establish an ordinary residence in a particular province.[57]

The jurisdictional requirements of section 3(1) of the *Divorce Act* cannot be waived or changed by consent of the spouses or by estoppel.[58]

Where neither spouse has been ordinarily resident in any single province for at least one year, no Canadian court can entertain an application for divorce.[59] It has been held that the term "ordinary residence" should not be construed too restrictively when it could create a jurisdictional vacuum.[60] No corresponding time limitation of one year applies with respect to variation proceedings under section 5(1). The residence requirement is a fundamental

---

53   *Marsellus v Marsellus* (1970), 2 RFL 53 (BCSC).

54   See *Anema v Anema* (1976), 27 RFL 156 (Man QB); *Quigley v Willmore*, [2008] NSJ No 144 (CA); *Lajoie v Woito*, [2009] OJ No 151 (Sup Ct); *Masse v Sykora* (1979), 13 RFL (2d) 68 (Que CS); *Cable v Cable* (1981), 130 DLR (3d) 381 (Sask QB).

55   *MacPherson v MacPherson* (1976), 28 RFL 106 (Ont CA); see also *Nowlan v Nowlan* (1970), 2 RFL 67 (NSSCTD); *Quigley v Willmore*, [2008] NSJ No 144 (CA); *Lajoie v Woito*, [2009] OJ No 151 (Sup Ct); *Wang v Lin*, 2013 ONCA 33.

56   *Re Beaton* (1980), 42 NSR (2d) 536 (TD); *Cadot v Cadot* (1982), 49 NSR (2d) 202 (TD); compare *Wrixon v Wrixon* (1982), 30 RFL (2d) 107 (Alta QB).

57   See *Blair v Chung*, [2006] AJ No 882 (QB); *Murphy v Wulkowicz*, [2003] NSJ No 324 (SC); *Jablonowski v Jablonowski* (1972), 8 RFL 36 (Ont SC); *Wood v Wood* (1987), 4 RFL (2d) 182 (PEISCTD); compare *Spek v Lawson* (1983), 43 OR (2d) 705 (CA).

58   *Byrn v Mackin* (1983), 32 RFL (2d) 207 (Que CS); *Quigley v Willmore*, [2007] NSJ No 426 (SC); *Lajoie v Woito*, [2009] OJ No 151 (Sup Ct); *NK c RV*, [2004] QJ No 8238 (CS); compare s 5(1) of the *Divorce Act*, RSC 1985 (2d Supp), c 3.

59   See *Winmill v Winmill* (1975), 47 DLR (3d) 597 (Fed CA); *Lietz v Lietz* (1990), 30 RFL (3d) 293 (NBQB).

60   RSQ c C-25. See *Droit de la famille — 1006*, [1986] RDF 81 (Que CS). See also *Mills v Butt* (1990), 82 Nfld & PEIR 42 (Nfld UFC).

condition and is unqualified by the effect of a delay in raising the issue under the Quebec *Code of Civil Procedure*.[61]

Section 3(1) of the *Divorce Act*, which imposes a minimum one-year period of ordinary residence, does not contravene section 6(2)(a) (mobility rights) or section 15 (equality rights) of the *Canadian Charter of Rights and Freedoms*. The imposition of the one-year ordinary residence requirement should also be upheld as a reasonable limit on guaranteed rights and freedoms under section 1 of the *Charter*, having regard to the ramifications of divorce, which go beyond the personal interests of the spouses.[62]

The period of ordinary residence required by section 3(1) of the *Divorce Act* is not limited to one year and may exceed it, but the required period of ordinary residence must continue without interruption for at least one year immediately preceding the commencement of the divorce proceedings.[63] An application for divorce that is presented before expiry of the minimum one-year period of ordinary residence must be dismissed, even though either or both spouses have been ordinarily resident in the province for more than one year at the time of a divorce hearing. Under these circumstances, however, a new application could be successfully launched without delay.[64]

In calculating the minimum one year of ordinary residence for the purposes of section 3(1) of the *Divorce Act*, the court may take account of premarital residence in the province. Section 3(1) is not confined to ordinary residence *qua* spouse.[65]

The requirements of section 3(1) may be satisfied if either spouse was ordinarily resident in the province for at least one year immediately preceding the commencement of the divorce proceeding, notwithstanding that such ordinary residence was abandoned before the application is adjudicated.[66]

---

61 See *Droit de la famille — 360*, [1987] RDF 171 (Que CS).

62 *Canadian Charter of Rights and Freedoms*, Part I of the *Constitution Act, 1982*, being Schedule B to the *Canada Act 1982* (UK), 1982, c 11. See *Koch v Koch* (1985), 23 DLR (4th) 609 (Sask QB); see also *Tit v Manitoba (Director of Vital Statistics)* (1986), 28 DLR (4th) 150 (Man QB) (application under the *Change of Name Act*, SM 1982–83–84, c 56).

63 See *Anema v Anema* (1976), 27 RFL 156 (Man QB); *Robichaud v Robichaud* (1974), 20 RFL 14 (NBQB); *Cullen v Cullen* (1969), 9 DLR (3d) 610 (NSTD).

64 *Anema v Anema* (1976), 27 RFL 156 (Man QB); *Stapleton v Stapleton* (1977), 1 RFL (2d) 190 (Man CA).

65 See *Navas v Navas*, [1969] 3 All ER 677; *Zoldester v Zoldester* (1974), 13 RFL 398 (BCSC).

66 See *Martin v Martin* (1970), 9 RFL 1 at 5 (NSWSC); *Battagin v Battagin* (1980), 28 AR 586 (QB); *Weston v Weston* (1972), 5 RFL 244 (BCSC); compare *Baia v Baia* (1970), 1 RFL 348 (Ont HCJ).

C. DIVORCE JUDGMENTS

1) Effective Date of Divorce Judgment; Appeals; Rescission of Divorce Judgment

Pursuant to section 12 of the *Divorce Act*, a divorce judgment normally takes effect on the thirty-first day after the day on which the judgment granting the divorce was rendered, or at such later date as all rights of appeal have been exhausted. A divorce is not effective until an appeal has been determined and the time for any further appeal from the appellate judgment has expired.[67] Pursuant to sections 12(3), 12(4), 12(5), and 21(2) of the *Divorce Act*, no appeal lies from a judgment granting a divorce on the expiry of the time fixed by law for instituting an appeal, unless an extension of the time for appeal has been granted prior to expiry of the normal period. Less restrictive conditions apply to appeals respecting corollary relief in divorce proceedings, as distinguished from the judgment on marital status. Pursuant to section 21(4), an appellate court or a judge thereof may, on special grounds, grant an extension of the time for appealing corollary relief even after expiry of the normal period. Although no appeal lies from a divorce judgment that has taken effect under section 12 of the *Divorce Act*, the judgment may be set aside where it was obtained by irregular or illegal means,[68] as, for example, where fraud is involved, where statutory provisions or rules of court are contravened, or where principles of natural justice are infringed. Infringement of principles of natural justice should not, however, render the divorce judgment void but only voidable, so that the court can do justice to all affected parties.[69] Any application for rescission is properly made to the trial court and not to the Court of Appeal. A court has the inherent jurisdiction to amend a divorce judgment so as to correct an error respecting the date of the marriage dissolved, notwithstanding that there is no ability to appeal the judgment and notwithstanding that the error goes beyond what can be corrected under the slip rule.[70] In *Rishi v Deo*,[71] the Saskatchewan Court of Appeal held that a divorce judgment may be vacated on appeal if the spouses have reconciled and the time for appeal has not expired.

---

67   *Bast v Bast* (1990), 30 RFL (3d) 181 (Sask CA).

68   *Geci v Gravel*, [1970] RP 402 (Que BR).

69   *Rivas v Rivas* (1977), 28 RFL 342 (Alta TD); *Luo v Yi*, 2012 BCSC 1201; *Harding v Harding* (1985), 47 RFL (2d) 52 at 57 (Man QB); *Chadderton v Chadderton* (1973), 8 RFL 374 (Ont CA); *Brown v Brown* (1980), 19 RFL (2d) 225 (PEITD).

70   *Tschudi v Tschudi*, [2007] BCJ No 2428 (SC), citing *Thynne v Thynne*, [1955] 3 All ER 129 (Eng CA).

71   2014 SKCA 54.

2) Expedition of Divorce Judgment

Section 12(2) of the *Divorce Act* empowers the court to reduce or eliminate the thirty-one day waiting period that must ordinarily elapse before the divorce judgment takes effect. The exercise of this jurisdiction is conditioned on (1) the existence of special circumstances[72] and (2) the agreement of the spouses and their undertakings that no appeal will be taken from the judgment or that any pending appeal has been abandoned.[73] Such agreement and undertakings may be oral[74] or they may be submitted to the court in writing without any requirement that the respondent appear personally before the court.[75] A divorce judgment cannot be expedited unless the parties positively agree to the abridgement and undertake not to appeal. Where a party cannot be found or refuses to agree, there can be no expedition of the divorce judgment.[76] Unlike the position under section 13(2) of the *Divorce Act, 1968*, section 12(2) of the current *Divorce Act* no longer requires the applicant to show that the public interest would be served by expediting the operative date of the divorce. Consequently, cases under the former *Divorce Act* that refused to expedite the divorce judgment must be viewed with circumspection.

Where the special circumstances were that reconciliation was impossible, the petition for divorce was not contested, no children were born of the marriage, the parties had reorganized their lives separately, and they agreed not to appeal, there were found to be sufficient reasons to expedite the granting of the divorce judgment.[77] Special circumstances may be found if the failure to waive the thirty-one day waiting period would cause a great deal of inconvenience, heartache, and possibly expense.[78]

If it is not waived by court order and either spouse attempts to remarry a third party before the thirty-one days have elapsed, the second marriage will be null and void. In law, the second marriage would be bigamous, although a criminal prosecution for bigamy would not result in a conviction if the remarriage occurred in ignorance of the thirty-one days requirement.

---

72 *Baia v Baia* (1970), 1 RFL 348 (Ont HCJ).

73 Compare *Bast v Bast* (1990), 30 RFL (3d) 181 (Sask CA).

74 *Dippel v Dippel* (17 February 1970) (Alta TD) [unreported].

75 *Cooper v Cooper* (1969), 1 RFL 338 (NSSC). Compare *Baia v Baia* (1970), 1 RFL 348 (Ont HCJ) wherein Wright J stated that although *viva voce* evidence can be given by the parties, the records of the court should in every case include a written agreement and undertaking properly attested.

76 *Baia v Baia* (1970), 1 RFL 348 (Ont HCJ).

77 *Bitard v Ritztallah*, [1981] RP 408 (Que CS).

78 *Mundle v Jurgaitis* (1994), 127 NSR (2d) 88 (TD).

Pursuant to section 12(2)(a) of the *Divorce Act*, the permissible range of judicial variation is within, not beyond, the general thirty-one-day effective date.[79]

3) National Effect of Divorce and Corollary Orders

Section 13 of the *Divorce Act* provides that a divorce granted pursuant to the Act shall have legal effect throughout Canada.[80] The recognition of foreign divorce judgments is independently regulated by section 22 of the *Divorce Act*. Pursuant to section 20(2) of the *Divorce Act*, 1968, any corollary order granted under the *Divorce Act*, other than a provisional order under section 18(2), also has legal effect throughout Canada.

4) Right to Remarry

Section 14 of the *Divorce Act* provides that "[o]n taking effect, a divorce granted under this Act dissolves the marriage of the spouses." A respondent's fundamental freedom to practise his or her own religion, which is guaranteed by section 2(a) of the *Canadian Charter of Rights and Freedoms*, is not violated by a divorce judgment granted to the petitioning spouse.[81]

D. RECOGNITION OF FOREIGN DIVORCES[82]

1) General Criteria

Consistent with the jurisdiction conferred on Canadian courts by section 3(1) of the *Divorce Act*, section 22(1) provides that recognition shall be afforded to a foreign divorce granted on or after the commencement of the Act if either spouse was ordinarily resident[83] in the foreign jurisdiction for at least one year immediately preceding the commencement of the proceedings for divorce.[84] In the common law provinces, at least, section 22(1) of the *Divorce Act* may be superfluous in light of the law as defined in *Robinson-Scott v Robinson-Scott*.[85]

---

79 *Pasiuk v Pasiuk*, 2011 BCSC 1312.

80 As to the impact of an extra-provincial divorce on an interim order for spousal support granted pursuant to *The Inter-jurisdictional Support Orders Act*, CCSM c I60, see *Richard v Richard*, 2012 MBQB 36.

81 *Gordon v Keyes* (1986), 72 NSR (2d) 172 (TD).

82 See James G McLeod, *The Conflict of Laws* (Calgary: Carswell, 1983) c 4.1.

83 *Kadri v Kadri*, 2015 ONSC 321. As to the significance of the term "ordinarily resident," see Section B(7), above in this chapter.

84 *Zhang v Lin*, 2010 ABQB 420.

85 [1958] P 71; see text below and see Julien D Payne, "Recognition of Foreign Divorce Decrees in Canadian Courts" (1961) 10 ICLQ 846. Compare *Droit de la famille — 1221*, [1989] RDF 161 (Que CS).

Sections 22(2) and 22(3) of the current *Divorce Act* substantially preserve the contents of section 6(2) of the *Divorce Act*, 1968. The continued recognition thereby afforded to foreign divorce decrees granted after 1 July 1968 on the jurisdictional basis of the wife's independent domicile reflects the provisions of section 6(1) of the *Divorce Act*, 1968, coupled with the doctrine of comity and reciprocity endorsed in *Travers v Holley*.[86] Section 22(3) of the *Divorce Act* expressly preserves pre-existing judge-made rules of law pertaining to the recognition of foreign divorces. It may be appropriate to summarize these rules.[87] Canadian courts will recognize a foreign divorce:

- where jurisdiction was assumed on the basis of the domicile of the spouses;[88]
- where the foreign divorce, though granted on a non-domiciliary jurisdictional basis, is recognized by the law of the domicile of the parties;[89]
- where the foreign jurisdictional rule corresponds to the Canadian jurisdictional rule in divorce proceedings;[90]
- where the circumstances in the foreign jurisdiction would have conferred jurisdiction on a Canadian court if they had occurred in Canada;[91]
- where either the petitioner or respondent had a real and substantial connection with the foreign jurisdiction wherein the divorce was granted;[92] and
- where the foreign divorce is recognized in another foreign jurisdiction with which the petitioner or respondent has a real and substantial connection.[93]

---

86 [1953] P 246 (Eng CA); see text below.

87 The following summary was endorsed in *Janes v Pardo*, [2002] NJ No 17 (SC), citing *Payne on Divorce*, 4th ed (Scarborough, ON: Carswell, 1996) at 110–11. See also *Orabi v El Qaoud*, [2005] NSJ No 76 (CA); *Zhang v Lin*, 2010 ABQB 420; *Marzara v Marzara*, 2011 BCSC 408; *Asghar v Doyle*, 2014 NBQB 254; *Nowacki v Nowacki*, 2014 ONSC 2052; *Essa v Mekawi*, 2014 ONSC 7409.

88 *Le Mesurier v Le Mesurier*, [1895] AC 517; *Kadri v Kadri*, 2015 ONSC 321.

89 *Armitage v Attorney General*, [1906] P 135.

90 *Travers v Holley*, [1953] P 246 (Eng CA).

91 *Robinson-Scott v Robinson-Scott*, [1958] P 71.

92 *Indyka v Indyka*, [1969] 1 AC 33 (HL); *Mayfield v Mayfield*, [1969] P 119; *Asghar v Doyle*, 2014 NBQB 254; *Martinez v Basail*, 2010 ONSC 2038; *Essa v Mekawi*, 2014 ONSC 7409.

93 *Mather v Mahoney*, [1968] 3 All ER 223. This criterion has been deemed applicable even though the foreign divorce was granted prior to that ruling: *Edward v Edward Estate* (1987), 8 RFL (3d) 370 (Sask CA).

If jurisdiction vests in the foreign court in accordance with the above criteria, the substantive ground for the foreign divorce is of no concern.[94]

Although the aforementioned rules were established by decisions of the English courts, they have generally been followed by Canadian courts, at least in those provinces that adhere to common law tradition.

Judicial recognition of a foreign divorce pursuant to section 22 of the *Divorce Act* does not imply that recognition automatically extends to any corollary order for financial relief granted in the foreign divorce judgment.[95]

2) Extra-Judicial Divorce

Canadian courts may recognize an extra-judicial foreign divorce.[96]

3) Substantive and Procedural Defects

The perpetration of fraud upon a foreign tribunal that goes to the question of jurisdiction will preclude recognition of the foreign divorce in Canada.[97] A foreign divorce may also be denied recognition where principles of natural justice have been contravened[98] or the divorce is contrary to Canadian public policy.[99]

4) Doctrine of Preclusion

A person who has invoked the jurisdiction of a foreign tribunal cannot be heard to question the validity of the foreign divorce so as to obtain a material or pecuniary advantage based on its invalidity in Canada. The foreign divorce is not validated for all purposes in such a case; it is merely recognized for the purpose of applying an estoppel.[100]

---

94   *Powell v Cockburn*, [1977] 2 SCR 218; *Pitre v Nguyen*, [2007] BCJ No 1708 (SC); *Sangi v Sangi*, 2011 BCSC 523.

95   *Vargo v Saskatchewan (Family Justice Services Branch)*, [2006] SJ No 350 (QB).

96   *Schwebel v Ungar* (1963), 42 DLR (2d) 622 (Ont CA), aff'd [1965] SCR 148; *Goldenberg v Triffon*, [1955] CS 341 (Que).

97   *Redl v Redl* (1983), 35 RFL (2d) 117 (Ont HCJ); see also *Powell v Cockburn*, [1977] 2 SCR 218; *Zhang v Lin*, 2010 ABQB 420; *Sangi v Sangi*, 2011 BCSC 523; *Nowacki v Nowacki*, 2014 ONSC 2052.

98   *Zhang v Lin*, 2010 ABQB 420; *Holub v Holub*, [1976] 5 WWR 527 (ManCA); *Orabi v El Qaoud*, [2005] NSJ No 76 (CA).

99   *Zhang v Lin*, 2010 ABQB 420; *Marzara v Marzara*, 2011 BCSC 408; compare *Essa v Mekawi*, 2014 ONSC 7409.

100 See *Downton v Downton Estate*, [1973] SCR 437; see also *Stephens v Falchi*, [1938] SCR 354; *Re Plummer*, [1941] 3 WWR 788 (Alta CA); *Sangi v Sangi*, 2011 BCSC 523; *Oliver v Oliver*, 2011 BCSC 1126.

E. MARRIAGE BREAKDOWN AS SOLE GROUND FOR DIVORCE

Section 8 of the *Divorce Act*[101] defines the ground for divorce. In light of its importance, it is appropriate to reproduce it in its entirety:

Divorce

8. (1) A court of competent jurisdiction may, on application by either or both spouses, grant a divorce to the spouse or spouses on the ground that there has been a breakdown of their marriage.

Breakdown of marriage

(2) Breakdown of a marriage is established only if

(a) the spouses have lived separate and apart for at least one year immediately preceding the determination of the divorce proceeding and were living separate and apart at the commencement of the proceeding; or

(b) the spouse against whom the divorce proceeding is brought has, since celebration of the marriage,

(i) committed adultery, or

(ii) treated the other spouse with physical or mental cruelty of such a kind as to render intolerable the continued cohabitation of the spouses.

Calculation of period of separation

(3) For the purposes of paragraph (2)(a),

(a) spouses shall be deemed to have lived separate and apart for any period during which they lived apart and either of them had the intention to live separate and apart from the other; and

(b) a period during which spouses have lived separate and apart shall not be considered to have been interrupted or terminated

(i) by reason only that either spouse has become incapable of forming or having an intention to continue to live separate and apart or of continuing to live separate and apart of the spouse's own volition, if it appears to the court that the separation would probably have continued if the spouse had not become so incapable, or

(ii) by reason only that the spouses have resumed cohabitation during a period of, or periods totalling, not more than ninety days with reconciliation as its primary purpose.

---

101 *Divorce Act*, RSC 1985 (2d Supp), c 3.

Pursuant to section 8 of the *Divorce* Act, there is only one ground for divorce in Canada, namely, a "breakdown of [the] marriage."[102] It is not sufficient for one or both spouses to simply assert that their marriage has irretrievably broken down. In order to obtain a divorce under the *Divorce Act*, breakdown of a marriage is established "only if" the spouses have lived separate and apart for at least one year immediately preceding the divorce judgment, or the spouse against whom the divorce is sought has since the celebration of the marriage committed adultery or treated the other spouse with physical or mental cruelty of such a kind as to render continued marital cohabitation intolerable.[103]

Same-sex couples who are legally married may invoke the primary and corollary relief provisions of the *Divorce Act*.[104]

It is important to bear in mind, however, that not all same-sex couples choose to marry. Only those who marry can avail themselves of the corollary relief provisions of the *Divorce Act* that relate to spousal support, child support, custody, and access. If same-sex couples, who cohabited but did not marry, wish to obtain any of the aforementioned types of relief, they must, like unmarried cohabitants of the opposite sex, have recourse to applicable provincial legislation. While this may be of little practical significance because applications for spousal support, child support, custody, and access usually generate the same result whether such relief is sought pursuant to provincial legislation or the *Divorce Act*, fundamental differences between same-sex married couples and same-sex unmarried couples may arise in the context of provincial statutory property rights on the breakdown of their relationships. For example, in Ontario, a same-sex married partner may obtain an equalization of the net spousal properties pursuant to Part I of the *Family Law Act*[105] as amended by the *Spousal Relationships Statute Law Amendment Act*.[106] However, in light of the judgment of the Supreme Court of Canada in *Nova Scotia (Attorney General) v Walsh*,[107] a same-sex former unmarried cohabitant cannot avail himself or herself of similar relief and must rest content with such relief as might be available at common law or by way of resulting or constructive trusts.

Section 8(1) of the *Divorce Act* provides that "either or both spouses" may apply for divorce. A joint petition for divorce may be based on marriage breakdown as manifested by the separation of the spouses within the meaning of

---

102   *Ibid*, s 8(1).
103   *Ibid*, s 8(2).
104   *HP v CTP*, 2014 BCSC 2024; *MH v JH*, [2004] OJ No 5314 (Sup Ct).
105   RSO 1990, c F.3.
106   SO 2005, c 5.
107   [2002] 4 SCR 325.

section 8(2)(a), but a joint petition cannot be brought where the facts relied upon, in whole or in part, involve the adultery or cruelty of the respondent as defined in section 8(2)(b).[108]

1) Spousal Separation as Proof of Marriage Breakdown

Spouses who rely on the one-year separation period in order to obtain their divorce are not required to wait until that period has expired before filing for divorce. A divorce petition can be filed on the day following the spousal separation but a divorce judgment cannot be obtained until the one-year period has elapsed. Once a divorce petition has been filed, either spouse may obtain interim corollary relief, such as support, custody, or access, to tide him or her over until the issues can be permanently resolved by a trial in open court or settled by the parties, with or without the aid of lawyers or mediators.

Subject to the provisions of section 8(3)(b) of the *Divorce Act*, the designated period of separation under 8(2)(a) must be continuous and uninterrupted up to the time when the divorce judgment is granted.

The words "living separate and apart" in section 8(2)(a) of the *Divorce Act* require proof of an intention to bring the marriage to an end in addition to the fact of separation. A spouse, who has the mental competence to manage her own affairs and instruct counsel, also has the mental capacity to form an intention to permanently live separate and apart from her husband, notwithstanding any delusions from which she may be suffering.[109] Subject to section 8(3)(b)(i) of the *Divorce Act*, the physical separation and the intention to end the marriage must co-exist for the requisite one-year period. Neither factor standing alone can satisfy the statutory requirements of section 8(2)(a).[110] No account will be taken of any period of physical separation that occurred prior to the formation of an intention to terminate the marriage.[111]

Section 8(2)(a) of the *Divorce Act* draws no distinction between deserted and deserting spouses. It is immaterial whether the separation occurred by consent of the spouses or by reason of an unjustifiable withdrawal from cohabitation by one of the spouses. In either event, it is open to one or both spouses to commence proceedings for divorce. Unilateral abandonment of

---

108 *Droit de la famille — 304*, [1986] RDF 589 (Que CS); *Droit de la famille — 471*, [1988] RDF 236 (Que CS).

109 *AB v CD*, 2009 BCCA 200.

110 *Raven v Raven* (1984), 30 Man R (2d) 71 (QB); *Shorten v Shorten* (1986), 65 NBR (2d) 429 (QB).

111 *Devani v Devani* (1976), 8 Nfld & PEIR 273 (Nfld TD); *Singh v Singh* (1976), 23 RFL 379 (Ont HCJ).

the matrimonial relationship is sufficient to satisfy the requirements of section 8 of the *Divorce Act*.[112]

Section 8(3)(b)(i) of the *Divorce Act* provides that the designated period of separation will not be interrupted or terminated by reason that either spouse has become incapable of forming or having an intention to live separate and apart, if it appears to the court that the separation would probably have continued in any event. Thus, supervening physical or mental illness that precludes a spouse from retaining a prior intention to treat the marriage as ended will not bar relief under section 8(2)(a). An enforced physical separation will satisfy the requirements of section 8(2)(a) of the *Divorce Act* but only if it is accompanied by a co-existing intention to end the marriage.[113]

Spouses may have been living "separate and apart" within the meaning of section 8(2)(a) of the *Divorce Act*, notwithstanding their continued residence under the same roof, provided that they have been living independent lives while sharing common accommodation.[114] In *Cooper v Cooper*,[115] Holland J of the Ontario Supreme Court pointed out that a finding that the spouses have been living separate and apart, albeit under the same roof, may be made where the following circumstances are present:

- occupation of separate bedrooms;
- absence of sexual relations;
- little, if any, communication between the spouses;
- the wife is providing no domestic services for her husband;
- meals eaten separately; and
- no social activities together.

It is not necessary, however, to establish all six elements and each case must stand or fall on its own merits.[116] In determining whether the spouses are living separate and apart within the meaning of section 8(2)(a) of the *Divorce Act*, the court must give greater weight to those matters that should

---

112 *Lachman v Lachman* (1970), 2 RFL 207 (Ont CA); *Thompson v St Croix*, 2014 NSSC 275.
113 *Dorchester v Dorchester* (1971), 3 RFL 396 (BCSC); *Norman v Norman* (1973), 12 RFL 252 (NSCA); *Burgoyne v Burgoyne* (1974), 14 RFL 92 (NSCA); *Lachman v Lachman* (1970), 2 RFL 207 (Ont CA).
114 *Rushton v Rushton* (1969), 1 RFL 215 (BCSC); *Galbraith v Galbraith* (1969), 1 RFL 77 (ManCA); *Dupere v Dupere* (1974), 19 RFL 270 (NBSC), aff'd (1975), 10 NBR (2d) 148 (CA); *Boulos v Boulos* (1980), 14 RFL (2d) 206 (Nfld SC); *Thompson v St Croix*, 2014 NSSC 275; *Williams v Williams*, [1991] NWTR 53 (SC); *Oswell v Oswell* (1992), 43 RFL (3d) 180 (Ont CA); *Hébert v Dame Houle*, [1973] CS 868 (Que); *Ginter v Ginter* (1988), 15 RFL (3d) 203 (Sask QB).
115 (1972), 10 RFL 184 (Ont SC); see also *Enman v McCafferty*, 2010 NBQB 118; *Ashworth v Ashworth* (1995), 15 RFL (4th) 379 (Ont Gen Div).
116 *Ibid*. See also *Bance v Bance* (1977), 18 NBR (2d) 262 (QB).

be peculiar to a husband and wife relationship, such as sexual relations, joint social ventures, communication, and discussion of family problems, rather than to the performance or non-performance of domestic chores.[117] Similarly, the payment of household expenses does not negate a finding that the spouses have been living separate and apart under the same roof where there were no activities of any kind as a family.[118]

The cessation of sexual intercourse is relevant but not conclusive on the issue whether the spouses have been living separate and apart within the meaning of section 8(2)(a) of the *Divorce Act*.[119] Where the spouses remain under the same roof and continue to discharge their marital responsibilities, the cessation of sexual intercourse will not suffice to justify a finding that the spouses are living separate and apart within the meaning of section 8(2)(a) of the *Divorce Act*.[120]

Isolated or casual acts of post-separation sexual intercourse between the spouses do not preclude a finding that they have continued to live separate and apart within the meaning of section 8(2)(a) of the *Divorce Act*, nor justify a finding that they have resumed cohabitation within the meaning of section 8(3)(b)(ii). In the absence of a mutual intention to become reconciled, the continuance or resumption of sexual intercourse between separated spouses is not to be equated with matrimonial cohabitation.[121] Just as sexual activity between separated spouses does not necessarily signify a resumption of the matrimonial relationship, so too, a resumption of cohabitation can occur even though sexual intercourse is restricted.[122]

Section 8(3)(b)(ii) of the *Divorce Act* confers a limited right on the spouses to resume cohabitation in an attempt to achieve a reconciliation without interrupting or terminating the period of separation that preceded the attempted reconciliation. The spouses are free to resume cohabitation on any number of occasions and are not confined to a single reconciliation attempt.

---

117 *McKenna v McKenna* (1975), 19 RFL 357 at 358 (NSCA). See also *Kobayashi v Kobayashi* (1972), 6 RFL 358 (Man QB); *Woolgar v Woolgar* (1995), 10 RFL (4th) 309 (Nfld UFC); *Smith v Smith* (1980), 28 Nfld & PEIR 99 (PEITD).

118 *Byzruki v Byzruki* (1982), 26 RFL (2d) 243 (Ont SC).

119 *Smith v Smith* (1970), 2 RFL 214 (BCSC); *Newman v Newman* (1971), 2 RFL 219 (Ont CA); *Seminuk v Seminuk* (1970), 72 WWR 304 (Sask CA).

120 *Cridge v Cridge* (1974), 12 RFL 348 (BCSC); *Davies v Davies* (1980), 29 NBR (2d) 207 (QB); *Burt v Burt* (1974), 7 RFL 155 (NSTD).

121 *Roadburg v Braut* (1994), 4 RFL (4th) 96 (BCCA); *Singh v Singh* (1982), 130 DLR (3d) 130 (Man QB); *Sampson v Sampson* (1994), 3 RFL (4th) 415 (NBQB); *KLS v DRS*, 2012 NBCA 16; *Deslippe v Deslippe* (1974), 16 RFL 38 (Ont CA); *Spinney v Spinney* (1982), 33 Nfld & PEIR 61 (PEICA); *Leaderhouse v Leaderhouse* (1971), 4 RFL 174 (Sask QB); see also *Oliver v Oliver*, 2011 BCSC 1126 (determination of spousal support).

122 *Sampson v Sampson* (1994), 3 RFL (4th) 415 at 421.

However, they have a maximum of ninety days during which they can resume cohabitation in any attempt(s) at reconciliation.[123]

2) Adultery and Cruelty as Proof of Marriage Breakdown: No Waiting Period

If either spouse has committed adultery or treated the other spouse with cruelty, a speedy divorce is obtainable without waiting for spousal separation to run for one year. A joint petition for divorce cannot be entertained by a court when only one of the spouses has committed adultery.[124]

Marriage breakdown as a ground for divorce where a spouse has committed adultery or cruelty is only available to the innocent spouse. The spouse who commits adultery or treats the other spouse with cruelty cannot petition for divorce on the basis of his or her own misconduct having caused a breakdown of the marriage. The guilty spouse can, nevertheless, invoke the no-fault separation criterion of marriage breakdown and obtain a divorce after the spouses have been separated for one year. In short, when separation is relied upon in proof of marriage breakdown, a mandatory one-year period must elapse before a divorce can be obtained by either spouse. With adultery or cruelty, the innocent spouse can proceed to obtain a divorce right away.

3) Marriage Breakdown: Adultery

Section 8(2)(b)(i) of the *Divorce Act* provides that marriage breakdown as a ground for divorce may be established if the spouse against whom the divorce proceeding is brought has committed adultery since the celebration of the marriage.

In the absence of any statutory definition, adultery has been traditionally defined by the courts as voluntary sexual intercourse between a married person and another person of the opposite sex other than his or her spouse.[125] Full and complete sexual intercourse is not required to prove adultery; partial penetration will suffice.[126] Masturbation or other activities that fall short of penetration of the male sexual organ into the female have been held not to constitute adultery, although such activities may lead to an inference that adultery has been committed.[127] Judicial opinion has been divided on the

---

123 *Enman v McCafferty*, 2010 NBQB 118; *Williams v Williams*, [1991] NWTR 53 (SC); *Thorogood v Thorogood* (1987), 11 RFL (3d) 82 (Ont UFC).

124 *Niyazov v Tkatch*, 2014 ONSC 5143.

125 *Orford v Orford* (1921), 49 OLR 15 (SC); *Kahl v Kahl*, [1943] OWN 558 (SC).

126 *Thompson v Thompson*, [1939] P 1; *Sapsford v Sapsford*, [1954] P 394; *Dennis v Dennis*, [1955] P 153.

127 *Sapsford v Sapsford*, [1954] P 394; *Dennis v Dennis*, [1955] P 153.

question of whether artificial insemination by a third party constitutes adultery.[128]

In *SEP v DDP*,[129] Garson J, of the British Columbia Supreme Court, observed that the *Civil Marriage Act*,[130] which has redefined "marriage, for civil purposes, as the lawful union of two persons to the exclusion of all others," reflects current values of our society consistent with the *Canadian Charter of Rights and Freedoms*. It therefore provides a guide to the current definition to be accorded to "adultery" in section 8(2)(b)(i) of the *Divorce Act*. Because same-sex couples can now marry and divorce, the common law definition of adultery would be anomalous if same-sex couples were not bound by the same legal and social restraints against extramarital sexual relationships that apply to heterosexual spouses. As Iacobucci J observed in *R v Salituro*,[131] "[j]udges can and should adapt the common law to reflect the changing social, moral and economic fabric of the country" but "the judiciary should confine itself to those incremental changes which are necessary to keep the common law in step with the dynamic and evolving fabric of our society." And as McLachlin CJ observed in *Retail, Wholesale and Department Store Union, Local 558 v Pepsi-Cola Canada Beverages*,[132] "the common law does not exist in a vacuum. The common law reflects the experience of the past, the reality of modern concerns and a sensitivity to the future. As such, it does not grow in isolation from the *Charter*." Garson J, in *SEP v DDP*, agreed with counsel for the wife and counsel for the Attorney General of Canada (who had intervened in the case) that it was unnecessary to undertake a section 15 *Charter* analysis to determine whether section 8(2)(b)(i) of the *Divorce Act* was discriminatory and therefore unconstitutional. Instead she accepted the submissions of both counsel that an incremental change in the definition of adultery, to include sexual acts between same-sex couples, was consistent with the *Civil Marriage Act*, the *Charter*, and the principles enunciated in *Salituro* and *Pepsi-Cola*, above. Having regard to the husband's admission of adultery with another man, Garson J did not consider it necessary or desirable to define what type of intimate sexual activity between persons of the same sex would constitute adultery, leaving this to be resolved over time on a case-by-case basis. It is submitted that the wiser course of action in *SEP v DDP* would have been for the court to strike down section 8(2)(b)(i) of the *Divorce Act* as a violation of section 15 of the *Canadian Charter of Rights and Freedoms*, leaving

---

128 See *Orford v Orford* (1921), 49 OLR 15 (SC); compare *MacLennan v MacLennan*, [1958] SC 105 (Scot).

129 [2005] BCJ No 1971 (SC).

130 SC 2005, c 33.

131 [1991] 3 SCR 654 at 670.

132 [2002] 1 SCR 156 at para 19.

it to Parliament to address the issue of whether (or what type of) sexual in-fidelity should continue to provide a basis for the dissolution of marriage on the ground of marriage breakdown. If this course of action had been pursued, it would have been open to Garson J to allow the wife petitioner to amend her pleadings to seek a divorce pursuant to section 8(2)(b)(ii) of the *Divorce Act* on the basis of her husband's cruelty. In its *Report on Family Law*,[133] the original Law Reform Commission of Canada proposed the abolition of matri-monial offences as grounds for divorce and the substitution of "marriage breakdown" as the sole criterion for divorce. The Commission envisaged that the dissolution process would be commenced by either spouse filing with the court a simple and non-accusatory notice of intention to seek dissolution of marriage and that marriage breakdown would be non-justiciable, being con-clusively established by the evidence of either spouse. Perhaps the time is ripe for Parliament to implement the Commission's proposal.

It is impossible to generalize about the circumstances that will warrant an inference of adultery being drawn by the court save to say that the circum-stances of the particular case must be such as to lead to a fair and reasonable inference of adultery.[134] Where the evidence of adultery is circumstantial, the circumstances must be such as would lead the guarded discretion of a reason-able and just person to the conclusion that adultery has been committed.[135] Evidence that creates only suspicion, surmise, or conjecture is insufficient.[136]

Adultery may be proved by the respondent's admission under oath.[137] The court may find that both spouses have committed adultery on the basis of their respective admissions.[138] The wife's evidence of the husband's out-of-court admissions of adultery may be sufficient to warrant a finding of adul-tery in divorce proceedings.

---

133 Law Reform Commission of Canada, *Report on Family Law* (Ottawa: Information Canada, March 1976).

134 *Stacey v Stacey*, [1977] 1 WWR 821 (Alta SC); *Furlong v Furlong* (1963), 49 MPR 377 (NBCA); *Harrison v Harrison* (1975), 12 NSR (2d) 149 (TD).

135 *Coates v Coates* (1974), 16 RFL 117 (NBQB), citing *MacCurdy v MacCurdy* (1971), 8 RFL 125 (NBCA).

136 *Carson v Carson* (1985), 46 RFL (2d) 102 at 105 (NBQB); *George v George*, [1950] OR 787 (CA); *Zawatsky v Zawatsky* (1976), 21 RFL 370 (Sask QB).

137 *d'Entremont v d'Entremont* (1992), 44 RFL (3d) 224 (NSCA); *Ewasiuk v Ewasiuk* (1969), 66 WWR 509 (NWTTC); *Mark v Mark* (1974), 15 RFL 73 (Ont HCJ); *Morice v Morice* (1972), 8 RFL 283 (Sask CA).

138 *Elligott v Elligott* (1977), 3 RFL (2d) 61 (Alta SC).

4) Marriage Breakdown: Cruelty

Section 8(2)(b)(ii) of the *Divorce Act* provides that marriage breakdown as a ground for divorce may be established if the spouse against whom the divorce proceeding is brought has, since the celebration of the marriage, treated the other spouse with physical or mental cruelty of such a kind as to render intolerable the continued cohabitation of the spouses.

Cruelty does not lend itself to any precise definition. Generally speaking, cruelty signifies a disposition to inflict suffering, to delight in or exhibit indifference to the pain and misery of others, mercilessness, or hard-heartedness as manifested by conduct.[139] It is impossible to categorize particular types of conduct as constituting mental or physical cruelty.[140] Cruelty is a question of fact and degree to be determined in light of the particular circumstances of each case.[141] Danger to life, limb, or health is not a prerequisite to a finding of cruelty under the *Divorce Act*.[142] The conduct complained of in the divorce petition must be grave and weighty; it must go beyond incompatibility of temperament between the spouses.[143]

Mere estrangement of the spouses or a breakdown of their marriage arising from incompatibility of temperament will not constitute cruelty within the meaning of the *Divorce Act*.[144] In the words of Schroeder JA, of the Ontario Court of Appeal:

> Care must be exercised in applying the standard set forth in . . . [the *Divorce Act*] that conduct relied upon to establish cruelty is not a trivial act, but one of a "grave and weighty" nature, and not merely conduct which can be characterized as little more than a manifestation of incompatibility of temperament between the spouses. The whole matrimonial relations must be considered, especially if the cruelty consists of reproaches, complaints, accusations, or constant carping criticism. A question most relevant for

---

139 See *Knoll v Knoll* (1970), 1 RFL 141 (Ont CA).

140 *Re Tremaine* (1968), 2 NSR 787 (SC).

141 *Stevens v Stevens* (1977), 17 NBR (2d) 656 at 659–60 (QB); *Ebenal v Ebenal* (1971), 3 RFL 303 (Sask CA).

142 *Zalesky v Zalesky* (1968), 67 WWR 104 (Man QB); *Knoll v Knoll* (1970), 1 RFL 141 (Ont CA); *Stevens v Stevens* (1977), 17 NBR (2d) 656 (QB).

143 *Zalesky v Zalesky* (1968), 67 WWR 104 (Man QB); *Knoll v Knoll* (1970), 1 RFL 141 (Ont CA); *Stevens v Stevens* (1977), 17 NBR (2d) 656 (QB).

144 *Takenaka v Takenaka* (1981), 24 BCLR 273 (SC); *Galbraith v Galbraith* (1969), 1 RFL 96 (Man QB); *Chouinard v Chouinard* (1969), 1 RFL 101 (NBCA), *White v White* (1971), 3 NBR (2d) 357 (CA); *MC v TC*, 2010 NBQB 192; *Goudie v Goudie* (1970), 2 RFL 128 (Nfld SC); *Hiltz v Hiltz9* (1971), 2 RFL 178 (NSTD), aff'd (1973) 11 RFL 35 (NSCA); *Knoll v Knoll* (1970), 1 RFL 141 (Ont CA); *Storey v Storey* (1973), 10 RFL 170 (PEITD); *Pawelko v Pawelko* (1970), 1 RFL 174 (Sask QB).

consideration is the effect of the conduct complained of upon the mind of the affected spouse. The determination of what constitutes cruelty in a given case must, in the final analysis, depend upon the circumstances of the particular case having due regard to the physical and mental condition of the parties, their character and their attitude towards the marriage relationship.[145]

It is not necessary that the allegedly cruel spouse acted with a culpable intention.[146] The impact of the alleged conduct on the victim is far more important.[147] Where the two spouses are of normal physical and mental health and the conduct of the respondent is so bad that the petitioner should not be called on to endure it, cruelty is established irrespective of the respondent's state of mind. It is immaterial whether the respondent's conduct was deliberately aimed at the petitioner or due to unwarranted indifference.[148] Malevolent intention, though not essential to cruelty, is a most important element where it exists.[149]

Where the conduct complained of would amount to cruelty in the absence of any culpable intention,[150] the insanity of the respondent is no answer to the charge of cruelty.[151]

The test of cruelty is largely subjective because the paramount question is whether "*this* conduct by *this* man towards *this* woman, or *vice versa*, is

---

145   *Knoll v Knoll* (1970), 1 RFL 141 at 150 (Ont CA), cited with approval in *Krause v Krause* (1975), 19 RFL 230, var'd (1976), 23 RFL 219 (Alta CA); *Edwards v Edwards* (1973), 12 RFL 35 (BCCA); *Zunti v Zunti* (1971), 15 DLR (3d) 369 (BCCA); *Shumila v Shumila* (1975), 21 RFL 110 (Man CA); *Aucoin v Aucoin* (1976), 28 RFL 43 (NSCA); *Horner v Horner* (1973), 13 RFL 117 at 126 (NSCA); *Pongor v Pongor* (1976), 27 RFL 109 (Ont CA); *Wittstock v Wittstock* (1971), 3 RFL 326 (Ont CA); *Cernic v Cernic*, 2012 ONSC 922; *Storey v Storey* (1973), 10 RFL 170 (PEITD); *Powell v Powell* (1972), 5 RFL 194 (Sask CA); *Ebenal v Ebenal* (1971), 3 RFL 303 (Sask CA); see also *Anderson v Anderson* (1972), 8 RFL 299 at 304 (Alta CA), aff'd (1973), 10 RFL 200 (SCC); *Stevens v Stevens* (1977), 17 NBR (2d) 656 (QB).

146   *Gollins v Gollins*, [1964] AC 644 (HL); *Williams v Williams*, [1964] AC 698 (HL).

147   *Gollins v Gollins*, [1964] AC 644 (HL); *Williams v Williams*, [1964] AC 698 (HL).

148   *Goldstein v Goldstein* (1970), 15 DLR (3d) 95 (Alta SC). See also *Gollins v Gollins*, [1964] AC 644 (HL); *Gollins v Gollins (No 2)* (1964), 108 SJ 941; *Rankin v Rankin* (1970), 13 DLR (3d) 630 (BCSC); *Martin v Martin* (1971), 1 RFL 154 (BCSC); *Schnerch v Schnerch* (1982), 13 Man R (2d) 277 (QB); *White v White* (1968), 69 DLR (2d) 60 (NS Div Ct); *Knoll v Knoll* (1970), 1 RFL 141 (Ont CA); *Wakefield v Schrogl*, [1976] CS 222 (Que).

149   *King v King*, [1953] AC 124 (HL); *Feldman v Feldman* (1970), 2 RFL 173 (Alta CA); *Krause v Krause* (1976), 23 RFL 219 at 222 (Alta CA); *Knoll v Knoll* (1970), 1 RFL 141 (Ont CA); *Wittstock v Wittstock* (1971), 3 RFL 326 (Ont CA).

150   *Gollins v Gollins*, [1964] AC 644 (HL); *Williams v Williams*, [1964] AC 698 (HL).

151   *Williams v Williams*, ibid; *Novak v Novak* (1969), 1 RFL 58 (BCSC); see also *Baker v Baker* (1970), 1 RFL 106 (BCSC); *McGrath v McGrath* (1977), 16 NBR (2d) 462 (QB); *Herman v Herman* (1969), 1 RFL 41 (NSTD); *MacKay v MacKay* (1978), 1 RFL (2d) 80 (PEICA); *Ifield v Ifield* (1976), 24 RFL 237 (Sask CA).

cruelty" such as renders matrimonial cohabitation intolerable.[152] The law has been aptly summarized by Disbery J, of the Saskatchewan Court of Queen's Bench, in the following observations:

> In dealing with the ingredient of cruelty it has been widely held that the conduct and actions of the respondent spouse upon which the petitioner relies must be conduct or acts of a serious, grave and weighty nature. Lesser marital misconduct such as rudeness, personal slovenliness, slovenly housekeeping, inability to hold steady employment, wasteful spending and the tit for tat irritations bestowed by each spouse upon the other are all part of the stresses and strains of marriage and, save for rare and exceptional cases, such conduct and actions do not constitute the kind of cruelty defined in [section 8(2)(b)(ii) of the *Divorce Act*]. Again incompatibilities, which of course include sexual incompatibility, resulting in an unhappy marriage do not constitute, *per se*, cruelty so defined in the said section . . . . Pearce J., in *Lauder v. Lauder*, [1949] P. 277 at p. 308; [1949] 1 All E.R. 76, said: "For in a cruelty case the question is whether this conduct by this man to this woman, or vice versa is cruelty." This subjective test has been approved and applied in this Province by the Court of Appeal in *Austin v Austin* (1970), 13 D.L.R. (3d) 498 at p. 500; 2 R.F.L. 136; 73 W.W.R. 289 at p. 291. . . . Having regard to the endless variations in the conduct, habits, dispositions, sensitivities, intelligence, temperaments and character of married persons, it immediately becomes apparent that when a divorce is sought on the ground of cruelty, each case must be determined on its own facts including, of course, the personalities of the spouses. Identical conduct and acts of a respondent spouse would [in one case] constitute cruelty within the ambit of [the section] having regard to the personality of the recipient spouse; while in another case identical acts and conduct would not suffice because of the different personality of the recipient spouse.[153]

The court has regard to the cumulative effect of the respondent's conduct on the petitioner.[154] The cumulative effect of the respondent's conduct may constitute cruelty although each of the individual incidents complained of would not, standing alone, be sufficiently grave and weighty to satisfy the requirements of section 8(2)(b)(ii) of the *Divorce Act*.[155]

---

152 *Lauder v Lauder*, [1949] P 277 at 308 (Eng); see also *Cernic v Cernic*, 2012 ONSC 922.

153 *Ifield v Ifield* (1976), 24 RFL 237 at 242–44 (Sask QB).

154 *Knoll v Knoll* (1970), 1 RFL 141 (Ont CA).

155 *Cochrane v Cochrane* (1976), 10 Nfld & PEIR 86 (Nfld TD); *Zwicker v Zwicker* (1973), 3 RFL 333 (NSTD); compare *Wyman v Wyman* (1971), 2 RFL 190 at 195 (Sask QB).

It is for the court and not the petitioner to determine whether the conduct of the respondent is sufficiently grave to warrant dissolution of the marriage pursuant to section 8(2)(b)(ii) of the *Divorce Act.*[156]

Diverse types of conduct may constitute cruelty, although whether cruelty actually exists will always depend on the facts of the particular case, having regard to the history of the marriage and the sensibilities of the spouses. Physique, temperament, culture, habits of verbal expression and of action, and the interaction of the spouses in their daily lives are vital considerations.[157] The court must have regard to the society in which the parties live — socially, morally, and materially.[158]

Cruelty may be established on the basis of commission or omission. The conduct of the respondent may be active or passive; it may consist of deliberate ill treatment, by word or deed, or it may arise from thoughtless neglect.[159]

A husband's violent assault committed on his wife on a single occasion may justify a finding of physical cruelty of such a kind as to render cohabitation intolerable within the meaning of the *Divorce Act.* Older cases that required repeated acts of physical violence for a finding of cruelty to be made[160] must be viewed with extreme caution in light of the current state of awareness concerning the battered wife syndrome. Courts have shown no hesitation in finding cruelty such as renders cohabitation intolerable within the meaning of the *Divorce Act* where there have been long-term or repeated incidents of violence[161] or where physical violence has been accompanied by other intolerable conduct.[162]

Verbal abuse,[163] false accusations of infidelity,[164] and domineering and demeaning conduct,[165] if of sufficient gravity, may constitute cruelty within

---

156   *Lake v Lake* (1983), 30 RFL (3d) 5 (BCSC); *B v B*, [1970] CS 212 (Que); *Summerfelt v Summerfelt* (1983), 31 RFL (2d) 240 (Sask QB).

157   *Watt v Thomas*, [1947] AC 484 at 488 (HL).

158   *Goudie v Goudie* (1970), 2 RFL 128 (Nfld TD).

159   *Ibid.*

160   See *Peskett v Peskett* (1980), 14 RFL (2d) 134 (BCSC); *McEvoy v McEvoy* (1984), 55 NBR (2d) 269 (QB).

161   *Curran v Curran* (1973), 3 Nfld & PEIR 395 (Nfld SC); *Betts v Betts* (1979), 25 NBR (2d) 478 (QB); *MacLeod v MacLeod* (1979), 32 NSR (2d) 137 (TD).

162   *Curran v Curran* (1973), 3 Nfld & PEIR 395 (Nfld SC); *MacLeod v MacLeod* (1979), 32 NSR (2d) 137 (TD).

163   *Chorney v Chorney* (1971), 4 RFL 347 (Alta CA); *Humeniuk v Humeniuk* (1970), 4 RFL 163 (Ont HCJ); *Giesbrecht v Giesbrecht* (1975), 16 RFL 399 (Sask QB).

164   *Chorney v Chorney* (1971), 4 RFL 347 (Alta CA); *Ivany v Ivany* (1971), 2 RFL 172 (BCSC); *Wakefield v Schrogl*, [1976] CS 222 (Que).

165   *Ratcliffe v Ratcliffe* (1977), 27 RFL 227 (BCSC); *Dowell v Dowell* (1978), 30 RFL 278 (Man QB); *Nichols v Nichols* (1968), 1 NSR (1965–69) 503 (TD); *Ells v Ells* (1971), 2 RFL 186 (NSTD); *Rowe v Rowe* (1977), 26 RFL 91 (Ont HCJ); *L v L*, [1970] CS 222 (Que).

the meaning of the *Divorce Act*. However, differences of opinion or verbal squabbles, even though accompanied by gross or vulgar language on isolated occasions, may fall short of satisfying the statutory requirements,[166] as may the respondent's continual complaints about the petitioner's absence from home in the discharge of professional responsibilities.[167]

Justice Stevenson, of the New Brunswick Court of Queen's Bench, has observed:

> When acts of cruelty relied upon take the form of abuse, quarrels, nagging, selfishness, etc. there is a greater danger of their being categorized as examples of incompatibility rather than of cruelty. However, where one spouse insists on totally dominating the other or deprives the other of his company or ridicules and belittles his spouse or is selfish and ignores his obligations of support he or she may be found guilty of cruelty. Similarly, threats of physical violence towards the petitioner, her children or towards the respondent himself, false accusations of theft, of non-support or of infidelity, vulgar abuse, constant nagging, and unseemly "scenes" before others, can amount to cruelty.[168]

Habitual drinking, drug-taking, or gambling does not necessarily constitute cruelty[169] but will be found to do so when it has a detrimental impact on the petitioner who finds continued cohabitation intolerable under those circumstances.[170]

Inattentiveness or insensitivity that is simply a manifestation of a spouse's personality ordinarily falls short of cruelty.[171]

A husband's addiction to work with consequential neglect of his wife and children may constitute cruelty within the meaning of the *Divorce Act*,[172] although the court may decline to make such a finding when the wife did not complain of his conduct until the last stage of their marriage and the conduct had continued from the very early stages of the marriage.[173]

A court may find cruelty by reason of the respondent's refusal to work and support the family.[174]

---

166 *B v R*, [1970] CS 21 (Que); see also *MC v TC*, 2010 NBQB 192.

167 *Turnbull v Turnbull* (1977), 28 RFL 92 (Man QB).

168 *Brewer v Brewer* (1978), 21 NBR (2d) 154 at 157 (QB).

169 *Kulyk v Kulyk* (1980), 5 Sask R 235 (QB).

170 *Le Blanc v Le Blanc* (1984), 54 NBR (2d) 388 (QB) (excessive drinking); *Bramley v Bramley* (1974), 15 RFL 152 (Ont Sup Ct) (heroin addiction); *Rauch v Rauch* (1976), 22 RFL 143 (Ont HCJ) (addiction to gambling).

171 *Cavalier v Cavalier* (1977), 25 RFL 118 (BCSC).

172 *Mark v Mark* (1974), 15 RFL 73 (Ont HCJ).

173 *Koch v Koch* (1978), 30 RFL 269 (Man Co Ct); see also *Kastrau v Kastrau* (1979), 7 RFL (2d) 318 (Ont UFC).

174 *Durant v Durant* (1971), 2 Nfld & PEIR 138 (PEITD).

Notwithstanding the wide diversity of standards between one married couple and another as to what is normal,[175] excessive demands for sexual intercourse,[176] or the persistent denial of sexual intercourse[177] may constitute cruelty within the meaning of the *Divorce Act*. Several courts have declined to find cruelty where the refusal of sexual intercourse was attributable to physical or psychological difficulties,[178] although it is doubtful whether any binding precedents have been thereby established.

The court may grant a divorce judgment to each spouse on the ground of mutual cruelty.[179]

The clear trend of the law is to remove fault from most spousal disputes. As it usually takes a year to bring a contested matter to trial, a divorce will usually be available on the basis of one year of separation. Where this is the case, a court should avoid dealing with any cruelty allegation that has been made and the divorce should be granted on the no-fault separation basis.[180] While a no-fault divorce is preferable where fault and no-fault bases for relief co-exist, there is no objection to a trial judge granting a divorce on the basis of cruelty, if the statutory one-year period of separation has not been fully satisfied at the time when the judgment was granted.[181]

F. BARS TO DIVORCE

Section 11 of the *Divorce Act* establishes the following four bars or impediments to divorce:

1)   collusion;
2)   connivance;
3)   condonation; and
4)   the absence of reasonable arrangements for child support.[182]

---

175   *M v M* (1974), 14 RFL 1 (Ont HCJ).

176   *Hock v Hock* (1971), 3 RFL 353 (BCCA).

177   *Lewis v Lewis* (1983), 44 NBR (2d) 268 (QB); *Delaney v Delaney* (1971), 5 RFL 44 (Ont CA); *Perry v Perry* (1971), 1 Nfld & PEIR 325 (PEISCTD).

178   *Anderson v Anderson* (1972), 8 RFL 299 (Alta CA), aff'd (1973), 10 RFL 200 (SCC); *Rouleau v Wells*, [1980] CS 915 (Que). Compare *Katapodis v Katapodis* (1980), 27 OR (2d) 711 (CA).

179   *Krause v Krause* (1976), 23 RFL 219 (Alta CA); *Hock v Hock* (1970), 2 RFL 333 (BCSC), aff'd (1971), 3 RFL 353 (BCCA); *Farkasch v Farkasch* (1972), 4 RFL 339 (Man QB); *McGrath v McGrath* (1977), 16 NBR (2d) 462 (QB); *MacNeil v MacNeil* (1976), 25 RFL 82 (NSCA).

180   *McPhail v McPhail*, 2001 BCCA 250; *BMD v CND*, 2010 BCSC 1785. Compare *HP v CTP*, 2014 BCSC 2024 (divorce granted on the basis of the respondent's adultery as well as the separation of the spouses for one year; religious factor taken into account).

181   *BKK v HD*, [2002] BCJ No 2683 (CA); *Paheerding v Palihati*, 2009 BCSC 557.

182   And see s 21.1 of the *Divorce Act*, RSC 1985 (2d Supp), c 3, as amended by SC 1990, c 18, and Section F(4), below in this chapter.

It expressly provides as follows:

Duty of court — bars

11. (1) In a divorce proceeding, it is the duty of the court

(a) to satisfy itself that there has been no collusion in relation to the application for a divorce and to dismiss the application if it finds that there was collusion in presenting it;

(b) to satisfy itself that reasonable arrangements have been made for the support of any children of the marriage, and, if such arrangements have not been made, to stay the granting of the divorce until such arrangements are made; and

(c) where a divorce is sought in circumstances described in paragraph 8(2)(b), to satisfy itself that there has been no condonation or connivance on the part of the spouse bringing the proceeding, and to dismiss the application for a divorce if that spouse has condoned or connived at the act or conduct complained of unless, in the opinion of the court, the public interest would be better served by granting the divorce.

Revival

(2) Any act or conduct that has been condoned is not capable of being revived so as to constitute a circumstance described in paragraph 8(2)(b).

Condonation

(3) For the purpose of this section, a continuation or resumption of cohabitation during a period of, or periods totalling, not more than ninety days with reconciliation as its primary purpose shall not be considered to constitute condonation.

Definition of "collusion'"

(4) In this section, "collusion" means an agreement or conspiracy to which an applicant for a divorce is either directly or indirectly a party for the purpose of subverting the administration of justice, and includes any agreement, understanding or arrangement to fabricate or suppress evidence or to deceive the court, but does not include an agreement to the extent that it provides for separation between the parties, financial support, division of property or the custody of any child of the marriage.

1) Collusion

A finding of collusion constitutes an absolute bar to divorce that compels a court to dismiss the divorce petition regardless whether the divorce is sought on the basis of no-fault separation, adultery, or cruelty.[183] Collusion will not be found unless there is an agreement or conspiracy to subvert the administration of justice, as for example, where there is an agreement to fabricate or suppress evidence or to deceive the court.[184] Spousal agreements to separate and to regulate the economic and parenting consequences of their separation are not collusive.[185] It is also not collusive for one spouse to co-operate with the other spouse by providing evidence that will substantiate the facts relied upon to establish marriage breakdown in the divorce proceeding.[186]

Judicial opinion is divided on the question whether collusion may be found where a marriage was entered into solely for the purpose of obtaining immigration or citizenship benefits and the spouses never intended to cohabit and went their separate ways after the marriage ceremony.[187] Although section 11(1)(a) of the *Divorce Act* imposes a duty on the court to satisfy itself that there has been no collusion, the role of the court is not inquisitorial. If the pleadings or evidence justify an inference of collusion, however, it falls upon the applicant to negate collusion and a mere denial of collusion does not discharge the burden of negating collusion.[188] Where the evidence is clear that the petitioner has been duped and was not a party to an agreement or conspiracy to circumvent the immigration laws of the country, or to any agreement that was collusive, he or she has satisfied any onus placed upon him or her by virtue of section 11(1)(a) of the *Divorce Act*.[189]

2) Connivance and Condonation

Connivance[190] and condonation[191] constitute provisional, rather than absolute, bars to divorce where marriage breakdown is sought to be proven by way of a spouse's adultery or cruelty. These bars have no application where the divorce petition is based on spousal separation for one year or more. Being provisional, and not peremptory or absolute bars to divorce, a court will

183 *Divorce Act*, RSC 1985 (2d Supp), c 3, s 11(1)(a).

184 *Ibid*, s 11(4); *Gillett v Gillett* (1979), 9 RFL (2d) 97 (Alta SCTD); *Sattar v Sattar* (1975), 26 RFL 127 (Ont HCJ).

185 *Gillett v Gillett* (1979), 9 RFL (2d) 97 (Alta SCTD); *Sattar v Sattar* (1975), 26 RFL 127 (Ont HCJ); see *Tannis v Tannis*, [1970] 1 OR 323 (HCJ).

186 *Milne v Milne*, [1970] 1 OR 381 (CA).

187 See *Johnson v Ahmad* (1981), 22 RFL (2d) 141 (Alta QB); *Ciresi v Ahmad* (1983), 31 RFL (2) 326 at 329 and 333–34 (Alta QB); *Singh v Singh* (1977), 25 RFL 20 (BCSC); *Fernandez v Fernandez* (1983), 34 RFL (2d) 249 (Man QB); *McKenzie v McKenzie* (1982), 26 RFL (2d) 310 at 312 (Ont CA); compare *Merchant v Dossani*, [2007] AJ No 815 (QB).

188 *Singh v Singh* (1977), 25 RFL 20 (BCSC).

189 *Gentles v Gentles* (1980), 12 RFL (2d) 287 (Ont CA).

190 *Divorce Act*, RSC 1985 (2d Supp), c 3, s 11(1)(c).

191 *Ibid*.

grant a divorce, notwithstanding the petitioner's connivance or condonation of the other spouse's adultery or cruelty, if the court is of the opinion that the public interest would be better served by granting the divorce.[192]

Connivance signifies that the petitioner has actively promoted or encouraged the commission of the offence complained of. A corrupt intention is an essential ingredient of connivance. If, for example, the petitioner has actively induced his or her spouse to commit adultery or has passively stood by and made no attempt to prevent the commission of the offence, connivance will be found.[193]

The basic principles of law respecting connivance are succinctly defined in *Maddock v Maddock*, wherein Laidlaw JA observed:

> It will be convenient and helpful to state certain propositions or principles of law respecting connivance, and which I extract from the following and other cases: *Rogers v. Rogers* (1830), 3 Hagg. Ecc. 57, at p. 59, *Gipps v. Gipps* (1864), 11 H.L. Cas. 1, *Lloyd v. Lloyd*, [1938] P. 174, *Churchman v. Churchman*, [1945] P. 44, *Woodbury v. Woodbury*, [1948] 2 All E.R. 684, *Mudge v. Mudge*, [1950] 1 All E.R. 607.
>
> 1. Connivance may consist of any act done with corrupt intention of a husband or wife to promote or encourage either the initiation or the continuance of adultery of his or her spouse, or it may consist of passive acquiescence in such adultery.
>
> 2. Corrupt intention of the husband or wife seeking a divorce is an essential ingredient of connivance, and the conduct of the husband or wife seeking the divorce must show that he or she, as the case may be, willingly consented to the adultery of the other spouse.
>
> 3. The issue is whether on the facts of the particular case, the husband or wife seeking the divorce was or was not guilty of the corrupt intention of promoting or encouraging either the initiation or the continuance of the adultery of the other spouse.
>
> 4. Acts done by a husband or wife seeking a divorce or by any person employed by him or her, as the case may be, to keep watch on the other spouse to see whether or not his or her suspicions of adultery are well-founded or unfounded, do not necessarily constitute connivance and, likewise, if one spouse does nothing without lulling into a sense of security, the other spouse about whom he or she, as the case may be, is suspicious, but merely watches her, he is not necessarily guilty of passive acquiescence amounting to connivance.

---

192 *Ibid.*
193 *Maddock v Maddock*, [1958] OR 810 at 818 (CA).

5. "The Court should not allow its judgment to be affected by importing, as principles of universal application, pronouncements made with regard to wholly different circumstances and be led to a conclusion contrary to the justice of the case": *Churchman v. Churchman*, [1945] P. 44, at p. 52.

6. There is a presumption of law against the existence of connivance and the court should not find a spouse guilty of connivance unless the evidence shows clearly that all the essential ingredients thereof exist in the particular facts under consideration.[194]

In determining whether the public interest would be better served by granting a divorce, notwithstanding the petitioner's connivance at the offence complained of, a court is more likely to excuse passive acquiescence than active procurement of the offence.[195]

Condonation arises where a divorce petitioner, with knowledge of his or her spouse's adultery or cruelty, forgives the offence and continues or resumes matrimonial cohabitation with the offending spouse. The essence of condonation is spousal reconciliation. Condonation requires a mutual intention to be reconciled coupled with a reinstatement of the guilty spouse to his or her former position.[196] It is not necessary for spouses to achieve the same degree of mutual devotion that they enjoyed when they were first married. The matrimonial relationship must, nevertheless, be restored to a settled rhythm in which the past offences, if not forgotten, no longer undermine the continued commitment of the spouses to each other.[197]

There can be no condonation of a matrimonial offence unless the innocent spouse has knowledge of all the material facts. It is the duty of the guilty spouse to make full disclosure of any factor that might reasonably weigh with the innocent spouse in deciding whether to remit the offence and reinstate the guilty spouse to his or her former position.[198] The innocent spouse may, however, expressly or impliedly waive the requirement of further knowledge of any material fact.[199]

Condonation requires a bilateral intention to be reconciled or to resume cohabitation. Although sexual intercourse is a significant factor to be considered in determining whether condonation exists, a continuation or

---

194   *Ibid*; cited with approval in *Fleet v Fleet* (1972), 7 RFL 355 (Ont CA).

195   See *Berger v Berger* (1974), 17 RFL 88 (BCSC).

196   *Mackrell v Mackrell*, [1948] 2 All ER 858 (Eng CA); *Leaderhouse v Leaderhouse* (1971), 4 RFL 174 (Sask QB).

197   *Mackrell v Mackrell*, [1948] 2 All ER 858 (Eng CA).

198   *Inglis v Inglis*, [1968] P 639; *Watkins v Watkins* (1980), 14 RFL (2d) 97 (Nfld TD).

199   *Inglis v Inglis*, [1968] P 639; *Watkins v Watkins* (1980), 14 RFL (2d) 97 (Nfld TD).

resumption of sexual intercourse is not a prerequisite to a finding of condonation. When the spouses engage in sexual intercourse without the slightest thought of reinstatement, no question of condonation can arise.[200]

Condonation is ordinarily manifested by a resumption of cohabitation that reflects a reconciliation of the spouses. Spousal residence under the same roof is not conclusive evidence of condonation and reconciliation will not be inferred from the mere continuation of an increasingly cold and sexless co-existence.[201] Spouses who are living independent lives, albeit under the same roof, will not be deemed to have continued or resumed cohabitation or to have achieved a spousal reconciliation.[202]

If spouses separate after one of them has committed adultery or matrimonial cruelty, subsequent attempts to reconcile do not necessarily constitute condonation so as to bar a divorce, if the reconciliation ultimately fails.[203] The *Divorce Act* encourages spousal reconciliation. Section 11(3) of the *Divorce Act* specifically provides that "a continuation or resumption of cohabitation during a period of, or periods totalling not more than ninety days with reconciliation as its primary purpose shall not be considered to constitute condonation." Consequently, spouses may attempt to reconcile on any number of occasions following the commission of adultery or cruelty provided that the aggregate period of cohabitation does not exceed ninety days.

Prior to the *Divorce Act*, 1968, the ecclesiastical doctrine of revival enabled a spouse to petition for divorce on the basis of a previously condoned offence. Condonation was conditional on future behaviour; if the guilty spouse misbehaved subsequent to the condonation, the condoned offence would be revived so as to constitute a ground for divorce. By virtue of section 11(2) of the current *Divorce Act*, the doctrine of revival no longer applies, but section 11(2) does not circumscribe the power of the court to grant a divorce

---

200 *Henderson v Henderson*, [1944] AC 49 (HL). See also Julien D Payne, "The Concept of Condonation in Matrimonial Causes: A Restatement of *Henderson v Henderson and Crellin*" (1961) 26 Sask Bar Rev 53. See also *Roschuk v Roschuk* (1979), 12 RFL (2d) 34 (Man QB); *Watkins v Watkins* (1980), 14 RFL (2d) 97 (Nfld TD); *Grandy v Grandy* (1972), 7 RFL 69 at 74 (NSCA); *Wood v Wood*, [1944] 1 DLR 493 at 494 (Ont HCJ), Robertson CJO: "To constitute condonation there must be an actual intention to forgive and be reconciled"; *H v H* (1978), 30 RFL 122 (Ont HCJ); *MacDougall v MacDougall* (1970), 3 RFL 174 (Ont CA); *Leaderhouse v Leaderhouse* (1971), 4 RFL 174 at 182 (Sask QB).

201 *Aucoin v Aucoin* (1976), 28 RFL 43 (NSCA).

202 *McAllister v McAllister* (1976), 14 NBR (2d) 552 (TD); *Aucoin v Aucoin* (1976), 28 RFL 43 (NSCA).

203 *Goldstein v Goldstein* (1970), 15 DLR (3d) 95 (Alta SC); *Nielsen v Nielsen* (1971), 2 RFL 109 (Ont HCJ).

pursuant to section 11(1)(c) of the *Divorce Act*, notwithstanding condonation, where the public interest so requires.[204]

In recent years, courts have rarely denied a divorce by reason of the petitioner's condonation of the offence complained of. To do so would tend to discourage attempts to reconcile. Furthermore, the public interest is best served by granting a divorce where the marriage has irretrievably broken down, rather than insisting that the parties preserve the mere legal shell of a marriage.[205]

3) Absence of Reasonable Arrangements for Child Support

Section 11(1)(b) of the *Divorce Act* requires that a judge must be satisfied that reasonable arrangements have been made for the support of any child of the marriage before a divorce will be granted. This is without any geographical limitation on where the child of the marriage resides.[206] Regardless of whether the divorce petition relies on adultery, cruelty, or no-fault separation, it is a statutory duty of the court to satisfy itself that reasonable arrangements have been made for the support of any children of the marriage. In determining whether reasonable arrangements have been made for the support of children of the marriage, the court has regard to the *Federal Child Support Guidelines*. If reasonable arrangements for child support could be but have not been made, the court cannot grant the divorce until such arrangements are made[207] but a court cannot discriminate between rich and poor by denying a divorce to spouses who have insufficient means to provide reasonable support for their children.[208] Furthermore, a court should not speculate about future contingencies, such as the impact of a non-custodial parent's remarriage, which could result in some reduction of the financial security provided for children of his or her dissolved marriage.[209] The reasonableness of arrangements for the support of children must be determined by the court in the particular circumstances of each case, which may include assistance

---

204 See JD Payne, "The *Divorce Act* (Canada), 1968" (1969) 7 Alta L Rev 1. See also *Raney v Raney* (1974), 13 RFL 156 at 158 (Ont HCJ). Compare *Grant v Grant* (1979), 9 BCLR 306 (SC), applying *Lyons v Lyons* (1971), 1 RFL 328 (NSTD).

205 See, generally, Kenneth L Kallish & Julien D Payne, "Current Controversies Concerning Condonation" in Julien D Payne, Freda M Steel, & Marilyn A Bégin, *Payne's Digest on Divorce in Canada, 1968–1980* (Don Mills, ON: R. De Boo, 1982) at 134, and especially at 141–43.

206 *Bullecer v Mayangat*, 2010 ABQB 680; *Roco v Roco*, 2010 ABQB 683.

207 *Divorce Act*, RSC 1985 (2d Supp), c 3, s 11(1)(b).

208 *F(RD) v F(SL)* (1987), 6 RFL (3d) 413 (BCSC); *Williams v Williams* (1971), 5 RFL 72 (NSSC); see also *Shore-Kalo v Kalo*, [2007] MJ No 297 (QB); *RJ v WJ*, 2011 NBQB 294.

209 *Williams v Williams* (1971), 5 RFL 72 (NSSC).

from other members of the family or friends, social assistance, and any other relevant circumstances.[210] Where, however, the divorcing spouses can afford to support their own children, this financial burden cannot be transferred by the parents to the welfare system.[211]

On a wife's motion to sever the husband's application for prospective and retroactive child support from a divorce action, Stevens J, of the Alberta Court of Queen's Bench, held in *Savoia v Savoia*[212] that severance was precluded by section 11(1)(b) of the *Divorce Act*, which requires a court to satisfy itself that reasonable arrangements have been made for the support of any children of the marriage and, if such arrangements have not been made, to stay the granting of the divorce until such arrangements are made. After a detailed review of relevant caselaw, Stevens J endorsed the following principles as governing the interpretation and application of section 11(1)(b) of the *Divorce Act*:

i)   counsel must realize that the court has a duty under s 11(1)(b). Therefore, prior to making a request for severance of corollary issues, counsel should be satisfied that maintenance for the children is adequate . . .

ii)   evidence of the parties' income is required. However, financial statements alone may be insufficient; evidence of the arrangements made for the support of any children of the marriage should be put before the court . . .

iii) quantum of support should not be in issue . . .

iv)   information pertaining to any social assistance payments is an important factor in determining the income available for child support. Such income is to be considered in determining whether reasonable arrangements for child support have been made . . .

v)   any agreement reached as to child support must be reasonable in the circumstances . . .

vi)   in negotiating a reasonable arrangement for child support, the parties must have regard to the Guidelines, as well as other relevant factors in terms of the circumstances of the children of the marriage . . .

vii) evidence as to whether reasonable arrangements for child support have been made should be fact based, as opposed to testimony reflecting subjective opinion . . .

viii) evidence as to the reasonableness of an arrangement need not be extensive; it needs to enable to [sic] the court to satisfy itself pursuant to s.11(1)(b) . . .

---

210 *F(RD) v F(SL)* (1987), 6 RFL (3d) 413 (BCSC).

211 *Simpson v Simpson* (1987), 8 RFL (3d) 216 at 219–20 (BCSC).

212 2009 ABQB 516, [2009] AJ No 965 at para 32; see also *Ballantyne v Nardone*, 2013 NWTSC 38.

ix) in certain limited circumstances, where it is impractical or inequitable to require an applicant to obtain financial information from a spouse with a view to establishing child support arrangements, a divorce may nonetheless be granted . . . .

Justice Stevens stated that the caselaw prescribes no set "test" for determining whether reasonable arrangements for child support have been made and that each case must be determined on its own particular facts. He further stated that the cases are clear that the court requires evidence as to income as well as evidence as to the proposed child support arrangements in order to discharge its statutory duty. In his opinion, there was insufficient evidence in the present case to satisfy the requirements of section 11(1)(b) of the *Divorce Act*. The wife's bald assertion that her husband earned a good income and had the ability to provide reasonable support for the two children of the marriage in his custody fell far short of satisfying the court that reasonable arrangements were made for the children's support. Justice Stevens acceded to the husband's argument that the wife's evidence not only failed to disclose the required financial information, it also failed to include any proposal respecting the future support of the two children of the marriage. As Stevens J observed, absent such a proposal, it would be difficult for a court to satisfy itself that reasonable arrangements for child support had been made. He acknowledged that evidence proposing a suitable arrangement need not be extensive. In most circumstances, a simple calculation of the applicable table amount of child support would suffice. In the present case, the wife's failure to provide the relevant financial evidence was, in itself, a basis for dismissing her severance application. Her affidavit evidence implied that she would not be making any support payments for the two children in her husband's custody, without providing adequate information as to her income or lack thereof.

A parent cannot escape the obligation to make reasonable arrangements for child support by voluntarily relinquishing well-paid employment. In such a case, reasonable arrangements for child support will be based on the respondent's earning capacity, not on a self-induced unemployed status. Consequently, if an agreed amount of child support is clearly insufficient in light of the respondent's earning capacity, the court must stay the granting of the divorce until reasonable arrangements are made.[213] The existence of a separation agreement or subsisting court order does not abrogate the duty of the court under section 11(1)(b) of the *Divorce Act* to satisfy itself that reasonable

---

213   *Eddy v Eddy* (1992), 39 RFL (3d) 339 (Alta QB).

arrangements are thereby provided for the support of the children of the marriage.[214]

In uncontested divorce proceedings where spouses rely on affidavits instead of appearing in person before a judge, the petitioner's affidavit must contain sufficient information to enable the court to discharge its statutory duty. It must include information concerning the spousal income and the number, age, and circumstances of the children so that the court can determine whether proposed arrangements for the support of the children are reasonable having regard to the applicable guidelines.[215] Bare assertions that the spouses have made reasonable arrangements for child support are not enough. If the court has insufficient information to determine whether the arrangements are suitable, it must withhold the divorce until this omission has been corrected. Consent by the divorcing parents to ignore the *Federal Child Support Guidelines* does not guarantee that section 11(1)(b) of the *Divorce Act* will be satisfied.[216]

The court can raise the bar created by section 11(1)(b) of the *Divorce Act* on its own motion.[217] In that event, either or both spouses must satisfy the court that reasonable arrangements have been made for the support of the children of the marriage or that any such arrangements are impracticable under the circumstances. Although the role of the court may be inquisitorial, there is no independent duty imposed on the court itself to make an order for child support that will guarantee the financial security of dependent children. If the court is not satisfied that reasonable efforts have been made to protect the financial security of the children of the marriage, the court must stay the granting of a divorce until reasonable arrangements are made for the support of any children of the marriage or the court is satisfied that the spouses cannot, by reason of the attendant circumstances, make any such arrangements.[218] Where an application for child support has been included in the divorce petition but the amount is insufficient, rather than imposing a stay under section 11(1)(b) of the *Divorce Act*, the court may allow amendment of the petition to reflect a proper amount of child support, provided

214 *K(LA) v K(GN)* (1987), 12 BCLR (2d) 9 (SC); *M(BJ) v M(JH)* (1987), 12 BCLR (2d) 16 (SC). Compare *Nagil v Nagil*, 2010 BCCA 533.

215 *F(RD) v F(SL)* (1987), 6 RFL (3d) 413 (BCSC); *Money v Money* (1987), 5 RFL (3d) 375 (Man CA); *MacKinnon v MacKinnon* (1986), 78 NSR (2d) 361 (SC); *Kendo v Kendo*, 2013 NWTSC 67.

216 *Walsh v Binet*, 2013 ABQB 686 at para 12, Viet J.

217 *Wallace v Wallace* (1973), 9 RFL 393 (Alta SCTD); *Money v Money* (1987), 5 RFL (3d) 375 (Man CA).

218 *Money v Money* (1987), 5 RFL (3d) 375 (Man CA); see also *Dumas v Dumas* (1992), 43 RFL (3d) 260 (Alta QB); *Acchione v Acchione* (1987), 9 RFL (3d) 215 (Ont Sup Ct).

that the obligor has notice of this and is given an opportunity to make submissions thereupon at trial.[219]

Failure to comply with section 11(1)(a) of the *Divorce Act* renders the divorce judgment voidable, not void. Where innocent third parties have acquired rights and interests in consequence of the ostensible validity of the divorce judgment and no party has any superior equity, it is thereafter too late to set the judgment aside.[220]

4) Barriers to Religious Remarriage

In some religions, one spouse may control the availability of religious divorce. The other spouse is powerless. State law does not interfere with religious doctrine. However, section 21.1 of the *Divorce Act* imposes legal sanctions on a spouse who unjustifiably refuses to remove a barrier to the religious remarriage of the other spouse. For example, a Jewish husband who refuses to deliver a *get* (a Jewish bill of divorcement) stands in the way of his wife's remarriage in the Jewish faith. If that husband were to seek a divorce or any corollary relief such as support or custody of the children from a Canadian court in proceedings instituted under the *Divorce Act*, his claim may be stayed unless and until he removes the barrier to his wife's religious remarriage. This sanction only applies where the removal of the barrier lies exclusively with a spouse, as distinct from a religious body or official. Its purpose is to prevent a spouse from withholding the right to a religious divorce or remarriage for the purpose of negotiating an unconscionable settlement of legal rights respecting spousal support, child support, child custody or access, or property division. Section 21.1 of the *Divorce Act* constitutes a temporary bar to the offending spouse's right to seek a divorce or corollary relief under the *Divorce Act*. If the offending spouse rectifies the situation by removing the obstacles to religious remarriage of the other spouse, the substantive claims of the previously offending spouse may proceed on their merits, although costs consequences may ensue for the spouse who acted improperly.[221]

In *Bruker v Marcovitz*,[222] the spouses negotiated a "Consent to Corollary Relief," which included an undertaking to obtain a Jewish divorce, or *get*,

---

219 *Almeida v Almeida* (1995), 11 RFL (4th) 131 (Alta QB); see also *Fowler v Szabo-Fowler*, [2006] SJ No 101 (CA).

220 *P v P*, [1971] 2 WLR 510 (Eng CA). See *Practice Direction*, [1970] 3 All ER 1023. And see *Wallin v Wallin* (1973), 13 RFL 305 at 311 (Ont HCJ), var'd (1975), 18 RFL 122 (Ont CA); see also *Rivas v Rivas*, [1977] 2 WWR 345 (Alta SC).

221 *Tanny v Tanny*, [2000] OJ No 2472 (Sup Ct) (wife not precluded from pursuing substantive relief under federal and provincial legislation where she withdrew her earlier refusal of consent to receive *get*).

222 [2007] 3 SCR 607.

from the rabbinical court (*Beth Din*) once their Quebec divorce became final. Under Jewish law, a wife cannot obtain a *get* unless her husband agrees to give it. So long as the husband refuses to give the *get*, his wife is unable to remarry under Jewish law and any children born after a civil marriage are illegitimate. In this case, the husband refused his wife's repeated requests to provide a *get* for fifteen years. The wife sought damages for breach of contract. The husband argued that his agreement to give a *get* was unenforceable under Quebec law and that he was protected from any liability for damages by his right to freedom of religion. The trial judge held the agreement to be a valid and binding contract that was enforceable by an award of damages in a Quebec court. The Court of Appeal allowed the husband's appeal, holding that the substance of his commitment was religious in character and was not enforceable by secular courts. On appeal to the Supreme Court of Canada, the majority judgment of seven to two held that the fact that a civil dispute involves a religious aspect does not, by itself, render it non-justiciable. The undertaking by the husband to provide a *get* was part of a voluntary exchange of promises that was intended to have legally enforceable consequences. The Court was not being asked to determine doctrinal religious issues and there is nothing in the *Civil Code*[223] to prevent someone from transforming his or her moral obligations into legal and binding obligations. Nor was the husband entitled to immunity from his contractual breach by invoking his freedom of religion under section 3 of the Quebec *Charter of Human Rights and Freedoms*.[224] Section 9.1 of the *Charter* confirms the principle that a claim to religious freedom must be reconciled with countervailing rights, values, and harm. Determining when such a claim must yield to a more pressing public interest is a complex, nuanced, fact-specific exercise. In this case, the husband's claim did not survive the balancing mandated by the Quebec *Charter* and by previous judgments of the Supreme Court of Canada. Any impairment of the husband's religious freedom was outweighed by the harm both to the wife personally and to the public's interest in protecting fundamental values such as equality rights and autonomous choice in marriage and divorce. These, as well as the public benefit in enforcing valid and binding contractual obligations, were among the interests that outweighed the husband's claim. The wife's appeal to the Supreme Court of Canada was accordingly allowed and the trial judge's award of damages was reinstated.

---

223   *Civil Code of Québec*, RSQ c C-1991.
224   RSQ c C-12.

CHAPTER 8

Spousal Support On or After Divorce

A. DEFINITION OF "SPOUSE" AND "SPOUSAL SUPPORT"

Pursuant to section 3 of the *Civil Marriage Act*,[1] "marriage, for civil purposes, is the lawful union of two persons to the exclusion of all others." Consequential on this parliamentary recognition of the validity of same-sex marriages, section 8(1) of the *Civil Marriage Act* has amended section 2(1) of the *Divorce Act* to provide that "'spouse' means either of two persons who are married to each other." A same-sex couple, who are married according to the law, may, therefore, invoke the primary and corollary relief provisions of the *Divorce Act*.[2]

The expression "spousal support" is somewhat misleading because it includes the payment of support to an ex-spouse. Furthermore, some provincial and territorial statutes impose "spousal" support obligations on unmarried cohabitants who have lived together for a designated period of time or who are the parents of a child.

B. FORMAL LEGAL EQUALITY BETWEEN SPOUSES

Formal legal equality exists between divorcing spouses insofar as support rights and obligations are concerned. A husband in need has just as much right to seek spousal support from his financially independent wife as she has if their financial situation is reversed.[3] In reality, divorcing or divorced husbands rarely seek or obtain spousal support.

---

1   SC 2005, c 33.
2   RSC 1985 (2d Supp), c 3. See *MM v JH*, [2004] OJ No 5314 (Sup Ct).
3   *Moge v Moge*, [1992] 3 SCR 813 at 849; *Rivard v Rivard*, 2011 ONSC 2988.

C. TYPES OF ORDERS

1) Diverse Types of Orders

The diverse types of spousal support orders that may be granted pursuant to subsection 15.2 of the *Divorce Act* are as follows:

- an order to secure a lump sum;
- an order to pay a lump sum;
- an order to secure and pay a lump sum;
- an order to secure periodic sums;
- an order to pay periodic sums; and
- an order to secure and pay periodic sums.

The court is not restricted to making only one type of order. A combination of the various types of orders may be accommodated. Any of the aforementioned orders may be granted by way of interim or permanent relief, although they are always subject to variation or rescission in the event of a material change of circumstances.

2) Nominal Orders; Final Orders

An order for nominal spousal support is not necessary for the purpose of preserving a future right to claim spousal support following a divorce.[4] Nominal orders have, nevertheless, been granted where the applicant establishes a present need but the respondent has no ability to pay or where there is no current need but there is a predictable future need. A nominal order for spousal support may be vacated on appeal where no current need has been demonstrated and any future need would be unrelated to the marriage.[5] According to the judgment of the British Columbia Court of Appeal in *Gill-Sager v Sager*,[6] the law is unsettled on the question whether the dismissal of an application for spousal support under section 15.2 of the *Divorce Act* precludes the applicant from ever succeeding on a subsequent application, regardless of a change in his or her circumstances. Only the Supreme Court of Canada can provide a definitive answer to this question. If the applicant is disentitled to spousal support at the time of the original application but might reasonably be subsequently entitled to relief in the event of a change of circumstances,

---

4   *Traversy v Glover*, [2006] OJ No 2908 (Sup Ct).
5   *Vickers v Vickers*, [2001] NSJ No 218 (CA). For the suggestion that nominal orders are not "support orders" within the meaning of the *Divorce Act*, see *Gill-Sager v Sager*, [2003] BCJ No 121 (CA). Compare *Labbe v Labbe*, 2009 BCSC 835.
6   *Gill-Sager v Sager*, [2003] BCJ No 121 (CA); see also *BGD v RWD*, [2003] BCJ No 1098 (CA). Compare *Tierney-Hynes v Hynes*, [2005] OJ No 2661 (CA).

for example, by reason of deteriorating health, an appropriate order should be couched in terms that do not preclude a subsequent application for spousal support.

3) Interim Support Orders

Section 15.2(2) of the *Divorce Act* empowers a court to grant an interim order requiring a spouse to secure and/or pay such lump sum and/or periodic sums as the court deems reasonable for the support of the other spouse. An interim spousal support order is intended to provide a reasonably acceptable short-term solution until a pre-trial conference allows for a more thorough and ju-dicious resolution of the issues[7] or the matter goes to trial when an in-depth examination can be undertaken.[8] The nature of interim spousal support dic-tates that the court does not have to embark upon a detailed examination of the merits of the claim for permanent spousal support.[9] Nevertheless, a *prima facie* entitlement to interim support must be established in accord-ance with the provisions of section 15.2 of the *Divorce Act*.[10] Section 15.2(2) of the *Divorce Act* includes no explicit reference to the variation of an interim spousal support order, but the court has an inherent jurisdiction to vary such an order in response to a material change of circumstances or when the assumptions on which the order was made later prove to have been clearly understated.[11] Where an interim order provides for periodic spousal support to be paid from the date of the filing of the application but payment of the instant arrears thereby created is to be deferred pending the resolution of outstanding monetary issues, the arrears may be subsequently expunged by a trial judge without proof of a change of circumstances since the granting of the interim order. In addressing the wife's contention that section 17(4.1) of the *Divorce Act* required the trial judge to find a change of circumstances before varying the interim spousal support order, the Newfoundland and Labrador Court of Appeal in *Whelan v Whelan*[12] observed that section 17(4.1)

---

7   *DMB v DBB*, 2012 SKQB 400, citing *Jacobson v Jacobson*, 2011 SKQB 402.

8   *Lapp v Lapp*, [2008] AJ No 208 (CA); *Kowalski v Grant*, [2007] MJ No 386 (QB); *Gabel v Gabel*, [2000] NWTJ No 54 (SC); *Knowles v Lindstrom*, 2015 ONSC 1408; *EAG v DLG*, 2010 YKSC 23.

9   *Squires v Squires*, 2014 NBQB 172.

10 *Dunn v Dunn*, 2009 ABQB 697; *Noonan v Noonan*, 2007 PEICAD 5; see also *Fong v Fong*, 2010 MBQB 5. Compare *Muchekeni v Muchekeni*, [2008] NWTJ No 19 (SC); *Balayo v Mead-ows*, 2013 ONSC 5321.

11 *Carvell v Carvell*, [1969] 2 OR 513 (CA); *Lipson v Lipson* (1972), 7 RFL 186 (Ont CA); *PLM v SYB*, 2014 NBQB 222; *Torres v Marin*, [2007] YJ No 94 (SC).

12 [2005] NJ No 134 (CA). See also *Janmohamed v Janmohamed*, 2014 BCSC 107; *Colter v Colter*, 2015 NSSC 2; *Damaschin-Zamfirescu v Damaschin-Zamfirescu*, 2012 ONSC 6689 at paras 18–20.

applies only when the court is considering an application to vary a "spousal support order," which is explicitly defined in section 2(1) of the *Divorce Act*. Since that definition stipulates that a "spousal support order" means an order made under section 15.2(1) of the *Divorce Act*, whereas interim spousal support orders are granted pursuant to section 15.2(2) of the *Divorce Act*, section 17(4.1) of the *Divorce Act* can have no application to the variation of interim orders. The Newfoundland and Labrador Court of Appeal further observed that the argument that finding a change of circumstance is required before a judge can grant a final order that is different from an interim order lacks any logical foundation. There would then be no difference between interim and final orders under the *Divorce Act* and both spouses would feel obliged to fully argue the whole case at the interim stage because of their concern that any subsequent adjustment would require a demonstrated change of circumstances. This would defeat Parliament's objective of enabling temporary orders to be made expeditiously pending a final determination of the issue of spousal support. The Newfoundland and Labrador Court of Appeal also rejected the wife's alternative contention that the trial judge had erred in failing to consider the five factors listed by Noonan J in *Tremblett v Tremblett*[13] as relevant to the remission of support arrears. In the opinion of the Newfoundland and Labrador Court of Appeal, these criteria relate to applications under section 17(4.1) of the *Divorce Act* to retroactively vary final orders for spousal support and have no application to original applications of the *Divorce Act*. In this latter context, the relevant factors to be applied are those specified in section 15.2(4) of the *Divorce Act*, namely, the condition, means, needs, and other circumstances of the spouses, which the Newfoundland and Labrador Court of Appeal found to have been properly applied by the trial judge in exercising his discretion to expunge the arrears under the interim order after a full and thorough review of the evidence.

However, Canadian courts have consistently asserted that interim support orders should only be varied when they are patently inappropriate. It is only where there has been a material change in circumstances since the prior interim order was made and the current circumstances provide a compelling reason, such as undue hardship, that a court will order variation of an interim order without awaiting trial.[14] Otherwise, any fine tuning or necessary adjustment can be accommodated at trial.[15] Parties with an interim order for

---

13   (1998), 75 Nfld & PEIR 175 (Nfld UFC).

14   *Simmons v Simmons*, 2011 ONSC 5020; *Savoy v Savoy*, 2014 SKQB 293.

15   *Owokalu v Owokalu*, [2000] AJ No 1519 (QB); *Burke v Burke*, 2010 BCSC 2 (spousal and child support); *Coley v Coley* (1981), 20 RFL (2d) 327 (Man CA); *Hope v Hope*, [2000] OJ No 4532 (Sup Ct) (child support); compare *Michaud v Kuszelewski*, 2009 NSCA 118; *Walter v Silvester-Purdon*, 2010 SKCA 40; *MacDonald v MacDonald*, 2010 SKCA 60. As to retroac-

support should move the matter forward to a settlement conference and, if necessary, a trial, to deal with any defect, real or perceived, in the temporary order, but the focus of the parties should be on settlement, and trial should be a last resort.[16]

Absent some reasonably sound prospect of success at trial, interim spousal support should be denied.[17] Interim spousal support should not be ordered in the face of conflicting affidavits on crucial issues relating to spousal support entitlement.[18] Because of the difficulty of applying the objectives set out in section 15.2(6) of the *Divorce Act* relating to compensatory spousal support when interim spousal support is in dispute, a court will ordinarily focus on the needs of the applicant and the respondent's ability to pay in light of the standard of living enjoyed prior to the spousal separation.[19] Need is a relative concept that is based on the standard of living that the parties were accustomed to during the marriage.[20] A court should not, at an interim stage, place too much emphasis on the applicant's failure at that point to achieve self-sufficiency.[21] Some courts have held that the amount of spousal support ordered on an application for interim spousal support should, absent exceptional circumstances, generally fall within the range suggested by the *Spousal Support Advisory Guidelines*.[22]

A court may impute income to a spouse for the purpose of determining interim spousal support. Although there is no express provision in the *Divorce Act* which sets out how this is to be done, courts may apply the same

tive adjustment of an interim spousal support order, see also *Lapp v Lapp*, [2008] AJ No 208 (CA); *Fisher v Fisher*, 2008 ONCA 11.

16   *Tomio v Armorer*, 2011 ONSC 5757; see also *Janmohamed v Janmohamed*, 2014 BCSC 107; *Huculak v Huculak* (1998), 103 BCAC 276 at paras 3–5.

17   *Howdle v Betteridge*, 2015 MBQB 12; *Belcourt v Chartrand*, [2006] OJ No 1500 (Sup Ct).

18   *Duder v Rowe*, [2006] AJ No 868 (QB); *MacKinnon v MacKinnon* (2005), 75 OR (3d) 175 (CA).

19   *Loesch v Walji*, 2008 BCCA 214; *Schilter v Schilter*, 2014 BCSC 2149; *Vauclair v Vauclair* (1998), 126 Man R (2d) 136 (CA); *Thomson v Thomson*, 2011 MBCA 28; *Betts v Betts*, 2014 NBQB 47; *Richards v Richards*, 2012 NSCA 7; *Muchekeni v Muchekeni*, [2008] NWTJ No 19 (SC); *Knowles v Lindstrom*, 2015 ONSC 1408; *Antonishyn v Boucher*, 2011 SKQB 147; *Larson v Larson*, 2014 SKQB 258; *EAG v DLG*, 2010 YKSC 23. Compare *Foster-Jacques v Jacques*, 2011 NSSC 43 and 2011 NSSC 124.

20   *Newcombe v Newcombe*, 2014 ONSC 1094, citing *Gardner v Gardner*, [2008] AJ No 954 (QB) at para 30.

21   *Pasta v Pasta*, 2013 MBQB 311; *Singh v Singh*, 2013 ONSC 6476. Compare *Babich v Babich*, 2015 SKQB 22.

22   *DRM v RBM*, 2006 BCSC 1921; *Crowther v Crowther*, 2014 BCSC 629; see also *Sydor v Sydor*, 2011 MBQB 38; *Simle v Borchuk*, 2014 NWTSC 80; *Dupuis v Desrosiers*, 2012 ONCJ 261 at para 21; *BDC v MCM*, 2014 ONSC 6064; *EAG v DLG*, 2010 YKSC 23. Compare *Sydor v Keough*, 2012 MBQB 241 at para 23; *Poirier v Poirier*, 2010 ONSC 920 at paras 113–16. See also *Ponkin v Werden*, 2015 ONSC 791.

methodology as is used under the *Federal Child Support Guidelines*.[23] In determining what amount of income to impute to a spouse on the basis of intentional unemployment or under-employment, the court must have regard to the spouse's capacity to earn income in light of such factors as employment history, age, education, skills, health, available employment opportunities, and the standard of living enjoyed during the spousal relationship. The court looks at the amount of income the party could earn if he or she worked to capacity.[24]

In cases where the parties are wealthy, the court can consider lifestyle in determining the wife's needs for the purposes of spousal support. Where there are the means available, the payee spouse is entitled to receive spousal support in an amount sufficient to enjoy a level of comfort beyond her basic needs.[25] Income that could be earned from capital is relevant to the quantification of interim spousal support, but the expenditure of capital is generally not required. There may be circumstances, however, where a support obligor ought reasonably to be compelled to utilize capital to pay interim spousal support. For example, where there has been a significant use of capital to support the marital lifestyle, the recipient of interim spousal support should not necessarily be relegated to a lifestyle based solely on the obligor's income.[26]

In *Robles v Kuhn*,[27] Master Keighley, of the Supreme Court of British Columbia, formulated the following useful list of principles governing applications for interim spousal support:

1. On applications for interim support the applicant's needs and the respondent's ability to pay assume greater significance.

2. An interim support order should be sufficient to allow the applicant to continue living at the same standard of living enjoyed prior to separation if the payor's ability to pay warrants it.

---

23 *Lahanky v Lahanky*, 2011 NBQB 220; *Koester v Koester*, 2014 NSSC 367; *Knowles v Lindstrom*, 2015 ONSC 1408 (income tax gross up). But compare *Richards v Richards*, 2012 NSCA 7, citing *Jean v Jean*, 2006 ABQB 938 at paras 108–9; see also *Gordon v Gordon*, 2014 ABQB 596 at paras 82–83 (reasoning in *Jean v Jean* applies to both payor and payee spouse). And see *Linke v Linke*, 2014 ABQB 668. See further, Professors Carol Rogerson and Rollie Thompson, *The Spousal Support Advisory Guidelines: A New and Improved User's Guide to the Final Version* (Ottawa: Department of Justice, 2010) at Part 5. Income.

24 *Poirier v Poirier*, 2010 ONSC 920; see also *Oliver v Oliver*, 2011 BCSC 1126; *Lahanky v Lahanky*, 2011 NBQB 220; *Gogas v Gogas*, 2011 ONSC 4571.

25 *Hodgkinson v Hodgkinson*, 2006 BCCA 158 at para 69; *Davis v Davis*, 2013 NBQB 115; *Knowles v Lindstrom*, 2015 ONSC 1408; *Scully v Scully*, 2013 SKQB 58.

26 *Colivas v Colivas*, 2013 ONSC 168; see also *Clapp v Clapp*, 2014 ONSC 4591.

27 2009 BCSC 1163; see also *Katchen v Katchen*, 2015 BCSC 103; *Foster-Jacques v Jacques*, 2011 NSSC 43; *Durden v Durden*, 2014 ONSC 3242.

3. On interim support applications the court does not embark on an in depth analysis of the parties' circumstances which is better left to trial. The court achieves rough justice at best.

4. The courts should not unduly emphasize any one of the statutory considerations above others.

5. On interim applications the need to achieve economic self-sufficiency is often of less significance.

6. Interim support should be ordered within the range suggested by the *Spousal Support Advisory Guidelines* unless exceptional circumstances indicate otherwise.[28]

7. Interim support should only be ordered where it can be said a *prima facie* case for entitlement has been made out.

8. Where there is a need to resolve contested issues of fact, especially those connected with a threshold issue, such as entitlement, it becomes less advisable to order interim support.

The relatively narrow perspective of needs and ability to pay is inevitable in the ordinary course of events for the following reasons:

- The marriage breakdown is usually recent. Consequently, the applicant, if unemployed prior thereto, will have been afforded insufficient opportunity to find suitable employment or obtain the requisite skills to become economically self-sufficient.
- The property of the spouses still remains to be divided.
- The nature of the hearing is such that insufficient evidence exists to determine issues of credibility and make the requisite findings of fact in light of statutorily designated factors and objectives that regulate spousal support entitlement.

Interim spousal support proceedings are, therefore, summary in nature and provide "rough justice" at best.[29] They are in the nature of a "holding order."[30] If a substantial period of time has elapsed between the spousal separation and the time of the application, a court may find it possible to determine whether the allegedly dependent spouse has made reasonable efforts to achieve economic self-sufficiency. Such a finding is easier to make if the court has the benefit of oral evidence instead of affidavit evidence. Where an interim order for spousal support is expressly declared subject to review after the filing and delivery of the Property and Financial Statement, a payor who seeks remission or reduction of the amount payable is not required to

---

28 Compare *Turner v Green*, 2014 NBQB 245 at para 42, Robichaud J.

29 *Squires v Squires*, 2014 NBQB 172; *Walker v Walker*, 2014 SKQB 270.

30 *Keyes v Keyes*, 2015 ONSC 1660 at para 61, Chiappetta J.

prove any material change of circumstances since the granting of the order. A reduction may be judicially perceived as appropriate where the recipient spouse is found capable of supplementing pension income through part-time employment.[31]

A trial judge is not bound by the interim award and, if necessary, can make adjustments to the permanent order, if one is made, to allow for any overpayment or underpayment involved in the interim award.[321]

Courts do not ordinarily impose time limits on interim spousal support orders but may do so in exceptional circumstances.[33] An interim order for spousal support for a fixed term is not binding on a trial judge at a subsequent final hearing.[34] Courts have repeatedly stated that successful appeals from interim orders will be rare and that such appeals are to be discouraged.[35] An appellate court should not interfere with an interim order for support, unless it is demonstrated that the interim order is clearly wrong and exceeds the wide ambit of reasonable solutions that are available on a summary interim proceeding.[36] This standard of appellate review reflects the following characteristics of interim support orders:

1) Interim orders are intended to provide short-term reasonable relief pending trial.

2) Interim orders are usually granted on the basis of affidavit evidence that is often conflicting or contradictory. This limited evidence renders interim orders more susceptible to error than permanent orders made after a trial.

3) Appeals from interim orders can provide an inappropriate means of deferring a trial and increasing the cost of litigation both financially and emotionally. Appeals from interim orders have been generally discouraged and will usually be dismissed, unless the trial date is so far in advance as to require immediate appellate review of an interim disposition.

4) Interim orders do not fetter the discretion of trial judges to determine the appropriate disposition after a full investigation of the facts. Where

---

31 *Threlfall v Threlfall*, [2001] BCJ No 2474 (SC).

32 *Grandbois v Grandbois* (1998), 131 Man R (2d) 110 (CA); *Carr v Anketell*, 2015 NBQB 51; *Colter v Colter*, 2015 NSSC 2; *Whelan v Whelan*, [2005] NJ No 134 (CA); *Ponkin v Werden*, 2015 ONSC 791.

33 *Kaytor v Unser*, 2014 SKQB 181 at para 36.

34 *Grant v Grant*, 2012 NBCA 101.

35 *Martin v Orris*, 2010 MBCA 59; *Droit de la famille — 142281*, 2014 QCCA 1692; *LaFreniere v LaFreniere*, 2014 SKCA 13.

36 *Loesch v Walji*, 2008 BCCA 214; *Sypher v Sypher*, [1986] OJ No 536 (CA); see also *Thomson v Thomson*, 2011 MBCA 28.

it is deemed appropriate, a trial judge may make a retroactive order to address any inequity or inadequacy arising under an interim order.[37]

As a general rule, retroactive spousal support preceding commencement of the proceedings ought not to be granted on an application for interim support.[38] The Manitoba Court of Appeal has held that, in the absence of evidence as to need or hardship, an interim order as to retroactive spousal support cannot be justified.[39]

4) Lump Sum Support Orders

Section 15.2(1) of the *Divorce Act* empowers a court to order a lump sum in addition to or in lieu of periodic sums for the support of a spouse.[40] The same statutory criteria apply to lump sum and periodic support orders.[41] When spousal support is granted, it is usually ordered to be paid on a periodic basis — weekly, fortnightly, or monthly. Because lump sum orders may not fairly anticipate future changes of circumstances, lump sum support is a solution that must be carefully weighed before implementation.[42] Lump sum support may be impractical by reason of the insufficient means of the obligor to pay.[43]

Although the court has a wide discretion to order a lump sum under section 15.2 of the *Divorce Act*, this discretion can only be exercised for the purpose of providing support in accordance with the provisions of the *Divorce Act*. Section 15.2 of the *Divorce Act* does not empower a court to redistribute property in the guise of lump sum support,[44] although an equitable distribution of the economic consequences of the marriage and its breakdown

---

37   See *Hartshorne v Hartshorne*, 2010 BCCA 327.

38   See *Kyle v Kyle*, 2014 SKQB 59.

39   *Sydor v Keough*, 2012 MBQB 241, citing *Dram v Foster*, [2009] MJ No 414 (CA). Compare *Burczynski v Burczynski*, 2013 MBQB 257.

40   *Mollot v Mollot*, 2007 ABCA 183.

41   *Waterman v Waterman* (1995), 16 RFL (4th) 10 (Nfld CA); *Vynnyk v Baisa*, [2008] OJ No 3747 (CA).

42   *Stricker v Stricker* (1991), 33 RFL (3d) 367 (Alta QB); *RB v IB*, [2005] NBJ No 134 (CA); *Litzenberger v Litzenberger*, 2012 SKQB 122.

43   *Ramantanis v Ramantanis*, [2004] MJ No 332 (CA); *Fraser v Fraser* (1994), 143 NBR (2d) 189 (CA); *Elliot v Elliot* (1993), 48 RFL (3d) 237 (Ont CA).

44   *Young v Young*, [1993] 4 SCR 3; *Newstone v Newstone* (1994), 2 RFL (4th) 129 (BCCA); *Werner v Werner*, 2013 NSCA 6; *Mannarino v Mannarino* (1992), 43 RFL (3d) 309 (Ont CA); *Davis v Crawford*, 2011 ONCA 294; *Tweel v Tweel* (1994), 7 RFL (4th) 204 (PEISCTD); *Droit de la famille — 1275*, 2012 QCCA 87; *Osborne v Osborne* (1973), 14 RFL 61 (Sask QB), var'd (1974), 23 RFL 358 (Sask CA). As to a court's jurisdiction to order lump sum spousal support to be paid out of money held in a LIRA, see *Brière v Saint-Pierre*, 2012 ONSC 421, citing *Belton v Belton*, 2010 ONSC 2400 at para 25.

may be achieved by a combination of property and support entitlements.[45] A lump sum support order may be granted notwithstanding a prior or contemporaneous property division,[46] but any substantial property entitlement affects the "means" and "needs" of the respective spouses for the purpose of subsection 15.2(4) of the *Divorce Act* and may render support unnecessary or inequitable.[47]

Some courts have expressed the view that lump sum orders should be the exception and not the rule.[48] This opinion is by no means universally held and each case must be decided on its merits.[49] Lump sum orders in divorce proceedings have not been confined to persons with very substantial capital assets, and a wide variety of circumstances may justify such a disposition.[50] In *Davis v Crawford*,[51] the Ontario Court of Appeal rejected the appellant's submission that its previous judgment in *Mannarino v Mannarino*[52] should be treated as restricting a court's ability to order lump sum spousal support to situations "where there is a real risk that periodic payments would not be made" or to "very unusual circumstances." It reasoned that the statutory authority conferred on a court to grant lump sum spousal support orders under both section 34 of the *Family Law Act*[53] and section 15.2 of the *Divorce Act*,[54] and the purposes underlying spousal support orders that are prescribed by section 33(8) of the *Family Law Act* and by section 15.2(6) of the *Divorce Act*, contain no restrictions of the type set out in *Mannarino*. These statutory provisions and the jurisprudence interpreting them provide substantial guidance as to the circumstances to be considered in determining whether a lump sum spousal support order is appropriate in any particular case. For example, it is undisputed that a lump sum spousal support order should not be granted

---

45   *Moge v Moge*, [1992] 3 SCR 813, 43 RFL (3d) 345 at 374.

46   *Cunningham v Cunningham* (1990), 30 RFL (3d) 159 (BCCA); *Smith v Smith* (1985), 55 Nfld & PEIR 85 (Nfld SC); *Wilson v Wilson* (1985), 66 NSR (2d) 361 (SC), rev'd (1985), 70 NSR (2d) 371 (CA); *Crawford v Crawford* (1987), 6 RFL (3d) 308 (Ont HCJ).

47   *Rafuse v Rafuse* (1984), 43 RFL (2d) 282 (NSSCAD); *Mannarino v Mannarino* (1992), 43 RFL (3d) 309 (Ont CA); see also *Newson v Newson* (1993), 45 RFL (3d) 115 (BCCA).

48   See, for example, *Krause v Krause*, [1976] 2 WWR 622 (Alta CA); *Rockall v Rockall*, 2010 ABCA 278; *Hauff v Hauff* (1994), 95 Man R (2d) 83 (CA); *Ramantanis v Ramantanis*, [2004] MJ No 332 (CA); *Powers v Powers* (1990), 92 NSR (2d) 337(SCTD); *Mannarino v Mannarino* (1992), 43 RFL (3d) 309 (Ont CA); *TAE v MEE*, [2003] OJ No 3300 (CA).

49   *Main v Main* (1978), 5 RFL (2d) 1 (Man CA); *Jensen v Jensen* (1986), 43 Man R (2d) 241 (CA); *Davis v Crawford*, 2011 ONCA 294.

50   *Raffin v Raffin*, [1972] 1 OR 173 (CA).

51   2011 ONCA 294; see also *Davis v Tatton*, 2013 BCSC 2126; *Racco v Racco*, 2014 ONCA 330; *Laframboise v Laframboise*, 2015 ONSC 1752.

52   (1992), 43 RFL (3d) 309 (CA).

53   RSO 1990, c F.3.

54   RSC 1985, c 3 (2d Supp).

for the purpose of achieving an equitable redistribution of property.[55] It is important, however, to differentiate the purpose of an award from its effect, because any lump sum order has the effect of redistributing assets between parties.[56] It is also well accepted that an obligor's ability to pay a lump sum is an important consideration. In addition, the perceived advantages of a lump sum order must be weighed against any presenting disadvantages. The Ontario Court of Appeal acknowledged that spousal support orders will typically take the form of periodic payments for very practical reasons, which include the absence of any justification for an immediate lump sum award and the ready ability of the obligor to pay periodic spousal support out of his or her recurring income, with the opportunity for variation in the event of a change in the financial circumstances of either party. But it rejected the notion that, as a matter of principle, lump sum spousal support orders are limited to "very unusual circumstances." In its opinion, which appears at paragraphs 75–76 of the judgment:

[75] Irrespective of whether the proposed support is periodic or lump sum, it is incumbent upon counsel to provide the judge deciding the matter with submissions concerning the basis for awarding and the method of calculating the proposed support, together with a range of possible outcomes. Further, it is highly desirable that a judge making a lump sum award provide a clear explanation of both the basis for exercising the discretion to award lump sum support and the rationale for arriving at a particular figure. Clear presentations by counsel and explanations by trial judges will make such an award more transparent and enhance the appearance of justice. Over time, this approach will undoubtedly foster greater consistency and predictability in the result.

[76] As part of this approach, where an award of lump sum spousal support is made as a substitute for an award of periodic support, it is preferable that, with the benefit of submissions from counsel, the judge consider whether the amount awarded is in keeping with the *Spousal Support Advisory Guidelines* (Ottawa, Department of Justice, 2008) (the "*Guidelines*"). If it is not, some reasons should be provided for why the *Guidelines* do not provide an appropriate result: *Fisher v. Fisher* (2008), 88 O.R. (3d) 241 (C.A.), at para. 103.[57]

---

55   *Zivic v Zivic*, 2014 ONSC 7262.

56   *Morrison v Morrison*, 2013 NSSC 358.

57   2011 ONCA 294. See also *Jones v Durston*, 2012 ONSC 3073; *Racco v Racco*, 2014 ONCA 330. As to the variables to be taken into account in quantifying lump sum spousal support orders, see *Pollitt v Pollitt*, 2011 ONSC 1186.

Diverse circumstances have justified orders for lump sum support.[58] For example, a lump sum payment may be appropriate where

- the obligor has substantial assets but a limited income;[59]
- periodic payments are plainly inadequate by themselves;[60]
- it is necessary to provide security;[61]
- there is a history of default with respect to periodic payments;[62]
- a lump sum would recoup unpaid periodic support;[63]
- the obligor has an unstable employment record;[64]
- the obligor's income is unpredictable,[65]
- the obligor's future employment prospects are uncertain;[66]
- there is evidence that the obligor will fritter away the capital;[67]
- the obligor is unlikely or unable to pay periodic support at all or for the appropriate length of time;[68] or
- the conduct of the obligor has been to unnecessarily protract litigation and force the dependent spouse to live on social assistance.[69]

When quantifying a lump sum spousal support order by reference to the capitalized value of periodic payments over a fixed period of time, a discounting for present value may be required and due account should also be taken of the different income tax consequences of lump sum and periodic spousal support payments.[70] Faced with inadequate reasons to justify a trial

---

58 For lists of relevant considerations, see *Rockall v Rockall*, 2010 ABCA 278; *KDRA v YJAA*, 2014 BCSC 2310; *Carter v Carter* (1978), 19 Nfld & PEIR 411 (Nfld SC); *Boland v Boland*, [2006] NJ No 206 (UFC); *Miller v Miller*, 2009 NSSC 294; *Davis v Crawford*, 2011 ONCA 294; *Beck v Beckett*, 2011 ONCA 559; see also *Hrenyk v Berden*, 2011 SKQB 305.

59 *Baker v Baker*, [2003] AJ No 778 (QB); *Maillet v Maillet* (1975), 25 RFL 126 (NBQB); *Battaglini v Battaglini* (1994), 4 RFL (4th) 235 (Ont Gen Div); see also *Waldick v Waldick*, 2011 NSSC 257 (lump sum payable out of obligor's matrimonial property entitlement).

60 *Stricker v Stricker* (1994), 4 RFL (4th) 29 (Alta CA).

61 *Rossiter-Forrest v Forrest* (1994), 129 NSR (2d) 130 (SC).

62 *Brodytsch v Brodytsch* (1977), 7 AR 541 (CA); *Verdun v Verdun* (1994), 9 RFL (4th) 54 at 67 (Ont Gen Div).

63 *Magne v Magne* (1990), 26 RFL (3d) 364 (Man QB); *Boland v Boland*, [2006] NJ No 206 (UFC).

64 *Clarke v Clarke* (1974), 14 RFL 190 (Alta SCTD), aff'd (1974), 15 RFL 115 (Alta CA); *Vanos v Vanos*, 2010 ONCA 876.

65 *Murphy v Murphy* (1989), 77 Nfld & PEIR 51 (Nfld UFC).

66 *Barker v Barker* (1993), 144 AR 314 (QB); *Bhatti v Bhatti* (1994), 45 BCAC 87; *Luehr v Luehr*, 2011 BCSC 359.

67 *Krause v Krause* (1976), 23 RFL 219 (Alta CA).

68 *Babowech v Von Como* (1989), 18 RFL (3d) 365 (BCCA); *Boland v Boland*, [2006] NJ No 206 (UFC); *Raymond v Raymond*, [2008] OJ No 5294 (Sup Ct).

69 *Droit de la famille — 1184*, [1988] RDF 272 (Que CS).

70 *Dudla v Lemay*, [2005] AJ No 117 (CA); *Rockall v Rockall*, 2010 ABCA 278; *Samoilova v Mahnic*, 2014 ABCA 65; *Robinson v Robinson*, 2012 BCCA 497; *KDRA v YJAA*, 2014 BCSC

judge's lump sum order, an appellate court may substitute an order for fixed-term periodic spousal support with the amount to be secured against the obligor's assets.[71]

Lump sum support may provide transitional financial relief to enhance a spouse's economic self-reliance[72] or to allow a spouse to become self-supporting where periodic support would serve as a disincentive to the recipient to make a genuine effort to obtain employment.[73] Lump sum spousal support should not be ordered in lieu of periodic payments when the timing and extent of the recipient's economic self-sufficiency is not reasonably ascertainable. However, lump sum payments to supplement periodic payments may be appropriate to facilitate a particular legitimate need for a larger immediate sum, for such purposes as education tuition, home repairs, and so on.[74]

Ongoing animosity between the spouses or other considerations such as the obligor's advanced age, which impacts security for the payee as well as on the obligor's ability to estate plan,[75] may justify a "clean break" by way of an order for lump sum support instead of periodic payments.[76] Similarly, where continued contact between the spouses would hamper a spouse's recovery from illness, a lump sum order promoting a clean break may be appropriate.[77]

Judicial opinion has been divided on whether the applicant must show that a lump sum is required for a specific or immediate purpose or project.[78] Lump sum orders have been granted to achieve a variety of objectives, many of which contain a compensatory element.[79] Lump sum orders may

- facilitate the purchase or repair of a residence;[80]
- provide reasonable accommodation for a custodial parent and child;[81]

2310; *Betts v Betts*, 2015 NBQB 19; *Hume v Tomlinson*, 2015 ONSC 843; compare *Dubreuil v Canada*, 2010 TCC 289; see also *Robinson v Robinson*, 2011 BCSC 1489; *Chapman v Chapman*, 2010 CanLII 18337 (Ont Sup Ct); *Edgar v Edgar*, 2012 ONCA 646; *Hrenyk v Berden*, 2011 SKQB 305; compare *Ludmer v Ludmer*, 2014 ONCA 827; *BP v AT*, 2014 NBCA 51; *Purdue v Purdue*, 2014 NBQB 262.

71 *Dudla v Lemay*, [2005] AJ No 117 (CA); *Rockall v Rockall*, 2010 ABCA 278.

72 *Boland v Boland*, [2006] NJ No 206 (UFC); *Tauber v Tauber*, [2003] OJ No 1083 (CA).

73 *Andrews v Andrews* (1995), 11 RFL (4th) 117 (BCSC).

74 *Maber v Maber*, [2007] NBJ No 128 at para 253 (QB).

75 *Yorke v Yorke*, 2010 NBQB 230.

76 See *Baker v Baker*, [2003] AJ No 778 (QB); *Carmichael v Carmichael* (1976), 27 RFL 325 (BCCA); *Foster v Foster*, 2007 BCCA 83; *Parish v Parish* (1993), 46 RFL (3d) 117 (Ont Gen Div).

77 *Poisson v Poisson* (1993), 46 RFL (3d) 105 (Ont Gen Div).

78 See *Jensen v Jensen* (1986), 5 RFL (3d) 346 (Man CA). Compare *Mosher v Mosher* (1995), 13 RFL (4th) 385 (NSCA); *Tweel v Tweel* (1994), 7 RFL (4th) 204 (PEISCTD).

79 *Sword v Sword* (1994), 118 Nfld & PEIR 69 at 74 (Nfld UFC).

80 *Krause v Krause* (1976), 23 RFL 219 (Alta CA); *Evans v Evans* (1988), 16 RFL (3d) 437 (Ont HCJ); compare *Gossen v Gossen*, [2003] NSJ No 113 (SC).

81 *Meltzer v Meltzer* (1989), 22 RFL (3d) 38 (Man QB); see also *Simms-Rideout v Rideout*, 2010 NSSC 276 (shared-parenting regime).

- enable a spouse to acquire furnishings for a new residence;[82]
- promote a spouse's economic self-sufficiency;[83]
- compensate a spouse for loss of career development or future earnings potential;[84]
- compensate a spouse for assuming the primary responsibility for child care;[85]
- compensate a spouse for assisting the other to further his or her education to the detriment of the contributing spouse's own education;[86]
- assist a spouse with education expenses or retraining for the labour market;[87]
- facilitate the purchase or repair of an automobile;[88]
- accommodate a spouse's temporary dislocation after separation and assist that spouse in reorganizing his or her life;[89]
- provide for transportation and relocation expenses in order for the spouse to return to his or her native country;[90]
- reimburse a spouse for household and other expenses incurred for the sake of the other spouse;[91]
- reimburse a spouse for post-separation debts[92] and facilitate the discharge of debts;[93] and
- pay for dental and medical needs.[94]

---

82 *Krause v Krause* (1976), 23 RFL 219 (Alta CA); *MacNaughton v MacNaughton* (1991), 32 RFL (3d) 312 (NSCA).

83 *Lacroix c Valois*, [1990] 2 SCR 1259; *Krause v Krause* (1976), 23 RFL 219 (Alta CA); *Amaral v Amaral* (1993), 50 RFL (3d) 364 (Ont Gen Div).

84 *Monks v Monks* (1993), 84 Man R (2d) 268 (QB), aff'd (1993), 88 Man R (2d) 149 (CA); *MacNeil v MacNeil* (1994), 2 RFL (4th) 432 (NSCA); *Henderson v Sharma-Henderson* (1993), 47 RFL (3d) 388 (Ont Gen Div).

85 *Wegert v Wegert* (1994), 6 RFL (4th) 430 (Man QB).

86 *Doiron v Doiron* (1994), 153 NBR (2d) 113 (QB).

87 *Baker v Baker*, [2003] AJ No 778 (QB); *KKC v APC*, [2003] BCJ No 1312 (CA); *Mosher v Mosher* (1995), 13 RFL (4th) 385 (NSCA); *Ross v Ross* (1993), 12 OR (3d) 705 (CA); compare *Gossen v Gossen*, [2003] NSJ No 113 (SC); *Rust v Rust*, [2003] SJ No 394 (CA).

88 *MacNaughton v MacNaughton* (1991), 32 RFL (3d) 312 (NSCA); *Gossen v Gossen*, [2003] NSJ No 113 (SC).

89 *Mroz v Mroz* (1987), 7 RFL (3d) 66 (Alta CA); *Nurmi v Nurmi* (1988), 16 RFL (3d) 201 (Ont UFC).

90 *Memisoglu v Memiche* (1994), 154 NBR (3d) 30 (QB).

91 *Desrochers v Desrochers* (1987), 47 Man R (2d) 135 (QB); *Van Stavern v Van Stavern* (1987), 10 RFL (3d) 354 (Sask QB).

92 *MacNeil v MacNeil* (1994), 2 RFL (4th) 432 (NSCA).

93 *Droit de la famille — 1115*, [1987] RDF 356 (Que CS); *Vieira v Vieira* (1987), 46 Man R (2d) 74 (QB); *Greenall v Greenall* (1984), 39 RFL (2d) 225 (Ont HCJ).

94 *Shaw v Shaw*, 2009 NSSC 353.

5) Security

Section 15.2(1) of the *Divorce Act* empowers a court to order a spouse to pay and/or secure such lump sum and/or periodic sums for the support of the other spouse. Support payments may be secured by way of a trust imposed on the obligor's property entitlement.[95] The power to order security does not extend to confer jurisdiction on the court to deprive a spouse of his or her property by ordering its transfer to the other spouse.[96] In *Milton v Milton*,[97] the New Brunswick Court of Appeal cautioned trial judges against making arbitrary orders securing support payments in the absence of some evidence establishing the amount of security necessary.[98] In determining whether court-ordered periodic spousal support payments should be secured pursuant to section 15.2 of the *Divorce Act*, caselaw has established that the court should consider

1)   whether the obligor has a history of dissipating assets;
2)   whether the obligor is likely to leave the jurisdiction and become an absconding debtor;
3)   whether the obligor has previously refused to discharge a support obligation;
4)   whether the obligor has a poor employment history or has indicated that he or she will leave his or her employment;
5)   the extent to which an order to secure interferes with the obligor's ability to manage his or her business affairs; and
6)   the availability of other substantial resources to enforce the support order.[99]

Section 15.2 of the *Divorce Act* empowers a court to order a spouse to secure a support payment against his interest in the former matrimonial home or the proceeds of sale thereof[100] but the court order does not, in and of itself, constitute a security interest. This stands to reason because the rationale behind the registration systems applicable to land and personal property

---

95   *Nand v Nand*, 2011 ABQB 324. Compare *Breed v Breed*, 2012 NSSC 285.

96   *Switzer v Switzer* (1969), 1 RFL 262 (Alta CA); *McConnell v McConnell* (1975), 11 NBR (2d) 19 (CA); *Slater v Slater*, 2010 NSSC 353. As to the enforcement of a spousal support order by means of a vesting order, see *Bargout v Bargout*, 2013 ONSC 29, citing *Lynch v Segal* (2006), 82 OR (3d) 641 (CA).

97   2008 NBCA 87; see also *Calvy v Calvy*, 2012 NBCA 47.

98   *Bradbury v Bradbury*, 2009 NBQB 78, MacDonald J; see also *HT v SS*, 2010 NBQB 312.

99   *Saleh v Saleh*, [2002] SJ No 426 (QB); see also *Green v Green*, 2013 ONSC 7265.

100 *RB v IB*, [2005] NBJ No 134 (CA).

under the *Land Titles Act*[101] and the *Personal Property Security Act*[102] is that persons claiming a security interest in particular property must give notice of that interest to other potential creditors in order to claim priority over them. A support order, without more, does not provide notice of its contents to persons other than those involved in the particular proceedings. Although there is provision in some provincial statutes, including the *Land Titles Act* and the *Maintenance Enforcement Act*,[103] for support orders to be registered so as to give notice to other potential creditors, in the absence of registration, a support order does not give rise to a secured interest that takes priority over other secured interests. Furthermore, even when registered, the support debtor will not have priority over previously registered secured creditors of the obligor.[104]

In *JM v LDM*,[105] Smith J, of the British Columbia Supreme Court, observed that it is not entirely clear whether a court has jurisdiction under section 15.2 of the *Divorce Act* to make an order securing spousal support against an obligor's estate. She further observed, however, that the judgment of the British Columbia Court of Appeal in *Waters v Conrad*[106] offers some support for the existence of such jurisdiction, while limiting the exercise of jurisdiction to cases wherein the support recipient is in extremely necessitous circumstances and the obligor is relatively affluent with assets available which could conveniently be charged with the payments. For the purpose of providing security for arrears and future payments of spousal support, the court may exercise its discretionary statutory jurisdiction to order the obligor to designate the obligee as the beneficiary under the obligor's life insurance policy. Orders of this nature have begun to be granted on a routine basis, even though no specific mention of life insurance policies is found in the provisions of sections 15.2(1), (2), and (3), and 17(3) of the *Divorce Act*, which relate to the court's jurisdiction to order security for spousal support payments.[107]

---

101 RSA 2000, c L-4.

102 RSA 2000, c P-7.

103 RSA 2000, c M-1.

104 *Minaei v Brae Centre Ltd*, [2004] AJ No 943 (QB).

105 2008 BCSC 1024; see also *Lippolt v Lippolt Estate*, 2015 ABQB 118.

106 2007 BCCA 230.

107 *Murphy v Murphy*, [2002] NSJ No 180 (SC); see also *KAP v KAMP*, 2012 BCSC 811; *Wiewiora v Wiewiora*, 2014 MBQB 218; *Katz v Katz*, 2014 ONCA 606 (child support); *Rebiere v Rebiere*, 2015 ONSC 1324. See also sections 170 and 171 of the *Family Law Act*, SBC 2011, c 25; *Joffres v Joffres*, 2014 BCSC 1778; *RM v NM*, 2014 BCSC 1755.

6) Fixed-Term Spousal Support Orders; Review Orders

Subsection 15.2(3) of the *Divorce Act* specifically empowers the court to make a support order for a definite or indefinite period or until the happening of a specified event, such as the retirement of the payor.

Orders for periodic spousal support for a fixed-term or on a sliding scale have been used as a means of promoting a dependent spouse's return to economic self-sufficiency where that spouse lacked occupational skills at the time of the divorce but could reasonably be expected to acquire or upgrade such skills in the foreseeable future. Such orders are improper where there is no evidence that the dependent spouse can secure employment within a stipulated period.[108] In these circumstances, a court may order the recipient spouse to furnish the payor with periodic sworn statements respecting employment efforts.[109] Time-limited orders have no place where a displaced homemaking spouse lacks marketable skills or has suffered a permanent economic disadvantage from the role assumed during a lengthy marriage.[110] Ongoing parental responsibilities may also render fixed-term support inappropriate.[111] In cases of long-term marriages, under-employment is best dealt with by imputing income, not by time-limited orders.[112]

It is unusual for a court to order time-limited spousal support on the breakdown of a marriage of significant duration.[113] However, the dissolution of a lengthy marriage does not inevitably signify that spousal support should be granted for an indefinite term as distinct from a fixed period of time.[114] Where both spouses have been in full-time employment during a long-term childless marriage, fixed-term spousal support may be appropriate to cushion the financial blow of the marriage breakdown to the lower income spouse.[115]

---

108 *Hudson v Hudson* (1989), 19 RFL (3d) 409 (BCCA); *Rayvals v Rayvals*, [2004] BCJ No 2538 (CA); *Nataros v Nataros* (2000), 4 RFL (5th) 290 (BCCA); *SC v JC*, [2006] NBJ No 186 (CA); *MacLennan v MacLennan*, [2003] NSJ No 15 (CA); *Chadder v Chadder* (1986), 2 RFL (3d) 433 (Ont CA); *Droit de la famille — 683*, [1989] RDF 390 (Que CA).

109 *Epstein v Epstein* (1988), 86 NBR (2d) 326 (QB), Supp reasons (1988), 91 NBR (2d) 98 (QB).

110 *Moge v Moge*, [1992] 3 SCR 813; *Jean v Jean*, [2006] AJ No 1687 (QB); *Tedham v Tedham*, [2005] BCJ No 2186 (CA); *Reisman v Reisman*, 2014 ONCA 109; *Beattie v Beattie*, 2013 SKQB 127 at para 40.

111 *Heimsoth v Heimsoth*, 2009 ABCA 129; *McEachern v McEachern*, 2006 BCCA 508.

112 *Moge v Moge*, [1992] 3 SCR 813; *Ripley v Ripley* (1991), 30 RFL (3d) 41 (BCCA); *Ross v Ross* (1993), 12 OR (3d) 705 (CA).

113 *Riad v Riad* (2002), 317 AR 201 (CA); *Thomas v Thomas and Abel v Abel*, [2005] AJ No 61 (CA); *Ickovich v Tonken*, [2005] AJ No 98 (CA); *Walsh v Walsh*, [2006] NBJ No 441 (QB); *Foran v Foran*, [2007] OJ No 1340 (Div Ct).

114 *Shields v Shields*, 2008 ABCA 213; *Mills v Mills*, 2010 NBCA 20; *Fisher v Fisher*, 2008 ONCA 11; *Rioux v Rioux*, 2009 ONCA 569.

115 *TBM v CJM*, 2009 BCSC 974; see also *Dobson v Dobson*, [2005] SJ No 722 (CA).

In the final analysis, every marriage is different and judges can reach different conclusions as to how to best achieve justice in the particular case. Provided that the trial judge has paid proper regard to the factors relevant to spousal support orders under section 15.2(4) of the *Divorce Act* and to the objectives of spousal support orders set out in section 15.2(6) of the Act, an appellate court should not disturb the trial judge's order for fixed-term support that is premised on findings that the recipient is capable of achieving economic self-sufficiency and has not been disadvantaged by the marriage, which changed from its original "traditional" character well before its breakdown.[116]

As the British Columbia Court of Appeal observed in *Foster v Foster*,[117] shorter-term marriages usually result in shorter-term spousal support orders, although exceptions are admitted based on the facts of the particular case, as, for example, where the dependent spouse assumes primary responsibility for the children or the marriage has dislocated a spouse from his or her country of origin and support networks there.

A useful and succinct summary of relevant Ontario cases dealing with situations in which time-limited spousal support orders have been granted and those in which such orders have been refused may be found in the judgment of Campbell J, of the Ontario Superior Court of Justice, in *Ramdatt v Ramdatt*,[118] who expressed the following opinions:

> Recent cases appear to decide that spousal support is more likely to be time-limited when the marriage is of short duration.
>
> . . .
>
> Cases also appear to suggest that spousal support is more likely to be time-limited where the party receiving the support is able to be self-sufficient.
>
> . . .
>
> Recent case law also seems to suggest that a court is not precluded from awarding indefinite spousal support for marriages of medium duration.
>
> . . .

---

116 *Spencer v Spencer*, [2002] BCJ No 984 (CA); compare *MacLean v MacLean*, [2004] NBJ No 363 (CA).

117 2007 BCCA 83.

118 [2004] OJ No 578 at paras 29, 30, 35, & 36 (Sup Ct). See also *Schmuck v Reynolds-Schmuck*, [1999] OJ No 3104 (Sup Ct), wherein Himel J also provides a succinct review of Ontario cases dealing with the issue of fixed-term spousal support orders. And see *Maber v Maber*, [2007] NBJ No 128 (QB). For a corresponding review of Nova Scotia caselaw by Goodfellow J, see *Bray-Long v Long*, [2000] NSJ No 10 (SC). And see *Rondeau v Kirby*, [2004] NSJ No 143 (CA), wherein Oland JA, delivering the opinion of the appellate panel, stated at para 7, that "[t]he time limitation in a spousal support order is to be decided on the facts of each case and not in accordance with facts which may or may not occur." See also *Palombo v Palombo*, 2011 ONSC 1796; *RB c NA*, [2004] AJ No 2778 (CA).

The unique circumstances of each of the parties in each case must be considered in determining whether spousal support should be time-limited, but courts at all appeal levels have indicated that spousal support should be time-limited only in unusual circumstances.

If a fixed-term spousal support order is granted on the assumption that the recipient spouse will become economically self-sufficient within the prescribed time period, the failure of the recipient to achieve that goal for reasons beyond his or her control can justify variation of the order by means of its renewal or extension.[119]

The special significance of a fixed-term order becomes apparent under subsection 17(10) of the *Divorce Act*, which imposes strict limitations on the discretionary jurisdiction of the court to vary a periodic order after expiry of the term therein defined.[120]

Fixed-term orders must not be confused with support orders that are declared subject to review on the application of either spouse after a specified period of time. The latter order is a mandate to revisit the issue of support after expiry of the designated period to determine again the right to, amount, and duration of a spousal support order. An order that is declared to be reviewable after a fixed period of time may be reconsidered without proof of any material change of circumstances.[121] The advantage of such orders is that, unlike variation applications, they enable a court to modify its order to take account of significant changes of circumstances that were anticipated at the time of the original order but about which there was no certainty. The disadvantage of review orders is that they generate an air of unfinished business and have the potential for unduly increasing litigation costs and suspending the ability of divorced spouses to get on with their lives.[122] Review orders are usually granted when there is a reasonable expectation that there will soon be changes or the payee will or should become partially or fully self-sufficient within the time set for review. They may also be granted to take account of an anticipated reduction in the payor's ability to pay ongoing spousal support

---

119 *Morgan v Morgan*, [2001] BCJ No 1244 (SC); *Fisher v Fisher*, 2008 ONCA 11, [2008] OJ No 38. See also *Palombo v Palombo*, 2011 ONSC 1796.

120 See *Bergeron v Bergeron*, [1999] OJ No 3167 (Sup Ct); and see Section R(2), below in this chapter.

121 *Leskun v Leskun*, [2006] 1 SCR 920; *Morck v Morck*, 2013 BCCA 186; *Chubey v Chubey*, 2011 MBQB 100; *Thurrott v Thurrott*, 2011 NBQB 125; *Beck v Beck*, 2012 NLTD(F) 34; *Hill v Hill*, 2003 NSCA 33 at para 26; *Strecko v Strecko*, 2014 NSCA 66; *Fisher v Fisher*, 2008 ONCA 11; *Heath v Heath*, 2012 SKQB 436. See also *Evans v Spicer*, 2014 NSSC 95.

122 *Tedham v Tedham*, [2005] BCJ No 2186 (CA).

in the amount originally ordered.[123] In *Leskun v Leskun*,[124] the Supreme Court of Canada affirmed the judicial jurisdiction to grant a review order pursuant to section 15.2(3) of the *Divorce Act* that enables the court to revisit the order after the occurrence of a specified event or the passage of a fixed period of time without any need for proof of a material change in circumstances. The Supreme Court of Canada observed that review orders are not to be routinely granted. Although they have a useful role, it is a very limited one. They are appropriate where either of the spouses lacks the ability to cope with the economic disadvantages arising from the marriage or its breakdown at the time of the divorce but his or her economic circumstances are reasonably expected to improve in the future. As Chappel J, of the Ontario Superior Court of Justice, observed in *VK v TS*,[125] "[a] spousal support review provision is only appropriate if the evidence indicates that specified uncertainties about the parties' circumstances will become certain within an identifiable time frame." Common examples of circumstances wherein review orders may be appropriate were identified by the Supreme Court of Canada in *Leskun*, namely, "the need to establish a new residence, start a program of education, train or upgrade skills, or obtain employment."[126] The Supreme Court of Canada asserted that "[i]nsofar as possible, courts should resolve the controversies before them and make an order which is permanent subject only to change under section 17 [of the *Divorce Act*] on proof of a change in circumstances."[127] Having regard to the fact that review orders impose no onus on either party to prove changed circumstances, and the risk that such orders may be perceived as an invitation to the parties to simply re-argue their case, the Supreme Court of Canada stated that any review order should identify the issue for future review and it should be "tightly delimited."[128] Given the examples provided by the Supreme

---

123 *Leskun v Leskun*, [2006] 1 SCR 920; *see also Aspe v Aspe*, 2010 BCCA 508; *Jendruck v Jendruck*, 2014 BCCA 320; *Wiewiora v Wiewiora*, 2014 MBQB 218; *Van Herweghe v Van Herweghe*, [2008] SJ No 582 (QB). See also *MacCarthy v MacCarthy*, 2014 BCSC 2229, citing Rollie Thompson, "To Vary, To Review, Perchance to Change: Changing Spousal Support" (2012) 31 Can Fam LQ 355 at 368. And see *Friesen-Stowe v Stowe*, 2015 ONSC 554, citing Justice David R Aston, "Review Orders: Let's Have Another Look" (2007) 26 Can Fam LQ 253.

124 *Leskun v Leskun*, [2006] 1 SCR 920 at para 7.

125 2011 ONSC 4305 at para 289; *see also Armstrong v Armstrong*, 2012 BCCA 166 (review after seven years deemed inappropriate).

126 [2006] 1 SCR 920 at para 36.

127 *Ibid* at para 39; *see also Litton v Litton*, [2006] BCJ No 2916 (CA); *Aspe v Aspe*, 2010 BCCA 508; *Thurrott v Thurrott*, 2011 NBQB 125; *Fisher v Fisher*, 2008 ONCA 11; *Greenglass v Greenglass*, 2010 ONCA 675.

128 See *RMS v FPCS*, 2011 BCCA 53; *Armstrong v Armstrong*, 2012 BCCA 166; *BJB v MKB*, 2014 NBQB 153; *Fisher v Fisher*, 2008 ONCA 11; *Linn v Frank*, 2014 SKCA 87. See also *Evans v Spicer*, 2014 NSSC 95.

Court of Canada as to the circumstances wherein review orders are appropriate, the role of review orders may not be unduly limited. Indeed, the listed circumstances reflect those that have been previously identified in appellate and trial judgments across Canada. However, the routine use of review orders is clearly impermissible since *Leskun*.[129] In the words of Tuck J, of the New Brunswick Court of Queen's Bench, in *Maber v Maber*,[130] "[t]he Supreme Court of Canada did not by any stretch signal the demise of review orders. Review orders are still with us; they still have a role. The court just emphasized the importance of using them on a principled basis when needed and not just as a matter of course." Review orders are only justified where there is a genuine and material uncertainty with regard to a particular matter at the time when a spousal support order is granted.[131] Furthermore, as Perkins J, of the Ontario Superior Court of Justice, observed in *Bemrose v Fetter*,[132] "[s]pousal support reviews are best conducted against stated goals and expectations." Given the wife's lack of any significant earning capacity in her previously chosen field, Perkins J coupled his spousal support order, which was declared subject to review after 1 May 2007, with a directive that the wife devise a realistic career plan and provide it to her husband within two months.

While a judicial direction that a periodic spousal support order should be reviewed after a designated period of time may be inappropriate on the dissolution of a long traditional marriage,[133] it may be appropriate for the court to direct the recipient of spousal support to keep the payor informed of the recipient's efforts to improve employment skills and find suitable employment.[134]

Trial issues are not to be re-litigated on court ordered reviews because the review is limited in scope to the reasons why it was ordered.[135] Reviewing an order involves a reconsideration of the issues in accordance with the scope of review granted in the previous order.[136] This involves considering whether, given the events since the previous order, the recipient is still entitled to support and, if so, whether the current level is still reasonable.[137] Where a review order clearly imposes a fixed term to give the support recipient an opportunity to find appropriate employment and become self-sufficient, it

---

129   *Long-Beck v Beck*, [2006] NBJ No 398 (QB).

130   [2007] NBJ No 128 at para 246 (QB); see also *RDJ v DJL*, 2013 NBQB 12.

131   *Parker v Vik*, [2006] BCJ No 1794 (SC); *Tsurugida v Romero*, [2006] BCJ No 3067 (SC); *Whelan v Whelan*, [2008] NJ No 269 (UFC); *Austin v Austin*, [2008] OJ No 421 (Sup Ct); *Holmes v Holmes*, [2009] OJ No 94 (Sup Ct); *Mehlsen v Mehlsen*, 2012 SKCA 55.

132   [2005] OJ No 3362 at para 44 (Sup Ct).

133   Compare *Litzenberger v Litzenberger*, 2012 SKQB 122.

134   *Rose v Ferguson*, [2001] BCJ No 2477 (SC); see also *AC v OF*, [2005] QJ No 5259 (CS).

135   *Beck v Beck*, 2012 NLTD(F) 34.

136   *Domirti v Domirti*, 2010 BCCA 472 at para 37; *Chubey v Chubey*, 2011 MBQB 100.

137   *Cleven v Cleven*, 2010 MBQB 279 at para 79; *Chubey v Chubey*, 2011 MBQB 100.

is incumbent on the recipient at the review hearing to establish that she was unable to become self-sufficient.[138] Absent such evidence, it is not open to a chambers judge at the review hearing to order ongoing spousal support on the basis of the respective incomes of the spouses, as found or imputed.[139]

The fact that the order is reviewable after a fixed period of time does not preclude an earlier application to vary the order pursuant to subsections 17(1)(a) and 17(4.1) of the *Divorce Act* if a material change does occur in the condition, means, needs, or other circumstances of either former spouse after the granting of the reviewable order.[140] Some years before the *Leskun* judgment, the Ontario Court of Appeal asserted that review orders should not be granted routinely, while acknowledging that a failure to make reasonable efforts to obtain full-time employment can constitute a material change of circumstances that will justify an application to vary an existing order.[141]

The judgment of the Supreme Court of Canada in *Leskun v Leskun*,[142] coupled with the *Spousal Support Advisory Guidelines*, may result in more frequent orders for fixed-term spousal support. Applying the duration formula under the *Without Child Support Formula* under the Guidelines, courts may be more inclined to order fixed-term support than has been their practice in the past.[143]

D. TERMS, CONDITIONS, AND RESTRICTIONS

Pursuant to section 15.2(3) of the *Divorce Act*, a court may order spousal support for a definite or indefinite period or until a specified event occurs, and the court may impose terms, conditions, and restrictions on its order.[144]

---

138 *Litzenberger v Litzenberger*, 2012 SKQB 122.

139 *Westergard v Buttress*, 2012 BCCA 38; *Williams v Williams*, 2010 SKCA 52.

140 *Lidstone v Lidstone* (1993), 46 RFL (3d) 203 (NSCA); *Bemrose v Fetter*, [2007] OJ No 3488 (CA); see also *Gossen v Gossen*, [2003] NSJ No 113 (SC); *Bergeron v Bergeron*, [1999] OJ No 3167 (Sup Ct).

141 *Andrews v Andrews* (1999), 45 OR (3d) 577 (CA); *Choquette v Choquette* (1998), 39 RFL (4th) 384 (Ont CA); see also *Greenglass v Greenglass*, 2010 ONCA 675.

142 [2006] 1 SCR 920; see also Section C(6), above in this chapter.

143 See, for example, *Bourque v Bourque*, 2008 NBQB 398; *Fisher v Fisher*, 2008 ONCA 11; *Gammon v Gammon*, [2008] OJ No 4252 (Sup Ct).

144 See, generally, *Re Muslake and Muslake* (1987), 58 OR (2d) 615 (UFC); see also *Torres v Marin*, [2007] YJ No 94 (SC) (obligor to pay periodic spousal support while earning employment income); *Lockyer v Lockyer*, [2000] OJ No 2939 (Sup Ct) (order for periodic spousal support declared subject to conditions whereby amount payable would be unaffected by either spouse earning an annual income below a specified amount). As to child support orders, see *Divorce Act*, RSC 1985 (2d Supp), c 3, s 15.1(4), as amended by SC 1997, c 1.

In appropriate circumstances, periodic spousal support may be ordered for the lifetime of the payee and made binding on the obligor's estate.[145] In the absence of any specific direction that the order shall survive the death of the payor, a spousal order terminates on the death of either spouse.[146]

E. RELEVANT FACTORS

Subsection 15.2(4) of the *Divorce Act* defines the "factors" that a court must consider in determining the right to, amount, and duration of spousal support. It provides that the court shall take into consideration the condition, needs, means, and other circumstances of each spouse, including (a) the length of time the spouses cohabited; (b) the functions performed by each spouse during cohabitation; and (c) any order, agreement, or arrangement relating to support of either spouse. These statutory criteria confer a virtually unfettered discretion on the court to have regard to any facts that the trial judge considers relevant, with the exception of matrimonial misconduct.[147]

Spousal support cases are fact-driven because terms such as "means" and "needs" in subsection 15.2(4) of the *Divorce Act* and "economic self-sufficiency" in subsection 15.2(6) of the *Divorce Act* have no absolute meaning. They must be interpreted and applied having regard to the circumstances of the particular spouses.[148]

---

145 See *Waters v Conrod*, 2007 BCCA 1024. See also Section C(5), above in this chapter; *Katz v Katz* (1983), 33 RFL (2d) 412 (Man CA), additional reasons (1983), 25 Man R (2d) 57 (CA); *Milton v Milton*, 2008 NBCA 87; *Celeste v Celeste*, 2013 NBQB 41; *Connelly v Connelly* (1974), 16 RFL 171 (NSCA); *Linton v Linton* (1990), 30 RFL (3d) 1 (Ont CA); *Katz v Katz*, 2014 ONCA 606 (child support); *Droit de la famille — 707*, [1989] RDF 614 (Que CA); compare *Hillhouse v Hillhouse* (1992), 43 RFL (3d) 266 (BCCA); *Donald v Donald* (1991), 33 RFL (3d) 196 at 217 (NSCA); and see *contra*: *Carmichael v Carmichael* (1992), 43 RFL (3d) 145 (NSCA); see also *Lippolt v Lippolt Estate*, 2015 ABQB 118; *Ross v Ross* (1994), 7 RFL (4th) 146 (BCCA); *Sinclair v McAuley*, 2012 MBCA 86; *Pick v Pick* (1987), 11 RFL (3d) 14 (Sask QB), var'd (1990), 25 RFL (3d) 331 (Sask CA).

146 *Despot v Despot Estate* (1992), 42 RFL (3d) 218 (BCSC); *Terry v Terry Estate* (1994), 1 BCLR (3d) 299 (SC) (specific direction found in this case); *Finnie v Rae* (1977), 16 OR (2d) 54 (HCJ); *Katz v Katz*, 2014 ONCA 606; compare *Family Law Act*, SBC 2011, c 25, sections 170–171; *Joffres v Joffres*, 2014 BCSC 1778; *Family Law Act*, RSO 1990, c F.3, s 34(4); see *contra*: *Chalmers Estate v Chalmers* (1990), 29 RFL (3d) 54 at 58–59 (Alta QB) (child support); see also *Droit de la famille — 324*, [1987] RJQ 149 (Que CS).

147 See *Racco v Racco*, 2014 ONCA 330.

148 *Beattie v Beattie*, 2013 SKQB 127 at para 41.

1) Definition of "Condition" of the Spouses

The "condition" of the spouses has been defined to include their age, health, needs, obligations, dependants, and the station in life of the parties.[149] Courts must look to the economic consequences of the marriage and its breakdown on a sick or disabled spouse and not simply to whether the illness or disability is causally connected to the marriage.[150] Consequently, previous judicial decisions that denied spousal support on the basis that the applicant's illness or disability had no causal connection to the marriage must be re-examined in light of the judgments of the Supreme Court of Canada in *Moge v Moge*[151] and *Bracklow v Bracklow*.[152] Illness does not equate to never-ending support entitlement.[153] As McLachlin J, as she then was, observed in the latter case,

> Divorce ends the marriage. Yet in some circumstances the law may require that the healthy party continue to support a disabled party, absent contractual or compensatory entitlement. Justice and considerations of fairness may demand no less.[154]

It does not follow that divorcing or divorced sick or disabled persons can always look to their healthy spouses or former spouses for support, without limitation as to the amount or duration of such support. As McLachlin J, as she then was, further observed in *Bracklow v Bracklow*,

> 53 The quantum awarded, in the sense of both amount and duration, will vary with the circumstances and the practical and policy considerations affecting particular cases. Limited means of the supporting spouse may dictate a reduction. So may obligations arising from new relationships in so far as they have an impact on means. Factors within the marriage itself may affect the quantum of a non-compensatory support obligation. For example,

---

149 *Moge v Moge*, [1992] 3 SCR 813; *Robichaud v Robichaud* (1988), 17 RFL (3d) 285 (BCCA); *Thomas v Thomas and Abel v Abel*, [2004] AJ No 30 (QB); *Bennett v Bennett*, [2005] AJ No 1824 (QB); *Robichaud v Robichaud* (1992), 124 NBR (2d) 332 (QB).

150 *Moge v Moge*, [1992] 3 SCR 813; *Hillhouse v Hillhouse* (1992), 43 RFL (3d) 266 (BCCA); *McKean v McKean* (1992), 38 RFL (3d) 172 (Man CA); *Tyler v Tyler*, 2011 NLTD(F) 20; *Schaldach v Schaldach*, 2015 ONSC 1574; *Currie v Currie* (1991), 32 RFL (3d) 67 (PEISCAD); *Hrenyk v Berden*, 2011 SKQB 305.

151 *Ibid.*

152 [1999] 1 SCR 420 at para 48. See also *Bracklow v Bracklow*, [1999] BCJ No 3028 (SC) (order for fixed-term support after matter remitted to trial court by Supreme Court of Canada).

153 *Hickey v Princ*, 2014 ONSC 5272.

154 *Bracklow v Bracklow*, [1999] 1 SCR 420 at para 48 (SCC). And see *Shen v Tong*, 2013 BCCA 519; *Aubé v Aubé*, 2013 NBQB 128; *Whitten v Whitten*, 2014 NLTD(F) 6.

it may be difficult to make a case for a full obligation and expectation of mutual support in a very short marriage. (Section 15.2(4)(*a*) of the *Divorce Act* requires the court to consider the length of time the parties cohabited.) Finally, subject to judicial discretion, the parties by contract or conduct may enhance, diminish or negate the obligation of mutual support. To repeat, it is not the act of saying "I do", but the marital relationship between the parties that may generate the obligation of non-compensatory support pursuant to the Act. It follows that diverse aspects of that marital relationship may be relevant to the quantum of such support. As stated in *Moge*, "[a]t the end of the day . . . , courts have an overriding discretion and the exercise of such discretion will depend on the particular facts of each case, having regard to the factors and objectives designated in the Act" (p. 866).

54 Fixing on one factor to the exclusion of others leads Mrs. Bracklow . . . to the false premise that if need is the basis of the <u>entitlement</u> to the support award, then the <u>quantum</u> of the award must meet the total amount of the need. It does not follow from the fact that need serves as the predicate for support that the quantum of the support must always equal the amount of the need. Nothing in either the *Family Relations Act* or the *Divorce Act* forecloses an order for support of a <u>portion</u> of the claimant's need, whether viewed in terms of periodic amount or duration. Need is but one factor to be considered. This is consistent with the modern recognition, captured by the statutes, of the variety of marital relationships in modern society. A spouse who becomes disabled toward the end of a very short marriage may well be entitled to support by virtue of her need, but it may be unfair, under the circumstances, to order the full payment of that need by the supporting spouse for the indefinite future.[155]

2) Definition of "Means"; Effect of Substantial Property Division

A substantial matrimonial property division with an income-generating potential will almost invariably affect a spousal support analysis. As a matter of law, therefore, the calculation of the division of assets and resulting equalization payment must always precede any support analysis.[156] While in some cases a division of property on marriage breakdown may address all or most of the objectives of spousal support defined in section 15.2(6) of the *Divorce Act* and thereby eliminate or reduce the need for a spousal support award,

---

155   *Ibid* at paras 53–54 (emphasis in original); see also *Rakhra v Rakhra*, 2012 NWTSC 33; *Rooke v Gallant*, 2013 ONSC 1150.

156   *Carr v Anketell*, 2015 NBQB 51; *Greenglass v Greenglass*, 2010 ONCA 675; *Jungwirth v Jungwirth*, 2012 SKQB 417.

that is not necessarily the case, particularly where the conceptual basis for support is predominantly compensatory. The impact of a division of property on a spouse's right to support is to be determined by the extent to which the property received has adequately compensated that spouse for the economic consequences of the marriage and its breakdown, including any claims for compensatory and non-compensatory support.[157] In high-end cases, a critical assessment of the means made available from a matrimonial property settlement must be undertaken in the context of the factors and objectives set out in subsections 15.2(4) and (6) of the *Divorce Act* to determine whether spousal support should be ordered and, if so, in what amount. A very substantial matrimonial property entitlement on the breakdown of marriage does not imply that a spousal support order is inappropriate.[158] In determining the impact of a matrimonial property entitlement on an application for spousal support, a distinction is to be drawn between income-producing assets derived from the settlement and assets such as a home and an automobile, which are not income-producing. The income-earning capacity of a matrimonial property settlement should be taken into account in determining the "means" factor under subsection 15.2(4) of the *Divorce Act*, and the pre-separation lifestyle of the spouses is pertinent to the "needs" factor under that subsection.[159] As was observed in *Moge v Moge*,[160] the longer a marriage endures, the greater the presumptive claim to equal standards of living on its dissolution.[161] But in the absence of an overriding compensatory factor, an onus remains on the applicant to prove need by establishing a shortfall between the amount required to cover a reasonable budget based on the pre-separation standard of living and the means available to the applicant from employment income and investment income from the matrimonial property settlement.[162]

In *Leskun v Leskun*,[163] the Supreme Court of Canada considered a divorced husband's contention that the chambers judge and the British Columbia Court of Appeal had both erred by having regard to his capital assets for the purpose of determining his obligation to pay ongoing periodic spousal support. The Court observed that section 15.2(4) of the *Divorce Act* empowers

---

157 *Bodine-Shah v Shah*, 2014 BCCA 191; see also *Hathaway v Hathaway*, 2014 BCCA 310; *Richards v Richards*, 2014 NSSC 270.

158 *Chutter v Chutter*, 2008 BCCA 507; *DLC v FMC*, 2011 BCCA 444; *Ouellette v Ouellette*, 2012 BCCA 145; *Parent v Morrissette*, 2013 NBQB 408; *Berta v Berta*, 2014 ONSC 3919; *Bergquist v Bergquist*, 2014 SKCA 20.

159 See *Richards v Richards*, 2014 NSSC 270.

160 [1992] 3 SCR 813.

161 See *McKenzie v McKenzie*, 2014 BCCA 381; compare *Lee v Lee*, 2014 BCCA 383. For criticism of these decisions, see Philip Epstein, Cases for the week of February 23, 2015.

162 *Spiers v Spiers*, [2003] AJ No 1223 (QB).

163 [2006] 1 SCR 920.

the court to have regard to the "means" of each spouse. On the authority of *Strang v Strang*,[164] which defines the term "means" to include all pecuniary resources,[165] capital assets,[166] income from employment or earning capacity,[167] and any other source from which a person received gains or benefits are received, together with, in certain circumstances, money that a person does not have in possession but that is available to such person, no error was found in the chambers judge's decision to have regard to the capital assets of the divorced husband in determining his capacity to pay ongoing periodic spousal support. Given that the doctrine of "double dipping" was inapplicable to the divorced husband's capital acquired after the dissolution of the marriage,[168] the Supreme Court of Canada observed that the failure of a court to take into account after-acquired capital assets in determining the right to and amount of spousal support can create the potential for injustice where a spouse attempts to shield his or her true worth to avoid paying spousal support, even though his or her financial position is far superior to that of the other spouse. In *Leskun*, wherein the ex-husband invested earned income in a bagel business, he was found by the chambers judge to have demonstrated a significant earning capacity[169] and to own assets worth approximately $1 million, and he enjoyed a lifestyle with his new wife that was far superior to that of his divorced wife. The Supreme Court of Canada agreed with the British Columbia Court of Appeal that the chambers judge was entitled to have regard to the husband's capital assets in determining his capacity to pay continued spousal support. As for the divorced husband's submission that the chambers judge had overestimated the value of his capital assets, the Supreme Court of Canada affirmed the right of the chambers judge to draw an adverse inference against the divorced husband as a result of his failure to make full and complete financial disclosure. In the words of Binnie J of the Supreme Court of Canada, "[i]f problems of calculation exist the appellant is

---

164   [1992] 2 SCR 112 at 119; see also *Milinusic v Milinusic*, 2015 ABQB 64; *Richards v Richards*, 2012 NSCA 7; *Thiyagarajah v Paramsothy*, 2011 ONSC 7368; *Farnsworth v Chang*, 2014 ONSC 1871; *Droit de la famille — 08316*, [2008] JQ no 872 (CA). As to imputing income on the basis of the obligor's failure to provide full and accurate disclosure of capital assets, see *Lahanky v Lahanky*, 2011 NBQB 220.

165   *Papasodaro v Papasodaro*, 2014 ONSC 30 (home insurance proceeds).

166   See *Scott v Scott*, 2011 NBCA 7; *Lahanky v Lahanky*, 2011 NBQB 220; *Colivas v Colivas*, 2013 ONSC 168 (interim support).

167   *Marquez v Zapiola*, 2013 BCCA 433; *Collingridge v Collingridge*, 2013 SKQB 305.

168   See text at Section P, below in this chapter.

169   For insight into the differing statutory and regulatory foundations for judicially imputing income for the purposes of spousal support and child support respectively, see *Jean v Jean*, 2006 ABQB 938, Greckol J.

largely the author of his own difficulties" and the court "would not interfere on that basis."[170]

Although the term "means" in sections 15.2(4) and 17(4.1) of the *Divorce Act* clearly encompasses capital assets, periodic spousal support is ordinarily payable out of the income of the obligor. This includes investment income from capital assets.[171] Where a spouse chooses to live off his or her capital rather than pursue available employment, income may be imputed to that spouse based on his or her unrealized earning capacity as well as on the basis of the actual or potential income yield of the capital assets.[172] If capital assets have already been divided pursuant to the provincial matrimonial property regime, the principle of "double dipping" or "double recovery" may preclude an order for spousal support or reduce the amount that would otherwise have been ordered.[173] "Means" under section 17(4.1) of the *Divorce Act* takes account of capital assets but the same standards apply to each former spouse in the overall evaluation of their financial circumstances.[174] A financially dependent wife who is incapable of achieving economic self-sufficiency will not be expected to erode her capital assets to support herself while her former spouse continues to build a retirement nest egg and preserve his asset base.[175] Conversely, a husband with insufficient income to pay spousal support is not obliged to erode his capital assets for the purpose of paying spousal support where the overall means of both spouses are relatively comparable.[176] In the final analysis, whether one or both spouses are required to use their capital for the purposes of supporting themselves or their (former) spouse will depend on the facts of the particular case. As is pointed out in *Moge v Moge*,[177] the overarching principle of the *Divorce Act* is to provide an equitable distribution of the economic consequences of the marriage and its breakdown. This may require either spouse to draw on their capital to support themselves or their former partner.[178]

---

170 *Leskun v Leskun*, [2006] 1 SCR 920 at para 34.

171 *Lane v Lane*, 2012 ABCA 2.

172 *Bartole v Parker*, [2006] SJ No 349 (QB) (application to vary child support order having regard to father's cessation of employment after winning a lottery). See also *Scott v Scott*, [2007] BCJ No 1863 (SC); *Thurrott v Thurrott*, 2011 NBQB 125; *Gainer v Gainer*, [2006] OJ No 1631 (Sup Ct).

173 *Puiu v Puiu*, 2011 BCCA 480. And see Section P, below in this chapter.

174 *Campese v Campese*, [2006] BCJ No 1412 (SC).

175 *Kranenburg v Kranenburg*, [1999] BCJ No 574 (CA); *Campese v Campese*, [2006] BCJ No 1412 (SC); *Petz v McNulty-Petz*, [2001] OJ No 1735 (Sup Ct). See also *TT v JMH*, 2014 BCSC 451.

176 *Wagstaff v Wagstaff*, [2002] NSJ No 527 (SC).

177 [1992] 3 SCR 813.

178 *Oliver v Oliver*, 2011 BCSC 1126.

For spousal support purposes, the meaning of income has generally been that used under section 16 of the *Federal Child Support Guidelines*, which is "the sources of income set out under the heading of 'Total Income' in the T1 General form issued by the Canada Revenue Agency."[179]

Income may be imputed to either spouse in determining the issue of spousal support, provided that a rational and solid evidentiary foundation has been laid. In developing a methodology for imputing income in spousal support cases, the courts have turned to an analysis based on the provisions of the *Federal Child Support Guidelines*.[180] It has been judicially asserted that while a spousal support obligation may be less compelling than a child support obligation, the difference is reflected at the entitlement and quantum stage of the analysis, not at the fact-finding level of determining an obligor's income.[181] In *Coady v Coady*,[182] however, Johnston J stated that there appears to be stronger policy reasons to impute income for child support rather than spousal support and the trend seems to be that courts are less prepared to attribute "pre-tax income" from an obligor's corporation as income for spousal support, compared to the readiness of courts to do so in cases of child support. If a spouse is intentionally unemployed or underemployed, support can be ordered based on his or her earning capacity.[183] A spouse is expected to take reasonable steps to obtain employment commensurate with such factors as his or her age, health, education, skills, and work history, and the availability of job opportunities.[184] As in the context of child support,[185] so too in the context of spousal support, a parent cannot justify under-employment by wanting to stay home with children who have no special needs.[186] In imputing income to a spouse, the court may take judicial notice of the official government web-

---

179   *Megson v Megson*, 2014 BCSC 2467; *Parent v Morrissette*, 2013 NBQB 408; *CLY v DGY*, 2013 ONSC 6550 at para 16.

180   *Richards v Richards*, 2013 ABQB 484; *Marquez v Zapiola*, 2013 BCCA 433; *McKenzie v McKenzie*, 2014 BCCA 381; *Carr v Anketell*, 2015 NBQB 51; *Shears v Shears*, 2014 NLTD(F) 20; *Richards v Richards*, 2012 NSCA 7; *Rebiere v Rebiere*, 2015 ONSC 1324; *Linn v Frank*, 2014 SKCA 87.

181   *Aelbers v Aelbers*, 2010 BCSC 1574. Compare *Thompson v Thompson*, 2013 ONSC 5500 at para 85.

182   2014 MBQB 182 at paras 74–75, citing *Martin v Orris*, 2009 MBQB 290. See also *Jean v Jean*, 2006 ABQB 938 at paras 108–9; *Linke v Linke*, 2014 ABQB 668, citing *Gordon v Gordon*, 2014 ABQB 596.

183   *Carr v Anketell*, 2015 NBQB 51; *Yeung v Silva*, 2014 BCSC 2436; *Ferguson v Ferguson*, 2014 NSSC 350; *Sobiegraj v Sobiegraj*, 2014 ONSC 2030.

184   *TN v JCN*, 2015 BCSC 439; *Carr v Anketell*, 2015 NBQB 51;*Younger v Younger*, [2007] OJ No 4659 at para 46 (Sup Ct); *Savonarota v Savonarota*, 2011 ONSC 4842; see also *Jordan v Jordan*, 2011 BCCA 518.

185   See *Llewellyn v Llewellyn*, 2002 BCCA 182 at para 31.

186   *RMS v FPCS*, 2011 BCCA 53; *MWB v ARB*, 2011 BCSC 1663.

site concerning employment insurance, which states that regular benefits are 55 percent of insurable income up to a maximum of $45,900 per annum.[187] To ensure consistency of treatment where a party's affairs are arranged to pay less tax on income, "grossing up" income in accordance with the *Child Support Guidelines* is commonly applied to spousal support scenarios.[188] For example, workers compensation benefits received by the support obligor may be grossed-up to take account of their tax-free status.[189] The pre-tax income of a private company may be attributed to a spousal support obligor.[190] As Forgeron J, of the Nova Scotia Supreme Court, points out in *Jenkins v Jenkins,*

> [S]everal themes have emerged from the case law as it relates to corporate holdings . . . . First, courts will access the pre-tax corporate income for support purposes . . . . Second, the onus of proof falls upon the director, officer, or shareholder to show that the pre-tax corporate income is not available for support purposes . . . . Third, minority share holders are not necessarily exempt from having pre-tax corporate income imputed to them for support purposes . . . . Fourth, personal benefits paid on behalf of a shareholder, officer, or director by a corporation will be considered in the calculation of income, often by adding that amount back into the pre-tax corporate income that thus becomes available as income for support purposes . . . . Fifth, negative inferences are correctly drawn when there is a lack of disclosure and a lack of relevant evidence before the court.[191]

The attribution of income to either spouse for expenses paid by his or her private company is supported by cases which indicate that these amounts should be grossed-up for the purposes of calculating spousal support.[192] Where a spouse's income fluctuates markedly from year to year, the court may consider more than the most recent annual income in accordance with section 17 of the *Federal Child Support Guidelines.*[193]

Veterans disability pension benefits are intended to replace income on an on-going basis and they should be included as income for spousal support

---

187   *Pinto v Pinto*, 2011 ONSC 7403.

188   *Knowles v Lindstrom*, 2015 ONSC 1408.

189   *Carr v Anketell*, 2015 NBQB 51.

190   *Ouellette v Ouellette*, 2012 BCCA 145; *Shears v Shears*, 2014 NLTD(F) 20; *Mayer v Mayer* 2013 ONSC 7099; *Hrenyk v Berden*, 2011 SKQB 305. See also *Milinusic v Milinusic*, 2015 ABQB 64.

191   2012 NSSC 117 at paras 21–25.

192   *Ragan v Ragan*, 2011 BCSC 766; *Richards v Richards*, 2012 NSCA 7; *Mariani v Mariani*, 2012 ONSC 4580.

193   *Oliver v Oliver*, 2011 BCSC 1126.

purposes. Because disability pension benefits are tax-free, it is not unusual to have them grossed up.[194]

3) Needs and Capacity to Pay; Economic Self-Sufficiency; Relevance of Cohabitational Standard of Living

a) General

Subsection 15.2(4) of the *Divorce Act* requires the court to have regard to the "needs" of each spouse. Needs is a flexible concept and is not confined to a subsistence lifestyle.[195] The "needs" of a spouse are relative and may be determined, at least in part, by reference to the lifestyle enjoyed by both spouses during long-term matrimonial cohabitation.[196] In determining entitlement to spousal support, the assessment of needs can in some circumstances look beyond basic financial obligations to consider the disproportionate effect of the marriage breakdown on the spouses' respective standard of living. As Frankel JA, of the British Columbia Court of Appeal, observed in *Kirton v Mattie*,[197] "[n]on-compensatory support can recognize the interdependency that may arise in marriages where there is a significant income disparity between the spouses. Non-compensatory support allows for transitional assistance to the lower-income earning spouse from the shared financial resources of the marriage to the financial realities of a single income." And in the words of Lang JA, of the Ontario Court of Appeal in *Fisher v Fisher*:

> 52   Section 15.2(6)(d) of the Divorce Act promotes the objective of economic self-sufficiency only if it is "practicable" to do so and where the objective can be realized "within a reasonable period of time".[198]
>
> 53   Self-sufficiency, with its connotation of economic independence, is a relative concept. It is not achieved simply because a former spouse can meet basic expenses on a particular amount of income; rather, self-sufficiency relates to the ability to support a reasonable standard of living. It is to be assessed in relation to the economic partnership the parties enjoyed and could sustain during cohabitation, and that they can reasonably an-

---

194 *Ste-Marie v Ste-Marie*, 2013 NBQB 375.

195 *Riad v Riad*, 2002 ABCA 254; *Yorke v Yorke*, 2010 NBQB 230.

196 *Moge v Moge*, [1992] 3 SCR 813; *Heimsoth v Heimsoth*, 2009 ABCA 129; *Chutter v Chutter*, 2008 BCCA 507; *Marquez v Zapiola*, 2013 BCCA 433; *Rémillard v Rémillard*, 2014 MBCA 101; *Boudreau v Brun*, [2005] NBJ No501 (CA); *Brown v Brown*, 2013 NBQB 369; *O v C*, [2004] NJ No 19 (SC); *Pettigrew v Pettigrew*, [2006] NSJ No 321 (CA); *Evans v Spicer*, 2014 NSSC 95; *Fisher v Fisher*, 2008 ONCA 11.

197 2014 BCCA 513 at para 49.

198 See also *Tedham v Tedham*, 2005 BCCA 502 at para 33; *Reisman v Reisman*, 2014 ONCA 109.

ticipate after separation. See *Linton v. Linton* (1990), 1 O.R. (3d) 1 (C.A.) at 27-28. Thus, a determination of self-sufficiency requires consideration of the parties' present and potential incomes, their standard of living during marriage, the efficacy of any suggested steps to increase a party's means, the parties' likely post-separation circumstances (including the impact of equalization of their property), the duration of their cohabitation and any other relevant factors.

54 Self-sufficiency is often more attainable in short-term marriages, particularly ones without children, where the lower-income spouse has not become entrenched in a particular lifestyle, or compromised career aspirations. In such circumstances, the lower-income spouse is expected either to have the tools to become financially independent or to adjust his or her standard of living.

55 In contrast, in most long-term marriages, particularly in traditional long-term ones, the parties' merger of economic lifestyles creates a joint standard of living that the lower-income spouse cannot hope to replicate, but upon which he or she has become dependent. In such circumstances, the spousal support analysis typically will not give priority to self-sufficiency because it is an objective that simply cannot be attained. See *Linton* at 27.[199]

One proxy for the marital standard of living is the combined incomes of the spouses at the time of separation.[200] The needs of a spouse may also be relative to the standard of living of the other spouse after their separation. Having regard to financial practicalities, it may not be possible for a spousal support order to provide the standard of living experienced during matrimonial cohabitation, but courts are unwilling to allow one party to a long marriage to maintain a substantially higher standard of living than the other party on the dissolution of their marriage. On the breakdown of a long marriage, there should not be a large discrepancy in the standard of living enjoyed by each spouse. An indefinite long-term order for spousal support may, therefore, be required to ensure that the benefits and detriments that were shared during the marriage continue to be shared on its dissolution. However, such an order does not negate the obligation of the recipient spouse to strive for some degree of self-support, where this is reasonable and practicable under the circumstances of the particular case. Where a support applicant needs to be encouraged to become self-sufficient, a step-down order

---

199 2008 ONCA 11 at para 53; see also *Carr v Anketell*, 2015 NBQB 51; *Knowles v Lindstrom*, 2015 ONSC 1408.

200 *Carr v Anketell*, 2015 NBQB 51 at para 29, Walsh J, citing *Scott v Scott*, 2011 NBCA 7.

may be appropriate.[201] In order to promote justice for both spouses and to avoid future litigation, the court may devise a formula whereby the amount of spousal support originally ordered shall be reduced by a designated amount when the recipient spouse's annual income exceeds a specified total. In order to retain an incentive for the support recipient spouse, the reduction may not be a dollar-for-dollar reduction.[202] The "needs" and entitlement of the obligor to a reasonable standard of living are also to be considered.[203] If the obligor is insolvent, in a precarious financial position, or in a worse financial position than the claimant, support may be modest or may be denied.[204]

b) Post-Separation Need

In *Fyfe v Jouppien*,[205] Chappel J, of the Ontario Superior Court of Justice, undertakes a useful review of Ontario caselaw dealing with the issue of whether non-compensatory spousal support may be ordered pursuant to section 15.2 of the *Divorce Act* under circumstances where the needs of the applicant arose several years after the separation. At paragraph 54 of her judgment, Chappel J formulates the following guiding principles for dealing with such cases:

a.   The starting point for analyzing non-compensatory support claims based on need arising post separation is whether there is evidence during the period prior to separation to rebut the presumption of mutuality and interdependence arising from the marriage relationship itself. Where there is no evidence to rebut this presumption, it may be reasonable to expect that the parties will support each other for a reasonable period of time in the event of need that does not exist at the time of separation but that arises at a later date.

b.   The existence of mutuality and interdependence prior to separation is not, however, a determinative factor favouring a spousal support obligation in the event of need arising post separation. As the Supreme Court of Canada stated in *Moge* and *Bracklow*, all of the objectives underlying a spousal support order must be considered, including the objective of promoting self sufficiency within a reasonable period of

---

201   *Reisman v Reisman*, 2012 ONSC 3148.

202   *Thomas v Thomas* and *Abel v Abel*, [2004] AJ No 30 (QB).

203   *Boyd v Boyd* (1992), 41 RFL (3d) 182 (BCCA); *Giorno v Giorno* (1992), 39 RFL (3d) 345 (NS-SCAD); *Hawkins v Hawkins* (1992), 40 RFL (3d) 456 (Ont CA); *Elliot v Elliot* (1993), 48 RFL (3d) 237 (Ont CA).

204   *Graham v Graham* (1988), 17 RFL (3d) 380 (BCSC); *Powers v Powers* (1990), 92 NSR (2d) 337 (SC); *Botchett v Botchett* (1990), 94 NSR (2d) 339 (SC).

205   2011 ONSC 5462; see also *Firth v Firth*, 2012 BCSC 857; *Jubinville v Jubinville*, 2013 BCSC 2262.

time. The question that must be determined is whether, taking into account all of the circumstances of the particular case, it is reasonable on an objective analysis to expect the parties to continue to be "safety nets" for each other in the event of post separation need, and if so, for how long.

c. The passage of time may be an important consideration, particularly where the parties both take steps post separation to unravel their interdependencies and to effect a clean break from each other. In these circumstances, the mutual obligation of support arising from the marriage itself may wane with the passage of time, and the objective of promoting self sufficiency within a reasonable time frame may come more to the forefront of the analysis. This would include an expectation that former spouses implement plans for their own care in the event of possible disability in the future.

d. On the other hand, the passage of time may be given less weight in the analysis of entitlement if, despite the passage of a number of years, the parties have not effected a clean break, and their relationship continues to be characterized by mutuality and interdependence. In such circumstances, an objective analysis of the situation may lead to the conclusion that the expectation of mutual support and dependency arising from the marriage relationship has continued.

e. Where the marriage was short lived, the objective of promoting self sufficiency may be given greater weight when considering the expectations of the parties.

f. Situations where a spouse has been awarded time limited compensatory support, and then suffers an unexpected disability which creates need on their part may need to be approached with a somewhat unique lens. In such cases, the passage of time from the date of separation may not be as compelling a consideration as in cases where no entitlement to support exists at the time of separation. Time limited compensatory awards are intended in part to provide the recipient with an opportunity to regroup and recover from the economic consequences of the marriage. If an intervening disability impedes their ability to do so, the objectives of the award are undermined, and the claimant spouse may remain disadvantaged as a result of the marriage. In these circumstances, the objectives set out in section 15.2(6) (a) and (b) of the *Divorce* Act may weigh more heavily than the objective of promoting self sufficiency.

Having regard to the interdependent financial relationship that had existed between the spouses during the course of their long marriage, Chappel J found that the husband had established a *prima facie* entitlement to interim spousal support seven years after their separation in 2004 in consequence of his disability arising from terminal T cell lymphoma, which was diagnosed three years after the separation. However, his wife had no capacity to pay because of significant debts incurred as a result of the responsibilities that she assumed to meet the children's needs following the separation. Accordingly, the application for interim spousal support was dismissed. Chappel J noted that once a *prima facie* entitlement is established, the *Spousal Support Advisory Guidelines* provide an ideal tool to assist judges on interim (temporary) support motions. However, the authors of the Guidelines recognize an exception to their application in circumstances where an obligor faces compelling financial circumstances that impact on the ability to pay interim spousal support.

4) Definition of "Other Circumstances"

It is impossible to catalogue all the "other circumstances" of the parties that might be deemed relevant under subsection 15.2(4) of the *Divorce Act*, although it has been stated that the circumstances must be "so nearly touching the matter in issue as to be such that a judicial mind ought to regard it as a proper thing to be taken into consideration."[206] "Other circumstances" have been said to include "a deficiency in language skills, the state of the employment market, a lack of professional qualifications, an innate shortage of skills, a shortfall of ambition and motivation, . . . mismanagement of funds," and the "likelihood of remarriage, cessation of employment, possibility of inheritance and many other unforeseen events."[207]

The short duration of the marriage is a "circumstance" that the courts have considered in denying spousal support, unless a significant sacrifice was made for the sake of the marriage.[208]

5) Post-Separation Income Increase[209]

In quantifying spousal support, post-separation increases in the obligor's income have to be analyzed in order to determine whether they are related to the marriage. There are a number of criteria that the court looks at in order

---

206   *Rogers v Rogers* (1962), 3 FLR 398 at 402 (NSWSC).

207   *Brockie v Brockie* (1987), 5 RFL (3d) 440 (Man QB), aff'd (1987), 8 RFL (3d) 302 (Man CA).

208   *South v South* (1992), 40 RFL (3d) 179 (Man CA); *Fleming v Fleming*, [2001] OJ No 1117 (Div Ct).

209   For a valuable summary of relevant principles, see *Thompson v Thompson*, 2013 ONSC 5500 at paras 100–3. As to post-separation need triggering a right to spousal support, see *Fyfe v Jouppien*, 2011 ONSC 5462, in Section E(3)(b), above in this chapter.

to decide whether to look at whether the obligor's post-separation income increases are to be used in determining spousal support. These criteria include the following:

1) Were the payor's skills and credentials from which he earns the increased income obtained during marriage?
2) Does the income of the payor flow from a job that is different from that which he had during marriage? Is the reason for the increase a career continuation or a new venture?
3) Was this a long-term marriage with a "complete integration of the parties' personal and economic lives"?
4) What is the time elapsed between the date of separation and the date of the income increase?
5) Is the support being awarded compensatory or non-compensatory.[210]

In *Hartshorne v Hartshorne*,[211] Leask J, of the British Columbia Supreme Court, provides the following valuable analysis of factors to consider in determining whether post-separation increases in the obligor's income should be included or ignored for the purpose of determining the amount of spousal support to be ordered:

> [110] ... As was observed by the authors of the *SSAG* at c 14.3, determining whether to consider post-separation increases in income involves a "complex, fact-based approach":
>
>> Some rough notion of causation is applied to post separation income increases for the payor, in determining both whether the income increase should be reflected in increased spousal support and, if it should by how much. *It all depends on the length of the marriage, the roles adopted during the marriage, the time elapsed between the date of separation and the subsequent income increase, and the reason for the income increase (e.g. new job vs. promotion within same employer, or career continuation vs. new venture).* The extent of sharing of these post-separation increases involves a complex, fact-based decision. [Emphasis added]

---

210 *Patton-Casse v Casse*, 2011 ONSC 4424 at para 136, McDermid J, aff'd 2012 ONCA 709.

211 2009 BCSC 698; see also *Sawchuk v Sawchuk*, 2010 ABQB 5; *O'Grady v O'Grady*, 2010 ABCA 109 (dissenting judgment of Martin JA); *Judd v Judd*, 2010 BCSC 153; *Pendleton v Pendleton*, 2010 BCSC 1167 (partial inclusion); *Cleven v Cleven*, 2010 MBQB 279; *Pettigrew v Pettigrew*, [2006] NSJ No 321 (CA); *Fisher v Fisher*, 2008 ONCA 11; *Patton-Casse v Casse*, 2012 ONCA 709; *Kovac v Kovac*, 2013 ONSC 4593.

[111] I have considered the authorities provided by the parties. The cases where post-separation increases in the payor's income are not considered, or are only partially considered, are distinguishable on their facts from the Hartshornes' situation. For example, they involve circumstances where the payor spouse changed positions or employers since separating, often making lifestyle sacrifices to do so [see *Chalifoux v. Chalifoux*, 2006 ABQB 535, rev'd on other grounds 2008 ABCA 70; *D.B.C. (v. R.M.W.*, 2006 ABQB 905); *Kelly (v. Kelly*, 2007 BCSC 227)]; the payor spouse's business underwent a reorganization requiring more work on the payor's part [see *Rozen v. Rozen*, 2003 BCSC 973, 37 R.F.L. (5th) 205]; the payor spouse had been given new career opportunities by virtue of luck or connections [see *Fletcher v Fletcher*, 2003 ABQB 890; *Robinson v Robinson*, 107 D.L.R. (4th) 78; 48 R.F.L. (3d) 265 (Ont. C.A.)]; the initial increase in income occurred long after the divorce [see *Bryant (v. Gordon*, 2007 BCSC 946); *Kelly*]; the recipient spouse was employed and/or was supported in her career aspirations by the payor during the relationship [see *Bryant*; *Kelly*]; or the recipient spouse had not made reasonable efforts to become self-sufficient [see *Bryant*; *Walsh v Walsh* (2006), 29 R.F.L. (6th) 164 (Ont. S.C.J.)].

On appeal,[212] the British Columbia Court of Appeal found no error on the part of the trial judge in ordering the divorced husband to pay lump sum retroactive spousal support based on post-separation income and by applying the high range of the *Spousal Support Advisory Guidelines* to the ten-year period commencing 1 January 2000. In response to the appellant husband's submission that there was no evidence that the respondent wife contributed to his acquisition of skills or credentials or to the advancement of his career in a manner that led to his ability to earn increased income, the British Columbia Court of Appeal held that the trial judge arrived at a fact-based decision that was entitled to deference. Speaking to the respondent's entitlement to compensatory spousal support, Smith JA stated:

> [58] The appellant acknowledges that the respondent has a significant claim for compensatory spousal support. The object of compensatory support is "to redress the economic disadvantage that arises from the marriage or the conferral of an economic advantage upon the other spouse" as well as "the economic advantages enjoyed by the other partner as a result of the recipient spouse's efforts": *Chutter v. Chutter*, 2008 BCCA 507 at paras. 50–51. The appellant's claim that the respondent made no contribution to the advancement of his career because he was an established lawyer when their relationship began, ignores the contribution the respondent made by

---

212   *Hartshorne v Hartshorne*, 2010 BCCA 327.

assuming the role of primary caregiver to the children, both during the marriage (between 1987 and 1998) and after separation (2000–2007), and how her assumption of that role gave him the opportunity to devote his time to the advancement of his professional development. It also ignores the sacrifice she made to her career by devoting her energies to the raising of the parties' children, which in turn significantly impacted her ability to advance her professional development.

[59] The trial judge concluded that consideration of each party's post-separation income would more accurately reflect the reality of the respondent's economic disadvantage arising from the breakdown of the marriage. He found that it would be to the financial benefit of the appellant because the appellant's income in 1999 (at $342,712) was higher than in each of the following years, and the respondent's lack of income in 1999 subsequently increased as a result of her continued employment as a lawyer from 2001 forward.

[60] . . . The effect of the spousal support award in *Hartshorne 1999* and *Hartshorne 2002* was to leave the respondent in a diminished financial state at a time when she had the greatest financial need. An award of compensatory spousal support had to "alleviate the economic consequences of marriage or marriage breakdown" (*Moge* at para. 47) for the respondent. In my view, the trial judge achieved that objective in crafting an award that fell at the high end of the quantum and duration ranges of *SSAG*.

[61] In my view, deference must be given to the trial judge's findings of fact, which informed the basis for his quantification of the lump sum award. I see no error in principle in his quantification of the lump sum award and would not accede to these grounds of appeal.

A similar conclusion was reached in *Judd v Judd*,[213] wherein the spouses separated in 2003 after a seventeen-year marriage. At that time, the husband earned an income of $105,000 per year. The spouses executed a separation agreement providing for a monthly amount of spousal maintenance, with provision for a review application after three years. The review application was delayed until September 2009, approximately three years after the last maintenance payment. At the review hearing, the husband contended that the amount of spousal maintenance payable should be calculated on the basis of his annual income for 2003, notwithstanding subsequent regular wage increases and a 7 percent increase due to his promotion in 2006. He argued that he obtained his professional qualifications prior to the marriage, that he had worked for the same employer throughout his career, and that the

---

213   2010 BCSC 153.

post-separation increases in his salary were unrelated to any contributions made by his wife. After listing a dozen cases dealing with post-separation increases in income and citing the observations of Leask J in *Hartshorne v Hartshorne*,[214] Punnett J stated:

> The resolution of the issue of post-separation wage increases is clearly fact based. The principle that appears to emerge from current case authority is that the connection the increase in salary has to the recipient's contribution during the marriage is determinative. If the increase in salary is founded in expertise and seniority established during the marriage and no intervening event or events are the cause of the increase, then the increase is to be included unless the recipient's role during marriage necessitates a different determination. If an event after separation is the reason for the increase, in whole or in part, then the increase may be excluded from consideration, also in whole or in part.[215]

Justice Punnett found that, although the husband was professionally trained before his marriage, he developed his expertise and seniority during the marriage while his wife subordinated her career to the needs of the family, by working part-time, by becoming a stay-at-home mother for several years, and by relocating the family for the benefit of the children to a place where there were limited employment opportunities for her. Quoting Leask J in *Hartshorne v Hartshorne*, Punnett J concluded that the spouses had "divide[d] their family responsibilities in such a way as to make a joint investment in one career."[216] He observed that the husband's post-separation salary increases fell into two basic categories, namely, regular salary increases and those arising from the husband's promotion. He noted that caselaw indicates that the portion arising from regular increases due to the husband's length of service with the same employer should be included in the review, taking into account the length of the marriage and the marital roles of the spouses. The increased salary attributable to the husband's promotion was viewed as more problematic in that it presumably required the husband to work longer hours and take on more responsibilities. In Punnett J's opinion, however, the promotion was, at least in part, attributable to the husband's length of service and experience, which was acquired during the marriage. It presumably recognized his abilities and performance both before and after the spousal separation. He, therefore, concluded that the husband's promotion

---

214   2009 BCSC 698.

215   2010 BCSC 153 at para 23. See *Pendleton v Pendleton*, 2010 BCSC 1167 (partial inclusion); see also *Cleven v Cleven*, 2010 MBQB 279; *AAM v RPK*, 2010 ONSC 930.

216   *Judd v Judd*, 2010 BCSC 153 at para 24.

was sufficiently connected to his wife's contributions as a wife and mother that the increased post-separation income should be included in determining the amount of spousal maintenance to be paid. He declined to include a one-year increase arising from the husband's additional duties with respect to the Olympics, as that short-lived increase was based on a unique event which was not connected to what transpired during the marriage. In the result, the husband's income was fixed at $164,000. Finding that the wife had taken reasonable steps to strive for economic self-sufficiency and that she was capable of earning $25,000 per year, Punnett J proceeded to consider the *Spousal Support Advisory Guidelines*, viewing them as a "useful tool" in review applications such as this, where entitlement was not in issue and the husband's post-separation wage increases were deemed relevant. With respect to the amount of spousal maintenance, Punnett J ordered the husband to pay $2,800 per month, which amount falls between the lower and middle ranges suggested by the Guidelines.

It is interesting to compare the judgment of the Alberta Court of Appeal in *Chalifoux v Chalifoux*,[217] wherein the trial judge determined the amount of ongoing spousal support payable to the wife by reference to the husband's pre-separation income. She found that his higher post-separation income was not the result of experience gained during the marriage; it was due to his decision to work in Yemen under burdensome conditions that were not shared by the wife. The Alberta Court of Appeal upheld this conclusion, being of the opinion that the trial judge had thoroughly reviewed the law and the factors that a court has to consider and had weighed all the evidence and could not be said to have misconstrued this husband's employment situation. There was, therefore, no justification for appellate court intervention on this matter. A similar decision was reached in *Sawchuk v Sawchuk*,[218] where the spouses were married for twenty-four years during which they were both employed. Neither spouse had established career paths before the marriage. After the birth of children, the wife reduced her hours of employment but she resumed full-time employment as the children grew older. At the time of the spousal separation, the wife, aged forty-three, earned a steadily increasing annual income of $44,000; the husband earned $65,000 per year. Four months after their separation, the husband changed his employment and his annual income dramatically increased to approximately $110,000. Dismissing the husband's argument that the wife was economically self-sufficient and not entitled to compensatory or non-compensatory support, Langston J

---

217 2008 ABCA 70.

218 2010 ABQB 5; see also *SDZ v TWZ*, 2011 ABQB 496; *Pollitt v Pollitt*, 2010 ONSC 1617; *Linn v Frank*, 2014 SKCA 87. Compare *Bujak v Bujak*, 2012 ABQB 458.

concluded that this was the type of spousal relationship referred to in *Moge v Moge*,[219] wherein it was ruled that long-term marriages result in a presumptive claim to equal standards of living. Having found that the wife was entitled to both compensatory and non-compensatory support by reason of the impact of the wife's homemaking responsibilities on her earning capacity and that of her husband, Langston J reviewed relevant cases, including *C(DB) v W(RM)*,[220] *Rozen v Rozen*,[221] and *Hartshorne v Hartshorne*,[222] that deal with post-separation increases in an obligor's income. Citing *C(DB) v W(RM)*, Langston J concluded that

> [i]n order to share in a former spouse's increased earnings post-separation, the Applicant must show that he or she has contributed to the acquisition of the other spouse's skills or credentials, thus contributing to the ability to earn the increased income.[223]

However, "[t]he requisite contribution need not be tangible and explicit, such as payment of the former spouse's tuition fees. Therefore, all circumstances which give rise to the current income level must be considered."[224] Responding to the wife's contention that she had contributed to her husband's ability to earn an increased post-separation income, Langston J found no supporting evidence. The wife had not sacrificed her own educational or career plans and there was no evidence of any steps taken by her to assist her husband in furthering his career. To the contrary, the evidence pointed to the husband acting on his own initiative by seeking a new job after the spousal separation and working overtime to increase his salary. To quote Langston J:

> To paraphrase the words of Leask J. in *Hartshorne*, I find there is no temporal link between the marriage and Mr Sawchuk's wage increase. Rather, the increase is due to an intervening change: Mr Sawchuk's decision to apply for a new job, and upon receiving it, Mr Sawchuk's decision to work overtime in order to increase his salary. I am not satisfied that Mrs. Sawchuk is entitled to increased support because Mr Sawchuk is working increased hours at a new job.[225]

In conclusion, Langston J held that the wife was entitled to an equalization of the spousal standards of living based on their pre-separation lifestyle,

---

219   [1992] 3 SCR 813.
220   2006 ABQB 905.
221   2003 BCSC 973.
222   2010 BCCA 327.
223   2010 ABQB 5 at paras 29–30; see also *RL v LAB*, 2013 PESC 24.
224   *Sawchuk v Sawchuk*, 2010 ABQB 5.
225   *Ibid* at para 51.

while bearing in mind that "both parties cannot, as individuals, separately enjoy the same standard of living they enjoyed as a married couple."[226] On the other hand, the wife was not entitled to any increased amount reflective of the husband's post-separation increased earnings. In the result, the husband was ordered to pay spousal support of $1,000 per month for a fixed term of eight years, the duration being set on the basis of an anticipated reduction in the husbands' future earning capacity due to age, the physical demands of employment, and potential retirement.

Since it is not a foregone conclusion that future increases in a spouse's income should be shared with a separated or divorced spouse and the *Spousal Support Advisory Guidelines* are not mandatory and do not have the force of law, the Alberta Court of Appeal in *Neighbour v Neighbour*[227] held that, absent consent, it was an error in principle to tie future support to a formula based on changes in the obligor's income.

In contrast to *Sawchuk v Sawchuk*, Weiler JA, of the Ontario Court of Appeal, stated in *Marinangeli v Marinangeli*:[228]

> In determining need, the court is to be guided by the principle that the spouse receiving support is entitled to receive the support that would allow her to maintain the standard of living to which she was accustomed at the time cohabitation ceased. In addition, there is jurisprudence to the effect that a spouse is entitled to an increase in the standard of living such as would have occurred in the normal course of cohabitation: See *MacDougall v. MacDougall* (1973), 11 R.F.L. 266 (Ont. Sup. Ct.) per Henry J. See also *Linton v. Linton* 1990 CanLII 2597 (ON C.A.), (1990), 1 O.R. (3d) 1 (C.A.). At the same time the court must guard against redistributing the payor's capital in the guise of support.

It is noteworthy, however, that Lang JA, of the Ontario Court of Appeal, in *Fisher v Fisher*,[229] quantified "non-compensatory" spousal support on the breakdown of a nineteen-year marriage by averaging the annual income of each spouse during the last three years of matrimonial cohabitation and during the year in which they separated. In *Thompson v Thompson*,[230] Chappel J, of the Ontario Superior Court of Justice, endorsed the following principles with respect to the treatment of post-separation increases in a support obligor's income in spousal support cases:

---

226 *Ibid* at para 59.
227 2014 ABCA 62.
228 (2003), 66 OR (3d) 40 at para 74 (CA); see also *Pollitt v Pollitt*, 2010 ONSC 1617.
229 2008 ONCA 11.
230 2013 ONSC 5500 at para 103; see also *Purdue v Purdue*, 2014 NBQB 262 at paras 115–16.

a)   A spouse is not automatically entitled to increased spousal support when a spouse's post-separation income increases.

b)   The right to share in post-separation income increases does not typically arise in cases involving non-compensatory claims, since the primary focus of such claims is the standard of living enjoyed during the relationship.[231]

c)   Compensatory support claims may provide a foundation for entitlement to share in post-separation income increases in certain circumstances. The strength of the compensatory claim and the nature of the recipient's contributions appear to be the major factors which may tip the balance either for or against an entitlement to share in the increased income.

d)   The recipient spouse may be permitted to share in post-separation increases in earnings if they can demonstrate that they made contributions that can be directly linked to the payor's post-separation success. The nature of the contributions does not have to be explicit, such as contribution to the payor's education or training. The question of whether the contributions made by the recipient specifically influenced the payor's post-separation success will depend on the unique facts of every case.

e)   A spousal support award is more likely to take into account post-separation income increases where the relationship was long-term, the parties' personal and financial affairs became completely integrated during the course of the marriage and the recipient's sacrifices and contributions for the sake of the family and resulting benefits to the payor have been longstanding and significant. When this type of long history of contribution and sacrifice by a recipient spouse exists, the court will be more likely to find a connection between the recipient spouse's role in the relationship and the payor's ability to achieve higher earnings following the separation.

f)   In determining whether the contributions of the recipient were sufficient, the court should consider such factors as whether the parties divided their family responsibilities in a manner that indicated they were making a joint investment in one career, and whether there was a temporal link between the marriage and the income increase with no intervening change in the payor's career.

g)   If the skills and credentials that led to the post-separation income increase were obtained and developed during the relationship while the recipient spouse was subordinating their career for the sake of the

---

231   See also *SRM v NGTM*, 2014 BCSC 442, citing *Kelly v Kelly*, 2007 BCSC 227.

family, there is a greater likelihood of the recipient deriving the benefit of post-separation income increases.

h) By contrast, the likelihood of sharing in such increases lessens if the evidence indicates that the payor spouse acquired and developed the skills and credentials that led to the increase in income during the post-separation period, or if the income increase is related to an event that occurred during the post separation period.

i) Assuming primary responsibility for child care and household duties, without any evidence of having sacrificed personal educational or career plans, will likely not be sufficient to ground an entitlement to benefit from post-separation income increases.

j) Evidence that the post-separation income increase has evolved as a result of a different type of job acquired post-separation, a reorganization of the payor's employment arrangement with new responsibilities, or that the increase is a result of significant lifestyle changes which the payor has made since the separation may militate against a finding that the recipient should share in the increase.

k) Where the payor's post-separation advancement is related primarily to luck or connections which they made on his own, rather than on contributions from the recipient, the claim for a share in post-separation income increases will be more difficult.

l) The court may also consider the amount of time that has elapsed since separation as an indicator of whether the recipient's contributions during the marriage are causally related to the post-separation income increases.

m) Evidence that the payor also made contributions to the recipient's career advancement, or that the recipient has not made reasonable steps towards achieving self-sufficiency are also factors that may preclude an award that takes into account post separation income increases.

The troublesome question of whether or when to exclude the obligor's post-separation income from the calculation of spousal support will undoubtedly continue to attract judicial attention. In the absence of exceptional circumstances, courts will probably be loath to introduce an income cut-off where "compensatory spousal support" is sought on original applications for spousal support involving marriages of long duration and marriages with young children. Different considerations may apply when a court is dealing with a variation application long after the spousal divorce. As the New Brunswick Court of Appeal observed in *Scott v Scott*:

> In *Boston v. Boston*, 2001 SCC 43, [2001] 2 S.C.R. 413, the Court made it
> clear that, when dealing with a variation application long after separation,

support is not to be determined in accordance with the payor's current standard of living, but the standard of living enjoyed by the parties during the marriage. Generally speaking, support should not be based on a reallocation of income according to the payor's current ability to pay.[232]

And in the words of Noble J, of the New Brunswick Court of Queen's Bench,

> 63 A spousal support order is intended to provide the dependant spouse with an income stream consonant with the income of the other spouse during the time prior to separation. As noted, post-separation income levels are generally taken into consideration in those instances when the income level is as a direct consequence of pre-separation efforts. In essence, to lay a claim to the income being generated after the marriage has been dissolved, the dependant spouse must establish this higher income had its roots in the period of the marriage.[233]

Whatever the outcome in the context of spousal support, prospective child support must be assessed on the basis of the obligor's current income. Section 2(3) of the *Federal Child Support Guidelines* expressly provides that "[w]here, for the purposes of these Guidelines, any amount is determined on the basis of specified information, the most current information must be used."

F. SPOUSAL CONDUCT

Section 15.2(5) of the *Divorce Act* provides that "the court shall not take into consideration any misconduct of a spouse in relation to the marriage" when considering an application for spousal support. Pursuant to section 17(6) of the *Divorce Act*, the same criterion applies to an application to vary an existing order. In addressing the impact of the husband's conduct on the wife's state of mind and her inability to strive for economic self-sufficiency, the Supreme Court of Canada in *Leskun v Leskun*[234] draws a distinction between misconduct, as such, which is irrelevant to the determination of spousal support, and the impact of such misconduct on a spouse's economic status, which is a relevant consideration under sections 15.2(4), 15.2(6), 17(4), and 17(7) of the *Divorce Act*. While courts have long since abandoned the notion that spousal

---

232   2011 NBCA 7 at para 37; see also *Reid v Gillingham*, 2014 NBQB 79. Compare *RL v NL*, 2012 NBQB 123 at para 49 and *BJB v MKB*, 2014 NBQB 153 at para 205.

233   *Hachey v Hachey*, 2011 NBQB 153 at para 63; *Reid v Gillingham*, 2014 NBQB 79.

234   [2006] 1 SCR 920; see also *Wiewiora v Wiewiora*, 2014 MBQB 218; *Menegaldo v Menegaldo*, 2012 ONSC 2915.

support orders are intended to punish the guilty and reward the innocent,[235] sections 15.2(5) and 17(6) of the *Divorce Act* do not preclude the court from taking account of the economic implications of spousal misconduct. Thus, the commission of a matrimonial offence, such as adultery[236] or cruelty or other misconduct that may have caused or contributed to the breakdown of the marriage, is *per se* irrelevant to the determination of spousal support under the *Divorce Act*. However, the economic implications of such conduct may be relevant in determining spousal support.[237] For example, the financial aspects of a spouse's "common-law relationship" may be taken into account in determining spousal support rights and obligations. Or, to use the example presented by the Supreme Court of Canada in *Leskun v Leskun*,

> [i]f . . . spousal abuse triggered a depression so serious as to make a claimant spouse unemployable, the consequences of the misconduct would be highly relevant (as here) to the factors which must be considered in determining the right to support, its duration and its amount. The policy of the 1985 Act however, is to focus on the consequences of spousal misconduct not the attribution of fault.[238]

Similarly, if spousal misconduct has caused a financial loss or assets have been depleted, these consequences of the misconduct may be relevant to the determination of spousal support.[239] The concealment of assets or the failure to make appropriate disclosure may also constitute relevant conduct.[240] Spouses may enhance, diminish, or negate their mutual support rights and obligations by their conduct. However, economic misconduct is only one consideration, and the nature and extent of any harm done will dictate its significance to the mandatory judicial review of all the factors and objectives to be considered on an application for spousal support pursuant to sections 15.2(4) and 15.2(6) of the *Divorce Act*.[241] In applying these criteria in *Sibbet v*

---

235 See *Connelly v Connelly* (1974), 16 RFL 171 at 176–78 (NSCA); *Hockey-Sweeney v Sweeney*, [2004] OJ No 4412 (CA).

236 See *Foster-Jacques v Jacques*, 2011 NSSC 43 (interim spousal support; motion to strike dismissed); *VK v TS*, 2011 ONSC 4305.

237 *VK v TS*, *ibid*. See also *TT v JMH*, 2014 BCSC 451; compare *Coughlan v Coughlan*, 2014 ABQB 471.

238 [2006] 1 SCR 920 at para 21; see also *Thurrott v Thurrott*, 2011 NBQB 125; *Foster-Jacques v Jacques*, 2011 NSSC 43.

239 See *Sibbet v Sibbet*, [2001] MJ No 181 (QB); *Cole v Luckman*, 2012 NSSC 118; *Racco v Racco*, 2014 ONCA 330; *Sparkes v Sparkes*, 2009 NLUFC 10; *AFA v AWG*, 2009 PESCTD 1.

240 *Mehlsen v Mehlsen*, 2012 SKCA 55.

241 *Sibbet v Sibbet*, [2001] MJ No 181 (QB); *Sparkes v Sparkes*, 2009 NLUFC 10; *AFA v AWG*, 2009 PESCTD 1.

Sibbet,[242] Little J, of the Manitoba Court of Queen's Bench, held that a wife who was suffering from ill-health should be denied a spousal support order where her deliberate misconduct in bringing the family business to an end placed ongoing burdens on her husband whom she had forced out of the business when it was a going concern. In addition, a spouse cannot sit idly by and expect to collect support. Each spouse must strive to attain financial self-sufficiency, if it is practicable to do so.[243]

A husband's cruel or abusive conduct, which impairs his divorced wife's ability to secure economic self-sufficiency through employment, may trigger a spousal support order, although the diminishing effect of the husband's misconduct on her earning capacity over a period of time may subsequently justify variation or termination of the order.[244]

Retroactive orders for spousal support and child support are not precluded by the husband/father's past imprisonment for assaulting his son and sexually assaulting his stepdaughter, and such conduct is not excluded from consideration in the context of spousal support by section 15.2(5) of the *Divorce Act*.[245]

In *Harris v Harris*,[246] a motion to strike the husband's pleadings because of his refusal to answer questions on an examination for discovery relating to his alleged alcoholism, was dismissed because the allegation of alcoholism was found irrelevant to the issues in the wife's claim for spousal support and for equalization of the spousal net family properties. Having determined that the wife's application for spousal support was governed by section 15.2 of the *Divorce Act* and the wife's alternative claim for spousal support under the Ontario *Family Law Act*[247] should be stayed, Olah J, of the Ontario Superior Court of Justice, found that the wife's pleadings did not support any correlation between the husband's alleged alcoholism and his ability to pay spousal support or the wife's entitlement thereto. After observing that section 15.2(5) of the *Divorce Act* precludes the court from taking into consideration "any misconduct of a spouse in relation to the marriage," Olah J concluded that the wife's argument, that the husband's alcoholism constituted a relevant "condition" to be considered pursuant to section 15.2(4) of the *Divorce Act*, was a thinly disguised attempt to circumvent section 15.2(5)

---

242 [2001] MJ No 181 (QB).

243 *Fisher v Fisher*, [2001] NSJ No 32 (CA).

244 *Kurcz v Kurcz* (1989), 20 RFL (3d) 206 (BCCA); *Martin v Martin* (1993), 50 RFL (3d) 77 (Sask CA); see also *Gainer v Gainer*, [2006] OJ No 1631 (Sup Ct).

245 *RB v IB*, [2005] NBJ No 134 (CA).

246 [2005] OJ No 1310 (Sup Ct).

247 RSO 1990, c F.3.

of the *Divorce Act*. Rule 20 of the Ontario *Family Law Rules*[248] allows wide latitude during questioning, so long as the questions have a semblance of relevance. Olah J concluded that this low threshold of relevance was not satisfied in the present case because the applicant had failed to establish that any economic consequences flowed from the husband's alleged alcoholism that would affect her entitlement to or the quantum of spousal support.

In *Menegaldo v Menegaldo*,[249] Chappel J, of the Ontario Superior Court of Justice, stated that "[m]isconduct on the part of a party considered in isolation, without regard to how the consequences of such misconduct impact on the objectives of spousal support, is irrelevant to the spousal support analysis regardless of whether the misconduct occurred before or after the marriage ended in divorce." She further concluded that "the phrase 'spousal misconduct in relation to the marriage' in sections 15.2(5) and 17(6) of the [*Divorce*] Act encompasses spousal misconduct relating to custody of and access to the children of the marital relationship, including parental alienation of the children."

There is no time limit under the *Divorce Act* for a former spouse to apply for a spousal support order. A provincial legislature lacks the constitutional authority to impose a limitation period with respect to any such application and neither laches nor the passage of time bars the application.[250] While there is no limitation period for making an application for support under the *Divorce Act*, a substantial delay may weaken or eliminate a claim for support, although there is no hard and fast rule barring such a claim.[251] In assessing entitlement in the context of delay, courts have focused on two primary factors, namely, the explanation for the delay and the prejudice to the possible payor spouse. Collateral factors that courts have considered include:

- the age of the parties;
- the length of marriage;
- the educational status of the parties;
- the role of the parties during the marriage;
- the existence of previous orders for child support and/or spousal support;
- the impact of a child support order on an award of spousal support;
- the likelihood of success had the spousal support been pursued in a timely fashion;

---

248   O Reg 114/99 (*Courts of Justice Act*).
249   2012 ONSC 2915.
250   *Desmoulin v Paul*, [2009] OJ No 1722 (Sup Ct).
251   *Miller v Miller*, 2009 NSSC 294; *Quackenbush v Quackenbush*, 2013 ONSC 7547 (interim spousal support); *Campbell v Campbell*, 2012 SKQB 39.

- the recipient's financial circumstances and the connection it has to the marriage;
- the payor's financial circumstances, including financial decisions made with the expectation that a spousal support award has not been requested or ordered;
- the degree of the payor's reliance on the absence of an order for spousal support or a request;
- circumstances since the separation or divorce that would impact on the decision, including delay;
- the prejudice to the potential payor given the financial circumstances and the effect of a retroactive and/or prospective order;
- special circumstances in the marriage, such as a child's illness or a parental illness; and
- evidence of duress in the marriage and efforts of the potential recipient to be self-sufficient.[252]

The *Spousal Support Advisory Guidelines* are of limited use in cases where a court is asked to fix an amount of support that will commence many years after separation. In such cases, the court is simply driven to the words of section 15.2(4)of the *Divorce Act*, which require the court to consider "the condition, means, needs and other circumstances of each spouse."[253]

G. FOUR OBJECTIVES OF SPOUSAL SUPPORT

Subsection 15.2(6) of the *Divorce Act* defines four objectives of spousal support orders. They are as follows:

1) to recognize any economic advantages or disadvantages arising from the marriage or its breakdown;
2) to apportion between the spouses any financial consequences arising from child care;
3) to relieve any economic hardship arising from the marriage breakdown; and
4) to promote the economic self-sufficiency of each spouse within a reasonable period of time, insofar as practicable.

Legislative endorsement of these four policy objectives manifests the realization that economic variables of marriage breakdown and divorce do not lend themselves to the application of any single objective. Long-term marriages

---

252 *Molloy v Molloy*, 2011 NSSC 390 at para 47, Legere-Sers J, aff'd 2012 NSCA 60.
253 *Donnelly v Descoteaux*, 2011 ONSC 5796, citing *van Rythoven v van Rythoven*, [2009] OJ No 3648 at para 75 (Sup Ct). See also *Jubinville v Jubinville*, 2013 BCSC 2262.

that ultimately break down may leave in their wake a condition of permanent financial dependence because wives have assumed the role of full-time
homemakers.[254] The legitimate objectives of spousal support in such a case
rarely coincide with the objectives that should be pursued with respect to
short-term childless marriages. Substantial periodic spousal support for
an indefinite term will customarily be granted to an older spouse whose
primary role during a long marriage was that of a homemaker or caregiver,
whereas a young able-bodied spouse with no children whose marriage was
of short duration is unlikely to be granted substantial or long-term spousal
support. Childless marriages cannot be treated in the same way as marriages
with dependent children. The two-income family cannot be equated with the
one-income family. A "clean break," with or without an order for lump sum
support in lieu of periodic spousal support, may provide a workable and desirable solution for a wealthy couple or for a two-income family where there
is no substantial difference between the spousal incomes, but is unlikely to
be feasible for most families on the dissolution of marriage. Quite apart from
the question of whether a spouse can afford to pay a lump sum, such an order
will not normally accommodate long-term needs, where they exist.

Periodic spousal support orders that are reviewable after a designated
period of time may be appropriate where rehabilitative support is required
until a dependent spouse returns to economic self-sufficiency by means of
gainful employment, although continued support may be appropriate to top
up the earned income of a recipient spouse who continues to suffer economic
disadvantages in consequence of the marriage and its breakdown. There can
be no fixed rules, however, whereby particular types of orders are tied to
the specific objectives sought to be achieved. In the final analysis, the court
must determine the most appropriate kind of order, having regard to the
attendant circumstances of the case, including the present and prospective
financial well-being of both the spouses and their dependent children. Much
of the above analysis was cited with approval in *Moge v Moge*.[255]

Judicial implementation of the statutorily defined objectives has, to
some degree, resulted in a shift from the former narrow perspective of a
"needs" and "capacity to pay" approach, particularly in cases where one of the
spouses has substantial means.[256] In the words of L'Heureux-Dubé J, of the
Supreme Court of Canada,

> The most significant change in the new Act when compared to the 1970 *Di-*
> *vorce Act* may be the shift away from the "means and needs" test as the

---

254 *Tyler v Tyler*, 2011 NLTD(F) 20.
255 [1992] 3 SCR 813, 43 RFL (3d) 345 at 375–76, L'Heureux-Dubé J.
256 *Moge v Moge*, [1992] 3 SCR 813; *Bracklow v Bracklow*, [1999] 1 SCR 420.

exclusive criterion for support to a more encompassing set of factors and objectives which requires courts to accommodate a much wider spectrum of considerations. This change, of course, does not signify that "means and needs" are to be ignored. Section 15(5) [now 15.2(4)] of the Act specifically states that "the court shall take into consideration the condition, means, needs and other circumstances of each spouse."[257]

In *Bracklow v Bracklow*,[258] McLachlin J, (as she then was), of the Supreme Court of Canada, observed that there are three bases upon which a court can make an award of spousal support, namely, compensatory; non-compensatory; and contractual. The dual operation of compensatory and needs-based considerations under the *Divorce Act* was specifically acknowledged by McLachlin J, who observed:

> In summary, nothing in the *Family Relations Act* or the *Divorce Act* suggests that the only foundations for spousal support are compensatory. Indeed, I find it difficult to confine the words of the statutes to this model. It is true that in 1986 the *Divorce Act* was amended to place greater emphasis on compensation. This represented a shift away "to some degree" from the "means and needs" approach of the 1968 Act: *Payne on Divorce*, supra, at p. 267. But while the focus of the Act may have shifted or broadened, it retains the older idea that spouses may have an obligation to meet or contribute to the needs of their former partners where they have the capacity to pay, even in the absence of a contractual or compensatory foundation for the obligation. Need alone may be enough. More broadly, the legislation can be seen as a sensitive compromise of the two competing philosophies of marriage, marriage breakdown, and spousal support.

The four objectives defined in the *Divorce Act* are not necessarily independent of each other. They may overlap or they may operate independently, according to the circumstances of the particular case.

All four of the objectives defined in the *Divorce Act* should be examined in every case wherein spousal support is claimed or an order for spousal support is sought to be varied. There is nothing in the *Divorce Act* to suggest that any one of the objectives has greater weight or importance than any other objective.[259] The fact that one of the objectives, such as economic

---

257 *Moge v Moge*, 43 RFL (3d) 345 at 374–75 (RFL).

258 [1999] 1 SCR 420.

259 *Moge v Moge*, [1992] 3 SCR 813; *Bracklow v Bracklow*, [1999] 1 SCR 420; *LMP v LS*, 2011 SCC 64 at para 49; *McCulloch v McCulloch*, 2013 ABQB 177; *Beck v Beck*, 2015 NLTD(F) 10; *Phinney v Phinney*, [2002] NSJ No 540 (CA); *Fisher v Fisher*, 2008 ONCA 11; *Berta v Berta*, 2014 ONSC 3919; *Heath v Heath*, 2012 SKQB 436.

self-sufficiency, has been attained, does not obviate the need to ascertain whether the remaining objectives have also been satisfied.[260]

The aforementioned objectives, which operate in the context of a wide judicial discretion under subsections 15.2(4) and 17(4.1) of the *Divorce Act*, provide opportunities for a more equitable distribution of the economic consequence of divorce between the spouses.[261] As has been stated by L'Heureux-Dubé J, of the Supreme Court of Canada in *Moge v Moge*,

> Equitable distribution can be achieved in many ways: by spousal and child support, by the division of property and assets or by a combination of property and support entitlements. But in many if not most cases, the absence of accumulated assets may require that one spouse pay support to the other in order to effect an equitable distribution of resources.[262]

Paragraphs 15.2(6)(a) and 17(7)(a) of the *Divorce Act* respectively provide that an original order for spousal support or a variation order should recognize any economic advantages or disadvantages to the spouses arising from the marriage or its breakdown. In the words of L'Heureux-Dubé J, of the Supreme Court of Canada in *Moge v Moge*,

> [T]he focus of the inquiry when assessing spousal support after the marriage is ended must be the effect of the marriage in either impairing or improving each party's economic prospects.[263]

Thus, a wife who has contributed to her husband's career development, or a wife whose earning potential has been eroded, restricted, or deferred by reason of the assumption of homemaking responsibilities, is entitled to have these circumstances taken into consideration in any determination of the right to, amount, and duration of spousal support.[264] It does not follow that a court must compensate for every economic disadvantage, no matter how minimal,[265] or that one spouse should shoulder the entire responsibility for redressing economic advantages or disadvantages arising from the

---

260 *Moge v Moge*, [1992] 3 SCR 813; *Travers v Travers*, [2003] AJ No 786 (CA); *Linton v Linton* (1990), 1 OR (3d) 1 (CA); *Allaire v Allaire*, [2003] OJ No 1069 (CA); *Mullin v Mullin* (1991), 37 RFL (3d) 139 at 148 (PEISCAD); *Schimelfenig v Schimelfenig*, 2014 SKCA 77.

261 *LMP v LS*, 2011 SCC 64; *McCulloch v McCulloch*, 2013 ABQB 177.

262 *Moge v Moge*, 43 RFL (3d) 345 at 374 (RFL); see also *Newson v Newson* (1993), 45 RFL (3d) 115 (BCCA); *Robinson v Robinson* (1993), 48 RFL (3d) 265 (Ont CA) (order for fixed-term support on sliding scale pursuant to *Family Law Act*, RSO 1990, c F.3).

263 *Moge v Moge*, 43 RFL (3d) 345 at 373 (RFL).

264 *Moge v Moge*, [1992] 3 SCR 813; *Rémillard v Rémillard*, 2014 MBCA 101; *Delaney v Delaney*, 2014 NLTD(F) 28; *Elliot v Elliot* (1993), 48 RFL (3d) 237 (Ont CA); *Cassidy v McNeil*, 2010 ONCA 218; *Schimelfenig v Schimelfenig*, 2014 SKCA 77.

265 *Grohmann v Grohmann* (1991), 37 RFL (3d) 71 at 83 (BCCA), Southin JA.

marriage or its breakdown.[266] Lack of resources may, of course, stand in the way of adequate compensation.[267]

Compensatory spousal support may be granted to a wife who has sacrificed her own earning potential by assuming primary responsibility for homemaking and child care during the marriage[268] or who has contributed to the career development of her husband.[269] Cultural dislocation on marriage that does not generate an economic loss will not justify a compensatory spousal support order.[270]

Financial consequences arising from the care of a child of the marriage that are personal to the custodial parent, in that they arise from the limitations and demands of parenting, are additional to the direct costs of raising the children that are addressed by means of the *Federal Child Support Guidelines*. Such personal financial consequences, therefore, fall properly within the ambit of paragraphs 15.2(6)(b) and 17(7)(b) of the *Divorce Act*, as well as subsections 15.2(4) and 17(4.1) of the Act.[271]

Paragraph 15.2(6)(c) of the *Divorce Act* provides that an order for spousal support should "relieve any economic hardship of the spouses arising from the breakdown of the marriage." The same criterion applies to variation proceedings pursuant to paragraph 17(7)(c) of the Act. As L'Heureux-Dubé J stated in *Moge v Moge*,

> Sections 15(7)(a) [now 15.2(6)(a)] and 17(7)(a) of the Act are expressly compensatory in character while ss 15(7)(c) [now 15.2(6)(c)] and 17(7)(c) may not be characterized as exclusively compensatory. These latter paragraphs may embrace the notion that the primary burden of spousal support should fall on family members *not* the state.[272]

---

266 *Moge v Moge*, 43 RFL (3d) 345 at 387; *Elliot v Elliot* (1993), 48 RFL (3d) 237 (Ont CA).

267 *Ibid.*

268 *Moge v Moge*, [1992] 3 SCR 813; *Bracklow v Bracklow*, [1999] 1 SCR 420; *Rémillard v Rémillard*, 2014 MBCA 101; *MacLean v MacLean*, [2004] NBJ No 363 (CA); *Scott v Scott*, 2011 NBCA 7; *Foster-Jacques v Jacques*, 2011 NSSC 124; *Caratun v Caratun* (1992), 10 OR (3d) 385 (CA); see also *Ross v Ross* (1993), 12 OR (3d) 705 (CA); *Elliot v Elliot* (1993), 48 RFL (3d) 237 (Ont CA); *Torrone v Torrone*, 2010 ONSC 661.

269 See *Rémillard v Rémillard*, 2014 MBCA 101; *MacLean v MacLean*, [2004] NBJ No 363 (CA); *Foster-Jacques v Jacques*, 2011 NSSC 124; *Caratun v Caratun* (1992), 10 OR (3d) 385; *Kovac v Kovac*, 2013 ONSC 4593.

270 *Dyal v Dyal*, [2000] BCJ No 1937 (CA).

271 *Moge v Moge*, [1992] 3 SCR 813; *Brockie v Brockie* (1987), 46 Man R (2d) 33 (QB), aff'd (1987), 8 RFL (3d) 302 (Man CA); *JHA v CGA*, [2008] MJ No 94 (QB); *Ray v Ray* (1993), 121 NSR (2d) 340 (SC); *DPO v PEO*, [2006] NSJ No 205 (SC).

272 *Moge v Moge*, [1992] 3 SCR 813 at 865 [emphasis in original].

A similar opinion is voiced by McLachlin J, as she then was, in *Bracklow v Bracklow*. She asserts:

> Section 15.2(6) of the *Divorce Act*, which sets out the objectives of support orders, also speaks to these non-compensatory factors. The first two objectives — to recognize the economic consequences of the marriage or its breakdown and to apportion between the spouses financial consequences of child care over and above child support payments — are primarily related to compensation. But the third and fourth objectives are difficult to confine to that goal. "[E]conomic hardship . . . arising from the breakdown of the marriage" is capable of encompassing not only health or career disadvantages arising from the marriage breakdown properly the subject of compensation (perhaps more directly covered in s 15.2(6)(a): see *Payne on Divorce*, *supra* at pp. 251–53), but the mere fact that a person who formerly enjoyed intra-spousal entitlement to support now finds herself or himself without it. Looking only at compensation, one merely asks what loss the marriage or marriage breakup caused that would not have been suffered but for the marriage. But even where loss in this sense cannot be established, the breakup may cause economic hardship in a larger, non-compensatory sense. Such an interpretation supports the independent inclusion of s 15.2(6)(c) as a separate consideration from s 15.2(6)(a). Thus, Rogerson sees s 15.2(6)(c), "the principle of compensation for the economic disadvantages of the marriage breakdown as distinct from the disadvantages of the marriage" as an explicit recognition of "non-compensatory" support ("Spousal Support After *Moge*", *supra*, at pp. 371–72).
>
> Similarly, the fourth objective of s 15.2(6) of the *Divorce Act* — to promote economic self-sufficiency — may or may not be tied to compensation for disadvantages caused by the marriage or its breakup. A spouse's lack of self-sufficiency may be related to forgoing career and educational opportunities because of the marriage. But it may also arise from completely different sources, like the disappearance of the kind of work the spouse was trained to do (a career shift having nothing to do with the marriage or its breakdown) or, as in this case, ill-heath.[273]

In addressing the economic advantages and disadvantages arising from the marriage and its breakdown and the economic implications of child-care responsibilities both before and after the marriage breakdown, as required by sections 15.2(6)(a) and (b) of the *Divorce Act*, judges are not excused from hearing relevant evidence and fully applying the law. However, as

---

273 (1999), 44 RFL (4th) 1 at 28–29 (SCC); see also *Thomas v Thomas* and *Abel v Abel*, [2004] AJ No 30 (QB).

L'Heureux-Dubé J observed in *Moge v Moge*,[274] adducing evidence to identify and quantify the economic consequences of marriage or marriage breakdown is an impossible task in most family law cases or one that is beyond the financial capability of litigating spouses. Consequently, trial judges should temper their expectations for detailed evidence and are encouraged to resort, where necessary, to judicial notice of certain realities. In the words of Richard JA in *MacLean v MacLean*,

> It is certainly amenable to judicial notice that one who has not been in the workforce for over 14 years will generally be less competitive on the job market than one who has acquired working experience over that same period. It is also evident that one who has foregone vocational pursuits for a significant period because of family priorities will not be able to re-enter the workforce at the level that he or she would likely have reached otherwise. It seems to me that these propositions are self-evident and that they ought to be properly considered in the complex and difficult analysis expected of trial judges when assessing a claim for spousal support.[275]

Although the objectives of spousal support, as defined in the *Divorce Act*, provide a legal foundation for fair and reasonable spousal support orders on or after divorce, they must be applied in light of the economic realities facing Canadians who divorce and thereafter enter into new family obligations. It is for that reason that many judges still tend to focus on needs and ability to pay as the fundamental basis of spousal support laws in Canada. Compensating a homemaking wife for her years of service in the home is not only appropriate, but may also be feasible when the courts are dealing with spouses, one of whom is a well-established professional or business man. It is more problematic when the husband is an unskilled labourer in receipt of a modest income or unemployment insurance. It does not follow that a

---

274 [1992] 3 SCR 813.

275 [2004] NBJ No 363 (CA). Compare *Sylvestre v Sylvestre*, [2004] BCJ No 1813 (SC). See also *Tweel v Tweel* (1994), 7 RFL (4th) 204 at 207 (PEISCTD), wherein DesRoches J remained "unconvinced that *Moge* stands for the proposition that a party can resort to judicial notice alone to quantify the economic advantages and disadvantages of marriage and its breakdown." And see Justice James Williams, "Grasping a Thorny Baton . . . A Trial Judge Looks at Judicial Notice and Courts' Acquisition of Social Science" (1996) 14 Can Fam LQ 179; LH Wolfson, "The Use of Judicial Notice after *Moge*" in The Law Society of Upper Canada, *Family Law à la* Moge (Toronto: The Law Society of Upper Canada, 1993) at Section D. Compare Madam Justice Claire L'Heureux-Dubé, "Re-examining the Doctrine of Judicial Notice in the Family Law Context" (1994) 26 Ottawa L Rev 551. And see Nicholas Bala, "Expert Evidence, Assessments and Judicial Notice: Understanding the Family Context" in Harold Niman & Anita Volikis, eds, *Evidence in Family Law*, looseleaf (Aurora, ON: Canada Law Book, 2010–).

divorced spouse can jettison support obligations owed to a former spouse by assuming new family obligations. Thus, in *Bracklow v Bracklow*, McLachlin J, as she then was, observed:

> Mr Bracklow makes a final policy argument. In an age of multiple marriages, he asserts, the law should permit closure on relationships so parties can move on. Why, he asks, should a young person whose marriage lasts less than a year be fixed with a lifelong obligation of support? When can a former spouse finally move on, knowing that he or she cannot be drawn back into the past by an unexpected application for support?
>
> Again the answer is that under the statutes, the desirability of freedom to move on to new relationships is merely one of several objectives that might guide the judge. Since all the objectives must be balanced, it often will not be possible to satisfy one absolutely. The respondent in effect seeks a judicially created "statute of limitations" on marriage. The Court has no power to impose such a limitation, nor should it. It would inject a rigidity into the system that Parliament and the legislatures have rejected. Marriage, while it may not prove to be "till death do us part", is a serious commitment not to be undertaken lightly. It involves the *potential* for lifelong obligation. There are no magical cut-off dates.[276]

If the economic plight of separated and divorced women is to be resolved, however, laws regulating spousal and child support rights and obligations are not sufficient. Federal and provincial governments must search for a more rational and cohesive system of income security for all needy families that reconstitutes the inter-relationship between spousal and child support payments, public assistance, and earned income.

Paragraphs 15.2(6)(d) and 17(7)(d) of the *Divorce Act* underline the responsibility of each spouse to become economically self-sufficient within a reasonable time to the extent that this is practicable. In determining what is practicable, regard must be had to all of the circumstances, including the age and gender of the spouse, her/his skills and education, or lack thereof, the opportunities for retraining, and the realistic prospect of the spouse being able to find not just a job, but one which enables her/him to become self-sufficient.[277] Although the court should not focus unduly on the recipient spouse's obligation to strive for economic self-sufficiency, given that this is only one of the four objectives of spousal support orders under section 15.2(6) of the *Divorce Act*, it remains a legitimate concern insofar as it is practicable and may justify the court granting an order for periodic spousal support

---

276 *Bracklow v Bracklow*, [1999] 1 SCR 420 at para 57.

277 See *Tedham v Tedham*, 2005 BCCA 502 at para 33; *Jendruck v Jendruck*, 2014 BCCA 320.

that is subject to review after a specified time.[278] A dependent spouse, who can reasonably be expected to acquire economic self-sufficiency, cannot assert a lifetime support entitlement, unless there is some ongoing economic disadvantage resulting from the marriage or its breakdown that compels financial redress in order to promote an equitable sharing of the economic consequences of the marriage and its dissolution.[279] A dependent spouse must be diligent in pursuing full-time employment and is not entitled to pursue a less economically advantageous career and look to the other spouse to make up the shortfall.[280] Where a spouse enters marriage with an education, a profession, and good health, and leaves it with these attributes intact, an order for spousal support may be inappropriate.[281]

Where both spouses have pursued their respective careers prior to the dissolution of their long-term marriage and there is no evidence of any significant economic advantage or disadvantage to either spouse arising from the marriage or its breakdown, an ongoing disparity between their professional incomes does not justify an order for spousal support in favour of the lower-income spouse.[282]

A court may order one spouse to furnish the other spouse with information concerning efforts to achieve economic self-sufficiency.[283] Economic self-sufficiency does not necessarily connote equality, although it should include fairness.[284] A dependent spouse's capacity to become self-sufficient must be examined in light of the particular case and have regard to the realities of the marketplace.[285] In *Moge v Moge*,[286] L'Heureux-Dubé J, of the Supreme Court of Canada, stressed the impracticability of applying a principle of economic self-sufficiency to many long-term homemaking spouses and the "unmitigated parsimony" of many courts in fixing the level of support that would reflect economic self-sufficiency for a dependent spouse.

---

278 *Gossen v Gossen*, [2003] NSJ No 113 (SC).

279 *Shields v Shields*, 2008 ABCA 213; see also *LeBlanc v Yeo*, 2011 ONSC 2741 (variation proceeding; fixed term order).

280 *Hedley v Hedley* (1989), 22 RFL (3d) 309 (BCCA).

281 *Zimmer v Zimmer* (1989), 90 NSR (2d) 243 (SC); see also *Penney v Pike*, 2009 NLTD 84 (modest lump sum deemed appropriate).

282 *Grams v Grams*, [2004] BCJ No 28 (SC); see also *Sylvestre v Sylvestre*, [2004] BCJ No 1813 (SC); *Droit de la famille — 1275*, 2012 QCCA 87.

283 *Romanoff v Romanoff* (1992), 41 RFL (3d) 433 (Man QB); *Melanson v Melanson* (1990), 98 NBR (2d) 357 (SC); see also *Walsh v Walsh* (1988), 16 RFL (3d) 8 (NBCA).

284 *Faulkner v Faulkner* (1986), 4 RFL (3d) 182 (BCSC); see also *Veres v Veres* (1987), 9 RFL (3d) 447 (Ont SC).

285 See *Messier v Delage*, [1983] 2 SCR 401.

286 [1992] 3 SCR 813.

Economic self-sufficiency does not signify a bare subsistence level of survival. Economic self-sufficiency is a relative term and its significance depends on the financial circumstances of the spouses during the marriage and at the time of the marriage breakdown. Subject to financial practicalities following divorce, a long-term spouse may be entitled to support sufficient to meet the cost of preserving a lifestyle not unlike that enjoyed during matrimonial cohabitation.[287] Where that is not feasible, as is frequently the case, a dependent long-term homemaking spouse should not be relegated to a significantly inferior standard of living than that enjoyed by the breadwinning spouse.[288]

Periodic spousal support will usually be denied to a young spouse who has no children and whose economic status was not materially affected by a marriage of short duration, although a modest lump sum may be ordered to compensate for any economic loss sustained.[289] The short duration of a marriage is no bar to periodic spousal and child support where a dependent spouse is unable to take full-time employment by reason of her responsibilities as the mother of a young child.

Economic self-sufficiency does not preclude an order for periodic spousal support where one of the spouses has suffered economic disadvantage in consequence of the marital role and the breakdown of the marriage. Gauging spousal support based on need is rather straightforward and arithmetically predictable. Fixing support on the basis of the amorphous notion of economic disadvantage where the disadvantage is not capable of calculation is extremely difficult, but the court must do the best it can.[290]

On the dissolution of a long traditional marriage that has had a detrimental impact on the lower-income spouse's earning capacity, the quantification of a spousal support order should promote similar lifestyles for both spouses until the economic disadvantages of the marriage and its breakdown can be overcome.[291]

An order for periodic spousal support, which provides for the future reduction of the designated monthly amount by one dollar for every dollar that the recipient earns in excess of $1,200 per month, provides no incentive for

---

287 *Ibid; Boudreau v Brun*, [2005] NBJ No 501 (CA); *Heinemann v Heinemann* (1989), 91 NSR (2d) 136 (SCAD); *Pettigrew v Pettigrew*, [2006] NSJ No 321 (CA); *Elliot v Elliot* (1993), 48 RFL (3d) 237 (Ont CA); *Fisher v Fisher*, 2008 ONCA 11; *Rioux v Rioux*, 2009 ONCA 569.

288 *Attwood v Attwood*, [1968] P 591 (Eng); *Marcus v Marcus*, [1977] 4 WWR 458 (BCCA); *Elias v Elias*, [2006] BCJ No 146 (SC).

289 See *Fisher v Giles* (1987), 75 NSR (2d) 395, 186 APR 395 at 398 (Fam Ct), Niedermayer FCJ, citing *Newman v Newman* (1979), 24 NSR (2d) 12, 35 APR 12 at 15 (SCAD).

290 *Higgins v Higgins*, [2001] OJ No 3011 (Sup Ct).

291 *Moge v Moge*, [1992] 3 SCR 813 at 870; *Ross v Ross* (1995), 168 NBR (2d) 147 at 158–59 (CA); *Adams v Adams*, [2003] NBJ No 51 (CA); *Ells-Hunter v Hunter*, 2011 NBQB 63.

the recipient to return to economic self-sufficiency. To provide such an incentive, an appellate court may substitute its own order whereby the reduction in the monthly amount of spousal support shall be by one dollar for every three dollars earned in excess of $1,200 per month.[292]

H. BROAD JUDICIAL DISCRETION

As McLachlin J, as she then was, observed in *Bracklow v Bracklow,*

> [T]he law recognizes three conceptual grounds for entitlement to spousal support: (1) compensatory; (2) contractual; and (3) non-compensatory. These three bases of support flow from the controlling statutory provisions and the relevant case law, and are more broadly animated by differing philosophies and theories of marriage and marital breakdown.[293]

As *Bracklow v Bracklow* further points out, the judicial role is not to select one particular model but to apply the relevant factors to the statutory objectives and strike a balance that best achieves justice in the particular case before the court.[294] Although *Moge v Moge* placed great emphasis on the concept that spousal support should seek to redress the advantages and disadvantages arising from the marriage or its breakdown, it does not seek to reduce the issue of spousal support to a simple equation conditioned on the notion of compensation. *Moge v Moge* confirms that there is a broad judicial discretion to determine the right to, amount, and duration of spousal support under the *Divorce Act.* This judicial discretion is exercisable having regard to the factors signified under sections 15.2(4) and 17(4.1) of the *Divorce Act* and having regard to all four of the policy objectives defined in sections 15.2(6) and 17(7). A court cannot bypass the statutory provisions nor formulate criteria that fly in the face of them. The authority to order both spousal[295] and child[296] support is statute-based. There is no single model or objective that underlies spousal support orders. The governing statute, be it the *Divorce Act* or provincial legislation, is central to the right to, duration, and amount of spousal support, if any, to be ordered. It is a discretion-driven analysis that is geared towards overall fairness.[297]

---

292 *Carmichael v Carmichael*, 2007 ABCA 3.

293 [1999] 1 SCR 420, 44 RFL (4th) 1 at 21. See also Bruce B Clark, "Spousal Support after *Bracklow*" (2001) 16 RFL (5th) 225.

294 *MacLean v MacLean*, [2004] NBJ No 363 (QB).

295 *Moge v Moge*, [1992] 3 SCR 813.

296 *Willick v Willick*, [1994] 3 SCR 670.

297 *Dreichel v Dreichel*, [2000] AJ No 664 (QB); *Mason v Mason*, [2006] NSJ No 227 (SC); *Pollitt v Pollitt*, 2010 ONSC 1617.

On the dissolution of a long marriage, a spouse is not automatically entitled to a spousal support order solely because that spouse stayed home with the children. The right to, duration, and amount of spousal support, if any, is dependent on all the circumstances of the particular case. Spousal support in Canada is frequently referred to as (1) compensatory; (2) contractual, or (3) non-compensatory. These categories reflect the combined operation of sections 15.2(4) and (6) of the *Divorce Act*. The law of spousal support continues to evolve, particularly with respect to the balancing of the factors and objectives contained in these subsections to determine whether, and how much, support should be ordered. The following principles may nevertheless be extrapolated from the judgments of the Supreme Court of Canada in *Moge v Moge*[298] and *Bracklow v Bracklow*:[299]

1) The focus of the inquiry is on the economic consequences of the marriage for each spouse.

2) There is no single model of support and no stipulated objective is paramount. The right to support and its quantum involve a balancing of all the factors and objectives specified in section 15.2 of the *Divorce Act*. This involves analysis of a wide range of issues, such as the length of the marriage, spousal contributions, means, needs, and self-sufficiency.

3) A fair distribution of the economic consequences of the marriage through the medium of spousal support does not require a detailed accounting of the spousal day-to-day financial and other contributions to their married life, nor does it require expert evidence as to the economic consequences of the marriage.[300]

Courts are entitled to take judicial notice of the economic effects of the division of labour during the marriage when the spouses divorce. A spouse's homemaking contributions and child-care responsibilities are highly relevant in terms of their ongoing economic impact on the spouses after the divorce, but they must be addressed in the context of all of the attendant circumstances that fall within the ambit of sections 15.2(4) and (6) of the *Divorce Act*. Applications for retroactive and prospective spousal support should take account of the assets, income, and earning capacity of the spouses following the breakdown of the marriage. Lump sum retroactive spousal support orders made after or contemporaneously with an order dividing matrimonial property can be especially problematic in that the payment of lump sum spousal support has an impact on the property that would or should have

---

298 [1992] 3 SCR 813.
299 [1999] 1 SCR 420.
300 *Richards v Richards*, 2014 NSSC 270 at para 70, Wood J.

been available for division. The global means and current net worth of the spouses must be considered when determining the right to and quantum of spousal support, if any, in light of the factors and objectives specified in sections 15.2(4) and (6) of the *Divorce Act*.[301] The characterization of support as either compensatory or non-compensatory may have an impact on the duration of the support order in that time limits can be imposed, even in a longish marriage, where support is non-compensatory in nature, whereas a compensatory support order, especially after a long marriage, starts from a premise of "indefinite" support.[302]

I.   OVERARCHING PRINCIPLE OF EQUITABLE SHARING

Moge v Moge provides a comprehensive rationale for all four of the statutory objectives of spousal support orders by endorsing the overarching principle of an equitable sharing of the economic consequences of the marriage and divorce.[303] This overarching principle, which applies not only to the amount of a spousal support order but also to its duration,[304] does not imply the equalization of the parties' net disposable income but the equalization of the economic consequences of the marriage or its breakdown.[305] An equitable sharing can be achieved by spousal property division, by spousal support, by child support, or by any combination thereof. In order to achieve an equitable distribution of economic resources on or after divorce, it is necessary to consider the circumstances of the parties as they existed during the marriage and at the time of the application for support or variation, and as they may reasonably be expected to emerge in the future.[306]

On an application for a spousal support order brought pursuant to section 15.2 of the *Divorce Act*, it may be unproductive to characterize the marriage as traditional or non-traditional. Instead, a functional analysis should be undertaken by examining the choices that the spouses made and their economic consequences. A wife who postponed her career aspirations to advance those of her husband may be entitled to substantial periodic spousal support for an indefinite term, where their marital roles resulted in ongoing economic disparity between the spouses in terms of their future earning capacity on the dissolution of their long marriage. The fact that the wife will

---

301   *Corbeil v Corbeil*, [2001] AJ No 1144 (CA).

302   *Firth v Allerton*, 2013 ONSC 2960 at para 42, Broad J.

303   *MacLean v MacLean*, [2004] NBJ No 363 (CA); *Richards v Richards*, 2014 NSSC 270; *Lepage v Lepage*, [1999] SJ No 174 (QB); *Riley v Riley*, [2009] SJ No 142 (QB).

304   *MacDonald v MacDonald*, 2004 NSCA 153.

305   *Armstrong v Armstrong*, 2012 BCCA 166 at para 69.

306   *Smyth v Smyth* (1993), 48 RFL (3d) 280 (Alta QB); *Beaulac v Beaulac*, [2005] SJ No 15 (QB).

continue to earn a reasonable annual income after the divorce does not preclude an order for permanent periodic spousal support because of her alleged self-sufficiency, where the economic consequences of the marriage and its breakdown continue to operate to the husband's advantage and to the wife's disadvantage after their divorce.[307]

J. NEEDS AND CAPACITY TO PAY NOT EXCLUDED BY COMPENSATORY MODEL

The judgment of L'Heureux-Dubé J in *Moge v Moge* endorses the concept of an equitable redistribution of resources, rather than a fixed compensation model. If the notion of compensation were regarded as paramount, this would fly in the face of the four objectives identified in the *Divorce Act* and could prove prejudicial rather than beneficial to spouses in certain cases, especially those where sickness or disability exists. It would also open the door to spousal misconduct, which is explicitly rejected as a relevant consideration by sections 15(6) and 17(6) of the *Divorce Act*.

As is amply demonstrated by *Bracklow v Bracklow*, needs and capacity to pay as the basis of spousal support have not been superseded by the notion of compensatory support. They have been complemented by it.[308] As *Moge v Moge* categorically points out, there are four objectives of spousal support set out in the *Divorce Act* — not one, not two, not three, but four. Every case must be reviewed in light of the potential applicability of each and all of these objectives. *Moge v Moge* pays special attention to the disservice to women that has resulted from undue emphasis being placed on the self-sufficiency objective defined in paragraphs 15.2(6)(d) and 17(7)(d) of the *Divorce Act*. Lawyers and judges must avoid moving from one extreme to another. A compensatory model of spousal support, like that of deemed self-sufficiency, if applied as the sole criterion of spousal support, would provoke more problems than solutions. The concept of compensatory support espoused in *Moge v Moge* was intended to foster a more equitable distribution of economic rights on divorce. It was not intended to provide a straitjacket where litigants, lawyers, and courts would debate the legitimacy of so-called expert valuations of the losses and gains flowing from marriage or its breakdown, nor was it intended to exclude the possibility of spousal support orders on bases other than compensation. Needs and means (or the ability to pay) have not been relegated to

---

307　*Allaire v Allaire*, [2003] OJ No 1069 (CA). Compare *Shields v Shields*, 2008 ABCA 213.

308　[1999] 1 SCR 420; see also *Boston v Boston*, [2001] 2 SCR 413; *Ross v Ross* (1995), 16 RFL (4th) 1 (NBCA); *Farrah v Farrah*, [2008] NBJ No 334 (QB); *Robinson v Robinson* (1993), 48 RFL (3d) 265 (Ont CA); *Tweel v Tweel* (1994), 7 RFL (4th) 204 (PEISCTD).

an inferior status by the notion of compensatory support.[309] Even if compensatory-based spousal support is no longer appropriate, ongoing needs-based spousal support may be required where a divorced wife would be left with no viable means of support and the divorced husband has the continuing ability to pay.[310] As McLachlin J, as she then was, observed in *Bracklow v Bracklow*,

> Judges must exercise their discretion in light of the objectives of spousal orders as set out in section 15.2(6), and after having considered all the factors set out in section 15.2(4) of the *Divorce Act*. By directing that the judge consider factors like need and ability to pay . . . , the new *Divorce Act* left in place the possibility of non-compensatory support.[311]

Professor Christine Davies has stated that "[c]ompensatory and needs-based support have different philosophical bases and should be kept apart."[312] This statement may be consistent with some, but not all, of the observations of McLachlin J in *Bracklow v Bracklow*.[313] It is open to question, however, whether such pigeon-holing is realistic, or even conceptually sound, under the express provisions of the *Divorce Act*, bearing in mind that, as Professor Davies correctly points out, "[s]pousal support is from first to last a matter of statutory interpretation."[314] That being the case, it is unfortunate that commentators and the courts have frequently failed to discriminate between the "factors" designated by section 15.2(4) of the *Divorce Act* that must be taken into consideration by the court and the "objectives" or goals that should be achieved by spousal support orders. Compensatory considerations do not so readily lend themselves to monetary assessment as needs-based support. Whether needs are measured by reference to a subsistence level, or by reference to the standard of living enjoyed during cohabitation, or by seeking to equalize the income of the spouses on the dissolution of marriage, there is a specific financial pool that can be readily divided in accordance with the governing criterion. The attribution of monetary values to perceived advantages and disadvantages arising from the marriage or its breakdown is much more

---

309 *Bracklow v Bracklow*, [1999] 1 SCR 420; see also *Colp (Silmarie) v Colp* (1994), 1 RFL (4th) 161 (NSCA) where, on an application to vary, Hallet JA found that, while the disadvantages and advantages arising from the marriage and its breakdown had been addressed, support was nevertheless appropriate based on the recipient spouse's dire need and the other spouse's ability to pay.

310 *Stier v Stier*, [2004] BCJ No 2343 (SC).

311 [1999] 1 SCR 420, 44 RFL (4th) 1 at 22.

312 Christine Davies, "Spousal Support under the *Divorce Act*: From *Moge* to *Bracklow*" (1999) 44 RFL (4th) 61 at 62.

313 [1999] 1 SCR 420, 44 RFL (4th) 1.

314 44 RFL (4th) 1 at 61 (RFL).

elusive, if not illusory, in most cases." And as Bastarache JA, as he then was, pointed out in *Ross v Ross*,

> It is in cases where it is not possible to determine the extent of the economic loss of the disadvantaged spouse that the court will consider need and standard of living as the primary criteria, together with the ability to pay of the other party.[315]

And those cases are the norm.

K. IMPLICATIONS OF CHILD CARE DURING MARRIAGE AND AFTER DIVORCE

Sections 15.2(6)(b) and 17(7)(b) of the *Divorce Act* seek to equitably apportion the financial consequences of child rearing between divorcing or divorced spouses by means of spousal support insofar as those consequences are not dealt with by child support orders. As L'Heureux-Dubé J observed in *Moge v Moge*,[316] a woman's ability to support herself after divorce is often significantly affected by her role as primary caregiver to the children both during the marriage and after the divorce. Her sacrifices include loss of training, workplace security and seniority, absence of pension and insurance plans, and decreased salary levels. These losses may arise from the woman's role as primary caregiver, regardless of whether she was employed outside the home.

L. ALLEVIATION OF FEMINIZATION OF POVERTY

On marriage breakdown and divorce, poverty is usually associated with parenting responsibilities, whether past or present. Divorced women often shoulder both economic and parenting burdens. This must be borne in mind with respect to spousal support under sections 15.2(6)(a), (b), and (c) and 17(7) (a), (b), and (c) of the *Divorce Act*. As L'Heureux-Dubé J has stated extra-judicially, "Through judicial discretion, these objectives must be interpreted and applied in a way that does not perpetuate the feminization of poverty and further diminish the economic condition of women after divorce."[317]

---

315 [1995] NBJ No 463 at para 15 (CA); see also *Boston v Boston*, [2001] 2 SCR 413, *Farrah v Farrah*, [2008] NBJ No 334 (QB).

316 [1992] 3 SCR 813 at 867–69, citing *Brockie v Brockie* (1987), 5 RFL (3d) 440 (Man QB), Bowman J, aff'd (1987), 8 RFL (3d) 302 (Man CA). See also *Gale v Gale*, [2002] MJ No 177 (CA); *Anderson v Anderson*, [2002] MJ No 176 (CA); *Snodgrass v Snodgrass*, [2004] NBJ No 27 (QB); *Torrone v Torrone*, 2010 ONSC 661. Compare *Shields v Shields*, 2008 ABCA 213.

317 Justice Claire L'Heureux-Dubé, "Economic Consequences of Divorce: A View from Canada" (1994) 31 Hous L Rev 451 at 489.

M. NO PAT FORMULA

For the purpose of determining the amount of spousal support to be ordered pursuant to section 15.2 of the *Divorce Act*, the court may impute income to one or both of the spouses. The court may find it appropriate to impute investment income to the applicant in light of the attendant circumstances, including rental income and tax write-offs relating thereto and a prospective equalization payment. However, the court may refuse to impute employment income where the applicant's historical and current child-care responsibilities render it impractical for her to pursue employment opportunities for some time, even though future part-time employment is judicially envisaged once the demands of the children have diminished.[318]

Section 18 of the *Federal Child Support Guidelines* empowers a court to include corporate profits in the income of a parent who has control over whether dividends are paid and what corporate earnings will be retained. There is no reason why the principles enunciated in section 18 of the Guidelines and in caselaw interpreting that section should not apply to spousal support as well. If a court decides to exercise its discretion to include corporate profits in the obligor's income for spousal support purposes, the extent to which such profits should be imputed to the obligor will be determined by the individual facts of the case.[319]

There is no general philosophy that spousal support should be assessed in an amount that will equalize the incomes of the spouses or their respective lifestyles. Any such general approach would impose a superficial response to a complex problem, whereas the law must seek to balance competing interests in light of the diverse factors and objectives specified in the applicable legislation.[320] Of course, an equalization of incomes may sometimes be appropriate after due regard is paid to the income, assets, means, and needs of the spouses. Such a result tends to occur more frequently on the dissolution of long traditional marriages involving spouses of low income who have little or no future earning potential. It may also be appropriate in circumstances involving middle-income spouses where the differential between their respective incomes is perceived as attributable to the career sacrifices made

---

318 *Brophy v Brophy*, [2002] OJ No 3658 (Sup Ct); compare *Marshall v Marshall*, [2002] OJ No 3653 (Sup Ct).

319 *Brophy v Brophy*, [2002] OJ No 3658 (Sup Ct); *Pollitt v Pollitt*, 2010 ONSC 1617.

320 *Lockyer v Lockyer*, [2000] OJ No 2939 (Sup Ct); see also *Shields v Shields*, 2008 ABCA 213; *Griffiths v Griffiths*, 2011 ABCA 359; *Lee v Lee*, 2014 BCCA 383; *Matthews v Gallant*, 2015 PESC 12.

by one spouse by virtue of homemaking and child-rearing responsibilities assumed during the marriage or on its dissolution.[321]

N. EFFECT OF SEPARATION AGREEMENT OR CONSENT ORDER ON SUBSEQUENT APPLICATION FOR SPOUSAL SUPPORT

By a majority of seven to two, the Supreme Court of Canada in *Miglin v Miglin*[322] endorsed the following principles to be judicially applied pursuant to section 15.2 of the *Divorce Act* when a spousal support order is sought that would override the provisions of a pre-existing spousal agreement.

1) The courts retain a supervisory jurisdiction to determine whether an order for spousal support should be granted pursuant to section 15.2 of the *Divorce Act* in the face of a purportedly final spousal agreement.[323]

2) The narrow test imposed by the *Pelech* trilogy under the 1968 *Divorce Act* is inappropriate under the 1986 *Divorce Act*. The provisions of a spousal agreement that limits the amount or duration of spousal support or waives any right to spousal support may be overridden by an order for spousal support granted pursuant to section 15.2 of the *Divorce Act* on grounds that are somewhat broader than those defined in the *Pelech* trilogy. It is no longer necessary for the applicant who seeks a support order under that section to prove there has been a radical and unforeseen change of circumstances that generates a need for spousal support that is causally connected to the roles assumed by the spouses during their marriage. The emphasis of the *Pelech* trilogy on economic self-sufficiency and a clean break is inconsistent with the current model of compensatory support espoused in *Moge v Moge*[324] and the conceptual analysis of compensatory and non-compensatory support in *Bracklow v Bracklow*.[325] Economic self-sufficiency, nevertheless, remains as one of the objectives

---

321 *Lockyer v Lockyer*, [2000] OJ No 2939 (Sup Ct); *Griffiths v Griffiths*, 2011 ABCA 359; compare *Pollitt v Pollitt*, 2010 ONSC 1617.

322 [2003] 1 SCR 303. See Carol Rogerson, "The Legacy of *Miglin*: Are Spousal Support Agreements Final?" and H Hunter Phillips, "The Legacy of *Miglin*: A Practitioner's Response" in The Law Society of Upper Canada, *Special Lectures 2006: Family Law* (Toronto: Irwin Law, 2007) at 119–34 and 135–52 respectively. For a critical review of the *Miglin* caselaw before *LMP*, and a brief postscript on *LMP*, see Carol Rogerson, "Spousal Support Agreements and the Legacy of *Miglin*" (2012) 31 Can Fam LQ 13.

323 *BGD v RWD*, [2003] BCJ No 1098 (CA); *Palombo v Palombo*, 2011 ONSC 1796.

324 [1992] 3 SCR 813.

325 [1999] 1 SCR 420.

of spousal support orders, and the policy of encouraging spouses to resolve their disputes by agreement remains of vital importance.

3) Although a material change in the condition, means, needs, or other circumstances of either of the former spouses is a threshold requirement on an application to vary a pre-existing spousal support order pursuant to section 17 of the *Divorce Act*, no similar prerequisite applies where an original order for spousal support is sought pursuant to section 15.2 of the *Divorce Act*. In the latter context, a change of circumstances since the execution of a pre-existing spousal agreement has no relevance except with respect to its impact when the court has regard to "any order, agreement or arrangement relating to support of either spouse" as required by section 15.2(4)(b) of the *Divorce Act*.

4) Where an application for spousal support under section 15.2 of the *Divorce Act* is inconsistent with a pre-existing spousal agreement, the court should examine the agreement in two stages. First, the agreement should be reviewed in light of the circumstances that existed at the time of its negotiation and execution. As of this date, the court should ascertain whether one spouse was vulnerable and whether the other spouse took advantage of that vulnerability. In assessing the issue of vulnerability, the court need not adhere to the stringent requirements of the doctrine of unconscionability that are applied to commercial transactions. Vulnerability and an imbalance of power should not be assumed, however, in the absence of evidence of a fundamental flaw in the negotiation process. The existence of emotional stress on separation or divorce should not be judicially perceived as negating the ability of the spouses to freely negotiate a mutually acceptable agreement. Any systemic imbalance of power between spouses will usually, but not always,[326] be overcome if each spouse has independent legal representation. After addressing the circumstances attendant on the execution of the agreement, the contents of the spousal agreement should be examined as of the date of its execution to see whether they substantially comply with the overall objectives of the *Divorce Act*, which include an equitable sharing of the economic consequences of the marriage and its breakdown in accordance with section 15.2(6) of the *Divorce Act* and the promotion of certainty, autonomy, and finality that is implicitly acknowledged by section 9(2) of the *Divorce Act*. Where the spousal agreement is unimpeachable as of the date of its execution, the court will pursue the second stage of its inquiry by examining the spousal agreement in light of the facts existing at the time of the application for a support order under section 15.2 of the *Divorce Act*. As of that date, the court should determine whether the

---

326 *Gauthier v Gauthier*, [2004] OJ No 4698 (CA); *Gammon v Gammon*, [2008] OJ No 603 (Sup Ct); see also *Rogerson v Rogerson*, [2004] NSJ No 152 (SC) (waiver of spousal support vitiated where wife not legally represented); *AAM v RPK*, 2010 ONSC 930 at paras 142–44.

applicant has established that the agreement no longer reflects the original intention of the spouses and whether it is still in compliance with the overall objectives of the *Divorce Act*.[327] In this context, the applicant must show that new circumstances have arisen that were not reasonably anticipated by the spouses when their agreement was executed and that these changes have led to a situation that cannot be condoned. Changes that occur in the ordinary course of people's lives, such as health problems, changes in the job market, business upswings or downturns, remarriage, or increased parenting responsibilities will not justify judicial interference with a final spousal settlement. It is only where the current circumstances represent a significant departure from the range of reasonable outcomes anticipated by the spouses, in a manner that puts them at odds with the overall objectives of the *Divorce Act*, that the court may be persuaded to give little weight to the agreement on the application for a spousal support order under section 15.2 of the *Divorce Act*.[328] The co-existence of diverse competing and conflicting objectives under the *Divorce Act* manifests Parliament's intention to vest a significant discretion in trial judges to assess the weight to be given to each objective against the particular backdrop of the spouses' circumstances. However, the objectives of spousal support orders that are set out in section 15.2(6) of the *Divorce Act* do not confer an unfettered discretion on trial judges to substitute their own view of what is required for that which the spouses found mutually acceptable. A court should be loath to interfere with a pre-existing spousal agreement, unless the court is convinced that the agreement does not comply substantially with the overall objectives of the *Divorce Act*. Courts should not condone spousal agreements that are manifestly prejudicial to one spouse but, equally important, they should not stand in the way of spouses bringing their personal concerns, desires, and objectives to the bargaining table in their negotiation of a mutually acceptable agreement that they regard as balancing economic fairness with the need for certainty and finality on the dissolution of their marriage. This is especially important when spousal support provisions constitute only one aspect of a comprehensive settlement that encompasses such interrelated matters as family property division and child support. In reviewing a comprehensive settlement, the court must look beyond the parameters of section 15.2(6) of the *Divorce Act*, which is written in permissive language and is expressly confined to defining the objectives of spousal support orders. *Moge v Moge* clearly affirms that an equitable sharing of the economic consequences of the marriage and its breakdown can be achieved by means of property division, spousal support, child support, or any combination thereof. A policy of promoting negotiated settlements is clearly endorsed by section 9(2) of the *Divorce Act*,

---

327   *DKN v MJO*, [2003] BCJ No 2164 (CA); *RSM v MSM*, [2006] BCJ No 1756 (CA); *AAM v RPK*, 2010 ONSC 930; *LLL v BAL*, 2010 BCSC 301.

328   *Borrett v Borrett*, [2006] BCJ No 1012 (SC); *Kerr v Kerr*, [2005] NSJ No 593 (SC).

which imposes a duty on every lawyer to discuss with his or her client the advisability of negotiating matters that may be the subject of a support or custody order. Certainty and finality that is achieved by means of freely negotiated settlements are fundamental objectives of the *Divorce Act* when it is viewed as a whole. If that were not the case and agreements could be lightly set aside, spouses would have little incentive to negotiate the economic consequences of their divorce.

Applying the aforementioned principles, the judgment of the Ontario Court of Appeal granting the wife periodic support for an indefinite term was reversed by the majority judgment of the Supreme Court of Canada, which vacated the order on the basis that the wife was bound by her waiver of spousal support, which constituted one aspect of a final spousal settlement. An agreement between the spouses need not specifically address all of the objectives and factors set out in the *Divorce Act*. So long as a fairly negotiated agreement that represents the intentions and expectations of the parties is in substantive compliance with the objectives of that legislation as a whole, it should be given considerable weight.[329]

Where a spousal support agreement includes no expiry or review date, public policy may compel a court to intercede where the contract leaves one party in penury, but there are no public policy grounds for disturbing a contract that pays too much support or tolerates the recipient's failure to secure full-time gainful employment.[330]

Whether the spousal support provisions of an agreement are contractually valid, and whether they are impeachable under the criteria defined by the Supreme Court of Canada in *Miglin v Miglin*, are questions to be determined in a single proceeding. In determining whether the spousal support provisions of a purportedly final settlement comply with the objectives of the *Divorce Act* as defined in *Miglin*, the court must guard against analyzing particular clauses in isolation; rather, the settlement must be viewed as a whole to determine whether the spousal support provisions comply with the statutory objectives.[331]

In the post-*Miglin* era, courts have experienced no difficulty in stating the principles to be applied when a spousal support order is sought under section 15.2 of the *Divorce Act* in the face of a purportedly final settlement previously negotiated by the spouses. Where difficulty may be encountered is in the application of those principles to the facts of the particular case. Although post-*Miglin* decisions have manifested a strong reluctance to inter-

---

329 *Strecko v Strecko*, 2014 NSCA 66 at para 24, Oland JA, citing *Miglin v Miglin*, 2003 SCC 24 at paras 4 and 66.

330 *Schultz v Schultz*, [2002] AJ No 1493 (CA).

331 *Megson v Megson*, 2014 BCSC 2467 at para 217; *SM c SK*, [2006] JQ no 778 (CA).

fere with final settlements,[332] the weighing of contractual autonomy, certainty, and finality as an objective of the *Divorce Act* against the objective of promoting an equitable distribution of the economic consequences of the marriage and its breakdown is not an easy task, even when both spouses are represented by competent lawyers throughout the entire negotiation process. If spouses have not previously sought independent legal advice, the finality of an unfair "kitchen table" agreement may be more readily disturbed by an order for spousal support on the basis that the agreement fails to reflect the financial objectives of spousal support orders under section 15.2(6) of the *Divorce Act.*

Departure from the ranges proposed by the *Spousal Support Advisory Guidelines* does not necessarily give rise to a conclusion that an agreement reached by the parties following extensive negotiations and with the benefit of experienced counsel is not in substantial compliance with the prescribed statutory objectives underlying spousal support orders.[333]

1) Finality of Spousal Agreement

The fundamental significance of the majority judgment in *Miglin* relates to purportedly final spousal agreements that either limit the amount or duration[334] of spousal support or waive it absolutely. Because final agreements envisage no future adjustments, spouses are expected to consider and guard against foreseeable changes, such as increases or decreases in income that may occur in the future, and changes of this nature cannot ordinarily be relied upon as a basis for the court to override the agreement by an order for spousal support that is inconsistent with its terms. However, if an agreement expressly provides that spousal support payments may be varied by reason of a material change of circumstances, the stringent criteria that attach to purportedly final settlements under *Miglin v Miglin* will be inapplicable.[335]

2) Applicability of *Miglin* to Payors

The principles formulated by the majority in *Miglin* are conceptually gender neutral, but men will fare better than women under *Miglin* because men are

---

332   Compare Professor Carol Rogerson in "Spousal Support Agreements and the Legacy of *Miglin*," (2013) 31 Can Fam LQ 13 cited in *Hume v Tomlinson*, 2014 ONSC 7195 at para 42.

333   See *Megson v Megson*, 2014 BCSC 2467 at paras 208 and 218.

334   *SP v RP*, 2011 ONCA 336.

335   *Stones v Stones*, [2004] BCJ No 378 (CA); *Marinangeli v Marinangeli*, [2003] OJ No 2819 (CA); *Pollitt v Pollitt*, 2010 ONSC 1617; *Poitras v Poitras*, [2006] SJ No 113 (QB); see also *Van Steinburg v Van Steinburg*, 2012 BCSC 1772; *Katz v Katz*, [2004] MJ No 206 (CA); *Henteleff v Henteleff*, 2005 MBCA 50; compare *Gobeil v Gobeil*, [2007] MJ No 19 (CA).

typically payors and women are typically payees, and finality usually favours the former group. In addition, the principles set out in *Miglin* are inevitably subject to the practicability of the payor's retention of an ability to pay. Because *Miglin* defined the principles to be applied where a spousal support order is sought by a financially dependent spouse to override the provisions of a spousal agreement, it would seem appropriate to adapt the principles set out therein to enable a paying spouse or former spouse to seek relief where, for reasons beyond his or her control, an inability to pay an agreed amount of spousal support supervenes. This may explain why the judgment of the Nova Scotia Court of Appeal in *Campbell v Campbell*,[336] in reducing the husband's previously agreed amount of spousal support, focused on the fundamental change in the husband's ability to pay rather than on the objectives of spousal support orders, both of which considerations are incorporated in stage two of a *Miglin* inquiry.

3) Non-cohabitation Covenants

In *Bakes v Bakes*,[337] the spouses executed a separation agreement whereby the husband's obligation to pay periodic spousal support would terminate upon the wife's "cohabiting in a common-law relationship." On the facts, Scanlan J, of the Nova Scotia Supreme Court, concluded that a "common-law relationship" existed so as to terminate the wife's right to contractual support. It became necessary, therefore, to consider her statutory entitlement, if any, to a spousal support order under section 15.2 of the *Divorce Act*, having regard to the two-step process defined by the Supreme Court of Canada in *Miglin v Miglin*. Applying the first step in *Miglin*, Scanlan J reviewed the separation agreement as a whole at the time of its negotiation and execution. After reviewing its terms, including those relating to the division of matrimonial assets, the assumption of debts, spousal support, and child support, Scanlan J concluded that the separation agreement was initially far more advantageous to the wife than to the husband who had assumed extremely onerous obligations to the subsequent prejudice of his physical and mental health. Consequently, the wife who, unlike the husband, had been legally represented during the negotiations, could not complain of oppression, pressure, or vulnerability at the time of the execution of the separation agreement. Scanlan J then proceeded to the second step articulated in *Miglin*, which requires the court to review the separation agreement at the time of the divorce in light of any changed circumstances and the objectives of the *Divorce Act*, which

---

336   2012 NSCA 86; see also *Blair v Stewart-Blair*, 2013 BCSC 927; *Stevens v Stevens*, 2013 BCSC 1899; *Droit de la famille — 142449*, 2014 QCCA 1791.

337   [2003] NSJ No 202 (SC). [appears as duplicate in review final.]

encompass the promotion of autonomy, certainty, and finality with respect to spousal agreements as well as an equitable sharing of the economic consequences of the marriage and its breakdown as envisaged by the four objectives of spousal support orders that are specifically identified in section 15.2(6) of the *Divorce Act*. In this case, there was one substantial change in circumstance that existed at the time of divorce. The wife's health had deteriorated to the point where it might have a long-term impact on her earning capacity. In this context, Scanlan J cited paragraph 89 in *Miglin* wherein the Supreme Court of Canada observed that negotiating spouses should know that their health may deteriorate and that such a change is unlikely to be sufficient for a court to override the terms of a purportedly final separation agreement by granting an order for spousal support pursuant to section 15.2 of the *Divorce Act*. After adverting to the fact that the wife's "common-law spouse" could be reasonably expected to make a greater contribution to their common household expenses, Scanlan J observed that there was nothing inherent in the twenty-year marriage or the roles assumed by the spouses during their marriage that warranted spousal support being paid to the wife indefinitely. Scanlan J then found that the terms of the separation agreement, which provided generous financial provision for the wife initially, while providing for the termination of spousal support when she formed a "common-law relationship," did not represent a significant departure from the range of reasonable spousal expectations so as to put them at odds with the objectives of the *Divorce Act*. Accordingly, the provisions of the separation agreement were judicially upheld and the husband's spousal support obligation was terminated in accordance with its terms.

4) Effect of Spousal Agreement on Interim Orders

Although similar considerations apply to both interim and permanent orders for corollary financial relief granted pursuant to section 15.2 of the *Divorce Act*, courts are especially reluctant to order interim support where a separation agreement has been freely entered into by the spouses and it provides a reasonable standard of living pending trial.[338]

Where the validity of the separation agreement is impugned and only a trial can resolve the matter, an order for interim spousal support is not precluded,[339] but a court must be careful not to prejudge the issue where, as

---

338 *Hubbell v Hubbell* (1984), 43 RFL (2d) 94 (BCCA), citing *Macy v Macy* (1984), 40 RFL (2d) 11 (Ont CA); *Trinchan v Trinchan* (1983), 34 RFL (2d) 331 (Ont CA); compare *Ziniuk v Ziniuk* (1986), 2 RFL (3d) 398 at 401 (BCCA); *Grieb v Grieb*, 2010 ONSC 2849.

339 *Desimone v Desimone* (1993), 48 RFL (3d) 161 (BCSC); *Krpan v Krpan*, 2013 BCSC 1020; *Carlsen v Carlsen* (1990), 25 RFL (3d) 461 (Ont HCJ); *Salzmann v Salzmann*, [2004] OJ

is often the case in interim proceedings, there is insufficient evidence for a proper *Miglin* analysis.[340] Interim spousal support can be ordered in the face of a release provided that there is a *prima facie* case that the agreement was not signed in unimpeachable circumstances as set out in *Miglin v Miglin* and that it did not otherwise meet the objectives of the *Divorce Act*.[341] In the words of Farrar JA, of the Nova Scotia Court of Appeal in *Burden v Burden*:

> [O]n an interim application for support, where there is a waiver of spousal support, it is necessary for the motions judge to look at all of the circumstances, recognizing that it is an interim motion, and determine whether the party seeking interim support has a reasonable chance of setting aside the waiver at trial. . . . Having made that determination, it was open to [the motion judge] to then go on to award interim spousal support.[342]

The objective of interim orders is to address the financial situations of the parties so that their immediate requirements are met with as little prejudice to the ultimate outcome as possible. An interim spousal support order may be refused because of a mutual waiver of spousal support in a comprehensive separation agreement, where there is no suggestion of fraud, duress, undue influence, or unconscionable conduct, and the applicant signed the agreement with the benefit of independent legal advice. Such preservation of the *status quo* under the separation agreement operates without prejudice to the applicant's right to have the agreement reviewed at trial for the purpose of determining whether a permanent order for spousal support is appropriate having regard to the criteria defined in *Miglin v Miglin*. If the applicant is successful at trial, the court may then adjust the equities between the spouses, including any hardship leading up to the trial.[343]

No 166 (Sup Ct); *Rempel v Androsoff*, 2010 SKQB 248; see also *Baudanza v Nicoletti*, 2011 ONSC 352 (cohabitation agreement).

340 *Palmer v Palmer*, 2003 SKQB 438; *Toon v Toon*, 2011 SKQB 281; compare *Evashenko v Evashenko*, 2011 SKCA 22; see also *McCain v McCain*, 2012 ONSC 7344; *Shachtay v Shachtay*, 2013 MBCA 17, citing *Kelly v Kelly*, [2004] OJ No 3108 (CA), wherein it was held that a motion for summary judgment under Rule 20 of the Ontario *Rules of Civil Procedure*, RRO 1990, Reg 194 (*Courts of Justice Act*) is often poorly suited to dispose of spousal support claims that must be resolved by applying the detailed two-stage analysis required by *Miglin v Miglin*, [2003] 1 SCR 303.

341 *Massai v Massai*, 2012 ONSC 6467 at para 20, McGee J. See also *Jubinville v Jubinville*, 2012 BCSC 1894 (stage two of *Miglin* test applied), and for subsequent proceedings, see *Jubinville v Jubinville*, 2013 BCSC 2262.

342 2013 NSCA 30 at para 38; see also *Marquis v Marquis*, 2013 SKQB 76, citing *Evashenko v Evashenko*, 2011 SKCA 22.

343 *Rodrigues v Rodrigues*, [2004] BCJ No 1353 (SC); see also *CMH v JRH*, 2012 NBCA 71 (interim spousal support denied).

In *CMH v JRH*,[344] interim spousal support was denied where the spouses had mutually waived their entitlement to spousal support under the terms of a prenuptial contract. By way of contrast, in *Chaitos v Christopoulos*,[345] the parties executed a marriage contract two days before their wedding under which they mutually released spousal property rights under the Ontario *Family Law Act* and any rights to spousal support. Applying the first stage of a *Miglin* analysis, Sachs J found that the circumstances attendant on the negotiation and execution of the marriage contract raised a serious issue as to its validity and enforceability. Applying the second stage of a *Miglin* analysis, Sachs J found that the marriage contract gave the husband the lion's share of the wealth accumulated by the spouses during their marriage and, in addition, the wife's earning capacity had been detrimentally affected by the marriage breakdown. Given these findings, Sachs J held that the marriage contract did not reflect any of the objectives set out in section 15.2(6) of the *Divorce Act*, which are applicable to interim spousal support orders. Indeed, the only objective under the *Divorce Act* that was achieved was that of certainty, finality, and autonomy, and this objective, while an important one, does not negate the significance of the other objectives. For these reasons, Sachs J determined that the waiver of spousal support in the marriage contract did not constitute a bar to the wife's application for interim spousal support. In addressing the amount of such support, having regard to the wife's needs and the husband's ability to pay, Sachs J observed that the wife should not be expected to deplete her capital in order to reduce the husband's liability to pay interim spousal support. The husband, whose annual income was determined to be $143,000, was ordered to pay $5,000 per month as interim spousal support.

5) Effect of Marriage Contract or Cohabitation Agreement

In *Miglin*, the majority judgment states that "the appeal raises the question of the proper weight to be given to any type of agreement"[346] that one of the spouses wishes to have modified by a spousal support order under section 15.2 of the *Divorce Act*. There is no "hard and fast" rule regarding the deference to be afforded to marriage agreements and cohabitation agreements as compared to separation agreements.[347] However, there are undoubtedly distinctions that can be drawn between prenuptial contracts and separation

---

344 *Ibid.*
345 [2004] OJ No 907 (Sup Ct).
346 [2003] 1 SCR 303 at para 2; see also *Varney v Varney*, [2008] NBJ No 465 at paras 25–26 (QB) (pre-nuptial cohabitation agreement).
347 *KK v AK*, 2012 NBQB 276 at para 86, citing *Hartshorne v Hartshorne*, 2004 SCC 22.

agreements drawn up on marriage breakdown. When spouses seek to regulate the economic consequences of an already existing marriage breakdown by negotiating a comprehensive separation agreement to determine their property rights and their support rights and obligations, courts legitimately exhibit a strong reluctance to isolate and interfere with the support provisions of that agreement.[348] Such an agreement will ordinarily have been negotiated at arm's length with independent legal advice and with knowledge of the capital assets and income-earning potential of both spouses. In contrast, where a marriage contract or cohabitation agreement is negotiated prior to the marriage, an election by the spouses in favour of economic independence on the breakdown of marriage is anticipatory and may not accommodate their condition, means, needs, or other circumstances at the time of divorce, or the policy objectives under the *Divorce Act*.[349] A prenuptial contract might, therefore, carry less weight with the court than a separation agreement, if a spousal support order is subsequently sought pursuant to section 15.2 of the *Divorce Act*. This result would ensue, however, not because of any judicial refusal to extend *Miglin* to marriage contracts but because the application of *Miglin* to marriage contracts would require the court to have regard to the different circumstances attendant upon the execution of a marriage contract and those attendant upon the execution of a separation agreement or minutes of settlement.

In *Culen v Culen*,[350] the wife's application for a spousal support order under section 15.2 of the *Divorce Act* was dismissed on the ground that such an order was inappropriate in the face of the waiver provisions of a prenuptial agreement executed with independent legal advice on the wife's initiative. In reaching this conclusion, Verville J, of the Alberta Court of Queen's Bench, applied the principles defined in *Miglin v Miglin*, being of the opinion that "the same principles should apply when considering pre-nuptial agreements as apply to separation agreements." The wife's current reliance on the public purse was found to provide no basis for an order in light of her waiver of spousal support and the absence of evidence before the court that the spouses had established an interdependent financial relationship during their nine years of matrimonial cohabitation. And in *Frazer v van Rootselaar*,[351] the British Columbia Court of Appeal found no error in the trial judge's refusal to order

---

348   See *Hartshorne v Hartshorne, ibid*; see also Chapter 4, Section A.

349   *Roberts v Salvador*, [2006] AJ No 715 at para 72 (QB); *Jenkins v Jenkins*, 2008 MBQB 271; *Varney v Varney*, [2008] NBJ No 465 (QB); see also *Stailing v Stailing*, 2011 NSSC 501 at paras 11–14.

350   [2003] AJ No 680 (QB).

351   [2006] BCJ No 875 (CA); *see also CMH v JRH*, 2012 NBCA 71 (interim spousal support denied).

spousal support where a waiver of such support was included in a marriage contract executed to protect the wife's capital assets.

Pursuant to section 53 of the Ontario *Family Law Act*, a cohabitation agreement shall be deemed to be a marriage contract if the cohabitants marry. Although a waiver of spousal support in the cohabitation agreement does not preclude a court order for spousal support under section 15.2 of the *Divorce Act*, the applicant's entitlement may be tempered by the provisions of the cohabitation agreement.[352]

6) Variation Orders

The majority judgment of the Supreme Court of Canada in *LMP v LS*,[353] delivered by Abella and Rothstein JJ, with whom Binnie, LeBel, and Deschamps JJ concurred, concludes that the *Miglin* approach is responsive to the specific provisions in section 15.2 of the *Divorce Act* and that it should not be imported into an analysis of section 17 of the *Divorce Act*. It perceives the *Miglin* approach as reflecting the express requirement under section 15.2(4)(c) of the *Divorce Act* that "the court shall take into consideration . . . any order, agreement or arrangement relating to support of either spouse." But no such express requirement is found in section 17 of the *Divorce Act*. That section simply provides that, before the court makes an order to vary an existing spousal support order, it must be satisfied that "a change in the condition, means, needs or other circumstances of either spouse has occurred since the making of the spousal support order or the last variation order." According to the majority judgment, the different language employed in sections 15.2 and 17 of the *Divorce Act* is recognized in *Miglin* as requiring different approaches to initial and variation applications. This flows from the fact that, while the *objectives* of initial orders under section 15.2(b) of the *Divorce Act* are virtually identical to the *objectives* of variation orders under section 17(7) of the *Divorce Act*, the *factors* that a court must consider under section 15.2(4) of the *Divorce Act* are significantly different from those specified as applicable to variation proceedings under section 17(4.1) of the *Divorce Act*. That is not to say that an agreement will be ignored in the latter context but its treatment will be different because sections 15.2 and 17 of the *Divorce Act* serve different purposes. The majority judgment asserts that the proper approach under section 17 of the *Divorce Act* is found in *Willick v Willick*[354] and *G(L)*

352 *Johnston v Burns*, [2002] OJ No 1805 (Sup Ct). Compare *LM v IM*, [2007] NJ No 379 (UFC). See also *Baudanza v Nicoletti*, 2011 ONSC 352.

353 2011 SCC 64; see also *RP v RC*, 2011 SCC 65; *McCulloch v McCulloch*, 2013 ABQB 177; *Menegaldo v Menegaldo*, 2012 ONSC 2915; *Van Wyk v Van Wyk*, 2012 ONSC 3280.

354 [1994] 3 SCR 670.

v B(G).[355] These judgments require the party seeking variation to establish a material change of circumstances since the making of the order which is sought to be varied. A "material change" signifies a change with some degree of continuity that, if known, would likely have resulted in different terms. It is presumed that the existing order is correct and that it met the objectives of the *Divorce Act* when it was granted. Consequently, the majority judgment holds that the threshold issue of a material change is the same whether or not the existing spousal support order incorporates an agreement. However, this does not mean that the incorporated agreement is irrelevant because, as Sopinka J observed in *Willick v Willick*, "where . . . the agreement is embodied in the judgment of the court, it is necessary to consider what additional effect is to be accorded to this fact."[356] Such "additional effect" will, of course, depend on the terms of the agreement viewed in the context of any alleged material change of circumstances. In the words of Abella and Rothstein JJ at paragraphs 38–42 of the majority judgment in *LMP*:

> 38 The agreement may address future circumstances and predetermine who will bear the risk of any changes that might occur. And it may well specifically provide that a contemplated future event will or will not amount to a material change.
>
> 39 Parties may either contemplate that a specific type of change will or will not give rise to variation. When a given change is specified in the agreement incorporated into the order as giving rise to, or not giving rise to, variation (either expressly or by necessary implication), the answer to the *Willick* question may well be found in the terms of the order itself. That is, the parties, through their agreement, which has already received prior judicial approval, have provided the answer to the *Willick* inquiry required to determine if a material change has occurred under s. 17(4.1). Even significant changes may not be material for the purposes of s. 17(4.1) if they were actually contemplated by the parties by the terms of the order at the time of the order. The degree of specificity with which the terms of the order provide for a particular change is evidence of whether the parties or court contemplated the situation raised on an application for variation, and whether the order was intended to capture the particular changed circumstances. Courts should give effect to these intentions, bearing in mind that the agreement was incorporated into a court order, and that the terms can therefore be presumed, as of that time, to have been in compliance with the objectives of the *Divorce Act* when the order was made.

---

355 [1995] 3 SCR 370.
356 [1994] 3 SCR 670 at 687. And see *Pustai v Pustai*, 2014 ONCA 422.

40 Alternatively, an agreement incorporated into an order may include a general provision stating that it is subject to variation upon a material change of circumstances, such as the agreement and subsequent order in *Hickey v. Hickey*, [1999] 2 S.C.R. 518. In such a case, the agreement incorporated into the s. 15.2 order does not expressly give the court any additional information as to whether a particular change would have resulted in different terms if known at the time of that order. The presence of such a provision will require a court to examine the terms of the s. 15.2 order and the circumstances of the parties at the time that order was entered into to determine what amounts to a material change.

41 Finally, an agreement incorporated into a s. 15.2 order may simply include a general term providing that it is final, or finality may be necessarily implied. But even where an agreement incorporated into an order includes a term providing that it is final, the court's jurisdiction under s 17 cannot be ousted (*Miglin; G. (L.); Leskun*). A provision indicating that the order is final merely states the obvious: the order of the court is final *subject to* s. 17 of the *Divorce Act*. Courts will always apply the *Willick* inquiry to determine if a material change of circumstances exists.

42 Ultimately, courts are tasked with determining if a material change of circumstances has occurred so as to justify a variation of a s. 15.2 order under s. 17. The analysis is always grounded in the actual circumstances of the parties and the terms of the s 15.2 order; what meaning a court will give any general statement of finality found in an order will be a question to be resolved on that basis. As we have explained, in some situations, the agreement incorporated into the order may help shape what is meant by a "material change of circumstances." Where a s. 15.2 order deals with a specific change, it assists courts by answering the *Willick* inquiry through its terms. Conversely, when the order is general, or simply purports to be final, these less specific terms provide less assistance to courts in answering the *Willick* inquiry. Sometimes, in such cases, the circumstances of the parties may be such that courts will give little weight to a general statement of finality and conclude that a material change exists. However, at other times, in such cases, the circumstances of the parties may also be such that the courts will give effect to a general statement of finality and conclude that a material change does not exist.[357]

The majority judgment expressly rejects the minority view of Cromwell J, with whom McLachlin CJ concurred, who were of the opinion that a pur-

---

357 *LMP v LS*, 2011 SCC 64. See also *RP v RC*, 2011 SCC 65 at paras 26–28; and see *Parent v Morrissette*, 2013 NBQB 408; *Dwyer v Dredge*, 2015 NLTD(F) 4; *Smith v Rand*, 2013 NSSC 369; *Droit de la famille — 132380*, 2013 QCCA 1504.

portedly final agreement is not just relevant to the determination of an application to vary an agreement-based spousal support order under section 17 of the *Divorce Act*; it must be given significant weight having regard to the principles defined in *Miglin*. In rejecting this opinion, the majority judgment opines that it "in effect raises the threshold necessary to establish a 'material change' under s. 17 when there is an agreement, and emphasizes legal certainty and finality at the expense of the statutory requirements of s. 17" and "[s]uch a result is reminiscent of the 'clean break' approach [that was] rejected in *Moge* and *Miglin* because it was held to be inappropriate in the context of the current *Divorce Act*" (paragraph 46).

The majority judgment then addresses the application of section 17 of the *Divorce Act* in the event that a material change is proven. It observes that given such proof, the court will take account of the material change and that it should limit itself to making only the variation justified by that change, having due regard to the objectives of variation orders set out in section 17(7) of the *Divorce Act*, which objectives guide the discretion of the court so as to provide opportunities for a more equitable distribution of the economic consequences of the divorce.

Many would accept that the minority reasoning of Cromwell J more closely corresponds to previous judicial responses to *Miglin* in the context of variation proceedings under section 17 of the *Divorce Act*. Consequently, the law has been changed by the majority judgment in *LMP*. How far the door has been opened to revisiting agreement-based spousal support orders under section 17 of the *Divorce Act* may largely depend on how well counsel delineate the circumstances that will or will not, in their opinion, constitute a material change of circumstances. The battle between the search for certainty and finality on the one hand and for the promotion of an equitable distribution of the economic consequences of divorce on the other hand will continue to be joined. But the results will be more unpredictable in advance than they would have been, had the *Miglin* approach been extended to variation applications.[358]

7) Effect of Spousal Agreement on Child Support

The *Miglin* criteria are inapplicable to child support.[359] Courts will not hesitate to order child support where a spousal agreement or settlement prejudicially affects the financial welfare of children. Child support, like access, is the

---

358 For a critical review of the *Miglin* caselaw before *LMP* and a brief postscript on *LMP*, see Carol Rogerson, "Spousal Support Agreements and the Legacy of *Miglin*" (2012) 31 Can Fam LQ 13.

359 *Turpin v Clark*, 2009 BCCA 530; *KK v AK*, 2012 NBQB 276.

right of the child, and neither parent has the authority to waive or restrict the statutory support obligations that each parent owes to his or her dependent children.[360] That is not to say that parents cannot negotiate settlements or other arrangements to stand in the place of child support payments that would otherwise be ordered pursuant to the *Federal Child Support Guidelines*. However, it is not open to parents to trade off child support against non-access to the children by the non-custodial parent.[361] The test of whether parents have made adequate provision for their child must be measured against the *Federal Child Support Guidelines* and the provisions of sections 15.1(5) to (8) (original applications) and sections 17(6.2) to (6.5) (variation applications) of the *Divorce Act*.[362]

8) Applications under Provincial Statute

In *Zimmerman v Shannon*,[363] the British Columbia Court of Appeal observed that the power of the court under section 15.2 of the *Divorce Act* is to order or refuse to order spousal support. It was not the intention of Parliament to supersede provincial legislative jurisdiction over contracts regulating spousal support, and the judgment of the Supreme Court of Canada in *Miglin v Miglin*[364] affirmed the jurisdiction to order spousal support inconsistent with a private contract without commenting on the effect of such an order on the enforceability of the private contract. Several provinces have enacted legislation whereby the support provisions of a separation agreement may be filed with a designated court and thereafter varied in the same way as a court order.

O. EFFECT OF SPONSORSHIP AGREEMENT

A sponsorship agreement entered into by one spouse to facilitate the other spouse's immigration defines obligations owed to the Canadian government rather than spousal support obligations arising pursuant to the *Divorce Act* or provincial statute. Though it may be deemed relevant on the issue of spousal

360 *Richardson v Richardson*, [1987] 1 SCR 857; *Willick v Willick*, [1994] 3 SCR 670; *Kopp v Kopp*, 2012 BCCA 140; *Jay v Jay*, [2003] PEIJ No 68 (CA). See also *GG v JTG*, 2013 ABQB 726.
361 *Black v Black* (1995), 19 RFL (4th) 442 (BCCA); *DAW v WMZ*, [2000] OJ No 2391 (Sup Ct).
362 *GG v JTG*, 2013 ABQB 726; *Gobeil v Gobeil*, [2007] MJ No 19 (CA); *Kudoba v Kudoba*, [2007] OJ No 3765 (Sup Ct); see, generally, Chapter 9, Section K.
363 [2006] BCJ No 2887 (CA).
364 [2003] 1 SCR 303.

support,[365] it is not determinative of the appropriate amount or duration of spousal support to be ordered.[366]

P. DOUBLE RECOVERY OR DOUBLE DIPPING

Court-ordered spousal support rights and obligations may survive the payor's retirement. In some instances, the payee will have received an equal share of the value of the payor's pension upon their separation or divorce, either by way of a lump sum or a trade-off of assets such as the pension against the matrimonial home. If that is the case, when addressing the issue of spousal support after the payor's retirement, the court should seek to avoid "double dipping" or "double recovery." Consequently, the court should not take account of an already divided pension, except insofar as its value to the pension-holding spouse may have increased since the separation or divorce.[367] A spouse who receives money or assets in satisfaction of his or her pension-sharing entitlement on separation or divorce must use those resources in a reasonable attempt to generate income, at least by the time pension benefits begin to be paid to the pensioned spouse. Failure to do so may result in the judicial imputation of income to the support payee, based on actuarial evidence. It is unfair to allow a support payee to reap the benefit of the pension both as a divisible asset and thereafter as a source of income to the payor, particularly when the payee previously received capital assets that have appreciated in value. To avoid double recovery, the court should, where practicable, focus on the portion of the payor's income and assets that have not been a part of the property division when the payee spouse's continuing need for support is shown. This would include the portion of the payor's pension earned after separation and not subject to equalization. Double recovery cannot always be avoided, and a pension previously divided can also be viewed as a maintenance asset where the payor has the ability to pay and the payee has made a reasonable effort to use equalized assets in an income-producing way and, despite this, economic hardship from the marriage or its breakdown persists. Subject to the obligor's ability to pay, double recovery may also be permitted in spousal support orders based upon need as opposed to compensation.[368]

---

365 *Singh v Singh*, 2013 ONSC 6476.

366 *Nathoo v Nathoo*, [2005] AJ No 255 (QB); *Paulina v Dudas*, [2005] BCJ No 172 (SC); *Gossen v Gossen*, [2003] NSJ No 113 (SC); *Gidey v Abay*, [2007] OJ No 3693 (Sup Ct).

367 *KH v AJS*, 2014 ABQB 427; *Truscello v Truscello*, 2014 ONSC 4590.

368 *Boston v Boston*, [2001] 2 SCR 413 (variation proceeding); see also *Alpugan v Baykan*, 2014 ABCA 152 (investment portfolio); *Jordan v Jordan*, 2011 BCCA 518; *Murphy v Murphy*, 2015 BCSC 408; *Senek v Senek*, 2014 MBCA 67; *Dwyer v Dredge*, 2015 NLTD(F) 4 (RRSPs and Canada Pension credits); *Flieger v Adams*, 2012 NBCA 39; *Meiklejohn v Meiklejohn*,

After reviewing the response to *Boston v Boston* in subsequent judicial decisions, Philp JA, who delivered the judgment of the Manitoba Court of Appeal in *Cymbalisty v Cymbalisty*,[369] expressed the following opinion:

> The general principles that the court enunciated in Boston were founded on unique factual circumstances that are not the fodder that usually feeds family law litigation. The goal of self-sufficiency is one that is not often attained following the break-up of a long-term marriage. Economic disadvantage or hardship will often persist. For this reason, it is not surprising that trial and appellate courts have found in the facts before them the circumstances that permit double recovery in spousal support orders/agreements. Balancing the needs of the wife who remains disadvantaged by the marriage and its breakdown against the right of the husband to enjoy his pension entitlement that had been equalized, the courts have come down, properly in my view, in favour of the wife.[370]

In *Litton v Litton*,[371] the principle of double dipping was held inapplicable to the husband's income earned from his business after a court-ordered division of property involved a trade-off of the matrimonial home and the business. But the double recovery problem is not limited to the pension situation; the fact that a payor spouse would have to deplete his share of the assets obtained as a result of the division of matrimonial property or use the "pension" income that he derives from those assets in order to be able to continue the support payments is a factor in determining whether or not a spousal support order should be terminated or reduced upon the payor's retirement.[372]

Double dipping issues are not taken into account in the formulas prescribed by the *Spousal Support Advisory Guidelines*.[373] Caution must, therefore, be exercised in applying the formulas set out in the *Spousal Support Advisory Guidelines* to a case where the sole source of income for the parties is income from assets that have already been divided pursuant to provincial matrimonial property legislation.[374] As the authors of the *Spousal Support Advisory*

[2001] OJ No 3911 (CA); *Hickey v Princ*, 2014 ONSC 5272; *MacQuarrie v MacQuarrie*, 2012 PECA 3; *Johnson v Johnson*, 2013 SKQB 57, citing Marie L Gordon, "Back to *Boston*: Spousal Support After Retirement" (2009) 28 Can Fam LQ 125.

369 [2003] MJ No 398 at para 37 (CA).

370 See also *Senek v Senek*, 2014 MBCA 67; *Coady v Coady*, 2014 MBQB 182.

371 2006 BCCA 494; see also *Biernacki v Biernacki*, 2014 ABQB 501; *Bozak v Bozak*, [2008] BCJ No 2080 (SC); *Jens v Jens*, 2008 BCCA 392; *ARJ v ZSJ*, 2009 BCSC 1662 (interim support); *Lazorek v Quinn*, 2010 BCSC 668; *Berta v Berta*, 2014 ONSC 3919; *Holmes v Matkovich*, 2008 YKCA 10. Compare *DLC v FMC*, 2011 BCCA 444.

372 *Peters v MacLean*, 2014 BCSC 990 at para 35, Joyce J.

373 *Flieger v Adams*, 2012 NBCA 39.

374 *Puiu v Puiu*, 2011 BCCA 480.

Guidelines point out, "the Advisory Guidelines on amount and duration do not change the law from *Boston v Boston* governing double-dipping, mostly from pensions. That law remains in place, as a possible constraint upon the amount of support, determining if some portion of income should be excluded from the formula because it has been previously shared under property division."[375]

Q. INCOME TAX AND RETROACTIVE ORDERS

Sections 56 and 60 of the *Income Tax Act*[376] provide that periodic spousal support payments made pursuant to an order of a competent tribunal or a written agreement after marriage breakdown are tax deductible by the payor and are taxable in the hands of the payee. Sections 56.1(3) and 60.1(3) of the *Income Tax Act* permit agreements for periodic payments of spousal support or an order for periodic spousal support to go back one prior calendar year but no farther.[377] However, a court cannot order that a retroactive support order be taxable/deductible even if the order relates to the current year and immediately preceding year, where the payments have not in fact been made in those years.[378] In contrast, lump sum spousal support payments are paid in after-tax dollars and are tax-free in the hands of the recipient. These basic principles are easy to state but not always easy to apply. For example, courts may order lump sum support to be payable in installments or alternatively may order periodic payments for a fixed period of time; or arrears of periodic support may be discharged by a lump sum that may or may not correspond to the aggregate of the arrears. The difference between lump sum and periodic support payments can, therefore, give rise to elusive distinctions with respect to income tax consequences. The particular language adopted in a separation agreement or court order may be important but is not decisive. In *R v McKimmon*,[379] Hugessen JA, of the Federal Court of Appeal, sets out a non-exhaustive list of eight factors to be taken into account for the purpose of differentiating between periodic spousal support payments and lump sum spousal support payable by instalments:

1.   the length of the periods at which the payments are made;

---

375   Department of Justice Canada, *Spousal Support Advisory Guidelines* (July 2008) at 12.6.3, online: www.justice.gc.ca/eng/rp-pr/fl-lf/spousal-epoux/spag/pdf/SSAG_eng.pdf. See also *MacQuarrie v MacQuarrie*, 2012 PECA 3.

376   RSC 1985, (5th Supp) c 1.

377   *Splett v Pearo*, 2011 ONSC 5329.

378   *Mayer v Mayer*, 2013 ONSC 7099 at para 136, Shaw J. Compare *Splett v Pearo*, 2014 ONSC 393 at paras 14 and 134–46.

379   [1990] 1 CTC 109 (Fed CA); see also *Berty v The Queen*, 2013 TCC 202.

2. the amount of payments in relation to the income and living standards of both payor and recipient;

3. whether the payments are to bear interest prior to their due date;

4. whether the amounts envisaged can be paid by anticipation at the option of the payor or can be accelerated as a penalty at the option of the recipient in the event of default;

5. whether the payments allow a significant degree of capital accumulation by the recipient;

6. whether the payments are stipulated to continue for an indefinite period or whether they are for a fixed term;

7. whether the agreed payments can be assigned and whether the obligation to pay survives the lifetime of either the payor or recipient;

8. whether the payments purport to release the payor from any future obligations to pay maintenance.

Periodic payments do not necessarily change in character merely because they are not made on time. Periodic spousal support payments that fall into arrears and are subsequently fully discharged by a lump sum payment may retain the characteristics necessary for their deductibility from the payor's income in the year when the lump sum payment is made and for their inclusion in the payee's taxable income for that year.[380] It has, nevertheless, been asserted that the quantification of retroactive spousal support cannot simply apply the *Spousal Support Advisory Guidelines* because those ranges are based upon periodic ongoing payments, which are presumed to be taxable by the recipient and deductible by the payor, whereas lump sum retroactive support amounts need to be "netted down" to reflect their non-tax inclusive status.[381] A more cautious approach was adopted in *Chapman v Chapman* by Belch J, who stated:

> [7] At the June 2009 hearing, the issue of personal tax relief, caused by a variation in the Order, was not addressed by either party. The December 17, 2009 Judgment results in arrears owing by the Respondent to the Applicant in the amount of $34,100.00. Had those payments been made pursuant to an existing agreement or court order, they would be deductible by the Respondent and included in the Applicant's income.
>
> [8] As the court did not discount the arrears to reflect tax consequences, it is the Court's belief the Respondent likely should be entitled to

---

380 *R v Sills*, [1985] 1 CTC 49 (Fed CA); *Laboret v Canada*, 2009 TCC 283.

381 *Betts v Betts*, 2015 NBQB 19; *AAM v RPK*, 2010 ONSC 930; but compare *Kerman v Kerman*, 2008 BCSC 852 and *Greenglass v Greenglass*, 2010 ONCA 675; and see *Dubreuil v Canada*, 2010 TCC 289; *Mayer v Mayer*, 2013 ONSC 7099; *Hume v Tomlinson*, 2015 ONSC 843.

tax relief and the Applicant entitled to some interest on the arrears. The parties nor the Court control what position will be taken by Canada Customs and Revenue Agency (CCRA) with respect to a lump sum payment of arrears. CCRA material handed to the Court on March 4, 2010 suggests that receipt by a payee of a retroactive lump sum is to be declared in the year it is received. The material suggests the taxpayer, however, can request his/her income tax return for previous years be reassessed to allocate the lump sum to the years the arrears relate to. Presumably, the payor of such a lump sum would be entitled to similar relief. Until such time as the parties learn of CCRA's decision, this Court cannot address whether the tax treatment impacted spousal support. The Court directs the tax treatment is grounds for a review of quantum of spousal support.[382]

Counsel should, therefore, address the income tax implications of any retroactive lump sum spousal support order that is being sought. If the submissions are inconsistent with a subsequent ruling by the Canada Revenue Agency, then the court may be asked to review its order in a variation proceeding, such as was contemplated by Belcher J in *Chapman v Chapman*.

Where, by prior agreement, the payor spouse agrees to pay directly to the recipient an amount equal to the recipient's tax liability on the support payments, that amount may be deducted from the payor's taxable income and must be included by the recipient spouse as income.[383]

Legal fees incurred in divorce proceedings by the applicant for spousal support are deductible claims against income.[384]

R. VARIATION AND TERMINATION OF SUPPORT ORDERS

1) General

Section 17(4.1) of the *Divorce* Act empowers a court to vary an existing order for spousal support upon proof of a substantial, unforeseen, and continuing change in the condition, means, needs, or other circumstances of either former spouse since the granting of the order that is sought to be varied.[385] An order for spousal support is subject to variation, rescission, or suspension on the application of either former spouse brought pursuant to section 17 of the *Divorce Act*.

---

382 2010 CanLII 18337 at paras 7–8 (Ont Sup Ct); see also *Hume v Tomlinson*, 2015 ONSC 843 at para 11.

383 *Guerin v R* (1994), 1 RFL (4th) 396 (TCC).

384 *Hutton v Hutton*, 2010 BCSC 923, citing *Gallien v The Queen*, [2001] 2 CTC 2676; see also Canada Revenue Agency, *Income Tax Folio S1-F3-C3: Support Payments*.

385 *LMP v LS*, 2011 SCC 64; *RP v RC*, 2011 SCC 65; *B(G) v G(L)*, [1995] 3 SCR 370.

Although interim orders are specifically authorized by subsections 15.1(2), 15.2(2), and 16(2) of the *Divorce Act*, no jurisdiction to grant interim orders is explicitly conferred by section 17 of the *Divorce Act*, which empowers a court to make an order varying, rescinding, or suspending, prospectively or retroactively, a permanent spousal support order, child support order, or custody order. In British Columbia and Saskatchewan, appellate courts have addressed the issue of whether interim variation orders could be granted under section 11 of the *Divorce Act*, 1968,[386] the predecessor to section 17 of the *Divorce Act*.[387] While acknowledging that there was no jurisdiction to grant interim orders on an application under section 11(2) of the *Divorce Act*, 1968 where variation was sought in respect of an existing permanent order for corollary financial relief, the judgments of *Burton v Burton*[388] and *Frey v Frey*[389] stated that an order could be varied pursuant to section 11(2) of the *Divorce Act*, 1968, and then varied again, if injustices might otherwise arise from delay prior to a full review of the attendant circumstances. On the other hand, in *Yeo v Yeo*,[390] the Prince Edward Island Court of Appeal concluded that injustices and hardships that can arise from delay in the full hearing of an application to vary an order under section 17(1) of the current *Divorce Act* cannot be addressed by successive orders, the first of which is merely transitional pending a full review of the attendant circumstances. Instead, injustices and hardships must be addressed by expedited hearings and/or by orders for retroactive variation, the latter jurisdiction being explicitly recognized by section 17(1) of the current *Divorce Act* but not by section 11(2) of the *Divorce Act*, 1968. Notwithstanding their different perspectives, the three aforementioned judgments have two features in common. First, they openly acknowledge that the relevant statutory provisions confer no jurisdiction on a court to grant an interim order varying an existing permanent order. Second, they acknowledge the need for the avoidance of injustices or hardships that might arise from delay. Where they differ is in the means whereby such avoidance is secured. Where the interests of children are concerned, some courts have purported to exercise their *parens patriae* jurisdiction as a means of securing the interim variation of a final order for child support.[391] There is, nevertheless, room for doubt whether such jurisdiction can properly be invoked in a proceeding relating to child support, as distinct

---

386 SC 1967–68, c 24 (RSC 1970, c D-4).

387 RSC 1985 (2d Supp), c 3.

388 (1982), 27 RFL (2d) 170 (BCCA).

389 (1987), 8 RFL (3d) 154 (Sask CA).

390 (1998), 42 RFL (4th) 418 (PEISCAD).

391 See *Dixon v Dixon* (1995), 13 RFL (4th) 160 (Alta QB); *Parlee v Lavallée* (1992), 42 RFL (3d) 58 (Ont Gen Div); *Bradley v Bradley* (1995), 15 RFL (4th) 33 (Ont Gen Div); *Daher v Daher*,

from a guardianship, custody, or adoption proceeding.[392] Even if such jurisdiction can be invoked to protect the economic interests of a child, there is
no reason to assume that it can be invoked to reduce pre-existing child support obligations for the benefit of a parent. Furthermore, the *parens patriae*
jurisdiction has no application in situations involving the variation of spousal support orders. As McQuaid J observed in *Yeo v Yeo*, "[t]he *parens patriae*
jurisdiction of the court, as broad as it may be, may only be invoked when
the person for whose benefit it is being invoked is incompetent. See: *Re Eve*
[(1986), 61 Nfld & PEIR 273 at para 36 (SCC)]."[393] After a detailed review of relevant caselaw in *Keogan v Weekes*,[394] RS Smith J, of the Family Law Division
of the Saskatchewan Court of Queen's Bench, found himself "in harmony
with the analytical chord struck by the Saskatchewan Court of Appeal in *Frey*
. . . [which] permits the court to address a manifest injustice but at the same
time respects the strictures of the *Divorce Act*."[395] Applying that approach,
Smith J concluded that changes in the children's parenting arrangements
were insufficient in themselves to justify an interim or temporary reduction
in the amount of child support payable under a pre-existing permanent order
in circumstances where the father's current income as a farmer could not be
resolved on affidavit evidence and required a *viva voce* hearing in which income issues and assertions could be tested by cross-examination.

On an application to vary a permanent spousal support order pursuant
to section 17(4.1) of the *Divorce Act*, the onus falls on the applicant to prove
a material change in the condition, means, needs, or other circumstances of
either former spouse. As Sopinka J observed in *Willick v Willick*,[396] a material
change is a change that was not contemplated by the court and that would
have led to different terms if the change had been known when the order was
granted. If the matter that is relied on as constituting a change was known at
the relevant time, it cannot be relied on as the basis for variation. The change
must be of a substantial, unforeseen, and continuing nature. In a variation
proceeding, the existing support order must be assumed to have been correct
when it was granted. Absent proof of a material change since then, the judge

---

[2002] OJ No 3671 (Sup Ct); *Clark v Vanderhoeven*, 2011 ONSC 2286 (application under
Ontario *Family Law Act*).

392 See *Harris v Harris* (1978), 90 DLR (3d) 699 (BCSC).

393 *Yeo v Yeo*, [1998] PEIJ No 97 at para 12 (SCAD).

394 [2005] SJ No 170 (QB).

395 *Ibid* at para 33.

396 [1994] 3 SCR 670; see also *B(G) v G(L)*, [1995] 3 SCR 370; *LMP v LS*, 2011 SCC 64; *RP v RC*,
2011 SCC 65; *Kowalski v Kowalski*, 2012 ABCA 60; *MacLanders v MacLanders*, 2012 BCCA
482; *Powell v Levesque*, 2014 BCCA 33; *Parent v Morrissette*, 2013 NBQB 408; *Daigle v
Daigle*, 2013 NSSC 205; *Bhandhal v Bhandhal*, 2015 ONSC 1152.

hearing a variation application has no jurisdiction to vary the order because he or she regards it as inappropriate or unrealistic. If a material change is established sufficient to warrant judicial intervention, the variation order should reflect that change in light of the objectives set out in section 17(7) of the *Divorce Act*.[397] An obligor cannot rely upon a future speculative financial change to justify variation of an order for spousal support.[398] The normal process of aging and the maturation of the family unit do not suffice as a change of circumstances.[399] A payor should not be estopped from seeking a variation in his spousal support obligations on the ground his retirement was "foreseeable" at the time of the original order. Courts routinely permit variations of spousal support orders if a payor retires. Courts should not look past a payor's decision to retire unless its purpose is to frustrate a support order.[400] Whether retirement constitutes a material change depends upon the attendant circumstances of the case.[401] The question to be asked is whether the court finds that the decision to retire is reasonable, given all the circumstances.[402] If an early retirement will severely prejudice a spousal support recipient, a court may impute income for spousal support purposes as though the obligor had not retired.[403]

The requirement of a material change within the meaning of section 17(4.1) of the *Divorce Act* is not met where the applicant, who seeks a reduction in the amount of spousal support, fails to explain a change in his or her employment status and provides no evidence that he or she has made reasonable efforts to find comparable employment commensurate with his or her earning capacity based on his or her education, skill, experience, age, and health. A self-

---

397 *LMP v LS*, 2011 SCC 64; *RP v RC*, 2011 SCC 65; *KD v ND*, 2014 BCCA 70; *Kordyban v Kordyban*, 2013 ABQB 500; *McMurchy v McMurchy*, [2002] BCJ No 2681 (CA); *Hepburn v Hepburn*, 2013 BCCA 383; *Winsor v Winsor*, [2002] NJ No 195 (CA); *Rondeau v Rondeau*, 2011 NSCA 5; *Smith v Rand*, 2013 NSSC 369; *Allaire v Lavergne*, 2014 ONSC 3653; *MacQuarrie v MacQuarrie*, 2012 PECA 3; *Droit de la famille — 141364*, 2014 QCCA 1144.

398 *Bhandhal v Bhandhal*, 2015 ONSC 1152.

399 *Kenyon v Kenyon*, 2011 BCSC 718, citing *Rondeau v Rondeau*, 2011 NSCA 5.

400 *Hickey v Princ*, 2014 ONSC 5272 at paras 32–33, Abrams J.

401 *Swales v Swales*, 2010 ABQB 187, rev'd 2010 ABCA 292; *McCulloch v McCulloch*, 2013 ABQB 177; *MacLanders v MacLanders*, 2012 BCCA 482; *Powell v Levesque*, 2014 BCCA 33; *Peters v MacLean*, 2014 BCSC 990; *Henteleff v Henteleff*, 2005 MBCA 50; *Flieger v Adams*, 2012 NBCA 39; *Sangster v Sangster*, 2014 NBCA 14; *Rondeau v Rondeau*, 2011 NSCA 5; *Cossette v Cossette*, 2014 ONSC 2678 (Div Ct).

402 *Oderkirk v Oderkirk*, 2014 NSSC 37 at para 22, Boudreau J. But compare *LeMoine v LeMoine*, [1997] NBJ No 31 (CA) and see *Vaughn v Vaughn*, 2014 NBCA 6.

403 *Holaday v Holaday*, 2012 SKQB 211 at para 24, citing *Moffatt v Moffatt* (2003), 67 OR (3d) 239 (Sup Ct) and *Fehr v Fehr*, 2006 BCSC 1440; see also *Way v Way*, 2014 BCSC 1587.

induced reduction in income does not satisfy the statutory requirement.[404] Similarly, self-induced increased needs cannot be relied upon to justify increased spousal support. A recipient spouse is not entitled to spend his or her way into a "change of circumstances" for the purposes of section 17 of the *Divorce Act*. Applying the above principles, the British Columbia Court of Appeal in *WCP v CP*[405] found no error on the part of the chambers judge who had dismissed the wife's application for increased spousal support because her increased expenses and reduced investment income were attributable to her lifestyle choice in purchasing a luxury condominium rather than more modest accommodation such as was envisaged by the trial judge when the original spousal support order was granted.

Changed circumstances may include not only the happening of something unexpected, but also the non-occurrence of an expected event.[406] A support recipient's failure to achieve anticipated economic self-sufficiency within a specified period of time may constitute a material change of circumstances that justifies extending the duration of the order.[407] The receipt of an inheritance is a relevant factor to consider in quantifying spousal support and may constitute a material change of circumstances that justifies variation order of a needs-based spousal support order.[408]

Where a bankrupt spouse is released from an equalization claim but retains an exempt pension asset, a support order might be used to redress the inequity.[409] Courts have recognized that a spouse's bankruptcy, with a consequential release from property equalization or matrimonial debt obligations, can be a material change in circumstances justifying variation of a spousal support order.[410]

Where a divorced wife has been adequately compensated for the economic disadvantages sustained in consequence of her previous marriage and its breakdown, and her new career and remarriage negate any continuing need for spousal support, an order for termination of the divorced husband's reviewable consensual spousal support obligation should be affirmed on appeal. A divorced wife has no proprietary interest in her divorced husband's

---

404 *Irvine v Irvine*, [1990] MJ No 392 (QB); *Parks v Parks*, [2000] OJ No 2863 (Sup Ct); *Poitras v Poitras*, [2006] SJ No 113 (QB). See also *Verschuren v Verschuren*, 2014 ONCA 518.
405 [2005] BCJ No 179 (CA).
406 *Morgan v Morgan*, 2001 BCSC 874 at para 25; *Fisher v Fisher*, 2008 ONCA 11; *Palombo v Palombo*, 2011 ONSC 1796.
407 *MMF v RB*, 2010 BCSC 1268; *Cottreau v Pothier*, [2002] NSJ No 556 (CA).
408 *LeBlanc v LeBlanc*, 2013 NBCA 22, citing *Mills v Mills*, 2010 NBCA 20 and *BS v LS*, 2011 NBCA 7. Compare *TT v RH*, 2011 BCSC 1920 (compensatory spousal support).
409 *Schreyer v Schreyer*, 2011 SCC 35; compare *Zivic v Zivic*, 2014 ONSC 7262.
410 *Ells-Hunter v Hunter*, 2011 NBQB 63; see also *Ross v Ross*, 2014 ONSC 1828.

increased earning capacity, and she cannot sustain a claim for ongoing support based simply on a substantial disparity between their current incomes. Economic self-sufficiency, which is one of the objectives of the *Divorce Act*, is to be determined by the divorced spouses' standard of living during their marriage, not by reference to the divorced husband's current income.[411] An appellate court should not overturn a support judgment unless the reasons disclose an error in principle or a significant misapprehension of the evidence, or unless the order is clearly wrong.[412] In *Roberts v Beresford*,[413] the British Columbia Court of Appeal found that the trial judge had considered all the relevant factors and objectives under the *Divorce Act* and had placed no undue emphasis on the objective of promoting economic self-sufficiency, due regard having been paid to the review clause in the prior spousal agreement that addressed the issues of economic self-sufficiency and the divorced husband's income. The British Columbia Court of Appeal declined to interfere with the trial judge's fixing of the date of the review as the appropriate termination date.

On an application to vary a spousal support order, section 17 of the *Divorce Act* requires the "means" of each divorced spouse to be addressed, and this includes their unrealized earning capacity[414] or capital assets.[415] Section 15.2(5) of the *Divorce Act* provides that "the court shall not take into consideration any misconduct of a spouse in relation to the marriage" when considering an application for spousal support. Pursuant to section 17(6) of the *Divorce Act*, the same criterion applies to an application to vary an existing order. These provisions do not disentitle a fifty-seven-year-old divorced wife to ongoing spousal support when she is incapable of achieving economic self-sufficiency due to her age, medical problems, and the emotional devastation that she suffered in consequence of her former husband's unilateral withdrawal from their twenty-year marriage and the death of close family members.[416]

In determining whether to vary a spousal support order pursuant to section 17 of the *Divorce Act*, the court must have regard to whether the alleged changes are of sufficient magnitude to warrant variation in light

---

411 *Purdue v Purdue*, 2014 NBQB 262 at para 84. But see Section E(5), above in this chapter.

412 *Hickey v Hickey*, [1999] 2 SCR 518 at para 11.

413 [2006] BCJ No 291 (CA).

414 *Hayward v Hayward*, [2006] NBJ No 283 (QB) (income imputed to spousal support recipient who failed to take reasonable steps to find employment; order for reduced amount); *House v House*, [2007] NJ No 383 (TD); *Walsh v Walsh*, [2006] OJ No 2480 (Sup Ct).

415 *Leskun v Leskun*, [2006] 1 SCR 920; *Walters v Walters*, 2011 BCCA 331.

416 *Leskun v Leskun*, [2006] 1 SCR 920.

of the conceptual basis of the original order. In *Bracklow v Bracklow*,[417] Mc-Lachlin J, as she then was, acknowledged three conceptual grounds for entitlement to spousal support: (1) compensatory; (2) contractual; and (3) non-compensatory. Where all three of these grounds are likely to have co-existed as bases for the original spousal support order on the dissolution of a twenty-two-year traditional marriage, the court may conclude that the changes largely resulting from the recipient's relatively new cohabitational relationship, namely, the sharing of household expenses and the sale of her former home—coupled with her modest earning capacity—are not material changes sufficient to warrant the elimination or reduction of her former husband's court-ordered spousal support obligation.[418]

Moge v Moge,[419] though decided under section 17 of the *Divorce Act* in the context of a variation proceeding, has produced its major impact on original applications for spousal support under section 15.2 of the *Divorce Act*. Although empirical evidence is lacking, legal practitioners throughout Canada acknowledge that *Moge v Moge* has strengthened the pre-existing trend towards higher amounts of spousal support and for longer periods of time. Fixed-term orders are no longer regarded as appropriate to address the economic consequences of long traditional marriages where the woman as wife and mother assumed the primary responsibility for homemaking and child care.

The impact of *Moge v Moge* on variation applications is explained in the following observations of Baker J, of the British Columbia Supreme Court, in *Patrick v Patrick*,[420] who sets out the evidential requirements faced by obligors in seeking to reduce or terminate spousal support orders:

> The *Divorce Act* does not rule out the possibility that an economically disadvantaged spouse may be only temporarily disadvantaged. As a result of post-divorce career developments, education or training, or other fortuitous circumstances, economic disadvantage may be reduced or even eliminated. Where the economic disadvantage sought to be remedied by the payment of spousal support has been eliminated or significantly reduced, termination or a reduction in support is envisioned by the Act. In my view, however, where an order for spousal support has been made with the primary objective of compensating the receiving spouse for economic disadvantage accruing during several years of marriage and expected to continue after divorce, a court should not readily reduce or terminate spousal support. The evidence on an application to vary a so-called "com-

---

417   [1999] 1 SCR 420.
418   *Goudy v Malbeuf*, [2002] SJ No 466 (QB).
419   [1992] 3 SCR 813.
420   (1994), 92 BCLR (2d) 50 (SC).

pensatory support" order must establish not only that there has been a significant change in the means and needs of the parties since trial but also that the factors which resulted in economic disadvantage during the marriage and after its breakdown no longer exist and that the lost advantage has been recovered.[421]

Many lawyers and judges assume that spousal support, like child support, should be reduced or eliminated once there are no longer any dependent children. Although it is appropriate to terminate child support when the child is economically self-sufficient, it does not follow that spousal support should be terminated, or even reduced, because the custodial parent's responsibilities for the child have ceased to exist. The economic consequences of child rearing for the custodial parent are often permanent and irreversible in terms of loss of employment potential, including loss of the fringe benefits usually associated with employment. As Palmeter ACJSC, of the Nova Scotia Supreme Court, observed in *Gillis v Gillis*,

> In my opinion, the fact that the two youngest children have left the respondent's home does not necessarily mean that maintenance has to be reduced on any pro rata basis, or even be reduced at all.[422]

On the same basis, it is submitted that, on an original application for spousal support or on a variation application, lawyers and judges should reject any assumption that short-term marriages warrant only short-term spousal support when these marriages have produced children. The notion that spousal support should terminate or be reduced when the youngest child is old enough to attend school is one that must be rejected if the observations of Bowman J in *Brockie v Brockie*,[423] which were quoted with approval in *Moge v Moge*,[424] are to have a real impact. Child-care responsibilities do not end when a child enters school, although the direct and hidden costs of child rearing may change.

2) Variation of Fixed-Term Orders

Subsection 17(10) of the *Divorce Act* provides that, where a spousal support order provides for support for a definite period or until a specified event occurs, a court may not vary that order after expiry of the period or the occurrence of the stipulated event for the purpose of resuming support, unless the

---

421 *Ibid* at 53–54.

422 (1994), 3 RFL (4th) 128 at 131 (NSSCAD). And see judgment of L'Heureux-Dubé J in *Willick v Willick*, [1994] 3 SCR 670, 6 RFL (4th) 161 at 216.

423 (1987), 5 RFL (3d) 440 at 447–48 (Man QB), aff'd (1987), 8 RFL (3d) 302 (Man CA).

424 [1992] 3 SCR 813, 43 RFL (3d) 345 at 388–89, L'Heureux-Dubé J.

court is satisfied that (1) a variation order is necessary to relieve economic hardship arising from a change in the condition, means, needs, or other circumstances of the spouse that is related to the marriage; and (2) the change, had it existed at the time when the current order was made, would likely have resulted in a different order.[425] The explicit requirement that the effect of the change must be causally connected to the marriage imposes a significant limitation on the jurisdiction of the court once an order has terminated by the effluxion of time or by the occurrence of the stipulated event. Given a material change, therefore, an application to vary should be brought before expiry of the order so as to avoid the explicit stringent requirements of subsection 17(10) of the *Divorce Act*.

The court hearing an application for variation should treat the first order as correct at the time it was made, and confine its role to examining whether subsequent changes justify its variation under section 17.[426] The change relied upon must be of a substantial, unforeseen, and continuing nature.[427] In an annotation of *Therrien-Cliché v Cliché*,[428] Professor James G McLeod identified two kinds of changed circumstances: "1) something happens that was not taken into account when the prior order was made; and 2) something that was expected to happen does not occur." This latter circumstance is exemplified in *O'Neill v Wolfe*,[429] wherein the wife was granted a spousal support order in the amount of $1,000 monthly for a fixed-term of two years in January 2001. The term was fixed in the expectation that she would recover from her depression, which had its origins in the marriage, and establish her economic self-sufficiency within the two-year period. This expectation was not realized but there was still hope that she would overcome her depression and that her acquisition of a bed and breakfast in a tourist centre would enable her to become economically self-sufficient at some future date. Having regard to this future potential and the fact that the business had enjoyed a significant capital gain, even though it had yet to earn a profit, Brooke J, of the British Columbia Supreme Court, granted a variation order to the wife but in the reduced amount of $750 monthly from the date of her application (1 April 2003) to 1 March 2004, with the amount to be further reduced to $500 monthly thereafter, and the amount to be reviewed in May 2005.

---

425   *Higgins v Higgins*, [2006] AJ No 1550 (QB); *Hancock v Hancock*, [2006] BCJ No 550 (SC); *Petroczi v Petroczi*, 2011 BCSC 1321; *Eidt v Eidt*, 2009 NBQB 152.

426   *Oakley v Oakley* (1985), 48 RFL (2d) 307 at para 16 (BCCA); *Aspe v Aspe*, 2010 BCCA 508.

427   *Carter v Carter* (1991), 34 RFL (3d) 1 (BCCA); *Hickey v Princ*, 2014 ONSC 5272.

428   (1997), 30 RFL (4th) 97 (Ont CA).

429   *O'Neill v Wolfe*, [2004] BCJ No 807 (SC).

3) Effect of Remarriage or Common Law Relationship

a) Effect of Remarriage

There is no express requirement in section 17 of the *Divorce Act* that the court shall vary or rescind a spousal support order in the event of the subsequent remarriage of either party. The remarriage of either divorced spouse is a relevant but not a decisive factor on any subsequent application to vary or discharge a subsisting order.[430] An obvious point of relevance is the extent to which remarriage or re-partnering impacts on a person's expenses or contributes to an improvement or diminution in one's standard of living.[431]

Remarriage of the obligor may either increase or reduce the ability to pay support under a pre-existing support order. Where the obligor has remarried and the new spouse contributes to their common household expenses, the obligor's ability to pay support for a former spouse is thereby increased and the amount of support may be varied in light of that factor.[432]

There have been conflicts of judicial opinion on the question of whether a divorced spouse should be relieved of court-ordered obligations to the first family by reason of newly acquired obligations owed to a second family.[433] Some courts have concluded that the primary responsibility is owed to the first family.[434] Other courts have held that the new family should take precedence where the obligor cannot support both families, because it is in the public interest for the new family to survive.[435] Still other courts have adopted

---

430 *B(G) v G(L)*, [1995] 3 SCR 370; *Ewing v Ewing* (1990), 26 RFL (3d) 115 (BCSC); *Richard v Richard*, 2012 MBQB 36 (interim spousal support order under interjurisdictional support orders legislation terminated by subsequent divorce); *Richards v Richards* (1972), 7 RFL 101 (Ont CA); *Freer v Freer*, 2012 ONSC 6269; *Ceulemans v Ceulemans* (1986), 50 Sask R 120 (CA); *Grainger v Grainger* (1992), 39 RFL (3d) 101 (Sask CA).

431 *Flieger v Adams*, 2012 NBCA 39; *Shurson v Shurson*, 2011 NSSC 163.

432 *Watson v Watson* (1991), 35 RFL (3d) 169 (BCSC); *Hersey v Hersey* (1993), 47 RFL (3d) 117 (NBCA); *Garwood v Garwood* (1995), 15 RFL (4th) 53 (NBCA); *Tyler v Tyler*, 2011 NLTD(F) 20; *Edwards v Edwards* (1994), 5 RFL (4th) 321 (NSCA); *Shurson v Shurson*, 2011 NSSC 163. Compare *Anderson v Anderson*, 2014 NSSC 7.

433 As to the effect of support obligations arising on a second divorce, see *Harvey v Harvey* (1995), 14 RFL (4th) 128 (BCCA).

434 *Doole v Doole* (1991), 32 RFL (3d) 283 (Alta QB); *Firth v Firth* (1991), 35 RFL (3d) 445 (BCSC); *Jenkins v Jenkins* (1993), 47 RFL (3d) 219 (BCSC); *Wallis v Wallis* (1989), 61 Man R (2d) 199 (QB); *Fournier v Fournier* (1990), 97 NBR (2d) 309 (QB); *Tyler v Tyler*, 2011 NLTD(F) 20; *Zinck v Zinck* (1989), 93 NSR (2d) 374 (Fam Ct); *Somers v Somers* (1990), 79 Nfld & PEIR 1 (PEITD); *Fredrickson v Fredrickson* (1993), 48 RFL (3d) 48 (Sask QB); see also *Greco v Levin* (1991), 33 RFL (3d) 405 (Ont Gen Div); *Burton v Burton* (1994), 9 RFL (4th) 108 (Ont Gen Div).

435 *Wolfe v Wolfe* (1995), 15 RFL (4th) 86 (BCSC); *Burt v Burt* (1990), 25 RFL (3d) 92 (Nfld TD); *Upshall v Janvier* (1994), 120 Nfld & PEIR 49 (Nfld TD); *L(GM) v L(VA)* (1993), 127 NSR (2d) 66 at 69–70 (Fam Ct); *Kelly v Kelly* (1992), 44 RFL (3d) 214 (PEITD).

a middle ground whereby no preference is given to either family.[436] In the final analysis, each case will be determined on its own facts.[437] The intractable problem of reconciling the respective interests of sequential families often produces a collision between questions of principle and economic realities. While it is proper for courts to recognize that a person should respect his or her obligations to the first family, children in the second family also have needs that should not be forgotten.[438] Human nature and the economic demands of children may wreak havoc with analytical doctrines or any cohesive philosophy that seeks to balance the legal rights of competing families. Courts are inescapably reduced, therefore, to making the best of a bad situation by seeking to promote a situation that is tolerable for the children of both families.[439] However, the judicial discretion is subject to the mandatory application of the *Child Support Guidelines*.

Different considerations apply where it is the divorced recipient spouse who remarries. In the absence of any direction to the contrary in the support order, the remarriage of a divorced spouse entitled to court-ordered support from a former spouse does not automatically justify the variation or discharge of a subsisting order for spousal or child support, but such remarriage is a relevant circumstance to be considered on any application for variation or discharge.[440] When it is the spouse receiving support that remarries, the burden falls on that spouse to demonstrate that, despite remarriage, there is a continuing basis for spousal support.[441] Where the parties to the second marriage are financially self-sufficient, courts have traditionally relieved the

436 *Koop v Polson* (1991), 31 RFL (3d) 1 (Man CA); *Pilon v Pilon* (1993), 48 RFL (3d) 99 (Man QB); *Ralph v Ralph* (1994), 7 RFL (4th) 238 (Nfld SC); *Smith v Smith* (1992), 40 RFL (3d) 316 (NS Fam Ct); *Grant-Hose v Grant-Hose* (1991), 32 RFL (3d) 26 (Ont UFC); *Greco v Levin* (1991), 33 RFL (3d) 405 (Ont Gen Div); *Wills v Wills* (1994), 9 RFL (4th) 78 (Ont Ct Prov Div) (balancing of family income in each household); *Cass v Cass* (1995), 15 RFL (4th) 436 (PEISCTD); see also *Willick v Willick*, [1994] 3 SCR 670, 6 RFL (4th) 161 at 217, L'Heureux-Dubé J.

437 *Jackson v Jackson*, [1993] OJ No 1713 (Gen Div); *Droit de la famille — 1404*, [1991] RJQ 1561 at 1566 (Que CA). See, generally, Judge Norris Weisman, "The Second Family in the Law of Support" (1984) 37 RFL (2d) 245.

438 *Young v Konkle* (1993), 1 RFL (4th) 211 (Alta QB).

439 *Smith v Smith* (1992), 40 RFL (3d) 316 at 318–19 (NS Fam Ct), Levy Fam Ct J; see also *Magder v Magder*, [1994] OJ No 1334 (CA).

440 See *Caron v Caron*, [1987] 1 SCR 892; *Stenhouse v Stenhouse*, 2011 ABQB 530; *Range v Range* (1995), 14 RFL (4th) 11 (BCSC); *Savoie v Savoie* (1999), 49 RFL (4th) 336 at 336 (Man CA); *Chubey v Chubey*, 2011 MBQB 100; *MacDougall v MacRae* (1989), 19 RFL (3d) 329 (NBQB); *Smith v Smith* (1992), 40 RFL (3d) 316 (NS Fam Ct); *Wilson v Wilson*, [2005] OJ No 3478 (Sup Ct); *Freer v Freer*, 2012 ONSC 6269; *Campbell v Rooney* (1995), 10 RFL (4th) 351 (PEIS-CTD); and see Judge Norris Weisman, "The Second Family in the Law of Support" (1984) 37 RFL (2d) 245.

441 *Rimmer v Adshead*, 2012 SKQB 500.

former spouse of any continuing obligation to support his or her divorced and remarried spouse.[442] In the final analysis, however, the effect of the obligee's remarriage on a subsisting spousal support order should be determined in light of the rationale upon which the order was based. A needs-based order for spousal support may be terminated or reduced by a court if the recipient remarries or enters into a non-marital cohabitational relationship,[443] but if the spousal support order was compensatory in nature, remarriage or unmarried cohabitation may not justify its termination.[444] In *LJH v JAZ*,[445] Brown J stated:

> 19 Broadly speaking, no one questions the principle that when the court considers an application to end spousal support and to vary child support, it should consider the earning capacity of the parties and the means of any new spouse: *Redpath v. Redpath*, 2008 BCSC 68, para. 44. See also, *Rakose v Rakose*, 2008 BCSC 1165; *Moreau v. Fliesen*, 2008 BCSC 1358; and *Chalmers v. Chalmers*, 2009 BCSC 517. While true, broadly speaking, the principle is subject to certain conditions, ones that bring us closer to the central issue, which is the extent to which the original award for spousal support was compensatory, non-compensatory, or contractual. The answer to this question largely decides whether, and to what extent, the spousal support order can be cancelled or varied in this case.
>
> . . .
>
> 35 In my opinion, the cases do not stand for a proposition that whenever a spousal support award includes a compensatory component, the financial benefits of a remarriage, no matter how great, become irrelevant. *Kelly* [*v. Kelly*, 2007 BCSC 227], for example, does not stand for that. Logically, the extent to which the financial benefits of remarriage have a voice in a variation application depends on how much compensatory considerations

---

442 *Wrobel v Wrobel* (1994), 8 RFL (4th) 403 (Alta QB); *Beaumont v Beaumont* (1988), 19 RFL (3d) 33 (NBQB); *Oxenham v Oxenham* (1982), 26 RFL (2d) 161 (Ont CA); *Bush v Bush* (1989), 21 RFL (3d) 298 (Ont UFC); *Droit de la famille — 1404*, [1991] RJQ 1561 (Que CA); *Impey v Impey* (1973), 13 RFL 240 (Sask QB).

443 *Wolters v Wolters*, 2013 ABQB 172; *Watkins v Watkins*, 2013 BCSC 1983; *Chubey v Chubey*, 2011 MBQB 100, *Lalonde v Lalonde*, 2014 ONSC 4925. See also *Qaraan v Qaraan*, 2014 ONCA 401.

444 *Rosario v Rosario* (1991), 37 RFL (3d) 24 (Alta CA); *Wolters v Wolters*, 2013 ABQB 172; *Murphy v Murphy*, 2007 BCCA 500; *Clarke v Clarke*, 2014 BCSC 824; *Savoie v Savoie* (1999), 49 RFL (4th) 336 (Man CA); *Lagacé v Lagacé*, [1999] NBJ No 556 (CA) (unmarried cohabitation); *TTB v PHD*, 2014 NBBR 164 (unmarried cohabitation); *Balazsy v Balazsy*, [2009] OJ No 4113 (Sup Ct); *Qaraan v Qaraan*, 2014 ONCA 401; *Beattie v Beattie*, 2013 SKQB 127 at para 43. Compare *Lockyer v Lockyer*, [2000] OJ No 2939 (Sup Ct).

445 2014 BCSC 1384 at paras 19 and 35–36.

figured in the original award, and on the nature and extent of the financial benefits remarriage conferred.

36   A result that would see either case of a recipient spouse with an only partially compensatory support order, now most advantageously remarried, but because of the compensatory part of the order, any variation of the order refused; or termination of the order granted because the remarriage had been so advantageous, the recipient wife holding an order almost wholly compensatory and only partly paid, would both be unreasonable.

Repartnering has an impact on needs-based spousal support simply because the recipient's needs are usually reduced in that current household expenses are shared by his or her new partner.[446] Addressing the effect of repartnering in *Colley v Colley*,[447] Quinn J, of the Ontario Superior Court of Justice stated:

69   When considering the implications upon a need-based spousal-support order of the re-partnering of a recipient spouse, there are two important questions to ask:
(a)   Does the recipient spouse have a present need for support?
(b)   Does her new partner have a legal obligation to contribute to her expenses?

70   Where the prior spousal-support order contains a compensatory component, the following questions are appropriate;
(a)   Has the recipient spouse overcome the economic disadvantages arising from her role in the marriage so that there is no basis for continuing compensatory support?
(b)   Have compensatory concerns been fully addressed as of the date of the variation?
(c)   Should the court reduce or eliminate the need-based portion of the prior order, while maintaining the compensatory portion?

A helpful list of issues to consider is also found in Marie Gordon's paper entitled "Glass Ceilings in Spousal Support."[448] The listed issues include:

1.   Does the recipient spouse still need support in view of her new relationship and the income of her new partner?
2.   Is there a way to terminate the periodic support obligation while acknowledging an ongoing entitlement (i.e. by a final lump sum payment)?
3.   Did the parties specify the reasons why support was being paid when they signed their agreement?

---

446   *Locke v Ledrew*, [2006] AJ No 759 (QB); *Smith v Smith*, [2007] MJ No 284 (QB).
447   2013 ONSC 5666 at paras 69–70.
448   Paper presented to the National Family Law Program, Whistler, BC, July 1998.

4. Was it foreseeable at the time of the agreement that the spouse would remarry or cohabit?

5. Can it be said with any degree of certainty that the new relationship will last?

6. What effort is the recipient spouse making to achieve economic self-sufficiency?

7. Will the new relationship compensate the recipient for the economic consequences of the first marriage?

To these considerations may be added:

8. Have the property claims been paid?

9. What are the respective obligations of the parties to the children, and will the children have post-secondary education costs?[449]

A spouse who wants to be able to argue that remarriage or cohabitation was foreseeable at the time of entering into minutes of settlement should assume the obligation to "lay that relationship on the table" at the time of signing the minutes of settlement. After reviewing the aforementioned issues in *Wilson v Wilson*,[450] the motion judge concluded that the wife's medical condition rendered part-time employment reasonable but that she continued to suffer an ongoing economic disadvantage from her homemaking role during her first marriage that was not eliminated by her remarriage. Having regard to the divorced husband's increased income and the divorced wife's reduced needs after her remarriage, the motion judge concluded that she should continue to receive indexed periodic spousal support, but in a reduced amount from that provided by the minutes of settlement. The remarriage of the recipient of spousal support does not constitute a material change of circumstances within the terms of minutes of settlement if the obligor was fully aware of the likelihood of his wife remarrying a wealthy friend who was known to both of them.[451]

b) Effect of Common Law Relationship

A divorced spouse who is under a court-ordered obligation to support his or her former spouse is not automatically released from that obligation because of voluntarily assumed new financial obligations arising from a common law relationship.[452] Where the divorced spouse's obligation to support the "common-law spouse" is legally recognized, the court may feel compelled to strike

---

449 *Jackson v McNee*, 2011 ONSC 4651.

450 [2005] OJ No 3478 (Sup Ct).

451 *Bhupal v Bhupal*, 2009 ONCA 521.

452 *Fiddler v Fiddler*, 2014 ONSC 4068.

a balance between the competing obligations owed to the respective families.[453] As with remarriage, each case will be determined on its own facts.[454] The fact that a divorced spouse shares expenses with a current partner is relevant to the ability to pay support to a former spouse, but the formulae under the *Spousal Support Advisory Guidelines* do not take this into account.[455]

The *Miglin* criteria apply where the terms of a comprehensive separation agreement, which includes a third-party non-cohabitation clause, are incorporated in a divorce judgment. In the absence of any express term or condition whereby court-ordered spousal support shall cease in the event that the recipient enters into a common law relationship,[456] the formation of such a relationship does not automatically justify termination of an order for spousal support.[457] However, when a recipient of spousal support enters into a cohabitational relationship that was not foreseen when the obligation to pay support was agreed or ordered, it can amount to a material change in the recipient spouse's circumstances that justifies the reduction or even termination of the spousal support obligation. Caselaw in British Columbia asserts that the recipient spouse bears the onus of demonstrating that, despite the material change, there is a continuing need for spousal support.[458] In *Juvatopolos v Juvatopolos*,[459] an order for compensatory spousal support granted to a homemaking wife on the dissolution of her traditional twenty-four-year marriage was found subject to reduction under section 17 of the *Divorce Act*, where the recipient failed to take reasonable steps to increase her earning capacity because of ongoing monthly payments that she received from her

---

453 *Cooper v Cooper* (1983), 33 RFL (2d) 359 (Ont Prov Ct); compare *McKinney v Polston* (1992), 42 RFL (3d) 141 (BCSC).

454 *Fiddler v Fiddler*, 2014 ONSC 4068. See Section R(3)(a), above in this chapter. As to the contributions of a "common-law spouse" to household expenses, see *Underwood v Underwood* (1994), 3 RFL (4th) 457 (Ont Gen Div).

455 *Chamberlain v Chamberlain*, 2003 NBCA 34; *Flieger v Adams*, 2012 NBCA 39; *Grant v Grant*, 2012 NBCA 101; *Mayer v Mayer*, 2013 ONSC 7099.

456 See *Caron v Caron*, [1987] 1 SCR 892; *Neufeld v Neufeld* (1986), 3 RFL (3d) 435 (Ont HCJ); *Rogers v Rogers* (1992), 42 RFL (3d) 410 (NBQB) (unsuccessful attempt to arrange affairs so as to stop short of "cohabitation"); see also *Gillham v Gillham* (1993), 48 RFL (3d) 156 (Alta CA) (separation agreement; onus of proof).

457 See *MFR v BPR*, 2010 BCSC 1063; *McMullen v McMullen* (1993), 141 NBR (2d) 297 at 304 (QB); *TTB v PHD*, 2014 NBBR 164; *Horlock v Horlock* (1984), 42 RFL (2d) 164 (Ont CA), aff'g (1983), 37 RFL (2d) 198 (Ont HCJ); *Ewart v Ewart* (1979), 10 RFL (2d) 73 (Ont CA); *Droit de la famille — 333*, [1987] RDF 45 (Que CA); *Campbell v Campbell*, 2012 SKQB 39; compare *Barnard v Barnard* (1982), 30 RFL (2d) 337 (Ont CA). See also *Janz v Harris* (1993), 86 Man R (2d) 300 (QB) (same-sex relationship; wife granted $50,000 lump sum for homemaking contributions to marriage).

458 See *Clarke v Clarke*, 2014 BCSC 824.

459 [2005] OJ No 4181 (CA); see also *KAM v PKM*, [2008] BCJ No 121 (SC); *Lalonde v Lalonde*, 2014 ONSC 4925.

current common law partner. Some cases indicate that re-partnering issues may be able to be addressed by some movement within the ranges calculated in accordance with the *Spousal Support Advisory Guidelines*.[460]

4) Finality of Orders

It is doubtful whether courts have a discretionary jurisdiction to direct that a support order shall be final and irrevocable.[461] Incidental to the above question is the jurisdiction, if any, of the court to vary a support order that has been completely discharged and has spent its force. Judicial opinions have been divided on this issue.[462] The objective of economic self-sufficiency defined in sections 15.2(6)(d) and 17(7)(d) of the *Divorce Act* implies that the courts may now direct that a spousal support order shall be final and irrevocable.[463] On the other hand, the jurisdiction of the court under section 4 to entertain an original application for support after the divorce, and the jurisdiction to vary a subsisting support order under section 17(1), regardless of its type and subject only to the express limitations of section 17(10), imply that the court has no jurisdiction to order a final settlement or preclude a future application for spousal support.[464] In *Tierney-Hynes v Hynes*,[465] in response to the appellant's request for a review of the principles hitherto endorsed by the Ontario Court of Appeal with respect to the finality of orders dismissing applications for spousal support, the Chief Justice appointed a five-judge panel to hear the appeal. In granting the divorced wife's appeal against a summary judgment that had dismissed her variation application, on the ground that the court had no jurisdiction to reinstate spousal support in the face of a prior variation order that had terminated an original order for spousal support granted at the time of divorce, the five-judge panel set out the following reasons. The question whether a court has jurisdiction to vary a prior denial, or a court-ordered termination, of spousal support is solely

---

460 *Rémillard v Rémillard*, 2014 MBCA 101 at para 88, Hamilton JA, citing *Flieger v Adams*, 2012 NBCA 39 and *Fisher v Fisher*, 2008 ONCA 11.

461 See *Gill-Sager v Sager*, [2003] BCJ No 121 (CA); *BGD v RWD*, [2003] BCJ No 1098 (CA); see also *Dipper v Dipper*, [1980] 2 All ER 722 (Eng CA), wherein such jurisdiction was denied, but this has since been abrogated by statutory provisions expressly conferring such jurisdiction on the English courts.

462 See *Collins v Collins* (1978), 2 RFL (2d) 385 (Alta SCTD); *Wyatt v Wyatt* (1986), 1 RFL (3d) 252 (Nfld UFC); *Droit de la famille — 382* (1988), 16 RFL (3d) 379 (Que CA); *A(C) v F(W)*, [1988] RDF 358 at 360 (Que CA). But see s 17(10) of the *Divorce Act*.

463 See *Smith v Smith* (1987), 5 RFL (3d) 398 (Man QB).

464 See *Droit de la famille — 382* (1988), 16 RFL (3d) 379 (Que CA).

465 [2005] OJ No 2661 (CA), leave to appeal to the SCC refused, [2005] SCCA No 424; see also *CAG v SG*, 2012 ABQB 529; *Gill-Sager v Sager*, [2003] BCJ No 121 (CA); *BGD v RWD*, [2003] BCJ No 1098 (CA); *Squires v Squires*, 2014 NBQB 172.

one of statutory interpretation. The judgments of the Ontario Court of Appeal in *Cotter v Cotter*[466] and *McCowan v McCowan*[467] have long supported the proposition that a court lacks jurisdiction under the *Divorce Act* to vary the prior dismissal of an application for spousal support. The economic self-sufficiency and finality objectives emphasized in *Cotter v Cotter* were endorsed by the Supreme Court of Canada in *Pelech v Pelech*,[468] *Caron v Caron*,[469] and *Richardson v Richardson*.[470] However, the language of section 17 of the current *Divorce Act* differs from its predecessor, and there has been a significant jurisprudential shift away from the former prioritization of the goals of finality, certainty, and self-sufficiency as a result of the judgments of the Supreme Court of Canada in *Moge v Moge*,[471] *Bracklow v Bracklow*,[472] *Miglin v Miglin*,[473] and *LMP v LS*.[474] Given significant changes in the legislative language and significant jurisprudential changes in the formulation of principles guiding spousal support, the judgments of the Ontario Court of Appeal in *Cotter v Cotter* and *McCowan v McCowan* are no longer authoritative. Under the current provisions of the *Divorce Act*, a court has jurisdiction to vary its previous denial of spousal support, whether such denial arose by dismissal of an original application brought pursuant to section 15.2 of the *Divorce Act* or by way of a variation order terminating a previous order providing spousal support. Such jurisdiction is inferentially supported by section 15.3 of the *Divorce Act*, which specifically contemplates an application for spousal support after an earlier dismissal of such a claim because of the priority accorded to child support orders. Section 15.3 provides powerful and persuasive support for the existence of a similar jurisdiction in analogous situations where the obligor previously lacked, but no longer lacks, the ability to pay, or where there was no previous need for spousal support, but a need currently exists that is related to the marriage or its breakdown. Another reason for allowing a court to revisit the issue of spousal support lies in the fact that the language of section 17(1)(a) of the *Divorce Act* does not distinguish between child support and spousal support in addressing variation applications, and courts have readily acknowledged their jurisdiction to vary a prior denial of child support. The right of a court to revisit the issue of spousal support is also

---

466 (1986), 53 OR (2d) 449 (CA).
467 (1995), 24 OR (3d) 707 (CA).
468 [1987] 1 SCR 801.
469 [1987] 1 SCR 892.
470 [1987] 1 SCR 857.
471 [1992] 3 SCR 813.
472 [1999] 1 SCR 420.
473 [2003] 1 SCR 303.
474 2011 SCC 64.

consistent with the structure and terms of the current *Divorce Act*, which was last amended in 1997 to accommodate the implementation of the *Federal Child Support Guidelines*. The current legislative provisions, particularly sections 15 and 17, differ substantially from the provisions in section 11 of the *Divorce Act* of 1968 and also introduce significant amendments to the *Divorce Act* of 1986.[475] In particular, the language of section 17(7) of the *Divorce Act* was amended in 1997 so that a court, in looking to the objectives of variation orders, is not confined to reviewing positive orders that previously provided for the support of a spouse. The current *Divorce Act* does not require a spouse to seek support at the time of divorce. Instead, it implements a structure that contemplates subsequent applications for spousal support. In addition, Parliament has provided the courts with broad jurisdiction to structure a wide range of support relief that includes the authority to order spousal support for a definite or indefinite term, to order support until a specified event occurs, and to impose any terms, conditions, or restrictions that are deemed appropriate. The broad range of options available on both original applications for spousal support and variation applications reflects parliamentary recognition that the courts require significant flexibility to tailor a just result for individual cases, given the multitude of circumstances in which spouses find themselves. The legislative changes and the expansive language used throughout the current legislation thus lead to the conclusion that a court now has the jurisdiction to vary the prior dismissal of an application for spousal support. This does not signify that the proverbial floodgates will open; applications to vary previous denials of spousal support will still be required to meet the threshold tests necessary to establish a meritorious claim. Furthermore, the spectre of adverse cost consequences will continue to discourage applications for relief that are without merit.

5) Interjurisdictional Variation of Support Orders

The *Divorce Act* provides two methods to vary a spousal or child support order when the parties do not reside in the same province. One method is the granting of a final variation order pursuant to sections 5 and 17 of the *Divorce Act*. Section 5(1) of the *Divorce Act* provides that a court has jurisdiction to determine a variation proceeding if (a) either former spouse is ordinarily resident in the province at the commencement of the proceeding or (b) both former spouses accept the jurisdiction of the court. Section 17 defines the substantive criteria that govern applications to vary support, whether spousal or child support, and specifically requires proof of a material change

---

475 See RSC 1985 (2d Supp), c 3.

of circumstances since the granting of the order which is sought to be varied. Pursuant to section 17.1 of the *Divorce Act*, where both former spouses are ordinarily resident in different provinces, a court of competent jurisdiction under section 5 of the *Divorce Act* may make a variation order on the basis of the submissions of the former spouses, whether presented orally before the court or by means of affidavits or any means of telecommunication, if both spouses consent thereto. The second method of variation is by way of bipartite provisional and confirmation orders under sections 18 and 19 of the *Divorce Act*.[476] A provisional order under section 18(2) of the *Divorce Act* can only be granted if (i) the respondent is ordinarily resident in another province; (ii) the respondent has not accepted the jurisdiction of the court; (iii) both former spouses have not consented to the application of section 17.1 of the *Divorce Act* in respect of the matter; and (iv) the court is satisfied that the issues can be adequately determined by proceeding by way of provisional and confirmation orders under sections 18 and 19 of the *Divorce Act*. All four conditions must be met.[477] An applicant who seeks a provisional order has the burden of satisfying the court that the issues can be adequately determined by the bipartite process of provisional and confirmation orders.[478] The complexity of the issues and the necessity of cross-examination may render it inappropriate for a court to determine a variation application by means of the bipartite process of provisional and confirmation orders, although the likelihood of contradictory evidence being given in the two different jurisdictions does not, of itself, militate against use of the bipartite process.[479] Section 18(3) of the *Divorce Act* sets out what documents must be transmitted by the court making the provisional order to the court conducting the confirmation hearing. It provides that, where a court in a province makes a provisional order, it shall send to the attorney general for the province three copies of the provisional order certified by a judge or officer of the court; a certified or sworn document setting out or summarizing the evidence given to the court; and a statement giving any available information respecting the identification, location, income, and assets of the respondent. This is then sent under section 18(4) to the province where the respondent resides. Should the confirmation court desire more evidence, it has the discretion under section 18(5) to remit the matter back to the court that made the provisional order.

The procedure under section 19 is not simply a rubber stamp approval of provisional orders; the court to which a provisional order is sent may accept

---

476   *Kennelly v Kennelly*, 2013 BCSC 1663.

477   *Dent v Flynn*, [2005] OJ No 1728 (Sup Ct).

478   *Davis v Leibel*, 2003 MBQB 75; *Foley v Foley* (1987), 8 RFL (3d) 98 (Nfld UFC); *DB c R(B)L*, [2003] QJ No 19844 (CS).

479   *Shindler v Shindler*, [1999] OJ No 932 (Gen Div); *Walsh v Walsh*, 2000 YTSC 13.

evidence upon which it refuses to approve the provisional order or it may confirm the order with a substantive variation.[480] At a confirmation hearing respecting a provisional order for support, variation may be ordered under section 19(7)(b) of the *Divorce Act*, or an issue may be remitted to the originating court under section 19(6) of the *Divorce Act* for further evidence to be adduced.[481] When a provisional order for the variation of an extra-provincial support order is remitted to the originating court for further evidence pursuant to section 19(8) of the *Divorce Act*, the remitting court may grant an order for interim support pursuant to section 19(10) of the *Divorce Act*. Such an order has legal effect throughout Canada and is enforceable in another province pursuant to sections 20(2) and 20(3) of the *Divorce Act*.[482] Section 19(7) of the *Divorce Act* expressly limits the range of options available at the confirmation hearing: the court must confirm the provisional order without variation, or confirm it with variation, or refuse confirmation.[483] The court also has jurisdiction under sections 19(6) and (8) of the *Divorce Act* to adjourn the application to confirm and to remit the matter back to the court that made the provisional order for further evidence before making any of the above orders.[484] Section 19(12)(c) of the *Divorce Act* requires written reasons to be provided for confirming a provisional order with variation.[485]

As is observed by Martinson J in *RDO v CJO*,[486] the existing process of provisional and confirmation hearings is "very time consuming, administratively complex and does not meet the needs of an increasingly mobile population." These deficiencies have been addressed by a simplified one-hearing process under provincial *Interjurisdictional Support Orders Acts*[487] but corresponding changes to the *Divorce Act* have not been implemented. The bipartite process set out in sections 18 and 19 of the *Divorce Act*, though cumbersome,

---

480 See *Smith v Smith* (1990), 25 RFL (3d) 256 (BCSC); *Watters v Watters* (1989), 78 Nfld & PEIR 339 (PEITD); *Stewart v Stewart*, 2012 NLTD(F) 1; *Kyler v Kyler*, [1992] SJ No 408 (QB).

481 *Turner v Turner*, [2000] AJ No 1162 (QB); *Kloczko v Kloczko*, [2000] BCJ No 160 (SC); *Matthews v Hancock*, [1998] SJ No 617 (QB); see also *Burke v Grant*, 2012 BCSC 76; *Koval v Brinton*, 2010 NSCA 78; *CAE v MD*, 2011 NBCA 17; *Kloczko v Kloczko*, [1999] SJ No 125 (QB).

482 *Bickford v Bickford*, [2000] AJ No 1512 (QB).

483 *Young v Young*, 2011 BCSC 1712.

484 *Ibid*; see also *Reid v Gillingham*, 2013 NBQB 338. For examples of circumstances where a court should remit back to the section 18 court, see *Cox v Cox*, 2009 BCSC 1609 at para 25; *Burke v Grant*, 2012 BCSC 76.

485 *CAE v MD*, 2011 NBCA 17.

486 [2003] BCJ No 1179 at para 45 (SC). See also *CAE v MD*, 2011 NBCA 17.

487 For an excellent summary of the legislative framework and correct steps to be followed under the statutory scheme created by the ISO legislation, see *Herriman v Beresford (Blais)*, 2012 BCCA 437 at paras 9–19.

expensive, and time-consuming, is structured to ensure that both parties have the opportunity to be fully heard before a final order is made and the statutorily prescribed processes must be followed.[488]

S. COST-OF-LIVING INDEXATION

In granting orders for periodic spousal support on separation or divorce, courts may order the payments to be annually adjusted in accordance with a designated cost-of-living index.[489] The support order may be indexed under the broad "terms and conditions" language of section 17(3) of the *Divorce Act*, and a formula established by provincial legislation may be used as a guideline for cost of living indexation.[490] Indexation eliminates the need for repeated applications to the court to increase the amount of support because of the impact of inflation on the purchasing power of the original order. It does not prevent either spouse from applying to vary an order by reason of changes of circumstances that are unconnected with the cost of living. The impact of inflation on the purchasing power of the amount of support ordered may itself constitute a material change that warrants an application for an increased amount.[491] Evidence should be adduced of any increase in the cost of living.[492] A court may decline to take judicial notice of this matter.[493] In the absence of wording to the contrary, an indexation clause will function notwithstanding that the obligor's income has increased at a lower rate than that set by the clause.[494]

---

488 *CAE v MD*, 2011 NBCA 17.

489 *Meiklejohn v Meiklejohn*, [2001] OJ No 3911 (CA); *Martin v Martin*, [2004] OJ No 5170 (Sup Ct). Compare *Yemchuk v Yemchuk*, [2005] BCJ No 1748 (CA), citing *LS v EP*, [1999] BCJ No 1451 (CA); *RT v DD*, [2008] BCJ No 1052 (SC); see also *Kerman v Kerman*, [2008] BCJ No 710 (SC) (review proceeding).

490 *Marquis v Marquis*, [1988] OJ No 921 (HCJ), varied (1991), 32 RFL (3d) 171 (Ont CA); *Gray v Gray*, 2014 ONCA 659; see also *Amsterdam v Amsterdam* (1991), 31 RFL (3d) 153 at 161 (Ont Gen Div); *Payne v Short* (1995), 10 RFL (4th) 257 (Ont Gen Div).

491 *France v France* (1987), 6 RFL (3d) 354 (Man CA); *Brickman v Brickman* (1987), 8 RFL (3d) 318 (Man QB); *Jayatilaka v Roussel* (1991), 36 RFL (3d) 447 (NBCA); *BJB v MKB*, 2014 NBQB 153 at para 190; *Single v Single* (1986), 5 RFL (3d) 287 at 292–293 (NS Fam Ct); *Caufield v Caufield* (1986), 4 RFL (3d) 312 at 314–315 (Ont HC); *Winsor v Winsor* (1992), 39 RFL (3d) 8 (Ont CA); *Droit de la famille — 1138*, [1988] RDF 29 (CS Qué), aff'd [1990] RDF 216 (CA Qué).

492 *Basque v Basque* (1988), 89 NBR (2d) 214 (QB).

493 *Schmidt v Schmidt* (1985), 37 Man R (2d) 245 at 246 (CA); compare *Will v Thauberger Estate* (1991), 34 RFL (3d) 432 (Sask QB), varied (1991), 38 RFL (3d) 68 (Sask CA); see also *Moge v Moge*, [1992] 3 SCR 813; *Willick v Willick*, [1994] 3 SCR 670, L'Heureux-Dubé J.

494 *Hennessey v Hennessey* (1993), 122 NSR (2d) 220 (TD).

T. RETROACTIVE SPOUSAL SUPPORT ORDERS

In *Quinn v Eusanio*,[495] it was held that a court has no jurisdiction to make a spousal support order retroactive to a date prior to the commencement of the divorce proceedings. It is highly questionable, however, whether this ruling has survived the judgment in *DBS v SRG; LJW v TAR; Henry v Henry; Hiemstra v Hiemstra*[496] wherein the Supreme Court of Canada held that "a court properly seized of a child support dispute between divorced parents will have the jurisdiction to order retroactive support to be payable from a date preceding the application for divorce."[497] Retroactive spousal support is not granted as a matter of course. Retroactive orders for spousal support are discretionary.[498] A party is expected to act in her own interests to promptly pursue an increase in support.[499] A court may deny an award of retroactive support where a party is aware of changed circumstances but delays in bringing an application.[500] Retroactive orders generally extend no more than three years before the date the paying spouse receives effective notice the other spouse is looking for more support.[501] In *Kerr v Baranow*,[502] the Supreme Court of Canada addressed the issue of the appropriate date for the commencement of spousal support. Observing that section 93(5)(d) of the *Family Relations Act* (British Columbia) conferred a discretion on the court to order "the payment of support in respect of any period before the order is made," the Supreme Court of Canada accepted that similar considerations to those set out in *DBS v SRG; LJW v TAR; Henry v Henry; Hiemstra v Hiemstra*[503] in the context of child support are also relevant to deciding the suitability of a retroactive award of spousal support. More specifically, the relevant factors are the financial circumstances of the claimant, the conduct of the obligor, the reason for the delay in seeking support, and any hardship a retroactive award might cause the obligor.[504] Regarding conduct, the courts have strongly condemned

---

495 2003 NBCA 1.

496 2006 SCC 37 at paras 91–93.

497 *Miller v Miller*, 2009 NSSC 294.

498 See *Scott v Scott*, 2004 NBCA 99; *Farnsworth v Chang*, 2014 ONSC 1871.

499 *Campbell v Campbell*, 2012 SKQB 39.

500 *Ellis v Ellis*, 2010 ONSC 1880, citing *Horner v Horner*, [2004] OJ No 4268 (CA).

501 *KSF v SMF*, 2011 BCSC 1563; *Rivard v Rivard*, 2011 ONSC 2988.

502 2011 SCC 10; see also *Aspe v Aspe*, 2010 BCCA 508; *Anderson v Sansalone*, 2015 BCSC 2; *Rémillard v Rémillard*, 2014 MBCA 101; *Aubé v Aubé*, 2013 NBQB 128; *Ferguson v Ferguson*, 2014 NSSC 350; *Van Wyk v Van Wyk*, 2012 ONSC 3280; *MacQuarrie v MacQuarrie*, 2012 PECA 3; *Bird v Bird*, 2013 SKQB 157.

503 2006 SCC 37; see Chapter 9, Section Q. See also *SDZ v TWZ*, 2011 ABQB 496; *Reis v Bucholtz*, 2010 BCCA 115 at para 66; *Mansoor v Mansoor*, 2012 BCSC 602; *Calder v Calder*, 2011 NSSC 328; *Stevens v Stevens*, 2012 ONSC 706.

504 See *Hallgren v Fry*, 2013 BCCA 15; *McKenzie v Perestrelo*, 2014 BCCA 161 at paras 105–106; *Graham v Graham*, 2013 MBCA 66; *Purdue v Purdue*, 2014 NBQB 262; *Toscano v Toscano*, 2015 ONSC 487; *Linn v Frank*, 2014 SKCA 87.

non-disclosure and late disclosure as constituting misconduct which will not be tolerated.[505] While the considerations for retroactive spousal and child support are largely similar, the court in *Kerr v Baranow* pointed out that the above factors must be considered and weighed in light of the different principles and objectives of these two kinds of support.[506] Concerns about notice, delay, and misconduct generally carry more weight in relation to claims for spousal support. Where the obligor's complaint is that spousal support could have been sought earlier but was not, there are two underlying interests at stake. The first relates to the certainty of the obligor's legal obligations; the second relates to inducing the applicant to proceed promptly.[507] In *Kerr v Baranow*, neither of these concerns carried much weight because the commencement of proceedings provided clear notice to the obligor that support was being sought and permitted him to plan for the contingency of a retroactive order from that date. Justice Cromwell noted[508] that the Ontario Court of Appeal in *MacKinnon v MacKinnon*[509] concluded that the date of the initiation of proceedings for spousal support is the "usual commencement date," absent a reason not to make the order effective as of that date. While asserting that the decision to order support for a period before the date of the order should be the product of the exercise of judicial discretion having regard to the attendant circumstances, Cromwell J stated that the fact that an order is sought effective from the commencement of proceedings will often be a significant consideration in how the relevant factors are weighed. In *DBS v SRG*, the applicants were seeking retroactive support payments reaching back to a period of time preceding their respective applications; that was not the case in *Kerr v Baranow*. Referring to the relevant considerations in *DBS v SRG*; *LJW v TAR*; *Henry v Henry*; *Hiemstra v Hiemstra*, Cromwell J emphasized the need for flexibility and a holistic approach in applications for both retroactive spousal support and retroactive child support. Having regard to these principles, the Supreme Court of Canada held that the British Columbia Court of Appeal in *Kerr v Baranow* made two material errors. First, it erred in finding that the circumstances of Ms Kerr were such that she had no need for support prior to the trial date. Second, it erred by faulting Ms Kerr for not bringing an interim

505 *PKC v JRR*, 2014 BCSC 932 at para 157, var'd on consent 2015 BCCA 179.

506 *Hallgren v Fry*, 2013 BCCA 15; *RLC v RGC*, 2014 BCSC 1852; *Betts v Betts*, 2015 NBQB 19; *Dufour v Dufour*, 2014 ONSC 166; *MacQuarrie v MacQuarrie*, 2012 PECA 3; see also *Vodden v Vodden*, 2014 ABQB 312 at para 5; *Doerksen v Houlahan*, 2012 MBQB 110; *Gidluck v Gidluck*, 2013 SKQB 304.

507 See *Toenjes v Toenjes*, 2012 ABQB 409; *Sinclair v Sinclair*, 2013 BCSC 2400; *Bastarache v Bastarache*, 2012 NBQB 75; *Molloy v Molloy*, 2011 NSSC 390, aff'd 2012 NSCA 60; *Stevens v Stevens*, 2012 ONSC 706; *Thompson v Thompson*, 2013 ONSC 5500 (claim must be specifically pleaded); *MacQuarrie v MacQuarrie*, 2012 PECA 3; *Mehlsen v Mehlsen*, 2012 SKCA 55.

508 2011 SCC 10 at para 211.

509 (2005), 75 OR (3d) 175 (CA); see also *Duggan v Duggan*, 2011 ONSC 1917; *Newcombe v Newcombe*, 2014 ONSC 1094 (interim spousal support order).

application, thereby attributing to her an unreasonable delay in seeking support for the period in question. Observing that Ms Kerr commenced her proceedings promptly after separation and that the trial occurred only thirteen months later, the Supreme Court of Canada concluded that she had diligently pursued the proceedings to trial. Furthermore, Mr Baranow had received clear notice that support was being sought and could readily take advice on the likely extent of his liability. Given the high financial, physical, and emotional costs of interlocutory applications, especially for a party with limited means and a significant disability such as Ms Kerr, Cromwell J opined that it was unreasonable for the British Columbia Court of Appeal to attach its denial of retroactive spousal support to the fact that an interim spousal support application was not pursued. As stated by Cromwell J, "[t]he position taken by the Court of Appeal to my way of thinking undermines the incentives which should exist on parties to seek financial disclosure, pursue their claims with due diligence, and keep interlocutory proceedings to a minimum. Requiring interim applications risks prolonging rather than expediting proceedings."[510] To summarize, the Supreme Court of Canada found that there was virtually no delay in Ms Kerr's applying for support, nor any inordinate delay between the date of the application and the date of trial. Ms Kerr was in need throughout the relevant period and her standard of living was far lower than it had been when she lived with Mr Baranow. He in turn had the means to provide support, had prompt notice of her application, and there was no indication that the trial judge's award would impose a hardship such as would render the retroactive award inappropriate. Accordingly, the British Columbia Court of Appeal erred in setting aside the portion of the trial judge's order for support between the commencement of proceedings and the beginning of the trial. The order of the trial judge making support payable from the commencement of proceedings was, therefore, restored.

The following non-exhaustive list of relevant considerations has been endorsed by the Ontario Court of Appeal as relevant to applications for retroactive spousal support orders:

1) the extent to which the claimant established past need (including any requirement to encroach on capital) and the payor's ability to pay;
2) the underlying basis for the ongoing support obligation;
3) the requirement that there be a reason for awarding retroactive support;
4) the impact of a retroactive award on the payor and, in particular, whether a retroactive order will create an undue burden on the payor or effect a redistribution of capital;
5) the presence of blameworthy conduct on the part of the payor, such as incomplete or misleading financial disclosure;

---

510 *Kerr v Baranow* and *Vanasse v Seguin*, 2011 SCC 10 at para 216.

6) notice of an intention to seek support and negotiations to that end;

7) delay in proceeding and any explanation for the delay; and

8) the appropriateness of a retroactive order predating the date on which the application for divorce was issued.[511]

These factors are consistent with the criteria spelled out in *DBS v SRG*; *LJW v TAR*; *Henry v Henry*; *Hiemstra v Hiemstra*.

A court may grant an order for lump sum retroactive spousal support, notwithstanding a prior interim order for spousal support, but such an order is the exception rather than the rule.[512] In determining whether an order for lump sum retroactive spousal support is appropriate, the court should carefully consider the impact it can have on the matrimonial property distribution.[513]

The quantification of retroactive spousal support cannot simply apply the *Spousal Support Advisory Guidelines* because those ranges are based upon periodic ongoing payments that are presumed to be taxable by the recipient and deductible by the payor. Retroactive support amounts need to be "netted down" to reflect their non-tax-inclusive status.[514]

Courts in British Columbia have held that the failure of a spouse to complain about a unilateral reduction in support for a significant period may be taken into account on an application for cancellation of arrears,[515] but a spouse's delay in enforcing arrears may be excused by the attendant circumstances.[516] In contrast, the New Brunswick Court of Appeal has imposed far more stringent criteria in *Brown v Brown*,[517] reasoning that there is "no valid policy reason for distinguishing between child and spousal support when it

---

511 *Bremer v Bremer*, [2005] OJ No 608 (CA); *Galeano v Dubail*, [2006] OJ No 5159 (CA); see also *Sinclair v Sinclair*, 2013 BCSC 2400; *Marinangeli v Marinangeli* (2003), 38 RFL (5th) 307 (Ont CA), citing *LS v EP* (1999), 67 BCLR (3d) 254 (CA); *Forrest v Forrest*, 2014 BCSC 343; *Aubé v Aubé*, 2013 NBQB 128; *Mayer v Mayer*, 2013 ONSC 7099 at paras 136–37; *MacQuarrie v MacQuarrie*, 2012 PECA 3; compare *Reis v Bucholtz*, 2010 BCCA 115, citing *DBS v SRG*, [2006] 2 SCR 231.

512 *Pettigrew v Pettigrew*, [2006] NSJ No 321 (CA), citing *Hauff v Hauff* (1994), 95 Man R (2d) 83 (CA) and *Elliot v Elliot* (1994), 15 OR (3d) 265 (CA).

513 *Corbeil v Corbeil*, [2001] AJ No 1144 (CA); *ES v JSS*, [2007] AJ No 832 (QB); see also *SDZ v TWZ*, 2011 ABQB 496.

514 *SDZ v TWZ*, ibid; *AAM v RPK*, 2010 ONSC 930; see also *Rockall v Rockall*, 2010 ABCA 278; *Samoilova v Mahnic*, 2014 ABCA 65; *Bastarache v Bastarache*, 2012 NBQB 75; *Chapman v Chapman*, 2010 CanLII 18337 (Ont Sup Ct); *Greenglass v Greenglass*, 2010 ONCA 675; *Hume v Tomlinson*, 2015 ONSC 843; compare *Dubreuil v Canada*, 2010 TCC 289. Compare *Ludmer v Ludmer*, 2014 ONCA 827; *BP v AT*, 2014 NBCA 51; *Purdue v Purdue*, 2014 NBQB 262.

515 *Cawker v Cawker* (1995), 18 RFL (4th) 268 (BCCA).

516 *Bains v Bains*, [1989] BCJ No 450 (SC); *Purvis v Purvis*, 2009 BCSC 1794.

517 2010 NBCA 5 at para 30; see Chapter 9, Section M(4). See also *Arbou v Robichaud*, 2012 NBQB 16; *Zenner v Zenner*, 2015 NSSC 16 at paras 34–36.

comes to the retroactive variation of arrears" because "the need for the distinction evaporates once it is accepted that delay in enforcement (the notion of fault) is no longer a relevant consideration when it comes to retroactive orders involving a decrease in support."

Section 17 of the *Divorce Act* empowers a court to remit all or part of spousal support arrears that have accrued[518] but, once remitted, they cannot be revived in the event of a subsequent improvement in the obligor's financial circumstances.[519] It is noteworthy that in the converse situation, where an application for the remission of support arrears has been dismissed, the doctrine of issue estoppel does not preclude a further application for retroactive variation and a consequential remission of arrears if a material change of circumstances has occurred since the dismissal of the previous application.[520]

U. *SPOUSAL SUPPORT ADVISORY GUIDELINES*[521]

1) Overview of the Guidelines

a) Introduction

In January 2005, the Department of Justice, Canada released a report entitled *Spousal Support Advisory Guidelines: A Draft Proposal*.[522] The report was written by Professor Carol Rogerson of the Faculty of Law at the University of Toronto and by Professor D Rollie Thompson of the Faculty of Law at Dalhousie University, who were retained by the Department of Justice in 2001 to prepare practical spousal support guidelines that could assist mediators, lawyers, and the courts in resolving spousal support disputes arising on divorce. In preparing the report, Professors Rogerson and Thompson engaged in a consultative process with an advisory working group of thirteen members composed of judges, lawyers, and mediators. As directors of the project, Professors Rogerson and Thompson engaged in consensus building but exercised the final decision-making authority when opinions were

---

518 See Chapter 9, Section M(4). See also *Dwyer v Dredge*, 2015 NLTD(F) 4 at para 81.

519 *Beninger v Beninger*, 2009 BCCA 145; *LBL v SB*, 2010 NBQB 339 (child support).

520 *DiFrancesco v Couto*, [2001] OJ No 4307 (CA).

521 See Rogerson and Thompson, *The Spousal Support Advisory Guidelines: A New and Improved User's Guide to the Final Version*, Department of Justice, Canada, March 2010; John-Paul Boyd, *Obtaining Reliable and Repeatable SSAG Calculations*, November 2009, online: www.justice.gc.ca/eng/fl-df/spousal-epoux/topic-theme/calc/pdf/orrssagc.pdf. For a short critical practitioner's review of the *Spousal Support Advisory Guidelines*, see Lorne Wolfson, "The Emperor's New Guidelines" (May 2005) 20:5 Money and Family Law 33.

522 Canada, Department of Justice, *Spousal Support Advisory Guidelines: A Draft Proposal*, by Carol Rogerson & Rollie Thompson (Ottawa: Department of Justice, 2005), online: www.law.utoronto.ca/documents/rogerson/spousal_draftreport_en.pdf.

divided. A final report was published by the Department of Justice in 2008. This final report incorporates revisions made to their original report by Professors Rogerson and Thompson.[523] The basic structure of the Guidelines as originally envisaged remains unchanged but the language and organization of the final report seek to clarify meaning, to incorporate the three years of experience with the Guidelines, and to focus attention on issues such as entitlement, application, using the ranges, restructuring, and exceptions. The following significant revisions to the 2005 report were endorsed in the 2008 report:

1) All social assistance is excluded from income for spousal support purposes,[524] although the Universal Child Care Benefit and other government child benefits are included in income under the *With Child Support Formula*.[525]

2) An additional formula has been recommended to address cases where child support is determined under section 3(2)(b) of the *Federal Child Support Guidelines* and there are no children for whom a table amount of child support is being paid.

3) The *Without Child Support Formula* has been modified so that the recipient of spousal support will never receive more than 50 percent of the couple's net disposable income.[526]

4) The *Shared Custody Formula* has been adjusted to always include an equal split of the couple's net disposable income.

The following summary highlights the major proposals of Professors Rogerson and Thompson.

b) Nature of the Guidelines

The Guidelines are informal, voluntary, and advisory. They have not been legislatively endorsed and are not legally binding. The report envisages that lawyers and mediators will use the Guidelines as a principled basis for negotiation or as a test for determining the reasonableness of offers to settle derived from a budgetary analysis. The report also envisages that judges will

---

523 See Canada, Department of Justice, *The Spousal Support Advisory Guidelines: A New and Improved User's Guide to the Final Version* by Carol Rogerson & Rollie Thompson (Ottawa: Department of Justice, 2010), which includes relevant caselaw and additional material to address new issues that have arisen since the Final Report was published in July 2008, online: www.justice.gc.ca/eng/fl-df/spousal-epoux/topic-theme/ug_a1-gu_a1/PDF/ug_a1-gu_a1.pdf.

524 *Cherry-Francey v Francey*, 2012 ONSC 2109; *Topper v Topper*, 2012 ONSC 3516.

525 *Thompson v Thompson*, 2013 ONSC 5500 at para 85.

526 See *Bentley v Bentley*, [2007] BCJ No 1780 (SC).

use the ranges established by the prescribed formulas in the Guidelines as a check or litmus test to assess the positions of the parties at pre-trial conferences or in argument at hearings and trials, and that the formulas will assist judges in adjudication by providing a structural approach to the exercise of the judicial discretion conferred by the *Divorce Act*.

c) Advantages and Disadvantages of the Guidelines

The following six potential advantages of the *Spousal Support Advisory Guidelines* [SSAG] are identified:

1. To provide a starting point for negotiations and decisions.
2. To reduce conflict and to encourage settlement.
3. To reduce the costs and improve the efficiency of the system.
4. To avoid budgets and to simplify the process.
5. To provide a basic structure for further judicial elaboration.
6. To create consistency and legitimacy.

The following five potential disadvantages of the Guidelines are identified:

1. They are too rigid.
2. Spousal support is too complicated.
3. Discretion allows intuitive reasoning.
4. Regional variations are too great.
5. Litigation will be foreclosed.

Given the inherent uncertainty of the present law of spousal support, Professors Rogerson and Thompson conclude that the advantages of the Guidelines far outweigh their disadvantages, especially in light of the inclusion of more than one formula in the Guidelines, the provision of ranges for the amount and duration of spousal support rights and obligations, and specified exceptions and other features of the Guidelines that balance consistency and certainty against the necessary flexibility that is permitted under the Guidelines.

d) Basic Structure and Application of the Guidelines
i) *Income-Sharing Regime Deemed Consistent with Spousal Support Criteria under the Divorce Act*

The most fundamental aspect of the Guidelines is that they are based on income sharing, as distinct from a budgetary analysis. Income sharing does not imply equal sharing of the combined income of the spouses. Mathematical formulas have been devised to determine the proportion of the spousal incomes to be shared. The authors of the report state that the income-sharing regime is consistent with existing legal principles and does not purport to change them. The report stipulates that the Guidelines do not deal with entitlement, but the authors assert that the post-*Bracklow* era has introduced a very expansive basis for entitlement to spousal support and "as a general matter, a significant income disparity will generate an entitlement to some support."[527] The report further states that the Guidelines do not empower a court to override final spousal support agreements, which continue to be governed by *Miglin v Miglin*.[528] The Guidelines are, nevertheless, expected to play an important role in the negotiation of spousal agreements by providing a more structured framework for negotiation and some benchmarks of fairness for determining the validity and enforceability of a purportedly final agreement.[529] They may also be applied where the spousal support provisions of an agreement envisage a review or variation, and in circumstances where an agreement is judicially set aside.

ii) Proposed Applicability of the Guidelines

The Guidelines are intended to apply to interim as well as final orders.[530] Although they may also be applied in variation proceedings based on an increase in the recipient's income or a decrease in the payor's income,[531] the Guidelines

---

527 See Canada, Department of Justice, *Spousal Support Advisory Guidelines*, by Carol Rogerson & Rollie Thompson (Ottawa: Department of Justice, 2008) c 4, "Entitlement," online: www.justice.gc.ca/eng/rp-pr/fl-lf/spousal-epoux/spag/pdf/SSAG_eng.pdf. See also *Duder v Rowe*, [2006] AJ No 868 (QB); *McKenzie v McKenzie*, 2014 BCCA 381; *Kirton v Mattie*, 2014 BCCA 513; *Eastwood v Eastwood*, 2006 NBQB 413; *Scheibel v Croft*, 2010 SKQB 439. Compare *Metcalfe v Metcalfe*, 2013 ABQB 356; *Lee v Lee*, 2014 BCCA 383.

528 [2003] 1 SCR 303; see also *Duder v Rowe*, [2006] AJ No 868 (QB); *KAM v PKM*, [2008] BCJ No 121 (SC); *New Brunswick (Attorney General) v Flanagan*, 2012 NBQB 49 (variation of pre-Guidelines order); *Carberry v Stringer*, 2008 NLUFC 1; *Vanderlinden v Vanderlinden*, 2007 NSSC 80; *Woodall v Woodall*, 2005 ONCJ 253.

529 See *Parent v Morrissette*, 2013 NBQB 408 (Cyr J), citing *The Spousal Support Advisory Guidelines: A New and Improved User's Guide to the Final Version*, Professor Carol Rogerson and Professor Rollie Thompson, March 2010), Chapter 3 at pages 9–10.

530 See *Pitamber v Pitamber*, 2014 BCSC 24; *Swarzynski v Swarzynski*, 2012 MBQB 13; *Betts v Betts*, 2014 NBQB 47; *Williams v Williams*, [2007] NJ No 257 (UFC); *Orach v Lukang-Orach*, 2011 NLTD(F) 21; *Fisher v Fisher*, 2008 ONCA 11; *Gammon v Gammon*, [2008] OJ No 4252 (Sup Ct); *Bot v Bot*, 2010 ONSC 3805; *Zdrill v Zdrill*, 2011 ONSC 2188; *Meggeson v Meggeson*, [2008] SJ No 478 (QB); compare *Van de Wint v McArthur*, 2009 BCSC 1283; *Wang v Seow*, [2008] MJ No 295 (QB); *Turner v Green*, 2014 NBQB 245 at para 42, Robichaud J; *BDC v MCM*, 2014 ONSC 6064.

531 *Beninger v Beninger*, 2007 BCCA 619; *Kelly v Kelly*, 2011 BCCA 173; *Scott v Scott*, 2011 MBCA 21; *Kelloway v Kelloway*, 2008 NSSC 261; *Favero v Favero*, 2013 ONSC 4216; *MacQuarrie v MacQuarrie*, 2012 PECA 3. As to review proceedings, see *Domirti v Domirti*, 2010 BCCA 472; *TH v RH*, 2011 BCSC 1920; *Chubey v Chubey*, 2011 MBQB 100; *Brooks v Brooks*, 2012 NBCA 50; *Beck v Beck*, 2012 NLTD(F) 34, citing Professors Carol Rogerson & Rollie Thompson, *The Spousal Support Advisory Guidelines: A New and Improved User's Guide to the Final Version* (Ottawa: Minister of Justice and Attorney General of Canada,

are not intended to be of general application in variation proceedings. Post-separation increases in the payor's income,[532] repartnering,[533] remarriage, and second families are left to be resolved under the evolving framework of existing law.[534] As Lauwers JA, of the Ontario Court of Appeal, stated in *Gray v Gray*, "[i]n such cases, the court must conduct an analysis of the facts of the specific case to assess whether the SSAG ranges are appropriate."[535]

Having regard to the legislative redefinition of "marriage" in the *Divorce Act* to include same-sex couples, the Guidelines apply to them in the same way as to opposite-sex divorcing or divorced couples.[536]

The Guidelines have been specifically developed for use under the *Divorce Act*. Their applicability to claims for spousal support under provincial or territorial legislation will depend on the extent to which such legislation endorses principles and a conceptual approach consistent with the *Divorce Act*.[537] Spousal support payments previously ordered and paid pursuant to provincial legislative authority are relevant to the application of the formulas prescribing the amount and duration of support under the *Spousal Support Advisory Guidelines* in subsequent divorce proceedings.[538]

iii) Two Basic Formulas — Marriages without and with Dependent Children

The Guidelines establish two basic mathematical formulas to determine both the amount and duration of spousal support.[539] The first formula, which applies to marriages without dependent children, is relatively simple, being based on the duration of marital and premarital cohabitation.[540] As the duration of the cohabitational relationship increases, so too does the amount and duration of spousal support. A more complex formula is devised to deal with marriages with dependent children. Both formulas provide ranges for

---

2010) at 49; *Trombetta v Trombetta*, 2011 ONSC 394; *Droit de la famille — 141364*, 2014 QCCA 1144.

532 *Beninger v Beninger*, 2007 BCCA 619; *Aelbers v Aelbers*, 2010 BCSC 1574; *Gray v Gray*, 2014 ONCA 659; *MacQuarrie v MacQuarrie*, 2012 PECA 3.

533 *KAM v PKM*, [2008] BCJ No 121 (SC); *Flieger v Adams*, 2012 NBCA 39; *Colley v Colley*, 2013 ONSC 5666 at para 74; *Gray v Gray*, 2014 ONCA 659.

534 *Lepp v Lepp*, [2008] BCJ No 640 (SC).

535 2014 ONCA 659 at para 45.

536 Compare *Scheibel v Croft*, 2010 SKQB 439.

537 See *McCulloch v Bawtenheimer*, [2006] AJ No 361 (QB); *Brown v Brown*, [2007] NBJ No 330 (QB); *Snyder v Pictou*, [2008] NSJ No 77 (CA); *Briand v Briand*, 2011 ONSC 6939.

538 *LMS v EJM*, 2008 NBQB 323.

539 *MacQuarrie v MacQuarrie*, 2012 PECA 3. For an excellent overview, see *Thompson v Thompson*, 2013 ONSC 5500.

540 *Sobiegraj v Sobiegraj*, 2014 ONSC 2030.

both the amount and duration of spousal support, rather than fixed amounts or periods.[541] The particularly wide ranges used in the *Without Child Support Formula* reflect regional variations and uncertainty in current practice, and could be refined after some period of experience under the Guidelines. For the purpose of applying both formulas, spousal income is defined in accordance with the criteria defined in the *Federal Child Support Guidelines*. However, the report opts to use different methods of calculating income under the two formulas. Under the *Without Child Support Formula*, gross income is used, whereas the *With Child Support Formula* relies upon net income calculations. Both formulas generate a gross amount of spousal support that remains subject to the current inclusion/deduction rules under the *Income Tax Act*. Severance payments and other termination payments are a form of replacement income and are therefore properly included in a party's income for SSAG purposes.[542]

iv) Floors and Ceilings

The Guidelines report sets out a provisional floor and ceiling for their application. Subject to exceptional circumstances, such as where the payor is living with parents or otherwise has significantly reduced expenses, the report does not envisage that the formulas would apply to payors until their gross annual income exceeds $20,000.[543]

In *Spousal Support Advisory Guidelines: A New and Improved Guide to the Final Version*,[544] Professors Carol Rogerson and Rollie Thompson state that "[f] or payor incomes between $20,000 and $30,000, there are ability to pay and work incentive concerns that may justify going below the formula ranges."[545] The formulas also are not to be automatically applied to the apportionment of income between the spouses insofar as the payor's gross annual income exceeds $350,000. Above-the-ceiling situations require an individualized

---

541 As to "Using the Ranges," see *Spousal Support Advisory Guidelines*, July 2008 at 9.1–9.7.

542 *O'Gorman v O'Gorman*, 2014 ONSC 3081 at para 30, Minnema J.

543 *ID v DD*, 2013 BCSC 45 at paras 63–72; *New Brunswick (Attorney General) v Flanagan*, 2012 NBQB 49; *Heywood v Heywood*, 2013 ONSC 58; *Torres v Marin*, [2007] YJ No 94 (SC).

544 Department of Justice, Canada, March 2010 at 11(a).

545 See *Matthews v Gallant*, 2015 PESC 12.

fact-specific analysis.[546] In instances where the payor's income is considerably more than \$350,000, a pure discretionary approach may be preferred.[547]

v)   Restructuring: Trade-Offs between Amount and Duration

The report provides for the possible restructuring of spousal support by trade-offs between the amount and duration of support. For example, the formula amount could be increased or reduced to reflect corresponding reductions or increases in the duration of spousal support, or a lump sum payment of spousal support could influence the amount and duration of periodic support.[548] The report states that the only limitation is that the overall value of the restructured award should remain within the global amount generated by the formulae when the amount is multiplied by the duration.[549] Restructuring is more likely under the *Without Child Support Formula* than under the *With Child Support Formula* because the duration of orders under the latter formula is often uncertain. The final report on the *Spousal Support Advisory Guidelines* suggests that restructuring may be appropriate in the following circumstances: (1) in shorter marriages without children; (2) where there is long-term disability after a medium-length marriage; and (3) in longer marriages where the formula generates a time limit but current practice dictates indefinite support.[550]

vi)   Exceptions

While acknowledging that the Guidelines are not binding, and departures are always possible on a case-by-case basis, the report provides a non-exhaustive list

---

546   *Loesch v Walji*, 2008 BCCA 214; *Smith v Smith*, 2008 BCCA 245; *JEH v PLH*, 2014 BCSC 125; *Betts v Betts*, 2015 NBQB 19; *Toscano v Toscano*, 2015 ONSC 487; *BLB v GDM*, 2015 PESC 1; *Linn v Frank*, 2014 SKCA 8; *Babich v Babich*, 2015 SKQB 22 (interim order); compare *Poirier v Poirier*, 2010 ONSC 920; *Fielding v Fielding*, 2014 ONSC 2272. And see *Saunders v Saunders*, 2014 ONSC 2459, citing Carol Rogerson & Rollie Thompson, "Complex Issues Bring Us Back to Basics: The SSAG Year in Review in BC" (2010) 28 Can Fam LQ 263 at 283–86.

547   *SRM v NGTM*, 2014 BCSC 442 at para 148, Butler J; see also *TT v JMH*, 2014 BCSC 451; but compare *Hathaway v Hathaway*, 2014 BCCA 310. And see *Volcko v Volcko*, 2015 NSCA 11 at para 79.

548   See, for example, *McCulloch v Bawtinheimer*, [2006] AJ No 361 (QB) (restructuring of spousal support payments under the *Family Law Act* (Alberta) by front-end loading to reflect the applicant's current unemployment and to promote her economic self-sufficiency within two years); *Pickford v Pickford*, [2008] BCJ No 548 (SC); *Fisher v Fisher*, 2008 ONCA 11 (amount higher; duration shorter); see also *RL v NL*, 2012 NBQB 123.

549   See *TAD v MKD*, 2010 BCSC 898.

550   Canada, Department of Justice, *Spousal Support Advisory Guidelines*, by Carol Rogerson & Rollie Thompson (Ottawa: Department of Justice, 2008), c 10, "Restructuring," online: www.justice.gc.ca/eng/rp-pr/fl-lf/spousal-epoux/spag/pdf/SSAG_eng.pdf.

of "recognized categories of departures" or "exceptions" where it might be inappropriate to apply the prescribed formulas.[551] By way of example, compensatory spousal support awards might exceed the prescribed formula in cases of shorter marriages that have generated disproportionate economic losses or gains to either spouse.[552] An inability to achieve economic self-sufficiency due to illness or disability might also justify deviation from the formulas,[553] as might a disproportionate responsibility for excessive or unusually high family debts,[554] support obligations to children and spouses from previous relationships,[555] or compelling financial circumstances at the interim stage.[556]

Additional specific exceptions have been introduced since the publication of the 2005 report. These relate to the following:

- reapportionment of property under the *Family Relations Act* (British Columbia);[557]
- inability of low-income recipients to meet basic needs in shorter marriages under the *Without Child Support Formula*;[558]
- special needs of a child under the *With Child Support Formula*;[559]
- inadequate spousal support under the *With Child Support Formula* due to the priority given to child support under section. 15.3 of the *Divorce Act*;
- non-taxable payor income;
- addition of a minimum duration to the *With Child Support Formula*; and
- non-primary parent to fulfill parenting role under the custodial parent formula[560]

---

551   See *Morrison v Barclay-Morrison*, [2008] OJ No 4663 (Sup Ct); *Pollitt v Pollitt*, 2010 ONSC 1617; *Stergios v Kim*, 2011 ONCA 836.

552   See *Ahn v Ahn*, [2007] BCJ No 1702 (SC); *RMS v FPCS*, 2011 BCCA 53; *Beardsall v Dubois*, [2009] OJ No 416 (Sup Ct).

553   *EET v ANT*, 2012 ABQB 298; *BJB v MKB*, 2014 NBQB 153 at para 211, Tuck J; *Gray v Gray*, 2014 ONCA 659; *Rakhra v Rakhra*, 2012 NWTSC 33; *Tscherner v Farrell*, 2014 ONSC 976; compare *Shen v Tong*, 2013 BCCA 519.

554   *Robles v Kuhn*, 2012 BCSC 752; *Aubé v Aubé*, 2013 NBQB 128; *Dunn v Dunn*, 2011 ONSC 6899.

555   *Pendleton v Pendleton*, 2010 BCSC 1167 (child support payments to ex-wife considered in *Spousal Support Advisory Guideline* analysis); see also *RMS v FPCS*, 2011 BCCA 53; *Ponkin v Werden*, 2015 ONSC 791.

556   *Kramchynsky v Kramchynsky*, 2013 MBQB 56; *Carrier v Ponn*, 2013 NBQB 146. Compare *Vanderlinden v Vanderlinden*, 2007 NSSC 80; see also *Rhynold v Rhynold*, [2009] OJ No 4339 (Sup Ct) (disability).

557   See *Hathaway v Hathaway*, 2014 BCCA 310. And see now *Family Law Act*, 2011 c 25, section 95.

558   *Thiyagarajah v Paramsothy*, 2011 ONSC 7368; see also *Ponkin v Werden*, 2015 ONSC 791.

559   *Hausmann v Klukas*, 2011 BCSC 1753 (duration).

560   See *RMS v FPCS*, 2011 BCCA 53; *Kelly v Kelly*, 2011 BCCA 173.

The parent who claims to fall within one of the specified exceptions bears the burden of proof.[561]

e) The *Without Child Support Formula*

The underlying premise of the *Without Child Support Formula*, which applies when there are no longer dependent children for whom child support is payable, is the concept of "merger over time." This signifies that as the duration of a marriage increases, the spouses merge their economic and non-economic lives to complement each other.[562]

The two essential elements of this formula relate to the gross income differential between the spouses and the duration of their cohabitational relationship. The report recommends as follows:

> The *Without Child Support Formula*
>
> *Amount* ranges from 1.5 to 2 percent of the difference between the spouses' gross incomes (the *gross income difference)* for each year of marriage, (or more precisely, years of cohabitation), up to a maximum of 50 percent. The range remains fixed for marriages twenty-five years or longer, at 37.5 to 50 percent of income difference.
>
> *Duration* ranges from .5 to one year for each year of marriage. However support will be *indefinite* if the marriage is *twenty years or longer* in duration *or*, if the marriage has lasted five years or longer, when years of marriage and age of the support recipient (at separation) added together total sixty-five or more (the *rule of 65).*[563]

Gross (i.e., pre-tax) income under this formula is based on the same definition of income as that in the *Federal Child Support Guidelines*, and courts are free to impute income to either spouse who unreasonably fails to achieve his or her earning potential. It is important to observe that the percentages in the formula are not percentages of the payor's annual income; they are percentages of the gross income difference between the spouses. Chapter 5 of the report sets out fact-specific examples to demonstrate the application of the formula and the ranges that it produces for marriages of different lengths and incomes.

---

561 *TAD v MKD*, 2010 BCSC 898; *Zdrill v Zdrill*, 2011 ONSC 2188.

562 *Roberts v Cantu-Roberts*, 2010 ONSC 1883.

563 Canada, Department of Justice, *Spousal Support Advisory Guidelines*, by Carol Rogerson & Rollie Thompson (Ottawa: Department of Justice, 2008) at vii, online: www.justice. gc.ca/eng/rp-pr/fl-lf/spousal-epoux/spag/pdf/SSAG_eng.pdf; see *Beck v Beck*, 2015 NLTD(F) 10; *Reisman v Reisman*, 2014 ONCA 109; *Djekic v Zai*, 2015 ONCA 25.

Although the ranges for the duration of spousal support are very broad, a tighter range was found to be unattainable because of uncertainties under the current law. The interrelationship between the amount and duration of spousal support is, nevertheless, regarded as of critical importance. As emphasized in the final report on the *Spousal Support Advisory Guidelines*, "[u]sing one part of the formula without the other undermines its integrity and coherence."[564] The proposed formula provides for spousal support awards of indefinite duration if cohabitation has lasted for twenty years or more or if the years of marriage plus the age of the support recipient at the time of separation equals or exceeds sixty-five (the so-called rule of 65).[565] Under the proposed formula, short childless marriages will generate very modest spousal support awards in terms of both amount and duration.[566] Medium-term childless marriages will generate transitional orders of varying amounts and duration that increase with the length of the relationship. Long childless marriages will generate generous spousal support for an indefinite term that provides comparable standards of living for each of the spouses. As under the current law, orders made under the Guidelines will be subject to variation in the event of a subsequent material change of circumstances and may also include provisions for review.[567]

f) The *With Child Support Formula*
i) *Reasons for Separate Model Where Dependent Children Involved;*
Parenting Partnership Model

Having regard to the impact of child support obligations on the ability to pay spousal support, the priority accorded to child support under section 15.3 of the *Divorce Act*, the income tax implications of child support (which differ radically from those governing periodic spousal support), and child-related federal and provincial benefits and credits, a separate formula has been devised for calculating spousal support in circumstances where child support is concurrently being paid by one spouse to the other. The underlying rationale of this formula is a "parental partnership model" premised on the compensatory notions espoused in both *Moge v Moge* and *Bracklow v Bracklow*. The parental partnership rationale looks not only at past loss but also at the continuing economic disadvantages that result from ongoing parenting responsibilities.

---

564 *Ibid* at 7.5.1; *Reisman v Reisman*, 2014 ONCA 109.
565 See *TT v JMH*, 2014 BCSC 451; *O'Brien v O'Brien*, 2011 NBQB 179; *Roberts v Cantu-Roberts*, 2010 ONSC 1883; *Stewart v Tudorachi*, [2008] OJ No 5111 (Sup Ct).
566 Compare *Refcio v Refcio*, [2009] OJ No 1539 (Div Ct).
567 See *Snyder v Pictou*, [2008] NSJ No 77 at para 25 (CA); see also *Michaud v Kuszelewski*, 2009 NSCA 118.

ii) Primary Differences between the Two Basic Formulas

There are three important differences between the *Without Child Support Formula* and the *With Child Support Formula*. First, the *With Child Support Formula* uses the net incomes of the spouses, not their gross incomes.[568] Second, it divides the pool of combined net incomes between the two spouses, instead of using the gross income difference. Third, the upper and lower percentage limits of net income division do not change with the length of the marriage.

iii) Summary of Basic With Child Support Formula

The following basic *With Child Support Formula* applies where the higher-income spouse is paying both child support and spousal support to the lower-income spouse, who is the parent with primary care of the child:

The Basic *With Child Support* Formula for Amount

(1) Determine the individual net disposable income (INDI) of each spouse:

- Guidelines Income *minus* Child Support *minus* Taxes and Deductions = Payor's INDI
- Guidelines Income *minus* Notional Child Support *minus* Taxes and Deductions *plus* Government Benefits and Credits = Recipient's INDI

(2) Add together the individual net disposable incomes. Determine the range of spousal support amounts that would be required to leave the lower income recipient spouse with between 40 and 46 percent of the combined INDI.[569]

Calculation of a spouse's individual net disposable income under this formula will require access to computer software. As Mitchell J, as he then was, of the Prince Edward Island Supreme Court, observed in *RL v LAB*, the " 'with child support formula' is fairly complicated and requires a computer analysis [whereas] [t]he 'without child support formula' is fairly straightforward and really does not require a computer printout."[570]

The *With Child Support Formula* seeks to isolate a pool of net disposable income available to the spouses after adjustment for child support obligations. In the interests of uniformity and efficiency, the same definition of income is used as that found in the *Federal Child Support Guidelines*. There is, however, one important variation under the formula. In calculating the recipient's individual net disposable income, the formula requires the inclusion

---

568 *KD v ND*, 2014 BCCA 70.

569 Canada, Department of Justice, *Spousal Support Advisory Guidelines*, by Carol Rogerson & Rollie Thompson (Ottawa: Department of Justice, 2008) at viii, online: www.justice. gc.ca/eng/rp-pr/fl-lf/spousal-epoux/spag/pdf/SSAG_eng.pdf.

570 2013 PESC 24 at para 60.

of government benefits and refundable credits, such as the Child Tax Benefit, the National Child Benefit, the GST credit, the refundable medical credit, and various provincial benefit and credit schemes.[571]

After undertaking the necessary steps to assign a Guidelines income to each spouse under the formula, the respective child support contributions of each spouse must be deducted. For the payor spouse, these contributions will typically comprise the applicable table amount of child support plus the payor's share of special and extraordinary expenses under section 7 of the *Federal Child Support Guidelines*. For the payee spouse, the deduction will be the notional table amount of child support payable by that spouse plus his or her contributions to section 7 expenses. The next stage in the calculations is to subtract income taxes and additional deductions from the income of each spouse to obtain his or her net incomes. These additional deductions include CPP contributions, EI contributions, medical and dental insurance premiums, group life insurance premiums, and other family benefit plans. Mandatory pension plan contributions are not an allowable deduction, although they might sometimes be used as a factor to justify fixing spousal support at the lower end of the formulaic range. Finally, with respect to the payee spouse, government benefits or credits such as those mentioned above must be included in the recipient's net disposable income.

After the individual net disposable income of each spouse has been ascertained, they must be added together, and hypothetical calculations will then be undertaken to determine the amount of spousal support that will provide the lower-income recipient spouse with between 40 and 46 percent of the combined pool of their individual net disposable incomes.

iv) Duration under the Basic Formula

Initial orders under the basic *With Child Support Formula* would be indefinite in form (i.e., duration not specified), but would be subject to outside time limits that would inform the processes of subsequent review or variation.[572]

While endorsing the criterion that the maximum duration of a spousal support order would be the longer of either one year of support for each year of the marriage or until the youngest or last child completed high school, Professors Rogerson and Thompson saw no reason to impose any kind of minimum duration in their 2005 report. However, lawyers and judges treated the maximum duration test as the norm, and this was never intended by

---

571 See *Kramchynsky v Kramchynsky*, 2013 MBQB 56. Compare *Janzen v Janzen*, 2014 BCSC 1374.

572 *KD v ND*, 2014 BCCA 70. But see *Depatie v Squires*, 2011 ONSC 1758 (fixed-term order where older stepchild).

Professors Rogerson and Thompson. Consequently, they introduced a minimum time limit for spousal support orders in their final report, namely, the longer of either one-half year of support for each year of marriage or until the date the youngest child starts attending school full-time.[573]

v) Shared and Split Custody

Split custody[574] and shared custody arrangements, which fall subject to sections 8 and 9 of the *Federal Child Support Guidelines* respectively, trigger adjustments to the computation of the individual net disposable income of each spouse under the basic *With Child Support Formula*.

In split custody arrangements, where one or more children are primarily resident with each parent, the report acknowledges the costs faced by each parent in supporting the child in his or her primary care by deducting a notional table amount of child support from the income of each parent, not just the recipient parent.

In cases of shared custody, Professors Rogerson and Thompson propose that, in computing the individual net disposable income of each spouse, the full table amount of child support, plus section 7 contributions, be deducted from the payor's income; and the notional table amount, plus any section 7 contributions, be deducted from the recipient's income, even though the child support actually paid and received is a straight set-off amount under section 9(a) of the *Federal Child Support Guidelines*.[575]

It is critical to determine which parent is receiving child-related government benefits before calculating the range for spousal support.

vi) Stepchildren

There is no specific formula dealing with stepchildren. Professors Rogerson and Thompson envisage that where, pursuant to section 5 of the *Child Support Guidelines*, a court orders a step-parent to pay less than the table amount of support for a stepchild, the *With Child Support Formula* should be applied using the full table amount rather than the reduced amount of child support.

---

573   See *Doucet v Doucet*, 2014 NBCA 63. As to the implications of very short marriages, see *Knezevich v Curtis*, 2013 BCSC 432 at paras 61–63, citing s 8.5.5. of the *Spousal Support Advisory Guidelines*, online: www.justice.gc.ca/eng/rp-pr/fl-lf/spousal-epoux/spag/pdf/ SSAG_eng.pdf.

574   *Jardine v Jardine*, 2013 NSSC 30.

575   See Professors Rogerson and Thompson, *The Spousal Support Advisory Guidelines: A New and Improved User's Guide to the Final Version*, Department of Justice, Canada, March 2010 at 8(a); *Swallow v De Lara*, [2006] BCJ No 2060 (SC); *Fell v Fell*, [2007] OJ No 1011 (Sup Ct). Compare *Mann v Mann*, 2009 BCCA 181; *RDLJ v BSJ*, 2014 BCSC 1566; *Matthews v Taylor*, 2012 NLTD(G) 24. As to the applicable formula where there is a hybrid of custody arrangements, see *Thompson v Thompson*, 2013 ONSC 5500.

To address concerns that the basic formula would generate too much spousal support in short step-parental relationships, they propose that courts should not lower the amount of spousal support but impose a time limit.[576]

vii) Hybrid Formula for Adult Children

A hybrid formula has been proposed to address cases where child support is determined under section 3(2)(b) of the *Federal Child Support Guidelines* and there are no children for whom a table amount of child support is being paid. Under this formula, once each spouse's contribution to the adult child's budget has been allocated under section 3(2)(b), those child support payments are grossed-up and deducted from each spouse's gross income. Then the *Without Child Support Formula* is applied, using the gross income disparity and the length of the marriage factor to determine the amount and duration of spousal support.

viii) Hybrid Formula Where Spousal Support Paid by Custodial Parent[577]

The basic *With Child Support Formula* is premised on the higher-income spouse's paying both child and spousal support to the lower-income parent. Cases do arise, however, where child support and spousal support flow in opposite directions. To address these cases, the report provides the following distinct formula:

Formula for Spousal Support Paid by Custodial Parent
(1) Reduce the payor spouse's Guidelines income by the *grossed-up notional table amount* for child support (plus a gross-up of any contributions to s. 7 expenses).
(2) If the recipient spouse is paying child support, reduce the recipient's Guidelines income by the *grossed-up amount of child support paid* (table amount plus any s. 7 contributions).
(3) Determine the *adjusted gross income difference* between the spouses and then quantum ranges from 1.5 percent to 2 percent for each year of marriage, up to a maximum of 50.
(4) *Duration* ranges from .5 to one year of support for each year of marriage, with the same rules for indefinite support as under the *Without Child Support Formula.*[578]

---

576 See *Collins v Collins*, 2008 NLUFC 31.

577 See *TT v JMH*, 2014 BCSC 451; *Brooks v Brooks*, 2014 NBCA 29; *Thompson v Thompson*, 2013 ONSC 5500; *Papasodaro v Papasodaro*, 2014 ONSC 30.

578 See *RMS v FPCS*, 2011 BCCA 53; *RL v NL*, 2012 NBQB 123; *Brooks v Brooks*, 2012 NBCA 50; *Puddifant v Puddifant*, [2005] NSJ No 558 (SC); *Cassidy v McNeil*, 2010 ONCA 218; *Zdrill v Zdrill*, 2011 ONSC 2188.

ix) Crossover between Formulas

The report provides for a crossover between the *With Child Support Formula* and the *Without Child Support Formula* after the children cease to be eligible for support.[579]

g) Narrowing the Range

As Walsh J, of the New Brunswick Court of Queen's Bench, points out in *RL v NL*,[580] lawyers and courts should avoid the tendency to "default" to the mid-range amount of spousal support. Fixing the ranges as to both amount and duration of spousal support is expected to be a more sophisticated exercise than that, at least according to the principal authors of the Guidelines. To assist in determining where spousal support should be fixed within the prescribed ranges, the Guidelines report lists the following seven circumstances for consideration:[581]

- A strong compensatory claim for spousal support might generate an award at the higher end of the range[582] whereas a non-compensatory claim based simply upon loss of the marital standard of living might result in an award at the lower end of the range.[583] Other things being equal, the longer the marriage, the more likely one might move towards the higher end of the range.[584]
- A recipient's needs arising because of age or disability might push an award to the higher end of the range.[585] Conversely, the absence of any compelling need might push the award to the lower end of the range.[586]
- The age, number, and needs of the children will affect placement within the *With Child Support Formula*. For example, the demands of very young children or special needs children may have a significant impact on the caregiving parent's earning potential, which would point to a higher-range award of spousal support. Generally speaking, when ability to pay is in issue, the larger the number of children, the less income is left available to pay spousal support, and the ranges will be lower consistent with section 15.3 of the *Divorce Act*. In these cases of

---

579 See *Hamdan v Hamdan*, 2012 NBQB 331; *Beck v Beck*, 2015 NLTD(F) 10; *Gray v Gray*, 2014 ONCA 659.

580 2012 NBQB 123 at para 43.

581 See *EET v ANT*, 2012 ABQB 298; *Triffonas v Triffonas*, 2011 BCSC 1090; *RL v NL*, 2012 NBQB 123; *Brown v Brown*, 2013 NBQB 369; *Freer v Freer*, 2012 ONSC 6269.

582 *Litzenberger v Litzenberger*, 2012 SKQB 122.

583 *Betts v Betts*, 2014 NBQB 47.

584 *Sarro v Sarro*, 2011 BCSC 1010; *MacQuarrie v MacQuarrie*, 2012 PECA 3.

585 *Squires v Squires*, 2014 NBQB 172; *MacQuarrie v MacQuarrie*, 2012 PECA 3.

586 *Cook v Cook*, 2011 ONSC 5920.

squeezed ranges for spousal support, there will be strong reasons to go higher in this "depressed" range, to generate some compensatory support for the primary parent.[587]

- The needs and ability of the payor spouse will have special importance at the lower end of the income spectrum, as, for example, where the payor is making mandatory pension deductions or incurring significant but reasonable costs in exercising access to the children. Thus, the needs and limited means of the payor spouse might push an award to the lower end of the range.

- The preservation of work incentives for the payor should be taken into account.[588]

- The absence of any property to be divided might trigger a spousal support order at the higher end of the range, whereas an unequal division of property in favour of the recipient could trigger a spousal support order at the lower end of the range. If spouses are at or approaching retirement and one spouse has a more pressing need to become and remain economically self-sufficient than the other, which need cannot be addressed through property reapportionment due to exempt or excluded assets, that factor may be considered in setting both the amount and duration of spousal support.[589]

- The need to promote the economic self-sufficiency of a recipient spouse could push in different directions. A spousal support award at the lower end of the range could be used to encourage a spouse to make greater efforts to achieve self-sufficiency. Alternatively, an award at the higher end of the scale might facilitate the recipient spouse's pursuit of retraining or education for the purpose of achieving economic self-sufficiency.[590]

h) Quebec

Professors Rogerson and Thompson perceive the basic *Without Child Support Formula* as readily applicable in Quebec. Although Quebec has its own *Child Support Guidelines*, which differ in some important ways from the *Federal Child Support Guidelines*, they foresee no obstacles to the application of the basic *With Child Support Formula* in Quebec after due account is taken of the differences between the provincial and federal *Child Support Guidelines*. Where one of the divorcing parents is ordinarily resident outside Quebec, the

---

587   *de Bruijn v de Bruijn*, 2011 BCSC 1546.

588   *MacQuarrie v MacQuarrie*, 2012 PECA 3. See also *Betts v Betts*, 2015 NBQB 19 (spousal support ordered below the SSAG ranges).

589   *Oliver v Oliver*, 2011 BCSC 1126.

590   *MacQuarrie v MacQuarrie*, 2012 PECA 3.

Federal Child Support Guidelines govern child support and no adjustments to the basic *With Child Support Formula* are necessary.

i) General Observations

It is evident from the above overview that the Guidelines are complex. Some of the terminology is new and the detailed commentary of the authors is vital to a proper understanding of the formulas. Professors Carol Rogerson and Rollie Thompson fully explain their rationale and the underlying bases of the formulas, as well as identify specific limitations and exceptions to their application. Many years ago, Justice Abella, now of the Supreme Court of Canada, observed that spousal support is a "Rubik's cube for which no one yet has written the Solution Book."[591] The highly sophisticated report prepared by Professors Rogerson and Thompson with input from their consultative group constitutes an important step towards providing a much needed Solution Book. However, progress towards achieving that objective is impeded by the fact that the Guidelines currently have no formal legal status. At this point in time, no steps have been taken to implement them by regulation pursuant to section 26(1) of the *Divorce Act*. Pending any such implementation or a judgment of the Supreme Court of Canada, the Guidelines have triggered differing responses from courts across Canada.

2) Judicial Responses to the *Spousal Support Advisory Guidelines*

A broad spectrum of differing judicial attitudes towards the *Spousal Support Advisory Guidelines* is manifested by the following cases from across Canada.

In *Lust v Lust*,[592] a decision of the Alberta Court of Appeal, the wife appealed the trial judge's order for spousal support of $700 per month for four years, pointing to the *Spousal Support Advisory Guidelines* as suggesting an order of $1,229 per month for ten years. In response to this contention, the Alberta Court of Appeal stated that, whereas the *Federal Child Support Guidelines* have the force of law and are mandatory, the *Spousal Support Advisory Guidelines* are not. While observing that the *Spousal Support Advisory Guidelines* "are instructive as to one route to proper exercise of discretion in arriving at an award," the Alberta Court of Appeal stated that "[t]hey do not fully fetter a trial judge's discretion."[593] Because the trial judge considered that his order would enable the appellant to acquire experience and training

---

591   Rosalie S Abella, "Economic Adjustment on Marriage Breakdown: Support" (1981) 4 Fam L Rev 1.

592   2007 ABCA 202.

593   *Ibid* at para 10.

to secure rewarding employment, and concluded that his order recognized the length of the marriage and its negative impact on the wife, and account was also taken of her receipt of $170,000 from matrimonial property, all of which were deemed to constitute proper factors in the setting of a spousal support order, the Alberta Court of Appeal concluded that, on the deferential standard of appellate review, there was no basis for interfering with the trial judge's award.

In *Lapp v Lapp*,[594] the Alberta Court of Appeal noted that, "although the Guidelines are not binding, they are a suggested measure of support that can be considered." However, "a guideline is just that — a guideline. It is always incumbent on a trial judge to look at all of the circumstances of the parties — their means, needs, and ability to pay. It is also necessary for the trial judge to consider the objectives of spousal support."

In *Sawatzky v Sawatzky*,[595] the husband appealed an interim order for on-going periodic spousal support. He argued that the chambers judge had failed to take into consideration the relevant factors and objectives of spousal support orders that are set out in sections 15.2(4) and (6) of the *Divorce Act* and fettered his discretion by using only the *Spousal Support Advisory Guidelines*. Citing appellate judgments from British Columbia, New Brunswick, Ontario, and Quebec, as well as its own previous judgment in *Lust v Lust*,[596] the Alberta Court of Appeal endorsed the following conclusions:

1. The Guidelines are not mandatory and do not have the force of law. They do not and cannot take the place of analysis of the applicable provisions of the *Divorce Act*.

2. The Guidelines have been characterized as a "useful tool" in determining the amount and duration of spousal support orders.[597] While they may be instructive as to one route to the proper exercise of discretion in arriving at an award, they do not and should not fetter a trial judge's discretion.[598]

3. Although it might be tempting to resort to a recipe for a mathematical formula instead of undergoing the difficult analysis required by the *Divorce Act*, such an approach is inconsistent with *Moge v. Moge*,[599]

---

594 2008 ABCA 15 at paras 23 and 33; see also *Lane v Lane*, 2012 ABCA 2; *De Winter v De Winter*, 2013 ABCA 311. For a useful review of relevant caselaw, see *Dowhaniuk v Dowhaniuk*, 2014 ABQB 217.

595 2008 ABCA 355; see also *Taylor v Taylor*, 2009 ABCA 354; *O'Grady v O'Grady*, 2010 ABCA 109; *Neighbour v Neighbour*, 2014 ABCA 62.

596 2007 ABCA 202.

597 *Yemchuk v Yemchuk* (2005), 16 RFL (6th) 430 at para 64 (BCCA).

598 *Lust v Lust*, 2007 ABCA 202.

599 [1992] 3 SCR 813.

wherein it was noted that there is no "magic recipe" or grid for determining spousal support.[600]

4. As the New Brunswick Court of Appeal observed in *S.C. v. J.C.*,[601] the Guidelines are best used as a "cross-check" or "starting point" for the determination of spousal support. However, they cannot be used as a software tool or a formula that calculates a specific amount of support for a set period of time.[602]

Applying these criteria, the Alberta Court of Appeal in *Sawatzky v Sawatzky* concluded that the chambers judge's reasons did not indicate that he had taken account of section 15.2 of the *Divorce Act*. Instead, he appeared to have used the *Spousal Support Advisory Guidelines* as a formula when he stated that he "[would] probably need some help with the spousal guidelines at the end of the day as far as plugging the right numbers into the right column."[603] Since there was nothing in the transcript or in the chambers judge's written memorandum of decision pointing to the use of anything other than the Guidelines to determine the amount of interim periodic spousal support, the Alberta Court of Appeal found an error of principle in that the chambers judge had fettered his discretion by his direct application of the Guidelines. Since the Alberta Court of Appeal could not be satisfied that the disposition would have been the same if the chambers judge had analyzed section 15.2 of the *Divorce Act*, this issue was remitted to the Court of Queen's Bench for reconsideration.

In *Rockall v Rockall*,[604] the Alberta Court of Appeal states:

> The fact that the support awarded arguably exceeds that recommended under the *Spousal Support Guidelines* is irrelevant. Those guidelines do not have the force of law. In any event, a trial judge cannot rely on the recommendations generated under them when his or her own proper analysis requires a different conclusion.

It is important, however, for lawyers and courts to realize that they should not confine their attention to the formulas prescribed by the report on the *Spousal Support Advisory Guidelines*. They must take account of textual commentary in the report. In Part 12.7 of their July 2008 report, Professors Rogerson and Thompson set out a list of exceptions to the application of the basic *Without Child Support Formula*. The facts in *Rockall v Rockall* would appear to

---

600 *GV c CG*, [2006] JQ no 5231 (CA).
601 [2006] NBJ No 186 at para 5.
602 *Fisher v Fisher*, 2008 ONCA 11 at para 94.
603 Cited in *Sawatzky v Sawatzky*, 2008 ABCA 355 at para 18.
604 2010 ABCA 278 at para 18.

fall within the basic needs/hardship exception set out in section 12.7 wherein the following statements appear:

> The *without child support* formula works well across a wide range of cases from short to long marriages with varying incomes. In some parts of the country and in some cases, there is a specific problem for shorter marriages where the recipient has little or no income. In these shorter-marriage cases, the formula is seen as generating too little support for the low income recipient to meet her or his basic needs for a transitional period that goes beyond any interim exception.[605]
>
> Restructuring in these cases will sometimes still not generate an amount or a duration that is sufficient, in the eyes of some, to "relieve any economic hardship of the spouses arising from the breakdown of the marriage", as stated in section 15.2(6)(c) of the *Divorce Act*. To complicate matters further, the amount required to meet basic needs will vary from big city to small city to town to rural area. Whether restructuring provides a satisfactory outcome, i.e. more support for a shorter time, will depend upon where the recipient lives. Thus the problem for these short-to-medium-marriage-low-income cases seems to be most acute in big cities.[606]
>
> We did not wish to change the structure of the formula itself for this one sub-set of cases. The best approach to these cases was to create a carefully tailored exception, the basic needs/hardship exception, leaving the basic formula intact for the vast majority of cases where the formula produces a reasonable range of outcomes.
>
> Other exceptions may avoid the need to resort to this basic needs/hardship exception. In some short marriages without children, the compensatory exception may apply, with more generous outcomes than under this exception. The basic needs/hardship exception is non-compensatory. In other cases, in shorter marriages, the compelling financial circumstances at the interim stage can provide for a higher amount of support for a transitional period, such that no further exception need be applied by the time of trial. Earlier, we made clear that basic needs/hardship exception should only be considered at the trial or initial determination stage, after a full review of the merits on all the evidence, including any interim exception granted.
>
> The basic needs/hardship exception applies under the *without child support* formula and the *custodial payor* formula, *only* in these circumstances:

---

605   See *Singh v Singh*, 2013 ONSC 6476.

606   For example, see *Simpson v Grignon*, [2007] OJ No 1915 (Sup Ct).

- the formula range, even after restructuring, will not provide sufficient income for the recipient to meet her or his basic needs
- the reason will be that the recipient's base or non-support income is zero or too low
- the marriage will typically be short to medium in length, e.g. 1 to 10 years
- the payor spouse will have the ability to pay.

We should be clear that this exception is only intended to ease the transition in these hardship cases. It is not intended to provide the marital standard of living, but only a standard of basic needs. And it is not intended to provide support for a long period of time after a shorter marriage, but only for a short transition period.

Summarizing the responses of the Alberta Court of Appeal to the *Spousal Support Advisory Guidelines*, Ross J, of the Alberta Court of Queen's Bench, has stated:

> 59 A review of the case law indicates that the Alberta Court of Appeal has consistently emphasized that the *Guidelines*, while not a mandatory consideration, can be a useful tool to determine the amount and duration of spousal support. Provided a trial judge has considered the factors and objectives required by the *Divorce Act*, the Court of Appeal has deferred to the trial judge's decision regarding whether or not to apply the *Guidelines*.[607]

Commenting on the diverse responses of Canadian appellate courts to the question whether a trial judge has a responsibility to explain why the Guidelines should not be applied, Ross J observes:

> 64 The Courts of Appeal in British Columbia and Ontario expect trial judges to provide reasons should they decide not to apply the *SSAG* (*Lightle v. Kotar*, 2014 BCCA 69, [2014] B.C.J. No. 294; *Fisher v. Fisher*, 2008 ONCA 11, [2008] O.J. No. 38). In *Lightle v. Kotar* at para 63, the BCCA described this expectation as "more of an obligation than a best practice."
>
> . . .
>
> 66 The Courts of Appeal in Manitoba, New Brunswick, and Quebec take a similar stance to the Alberta Court of Appeal. Failure to follow or refer to the *SSAG* is not an error of law or an error in principle (*Kynoch v. Kynoch*, 2013 MBCA 73, 294 Man R (2d) 250; *Droit de la famille - 112606*, 2011 QCCA 1554, [2011] Q.J. No. 11097).[608] The fact that a spousal support award is outside the *SSAG* range without any exceptional circumstances to justify

---

607 *Dowhaniuk v Dowhaniuk*, 2014 ABQB 217 at para 59.
608 See also *Droit de la famille — 141364*, 2014 QCCA 1144.

the departure, is not a reviewable error in itself (*Smith v. Smith*, 2011 NBCA 66, [2011] N.B.J. No. 245).

Extremely strong judicial endorsement of the Rogerson/Thompson 2005 and 2008 reports on *Spousal Support Advisory Guidelines* is found in judgments of the British Columbia Court of Appeal.[609] In *Yemchuk v Yemchuk*,[610] the first appeal on the issue, the British Columbia Court of Appeal expressed the following conclusions. The Rogerson/Thompson report is a useful tool to assist judges in assessing the amount and duration of spousal support. While decisions undoubtedly exist in which the result differs from the Guidelines, the report and its formulas seek to build upon current law rather than devise an entirely new approach to the determination of spousal support. The Guidelines do not operate to displace judicial reliance on decided cases to the extent that they are forthcoming, but to supplement relevant caselaw. In that regard, they do not constitute evidence but are properly considered as part of counsel's submissions. The ranges of spousal support set out under the applicable formula in the Guidelines are appropriate for consideration when the court attempts to give effect to the principles espoused in *Moge v Moge*[611] and *Bracklow v Bracklow*[612] in light of the overall financial circumstances of the particular spouses.

In the subsequent judgment of the British Columbia Court of Appeal in *Redpath v Redpath*,[613] it was held that an award of spousal support that is substantially lower or higher than the range established by the *Spousal Support Advisory Guidelines* may constitute an error of law in the absence of exceptional circumstances.

The authors of the *Spousal Support Advisory Guidelines*, Professors Rogerson and Thompson, have identified certain situations where the Guidelines

---

609   *Yemchuk v Yemchuk*, [2005] BCJ No 1748 (CA); *Tedham v Tedham*, [2005] BCJ No 2186 (CA); *Kopelow v Warkentin*, [2005] BCJ No 2412 (CA); *Toth v Kun*, [2006] BCJ No 739 (CA); *Redpath v Redpath*, [2006] BCJ No 1550 (CA); *Stein v Stein*, [2006] BCJ No 2020 (CA); *McEachern v McEachern*, [2006] BCJ No 2917 (CA); *Foster v Foster*, [2007] BCJ No 244 (CA); *Beninger v Beninger*, 2007 BCCA 619; *Shellito v Bensimhon*, [2008] BCJ No 425 (CA); *Loesch v Walji*, 2008 BCCA 214; *Chera v Chera*, 2008 BCCA 374; *Jens v Jens*, 2008 BCCA 392; *Beese v Beese*, 2008 BCCA 396; *Chutter v Chutter*, 2008 BCCA 507; *Gonabady-Namadon v Mohammadzadeh*, 2009 BCCA 448; *Beninger v Beninger*, 2009 BCCA 458; *Hartshorne v Hartshorne*, 2010 BCCA 327; *Domirti v Domirti*, 2010 BCCA 472; *Stace-Smith v Lecompte*, 2011 BCCA 129; *Kelly v Kelly*, 2011 BCCA 173.

610   *Yemchuk v Yemchuk*, [2005] BCJ No 1748 (CA).

611   [1992] 3 SCR 813.

612   [1999] 1 SCR 420.

613   [2006] BCJ No 1550 at para 38 (CA). See also *McEachern v McEachern*, [2006] BCJ No 2917 (CA); *Stein v Stein*, [2006] BCJ No 2020 (CA); *Bodine-Shah v Shah*, 2014 BCCA 191. Compare *JHA v CGA*, [2008] MJ No 94 (QB).

apply on review and variation applications, including increases in the recipient's income and decreases in the payor's income. Other situations, such as post-separation increases in the payor's income, repartnering, remarriage, and second families, were left to be resolved by the exercise of judicial discretion because of the uncertain state of current substantive law in these contexts and the threshold issue of entitlement that may arise in these situations.[614] In *Beninger v Beninger*,[615] the British Columbia Court of Appeal found that the complications, referred to by Professors Rogerson and Thompson as arising on a variation application, were not a barrier to using the Guidelines as a tool in determining the amount and duration of spousal support. At the time of the original order, the Guidelines were not available and, therefore, played no part in the spousal support determination. It was apparent, however, that the criteria applied under section 15.2 of the *Divorce Act*, which are mirrored on variation applications under section 17 of the *Divorce Act*, led the trial judge to conclude that the wife was entitled to substantial spousal support for an indefinite term on both compensatory and non-compensatory principles. While there was some prospect of the wife's obtaining employment thereafter, this expectation was not realized due to the wife's marital role and her persistent and increasing health problems. On the other hand, the divorced husband's increased income was directly related to the career that he embarked on during the marriage while his wife assumed the role of a full-time homemaker and relinquished her own career prospects. Given these circumstances, and the fact that the divorced wife continued to struggle with the adverse economic consequences of the marriage breakdown, the British Columbia Court of Appeal concluded that almost all of the same factors that were relevant on the wife's original application for spousal support continued to apply with equal force to the current variation application. In these circumstances, the British Columbia Court of Appeal held that it would be appropriate to apply the Guidelines as a guide to the appropriate level and duration of support. At the same time, the British Columbia Court of Appeal made it clear that the decision whether to use the Guidelines as a guide on variation applications will have to be made cautiously and on a fact-specific basis.

In *Kontogiannis v Langridge*,[616] Russell J, of the British Columbia Supreme Court, provided the following synopsis of the responses of the British Columbia Court of Appeal to the *Spousal Support Advisory Guidelines*:

---

614 *Wegler v Wegler*, 2012 ONSC 5982.

615 2007 BCCA 619. For subsequent variation proceedings, see *Beninger v Beninger*, 2009 BCCA 458 and *Beninger v Beninger*, 2011 BCSC 302; see also *Jens v Jens*, 2008 BCCA 392; *Domirti v Domirti*, 2010 BCCA 472 (review proceeding); *Kelly v Kelly*, 2011 BCCA 173; compare *Lepp v Lepp*, 2008 BCSC 448; *Thompson v Thompson*, 2013 ONSC 7561.

616 2009 BCSC 1545 at para 37.

While the Guidelines are not legislated and are therefore only advisory, it has been repeatedly stated by the courts of this province that the Guidelines are a "useful tool" in determining issues of quantum and duration of spousal support and have been deemed to reflect the state of law in British Columbia: *Yemchuk v. Yemchuk*, 2005 BCCA 406, 44 B.C.L.R. (4th) 77; and *Chutter v. Chutter*, 2008 BCCA 507, 301 D.L.R. (4th) 297. In *Dunnigan v Park*, 2007 BCCA 329, 38 R.F.L. (6th) 241, the court described the Guidelines as providing a range of awards. In *Redpath v. Redpath*, 2006 BCCA 338, 62 B.C.L.R. (4th) 233 [*Redpath*], the court stated that it is not an error in law to fail to apply the Guidelines when assessing a claim for spousal support, but where an award is substantially above or below the suggested range of appropriate maintenance awards, it may be an error in law in the absence of exceptional circumstances (*Redpath*) or at least a reasonable explanation: *McEachern v. McEachern*, 2006 BCCA 508 at para. 64, 62 B.C.L.R. (4th) 95. Appellate review will be assisted by the inclusion of reasons explaining why the Guidelines do not provide an appropriate result: *Redpath*. The Court has upheld awards outside the proposed range when it was clear that the trial judge considered the Guidelines, but chose not to apply them for reasons specific to the facts of the case: *Shellito v. Bensimhon*, 2008 BCCA 68 at para. 24, 79 B.C.L.R. (4th) 45.

In *Scott v Scott*,[617] the Manitoba Court of Appeal held that, although the motion judge might usefully have referred to the *Spousal Support Advisory Guidelines* in his reasons, his failure to do so did not justify appellate intervention with his variation order reducing the amount of spousal support payable from $700 to $400 monthly. Dealing with the motion judge's failure to refer to the *Spousal Support Advisory Guidelines*, Monnin JA stated:

> 11 I deal lastly with the motions judge's failure to refer to the *SSAG*. Although it might be useful, in certain cases, to refer to the *SSAG*, one must not forget that they are not legislated guidelines, they are not binding on courts and, as of yet, they have not replaced the inherent discretion of a judge to determine what he or she considers an appropriate quantum to be awarded.
>
> 12 I am aware that in some jurisdictions it has been decreed that heavy reliance is to be placed on the *SSAG*. I prefer the approach taken by the Ontario Court of Appeal in *Fisher v Fisher*, 2008 ONCA 11, 288 DLR (4th) 513, where Lang J.A., writing for the court, stated (at paras. 94–98):

---

617   2011 MBCA 21; see also *Thomson v Thomson*, 2011 MBCA 28; *Swarzynski v Swarzynski*, 2012 MBQB 13; *Belot v Connelly*, 2013 MBQB 98.

The Guidelines were drafted under the aegis of the federal Department of Justice by the highly-regarded family law professors, Carol Rogerson and Rollie Thompson. The objective of the Guidelines is to bring certainty and predictability to spousal support awards under the *Divorce Act*. For this purpose, they employ an income-sharing model of support, that if proven viable, will reduce the need to rely on the labour-intensive, and thus expensive, budget-based evidence employed in a typical case. In this way, in a manner quite different from the *Federal Child Support Guidelines*, SOR/97 (CSGs), the Guidelines aspire to reduce the expense of litigation of spousal support by promoting resolution for the average case.

In the seminal case of *Yemchuk v. Yemchuk* (2005), 16 R.F.L. (6th) 430, 257 D.L.R. (4th) 476 (B.C.C.A.), at para. 64, Prowse J.A. aptly characterized the Guidelines as a "useful tool." She recognized that, unlike the CSGs, the Guidelines are neither legislated nor binding; they are only advisory. The parties, their lawyers, and the courts are not required to employ them. As well, the Guidelines continue to evolve; they are a "work in progress" subject to revision. Those revisions, as with the Guidelines themselves, will follow after broad consultation by the authors with a wide range of interested constituents.

Importantly, the Guidelines do not apply in many cases. They specifically do not apply at all in certain enumerated circumstances, including where spouses earn above $350,000 or below $20,000. Furthermore, they only apply to initial orders for support and not to variation orders. They are thus prospective in application. They do not apply in cases where a prior agreement provides for support and, obviously, in cases where the requisite entitlement has not been established. They will not help in atypical cases.[618] As well, there will be regional variations, as well as rural and urban variations, that may be seen to merit divergent results based on variations in cost of living or otherwise. Importantly, in all cases, the reasonableness of an award produced by the Guidelines must be balanced in light of the circumstances of the individual case, including the particular financial history of the parties during the marriage and their likely future circumstances.

Accordingly, the Guidelines cannot be used as a software tool or a formula that calculates a specific amount of support for a set

---

618 See *Singh v Singh*, 2013 ONSC 6476, citing *Fisher v Fisher*, 2008 ONCA 11.

period of time. They must be considered in context and applied in their entirety, including the specific consideration of any applicable variables and, where necessary, restructuring.

Importantly, the Guidelines do not impose a radically new approach. Instead, they suggest a range of both amount and duration of support that reflects the current law. Because they purport to represent a distillation of current case law, they are comparable to counsel's submissions about an appropriate range of support based on applicable jurisprudence. However, if the Guidelines suggest a range that conflicts with applicable authorities, the authorities will prevail.

13 This court is aware that the comments of Lang J.A., in the above quote, to the effect that the *SSAG* are not applicable to variation orders may not be the case in all situations, nor accepted by all courts. See, for example, *Beninger v. Beninger*, 2007 BCCA 619, 47 R.F.L. (6th) 11 at para. 51. However, we need not decide that issue in this case. For our purposes, it is sufficient to say that, although given counsels' reference to the *SSAG* in their submissions, it might have been useful for the motions judge to have referred to them in his reasons. His failure to do so is not an error in law justifying appellate intervention.

In *Kynoch v Kynoch*,[619] Steel JA, who delivered the opinion of the Manitoba Court of Appeal, noted that the wife had referred to the *Spousal Support Advisory Guidelines* and the trial judge, having acknowledged that courts use them, did not consider them and did not explain how he arrived at the quantum of $250 per month. Speaking to the Guidelines, Steel JA expressed the following opinion:

> [45] The SSAG were finalized in 2008. Their acceptance seems to be growing among lawyers and the judiciary, as everyone becomes more familiar with their use and the computer programs that make their application easier to adopt. (Annual review of Family Law, 2011, James G. McLeod and Alfred A. Mamo, Carswell (2012), p. 454)
>
> [46] I am well aware that the SSAG, although certainly part of the legal landscape at this point in time, are not legislated or binding, are only advisory and do not replace judicial discretion. The parties, their lawyers and the courts are not required to employ them. This court in *Scott v. Scott*, 2011 MBCA 21 (CanLII), 2011 MBCA 21, 262 Man.R. (2d) 237, has adopted the approach taken by the Ontario Court of Appeal in *Fisher v. Fisher*, 2008 ONCA

---

619   2013 MBCA 73 at paras 45–49; see also *Pasta v Pasta*, 2013 MBQB 311; *Rémillard v Rémillard*, 2014 MBCA 101 (*SSAG* used as "litmus test")

11 (CanLII), 2008 ONCA 11, 88 O.R. (3d) 241, and has held that the SSAG have not replaced the inherent discretion of a judge to determine what he or she considers an appropriate quantum to be awarded. Failure to refer to the SSAG or failure to follow them is not an error in principle.

[47] The SSAG must be used with care and understanding as to their structure and the limitations of determining spousal support based on a formula. As the Ontario Court of Appeal explained in *Fisher*, the formulas in the guidelines do not create new law, but reflect the result and the preponderance of decisions under the existing jurisprudence. The guidelines do not apply in many cases and must not be used in substitution for a consideration of the individual circumstances of the parties in front of the court.

[48] Having repeated the cautions expressed in the *Scott* case, I also acknowledge that the SSAG can bring some measure of consistency and predictability to a sorely inconsistent area and thereby encourage settlement. After considering the individual facts of a case, testing the quantum of support against the range suggested by the SSAG to see whether it falls within or close to that range is a reasonable method of double-checking the validity of the quantum of spousal support. This is especially so, in a case such as this, where the trial judge did not explain how he arrived at the figure of $250, and failed to take into account certain other considerations as mentioned above. As a matter of fact, at trial, even counsel for the husband suggested a higher quantum of spousal support of $300. In effect, the SSAG can act as a "litmus test" to determine whether the quantum of spousal support is so low as to be unjust or clearly wrong.

[49] In this case, reference to the SSAG confirm, in my view, that $250 per month is too low in the circumstances of this case. The SSAG shows a spousal support award in the range of between $878 to $1,134, with a mid-range of $1,006. While I understand the trial judge's desire to adjust the quantum of spousal support to take into account the fact that the wife owns a house and the husband has no assets, the reality is still that the husband's present income is double that of the wife's, as a result of training he obtained during the marriage. While I agree that some allowance should be made for the fact that the wife owns a home, I disagree with the quantum arrived at by the trial judge for the reasons listed above. Instead, I would substitute an award that is below the low end of the range in the amount of $600 per month.

In *Smith v Smith*,[620] the New Brunswick Court of Appeal reviewed its own previous rulings on the *Spousal Support Advisory Guidelines* and Quigg JA formulated the following principles in response to "the question of whether a trial judge errs in law, if he or she disregards the range of payments that would apply if the *Spousal Support Advisory Guidelines* were followed, without providing an explanation as to why they were not followed":

1) A trial judge's exercise of the judicial discretion conferred by section 15.2 (1) of the *Divorce Act* in fashioning an appropriate spousal support order is not constrained by the Guidelines.

2) Although the authors of the Guidelines identify certain exceptional situations where the ranges in the Guidelines may be considered inappropriate, they acknowledge that their list is not exhaustive. More importantly, no such list exists at law.

3) Previous SSAG judgments of the New Brunswick Court of Appeal do not support the argument that courts are bound by the Guidelines range, unless exceptional circumstances exist. While the New Brunswick Court of Appeal in *DLM v JAM*[621] held that judges "should" apply the Guidelines, it approved *Yemchuk v Yemchuk*[622] wherein it was observed that the Guidelines are intended to reflect the current law and are a useful tool to assist judges in assessing the quantum and duration of spousal support. They do not operate to displace the courts' reliance on decided authorities (to the extent that relevant authorities are forthcoming) but to supplement them. The judgment in *SC v JC*[623] is to similar effect.

4) There is a great difference between demanding that a court order support in accordance with the Guidelines ranges and suggesting that the ranges may be properly considered by a court. Relevant case law offers no support for the mandatory application of the Guidelines ranges.

5) Nor can a litigant rely on *Cassidy v McNeil*[624] to suggest that "not only must the *Guidelines* be respected, selection of the support amount within the ranges must be explained." This judgment does not support mandatory application of the Guidelines ranges.

6) While the Guidelines are not law *per se*, following them can enhance the legitimacy of a spousal support award, as the Guidelines promote consistency and therefore aid in the avoidance of arbitrary decision-making. Although the Guidelines have been considered in more than 400 deci-

---

620   2011 NBCA 66. See also *Purdue v Purdue*, 2014 NBQB 262; *Betts v Betts*, 2015 NBQB 19.
621   2008 NBCA 2.
622   2005 BCCA 406.
623   2006 NBCA 46; see also *Brooks v Brooks*, 2014 NBCA 29.
624   2010 ONCA 218.

sions nationwide, they are still a relatively recent development and con-
straining the discretion conferred upon judges by the *Divorce Act* with
regard to spousal support awards is best left to Parliament. It is too early
to know whether an over-dependence on the Guidelines may present
problems. This is not to say that the Guidelines may not be included at
some point in the legislation, or incorporated into the common law.

7)   While judges would be wise to follow the Guidelines, and usually do so,
     they should not be mandated to do so even when their reasons for decision
     do not bring into play an exception listed in Chapter 12 of the Guidelines.[625]

8)   In order to avoid the appearance of arbitrary decision-making, a trial
     judge should give reasons for spousal support awards above or below the
     Guidelines amounts.[626] Failing to give reasons or giving reasons based on
     erroneous fact-finding subjects trial decisions to appellate review.

9)   Where a marriage has lasted well over twenty years, indefinite (without
     specified duration) support is appropriate. The Guidelines' recommen-
     dations concerning indefinite support reflect New Brunswick jurispru-
     dence in long-term marriages.

In *BP v AT*,[627] Larlee JA, of the New Brunswick Court of Appeal, observed
that, while giving reasons for departure from the Guidelines avoids the appearance of arbitrariness, "this court has not gone so far as to say one range
(low, middle or high) is the default position and reasons should be given for
deviating from it. I am not prepared to do so now on the facts of this case."

In *Morgan v Morgan*,[628] LeBlanc J, of the Newfoundland and Labrador
Supreme Court, examined several aspects of the *Spousal Support Advisory
Guidelines* with a critical eye. Reviewing the "parental partnership rationale"
as the basis of spousal support obligations under the Guidelines, LeBlanc J
stated that the rationale is not applicable in every case. There will be cases
where the pre-separation and post-separation arrangements involving the
children will not create any ongoing economic disadvantage or negative financial consequences, as for example, where both parents have established
careers during the marriage, which are not materially affected by child-care
responsibilities. Cases will also arise where the duration of the spousal relationship will be so short that the presence of children will make no differ-

---

625   *Betts v Betts*, 2015 NBQB 19.

626   *Flieger v Adams*, 2012 NBCA 39; *Grant v Grant*, 2012 NBCA 101.

627   2014 NBCA 51.

628   [2006] NJ No 9 (SC); compare *Collins v Collins*, 2008 NLUFC 31. For two Newfoundland
      and Labrador judgments wherein the *Spousal Support Advisory Guidelines* were consid-
      ered on applications to vary an existing order for spousal support, see *Upshall v Upshall*,
      [2006] NJ No 23 (UFC), Dunn J and *Walsh v Walsh*, [2006] NJ No 33 (UFC), Cook J. See
      also *Puddifant v Puddifant*, [2005] NSJ No 558 (SC), Gass J.

ence to spousal support. In LeBlanc J's opinion, the parenting partnership rationale will most likely constitute the basis of spousal support entitlement where, due to the needs of the children, their age, or other special circumstances, one parent ends up having restricted employment or educational opportunities. A parent who has flexibility in his or her employment and educational opportunities may not face the same limitations or restrictions. Consequently, the fact that the spouses have cohabited for a period of time and have children will not, of itself, be determinative as to the applicability of the parenting partnership rationale. Each case must be determined on its own facts. In *Morgan v Morgan*, LeBlanc J found that the wife's parenting responsibilities, including those relating to a special-needs child, established a clear entitlement to spousal support. If the *With Child Support Formula* under the *Spousal Support Advisory Guidelines* had been applied, the husband would have been required to pay monthly spousal support in the range of $329 to $546. However, after reviewing the husband's net income after the payment of child support and having regard to his monthly expenses, including housing and automobile expenses, which were not excessive and were affected by his exercise of access to the children, LeBlanc J concluded that the husband lacked the capacity to pay any spousal support. In this context, it is noteworthy that the *Spousal Support Advisory Guidelines* suggest that no spousal support should be payable until the obligor's gross annual income exceeds $20,000, and in cases where his or her gross annual income falls between $20,000 and $30,000, "consideration should be given to the percentages sought under the applicable formula, the net disposable income left to the payor spouse, and the impact of a spousal support payment upon the work incentives and marginal gains of the payor."[629] While conceding that the Rogerson/Thompson proposal might constitute an appropriate floor in most cases, LeBlanc J concluded that it was too low in the present case and it would be preferable to have the father continue in his present lifestyle, which was not excessive or extravagant, with him meeting his child support and access obligations rather than risk placing him in such poor financial shape as to jeopardize his child support obligations and his relationship with the children. LeBlanc J also expressed reservations about the Rogerson/Thompson proposals respecting the duration of child support when there are young children residing with the applicant spouse and the spousal relationship is of short duration. In the present case, LeBlanc J would have been inclined to favour a short period of time-limited spousal support whereas the maximum

---

629 Canada, Department of Justice, *Spousal Support Advisory Guidelines*, by Carol Rogerson & Rollie Thompson (Ottawa: Department of Justice, 2008) at 11.4, online: www.justice. gc.ca/eng/rp-pr/fl-lf/spousal-epoux/spag/pdf/SSAG_eng.pdf.

duration under the *Spousal Support Advisory Guidelines* would have been up to the date when the youngest child finished high school. In LeBlanc J's opinion, such an order would require exceptional circumstances under the current law in Newfoundland and Labrador.

In the more recent case of *Whitten v Whitten*,[630] Fowler J of the Newfoundland and Labrador Supreme Court, has stated:

> In determining the amount of spousal support, I will be relying on the *Spousal Support Advisory Guidelines* ("SSAG"), which now seem to have been accepted throughout Canada as a fair and accurate method of such calculations.

And in reviewing the *Spousal Support Advisory Guidelines* in *Collins v Johnson*, Fry J, of the Newfoundland and Labrador Supreme Court, has stated:

> 40   The *SSAG*, while advisory only, are a useful tool to assist in providing a range of either spousal or partner support in a variety of circumstances. The *SSAG* are particularly helpful because of the various formulae which are embedded in the software program used to establish a low, middle and high range of spousal support payments based on *Guideline* incomes, taking into account the taxes and deductions available to payors as well as taxes, deductions, government benefits and credits available to recipients. These formulae are updated regularly with new tax information on a province by province basis.
>
> 41   . . . Unlike child support, partner support does not vary from year to year as income fluctuates, so once determined as a final order it will only be subject to variation when and if a material change in circumstances can be demonstrated.[631]

In *Phinney v Phinney*,[632] Warner J, of the Nova Scotia Supreme Court, observed:

> The prerequisite to the determination of the quantum of spousal support is entitlement. While the draft proposal for the *Spousal Support Advisory Guidelines* states that the Guideline amounts are premised on a finding by a court that entitlement exists, the application of the ranges, and the basis for the calculation of quantum, does not appear to fully take into account circumstances where entitlement, based on the objectives in s 15.2(6), is weak.

In *Phinney*, Warner J reviewed the four objectives of spousal support orders under section 15.2(6) of the *Divorce Act* in concluding that the wife was

---

630   2014 NLTD(F) 6.
631   2014 NLTD(F) 16 at paras 40–41.
632   [2005] NSJ No 224 at para 26 (SC).

disentitled to spousal support after September 2004. Warner J held that no foundation had been established for compensatory spousal support and any right to non-compensatory support based on the wife's needs was negated by her earning capacity and her entry into a stable common law relationship with a man whose income significantly exceeded that of the husband. In addressing section 15(2)(6)(d) of the *Divorce Act*, whereby the fourth objective of spousal support orders is to promote the economic self-sufficiency of each of the spouses, insofar as is practicable, Warner J observed that economic self-sufficiency does not have to be achieved through employment income. Alternative means of achieving economic self-sufficiency include good fortune, investments, inheritance, or entering into a new partnership with a person with a significant and secure financial status.

In *Vanderlinden v Vanderlinden*,[633] Campbell J, of the Nova Scotia Supreme Court, set aside a separation agreement negotiated by the spouses with minimal legal advice on the ground that the spouses had mistakenly applied the *Spousal Support Advisory Guidelines* in effectuating a trade-off between spousal support and the future discharge of family and personal debts and thereby produced an agreement that was not even remotely affordable by the husband.

In *Pettigrew v Pettigrew*,[634] the appellant husband argued that the trial judge erred in setting the amount of spousal support by applying the *Spousal Support Advisory Guidelines* instead of assessing the evidence and applying the law. The Nova Scotia Court of Appeal held that the trial judge had only referred to the Guidelines as a cross-check and, applying the customary standard of appellate review, was not satisfied that the trial judge erred in law, misapprehended the evidence, or was clearly wrong in determining the amount of spousal support to be paid. In *Michaud v Kuszelewski*,[635] the Nova Scotia Court of Appeal found it to be appropriate in the circumstances of the case for the trial judge to rely on the *Spousal Support Advisory Guidelines* to determine that the award should be indefinite as a result of the mother's continuing care of dependent children. But in *Strecko v Strecko*,[636] wherein the trial judge declined to apply the Guidelines in addressing the impact of minutes of settlement on the wife's claim for ongoing spousal support, the Nova Scotia Court of Appeal held that the Guidelines are not law; they are only advisory and the trial judge was not obliged to apply them.

---

633   2007 NSSC 80. See also *Evans v Spicer*, 2014 NSSC 95.
634   [2006] NSJ No 321 (CA).
635   2009 NSCA 118; compare *Werner v Werner*, 2013 NSCA 6.
636   2014 NSCA 66.

In *Fisher v Fisher*,[637] the Ontario Court of Appeal sought to provide the wife with a reasonable financial transition after the breakdown of her nineteen-year marriage. Lang JA, with whom Doherty and Goudge JJA concurred, concluded that the wife should receive support for seven years running from the date of spousal separation to facilitate her attainment of economic self-sufficiency, either by earning a higher income or by adapting her lifestyle to her earned income. With respect to the trial judge's refusal to revisit the amount of interim spousal support, Lang JA stated that "retroactive support should be available when the recipient establishes at trial that he or she was entitled to a greater amount of interim support, the respondent had the ability to pay, and the imposition of retroactive support would not create undue hardship for the payor."[638] Lang JA further stated that this approach accords with the structure of the *Spousal Support Advisory Guidelines*, which apply to both interim and permanent orders, and it avoids distortions that would otherwise arise under the Guidelines in determining the interdependent issues of the amount and duration of spousal support orders. To achieve an equitable outcome in determining the amount of spousal support, Lang JA averaged the annual income of each spouse during the last three years of matrimonial cohabitation and during the year in which they separated. This produced an average annual income of $89,825 for the husband and $35,500 for the wife. Based on these averages, Lang JA concluded that the wife should receive spousal support in the amount of $3,000 per month for three and one-half years from the date of the interim order, followed by monthly spousal support of $1,500 for a further three and one-half years, whereafter spousal support would terminate. Although she assessed the amount and duration of spousal support on the basis of the circumstances of the case, Lang JA stated that "it is helpful to consider the reasonableness of this award by reference to the Guidelines."[639] After referring to "the seminal case" of *Yemchuk v Yemchuk*,[640] wherein the *Spousal Support Advisory Guidelines* were characterized as a "useful tool," and after identifying specified circumstances wherein their application is limited or excluded, Lang JA expressed the following general conclusion:

---

637 2008 ONCA 11; see also *Topper v Topper*, 2012 ONSC 3516; *Firth v Allerton*, 2013 ONSC 2960. And see *JHA v CGA*, [2008] MJ No 94 (QB); *Rakhra v Rakhra*, 2012 NWTSC 33. Compare *Refcio v Refcio*, [2009] OJ No 1539 (Div Ct). See also Mary Jo Maur, "How Have Ontario Courts Interpreted *Fisher*?" AFCC Ontario Inaugural Event (3 April 2009); Rollie Thompson, "Following *Fisher*: Ontario Spousal Support Trends 2008–09" (2009) 28 Can Fam LQ 241.

638 2008 ONCA 11 at para 76; see also *Hartshorne v Hartshorne*, 2010 BCCA 327.

639 *Fisher v Fisher*, 2008 ONCA 11 at para 92.

640 [2005] BCJ No 1748 (CA).

[96] Importantly, in all cases, the reasonableness of an award produced by the Guidelines must be balanced in light of the circumstances of the individual case, including the particular financial history of the parties during the marriage and their likely future circumstances.

[97] Accordingly, the Guidelines cannot be used as a software tool or a formula that calculates a specific amount of support for a set period of time. They must be considered in context and applied in their entirety, including the specific consideration of any applicable variables and, where necessary, restructuring.[641]

Lang JA further observed:

[98] Because they purport to represent a distillation of current case law, they are comparable to counsel's submissions about an appropriate range of support based on applicable jurisprudence. However, if the Guidelines suggest a range that conflicts with applicable authorities, the authorities will prevail.[642]

She noted that counsel had advised her that the Guidelines are widely used by lawyers "as a starting point for the purpose of assessing an appropriate level of spousal support, or for checking the validity of a proposed settlement."[643] And she stated:

[103] In my view, when counsel fully address the Guidelines in argument, and a trial judge decides to award a quantum of support outside the suggested range, appellate review will be assisted by the inclusion of reasons explaining why the Guidelines do not provide an appropriate result. This is no different than a trial court distinguishing a significant authority relied upon by a party.[644]

Applying the Guidelines to the *Fisher* marriage, Lang JA found that the amount proposed under the *Without Child Support Formula* ranged from $1,290 to $1,720 monthly and the duration formula would provide support for a period ranging from nine and one-half years to nineteen years. Since the award deemed appropriate by the Ontario Court of Appeal exceeded the range for the amount of spousal support and fell well below the range for the

---

641   *Fisher v Fisher*, 2008 ONCA 11 at paras 96–97; see also *Topper v Topper*, 2012 ONSC 3516. Compare *Refcio v Refcio*, [2009] OJ No 1539 (Div Ct).

642   *Fisher v Fisher*, 2008 ONCA 11 at para 98.

643   *Ibid* at para 99; see also *Rapoport v Rapoport*, 2011 ONSC 4456; compare *JHA v CGA*, [2008] MJ No 94 at paras 159–63 (QB).

644   *Fisher v Fisher*, 2008 ONCA 11 at para 103. See also *Gagne v Gagne*, 2011 ONCA 188; *Davis v Crawford*, 2011 ONCA 294; *Djekic v Zai*, 2015 ONCA 25.

duration of spousal support, Lang JA applied the restructuring concept endorsed in the *Spousal Support Advisory Guidelines* report, which allows amount and duration to be traded off against each other, as long as the overall value of the restructured award remains within the global amount generated by the formulas when the amount is multiplied by the duration of the award. After undertaking the necessary arithmetical calculations, Lang JA observed that the global amount under the spousal support order was $189,000, an amount that fell within the Guidelines global range of a low of $147,000 to a high of $392,236.[645]

Commenting on the manner in which counsel should address the *Spousal Support Advisory Guidelines* in *Cassidy v McNeil*,[646] Lang JA stated:

[I]n *Fisher v. Fisher* (2008), 88 O.R. (3d) 241 (C.A.), at para. 103, I commented about counsel "fully" addressing the *SSAG*. In my view, a "full" argument on the application of the *SSAG* would generally include provision of calculator worksheets for various scenarios. Those scenarios should be provided to the trial judge and marked as exhibits or aids to the court so that they are available on appeal. When counsel do not provide the trial court with worksheets, or fail to have those calculations before the appellate court, the court cannot be expected to do the calculations on their behalf.

In *Jessop v Wright*,[647] the Ontario Court of Appeal held that the motion judge was not in error in failing to apply the *Spousal Support Advisory Guidelines* when ranges under the Guidelines had not been presented to him. The motion judge was found in error, however, in failing to provide any reason why spousal support in the amount of $2,000 per month should be paid both in years when the wife earned no income and in years when her annual income was between $28,000 and $38,000. Having regard to the respective annual incomes of the spouses from 2005 to 2007, the Ontario Court of Appeal reduced the amount of monthly spousal support to $1,700 during the period when the wife was earning income. This amount was said to fit within the one Guidelines example that had been provided in the husband's factum. The Ontario Court of Appeal saw no reason to interfere with the motion judge's award of $2,000 per month from 1 December 2007, which amount had been sought by the respondent wife in her notice of motion and appeared to fall at the low end or even below the suggested Guidelines range, given the wife's current unemployment.

---

645 See also *Grinyer v Grinyer*, [2008] OJ No 290 (Sup Ct).
646 2010 ONCA 218 at para 61.
647 2008 ONCA 673.

Accepting that the *Spousal Support Advisory Guidelines* are advisory, and not mandatory,[648] the Prince Edward Island Court of Appeal in *MacQuarrie v MacQuarrie*[649] observed that their authors, Professors Rogerson and Thompson, envisaged that the Guidelines would apply to variation orders in straightforward situations where there was an increase or decrease in the income of a spouse, but they would not necessarily apply in situations involving remarriage, repartnering, or post-separation income increases, all of which can give rise to questions of entitlement.[650] Finding no reason why the husband's post-separation income increases should not be taken into account in quantifying the amount of spousal support, the Prince Edward Island Court of Appeal concluded that the motion judge was entitled to award retroactive spousal support in the pre-retirement amount of $4,000 per month and in the post-retirement amount of $1,100 per month, which amounts represented the highest point in the ranges presented under the *Spousal Support Advisory Guidelines*. The appellate court noted that Chapter 9 of the SSAG final report highlights several factors that can be taken into account in using the ranges to determine the amount and duration of spousal support. These factors include the strength of any compensatory claim, the needs of the recipient, the needs and ability of the payor, and self-sufficiency incentives. Finding that the motion judge had considered these factors, the Prince Edward Island Court of Appeal determined that the motion judge did not err in determining the amount of spousal support payable either retroactively or subsequent to the husband's retirement. Nor was any error found insofar as the motion judge did not apply the Guidelines in establishing the duration of spousal support either retroactively or post-retirement. In the opinion of the appellate court, the Guidelines would not be applicable in establishing the duration of retroactive support as this was established in accordance with the applicable caselaw.

The judgment of the Quebec Court of Appeal in *Droit de la famille — 112606*[651] reflects a similar cautionary approach to the *Spousal Support Advisory Guidelines* as that adopted by the Alberta Court of Appeal in *Sawatzky v Sawatzky*.[652] It explicitly rejected the presumptive approach to the Guidelines suggested by Newbury JA, of the British Columbia Court of Appeal, in *Redpath v Redpath*[653] and endorsed by Lang JA, of the Ontario Court of Appeal, in

---

648   See *BLB v GDM*, 2015 PESC 1; *KDM v JDM*, 2015 PESC 8.
649   2012 PECA 3.
650   See *Beninger v Beninger*, 2007 BCCA 619.
651   2011 QCCA 1554.
652   2008 ABCA 355.
653   2006 BCCA 338.

Fisher v Fisher,[654] indicating that the ranges specified in the Guidelines should be applied in the absence of articulated reasons explaining why the Guidelines do not provide an appropriate result. Stated briefly, the Quebec Court of Appeal asserted that determination of the amount and duration of a spousal support order requires a close examination of the facts of each case in light of the applicable legal criteria defined in section 15.2 of the *Divorce Act* as interpreted and applied in *Moge v Moge*[655] and *Bracklow v Bracklow*.[656] By way of elaboration, Marie-France Bich JCA, with whom Allen R Hilton JCA concurred, enunciated the following principles:

1. The Guidelines do not determine the right to spousal support. Entitlement to spousal support must first be established. Only then can the Guidelines be invoked to facilitate a determination of the amount and duration of spousal support.

2. Income disparity between the spouses does not, of itself, confer any entitlement to spousal support.

3. The Guidelines are not intended to exclude a judicial analysis of the particular facts having regard to the relevant factors and the objectives of spousal support orders that are set out in section 15.2(4) and (6) of the *Divorce Act*. Nor do the Guidelines displace the judicial discretion that section 15.2 confers on the court.

4. The judicial discretion is exercisable not only in determining entitlement; it is also exercisable in fixing the amount and duration of spousal support and in determining whether the ranges provided by the Guidelines are appropriate in the particular circumstances of the case.

5. The Guidelines are intended to minimize unpredictability and arbitrary subjectivity in spousal support cases. They are based on a comprehensive review of Canadian case law and their authors strive to avoid simplistic solutions by providing commentary to explain and qualify the mathematical calculations. Questions, nevertheless, remain concerning the choices made by the authors. For example, the Guidelines are based on a concept of income sharing that reflects a traditional view of marriage. In the case of marriages without children, undue weight is placed on the duration of cohabitation. The notion that spouses lives become progressively more economically interdependent with the passage of time, though true in long-term traditional marriages with children, may not be true in non-traditional marriages or in childless marriages. The concept of income sharing may also be

---

654 2008 ONCA 11.
655 [1992] 3 SCR 813.
656 [1999] 1 SCR 420.

inappropriate for short marriages. Although the Guidelines may provoke controversy, they cannot be criticized as being too mechanical. They are subtle and encompass differing situations. Furthermore, they do not ignore the judge's discretion. They also have the advantage of providing predictability and consistency in cases of "compensatory support" in which specific quantification by the court is often elusive.

6. Courts in several provinces have acknowledged that the Guidelines constitute a useful tool in determining the amount and duration of spousal support. As Professor Goubau has observed, the Guidelines do not replace the law or the authority of the court, but they may well facilitate the implementation of the law and the exercise of judicial authority.

7. As was pointed out in the previous judgment of the Quebec Court of Appeal in *G.V. v. C.G.*,[657] the Guidelines do not provide a recipe or grid for the judge to apply instead of analyzing the factors and objectives set out in section 15.2(4) and (6) of the *Divorce Act*. The Guidelines are not law, nor do they carry the weight of expert evidence, even though they were produced by academics with expertise in family law who had undertaken an extensive empirical study of relevant Canadian case law. The Guidelines constitute a secondary source of legal opinion that can be used to verify or support a conclusion but they are not, in themselves, decisive. A judge may consult them, as he or she might consult books or previous judgments to learn about the practices or ranges adopted in similar cases. In short, the Guidelines are an extra tool that can enable the court to quantify spousal support.

8. In Quebec, some courts have interpreted *G.V. v. C.G.*, above, as prohibiting the use of the Guidelines. But the Guidelines were not wholly rejected by the Quebec Court of Appeal in that case, although the need for caution was acknowledged and it was concluded that the Guidelines cannot displace the required analysis under section 15.2 of the *Divorce Act*. In Quebec, as in the rest of Canada, the Guidelines are a useful tool. However, they are not mandatory and cannot substitute for an analysis under section 15.2 of the *Divorce Act*. As Lang J.A. observed in *Fisher v. Fisher*, with time and experience, they will prove to be a "reliable tool" for resolving the amount and duration of spousal support while taking due account of the particular circumstances of the case.

9. The Guidelines, introduced in 2005 and finalized in 2008, have been widely tested and are no longer in an exploratory state. However, that

---

657 [2006] RJQ 1519.

does not signify that caution in their application is no longer appropriate or that courts can blindly rely on them. They do not fetter the judicial discretion conferred by section 15.2 of the *Divorce Act*, which allows the trial judge to craft a solution that reflects the particular circumstances of the spouses. But they may be used by Quebec courts to avoid arbitrary decision making.

10. The suggestion of Newbury J.A. in *Redpath v. Redpath*, above, and of Lang J.A. in *Fisher v. Fisher* that trial judges should not depart from the ranges specified in the Guidelines without providing reasons for doing so is unacceptable. It cannot be an error of law for a trial judge not to consider the Guidelines, if he or she has undertaken an analysis in accordance with section 15.2 of the *Divorce Act*. In the converse situation, however, a trial judge will err in law or in principle, if he or she bases a decision solely on the Guidelines without conducting an analysis under section 15.2 of the *Divorce Act*, unless the spouses consent to such a course of action. Unless and until Parliament renders the use of the Guidelines mandatory, they can provide no more than supplementary assistance in the application of section 15.2 of the *Divorce Act*. But such supplementary guidance should be welcomed in Quebec as it is in other Canadian provinces. Litigants are free to use the Guidelines in pursuing negotiations for a settlement or in seeking a spousal support order from the court.

11. Although the Guidelines may be referred to in final submissions, it can be advantageous to include their potential relevance in the initial pleadings. This may facilitate agreement, reduce the scope of legal argument, or prompt a party into submitting relevant evidence.

12. The Guidelines provide an overview of previous decisions against which a judge may review his or her findings under section 15.2 of the *Divorce Act*. However, as stated by the Alberta Court of Appeal in *Rockall v. Rockall*,[658] "a trial judge cannot rely on the recommendations generated under [the Guidelines] when his or her own proper analysis requires a different conclusion."

13. If the parties do not raise the Guidelines, the trial judge is not bound to consider them. Trial judges, who are immersed in the day-to-day adjudication of spousal support applications and who are familiar with the levels of spousal support, are best equipped to assess the usefulness of the guidelines in any particular case. They can correlate the

---

658   2010 ABCA 278 at para 18.

presentations on the facts before them to the Guidelines and choose to use the Guidelines or to depart from them.[659]

Having endorsed the aforementioned principles, the Quebec Court of Appeal found no error on the part of the trial judge in quantifying spousal support without regard to the *Spousal Support Advisory Guidelines*. The appellate court, nevertheless, increased the amount of spousal support from $3,500 to $6,250 per month. In ordering this increase, the Quebec Court of Appeal reviewed the facts of the case in light of section 15.2 of the *Divorce Act*, finding that this was a traditional marriage that lasted twenty-four years during which the wife was the primary homemaker and child caregiver while the husband advanced his career. Given their respective marital roles, the wife's responsibility for the care of the children after the spousal separation, and the current annual income of each spouse (the husband earning $363,000 and the wife earning $45,150), the Quebec Court of Appeal concluded that it would be appropriate for the husband to pay spousal support in the monthly amount of $6,250, this amount being somewhat lower than the range under the *Spousal Support Advisory Guidelines*. During the course of her judgment, Bich JCA cited the following observations that appeared in a previous edition of this book:

By way of an overview of Canadian caselaw, the following opinions are tendered:

1) Absent statutory or regulatory adoption, the Guidelines are informal and advisory. Blind adherence to the ranges established by the formulas under the Guidelines is not endorsed by the authors of the report, nor by the courts. In the opinion of the majority of courts that have considered the Guidelines, the prescribed formulas provide a useful supplementary tool to assist the court in determining the amount and duration of spousal support orders after the evidence has been reviewed in light of the statutory and judicial criteria governing such orders, which are elucidated in *Moge v Moge*[660] and *Bracklow v Bracklow*.[661]

2) Even if the formulas in the Guidelines can be used as a starting point, as proposed by Professors Rogerson and Thompson[662] and endorsed by Sullivan J in *McCulloch v Bawtinheimer*[663] and by Heeney J in *Hesketh v*

---

659   For a useful review of relevant Canadian caselaw, see *Dowhaniuk v Dowhaniuk*, 2014 ABQB 217.

660   [1992] 3 SCR 813.

661   [1999] 1 SCR 420.

662   See *Fisher v Fisher*, 2008 ONCA 11 at para 99; *Rapoport v Rapoport*, 2011 ONSC 4456 at para 505; *Benvenuto v Whitman*, 2012 ONSC 2696; compare *Bruni v Bruni*, 2010 ONSC 6568.

663   [2006] AJ No 361 (QB).

Hesketh,[664] but opposed by Trussler J in *VS v AK,*[665] they are no substitute for a factual analysis of evidence and a legal analysis of the factors and objectives that are prescribed as relevant by the governing statute and relevant case law.[666]

3) On the breakdown or dissolution of long-term marriages in which the wife has assumed the primary homemaking and child caregiving roles, income splitting under the *Spousal Support Advisory Guidelines* substantially accords with *Moge v Moge*, wherein L'Heureux-Dubé J observed that "[a]s marriage should be regarded as a joint endeavour, the longer the relationship endures, the closer the economic union, the greater will be the presumptive claim to equal standards of living upon its dissolution."[667]

4) Although Professors Rogerson and Thompson perceive an interdependence between the amount and duration of spousal support orders, especially under the *Without Child Support Formula,*[668] courts use the Guidelines more frequently when addressing the amount of support to be ordered than in addressing the duration of the order.

5) The Guidelines are inapplicable until an entitlement to spousal support is established.[669] In exceptional circumstances, the Guidelines may operate to negate any entitlement to spousal support.[670]

6) Given the informal, voluntary, and advisory status of the Guidelines, courts are disinclined to apply the proposed formulas as the sole or primary determinant of the amount and duration of spousal support orders. Courts have, nevertheless, accepted the Guidelines as providing an appropriate benchmark for the judicial determination of spousal support orders, whether made pursuant to the *Divorce Act* or provincial legislation.[671]

---

664 [2005] OJ No 4053 (Sup Ct); see also *Bruni v Bruni*, 2010 ONSC 6568.

665 [2005] AJ No 1357 (QB).

666 *VS v AK, ibid; JHA v CGA*, [2008] MJ No 94 (QB); *Saunders v Saunders*, 2010 NSSC 304; *Fisher v Fisher*, 2008 ONCA 11; *Morash v Morash*, [2005] SJ No 618 (QB); *Nasby v Nasby*, [2005] SJ No 619 (QB); *McCorriston v McCorriston*; [2006] SJ No 277 (QB); *Rudyk v Rudyk*, 2010 SKQB 315.

667 [1992] 3 SCR 813 at 870; see also *Betts v Betts*, 2015 NBQB 19.

668 See *Domirti v Domirti*, 2010 BCCA 472; *Fisher v Fisher*, 2008 ONCA 11.

669 *Metcalfe v Metcalfe*, 2013 ABQB 356; *Dubey v Dubey*, [2008] BCJ No 605 (SC); *Eastwood v Eastwood*, [2006] NBJ No 513 (QB).

670 *Rossi v Rossi*, [2005] OJ No 4136 (Sup Ct); see also *Bains v Bains*, [2008] AJ No 537 (QB).

671 See, for example, *Modry v Modry*, [2005] AJ No 442 (QB), Germain J; *JHA v CGA*, [2008] MJ No 94 (QB), Little J; *Scott v Scott*, 2011 MBCA 21; *Chubey v Chubey*, 2011 MBQB 100; *Simmonds v Simmonds*, [2005] NJ No 144 (UFC), Handrigan J; *Garland v Garland*, [2005] NJ No 139 (UFC), Cook J; *Barter v Barter*, [2006] NJ No 52, BG Welsh JA (CA); *Harding v Harding*, [2006] NJ No 64 (SC), Fowler J; *Denton v Denton*, [2005] NSJ No 245 (SC), Moir

7)   Since computer software on the *Spousal Support Advisory Guidelines* has become available, their application as benchmarks or cross-checks has been more frequent. Lawyers and judges are cautioned against attempting to apply the prescribed *With Child Support Formula* under the *Spousal Support Advisory Guidelines* without recourse to available computer software.

8)   Although they have not gained universal acceptance as a "cross-check," "benchmark," "litmus test," or starting point in the judicial assessment of the amount and duration of spousal support orders, many judges now appear to have established a comfort level with the formulas and principles presented by Professors Rogerson and Thompson. It is becoming increasingly frequent for courts to look beyond the prescribed formula by examining the underlying principles set out in the Rogerson/Thompson report.

9)   Some previous judicial reservations about applying the *Spousal Support Advisory Guidelines* because they are a "work in progress" have been laid to rest since the Department of Justice, Canada released a final version of the Rogerson/Thompson report in 2008. However, that version introduces no major substantive changes. The differing responses of Canadian appellate courts to the *Spousal Support Advisory Guidelines* will, therefore, continue until such time as the Supreme Court of Canada addresses the issue.

In *Linn v Frank*,[672] Jackson JA, of the Saskatchewan Court of Appeal, set out the following principles as governing the response of the Saskatchewan Court of Appeal to the *Spousal Support Advisory Guidelines* :

> 82   First, when a court of appeal reviews a spousal support order, where the application of the *Guidelines* has been put in issue, the court refers to the usual standard of review first stated authoritatively by L'Heureux-Dubé J. for the Court in *Hickey v. Hickey*, [1999] 2 S.C.R. 518 . . . .
>
> 83   Within the confines of the standard of review analysis as articulated in *Hickey*, the issue for an appeal court then becomes the extent to which a failure to follow or apply the *Guidelines* gives rise to "material error" or "an error of law" permitting or requiring appellate intervention.
>
> 84   Second, the starting point for any analysis of the appropriate level of spousal support continues to be the legislative obligations prescribed by the applicable legislation. A court referring to the *Guidelines* must still perform the analysis prescribed by *Moge v. Moge*, [1992] 3 S.C.R. 813 and *Brack-*

J; *Kerr v Kerr*, [2005] OJ No 1966 (Sup Ct), Blishen J; and *Fleming v Fleming*, [2005] SJ No 251 (QB), Sandomirsky J. Compare *Large v Large*, [2005] PEIJ No 43 (SC), Mitchell CJPEI.
672 2014 SKCA 87 at paras 82–90.

low v. Bracklow, [1999] 1 S.C.R. 420. If the trial judge does not perform that analysis, it may not be possible to sustain the decision on appeal whether or not the *Guidelines* are applied (see *Sawatzky v. Sawatzky*, 2008 ABCA 355 at para 16, 59 R.F.L. (6th) 88). A complete factual analysis is also important to determine which of the amounts suggested by the appropriate range apply or to determine whether to give effect to one of the exceptions — or indeed whether to fix an amount suggested by the *Guidelines* at all (see *Deringer v. Hill*, 2007 SKQB 206 at para. 16, 308 Sask. R. 122).

85 Third, it is critically important to understand that the *Guidelines* require more analysis than inserting a few numbers into a formula to obtain a number, which is then considered to be the ideal and immutable amount of spousal support. The *Guidelines* recognize the considerable discretion enjoyed by trial judges. *The Spousal Support Advisory Guidelines: A New and Improved User's Guide to the Final Version* ([Ottawa]: Department of Justice, 2010) also make it clear that a sophisticated analysis of the parties' needs and means is required to arrive at the best possible spousal support order in the circumstances of each case. This principle is fully understood in the many decisions of the Court of Queen's Bench to date (see, for example, *Billett v. Billett*, 2013 SKQB 269 at para. 63, 425 Sask. R. 217; *Verhelst v. Verhelst*, 2013 SKQB 12 at para. 52, 415 Sask. R. 17; *Sangray v. Sangray*, 2012 SKQB 455 at para. 6, 407 Sask. R. 149; *Geransky v. Geransky*, 2012 SKQB 218 at para. 25).

86 Fourth, when counsel makes a submission with respect to the *Guidelines* in the trial court, it is expected, as a matter of good judicial decision-making, that the trial judge's reasons explain why the *Guidelines* were or were not followed. This would be so in relation to any significant argument seriously made to a court at any level (see *Fisher v. Fisher*, 2008 ONCA 11 at para. 103, 288 D.L.R. (4th) 513).

87 Fifth, with the passage of time, more and more of the reported decisions are awarding an amount derived from the application of the *Guidelines* such that future compliance with them will become more typical. They will become a "litmus test," to use the words of Steele J.A. in *Kynoch v. Kynoch*, 2013 MBCA 73 at para. 48, 294 Man. R. (2d) 250, for what constitutes an "equitable sharing of the economic consequences of marriage or marriage breakdown" (*Moge* at p. 866). See also *De Winter v. De Winter*, 2013 ABCA 311 at paragraph 28 where the Court referred to the *Guidelines* as being "a useful tool when determining spousal support . . . and the need to view the award through the lens of the criteria set forth in the *Divorce Act*."

88 Sixth, over time it can only be expected that the *Guidelines* will influence judicial thinking about what is a clearly wrong award. As the Court stated in *Fisher*, "when considered in their entirety and subject to their limitations, the *Guidelines* also assist in informing an appellate standard of

review" (at para. 102). This will permit the use of the *Guidelines* to ensure consistency in situations when the parties do not wish to use the courts to resolve the question of spousal support (see: *S.C. v. J.C.*, 2006 NBCA 46, 27 R.F.L. (6th) 19 at para. 5, leave to appeal refused, [2006] S.C.C.A. No. 246).

89   In sum, the role of the appellate court reviewing a spousal support order in 2014 remains the same as under *Hickey*: i.e., a court of appeal will intervene only if it finds a material error, a serious misapprehension of the evidence, or an error in law. A court of appeal will show considerable deference to the decision under appeal, but if the *Guidelines* have been fully argued by counsel, an appeal court may intervene if reasons are not or cannot be given to support the trial judge's disposition in relation to them.

90   It is important to stress that the foregoing points are broad observations only. They do not prescribe when this court will intervene. In the pre-*Guidelines* era, it was not possible to determine the precise point at which an appellate court would intervene. This was so because many factors entered the equation; evidence and individual circumstances, as well as the particular issue the appellate court is asked to address, influence outcomes. The same can be said in the *Guidelines* era. The *Divorce Act* and *The Family Maintenance Act, 1997* continue to grant considerable discretion to judges of first instance.

V.   APPEALS

The role of appellate courts in reviewing spousal support orders is clearly defined by L'Heureux-Dubé J in *Hickey v Hickey*.[673] Because the application of the relevant factors and objectives governing spousal support orders under sections 15.2(4) and (6) (original orders) and sections 17(4.1) and (7) of the *Divorce Act* (variation orders) necessarily involves the exercise of a broad judicial discretion, appellate courts afford considerable deference to the decisions of trial judges. In the words of L'Heureux-Dubé J, appellate courts "should not overturn support orders unless the reasons disclose an error in principle, a significant misapprehension of the evidence, or unless the award is clearly wrong."[674] The fact that the appellate court finds the amount of spousal support to be relatively low is insufficient, in itself, to warrant appellate intervention. It is only when the decision of the application judge falls outside the general ambit within which reasonable disagreement is possible

---

673   [1999] 2 SCR 518 at paras 11–12.

674   See, for example, *FCW v BEW*, [2005] AJ No 143 (CA); *RMS v FPCS*, 2011 BCCA 53; *Scott v Scott*, 2011 NBCA 7; *Rondeau v Rondeau*, 2011 NSCA 5; *Heard v Heard*, 2014 ONCA 196; *MacQuarrie v MacQuarrie*, 2012 PECA 3; *Riley v Riley*, 2011 SKCA 5.

and the order is, in fact, plainly wrong, that an appellate court is entitled to interfere.[675]

---

675   *Silver v Silver* (1985), 54 OR (2d) 591 (CA); *Juvatopolos v Juvatopolos*, [2005] OJ No 4181 (CA).

CHAPTER 9

Child Support On or After Divorce[1]

A. GENERAL OBSERVATIONS

Fundamental changes to child support laws in Canada occurred on 1 May 1997, when the *Federal Child Support Guidelines*[2] were implemented. These Guidelines, as amended, regulate the jurisdiction of the courts to order child support in divorce proceedings or in subsequent variation proceedings.

B. INCOME TAX — CHILD SUPPORT

Periodic child support payments under agreements or orders made after 1 May 1997 are free of tax. They are not deductible from the taxable income of the payor, nor are they taxable in the hands of the recipient. This represents a radical change from the former income tax regime, which applied similar criteria to both periodic spousal support and periodic child support in that periodic payments were deductible from the payor's taxable income and were taxable as income in the hands of the payee.

C. PRESUMPTIVE RULE; TABLE AMOUNT OF CHILD SUPPORT; SECTION 7 EXPENSES

In the absence of specified exceptions, section 3(1) of the *Federal Child Support Guidelines* requires the court to order the designated monthly amount of child support set out in the applicable provincial table. The table amount of child

---

1   See generally, Julien D Payne, "Child Support Guidelines – Some Landmark Cases" (2014), 42 Adv Q 309.

2   SOR/197-175 (*Divorce Act*).

support is fixed according to the obligor's annual income and the number of children in the family to whom the order relates. Where the obligor resides in Canada, the applicable provincial or territorial table is that of the province or territory in which the obligor resides.[3] If the obligor's residence is outside of Canada, the applicable table is that of the province or territory wherein the recipient parent resides. Section 3(1) of the Guidelines also empowers a court to order a contribution to be made towards necessary and reasonable special or extraordinary expenses that are specifically listed under section 7 of the Guidelines. Although the court has discretion in ordering section 7 expenses, it has no corresponding discretion with respect to ordering the table amount. It must order the table amount except where the Guidelines or the *Divorce Act*[4] expressly provide otherwise. The onus is on a parent seeking special expenses to prove that the claimed expenses fall within one of the categories and are reasonable and necessary.[5]

In determining a father's concurrent obligations to pay court-ordered support for his two children born of different mothers, where neither child is living with the father, section 3(1) of the *Federal Child Support Guidelines* requires the court to separately determine the table amount of support payable for each child. It is not open to the court to treat the children as members of the same family unit by using the column in the applicable provincial table for the total number of children and then dividing the specified amount so that each child receives an equal share. In *ML v RSE*,[6] Sullivan J granted two orders that required the father, whose annual income was $22,900, to pay the full table amount of $203 to each of his two children, in addition to specified section 7 expenses. Because the table amounts of child support reflect economies of scale as the number of children residing in the same household increases, but no such economies apply when two children reside in different households, Sullivan J held that, in fixing the table amount of child support, the two children must be treated as members of distinct family units, and the two families could not be treated as a single unit by determining the table amount payable for two children and then dividing this equally between the two children. The Alberta Court of Appeal found no error in Sullivan J's order respecting the full table amount of child support being payable for each child in addition to the specified section 7 expenses. Given the obligor's limited means, however, the Alberta Court of Appeal stayed the monthly payment of child support arrears ordered by Sullivan J, but directed

---

3   *Federal Child Support Guidelines*, SOR/97-175 (*Divorce Act*), s 3(3).

4   RSC 1985 (2d Supp), c 3.

5   *Bhandari v Bhandari*, 2012 ONSC 3386, citing *Park v Thompson* (2005), 77 OR (3d) 601 (CA).

6   [2006] AJ No 642 (CA); see also *Ewing v Mallette*, [2009] AJ No 346 (CA); *WL v NDH*, 2014 NBQB 214.

that the parties were at liberty to apply to the Court of Queen's Bench to lift the stay in the event of a change of circumstances.

D. EXCEPTIONS TO PRESUMPTIVE RULE

The presumptive rule endorsing orders for the applicable table amount of child support may be deemed inapplicable in the following circumstances:

- where child support is sought from a person who is not a biological parent but who stands in the place of a parent;
- where a child is over the provincial age of majority;
- where the obligor earns an income of more than $150,000;
- in split custody arrangements whereby each parent has custody of one or more of the children;
- in shared custody or access arrangements where a child spends not less than 40 percent of the year with each parent;
- where undue hardship arises and the household income of the party asserting undue hardship does not exceed that of the other household;
- where there are consensual arrangements in place that attract the operation of sections 15.1(5), (7), and (8) or sections 17(6.2), (6.4), and (6.5) of the *Divorce Act*.

E. OBLIGATION OF *DE FACTO* PARENT

1) Relevant Statutory Provisions

The definition of "child of the marriage" in section 2(2) of the *Divorce Act* reads as follows:

> 2(2) For the purposes of the definition of "child of the marriage" in subsection (1), a child of two spouses or former spouses includes:
>
> (a) any child for whom they both stand in the place of parents; and
>
> (b) any child of whom one is the parent and for whom the other stands in the place of a parent.

A divorcing spouse can, therefore, be ordered to pay child support even though he or she is not the biological parent of the child. For example, a divorcing step-parent, who stands "in the place of a parent" to his or her spouse's children from a previous marriage, may be ordered to support those children.[7]

---

7   *Chartier v Chartier*, [1998] SCJ No 79. See, generally, Nicholas Bala, "Who Is a 'Parent'? 'Standing in the Place of a Parent' and Section 5 of the *Child Support Guidelines*" in The

A spouse stands in the place of a parent within the meaning of section 2(2) of the *Divorce Act* when that spouse by his or her conduct manifests an intention of placing himself or herself in the situation ordinarily occupied by the biological parent by assuming the responsibility of providing for the child's economic and parenting needs. Judicial opinion is divided on the question whether the requisite intention can exist when a husband who is alleged to be standing in the place of the parent erroneously believes that he is the father of the child.[8] In *Peters v Graham*,[9] Boudreau J, of the Nova Scotia Supreme Court, concluded that a husband, who unknowingly stands in the place of a parent to his wife's children because he erroneously believes that he is their biological father, may be ordered to support the children but the amount of support to be paid may be reduced pursuant to section 5 of the *Federal Child Support Guidelines* in light of the concurrent obligations owed by the children's biological father and the wife's "common-law spouse" who currently stands in the place of a parent to the children.

While financial contribution towards the support of the child is a material consideration, it is not decisive in determining whether the contributor stands in the place of a parent. Accordingly, a step-parent is not liable to pay support where his or her relationship with the stepchildren "never jelled into a family unit," even though he or she made indirect contributions to an educational trust for the children by way of contributions being paid out of joint family accounts.[10] Evidence of financial support may simply be indicative of kindness and compassion and is insufficient in itself to justify a finding that a spouse stands in the place of a parent where there is no evidence of any relationship akin to that of parent and child.[11] Such a status implies an intention on the part of the person alleged to stand in the place of a parent to fulfill the office and duty of a parent in both a practical and legal sense.[12] Courts look to a variety of objective factors for the purpose of determining intention. For example, they may consider the duration of the relationship, the age of the children, whether psychological parenting has

---

Law Society of Upper Canada, *Special Lectures 2006: Family Law* (Toronto: Irwin Law, 2007) 71.

8   See *TA v RCA*, [1999] BCJ No 1382 (SC); *Aksugyuk v Aksugyuk* (1975), 17 RFL 224 (NWTSC); compare *Day v Weir*, 2014 ONSC 5975. See also *DRD v SEG*, [2001] OJ No 320 (Sup Ct); *HR v RP*, [2001] OJ No 4374 (Sup Ct) (portions of statement of claim for damages against wife and alleged father of child struck out); *SE v DE*, [1998] SJ No 223 (QB).

9   [2001] NSJ No 452 (SC); see also *JS v DW*, [2005] AJ No 8 (QB).

10 *Fair v Jones*, [1999] NWTJ No 17 (SC); see also *Henderson v Henderson*, [1999] BCJ No 2938 (SC).

11 *Fournier v Fournier*, [1997] BCJ No 2299 (SC).

12 *Wuzinski v Wuzinski* (1987), 10 RFL (3d) 420 (Man QB); *Andrews v Andrews* (1992), 38 RFL (3d) 200 (Sask CA); *Anderson v Lambert*, [1997] SJ No 725 (QB).

taken place, day-to-day care of the children, involvement in vital activities such as the child's education or discipline, how the child and the person in question acknowledge each other in their daily roles, as well as any financial contribution to the children.[13] In *Chartier v Chartier*, Bastarache J, speaking for the Supreme Court of Canada as a whole, observed:

> 39 Whether a person stands in the place of a parent must take into account all factors relevant to that determination, viewed objectively. What must be determined is the nature of the relationship. The *Divorce Act* makes no mention of formal expressions of intent. The focus on voluntariness and intention in *Carignan* [*v Carignan* (1989), 64 DLR (4th) 119 (Man CA)], was dependent on the common-law approach discussed earlier. It was wrong. The Court must determine the nature of the relationship by looking at a number of factors, among which is intention. Intention will not only be expressed formally. The court must also infer intention from actions, and take into consideration that even expressed intentions may sometimes change. The actual fact of forming a new family is a key factor in drawing an inference that the step-parent treats the child as a member of his or her family, i.e., a child of the marriage. The relevant factors in defining the parental relationship include, but are not limited to, whether the child participates in the extended family in the same way as would a biological child; whether the person provides financially for the child (depending on ability to pay); whether the person disciplines the child as a parent; whether the person represents to the child, the family, the world, either explicitly or implicitly, that he or she is responsible as a parent to the child; the nature or existence of the child's relationship with the absent biological parent. The manifestation of the intention of the step-parent cannot be qualified as to duration, or be otherwise made conditional or qualified, even if this intention is manifested expressly. Once it is shown that the child is to be considered, in fact, a "child of the marriage", the obligations of the step-parent towards him or her are the same as those relative to a child born of the marriage with regard to the application of the *Divorce Act*. The step-parent, at this point, does not only incur obligations. He or she also acquires

---

13   *Motuzas v Yarnell*, [1997] MJ No 520 (QB); *BP v AT*, 2013 NBQB 309; *Laframboise v Laframboise*, 2015 ONSC 1752; *Halliday v Halliday*, [1998] SJ No 53 (QB); *Campbell v Campbell*, [1998] SJ No 180 (QB); see also *McDonald v McDonald*, [1998] BCJ No 3150 (SC); *A(DR) v M(RM)* (1997), 30 RFL (4th) 269 (Ont Gen Div) (application under *Family Law Act*); *Do Carmo v Etzkorn* (1995), 16 RFL (4th) 341 (Ont Gen Div) (application under *Family Law Act*); *Cassar-Fleming v Fleming* (1996), 20 RFL (4th) 201 (Ont Gen Div) (application under *Family Law Act*); *Prieur v Prieur*, [1998] OJ No 5378 (Gen Div); *Marud v Marud*, [1999] SJ No 478 (QB).

certain rights, such as the right to apply eventually for custody or access under s 161(1) of the *Divorce Act*.

40 Nevertheless, not every adult-child relationship will be determined to be one where the adult stands in the place of a parent. Every case must be determined on its own facts and it must be established from the evidence that the adult acted so as to stand in the place of a parent to the child.

41 Huband J.A., in *Carignan*, [above,] expressed the concern that individuals may be reluctant to be generous towards children for fear that their generosity will give rise to parental obligations. I do not share those concerns. The nature of a parent relationship is complex and includes more than financial support. People do not enter into parental relationships with the view that they will be terminated.[14]

A spouse's subjective feelings[15] and motivation[16] are not relevant when his or her objective behaviour has manifested an intention to treat the child as a member of his or her family.[17]

The judgment in *Chartier v Chartier* leaves open the question whether a person can or should be deemed to stand in the place of a parent in circumstances where both biological parents continue to play a significant role in their child's life. This question was examined by Campbell J, of the Supreme Court of Nova Scotia, in *Cook v Cook*.[18] He concluded that Parliament endorsed the use of the words "in the place of" to indicate that parental status, with its concomitant child support obligations and the right to apply for custody of or access to the child, would arise only when a person has "substantially replaced the natural parent with respect to the various needs of the [child]." Campbell J acknowledged that the judgment of the Supreme Court of Canada "clearly implies that both the biological parent and the step-parent can be required to pay support in appropriate circumstances" and that there are circumstances where concurrent payments would be appropriate, as, for example, where the biological parent is paying inadequate support and the step-parent has provided "financial, emotional and physical support and guidance over a sufficient period of time in substitution for the natural parent."

---

14 [1999] 1 SCR 242.

15 *Cassar-Fleming v Fleming* (1996), 20 RFL (4th) 201 (Ont Gen Div); *Seeley v McKay*, [1998] OJ No 2857 (Gen Div).

16 *F(RL) v F(S)* (1996), 26 RFL (4th) 393 (Ont Gen Div) (application under *Family Law Act*).

17 *A(DR) v M(RM)* (1997), 30 RFL (4th) 269 (Ont Gen Div) (application under *Family Law Act*), citing *Spring v Spring* (1987), 61 OR (2d) 743 (Gen Div).

18 [2000] NSJ No 19 at para 37 (SC); see also *Lewcock v Natili-Lewcock*, [2001] OJ No 2051 (Sup Ct); *Anderson v Lambert*, [1997] SJ No 725 (QB); compare *Hearn v Bacque*, [2006] OJ No 2385 (Sup Ct); *Widdis v Widdis*, [2001] SJ No 614 (QB).

Both before and after the implementation of the *Federal Child Support Guidelines* on 1 May 1997, several courts have shared the opinion expressed by Campbell J in *Cook v Cook*, above, and have been disinclined to impose long-term child support obligations on cohabitants who assume parental responsibilities during a relatively brief relationship with the child's custodial parent.[19] However, it should not be overlooked that the parties in *Chartier v Chartier*[20] lived together in premarital cohabitation and marital cohabitation for an aggregate period of less than three years and the marriage itself lasted only fifteen months.

On the stepfather's application to vary an existing order in *Swindler v Belanger*,[21] the mother's renewal of her relationship with the biological father did not release the stepfather from his obligation to support his stepchild in addition to his biological child born of the same mother. In fixing the amount of support payable for the two children, the Saskatchewan Court of Appeal took account of the fact that the biological father earned no income but, in the exercise of the discretion conferred with respect to the stepchild by section 5 of the *Federal Child Support Guidelines*, the stepfather was ordered to pay the full table amount of support for his biological child and an additional one-half of the differential between that amount and the full table amount normally payable for two children. The stepfather's application to remit the support arrears that had accrued under the original order was dismissed where there was no evidence that he was unable to pay the arrears and the mother had taken reasonable steps to enforce the arrears, but with little success. The Saskatchewan Court of Appeal acceded to the stepfather's request that he be granted reasonable access to his stepchild in addition to his biological child.

The uncertainties that continue to exist after *Chartier v Chartier* have been explained by a Saskatchewan legal practitioner in the following words:

> In summary, although the *Chartier* case has outlined the principles which should be applied in determining whether or not a person stands in the place of a parent, it is still not clear how those principles will be applied to future cases. The result will depend very much on the amount of evidence and how this evidence is presented to the court. It may also depend on the judge's own beliefs whether a high or low threshold test should be applied. The finding will be in the judge's discretion and will likely not be subject to

---

19   See, for example, *Weicholz v Weicholz* (1987), 81 AR 236 (QB); *Gavigan v Gavigan* (1990), 30 RFL (3d) 314 (Alta QB); *M(CF) v M(MF)* (1996), 23 RFL (4th) 55 (NBQB); *Sloat v Sloat* (1990), 102 NBR (2d) 390 (QB).

20   [1998] SCJ No 79 at para 2.

21   [2005] SJ No 709 (CA).

an appeal providing the principles as set out in the *Chartier* case have been applied.[22]

2) Termination of Parent-Child Relationship: Impact on Child Support

The time for determining whether a person stands in the place of a parent for the purpose of ascertaining child support rights and obligations under the *Divorce Act* or under provincial-territorial statute is the time when the parties were cohabiting as a family unit.[23] A person who has established an enduring parent-child relationship during matrimonial cohabitation cannot be permitted to escape the statutory child support obligations that flow from that relationship simply by a unilateral abandonment of the relationship after the separation of the spouses.[24]

Although a person who has stood in the place of a parent cannot unilaterally sever the relationship and thereby avoid child support obligations, the question arises whether a parent can or should be required to support a child who is instrumental in severing the parent-child relationship. In *Cox v Cox*,[25] Adams J of the Newfoundland Unified Family Court concluded on the basis of *Chartier v Chartier* that the obligation to support a child is not discharged, even if the child is responsible for severing the parent-child relationship. However, in *Ollinger v Ollinger*,[26] Sandomirsky J, of the Saskatchewan Court of Queen's Bench, held that standing in the place of a parent is not static and such a relationship, with its attendant rights and obligations, can cease when a stepchild of sufficient maturity unilaterally withdraws from the stepparent or where there is a bilateral or mutual withdrawal from each other.

---

22   Marcia E Jackson, "Multiple Parents" (Paper presented to Saskatchewan Legal Education Society Inc, University of Saskatchewan College of Law, and Law Foundation of Saskatchewan, Family Law Conference: Economic and Parenting Consequences of Separation and Divorce, Saskatoon, 31 March and 1 April 2000) at 5–6.

23   *Chartier v Chartier*, [1998] SCJ No 79; *Dutrisac v Ulm*, [1999] BCJ No 591 (SC); *H(UV) v H(MW)*, 2008 BCCA 177; *M(CF) v M(MF)* (1996), 23 RFL (4th) 55 (NBQB) (application under *Family Services Act*); *LMA v PH*, 2014 ONSC 1707; *Swindler v Belanger*, [2005] SJ No 709 (CA).

24   *Chartier v Chartier*, [1998] SCJ No 79.

25   [1999] NJ No 242 (UFC); see also *Necemer v Necemer*, [1999] BCJ No 3023 (SC).

26   2006 SKQB 433.

3) Respective Obligations of Biological and Adoptive Parents and of Persons Who Stand in the Place of Parents

Section 26.1(2) of the *Divorce Act* provides that the *Federal Child Support Guidelines* "shall be based on the principle that spouses have a joint financial obligation to maintain the children of the marriage in accordance with their relative abilities to contribute to the performance of that obligation."

Section 5 of the *Federal Child Support Guidelines* provides as follows:

> Where a spouse against whom a child support order is sought stands in the place of a parent for a child, the amount of the child support order is, in respect of that spouse, such amount as the court considers appropriate, having regard to these Guidelines and any other parent's legal duty to support the child.

It is noteworthy that *Chartier v Chartier* does not address the implications of section 5 of the *Federal Child Support Guidelines*.[27] Courts have employed a variety of techniques, such as time-limited support, apportionment, percentages, and top ups to fix the amount of child support payable by the step-parent and the reasons employed by the courts vary.[28] In determining the respective child support obligations of the natural father and the stepfather in *H(UV) v H(MW)*,[29] the judgment of the British Columbia Court of Appeal endorsed the following principles:

1)   A non-custodial natural parent cannot invoke section 5 of the Guidelines even though a non-custodial step-parent is concurrently liable to pay child support.[30] There can be no "balancing" or "apportionment" of the table amount of child support payable by the non-custodial natural parent by reason of the non-custodial step-parent's concurrent liability. The obligation of the non-custodial natural parent to pay the applicable table amount of child support, pursuant to section 3(1) of the Guidelines, can only be modified or affected by the obligation of the step-parent in those discretionary situations specified by the Guidelines, namely, in circumstances involving children over the provincial age of majority (section 3(2)

---

27   *Dutrisac v Ulm*, [2000] BCJ No 1078 (CA); *H(UV) v H(MW)*, 2008 BCCA 177, [2008] BCJ No 717 (CA); *Boivin v Smith*, 2013 ONCJ 426; *Marud v Marud*, [1999] SJ No 478 (QB).

28   *LMA v PH*, 2014 ONSC 1707 at para 159, Horkins J.

29   2008 BCCA 177; see also *Johnston v Embree*, 2013 BCCA 74; *Shen v Tong*, 2013 BCCA 519; *LMA v PH*, 2014 ONSC 1707.

30   See also *Wright v Zaver*, [2002] OJ No 1098 (CA).

(b)), incomes over $150,000 (section 4), special or extraordinary expenses (section 7), shared custody (section 9), or undue hardship (section 10).[31]

2) A non-custodial natural parent is not released from his or her obligation to pay the applicable table amount of child support by a prior consensual undertaking on the part of the step-parent to shoulder primary responsibility for supporting the natural parent's children.

3) The non-custodial natural parent's legal obligation to pay the applicable table amount of child support is not discharged by voluntary payments of his own choosing made for the benefit of the children.

4) As was stated by the British Columbia Court of Appeal in *Dutrisac v Ulm*,[32] in the context of the provincial *Child Support Guidelines*, the judgment of the Supreme Court of Canada in *Chartier v Chartier*[33] does not preclude a court from concluding that a step-parent should pay a reduced amount or no amount of child support, if that is deemed appropriate in the exercise of the judicial discretion conferred by section 5 of the Guidelines.

5) Where it is practicable to do so, the amount of child support payable by the non-custodial natural parent must be determined in order to determine the appropriate amount of child support to be paid by the non-custodial step-parent. Once the former amount has been ascertained, the step-parent's obligation should be determined in light of that amount and the notional amount of child support payable by the custodial parent, having regard to the objectives specified in section 1 of the Guidelines. In the words of Newbury JA, in *H(UV) v H(MW)*,

> Thus a "fair standard of support", objectivity of calculation, and reduction of conflict between parents are relevant to the determination of "appropriate" support by the stepparent. On the other hand, s 5 does not, in my view, confer a discretion that is so broad as to encompass *"all"* the circumstances of a case . . . or "fairness" to the father arising from a kind of promissory estoppel against the stepparent (as was suggested by the chambers judge in this case).
>
> Given the "children-first" perspective of the Guidelines . . . , primacy should be given to the children's standard of living.[34] Where for example the stepparent provided a standard to the children during the period of cohabitation that was materially higher than that which the natural parents can provide by means of their Guidelines amounts, a court might find it appropriate to make an order against the stepparent that is designed

---

31 See also *PRR v JCG*, 2013 NBQB 405; *Pevach v Spalding*, [2001] SJ No 469 (QB).

32 [2000] BCJ No 178 (CA).

33 [1998] 1 SCR 242.

34 *LMA v PH*, 2014 ONSC 1707.

to provide the higher standard, or something approximating it, "on top of" the other parents' support. However, where the "piling" of Guidelines amounts would result in a standard beyond one that is reasonable in the context of the standard the children have previously enjoyed, such a "windfall" or "wealth transfer" . . . is unlikely to be "appropriate". At the other end of the spectrum, where the three (or more) parents' Guidelines "contributions" together are needed to provide the children with a reasonable standard of living, then both the stepparent and the non-custodial parent(s) may well be required to pay full Guidelines amounts. Or, where one of the natural or adoptive parents is not present or is unable to pay any support, the step-parent may well have to pay his or her full table amount.[35] The Legislature has left it to the judgment of trial and chambers judges in the first instance to fashion orders that are "appropriate" under s 5. At the same time, the Guidelines system is not thereby jettisoned in favour of a "wide open" dis-cretion. The inquiry must, like the Guidelines themselves, focus on the chil-dren and their needs.[36]

Applying the above criteria to the facts of the case, the British Colum-bia Court of Appeal held that, notwithstanding the stepfather's prior con-sensual undertaking to support the children, the chambers judge erred in his approach to determining the stepfather's child support obligation under section 5 of the *British Columbia Child Support Guidelines* without due regard for the natural father's obligation under section 3 of the Guidelines. Where he erred was in approaching the father's obligation as a secondary obliga-tion, and losing sight of the father's non-discretionary obligation to pay the table amount of child support pursuant to section 3 of the Guidelines. In the result, the British Columbia Court of Appeal set aside the chambers judge's order that the stepfather pay the full table amount of child support based on his income while requiring the natural father to pay substantially less than his table amount. In its place, the British Columbia Court of Appeal substi-tuted an order whereby the natural father was required to pay the full table amount of child support and the stepfather was ordered to pay a designated "top up" amount as his contribution towards the custodial mother's child-related expenses.

A similar approach was endorsed in the following observations of Aston J in *MacArthur v Demers*:

---

35   See *Janes v Janes*, [1999] AJ No 610 (QB); *Shen v Tong*, 2013 BCCA 519; *LMA v PH*, 2014 ONSC 1707; compare *Cook v Kilduff*, [2000] SJ No 482 (QB); see also *Boyko v Boyko*, 2010 SKQB 247.

36   2008 BCCA 177 at paras 40–41; see also *LMA v PH*, 2014 ONSC 1707.

[para 28] Section 5 of the guidelines only applies if the respondent is not the child's biological parent. The following step-by-step approach offers one way of structuring the exercise of judicial discretion under section 5:

1. Determine the guideline amount payable by the respondent. This will involve consideration of the table amount, any section 7 add-ons and any undue hardship adjustment.

2. Determine the "legal duty" of any other non-custodial parent to contribute to the support of the child. As noted above, this will be established by a pre-existing order or agreement or by a guideline calculation. The words in section 5 "any other parent's legal duty to support the child" would include the custodial parent, but the guideline scheme assumes the custodial parent meets this duty by sharing his or her household standard of living with the child.

3. In considering whether it is "appropriate" to reduce the respondent's obligation under the guidelines, once the non-custodial parent establishes that another non-custodial parent (or parents) has (have) a legal duty to support the child, the onus ought to shift to the custodial parent to demonstrate why the respondent's obligation should not be reduced by that of other non-custodial parent(s).

[para 29] The custodial parent might satisfy that onus, in whole or in part, by demonstrating that

(a) the "legal duty" of the other non-custodial parent(s) is (are) unenforceable, or

(b) such a reduction is inconsistent with the stated objectives in section 1 of the guidelines.[37]

In *McBride v McBride*,[38] Vertes J, of the Northwest Territories Supreme Court, concluded that a non-custodial step-parent, against whom a child support order is sought, may initiate a concurrent application for child support under provincial statute against the non-custodial biological parent. If this is done, the court may order the non-custodial biological parent to pay the applicable table amount of child support and may then proceed to determine whether the step-parent's child support obligation should be reduced because of the non-custodial biological parent's court-ordered child support payments. Justice Vertes further observed that a court should not order the full table amount of child support to be paid by the non-custodial step-parent

---

37   [1998] OJ No 5868 (Gen Div); see also *RAV v SMIV*, [2007] BCJ No 2808 (SC); *Robinson v Cleary*, 2009 NLUFC 29; *GNP v LAG*, 2001 NSSC 165; *Hari v Hari*, 2013 ONSC 5562; *Boyko v Boyko*, 2010 SKQB 247.

38   [2001] NWTJ No 69 (SC); see also *Snow v Snow*, 2013 ABQB 146.

as a matter of course. Evidence should be adduced as to the needs and circumstances of the child so that the appropriate amount of child support to be paid by the non-custodial step-parent can be determined.

F. CHILDREN OVER PROVINCIAL AGE OF MAJORITY

1) Relevant Provisions of *Divorce Act* and *Federal Child Support Guidelines*

For the purpose of determining the right of adult children to child support, section 2(1) of the *Divorce Act* defines "age of majority" and "child of the marriage" as follows:

Definitions
2. (1) In this Act,

"age of majority"
"age of majority", in respect of a child, means the age of majority as determined by the laws of the province where the child ordinarily resides, or, if the child ordinarily resides outside of Canada, eighteen years of age; . . .

"child of the marriage"
"child of the marriage" means a child of two spouses or former spouses who, at the material time,
(a) is under the age of majority and who has not withdrawn from their charge, or
(b) is the age of majority or over and under their charge but unable, by reason of illness, disability or other cause, to withdraw from their charge or to obtain the necessaries of life;

In determining an adult child's right, if any, to child support, sections 3 and 7 of the *Federal Child Support Guidelines* are the key provisions. The relevant provisions read as follows:

Amount of Child Support

Presumptive rule
3. (1) Unless otherwise provided under these Guidelines, the amount of a child support order for children under the age of majority is
(a) the amount set out in the applicable table, according to the number of children under the age of majority to whom the order relates and the income of the spouse against whom the order is sought; and
(b) the amount, if any, determined under section 7.

Child the age of majority or over

(2) Unless otherwise provided under these Guidelines, where a child to whom a child support order relates is the age of majority or over, the amount of the child support order is

(a) the amount determined by applying these Guidelines as if the child were under the age of majority; or

(b) if the court considers that approach to be inappropriate, the amount that it considers appropriate, having regard to the condition, means, needs and other circumstances of the child and the financial ability of each spouse to contribute to the support of the child.

Special or extraordinary expenses

7. (1) In a child support order the court may, on either spouse's request, provide for an amount to cover the following expenses, or any portion of those expenses, taking into account the necessity of the expense in relation to the child's best interests and the reasonableness of the expense, having regard to the means of the spouses and those of the child and to the family's spending pattern prior to the separation:

. . .

(e) expenses for post-secondary education; and

. . .

Sharing of expense

(2) The guiding principle in determining the amount of an expense referred to in subsection (1) is that the expense is shared by the spouses in proportion to their respective incomes after deducting from the expense, the contribution, if any, from the child.

Subsidies, tax deductions, etc.

(3) In determining the amount of an expense referred to in subsection (1), the court must take into account any subsidies, benefits or income tax deductions or credits relating to the expense, and any eligibility to claim a subsidy, benefit or income tax deduction or credit relating to the expense.

2) Status of Applicant; Payment to Parent or Child

An application for a child support order or for variation thereof can only be brought under the *Divorce Act* by either or both spouses or former spouses.[39]

---

39   *Divorce Act*, RSC 1985 (2d Supp), c 3, s 15.2(1) (original application), s 17(1)(a) (variation application).

An adult child has no standing to bring an application for support under the *Divorce Act* on his or her own behalf.[40]

On the application of either or both of the spouses, a court may order support to be paid directly to the child. Such orders are relatively unusual, even for adult children. Where a child resides with a parent who provides his or her basic needs, a court should not order support payments to be made directly to the child, unless that parent consents or there are exceptional circumstances.[41] On the other hand, direct payments to an adult child may be deemed appropriate where the child attends an out-of-town college or university.[42]

Where child support is ordered to be paid to the custodial parent, the obligor is not entitled to make payments to the child instead or to purchase things for the child in partial discharge of the support obligation.[43]

3) Statutory Definition of "Child of the Marriage"; Eligibility of Adult Children for Child Support

a)   General

A divorcing spouse may be ordered to pay support for a child under the age of provincial majority (which is either eighteen or nineteen years of age according to the province or territory in which the child ordinarily resides) or for an adult child who is unable to achieve self-sufficiency by reason of "illness, disability or other cause." Determining where a child is "ordinarily resident" for the purpose of the definition of "child of the marriage" in section 2(1) of the *Divorce Act* is a question of fact to be determined in light of the attendant circumstances.[44]

Children under the provincial age of majority who are financially dependent while they continue with their schooling satisfy the definition of "children of the marriage" under section 2(1) of the *Divorce Act*, even though they are estranged or alienated from the non-custodial parent who is called upon to pay child support.[45] The definition of "child of the marriage" in section 2(1)

---

40   *Tapson v Tapson* (1970), 2 RFL 305 (Ont CA); *Skolney v Herman*, [2008] SJ No 73 (QB).

41   *Morgan v Morgan*, [2006] BCJ No 1795 (SC); *Tobias v Meadley*, 2011 BCCA 472 (retroactive child support); *Marshall v Marshall*, [1998] NSJ No 311 (SC); *Lu v Sun*, [2005] NSJ No 314 (CA); *Glaspy v Glaspy*, 2011 NBCA 101.

42   *Wesemann v Wesemann*, [1999] BCJ No 1387 (SC); *Chapple v Campbell*, [2005] MJ No 323 (QB); *O'Donnell v O'Donnell*, 2011 NBQB 56; *Merritt v Merritt*, [1999] OJ No 1732 (Sup Ct); *Burzminski v Burzminski (Lewis)*, 2010 SKCA 16.

43   *Haisman v Haisman*, [1994] AJ No 553 (CA).

44   See *RJM v EM*, 2015 BCSC 414.

45   *Marsh v Marsh*, [2006] BCJ No 615 (CA).

of the *Divorce Act* is not simply one of age; it is one of dependence.[46] The mere fact that an adult child lacks the ability to withdraw from parental charge or to obtain the necessaries of life is not determinative of the child's eligibility for support; the inability must be shown on the evidence to have arisen or to continue by reason of an illness, disability, or other cause recognized by the *Divorce Act*.[47] In *AAC v MAB*,[48] an adult child, who was pursuing post-secondary education that was largely financed by summer-employment income, scholarships, and student loans, was held disentitled to ongoing child support from her parent once she married. Justice MacDonald observed that the marriage, which would take place in July 2006, constituted a declaration of independence and a "withdrawal from [parental] charge" under the definition of "child of the marriage" in section 2(1) of the *Divorce Act*. It is noteworthy that an adult child who lives with his girlfriend or boyfriend while pursuing university studies does not automatically cease to be a "child of the marriage" where the adult child remains economically dependent on his or her parents.[49] In *Karol v Karol*,[50] an adult child, who withdrew from her mother's home because of overcrowding, was not disentitled to child support while pursuing post-secondary education, merely because she was sharing household expenses with a common law partner. Justice Wilkinson undertook a review of the caselaw and identified the following factors as relevant in determining the impact of an adult child's common law relationship upon his or her eligibility for child support to meet the costs of post-secondary education:

> [19] Similarly, the fact that Sharla resides in a common-law relationship does not automatically disqualify her for support. A review of the case law shows mixed results, depending on a number of factors, including the child's age, whether the parents approved the relationship, how long the common-law relationship has lasted, and whether the common-law partner is working full-time or part-time or attending school and without income. Other considerations are how long the child has been in school, how much the child has been able to contribute from other sources, and whether the parents would provide assistance in any event, whether ordered to or not. Another relevant consideration is whether the parents had provided

---

46   *Ivany v Ivany* (1996), 24 RFL (4th) 289 (Nfld SC); *Martell v Height* (1994), 3 RFL (4th) 104 (NSCA).

47   *Ethier v Skrudland*, 2011 SKCA 17.

48   [2006] NSJ No 169 (SC).

49   See *Robertson v Hibbs*, [1997] BCJ No 1305 (SC); *Taylor v Taylor*, [2002] NJ No 52 (SC); *Crowdis v Crowdis*, [2003] SJ No 371 (QB); compare *Hrechka v Andries*, [2003] MJ No 114 (QB); *Ritchie v Ritchie*, [2003] SJ No 326 (CA).

50   [2005] SJ No 349 (QB).

any financial assistance at all towards the child's post-secondary training and, if so, for how long.

Child support is transitional; it is not an income security plan for the indolent child or the perennial student. A court must be careful not to be carried away with claims on behalf of the would-be "hanger on" in perpetuity.[51]

b) Sick or Disabled Children

Adult children who are incapable of economic self-sufficiency because of illness or disability fall within the definition of "child of the marriage" under section 2(1) of the *Divorce Act*.[52] State subsidized financial assistance for special-needs adult children does not necessarily absolve parents of their child support obligation.[53] In some cases, the subsidies will be sufficient to eliminate or significantly reduce child support otherwise payable. In other cases where the government funding only subsidizes extraordinary expenses related to the child's disability, the table amount of child support may be unaffected.[54] In *Krangle (Guardian ad litem of) v Brisco*,[55] McLachlin CJ, of the Supreme Court of Canada, addressed the issue of a disabled adult child's withdrawal from the charge of his parents in the context of an action for damages for medical malpractice. She observed that the relevant statutory amendments "were not aimed at shifting the burden of caring for adult children from the state to parents, but rather with ensuring that in situations where one parent is charged with the care of an adult disabled child, the other parent is obliged to assist." A similar approach is tenable when interpreting federal or provincial legislation dealing with the support of adult disabled children.[56] In *Carpenter v March*,[57] Handrigan J, of the Family Division of the Newfoundland and Labrador Supreme Court, provided the following list

---

51   *Yashuk v Logan* (1992), 39 RFL (3d) 417 at 438 (NSCA), Chipman JA.

52   *Carpenter v March*, 2012 NLTD(F) 11 at para 7; see also *Pitcher v Pitcher*, 2013 NLTD(F) 11; *Harris v Harris*, [2006] NSJ No 257 (CA); compare *Hartshorne v Hartshorne*, 2010 BCCA 327. Compare also s 46(b) of the *Family Law Act*, SA 2003, c F-4.5 (effective 1 October 2005); *LLM v WLK*, [2007] AJ No 1424 (QB).

53   *Hellinckx v Large*, [1998] BCJ No 1462 (SC); *Lougheed v Lougheed*, [2007] BCJ No 1648 (CA); compare *Harrington v Harrington* (1981), 22 RFL (2d) 40 (Ont CA); *Hill v Davis*, [2006] NSJ No 331 (SC).

54   *Misner v Misner*, 2010 ONSC 2284.

55   [2002] 1 SCR 205 at para 35.

56   *Hill v Davis*, [2006] NSJ No 331 (SC); *Hanson v Hanson*, [2003] SJ No 514 (QB); *Briard v Briard*, 2010 BCCA 431.

57   2012 NLTD(F) 11 at para 7. See also *Steidinger v Morrell*, 2013 MBQB 143. And see Christine Dobby, "Whose Responsibility?: Disabled Adult 'Children of the Marriage' Under the *Divorce Act* and the Canadian Social Welfare State" (2005) 20 Windsor Rev Legal Soc Issues 41.

of relevant principles that may assist courts in determining when an adult child with disabilities is entitled to support pursuant to the *Divorce Act* and the *Federal Child Support Guidelines*:

- A child over the provincial age of majority who is unable to work due to illness or disability may be a "child of the marriage" within the meaning of section 2(1) of the Divorce Act.
- The onus of proving that an adult child remains a "child of the marriage" is on the parent making the claim.
- State-subsidized financial assistance does not relieve parents of their child support obligations.
- Child support set under section 3(2)(b) of the Guidelines for an adult child who is still a "child of the marriage" because of illness or disability may take into account subsidies and other disability benefits the adult child or custodial parent receives from the province, such as subsidized housing and respite care.
- A disabled adult child may be entitled to child support if the child receives a monthly disability payment, even if the child stays in a foster home five nights a week.
- Proof of an adult child's disability alone does not justify a child support order if there is no indication that the disability prevents the child from being gainfully employed — evidence of financial dependence is required.
- It may be premature to limit the duration of support for a disabled adult child at the time when the child support order is made.
- Parental responsibility to support a permanently disabled child may last for the rest of the child's life.

An adult child, with serious addictions that are treatable, must make reasonable efforts to achieve economic independence. Although addiction is a disease, courts have not condoned chronic financial dependence in cases where individuals refuse to help themselves. An addicted child, who has squandered opportunities to overcome the disease and become economically self-sufficient, may cease to be a "child of the marriage" within the meaning of section 2(1) of the *Divorce Act*. Even if that status were deemed to continue, the adult child cannot look to a parent to continue to underwrite the costs of the post-secondary education or training, where the adult child has already wasted several opportunities in the past and has demonstrated no aptitude for a proposed new field of study. Section 4 of the *Federal Child Support Guidelines* empowers a court to deviate from the applicable table amount of child support insofar as a parent's annual income exceeds $150,000, where the reasonable needs of the adult child are already being met and anything other than a modest lifestyle would be an obstacle to recovery.[58]

c) Unemployed Adult Children

Some courts have held that a child's inability to obtain employment, which does not result from illness or disability but from restrictions on job availability, falls outside the meaning of "other cause" in section 2(2) of the *Divorce Act*. Given this interpretation, parents cannot be ordered to support a child who cannot withdraw from the charge of his or her parents or provide himself or herself with the necessities of life because of the state of the labour market.[59] Other courts have opted for a broader interpretation of "other cause" and have ordered child support in cases where the economic climate makes it impossible for a diligent child to find employment and become self-supporting.[60] Such orders are typically transitional, rather than long-term.[61]

4) Post-Secondary Education or Training

a) General

Pursuit of post-secondary education or training constitutes "other cause" within the meaning of the definition of "child of marriage" in section 2(1) of the *Divorce Act*, thus rendering an adult child eligible for support in appropriate circumstances.[62]

Post-secondary education or training is not confined to pursuit of a university degree. It includes vocational training[63] and may extend to an adult child's pursuit of a career in professional sport, where the child has the requisite aptitude and realistic career aspirations.[64]

Where support is sought for an adult child pursuing post-secondary education or vocational training, the onus of demonstrating that the child cannot

---

58   *RWG v SIG*, [2002] SJ No 231 (QB), var'd [2003] SJ No 250 (CA).

59   See, for example, *Gartner v Gartner* (1978), 5 RFL (2d) 270 at 274 (NSSC); *Sproule v Sproule* (1986), 2 RFL (3d) 54 (NSCA); *Murray v Murray* (1982), 30 RFL (2d) 222 (Sask QB).

60   See, for example, *Baker v Baker* (1994), 2 RFL (4th) 147 at 155–56 (Alta QB); *Bruehler v Bruehler* (1985), 49 RFL (2d) 44 (BCCA); *McAdam v McAdam* (1994), 8 RFL (4th) 252 at 255–56 (Man QB).

61   *CLB v BTC*, [2006] BCJ No 3112 (SC).

62   *Sherlow v Zubko*, [1999] AJ No 644 (QB); *O'Donnell v O'Donnell*, 2011 NBQB 56.

63   *Blake v Blake* (1994), 121 Nfld & PEIR 263 (Nfld SC) (technical college); *Van Wynsberghe v Van Wynsberghe*, [1997] OJ No 2566 (Gen Div) (film school).

64   *Olson v Olson*, [2003] AJ No 230 (CA); *Thompson v Thompson*, [1999] SJ No 317 (QB); see also *Maxwell v Maxwell*, [2007] BCJ No 43 (SC); *Hnidy v Hnidy*, 2015 SKQB 1, citing *Ethier v Skrudland*, 2011 SKCA 17.

provide for himself or herself and is, therefore, unable to withdraw from the parents' charge, rests with the applicant seeking child support.[65]

Relevant considerations in determining the right to child support include the following:

- the age of the child;
- his or her academic achievements;
- the ability to profit from further education;
- the possibility of securing employment having regard to the standard of education already achieved and the state of the labour market; and
- the capacity of the parents to bear the costs of a college education for a child who evinces an aptitude therefor.[66]

Additional considerations include the following:

- whether the child is a full-time or part-time student;
- whether the child is eligible for student loans or other financial assistance;
- whether the child has reasonable career plans;
- the ability of the child to contribute to his or her own support through part-time employment;
- parental plans for the child's education, particularly those made during cohabitation; and
- (at least in the case of a mature child who has reached the age of majority,) whether the child has unilaterally terminated his or her relationship with the parent from whom child support is sought.[67]

Evidence need not be adduced on all the aforementioned considerations in order for an application for child support to be successful.[68] Although relevant authorities have developed lengthy lists of factors relevant to determining whether an adult child remains a "child of the marriage" for support

---

65 *Albo v Albo*, [2006] AJ No 1330 (QB); *Jean v Jean*, [2006] AJ No 1687 (QB); *Wionzek v Magyar*, 2013 SKQB 194, citing *Geran v Geran*, 2011 SKCA 55 at para 21.

66 *Douglas v Campbell*, [2006] NSJ No 350 (SC); *Wionzek v Magyar*, 2013 SKQB 194. see also *Albert v Albert*, [2007] OJ No 2964 (Sup Ct).

67 *Farden v Farden* (1993), 48 RFL (3d) 60 (BCSC); see also *Miller v Joynt*, 2007 ABCA 214; *Darlington v Darlington*, [1997] BCJ No 2534 (CA); *YHB v JPB*, 2014 BCSC 618; *O'Donnell v O'Donnell*, 2011 NBQB 56; *Green v Green*, [2005] NJ No 165 (CA); *PRR v JCG*, 2013 NBQB 405; *Durso v Mascherin*, 2013 ONSC 6522; *Bradley v Zaba* (1996), 137 Sask R 682 (CA); *Wionzek v Magyar*, 2013 SKQB 194. .

68 *Albo v Albo*, [2006] AJ No 1330 (QB); *Darlington v Darlington*, [1997] BCJ No 2534 (CA); *Brandner v Brandner*, [2002] BCJ No 1398 (CA); *Morgan v Morgan*, [2006] BCJ No 1795 (SC); *MacDonald v Rasmussen*, [2000] SJ No 660 (QB).

purposes,[69] such lists, helpful though they are, must not be used in place of the language of the statute,[70] nor should they be invoked to impose a burden on parents to call evidence about the obvious, or on judges to address non-issues in their reasons for judgment. Judges are entitled to draw reasonable, common-sense inferences from the proven facts and may take into account notorious facts, such as, that post-secondary education is expensive, that well-paid part-time employment for full-time students is scarce, and that the demands of a full-time course load limit the time available for part-time work.[71]

The governing principle in determining whether child support should be ordered is reasonableness.[72] There is no arbitrary cut-off point based on age or academic achievement,[73] although the onus of proving a child's continued financial dependence on his or her parents grows heavier as these increase.[74] There must be some degree of congruency between the financial circumstances of the parents and the child's educational plans.[75] Parents of modest means may not be able to afford to underwrite their children's post-secondary education. Middle-class parents may be called on to make some sacrifice to put their children through college, but they are not required to assume more debt than they can repay or sell capital assets if their estates are modest. They may, nevertheless, be expected to make reasonable adjustments to their lifestyle by reducing their consumption of luxuries.[76]

Academically qualified children with reasonable expectations of undertaking post-secondary education will normally receive support to permit their completion of an undergraduate university degree or college diploma, provided that their parents have the means to pay.[77] The parental support obligation does not necessarily extend to postgraduate or professional education or training,[78] although it may do so in appropriate circumstances.[79] As a

---

69 See, for example, *Farden v Farden* (1993), 48 RFL (3d) 60 (BCSC); *Rebenchuk v Rebenchuk*, 2007 MBCA 22; *Cole v Cole*, [1995] NSJ No 362 (Fam Ct).

70 *RJM v EM*, 2015 BCSC 414 at para 50.

71 *MacLennan v MacLennan*, [2003] NSJ No 15 (CA); *TTB v PHD*, 2014 NBQB 164.

72 *RYW v DWW*, 2013 BCSC 472; *Ivany v Ivany* (1996), 24 RFL (4th) 289 (Nfld SC); *Hiebert v Hiebert*, [2007] SJ No 569 (QB).

73 *RYW v DWW*, 2013 BCSC 472; *Ivany v Ivany* (1996), 24 RFL (4th) 289 (Nfld SC); *Martell v Height* (1994), 3 RFL (4th) 104 (NSCA); *Erickson v Erickson*, [2007] NSJ No 483 (SC).

74 *McArthur v McArthur*, [1998] AJ No 1522 (QB); *Penn v Penn*, 2014 ONSC 6321.

75 *RYW v DWW*, 2013 BCSC 472; *Jarzebinski v Jarzebinski*, [2004] OJ No 4595 (Sup Ct).

76 *JCR v JJR*, [2006] BCJ No 2150 (SC).

77 *Rebenchuk v Rebenchuk*, 2007 MBCA 22; *Matwichuk v Stephenson*, [2007] BCJ No 2347 (SC); *Holizki v Reeves*, [1997] SJ No 746 (QB).

78 *Rebenchuk v Rebenchuk*, 2007 MBCA 22; *Smith v Smith* (1990), 27 RFL (3d) 32 (Man CA).

79 *RYW v DWW*, 2013 BCSC 472; *Jamieson v Jamieson* (1995), 14 RFL (4th) 354 (NBCA); *Martell v Height* (1994), 3 RFL (4th) 104 (NSCA); *Penn v Penn*, 2014 ONSC 6321; *DJF v EK*, 2005 SKQB 131.

general rule, parents of a *bona fide* adult student remain financially responsible until the child has reached a level of education commensurate with his or her demonstrated abilities that fits the child for entry-level employment in an appropriate field within a reasonable period of time.[80] In making this determination, the court must be aware of prevailing socio-economic conditions whereby an undergraduate degree no longer assures economic self-sufficiency,[81] although this awareness must be tempered by the realization that the majority of children find their place in the world without the benefit of any post-secondary education.[82] Additional considerations include the means and standard of living of the parent and the legitimate expectations of the children.[83]

Full-time post-secondary education by means of correspondence courses may render an adult child eligible for support.[84] Post-secondary education that is pursued on a part-time basis by an adult child with a clear career plan may entitle the child to support where his or her income from employment is insufficient to enable the child to fully withdraw from the charge of his or her parents.[85] The failure of an adult child to obtain exemplary grades in his or her university studies is not a sufficient basis in itself to justify a finding that the child is no longer a "child of the marriage" within the meaning of the *Divorce Act*, where the evidence does not support allegations that the child is taking advantage of the situation and is not serious in his or her studies.[86] A court may conclude that a financially contributing parent should be kept informed of the child's marks and academic progress,[87] and a condition to this effect may be imposed on the child support order pursuant to section 15.1(4) of the *Divorce Act*.[88]

It has been judicially asserted that an estranged relationship between an adult child and the paying parent may not justify the immediate denial or reduction of child support, but that the child may ultimately be called upon to bear the consequence of persisting in the estrangement and that consequence may be cessation of child support.[89] As the Manitoba Court of

---

80 *WPN v BJN*, [2005] BCJ No 12 (CA); *Martell v Height* (1994), 3 RFL (4th) 104 (NSCA); *Erickson v Erickson*, [2007] NSJ No 483 (SC).

81 *Martell v Height* (1994), 3 RFL (4th) 104 (NSCA).

82 *Jonasson v Jonasson*, [1998] BCJ No 726 (SC).

83 *Douglas v Campbell*, [2006] NSJ No 350 (SC).

84 *Kirkpatrick v Kirkpatrick*, [1997] SJ No 212 (QB).

85 *Kovich v Kreut*, [1998] BCJ No 2586 (SC).

86 *Budyk v Sol*, [1998] MJ No 252 (CA).

87 *Ciardullo v Ciardullo* (1995), 15 RFL (4th) 121 (BCSC).

88 *Brown v Brown* (1993), 45 RFL (3d) 444 (BCSC).

89 *Fraser v Jones* (1995), 17 RFL (4th) 218 (Sask QB); see, generally, *Farden v Farden* (1993), 48 RFL (3d) 60 (BCSC); *Bradley v Zaba* (1996), 137 Sask R 682 (CA); *Hamel v Hamel*, [2001] SJ No 692 (CA).

Appeal observed in *Rebenchuk v Rebenchuk*, parent-child estrangement is a particularly difficult issue.

> [S]elfish or ungrateful children who reject the non-custodial parent without justification should not expect to be supported through their years of higher education. But this factor rarely stands alone as the sole ground for denying support unless the situation is "extremely grave" (*Pepin v. Jung*, [2003] O.J. No. 1779 (S.C.J.).[90]

A parent is not relieved of the obligation to support an adult child pursuing post-secondary education or training at an accredited institution merely because the parent disapproves of the child's career choice.[91]

There is nothing in the *Divorce Act* to suggest that a child may not move from being a child of the marriage to being outside the category and thereafter within it again.[92] An adult child who has ceased to be a "child of the marriage" under the *Divorce Act* and the *Federal Child Support Guidelines* may regain that lost status by reason of the pursuit of further education.[93] Whether the status has been regained is a question of fact that may be determined by whether the educational program and the resources of the parent render such a course realistic. When the child in respect of whom support is brought has already been provided with the means to be independent, and the parent against whom support is sought has assumed new obligations to a second family, a court may conclude that the parent should not be called upon to support an adult child's pursuit of postgraduate professional training.[94]

b) Options Available to the Court under Section 3(2) of the *Federal Child Support Guidelines*

Section 3(2) of the *Federal Child Support Guidelines* stipulates that, unless otherwise provided under the Guidelines, where a child who is entitled to support is the age of majority or over, the amount of the child support order is

---

90   2007 MBCA 22 at para 56; see also *O'Donnell v O'Donnell*, 2011 NBQB 56; *Broaders v Broaders*, 2014 NLTD(F) 13; *Droit de la famille — 121520*, 2012 QCCA 1143; *Olszewski (Willick) v Willick*, 2009 SKCA 133 at para 34.

91   *Evans v Evans*, [1998] SJ No 91 (QB).

92   *Stocchero v Stocchero* (1997), 29 RFL (4th) 223 (Alta CA); *Prince v Soenen*, 2015 MBQB 31; *MV v DV*, [2005] NBJ No 505 (QB); *Morin v Leclerc*, 2012 ONSC 2320; *Olsen v Olsen*, [1997] SJ No 476 (QB).

93   *Horvath v Horvath*, [2000] MJ No 428 (CA); *Doerksen v Houlahan*, 2012 MBQB 110; *O'Donnell v O'Donnell*, 2011 NBQB 56; *Leonard v Leonard* (1996), 29 RFL (4th) 237 (NWTSC).

94   *Jonasson v Jonasson*, [1998] BCJ No 726 (SC).

(a) the amount determined by applying the Guidelines as if the child were under the age of majority; or

(b) if the court considers that approach to be inappropriate, the amount that it considers appropriate, having regard to the condition, means, needs and other circumstances of the child and the financial ability of each spouse to contribute to the support of the child.

Pursuant to the presumptive rule established by section 3(1) of the *Federal Child Support Guidelines*, a child under the age of majority is entitled to the applicable provincial table amount of basic child support and to such special or extraordinary expenses as may fall within section 7 of the Guidelines. If section 3(1)(a) of the Guidelines is deemed applicable, the basic amount of child support fixed by the applicable provincial table cannot be reduced to reflect the child's ability to contribute to his or her own support, but any supplementary amount ordered pursuant to section 7 of the Guidelines will be determined having regard to the guiding principle set out in subsection 7(2), whereby the expense is shared by the spouses in proportion to their respective incomes after deducting from the expense the contribution, if any, from the child.[95]

If a child under the age of majority is pursuing post-secondary education away from home, a court has no authority to deviate from the presumptive rule,[96] unless the attendant circumstances trigger the discretionary jurisdiction of the court by reason of a parent's annual income exceeding $150,000 (Guidelines, section 4), split or shared custody arrangements (Guidelines, sections 8 and 9), or undue hardship (Guidelines, section 10). A court cannot refuse to apply the presumptive rule by invoking section 3(2)(b) of the Guidelines simply because the parents are agreeable to this course of action, even though the child is under the provincial age of majority. In quantifying the living expenses associated with the child's post-secondary education, clothing expenses, spending money, and personal expenses will be excluded from the allowable expenses under section 7 of the Guidelines. This consequence ensues from the fact that these expenses are incorporated in the applicable table amount of child support and they are moveable and not dependent on "economy of scale" when the applicable table amount relates to two or more children. Some, but not all, of the child's food costs are also covered by the applicable table amount of child support, so an adjustment of these expenses is warranted under section 7 of the Guidelines. However, the same is not true of the child's out-of-town accommodation costs, which are allowable under

---

95   *Glen v Glen*, [1997] BCJ No 2806 (SC).

96   *Hodgson v Hodgson*, 2014 BCSC 1372 at para 35; *Merritt v Merritt*, [1999] OJ No 1732 (Sup Ct); *JC v SAW*, 2013 YKSC 1.

section 7 of the Guidelines to the extent that they are reasonable. In fixing the respective parental contributions to the child's post-secondary education expenses, including tuition, books, and incidental fees, as well as the aforementioned expenses, the court may have regard to money previously set aside or otherwise available to defray the costs of the child's post-secondary education, including scholarship funds and any income tax refund received by a parent as a tuition and education tax credit.[97] In *Lu v Sun*,[98] the Nova Scotia Court of Appeal held that the trial judge had erred in apportioning the child's overall university expenses, including accommodation and food costs, between the parents in accordance with their respective incomes, given that the mother also received the full table amount of child support (which includes provision for accommodation and food) during the months that the child was living away from home while attending university. The father's contribution to the child's section 7 expenses was accordingly reduced on appeal. No error was found in the trial judge's order that the father pay one-half of the table amount of child support in addition to a parental income-based proportionate contribution to section 7 expenses for the second and subsequent years of the child's attendance at university, such attendance occurring after the child had attained the provincial age of majority, thus triggering a permissible discretionary deviation from the aforementioned presumptive rule pursuant to section 3(2)(b) of the *Federal Child Support Guidelines*. The Nova Scotia Court of Appeal accepted the trial judge's finding that the attendant circumstances justified the child's attendance at an out-of-town university, even though her estranged father had not been consulted on this matter.

The problem of applying section 3(1) of the *Federal Child Support Guidelines* to children under the age of majority who are attending college or university away from home is particularly acute in provinces where the age of majority is nineteen years. This problem is not addressed in *Children Come First: A Report to Parliament Reviewing the Provisions and Operation of the Federal Child Support Guidelines*.[99] Provincial representations to the federal Minister of Justice might elicit a response. In the meantime, some courts may opt to depart from the "guiding principle" of a *pro rata* sharing of allowable expenses based on the respective parental incomes under section 7 of the

---

97   *Callaghan v Callaghan*, [2002] NJ No 117 (SC). Had a step-parent been involved in *Callaghan v Callaghan*, the discretionary provisions of s 5 of the Guidelines might have been invoked. As to additional circumstances where a court may deviate from the *Federal Child Support Guidelines*, see *Divorce Act*, ss 15.1(5)–(8) and 17(6.2)–(6.5).

98   [2005] NSJ No 314 (CA).

99   Canada, Department of Justice, *Children Come First: A Report Reviewing the Provisions and Operation of the Federal Child Support Guidelines* (Ottawa: Department of Justice, 2002).

Federal Child Support Guidelines, if a forced payment of the applicable table amount of child support under section 3(1) of the Guidelines generates financial inequity between the parents.

Section 3(2) of the Guidelines involves a two-stage analysis where a child has attained the provincial age of majority. The initial approach involves a determination of the applicable table amount, together with such amounts for special or extraordinary expenses as may be justified under section 7 of the Guidelines. Only when the court considers that approach inappropriate can the court invoke the broader discretionary jurisdiction that is exercisable under section 3(2) of the Guidelines, having regard to the condition, means, needs, and other circumstances of the child and the financial ability of each spouse to contribute to the support of the child.[100] The words "inappropriate approach" in section 3(2)(b) of the Guidelines may be interpreted as signifying an unreasonable amount of child support. If section 3(2)(b) of the Guidelines is triggered, the court must undertake the budget-driven approach that was in vogue before implementation of the Guidelines.[101]

The party who invokes section 3(2)(b) of the *Federal Child Support Guidelines* has the onus of establishing that the application of section 3(2)(a) of the Guidelines would be inappropriate.[102]

It is a reasonable expectation of a parent that an adult child will pursue post-secondary education at their home-town university if the desired source of study is available there. If the child wishes to pursue studies elsewhere, reasonable evidence should be offered to justify that decision; for example, evidence that the chosen university offers a program that better accommodates the child's anticipated career path.[103]

Double counting must be avoided. If the applicable provincial table amount is deemed appropriate for a child attending college, it will be necessary to exclude the residence, meals, and other costs that are subsumed in the table amount from any supplementary order for post-secondary expenses under section 7 of the *Federal Child Support Guidelines*.[104]

There is insufficient judicial consistency of approach to lay down any hard and fast rules with respect to adult children who are pursuing university studies while living at home or away from home. Helpful guidance has been

---

100 *O'Donnell v O'Donnell*, 2011 NBQB 56; *SDP v PW*, [1998] NSJ No 565 (Fam Ct); *MacDonald v Rasmussen*, [2000] SJ No 660 (QB); *Hiebert v Hiebert*, [2007] SJ No 569 (QB).

101 *Welsh v Welsh*, [1998] OJ No 4550 (Gen Div).

102 *Glen v Glen*, [1997] BCJ No 2806 (SC); *Rebenchuk v Rebenchuk*, 2007 MBCA 22; *MV v DV*, [2005] NBJ No 505 (QB); *JC v AMM*, [2007] OJ No 3887 (Sup Ct); *MacDonald v Rasmussen*, [2000] SJ No 660 (QB). Compare *Canada v Canada-Somers*, 2008 MBCA 59 (CA).

103 *Woods v Woods* (1998), 42 RFL (4th) 123 (Sask QB); *Krueger v Tunison*, [1999] SJ No 482 (QB).

104 *Degagne v Sargeant*, [1999] AJ No 506 (CA); see also *Lu v Sun*, [2005] NSJ No 314 (CA).

furnished, however, by the following analysis of Martinson J, of the Supreme Court of British Columbia, in *Wesemann v Wesemann*.[105] The law relating to adult children involves a four-step process. The court must first determine whether an adult child falls within the definition of a "child of the marriage" under section 2(1) of the *Divorce Act*. Second, the court must determine whether the approach of applying the Guidelines as if the child were under the age of majority is challenged. If not, the court shall apply the same criteria as those applicable to children under the age of majority. Third, if this approach is challenged, the court must determine whether the challenger has satisfied the burden of proving that it is inappropriate. If not, the usual Guidelines apply. Fourth, if the usual Guidelines approach is proven to be inappropriate, the court must decide what amount is appropriate, having regard to the condition, means, needs, and other circumstances of the child and the financial ability of each parent to contribute to the support of the child. Where it is appropriate to apply the same approach under the Guidelines to adult children as that applied to children under the age of provincial majority, this can result in an order for the applicable table amount or an order for the applicable table amount and an additional amount under section 7 of the Guidelines for the expenses of post-secondary education. Justice Martinson suggests a third alternative, whereby an order could be made under section 7 of the Guidelines without any table amount, but this suggestion negates the significance of the word "and" that links paragraphs (a) and (b) in section 3(1) of the Guidelines. This third alternative would be available, however, by recourse to section 3(2) (b) of the Guidelines in circumstances where the concurrent allocation of the applicable table amount is inappropriate. Section 3(2) of the Guidelines does not inform a court how to determine whether the usual Guidelines approach is appropriate. The usual Guidelines approach is based on certain factors that normally apply to children under the age of majority; namely, they reside with one or both parents, are not earning an income, and are financially dependent on their parents. The closer the circumstances of an adult child are to those upon which the usual Guidelines approach is based, the less likely it is that the usual Guidelines will be found inappropriate. The opposite is also true. Children over the age of majority may reside away from home and/or earn a significant income. In these circumstances, the adult child's expenses will be quite different from those of a typical child under the age of majority. In exercising the discretion to move away from the usual approach under the Guidelines, a court will find it helpful to consider the following:

---

105 [1999] BCJ No 1387 (SC); see also *Pollock v Rioux*, [2004] NBJ No 467 (CA); *Simon v Adey*, 2012 NBCA 63. But see *WPN v BJN*, [2005] BCJ No 12 (CA), discussed below in this section; *Rebenchuk v Rebenchuk*, 2007 MBCA 22.

1) the reasonable needs of the child;
2) the ability and opportunity of the child to contribute to those needs; and
3) the ability of the parents to contribute to those needs.

The reasonable needs of the child has two aspects, namely,

1) the child's needs for accommodation, food, clothing, and miscellaneous expenses; and
2) the child's actual post-secondary expenses.

Children have an obligation to make a reasonable contribution to their own post-secondary education or training. This does not signify that all of a child's income should be applied to the costs of the child's further education. A child should be entitled to some personal benefit from the fruits of his or her labours. It is not appropriate to require a child to pursue part-time employment during the academic year where that would interfere with the child's academic progress, nor should the availability of student loans automatically require the child to obtain such loans. Student loans are not to be equated with bursaries, grants, or scholarships. A student loan delays the payment of expenses, rather than defraying them. After considering the ability of both parents to contribute to an adult child's reasonable needs, the court may choose to apportion the parental contributions in accordance with their respective incomes.[106] Courts have a very broad discretion in determining how to balance the many competing considerations relevant to determining the respective responsibilities of the parents and the child to cover the post-secondary education costs of an adult child still considered to be a child of the marriage for the purpose of the *Child Support Guidelines*. Relevant cases indicate that there is a growing trend to impose one-third to one-half of the responsibility on the adult child, to be met by part-time employment, scholarships, or student loans, depending on the talents and choices of the child, and the balance on the parents, proportional to their respective incomes. This is far from invariable, and depends on the incomes and circumstances of the parties.[107]

After reviewing relevant caselaw, including *Wesemann v Wesemann*,[108] the British Columbia Court of Appeal in *WPN v BJN*[109] concluded that, even when

---

106 *Jordan v Stewart*, 2013 ONSC 902.

107 *Fleming v Boyachek*, 2011 SKCA 11; compare *PHH v NRY*, 2015 BCSC 320, citing *Semancik v Saunders*, 2011 BCCA 264 (10 to 50 percent); see also *Wiewiora v Wiewiora*, 2014 MBQB 218.

108 [1999] BCJ No 1387 (SC).

109 [2005] BCJ No 12 (CA); see also *Roberts v Beresford*, [2006] BCJ No 291 (CA); *Rebenchuk v Rebenchuk*, 2007 MBCA 22; *Park v Thompson*, [2005] OJ No 1695 (CA); *Lewi v Lewi*, [2006] OJ No 1847 (CA); *Royko v Royko*, [2008] SJ No 155 (QB). Compare *De Beck v De Beck*, 2012

a party has not challenged the appropriateness of applying the presumptive rule pursuant to section 3(2)(a) of the Guidelines, it is open to the court to find the application of the presumptive rule to be inappropriate on the facts of the particular case, in which event the court should apply section 3(2)(b) of the Guidelines and order an appropriate amount of child support having regard to the condition, means, needs, and other circumstances of the child and the financial ability of each parent to contribute to the support of the child. Given a reasonable expectation that an adult child will contribute to his or her own expenses and the fact that the table amount is based solely on the obligor's income and can take no account of the child's contribution, the British Columbia Court of Appeal stated that, in principle, support for an adult child who is in attendance at a post-secondary institution should generally be determined under section 3(2)(b) of the Guidelines. The British Columbia Court of Appeal further concluded that concurrent orders may be made under section 3(2)(b) and section 7 of the Guidelines and suggested that a separation agreement providing for specific expenses might lead to such an approach. It is noteworthy that in *De Beck v De Beck*,[110] Smith JA, of the British Columbia Court of Appeal, qualified the observations of Levine JA in *WPN v BJN* by stating that

> [j]ust as the absence of a challenge to the 'usual *Guidelines* approach' under s. 3(2)(a) should not preclude a consideration of s. 3(2)(b), similarly the fact that an adult child is attending a post-secondary institution while living at home should not in my view foreclose a consideration of the approach under s. 3(2)(a). In each case, the choice between applying s. 3(2)(a) and s. 3(2)(b) will be a discretionary one that will be governed by the circumstances of that case.

A court is more likely to order the applicable table amount of support with respect to an adult child attending university where that child is pursuing his or her studies while living at home with a parent and any other siblings.[111] In addition to ordering the table amount of basic child support in these circumstances, the court may order a contribution towards tuition, books, and incidental expenses pursuant to section 7 of the Guidelines, unless the child can

---

BCCA 465 at paras 54–58; *Pollock v Rioux*, [2004] NBJ No 467 (CA); *Simon v Adey*, 2012 NBCA 63; *Wionzek v Magyar*, 2013 SKQB 194.

110   *De Beck v De Beck*, 2012 BCCA 465 at para 56. See also *Lerner v Lerner*, 2013 BCSC 239 at paras 43–44; *YHB v JPB*, 2014 BCSC 618.

111   *Sherlow v Zubko*, [1999] AJ No 644 (QB) (support to be reviewed if children pursued post-secondary education away from home); *Morgan v Morgan*, [2006] BCJ No 1795 (SC); *Lewi v Lewi*, [2006] OJ No 1847 (CA); *Coghill v Coghill*, [2006] OJ No 2602 (Sup Ct); *Hiebert v Hiebert*, [2007] SJ No 569 (QB).

reasonably be expected to meet these expenses.[112] The table amount of support under the Guidelines may be deemed inappropriate for an adult child attending a home-town university, where the child is capable of contributing to his or her own support from earned income, in which event the court should invoke its discretionary jurisdiction under section 3(2)(b) of the Guidelines.[113] The table amount of child support is usually inappropriate in cases where children are attending post-secondary education programs away from home or where the child has the ability through their own means to pay not only for post-secondary education expenses but also a portion of their living costs.[114] Where children attend university away from home, courts do not normally resort to the provincial table amount, but to the means and needs approach set out in section 3(2)(b) of the *Federal Child Support Guidelines*.[115] Economies of scale, which are reflected in the provincial and territorial tables under the *Federal Child Support Guidelines* where several children are residing in the same household, are inapplicable where one or more of the children are residing elsewhere while pursuing post-secondary education. It is, therefore, more appropriate to calculate the actual costs of providing for the needs of any child in another residence, factoring in a contribution towards the cost of maintaining the family home to return to on weekends or college breaks where appropriate, and apportioning that between the spouses on a means and needs basis after considering the child's own ability to contribute.[116]

c)   Expenses for Post-Secondary Education under Section 7 of the *Federal Child Support Guidelines*

Section 7(1)(e) of the *Federal Child Support Guidelines* empowers a court to provide for the payment of some or all of post-secondary education expenses. Post-secondary education expenses do not have to be "extraordinary" in order to satisfy section 7 of the Guidelines.[117]

Expenses for post-secondary education may include tuition, books and other supplies, and transportation costs.[118] Where the table amount of basic child support is deemed inappropriate because the adult child is living away

---

112   *Mills v Mills*, [1999] SJ No 177 (QB).

113   *Phillipchuk v Phillipchuk*, [1999] AJ No 438 (QB); *Hagen v Rankin*, [2002] SJ No 15 (CA); *Geran v Geran*, 2011 SKCA 55.

114   *Meyer v Content*, 2014 ONSC 6001. Compare *RJM v EM*, 2015 BCSC 414.

115   *WPN v BJN*, [2005] BCJ No 12 (CA); *Rebenchuk v Rebenchuk*, 2007 MBCA 22; *Lewi v Lewi*, [2006] OJ No 1847 (CA); *Coghill v Coghill*, [2006] OJ No 2602 (Sup Ct); *Krueger v Tunison*, [1999] SJ No 482 (QB); see also *Power v Hunt*, [2000] NJ No 315 (UFC). Compare *Pollock v Rioux*, [2004] NBJ No 467 (CA); *Simon v Adey*, 2012 NBCA 63.

116   *Merritt v Merritt*, [1999] OJ No 1732 (Sup Ct).

117   *Odermatt v Odermatt*, [1998] BCJ No 55 (SC).

118   *St Amour v St Amour*, [1997] NSJ No 363 (SC).

from home while attending university, the post-secondary education expenses under section 7 of the Guidelines will include tuition and institutional expenses, room and board or equivalent expenses, and books, travel, and miscellaneous expenses reasonably attributable to the pursuit of that education.[119]

There are a number of things that the court is required to consider in relation to post-secondary education expenses. The court must determine whether the expenses are reasonable having regard to the means of the spouses and child and the family's spending pattern before separation. It is also necessary to determine whether an expense has arisen solely as a result of post-secondary education or whether some portion is already factored into the basic amount provided by the applicable provincial or territorial table. Contributions of the child made possible from his or her earnings or available student loans may be deducted from the expenses. The court must also take into account subsidies, benefits, and income tax deductions or credits relating to the expenses.[120]

Adult children have an obligation to make a reasonable contribution towards the costs of their post-secondary education or training, whether by scholarships, bursaries, loans, or summer employment, but availability for part-time employment while at college is to be determined in light of the academic demands for successful completion of the program.[121] The extent to which an adult child can reasonably be expected to contribute to his or her living or post-secondary education expenses should be determined by seeking to achieve a fair balance between the child's means and capabilities and those of the parents.[122] Support may be denied where a child who attends university can totally finance his or her own studies through savings and student loans, or employment income.[123] Gifts received by the child may also be taken into account, although it does not follow that the child should exhaust his or her savings before seeking support from a parent.[124] Although a court lacks jurisdiction to compel adult children to expend trust funds to underwrite the costs of their post-secondary education, the amount of support payable by a parent may be reduced to reflect the children's ability to

---

119 *Johnson v Johnson*, [1998] BCJ No 1080 (SC).

120 *Magnes v Magnes*, [1997] SJ No 407 (QB). Compare *Koback v Koback*, 2013 SKCA 91 at paras 16–24.

121 *Matwichuk v Stephenson*, [2007] BCJ No 2347 (SC); *Rebenchuk v Rebenchuk*, 2007 MBCA 22; *Selig v Smith*, 2008 NSCA 54; *Coghill v Coghill*, [2006] OJ No 2602 (Sup Ct); *Zaba v Bradley* (1996), 140 Sask R 297 at 300 (QB), Archambault J.

122 *Whitley v Whitley*, [1997] BCJ No 3116 (SC); *Selig v Smith*, 2008 NSCA 54; *Barbeau v Barbeau*, [1998] OJ No 3580 (Gen Div); *MacDonald v Rasmussen*, [2000] SJ No 660 (QB).

123 *Clark v Clark*, [1998] BCJ No 1934 (SC); *Evans v Evans*, [1998] SJ No 91 (QB).

124 *Griffiths v Griffiths*, [1998] BCJ No 2000 (SC); *Lewi v Lewi*, [2006] OJ No 1847 (CA).

use their trust funds or a reasonable portion thereof as a contribution to-wards the costs of their post-secondary education. The term "means," which appears in both sections 3(2)(b) and 7 of the Guidelines, includes both capital assets and income, and requires the means of the children as well as those of the parents to be considered in determining the parental contributions towards the costs of the post-secondary education of adult children. In *Lewi v Lewi*,[125] the motions judge was found to have erred in confining the adult children's contribution to their post-secondary education expenses to their summer employment income, while disregarding trust funds of approxi-mately $41,820 for each child that had been provided by their grandfather. In determining the respective contributions to be made by each of the children, Juriansz JA, delivering the majority judgment of the Ontario Court of Ap-peal, observed that there is no provision in the Guidelines that implies that children over the age of majority should contribute all their capital assets towards their post-secondary education before their parents will be required to provide support, or that such children should not have to make any con-tribution out of their capital. As a general rule, however, the amount of child support that a parent is ordered to pay should be determined in the expect-ation that a child with means, such as independent assets, will contribute something from those means towards his or her post-secondary education. The extent of the contribution expected depends on the circumstances of the case. Neither section 3(2)(b) nor section 7 of the Guidelines contains any indication whatsoever of the level of contribution an adult child with capital should be expected to make to his or her post-secondary education expenses. There is no standard formula. Under both provisions, the question is largely a matter of discretion for the trial judge. In *Roth v Roth*,[126] Ricchetti J, of the Ontario Superior Court of Justice, provided the following useful summary of principles governing the allocation of post-secondary education expenses and an adult child's obligation to contribute towards the expenses pursuant to section 7 of the *Federal Child Support Guidelines*:

a)   Generally, post secondary education is considered a necessary expense in the best interests of the children . . . .

b)   The reasonableness of the expense considers the means of the spouses or former spouses <u>and</u> the means of the child.

c)   Children have an obligation to make a <u>reasonable contribution</u> to their own post-secondary education or training. This does not mean that all of a child's income should necessarily be applied to the costs of the

---

125   *Ibid.* For an excellent detailed summary of the principles espoused in *Lewi v Lewi*, see *Razavi-Brahimi v Ershadi*, [2007] OJ No 3736 (Ct J), Murray J.

126   [2010] OJ No 1934 at para 16; see also *Lee-Broomes v Broomes*, 2012 ONSC 2195.

child's further education. The court should consider whether the child should be entitled to some personal benefit from the fruits of his or her labours.

d) Grants, scholarships and bursaries are generally treated as a reduction of the education expense as they involve a net transfer of resources to the child without any obligation of repayment.

e) A student loan is not a "benefit" within the meaning of section 7(3) of the Guidelines that must be automatically taken into account in determining the amount to be ordered in respect of s 7 expenses. A student loan may constitute, in whole or in part, a "contribution . . . from the child" to post-secondary education expenses within the meaning of section 7(2) of the Guidelines and thereby exclude or reduce the need for any parental contribution. This turns on the reasonableness of taking account of any such loans in the circumstances of the case.

f) In determining the amount of an expense or the contribution thereto under section 7 of the *Federal Child Support Guidelines*, the guiding principle is that, once the court has determined the appropriate amount of contribution by the spouses or former spouses, the spouses or former spouses should share the expense in proportion to their respective incomes after deducting any contribution from the child, or other liable parent.

The applicant and child may be judicially required to keep the payor parent fully informed about the child's educational progress and expenses and about the child's employment income and student loans.[127]

Section 7 of the *Federal Child Support Guidelines* confers a discretion on the court to order a parent to make a contribution to a child's post-secondary education expenses. The court is under no compulsion to make such an order and may conclude that any contribution would be inappropriate, having regard to the parent's inability to pay.[128]

G. INCOMES OVER $150,000

Obligors with annual incomes exceeding $150,000 must pay the basic table amount of child support on the first $150,000. With respect to the income over $150,000, the court has one of two alternatives. It can order the additional amount prescribed by a percentage formula in the applicable provincial or

---

127 *Adams v Adams*, [1997] MJ No 621 (QB); *Evans v Evans*, [1998] SJ No 91 (QB); *Rosenberg v Rosenberg*, [2003] OJ No 2962 (Sup Ct).

128 *Giebelhaus v Bell*, [1998] BCJ No 627 (SC); *Jarzebinski v Jarzebinski*, [2004] OJ No 4595 (Sup Ct).

territorial table. Or, if it finds that additional amount "inappropriate," the court can exercise its discretion to order a different amount, having regard to the child's condition, means, needs, and other circumstances and the financial ability of each parent to contribute to the support of the child. Deviation from the table formula presupposes a finding that the amount thereby prescribed is "inappropriate." In *Francis v Baker*,[129] the Supreme Court of Canada concluded that the word "inappropriate" in section 4(b) of the *Federal Child Support Guidelines* does not mean "inadequate"; it bears its ordinary dictionary meaning of "unsuitable" or "inadvisable." Consequently, insofar as the obligor's annual income exceeds $150,000, a court has the discretion to increase, decrease, or confirm the amount of child support prescribed by a strict application of the table formula. A point may be reached where the overall table amount is so far in excess of the child's reasonable needs as to justify the court ordering a lower supplementary amount than that prescribed by the table formula relating to the obligor's income in excess of $150,000. Some obligors, such as sports stars, may have astronomic incomes but short professional careers. In *Bachorick v Verdejo*,[130] the Saskatchewan Court of Appeal concluded that a court has no jurisdiction to build a fund to cover future contingencies, such as a child's education, out of monthly table amounts of child support. Any judicial direction to such effect would negate the underlying premise of the *Federal Child Support Guidelines* that the amount of child support ordered reflects the current needs of the children. It would also constitute an unwarranted intrusion on the spending priorities of the custodial parent.

The relevant principles that were laid down in *Francis v Baker* are aptly summarized as follows by Finch JA (now Finch CJ) in *Metzner v Metzner*:

1) It was Parliament's intention that there be a presumption in favour of the table amount in all cases.

2) The Guidelines figures can only be increased or reduced under s 4 if the party seeking such a deviation has rebutted the presumption that the applicable table amount is appropriate.

3) There must be clear and compelling evidence for departing from the Guidelines figures.

4) Parliament expressly listed in s 4(b)(ii) the factors relevant to determining both appropriateness and inappropriateness of the table amount or any deviation therefrom.

---

129 [1999] 3 SCR 250.
130 [1999] SJ No 450 (CA); see also *Simon v Simon*, [1999] OJ No 4492 (CA).

5) Courts should determine table amounts to be inappropriate and so create more suitable awards only after examining all circumstances including the factors expressly set out in s 4(b)(ii).

6) Section 4(b)(ii) emphasizes the "centrality" of the actual situation of the children. The actual circumstances of the children are at least as important as any single element of the legislative purpose underlying the section. A proper construction of s 4 requires that the objectives of predictability, consistency and efficiency, on the one hand, be balanced with those of fairness, flexibility and recognition of the actual "condition, means, needs and other circumstances of the children" on the other.

7) While child support payments unquestionably result in some kind of wealth transfer to the children which results in an indirect benefit to the non-paying parent, the objectives of child support payments must be kept in mind. The Guidelines have not displaced the *Divorce Act* which has as its objective the maintenance of children rather than household equalization of spousal support.

8) The court must have all necessary information before it in order to determine inappropriateness under s 4. If the evidence provided is a child expense budget then "the unique economic situation of high income earners" must be considered.

9) The test for reasonableness of expenses will be a demonstration by the paying parent that the budgeted expense is so high as to exceed the generous ambit within which reasonable disagreement is possible.[131]

And in *Ewing v Ewing*,[132] Conrad JA, of the Alberta Court of Appeal summarized the guiding principles emerging from *Francis v Baker* as follows:

i. There is a presumption that the Table applies to all incomes, including incomes over $150,000. A party seeking to deviate from the Table has the onus of rebutting the presumption. (paras. 41, 43)

ii. Children can expect the Table amount on the first $150,000 and a fair additional amount for that portion that exceeds $150,000. The closer the amount is to $150,000, the more likely it is that the Table amount will be awarded. (para. 41)

---

131 [2000] BCJ No 1693 (CA); see also *Hollenbach v Hollenbach*, [2000] BCJ No 2316 (CA); *Hathaway v Hathaway*, 2014 BCCA 310; *Rémillard v Rémillard*, 2014 MBCA 101; *Mercer v Rosenau*, 2014 NLTD(F) 7; *Debora v Debora*, [2006] OJ No 4826 (CA); *Kristmanson v Kristmanson*, 2013 SKQB 387. For a review of Ontario appellate judgments dealing with the child support of parents with annual incomes exceeding $150,000, see *R v R*, [2002] OJ No 1095 (CA).

132 2009 ABCA 227 at para 46 [emphasis in original]; see also *Klette v Leland*, 2014 SKCA 122.

iii. Where the presumption is rebutted, the *Guideline* figures can be increased or reduced under section 4. (para. 42)

iv. The test for deviation from the Table amount is that the evidence in its entirety must be sufficient to *raise a concern* that the Table amount is inappropriate. The evidence for departure from the *Guidelines* must be clear and compelling. A party seeking deviation is not required to testify or adduce evidence and no unfavourable conclusion should be drawn from a failure to do so. It is recognized that a party may not possess the required relevant evidence. (para. 43)

v. The actual situation of the children is central, and the condition, means, needs and other circumstances of the children must be considered in the assessment of the initial determination of inappropriateness and the determination of appropriate support. (para. 44) No single element of legislative purpose is to be given more weight than the actual circumstances of the children. (para. 39) A proper construction of section 4 requires that the objectives of predictability, consistency and efficiency on the one hand, be balanced with those of fairness, flexibility and recognition of the actual "condition, means, needs and other circumstances of the children" on the other. (para. 40)

vi. To determine appropriateness the court must be armed with sufficient information, and trial judges have discretion to determine on a case-by-case basis whether a child expense budget is required to provide that information and they have the power to order it. (para. 45) Custodial parents are not required to produce child expense budgets in all cases under section 4.

vii. Although frequently child support results in a benefit to the wife, the legislative objective is maintenance for the children rather than household equalization or spousal support. (para. 41)

viii. While standard of living can be considered in assessing need, at some point support payments will meet even a wealthy child's reasonable needs. When the Table amount is so in excess of the child's reasonable needs it must be considered a functional wealth transfer to a parent, or *de facto* spousal support. (para. 41)

ix. The test for whether expenses are reasonable will be met by the paying parent if the budgeted expenses are so high as to "excee[d] the generous ambit within which reasonable disagreement is possible": *Bellenden v. Satterthwaite*, [1948] 1 All E.R. 343 (Eng. C.A.). (para. 49)

Citing the judgment of Rosenberg JA in *Tauber v Tauber*,[133] Conrad JA further observed that a *prima facie* case may be sufficient to rebut the presumption in

---

133 (2000), 48 OR (3d) 577 (CA) at para 39.

favour of the full table amount, and the payee's failure to adduce evidence on the subject may well result in an unfavourable determination — as a matter of common sense rather than evidentiary burden.

In *Hodgkinson v Hodgkinson*,[134] wherein the father's annual income exceeded $150,000, the trial judge awarded the table amount of child support ($2,415 per month) pursuant to section 4 of the *Federal Child Support Guidelines*. In addressing the presumptive rule in favour of the full table amount of child support under section 4, the Supreme Court of Canada in *Francis v Baker*[135] observed that, where the table amount is "inappropriate" with respect to the portion of the parent's annual income that exceeds $150,000, the court has "the discretion to both increase and reduce the [full table] amount." In *Hodgkinson v Hodgkinson*, the British Columbia Court of Appeal accepted the wife's submission that the trial judge had erred by viewing the discretion conferred by section 4 as being triggered only when the overall table amount is excessive. Having regard to the trial judge's finding that the expenses in relation to the child totaled $2,716, all of which were reasonable, and having regard also to the vast discrepancy between the parental incomes, the British Columbia Court of Appeal held that the trial judge's order, in failing to cover all the reasonable expenses of the child, was "inappropriate," which, according to *Francis v Baker*, means "unsuitable." Consequently, the British Columbia Court of Appeal in *Hodgkinson v Hodgkinson* increased the amount of the trial judge's child support order by $300 per month, retroactive to the date of the order.

H. SPLIT CUSTODY; SECTION 8 OF GUIDELINES[136]

Section 8 of the *Federal Child Support Guidelines* provides that, where each spouse or former spouse has custody of one or more children, the amount of a child support order is the difference between the amount that each would otherwise pay if a child support order were sought against each of them.[137] Given possible future changes in the parental incomes, the parents may be

---

134 [2006] BCJ No 678 (CA).

135 [1999] 3 SCR 250 at para 40.

136 See, generally, Carol Rogerson, "Child Support under the Guidelines in Cases of Split and Shared Custody" (1998) 15 Can J Fam L 11 (on Quicklaw under Commentary, Syrtash Collection of Family Law Articles, SFLRP/1999-003).

137 *SEH v SRM*, [1999] BCJ No 1458 (SC) (split custody involving biological child and stepchild; set-off under s 8 of *Federal Child Support Guidelines*); *Fitzpatrick v Fitzpatrick*, [2000] NJ No 62 (UFC); *Watson v Watson*, [1999] NSJ No 272 (SC); *Bergman-Illnik v Illnik*, [1997] NWTJ No 93 (SC); *JP v BG*, [2000] OJ No 1753 (Sup Ct); *MacLean v MacLean*, [2003] PEIJ No 16 (SCTD); *Hladun v Hladun*, [2002] SJ No 476 (QB). Compare *Dudka v Dudka*, [1997] NSJ No 526 (TD).

judicially directed to exchange complete copies of their income tax returns by 15 May of each year.[138] Where the parents earn the same income and each is responsible for the support of a child of the marriage, the court may decline to make any order for child support.[139] Bilateral orders may be granted for child support where each parent had custody of one or more children of the marriage.[140] Section 8 of the *Federal Child Support Guidelines*, unlike section 9, provides no judicial discretion in the assessment of child support.[141]

Section 8 of the *Federal Child Support Guidelines* may be applied where each of the parents provides a home for one or more of their dependent children, even though one of the children is an adult attending university in respect of whom "neither parent has custody."[142] Section 8 of the Guidelines will not be satisfied, however, where the evidence is insufficient to establish that the adult child is a "child of the marriage" within the meaning of the *Divorce Act*.[143]

Where parents have a split custody arrangement but the income of one of the parents falls short of the minimum threshold under the applicable provincial table, the other parent will be required to pay the full table amount of support for the child in the custody of the low- or no-income parent.[144]

In addition to ordering payment of the differential between the two table amounts pursuant to section 8 of the *Federal Child Support Guidelines*, a court may order a sharing of special or extraordinary expenses under section 7 of the Guidelines in proportion to the respective parental incomes,[145] or in such other proportion as the court deems reasonable.[146]

---

138 *Hladun v Hladun*, [2002] SJ No 476 (QB).

139 *Cram v Cram*, [1999] BCJ No 2518 (SC).

140 *Mayer v Mayer*, [1999] OJ No 5286 (Sup Ct) (cost-of-living indexation of orders); *Holman v Bignell*, [2000] OJ No 3405 (Sup Ct).

141 *Wright v Wright*, [2002] BCJ No 458 (SC); *Kavanagh v Kavanagh*, [1999] NJ No 358 (SC).

142 *Khoee-Solomonescu v Solomonescu*, [1997] OJ No 4876 (Gen Div); see also *Sutcliffe v Sutcliffe*, [2001] AJ No 629 (QB); *Davis v Davis*, [1999] BCJ No 1832 (application of s 8 of *Federal Child Support Guidelines* in circumstances involving split custody over summer months when adult child not away at university); *Kavanagh v Kavanagh*, [1999] NJ No 358 (SC).

143 *Tanner v Simpson*, [1999] NWTJ No 71 (SC).

144 *Estey v Estey*, [1999] NSJ No 226 (SC); *Fraser v Gallant*, [2004] PEIJ No 5 (SCTD); *Hamonic v Gronvold*, [1999] SJ No 32 (QB). Compare *KO v CO*, [1999] SJ No 29 (QB) (shared custody).

145 *Sutcliffe v Sutcliffe*, [2001] AJ No 629 (QB); *Patrick v Patrick*, [1999] BCJ No 1245 (SC); *Sayong v Aindow*, [1999] NWTJ No 63 (SC); *Fraser v Fraser*, [2001] OJ No 3765 (Sup Ct); *Fransoo v Fransoo*, [2001] SJ No 121 (QB).

146 Compare *Tooth v Knott*, [1998] AJ No 1395 (QB); and see Section I, below in this chapter.

I. SHARED CUSTODY: 40 PERCENT RULE

Section 9 of the *Federal Child Support Guidelines* permits a court to deviate from the normal guidelines amount of child support where a parent exercises access to or has physical custody of a child for not less than 40 percent of the time over the course of a year. Shared custody or access for 40 percent of the time over the course of a year is the equivalent of 146 days[147] or 3,504 hours[148] of the year. Judicial opinions have differed on how to determine whether the 40 percent threshold has been met. Some courts have favoured a strictly mathematical approach that may even involve hourly calculations.[149] Other courts have placed emphasis on the functioning of the particular shared parenting regime. These differences of approach arise from the fact that the relevant criterion under section 9 of the Guidelines is the amount of time that the children are in the care and control of a parent, not the amount of time that the parent is physically present with the children. After reviewing relevant appellate decisions from across Canada, the Manitoba Court of Appeal in *Mehling v Mehling*[150] favoured a functional approach but concluded that a decision as to the proper approach falls within the discretion of the presiding judge. Irrespective of the methodology favoured, the 40 percent criterion must be satisfied before section 9 of the Guidelines is triggered.[151] Time spent by a child sleeping, in daycare, or at school is credited to the parent who has care and control over the child at that time.[152] Parents who exercise access for part of a day, such as midweek evening access, cannot be credited with a full day when the custodial parent would be called upon if anything happened while the child was at school.[153] A custodial parent will ordinarily be credited with time that a child spends sleeping, or at daycare, or at school,[154] except for those hours when the non-custodial parent is actually exercising rights of access or the child is sleeping in that parent's home.[155] The existence of an order or agreement for joint guardianship or joint legal

---

147   *Handy v Handy*, [1999] BCJ No 6 (SC); *Gardiner v Gardiner*, [2007] NSJ No 367 (SC).

148   *Claxton v Jones*, [1999] BCJ No 3086 (Prov Ct); *D'Urzo v D'Urzo*, [2002] OJ No 2415 (Sup Ct).

149   *Arlt v Arlt*, 2014 ONSC 2173.

150   2008 MBCA 66; see also *Maultsaid v Blair*, 2009 BCCA 102; *Probert v Andres*, 2008 SKQB 361. Compare *Desjardins v Bouey*, 2013 ABQB 714 (hours calculation preferred).

151   *LC v ROC*, 2007 ABCA 158; *Campolin v Campolin*, [2007] BCJ No 2090 (SC); *Ransom v Coulter*, 2014 NWTSC 55; *Probert v Andres*, 2008 SKQB 361.

152   *Arlt v Arlt*, 2014 ONSC 2173.

153   *McGrath v McGrath*, [2006] NJ No 201 (UFC); *Lepage v Lepage*, [1999] SJ No 174 (QB).

154   *Gardiner v Gardiner*, [2007] NSJ No 367 (SC); *Cross v Cross*, [2004] OJ No 2341 (Sup Ct); *Jarocki v Rice*, [2003] SJ No 178 (QB).

155   *Cusick v Squire*, [1999] NJ No 206 (SC); *Jarocki v Rice*, [2003] SJ No 178 (QB). See also *Maultsaid v Blair*, 2009 BCCA 102 (joint guardianship).

custody is not a criterion for the application of section 9. The 40 percent criterion is quantitative as applied to one of two aspects of the relationship between the child and the parents, namely access or physical custody.[156]

The amount of child support to be paid pursuant to section 9 of the *Federal Child Support Guidelines* when the minimum 40 percent criterion has been satisfied must be determined by taking into account (a) the amounts set out in the applicable tables for each spouse; (b) the increased costs of shared custody; and (c) the conditions, means, needs, and other circumstances of each spouse and of any child for whom support is sought.[157] A court is not compelled to make a formal finding of the precise percentage of time that each parent is responsible for the child. There is nothing in section 9 of the Guidelines to suggest that the amount of child support must invariably reflect the percentages of shared parenting. A contextual approach that does not place undue reliance upon percentages or formulas is required. Shared parenting is usually expensive for both parents and it cannot be assumed that, once the 40 percent threshold is met, the parent who spends more time with the child will have higher costs than the parent who spends less time with the child. Even if a finding is made with respect to the percentage of the year that each parent is responsible for the child, this neither avoids nor assists in the financial analysis that must be undertaken pursuant to sections 9(b) and (c) of the Guidelines, which respectively require the court to have regard to any proven increased costs of the shared-parenting regime and to the relative standards of living available in the two households and the ability of each parent to absorb the costs required to maintain an appropriate standard of living.[158]

In *Contino v Leonelli-Contino*,[159] the Supreme Court of Canada, by a majority of eight to one, held that section 9 of the Guidelines promotes flexibility and fairness by ensuring that the economic reality and particular circumstances of each family are accounted for. The three listed factors all structure the exercise of judicial discretion and no single factor prevails. The weight given to each of the three factors will vary according to the particular circumstances of each case. There is no presumption in favour of awarding at least the amount prescribed by section 3 of the Guidelines. Nor is there any presumption in favour of reducing a parent's child support obligation below

---

156 *Maultsaid v Blair, ibid.*

157 *Ferris v Longhurst*, 2014 SKQB 294.

158 *Stewart v Stewart*, 2007 MBCA 66.

159 2005 SCC 63. For an excellent detailed summary of the criteria defined by the Supreme Court of Canada in *Contino v Leonelli-Contino* with respect to the calculation of child support in shared-parenting situations falling within s 9 of the *Federal Child Support Guidelines*, see the judgment of Chappel J, of the Ontario Superior Court of Justice, in *Kerr v Pickering*, 2013 ONSC 317 at para 32.

that amount, because after an analysis of all three factors in section 9, a court may conclude that the normal Guidelines amount should be paid in full under the circumstances of the particular case.[160] A simple set-off between the table amounts payable by each parent is an appropriate starting point under section 9(a), but it must be followed by an examination of the continuing ability of the recipient parent to meet the financial needs of the child, especially in light of the fact that many costs are fixed. Where both parents are making effective contributions, it is necessary to verify how each parent's actual contribution compares to the table amount that is provided for each of them. This will provide the judge with better insight when deciding whether the adjustments to be made to the set-off amount are based on the actual sharing of child-related expenses. The court retains the discretion to modify the set-off amount where, considering the financial situation of the parents, it would lead to a significant variation in the standard of living experienced by the children as they move between the respective households. Section 9(b) of the *Federal Child Support Guidelines* recognizes that the total cost of raising children may be greater in shared-custody situations than in sole-custody situations. The court will examine the budgets and actual expenditures of both parents in addressing the needs of the children and determine whether shared custody has resulted in increased costs globally. These expenses will be apportioned between the parents in accordance with their respective incomes. Lastly, section 9(c) vests the court with a broad discretion to analyze the resources and needs of both the parents and the children. It is important to keep in mind the objectives of the Guidelines that require a fair standard of support for the child and fair contributions from both parents. The court will look at the standard of living of the child in each household and the ability of each parent to absorb the costs required to maintain the appropriate standard of living in the circumstances.[161] Financial statements and/or child-expense budgets are necessary for a proper evaluation of section 9(c).[162] There is no need to resort to section 10 and section 7[163] of the Guidelines either to increase or to reduce support, since the court has full discretion under section 9(c) to consider "other circumstances" and order the payment of any amount above or below the table amounts. It may be that section 10 would find application in an extraordinary situation. It is important that the parties lead evidence relating to sections 9(b) and 9(c), and courts should demand information from the parties when the evidence is deficient. A court

---

160 *Schick v Schick*, 2008 ABCA 196.
161 *Dagg v Chenier*, 2014 ONSC 336; *Amos v Fischer*, 2013 SKQB 49.
162 *Wilkie v Wilkie*, 2009 SKQB 119.
163 *RM v NM*, 2014 BCSC 1755 at para 66; *Stewart v Stewart*, 2007 MBCA 66.

should neither make "common-sense" assumptions about costs incurred by the payor parent, nor apply a multiplier to account for the fixed costs of the recipient parent, such as has been done by some courts in the past. Although the Comparison of Household Standards of Living Test in Schedule II of the Guidelines, which is included in Child View Calculations, is normally used in the context of the undue hardship provisions of section 10 of the Guidelines, its use in the broad discretionary context of section 9(c) of the Guidelines is neither required nor precluded. In some situations it will provide assistance. Provided that it is not overemphasized at the expense of the required consideration of the relevant personal factors applicable to the parties under section 9(c) of the Guidelines, its use by the trial judge does not constitute a reviewable error.

The majority judgment in *Contino v Leonelli-Contino* denounces a strict formulaic approach to the determination of child support in shared-parenting situations, and emphasizes the need for relevant financial evidence to be adduced so that the court can address the factors specified in paragraphs 9(b) and (c) of the Guidelines, in addition to taking account of the table amount payable by each parent, as required by paragraph 9(a). After reviewing diverse formulas that had previously been applied, especially in British Columbia, the Supreme Court of Canada in *Contino v Leonelli-Contino* rejects the use of prorated set-offs between the applicable table amounts of child support payable by each parent, which have been frequently used in the past in situations involving unequal time-sharing arrangements falling within section 9 of the Guidelines. The Supreme Court of Canada also discredits the judicial application of a multiplier (usually 1.5 times the determined set-off amount), which some courts previously applied on the assumption that part of the recipient parent's costs are fixed and unaffected by increased time that the child spends with the payor parent. The majority judgment in *Contino v Leonelli-Contino*, nevertheless, accepts that a simple set-off between the full table amount of child support payable by each parent is a useful starting point in shared-parenting situations, but emphasizes the need for a facts-based and child-related budgetary analysis that reflects the factors specified in paragraphs 9(b) and (c) of the Guidelines.[164] Given the Supreme Court of Canada's assertion that a child should not suffer a noticeable decline in his or her standard of living from any change in the parenting regime, a distinction may need to be drawn between original applications for child support and variation applications, which can trigger the so-called cliff effect, in that a modest increase in the time spent with the child could result in an unjustifiable reduction in the amount of child support payable if a strict formulaic

---

164 *Muller v Muller*, 2015 BCSC 370; *Amos v Fischer*, 2013 SKQB 49.

approach were applied.[165] The cliff effect can only be resolved by the court paying due regard to the criteria specified in paragraphs 9(b) and (c) of the Guidelines. If evidence relating to these criteria is not initially adduced, the court may grant an adjournment to permit the necessary evidence to be provided. It is not open to the court to make unsubstantiated assumptions as to the increased costs of a shared-custody arrangement or to apply any arbitrary multiplier to the set-off amount instead of requiring relevant evidence to be adduced. While mandatory financial statements and child-related budgets may be fraught with difficulties, as parents confuse necessary expenditures with their preferred wish lists, trial judges are well-placed to resolve any such conflict.[166] The majority judgment in *Contino v Leonelli-Contino* states that the broad discretion conferred by paragraph 9(c) of the Guidelines empowers the court to order an overall amount of child support that includes special or exceptional expenses that would otherwise fall within section 7 of the Guidelines.[167] As was observed in *Slade v Slade*,[168] special or extraordinary expenses may be ordered in shared-parenting situations pursuant to section 7 of the Guidelines, or they may be considered under the broad provisions of paragraph 9(c) of the Guidelines. Neither option is foreclosed by the majority judgment in *Contino v Leonelli-Contino*, and a severance of the basic amount of child support from allowable section 7 expenses may be advantageous in facilitating future variations. The majority judgment of the Supreme Court of Canada in *Contino v Leonelli-Contino* represents a balanced approach to reconciling the inherent flexibility of the judicial discretion conferred by section 9 of the *Federal Child Support Guidelines* with the objective of providing some measure of consistency and predictability. If there is limited information available to the court and the incomes of the parents are not widely divergent, a simple set-off between the table amounts of child support may be deemed appropriate.[169] Where there is a substantial disparity between the parental incomes, and the child's standard of living would be significantly reduced by a simple set-off approach, it behooves the court to adjourn the proceeding so that requisite evidence can be provided that will enable the court to apply the criteria defined in paragraphs 9(b) and (c) of the Guidelines. In addressing the application of section 9 to the shared-parenting arrangement that existed in *Dillon v Dillon*,[170] the Nova Scotia Court of Appeal found no error on the part of the trial judge who fixed child support at the

---

165   *Martin v Martin*, [2007] MJ No 449 (QB); *Costa v Petipas*, [2006] PEIJ No 39 (SCTD).

166   *JC v MC*, 2014 NBQB 161.

167   *Stewart v Stewart*, 2007 MBCA 66.

168   [2001] NJ No 5 (CA); see also *Costa v Petipas*, [2006] PEIJ No 39 (SCTD).

169   *JC v MC*, 2014 NBQB 161; *Ferris v Longhurst*, 2014 SKQB 294.

170   [2005] NSJ No 548 (CA).

set-off amount created by the differential between the table amount of child support payable by each parent. In upholding the set-off amount, the Nova Scotia Court of Appeal held that the judgment of the Supreme Court of Canada in *Contino v Leonelli-Contino* does not rule out the fixing of child support on the basis of a simple set-off of the respective table amounts, provided that, in so doing, the additional factors in sections 9(b) and (c) of the *Federal Child Support Guidelines* are considered.

In a summary of their review of post-*Contino* cases published in June 2006, Justice Jennifer Blishen and Michèle Labrosse, a family law practitioner, express the following conclusion:

> Given the Supreme Court of Canada's emphasis on a discretionary rather than a "formulaic" or "mathematical" approach to calculating child support under s 9 of the *Child Support Guidelines*, it is not surprising that recent cases have widely differing results depending on their circumstances. The results range from a determination that no child support was payable (see *Lowe v. Lowe*, [2006] O.J. No. 128 (S.C.J.)), to the use of a straight set-off (see *Dillon v. Dillon*, [2005] N.S.J. No. 548 (C.A.)), to orders for the full Table amount or close to it in situations where there is a significant disparity in the incomes, assets and/or expenses of the parties (see *Kennedy v. Kennedy*, [2006] B.C.J. No. 509 (S.C.), *Elliot v. MacAskill*, [2005] N.S.J. No. 479 (Fam. Ct.), *Mendler v Mendler*, [2006] O.J. No. 878 (S.C.J.) and *Easton v. McAvoy*, [2005] O.J. No. 5479 (O.C.J.)).[171]

In *Dagg v Chenier*,[172] Cornell J, of the Ontario Superior Court of Justice, refers to a more recent study undertaken by Professor Rollie Thompson wherein the following findings and conclusions were expressed:

> 24   In an article entitled "The TLC of Shared Parenting: Time, Language and Cash," presented at the Law Society of Upper Canada's *7th Annual Family Law Summit 2013*, Professor Thompson undertook a review of the 2012 cases which considered *Contino*. He found that of the thirty-two reported decisions, twenty ended up at the straight set-off amount, five were above the set-off and five were below the set-off amount. He summarizes his findings at p. 21 as follows:
>
> > What this brief survey reveals is that the straight or simple set-off has become the default solution in many s. 9 cases, despite the wide discretion

---

171   Justice Jennifer Blishen & Michèle Labrosse, "Shared Custody and Child Support after *Contino*" (Paper presented to the County of Carleton Law Association, 15th Annual Institute of Family Law, 2 June 2006) at tab 1cii.

172   2014 ONSC 336.

espoused by *Contino*. Child expense budgets are avoided. Section 7 expenses are dealt with separately. Courts make adjustments up or down from the set-off based upon some sense of "fairness". Only rarely do courts appear to consider net disposable income or other measures of household standard of living, despite the Supreme Court's emphasis upon that concern. We do not see the emergence of any formulaic solution in the cases to date, hardly surprising given the holdings in *Contino*.

Canadian caselaw has manifested divergent approaches to the application of section 9 of the *Federal Child Support Guidelines* when there is a hybrid of parenting arrangements in that different time-sharing regimes apply to different children in the family.[173] In *Wouters v Wouters*,[174] the oldest of three children lived with the mother, and the two younger children spent equal time with each parent. Justice M-E Wright, of the Saskatchewan Court of Queen's Bench, concluded that a two-stage analysis should be undertaken to determine the amount of child support to be ordered. First, child support should be fixed for the oldest child whose custody was not shared. After determining the table amount payable with respect to this child in accordance with the presumptive rule under section 3(1) of the Guidelines, Wright J turned to support for the two children whose custody was shared. Their entitlement was determined by ordering a set-off between the table amount of support payable by each parent when there are two children. In *Hofsteede v Hofsteede*,[175] Marshman J, of the Ontario Superior Court of Justice, conceded that the wording of the Guidelines might, at first blush, dictate that the approach in *Wouters v Wouters* is the proper one. However, Marshman J accepted the reasoning of Vogelsang J in *Burns v Burns*,[176] who observed that the table amounts prescribed by the Guidelines recognize the principle of economies of scale when children are residing under the same roof. Thus, the table amount for three children is less than the table amount for one child plus the table amount for two children before any *Contino* adjustment is made by virtue of a set-off or the application of paragraphs 9(b) and (c) of the Guidelines. Applying the reasoning in *Burns v Burns* to the facts in *Hofsteede v Hofsteede*, wherein the older of two children resided primarily with the mother and the younger child spent equal time with both parents,

---

173 See, for example, *Ferster v Ferster*, [2002] BCJ No 172 (SC); *RB v LML*, 2014 BCSC 134; *JC v MC*, 2014 NBQB 161; *Seguin v Masterson*, [2004] OJ No 2176 (Sup Ct); *Dagg v Chenier*, 2014 ONSC 336; *Tweel v Tweel* (2000), 186 Nfld & PEIR 99 (PEISCTD); *Costa v Petipas*, [2006] PEIJ No 39 (SCTD).

174 (2001), 205 Sask R 215 (QB). See also *Shoukri v Mishriki*, 2012 ONSC 7336.

175 [2006] OJ No 304 (Sup Ct); see also *RB v LML*, 2014 BCSC 134; *JC v MC*, 2014 NBQB 161; *Murphy v Murphy*, 2012 ONSC 1627.

176 (1998), 40 RFL (4th) 32 (Ont Gen Div).

Marshman J found it more appropriate to apply sections 8 (split custody) and 9 (shared custody) to the situation rather than sections 3 and 9. Consequently, in calculating the child support to be paid, Marshman J first determined the father's table amount of support for the two children and the wife's table amount of support for one child and effectuated a set-off between these two amounts. Justice Marshman then reviewed the children's budgets prepared by both parents and increased the set-off amount to reflect the increased costs of the shared-parenting arrangement with respect to the younger child and the mother's assumption of a disproportionate share of the overall child-related expenses. In *Thompson v Thompson*,[177] Chappel J, of the Ontario Superior Court of Justice, stated:

> Turning to the principles that apply in hybrid child care arrangements, a review of the current case-law reveals broad support for the approach which Zisman J adopted in the case of *Sadkowski v Harrison-Sadkowski*.[178] In that case, the court described two possible approaches to hybrid claims, namely the "two-step" analysis and the "economies of scale" analysis. The former approach involves first calculating the child support owing relating to the children whose custody is not shared, based on section 3 of the *Guidelines*, then separately calculating the support owed for the child in a shared custody arrangement using a straight set-off amount, and adding the two sums. The latter "economies of scale" involves calculating the full *Table* amount owed by the parent with shared care of children for the total number of children in the care of the parent who has both primary and shared care of children, and setting that amount off by the full *Table* amount payable by the parent with both primary and shared care for the total number of children with the parent who has shared care. Zisman J held that the set-off calculation using the "economies of scale" approach is the proper starting point for the analysis of hybrid claims. She concluded that this set-off calculation serves only as a starting point for the child support analysis, and is not presumptive. The second step in determining hybrid claims is to carry out a *Contino* inquiry to determine whether adjustments are necessary in order to achieve the goal of establishing fair levels of support for the children from both parents. This step involves the court examining the budgets and actual expenditures of each parent to determine whether adjustments are necessary in order to ensure that the children enjoy relatively comparable standards of living in each household. The approach which Zisman J described in this case has since been followed

---

177 2013 ONSC 5500 at para 42; see also *JC v MC*, 2014 NBQB 161; *Clark v Leska*, 2014 ONSC 268.
178 2008 CarswellOnt 1425 (Ct Just); see also *Dagg v Chenier*, 2014 ONSC 336.

in subsequent cases, including *Murphy v Murphy*[179] and *Lalonde v Potier*.[180] I conclude that this approach is the appropriate one to follow, as it recognizes the economies involved when fixed costs are shared between more than one child, and accords with the general principles which the Supreme Court of Canada adopted in *Contino* in the case of shared custody arrangements.

In *Doyle v Doyle*,[181] the British Columbia Court of Appeal found that the chambers judge had erred by failing to apply the *Federal Child Support Guidelines* on a variation application after finding that a change of circumstances had occurred in consequence of the older of two children taking up residence with the father and thereby changing the equal time-sharing regime that had previously been implemented with respect to both of the children. After reviewing the submissions of both parties with respect to the potential application of sections 8 and 9 of the Guidelines, the British Columbia Court of Appeal concluded that additional evidence was required, and the application to vary should be remitted to the British Columbia Supreme Court for a new hearing to enable both parents to provide the necessary evidence and to permit a proper determination to be made as to whether the parenting arrangements fell within section 8 or 9 of the Guidelines, or some combination thereof and, if within section 9, to consider and weigh each of the factors listed in paragraphs (a), (b), and (c). It is noteworthy that *Wouters v Wouters* predates the judgment of the Supreme Court of Canada in *Contino v Leonelli-Contino*. Given the broad discretion conferred by section 9, and especially 9(c) of the Guidelines, as manifested by *Contino v Leonelli-Contino*, equitable and reasonably consistent results can be reached regardless of whether courts prefer the *Wouters v Wouters* or the *Hofsteede v Hofsteede* approach. A similar approach to *Wouters v Wouters* was endorsed by Vertes J in *McBride v McBride*,[182] wherein the following conclusions were expressed. If there is a hybrid of custody arrangements whereby one child is living in a shared-parenting arrangement but a second child is not, the court must segregate the determination of support for each child. A hybrid of custody arrangements calls for the application of different formulas under the *Federal Child Support Guidelines*. The court cannot simply mix different arrangements into a mélange and then apply one formula. Where section 9 of the Guidelines is triggered with respect to one child and section 5 of the Guidelines applies to the other child, the court cannot simply pull a number out of the air that appears to be fair. Although both sections 9 and 5 of the Guidelines confer a

---

179 2012 CarswellOnt 3465 (Sup Ct).
180 2013 ONSC 211.
181 [2006] BCJ No 523 (CA). See also *RB v LML*, 2014 BCSC 134.
182 [2001] NWTJ No 69 (SC).

discretion on the court, different factors must be taken into account under each section. In the more recent case of *TLR v RWR*,[183] wherein a shared-parenting arrangement involved the defendant's biological child and his step-child, Taylor J first examined section 5 of the *Federal Child Support Guidelines*. Having observed that the full table amount payable by the defendant for the two children would be $678 per month and for the one child would be $415 per month, Taylor J stated that the primary consideration in exercising the discretion conferred by section 5 to reduce a step-parent's obligation to support a child because of the biological parent's concurrent support obligation is fairness and societal expectations. Having regard to the defendant's close relationship with his stepchild, which would continue under a joint-custody and joint-guardianship order, and the absence of the biological father's involvement in the life of the child and his failure to pay court-ordered support, Taylor J concluded that the defendant's obligation to pay support for his stepchild should be reduced by only 10 percent of $263 per month, which total amount represents the difference between the table amount that he would be required to pay for his biological child and the additional amount that would be payable for a second child, his stepchild. The full table amount of child support was, therefore, reduced by $26 per month, leaving his Guidelines obligation for the two children at $652 per month. Justice Taylor then proceeded to apply section 9 of the Guidelines in light of *Contino v Leonelli-Contino* by effectuating a set-off of the table amount payable by the mother for her two biological children and thereafter increasing the balance pursuant to paragraphs (b) and (c) of section 9 of the Guidelines to take account of the fact that the children spent more time with their mother, who had the primary financial responsibility for them notwithstanding that she had fewer resources than the defendant, and to accommodate a comparable standard of living for the children in each of the two households.

J. UNDUE HARDSHIP

Section 10 of the *Federal Child Support Guidelines* confers a discretion on the court to deviate from the normal Guidelines amount of child support in cases of undue hardship. Undue hardship is a tough threshold to meet. Hardship is not sufficient. It must be hardship that is excessive, extreme, improper, unreasonable, or unjustified.[184] Absent a finding of undue hardship within

---

183 [2006] BCJ No 409 (SC).

184 *Hanmore v Hanmore*, [2000] AJ No 171 (CA); *Van Gool v Van Gool*, [1998] BCJ No 2513 (CA); *Schenkeveld v Schenkeveld*, [2002] MJ No 69 (CA); *Green v Green*, [2005] NJ No 165 (CA); *Locke v Goulding*, 2012 NLCA 8; *Barber v Barber*, 2011 SKQB 131.

the meaning of section 10 of the *Federal Child Support Guidelines*, bankruptcy does not relieve the obligor of child support obligations.[185] The undue hardship provisions of section 10 of the Guidelines may be invoked to increase or reduce the amount of child support that would otherwise be payable.[186] However, courts must be cautious where undue hardship is pleaded by a recipient spouse because of the potential for its abuse as an indirect vehicle for the payment of spousal support or for imposing the child support obligation on other members of the obligor's household.[187] The undue hardship provisions of section 10 of the Guidelines are inapplicable to claims for special or extraordinary expenses under section 7 of the Guidelines, being unnecessary to such claims by virtue of the broad discretion conferred on the court by that section.[188] The judgment of the Newfoundland and Labrador Court of Appeal in *Locke v Goulding*[189] provides an excellent review of the judicial discretion to deviate from the presumptive rule under section 3(1) of the *Federal Child Support Guidelines* in favour of the applicable table amount of child support on the basis of a finding of undue hardship within the meaning of section 10 of the Guidelines in circumstances where the support obligor is required to support children from successive marriages. The following principles have been distilled from the judgment:

1) Section 3(1)(a) of the Guidelines prescribes a presumptive rule in favour of the applicable table amount of child support.

2) A court may deviate from the table amount of child support on the basis of undue hardship if the requirements of section 10 of the Guidelines are satisfied.

3) In the absence of a finding of undue hardship under section 10 of the Guidelines, a court has no jurisdiction to reduce the applicable provincial table amount of support payable to children of the parent's first marriage by taking account of his or her legal obligation to support children born of a second marriage. Before a court can find undue hardship under section 10(2)(d) of the Guidelines on the basis that a parent must also support the children of a second marriage, there must be cogent and persuasive evidence that undue hardship would result from an order for the table amount of child support to be paid for the children of the first marriage. If a parent remarries and has more children when he or she already has a responsibility to support the children from a previous marriage,

---

185   *Court v McQuaid*, [2005] PEIJ No 24 (SCTD).
186   *Gandy v Gandy*, [2000] BCJ No 2294 (SC).
187   *Middleton v MacPherson*, [1997] AJ No 614 (QB).
188   *Dean v Friesen*, [1999] SJ No 424 (QB).
189   2012 NLCA 8.

that parent is ordinarily expected to organize his or her affairs so as to honour the pre-existing obligation.

4) A claim of undue hardship under section 10 of the Guidelines should be included in the pleadings and supported by full financial disclosure.

5) The onus of proving undue hardship falls upon the party who invokes section 10 of the Guidelines.

6) A judicial determination under section 10 of the Guidelines presupposes a consideration of all relevant evidence, findings of fact being made, and the application of the criteria set out in that section.

7) An undue hardship analysis involves several steps. The table amount of child support payable under section 3(1) of the Guidelines must first be determined. Then, the evidence in support of the claim for undue hardship must be evaluated in relation to the circumstances listed under section 10(2) of the Guidelines or any other circumstances (as the list is not exhaustive) that reasonably invite consideration of undue hardship. This evaluation must recognize that undue hardship is a high threshold to meet. It goes beyond difficulty or inconvenience; the hardship must be "excessive, extreme, improper, unreasonable, [or] unjustified." Section 10(2) of the Guidelines sets out circumstances that *may* constitute undue hardship within the meaning of section 10(1) of the Guidelines. Merely showing that one of the circumstances listed in section 10(2) exists is not sufficient to meet the requirement of establishing undue hardship. The applicant must show that the circumstances relied upon *will* create undue hardship if the table amount of child support is ordered. The claimant must prove that his or her obligations and expenses cannot be reasonably managed so as to enable him or her to pay the table amount of child support and how and why it is that he or she will suffer undue hardship if ordered to pay the table amount of child support. If the claimant is unable to prove this, his or her claim of undue hardship must fail at this stage. A general reference to the overall expense of a new household will not suffice to support a claim of undue hardship; there must be full disclosure of the support obligor's household income and expenses.

8) If the evidence supports a finding of undue hardship under section 10(2) of the Guidelines, the court *must* undertake a standards-of-living comparison under section 10(3) of the Guidelines. A comparison of the standard of living of the two households will be undertaken pursuant to section 10(3) of the Guidelines only when there has been a prior determination of undue hardship.

9) An optional test for conducting a standards-of-living comparison is found in Schedule II of the Guidelines. Without attempting to catalogue the factors that inform a standards-of-living comparison, it involves

more than a straightforward comparison of household incomes. Even Schedule II contemplates imputing income to any member of the household, which includes the spouse of a payor parent. But Schedule II does not account for all factors relevant to one's standard of living. The value of a two-parent household as opposed to a single-parent household, high medical costs, or a multitude of other circumstances could well inform a standards-of-living comparison.

10) If the court determines that, after paying the table amount of child support, the standard of living of the support obligor's household would remain higher than (or perhaps equal to) that of the recipient household, the claim must be denied. Furthermore, the use of the word "may" in section 10(1) of the Guidelines clearly demonstrates that any deviation from the table amount of child support is discretionary, even if the court finds undue hardship and a lower standard of living in the obligor's household.

11) If a court ultimately exercises its discretion and grants the claim for undue hardship, section 10(6) of the Guidelines requires the court to record its reasons for doing so.

Section 10(2) of the Guidelines sets out the following non-exhaustive list of five circumstances that may constitute undue hardship:

(a) the spouse has responsibility for an unusually high level of debts reasonably incurred to support the spouses and their children prior to the separation or to earn a living;

(b) the spouse has unusually high expenses in relation to exercising access to the child;

(c) the spouse has a legal duty under a judgment, order or written separation agreement to support any person;

(d) the spouse has a legal duty to support any child, other than a child of the marriage, who is
   (i) under the age of majority, or
   (ii) the age of majority or over but is unable, by reason of illness, disability, or other cause to obtain the necessaries of life; and

(e) the spouse has a legal duty to support any person who is unable to obtain the necessaries of life due to an illness or disability.

Undue hardship may arise from a combination of the circumstances listed under paragraphs (a) to (e) of subsection 10(2) of the *Federal Child Support Guidelines*[190] or from a combination of circumstances, some of which fall

---

190   *MacFarlane v MacFarlane*, [1999] BCJ No 3008 (SC); *Deveau v Groskopf*, [2000] SJ No 281 (QB); *Kaatz v Kaatz*, [2001] SJ No 661 (QB).

within the categories listed while others fall outside.[191] All five circumstances listed under section 10(2) of the Guidelines relate in one way or another to the financial costs associated with past or present obligations to children or other family members. The circumstances listed in section 10(2) of the Guidelines are not exhaustive, nor does their existence mandate a conclusion that undue hardship exists. Before adding to the list, however, a court must be satisfied that the circumstances pleaded as constituting undue hardship are as serious, exceptional, or excessive as those listed in section 10(2) of the Guidelines.[192] Obligors have frequently asserted undue hardship as a consequence of their assumption of new family support obligations. Subjective perceptions of undue hardship do not satisfy the requirements of section 10 of the Guidelines. Sequential families may inevitably introduce some degree of hardship, but undue hardship is not to be equated with financial difficulty, budgetary cutbacks, or financial restraints or re-evaluations. As stated previously, the hardship must be excessive or extreme. The fact that the standard of living in the obligor's household is lower than that in the recipient household does not, of itself, constitute evidence of undue hardship.[193]

Where undue hardship is found, a court should seek to ensure as much as possible that the children of both families are treated equitably.[194] In the absence of undue hardship as defined above, the "first in time prevails" as between the children of sequential families.[195]

Pursuant to section 10(5) of the *Federal Child Support Guidelines*, where the court orders a different amount of child support after making a finding of undue hardship under section 10(1) of the Guidelines, it may specify, in the child support order, a reasonable time for the satisfaction of any obligation arising from the circumstances that cause undue hardship and the amount payable at the end of that time. This provision is likely to be most frequently invoked in situations where unusually high family debts are the cause of the hardship[196] but it is by no means expressly confined to those

---

191 *Goudie v Buchanan*, [2001] NJ No 187 (UFC) (application under *Newfoundland Child Support Guidelines*); *Hollett-Collins v Hollett*, [2002] NJ No 292 (SC); *Wainman v Clairmont*, [2004] NSJ No 69 (SC).

192 *Adams v Loov*, [1998] AJ No 660 (QB); *Goudie v Buchanan*, [2001] NJ No 187 (UFC).

193 *Van Gool v Van Gool*, [1998] BCJ No 2513 (CA); *Schenkeveld v Schenkeveld*, [2002] MJ No 69 (CA); *Steele v Koppanyi*, [2002] MJ No 201 (CA); *Locke v Goulding*, 2012 NLCA 8; *Gaetz v Gaetz*, [2001] NSJ No 131 (CA); *Ross v Ross*, [2001] NSJ No 171 (CA); *Birss v Birss*, [2000] OJ No 3692 (Div Ct); *Messier v Baines*, [1997] SJ No 627 (QB); *Barber v Barber*, 2011 SKQB 131.

194 *Messier v Baines*, [1997] SJ No 627 (QB); *Douglas v Ward*, [2006] SJ No 57 (QB).

195 *Schenkeveld v Schenkeveld*, [2002] MJ No 69 (CA); *Steele v Koppanyi*, [2002] MJ No 201 (CA); *Locke v Goulding*, 2012 NLCA 8.

196 *Aker v Howard*, [1998] OJ No 5562 (Gen Div).

situations. In *Bourque v Phillips*,[197] undue hardship was found under section 10(2)(c)of the *Nova Scotia Child Support Guidelines*, where the father was obliged to pay fixed-term spousal support under a separation agreement, but the court concluded that the undue hardship would cease to exist once the time-limited spousal support obligation terminated.

A reduction of the applicable table amount of child support on the basis of unusually high access expenses is permissible under the undue hardship provisions of section 10 of the *Federal Child Support Guidelines*. Nothing in the Guidelines, however, authorizes a court to order a custodial parent to make a financial contribution towards access costs.[198] Prior to the implementation of the *Federal Child Support Guidelines* on 1 May 1997, a court could make an order for the payment of access costs pursuant to either section 15(4) or section 16(6) of the *Divorce Act*.[199] It is questionable whether section 10 of the *Federal Child Support Guidelines* impliedly limits this jurisdiction, given that the provisions of section 15(4) are currently mirrored in section 15.1(4) of the *Divorce Act*, as amended by the SC 1997, c 1, and section 16(6) of the *Divorce Act* is unaffected by the 1997 amendments.[200] This issue was not specifically addressed in *Curniski v Aubert*,[201] wherein the custodial parent was ordered to pay the transportation expenses of the children to enable them to visit the non-custodial parent, but the court refused to set off these expenses against the court-ordered child support payments. In *Holtskog v Holtskog*,[202] the Saskatchewan Court of Appeal concluded that the trial judge erred in ordering the custodial parent to contribute one-half of the monthly airfare arising from extraprovincial access in light of the non-custodial parent's failure to substantiate the plea of unusually high access expenses generating undue hardship within the meaning of section 10 of the Guidelines. In *RBN v MJN*,[203] Campbell J, of the Nova Scotia Supreme Court, questioned whether *Holtskog v Holtskog* precluded an order for the payment or sharing of access costs in the absence of a finding of undue hardship. In ordering the custodial parent to pay all of the extraprovincial access transportation costs resulting from her relocation of the children, Campbell J stated that the authority to order a contribution to access costs comes from the *Divorce Act* itself, both under section 15.1(4), which permits the court to impose terms, conditions,

---

197 [2000] NSJ No 13 (SC).

198 *South v South*, [1998] BCJ No 962 (SC).

199 RSC 1985 (2d Supp), c 3.

200 See *Ruel v Ruel*, [2006] AJ No 621 (CA); *Lebouthillier v Manning*, 2014 ONSC 4081; *MacPhail v MacPhail*, [2000] PEIJ No 41 (SCTD). Compare *Greene v Greene*, 2010 BCCA 595.

201 [1998] SJ No 825 (QB).

202 [1999] SJ No 304 (CA). See also *Greene v Greene*, 2010 BCCA 595.

203 [2002] NSJ No 530 (SC); see also *Morrone v Morrone*, [2007] OJ No 5341 (Sup Ct).

or restrictions in connection with a support order, and under section 16(6) of the *Divorce Act*, which provides a similar jurisdiction with respect to a custody order. As Campbell J observes, "there is no logical reason to deny a claim for a contribution or full payment of access costs by the custodial parent merely because the undue hardship claim failed."[204]

K. EFFECT OF ORDER OR AGREEMENT

Contractual covenants do not suffice to negate child support obligations that would otherwise ensue from the parent-child relationship.[205] Where a separation agreement purports to fix the amount of child support payable, a material change since the execution of the agreement is not required before a judicial review of child support can be undertaken in accordance with the *Federal Child Support Guidelines*.[206] Sections 15.1(5) to (8) and sections 17(6.2) to (6.5) of the *Divorce Act* confer limited powers on parents to deviate from their child support obligations as set out in the *Federal Child Support Guidelines*.[207]

Given that these provisions are substantially similar, except insofar as section 15.1 relates to applications for an original child support order whereas section 17 relates to applications for the variation of an existing order, it will suffice for the purposes of this analysis if section 15.1 is reproduced. Section 15.1 reads as follows:

Child support order

15.1 (1) A court of competent jurisdiction may, on application by either or both spouses, make an order requiring a spouse to pay for the support of any or all children of the marriage.

Interim order

(2) Where an application is made under subsection (1), the court may, on application by either or both spouses, make an interim order requiring a spouse to pay for the support of any or all children of the marriage, pending the determination of the application under subsection (1).

---

204 *RBN v MJN*, [2002] NSJ No 530 (SC) at para 37.
205 See *Chartier v Chartier*, [1998] SCJ No 79; *Richardson v Richardson*, [1987] 1 SCR 857; *Doe v Alberta*, 2007 ABCA 50; *Kopp v Kopp*, 2012 BCCA 140; *NC v ES*, 2014 NBQB 272; *CMM v DGC*, 2015 ONSC 1815 (application by child under *Family Law Act*); *Denis v Denis*, 2012 SKQB 49. And see Chapter 8, Section N(7).
206 *Kopp v Kopp*, 2012 BCCA 140.
207 *Gobeil v Gobeil*, [2007] MJ No 19 (CA); *Kudoba v Kudoba*, [2007] OJ No 3765 (Sup Ct).

424 CANADIAN FAMILY LAW

Guidelines apply

(3) A court making an order under subsection (1) or an interim order under subsection (2) shall do so in accordance with the applicable guidelines.

Terms and conditions

(4) The court may make an order under subsection (1) or an interim order under subsection (2) for a definite or indefinite period or until a specified event occurs, and may impose terms, conditions or restrictions in connection with the order or interim order as it thinks fit and just.

Court may take agreement, etc., into account

(5) Notwithstanding subsection (3), a court may award an amount that is different from the amount that would be determined in accordance with the applicable guidelines if the court is satisfied

(a) that special provisions in an order, a judgment or a written agreement respecting the financial obligations of the spouses, or the division or transfer of their property, directly or indirectly benefit a child, or that special provisions have otherwise been made for the benefit of a child; and

(b) that the application of the applicable guidelines would result in an amount of child support that is inequitable given those special provisions.

Reasons

(6) Where the court awards, pursuant to subsection (5), an amount that is different from the amount that would be determined in accordance with the applicable guidelines, the court shall record its reasons for having done so.

Consent orders

(7) Notwithstanding subsection (3), a court may award an amount that is different from the amount that would be determined in accordance with the applicable guidelines on the consent of both spouses if it is satisfied that reasonable arrangements have been made for the support of the child to whom the order relates.

Reasonable arrangements

(8) For the purposes of subsection (7), in determining whether reasonable arrangements have been made for the support of a child, the court shall have regard to the applicable guidelines. However, the court shall not consider the arrangements to be unreasonable solely because the amount of support agreed to is not the same as the amount that would otherwise have been determined in accordance with the applicable guidelines.

It is not clear whether the term "special provisions" in sections 15(1)(5)(a) and 17(6.2)(a) of the *Divorce Act* means "particular" or "out of the ordinary or unusual."[208] It has been generally acknowledged, however, that "special provisions" must be of a nature that, in whole or in part, replace the need for ongoing child support.[209]

Courts will be called upon to examine a wide variety of agreements to determine whether they contain "special provisions" within the meaning of sections 15.1(5) and 17(6.2) of the *Divorce Act*. Some agreements will have been prepared by legal counsel; others will not. Some will have been entered before, and others after, the Guidelines were implemented. Some will expressly purport to set out "special provisions"; others will not. Some agreements will provide more, others will provide less, than the amounts payable under the Guidelines. The particular circumstances facing each family and their children will obviously differ from case to case. Consequently, the determination whether an agreement contains "special provisions" will depend on the unique circumstances of the individual case.[210]

An agreement made, with knowledge of the Guidelines, that provides for child support in an amount greater than the amount payable under the Guidelines may, in itself, be a "special provision."[211]

The term "inequitable" in sections 15(1)(5)(b) and 17(6.2)(b) of the *Divorce Act* is capable of several meanings depending on the subject of comparison. It could refer to inequity as between the parties, or as between a child and parent, or as between these parties and others in the community to whom the Guidelines apply. The last construction is raised by section 1(d) of the Guidelines, which defines one of their objectives as being "to ensure consistent treatment of spouses and children who are in similar circumstances." Notwithstanding this declared objective, the term "inequitable" relates to the parties and requires consideration of both the circumstances giving rise to the written agreement or order and their circumstances at the time of the application. This interpretation recognizes the give and take of settlement negotiations and the interrelationship of the terms reflected in an agreement or order.[212]

---

208 *Wang v Wang*, [1997] BCJ No 1678 (SC), Saunders J, aff'd [1998] BCJ No 1966 (CA); compare *Wright v Zaver*, [2002] OJ No 1098 (CA); see also *Danchuk v Danchuk*, [2001] BCJ No 755 (CA).

209 *Wright v Zaver*, [2002] OJ No 1098 (CA).

210 *Finney v Finney*, [1998] BCJ No 1848 (SC).

211 *Ibid*; compare *Biggar v Biggar*, [1998] SJ No 570 (QB).

212 *Wang v Wang*, [1997] BCJ No 1678 (SC); *Eilers v Eilers*, [1998] BCJ No 1021 (SC); *Epp v Robertson*, [1998] SJ No 684 (QB).

In the absence of evidence of undue hardship within the meaning of section 10 of the *Federal Child Support Guidelines*, a pre-existing spousal agreement with special provisions that benefit the children constitutes no bar to the application of the Guidelines where the needs and circumstances of the children have changed since the agreement and where no inequitable consequences would ensue from the application of the Guidelines in these circumstances.[213]

A lump sum payment, which purports to constitute a final and binding resolution of child support rights and obligations, does not preclude a subsequent application for periodic support under the Guidelines, although it may constitute a "special provision" for the benefit of the child that renders inequitable an order for the future payment of the full monthly table amount of child support under the Guidelines.[214]

In addressing sections 15.1(5) and 17(6.2) of the *Divorce Act*, whereby special provisions in a written agreement or order that directly benefit a child may justify deviation from the *Federal Child Support Guidelines* but only if the application of the Guidelines would be inequitable having regard to the special provisions, the court must first decide whether it should exercise its discretion not to apply the *Federal Child Support Guidelines*. If it concludes that the Guidelines should be applied, the court must then decide whether an amount less than that required by the Guidelines should be ordered on the basis that the written agreement contains special provisions that directly or indirectly benefit the child so as to render application of the Guidelines inequitable within the meaning of section 15.1(5) of the *Divorce Act*. A six-step procedure has been formulated by Martinson J, of the British Columbia Supreme Court, to address these two issues:

1) identify the child support provisions in the agreement;
2) identify any special provisions in the agreement as defined in section 15.1(5) of the *Divorce Act*;
3) determine the Guidelines amount as though there were no separation agreement;
4) compare the Guidelines amount to the provisions of the separation agreement to see whether reasonable arrangements have been made in light of the Guidelines standard;
5) if reasonable arrangements have been made, the court will decline to make an order under the Guidelines, and the terms of the separation

---

213   *Fisher v Heron*, [1997] PEIJ No 77 (SCTD). See also *Greene v Greene*, 2010 BCCA 595.
214   *MacKay v Bucher*, [2001] NSJ No 326 (CA); *Wright v Zaver*, [2002] OJ No 1098 (CA).

agreement will prevail; if reasonable arrangements have not been made, the Guidelines should be addressed;

6) in addressing the Guidelines, compare the Guidelines amount to the special provisions and child support provisions to see if an order different from the Guidelines amount should be ordered; if it should be, decide what amount is appropriate; if it should not be, apply the Guidelines amount determined in the third step.[215]

Spousal reapportionment of property, transfers of property, or the payment of a substantial lump sum may constitute examples of "special provisions" that benefit the children and justify deviation from the Guidelines under sections 15.1(5) and 17(6.2) of the *Divorce Act*.[216] Such deviation will only be justified, however, where the special provisions replace or reduce the need for ongoing child support.[217]

A custodial parent's willingness to accept less child support than the amount provided by the Guidelines cannot justify a court deviating from the Guidelines where no compensatory benefits are conferred on the children.[218]

The phrase "or that special provisions have otherwise been made for the benefit of the child" in sections 15.1(5)(a) and 17(6.2)(a) of the *Divorce Act* does not specifically require that special provisions be made by the divorcing or divorced spouses. A family trust established by a parent[219] or by a grandparent[220] may satisfy either section.

Where a court deviates from the Guidelines pursuant to section 15.1 (5) or section 17(6.2) of the *Divorce Act*, the court must record its reasons for doing so.[221]

Sections 15.1(7) and (8) and 17(6.4) and (6.5) of the *Divorce Act* empower a court to grant a consent order for child support that deviates from the *Federal Child Support Guidelines* if the court is satisfied that reasonable arrangements have been made for the support of the child to whom the order relates. It has been suggested that a court should be loath to change negotiated child support arrangements to which the parents wish to adhere, even though they provide an amount of support modestly lower than the applicable table amount under the Guidelines.[222] It is submitted, however, that

---

215 *Baum v Baum*, [1999] BCJ No 3025 (SC).

216 *Fonseca v Fonseca*, [1998] BCJ No 2772 (SC); *Handy v Handy*, [1999] BCJ No 6 (SC).

217 *Hall v Hall*, [1997] BCJ No 1191 (SC); *Garard v Garard*, [1998] BCJ No 2076 (CA); *Wright v Zaver*, [2002] OJ No 1098 (CA).

218 *Howe v Kendall*, [1997] NSJ No 310 (SC).

219 *Davidson v Davidson*, [1998] AJ No 1040 (QB).

220 See *Tauber v Tauber*, [1999] OJ No 359 (Gen Div).

221 *Divorce Act*, RSC 1985 (2d Supp), c 3, ss 15.1(6) and 17(6.3).

222 *McIllwraith v McIllwraith*, [1999] NBJ No 129 (QB).

courts should be cautious about allowing parents the freedom to pay or receive lower periodic child support payments than those required by the applicable provincial or territorial table, unless there are circumstances other than the agreement itself that warrant deviation from the table amount. On the other hand, the Guidelines should not blind the courts to the realities of comprehensive negotiations, which lead the parties to a complex settlement of their financial affairs in which the components are finely balanced, and alteration of one term may upset the balance and thereby render the remaining terms unfair.[223]

With respect to consent orders, a finding under section 15.1(7) of the *Divorce Act* that reasonable arrangements have been made for the support of a child to whom the order relates presupposes that adequate information has been provided to the court about the economic and other circumstances of the spouses and the children, including any special or extraordinary expenses likely to be incurred on behalf of the children. Sufficient evidence must be presented to the court to enable it to make an informed judgment. A bald assertion that reasonable arrangements have been made for the support of a child does not warrant a consent order that deviates from the Guidelines. Such a bald assertion is not evidence but a conclusion to be determined by the court after an evaluation of any supporting evidence.[224]

L. SPECIAL AND EXTRAORDINARY EXPENSES[225]

1) General

Section 7 of the *Federal Child Support Guidelines* empowers a court to grant an order for designated special or extraordinary expenses relating to a child of the marriage. An order for contribution to special and extraordinary expenses under section 7 of the Guidelines is discretionary as to both entitlement and amount.[226] The list of expenses under section 7 of the Guidelines is exhaustive. Expenses that fall outside the categories specified cannot be the subject of any order. The expenses must be necessary in light of the child's

---

223 *Eilers v Eilers*, [1998] BCJ No 1021 (SC).

224 Compare *Dumas v Dumas* (1992), 43 RFL (3d) 260 (Alta QB), applying *Divorce Act*, s 11(1)(b); see, generally, Chapter 7, Section F(3).

225 See Elizabeth Jollimore, "A Practitioner's Guide to Presenting Applications under Section 7 of the *Federal Child Support Guidelines*" (Paper presented to Federation of Law Societies, National Family Law Program, Muskoka, Ontario, July 2008). See also Len Fishman, "2006 Amendments to the *Federal Child Support Guidelines*," Department of Justice Canada, online: www.justice.gc.ca/eng/fl-df/spousal-epoux/topic-theme/fed1.html.

226 *Terry v Moyo*, 2013 ONCJ 364.

best interests.[227] The expenses must also be reasonable, having regard to the means of the spouses and child and the family's previous spending pattern.[228] The family's pre-separation spending pattern may need to be re-assessed in light of the increased costs generated by the split into two households. Relevant factors to be considered in determining whether special or extraordinary expenses are reasonable include (1) the combined income of the parents; (2) the fact that two households must be maintained; (3) the extent of the expenses in relation to the combined income level of the parents; (4) the debts of the parents; (5) any prospect for a decline or increase in the parents' means in the near future; and (6) whether the other parent was consulted prior to the expenses being incurred.[229]

Child-care expenses, dental and medical insurance premiums, health care expenses, and post-secondary education expenses, if necessary and reasonable, will be ordinarily shared in proportion to the respective parental incomes. These expenses need not be "extraordinary" in order to satisfy the requirements of section 7 of the Guidelines.[230] Expenses relating to primary or secondary school or special educational needs and expenses for extracurricular activities must be "extraordinary" in order to trigger an order under section 7 of the Guidelines.[231] A contribution to affordable "special" (as distinct from "extraordinary") expenses listed under section 7(1) of the *Federal Child Support Guidelines* is generally ordered more or less as a routine matter where these expenses are sought in a child support proceeding.[232]

The test for awarding section 7 expenses was described by the Ontario Court of Appeal in *Titova v Titov* as follows:

> In awarding s. 7 special and extraordinary expenses, the trial judge calculates each party's income for child support purposes, determines whether the claimed expenses fall within one of the enumerated categories of s. 7 of the Guidelines, determines whether the claimed expenses are necessary "in relation to the child's best interests" and are reasonable "in relation to the means of the spouses and those of the child and to the family's spending pattern prior to the separation." If the expenses fall under s. 7(1)(d) or

---

227 *Holeman v Holeman*, [2006] MJ No 456 (QB) (private school); *JC v MC*, 2014 NBQB 161; see also *Fritz v Tate*, [2006] NJ No 336 (UFC).

228 *JC v MC*, 2014 NBQB 161; *TH v WH*, [2007] NSJ No 27 (SC); *Park v Thompson*, [2005] OJ No 1695 (CA); *Jones v Durston*, 2012 ONSC 3073.

229 *Holeman v Holeman*, [2006] MJ No 456 (QB), citing *Bland v Bland*, [1999] AJ No 344 (QB) and *Correia v Correia*, [2002] MJ No 248 (QB).

230 *MacKinnon v MacKinnon*, [2005] OJ No 1552 (CA).

231 See Section L(5), below in this chapter.

232 *Slade v Slade*, [2001] NJ No 5 (CA); *Sharf v Sharf*, [2000] OJ No 4052 (Sup Ct).

(f) of the Guidelines, the trial judge determines whether the expenses are "extraordinary".[233]

In the past, there has been a lack of judicial consistency in the interpretation accorded to the term "extraordinary expenses" under paragraph 7(1)(d) (extraordinary education expenses) and paragraph 7(1)(f) (extraordinary expenses for extracurricular activities) of the *Federal Child Support Guidelines*.[234] To promote clarity and consistency, section 7 of the *Federal Child Support Guidelines* has been amended as of 1 May 2006 by SOR/2005-400, to include subsection 7(1.1), which sets out a specific two-part definition of "extraordinary expenses."[235] Pursuant to paragraph 7(1.1)(a), expenses are extraordinary if they exceed an amount that the requesting spouse can reasonably cover, taking into account that spouse's income and the basic amount of child support received (usually the applicable table amount). Where paragraph 7(1.1) (a) is inapplicable because the expenses do not exceed the amount that the requesting spouse can reasonably cover, paragraph 7(1.1)(b) directs the court to determine whether the expenses are extraordinary having regard to the following five factors:

(i)   the amount of the expense in relation to the income of the spouse requesting the amount (including the child support amount);

(ii)   the nature and number of the educational programs and extracurricular activities;

(iii) any special needs and talents of the child or children;

(iv)   the overall costs of the programs and activities; and

(v)   any other similar factor that the court considers relevant.

The definition of "extraordinary expenses" under section 7(1.1) of the amended *Federal Child Support Guidelines* largely mirrors the definition adopted in 2001 under paragraph 7(1.1) of the *Manitoba Child Support Guidelines*.[236] The additional requirements of necessity and reasonableness within the meaning of subsection 7(1) of the *Federal Child Support Guidelines* are unaffected by

---

233   2012 ONCA 864; see also *Williams v Steinwand*, 2014 NWTSC 74; *MacNeil v MacNeil*, 2013 ONSC 7012.

234   See Julien D Payne & Marilyn A Payne, *Child Support Guidelines in Canada, 2012* (Toronto: Irwin Law, 2012) at 286–87.

235   As to ongoing judicial uncertainty and lack of consistency, see *Simpson v Trowsdale*, [2007] PEIJ No 7 (SCTD), MacDonald J.

236   See Len Fishman, "2006 Amendments to the *Federal Child Support Guidelines*," Department of Justice Canada, online: www.justice.gc.ca/eng/fl-df/spousal-epoux/topic-theme/fed1.html. See *Correia v Correia*, [2002] MJ No 248 (QB); *Holeman v Holeman*, [2006] MJ No 456 (QB); *Gard v Gard*, 2013 MBQB 128. See also *DMCT v LKS*, 2008 NSCA 61, *Simpson v Trowsdale*, 2007 PESCTD 3.

the explicit definition of "extraordinary expenses" under paragraph 7(1.1) of the Guidelines. Only if the court concludes that an expense is extraordinary, will the court turn its attention to the additional requirements of necessity and reasonableness within the meaning of subsection 7(1) of the *Federal Child Support Guidelines.*[237]

In determining the amount of an expense, section 7(3) of the Guidelines requires the court to take into account any subsidies, benefits, and income tax deductions or credits that are available with respect to the expense. Contributions to expenses made by family relatives or community groups are taken into account.[238] Eligibility for income tax relief must be taken into account, even if such relief is not sought by the recipient spouse.[239] Although a court must take the income tax implications into account, it may be impossible to quantify this until the end of the tax year. One way of addressing this problem is for the court to direct each parent to pay his or her proportionate share of the expenses when they fall due and to later share in the tax benefit on the same proportionate basis, when it is ascertained.[240] In order to accommodate this result, the court may direct the parties to exchange their income tax returns within a specified time after filing.[241]

Pursuant to section 13(e) of the *Federal Child Support Guidelines*, where a court orders the payment of special or extraordinary expenses, the particulars of the expense must be specified in the order, including the child to whom the expense relates, the amount of the expense, or where the amount cannot be determined, the proportion to be paid in relation to the expenses.[242]

An order for the payment of special or extraordinary expenses need not specify periodic payments on a regular basis. The expenses may be isolated, sporadic, or recurring at irregular intervals. Pursuant to section 11 of the *Federal Child Support Guidelines*, a court may require expenses to be discharged on a periodic basis or by a lump sum or by a combination of both. Where the expenses cannot be predetermined, a court may simply order that all or a fixed percentage of the expenses shall be paid after a proper account is presented, although such an order may trigger difficulty if automatic enforcement processes are invoked to secure due compliance with the order.

---

237 *Chambers v Chambers*, [2004] MJ No 397 (QB); *Gard v Gard*, 2013 MBQB 128.

238 *Giles v Villeneuve*, [1998] OJ No 4492 (Gen Div).

239 *Laskosky v Laskosky*, [1999] AJ No 131 (QB); *Skiba v Skiba*, [2000] OJ No 76 (Sup Ct); *Leibel v Davis*, [2001] SJ No 208 (QB); compare *Mundle v Mundle*, [2001] NSJ No 111 (SC).

240 *Murphy v Murphy*, [1998] NJ No 304 (SC); compare *Jackson v Punga*, [1998] SJ No 633 (QB) (order for adjustment of payments either by additional disbursement or rebate after requisite tax calculations).

241 *Murphy v Murphy*, [1998] NJ No 304 (SC).

242 See *MacKinnon v MacKinnon*, 2015 NBQB 55.

2) Child-Care Expenses

Section 7 of the *Federal Child Support Guidelines* confers a discretion on the court to order the payment of all or part of child-care expenses incurred as a result of the custodial parent's employment, illness, disability, or education or training for employment. No corresponding discretion is conferred on the court where child-care expenses are incurred for the above reasons by a non-custodial parent.[243] Child-care expenses may be denied under section 7 of the Guidelines where the non-custodial parent's family is able to provide child care,[244] although a court may refuse to disturb existing daycare arrangements that have worked well for a substantial period of time.[245] Section 7 of the Guidelines does not cover babysitting expenses that are incidental to a custodial parent's recreational activities.[246] A contribution to child-care expenses may be reduced to take account of child-connected expenses incurred by the contributing spouse.[247] In situations where resources are available, the court will allow child-care costs for an employed parent as a legitimate expense.[248] Even though child care may be a necessity, the amount of the non-custodial parent's contribution may be limited by the ability to contribute.[249] A court should refuse to order a contribution towards childcare expenses where the non-custodial parent lacks the financial ability to meet this additional obligation.[250] An application for a contribution to childcare costs may also be denied because of the non-custodial parent's access costs.[251] Where child-care costs are found excessive, the court may reduce the amount before calculating the respective contributions of each spouse or former spouse to these costs.[252] A claim for child-care expenses may be denied where the child is twelve years of age and, therefore, old enough to care for himself or herself,[253] but a twelve-year-old child should not be expected to regularly babysit a younger sibling in order to reduce child-care expenses.[254] Child-care expenses, like health-related expenses and expenses for

---

243   *SM v RP*, [1998] QJ No 4119 (SC).

244   *Shipka v Shipka*, [2001] AJ No 213 (QB); compare *ECH v WEH*, [2003] BCJ No 715 (SC).

245   *Erickson v Erickson*, [2001] BCJ No 71 (SC).

246   *Forrester v Forrester*, [1997] OJ No 3437 (Gen Div).

247   *Enman v Enman*, [2000] PEIJ No 48 (SCTD).

248   *Murray v Murray* (1991), 35 RFL (3d) 449 (Alta QB).

249   *Zsiak v Bell*, [1998] BCJ No 2233 (SC); *Wedsworth v Wedsworth*, 2000 NSCA 108.

250   *Kennedy v Kennedy*, [1997] NSJ No 450 (Fam Ct).

251   *Chaput v Chaput*, [1997] OJ No 4924 (Gen Div); *Keller v Black*, [2000] OJ No 79 (Sup Ct).

252   *Tallman v Tomke*, [1997] AJ No 682 (QB); *Kramer v Kramer*, [1999] MJ No 338 (QB).

253   *Acorn v DeRoche*, [1997] PEIJ No 82 (SCTD); compare *Gormley v Gormley*, [1999] PEIJ No 83 (SCTD) (contribution to child-care expenses for eleven-year-old child deemed appropriate).

254   *Levesque v Levesque*, [1999] OJ No 3056 (Sup Ct).

post-secondary education, do not need to be extraordinary in order to satisfy the requirements of section 7(1)(a) of the *Federal Child Support Guidelines*.[255] Child-care costs can vary substantially according to the age of the child, the type of care, whether the care is full-time or part-time, and the ability to pay, but they must be reasonable and necessary. Section 7(1) of the *Federal Child Support Guidelines* specifically limits the judicial discretion to provide for the payment of all or any expenses by requiring the court to take into account the necessity of the expense in relation to the child's best interests and the reasonableness of the expense, having regard to the means of the spouses and those of the child and to the family's spending pattern before the separation.[256] Notwithstanding the last mentioned consideration, courts will, no doubt, take account of reasonable and necessary child-care expenses triggered by the fact of separation.

3) Medical and Dental Insurance; Medical, Dental, or Health-Related Expenses

Section 6 of the *Federal Child Support Guidelines* provides that, in making a child support order, where medical or dental insurance coverage is available to either or both[257] of the spouses or former spouses through his or her employer or otherwise at a reasonable rate, the court may order that coverage be acquired or continued.[258] Child support orders normally include a provision whereby health insurance coverage will be maintained for eligible dependants. Where this is placed at risk by an obligor's threat to quit employment, the court may order an additional amount of support to replace the health insurance coverage.[259]

Where there is existing medical and dental insurance coverage through employment, its continuance should be virtually automatic.[260] The court may grant an order under section 6 of the *Federal Child Support Guidelines* for

---

255 *Tang v Tang*, [1998] BCJ No 2890 (SC); *Crawley v Tobin*, [1998] NJ No 293 (SC); *Smith v Smith*, [2001] NSJ No 505 (SC).

256 *Wait v Wait*, [2000] BCJ No 1282 (CA) (custodial parent entitled to contribution from non-custodial parent towards child's daycare expense but not entitled to incur higher expenses by enrolling child in Montessori school); *Kramer v Kramer*, [1999] MJ No 338 (QB).

257 *Young v Vincent*, [1997] NSJ No 163 (TD).

258 *Colbourne v Colbourne*, 2014 ABQB 547; *Dempsey v Dempsey*, [1997] NSJ No 327 (TD); *Kingston v Kelly*, [1999] PEIJ No 52 (SCTD) (order under *PEI Child Support Guidelines*); *Martel v Martel*, [2000] SJ No 322 (QB); compare *MDL v CR*, [2004] SJ No 326 (QB).

259 *Dickinson v Dickinson*, [1998] OJ No 4815 (Gen Div).

260 *Robski v Robski*, [1997] NSJ No 444 (TD).

the reinstatement of cancelled medical and dental insurance available to a spouse through employment.[261]

Section 6 is complemented by sections 7(1)(b) and (c) of the *Federal Child Support Guidelines*, which provide that in a child support order the court may, on either spouse's or former spouse's request, provide for the payment of all or a portion of the following expenses, taking into account the necessity of the expenses in relation to the child's best interests and the reasonableness of the expenses, having regard to the means of the spouses and the family's pre-separation spending pattern:

(b) that portion of the medical and dental insurance premiums attributable to the child;[262] and

(c) health-related expenses that exceed insurance reimbursement by at least $100 annually,[263] including orthodontic treatment;[264] professional counselling provided by a psychologist, social worker, psychiatrist, or any other person;[265] physiotherapy, occupational therapy, speech therapy;[266] and prescription drugs, hearing aids, glasses, and contact lenses . . . .

Section 6 of the *Federal Child Support Guidelines* should be utilized whenever possible before resorting to section 7 of the Guidelines, because section 6 provides a significant benefit to children at little or no expense to the parents in that the insurance premiums, if any, will normally be significantly less than the amount of the expenses that would otherwise be incurred if no insurance coverage were available.[267] Any expenses in excess of those reimbursed through a medical or dental insurance plan may be ordered to be shared proportionately in accordance with the respective spousal incomes.[268] Reciprocal obligations may be imposed on the parents to maintain coverage for the children under their employment health and dental plans, with any

---

261 *Jackson v Holloway*, [1997] SJ No 691 (QB).

262 *Rudulier v Rudulier*, [1999] SJ No 366 (QB).

263 *Federal Child Support Guidelines*, s 7(1)(c), as amended by SOR/2000-337, s 1; *Colbourne v Colbourne*, 2014 ABQB 547; *Corkum v Clarke*, [2000] NSJ No 285 (Fam Ct); *Baram v Bakshy*, [2000] OJ No 2349 (Sup Ct); *Woode v Woode*, [2002] SJ No 55 (QB).

264 *Moss v Moss*, [1997] NJ No 299 (SC); *Kennedy-Dalton v Dalton*, [2000] NJ No 41 (UFC); *O'Brien v O'Brien*, [1999] NWTJ No 56 (SC); *Bell v Griffin*, [1997] PEIJ No 86 (SCTD).

265 *Massler v Massler*, [1999] AJ No 206 (QB); *Moss v Moss*, [1997] NJ No 299 (SC) (need for counselling not established); *Sharf v Sharf*, [2000] OJ No 4052 (Sup Ct) (counselling expenses deemed excessive).

266 *Tubbs v Phillips*, [2000] SJ No 282 (QB).

267 *Hansvall v Hansvall*, [1997] SJ No 782 (QB); see also *Budden v Combden*, [1999] NJ No 199 (SC).

268 *MacLellan v MacLellan*, [1998] NSJ No 349 (TD); *Hansvall v Hansvall*, [1997] SJ No 782 (QB).

expenses not covered being shared proportionately in accordance with the respective parental incomes.[269]

Medical expenses may be viewed as a whole, rather than individually, in determining whether they are reasonable and necessary within the meaning of section 7(1) of the *Federal Child Support Guidelines*.[270]

With respect to necessary health-related expenses, ability to pay is the deciding factor.[271] Expenses for private nursing care will be denied where there is no money available to meet such expenses.[272]

As was observed by Johnstone J, of the Alberta Court of Queen's Bench, in *ALY v LMY*,[273] Canadian judgments are divided on the question whether respite care provided for the benefit of the parent of a special needs child can constitute a child-care-related expense or health-related expense under sections 7(1)(a) and (c) respectively of the *Federal Child Support Guidelines*. While disallowing the expense under either of these two headings, Johnstone J concluded that it would be appropriate for the court to address the issue of respite care through a spousal support order premised on section 15(2)(6)(b) of the *Divorce Act*.

4)   **Extraordinary Educational Expenses; Private School**[274]

Section 7(1)(d) of the *Federal Child Support Guidelines* confers a discretion on the court to provide for the payment of all or part of extraordinary expenses for primary or secondary school education or for any educational programs that meet the child's particular needs.[275] The expenses must satisfy the tests of reasonableness and necessity under section 7(1) of the Guidelines.[276]

---

269   *Bellman v Bellman*, [1999] BCJ No 1196 (SC).

270   *Giles v Villeneuve*, [1998] OJ No 4492 (Gen Div).

271   *Bell v Griffin*, [1997] PEIJ No 86 (SCTD); *Sharf v Sharf*, [2000] OJ No 4052 (Sup Ct).

272   *Van Harten v Van Harten*, [1998] OJ No 1299 (Gen Div).

273   [2001] AJ No 506 (QB).

274   For a revised definition of "extraordinary expenses," see Section L(1), above in this chapter, citing SOR/2005-400.

275   *Crofton v Sturko*, [1997] BCJ No 38 (SC); *Hogan v Johnston*, [1998] BCJ No 2055 (SC); *Hoover v Hoover*, [1997] NWTJ No 43 (SC); *McCoy v Hucker*, [1998] OJ No 4982 (Gen Div); *Andrews v Andrews*, [1999] OJ No 3578 (CA) (application under Ontario *Family Law Act* and Ontario *Child Support Guidelines*); *Jonas v Jonas*, [2002] OJ No 2117 (Sup Ct) (partial contribution); *Tubbs v Phillips*, [2000] SJ No 282 (QB) (tutoring expenses); *Wurmlinger v Cyca*, [2003] SJ No 247 (QB).

276   *Piwek v Jagiello*, 2011 ABCA 303; *NMM v NSM*, [2004] BCJ No 642 (SC) (fees to be paid until end of current school year); *JC v MC*, 2014 NBQB 161; *Casals v Casals*, [2006] OJ No 5602 (Sup Ct).

Extraordinary education expenses are those that extend beyond the basic school program.[277] Routine school fees, general school supplies, and normal transportation are regarded as "usual expenses" rather than "extraordinary expenses" within the meaning of section 7 of the *Federal Child Support Guidelines*.[278]

Laura W Morgan, an American commentator,[279] has identified the following factors as relevant to the provision of expenses for private schooling:

> whether one or both parents attended private school; whether the child has been enrolled in a private school prior to the divorce;[280] whether there has been an expectation that the child would have a private education, by express agreement or otherwise;[281] whether the parents can afford a private education;[282] and whether the child has a special need for private school that public schools cannot provide,[283] making private education in the best interests of the child.[284]

She further asserts that these "considerations would also justify ... [expenses] for music lessons or other cultural activities" and that when "private education costs are awarded, the court should award such expenses only to the extent that they are actually incurred and not paid from other sources."[285]

In determining the extent, if any, to which a parent should contribute to private school expenses of children of the marriage, the court may assess each child independently and thereby reach differing outcomes.[286] However, a court should not lightly deny one child the same benefits of private school

---

277 *Middleton v MacPherson*, [1997] AJ No 614 (QB); *Lavoie v Wills*, [2000] AJ No 1359 (QB); *Ebrahim v Ebrahim*, [1997] BCJ No 2039 (SC).

278 *Cowan v Cowan*, [2001] AJ No 669 (QB); *Smith v Smith*, [2001] AJ No 1420 (CA); *Callaghan v Brett*, [2000] NJ No 354 (SC); *McEachern v McEachern*, [1998] SJ No 507 (QB).

279 Laura W Morgan, *Child Support Guidelines: Interpretation and Application*, loose-leaf (New York: Aspen Law and Business, 1996–2004) at § 4.05[b]; see also *Andrews v Andrews*, [1999] OJ No 3578 (CA).

280 *Van Deventer v Van Deventer*, [2000] BCJ No 37 (CA); *Rivett v Bylund*, [1998] OJ No 325 (Gen Div); compare *BAC v DLC*, [2003] BCJ No 1303 (SC).

281 *Barker v Barker*, [2000] BCJ No 388 (SC).

282 *Stelter v Klingspohn*, [1999] BCJ No 2926 (SC); *Steele v Koppanyi*, [2002] MJ No 201 (CA); *Grierson v Brunton*, [2004] OJ No 3043 (Sup Ct); *Maloney v Maloney*, [2004] OJ No 5828 (Div Ct).

283 *Greenwood v Greenwood*, [1998] BCJ No 729 (SC); *Shankman v Shankman*, [2001] OJ No 3798 (Sup Ct).

284 See *LHMK v BPK*, 2012 BCSC 435; *JD v YP*, 2015 BCSC 321.

285 Laura Morgan, *Child Support Guidelines: Interpretation and Application*, loose-leaf (New York: Aspen Law and Business, 1996–2004) at § 4.05[b].

286 *Burton v Burton*, [1997] NSJ No 560 (TD); see also *Ostlund v Ostlund*, [2000] BCJ No 1158 (SC).

as those enjoyed by another sibling, where there are no financial obstacles to the payment of the requisite costs.[287] Private school expenses, though reasonable for a short period of transition, may become unreasonable in the long term, especially where a change in circumstances reduces the parental income.[288] In *Delichte v Rogers*,[289] Steel JA, who delivered the judgment of the Manitoba Court of Appeal, provided an excellent summary of many of the principles that govern applications for extraordinary expenses for schooling and for extracurricular activities under section 7 of the *Federal Child Support Guidelines*. The following eighteen considerations have been extracted, often verbatim, from her reasons for judgment:

1) The table amount of child support covers all ordinary expenses of child-rearing. Any special or extraordinary expenses are governed by section 7 of the *Federal Child Support Guidelines*. Section 7 of the *Guidelines* provides some flexibility because not all family needs are the same. See (1998), *Andries v. Andries* (1998), 126 Man.R. (2d) 189 (at para. 11) (Twaddle, J.A.).

2) Although child care expenses, medical and dental insurance, health-related expenses and post-secondary educational expenses need not be extraordinary under section 7(1)(a), (b), (c) and (e) of the *Federal Child Support Guidelines* in order to warrant a judicial order, expenses for primary or secondary school education or for any educational programs that meet a child's particular needs under section 7(1)(d) of the Guidelines and expenses for extracurricular activities under section 7(1)(f) of the Guidelines must be extraordinary in order to be allowable.

3) Pursuant to section 7(1.1)(a) of the Guidelines, expenses are extraordinary if they exceed an amount that the requesting parent can reasonably cover, taking into account the income of the requesting spouse and any child support received. Thus, the term "extraordinary expense" must be understood within the particular family's means and circumstances. See *Correia v. Correia*, 2002 MBQB 172 at paras. 7, 10, 165 Man.R. (2d) 134; and *Holeman v. Holeman*, 2006 MBQB 278 at para. 42, 209 Man.R. (2d) 299. If the expenses do not exceed an amount the requesting spouse can reasonably cover, then the court will consider the five factors listed in section 7(1.1)(*b*) to determine whether the expenses can still be classified as extraordinary in the circumstances. The five factors to consider under section 7(1.1)(*b*) are: (i) the amount of the expense in relation to the income of the spouse requesting the amount, including the amount of child support received, (ii) the nature and number of the educational

---

287 *Bell-Angus v Angus*, [2000] OJ No 2074 (Sup Ct).
288 *McDonald v McDonald*, [2001] BCJ No 2570 (BCCA).
289 2013 MBCA 106.

programs and extracurricular activities, (iii) any special needs and talents of the child or children, (iv) the overall cost of the programs and activities, and (v) any other similar factor that the court considers relevant.

4) On an initial application, the onus is upon the applicant to prove that the claimed expenses fall within one of the categories listed under section 7(1) since the categories listed are exhaustive (*Graham v. Graham*, 2008 MBQB 25 at para. 62, 224 Man.R. (2d) 141).

5) Extracurricular activities have been broadly held to include any activity outside the regular school curriculum, although not activities such as family vacations: *Raftus v. Raftus* (1998), 166 N.S.R. (2d) 179 at para. 22 (C.A.). Everyday clothing does not fall within section 7 expenses, although the costs of equipment and uniforms which related to an extracurricular activity may qualify: *Walsh v. Walsh*, 2006 NLUFC 7 at paras. 62–64, 254 Nfld. & P.E.I.R. 338.

6) When the actual amount of the expense is difficult to ascertain, the expenses may be estimated; however, there must be some evidence to support the estimation of the expenses, otherwise the court cannot determine whether the requesting spouse is able to reasonably cover a totally unknown expense. See *Ferguson v. Thorne*, 2007 NBQB 66 at paras. 63–65, 316 N.B.R. (2d) 18.

7) Where a court determines that an amount to cover extraordinary expenses should be awarded, the contribution generally will be in proportion with the spouses' respective incomes (section 7(2)), but not always. The court may order a different contribution, depending on the specific circumstances of the case. See *E.K.R. v. G.A.W.* (1997), 122 Man.R. (2d) 120 at paras. 15–17 (Q.B.). For example, the courts have occasionally departed from the general rule of contribution in accordance with the parties' respective incomes in situations where the payor's access costs are unusually high: *Carmichael v. Douglas*, 2008 SKQB 320 at paras. 31–32, 56 R.F.L. (6th) 420; *Brown v. Hudon*, 2004 SKQB 294 at para. 24, 267 Sask.R. 53. Or a court may depart from the general principle of an income-based *pro rata* sharing of the child's expenses where the parents have agreed to equally share the expenses, or where there is a substantial disparity between the parental incomes, as for example, where one parent's income is barely sufficient to provide for his or her own needs and the other parent has ample ability to shoulder the expense . . .

8) Even if the expenses fall within one of the categories listed in section 7(1), the court must still be satisfied that the expenses are reasonable and necessary before ordering the sharing of the expenses.

9) In determining whether the two-part test of necessity and reasonableness outlined in s. 7(1) has been satisfied, the court is to take the following factors into account: (i) the necessity of the expense in relation to the child's best interests; (ii) the reasonableness of the expense in relation to the means of the spouses and those of the child; and (iii) the family's spending pattern prior to the separation.

10) Courts have generally considered that the test of necessity does not connote only the necessities of life, but, rather, may include things that are "suitable to or proper for his station in life bearing in mind his requirements at the time." See *Hiemstra v. Hiemstra*, 2005 ABQB 192 at paras. 52–53, 13 R.F.L. (6th) 169. Courts have looked to activities that have aided the child's development and health. So, for example, participation in sports activities has been held to be necessary in relation to the child's best interests. See *Fong v. Charbonneau*, 2005 MBQB 92, 194 Man.R. (2d) 45, and *Correia*.

11) With regard to private schooling, the British Columbia Court of Appeal has held that a trial judge correctly considered private schooling to be necessary where both parties affirmed the importance of private Catholic school for their daughters and had serious reservations about public school. This agreement was determined to be "strong evidence to support a finding of necessity in relation to the children's best interests" (*McDonald v. McDonald*, 2001 BCCA 702 at para. 27, 161 B.C.A.C. 310). In other cases, the court has been stricter about proving necessity, in particular with regard to tuition for private school. For example, in *Steele v. Koppanyi*, 2002 MBCA 60, 163 Man.R. (2d) 268, Helper J.A. determined that "[t]here is no evidence to support a finding that [the child's] best interests necessitate his attending a private school" (at para. 46), despite the fact that the child had attended private school for several years.

12) In many cases, the issue of necessity is not really discussed. The lack of discussion about "necessity" was commented upon by MacDonald J. in *T.L.S. v. D.J.M.*, 2009 NSSC 79, 275 N.S.R. (2d) 357, as follows (at para. 48):

> . . . . The requirement for evidence from which a conclusion of "necessity" can be made is generally overlooked and this may occur because many parents agree, after separation, to share these expenses proportionally. This prior agreement may remove the prerequisite that the court determine whether a particular expense is "necessary".

13) Furthermore, in many cases, it quickly becomes apparent that the "real" issue is whether the expense is reasonable in relation to the means of the spouses, and whether the expense is reasonable in light of the parties' spending pattern pre-separation. In that regard, it is necessary to focus

on the <u>means</u> of the parties, not just their incomes. Case law indicates that the means of the parties should be interpreted broadly to include a consideration of all financial resources, including capital assets, income distribution, debt load, third-party resources which impact upon the parties' means, access costs, obligations to pay spousal or other child support orders, spousal support received, and any other relevant factors (see *Leskun v. Leskun*, 2006 SCC 25 at para. 29, [2006] 1 S.C.R. 920).

14) The courts have indicated that the following matters can be considered when assessing the reasonableness of the expense in relation to the means of the spouses:

- the combined income of the parties;
- the fact that two households must be maintained;
- the extent of the expense in relation to the parties' combined level of income;
- the debt of the parties;
- any prospect for a decline or increase in the parties' means in the near future; and
- whether the non-custodial parent was consulted regarding the expense prior to the expense being incurred.

15) The reasonableness of the expense in relation to the family's spending pattern prior to the separation is also a factor which the court is required to take into account (section 7(1)). In *Correia*, Allen J. indicated that "[a]n examination of this factor helps to see if the activity was one which would have been likely to be supported by the parents when together and thus considered by both to be in the child's best interests" (at para. 25). See also *Van Deventer v. Van Deventer*, 2000 BCCA 9, 132 B.C.A.C. 186, (at para. 17) (Prowse J.A.). In fact, the pre-separation pattern of spending may assist the court on the issue of reasonableness and necessity even where the expense seems relatively excessive. See, for example, *Winseck v. Winseck* (2008), 235 O.A.C. 38 at paras. 30–31 (S.C.J.). The court should, therefore, consider the family's lifestyle and activities prior to the separation, although the weight given to this factor may have to be re-evaluated in light of the dissolution of the marriage, the fact that there will now be two households to support, and the decreased means of the parties (*N.M.M. v. N.S.M.*, 2004 BCSC 346 at paras. 111–113, [2004] B.C.T.C. 346). Obviously, where the means of the parties have dropped substantially after separation, judicial reliance on the family's pre-separation spending pattern will be less appropriate.

16) Where there has been a history of spending for an extraordinary expense, but that expense has increased to what could be considered an unreasonable level, the court may order the payor to contribute to a portion of the expense in recognition of the prior history of spending (*Doherty v. Doherty* (2001), 19 R.F.L. (5th) 46 (Ont. S.C.J.); *Abelson v. Mitra*, 2008 BCSC 1197 at para. 95, 59 R.F.L. (6th) 364; and *Magee v. Faveri*, [2007] O.J. No. 4826 at para. 42 (QL) (S.C.J.)). Also see *Iddon v. Iddon*, [2006] O.J. No. 237 at paras. 72–80 (QL) (S.C.J.), wherein Corbett J. set a cap of $7,000 annually on the amount of the private school expense prior to ordering its apportionment between the parties, and *B.B.W.-B. v. D.M.B.*, 2005 SKQB 462 at paras. 35–38, 271 Sask.R. 151, wherein Smith J. set a cap of $75 per month on the amount the payor had to contribute to extracurricular activities.

17) While it is clear that a lack of consultation with the other spouse does not automatically preclude the proper apportionment of an extraordinary expense, it is a factor the judge can take into account when exercising his or her discretion. In some cases, the courts have reduced the payor's contribution due to the lack of consultation. See *Pepin v. Jung*, [1997] O.J. No. 4604 (Gen. Div.).

18) Ultimately, the decision as to whether a particular expense will be considered necessary and reasonable depends on the facts of the particular case and the hearing judge's discretion.

5) Extraordinary Expenses for Extracurricular Activities[290]

Section 7(1)(f) of the *Federal Child Support Guidelines* confers a discretion on the court to provide for the payment of all or part of any extraordinary expenses for extracurricular activities. Section 7(1.1) of the *Federal Child Support Guidelines* sets out a two-part definition of "extraordinary expenses."[291] First, pursuant to paragraph 7(1.1)(a), expenses are extraordinary if they "exceed those that the spouse requesting an amount for the extraordinary expenses can reasonably cover." This is determined having regard to the income of the requesting spouse as well as any child support received. This element of the definition relates to the requesting spouse's ability to pay for the expenses. If the expenses exceed those that the requesting spouse can reasonably cover, they are extraordinary. The tests of necessity and reasonableness set out in section 7(1) of the Guidelines continue to apply to extraordinary expenses

---

290 See *Delichte v Rogers*, 2013 MBCA 106.

291 SOR/2005-400, s 1 (28 November 2005), published in *Canada Gazette*, Vol 139, No 25 (14 December 2005).

under sections 7(1)(d) and 7(1)(f). Where paragraph 7(1.1)(a) does not apply (because the expense does not exceed the amount that the requesting spouse can reasonably cover), the second part of the definition, set out in paragraph 7(1.1)(b), applies. Paragraph 7(1.1)(b) directs the court to determine whether the expenses are extraordinary having regard to the following five factors:

- the amount of the expense in relation to the income of the spouse requesting the amount (including the child support amount);
- the nature and number of the educational programs and extracurricular activities;
- any special needs and talents of the child or children;
- the overall costs of the programs and activities; and
- any other similar factor that the court considers relevant.

It is impossible to list specific categories of expenses as falling within the ambit of section 7(1)(f) of the Guidelines. Although the table amounts of child support under the *Federal Child Support Guidelines* apparently include some allowance for expenditures incurred for the extracurricular activities of children, there is no readily available information to indicate what portion of the applicable table amount is allocated to meet these expenses. Accordingly, courts lack any clear guidance as to when expenses for extracurricular activities are ordinary and when they are extraordinary. As Veit J, of the Alberta Court of Queen's Bench, observed in *MacIntosh v MacIntosh*, "it would be helpful if some guideline, based perhaps on a percentage of the total income of the parents, could help identify which extracurricular activities belong in the 'extraordinary' category."[292] Given the absence of any such guidance, there is a substantial lack of consistency in the judicial disposition of applications for extraordinary expenses for extracurricular activities under section 7(1)(f) of the *Federal Child Support Guidelines*.

Not all expenses for extracurricular activities will qualify for sharing between the spouses or former spouses. The expenses must be "extraordinary" in order to qualify under section 7 of the *Federal Child Support Guidelines*.[293] Basic expenses, such as the costs of registration in a community sports league, or normal costs commonly associated with sport, such as the purchase of ordinary equipment and minimal travel costs, are not extraordinary expenses and should be discounted from any exceptional expenses.[294] In determining whether a child support order should provide for an amount

---

292 [2003] AJ No 728 at para 42 (QB).

293 *Lavoie v Wills*, [2000] AJ No 1359 (QB); *Pomroy v Greene*, [2000] NJ No 38 (UFC); *Pitcher v Pitcher*, [2002] NJ No 358 (UFC); *Cane v Newman*, [1998] OJ No 1776 (Gen Div); *Kofoed v Fichter*, [1998] SJ No 338 (CA); *Fransoo v Fransoo*, [2001] SJ No 121 (QB).

294 *Bruno v Bruno*, [2000] OJ No 3057 (Sup Ct).

to cover all or some extraordinary expenses for extracurricular activities, the court takes into account the necessity of the expense in relation to the child's best interests and the reasonableness of the expense, having regard to the current means of the spouses and those of the child and to the family's spending pattern prior to the separation.[295] The test of necessity relates to the best interests of the child and is not one of strict necessity;[296] money spent on a child will usually benefit that child and thereby satisfy the necessity criterion imposed by section 7(1) of the Guidelines.[297] A child does not require any special talent for an activity's expenses to qualify as necessary.[298] Expenses may be deemed necessary when they relate to activities, such as sports, that aid in the development of the child's character and health to their full potential.[299] The issue of whether expenses are reasonable, given the means of the spouses and those of the child, and the family's established spending pattern before separation, will depend on the circumstances of the particular case.[300] Although each case should be determined on its own facts, orders for such expenses should be the exception, not the rule;[301] they should not be routinely included in an order for child support.[302] Even if a child is extremely talented, an order for a contribution to the extraordinary expenses of that activity will be denied where the cost is not reasonable in light of the modest means of the parents.[303]

Having regard to the fact that the table amount of child support builds in a certain amount for extracurricular expenses,[304] the norm for what are ordinary expenses increases as the family income increases;[305] ordinary expenses for a family income of $30,000 are less than what is normal for a

---

295 *Trueman v Trueman*, [2000] AJ No 1301 (QB); *Ackland v Brooks*, [2001] BCJ No 1733 (SC); *Myers v Myers*, [2000] NSJ No 367 (SC); *Doherty v Doherty*, [2001] OJ No 2400 (Sup Ct); *Fransoo v Fransoo*, [2001] SJ No 121 (QB).

296 *Omah-Maharajh v Howard*, [1998] AJ No 173 (QB); *Stewart v Stewart*, [2004] AJ No 362 (QB).

297 *Trueman v Trueman*, [2000] AJ No 1301 (QB).

298 *Omah-Maharajh v Howard*, [1998] AJ No 173 (QB); *Raftus v Raftus*, [1998] NSJ No 119 (CA).

299 *DiPasquale v DiPasquale*, [1998] NWTJ No 58 (SC); *Yeo v Yeo*, [1998] PEIJ No 100 (SCTD).

300 *Omah-Maharajh v Howard*, [1998] AJ No 173 (QB); *Morrissette v Ball*, [2000] BCJ No 73 (SC); *DiPasquale v DiPasquale*, [1998] NWTJ No 58 (SC).

301 *Johnston v Johnston*, [2004] AJ No 333 (QB); *McEachern v McEachern*, [1998] SJ No 507 (QB); *Fransoo v Fransoo*, [2001] SJ No 212 (QB).

302 *Yeo v Yeo*, [1998] PEIJ No 100 (SCTD).

303 *Bland v Bland*, [1999] AJ No 344 (QB). Compare *Strickland v Strickland*, [1998] OJ No 5869 (Gen Div) (interim order for contribution to extremely high costs of teenage Olympic hopeful; fixed-term order; payment conditioned upon other parent's undertaking to reimburse payor for one-half of mortgage payments and municipal taxes on matrimonial home).

304 *Nataros v Nataros*, [1998] BCJ No 1417 (SC); *Shambrook v Shambrook*, [2004] BCJ No 1410 (SC).

305 *Nataros v Nataros*, [1998] BCJ No 1417 (SC); *Yeo v Yeo*, [1998] PEIJ No 100 (SCTD).

family income of $60,000.[306] It may be difficult to determine where ordinary expenses for extracurricular activities end and extraordinary expenses begin, but the court must make that determination based on the facts of each particular case.[307] To the extent that extracurricular expenses are found to be extraordinary, the court still retains a discretion whether to order any contribution to be paid, having regard to the necessity of the expenses and their reasonableness as defined in section 7 of the *Federal Child Support Guidelines*.[308] In most middle-income families, the expenses of extracurricular activities are ordinary and largely covered by the applicable table amount. The same expenses for a low-income family would be extraordinary because the applicable table amount of child support would be required to meet basic needs.[309]

M. VARIATION OF CHILD SUPPORT ORDERS[310]

Pursuant to section 17(4) of the *Divorce Act* and section 14 of the *Federal Child Support Guidelines*, a court may vary an order for child support in any one of the following circumstances:

(a) an order providing the applicable table amount of child support is variable on proof of any change of circumstances that would result in a different disposition;

(b) an order that does not include any table amount of child support is variable on proof of any change in the condition, means, needs or other circumstances of either spouse or of any child who is entitled to support;

(c) any order granted before the implementation of the *Federal Child Support Guidelines* on 1 May 1997 may be varied in light of their implementation.

A court has jurisdiction to hear a variation application even when the subject order is under appeal.[311]

1) Variation of Amount of Child Support Made under Applicable Table

Pursuant to section 17(4) of the *Divorce Act* and section 14(a) of the *Federal Child Support Guidelines*, a court may vary a child support order whenever the

---

306 *Campbell v Martijn*, [1998] PEIJ No 33 (SCTD).

307 *Nataros v Nataros*, [1998] BCJ No 1417 (SC).

308 *Ibid.*

309 *Trueman v Trueman*, [2000] AJ No 1301 (QB); *DiPasquale v DiPasquale*, [1998] NWTJ No 58 (SC).

310 As to the interjurisdictional variation of child support orders, see Chapter 8, Section R(5).

311 *Labrecque v Labrecque*, 2012 SKQB 320.

amount of child support was determined in accordance with the applicable provincial or territorial table and any change has occurred that would result in a different child support order. Any change that triggers a different order, whether it is a change in form, in substance, or in dollar amounts, is sufficient justification for a variation application.[312] Such a change will occur when the obligor's annual income and consequential capacity to pay child support has increased[313] or has deteriorated for reasons beyond his or her control.[314] An obligor who seeks to retroactively and prospectively reduce the amount of child support payable must provide reliable and credible evidence that his annual income is less than the amount previously attributed to him.[315] The basic amount of child support payable under the applicable provincial or territorial table is unaffected by a reduction in the payee's income, unless such reduction triggers a successful claim of undue hardship under section 10 of the *Federal Child Support Guidelines*.[316] The judicial jurisdiction to vary an order for child support based on a provincial or territorial table is not confined to circumstances where the obligor's income has increased or decreased. For example,

- a complementary provision could be included with respect to newly encountered special or extraordinary expenses; or
- a reconstitution of either household might justify a claim of undue hardship under subsections 10(1) and 10(3) of the Guidelines; or
- the residence of the obligor might change so as to trigger the application of a different provincial or territorial table under section 3(3)(a) of the Guidelines; or
- the accumulation of arrears might warrant the variation of an order for periodic support into an order for lump sum support in accordance with section 11 of the Guidelines; or
- the implementation of revised table amounts of child support may necessitate variation of the amount previously ordered.

Section 14(a) of the *Federal Child Support Guidelines* deems that there is a change in circumstances for the purposes of section 17(4) of the *Divorce Act* if section 9 of the Guidelines is triggered.[317]

---

312 *Blais v Blais*, [2001] SJ No 468 (SC).
313 *ADB v SAM*, [2006] NSJ No 252 (SC); *Khoee-Solomonescu v Solomonescu*, [2000] OJ No 743 (Div Ct).
314 *ADB v SAM*, [2006] NSJ No 252 (SC); *Guillet v Guillet*, [1999] SJ No 266 (QB).
315 *Murphy v Murphy*, 2007 BCCA 500, [2007] BCJ No 2258.
316 *Saby v MacIntosh*, [2002] BCJ No 1813 (SC); *Williams v Williams*, [1997] NWTJ No 49 (SC).
317 *Kolada v Kolada*, [2000] AJ No 342 (QB).

2) Variation Where Amount of Child Support Not under Provincial or Territorial Table

Variation of an order for child support under section 14(b) of the *Federal Child Support Guidelines*, where the amount of child support was not determined under a provincial or territorial table, may be granted when there has been a change in the condition, means, needs, or other circumstances of either spouse or former spouse or a change in the condition, means, needs, or other circumstances of any child who is entitled to support.[318] The terms "condition," "means," "needs," and "other circumstances" of either former spouse provide an extremely wide range of relevant considerations that leave the court with an extremely broad discretionary jurisdiction to vary, rescind, or suspend a support order.[319] In determining the obligor's available means, the nature and source of those means (whether salary, pension, other income, or capital) are not material.[320] Income may be imputed to a spouse in the context of an application to vary child support for the purpose of determining whether a material change of circumstances has occurred within the meaning of section 14(b) of the Guidelines.[321]

A material change has been defined by the Supreme Court of Canada in *Willick v Willick*[322] as being a change of such magnitude that, if the court had known of the changed circumstances at the time of the original order, it is likely that the order would have been made on different terms.[323] The change must be significant and long lasting.[324] It must also be involuntary; a self-induced change of circumstances will not suffice.[325] A parent has a continuing obligation to support his or her children in spite of temporary unemployment,[326] or a fluctuating income; some degree of budgeting may be required.[327] If the change was known at the relevant time, it cannot be relied

318 *Birks v Birks*, [2003] BCJ No 949 (SC); *Sikler v Snow*, [2000] SJ No 271 (QB).

319 *Willick v Willick*, [1994] 3 SCR 670.

320 *Bartlett v Bartlett* (1994), 2 RFL (4th) 202 (Nfld UFC).

321 *Daku v Daku*, [1999] SJ No 330 (QB).

322 [1994] 3 SCR 670.

323 *Bushell v Bushell*, [2000] AJ No 1499 (QB); *Meuser v Meuser*, [1998] BCJ No 2808 (CA); *MLP v MJM*, 2012 BCCA 395; *AC v RR*, [2006] NBJ No 204 (CA); *Collins v Collins*, [2003] NJ No 278 (SC); *ADB v SAM*, [2006] NSJ No 252 (SC); *Osmar v Osmar*, [2000] OJ No 2060 (Sup Ct); *Vezina v Vezina*, [2006] SJ No 105 (CA).

324 *Bushell v Bushell*, [2000] AJ No 1499 (QB); *Pagani v Pagani*, [1999] BCJ No 3051 (SC); *Martin v Martin*, [2000] BCJ No 303 (SC); *Birks v Birks*, [2003] BCJ No 949 (SC); *Cook v McManus*, [2006] NBJ No 334 (QB).

325 *MLP v MJM*, 2012 BCCA 395; see also *Verschuren v Verschuren*, 2014 ONCA 518.

326 *NB v KJB*, [1999] BCJ No 1584 (SC).

327 *Pagani v Pagani*, [1999] BCJ No 3051 (SC).

on as the basis for variation.[328] Subject to the express provisions of section 14 of the *Federal Child Support Guidelines*, the principles of *Willick v Willick* continue to apply to the variation of child support orders under the *Federal Child Support Guidelines*.[329]

An obligor cannot reduce an existing child support obligation by a self-imposed reduction of income.[330] It may be otherwise if an obligor's change of employment that resulted in a reduced income was not made for selfish or illogical reasons and could prove sensible in the longer term.[331] Parents who are subject to support obligations are entitled to make decisions in relation to their careers so long as the decisions are reasonable at the time having regard to all the circumstances. Those circumstances include the age, education, experience, skills, historical earning capacity and health of the payor, the standard of living experienced during marriage, the availability of work, the payor's freedom to relocate, the reasonableness of the career aspirations and of the motives behind any change, as well as any other obligations of the payor.[332]

3) Variation of Orders Predating Implementation of Guidelines[333]

Appellate rulings in Canada are divided on the question whether the implementation of the *Federal Child Support Guidelines* on 1 May 1997 compels a court to vary a pre-Guidelines agreement or order for child support or whether a residual discretion vests in the court to leave the order unchanged so as to retain the income tax inclusion and deductibility rules that continue to apply to pre-Guidelines agreements and orders.[334]

---

328 *Meuser v Meuser*, [1998] BCJ No 2808 (CA); *MLP v MJM*, 2012 BCCA 395.

329 *Bushell v Bushell*, [2000] AJ No 1499 (QB); *Khoee-Solomonescu v Solomonescu*, [2000] OJ No 743 (Div Ct).

330 *Aziz v Aziz*, [2000] BCJ No 1134 (CA); *Donovan v Donovan*, [2000] MJ No 407 (CA) (application under *Manitoba Child Support Guidelines*); *Hart v Neufeld*, [2004] SJ No 232 (CA).

331 *Darvill v Chorney*, [1999] SJ No 551 (QB).

332 *Kozub v Kozub*, [2002] SJ No 407 (QB).

333 See Carol Rogerson, "Of Variation, 'Special Provisions' and 'Reasonable Arrangements' — The Effect of Prior Orders and Agreements on Child Support Determinations under the Guidelines" (available on Quicklaw, Commentary, Syrtash Collection of Family Law Articles, SFLRP/1998-012).

334 For a detailed review of this subject, see Julien D Payne & Marilyn A Payne, *Child Support Guidelines in Canada, 2012* (Toronto: Irwin Law, 2012) at 500–2.

4) Remission of Arrears

In *Earle v Earle*,[335] Martinson J, of the Supreme Court of British Columbia, set out the following propositions with respect to applications to reduce or cancel child support arrears:

Basic Principles
a. There is a heavy duty on the person asking for a reduction or a cancellation of arrears to show that there has been a significant and long lasting change in circumstances. Arrears will not be reduced or cancelled unless it is grossly unfair not to do so.
b. If arrears are not reduced or cancelled, the court can order a payment plan over time if convinced the arrears cannot be paid right away.

Examples
a. Arrears will only be cancelled if the person is unable to pay now and will be unable to pay in the future.
b. A reduction or a cancellation requires detailed and full financial disclosure, under oath (usually in the form of an affidavit) that at the time the payments were to be made:
    i.   the change was significant and long lasting and
    ii. the change was real and not one of choice and
    iii. every effort was made to earn money (or more money) during the time in question, and those efforts were not successful.
c. Responsibility for a second family cannot relieve the parent of his or her legal obligation to support the first family.
d. Delay in enforcement is generally not a legal basis to cancel or reduce child support arrears.[336]
e. Judges will not cancel arrears because the other party gets a lot of money at once. Otherwise, people would be encouraged to not pay maintenance and be rewarded for not paying maintenance.
f. Judges will not cancel arrears because the children were looked after in spite of the non-payment.
g. Nor will judges cancel arrears because the children no longer need the money. The children should be compensated for what they missed.
h. An agreement between parents that the maintenance for the children does not have to be paid will not be considered.[337]

---

335 [1999] BCJ No 383 (SC); see also *Ghisleri v Ghisleri*, 2007 BCCA 512; *Luney v Luney*, 2007 BCCA 567; *Nielsen v Nielsen*, 2007 BCCA 604; *Jacobs v Jacobs*, 2015 BCSC 94.
336 Compare *Burgie v Argent*, 2014 BCSC 364.
337 But see *Llewellyn v Llewellyn*, 2002 BCCA 182 at para 19; *Burgie v Argent*, 2014 BCSC 364.

i.   Lack of access between a parent and child is not a legal reason to reduce or cancel arrears.

j.   Judges will not reduce or cancel arrears because other money has been spent to buy things for the children.

k.   The fact that a person did not have legal advice when the order was made or during the time when the arrears added up, is not, by itself, a reason to reduce or cancel arrears.

In *Sewell v Grant*,[338] Gower J, of the Yukon Territory Supreme Court, questioned the validity of several of the principles set out in *Earle v Earle*, above, in concluding that the court has no discretion to refuse to reduce arrears of child support where the payor's income is less than that previously judicially imputed to him. And in *Turecki v Turecki*,[339] judicial remission of child support arrears was deemed appropriate because the custodial parent deliberately refrained from enforcing court-ordered child support payments so as to avoid disclosing her whereabouts, thereby denying the non-custodial parent court-ordered access to which both he and the child were entitled. The British Columbia Court of Appeal reasoned that a custodial parent, who has been required to draw on his or her own resources to properly maintain the children of the marriage, is entitled to recover child support arrears from the non-custodial parent, but this reasoning does not apply where the encroachments are self-induced. In the ordinary course of events, however, both parents have a joint legal obligation to support their children according to their respective abilities. Courts must avoid giving the appearance of favouring non-custodial parents who fail to discharge their support obligations diligently, thereby casting additional financial burdens on the more diligent custodial parents.[340] The "grossly unfair" principle which is legislatively endorsed in section 174 of the British Columbia *Family Law Act* has been found appropriate for consideration on variation applications under the *Divorce Act*.[341]

In *Haisman v Haisman*,[342] the Alberta Court of Appeal drew an important distinction between child support and spousal support arrears. It concluded

---

338 [2005] YJ No 37 (SC).

339 (1989), 19 RFL (3d) 127 (BCCA); see also *Misener v Muir*, [2007] BCJ No 2029 (SC).

340 *Labell v Labell*, [2006] BCJ No 185 (CA), citing *Longstaff v Longstaff* (1993), 49 RFL (3d) 1 at para 54 (BCCA).

341 *Hodgson v Hodgson*, 2014 BCSC 1372 at para 20, Ross J; *Jacobs v Jacobs*, 2015 BCSC 94.

342 (1994), 7 RFL (4th) 1 (Alta CA), leave to appeal to SCC refused (1995), 15 RFL (4th) 51 (SCC); see also *Blyth v Brooks*, [2008] AJ No 100 (CA); *EMV v TDHV*, [2008] AJ No 328 (CA); *Johnston v Johnston*, [1997] BCJ No 418, 26 RFL (4th) 131 (CA); *Heiden v British Columbia (Director of Maintenance Enforcement)* (1995), 19 RFL (4th) 320 (BCCA); *AE v MG*, [2004] NWTJ No 8 (SC); *Filipich v Filipich*, [1996] OJ No 3081 (CA); *Mondino v Mondino*,

that a child should not be penalized by a custodial parent's delay in enforcing a child support order, and the obligor should not be allowed to shift the burden of child support to the custodial parent or to the public purse unless there was an inability to pay over a substantial period of time during which the child support payments fell due, and this inability would have necessitated a suspension of the child support order or a reduction in the amount of the order, had a timely application for variation or rescission been instituted. A present inability to pay child support arrears does not itself warrant judicial remission of the arrears, although it may justify a suspension of their enforcement for a limited term or an order for instalment payments against the arrears.[343] In appropriate circumstances, an indefinite suspension of the enforcement of child support arrears may be ordered.[344] The court is not precluded from relieving an obligor of his or her obligation to discharge support arrears because it dismissed a previous application, but a material change of circumstances must have occurred since the previous application.[345]

In determining whether to remit arrears of child support, courts in Ontario and Saskatchewan consider

- the nature of the support obligation sought to be varied;
- the obligor's ability to pay the arrears when they fell due;
- the ongoing financial capacity of the obligor;
- the ongoing needs of the payee and child;
- unreasonable and unexplained delay by the payee in enforcing the arrears;
- unreasonable and unexplained delay by the payor in seeking relief from the support obligation; and
- whether enforcement of payment will cause hardship to the payor.

The court is at liberty to consider whether hoarding has occurred or whether the payee has rested on his or her rights in such a manner as to mislead the payor, but the court is not bound to discharge any arrears solely because they have been outstanding for more than one year.[346] Relevant factors that have

---

2013 ONSC 7051; *White v Gallant*, [2001] PEIJ No 115 (SCTD); *Diebel v Diebel*, [1997] SJ No 165 (QB); *MLC v GCC*, [2000] YJ No 114 (SC).

343 *Haisman v Haisman* (1994), 7 RFL (4th) 1 (Alta CA); *Wasswa v Wasswa*, 2012 NWTSC 88; *DiFrancesco v Couto*, [2001] OJ No 4307 (CA); *Ross v Vermette*, [2007] SJ No 483 (QB).

344 *CAG v SG*, 2012 ABQB 529.

345 *Ibid.*

346 *Gray v Gray* (1983), 32 RFL (2d) 438 at 440 (Ont HCJ); *Filipich v Filipich*, [1996] OJ No 3081 (CA); *DiFrancesco v Couto*, [2001] OJ No 4307 (CA); *Mondino v Mondino*, 2013 ONSC 7051; *Loshney v Hankins* (1993), 48 RFL (3d) 67 (Sask QB) (wherein the court also identifies the evidence that must be adduced when remission of arrears is sought); *Ross v Vermette*, [2007] SJ No 483 (QB); *Ford v Ford*, 2013 SKQB 48.

been singled out by courts in Newfoundland and Labrador include whether there is a reasonable explanation for the delay, the obligor's efforts to comply with the order, the ability of the obligor to pay, the creditor's means and needs, whether denial of retroactive variation would result in a windfall hoarding, whether the obligor was lulled by the creditor into believing that the order would not be enforced, and the futility of making an order that would be impossible to perform.[347] A failure to enforce a child support order without more is not evidence of waiver.[348]

In *Brown v Brown*,[349] Robertson JA, of the New Brunswick Court of Appeal, provided the following overview of the principles to be applied in New Brunswick in variation proceedings wherein the judicial remission of arrears of child support and/or spousal support is sought:

> 2 The jurisdiction to issue retroactive variation orders that reduce or cancel arrears of support has been carefully circumscribed under both the provincial and federal legislation. In each instance, the order is contingent on the court finding a "change in circumstances" of one of the parties, or a child, between the time of the original order and the application for variation. Invariably, the law requires the change to be "material". Actually, the court must rule on two discrete questions: Was there a material change in circumstances during the period of retroactivity and, having regard to all other relevant circumstances during this period, would the applicant have been granted a reduction in his or her support obligation but for his or her untimely application? The concept of material change in circumstances has always been interpreted broadly. As a general proposition, the court will be asking whether the change was significant and long lasting; whether it was real and not one of choice.
>
> 3 When deciding whether to grant a full or partial remission of arrears, courts need not be concerned with several factors often explored in the jurisprudence of other jurisdictions. Specifically, the court need not address why the applicant failed to make a timely application for retroactive variation. Correlatively, the court need not be concerned with the reasons underscoring the support recipient's failure to pursue timely enforcement measures thereby thwarting the accumulation of arrears. In short, the notion of "fault" plays no role in the decision to grant retroactive variation orders involving support arrears. Admittedly, this narrowed approach appears to

---

347 *Hawko v Knapp*, [2001] NJ No 300 (UFC); *Lynch v Lundrigan*, [2002] NJ No 185 (SC).

348 *Boehmer v Boehmer*, [1997] AJ No 69 (QB); *Poyntz Estate v Poyntz*, [1998] OJ No 1024 (Gen Div).

349 2010 NBCA 5; see also *Thomas v Thomas*, 2014 ABQB 481 at para 56; *Bowen v Halliday*, 2014 NBQB 189; *Poirier v Poirier*, 2013 NSSC 314.

deviate from the analytical framework set down in *D.B.S. v. S.R.G.*, [2006] 2 S.C.R. 231, [2006] S.C.J. No. 37 (QL), 2006 SCC 37. In that case, the Supreme Court outlined four factors to be considered when deciding whether to order a retroactive *increase* in child support, including the two factors just cited. But the present case involves a retroactive order to *reduce* both spousal and child support. The distinction between the two orders is not without difference and one which did not escape the Supreme Court. It is one thing to demand immediate payment of monies with respect to a past obligation that only recently matured and quite another to seek an order that recalculates and reduces the amount owing with respect to a debt never paid.

4 As will be explained, the understanding that "fault" plays no role in the adjudication of applications for retroactive variation of support arrears is consistent with both the majority and minority opinions delivered in *D.B.S. v. S.R.G.* Moreover, once the law disposes of the need to consider the reasons underscoring the support recipient's failure to pursue timely enforcement measures, there is no room for the antediluvian rule against support recipients "hoarding" arrears and the corollary rule limiting arrears to "one year". In recent times, other courts have soundly rejected the validity of these rules. The jurisprudence of this Province should reinforce that understanding of the law. Similarly, there is no room in the law for retroactive variation orders that reduce or eliminate support arrears based on misconceived notions of "laches", "acquiescence" and "waiver" on the part of the support recipient.

5 These reasons do not subscribe to the understanding that courts possess a residual discretion to forgive arrears. In cases where the applicant is unable to establish a material change in circumstances, there is no residual discretion to either reduce or cancel arrears based on the interlocking pleas of "inability to pay" and "hardship". As a matter of statutory interpretation, neither the provincial nor federal legislation expressly contemplates the exercise of such discretion, nor can it be reasonably inferred as being a necessary incident of the power to issue retroactive orders. Indeed, other statutory provisions undermine the notion of a residual discretion to forgive arrears.

6 Finally, these reasons do not stand for the proposition that the ability to pay arrears is never relevant. It is relevant when it comes to the matter of arrears enforcement. If payers of support truly lack the present and future financial resources to address the arrears problem, the court cannot be expected to craft an enforcement order that ignores the adage: "one cannot draw blood from a stone". In this limited sense, the pleas of inability to pay and hardship cannot be ignored. But the pleas must fall deafly on

judicial ears when the relief sought is a forgiveness of arrears.[350] As a matter of law, support recipients are entitled to cling to the faint hope of a future ability to pay.

The distinction between a variation order for the remission of arrears and a judicial refusal to enforce arrears, which is drawn by Robertson JA in paragraph 6 above, is important because once arrears have been remitted by court order, they cannot be subsequently reinstated.[351]

Applying the above principles to the facts of the case, Robertson JA noted that the husband brought a motion for a retroactive variation order to reduce or eliminate arrears of child support and spousal support totalling $132,965 that had accrued since 2004. The motion judge ordered a reduction of $14,100 in the child support arrears on the basis that the child had lived with the husband for fifteen months during the years when the arrears accrued. The motion judge refused to order any additional remission of the overall arrears, reasoning that a retroactive variation to decrease or eliminate support was not justified because there was "limited knowledge as to what, if any, impact a reduction in the existing accrued ordered arrears might have upon [Ms Brown's] lifestyle." Finally, "the motion judge held that there was no support in law for the proposition that a recipient's failure to enforce the payment of her right to support or that of the child was sufficient basis for cancelling outstanding arrears." The New Brunswick Court of Appeal found no error in the motion judge's remission of the arrears of child support that accrued during the months that the child resided with the husband. However, it found some merit in the husband's argument that the motion judge erred by narrowing the scope of the remaining issues to whether the support arrears should be reduced or eliminated because of the wife's failure to pursue timely enforcement measures. In its opinion, the husband's belated filing of financial information on the eve of the motion did not relieve the motion judge from examining, if necessary after an adjournment for cross-examination on the husband's affidavit, whether there had been a material change of circumstances involving a decline in the husband's income during the years when the support arrears accrued, and whether the husband's application for a reduction of his support obligations would have been granted but for the untimely nature of his application. As a result, the New Brunswick Court of Appeal remitted the case to the motion judge for a hearing and determination in accordance with its reasons for judgment.

---

350 See also *Lamarche v Lamarche*, 2011 NSSC 72; *NSC v DC*, 2011 NBQB 229.

351 *Beninger v Beninger*, 2009 BCCA 145 (spousal support); *LBL v SB*, 2010 NBQB 339 (child support); *Scurci v Scurci*, 2013 ONSC 7199 (child support).

In *Brown v Brown*, Robertson JA acknowledged that "the legal proposition holding it unnecessary to examine a host of factors before deciding on whether to grant a retroactive order to reduce a support obligation is contrary to a substantial body of jurisprudence"[352] but in his opinion, these cases, many of which were decided before the Supreme Court of Canada's decision in *DBS v SRG*, "must be re-evaluated in light of that decision."[353] Robertson JA also acknowledged that *DBS v SRG* deals with child support but he perceives "no valid policy reason for distinguishing between child and spousal support when it comes to the retroactive variation of arrears" because "the need for the distinction evaporates once it is accepted that delay in enforcement (the notion of fault) is no longer a relevant consideration when it comes to retroactive orders involving a decrease in support."[354] His elimination of any distinction between child support and spousal support runs contrary to caselaw elsewhere in Canada, which suggests that child support arrears are less likely to be remitted, because parents cannot waive their child's right to support and the conduct of a parent should not prejudice the rights of the child.[355] It is noteworthy, however, that Robertson JA stated that

> [t]here may be cases where the support recipient expressly agrees to waive spousal support or acts such that the payer reasonably believes that the support obligation will not be enforced and the payer relies, to his or her detriment, on the recipient's representations or inducements. If that should be the case, the payer is entitled to plead a material change of circumstances as of the time of the representation or inducement.[356]

Since *DBS v SRG* does not specifically address the criteria to be applied on a variation application seeking remission of child support arrears, the doctrine of *stare decisis*, whereby courts of first instance are bound by decisions of appellate courts from the same jurisdiction, may preclude courts elsewhere in Canada from adopting the principles articulated in *Brown v Brown*. Robertson JA expressly acknowledged that obstacles to the application of *Brown v Brown* extend to courts in British Columbia by reason of the express provisions of the *Family Relations Act*. He states:

---

352 2010 NBCA 5 at para 29.
353 *Ibid.*
354 *Ibid* at para 30.
355 See, for example, *Haisman v Haisman* (1994), 7 RFL (4th) 1 (Alta CA), leave to appeal to SCC refused (1995), 15 RFL (4th) 51 (SCC). See also *Thomas v Thomas*, 2014 ABQB 481 at para 56; *Scurci v Scurci*, 2013 ONSC 7199, citing *Cole v Freiwald and Freiwald*, 2011 ONCJ 395.
356 2010 NBCA 5 at para 37.

I cannot deny the existence of a large body of jurisprudence supporting the commonly held understanding that courts retain the jurisdiction to reduce or cancel arrears in circumstances where there is a present and future inability to pay on the part of the delinquent payer. I am also aware of the existence of legislation which expressly authorizes the remission of arrears on broad grounds. The British Columbia *Family Relations Act*, R.S.B.C. 1996, c 128, s 96(2) and (3), authorizes the court to forgive arrears if it is satisfied that it would be "grossly unfair" not to do so.[357] The legislation also introduces the notion of fault when it comes to the decision to rescind: see: *Girard v Girard*, [2006] B.C.J. No. 2810 (QL), 2006 BCCA 482. Neither the federal nor New Brunswick legislation contains equivalent provisions.[358]

Although it may be legally improper to "directly" apply provincial statutory criteria to a variation proceeding that falls suspect to section 17 of the *Divorce Act*, they may be of assistance to a court in the exercise of its discretion under section 17 of the *Divorce Act*. It would be inequitable if the judicial remission of arrears were to depend on whether they accrued under an order granted pursuant to provincial statute or an order granted pursuant to the federal *Divorce Act*.

Since it may be impossible to reconcile the reasons for judgment in *Brown v Brown* with those of appellate judgments in other provinces,[359] the final resolution of any conflict must await a ruling from the Supreme Court of Canada. In an attempt to resolve the apparent conflict, Chappel J, of the Ontario Superior Court of Justice, in *Corcios v Burgos*[360] ventured the following opinion:

> I find that the following principles apply on a motion to change a child support order where the child support payor requests that the support be decreased on a retroactive basis, or that child support arrears be reduced or rescinded:
>
> 1. In dealing with these claims, the court must consider the following fundamental principles relating to child support which the Supreme Court of Canada set out in *D.B.S., supra:*
>   i. Child support is the right of the child that arises upon the child's birth and exists independent of any statute or court order. It survives the breakdown of the parents' relationship.

---

357   See now *Family Law Act*, SBC 2011, c 25, s 174, effective 18 March 2013.

358   *Brown v Brown*, 2010 NBCA 5 at para 39.

359   See *Scurci v Scurci*, 2013 ONSC 7199; compare *Thomas v Thomas*, 2014 ABQB 481 at para 56. And see *Corcios v Burgos*, 2011 ONSC 3326.

360   2011 ONSC 3326 at para 55.

ii. Child support should, as much as possible, provide children with the same standard of living they enjoyed when their parents were together. The amount of child support owed will vary based upon the income of the payor parent.

iii. The provincial power to regulate child support matters in contexts not involving divorce remains unfettered. Accordingly, when retroactive child support is sought, the court must analyze the statutory scheme in which the application is brought.

iv. The child support analysis must not lose sight of the fact that child support is the right of the child. Accordingly, the child should not be left to suffer if one or both parents fail to monitor child support payments vigilantly.

v. Ultimately, the goal in addressing child support issues is to ensure that children benefit from the support they are owed when they are owed it, and any incentives for payor parents to be deficient in meeting their child support obligations should be eliminated.

vi. The specific amounts of child support owed will vary based upon the income of the payor parent. As income levels increase or decrease, so will the parents' contributions to the needs of the child.

2. A distinction must be drawn between cases where the child support payor had the ability to pay child support when arrears accrued, and then asks for relief from payment of the arrears based on current inability to pay, as opposed to those cases where arrears accumulated due to a change in the payor's circumstances that affected the payor's ability to make the child support payments when they came due.

3. The mere accumulation of child support arrears and current inability to pay, without evidence that the payor was unable to make the child support payments when they became due because of a change in circumstances at that time, does not typically justify a rescission or reduction of arrears. In this situation, the court should enforce the outstanding court order, unless there are compelling reasons not to do so. Generally, a reduction or rescission of arrears should only be considered in this type of case where the payor has established on a balance of probabilities that they cannot pay and will not ever in the future be able to pay the arrears (*Haisman v. Haisman, supra*; *Gray v. Gray, supra*).

4. Where the payor cannot establish a change in circumstances at the time that the arrears accumulated that affected their ability to pay at the time, evidence that the recipient agreed to non-payment of the support is irrelevant, as child support is the right of the child and cannot be bargained away by the recipient parent.

5. Where the child support payor can establish a change in circumstances during the time that arrears were accumulating which rendered them unable for a substantial period of time to make child support payments, the court may provide relief to the payor in a later proceeding to vary the child support order or rescind arrears. In these circumstances, the court may determine that it is appropriate to retroactively suspend enforcement of the support order during the time when the payor was unable to pay, or decrease the amount of child support owed during that time and reduce or rescind the arrears owing accordingly (*see Haisman v. Haisman, supra*). There is no fixed formula for how the court should exercise its discretion in these circumstances, but the relevant factors and considerations include the following:

   i. The nature of the obligation to support, whether contractual, statutory or judicial. (*Gray v. Gray, supra*; *Filipich v. Filipich, supra*; *DiFrancesco v. Couto, supra*).

   ii. Whether there is a reasonable excuse for the child support payor's delay in applying for relief. (*D.B.S., supra*; *Gray v. Gray, supra*; *Filipich v. Filipich, supra*; *DiFrancesco v. Couto, supra*). While unreasonable delay may not negate all potential relief, it is a factor to consider in determining whether the court should exercise its discretion to grant relief and if so, how the remedy should be crafted. (*M.(D.) v. A.(S.), supra*). Even in cases where the child support payor gives the recipient notice of a change in circumstances, delay in actually initiating a court proceeding may be a relevant factor in determining whether to grant relief to the payor. This could arise, for instance, if the payor does not provide the recipient with disclosure which the recipient may need to independently assess the payor's claim that child support should be changed.

   iii. The ongoing financial capacity of the child support payor, and in particular, their ability to make payments towards the outstanding arrears. (*Gray v. Gray, supra*; *Filipich v. Filipich, supra*; *DiFrancesco v. Couto, supra*; *Malleye v. Brereton, supra*; *Vaughan v. Vaughan*, [2007] O.J. No. 138, 2007 CarswellOnt 184 (S.C.J.)).

   iv. The ongoing need of the child support recipient and the child. (*D.B.S., supra*; *Gray v. Gray, supra*; *Filipich v. Filipich, supra*; *DiFrancesco v. Couto, supra*; *Malleye v. Brereton, supra*; *Vaughan v. Vaughan, supra*).

   v. The conduct of the child support payor, including whether they have made any voluntary payments on account of arrears, whether they have cooperated with enforcement agencies in addressing the issue of child support, whether they have kept the recipient fully apprised of the changes in their circumstances over time as these changes occurred, whether they have complied with obligations and requests for financial disclosure to the child support recipient in an effort to address the child support issue, and any evidence respecting their willingness to support the child or alternatively to avoid their child support obligation. Behaviour that indicates wilful non-compliance with the terms of the order or failure to work cooperatively to address the child support issue is a factor that militates against even partial rescission of or reduction of arrears. (*D.B.S.*, *supra*; *DiFrancesco v. Couto*, *supra*). Further, failure to disclose a material change in circumstance to the recipient for an extended period of time may also be relevant (*M.(D.) v. A.(S.)*, *supra*).

vi. Delay on the part of the child support recipient, even a long delay, in enforcing the child support obligation, is not relevant and does not in and of itself constitute a waiver of the right to claim arrears. (*Haisman v. Haisman*, *supra*; *Brown v. Brown*, *supra*).

vii. Any hardship that may be occasioned by a retroactive order reducing arrears or rescinding arrears, or by an order requiring the payment of substantial arrears. (*Gray v. Gray*, *supra*; *Filipich v. Filipich*, *supra*; *DiFrancesco v. Couto*, *supra*; *D.B.S.*, *supra*). For example, if a retroactive order reducing child support would result in the child support recipient having to repay money to the child support payor, this may militate against making the order, particularly if the payor has not given the recipient notice of the change in their circumstances, has not provided appropriate disclosure to support their claim for an adjustment to the child support, or has delayed initiating court proceedings to change the order (*M.(D.) v. A.(S.)*, 2008 CarswellNS 367 (N.S.F.C.)). Where the order that the court considers to be appropriate involves payment of substantial arrears and could result in significant hardship to the payor, it may be necessary to retroactively decrease the child support payable, suspend enforcement of arrears for a period of time or establish a schedule for the payment of arrears that is realistic having regard for the payor's financial situation. (*Haisman v. Haisman*, *supra*; *(M.D.) v. A.(S.)*, *supra*).

6. If the court determines that a retroactive reduction of child support is appropriate, it must determine the date from which the change should be retroactive and the extent of the reduction. The Supreme Court of Canada in *D.B.S.*, *supra*, has established that generally, a retroactive child support Order should commence as of the date of effective notice

that a request is being made for an adjustment to child support. It further held that in most cases, it will be inappropriate to make a support award retroactive to a date more than three years before formal notice was given to the payor parent. These principles apply equally to claims for retroactive downward variation of child support, to the extent of determining how far back a court should consider making adjustments to the order.[361] The effective date of notice is "any indication by the payor parent that child support requires a review and adjustment. Effective notice does not require the payor parent to take legal action; what is required is that the topic be broached." (*M.(D.) v. A. (S.), supra*).

7. However, in the case of retroactive child support reduction or rescission claims, the payor is the party who has the information to support the claim, and therefore effective notice in these cases also entails providing reasonable proof to support the claim for a change to the Order, so that the recipient can independently assess the situation in a meaningful way and respond appropriately. A child support recipient is entitled to expect that the existing order will be complied with, and to arrange their financial affairs respecting their children accordingly, unless they are in receipt of reasonable proof that a relevant change in the payor's circumstances has occurred. The absence of a disclosure requirement on the payor in these cases would unfairly impose a burden on the support recipient to attempt to confirm the alleged change in circumstances in order to decide how to respond to the payor's claim for an adjustment.

8. Once effective notice is given, a reasonable opportunity should be granted for the parties to enter into negotiations. However, the payor has a duty to initiate proceedings in a timely manner to address the issue if these negotiations are not successful and failure to do so may militate against relief for the Respondent, particularly where the Respondent has failed to provide disclosure of relevant materials to the recipient. (*M.(D.) v. A(S.), supra*).

9. In the case of retroactive reduction or rescission claims, the payor's circumstances may continue to change from time to time after the date when the initial change in circumstance arose. There is an ongoing obligation on the child support payor to engage in dialogue with the recipient about those changes as they arise, and to provide disclosure of relevant information respecting the Respondent's circumstances so that the recipient can continue to independently assess the situation and react appropriately. Thus, in these cases, the effective date of notice of

---

361 But see *Trembley v Daley*, 2012 ONCA 780; *Abballe v Abballe*, 2014 ONSC 4244.

the initial change of circumstance may determine the date from which relief for the payor may begin, but there are ongoing notice and disclosure obligations about subsequent changes which, if not satisfied, may impact on the remedy which the court crafts.

10. With respect to the quantum of any retroactive child support order, the *Child Support Guidelines* apply, provided that the date of retroactivity is not prior to the date when the *Guidelines* came into force, and subject to the principles set out in the statutory scheme under which the Court is operating (*D.B.S., supra; M.(D.) v. A.(S.), supra*).

It remains to be seen whether appellate courts in Canada will accept Chappel J's rationalization of the relevant caselaw.[362]

The court has jurisdiction to order the payment of arrears in an orderly manner. A schedule for payment must be realistic, having regard to the potential for compliance and its sufficiency in addressing the needs of the children for whose benefit the payments are being made. Enforcement of some or all of the arrears may be postponed with a direction for them to be discharged by future instalments.[363]

Full or partial remission of arrears may be granted for a variety of reasons, the most compelling of which is the obligor's inability to pay by reason of unemployment, reduction of income, or illness,[364] or termination of the child's entitlement to support. Lack of knowledge of the relevant facts may entitle a payor to reimbursement of overpayments of child support by means of a retroactive variation order, but such relief should not be granted to a payor who knew the facts but failed to take timely action to remedy the situation.[365]

---

362 Compare *Trembley v Daley*, 2012 ONCA 780 at para 15.

363 *Young v Konkle* (1993), 1 RFL (4th) 211 (Alta QB); *Sampson v Sampson*, [1998] AJ No 1214 (QB); *BL v SS*, [2003] AJ No 696 (QB); *Beaudoin v Beaudoin* (1993), 45 RFL (3d) 412 (BCSC); *PH v PH*, [2008] NBJ No 52 (CA); *Delorme v Woodham* (1993), 89 Man R (2d) 16 (QB); *Adamson v Steed*, [2006] OJ No 5306 (Sup Ct); *Stewart v Stewart*, [2000] SJ No 149 (QB).

364 *Doole v Doole* (1991), 32 RFL (3d) 283 (Alta QB); *Smith v Smith* (1990), 27 RFL (3d) 32 (Man CA); *Domanski v Domanski* (1992), 83 Man R (2d) 161 (CA); *Klassen v Klassen* (1993), 44 RFL (3d) 443 (Man CA); *Stacey v Hacking* (1993), 142 NBR (2d) 99 (QB); *Pidgeon v Hickman*, [2000] NJ No 44 (SC); *Rector v Hamilton* (1989), 94 NSR (2d) 284 (Fam Ct); *Propper v Vanleeuwen*, [1999] OJ No 2297 (Sup Ct); *Stewart v Stewart*, [2000] SJ No 149 (QB); *Turnbull v Turnbull*, [1998] YJ No 145 (SC); see also *Bernard v Bernard*, [2008] AJ No 302 (QB) (partial remission of arrears accrued during obligor's imprisonment).

365 *Collison v Collison*, [2001] BCJ No 2080 (SC); see also *GMW v DPW*, 2014 BCCA 282; *Poirier v Poirier*, 2013 NSSC 314.

N. DETERMINATION AND DISCLOSURE OF INCOME

The obligor's income is the foundation on which the provincial and territorial tables in the *Federal Child Support Guidelines* fix the monthly amount of basic child support. The recipient parent's income or that of the child only becomes relevant in those cases where the court is empowered to deviate from the table amount.[366]

Justice Martinson, of the Supreme Court of British Columbia, has formulated the following step-by-step guide to the determination of a parent's income under the *Federal Child Support Guidelines*.[367] The steps are divided in two parts, each of which has four steps. The following summary is extracted from her judgment:

Part I — Actual Earnings
- *Step One*: Gather mandatory information pursuant to financial disclosure requirements.
- *Step Two*: Examine separately each source of income identified in the CRA T1 General form and use the most current information available to predict the parent's prospective annual earnings from each source.
- *Step Three*: Review historical patterns of income over the last three taxation years to determine whether the predicted income under Step Two is the fairest determination of annual income from each source. If it is not, the historical pattern of earnings can be used to predict the parent's prospective annual income from each source.
- *Step Four*: Total the predicted income from each source.

Part II — Imputing Income
- *Step Five*: Assess the parent's earning capacity in light of whether a parent is under-employed, unreasonably deducts expenses from income, is not using property to generate income, or is hiding income behind a corporate veil.
- *Step Six*: Determine whether the parent receives any income tax benefits or concessions or benefits under a trust.
- *Step Seven*: Decide whether a parent is seeking to avoid the payment of child support by diverting income or not making full financial disclosure.
- *Step Eight*: Decide whether any other supplemental income should reasonably be attributed to the parent.

---

366 See Section D, above in this chapter.
367 *Murphy v Murphy*, [2000] BCJ No 1253 (SC); *Hamilton v Pearce*, [2000] BCJ No 1953 (SC).

Sections 16 to 20 of the *Federal Child Support Guidelines* define how income is to be determined for the purpose of applying the Guidelines.[368]

Section 16 of the *Federal Child Support Guidelines* provides that, subject to sections 17 to 20 of the Guidelines, a spouse's annual income is determined by reference to the sources of income set out under the heading "Total income" in the Canada Revenue Agency's T1 General form, with adjustments being made in accordance with sections 1 to 10 of Schedule III of the Guidelines.[369] The T1 General form identifies the sources that make up total income, including:

(a)   employment income;

(b)   other employment income;

(c)   Old Age Security pension;

(d)   Canada or Quebec Pension Plan benefits;

(e)   disability benefits;

(f)   other pensions or superannuation;

(g)   Employment Insurance benefits;

(h)   dividends;

(i)   interest and other investment income;

(j)   partnership income;

(k)   rental income;

(l)   capital gains;

(m)   registered retirement savings plan income;

(n)   other income;

(o)   business income;

(p)   professional income;

(q)   commission income;

(r)   farming income;

(s)   fishing income;

(t)   workers' compensation benefits;

(u)   social assistance payments; and

(v)   net federal supplements.[370]

---

368   For an excellent detailed analysis of this topic, see V Jennifer MacKinnon, "Determining Income under the *Child Support Guidelines*" in The Law Society of Upper Canada, *Child Support Guidelines: Recent and Important Caselaw* (16 December 1998). See also Aaron Franks, "Deferred Compensation versus Current Support Obligations" in The Law Society of Upper Canada, *Special Lectures 2006: Family Law* (Toronto: Irwin Law, 2007) 273.

369   *Lavergne v Lavergne*, 2007 ABCA 169; *Caverley v Stanley*, 2015 ONSC 647.

370   *Strecko v Strecko*, 2013 NSSC 49 at para 68, citing the *Income Tax Act*, RSC 1985 (5th Supp), c 1 as amended, Part 1 — Income Tax: Division B — Computation of Income.

Specified adjustments to the spouse's income provided under Schedule III of the Guidelines include the following:

- the spouse's employment expenses that would be deductible under paragraphs 8(1)(d) to (j) and (n) to (q) of the *Income Tax Act* are deducted;[371]
- CPP contributions and Employment Insurance premiums under section 8(1)(l.1) of the *Income Tax Act* are deducted if paid in respect of another employee who has acted as an assistant or substitute for the spouse;[372]
- child support that is included to determine total income in the T1 General form issued by the Canada Revenue Agency is to be deducted;
- spousal support received from the other spouse is deducted in calculating income for the purpose of determining the amount of child support under the applicable provincial or territorial table;[373]
- spousal support paid to the other spouse is deducted in calculating income for the purpose of determining an amount respecting special or extraordinary expenses under section 7 of the Guidelines;[374]
- social assistance income is adjusted to include only the amount determined to be attributable to the spouse;[375]
- the taxable amount of dividends from Canadian corporations received by the spouse is replaced by the actual amount of those dividends received by the spouse;[376]
- the taxable capital gains realized in a year by the spouse are replaced by the actual amount of capital gains realized by the spouse in excess of actual capital loss suffered by the spouse in that year;[377]
- the actual amount of business investment losses suffered by a spouse during the year is deducted;[378]

---

371 *Jarbeau v Pelletier*, [1998] OJ No 3029 (Prov Div) (meals and lodgings of railway employee held deductible under *Income Tax Act*, paragraph 8(1)(e); union dues deductible under paragraph 8(1)(i); motor vehicle expenses deductible under paragraph 8(1)(j)); *Haimanot v Haimanot*, [2002] SJ No 12 (CA) (union dues).

372 *Guidelines to Amend the Federal Child Support Guidelines*, SOR/97-563, s 12 amending SOR/97-175, para 1(i) of Schedule III.

373 *Moro v Miletich*, [1998] OJ No 1799 (Gen Div); *Schick v Schick*, [1997] SJ No 447 (QB). See also *Henderson v Casson*, 2014 ONSC 720.

374 *Russell v Russell*, [2002] BCJ No 1983 (SC); *Galloway v Galloway*, [2008] BCJ No 94 (CA); *Margee v Magee*, [1997] SJ No 468 (QB).

375 *Martell v Martell*, [2001] OJ No 759 (Ct Just).

376 But see *DE v LE*, 2014 NBCA 67.

377 *Kendry v Cathcart*, [2001] OJ No 277 (Sup Ct); *Andersen v Andersen*, [1997] BCJ No 2496 (SC); *Coghill v Coghill*, [2006] OJ No 2602 (Sup Ct); see also *Schick v Schick*, 2008 ABCA 196.

378 *Omah-Maharajh v Howard*, [1998] AJ No 173 (QB).

- the spouse's carrying charges and interest expenses that are paid by the spouse and that would be deductible under the *Income Tax Act* are deducted;[379]
- where the net self-employment income of the spouse is determined by deducting an amount in respect of salaries, wages or management fees, or other payments, paid to or on behalf of persons with whom the spouse does not deal at arm's length, that amount shall be added, unless the spouse establishes that the payments were necessary to earn the self-employment income and were reasonable in the circumstances;[380]
- where the spouse reports income from self-employment that includes income for the reporting year plus a further amount earned in the prior year, the spouse may deduct the amount earned in the prior period, net of reserves;
- spousal income includes any deduction for an allowable capital cost allowance with respect to real property;
- where the spouse earns income from a partnership or sole proprietorship, any amount included in income that is properly required by the partnership or sole proprietorship for purposes of capitalization shall be deducted from the spouse's income;[381]
- where the spouse has received, as an employee benefit, stock options to purchase shares of a Canadian-controlled private corporation, or a publicly traded corporation that is subject to the same tax treatment as a Canadian-controlled private corporation, and has exercised the options during the year, the difference between the value of the shares at the time the options are exercised and the amount paid for the shares and any amount paid to acquire the options is added to the spouse's income for the year in which the options are exercised;[382] and
- if a spouse is deemed to have received a split-pension amount under paragraph 60.03(2)(b) of the *Income Tax Act* that is included in that

---

379 *Tynan v Moses*, [2002] BCJ No 197 (SC); *Andres v Andres*, [1999] MJ No 103 (CA) (mortgage payments respecting rental property; principal not deductible under s 18(1)(b) of *Income Tax Act*; interest deductible under s 20(1)(c) of *Income Tax Act*); *Haimanot v Haimanot*, [2002] SJ No 12 (CA).

380 *Holtby v Holtby*, [1997] OJ No 2237 (Gen Div); *Finn v Levine*, [1997] OJ No 2201 (Gen Div); *Stewart v Stewart*, [2000] SJ No 149 (QB).

381 *Austin v Austin*, [2007] OJ No 4283 (Sup Ct).

382 See Aaron Franks, "Deferred Compensation versus Current Support Obligations," in The Law Society of Upper Canada, *Special Lectures 2006: Family Law* (Toronto: Irwin Law, 2007) 273.

spouse's total income in the T1 General form issued by the Canada Revenue Agency, that amount is to be deducted.[383]

Pursuant to SOR/2007-59, which became effective on 1 April 2007, the *Federal Child Support Guidelines* have been amended to address the impact of the Universal Child Care Benefit (UCCB). Although the UCCB does not constitute spousal income for the purpose of determining the table amount of child support, it must be taken into account in determining the reasonableness of section 7 expenses and in apportioning those expenses between the spouses insofar as the UCCB is paid for the child in respect of whom section 7 expenses are ordered.[384]

The calculation of income under sections 16 to 20 of the *Federal Child Support Guidelines* can be exceedingly complex, and the problems are compounded by the fact that accounting procedures applicable under the *Income Tax Act* are not necessarily the same as those applicable under the Guidelines.

Judicial determination of the income of wage earners is relatively simple, because they usually have only one source of income and their income tax returns are likely to provide a true reflection of their annual income. Where spouses are self-employed, the net income reported on their income tax return is not necessarily a true reflection of their income for the purpose of determining their child support obligations. Business expenses that may be legitimately deducted under the *Income Tax Act* are not necessarily allowed under the *Federal Child Support Guidelines*.[385] For example, capital cost allowances permitted for the depreciation of business equipment may be permissible for income tax purposes, but disallowed in whole or in part for the purpose of determining a spouse's income under the *Federal Child Support Guidelines*.[386]

Section 2(3) of the *Federal Child Support Guidelines* requires a court to use "the most current information" to determine a spouse's annual income.[387] Historical information, based on personal or corporate tax returns or other available data, is often predictive of a spouse's current annual income and may be relied upon in the absence of any contrary indication.[388] Reliable current information should be used where it conflicts with historical information

---

383 *Guidelines Amending the Federal Child Support Guidelines*, SOR/2009-181 (11 June 2009).

384 For the specific language of the amendments and an excellent "Regulatory Impact Analysis Statement," see *Canada Gazette*, Vol. 141, No 7 (4 April 2007), online: http://publications.gc.ca/gazette/archives/p2/2007/2007-04-04/pdf/g2-14107.pdf.

385 *Cook v McManus*, [2006] NBJ No 334 (QB).

386 *Andries v Andries*, [1999] MJ No 103 (CA); see also *Huber v Yaroshko*, [2000] SJ No 201 (QB).

387 *Lavergne v Lavergne*, 2007 ABCA 169; *TM v DM*, 2014 NBQB 132; *Koester v Koester*, 2014 NSSC 367.

388 *Rasmussen v MacDonald*, [1997] SJ No 667 (QB).

because child support is payable out of current and future income, not out of past earnings.[389] In determining a spouse's (parent's) income for the purpose of determining child support, section 2(3) of the *Federal Child Support Guidelines* mandates the use of the most current information, but this is only appropriate when the most recent information is likely to accurately reflect the spouse's prospective annual income. In *LAK v AAW*,[390] Johnstone J found that the father's pay stubs from January through May 2005 were not necessarily reflective of his anticipated annual income. Accordingly, the father's income for 2005 was determined by reference to his income tax return for 2004. In *Green v Green*,[391] the father contended that ill-health would continue to reduce his prospective annual income, as it had over the preceding three years. The applications judge, nevertheless, calculated the father's prospective annual income by extrapolation from his year-to-date earnings. The Newfoundland and Labrador Court of Appeal concluded that the applications judge had made no palpable and overriding error in determining the father's annual income for 2004 in this manner because, if his income continued to decrease due to ill-health, the father could apply to vary the amount of child support payable.

Section 17 of the *Federal Child Support Guidelines* provides various means whereby a court can address erratic or fluctuating annual incomes. The most widely used means of dealing with this problem under section 17 of the Guidelines is by way of averaging the annual income over the three most recent taxation years. It is inappropriate to rely on the averaging provisions of section 17 of the Guidelines to reduce an obligor's income where his or her current income is known and will not decrease in future years.[392] Section 17 of the Guidelines confers discretionary, not mandatory, powers on the court that are exercisable in the search for the fairest determination of a spouse's income.[393] When averaging a parent's income over the three preceding taxation years pursuant to section 17 of the *Federal Child Support Guidelines*, section 16 of the Guidelines does not require the court to rely on the pattern of income revealed in the parent's income tax returns. Additional income may be imputed to the parent pursuant to section 19 of the Guidelines before the averaging of the last three years of income is undertaken. While section 16 of the Guidelines permits recourse to sections 17 and 19 of the Guidelines to enable

---

389 *Halley v Halley*, [1998] NJ No 104 (SC); *Lee v Lee*, [1998] NJ No 247 (CA); *Coghill v Coghill*, [2006] OJ No 2602 (Sup Ct); *Luckett v Luckett*, [2002] SJ No 232 (QB).

390 [2005] AJ No 1140 (QB).

391 [2005] NJ No 165 (CA).

392 *Johnson v Checkowy*, [1997] SJ No 451 (QB).

393 *Wilson v Wilson*, [1998] SJ No 236 (QB); *Schnell v Schnell*, [2001] SJ No 704 (CA); *Luckett v Luckett*, [2002] SJ No 232 (QB).

a court to make the fairest determination of the parent's prospective annual income, section 16 does not treat sections 17 and 19 as mutually exclusive.[394]

Pursuant to section 18 of the *Federal Child Support Guidelines*, income may be attributed to a spouse whose income is artificially low because of low draws from a personal corporation.[395] Section 18 of the Guidelines can be invoked whenever a spouse's income, as determined under section 16 of the Guidelines, does not fairly reflect all the money that ought reasonably to be available for child support, after the legitimate needs of the corporation are taken into account. Given such a finding, the court has the discretionary jurisdiction under section 18(1) of the Guidelines to consider the spouse's income as including (a) all or part of the pre-tax income of the corporation; or (b) an amount commensurate with the services rendered to the corporation provided that the amount does not exceed the corporation's pre-tax income.[396] Only the pre-tax income of a corporation for the most recent taxation year may be included in a spouse's annual income under section 18(1)(a) of the Guidelines.[397] Section 18 is not directed at retained corporate earnings over several years, although such retained earnings could result in an imputation of income to a spouse under section 19 of the Guidelines.[398] In determining the pre-tax income of a corporation, money paid to persons with whom the corporation does not deal at arm's length must be added to the pre-tax income, unless the payment is shown to be reasonable in the circumstances.[399]

Three appellate judgments from British Columbia, Newfoundland and Labrador, and Manitoba offer significant guidance as to the interpretation to be accorded to section 18 of the Guidelines. The first is *Kowalewich v Kowalewich*,[400] wherein the British Columbia Court of Appeal formulated the following principles:

- A court need not look for signs of bad faith or undeclared personal benefits before imputing income to a parent pursuant to sections 17 or 18 of the Guidelines. Nor should a court look only to section 18(1)(b) of the Guidelines to determine the value of the parent's services to a company that the parent owns or controls.
- The attribution of pre-tax corporate income to a parent pursuant to section 18(1)(a) of the Guidelines does not strip that parent or his or

394 *Schnell v Schnell*, [2001] SJ No 704 (CA).
395 *Bhopal v Bhopal*, [1997] BCJ No 1746 (SC).
396 *Bear v Thompson*, 2014 SKCA 111.
397 *Ibid.*
398 *Morley v Morley*, [1999] SJ No 31 (QB).
399 *Federal Child Support Guidelines*, s 18(2); *Needham v Needham*, [1998] BCJ No 202 (SC).
400 [2001] BCJ No 1406 (CA).

her corporation of the income attributed. It is simply used as a measuring rod for the purpose of fixing the parent's annual income on the
basis of which the amount of child support will be determined.

- The purpose of section 18 of the Guidelines is to allow the court to lift
the corporate veil to ensure that money received as income by the paying parent fairly reflects all of the income reasonably available for the
purpose of assessing child support. A court's effort to ensure fairness
does not require a court to second-guess business decisions. What it
does require is that a parent's allocation of pre-tax corporate income
between business and family purposes be assessed for fairness by an
impartial tribunal when parents cannot reach agreement on priorities
as they would in an intact family. To determine whether "Total income"
in the T1 General form issued by the Canada Revenue Agency fairly
reflects a parent's income in the context of child support, a court might
ask what a reasonable and well-informed parent would make available
for child support in the circumstances of the particular business over
which the parent exercises control, having regard to the objectives
under section 1 of the Guidelines, the underlying parental obligation
to support children in accordance with parental means under section
26(2) of the *Divorce Act*, and any applicable situation arising from income fluctuations or non-recurring gains or losses under section 17 of
the Guidelines.

- No explicit guidance is provided as to how a parent or a court might go
about choosing whether to use the corporate income method of attribution under section 18(1)(a) of the Guidelines or the personal services
attribution method under section 18(1)(b) of the Guidelines. Section
18 suggests, however, two considerations in the pre-conditions for its
application: (1) which method produces an annual income that more
fairly reflects all the income available for the assessment of child support?, and (2) which method does the nature of the parent's relationship with the corporation support? Section 18 also permits reference
to the "situations described in section 17" and thus to the parent's income pattern over the preceding three years. The nature of the parent's
relationship with the corporation may sometimes be decisive. Section
18 of the Guidelines applies not only to a parent who wholly controls
a corporation; it also applies to a parent who shares corporate ownership and control with others. Where a parent wholly owns a corporation, the attribution of corporate income under section 18(1)(a) of the
Guidelines is likely to be the fairer method of determining parental income, because it allows a court to include not only reasonable payment
for personal services rendered to the corporation but also a reasonable

return on the parent's entrepreneurial capacity and investment. These are sources of income that an intact family would utilize. Moreover, it not only permits but requires the inclusion of the income of companies related within the meaning of the *Income Tax Act* and of non-armslength payments made without value to the company.

- There may be factors in particular cases that will recommend to the court the personal services method of attributing income under section 18(1)(b) of the Guidelines, as for example, where the corporation's only business is the provision of the personal services of its owner. There may also be cases where stability of income will persuade a trial judge to use the personal services method, having regard to situations under section 17 of the Guidelines.
- Section 18(1)(a) of the Guidelines allows a court to include all the pretax income of a corporation for the most recent taxation year in a parent's annual income for Guidelines purposes, but this is not required and courts should not make the inclusion of pretax corporate income the default position.
- The only explicit guidance provided as to how much of a corporation's pretax income should be included in the parent's annual income is found in the words "the court may consider the situations described in section 17." That section refers to the historical income pattern of a spouse and to non-recurring gains and losses. Regard should also be paid to the nature of the corporation's business and any evidence of legitimate calls on its corporate income for the purposes of that business. Money needed to maintain the value of the business as a viable going concern will not be available for support purposes and should not be included in determining a parent's annual income.
- Although an appellate court should not tinker with a trial judge's exercise of discretion, it may reduce the amount of corporate income attributed to a parent where the trial judge has paid insufficient regard to the evidence of legitimate business needs in determining what portion of pretax corporate income to include in the parent's annual income.

The second important appellate decision interpreting and applying section 18 of the Guidelines is *Gosse v Sorensen-Gosse*,[401] wherein the Newfoundland and Labrador Court of Appeal, building on and reiterating many of the principles set out in *Kowalewich v Kowalewich*, above, expressed the following opinion on the interpretation and application of section 18(1)(a) of the *Federal Child Support Guidelines*:

---

401 2011 NLCA 58.

- Section 18(1)(a) of the Guidelines provides that where a spouse is a shareholder, director, or officer of a corporation and the court is satisfied that the spouse's T1 Income Tax form does not fairly reflect all the money available to the spouse for the payment of child support, the court may include all or part of the pre-tax income of the corporation for the most recent taxation year in the spouse's annual income for the purpose of determining the appropriate amount of child support to be paid.

- The pre-tax income of the corporation will be adjusted pursuant to section 18(2) of the Guidelines to add non–arm's-length payments and benefits, unless they were reasonable under the circumstances.

- The pre-tax income of the corporation may be adjusted having regard to capital cost allowances claimed by the corporation.[402]

- Determining the annual income for child support purposes of a spouse who is a shareholder has nothing to do with the retained earnings of the corporation. Such a determination does not require paying out retained earnings. Whether the corporation has a pot of money, and whether the child of the parties was deprived of anything, is totally irrelevant to determining the income available to a spouse for child care.

- Section 18(1)(a) of the Guidelines does not make clear whether the discretion to impute "all" or "part" of the pre-tax corporate income is a general discretion, applicable to any corporation in which the spouse is a shareholder, or whether the discretion to impute all of the income arises only where the spouse is the sole shareholder and a part of the income, proportionate to the shareholding, where the spouse owns only part of the shares. It is reasonable to conclude that the latter is the correct interpretation.[403]

- Many professionals manage their practices through corporations, either as sole shareholders or as one of several shareholders. The necessity of imputing Guidelines income on the basis of shareholdings in these circumstances is obvious. It is equally obvious that the fact that a doctor or lawyer or engineer chooses to record his or her professional income through a wholly owned corporation does not justify reducing the pre-tax corporate income by factors that would not warrant reducing an unincorporated professional's income.

- The attribution of pre-tax corporate income to a spouse pursuant to section 18(1)(a) of the Guidelines does not strip that spouse or his or her corporation of the income attributed. It is simply used as a measuring

---

402   See also *Gossen v Gossen*, [2003] NSJ No 113 at para 83 (SC).
403   See, to like effect, *Chapman v Summer*, 2010 BCCA 237; *REG v TWJG*, 2011 SKQB 269.

rod for the purpose of fixing the spouse's annual income on the basis of which the amount of child support will be determined. Neither imputing pre-tax corporate income to a shareholder, nor adjusting the amount shown as pre-tax corporate income to offset non-cash expensing, in the course of establishing the basis for calculating child support obligations under the Guidelines, requires the corporation to alter its financial records or its business decisions in any manner. It does not require the actual transfer of any of its financial resources to the sole shareholder. That remains a decision of the corporation, as guided and directed by the sole shareholder. The corporation is not a party to the action and no order is directed at the corporation. In the case of a sole shareholder, the effect is, essentially, to ignore the corporate structure, for Guidelines income assessment purposes only, and to treat the shareholding spouse in the same manner as that spouse would be treated if the business were carried on in the name of that spouse personally.

- A court need not look for signs of bad faith or undeclared personal benefits before imputing income to a spouse pursuant to section 18(1)(a) of the Guidelines.
- The purpose of section 18 of the Guidelines is to allow the court to lift the corporate veil to ensure that money received as income by the paying spouse fairly reflects all of the income reasonably available for the purpose of assessing child support. A court's effort to ensure fairness does not require a court to second-guess business decisions nor "place the largest available shovel in the company store." What it does require is that a spouse's allocation of pretax corporate income between business and family purposes be assessed for fairness by an impartial tribunal when the spouses cannot reach agreement on priorities as they would in an intact family.
- To determine whether "total income" in the T1 General form issued by the Canada Revenue Agency fairly reflects a spouse's income in the context of child support, a court might ask what a reasonable and well-informed parent would make available for child support in the circumstances of the particular business over which the spouse exercises control, having regard to the objectives under section 1 of the Guidelines, the underlying obligation to support children in accordance with one's means under section 26(2) of the *Divorce Act*, and any applicable situation arising from income fluctuations or non-recurring gains or losses under section 17 of the Guidelines.
- The corporation's pre-tax income will be assumed to be available to the shareholding spouse for the payment of child support, unless there

is clear evidence led by that spouse to support the conclusion that re-investment is necessary to sustain the company as a viable enterprise. It is not open to a judge to speculate about the needs of the corporation in the absence of any supporting evidence.

- Where the spouse is a shareholder of a corporation, the test is whether or not the income, calculated in accordance with the Canada Revenue Agency T1 General form, "clearly reflect[s] all the money available to the spouse for the payment of child support." Section 18(1)(a) of the Guidelines provides that "the court may consider the situations de-scribed in section 17," namely, a fluctuating income pattern and non-recurring gains and losses. Pursuant to the options available under section 17, this could result in adding, solely for purposes of calculat-ing child support obligations, to the corporation's stated income, any capital losses used to set off capital gains during that year, or even the ignoring of business investment losses (see Guidelines, section 17 and Schedule III, paragraphs 6 and 7). It does not and cannot alter the corporation's stated income or affect any decision relevant to the de-termination of its income.

- Subject to the exclusion of amounts necessary to meet legitimate busi-ness calls substantiated by the evidence, the Guidelines are clearly in-tended to include as income available for child support all income over which the spouse has discretionary control, whether that income is recorded as being received personally or by a corporation. Where the corporation is wholly owned by the spouse, that can only mean 100 percent of the pre-tax income that is not subject to a retention require-ment to meet existing legitimate obligations of the corporation.

The third important appellate judgment interpreting section 18 of the *Federal Child Support Guidelines*, and its provincial counterpart under the *Manitoba Child Support Guidelines* whereunder subtle differences exist, is *Nesbitt v Nesbitt*,[404] wherein the Manitoba Court of Appeal formulated the following conclusions: Some cases assert that section 18 of the *Federal Child Support Guidelines* and their provincial counterparts should be applied only where a parent deliberately seeks to avoid child support obligations by, for example, artificially reducing income by leaving funds in his or her private company, or charging personal or living expenses to the company. Other cases interpret section 18 of the Guidelines more broadly to encompass situations where the parent's income, as determined under section 16 of the Guidelines, is perceived as not "fairly" reflecting all the income available to

---

404   [2001] MJ No 291 (CA); see also *Gossen v Gossen*, [2003] NSJ No 113 (SC).

the parent for the purpose of determining child support. A parent in control of a corporation who chooses to build up retained corporate earnings, rather than take the money out as personal income, has the onus of proving that there are legitimate business reasons for leaving the earnings in the corporation. If this onus is not discharged, a court may impute all the retained corporate earnings for the most recent taxation year to the parent for the purpose of applying the Guidelines. Pursuant to section 17 of the Guidelines, a court may average corporate income over the last three years to determine the annual income "that is fair and reasonable" to impute to the parent for the purpose of determining support under the Guidelines.[405] Although section 18 of the Guidelines allows the court to attribute corporate income to a parent only for the immediately preceding year, it may be possible to apply section 19(1)(e)[406] of the Guidelines as an additional potential source to impute retained corporate earnings to a parent. In *Bear v Thompson*,[407] Klebuc JA, of the Saskatchewan Court of Appeal observed that there are conflicting decisions on the interpretation to be accorded to section 18(1)(a) of the *Federal Child Support Guidelines* in circumstances where section 17(1) of the Guidelines is applied. One line of cases, including *Nesbitt v Nesbitt*, above, interprets the conjoint operation of sections 18(1)(a) and 17(1) of the Guidelines as entitling the court to attribute to the shareholding parent an annual sum equal to the average of the pre-tax income of a corporation during the preceding three years, even if that sum exceeds the corporation's pre-tax income for its most recent tax year. The second line of cases interprets the conjoint operation of sections 18(1)(a) and 17(1) of the *Federal Child Support Guidelines* in a manner that limits the authority of the court to attribute to the parent no more than the pre-tax income of a corporation for its most recent taxation year. Klebuc JA's closely reasoned analysis of the conflicting judicial decisions and his endorsement of the second line of cases is highly persuasive; it provides that a court should consider section 17 as part of the process of assessing whether "all or part of the pre-tax income of the corporation . . . for the most recent taxation year" should be attributed to the parent. In *O'Neill v O'Neill*,[408] Harvison Young J, in endorsing the first line of cases, stated that " [a] literal and restrictive interpretation of section 18(1)(a) would create an incentive for litigants seeking to avoid or minimize support obligations to manipulate the success or lack thereof of the corporation for the year preceding the trial." Any such manipulation, however, could be addressed by

---

405 Compare *Bear v Thompson*, 2014 SKCA 111.

406 Section 19 of the *Federal Child Support Guidelines* empowers a court to impute income to a parent whose "property is not reasonably utilized to generate income."

407 2014 SKCA 111.

408 [2007] OJ No 1706 (Sup Ct).

applying section 19 of the *Federal Child Support Guidelines*.[409] Although section 18 of the Guidelines allows the court to attribute corporate income to a parent only for the immediate preceding year, it may be possible to apply section 19(1)(d) or (e) of the Guidelines as an additional potential source to impute retained corporate earnings to a parent.[410] The accumulation of retained earnings in a corporation may result in an imputation of income pursuant to section 19 of the Guidelines where an obligor is not properly utilizing his or her property to generate income by, for example, failing to declare dividends when it is appropriate to do so.[411]

Speaking to factors relevant to determining whether corporation pre-tax income should be attributed to a parent under section 18 of the *Child Support Guidelines*, Chappel J, of the Ontario Superior Court of Justice, in *Thompson v Thompson*[412] stated:

> 92 A review of the case-law relating to section 18 indicates that courts have considered the following factors in determining whether all or a portion of a corporation's pre-tax income should be included in a party's income:
>
> a)   The historical pattern of the corporation for retained earnings.
> b)   The restrictions on the corporation's business, including the amount and cost of capital equipment that the company requires.
> c)   The type of industry the corporation is involved in, and the environment in which it operates.
> d)   The potential for business growth or contraction.
> e)   Whether the company is still in its early development stage and needs to establish a capital structure to survive and growth [sic].
> f)   Whether there are plans for expansion and growth, and whether the company has in the past funded such expansion by means of retained earnings or through financing.
> g)   The level of the company's debt.

---

409 Compare, for example, *Goett v Goett*, 2013 ABCA 216 wherein the pre-tax income of a corporation was imputed to a parent for child support purposes under the conjoint operation of sections 18 and 19 of the *Federal Child Support Guideline* when the parent was not a shareholder, director, or officer of the corporation but was the controlling mind and *de facto* owner of the corporation.

410 *Nesbitt v Nesbitt*, [2001] MJ No 291 (CA); *Verwey v Verwey*, 2007 MBCA 102; *Dyck v Dyck*, 2008 MBCA 135; *Cook v McManus*, [2006] NBJ No 334 (QB); see also *Giene v Giene* (1998), 234 AR 355 (QB); *Hodgkinson v Hodgkinson*, 2011 BCSC 634 at paras 38–42; *O'Neill v O'Neill*, [2007] OJ No 1706 (Sup Ct); but compare *C v S*, 2010 NBQB 252; *Bear v Thompson*, 2014 SKCA 111.

411 *Trueman v Trueman*, [2000] AJ No 1301 (QB); *Morley v Morley*, [1999] SJ No 31 (QB).

412 2013 ONSC 5500 at para 92.

h)   How the company obtains it [sic] financing and whether there are banking or financing restrictions.

i)   The degree of control exercised by the party over the corporation, and the extent if any to which the availability of access to pre-tax corporate income is restricted by the ownership structure.

j)   Whether the company's pre-tax corporate income and retained earnings levels are a reflection of the fact that it is sustained primarily by contributions from another related company.

k)   Whether the amounts taken out of the company by way of salary or otherwise are commensurate with industry standards.

l)   Whether there are legitimate business reasons for retaining earnings in the company. Monies which are required to maintain the value of the business as a going concern will not be considered available for support purposes. Examples of business reasons which the courts have accepted as legitimate include the following:

   i)   The need to acquire or replace inventory;

   ii) Debt-financing requirements;

   iii) Carrying accounts receivable for a significant period of time;

   iv) Cyclical peaks or valleys in cash flow;

   v)   Allowances for bad debts;

   vi) Allowances for anticipated business losses or extraordinary expenditures; and

   vii) Capital acquisitions.

In determining the annual income of a spouse or former spouse, section 19 of the *Federal Child Support Guidelines* entitles the court to impute such income to the spouse or former spouse as it considers appropriate in specified circumstances. The listed circumstances include the following:

(a)   the spouse [or former spouse] is intentionally under-employed or unemployed, other than where the under-employment or unemployment is required by the needs of a child of the marriage or any child under the age of majority or by reasonable educational or health needs of the spouse [or former spouse];

(b)   the spouse [or former spouse] is exempt from paying federal or provincial income tax;

(c)   the spouse [or former spouse] lives in a country that has effective rates of income tax that are significantly lower than those in Canada;

(d)   it appears that income has been diverted that would affect the level of child support to be determined under the Guidelines;

(e)   the property of the spouse [or former spouse] is not reasonably utilized to generate income;

(f) the spouse [or former spouse] has failed to provide income information when under a legal obligation to do so;[413]

(g) the spouse [or former spouse] unreasonably deducts expenses from income;

(h) the spouse [or former spouse] derives a significant portion of income from dividends,[414] capital gains, or other sources that are taxed at a lower rate than employment or business income; and

(i) the spouse [or former spouse] is a beneficiary under a trust and has been or may be in receipt of income or other benefits from the trust.

The list of circumstances under section 19 of the Guidelines that entitles a court to impute income to a spouse is not comprehensive and does not purport to limit the power of a court to impute income in other circumstances.[415] However, a court should decline to attribute income to an obligor on the basis of his or her lifestyle, insofar as that lifestyle is enhanced by the independent income of the obligor's new spouse.[416] Income may, nevertheless, be imputed to an obligor who diverts income to his or her spouse or common law spouse by means of a corporate entity that engages in non-arm's-length transactions.[417] Although income has been attributed to an obligor whose household expenses are shared by a new wife or an unmarried cohabitant,[418] widespread adoption of this practice would undermine the predictability and certainty sought to be achieved by the provincial and territorial tables under the *Federal Child Support Guidelines*. Different considerations apply, however, in those situations where the Guidelines expressly confer a judicial discretion, in the exercise of which the court is required to take account of the means or ability to pay of the parties.

Section 19(1)(a) of the *Federal Child Support Guidelines* empowers a court to impute such income as it deems appropriate to a spouse who "is intentionally under-employed or unemployed, other than where the under-employment or unemployment is required by the needs of a child of the marriage or any child under the age of majority or by reasonable educational or health

---

413 *Snyder v Pictou*, [2008] NSJ No 77 (CA); *Graham v Bruto*, 2008 ONCA 260.

414 *DE v LE*, 2014 NBCA 67; *Austin v Austin*, [2007] OJ No 4283 (Sup Ct).

415 *Charles v Charles*, [1997] BCJ No 1981 (SC); *DLM v JAM*, 2008 NBCA 2; *Bak v Dobell*, 2007 ONCA 304.

416 *Risen v Risen*, [1998] OJ No 3184 (Gen Div). As to parental gifts, see *Bak v Dobell*, 2007 ONCA 304.

417 *Kowalewich v Kowalewich*, [2001] BCJ No 1406 (SC).

418 See, for example, *Courchesne v Charlebois*, [1998] OJ No 2625 (Prov Ct); *Chace v Chace*, [1998] PEIJ No 64 (SCTD).

needs of the spouse."[419] Appellate courts in British Columbia,[420] Manitoba,[421] Newfoundland and Labrador,[422] Nova Scotia,[423] Ontario,[424] Quebec,[425] and Saskatchewan[426] have concluded that section 19(1)(a) of the Guidelines is not confined to circumstances where a parent deliberately seeks to evade his or her child support obligations or recklessly disregards his or her children's financial needs while pursuing his or her personal choice of employment or lifestyle. Although such deliberate or reckless conduct, where it exists, weighs heavily in the exercise of the court's discretion to impute income to a parent, the proper test for the judicial imputation of income to a parent pursuant to section 19(1)(a) of the Guidelines is perceived in the aforementioned appellate judgments as being a test of reasonableness. According to this criterion, the court must have regard to the parent's capacity to earn in light of such factors as employment history, age, education, skills, health, available employment opportunities, and the standard of living enjoyed during the marriage. This criterion was accepted in the dissenting opinion of Picard JA, of the Alberta Court of Appeal, in *Hunt v Smolis-Hunt*.[427] A contrary opinion was voiced, however, by Berger JA, with whom Wittmann JA concurred.[428] Their majority judgment spoke of two irreconcilable lines of authority interpreting section 19(1)(a) of the Guidelines. The one line of authority would allow a court to impute income to parents only when they have engaged in a deliberate course of conduct for the purpose of undermining or avoiding their child support obligations. The second line is reflected in the test of reasonableness previously outlined. The majority judgment's endorsement of a test based on the deliberate evasion of child support obligations is difficult to reconcile with the overall content of section 19(1)(a) of the *Federal Child Support Guidelines*.

---

419   See DA Rollie Thompson, "Slackers, Shirkers, and Career-Changers: Imputing Income for Under/Unemployment" (2007) 26 Fam LQ 135.

420   *Watts v Willie*, [2004] BCJ No 2482 (CA); *TK v RJHA*, 2015 BCCA 8.

421   *Donovan v Donovan*, [2000] MJ No 407 (CA); *Schindle v Schindle*, [2001] MJ No 564 (CA); *Steele v Koppanyi*, [2002] MJ No 201 (CA).

422   *Duffy v Duffy*, 2009 NLCA 48.

423   *Montgomery v Montgomery*, [2000] NSJ No 1 (CA); see also *Lamarche v Lamarche*, 2011 NSSC 72.

424   *AMD v AJP*, [2002] OJ No 3731, (*sub nom Drygala v Pauli*) (2002), 29 RFL (5th) 293 (CA); *Riel v Holland*, [2003] OJ No 3901 (CA); *Lawson v Lawson*, [2006] OJ No 3179 (CA). For an excellent summary of relevant principles and Ontario caselaw, see *Tillmanns v Tillmanns*, 2014 ONSC 6773 at paras 48–81.

425   *Droit de la famille — 1275*, 2012 QCCA 87.

426   *Pontius v Murray*, 2011 SKCA 121; see also *Tessman v Tessman*, 2012 SKQB 11.

427   [2001] AJ No 1170 (CA).

428   See also *PEK v BWK*, [2003] AJ No 1706 (CA); *Demers v Moar*, [2004] AJ No 1331 (CA); *Taylor v Taylor*, 2009 ABCA 354; *Normandin v Kovalench*, [2007] NWTJ No 105 (SC). Compare *Thomas v Thomas*, 2014 ABQB 481.

As Veit J, of the Alberta Court of Queen's Bench, has observed, section 19(1)(a) of the Guidelines, when read in its entirety, appears to negate any requirement that a parent intend to evade his or her child support obligations. If such an intention were required, it would not have been necessary to create an express exemption in section 19(1)(a) of the Guidelines for a parent who is underemployed or unemployed because of the needs of a child or because of the reasonable educational or health needs of the parent.[429]

In *Donovan v Donovan*,[430] Steele JA, of the Manitoba Court of Appeal, endorsed the following six principles as relevant when determining whether income should be imputed to a parent pursuant to section 19(1)(a) of the *Federal Child Support Guidelines*:

1. There is a duty to seek employment in a case where a parent is healthy and there is no reason why the parent cannot work. It is "no answer for a person liable to support a child to say he is unemployed and does not intend to seek work or that his potential to earn income is an irrelevant factor" (*Van Gool v. Van Gool* (1998), 113 B.C.A.C. 200; 184 W.A.C. 200; 166 D.L.R. (4th) 528 (C.A.)).

2. When imputing income on the basis of intentional under-employment, a court must consider what is reasonable under the circumstances. The age, education, experience, skills and health of the parent are factors to be considered in addition to such matters as availability of work, freedom to relocate and other obligations.

3. A parent's limited work experience and job skills do not justify a failure to pursue employment that does not require significant skills, or employment in which the necessary skills can be learned on the job. While this may mean that job availability will be at the lower end of the wage scale, courts have never sanctioned the refusal of a parent to take reasonable steps to support his or her children simply because the parent cannot obtain interesting or highly paid employment.

4. Persistence in unremunerative employment may entitle the court to impute income.

---

429 *Phipps v Phipps*, [2001] AJ No 1206 (QB). See also *Barker v Barker*, [2005] BCJ No 687 (CA).

430 (2000), 150 Man R (2d) 116 at para 21 (CA); see also *Thomas v Thomas*, 2014 ABQB 481; *Hanson v Hanson*, [1999] BCJ No 2532 (SC); *Watts v Willie*, [2004] BCJ No 2482 (CA); *McCaffrey v Paleolog*, 2011 BCCA 378; *DLM v JAM*, 2008 NBCA 2; *ML v BH*, 2012 NBQB 233; *Lambert v Lambert*, 2008 NLUFC 38; *Smith v Helppi*, 2011 NSCA 65; *Favero v Favero*, 2013 ONSC 4216; *Tessman v Tessman*, 2012 SKQB 11. For a more detailed summary of the principles applicable under s 19(1)(a) of the *Federal Child Support Guidelines*, see *Algner v Algner*, [2008] SJ No 182 (QB); see also *Daniel-DeFreitas v Francis*, 2012 ONSC 515 at paras 57–58.

5. A parent cannot be excused from his or her child support obligations in furtherance of unrealistic or unproductive career aspirations.

6. As a general rule, a parent cannot avoid child support obligations by a self-induced reduction of income.

Delivering the opinion of the Newfoundland and Labrador Court of Appeal in *Duffy v Duffy*,[431] Welsh JA elicited the following principles from relevant caselaw dealing with the judicial imputation of income to a parent under the *Federal Child Support Guidelines*:

1. The fundamental obligation of a parent to support his or her children takes precedence over the parent's own interests and choices.

2. A parent will not be permitted to knowingly avoid or diminish, and may not choose to ignore, his or her obligation to support his or her children.

3. A parent is required to act responsibly when making financial decisions that may affect the level of child support available from that parent.

4. Imputing income to a parent on the basis that the parent is "intentionally under-employed or unemployed" does not incorporate a requirement for proof of bad faith. "Intentionally" in this context clarifies that the provision does not apply to situations beyond the parent's control.

5. The determination to impute income is discretionary, as the court considers appropriate in the circumstances.

6. Where a parent is intentionally under-employed or unemployed, the court may exercise its discretion not to impute income where that parent establishes the reasonableness of his or her decision.

7. A parent will not be excused from his or her child support obligations in furtherance of unrealistic or unproductive career aspirations or interests. Nor will it be acceptable for a parent to choose to work for future rewards to the detriment of the present needs of his or her children, unless the parent establishes the reasonableness of his or her course of action.

8. A parent must provide proper and full disclosure of financial information. Failure to do so may result in the court drawing an adverse inference and imputing income.

Welsh JA further stated that the amount of imputed income must be supported by the evidence, although some degree of imprecision may be inevitable.

---

431 2009 NLCA 48 at para 35.

A father, who is currently earning far less than the annual income previously earned, must provide a satisfactory explanation for the change or run the risk that income will be imputed to him on the basis of his previously demonstrated earning capacity.[432]

Courts have frequently declined to impute income to mothers who have temporarily withdrawn from the work force so as to provide stay-at-home care for their child of a second family. In *Burke v Burke*,[433] the father sought to reduce the amount of child support payable under a separation agreement in consequence of his subsequent retirement from the military at the age of forty-two. At the time of the application, which was joined with a divorce proceeding, the father was living with his common law spouse and their infant son. His common law spouse's earning capacity exceeded that of the father when he was in the military and they decided that he would be a "stay-at-home dad" for their child. In addressing his application to reduce the agreed amount of child support to reflect his current retirement income, Coady J found that the father's decision to retire after twenty-two years in the military was reasonable, as was his decision to personally provide primary daily care for his infant son. Consequently, Coady J refused to impute income to the father under section 19(1)(a) of the Guidelines, being of the opinion that to do so would constitute a gender-based double standard. In the result, child support was fixed on the basis of the retirement income being received by the father.

Income may be judicially imputed to a parent on a stepped-up basis over several years where the court is not satisfied that parent has made reasonable efforts to realize his or her income earning capacity.[434]

A judge cannot act on personal or privately acquired information. Furthermore, a judge cannot take judicial notice of a fact unless (1) the matter is so notorious as to be indisputable by reasonable people; or (2) the matter is capable of immediate accurate demonstration by resort to readily reliable sources of indisputable accuracy. A judge should proceed with the utmost caution if he or she is tempted to take judicial notice of a fact that is vital to the resolution of the case, especially where counsel has not been afforded an opportunity to speak to the matter. Where a self-employed parent has provided unchallenged evidence of his or her annual earnings and business expenses and there is no evidence that the parent is intentionally underemployed, or that his or her property is underutilized, or that he or she has unreasonably deducted business expenses, a court is not entitled to impute additional

---

432   *Steele v Koppanyi*, [2002] MJ No 201 (CA).

433   [2005] NSJ No 74 (SC).

434   *Cipriano v Hampton*, 2015 ONSC 349 at para 15.

income to that parent by relying on information that the judge possesses with respect to the income earned and the cost of services rendered by people in similar occupations to the parent. Should a judge pursue such a course of action, it constitutes a palpable and overriding error that warrants reversal on appeal.[435]

An appellate court should not interfere with a trial judge's conclusion that a parent acted reasonably in seeking lesser-paid employment in order to spend more time with his children, where the trial judge chose to accept the husband's explanation for the change of employment. The fact that the appellate court is troubled by the finding of the trial judge is an insufficient basis for overturning it. An appellate court may intervene only where there is a material error, a serious misapprehension of the evidence, or an error in law. An appellate court cannot overturn a support order simply because it would have made a different decision or balanced the factors differently.[436]

The *Federal Child Support Guidelines* base support payments on the payor's gross taxable income. One of the objectives of the Guidelines is to ensure "consistent treatment" of those who are in "similar circumstances." Thus, there are provisions to impute income where a parent is exempt from paying tax, lives in a lower taxed jurisdiction, or derives income from sources that are taxed at a lower rate. Where a parent arranges his or her affairs to pay substantially less tax on income, the income must be grossed up before the table is applied. This is the only way to ensure the consistency mandated by the legislation.[437] In addition to the express powers to impute income under section 19 of the *Federal Child Support Guidelines*, a failure to file income tax returns and other financial data, as required by section 21(1) of the *Federal Child Support Guidelines*, entitles the other spouse to have an application for child support set down for a hearing in accordance with section 22(1)(a) of the Guidelines and, at such a hearing, the court may, pursuant to section 23 of the Guidelines, impute income to the offending spouse in such amount as is considered appropriate.[438] The inadequacy of the income information provided by the obligor may entitle the court to impute an income based on all of the evidence presented. The court may take cognizance that the lifestyle of the obligor indicates a higher income than that indicated.[439] Income may be

---

435 *Dean v Brown*, [2002] NSJ No 439 (CA).

436 *Schindle v Schindle*, [2001] MJ No 564 (CA).

437 *Orser v Grant*, [2000] OJ No 1429 (Sup Ct); *Manis v Manis*, [2000] OJ No 4539 (Sup Ct).

438 *Cole v Cole*, [2000] NSJ No 74 (SC); *Guillena v Guillena*, [2003] NSJ No 76 (SC); *Alexander v Alexander*, [1999] OJ No 3694 (Sup Ct).

439 *Davari v Namazi*, [1999] BCJ No 116 (SC); *Motyka v Motyka*, [2001] BCJ No 52 (CA); *Manis v Manis*, [2000] OJ No 4539 (Sup Ct); *Muir-Lang v Lang*, [2002] OJ No 869 (Sup Ct); *Jonas*

imputed to a parent whose banking records are indicative of a higher income than that asserted.[440]

Section 19(1)(g) of the *Federal Child Support Guidelines* empowers a court to impute income to a parent who unreasonably deducts expenses from income. Section 19(2) of the Guidelines provides that the reasonableness of an expense deduction is not solely governed by whether the deduction is permissible under the *Income Tax Act*.[441] Although there may be good reason to look behind the income tax return of a self-employed spouse to determine whether business expenses should be allowed in the context of the Guidelines, a court is fully entitled to find that the expenses are reasonable and should not be added back into the spouse's income for the purpose of determining the child support to be paid.[442] Various courts in Canada have addressed the question whether capital cost allowances (CCA) for farming or business equipment should be allowed when determining a parent's income under the *Federal Child Support Guidelines* or their provincial counterparts. The leading case in this context is *Cornelius v Andres*,[443] wherein the Manitoba Court of Appeal listed the following factors as relevant for consideration in deciding whether capital cost allowances should be imputed back into income.

1. Was the CCA deduction an actual expense in the year?
2. Was the CCA deduction greater than or less than the cost of acquisitions during the same time period?
3. Was the CCA deduction greater than or less than the repayments of principal with respect to chattels in question?
4. Was the CCA deduction the maximum allowable CCA deduction?
5. Was it necessary to take the CCA deduction in that year?
6. How much of a loss in a business year resulted in that year?
7. Are the chattels for which the CCA was claimed truly needed for business purposes?
8. [Have] the chattels for which the CCA was claimed truly depreciated?
9. Is it foreseeable that future chattel purchases will not be required?
10. Is there a pattern of spending which establishes a greater real income than income tax returns indicate?

---

v Jonas, [2002] OJ No 2117 (Sup Ct); *Scholes v Scholes*, [2003] OJ No 3432 (Sup Ct); *Arlt v Arlt*, [2003] SJ No 713 (QB); *Kelly v Lyle*, [2001] YJ No 90 (SC).

440 *Schluessel v Schluessel*, [1999] AJ No 1555 (QB); *Van Deventer v Van Deventer*, [2000] BCJ No 37 (CA).

441 *Hall v Hall*, [2006] AJ No 563 (QB); *PCJR v DCR*, [2003] BCJ No 792 (CA); *Cook v McManus*, [2006] NBJ No 334 (QB); *Guderyan v Meyers*, [2006] SJ No 797 (QB).

442 *Gossen v Gossen*, [2003] NSJ No 113 (SC); *TH v WH*, [2007] NSJ No 27 (SC).

443 *Cornelius v Andres* (1999), 45 RFL (4th) 200, (*sub nom Andres v Andres*) [1999] MJ No 103 at para 29 (CA).

11. If the children were living with the spouse, would they benefit from the actual income earned by the spouse?

12. Is there a dire need for child support?

After enumerating these factors, the Manitoba Court of Appeal affirmed that no general rule can be readily established as to when capital cost allowances should be imputed as income under section 19 of the Guidelines. Each case must be decided on its own merits, after scrutinizing the business in respect of which the capital cost allowance is being claimed, the equipment on which the deduction is being claimed, and the capital cost allowances claimed in the past years, as well as the justification advanced by the party making the claim.[444] Where capital cost allowance deductions are made through a private corporation in which the parent is the sole shareholder, the court may pierce the corporate veil in the interests of achieving justice under the Guidelines and add back the deductions into the parent's personal income for the purpose of applying the Guidelines.[445] As was observed by the Prince Edward Island Court of Appeal in *Koren v Blum*,[446] where the determination of a parent's income under the Guidelines involves capital cost adjustments or optional inventory adjustments, such as are available to farmers, the parent claiming the expenses must justify the deductions, and this requires much more than merely providing copies of relevant income tax returns as required by section 21 of the Guidelines. However, a strong case can be made for the view that, where a parent has made full financial disclosure in accordance with the *Federal Child Support Guidelines* and relevant provincial Rules of Court, an onus falls on the parent asserting the "unreasonableness" of the expense to establish a *prima facie* case, in the absence of which the court should not disallow or adjust the expense in determining the parent's Guidelines income.[447]

While offsetting farm losses may lower the obligor's income tax payable on off-farm income, it does not follow that such losses will be allowed to reduce the obligor's income for the purposes of the *Federal Child Support Guidelines*. Some courts have allowed such losses, at least in part;[448] others

---

444 See also *Trueman v Trueman*, [2000] AJ No 1301 (QB); *Balaban v Balaban*, [2001] AJ No 505 (QB); *Egan v Egan*, [2002] BCJ No 896 (CA); *Blaine v Sanders*, [2000] MJ No 149 (QB); *Koren v Blum*, [2000] PEIJ No 121 (SCAD); *Rush v Rush*, [2002] PEIJ No 29 (SCTD); *Huber v Yaroshko*, [2000] SJ No 201 (QB); *Shillington v Shillington*, [2007] SJ No 241 (QB).

445 *Trueman v Trueman*, [2000] AJ No 1301 (QB); *Rudachyk v Rudachyk*, [1999] SJ No 312 (CA).

446 [2000] PEIJ No 121 (SCAD).

447 *Rush v Rush*, [2002] PEIJ No 29 (SCTD); see also *Egan v Egan*, [2002] BCJ No 896 (CA), concurring judgment of Newbury JA; *Monney v Monney*, [1999] MJ No 17 (QB).

448 *Cole v McNeil*, [2001] NBJ No 37 (QB); *Dreger v Dreger*, [2000] SJ No 11 (QB).

have asserted that such losses should not normally be allowed.[449] In the final analysis, the issue would appear to be one of reasonableness. Consequently, in *Myketiak v Myketiak*,[450] the Saskatchewan Court of Appeal concluded that a court may impute income under the Guidelines to a parent who sets off farm losses against his or her taxable income from other sources, where the losses are likely to continue unless the parent reorganizes his or her affairs, as for example, by renting the farm to third parties.

Where business expenses are added back into a parent's income under the *Federal Child Support Guidelines*, they should be grossed up to reflect their tax-free status to the parent.[451]

Section 20(1) of the *Federal Child Support Guidelines* provides that where a parent is a non-resident of Canada, the parent's annual income is determined as though the parent were a resident of Canada.[452] Section 20(2) of the Guidelines provides that where a parent is a non-resident of Canada and resides in a country that has effective rates of income tax that are significantly higher than those applicable in the province in which the other parent resides, the non-resident parent's annual income is the amount which the court determines to be appropriate taking the higher rates into consideration. A parent cannot invoke section 20 of the Guidelines to reduce the annual income to be attributed to him by asserting a high cost of living in the foreign country, although such an assertion might be examined in the context of section 19(1)(c) of the Guidelines, which empowers but does not compel a court to impute additional income to a spouse whose foreign income generates significantly lower income tax liabilities than those applicable in Canada. Absent undue hardship, the court cannot deviate from the applicable table amount of child support under the Guidelines on the basis of the high cost of living in the foreign country.[453] Where income is earned in a foreign jurisdiction, section 20 of the Guidelines requires its conversion into Canadian dollars in light of the applicable currency exchange rate.[454] Because there can be wide and rapid

---

449 *LAK v AAW*, [2005] AJ No 1140 (QB); *TLK v DNK*, [1999] SJ No 401 (QB); see also *Botha v Botha*, [2000] AJ No 1533 (QB); *Hollett v Vessey*, [2005] NSJ No 538 (SC).

450 [2001] SJ No 85 (CA).

451 *Cabernel v Cabernel*, [1997] MJ No 375 (QB); *Voth v Voth*, [2004] MJ No 137 (QB); *Riel v Holland*, [2003] OJ No 3901 (CA); see also *Sarafinchin v Sarafinchin*, [2000] OJ No 2855 (Sup Ct); *Iselmoe v Iselmoe*, [2003] OJ No 4078 (Sup Ct); *Naidoo v Naidoo*, [2004] OJ No 1458 (Sup Ct); compare *Johnson v Johnson*, [2000] BCJ No 2065 (SC).

452 *Bennett v Bonatsos*, 2014 ONSC 1048.

453 *JGT v TN*, [2001] AJ No 1426 (QB); *ADB v SAM*, [2006] NSJ No 252 (SC); *Connelly v McGouran*, [2006] OJ No 993 (CA).

454 *EKR v GAW*, [1997] MJ No 501 (QB); *Hare v Kendall*, [1997] NSJ No 310 (TD); *Mascarenhas v Mascarenhas*, [1999] OJ No 37 (Gen Div), aff'd (2000) 18 RFL (5th) 148 (Ont Div Ct) (caveat added).

fluctuations in currency exchange rates, it may be desirable to determine the rate of exchange on the basis of the average or median rate over the preceding year, thereby avoiding unnecessary applications where there are frequent fluctuations in the exchange rate.[455] A court may order financial disclosure in the face of a separation agreement that purports to specify that the agreed amount of child support shall be final and not subject to variation and that purports to waive any future right to financial disclosure. While it might be superficially persuasive that a parent should not be required to provide any financial information when he or she has conceded the ability to pay anything the court orders, such an approach is inconsistent with the legal framework of the *Federal Child Support Guidelines* and would not allow a court to make the appropriate analysis to determine whether to vary the support or to determine quantum. The Guidelines provide for mandatory disclosure regardless of any purported waiver by the parents. Where there is a legitimate concern that full financial disclosure would be costly and potentially prejudicial, the court may limit the amount of disclosure and seal sensitive information, provided that the financial disclosure ordered is sufficient to enable the court to determine the amount of support required to meet the children's reasonable needs. In *Quinn v Keiper*,[456] the father, who conceded that his annual income exceeded $5 million, was ordered to provide the information required by sections 21(1)(a) and (b) of the Guidelines and complete a financial statement as required by Ontario Rule 13. In addition to his income tax returns for 2002, 2003, and 2004, he was ordered to disclose the amounts that he paid in meeting 100 percent of the children's special expenses that he undertook to pay under the terms of the 2001 separation agreement, which also provided for basic monthly support in the indexed amount of $5,000. Accepting that detailed additional financial disclosure in this case would have limited relevance and would be difficult, time-consuming, and expensive, the court was not satisfied that all the information in sections 21(1)(c) to (g) of the Guidelines was necessary to determine the amount of child support to be ordered; consequently, it declined to order the father to provide additional back-up documentation with respect to partnerships or companies and with respect to values set out in his financial statement. The court reserved the right to order additional financial disclosure if the need should become apparent in the future. Because public disclosure of the father's investment and

---

455 *Ward v Ward*, [2001] BCJ No 1206 (SCJ); *ADB v SAM*, [2006] NSJ No 252 (SC); *Bennett v Bonarsos*, 2014 ONSC 1048; *LSP v JRP*, [2002] SJ No 35 (QB); compare *Horton v Horton*, [1999] OJ No 4855 (Sup Ct) (trial judge opted for the average of the over-the-counter rate and the rate reported at the date of the hearing). See also *Kelly v White*, [2002] OJ No 5397 (Sup Ct); *Pawlus v Pawlus*, [2004] OJ No 5706 (Sup Ct).

456 [2005] OJ No 5034 (Sup Ct).

trading strategies would be prejudicial to him and contrary to the best interests of the children in terms of his ongoing earning capacity, the court issued a sealing order with respect to the father's financial statement and income tax returns for a period of twelve months, with a reserved right for him to apply for an extension thereafter.

Sections 21 to 26 of the *Federal Child Support Guidelines* set out detailed provisions with respect to the acquisition and disclosure of information concerning spousal income and sanctions for non-disclosure. These sections provide a new minimum standard of financial disclosure in child support proceedings. They are complemented by section 10(4) of the *Federal Child Support Guidelines*, which together with Schedule II of the Guidelines, requires additional financial disclosure to enable a court to undertake a comparison of the household living standards in cases where undue hardship exists.[457] The disclosure requirements of the *Federal Child Support Guidelines* may be supplemented by different, but not conflicting, provincial rules of practice and procedure.[458]

O. DISABILITY PAYMENTS AND CHILD SUPPORT

As illustrated in *Vickers v Vickers*,[459] given that the table amount of child support is determined solely by reference to the obligor's income, federal or provincial monthly benefits paid to or for a child of a disabled parent are not deductible from the applicable table amount of child support that is payable under the *Federal Child Support Guidelines*. The income of the custodial parent or child is relevant only where there are special or extraordinary expenses within the meaning of section 7 of the Guidelines or where the court has a discretion,[460] such as under section 3(2) of the Guidelines if the child has attained the provincial age of majority,[461] or under section 4 insofar as the

---

457 *Buhr v Buhr*, [1997] MJ No 565 (QB).

458 *Le Bourdais v Le Bourdais*, [1998] BCJ No 2488 (SC).

459 [2001] NSJ No 218 (CA). For decisions to similar effect, see *Trehearne v Trehearne*, [2000] AJ No 1632 (QB); *Kaupp v Kaupp*, 2008 ABQB 372; *Wadden v Wadden*, [2000] BCJ No 1287 (SC); *Callaghan v Brett*, [2000] NJ No 354 (SC); *Sayong v Aindow*, [1999] NWTJ No 43 (SC); *St Croix v Maxwell*, [1999] OJ No 4824 (Sup Ct); *Sipos v Sipos*, [2007] OJ No 711 (CA); *Rousseau v Rousseau*, [1999] SJ No 76 (QB); *Jones v Jones*, [2005] SJ No 284 (QB); *Peterson v Horan*, [2006] SJ No 333 (CA); see *contra*: *Mullen v Mullen*, [1998] NBJ No 338 (QB).

460 *Vickers v Vickers*, [2001] NSJ No 218 (CA); *Jones v Jones*, [2005] SJ No 284 (QB); *Peterson v Horan*, [2006] SJ No 333 (CA).

461 *BGM v PGM*, 2013 ABQB 67; *Burhoe v Goff*, [1999] NBJ No 296 (QB); *Senos v Karcz*, 2014 ONCA 459; see also *Rémillard v Rémillard*, 2014 MBCA 101 at paras 64–68. And see also *Klette v Leland*, 2014 SKCA 122 (adult disabled child not entitled to full table amount from father whose annual income exceeded $150,000).

obligor's income exceeds $150,000,[462] or under section 5 of the Guidelines, which relates to the child support obligation of a spouse who stands in the place of a biological or adoptive parent,[463] or in shared-parenting arrangements under section 9 of the Guidelines,[464] or under section 10 of the Guidelines in circumstances of undue hardship.[465] On an application for special or extraordinary expenses under section 7 of the Guidelines, an obligor is not entitled to be credited dollar for dollar with respect to Canada Pension Plan payments made to children in consequence of the obligor's disability, but the amount received by the other parent will be included in that parent's income for the purpose of determining the proportionate parental contributions towards the expenses.[466] In Saskatchewan, the benefits payable under the Canada Pension Plan to the children of a disabled parent have been held not to constitute "special provisions" for the benefit of the children within the meaning of section 3(4)(a) of the *Family Maintenance Act, 1997*,[467] and similar reasoning can be applied to sections 15.1(5) and 17(6.2) of the *Divorce Act*.

P. TYPES OF ORDERS

1) Interim Orders

Section 15.1(3) of the *Divorce Act* empowers a court to grant an interim order for child support. Interim and permanent orders fall subject to the same criteria under the *Divorce Act* and the *Federal Child Support Guidelines*. An interim order continues in force until a permanent order is granted and is not automatically terminated by divorce.[468] Although section 17 of the *Divorce Act* relates only to applications to vary permanent orders and section 15.1 of the *Divorce Act* includes no express provision for the variation of interim orders, a court has an inherent jurisdiction to vary an interim order.[469] In the words of Voith J, of the British Columbia Supreme Court:

> A compelling change of circumstances justifying variation of an interim order is a change that arises subsequent to the making of an order such that

---

462 *Rémillard v Rémillard*, 2014 MBCA 101; compare *Klette v Leland*, 2014 SKCA 122.

463 *Fedoruk v Jamieson*, [2002] BCJ No 503 (SC).

464 *Jones v Jones*, [2005] SJ No 284 (QB).

465 *Alfaro v Alfaro*, [1999] AJ No 1062 (QB); *Dixon v Fleming*, [2000] OJ No 1218 (Sup Ct).

466 *MJB v WPB*, [1999] MJ No 314 (QB).

467 SS 1997, c F-6.2. See *Peterson v Horan*, [2006] SJ No 333 (CA).

468 *Boznick v Boznick* (1993), 45 RFL (3d) 354 (BCSC).

469 See *Stannard v Stannard*, [1991] AJ No 679 (Alta QB); *Janmohamed v Janmohamed*, 2014 BCSC 107; *Colter v Colter*, 2015 NSSC 2; *Lipson v Lipson* (1972), 7 RFL 186 (Ont CA); *Carvell v Carvell*, [1969] 2 OR 513 (CA); *Ford v Ford*, 2015 SKCA 23.

one or both parties would be seriously prejudiced by waiting until trial or a final order (*Hama v. Werbes*, [1999] B.C.J. No. 2558 at para. 10, 2 R.F.L. (5th) 203 (S.C.)). The court may consider a number of factual matters in deciding whether to vary an interim support order, including the completeness of the information on the application, the proximity of the trial date, whether the trial has been adjourned, the length of time since separation, the provision of correct, better or additional financial information, and a change in the means or needs of the payor and payee spouse respectively (*Kirk v. Kirk et al.*, 2007 BCSC 67 at para. 60).

In ordering permanent child support, a trial judge is not bound by a preexisting order for interim child support.[470] An amount payable under an interim order may be adjusted retroactively by a trial judge, if an erroneous assumption was made concerning the obligor's income.[471] However, a trial judge is not compelled to top up a pre-existing interim support order by a lump sum or supplementary periodic payments in light of a subsequent attribution of income.[472] Appellate courts have endorsed a general policy of not disturbing interim orders, unless there is a manifest error that requires immediate correction.[473] Interim variation orders, even though permissible under sections 15.1, 15.2, 16, and 17 of the *Divorce Act*, are not available as a matter of course. They should be regarded as exceptional. Courts generally frown upon multiplying interim proceedings and seek to encourage the parties to move without delay to a final resolution. If any inequities ensue, they can be addressed at trial.[474]

2) Periodic and Lump Sum Orders

Section 11 of the *Federal Child Support Guidelines* empowers a court to order payments under a child support order to be made by way of periodic sums, a lump sum, or a combination of both. Given that the provincial and territorial tables under the Guidelines fix a monthly sum for child support based on the obligor's annual income and the number of children, there appear to be significant limitations of the right of a court to order lump sum child support,

---

470 *Thomas v Thomas*, 2014 ABQB 481 at para 48; *Colter v Colter*; 2015 NSSC 2; *Ford v Ford*, 2015 SKCA 23.

471 *Lewkoski v Lewkoski*, [1998] OJ No 1736 (Gen Div); *Ford v Ford*, 2015 SKCA 23. See also *Durocher v Klementovich*, 2013 ABCA 115; *Graham v Graham*, 2013 MBCA 66.

472 *L'Heureux v L'Heureux*, [1999] SJ No 437 (QB).

473 *Phillips v Phillips* (1985), 43 RFL (2d) 462 (BCCA); *Chevalier v Chevalier*, 2007 MBCA 131.

474 *Hayden v Stockwood*, [2006] NJ No 97 (UFC); *Connell v Connell*, [2006] PEIJ No 12 (SCTD). Compare *Werden v Werden*, [2005] OJ No 5257 (Sup Ct).

although no corresponding limitations apply to orders for spousal support.[475] In the rare case where a lump sum order for basic child support is granted, the court should capitalize the periodic payments that would otherwise have been ordered.[476] Such capitalization may warrant actuarial evidence being adduced.[477] Capitalization of child support payments is exceptional, but may be found appropriate where a parent has previously failed to discharge support obligations or is likely to do so in the future[478] or where the parent has a history of irresponsible money management.[479] An order for retroactive lump sum child support may be appropriate, where a non-custodial parent has failed to assume his or her fair share of financial responsibility for a child following spousal separation, thereby shifting an undue burden of child support to the custodial parent.[480] A lump sum may also be appropriate when a parent is ordered to make a contribution to special or extraordinary expenses falling within the ambit of section 7 of the *Federal Child Support Guidelines*.[481] Unless there has been a failure to recognize an obvious obligation or an attempt to avoid it, a parent should not ordinarily be ordered to pay a lump sum amount for child support on an interim basis.[482] Undue hardship within the meaning of section 10 of the *Child Support Guidelines* may justify an order for lump sum child support.[483]

Adult children who pursue post-secondary education may be entitled to lump sum support payable out of a deceased parent's modest estate. Such an order may be granted pursuant to the Ontario *Family Law Act*, even if a corollary relief claim is unavailable under the *Divorce Act* following the respondent's death. The jurisdiction of a court to order lump sum support in the above circumstances is exercisable pursuant to the conjoint operation of sections 3(2)(b) and 11 of the *Federal Child Support Guidelines*. In assessing the amount of lump sum child support to be paid, the child support obligation

---

475 *Finlay v Finlay*, [2004] NBJ No 448 (QB); *Scorgie v Scorgie*, [2006] OJ No 225 (Sup Ct), Timms J; *Chamanlall v Chamanlall*, [2006] OJ No 251 (Sup Ct), Timms J. For a more detailed analysis of lump sum child support orders, see Julien D Payne & Marilyn A Payne, *Child Support Guidelines in Canada, 2012* (Toronto: Irwin Law, 2012) at 408–14.

476 See, for example, *Megaval v Megaval*, [1997] BCJ No 2454 (SC); *Venco v Lie*, 2009 BCSC 831 (lump sum prepayment of table amount of child support for three years).

477 *Assinck v Assinck*, [1998] OJ No 875 (Gen Div).

478 *Megaval v Megaval*, [1997] BCJ No 2454 (SC); *Bartole v Parker*, [2006] SJ No 349 (QB).

479 *Lobo v Lobo*, [1999] AJ No 113 (QB).

480 *Lackie v Lackie*, [1998] OJ No 888 (Gen Div); *Krawczyk v Krawczyk*, [1998] OJ No 2526 (Gen Div).

481 *Harrison v Harrison*, [1998] BCJ No 3090 (SC).

482 *Letourneau v Letourneau* (1998), 131 Man R (2d) 123 (CA); *Chevalier v Chevalier*, 2007 MBCA 131.

483 *Trebilcock v Trebilcock*, 2012 ONCA 452.

takes priority over the rights of ordinary creditors and the declared benefici-aries of the deceased's estate. Due account must be taken, however, of the federal Crown's superior right to enforce the deceased's tax liabilities.[484]

3) Orders to Pay and Secure Child Support

Section 12 of the *Federal Child Support Guidelines* expressly empowers a court to order that child support be paid or secured, or paid and secured, in the manner specified in the order. The mutual exclusivity of orders to pay child support and orders to secure the payments, which was endorsed by the Su-preme Court of Canada in *Nash v Nash*,[485] no longer prevails under section 12 of the Guidelines. A court may now grant an order for the payment of child support, combined with an order to secure those payments. When granting an order to secure child support, a court should make it abundantly clear that the order is an order "to pay and secure" the child support ordered. Or-ders for security may be made against real or personal property but should only be granted when there is a risk of default. An obligor may be ordered to acquire life insurance to secure child support payments even though no policy existed on the date when relief was sought.[486]

Q. RETROACTIVE CHILD SUPPORT ORDERS UNDER THE *DIVORCE ACT*[487]

Prior to the judgments of the Supreme Court of Canada in *DBS v SRG; LJW v TAR; Henry v Henry; Hiemstra v Hiemstra*,[488] provincial appellate courts in Canada were divided on two fundamental issues relating to retroactive child support orders. The first issue related to whether Canadian courts could or-der retroactive child support to be paid for a period of time that preceded the commencement of divorce proceedings.[489] The second issue related to the criteria to be applied in determining whether retroactive child support

---

484 *Hillock v Hillock*, [2001] OJ No 3837 (Sup Ct). As to the effect of the child support obli-gor's death on the enforcement of a consent order to pay lump sum child support in instalments, see *McLeod v McLeod*, 2013 BCCA 552.

485 [1975] 2 SCR 507.

486 See *Laczko v Laczko*, [1999] OJ No 2577 (Sup Ct); *Katz v Katz*, 2014 ONCA 606 at para 73. Compare *RM v NM*, 2014 BCSC 1755 at paras 213–214 (spousal support) applying section 170 of the *Family Law Act*, SBC 2011, c 25; see also *Joffres v Joffres*, 2014 BCSC 1778.

487 See D Smith, "Retroactive Child Support: An Update" (2007) 26 Fam LQ 209.

488 2006 SCC 37. For an excellent detailed summary of the principles defined by the Supreme Court of Canada, see the judgment of Skilnick Prov Ct J in *DMP v GEA*, 2013 BCPC 117 at paras 10–11.

489 For a review of the conflicting provincial appellate rulings, see *Mellway v Mellway*, [2004] MJ No 300 (CA); compare *Dickson v Dickson*, 2011 MBCA 26.

should be ordered in the diverse situations where such jurisdiction is possessed by the court.[490] On the first issue, the Supreme Court of Canada has accepted the reasoning of the majority judgment of the Alberta Court of Appeal in *Hunt v Smolis-Hunt*[491] that "[a]n order for retroactive child support pre-dating the issuance [of] a petition for divorce is . . . a necessary incident to the dissolution of a marriage" and falls within the legislative authority of the Parliament of Canada. On the second issue, the Supreme Court of Canada was divided four to three. Subject to a potential finding of "undue hardship" within the meaning of section 10 of the *Federal Child Support Guidelines*, the minority judgment was disposed to holding parents fully accountable for any failure to pay increased child support in accordance with the Guidelines as and when their incomes materially increased. The majority judgment adopted a somewhat more conservative approach in endorsing the following conclusions:

1) So-called retroactive orders for child support are not truly retroactive. They simply enforce the pre-existing legal obligation of parents to pay an amount of child support commensurate with their income.

2) When an application for retroactive child support is brought, it is incumbent on the court to analyze the federal or provincial statutory scheme under which the application is brought. Different policy choices by the federal and provincial governments must be judicially respected.

3) The propriety of a retroactive award can only be evaluated after a detailed examination of the facts of the particular case.

4) Retroactive orders should not be regarded as exceptional orders to be granted only in exceptional circumstances. Although the propriety of a retroactive order should not be presumed, it is not confined to rare cases.

5) Child support is a right of the child that cannot be bargained away by the parents. Sections 15.1(5) to (8) and 17(6.2) to (6.5) of the *Divorce Act* control the extent to which parents can consensually determine their child obligations and the criteria defined therein take account of the standards prescribed by the *Federal Child Support Guidelines*. Corresponding legislation is to be found under provincial child support regimes. Courts may order retroactive child support where circumstances have changed or were not as they appeared when a prior parental agreement was reached or court order was made.

---

490 See, for example, *LS v EP*, [1999] BCJ No 1451 (CA); *Cabot v Mikkelson*, [2004] MJ No 240 (CA); *Lu v Sun*, [2005] NSJ No 314 (CA); *Marinangeli v Marinangeli*, [2003] OJ No 2819 (CA); compare the Alberta Court of Appeal judgments in *DBS v SRG*, [2005] AJ No 2 (CA); *LJW v TAR*, [2005] AJ No 3 (CA); *Henry v Henry*, [2005] AJ No 4 (CA); *Hiemstra v Hiemstra*, [2005] AJ No 27 (CA).

491 [2001] AJ No 1170 at para 32 (CA); see also *S v S*, [2007] NBJ No 422 (QB).

6) The underlying premise of both federal and provincial child support guidelines is that the amount of child support should reflect the obligor's income.

7) Quite independently of any court order or any steps taken by the prospective recipient, there is a free-standing obligation on parents to support their children commensurate with their income. A parent who fails to do so will have failed to fulfill his or her child support obligation. Consequently, a parent has an obligation to increase the child support payments when his or her income increases.

8) Although the Guidelines do not impose a direct obligation on an obligor to automatically disclose income increases and adjust child support payments accordingly, this does not mean that a parent will satisfy his or her child support obligation by doing nothing. If his or her income increases without an appropriate increase in the amount of child support paid, there exists an unfulfilled legal obligation that may subsequently merit enforcement by means of a retroactive child support award.

9) The obligor's interest in certainty must be balanced with the need for fairness and flexibility. Relevant factors for consideration in determining whether a retroactive child support award is justified include whether there is a reasonable excuse why support was not sought earlier by the obligee; the conduct, blameworthy or otherwise, of the obligor; the circumstances of the child; and hardship that would be occasioned by a retroactive award. None of these factors is, in itself, determinative; the court should take a holistic approach.

10) An unreasonable delay in seeking support militates against a retroactive child support award, but the court must bear in mind that child support is the right of the child and cannot be waived by parental agreement. Courts should not hesitate to find a reasonable excuse for the delay where the applicant harbours fears about a vindictive response from the obligor or lacks the financial or emotional means to bring an application or was given inadequate legal advice. Conversely, a parent who discloses income increases in a timely manner and who does nothing to pressure or intimidate the applicant will have gone a long way towards ensuring that the delay is characterized as unreasonable. Such a characterization does not inevitably preclude a retroactive award. It is simply one factor to consider when the court seeks to balance the obligor's interest in certainty with fairness to the children.

11) Blameworthy conduct, though not a prerequisite to retroactivity, is an important factor to consider in determining the propriety of a retroactive child support award. Blameworthy conduct is accorded an expansive definition and arises whenever a parent knowingly chooses to ignore

or evade his or her child support obligations. An obligor who does not automatically increase his or her child support payments to reflect his or her increased income is not necessarily engaging in blameworthy conduct, but objective factors can be used to determine whether the obligor had a reasonable belief that he or she was meeting his or her child support obligations. Breach of contractual undertakings to disclose income increases and adjust the amount of child support to conform to the requirements of the *Federal Child Support Guidelines* constitutes compelling evidence of blameworthy conduct.[492]

12) In assessing the obligor's conduct, the court is not confined to looking at blameworthy conduct. Sometimes, an obligor's positive conduct will militate against a retroactive child support award. For example, an obligor who contributes to specific child-related expenses over and above his or her statutory obligations may be deemed to have met any increased child support obligation, although it must be borne in mind that the obligor is not free to decide how his or her child support obligation shall be discharged. A court may, nevertheless, conclude that such contributions negate any justification for a retroactive child support award.

13) In determining whether a retroactive child support award is justified, the court should have regard to the circumstances of the child as they exist at the time of the application, as well as the circumstances of the child as they existed at the time when the support should have been paid. For example, a child who is currently enjoying a relatively high standard of living may benefit less from a retroactive award than a child who is currently in need. And a child who suffered hardship in the past may be compensated through a retroactive award, although trial judges should not delve into the past to remedy all old familial injustices, such as the sacrifices made by a custodial parent on behalf of the child.

14) Hardship to the obligor and his or her new family dependants is a relevant factor to be considered in determining whether a retroactive child support award is justified. The minority judgment clearly spells out that the hardship must be "undue hardship" that satisfies the requirements of section 10 of the Child Support Guidelines. While the majority judgment accepts the premise that the Guidelines govern both retroactive and prospective child support orders, Bastarache J's analysis with respect to the impact of hardship[493] is not so clearly defined as to expressly confine its application to circumstances in which the very stringent

---

492 *Goulding v Keck*, 2014 ABCA 138.

493 *DBS v SRG; LJW v TAR; Henry v Henry; Hiemstra v Hiemstra*, 2006 SCC 37 at paras 114–16 [*DBS*]; see also *Locke v Goulding*, 2012 NLCA 8 and compare *BW v JG*, 2014 NLCA 5.

requirements of section 10 of the Guidelines are satisfied. He does volunteer the statement that "[w]hile hardship for the payor parent is much less of a concern where it is the product of his/her blameworthy conduct, it remains a strong one where this is not the case."[494] He also acknowledges that courts should craft their retroactive awards so as to minimize hardship, for example, by ordering periodic payments over a period of time to discharge the overall amount due.[495] The exercise of this jurisdiction is consistent with section 11 of the *Federal Child Support Guidelines*.[496] Furthermore, if a court wishes to defer the payment of retroactive support or order payment by instalments, it may do so pursuant to sections 15.1(4) (original child support orders) or 17(3) of the Divorce Act (variation orders), which empower the court to impose "terms, conditions or restrictions" on its orders.

15) There are two aspects to the judicial determination of the amount of any retroactive child support award. First, the court must determine the date to which the award should be retroactive. Second, the court must determine the dollar value of its order.

   a) *Date of Retroactivity*
      The majority judgment examines four options as to the appropriate date when retroactive child support becomes payable, namely (1) the date when the application was made to the court; (2) the date when formal notice was given to the obligor; (3) the date when effective notice was given to the obligor; and (4) the date when the amount of child support should have increased. Given the desirability of parents resolving the issue of child support promptly and without recourse to costly and emotionally draining litigation, the majority judgment favoured the third option. This option does not require the applicant to take any legal action. All that is required is that the topic be broached. After that, the obligor can no longer assume that the *status quo* is fair to the child, and his or her interest in certainty in the management of his or her financial affairs is less compelling. While the date of effective notice will usually signal the applicant's attempt to change the child support obligation, an unwarranted, prolonged period of inactivity should not be ignored. Consistent with this approach and with section 25(1)(a) of the *Federal Child Support Guidelines*, which limits an applicant's request for financial

---

494   *DBS*, 2006 SCC 37 at para 116; see also *WL v NDH*, 2014 NBQB 214; *LMA v PH*, 2014 ONSC 1707; *Koback v Koback*, 2013 SKCA 91 at paras 80–87.
495   *LMA v PH*, 2014 ONSC 1707.
496   *Goulding v Keck*, 2014 ABCA 138.

disclosure by the obligor to the preceding three years, the majority judgment states that "it will usually be inappropriate to make a support award retroactive to a date more than three years before formal notice was given to the obligor." However, the date when increased support should have been paid will sometimes be a more appropriate date from which the retroactive order should start. Such will be the case where the obligor engages in blameworthy conduct, such as intimidation or misrepresentation, and a failure to disclose a material income increase itself constitutes blameworthy conduct. Given such conduct, the presumptive date of retroactivity can be moved back to the time when the obligor's circumstances materially changed. In the final analysis, a retroactive award must fit the circumstances of the case, and the date of retroactivity can be adjusted to affect the quantum of the award so as to ensure that the award is appropriate.

b) *Amount*

The *Divorce Act* confers a discretion on the courts to determine whether a child support order should be granted, but the amount of any order after 1 May 1997 must be "in accordance with the applicable guidelines."[497] However, blind adherence to the table amounts set out in the Guidelines is neither required nor recommended. The first method whereby the court may deviate from the table amount of child support arises where undue hardship is established within the meaning of section 10 of the Guidelines. In addition to cases of undue hardship, courts may exercise their discretion with respect to amount in the diverse circumstances prescribed by sections 3(2) (adult children), 4 (parental annual income in excess of $150,000), and 9 (shared custody) of the Guidelines. A second method of adjusting the amount of support payable is exercisable by altering the time period encompassed by the retroactive award. For example, where a court finds that there has been an unreasonable delay after effective notice of the child support claim was first given, the period of excessive delay might be excluded in calculating the retroactive award. Unless the statutory provisions mandate a different outcome, a court should not order retroactive child support in an amount that it considers unfair in light of all the attendant circumstances of the case.

16) The use of the phrase "at the material time" in the definition of "child of the marriage" in section 2(1) of the *Divorce Act* refers to the time of the application. Consequently, a child who is over the provincial age of

---

497 See *Divorce Act*, RSC 1985 (2d Supp), c 3, ss 15.1(3) and 17(6.1).

majority and no longer economically dependent on his or her parents at the time of the application is ineligible for a retroactive child support award. An exception may arise if a Notice to Disclose/Notice of Motion was filed prior to the application for retroactive support.[498] Furthermore, the fact that an application for the enforcement or variation of child support arrears under an existing order is brought after the children have ceased to be eligible for support does not necessarily preclude the recovery of, or the remission of, arrears that accrued prior thereto, although it may be a relevant consideration.[499]

17) The aforementioned principles are inapplicable to the issue of retroactivity in the context of the cancellation of child support arrears,[500] at least in the absence of a material change in circumstances prior to the accumulation of the arrears.[501] The *DBS* judgment, nevertheless, reiterates some principles of child support that are generally applicable, namely, the cardinal principle that support is the right of the child, and both parents are obligated to support their children and monitor child support payments. In *GMW v DPW*,[502] the British Columbia Court of appeal reviewed and applied the aforementioned four factors in *DBS v SRB* in rejecting a child support obligor's application for the reimbursement of overpayments of child support.

As a preventative measure that could significantly reduce the number of future claims for retroactive child support, the Alberta Court of Appeal in *DBS v SRG*[503] stated that court orders and negotiated agreements should

---

498   *Calver v Calver*, 2014 ABCA 63 at para 28; *VanSickle v VanSickle*, 2012 ONSC 7340; See also *Gordashko v Boston*, [2009] AJ No 404 (QB)(use of CRS process prior to application; blameworthy conduct of obligor); *JDG v JAB*, 2012 NSSC 20.

499   *Hussey v Hussey*, 2014 ABQB 656; *MacCarthy v MacCarthy*, 2014 BCSC 2229; *Poirier v Poirier*, 2013 NSSC 314; *Ross v Vermette*, [2007] SJ No 483 (QB); *Ross v Welsh*, 2009 SKQB 483; compare *McDonald v McDonald*, [2008] BCJ No 1694 (SC); *Meyer v Content*, 2014 ONSC 6001; *Millar v Millar*, 2007 SKQB 25.

500   *DBS v SRG; LJW v TAR; Henry v Henry; Hiemstra v Hiemstra*, [2006] 2 SCR 231 at para 98; *HN v SB*, 2013 BCSC 1509; *Brown v Brown*, 2010 NBCA 5; *Smith v Helppi*, 2011 NSCA 65; *Poirier v Poirier*, 2013 NSSC 314; *Scarrow v Cowan*, 2014 ONSC 955; *Hnidy v Hnidy*, 2015 SKQB 1; *Matthews v Matthews*, [2007] YJ No 12 (SC). Compare *NDC v JLC*, 2010 BCSC 1803; *Smith v Oake*, 2012 NSSC 100; *Mondino v Mondino*, 2013 ONSC 7051; *JC v SAW*, 2013 YKSC 1. For a discussion of relevant Ontario cases, see *Scurci v Scurci*, 2013 ONSC 7199.

501   See *Corcios v Burgos*, 2011 ONSC 3326, especially paras 41–55, wherein a distinction is drawn between cases where the obligor has the ability to pay child support when the arrears accrued and cases where the arrears accumulated due to a change in the obligor's circumstances that impaired his or her ability to make the child support payments when they became due. And see, generally, Section M(4), above in this chapter.

502   2014 BCCA 282.

503   [2005] AJ No 2 (CA).

expressly provide an appropriate mechanism for the future variation of child support obligations to reflect changes in parental income. It is incumbent on courts to ensure the recalculation of child support on a regular basis. At a minimum, orders for child support should routinely include the following provisions unless the attendant circumstances render them inappropriate. First, the payor should be required to annually disclose the financial information, including income tax returns, outlined in section 25 of the *Federal Child Support Guidelines*. Second, the court order should specify that the amount is subject to annual recalculation based on the then current income or as agreed upon between the parents. Third, the court order should provide that, if the parents are unable to agree on the amount of child support payable or the date when the adjusted payments will commence, then either parent may apply to the court to resolve the issues and/or make use of available alternative dispute resolution services. The current practice in Alberta requires a mandatory annual disclosure clause in every support order, thereby highlighting the importance of ensuring that financial disclosure is kept up to date.[504]

A child support order may provide for a retroactive contribution to allowable expenses under section 7 of the *Federal Child Support Guidelines*.[505] Whether such provision should be ordered will depend on the circumstances of the case, including but not limited to voluntary arrangements between the parents, the extent to which the expenditures were known, the custodial arrangements for the children, and the date of the application.[506] Many of the policy issues and factors that are addressed in relation to retroactive basic child support are also applicable to claims for a contribution to section 7 expenses under the *Federal Child Support Guidelines*. However, there is one fundamental difference. Basic child support reflects the right of the child to have his or her essential needs met. Extraordinary expenses for extracurricular activities are not a basic right of the child, and there is no inherent obligation on the parents to pay for such activities. An order for a retroactive contribution to such expenses may be deemed unfair where the father had no knowledge of these expenses and no idea that he might ultimately be called upon to contribute towards them.[507]

Motions for interim (i.e., temporary) orders are not well-suited to dealing with retroactive claims where there is a lack of clarity on factual and financial issues due to competing affidavits. These issues are better determined by

---

504 *Roseberry v Roseberry*, 2015 ABQB 75 at para 64.
505 *Selig v Smith*, 2008 NSCA 54.
506 *PCJR v DCR*, [2003] BCJ No 792 (CA); see also *Clegg v Downing*, [2004] AJ No 1511 (QB).
507 *Clegg v Downing, ibid.*

the give and take of the negotiation process or, if necessary, by trial with oral testimony and cross-examination.[508]

R.   PRIORITY OF CHILD SUPPORT OVER SPOUSAL SUPPORT; EFFECT OF CHILD SUPPORT ORDER ON ASSESSMENT OF SPOUSAL SUPPORT[509]

1)   Relevant Statutory Provisions

Section 15.3 of the *Divorce Act* provides as follows:

Priority to child support

15.3 (1) Where a court is considering an application for a child support order and an application for a spousal support order, the court shall give priority to child support in determining the applications.

Reasons

(2) Where, as a result of giving priority to child support, the court is unable to make a spousal support order or the court makes a spousal support order in an amount that is less than it otherwise would have been, the court shall record its reasons for having done so.[510]

Consequences of reduction or termination of child support order

(3) Where, as a result of giving priority to child support, a spousal support order was not made, or the amount of a spousal support order is less than it otherwise would have been, any subsequent reduction or termination of that child support constitutes a change of circumstances for the purposes of applying for a spousal support order, or a variation order in respect of the spousal support order, as the case may be.

2)   Commentary

Section 15.3 of the *Divorce Act* addresses the situation where the application for child support and the application for spousal support involve members of the same family.[511] It does not establish priorities as between sequential families. For example, a former divorced wife's order for spousal support will not be subject to a statutory priority in favour of the obligor's children from

---

508   *Douglas v Faucher*, 2014 ONSC 4045 at para 11, James J.

509   See DA Rollie Thompson, "The Chemistry of Support: The Interaction of Child and Spousal Support" (2006) 25 Can Fam LQ 251.

510   See *Pitt v Pitt*, [1997] BCJ No 1949 (SC), wherein the judgment was amended to reflect s 15.3(2) of the *Divorce Act*.

511   *Hilborn v Hilborn*, [2007] OJ No 3068 (Sup Ct).

a second subsequently dissolved marriage. The difficulties that have plagued the courts respecting the competing claims of sequential families remain unresolved.

In consequence of the priority accorded to child support by section 15.3 of the *Divorce Act*, a court may be unable to grant a spousal support order because the obligor has no ability to pay any amount to satisfy the demonstrated need of the other spouse.[512] In granting an order for periodic spousal support, a court may acknowledge the amount to be less than would have been ordered but for the priority to be accorded to the needs of the children under section 15.3 of the *Divorce Act*.[513] A similar acknowledgment of the priority accorded to child support may be made where an order for lump sum spousal support is granted,[514] or where an order for spousal support is denied.[515]

Although periodic spousal support may be reduced or denied where child support obligations impair the obligor's ability to pay,[516] a lump sum spousal support payment may be practical.[517] In granting a lump sum order for spousal support, the court may expressly acknowledge a potential future right to periodic spousal support under section 15.3(3) of the *Divorce Act*.[518] Where the amount of spousal support has been reduced to accommodate child support payments, spousal support may be increased when these obligations cease.[519] A court may direct that an order for periodic spousal support shall be increased by the amount by which child support is reduced when each of the children ceases to be entitled to support.[520] Before making any order, it is important to keep in mind that periodic payments for child support that

---

512 *Bell v Bell*, [1997] BCJ No 2826 (SC); *Falbo v Falbo*, [1998] BCJ No 1497 (SC) (application for interim spousal support adjourned indefinitely); *Miao v Chen*, [1998] BCJ No 1926 (Prov Ct); *Cooper v Cooper*, [2002] SJ No 226 (QB).

513 *Langois v Langois*, [1999] BCJ No 1199 (SC); *Beatty v Beatty*, [2000] OJ No 1755 (Sup Ct); *Whalen v Whalen*, [2000] OJ No 2658 (Sup Ct). See also *Gray v Gray*, 2014 ONCA 659.

514 *Lepage v Lepage* (1999), 179 Sask R 34 (QB).

515 *Falbo v Falbo*, [1998] BCJ No 1497 (SC).

516 *D'Entremont v D'Entremont*, [2001] NSJ No 586 (SC); *Norlander v Norlander* (1989), 21 RFL (3d) 317 (Sask QB); see also *Hunt v Smolis-Hunt*, [2001] AJ No 1170 (CA) (spousal support to be revisited by trial court in light of appellate court's disposition of appeal respecting child support); *Kenning v Kenning* (1995), 11 RFL (4th) 216 (BCSC).

517 *Amaral v Amaral* (1993), 50 RFL (3d) 364 (Ont Gen Div); *Kapogianes v Kapogianes*, [2000] OJ No 2572 (Sup Ct); *Lepage v Lepage*, [1999] SJ No 174 (QB); compare *Whalen v Whalen*, [2000] OJ No 2658 (Sup Ct).

518 *Lepage v Lepage*, [1999] SJ No 174 (QB).

519 *Sneddon v Sneddon* (1993), 46 RFL (3d) 373 (Alta QB); *Peters v Peters*, [2002] NSJ No 413 (SC); *MacArthur v MacArthur*, [2004] NSJ No 209 (SC); *Gray v Gray*, 2014 ONCA 659.

520 *McLean v McLean*, [1997] OJ No 5315 (Gen Div); see also *Smith v Smith* (1998), 36 RFL (4th) 419 at 425 (Ont Gen Div); *Gritti v Gritti*, [2001] OJ No 1363 (Sup Ct); *Cusack v Cusack*, [1999] PEIJ No 90 (SCTD).

are ordered after 1 May 1997 are tax-free, whereas periodic spousal support payments are deductible from the payor's taxable income and are taxable in the hands of the recipient spouse.[521] Courts must not overlook this difference when ordering what is, in effect, the conversion of child support payments into spousal support payments at some future date. An order whereby spousal support will be increased to a designated monthly amount on termination of the obligor's duty to pay court-ordered child support may be expressly declared to be subject to further variation by reason of a material change of circumstances,[522] although such a declaration is presumably unnecessary.

Although section 15.3(1) of the *Divorce Act* requires the court to give priority to child support over spousal support, this does not signify that special or exceptional expenses should be ordered under section 7 of the *Federal Child Support Guidelines* to supplement the basic amount of child support payable under the applicable provincial or territorial table, where such a supplementary allocation would render the custodial spouse destitute.[523] The priority of child support, including section 7 expenses,[524] over spousal support that is mandated by section 15.3 (1) of the *Divorce Act* does not preclude the court from giving consideration to spousal support and looking at the overall picture in determining the appropriate contribution, if any, to be made to special or extraordinary child-related expenses.[525]

A non-custodial parent who is ordered to pay periodic child support is not thereby disqualified from obtaining an order for periodic spousal support. Child support and spousal support, though necessarily intertwined, are separate concepts. The fact that the receipt of one may offset the payment of the other does not preclude an order for both kinds of relief in appropriate circumstances.[526]

---

521 See *Rondeau v Kirby*, [2003] NSJ No 436 (SC).

522 *Lackie v Lackie*, [1998] OJ No 888 (Gen Div).

523 *Lyttle v Bourget*, [1999] NSJ No 298 (SC); *Kaderly v Kaderly*, [1997] PEIJ No 74 (SCTD); see also *Cameron-Masson v Masson*, [1997] NSJ No 207 (Fam Ct).

524 *Andrews v Andrews*, [1999] OJ No 3578 (CA) (priority over spousal support given to extraordinary expenses for children's schooling pursuant to s 38.1(i) of Ontario *Family Law Act*).

525 *Nataros v Nataros*, [1998] BCJ No 1417 (SC).

526 *Richter v Vahamaki* (2000), 8 RFL (5th) 194 (Ont Sup Ct) (mother with annual income of $42,000; father with annual income of $104,000 and perhaps much more; father ordered to pay $1,000 per month as interim periodic spousal support; mother ordered to pay $605 per month for interim support of two children living with their father; child-care expenses to be totally assumed by father); see also *Varcoe v Varcoe*, [2000] OJ No 229 (Sup Ct) (interim orders).

Section 15.3 of the *Divorce Act* applies to both custodial and non-custodial parents.[527] Consequently, a custodial parent's obligation to provide financially for a child of the marriage takes priority over the obligation to pay spousal support to the non-custodial parent and may result in a reduction of the amount of spousal support that would otherwise be ordered.[528] A custodial parent cannot avoid the obligation to pay a reasonable amount of spousal support on the dissolution of a long marriage by calling upon the non-custodial parent to live at below the poverty level in order for the custodial parent to provide a child of the marriage with luxuries.[529]

Where a child has special needs due to a chronic illness, this may be taken into account in determining the ability to pay spousal support when the obligor is already committing significant resources to the child.[530]

Judicial opinions vary on the question whether it is appropriate or desirable to grant a nominal order for spousal support in circumstances where a substantial order is precluded by the priority accorded to a child support order. Some courts have ordered the nominal sum of $1 per year as spousal support because of the priority placed on child support obligations.[531] It has, nevertheless, been concluded that, where a parent with custody is unable to afford spousal support and the non-custodial parent is unable to pay child support, a court should decline to make any support order because "in case" nominal orders serve no useful purpose in that the parties are free to reapply in the event of a change of circumstances.[532]

Where the spousal incomes are approximately equal after the payment of child support, a court may refuse to order spousal support until the child support obligation is eliminated.[533]

The cessation of child support payments does not inevitably justify an increase in the amount of spousal support payments.[534]

Where the combined income of the two spousal households has been substantially diminished in consequence of the application of the *Federal Child Support Guidelines* and accompanying amendments of the *Income Tax Act*, which took effect on 1 May 1997, a court may conclude that this constitutes a

---

527 *Lockyer v Lockyer*, [2000] OJ No 2939 at para 52 (Sup Ct).
528 *Schick v Schick*, [1997] SJ No 447 (QB).
529 *Reyher v Reyher* (1993), 48 RFL (3d) 111 (Man QB).
530 *Broder v Broder* (1994), 93 Man R (2d) 259 (QB).
531 *Comeau v Comeau*, [1997] NSJ No 409 (TD); *Young v Young*, [1999] NSJ No 63 (SC).
532 *Frydrysek v Frydrysek*, [1998] BCJ No 394 (SC); see also *Gill-Sager v Sager* (2003), 36 RFL (5th) 369 (BCCA) and *Tierney-Hynes v Hynes*, [2005] OJ No 2661 (CA); see Chapter 8, Sections C(2) and R(4).
533 *Rupert v Rupert*, [1999] NBJ No 5 (QB).
534 *Davis v Davis*, [2000] NSJ No 86 (SC).

change of circumstances that warrants a reduction of the amount of spousal support under a pre-existing order so that the overall reduction in total income may be shared on some equitable basis by the former spouses.[535] On an application to vary the spousal support order on this basis, the court must be provided with accurate information concerning the after-tax income of the spouses before and after 1 May 1997.[536] In the absence of such information, an appellate court may conclude that a trial judge's order for a substantial reduction in the amount of court-ordered spousal support cannot be sustained, having regard to the financial disparity and apparent inconsistency between the old and new orders for spousal and child support, and may direct a new hearing on the issue of the amount of spousal support.[537]

Section 15.3(2) of the *Divorce Act* provides that, where a court is unable to make a spousal support order or makes an order in a reduced amount because of the priority accorded to child support, the court "shall record its reasons for having done so."[538] Thomas Bastedo, a senior family law practitioner from Toronto, has concluded that "it is difficult to accept that the court will insist on section 15.3(2) as a precondition for its exercise of jurisdiction under subsection (3)."[539] But, as B Lynn Reierson, a Halifax family law practitioner, has shrewdly observed,

> Although s. 15.3(3) of the *Divorce Act* establishes an automatic variation threshold, where the child support order relates to young children the opportunity to apply s. 15.3(3) to a spousal support variation application may not arise for many years. Entitlement on a compensatory basis, where need is not acute, may be very difficult to revisit at that future time.[540]

In the final analysis, there appear to be few, if any, distinct criteria to assist Canadian courts in balancing competing demands for child support and spousal support. Although the applicable table amount of periodic child support will normally be accorded priority over compensatory or even non-compensatory periodic spousal support, and the same priority may be ac-

---

535   *Desjardins v Desjardins*, [1999] MJ No 70 (CA) (minority opinion of Huband J. The majority opinion of Scott CJM, with Monnin JA concurring, expressly declined to speculate on this issue).

536   *Ibid.*

537   *SAJM v DDM*, [1999] MJ No 118 (CA).

538   *Lepp v Lepp*, 2008 BCSC 448.

539   Thomas Bastedo, "Impact of *Child Support Guidelines* on Spousal Support" (November 1999) 11:3 *Matrimonial Affairs, CBAO Family Law Section Newsletter* 1 at 27.

540   B Lynn Reierson, "The Impact of *Child Support Guidelines* on Spousal Support Law and Practice" (Paper presented to Federation of Law Societies and Canadian Bar Association, The 2000 National Family Law Program, St John's, Newfoundland 10–13 July 2000) c 23-1 at 1.

corded to necessary "special" expenses falling within section 7 of the *Federal Child Support Guidelines*, courts appear to be much less likely to accord priority to "extraordinary" expenses falling within the ambit of section 7 of the Guidelines where there are insufficient funds to meet those expenses and also provide a basic level of necessary spousal support.

The impact of the *Federal Child Support Guidelines* on spousal support is not confined, however, to their substantive significance in light of section 15.3 of the *Divorce Act*. The effect of specific disclosure requirements under sections 21 to 26 of the *Federal Child Support Guidelines* has spread over into the context of spousal support.[541]

---

541 *Ibid* at 10–11.

CHAPTER 10

Parenting Arrangements After Divorce[1]

A. INTRODUCTION

Since 1968, more than 1 million Canadian children have been affected by the divorce of their parents. More than 100,000 of these children have witnessed the breakdown of a second long-term relationship of their custodial parent.

Divorced mothers and their children have a higher risk of living in poverty. Children who are raised in poverty by a single parent often encounter nutritional, health, and educational problems that significantly affect their adult lives.

Less than 4 percent of all divorce proceedings result in full-blown contested trials and, of these, very few involve disputes concerning the children. Less than 1 percent of contested divorce cases are confined to custody and access disputes.

Contested custody litigation is often a reflection of continued and unresolved personal hostility between the spouses. Custody litigation may also disguise an issue relating to money and property, rather than the children. A custodial parent may, for example, obtain an order for exclusive possession of the matrimonial home or an order for spousal support that would be unavailable if custody were denied to that parent. Or a non-custodial parent may seek an order for shared parenting in order to reduce the amount of child support payable.

A custodial parent has the authority to make decisions that affect the growth and development of a child[2] but is expected to exercise that authority

---

1   For sweeping proposals to change the law, see Canada, Parliament, Report of the Special Joint Committee on Child Custody and Access, *For the Sake of the Children* (Ottawa: Senate and House of Commons, December 1998), Summary of Recommendations 1–48 at xvii–xxiii.

2   *MP v NM*, 2008 BCSC 1501.

in the best interests of the child. Where the parents disagree, either of them may institute legal proceedings to have the dispute resolved by a court.

B. DEFINITION OF "CUSTODY ORDER"

Section 2(1) of the *Divorce Act*[3] provides that "custody order means an order made under subsection 16(1)" of the Act. Having regard to the provisions of section 16(1), the term "custody order" includes an order for access.[4] It does not include, however, an interim order for custody or access made pursuant to section 16(2) of the *Divorce Act*. The distinction between interim and permanent orders for custody or access is of special significance with respect to the jurisdiction of the courts to vary, rescind, or suspend such orders.[5] It may also prove to be of significance with respect to appellate proceedings insofar as these proceedings are governed by provincial rules of practice and procedure.[6]

C. DEFINITIONS OF "CUSTODY" AND "ACCESS"

Section 2(1) of the *Divorce Act* provides that "custody" includes care, upbringing, and any other incident of custody. The reference to "any other incident of custody" in the statutory definition of "custody" facilitates a court-ordered division of the various incidents of custody between the respective claimants, where an order for custody or any variation thereof is made pursuant to section 16 or section 17 of the *Divorce Act*.[7] Section 2(1) of the *Divorce Act* provides no definition of "access" in the English language, but the French version provides as follows: "'Accès' comporte le droit de visite." Section 16(5) of the *Divorce Act* qualifies this definition of "accès" by entitling a spouse who is granted access privileges to make inquiries and receive information concerning the health, education, or welfare of the child. This right exists in the absence of a court order to the contrary. It does not extend to any person other than a spouse who has been granted access privileges. Section 16(5) entitles a spouse who is granted access privileges to direct relevant inquiries to the custodial parent or to a third party, such as the child's doctor or school principal. This right may not extend to being entitled to be involved in school activities.[8]

---

3   RSC 1985 (2d Supp), c 3.
4   See *Chisholm v Bower* (1987), 11 RFL (3d) 293 (NS Fam Ct).
5   See Section L, below in this chapter.
6   *Divorce Act*, s 21(6).
7   *Crawford v Crawford* (1991), 36 RFL (3d) 337 at 341 (Ont Gen Div).
8   *Moss v Boisvert* (1990), 74 Alta LR (2d) 344 (Master); see also *Boyd v Wegrzynowicz* (1991), 35 RFL (3d) 421 (BCSC); *Amaral v Myke* (1992), 42 RFL (3d) 322 (Ont UFC); and see

The onus is on the non-custodial spouse to seek the relevant information[9] unless the court specifically directs that custodial parent to provide the information.[10] Section 16(5) does not expressly require the custodial parent to consult with the spouse who has access privileges before decisions are taken that affect the child's health, education, and welfare.[11] If, for example, the parents cannot agree on where their child should go to school, the custodial parent has the ultimate decision-making power,[12] subject to a court's right to override that decision.[13]

The term "custody" is imprecise and has in the past been used in both a wide and a narrow sense. In *Hewar v Bryant*,[14] Sachs LJ, of the Court of Appeal in England, observed that in its wide sense, custody is virtually equivalent to guardianship, whereas in its narrow sense, custody refers to the power to exercise physical control over the child. In Canadian divorce proceedings, case-law tends to support the conclusion that, in the absence of directions to the contrary, an order granting sole custody to one parent signifies that the custodial parent shall exercise all the powers of the legal guardian of the child.[15] The non-custodial parent with access privileges is thus deprived of the rights and responsibilities that previously vested in that parent as a joint custodian of the child.[16] Although a parent who has been granted access privileges may have some limited powers to make decisions where an emergency necessitates action and the custodial parent is unavailable, these limited powers fall short of a fundamental right to equally participate in decisions affecting

---

Hamilton v Hamilton (1992), 43 RFL (3d) 13 at 23 (Alta QB) (express waiver of right to contact third parties upheld by court).

9   *Hume v Hume* (1989), 79 Nfld & PEIR 114 (PEISCTD). Compare *Perillo v Perillo* (1994), 6 RFL (4th) 29 (Alta QB).

10 *McLean v Goddard* (1994), 129 NSR (2d) 43 (Fam Ct) (custodial parent required to provide a monthly list of the child's upcoming events); *Hess v Hess* (1994), 2 RFL (4th) 22 (Ont Gen Div) (onus placed on custodial parent to give access parent "full and meaningful notice" of children's activities).

11 See *Anson v Anson* (1987), 10 BCLR (2d) 357 (Co Ct); compare *Abbott v Taylor* (1986), 2 RFL (3d) 163 at 169 (Man CA); and see Berend Hovius, "The Changing Role of the Access Parent" (1993) 10 Can Fam LQ 123.

12 *Ducas v Varkony* (1995), 16 RFL (4th) 91 (Man QB).

13 See *Perron v Perron*, 2012 ONCA 811.

14 [1970] 1 QB 357 at 372–73 (Eng CA). But compare *Dipper v Dipper*, [1981] Fam 31 (Eng CA).

15 See *JR v NR*, 2013 BCSC 2139, citing *Young v Young*, [1993] 4 SCR 3 at paras 40–41; see also *BDM v AEM*, 2014 BCSC 453; *JM v JA*, 2014 NBQB 233. But see contra: *Walsh v Binet*, 2013 ABQB 686, citing *VL v DL*, [2001] AJ No 1259 (CA) at paras 48–56. And see John-Paul Boyd, "A Regime of Peaceful Coexistence, Part 2, Disentangling Custody and Guardianship Under the *Divorce Act* and *The Family Law Act*" (2013) 71:3 The Advocate 359 at 366 (Hein Online), cited with approval in *Rana v Rana*, 2014 BCSC 530.

16 *Young v Young*, [1993] 4 SCR 3, L'Heureux-Dubé J; *Ross v Ross*, 2004 BCSC 637.

the child's welfare and development.[17] The provisions of the *Divorce Act*, and particularly the definitions of "custody" and "accès" in section 2(1), apparently preclude Canadian courts from adopting a narrow definition of custody. Pursuant to section 2(1), "'custody' includes care, upbringing and any other incident of custody" and "'accès' comporte le droit de visite." The use of the word "includes" in the definition of "custody" implies that the term embraces a wider range of powers than those specifically designated in section 2(1).[18] It is legitimate to deduce, therefore, that the term "custody" is to be regarded as virtually synonymous with guardianship of the person.[19] Consequently, in the absence of an order for joint custody or for shared parenting[20] or a court-ordered division of the incidents of custody,[21] a non-custodial spouse with access privileges remains a very interested observer who gives love and support to the child but whose opinions cannot undermine the custodial parent's ultimate decision-making authority in matters relating to the child's welfare, growth, and development. This remains true notwithstanding that section 16(10) of the *Divorce Act* provides that the court shall promote "maximum contact" between the child and the non-custodial parent to the extent that this is consistent with the best interests of the child.[22] It is always open to a court, however, to grant an order for shared parenting or adjudicate the diverse incidents of custody individually on an evidentiary basis and thus avoid an order for sole custody that places absolute control in one of the two parents.[23]

---

17 See *Young v Young*, [1993] 4 SCR 3; *Anson v Anson* (1987), 10 BCLR (2d) 357 at 368 (Co Ct); *BDM v AEM*, 2014 BCSC 453; *DM v SM*, 2014 NBQB 268; *Glasgow v Glasgow (No 2)* (1982), 51 NSR (2d) 13 at 24–25 (Fam Ct); *Gubody v Gubody*, [1955] OWN 548 (HCJ); *Misch v Pfister*, 2012 ONSC 5278; *Gunn v Gunn* (1975), 24 RFL 182 at 185–86 (PEISCTD); *Droit de la famille — 301* (1986), 3 RFL (3d) 65 at 78 (Que CS), rev'd (1988), 14 RFL (3d) 185 (Que CA); *Bannman v Bannman* (1992), 106 Sask R 219 (QB). Compare *Gordon v Goertz*, [1996] 2 SCR 27.

18 See *Anson v Anson* (1987), 10 BCLR (2d) 357 at 365 (Co Ct); see also *Clarke v Clarke* (1987), 7 RFL (3d) 176 (BCSC).

19 *Young v Young*, [1993] 4 SCR 3, 49 RFL (3d) 117 at 184; compare *Gordon v Goertz*, [1996] 2 SCR 27.

20 See *Da Costa v Da Costa* (1990), 29 RFL (3d) 422 (Ont Gen Div), aff'd on other grounds (1992), 40 RFL (3d) 216 (Ont CA).

21 See *Hines v Hines* (1992), 40 RFL (3d) 274 (NSTD); *Ganie v Ganie*, 2014 ONSC 7500.

22 *Young v Young*, [1993] 4 SCR 3, 49 RFL (3d) 117 at 184, L'Heureux-Dubé J; *BDM v AEM*, 2014 BCSC 453; *Scanlan v Tootoo* (1994), 152 NBR (2d) 304 (QB); *Misch v Pfister*, 2012 ONSC 5278. Compare *Pang v Pang*, 2013 ONSC 2564 at paras 123–24.

23 *Young v Young*, [1993] 4 SCR 3; *Hines v Hines*, (1992), 40 RFL (3d) 274 (NSTD).

D. JURISDICTION

1) Constitutional Authority of Parliament of Canada

The provisions of the *Divorce Act*, insofar as they relate to the custody of a "child of the marriage," are within the legislative competence of the Parliament of Canada.[24] Although the matter is not beyond dispute, it is submitted that the jurisdiction to make third party orders pursuant to section 16 of the *Divorce Act* falls within the federal legislative domain where such claims arise on or after divorce.[25]

2) Definition of "Court"

Sections 16 and 17 of the *Divorce Act* empower a "court of competent jurisdiction" to grant interim, permanent, and variation orders respecting the custody of and access to the children of the marriage. In determining whether a court is "a court of competent jurisdiction," the definition of "court" in section 2(1) applies, and the court must be presided over by a federally appointed judge. If this definition is satisfied, sections 3 to 6 of the *Divorce Act* determine the province or territory wherein proceedings under sections 16 or 17 shall be instituted.[26]

3) Competing Jurisdictions under Federal and Provincial Legislation

An existing custody order made under provincial legislation does not bar the matter of custody from being re-opened in subsequent divorce proceedings, but a custody order granted pursuant to the *Divorce Act* precludes a subsequent order being granted pursuant to provincial legislation by virtue of the doctrine of paramountcy.[27]

4) National Effect of Custody or Access Order; Extra-Provincial Registration and Enforcement

A custody or access order made under section 16 of the *Divorce Act* has legal effect throughout Canada and may be extra-provincially registered and enforced pursuant to sections 20(2) and (3) of the *Divorce Act*.

---

24   *Papp v Papp*, [1970] 1 OR 331 (CA).

25   See *Kerr v McWhannel* (1974), 16 RFL 185 (BCCA); compare *Clarke v Hutchings* (1976), 24 RFL 328 (Nfld CA).

26   See, generally, Chapter 7, Section B, for a discussion of jurisdiction over divorce.

27   *Adamson v Adamson* (1979), 15 BCLR 195 (SC); *McKay v McKay* (1982), 30 RFL (2d) 463 (Ont HCJ).

E. TYPES OF ORDERS

1) General

Courts have an extremely wide discretion in making custody and access orders and attaching conditions thereto. They may grant interim or temporary orders, consent orders, joint custody orders, third-party custody and access orders, orders dividing the incidents of custody, non-molestation or restraining orders, supervision orders, orders restricting mobility or providing for notice of any intended change of residence, orders for the tracing of missing children, orders for the apprehension of children to prevent parental abduction, orders for the return of a child from outside the province or territory, orders for the enforcement of custody and access arrangements, and orders for the variation and termination of custody and access.

2) Interim Custody Orders

Section 16(2) of the *Divorce Act* expressly confers a discretionary jurisdiction on a court of competent jurisdiction to grant an interim order for the custody of or access to any child of the marriage pending a final determination.[28] A final determination can be made under the *Divorce Act* only upon the granting of a divorce judgment.[29] Any subsisting interim order made under section 16(2) of the *Divorce Act* will expire in the unlikely event of a dismissal of the divorce petition.[30] In *SMS v TMP-S*,[31] Walsh J, of the New Brunswick Court of Queen's Bench Family Division, characterized applications for interim custody in the following words:

> Interim hearings such as this are different. They are limited by time and the nature of the evidence before it. The evidence is in affidavit form, and as usual, there is great conflict in the competing affidavits. In these circumstances, our Court of Appeal has directed judges to try to find "a reasonable temporary solution" to a very difficult problem from a host of options, pending the full hearing (See: *Legault v. Rattray* [2003] N.B.J. No. 442 (C.A.) at para. 4).

---

28 As to the nature and purpose of interim custody/access orders, see *Wiktorowski v Ramsay*, 2011 SKQB 348 at paras 22–24. And see, generally, Julien D Payne, *Payne on Divorce*, 4th ed (Scarborough, ON: Carswell, 1996) c 12 at 381–88.

29 *Yu v Jordan*, 2012 BCCA 367; compare *Bridgeman v Balfour*, 2012 ONSC 6583.

30 *Papp v Papp*, [1970] 1 OR 331 (CA); see also *Yu v Jordan*, 2012 BCCA 367; and compare *Bridgeman v Balfour*, 2012 ONSC 6583.

31 2010 NBQB 329 at para 4; see also *Coe v Tope*, 2014 ONSC 4002 at para 25.

Although the best interests of the child is the sole consideration in proceedings for interim and permanent custody or access, preservation of the *status quo* plays a more significant role in proceedings for interim custody than in proceedings for permanent custody. In the absence of material evidence that the child's best interests demand an immediate change, the *status quo* will ordinarily be maintained until trial.[32] In the words of Laskin JA in *Papp v Papp*,[33] the "evidence to warrant an order for interim custody must more cogently support disturbance of the *de facto* situation than evidence to support an order for custody after a trial on the merits." Courts do not like to disturb the *status quo* on a temporary basis because they do not want to give one parent an advantage in the litigation and because it is disruptive for children to go back and forth between different parenting regimes.[34] Where a motion judge is faced with untested evidence and incomplete investigations, coupled with the imminence of a trial date, it is unnecessary or even undesirable to make rulings that may be significantly altered when the full picture is available. Therefore, these matters should be left to the trial judge.[35] Applications to vary interim custody orders are discouraged when a trial of the issues will take place in the near future. Courts have an inherent jurisdiction to vary interim custody orders under the *Divorce Act* but such variations are not granted lightly and they are rare. There is a heavy onus on the person who, rather than wait for the trial, brings on a variation motion.[36] Appeals from interim custody orders are similarly discouraged.[37] An interim order is not binding on a trial judge.[38] In the words of Slatter JA, of the Alberta Court of Appeal, in *Olson v Olson*:

> An interim order in a family matter can be varied by the court if there is a change in circumstances. Further, after a trial the trial judge may make a different order, and can vary the interim terms previously ordered: *MacMinn v. MacMinn* (1995), 174 AR 261, 17 RFL (4th) 88 (CA); *Hartley v. Del Pero* at para. 9. This allows the court to promote the best interests of the child

---

32   *JV v ES*, 2014 NBQB 210; *Tran v Tran*, 2013 NSSC 280; *Ganie v Ganie*, 2014 ONSC 7500; *Babich v Babich*, 2015 SKQB 22; compare *Peet v Zolob*, 2014 ONSC 5748.

33   [1970] 1 OR 331 at 344–45 (CA).

34   *Shotton v Switzer*, 2014 ONSC 843 at para 15, Van Melle J; *Coe v Tope*, 2014 ONSC 4002.

35   *Zaidi v Qizilbash*, [2013] OJ No 4406 (Sup Ct).

36   *PLM v SYB*, 2014 NBQB 222 at para 27, d'Entremont J; see also *Simle v Borchuk*, 2014 NWTSC 80.

37   *TN v JCN*, 2013 BCCA 432; *Fitzgibbon v Fitzgibbon*, 2014 BCCA 403 (interim order for supervised access); *DA v JR*, 2012 NBCA 38; *Bolan v Bolan*, 2013 SKCA 97. See also Section L, below in this chapter.

38   See *CMH v TTH*, 2014 MBQB 65, citing *Skinner v Skinner* (1999), 134 Man R (2d) 313 at para 5. See also *VMB v KRB*, 2014 ABCA 334.

on an interim basis, based on what is often an incomplete or inadequate record. Before permanent arrangements are put in place, the parties are entitled to a reasonable opportunity to marshal their evidence, gather documents, consult experts, and testify *viva voce* on contested issues.[39]

F. PRESERVATION OF FAMILY BONDS; JOINT CUSTODY; MAXIMUM CONTACT PRINCIPLE

1) General Application

The history of custody during the last century has witnessed a radical judicial shift from a strong paternal preference, through a strong maternal preference, to the present-day philosophy that both parents are forever and marriage breakdown and divorce should not preclude continuing meaningful relationships between the child and both parents. Increased legal recognition of the importance of preserving the child-parent bond that evolved during the marriage is manifested by changes in orders for joint custody and access that have evolved over several decades.[40] Before the first dominionwide *Divorce Act*[41] came into force in 1968, orders for joint custody were statistically insignificant. In recent years, courts have moved away from their former practice of granting sole responsibility for the children of separated or divorced parents to one of the parents and granting only access rights to the non-custodial parent. Today, some form of joint custody disposition is found in more than 40 percent of divorce cases, and a non-custodial parent is likely to be granted access privileges on one evening every week in addition to overnight access from Friday to Sunday on alternate weekends. During the summer vacation, a non-custodial parent is frequently granted access for two to four weeks, and other vacations and statutory holidays are often equally shared between the parents on a rotational basis.

Subsections 16(4), (5), and (10) of the *Divorce Act*[42] go some way towards recognizing that divorce should not undermine the family bonds that a child develops during the marriage of his or her parents.

Subsection 16(4) of the *Divorce Act* empowers the court to make orders "granting custody of, or access to, any or all children of the marriage to any

---

39 2014 ABCA 15 at para 5.

40 For an excellent overview of changes in the judicial approach to custody litigation, in particular, the shift in emphasis from the need of the child to have an attachment to one "psychological parent" to the need for children to maintain relationships with both parents, see *Moreira v Garcia Dominguez*, 2012 ONCJ 128.

41 SC 1967–68, c 24.

42 RSC 1985 (2d Supp), c 3.

one or more persons." This subsection is of fundamental importance in that it recognizes a place for joint custody arrangements; it also entitles third parties, such as grandparents or other relatives, to enjoy access to the children of divorcing or divorced parents. Third-party applications for custody and access can only be brought under the *Divorce Act* by leave of the court. Courts will only allow third-party applications to be brought by persons who have been previously involved in the child's life. Third-party custody orders are rare. Applications for access privileges by third parties, especially grandparents, are far more likely to be favourably received by the courts, especially when such access will provide a measure of ongoing stability for the child. Grandparents have no presumptive right of access to their grandchildren and must discharge the onus of proving that they should have a continuing relationship with the child, notwithstanding the opposition of the custodial parent to access.[43]

Subsection 16(5) of the *Divorce Act* entitles a spouse who is granted access to make inquiries and to be given information concerning the health, education, and welfare of the children. Although subsection 16(5) falls short of giving equal participatory rights in the upbringing of the child to the non-custodial and the custodial parent,[44] it provides the foundation for an exchange of opinions that may facilitate the non-custodial parent's meaningful involvement in decision making. While section 16(5) of the *Divorce Act* does not confer decision-making authority on the non-custodial parent,[45] an equal right to participate in major decisions respecting a child's health, education, or welfare may be conferred by a joint custody order under section 16(4) of the *Divorce Act*, notwithstanding that one of the parents is contemporaneously granted primary day-to-day care and control of the child.

Joint custody is a term that generates confusion. It may signify that separated or divorced parents will continue to share in making all major decisions concerning their child's health, education, and upbringing. In this context, it is sometimes called "joint legal custody" to differentiate it from "joint physical custody," which signifies that the child will reside with each parent for substantial periods. Joint physical custody may, but does not automatically, involve equal time-sharing,[46] such as three and one-half days a week with each parent, or alternating weeks or months or years[47] with each parent. "Joint legal custody" usually exists when the parents have joint

43   *CML v RST*, [2000] SJ No 362 (QB).

44   *Misch v Pfister*, 2012 ONSC 5278, citing *Young v Young*, [1993] 4 SCR 3 at para 41.

45   *TLMM v CAM*, 2011 SKQB 326, citing L'Heureux-Dubé J's judgment in *Young v Young*, [1993] 4 SCR 3 at para 42.

46   *Strong v Strong*, 2014 MBQB 176.

47   *Auigbelle v King*, 2008 ABCA 295.

physical custody, but "joint legal custody" can also exist independently of "joint physical custody."[48] Joint legal custody may extend across provincial boundaries or international borders.[49] Negotiated settlements and court orders should spell out parenting arrangements in unambiguous words that everyone can understand. This eliminates the risk that legal jargon such as "joint custody" will be misunderstood.[50]

There are no presumptions, either factual or legal, in favour of sole custody or joint custody; each case must be determined on its own unique circumstances.[51] As Goepel J, of the British Columbia Supreme Court, pointed out in *KDP v ARK*, "there are no presumptions for or against joint custody, nor is there a threshold test to establish when joint custody is feasible," and while communication is an important factor, it is also important to "balance and preserve the relationship of the child with both parents."[52] Notwithstanding the lack of any presumptions, joint legal custody is usually ordered by the courts unless there exists an insurmountable inability to communicate appropriately so as to be able to jointly make decisions with regard to a child or where there is found to be a history of abuse in the family and/or where there is disinterest by one parent as regards the care of the child that suitability of a joint legal custody arrangement likely will not be present.[53] But shared parenting arrangements should not be ordered where the parties are in substantial conflict with each other; nor should such orders be made by way of interim relief before trial if there is significant disagreement on the evidence.[54] On a shared parenting application, each parent bears the evidential burden of his or her position.[55]

Courts have recognized changing parenting roles in the two-income family by means of orders for joint custody.[56] In *Gibney v Conohan*, O'Neil ACJ,

---

48   *CM v DJL*, 2012 NBQB 188; *Rowe v Coles*, 2012 NLTD(F) 24; *Schick v Woodrow*, 2012 SKCA 1; *Richardson v Biggs*, 2012 SKQB 162. For the most comprehensive judicial analysis in Canada of expert evidence relating to joint custody, see *GCV v GE*, [1992] QJ No 337 (CS).

49   *PLG v RJM*, 2010 NBQB 435 at para 47.

50   As to the inherent vagueness of the term "joint custody," see *Lennox v Frender* (1990), 27 RFL (3d) 181 at 185 (BCCA); *JRC v SJC*, 2010 NSSC 85; *Vojan v Lauzon*, 2015 ONSC 987.

51   *Robinson v Filyk* (1996), 28 BCLR (3d) 21 (CA); *ELS v CAS*, 2012 BCSC 1224; *Kopp v Burke*, 2014 MBQB 247; *FFR v KF*, 2013 NLCA 8; *Gagnon v Gagnon*, 2011 NSSC 486; *JAW v CFCR*, 2012 SKQB 46; *Ackerman v Ackerman*, 2014 SKCA 86 at para 48.

52   2011 BCSC 1085 at para 148, cited with approval by Warren J in *NU v GSB*, 2015 BCSC 105 at para 130.

53   *Butt v Major*, 2013 NLTD(F) 5, LeBlanc J. See also *JM v JA*, 2014 NBQB 233.

54   *Rensonnet v Uttl*, 2014 ABCA 304 at para 9, citing *Richter v Richter*, 2005 ABCA 165; *CEC v MPC*, 2006 ABCA 118.

55   *Wickens v Wickens*, 2012 ABQB 441.

56   *Gibney v Conohan*, 2011 NSSC 268 at para 45. As to the increased incidence of joint custody and shared parenting arrangements, see Rachel Birnbaum, John-Paul Boyd,

of the Nova Scotia Supreme Court, identified the following factors for consideration in determining whether a child's best interests might be served by a shared parenting arrangement:

a. the proximity of the parents' homes;

b. the daily availability of parents and others in the child's extended family;

c. each parent's motivation and capability;

d. the number of transitions between homes required of the parenting schedule;

e. the ease of mid-week contact;

f. each parent's interest in shared decision-making;

g. the ease of developing a routine in each home;

h. each parent's willingness to share the parenting burden;

i. the benefits to each parent of sharing the parenting burden;

j. any improvements to the parents' standards of living as a result of sharing the parenting burden;

k. the parents' willingness to access professional advice on parenting issues;

l. "the elephant in the room"; and

m. each parent's style of parenting.[57]

But decisions on shared parenting applications are fact-specific[58] and not all of the factors identified in *Gibney v Conohan* will be relevant in all cases.[59]

Courts have moved away from presuming that if parties have difficulty communicating, all forms of joint custody are inappropriate.[60] As Baird J, of the New Brunswick Court of Queen's Bench, observed in *DLG v GDR*:

> 279 Judges are becoming far more receptive to joint custody orders in high conflict situations.
>
> . . .
>
> 281 Recent *jurisprudence* has challenged the oft repeated principle that joint custody orders should only be granted in cases where the parents can effectively communicate with each other. In fact, judges are resorting to

---

Nicholas Bala, and Lorne Bertrand, "Shared Parenting is the new norm: Legal Professionals agree on the need for reform", *The Family Way*, October 2014 – The CBA National Family Law Section Newsletter.

57 *Gibney v Conohan*, 2011 NSSC 268 at para 92; see also *MSC v TLC*, 2013 NSSC 378; compare *LeBlanc v Brown*, 2013 NSSC 429.

58 *Matthews v Taylor*, 2012 NLTD(G) 24; *SB v TO*, 2013 NSSC 243; *MacNutt v MacNutt*, 2013 NSSC 267.

59 *Conrad v Skerry*, 2012 NSSC 77.

60 *Landa-McAuliffe v Boland*, 2012 BCSC 465; *Kopp v Burke*, 2014 MBQB 247; *Droit de la famille — 132434*, 2013 QCCA 1530; *Gagnon v Gagnon*, 2011 NSSC 486; *JAW v CFCR*, 2012 SKQB 46.

creative alternatives as an attempt to maintain a meaningful role for the access parent. These alternatives in high conflict situations include, but are not exclusive to, parallel parenting orders, parenting coordinators, therapeutic intervention, deprogramming of children such as is offered by the Warshak and Rand Clinic in the United States, transfer of custody from the alienating parent to the other parent or a combination of joint and shared custody orders with specified parenting clauses.[61]

Although ongoing parental conflict is not an automatic bar to some form of joint custody or shared parenting order, the degree of conflict may be sufficiently high to preclude any such order.[62] In the words of Pentelechuk J in *AJU v GSU*,[63] "[c]ommunication issues and lack of cooperation for a couple caught in the turbulence of divorce should not be compared to an impossible standard that does not exist in the most functional of families." The nature and extent of the conflict must be analyzed.[64] There must be an evidentiary basis for the belief that joint custody will be feasible.[65] For shared parenting to work, the parents must both be involved in their children's lives.[66] However, one parent cannot create problems with the other parent and claim sole custody on the basis of a lack of co-operation.[67] Joint custody may be appropriate to preserve a parent's relationship with the children in cases where the primary caregiver objects to joint custody without just cause and there is a risk that he or she will try to marginalize the other parent's involvement with the children.[68] The fact that one parent is opposed to sharing

---

61 2012 NBQB 177. See also *MacDonald v Ross*, 2013 NSSC 117, citing *Baker-Warren v Denault*, 2009 NSSC 59 at para 26. And see *Hsiung v Tsioutsioulas*, 2011 ONCJ 517 at para 17.

62 *CEC v MPC*, [2006] AJ No 383 (CA) (interim proceeding), citing *Richter v Richter*, [2005] AJ No 616 at para 11 (CA); see, generally, *AJU v GSU*, 2015 ABQB 6; *Robinson v Filyk*, (1996), 84 BCAC 290; *Javid v Kurytnik*, [2006] BCJ No 3195 (CA); *Kopp v Burke*, 2014 MBQB 247; *MDC v TC*, 2012 NBQB 376; *FFR v KF*, 2013 NLCA 8; *Hustins v Hustins*, 2014 NSSC 185; *Yasinchuk v Farkas*, 2012 ONSC 2056; *JAW v CFCR*, 2012 SKQB 46; *CMS v MRJS*, 2009 YKSC 32; compare *CS v SN*, 2008 YKSC 22; see also *Children's Act*, RSY 2002, c 31, s 30(4). See also *Wardell v Perreault*, 2011 ONCJ 288, citing Justice Harvey Brownstone, *Tug of War: A Judge's Verdict on Separation, Custody Battles, and the Bitter Realities of Family Court* (Toronto: ECW Press, 2009) at 96.

63 2015 ABQB 6 at para 76.

64 *Kopp v Burke*, 2014 MBQB 247; *MAB v LAB*, 2013 NSSC 89.

65 *May-Iannizzi v Iannizzi*, 2010 ONCA 519.

66 *Kopp v Burke*, 2014 MBQB 247; *KCWV v KLP*, 2010 NBCA 70; *RJ v WJ*, 2011 NBQB 294; *BP v AT*, 2014 NBCA 51 at para 14.

67 *Hestbak v Hestbak*, 2012 ABQB 633; *DLG v GDR*, 2012 NBQB 177; *Lawson v Lawson*, [2006] OJ No 3179 (CA); *Caverley v Stanley*, 2015 ONSC 647; *Ackerman v Ackerman*, 2014 SKCA 86. See also *AJU v GSU*, 2015 ABQB 6 at paras 70–73.

68 *Vendetti v Mackenzie*, 2014 ONSC 4846 at para 15, citing *Kaplanis v Kaplanis*, [2005] OJ No 275 (CA) and *Ladisa v Ladisa*, [2005] OJ No 276 (CA), see text at notes 70 and 71.

major decision-making authority over the children does not preclude an order for joint custody. If the court is satisfied that the parents are capable of communicating and that the child would not be adversely affected, an order aimed at enhancing parental involvement in the child's life would generally seem consistent with the best interests of the child.[69]

In *Jordan v Jordan*,[70] Joyce J, of the British Columbia Supreme Court, discussed factors to be considered by a court in relation to a joint custody order:

> [279] ... I am satisfied that the ability of the parents to communicate and cooperate remains an important factor when considering the best interests of a child. That is apparent from the decision in *Robinson v Filyk* itself as well as from the decision in *Ness v Ness* (1999) 43 R.F.L. (4th) 363 (B.C.C.A.). It is not the only factor to be considered, however.
>
> [281] In my view, some other factors that are relevant to this enquiry include: (i) the ability of each parent to make proper decisions for the child; (ii) the extent to which the child will reside with each parent; (iii) the geographic distance between the parents' homes; (iv) the extent to which the parties' "parenting styles" may differ and, consequently, the extent to which their different parenting styles may provide the opportunity for disagreement; (v) the harm that may be caused to the child if the parents' disagreement on issues creates an atmosphere of conflict; and (vi) the nature of the disagreements in the past, particularly whether they relate to "access issues" that are likely to be resolved by the court order or whether they concern matters of child rearing that are likely to continue to arise. These are not necessarily all of the factors that have a bearing on what sort of custody order is in the best interests of the particular child but they are, I think, some of the important ones.

In *Ladisa v Ladisa*,[71] the Ontario Court of Appeal upheld the trial judge's order for joint custody, which provided for the two younger siblings, aged thirteen and nine at the time of the appeal, to spend alternate weeks in each parental home. In dismissing the appeal in the absence of any demonstrated

---

69 *VL v DL*, [2001] AJ No 1259 (CA); *Kopp v Burke*, 2014 MBQB 247; *JAW v CFCR*, 2012 SKQB 46. In Ontario, guardianship of the person of a child is subsumed under "custody" of that child. "Guardianship" is a term that is confined to the guardianship of the property of a child: see *Children's Law Reform Act*, RSO 1990, c C.12, Part III, especially ss 20, 47–58, and 61.

70 2001 BCSC 1058; see also *Marino v Marino*, 2008 BCSC 1402; *Haigh v Spence*, 2010 BCSC 270; *CLH v RJJS*, 2012 BCSC 579; *Merritt v Merritt*, 2010 ONSC 4959; see also *Hammond v Nelson*, 2012 NSSC 27 at para 68.

71 [2005] OJ No 276 (CA); see also *Ursic v Ursic*, [2006] OJ No 2178 (CA); *Cook v Sacco*, [2006] OJ No 4379 (CA); *May-Iannizzi v Iannizzi*, 2010 ONCA 519; *Madott v Macorig*, 2010 ONSC 5458; *Walters v Walters*, 2012 ONSC 1845.

palpable and overriding error, the Ontario Court of Appeal observed that the trial judge's exercise of discretion properly took account of the history of co-parenting during the marriage, the wishes of the thirteen-year-old child, the absence of any compelling reason to separate the siblings, expert evidence presented by the Children's Lawyer who recommended joint custody, the evidence of third parties respecting the parents' interaction with the children, and the ability of the parents to communicate effectively and put their children's interests ahead of their own, notwithstanding ongoing parental strife. The provisions of the trial judge's order with respect to an older child, who was almost seventeen years of age at the time of the appeal, were vacated by the Ontario Court of Appeal on the basis that this child was now old enough to determine with whom she would live.

The judgment in *Ladisa v Ladisa* may be compared with that of the same panel of judges of the Ontario Court of Appeal in *Kaplanis v Kaplanis*.[72] In the latter case, the trial judge was found in error in granting an order for joint legal custody of a two-and-a-half-year-old child in the face of ongoing spousal conflict but in the hope parental co-operation would improve in the future after the parents received counselling. The trial judge was also found in error in ordering mandatory counselling for the parents with the un-named counsellor being empowered to make decisions respecting the child's schools, activities, and hobbies, if the parents were unable to agree. While acknowledging that it might be desirable for parents to have recourse to a counsellor or parenting coach to resolve their disputes, the Ontario Court of Appeal stated that the counselling provisions of the order of the trial judge were problematic. In particular, the Ontario Court of Appeal observed that the legislation does not specifically authorize the court to order counselling,[73] although some trial judges have held that such orders may be granted in the exercise of the court's inherent jurisdiction.[74] In the present case, however, there was no evidence that the parties would be able to agree upon a counsellor and no agreed procedure was established for appointing a counsellor if the parents could not agree; nor was there any evidence that the parents

72 [2005] OJ No 275 (CA); see also *Roy v Roy*, [2006] OJ No 1872 (CA); *Giri v Wentges*, 2009 ONCA 606; *BV v PV*, 2012 ONCA 262. And see Martha Shaffer, "Joint Custody, Parental Conflict and Children's Adjustment to Divorce: What the Social Science Literature Does and Does Not Tell Us" (2007) 26 Fam LQ 285; Martha Shaffer, "Joint Custody Since *Kaplanis* and *Ladisa*: A Review of Recent Ontario Case Law" (2007) 26 Fam LQ 315; Martha Shaffer, "Experiments in Custody Reform" in The Law Society of Upper Canada, *Special Lectures 2006: Family Law* (Toronto: Irwin Law, 2007) at 373.

73 But see *contra*, *Marquez v Zapiola*, 2013 BCCA 433 at para 66, citing section 16(6) of the *Divorce Act*.

74 See also *LM v TM*, 2012 NBQB 238, citing s 129(2) of the *Family Services Act*, SNB 1980, c F-2.2; see also s 16(6) of the *Divorce Act*.

were willing to have their disputes resolved by a counsellor outside the court process envisaged by the *Divorce Act* and without recourse to it. In addressing the broader issue of joint custody, the Ontario Court of Appeal expressed the opinion that the ongoing needs of the child require some evidence to be presented to the court that the parents, despite their differences, can effectively communicate with each other. Where such evidence is lacking or the evidence points to a parental inability to communicate, the hope that communication will improve once the litigation is over is an inadequate basis for making a joint custody order. Given its finding that this is what occurred in *Kaplanis v Kaplanis*, the Ontario Court of Appeal substituted its own order for sole custody in favour of the mother and directed a rehearing of the issue of access, with the hope that the Children's Lawyer would become involved.

Where a court is concerned about the disruption caused by the children's frequent moves between the two parental households, the court may reduce the frequency of the exchanges by substituting an alternate weekly parenting regime for daily exchanges.[75] Exceptionally, a court may grant a "bird's nest" order whereby the children will reside in the home of one of the parents and each of the parents will be allotted specific blocks of time to spend with the children in that home.[76] Although the benefits of a "bird's nest" order under which the parents visit the children rather than *vice versa* are best achieved where the children are able to stay in the matrimonial home, particularly if it is the only residence that they have known, all benefits are not lost merely because the matrimonial home has been sold and the parents have acquired separate residences.[77] As an alternative to an order whereby the children continue to reside in the matrimonial home and each parent lives in the home with the children at different periods of time, a court may grant exclusive possession of the home to one spouse but provide for specified access periods within the home by the non-custodial parent, during which time the custodial parent must vacate the premises.[78] Given privacy concerns and the financial costs involved, "bird's nest" orders are exceptional even on a temporary basis, save in circumstances where the parents are agreeable to that form of order. Such orders, nevertheless, constitute one of the options available to promote shared parenting responsibilities.

Faced with a pattern of previous parental conflict, expert opinions may differ on the question whether the best interests of a child of separated or divorced parents will be served by a shared parenting regime. Judges in Quebec

---

75   *Zukerman v Villalobos-Cardeilhac*, 2009 BCSC 1223.

76   *Hughes v Erickson*, 2014 BCSC 1952.

77   *Hatton v Hatton*, [1993] OJ No 2621 (Gen Div); *Greenough v Greenough*, [2003] OJ No 4415 (Sup Ct).

78   *Stefanyk v Stefanyk* (1994), 1 RFL (4th) 432 (NSSC).

are inclined to grant orders for shared parenting only when the following conditions co-exist: (1) adequate parenting capacity; (2) some minimal functional ability in the parents to communicate and co-operate; and (3) geographic proximity of the two households. In a high-conflict situation where the expert evidence of a psychologist supports a finding that the parents are incapable of reaching a viable parenting plan that will meet the developmental needs of their child, the trial judge's refusal to grant an order for shared parenting should be upheld on appeal.[79]

Although many Canadian courts have been traditionally averse to granting any form of joint custody order where the parents have a history of ongoing substantial conflict after their separation, some courts have endorsed the concept of "parallel parenting" in cases where the parents are openly hostile and uncooperative.[80] Indeed, the conventional wisdom that joint custody and joint guardianship orders should only be granted when the parents can co-operate and communicate relatively well is being challenged in more and more cases, especially in Alberta,[81] British Columbia,[82] Ontario,[83] and Saskatchewan.[84] The following characteristics of parallel parenting orders have been identified:

- A parent assumes responsibility for the children during the time they are with that parent.
- A parent has no say or influence over the actions of the other parent while the children are in the other parent's care.
- There is no expectation of flexibility or negotiation.
- A parent does not plan activities for the children during the other parent's time.
- Contact between the parents is minimized.
- Children are not asked to deliver verbal messages.

---

79 *TPG c DM*, [2004] JQ no 5040 (CA); *Droit de la famille — 091541*, [2009] JQ no 6461 (CA).

80 For a summary of the evolution of caselaw on joint custody in Alberta and Ontario, see *VL v DL*, [2001] AJ No 1259 (CA); *VK v TS*, 2011 ONSC 4305; see also *Frame v Frame*, [2007] MJ No 344 (CA); *MacDonald v MacDonald*, 2011 NSSC 317; *Sgroi v Socci*, [2007] OJ No 5801 (Sup Ct); *Howard v Howard*, [2007] SJ No 489 (CA). Compare the use of the "Joyce" style of joint guardianship order in *Jordan v Jordan* (elsewhere known as "joint legal custody"), which is frequently used in British Columbia, with or without a substantial child-parent time-sharing regime ("joint physical custody"): see, for example, *SDN v MDN*, [1997] BCJ No 3027 (SC); *DCR v TMR*, [2007] BCJ No 1684 (SC); compare *Cavanaugh v Balkaron*, 2008 ABCA 423; *ANH v MKC*, 2010 NBQB 120. See also *Koeckeritz v Secord*, 2008 SKQB 502.

81 *McCurry v Hawkins*, [2004] AJ No 1290 (QB); *Roberts v Salvador*, [2006] AJ No 715 (QB).

82 *Carr v Carr*, [2001] BCJ No 1219 (CA); *JR v SHC*, [2004] BCJ No 2444 (Prov Ct); compare *Javid v Kurytnyk*, [2006] BCJ No 3195 (CA).

83 See *VK v TS*, 2011 ONSC 4305, wherein several Ontario Court of Appeal cases are reviewed.

84 *McMartin v Fraser*, 2014 SKQB 243.

- Information about health, school, and vacations is shared in writing, usually in the form of an access book.[85]

Cases involving high conflict, including suspected parental alienation, may be candidates for a parallel parenting regime.[86] Parallel parenting orders do not depend upon cooperative working relationships or even good communication between the parents.[87]

In *VL v DL*,[88] the Alberta Court of Appeal summarized various judicial and legislative efforts to ensure that the children of separated or divorced parents continue to benefit from the input of both parents on the breakdown of the family unit. The task of the court is to find a parenting arrangement that optimizes the children's best interests. In some, but not all, cases in which the parents can no longer co-operate, an order for parallel parenting may constitute a viable option. Such an order has three advantages. First, it allows the court to make decisions on disputed evidence because an order for parallel parenting typically requires the parents to maintain a communications record, thereby enabling the court to decide which of the parents is unreasonable, controlling, or obstructive. Second, and more important, it gives primacy to the children's best interests rather than to the dispute between the parents. A parallel parenting regime avoids a destructive result in that it enables both parents to have continuing input into their children's lives, rather than have one of them reduced to the role of a passive observer or babysitter as a result of ongoing hostility and lack of co-operation between the parents. Because custody and access orders are never final, a parallel parenting order can always be revisited if it fails to accommodate the best interests of the children. In granting its initial order, therefore, a court does not have to make a permanently binding choice between optimism and prudence. It is well placed to monitor the effects of a parallel parenting regime and, if it becomes satisfied that an ongoing poor relationship between the parents is having a detrimental effect on the children, the parenting regime can be

---

85   *JEB v CB*, 1998 ABQB 774 at para 18; *McCurry v Hawkins*, [2004] AJ No 1290 (QB); *Hensell v Hensell*, [2007] OJ No 4189 (Sup Ct); *JAW v CFCR*, 2012 SKQB 46. And see Peter G Jaffe et al, "Custody Disputes Involving Allegations of Domestic Violence: Toward a Differentiated Approach to Parenting" (2008) 46 Fam Ct Rev 500 at 516.

86   *DJG v JRG*, [2008] NBJ No 516 at para 115 (QB); *AL v CM*, 2010 NBQB 46. Compare *AA v GG*, 2010 ONSC 1261 at paras 238–41; *Seed v Desai*, 2014 ONSC 3329; see also *Madott v Macorig*, 2010 ONSC 5458, citing *Andrade v Kennelly*, [2007] OJ No 5004 (CA); *Ladisa v Ladisa*, [2005] OJ No 276 (CA); *Ursic v Ursic*, [2006] OJ No 2178 (CA).

87   *Askin v Askin*, 2011 BCSC 1779; *Barnes v Parks*, [2001] OJ No 643 (CA); *TGM v PGM*, [2002] OJ No 398 (Sup Ct); compare *JDL v RJJL*, 2012 NBQB 378; *Ryan v Scott*, 2011 ONSC 3277.

88   [2001] AJ No 1259 (CA). For a useful and succinct review of the increasing use of "parallel parenting" orders in high-conflict custody disputes, see *JR v SHC*, [2004] BCJ No 2444 (Prov Ct), Tweedale Prov Ct J; see also *JAW v CFCR*, 2012 SKQB 46.

changed. The third advantage of parallel parenting is that it nurtures the objective of ensuring, insofar as is practicable, maximum contact between the children and their two parents, a legislative objective that has been endorsed by the Parliament of Canada in the *Divorce Act* and by provincial legislation that deals with both married and unmarried parents.

In *VK v TS*,[89] Chappel J, of the Ontario Superior Court, listed the following factors as particularly relevant in determining whether a parallel parenting regime, rather than sole custody, is appropriate:

a) The strength of the parties' ties to the child, and the general level of involvement of each parent in the child's parenting and life. In almost all cases where parallel parenting has been ordered, both parents have consistently played a significant role in the child's life on all levels.

b) The relative parenting abilities of each parent, and their capacity to make decisions that are in the child's best interests.[90] Where one parent is clearly more competent, responsible and attentive than the other, this may support a sole custody arrangement. On the other hand, where there is extensive conflict between the parties, but both are equally competent and loving parents and are able at times to focus jointly on the best interests of the child, a parallel parenting regime may be ordered.

c) Evidence of alienation by one parent. If the alienating parent is otherwise loving, attentive, involved, competent and very important to the child, a parallel parenting arrangement may be considered appropriate as a means of safeguarding the other party's role in the child's life. On the other hand, if the level of alienation is so significant that a parallel parenting order will not be effective in achieving a balance of parental involvement and will be contrary to the child's best interests, a sole custody order may be more appropriate.

d) Where both parties have engaged in alienating behaviour, but the evidence indicates that one of them is more likely to foster an ongoing relationship between the child and the other parent, this finding may tip the scale in favour of a sole custody order.

e) The extent to which each parent is able to place the needs of the child above their own needs and interests. If one of the parties is unable to focus on the child's needs above their own, this may result in a sole

---

89   2011 ONSC 4305 at para 96; see also *Denninger v Ross*, 2013 NSSC 237; *Pang v Pang*, 2013 ONSC 2564 at paras 123–124. For additional factors, see *KH v TKR*, 2013 ONCJ 418 at paras 51–54. And see *Batsinda v Batsinda*, 2013 ONSC 7869 (interim orders); *Ganie v Ganie*, 2014 ONSC 7500.

90   See *HD v PED*, 2012 NBQB 315 at paras 143–151.

custody order, even if that parent is very involved with the child and otherwise able to meet the child's day to day needs.

f) The existence of any form of abuse, including emotional abuse or undermining behaviour, which could impede the objective of achieving a balance of roles and influence through parallel parenting.

As Chappel J further observed, parallel parenting orders, like orders for sole custody or joint custody, may address incidents of custody beyond the residential schedule.[91] In the particular circumstances of the case, she concluded that the ongoing high conflict between the parents could be effectively managed by a parallel parenting order for equal time sharing, with sole decision-making authority over the child's education being granted to the father and sole decision-making authority on matters relating to the child's medical and health needs being given to the mother. Cases that support joint custody even when there is a high degree of conflict generally include clauses for parallel parenting and contain multidirectional orders.[92] In some cases, a parallel parenting order provides that each parent has the final decision-making authority with respect to a different area. In other cases, parallel parenting means that each parent has the right to make major decisions respecting the child when the child is with that parent.[93]

Subsections 16(10) and 17(9) of the *Divorce Act* extol the virtues of preserving the parent-child bond after divorce. They expressly require the court, in making an order for custody or access, or a variation order relating thereto, to give effect to the principle that a child of the marriage should have as much contact with each spouse or former spouse as is consistent with the best interests of the child and, for that purpose, shall take into consideration the willingness of the person for whom custody is sought to facilitate such contact.[94] The maximum contact principle is mandatory but not absolute. The *Divorce Act* only obliges the judge to respect it to the extent that such contact is consistent with the child's best interests; if other factors show that it would not be in the child's best interests, the court can and should restrict contact.[95] The

91 See also *South v Tichelaar*, [2001] OJ No 2823 (Sup Ct); *Hodgins v Durnford*, 2011 ONSC 4580.

92 *Quercia v Francioni*, 2011 ONSC 6844 at para 8.

93 *MB v DT*, 2012 ONSC 840; *Pang v Pang*, 2013 ONSC 2564 at para 136; *KH v TKR*, 2013 ONCJ 418.

94 See *Young v Young*, [1993] 4 SCR 3 at para 17; *Lust v Lust*, [2007] AJ No 654 (CA); *DME v RDE*, 2015 ABQB 47; *RMS v FPCS*, 2011 BCCA 53; *SS v DS*, 2013 NSSC 384; *BV v PV*, 2012 ONCA 262; *Magnus v Magnus*, [2006] SJ No 510 (CA).

95 *Young v Young*, 49 RFL (3d) 117 at 117–18 (RFL), McLachlin J; see also *SLT v AKT*, 2009 ABQB 13; *RMS v FPCS*, 2011 BCCA 53; *KM v SM*, 2011 NBQB 369; *MacRae v Hubley*, 2011 NSCA 25; *AF v JW*, 2013 ONSC 4272.

maximum contact principle does not, of itself, provide a sufficient basis upon which to order shared parenting,[96] although such an order may be deemed appropriate in light of the attendant circumstances.[97]

Where a joint custody order is inappropriate, an access order will enable the child and parent to develop or maintain a positive relationship and facilitates the parent's ongoing contribution to the child's development during his or her formative years.[98]

2) Maximum Contact: Infants and Toddlers[99]

Recent Canadian caselaw affirms that orders whereby infants and toddlers enjoy overnight access to their non-custodial parent should no longer be regarded as exceptional. It has been asserted that the view formerly held by social scientists that overnight access for infants is undesirable, reflects an outdated perception of parent-child relationships and is inconsistent with more recent research on child development. Current opinion suggests that infants readily adapt to the different household environments, provided that feeding and sleeping routines are similar in each household to ensure stability.[100] Consistent with this approach and with a recommendation that the father accept the primary-caregiving mother's advice respecting the child's routines and schedules, Wilson J in *Lygouriatis v Gohm*[101] granted the father interim access to a three-month-old child that included specified overnight access on alternate weekends. Different considerations apply where a sub-

---

96 *SLT v AKT*, 2009 ABQB 13; *Dempsey v Dempsey*, [2004] BCJ No 2400 (SC); *FFR v KF*, 2013 NLCA 8; *Bromm v Bromm*, 2010 SKCA 149.

97 *Moreau v Moreau*, [2004] AJ No 1296 (QB).

98 *MEE v TRE*, [2002] NSJ No 425 (SC); compare *KRC v CAC*, [2007] NSJ No 314 (SC). See also *Richardson v Biggs*, 2012 SKQB 162.

99 For an insightful detailed analysis of this issue that examines mental health research and relevant legal judgments, see Melanie Kraft, "Things You Need To Know About Parenting Plans for Children under 3 Years Old" (Paper presented to Law Society of Upper Canada, 2011 Six-Minute Family Law Lawyer, Toronto, 1 December 2011).

100 See *Cooper v Cooper*, [2002] SJ No 226 (QB), citing Joan B Kelly & Michael E Lamb, "Using Child Development Research to Make Appropriate Custody and Access Decisions for Young Children" (July 2000) 38:3 Family and Conciliation Courts Review 297 at 308–9. See also *Marsden v Murphy*, [2007] AJ No 830 (QB); *JV v ES*, 2014 NBQB 210; *Hann v Elms*, 2011 NLTD(F) 45; *MT v MG*, 2010 NSSC 89; *Ryan v Scott*, 2011 ONSC 3277; *Hasan v Khalil*, 2012 ONSC 7264. But compare *Perchaluk v Perchaluk*, 2012 ONCJ 525 at paras 36–43. And see Nicholas Bala, "Expert Evidence, Assessments and Judicial Notice: Understanding the Family Context" in Harold Niman & Anita Volikis, *Evidence in Family Law*, loose-leaf (Aurora, ON: Canada Law Book, 2010–).

101 [2006] SJ No 609 (QB); As to breast-fed child, see also *Squires v Smith*, 2015 NLTD(F) 6, leave to appeal denied, 2015 NLCA 25 at para 37, Hoegg JA; *Stewart v Abedi*, 2015 ONSC 1870.

stantial block of summer access is sought. In *Ursic v Ursic*,[102] Laskin JA, of the Ontario Court of Appeal, accepted the opinion of an expert witness that the father's access to a three-year-old child for a full, uninterrupted month during the summer would be inappropriate, having regard to the child's age and state of development, and would likely be harmful to the child's sense of security and primary attachments. And in *Richardson v Biggs*,[103] Smith J, of the Saskatchewan Court of Queen's Bench, held that an alternating weekly shared parenting regime was inappropriate for a three-year-old child.

In *Chaisson v Williams*, MacDonald J, of the Nova Scotia Supreme Court, stated:

> 9 This is a very young child. I do not think it is controversial to say that children under five generally require relatively frequent contact with each of his or her parents to establish and maintain healthy attachments. The *Divorce Act*, R.S.C. 1985, c. 3 specifically directs that a child is to be provided as much contact with each of that child's parents as is consistent with that child's best interests. Although this requirement does not specifically appear in the *Maintenance and Custody Act*, R.S.N.S. 1989, c. 160, the *Act* under which this application had been commenced, this principle is recognized and applied. This is because it has now been understood both parents play a significant role in developing a healthy well adjusted child. Negative consequences can result from infrequent contact with one of the child's parents.
>
> . . .
>
> 16 There appears to be some consensus amongst those who study child development that children younger than two or three should have an opportunity to interact with both parents every day or every other day (if at all possible) in a variety of functional contexts such as feeding, play, discipline, basic care, limit setting, and putting the child to bed. Most children who have a secure attachment to their parents can move from one parent to the other without concern about psychological distress. They may still exhibit transition stress reactions typical for their age but generally these cause no long term damage if properly managed by the child's parents. After the age of two it is generally recognized many children can manage 2 consecutive overnights with one parent in the absence of the other. After age 3 many children tolerate 3 to 4 consecutive days absence from one parent while in the care of the other parent and they may be able to be quite happy for several consecutive days with that parent when they are in a stimulating situation, going on a special trip for example. Many child psychologists

---

102 [2006] OJ No 2178 (CA). Compare *Bolan v Bolan*, 2013 SKCA 97 (interim order).
103 2012 SKQB 162. Compare *Parsons v Parsons*, 2014 ABQB 586.

would not recommend a child to be absent from the care of one of his or her parents for as long as two consecutive weeks until that child reaches six years of age. These are general recommendations. Whether they should apply to a particular child will depend upon many factors including the personality and temperament of the child and the personality, temperament, and parenting skills of the parent.[104]

Reviewing the conference of the Association of Family and Conciliation Courts on Divorce Custody and Attachments held in Chicago in June 2012, Bill Eddy, a lawyer, mediator, and author from San Diego, California, states:

> The issue of when to start overnights and how many nights to have with the other parent remains controversial during these first three years. Research was presented that showed that one or more overnights a week away from the primary attachment parent is distressing to the child during the first two years. What seems to be agreed upon is that the gender of the "primary attachment" is not the biggest factor, and that shared parenting up to 50-50 after about age 4–5 generally can work well.[105]

G. TERMS AND CONDITIONS

1) General

Subsections 16(6) and 17(3) of the *Divorce Act* confer a broad discretion on the court to grant custody or access orders for a definite or indefinite period and subject to any such terms, conditions, or restrictions as the court thinks fit.[106] These subsections are broad enough to permit a court to incorporate a peace officer assist clause in a custody or access order.[107]

Custody orders can be reviewable or varied after a specific period of time.[108] Review orders, unlike variation orders under section 17 of the *Divorce Act*, do not require proof of a change of circumstances to justify modification of an existing custody or access order.[109] It is appropriate that the court order

---

104 2012 NSSC 224 at paras 9 and 16.

105 Bill Eddy, Online Blog, online: http://highconflictinstitute.com/blog. But see *Parsons v Parsons*, 2014 ABQB 586.

106 *Lust v Lust*, [2007] AJ No 654 (CA) (interim custody order coupled with judicial directions for counselling); *Marquez v Zapiola*, 2013 BCCA 433 (counselling); *JDL v RJJL*, 2012 NBQB 378 (diverse conditions imposed); *Crewe v Crewe*, 2008 NSCA 115 (restrictions on access); *Gagnon v Gagnon*, 2011 NSSC 486; see also *Perron v Perron*, 2012 ONCA 811 (minority language education rights).

107 *DJS v JMD*, 2013 BCSC 2302.

108 *LG v RG*, 2012 BCSC 1365; *LES v MJS*, 2014 NSSC 34; *Noah v Bouchard*, 2013 ONCA 383.

109 *MWB v ARB*, 2011 BCSC 1663; *LES v MJS*, 2014 NSSC 34; *Chernoff v Chernoff*, 2014 SKQB 139.

a review where there is uncertainty as to what the final disposition of a matter should be, and when and how the trial judge anticipates the uncertainty will be resolved.[110] A review order is also appropriate in situations where serious uncertainty may arise and require case management of transitions for limited purposes.[111]

Although courts are generally averse to attaching conditions to a custody order that limit the powers of the custodial parent,[112] it is not that unusual for a court to impose restrictions on an access order that restrain the noncustodial parent from engaging in conduct that is detrimental to a child.[113] In determining what restrictions, if any, should be placed on a custodial parent, a court should be wary about interfering with the custodial parent's right to decide what is best for the child. A court should defer to the decision-making responsibilities of the custodial parent unless there is substantial evidence that the child's long-term welfare will be impaired.[114] There are two notable exceptions where courts will impose restrictions on a custodial parent.[115] The first arises in mobility cases wherein the court determines that restrictions should be imposed on a custodial parent's right to relocate with the children.[116] The second arises in high-conflict parental disputes wherein the court directs one or both parents to undergo counselling.[117] These orders are becoming increasingly common. While enforcement of court-ordered counselling by means of contempt proceedings may not be permissible, it is not improper for a court to draw an adverse inference against a parent who refuses to comply with such an order, and this may result in a court-ordered variation of the parenting regime. By analogy to court-ordered blood tests in disputed paternity cases that may result in an adverse inference being drawn against a person who refuses to undergo the test, a parent who refuses to

---

110   *Zaidi v Qizilbash*, 2014 ONSC 201 at paras 166–68.

111   *Ross-Johnson v Johnson*, 2010 NSSC 262; see also *Sather v McCallum*, [2006] AJ No 1241 (CA). Compare *EKI v MGS*, 2013 NBQB 406; *Moore v Moore*, 2013 NSSC 252.

112   Compare *Martin v Martin*, 2014 ONSC 7530 at paras 199–200.

113   See, for example, *Hannigan v Flynn*, 2010 ONSC 4076.

114   *MacGyver v Richards* (1995), 11 RFL (4th) 432 at 445 (Ont CA), Abella JA, as she then was.

115   *Perron v Perron*, 2012 ONCA 811, introduces the possibility of an additional exception in cases where the preservation of minority language rights and culture is an issue between Anglophone and Francophone parents.

116   See Section G(2), below in this chapter.

117   See *NL v RL*, 2008 NBCA 79; compare *Kaplanis v Kaplanis*, [2005] OJ No 275 (CA); see also *SC v ASC*, 2011 MBCA 70; *Kramer v Kramer* (2003), 37 RFL (5th) 381 at para 38 (Ont Sup Ct); *Kozachok v Mangaw*, 2007 ONCJ 70 at para 25; *JKL v NCS*, [2008] OJ No 2115 at para 192 (Sup Ct); *Faber v Gallicano*, 2012 ONSC 764.

undergo counselling is unlikely to be successful in any *Charter* challenge of the court's order.[118]

In the absence of spousal hostility, courts will often order specified mid-week, alternate weekend, and summer access. When spouses are still at war and cannot work out an access schedule, the court will step in to fill the vacuum by stipulating detailed access arrangements. Detailed specifications are usually imperative in high-conflict situations.[119]

Where appropriate, a court may order supervised access, which signifies that a third party will be present when access privileges are being exercised.[120] Supervised access may be ordered when some risk to the child is envisaged.[121] Supervised access creates an artificial environment that inhibits the development of a natural, healthy parent-child relationship. Consequently, it should only be imposed by a court in exceptional circumstances.[122] Because of their inevitable limitations, the exercise of access at a supervised access centre should be avoided unless a suitable access supervisor cannot be found or there are serious and current safety issues which can only be addressed through institutional supervised access.[123] Supervised access may be found appropriate where there is reason to question a non-custodial parent's fitness to parent, or ability to protect the child if domestic violence, child abuse, or parental alienation has occurred, or if there has been no contact between the parent and child for an appreciable length of time. Supervised access is used as a last resort and should not become a permanent feature of a child's life. It is intended to provide a temporary and time-limited means of resolving a parental impasse over access and should not ordinarily be used as a long-term solution.[124] It is typically ordered when children require gradual reintroduction to a parent or until a parent is sufficiently rehabilitated so that the

---

118 For relevant *Charter* cases on court-ordered blood tests in affiliation proceedings, see *Crow v McMynn*, [1989] BCJ No 1233 (SC); *LLDS v WGF*, [1995] OJ No 418 (Gen Div); *KP v PN* (1988), 15 RFL (3d) 110 (Ont HCJ).

119 See *RMS v FPCS*, 2011 BCCA 53 at para 50; see also *MacFarlane v Ferron*, 2011 ONSC 2053.

120 As to various levels of supervision, see *LES v MJS*, 2014 NSSC 34 at paras 87–91.

121 *BP v AT*, 2014 NBCA 51.

122 *C(RM) v C(JR)* (1995), 12 RFL (4th) 440 (BCSC); *EAM v ADM*, 2014 NBQB 216; *Price v Laflamme*, 2012 MBQB 145; *CRJ v DJ*, 2013 ONSC 1280; *Guenther v Vanderhoof*, 2014 SKQB 296.

123 *APGP v MSP*, 2013 ONSC 6595.

124 *M(BP) v M(BLDE)* (1992), 42 RFL (3d) 349 (Ont CA), citing Judge Norris Weisman, "On Access after Parental Separation" (1992) 36 RFL (3d) 35 at 74, leave to appeal to SCC refused (1993), 48 RFL (3d) 232 (SCC). See also *LAMG v CS*, 2014 BCPC 172 at paras 35–36; *TAF v MWB*, 2013 MBQB 213; *HD v PED*, 2012 NBQB 315; *MT v MG*, 2010 NSSC 89; *Folahan v Folahan*, 2013 ONSC 2966; *RHM v CH*, 2014 ONSC 521; *TLMM v CAM*, 2011 SKQB 326.

child is no longer in danger of physical or emotional harm.[125] But in *Merkand v Merkand*,[126] the Ontario Court of Appeal dismissed the appellant's submission that the trial judge had erred in law by ordering supervised access to the children for an indefinite term, being of the opinion that the trial judge was aware that her order was exceptional in that it included no provision for a transition to unsupervised access nor any prescribed review date. While acknowledging that such an order should only be made in rare circumstances, the Ontario Court of Appeal found that the record fully supported the trial judge's decision to order the continuation of supervised access because of the appellant's attempts to manipulate the children and pressure them into living with him. In rejecting the appellant's submission that the order of the trial judge rendered it practically impossible for the appellant to obtain a future order for unsupervised access, the Ontario Court of Appeal pointed out that the trial judge's order in no way precluded a future application to vary the terms of access upon proof of a material change of circumstances. Orders for supervised access to a teenager are rare but the circumstances of a particular case may justify a determination that it is in the child's best interests to have long-term supervised access, notwithstanding the age and wishes of the child.[127] Although supervised access is not a remedy the law looks on with favour, particularly over the long term, termination of access is obviously an even more drastic remedy, rarely invoked unless absolutely required in a child's best interests.[128] In appropriate circumstances, a court may suspend access pending the submission of an acceptable parenting plan.[129]

2) Intended Change of Residence; Mobility Rights

Pursuant to subsection 16(7) of the *Divorce Act*, any person granted custody of a child may be required to give notice of any change of residence to any other person who has been granted access privileges.[130] In the absence of any specified period to the contrary, such notice must be given thirty days in advance of the change of residence. Given such notice, the person with access privileges may apply to the court to challenge the intended change of residence of the child or seek variation of the custody or access arrangements in order to preserve meaningful contact with the child.

---

125 *Tuttle v Tuttle*, 2014 ONSC 5011 at para 15, Robertson J.
126 [2006] OJ No 528 (CA). See also *LAMG v CS*, 2014 BCPC 172; *Tuttle v Tuttle*, 2014 ONSC 5011; *VSG v LJG*, [2004] OJ No 2238 (Sup Ct); and see Section L, below in this chapter.
127 *Tuttle v Tuttle*, 2014 ONSC 5011.
128 *BC v JC*, 2014 NBQB 59 at para 7, Walsh J; see also *LAMG v CS*, 2014 BCPC 172 at para 36, Woods Prov Ct J.
129 *Zanewycz v Manryk*, 2010 ONSC 1168.
130 *KK v AK*, 2012 NBQB 276.

The issue of mobility rights was addressed by the Supreme Court of Canada in *Gordon v Goertz*,[131] wherein the custodial parent, the mother, intended to move to Australia and wished to take her daughter with her. Upon learning this, the non-custodial parent, the father, applied for custody of the child or, alternatively, an order restraining the mother from removing the child. The mother cross-applied to vary access so as to permit her to change the child's residence to Australia. In the majority judgment of McLachlin J, as she then was, which represented the opinion of seven of the nine judges, the law was summarized as follows:

1. The parent applying for a change in the custody or access order must meet the threshold requirement of demonstrating a material change in the circumstances affecting the child.[132]

2. If the threshold is met, the judge on the application must embark on a fresh inquiry into what is in the best interests of the child, having regard to all the relevant circumstances relating to the child's needs and the ability of the respective parents to satisfy them.

3. This inquiry is based on the findings of the judge who made the previous order and evidence of the new circumstances.

4. The inquiry does not begin with a legal presumption in favour of the custodial parent, although the custodial parent's views are entitled to great respect.[133]

5. Each case turns on its own unique circumstances. The only issue is the best interests of the child in the particular circumstances of the case.

6. The focus is on the best interests of the child, not the interests and rights of the parents.

7. More particularly the judge should consider, *inter alia*:
   (a) the existing custody arrangement and relationship between the child and the custodial parent;

---

131 [1996] 2 SCR 27 at paras 49–50; see also *Spencer v Spencer*, [2005] AJ No 934 (CA); *RL v MP*, 2008 ABCA 313; *CLR v RAR*, [2006] BCJ No 945 (CA); *Orring v Orring*, [2006] BCJ No 2996 (CA); *Chera v Chera*, 2008 BCCA 374; *Falvai v Falvai*, [2008] BCJ No 2365 (CA); *SSL v JWW*, 2010 BCCA 55; *EAL v HMG*, 2011 BCCA 167; *Hejzlar v Mitchell-Hejzlar*, 2011 BCCA 230; *Delichte v Rogers*, 2011 MBCA 50, subsequent proceedings, 2012 MBCA 105; *NT v RWP*, 2011 NLCA 47; *Harris v Mouland*, [2006] NSJ No 404 (CA); *Cameron v Cameron*, [2006] NSJ No 247 (CA); *Burgoyne v Kenny*, 2009 NSCA 34; *KC c NP*, [2006] QJ No 8697 (CA); *Olfert v Olfert*, 2013 SKCA 89.

132 *Bachorcik v Bachorcik*, 2014 SKQB 235.

133 As to the importance of the views of the custodial parent, see *Delichte v Rogers*, 2011 MBCA 50. Compare *Rink v Rempel*, 2011 SKQB 472. See also *Sferruzzi v Allan*, 2013 ONCA 496.

(b) the existing access arrangement and the relationship between the child and the access parent;

(c) the desirability of maximizing contact between the child and both parents;[134]

(d) the views of the child;[135]

(e) the custodial parent's reason for moving, only in the exceptional case where it is relevant to that parent's ability to meet the needs of the child;[136]

(f) disruption to the child of a change in custody;

(g) disruption to the child consequent on removal from family, schools, and the community he or she has come to know.[137]

In the end, the importance of the child remaining with the parent to whose custody it has become accustomed in the new location must be weighed against the continuance of full contact with the child's access parent, its extended family and its community. The ultimate question in every case is this: what is in the best interests of the child in all the circumstances, old as well as new?

In applying the above criteria to the facts of the case, the Supreme Court of Canada, in both its majority and dissenting judgments, concluded that the mother's custody of the child should be continued, notwithstanding her intended move to Australia. However, the access arrangements were varied to provide for access to be exercisable in Canada so that the father's limited time with the child would be more natural and the child could maintain contact with friends and the extended family.

In determining whether a custodial parent should be entitled to relocate with the children, Burnyeat J, of the British Columbia Supreme Court, has identified the following twelve factors as relevant, together with pertinent jurisprudence dealing with each of them:

1) the parenting capabilities of and the children's relationship with their parents and new partners;

2) the employment security and the prospects of each parent and, where appropriate, their partner;

3) access to and support of extended family members;

---

134 *Berry v Berry*, 2011 ONCA 705.

135 *Seymour v Seymour*, 2012 SKQB 161.

136 See *MacPhail v Karasek*, [2006] AJ No 982 (CA); *Nunweiler v Nunweiler*, 2000 BCCA 300 at para 28; *Zacharias v Zacharias*, 2012 MBQB 199; *Berry v Berry*, 2011 ONCA 705; *Trisolino v De Marzi*, 2013 ONCA 135.

137 See *Sferruzzi v Allan*, 2013 ONCA 496.

4) any difficulty in exercising the proposed access and the quality of the proposed access if the move is allowed;

5) the effect upon the children's academic situation;

6) the psychological/emotional well-being of the children;

7) disruption of the children's existing social and community support and routines;

8) the desirability of the proposed new family unit for the children;

9) the relative parenting capabilities of each parent and their respective ability to discharge parenting responsibilities;

10) the child's relationship with both parents;

11) any separation of siblings; and

12) retraining/educational opportunities for the moving parent.[138]

In *NDL v MSL*,[139] MacDonald J, of the Nova Scotia Supreme Court, set out the following list of factors to consider in mobility cases:

- the number of years the parents cohabited with each other and with the child
- the quality and the quantity of parenting time
- the age, maturity, and special needs of the child
- the advantages of a move to the moving parent in respect to that parent's ability to better meet the child's needs
- the time it will take the child to travel between residences and the cost of that travel
- feasibility of a parallel move by the parent who is objecting to the move
- feasibility of a move by the moving parent's new partner
- the willingness of the moving parent to ensure access or [sic] will occur between the child and the other parent
- the nature and content of any agreements between the parents about relocations
- the likelihood of a move by the parent who objects to the relocation
- the financial resources of each of the family units
- the expected permanence of the new custodial environment
- the continuation of the child's cultural and religious heritage
- the ability of the moving parent to foster the child's relationship with the other parent over long distances

---

138 *One v One*, [2000] BCJ No 2178 (SC); see also *CAP v MSP*, 2015 BCSC 183. For additional factors, see *Chepil v Chepil*, 2014 SKQB 341 at para 40, Megaw J.

139 2010 NSSC 68 at para 9; see also *Gibney v Conohan*, 2011 NSSC 268 at para 92; *Rink v Rempel*, 2011 SKQB 472. For additional factors, see *SL v CB*, 2013 SKQB 333.

Although such specified factors may be useful, *Gordon v Goertz*[140] makes clear that the best interests of the child inquiry must relate to the particular child's needs and the ability of his or her parents to satisfy that child's needs. The inquiry is individualized. Decided cases are of limited assistance, although they provide guidance to the application of governing principles.[141]

Gordon v Goertz sets out the legal framework for analyzing cases involving a provincial change of residence by a custodial parent. The primary issue is not the appropriateness of the move, unless there is evidence of the underlying purpose being to interfere with access by the non-custodial parent. Rather, where the move constitutes a material change of circumstances, the issue becomes a reconsideration of which parent is better qualified to have custody of the child under the present circumstances.[142] *Gordon v Goertz* acknowledges that a trial judge is entitled to give some weight to the existing custody order in determining whether the best interests of the child will be served by allowing the custodial parent to relocate with the child. Where the moving parent, after a reconsideration of all relevant factors, is still found to be the appropriate custodial parent, variation of the terms of access may be justified so as to reflect the new realities. If access problems have been encountered in the past, it may be necessary to spell out where access shall be exercised and at whose expense so that the maximum contact principle under section 17(9) of the *Divorce Act* can be accommodated.[143] In determining whether a custodial parent should be entitled to relocate with the child to another country, the custodial parent's perceptions of his or her personal academic and professional interests should not be confused with a detached appreciation of the child's best interests.[144]

In *Spencer v Spencer*,[145] the Alberta Court of Appeal expressed concern about the "double bind" faced by custodial parents who acknowledge that they would abandon their relocation plans if the children were unable to accompany them. It observed that if a custodial mother, in response to an inquiry, states that she is unwilling to remain behind with the children, her answer raises the prospect of her being regarded as selfish in placing her own interests ahead of the best interests of the children. If, on the other hand,

---

140 [1996] 2 SCR 27.

141 *Hannan v Hannan*, 2010 BCSC 1626.

142 *DHP v PLP*, 2012 NBQB 345.

143 *Brink v Brink*, [2002] PEIJ No 7 (CA).

144 *KC c NP*, [2006] QJ No 8697 (CA). Compare *MacPhail v Karasek*, [2006] AJ No 982 (CA). See also *CS v EL*, 2010 ABQB 285; *HS v CS*, [2006] SJ No 247 (CA).

145 [2005] AJ No 934 (CA); see also *Milton v Letch*, 2013 ABCA 248; *Sangha v Sandhar*, 2013 ABCA 259; *RJF v CMF*, 2014 ABCA 165; *SSL v JWW*, 2010 BCCA 55; *NT v RWP*, 2011 NLCA 47; *DP v RB*, 2009 PECA 12; *Droit de la famille — 091332*, 2009 QCCA 1068.

she is willing to forego the relocation, her willingness to stay behind "for the sake of the children" renders the *status quo* an attractive option for the presiding judge to favour because it avoids the difficult decision that the application otherwise presents.[146] In *Spencer v Spencer*, the chambers judge was found to have erred in failing to address the effect on the children if they were left in Calgary without their mother, their stepfather, and their soon-to-be-born sibling, and the effect on them if they were left in the care of their father, who the chambers judge found was unable to assume primary care or even significant responsibility for the children. The mother's appeal was allowed and the order prohibiting her from taking the children to Victoria was set aside. Failing parental agreement on access, this issue was ordered to be returned to the Alberta Court of Queen's Bench for determination. In *Stav v Stav*, Prowse JA expressed the following opinion with respect to the "double bind":

> [64] I should observe, however, that I perceive a problem with the stricture against courts expressly taking into account evidence of what one or the other parent would do depending on the decision made by the trial judge in relation to mobility. It is arguable that avoidance of questions giving rise to the double-bind is directed more to the interests of the parents than it is to the interests of the children. It may be unfair to place either or both of the parents in the double-bind, but is it unfair to the children? Is it contrary to their best interests? Arguably, the answer is that it is only by asking this question of both parents and assessing their answers, that the court can make a determination in the children's best interests, cognizant of all of the options.[147]

In *SSL v JWW*,[148] the British Columbia Court of Appeal held that where one parent wishes to relocate with the children to another city or province, the court's task is to analyze the evidence in the context of four possible alternatives: (1) primary residence with the mother; (2) primary residence with the father; (3) shared parenting in the mother's chosen place of residence; and (4) shared parenting in the father's chosen place of residence. However, the

---

146   See also *Hejzlar v Mitchell-Hejzlar*, 2011 BCCA 230; *NT v RWP*, 2011 NLCA 47.

147   2012 BCCA 154 at para 64; see also *De Jong v Gardner*, 2013 BCSC 1303; *TK v RJHA*, 2015 BCCA 8. Compare *MM v CJ*, 2014 BCSC 6 at para 45 wherein Jenkins J concluded that section 69(7) of the *Family Law Act* prohibits a consideration of whether a parent would still relocate without the child. See also *CMB v BDG*, 2014 BCSC 780; *Fotsch v Begin*, 2015 BCSC 227.

148   2010 BCCA 55; see also *Stav v Stav*, 2012 BCCA 154; *McIntosh v Kaulbach*, 2014 BCCA 299; *DAM v EGM*, 2014 BCSC 2091; *Fotsch v Begin*, 2015 BCSC 227. Compare *Sangha v Sandhar*, 2013 ABCA 259.

court's first task is to determine which parent should provide the primary residence. Where the question of primary residence is evenly balanced and the court finds that the best interests of the children require both parents to be in the same area, the court must then choose between the shared parenting options proposed by each parent without presuming that the current regime is the preferred one. And in *Olfert v Olfert*, Caldwell JA , of the Saskatchewan Court of Appeal, stated that "it would be best practice for a court of first instance to consider all of the possible scenarios in any mobility application which comes before it."[149] But in *Walker v Maxwell*,[150] Kent J, of the British Columbia Supreme Court, observed:

> 57 It will be noted that s. 46(2)(b) and s. 69(7) of the *Family Law Act*[151] expressly prohibit the court considering whether the parent who is planning to move would still do so if the child's relocation were not permitted. These provisions were designed to remedy the so-called "double bind" dilemma referred to above but they can also introduce an element of artificiality into any "four scenario" analysis of the sort posited in *S.S.L. v. J.W.W.*

The criteria in *Gordon v Goertz* apply whether mobility rights arise on an original application for custody or on an application to vary an existing custody order.[152] They also apply not only to proceedings under the *Divorce Act* but also to proceedings under provincial legislation.[153] Geographically distant interprovincial relocations as well as extra-provincial relocations fall subject to the same criteria. The principles defined in *Gordon v Goertz* do not provide a precise formula; each case must ultimately be determined on its own facts.[154] It is, nevertheless, possible to distill the following propositions from the judgment of the New Brunswick Court of Appeal in *LDD v JAD*[155] that are transmissible to diverse fact situations:

---

149 2013 SKCA 89 at para 22.

150 2014 BCSC 2357 at para 57, aff'd 2015 BCCA 282.

151 SBC 2011, c 25, see text to note 149.

152 *Nunweiler v Nunweiler* (2000), 5 RFL (5th) 442 (BCCA); *Mai v Schumann*, 2013 BCCA 365; *LDD v JAD*, 2010 NBCA 69; *Droit de la famille — 091332*, 2009 QCCA 1068; *DP v RB*, 2009 PECA 12; *Seymour v Seymour*, 2012 SKQB 161.

153 *McWilliams v Couture*, 2014 NBQB 86; *Borgal v Fleet*, 2014 NSSC 16.

154 *Sulatyski-Waldack v Waldack*, [2000] MJ No 412 (QB).

155 2010 NBCA 69; see also *ADE v MJM*, 2012 NBQB 260 (interim order); *Olfert v Olfert*, 2013 SKCA 89. And see *Mantyka v Dueck*, 2012 SKCA 109 (unilateral removal of children to nearby community; denial of interim order for their return); *Alix v Irwin*, 2014 SKCA 46; compare *Jochems v Jochems*, 2013 SKCA 81.

1) Although the aforementioned seven principles in *Gordon v Goertz*[156] were formulated in the context of a variation proceeding, the considerations set out in paragraphs 4 to 7 are equally applicable to initial applications for custody where the prospective relocation of a child arises as an issue. In such cases, courts should adopt a blended approach that examines the proposed relocation in the broader context of the competing custody claims of the parents.

2) In order to put the best interests of the child test in a proper context in mobility situations, courts must review the pertinent legislation as well as jurisprudence relating to this issue. *Gordon v Goertz* prescribes the minimum criteria to be considered when determining the best interests of the child in mobility cases.

3) Since the *Divorce Act* does not provide a definition of "best interests of the child," courts may look to provincial legislation for guidance where such legislation defines that concept or lists relevant factors to be considered in determining the best interests of a child.

4) The principle in sections 16(10) and 17(9) of the *Divorce Act* that a child of divorcing or divorced parents should have maximum contact with each of his or her parents is not absolute; it is qualified by the condition that such maximum contact is in the best interests of the child. Disruption of the child's relationship with his or her primary caregiver may be more detrimental to the child than reduced contact with the non-custodial parent.[157]

5) The general trend of the jurisprudence since *Gordon v Goertz* has been to grant approval for a proposed move in cases where there is a clear primary caregiver for the child or children. A proposed move is less likely to be approved where caregiving and physical custody have been equally shared between parents.[158]

6) Absent any culpable intention or any consequential impairment of the custodial parent's ability to meet the needs of the child, courts are not concerned with the custodial parent's reasons for the proposed relocation. Their concern is with the potential impact of the proposed relocation on the child's life and, in particular, the child's relationship with both of the parents, with siblings, and with members of the child's extended family.

Although relocation issues typically turn upon the facts of the particular case, and previous caselaw is only of limited assistance, it is generally acknowledged that there should be a pressing reason for an immediate move

---

156 See text to notes 131–37, above in this chapter.
157 See *RJF v CMF*, 2014 ABCA 165.
158 Compare *Thurston v Maystrowich*, 2010 SKCA 113.

before a court permits the relocation of children on a motion for interim relief. There are two primary reasons for this. First, an interim relocation may create a new *status quo* and sometimes can effectively decide the outcome of the trial. Second, the interim application is usually based on affidavits, which are incomplete or limited in scope and frequently conflict with each other. As a result, interim relocations by a custodial parent are generally allowed only in compelling circumstances.[159] In *DA v JR*,[160] Larlee JA, of the New Brunswick Court of Appeal, stated that "the *status quo* may be favoured on an interim basis unless there are compelling or urgent circumstances which dictate a move before a full hearing: relocation to live with new partner; child starting school; urgency in the move to preserve a job that would be lost; or the move may result in a financial benefit to the family unit, which will be lost if the matter awaits a trial." And in *Plumley v Plumley*, Marshman J, of the Ontario Superior Court of Justice, listed the following three factors as important:

1) A court is more reluctant to disturb the *status quo* by permitting the move on an interim basis where there is a genuine issue for trial.

2) There can be compelling circumstances that warrant relocation where, for example, financial benefits would be lost if relocation awaited a trial or the best interests of the children dictate that they commence school at a new location.

3) Although there may be a genuine issue for trial, the relocation may be authorized on an interim basis if there is a strong probability that the custodial parent's position will prevail at trial.[161]

In *MB v DAC*,[162] Sherr J, of the Ontario Court of Justice, provided the following more detailed list of relevant considerations:

---

159   *Klinger v Klinger*, 2013 SKQB 59 at para 11; *McKerracher v Morgan*, 2013 SKQB 207, citing *Mantyka v Dueck*, 2012 SKCA 109.

160   2012 NBCA 38 at para 14; see also *Mantyka v Dueck*, 2012 SKCA 109.

161   The three factors identified in *Plumley v Plumley*, [1999] OJ No 3234 (Sup Ct) have been endorsed in numerous cases: see, for example, *Hunter v Hunter*, 2013 NSSC 417; *Ivens v Ivens*, [2008] NWTJ No 11 (SC); *Crewson v Crewson*, 2014 ONSC 4372; *Smith v Pozzo*, 2015 ONSC 1284; *DP v RB*, [2007] PEIJ No 53 (SCAD); *Harding v Harding*, 2013 SKQB 285; see also *SMK v OAJ*, 2012 ABCA 49. For cases wherein relocation was permitted on an interim basis, see *Lawrence v Lawrence*, 2012 BCSC 1315; *Zacharias v Zacharias*, 2012 MBQB 199; *EKI v MGS*, 2013 NBQB 274; *EL v AN*, 2014 NBQB 200; *SS v TT*, 2012 NUCJ 17; *Boone v Boone*, 2014 NSSC 227; *Mercredi v Hawkins*, 2008 NWTSC 57; *Alcaniz v Willoughby*, 2010 ONSC 5266; *Ayadi v Somerset-Paddon*, 2014 SKQB 395.

162   2014 ONCJ 273 at para 26; see also *Noseworthy v Morin*, 2014 SKQB 206; *MDT v MLSM*, 2014 SKQB 209.

a) The burden is on the parent seeking the change to prove compelling circumstances exist that are sufficient to justify the move. See: *Mackenzie v. Newby*, [2013] O.J. No. 4613 (OCJ).

b) Courts are generally reluctant to permit relocation on a temporary basis. The decision will often have a strong influence on the final outcome of the case, particularly if the order permits relocation. The reality is that courts do not like to create disruptions in the lives of children by making an order that may have to cause further disruption later if the order has to be reversed. See: *Goodship v. McMaster* [2003] O.J. No. 4255 (OCJ).

c) Courts will be more cautious about permitting a temporary relocation where there are material facts in dispute that would likely impact on the final outcome. See: *Fair v. Rutherford-Fair* 2004 CarswellOnt 1705 (Ont. S.C.J.). In such cases, the court requires a full testing of the evidence. See: *Kennedy v. Hull*, [2005] ONCJ 275.

d) Courts will be even more cautious in permitting a temporary relocation when the proposed move involves a long distance. It is unlikely that the move will be permitted unless the court is certain that it will be the final result. See my comments in: *Downey v. Sterling* [2006] O.J. No. 5043 (OCJ) and *Costa v. Funes* [2012] O.J. No. 3317 (OCJ).

e) Courts will be more cautious in permitting a temporary relocation in the absence of a custody order. See: *Mackenzie v. Newby, supra*.

f) Courts will permit temporary relocation where there is no genuine issue for trial (see: *Yousuf v. Shoaib*, [2007] O.J. No. 747 (OCJ)), or where the result would be inevitable after a trial (see: *Mackenzie v. Newby, supra*, where the court observed that the importance of the father's contact with the child could not override the benefits that the move would have on the child).

g) In assessing . . . the three considerations in *Plumley*, the court must consider the best interest factors set out in subsection 24 (2) of the *Children's Law Reform Act* (the Act) and any violence and abuse in assessing a parent's ability to act as a parent as set out in subsections 24 (3) and (4) of the Act as well as the leading authority on mobility cases, *Gordon v. Goertz*, [1996] 2 S.C.R. 27 (S.C.C.).

h) These principles apply with necessary modifications to an initial consideration of custody and access and not just to a variation of access. See: *Bjornson v. Creighton* (2002), 31 R.F.L. (5th) 242 (Ont.C.A.).

i) The financial security of the moving parent is a relevant factor in mobility cases. See: *Greenfield v. Garside*, 2003 CarswellOnt1189 (Ont. SCJ).

j) Several cases have recognized that requiring a parent to remain in a community isolated from his or her family and supports and in difficult financial circumstances will adversely impact a child. The economic and financial benefits of moving to a community where the parent will have supports, financial security and the ability to complete their education and establish a career are properly considered in assessing whether or not the move is in the child's best interests. See: *MacKenzie v. Newby, supra,* . . . *Lebrun v. Lebrun* [1999] O.J. No. 3393 (SCJ) . . . .

k) There is case law that says that if a primary caregiver is happier, this will benefit the child. See: *Del Net v. Benger,* 2003 CarswellOnt 3898 (Ont. SCJ).

l) The level of co-operation that the moving parent will provide in facilitating access to the other parent is also a relevant consideration in a mobility application. See: *Orrock v. Dinamarea,* 2003 CarswellBC 2845 (B.C.S.C.).

Commenting on Ontario relocation trends in his review of the decision of the Ontario Court of Appeal in *Berry v Berry*,[163] Professor DA Rollie Thompson, Canada's leading authority on mobility cases, has noted

> the prevalence of interim relocation cases in Ontario (thanks to an overburdened and slow-moving system) and the clear division in decisions between the "proceduralists" (who apply *Plumley*) and the "deciders" . . . who just make a "final-type" decision at the interim stage. This means that many Ontario interim cases should be treated "with great caution," to quote Jay McLeod."[164]

An explanation for "final-type" decisions at the interim stage may well be found in the observations of Campbell J, of the Prince Edward Island Supreme Court, in *GER v HJR*,[165] who notes that interim orders become *de facto* final orders in many cases because very few cases ever reach the trial stage due to the delay and cost involved.

A court is not bound by the terms of a prior separation agreement in determining whether to permit the primary residential parent to relocate with the children, nor is an unforeseen material change of circumstances since the execution of the agreement a prerequisite to a court order that varies the terms of the agreement.[166]

With the increasing mobility of Canadian families, non-removal clauses have become fashionable in separation agreements and court orders regulating

---

163 (2011), 7 RFL (7th) 1; see Rollie Thompson, "*Berry v Berry*: Recent Ontario Relocation Trends" (2012) 7 RFL (7th) 10.

164 Private correspondence received by the authors from Professor Thompson.

165 2012 PESC 24. See also Section L, below in this chapter.

166 *CRH v BAH,* [2005] BCJ No 1121 (CA); *Betz v Joyce,* 2009 BCSC 1199.

the custody of and access to children on the breakdown of spousal relationships. These clauses have been used to flag the notion that extra-provincial removal of the children must not occur without parental consent or a court order. The practical significance of such an express clause is that the task falls on the custodial parent to initiate an application to the court, if relocation is sought without the consent of the non-custodial parent. If a separation agreement or court order is silent with respect to removal, the non-custodial parent has the responsibility of bringing the matter to court to prevent the custodial parent's proposed removal of the children. In either situation, the court has the clear jurisdiction to determine whether the children can leave the province. When the agreement or court order is silent and the custodial parent chooses not to notify the non-custodial parent until after the relocation has occurred, the custodial parent runs a significant risk of incurring substantial expenses and losses in consequence of a subsequent court order requiring the children to reside in the province from which they have been unilaterally removed. Custodial parents who are not legally represented might not understand that they have a moral obligation to notify the non-custodial parent of any proposed relocation of the children, but common sense dictates that they should do so no matter how inconvenient it might be for the custodial parent to remain in the province and seek the necessary court approval.[167] The *Divorce Act* does not expressly authorize a court to order the return of children or to order a divorced parent to live in a particular location. However, these consequences may ensue pursuant to sections 16(6) and 17(3) of the *Divorce Act*, which empower the court on an original application for custody or on an application to vary a custody order to impose such "terms, conditions or restrictions in connection therewith as it thinks fit and just." Consequently, the court can make a contingent custody and access order that is dependent on where a parent chooses to live.[168]

In custody cases involving mobility, the task of balancing the various factors that would affect the children's best interests in reaching a decision whether to permit the relocation of the children is an almost impossible one. The one tool available to the court in finding a balance is the ability to

---

167 *PLG v RJM*, 2010 NBQB 435.

168 *Decaen v Decaen*, 2013 ONCA 218; *Jochems v Jochems*, 2013 SKCA 81; *Alix v Irwin*, 2014 SKCA 46. And see *Reeves v Reeves*, 2010 NSCA 35 wherein the trial judge granted custody of three children to their mother, subject to the condition that she relocate with the children to a community in the Halifax Regional Municipality that was closer to their father; see also *MacRae v Hubley*, 2011 NSCA 25. Compare *Droit de la famille — 13328*, 2013 QCCA 277 and see section 6 of the *Canadian Charter of Rights and Freedoms*, which guarantees mobility rights to adult Canadians. Any court order that directly requires a parent to personally relocate would appear to contravene section 6 of the *Charter*. And see *McIntosh v Kaulbach*, 2014 BCCA 299.

order block access. A relocation, no matter how valid the reasons, should not result in a termination of the relationship between the children and their non-custodial parent. Regular and frequent access is usually not possible when divorced parents live in different provinces or countries. Block access is often the only solution under these circumstances. A custodial parent may be required to accept a considerable amount of inconvenience and expense to facilitate block access, if the custodial parent seeks judicial approval of an extraprovincial relocation of the children. Having regard to the superior financial means of the custodial parent and the obligation of the non-custodial parent to pay the applicable table amount of child support, the court may order the custodial parent to cover all the transportation costs associated with the blocks of access ordered by the court.[169]

In the opinion of Professor DA Rollie Thompson, who has reviewed hundreds of judicial decisions on mobility since *Gordon v Goertz*, "over time, the caselaw has become less predictable, not more so."[170] In later publications, Professor Thompson has spoken of a *de facto* presumption in favour of allowing the primary parent to relocate with the child(ren)[171] and a reverse presumption against relocation in cases of shared parenting.[172] In *PRH v MEL*,[173] Larlee JA, of the New Brunswick Court of Appeal, ventured the following opinion:

> 18 The general trend of the jurisprudence since *Gordon v Goertz* has been to grant approval for a proposed move, so long as it is proposed in good faith and is not intended to frustrate the access parent's relationship with the child. However, the relocating parent must generally also be willing to accommodate the interests of both the child and the access parent. This will generally require a restructuring of access, with the relocating parent possibly incurring the increased costs of access in the new arrangement, sometimes by way of an alteration of the child support obligations.

169 *RBN v MJN*, [2002] NSJ No 529 (SC), supplementary reasons [2002] NSJ No 530 (SC), aff'd [2003] NSJ No 192 (CA).

170 "Movin' On: Mobility and Bill C-22" (Paper presented to 12th Annual Institute of Family Law, 2003, County of Carleton Law Association, Ottawa, 6 June 2003).

171 See *REQ v GJK*, 2012 BCCA 146 at paras 57–59, Newbury JA, citing Professor Thompson's papers: "Ten Years after *Gordon*: No Law, Nowhere" (2007) 35 RFL (6th) 307 at 315 and "Where is BC Law Going? The New Mobility" prepared for the Continuing Legal Education Society of British Columbia's Family Law — 2011 Update at 8.2.7. See also "*Berry v Berry*: Recent Ontario Relocation Trends" (2012) 7 RFL (7th) 10. And see *Droit de la famille — 121505*, 2012 QCCA 1131. Compare *MO v CO*, 2012 ABCA 297.

172 See *SJRC v CAL*, 2014 NBQB 113, Wooder J, citing Rollie Thompson, "Heading for the Light: International Relocation from Canada" (2011) 30 Can Fam LQ 1.

173 2009 NBCA 18; see also *LDD v JAD*, 2010 NBCA 69; *AFG v DAB*, 2011 NBCA 100; *TDL v AL*, 2014 NBCA 57; compare *Parent v MacDougall*, 2014 NSCA 3.

However, this general trend is most evident in cases where there is a clear primary caregiver for the child or children. A proposed move is less likely to be approved where caregiving and physical custody have been equally shared between parents. Furthermore, no such trend is evident in cases where the proposed move would result in a separation of siblings who have, prior to that point, lived together. The court-imposed separation of siblings remains exceptional.

A presumptive approach to relocation issues is addressed in Division 6 of the British Columbia *Family Law Act*,[174] which received Royal Assent in November 2011 and came into effect on 18 March 2013.[175] However, these provisions do not extend beyond the provincial boundaries of British Columbia and have no direct application even in that province when the relocation issue falls to be determined under the provisions of the *Divorce Act*.[176] Given the current nation-wide unpredictability of relocation applications, it is time for the Government of Canada to consult with its provincial counterparts for the purpose of amending the *Divorce Act* as well as provincial legislation so as to more precisely define the ground rules to be applied in relocation cases.

Parliament and the provincial legislatures have devised a comprehensive scheme for dealing with child custody disputes, and there is no ancillary right at common law for seeking damages in tort for a denial of access[177] or a parent's alleged wrongful relocation of a child.[178]

H. BEST INTERESTS OF CHILD

Where custody and access issues arise on or after divorce, whether by way of an original application or an application to vary an existing order, the court must determine the application by reference only to the best interests of the child.[179] A trial judge is not bound by a prior interim order and has an unfettered discretion to re-examine the facts for the purpose of determining

---

174 SBC 2011, c 25.

175 See *SLS v JAS*, 2013 BCSC 1775; *HDM v SWT*, 2013 BCSC 1863; *CMB v BDG*, 2014 BCSC 780; *RM v NM*, 2014 BCSC 1755; *Walker v Maxwell*, 2014 BCSC 2357, aff'd 2015 BCCA 282; compare *SJF v RMN*, 2013 BCSC 1812.

176 See *TK v RJHA*, 2013 BCSC 2112 at paras 38–39, Verhoeven J, aff'd 2015 BCCA 8. Compare *AJD v EAE*, 2013 BCSC 2160; *MM v CJ*, 2014 BCSC 6; see also *DAM v EGM*, 2014 BCSC 2091; *CAP v MSP*, 2015 BCSC 183; *Fotsch v Begin*, 2015 BCSC 227.

177 *Frame v Smith*, [1987] 2 SCR 99; *Ludmer v Ludmer*, 2014 ONCA 827.

178 *Curle v Lowe*, [2004] OJ No 3789 (Sup Ct).

179 *Divorce Act*, RSC 1985 (2d Supp), c 3, s 16(8) (original application), s 17(5) (variation proceeding). See *Doncaster v Field*, 2014 NSCA 39 (denial of access).

the best interests of the child.[180] The "best interests of a child" criterion does not constitute a denial of a parent's freedom of association under section 2(d) of the *Canadian Charter of Rights and Freedoms*,[181] nor does it contravene equality rights under section 15 of the *Charter*.[182] The "best interests of the child" test has been described as one with an inherent indeterminacy and elasticity.[183] The "best interests of the child" is a fluid and all-embracing concept that encompasses the physical, emotional, intellectual, moral, and social well-being of the child.[184] The court must look not only at the day-to-day needs of the child but also to the longer-term growth and development of the child.[185] What is in the child's best interests must be examined from the perspective of the child's needs with an examination of the ability and willingness of each parent to meet those needs.[186]

Although many factors have been identified as appropriate for consideration in custody and access disputes, few attempts have been made to measure the relative significance of individual factors. The outcome of any trial may be largely influenced, therefore, by the attitudes and background of the presiding judge. Three factors have traditionally been regarded as of special importance where, as in most cases, either parent would be capable of raising the child. First, courts have frequently stated that preservation of the *status quo* is a compelling circumstance as a temporary measure in proceedings for interim custody but it is of less significance after a trial of the issues in open court,[187] although it may still be important in the latter situation where it has been of long standing.[188] And an interim or temporary order is significant because it will frequently influence or form the basis for a final order.

---

180 *RGN v MJN*, [2003] NSJ No 192 at paras 15–16 (CA); *MacKinnon v MacKinnon*, 2009 NSSC 278.

181 *The Constitution Act, 1982*, being Schedule B to the *Canada Act 1982 (UK), 1982, c 11*.

182 *Green v Millar*, [2004] BCJ No 2422 (CA).

183 *MacGyver v Richards*, (1995), 22 OR (3d) 481 at paras 27–29 (CA).

184 *CDMZ v REH-Z*, 2013 NSSC 242.

185 *Gordon v Goertz*, [1996] 2 SCR 27 at para 120; *Gagnon v Gagnon*, 2011 NSSC 486; *Lubin v Lubin*, 2012 NSSC 31; *Cooke v Cooke*, 2012 NSSC 73; *Pinto v Pinto*, 2011 ONSC 7403; *Schick v Woodrow*, 2009 SKQB 167.

186 *Gagnon v Gagnon*, 2011 NSSC 486 at para 13, MacDonald J; see also *DAM v DMT*, 2013 BCSC 359, citing *Gordon v Goertz*, [1996] 2 SCR 27 at para 69; *Steever v McCavour*, 2009 NBQB 169.

187 See *Kastner v Kastner* (1990), 109 AR 241 (CA); *Richter v Richter*, [2005] AJ No 616 (CA); *MAG v PLM*, 2014 BCSC 126; *GH v JL* (1996), 177 NBR (2d) 184 (CA); *ADE v MJM*, 2012 NBQB 260; *FFR v KF*, 2013 NLCA 8; *MacDonald v MacNeil*, 2012 NSSC 171; *Homsi v Zaya*, 2009 ONCA 322; *Batsinda v Batsinda*, 2013 ONSC 7869; *JDF v JLJF*, 2009 PESC 28; compare *Johal v Johal*, [2009] BCJ No 1874 (CA); *HD v PED*, 2012 NBQB 315; *Horton v Marsh*, [2008] NSJ No 306 (SC); *Kerr v Hauer*, 2010 ONSC 1995; *Haider v Malach* (1999), 177 Sask R 285 (CA); *Chernoff v Chernoff*, 2014 SKQB 139.

188 *WL v NDH*, 2014 NBQB 214 at paras 21–22. Compare *Ackerman v Ackerman*, 2014 SKCA 86.

Once a child has settled into a life or routine with a parent on a temporary basis, the final order will frequently reflect that it is not in the child's best interests to disrupt or significantly change the temporary arrangement.[189] As Pentelechuk J aptly stated in *AJU v GSU*, "there is no presumption in favour of the pre-trial *status quo*. Instead the *status quo* is a factor to be weighed in determining the best interest of the child."[190] The *status quo* does not refer only to geographic locations but to relationships and a way of life established for the child.[191] The *status quo* that is relevant is that which existed just prior to the parties' separation, except in circumstances where there is clear and unequivocal evidence that the parties agreed to a different decision-making and residence arrangement following the separation.[192] A second important factor is the strong inclination of courts to grant day-to-day custody of a child to the parent who was the primary caregiver during the marriage.[193] However, as Walsh J, of the New Brunswick Court of Queen's Bench (Family Division), observed in *MAS v JSS*,[194] "it does not necessarily follow that because one parent has been a primary caregiver [in the past] that that parent is the 'psychological parent' of the child." Furthermore, as Roscoe JA, of the Nova Scotia Court of Appeal, observed in *Burns v Burns*,[195] the actual period of time spent with the children is not the only determinant. More important is which parent has taken primary responsibility for all the important decisions concerning the health, safety, education, and overall welfare of the children since the parents separated. In addition to major concerns, the primary caregiver is the parent who deals with the countless less significant but necessary arrangements for the children's clothing, haircuts, hygiene, extracurricular activities, and mundane affairs such as birthday parties, dental and medical appointments, and attendance at parent-teacher interviews. In *NDL v MSL*,[196] MacDonald J, of the Nova Scotia Supreme Court, formulates an insightful list of questions to be answered in reviewing the nature and quality of a child's relationship with each parent for the purpose of determining which parent should be given the primary caregiving role. The primary

---

189 *Rifai v Green*, 2014 ONSC 1377 at para 17, Pazaratz J.

190 2015 ABQB 6 at para 50.

191 *Johal v Johal*, [2009] BCJ No 1874 (CA).

192 *Batsinda v Batsinda*, 2013 ONSC 7869 at para 28, Chappel J.

193 See *MAG v PLM*, 2014 BCSC 126; *Warcop v Warcop*, [2009] OJ No 638 at para 85 (Sup Ct); *Haider v Malach* (1999), 177 Sask R 285 (CA); *Chernoff v Chernoff*, 2014 SKQB 139; compare *DSW v DLW*, 2009 ABQB 279; *Ackerman v Ackerman*, 2014 SKCA 86, citing *Gilles v Gilles*, 2008 SKCA 97.

194 2012 NBQB 285 at para 61.

195 2000 NSCA 1.

196 2010 NSSC 68; see also *Marchand v Marchand*, 2011 NSSC 138; *Gibney v Conohan*, 2011 NSSC 268.

caregiver is of particular importance to very young children, for that is the person to whom children initially form a secure attachment, but the importance of being the primary caregiver decreases with the age of the children.[197] And in many two-income families, neither parent can be classified as the primary caregiver because both parents will have been actively involved, though not necessarily equally every day.[198] A third important factor is the disinclination of courts to split siblings between the parents.[199] The law not only seeks to foster the relationship between siblings but also between step-siblings.[200] It is absolutely vital to keep in mind, however, that in the final analysis, the above three factors will be taken into account only insofar as they reflect the best interests of the children in the overall context of the evidence presented in the particular case. Custody and access cases require an integrated assessment of all relevant factors and circumstances in order to determine the best interests of the child.[201] With the passage of time, the relevance or significance of any particular factor may change as new attitudes and standards emerge.[202] For example, the principle under sections 16(10) and 17(9) of the *Divorce Act* that a child should have as much contact with each parent as is consistent with the child's best interests now carries very substantial weight in contested custody proceedings.[203] The views and preferences of children are also an important consideration. On the other hand, religion plays a far less important role than it did many years ago. Although isolated cases may centre upon the religious upbringing of a child,[204] most custody and access disputes pay little or no attention to religious matters, although ethnic and cultural diversity, including minority language educational rights,[205] have

---

197 *AMIH v JNM*, 2009 SKQB 501.

198 *Gagnon v Gagnon*, 2011 NSSC 486.

199 *MacPhail v Karasek*, 2006 ABCA 238 at para 33; *Funk v Funk*, 2004 BCSC 1800; *CMH v TTH*, 2014 MBQB 65; *PRH v MEL* (2009), 343 NBR (2d) 100 (CA); *JM v JA*, 2014 NBQB 233; *Greene v Lundrigan*, 2011 NLTD(F) 55; *Hill v Hill*, [2008] OJ No 4730 (Sup Ct); *Edmonds v Green*, 2012 SKQB 307.

200 *MDC v TC*, 2012 NBQB 376, citing *KK v AK*, 2012 NBQB 276 at para 67. Compare *WL v NDH*, 2014 NBQB 214.

201 *Gordon v Goertz*, [1996] 2 SCR 27, 19 RFL (4th) 177 at 197; *Rail v Rail* (1999), 180 DLR (4th) 490 (BCCA), citing *Poole v Poole* (1999), 173 DLR (4th) 299 (BCCA); *Harraway v Harraway*, 2010 BCSC 679; *CM v DJL*, 2012 NBQB 188; *Ackerman v Ackerman*, 2014 SKCA 86.

202 As to the impact of dual-income parents and shared child caregiving responsibilities on preservation of the *status quo*, see *Dunn v Dunn*, 2010 NSSC 321, MacDonald J.

203 See *Gallant v Gallant*, 2009 NSCA 56; *Hackett v Hackett*, 2009 NSSC 131.

204 See, for example, *Young v Young*, [1993] 4 SCR 3; *Hockey v Hockey* (1989), 21 RFL (3d) 105 (Ont Div Ct).

205 *Perron v Perron*, 2012 ONCA 811 (parental dispute on French-language schooling in light of s 23 of the *Canadian Charter of Rights and Freedoms*); see also *Horvath v Thibouthot*, 2014 ONSC 5150. Compare *Bamford v Peckham*, 2013 ONSC 5241.

emerged as a contemporary issue.[206] However, a child's racial and cultural heritage that is attributable to one but not both parents is only one factor—albeit an important factor—to consider in determining the best interests of a child for the purpose of granting a custody/access order.[207] Where no evidence is adduced at the trial to indicate that race is an important consideration, a court, and especially an appellate court, is not entitled to treat the child's race as of paramount importance in determining which parent shall have custody of the child.[208]

It has been widely accepted by courts across Canada that provincial and territorial statutory criteria of the "best interests of the child" can provide useful guidance in custody cases arising under the *Divorce Act*.[209] Given the inherent vagueness of the concept of the "best interests of a child" in custody disputes, some courts have formulated lists of relevant considerations to complement those found in provincial or federal legislation. The following factors have been judicially identified in Alberta[210] and Newfoundland and Labrador[211] as relevant to determining the best interests of a child, but they do not purport to constitute a comprehensive list:

- the provision of the necessaries of life, including physical and health care and love;
- stability and consistency and an environment that fosters good mental and emotional health;
- the opportunity to learn good cultural, moral, and spiritual values;
- the necessity of setting realistic boundaries on conduct and fair and consistent discipline in teaching appropriate behaviour and conduct;
- the opportunity to relate to and love and be loved by immediate and extended family and the opportunity to form relationships;
- the opportunity to grow and fulfill his or her potential with responsible guidance;
- to have optimal access to the non-custodial parent in order to encourage and foster a good relationship;

---

206 See, generally, John T Syrtash, *Religion and Culture in Canadian Family Law* (Markham, ON: Butterworths, 1992).

207 *Van de Perre v Edwards*, [2001] 2 SCR 1014; *Pigott v Nochasak*, 2011 NLTD(F) 26; *O'Connor v Kenney*, [2000] OJ No 3303 (Sup Ct); *Sawatzky v Campbell*, [2001] SJ No 317 (QB).

208 *Van de Perre v Edwards*, [2001] 2 SCR 1014.

209 *DME v RDE*, 2015 ABQB 47; *SRM v NGTM*, 2014 BCSC 442 (appointment of parenting coordinator); *NU v GSB*, 2015 BCSC 105; *Holt v Holt*, 2014 MBQB 56; *NER v JDM*, 2011 NBCA 57; *Fowler v Fowler*, 2014 NLTD(F) 25; *MC v JC*, 2012 NUCJ 16; *Ganie v Ganie*, 2014 ONSC 7500; *Chernoff v Chernoff*, 2014 SKQB 139.

210 *Calahoo v Calahoo*, [2000] AJ No 815 (QB).

211 *Rowe v Coles*, 2012 NLTD(F) 24, citing *Lane v Hustins-Lane*, 2005 NLUFC 42.

- to be with the parent best able to fulfill the child's needs; and
- the provision of an environment that is safe, secure, free of strife and conflict, and that positively guides the child in development.[212]

Courts in New Brunswick often look to the definition of the "best interests of the child" in the *Family Services Act* for useful guidance in custody cases arising under the *Divorce Act*.[213] It provides as follows:

"best interests of the child" means the best interests of the child under the circumstances taking into consideration

(a) the mental, emotional and physical health of the child and his need for appropriate care or treatment, or both;

(b) the views and preferences of the child, where such views and preferences can be reasonably ascertained;

(c) the effect upon the child of any disruption of the child's sense of continuity;

(d) the love, affection and ties that exist between the child and each person to whom the child's custody is entrusted, each person to whom access to the child is granted and, where appropriate, each sibling of the child and, where appropriate, each grandparent of the child;

(e) the merits of any plan proposed by the Minister under which he would be caring for the child, in comparison with the merits of the child returning to or remaining with his parents;

(f) the need to provide a secure environment that would permit the child to become a useful and productive member of society through the achievement of his full potential according to his individual capacity; and

(g) the child's cultural and religious heritage.[214]

There are additional matters relating to or arising out of this definition of which the court may take cognizance on a case-by-case basis. Among them are the following:

- Which parent offers the most stability as a family unit?
- Which parent appears most prepared to communicate in a mature and responsible manner with the other parent?

---

212   *Calahoo v Calahoo*, [2000] AJ No 815 (QB), citing *Starko v Starko* (1990), 74 Alta LR (2d) 168 (QB); see also *MS v JS*, 2010 ABQB 127; *MD v RD*, 2013 NLTD(G) 184. For additional factors, see *DLS v DES*, [2001] AJ No 883 (QB). And see *Family Law Act*, SA 2003, c F-4.5, s 18.

213   *NER v JDM*, 2011 NBCA 57; *HD v PED*, 2012 NBQB 315; *NL v AP*, 2015 NBQB 57.

214   *Family Services Act*, SNB 1980, c F-2.2, s 1.

- Which parent is more able to set aside personal animosity and be generous with access arrangements?
- Which parent shows promise of being an appropriate role model for the children, and exhibits a sense of values and directions?
- Which parent is more prepared to broaden the scope of the child's life with learning, associations, and challenges?
- Are the extended families on either side polarized or are they generous of attitude with the opposite parent?
- Which parent provides the best cushion for the child against the stresses of marriage breakdown?
- Does the child have physical or mental problems that require special attention and care (for example, attention deficit disorder or asthma)?
- Does one parent play mind games with the child and carelessly expose the child to domestic turmoil?
- Where will the overall long-term intellectual and security interests of the child best be served?
- Will there be material provisions that meet at least minimal standards?
- Which parent appears most prepared to give priority to the child's best interests over and above his own?
- Which parent exhibits the most maturity and ability to accept and deal with responsibility?
- Does either parent appear more prone to litigate than to communicate or negotiate?
- Is there a positive or negative effect with respect to the involvement of third parties with either parent on the welfare of the child, and is such effect financial or emotional?
- Does the evidence disclose a more substantial bonding between the child and one parent or the other?
- In consideration of the potential for joint custody, does the evidence reveal a couple with the maturity, self-control, ability, will, and communication skills to make proper joint decisions about their children.[215]

In *Foley v Foley*,[216] Goodfellow J, of the Nova Scotia Supreme Court, formulated the following list of seventeen factors to consider in determining the best interests of a child, namely,

---

215   *Shaw v Shaw*, [1997] NBJ No 211 (QB), Graser J; see also *LDW v KDM*, 2011 ABQB 384; *LDD v JAD*, 2010 NBCA 69; *KCWV v KLP*, 2010 NBCA 70; *McWilliams v Couture*, 2014 NBQB 86.
216   [1993] NSJ No 347 (SC). See also *NL v AP*, 2015 NBQB 57; *Chafe v Chaisson*, 2013 NLTD(F) 19; *Burgoyne v Kenny*, 2009 NSCA 34; *Reeves v Reeves*, 2010 NSCA 35; *Hustins v Hustins*,

1) statutory direction;
2) physical environment;
3) discipline;
4) role model;
5) wishes of the children;
6) religious and spiritual guidance;
7) assistance of experts, such as social workers, psychologists, and psychiatrists;
8) time availability of parent for a child;
9) the cultural development of a child;
10) the physical and character development of the child by such things as participation in sports;
11) the emotional support to assist in a child developing self-esteem and confidence;
12) the financial contribution to the welfare of a child;
13) the support of an extended family, including uncles, aunts, and grandparents;
14) the willingness of a parent to facilitate contact with the other parent;
15) the interim and long-range plan for the welfare of the children;
16) the financial consequences of custody; and
17) any other relevant factors.

This list does not purport to be exhaustive, nor will all factors be relevant in every case. Determining a child's best interests is not simply a matter of scoring each parent on a generic list of factors. Each case must be decided on the evidence presented.[217] The listed factors in *Foley v Foley* merely serve as indicia of the best interests of the child. By their very nature, custody and access applications are fact-specific. The listed factors may, therefore, expand, contract, or vary, depending upon the circumstances of the particular case as manifested by the totality of the evidence. Courts must approach each decision with great care and caution. They must be mindful that there is no such thing as a "perfect parent" and they should not be quick to judge litigants for common parenting mistakes.[218] In *JRC v SJC*,[219] MacDonald J, of the Nova Scotia Supreme Court, listed the following questions as relevant in assessing what parenting plan was best for the child:

2014 NSSC 185. And see *CM v RL*, 2013 NSFC 29 and *Myer v Lyle*, 2014 NSSC 233, citing 2013 amendments to the Nova Scotia *Maintenance and Custody Act*.

217 *Burgoyne v Kenny*, 2009 NSCA 34; *NL v AP*, 2015 NBQB 57.
218 *MEE v TRE*, [2002] NSJ No 425 (SC).
219 2010 NSSC 85 at para 12.

1. What does the parent know about child development and is there evidence indicating what is suggested to be "known" has been or will be put into practice?

2. Is there a good temperamental match between the child and the parent? A freewheeling, risk taking child may not thrive well in the primary care of a fearful, restrictive parent.

3. Can the parent set boundaries for the child and does the child accept those restrictions without the need for the parent to resort to harsh discipline?

4. Does the child respond to the parent's attempts to comfort or guide the child when the child is unhappy, hurt, lonely, anxious, or afraid? How does that parent give comfort and guidance to the child?

5. Is the parent empathic towards the child? Does the parent enjoy and understand the child as an individual or is the parent primarily seeking gratification of his or her own personal needs through the child?

6. Can the parent examine the proposed parenting plan through the child's eyes and reflect what aspects of that plan may cause problems for, or be resisted by, the child?

7. Has the parent made changes in his or her life or behaviour to meet the child's needs, or is he or she prepared to do so for the welfare of the child?

And in *Westhaver v Howard*,[220] Williams J, of the Nova Scotia Supreme Court, endorsed the following principles as applicable when a court is reviewing the issue of access:

1) While contact with each parent will usually promote the balanced development of the child, it is a consideration that must be subordinate to the determination of the best interests of the child.

2) While the burden of proving that access to a parent should be denied rests with the parent who asserts that position, it is not necessary to prove that access by a parent would be harmful to the children. The extent of the burden is to prove that the best interests of the children would be met by making such an order.

3) It is appropriate for a trial judge to consider the possible adverse effect on the mother of the father's behaviour, if the father were to be granted access.

4) The court must be slow to deny or extinguish access unless the evidence dictates that it is in the best interests of the child to do so.[221]

---

220 [2007] NSJ No 499 (SC).
221 *Ibid* at para 5.

In Prince Edward Island, the following list of factors have been endorsed as relevant to the determination of the best interests of a child:

(1) The wishes of the parents;

(2) The proposals of the parents for the maintenance, education and religious upbringing of the children;

(3) The parents' stations, aptitude and prospects in life;

(4) Pecuniary circumstances of the parents, not in the context that the richer shall receive custody, but to assist in the apportionment of the maintenance payments;

(5) The age and sex of the children;

(6) The conduct of the parents;

(7) Where the sense of love, affection and security of the child is directed;

(8) The home situation in which the child will be living;

(9) The requirements of the child and which parent is best equipped to meet the needs of that child;

(10) The length of time that the child has lived with a particular parent to the exclusion of the other parent;

(11) The bond that may exist between the children in a family with the intent that where a bond exists, the court should be reluctant to separate the children;

(12) The views and preferences of the child, where such views and preferences can reasonably be ascertained.[222]

I. CONDUCT

1) General

Subsections 16(9) and 17(6) of the *Divorce Act* stipulate that the court, in making or varying an order for custody or access,[223] shall not take into consideration the past conduct of a person, unless the conduct is relevant to the ability of that person to act as a parent.[224]

---

222 *JDF v JLJF*, 2009 PESC 28 at para 14.

223 *MJT v SAT*, 2010 NBQB 268; *Poirier v Poirier*, 2011 SKQB 298.

224 See *Gordon v Goertz*, [1996] 2 SCR 27 at para 21; *DPO v PEO*, [2006] NSJ No 205 (SC) (joint custody negated by spousal abuse); compare *Somerville v Somerville*, 2007 ONCA 210, [2007] OJ No 1079 (husband's deceit at time of marriage breakdown not reflective of his parenting capacity). *BJG v DLG*, 2010 YKSC 33 (joint guardianship negated by father's controlling behavior); see also *Gallant v Gallant*, 2009 NSCA 56; *Mertz v Symchyck*, 2007 SKCA 121 (application under the *Children's Law Act, 1997)* For a useful summary of conduct that may be deemed relevant to the determination of a child's best interests, see *TT v CG*, 2012 BCSC 1205 at para 39, citing the *Family Law Sourcebook for British*

Perceptions of morality have changed. In past generations, a parent living in an adulterous relationship would be automatically denied custody. Today, spousal conduct, which does not overtly reflect on parenting ability, is generally disregarded. A court may be concerned with the viability of a parent's non-marital cohabitational relationship but is unconcerned with historical perceptions of the morality of the relationship. Contemporary issues of misconduct are more likely to focus on domestic violence[225] or parental alienation.[226] On an application to change the custody and guardianship of a child on the basis of the custodial parent's intransigent conduct in alienating the child from the non-custodial parent, the immediate detrimental impact on the child of a court-ordered change of custody may be outweighed by the long-term detrimental impact that will be suffered by the child if the parental alienation continues unabated.[227]

Subsections 16(9) and 17(6) of the *Divorce Act* will not eliminate acrimonious custody or access litigation unless lawyers and parents jointly pursue other avenues for resolving parenting disputes on or after divorce. The strategic use of mediation and court-ordered independent custody assessments can reduce the potential for protracted no-holds-barred litigation.

2) Child Sexual Abuse Allegations

In contested custody or access proceedings, a parent who alleges that the other parent has sexually abused their child has the burden of proving the allegation on the balance of probabilities. If the evidence clearly establishes sexual abuse, such conduct will usually be determinative of future parenting arrangements. If the evidence leaves it uncertain whether sexual abuse occurred in the past, the court must still go on to assess the risk of future abuse.

Columbia (2011 Update), published by the Continuing Legal Education Society of British Columbia at 2-26 and 2-27.

225 For insights into the appropriate judicial response to allegations of domestic violence, which may range from an isolated incident to a recurring pattern of spousal abuse that controls and disempowers the victim, see Peter G Jaffe *et al*, "Custody Disputes Involving Allegations of Domestic Violence: Toward a Differentiated Approach to Parenting Plans" (2008) 46:3 Fam Ct Rev 500. And see *CDG v DJP*, 2010 BCSC 1216; *MAB v LAB*, 2013 NSSC 89; *Ganie v Ganie*, 2014 ONSC 7500; *CRL v REL*, [1998] SJ No 20.

226 *Ottewell v Ottewell*, 2012 ONSC 5201.

227 *AA v SNA*, [2007] BCJ No 1474 (CA); see also *LDW v KDM*, 2011 ABQB 384; *AA v SNA*, [2007] BCJ No 1475 (CA); *CLH v RJJS*, 2012 BCSC 579; *SC v ASC*, 2011 MBCA 70; *McAlister v Jenkins*, [2008] OJ No 2833 (Sup Ct), citing Nicholas Bala *et al*, "Alienated Children and Parental Separation: Legal Responses in Canada's Family Courts" (2007) 33 Queen's LJ 79. For a useful summary of research findings on the impact of high parental conflict on the children of separated or divorced parents, see *Jackson v Jackson*, [2008] OJ No 342 (Sup Ct), JC Murray J. And see Section R, below in this chapter.

As was stated by Green J, of the Newfoundland Unified Family Court, in *CC v LB*,[228] "the issue in a custody and access case where sexual abuse is alleged is not whether abuse did occur in the past but whether there is a real risk to the child in the future and, if so, whether that factor, when weighed against all the other factors bearing upon the best interests of the children, mandates a particular result." Hearsay evidence respecting statements made by young children may be admitted where sexual abuse is alleged in a custody or access dispute, provided that such evidence satisfies the criteria of necessity and reliability set out in *R v Khan*.[229] In the words of Fisher J, of the British Columbia Supreme Court, in *DAM v DMT*:

> 23 In a family law case involving allegations of physical and sexual abuse against children, hearsay evidence of statements made by the children may be admitted under the principled exception to the hearsay rule. This exception requires that the evidence is both necessary and reliable. Children do not normally testify in proceedings of this nature, particularly young children, as to do so may be very harmful to them. For this reason, the hearsay evidence meets the necessity requirement: see *J.K.F. v. J.D.F.*, [1988] B.C.J. No. 278 (C.A.); *R. v Khan*, [1990] 2 S.C.R. 531; *S.F.R. v. E.C.R.* (1997), 41 B.C.L.R. (3d) 239 (S.C.); *P.V. v. D.B.*, 2007 BCSC 237; and *J.P. v. B.G.*, 2012 BCSC 938.
>
> 24 Reliability for the purpose of admissibility, or threshold reliability, is aimed at identifying circumstances where the inability to test the hearsay evidence is sufficiently overcome to justify receiving it as an exception to the general exclusionary rule. This requirement may be met by showing that sufficient trust can be put in the truth and accuracy of the statement because of the way in which it came about, or by showing that in the circumstances the judge will be able to sufficiently assess its worth. The presence of corroborating or conflicting evidence may also be considered: see *R. v. Khan; R. v. Khelawon*, [2006] 2 S.C.R. 787.
>
> 25 In *S.F.R.*, the indicia of reliability in cases involving allegations of sexual abuse were held to include the following factors: timing of the statement; demeanour and personality of the child; intelligence and understanding of the child; absence of motive of the child to fabricate; absence of motive or bias of the person who reports the child's statement; spontaneity; statement in response to non-leading questions; absence of suggestion, manipulation, coaching, undue influence or improper influence; corroboration by

---

228 (1995), 136 Nfld & PEIR 296 at para 85 (Nfld UFC); see also *DAM v DMT*, 2013 BCSC 359; *CMB v WSB*, 2011 ONSC 3027.

229 [1990] 2 SCR 531.

real evidence; consistency over time; and whether the statement was equally consistent with other hypothesis or alternative explanation.

26 If the hearsay evidence meets the test of threshold reliability, it can be admitted for its truth and its ultimate reliability is to be assessed with the rest of the evidence.[230]

The receipt of hearsay evidence is subject to judicial evaluation as to the weight to be accorded to it. In *JAG v RJR*,[231] Robertson J, of the Ontario Court, General Division, formulated the following list of factors to consider in weighing the evidence to determine whether a young child was sexually abused by a parent:

1) What were the circumstances of disclosure — to whom, and where?
2) Did the disclosure of evidence of alleged abuse come from any disinterested witnesses?
3) Were the statements made by the child spontaneous?
4) Did the questions asked of the child suggest an answer?
5) Did the child's statement provide context such as a time frame or positioning of the parties?
6) Was there progression in the story about events?
7) How did the child behave before and after disclosure?
8) Is there physical evidence that would be available by medical examination? If so, and no medical report has been filed, is there a sufficient explanation for its lack?
9) Was there opportunity?
10) What investigative or court action was taken by the parent alleging abuse?
11) Who provided background information to the experts and investigators, and is it accurate, complete, and consistent with both parties' recollections?
12) Was there other evidence supporting the allegations of sexual abuse?
13) Was the custodial parent co-operative regarding access, or was access resisted on other grounds prior to the allegations and after disclosure?
14) Was there harmony between the evidence of one witness and another, and between the evidence of the experts?
15) Was there consistency over time of the child's disclosure?
16) Did the child use wording in statements which appeared to be prompted, rehearsed, or memorized?

---

230 2013 BCSC 359; see also *Ganie v Ganie*, 2014 ONSC 7500 (domestic violence).
231 [1998] OJ No 1415 (Gen Div); see also *KB v CA*, 2012 MBQB 115.

17) Was the language used by the child consistent and commensurate with the child's language skills?

18) Was the information given by the child beyond age-appropriate knowledge?

19) What was the comfort level of the child to deal with the subject matter, in particular with respect to the offering of detail?

20) Did the child exhibit sexualized behaviour?

21) Was there evidence of pre-existing inappropriate sexual behaviour by the alleged perpetrator?

22) Was a treatment plan put forth by either parent?

23) Was the child coached or prompted?

24) Did the evidence of the expert witnesses, as accepted by a trial Judge, support the allegations of sexual abuse?

Lists such as this may be helpful, but only when they are tailored to the facts of the particular case. There is no single list that can be used for all cases involving alleged sexual abuse. Nicholas Bala and John Schuman, in their commentary entitled "Allegations of Sexual Abuse When Parents Have Separated,"[232] observe that, given the distinction between the rules of evidence and the standard of proof in criminal and civil proceedings, "it seems inappropriate for a family law judge to place much weight on the decision of police not to charge or on a criminal court acquittal" of a parent against whom allegations of child sexual abuse have been made.

Bala and Schuman further observe that abused children often feel an attachment to the abusing parent, notwithstanding the abuse. Consequently, a "family law court" may allow access by the former abusing parent, if it is satisfied that such access is in the best interests of the child. The judge must be satisfied, however, that the child is not at risk, and this may require supervised access in a neutral setting, before access in the home of the non-custodial parent is allowed.

A five-year-old child is not a competent witness where sexual abuse of the child is alleged in contested custody or access proceedings, and the reception of hearsay evidence as to statements made by the child may, therefore, be "reasonably necessary" to make a proper determination. The reliability of the child's statements is to be evaluated and weighed along with the evidence provided by other witnesses. Where "prompting" has definitely occurred and "coaching" may have occurred, this will adversely affect the reliability to be accorded to the child's disclosures and demonstrations. Circumstantial physical evidence that is relied upon to support the allegation of sexual

---

232 (1999) 17 Can Fam LQ 191.

abuse may be discounted where there is a reasonable and plausible explanation provided for the physical condition. Past incidents in which the child "made up stories" are also relevant to the issue of reliability of the hearsay evidence. Where a review of all the relevant and admissible evidence leads the court to conclude, not only that the burden of proving sexual abuse has not been satisfied, but also that the facts do not support a finding that there is a substantial possibility of future sexual abuse, the "maximum contact" principle should be applied and an order for joint custody with shared decision-making authority and for unsupervised access on alternate weekends is appropriate.[233]

In proceedings for interim custody and access wherein the custodial parent alleges that the non-custodial parent has sexually abused the children, the adage about erring on the side of caution has its place, but it does not merit absolute application. Allegations of sexual abuse are always troubling, but the court should not abdicate its responsibility by postponing a determination until trial and granting the non-custodial parent supervised access to the children in the meantime. Supervised access creates an artificial and stilted environment for the children and the parent and may undermine the preservation of a close bond such as the child enjoys with the custodial parent. Supervised access may be better than no access but it is not much better. Consequently, it should only be ordered when there is no reasonable alternative. Given that the *Divorce Act* endorses the principle that it is in the best interests of children to enjoy a relationship with both parents to the extent reasonably possible, access to a non-custodial parent should not be denied or restricted in the absence of a compelling reason. Instead of deferring the issue until trial, the court, on an interim application, should examine the sexual abuse allegations with care and objectivity. Where the descriptions of the alleged abuse are vague, where they were elicited by the custodial parent as opposed to being volunteered, where the children made no incriminating disclosures to third-party professionals, including a social services agency and the police who looked into the custodial parent's allegations, and where an examination of the children by a licensed physician finds no evidence of sexual abuse and provides a clinical explanation of their physical condition, an order for unsupervised access to the children by the non-custodial parent may be granted.

When the custodial parent has been the children's primary caregiver, a more fundamental change in the parental roles may be inappropriate having regard to the best interests of the children, notwithstanding that the custodial parent has relocated with the children in contravention of a court

233 *BS v RT*, [2002] NJ No 101 (SC), Cook J.

order that is currently under appeal. Although such relocation might justify a change of custody in other circumstances, Gerein CJ, of the Saskatchewan Court of Queen's Bench, in *TGF v DSV*,[234] concluded that it would constitute an improper punitive sanction in this case and it would be contrary to the best interests of the children. However, for the purposes of achieving continued meaningful involvement of the non-custodial parent in the children's lives, Gerein CJ, while conceding that such a disposition was unusual, granted the non-custodial parent access to the children for the entire and every weekend.

Determination of the credibility of witnesses is a function of the trier of fact, not an expert witness. The majority judgment of the Supreme Court of Canada in *R v Béland*[235] renders polygraph evidence inadmissible in a criminal proceeding because it contravenes certain basic rules of evidence, namely (1) the rule against oath-helping; (2) the rule against the admission of past out-of-court consistent statements by a witness; (3) the rule relating to character evidence; and (4) the expert evidence rule. These rules of evidence, which were relied upon in *R v Béland* to exclude the admission of polygraph evidence that was sought to be used to determine the credibility of the accused, are equally applicable to a contested guardianship, or custody and access proceeding, wherein a parent seeks to negate allegations of child sexual abuse by introducing polygraph evidence.[236]

J. EFFECT OF AGREEMENT

An agreement between parents or between parents and third parties respecting a child's upbringing cannot oust the statutory obligation of a court to grant a custody order that reflects a full and balanced consideration of all factors relevant to a determination of the child's best interests. A prior parenting agreement between the disputants is only one factor to be considered, albeit an important factor.[237] As Nightingale J, of the Ontario Superior Court of Justice, remarked in *Todoruck v Todoruck*, "a parent who has agreed to a child care arrangement should be prepared to explain why what he or she felt was appropriate earlier on is no longer appropriate."[238] Parents cannot oust

---

234 [2005] SJ No 582 (QB).

235 [1987] 2 SCR 398.

236 *EW v DW*, [2005] BCJ No 1345 (SC).

237 *AL v DK*, 2000 BCCA 455 at para 11; *Sabbagh v Sabbagh* (1994), 2 RFL (4th) 44 (Man CA); *LW v PA*, 2010 NBQB 201; *Blois v Gleason*, [2009] OJ No 1884 (Sup Ct); *Holliday v Hansen*, 2010 SKQB 350; *BL v ML*, 2010 YKSC 41; see also *MEO v SRM*, [2004] AJ No 202 (CA) and *Hearn v Hearn*, [2004] AJ No 105 (QB) and *AL v CC*, 2011 ABQB 819, applying *Miglin v Miglin*, [2003] 1 SCR 303.

238 2014 ONSC 6983 at para 43, citing *Summers v Summers* [1999] OJ No 3082.

the statutory jurisdiction of the court to order child support and access by contracting to trade off child support and access.[239]

Although a separation agreement may include provisions whereby its terms shall only be varied in the event of a material change of circumstances, such provisions cannot oust the jurisdiction of a court to grant orders for custody and child support in subsequent divorce proceedings. In allowing an appeal in *Jay v Jay*[240] because the chambers judge had erred by concluding that his jurisdiction under the *Divorce Act* was limited by the provisions of the separation agreement, the Appeal Division of the Prince Edward Island Supreme Court expressed the following opinion:

> Irrespective of the terms of any agreement between the parties, the court has the jurisdiction in a motion for corollary relief in connection with divorce proceedings to hear and deal with all issues of custody and child support. An agreement between the parties is only one factor to be taken into consideration when deciding upon the best interests of the child. While such an agreement provides strong evidence of what the parties accepted at the time as meeting the best interests of the child, it does not relieve the court of its responsibility under s 16 of the *Divorce Act* to make an independent assessment of the best interests of the child. (See: *Willick v. Willick*, [1994] 3 S.C.R. 670.)[241]

In the context of custody and access orders, the above observations are clearly consistent with established caselaw and with the express provisions of section 16(8) of the *Divorce Act* whereby "[i]n making an order under this section, the court shall take into consideration only the best interests of the child of the marriage as determined by reference to the condition, means, needs and other circumstances of the child."

K. RELIGIOUS UPBRINGING OF CHILD

Although an order for sole custody under section 16 of the *Divorce Act* empowers the custodial parent to determine the religious upbringing of the child, such an order does not necessarily entitle the custodial parent to prevent the noncustodial parent from sharing religious views and practices with

---

239 *Kroupa v Stoneham*, 2011 ONSC 5824 (variation of consent order).
240 [2003] PEIJ No 68 (CA); see also *Cooke v Cooke*, 2012 NSSC 73.
241 *Jay v Jay*, [2003] PEIJ No 68 (CA) at para 4.

the child.[242] Religion will not be a critical factor in custody proceedings where the parents are not practising their religion and the child is of a young age.[243]

In custody and access disputes, a court should not seek to determine whether one religion is better than the other. The religious upbringing of children concerns the court only insofar as it affects their well-being and their relationships with both the custodial and non-custodial parent.[244] A court will only encroach upon the personal domain of religious freedom where the failure to do so is shown to place a child at substantial risk of harm.[245] A court will not usually object to or interfere with the religious instruction of a child by the parents;[246] indeed, exposure to different religious beliefs will often be of value to the child.[247] The court may have to strike a compromise between the parties and their wish to provide a child with a religious education. The court may direct the parents to tolerate and respect each other's religion.[248]

In *ASK v MABK*, Baird J, of the New Brunswick Court of Queen's Bench, stated:

> [122] The child's religious heritage, like racial or cultural heritage, is one factor in his or her personal identity. In making a best interest[s] decision, a court must consider that factor but it is not determinative . . . . What is more important is the child's right to make his or her own decision on religious affiliation . . . The best way to preserve that right is by not foreclosing any future options and allowing both parents to share their religious heritage with the child . . . .

---

242   *Young v Young*, [1993] 4 SCR 3; see also *MW v SEM*, 2010 NBQB 26. Compare *Boudreau v Boudreau* (1994), 143 NBR (2d) 321 at 328 (QB) wherein the court stated that the custodial parent had no right to impose her religious views on the children. For further analysis of the significance of parents' religious persuasions, see *Barrett v Barrett* (1988), 18 RFL (3d) 186 (Nfld TD) wherein Bartlett J cites with approval copious extracts from a didactic brief filed by David Day, QC; see also Vittorio Toselli, "Religion in Custody Disputes" (1990) 25 RFL (3d) 261; John T Syrtash, *Religion and Culture in Canadian Family Law* (Toronto: Butterworths, 1992).

243   *White v White* (1990), 28 RFL (3d) 439 (BCSC) (two-year-old child); *Tyabji v Sandana* (1994), 2 RFL (4th) 265 at 280–81 (BCSC).

244   *Young v Young*, [1993] 4 SCR 3, 49 RFL (3d) 117 at 217; *ASK v MABK*, [2008] NBJ No 332 (QB); *Solomon v Solomon* (1990), 100 NSR (2d) 73 (TD), aff'd (1991), 106 NSR (2d) 28 (CA); *Hines v Hines* (1992), 40 RFL (3d) 274 (NS Fam Ct); *Voortman v Voortman* (1994), 4 RFL (4th) 250 (Ont CA); *Harvey v Lapointe* (1988), 13 RFL (3d) 134 (Que CS); *Travis v Travis*, 2011 SKQB 307.

245   *Rosenberg v Minster*, 2011 ONSC 4758.

246   *Droit de la famille — 353* (1987), 8 RFL (3d) 360 (Que CA).

247   *Young v Young*, [1993] 4 SCR 3; *Voortman v Voortman* (1994), 4 RFL (4th) 250 (Ont CA).

248   *Jaillet v Jaillet* (1988), 91 NBR (2d) 351 (QB); *Avitan v Avitan* (1992), 38 RFL (3d) 382 (Ont Gen Div).

[123] The freedom to provide religious instruction to their children, however, cannot be used as an opportunity to undermine the children's love and respect for the other parent. In other words, there is no right or wrong religion and the children should not be taught that the other parent is somehow evil or bad because they are not practicing Christians or for some other reason.

. . .

[125] The age at which a court will deem a child mature enough to have established religious convictions will depend on the individual child and the facts of each case.[249]

And in *Langille v Dossa*, Wilson JFC, of the Nova Scotia Family Court, held that:

Where there is conflict between the rights of a custodial parent to share her life with the child and the [tenets] of any particular religion, I must hold that the rights of the child to know their parent must take precedence . . . . To allow one party . . . to attack the morality of the other parent cannot be in the best interests of the child.[250]

A court may stipulate that a non-custodial parent is not entitled to object to the religious practices of the custodial parent,[251] and a custodial parent's objection to the non-custodial parent's religious beliefs is no bar to granting the non-custodial parent access.[252] Custody may, however, be granted to one parent if the other parent places his or her commitment to church over and above his or her responsibility to promote the best interests of the children.[253] Where a custodial parent's religious beliefs and practices are found to be detrimental to the children's welfare, custody may be granted to the other parent and an order may be made prohibiting the former custodial parent from engaging in future religious indoctrination of the children.[254] Limitations may be imposed on the non-custodial parent with respect to religious

---

249 [2008] NBJ No 332 (QB); see also *MW v SEM*, 2010 NBQB 26; *MP v ADA*, 2011 NBQB 351.

250 (1994), 136 NSR (2d) 180 at 189 (Fam Ct) (application under *Family Maintenance Act*, RSNS 1989, c 160).

251 *Droit de la famille — 1114*, [1987] RDF 366 (Que CS).

252 *Friesen v Friesen* (1989), 56 Man R (2d) 303 (QB); *Smith v Smith* (1989), 92 NSR (2d) 204 (TD); *Avitan v Avitan* (1992), 38 RFL (3d) 382 (Ont Gen Div).

253 *Schulz v Schulz* (1987), 12 RFL (3d) 141 (BCSC); compare *McNeil v McNeil* (1989), 20 RFL (3d) 52 (BCSC), wherein a mother's adherence to a fundamental church was found not to be detrimental to the children's best interests.

254 *Moseley v Moseley* (1989), 20 RFL (3d) 301 (Alta Prov Ct).

practices when the child is in his or her care.[255] Where the best interests of the children are thereby served, the court may impose restrictions on a parent to prevent the religious indoctrination of a child or to prohibit a non-custodial parent from involving the children in his or her religious activities, even in the absence of demonstrable harm to the child.[256] Such restrictions do not contravene section 2 of the *Canadian Charter of Rights and Freedoms*,[257] but in the absence of compelling evidence that the sharing of religious beliefs and practices with the child or the exposure of the child to two religions is contrary to the best interests of a child, the *Divorce Act* should be interpreted in a manner consistent with the freedom of religion guaranteed by the *Canadian Charter of Rights and Freedoms*.[258]

Where one parent suggests a change to or from a religious school over the objections of the other parent, it must be demonstrated on the evidence that the change will be in the best interests of the child.[259]

L. VARIATION AND RESCISSION OF INTERIM AND PERMANENT CUSTODY AND ACCESS ORDERS

On the issue of the variation of interim custody orders, Schwann J, of the Saskatchewan Court of Queen's Bench, observed in *Rue v Babyak*:

> 15 As a starting point, this Court's reluctance to vary interim custody orders must again be emphasized. In the absence of any credible evidence the child is in danger or compelling evidence calling for a change, no change should be made to interim orders. (See *MacEwen v. MacEwen*, 2004 SKQB 271, [2004] S.J. No. 419 (QL); *Salisbury v. Salisbury*, 2011 SKQB 258, 376 Sask. R. 276 and *Guenther v. Guenther* (1999), 181 Sask. R. 83, [1999] S.J. No. 120 (QL) (Q.B.)). In fact *Guenther* goes so far as to describe it as a "... reversible error in law to vary interim arrangements pending trial ..." (para 8).

---

255   *Borris v Borris* (1991), 37 RFL (3d) 339 (Alta QB); *LCM v BAC*, 2010 NBQB 127; *Droit de la famille — 1150*, [1988] RDF 40 (Que CS), aff'd (1990), [1991] RJQ 306 (Que CA), aff'd [1993] 4 SCR 141.

256   *Young v Young*, [1993] 4 SCR 3.

257   *Young v Young*, ibid; *Fougère v Fougère* (1986), 70 NBR (2d) 57 at 75–76 (QB), var'd (1987), 6 RFL (3d) 314 (NBCA); *Droit de la famille — 260* (1986), 50 RFL (2d) 296 (Que CS); *Droit de la famille — 353* (1987), 8 RFL (3d) 360 (Que CA); see also *Moseley v Moseley* (1989), 20 RFL (3d) 301 (Alta Prov Ct); *Schulz v Schulz* (1987), 12 RFL (3d) 141 (BCSC); *Jaillet v Jaillet* (1988), 91 NBR (2d) 351 (QB); *Ryan v Ryan* (1986), 3 RFL (3d) 141 (Nfld TD).

258   *Hockey v Hockey* (1989), 21 RFL (3d) 105 (Ont Div Ct); *Avitan v Avitan* (1992), 38 RFL (3d) 382 (Ont Gen Div).

259   *Travis v Travis*, 2011 SKQB 307, citing *Stephanson v Schulte*, 2000 SKQB 341.

16 The purpose of an interim custody/access order is to stabilize the parenting situation and the children's lives, usually by preserving the *status quo*, in order to provide an acceptable solution to difficult problems pending trial. For that reason, and to bring finality to litigation, interim orders are not lightly disturbed. As stated in *Harden v. Harden* (1987), 54 Sask. R. 155, 6 R.F.L. (3d) 147 (Sask. C.A.) " . . . interim custody is just that: a makeshift solution until the correct answer can be discovered . . . designed to minimize conflict between parents and cause the least harm to the child and determination of the cause."[260]

And Boswell J, of the Ontario Superior Court of Justice, stated in *Lamoureux v Lamoureux*:

29 I am also governed by a number of principles that have developed in relation to motions to vary interim orders. Interim, or temporary orders, are by their nature imperfect solutions to often complex problems. They are based on limited evidence, typically in affidavit form. They are meant to provide "a reasonably acceptable solution to a difficult problem until trial": see *Chaitas v. Christopoulos*, [2004] O.J. No. 907 (S.C.J.) per Sachs J.

30 Variations of temporary orders are not encouraged. They should not become the focus of the parties' litigation: *Cutaia-Mahler v. Mahler*, 2001 CarswellOnt 3054 (S.C.J.) per Benotto J. There is, therefore, a heavy onus on a party who seeks to vary a temporary order — essentially replacing one imperfect solution with another imperfect solution — pending trial: *Boissy v. Boissy*, 2008 CarswellOnt 4253 (S.C.J.) per Shaw J. A substantial change in circumstances is typically necessary before a variation to a temporary order will be granted: *Biddle v. Biddle*, [2005] O.J. No. 737 (S.C.J.) per Blishen J.[261]

The above opinions may be compared to the following opinion of Campbell J, of the Prince Edward Island Supreme Court, in *GER v HJR*:

The practice of law has evolved greatly over the last number of years. The time between the start of an action and the trial, which used to be measured in months, is now often measured in years. Considerably fewer matters ever reach the trial stage. Interim orders, which used to be viewed as being "temporary" have now become the *de facto* final orders in many cases. While parties are free to go to trial in any case, the vast majority choose not

---

260 2012 SKQB 541 at paras 15–16. As to the disinclination of appellate courts to disturb an interim custody order, see *HEK v MLK*, 2013 SKCA 14, citing *Mantyka v Dueck*, 2012 SKCA 109.

261 2010 ONSC 4488; see also *Daley v Daley*, 2011 NLTD(F) 35; *Lafferty v Larocque*, 2013 NWTSC 10.

to do so. Cost is often a significant factor in those decisions. The desire of the parties to gather evidence by way of an independently prepared home study is another factor which extends the time required between any interim order and an order following trial. Interim orders, varied from time to time as the need arises, have largely replaced the so-called "final" order after trial. Having stable and predictable custodial arrangements can be of great value to a child. However, given the significant changes in the use and duration of "interim" orders, courts must retain the ability to adjust interim orders to reflect developments impacting the best interests of the child. Preservation of the *status quo* should not be seen as a goal in and of itself, but only as one factor, albeit a significant one, affecting the best interests of the child.[262]

Although it is rare for a motions judge to vary an interim order granted pursuant to the *Divorce Act*, a judge always has the jurisdiction to decide the custody of a child as it relates to the best interests of that child, particularly where it can be demonstrated that there has been a change of circumstances raising concerns about the child's welfare. However, there must be compelling reasons that militate in favour of immediate action rather than waiting for a hearing on the matter and a final order.[263] There is no section in the *Divorce Act* that expressly authorizes the court to vary an interim order. If it was the intention of Parliament to prohibit such variation orders, it surely would have included a provision to indicate its clear intention. Where there is a gap in the legislation that the court is required to apply, the *parens patriae* jurisdiction of the court may be exercisable. The court may draw upon its inherent jurisdiction whenever it is just or equitable to do so, and the exercise of the court's inherent jurisdiction to vary an interim order does not contravene any provision of the *Divorce Act*.[264]

Although interim custody orders ordinarily preserve the *status quo* and any subsequent variation is unusual in the absence of evidence of risk to the child or some other compelling reason,[265] special circumstances may warrant such variation. In *Lewis v Lewis*,[266] the mother was granted sole custody of the children and the father supervised access pursuant to an interim consent order triggered by the mother's allegations of abuse. Subsequently, the court rejected these allegations and the mother's contention that she was a pawn who was being controlled by the father. For example, the court found that

---

262 2012 PESC 24 at para 22; see also *Lafferty v Larocque*, 2013 NWTSC 10 at para 25.
263 *Cloutier-Chudy v Chudy*, 2008 MBQB 155.
264 *DG v HF*, [2006] NBJ No 158 (CA).
265 *Napper-Whiting v Whiting*, 2014 SKCA 33.
266 [2005] NSJ No 368 (SC).

the parents' involvement in "phone sex" and watching pornographic movies was a joint and consensual adult activity that did not affect their parenting abilities or the best interests of the children and was therefore irrelevant to the issues of custody and access. Finding that an order for joint custody would be unworkable because of the parents' inability to communicate, the mother was granted sole custody of the children and the father was granted unsupervised access on specified terms.

Section 17 of the *Divorce Act* regulates the jurisdiction of the court to vary, rescind, or suspend a permanent custody order or any provision thereof. It involves a two-stage analysis. Before entering on the merits or an application to vary a custody order, the judge must be satisfied of a change in the condition, means, needs, or circumstances of the child, and/or the ability of the former spouses to meet the parenting needs of the child. A material change in circumstances is one which (1) amounts to a change in the condition, means, needs, or circumstances of the child and/or the ability of the parents to meet the needs of the child; (2) materially affects the child; and (3) was either not foreseen or could not have been reasonably contemplated by the judge who made the order that is sought to be varied.[267] If an applicant fails to meet this threshold requirement, the inquiry can go no further.[268] A court must make a finding of a material change in circumstances even when both parents request a variation.[269] If the threshold condition of a material change is established, the court should reassess the parenting arrangements in light of all the circumstances existing at the time of the variation proceeding. The court should consider the matter afresh without defaulting to the existing arrangements and must make its determination having regard only to the best interests of the child.[270] Although section 17(5) of the *Divorce Act* directs the court to consider the child's best interests by reference to the material change in

---

267 *Gordon v Goertz*, [1996] 2 SCR 27; *Ryan v Ryan*, [2008] AJ No 128 (CA); *Boychuk v Singleton*, 2008 BCCA 355; *Heisler v Heisler*, 2012 BCSC 753; *Kitt v Kitt*, 2011 MBQB 208; *KCWV v KLP*, 2010 NBCA 70; *SLB v PJO*, 2013 NBCA 52; *Pope v Janes*, 2014 NLTD(F) 27; *Mahaney v Malone*, 2013 NSSC 400; *Brown v Lloyd*, 2015 ONCA 46; *Talbot v Henry* (1990), 25 RFL (3d) 415 (Sask CA); *Gray (formerly Wiegers) v Wiegers*, 2008 SKCA 7; *DMM v TBM*, 2009 YKSC 50; see also *MW v SEM*, 2010 NBQB 26 at paras 165–66.

268 *Litman v Sherman*, 2008 ONCA 485; *Greene v Lundrigan*, 2011 NLTD(F) 55; *Persaud v Garcia-Persaud*, 2009 ONCA 782.

269 *Persaud v Garcia-Persaud*, ibid.

270 See cases cited above at note 242. See also *DEC v SCC*, 2012 ABCA 252; *Baynes v Baynes* (1987), 8 RFL (3d) 139 (BCCA); *West v West* (1994), 92 Man R (2d) 164 (CA); *Gill v Chiang*, 2011 ONSC 6803; *Talbot v Henry* (1990), 25 RFL (3d) 415 (Sask CA); *Wilson v Grassick* (1994), 2 RFL (4th) 291 (Sask CA), leave to appeal to SCC refused (1994), 7 RFL (4th) 254 (SCC); compare *Magnus v Magnus*, [2006] SJ No 510 (CA) (variation of shared parenting regime should not be disproportionate to the proven change).

circumstances, the inquiry cannot be confined to that change alone, isolated from the other factors bearing on the child's best interests.[271]

Section 17(1)(b) of the *Divorce Act* empowers a court to grant an interim order varying or suspending the provisions of an existing permanent custody/access order. A distinction is to be drawn between the existence of such jurisdiction and the exercise of such jurisdiction. Before granting an interim variation order, the court must be satisfied (1) that a *prima facie* case has been made out pointing to a change of circumstances of sufficient import as might well result in variation of the custody/access order at the final hearing; and (2) that the best interests of the child lie in making an interim order of the nature of that being contemplated. The court should also have regard to the principle that a child should have as much contact with each parent as is consistent with the child's best interests. The court should exercise its jurisdiction to grant an interim variation order sparingly and solely in the best interests of the child, bearing in mind that a final order will be forthcoming and even a temporary change can be unsettling.[272] Applying these principles to the facts in *Dorval v Dorval*,[273] wherein the interim variation order prohibited the mother from relocating the child, the Saskatchewan Court of Appeal found no tenable reason for interfering with the order. Addressing the incidental question of appeals challenging interim orders of limited duration, the Saskatchewan Court of Appeal stated that, while a right of appeal exists, the appellate court will exercise its powers sparingly and only in extraordinary circumstances. The reasons for this are obvious. Such appeals generate additional costs and delay, even when they are heard on an expedited basis, whereas it is in everybody's best interests that the matter proceed to a final determination as soon as is practicable. The judgment in *Dorval v Dorval* does not purport to resolve the "controversy" relating to the interim variation of spousal support orders. It rests content with the statement that "even in those cases in which it has been held that the courts are not empowered to make interim orders on applications under section 17 or its equivalent, allowance is consistently made for the *parens patriae* jurisdiction of the courts when it comes to children and their interests."[274] In *Sundara v Sundara*,[275] on

---

271   *KRD v CKK*, 2013 NBQB 211; *Bromm v Bromm*, 2010 SKCA 149.

272   *Landry v Welsh*, 2013 NBQB 347.

273   [2006] SJ No 94 (CA); compare *Welch v George*, 2011 SKCA 33; see also *Carey v Hanlon*, 2007 ABCA 391; *Vargas v Berryman*, 2009 BCCA 588; *Moore v Moore*, 2013 NSSC 252; *Huliyappa v Menon*, 2012 ONSC 5668; *Jones v Bahr*, 2010 SKCA 41; see also *Caparelli v Caparelli*, [2009] OJ No 5640 (Sup Ct) (access).

274   [2006] SJ No 94 at para 21 (CA); compare *Vargas v Berryman*, 2009 BCCA 588; *Welch v George*, 2011 SKCA 33.

275   2010 SKQB 313.

an application for an interim order to vary a consent order for co-parenting when a material change of circumstances has been established within the meaning of section 17 of the *Divorce Act*, Maher J, of the Saskatchewan Court of Queen's Bench, identified the following three options available to him:

1. In exceptional circumstances without *viva voce* evidence I can make a determination of the appropriate new parenting arrangement in light of the change of circumstance;

2. If a *prima facie* case pointing to a change of circumstance has been established, I may refer the matter to a pre-trial conference and if the matters are not resolved at that stage the matter will proceed to trial;

3. If I am satisfied there is a *prima facie* case pointing to a change of circumstances, I may order that there be a pre-trial conference and make an interim variation order which would be in place until trial.

Given the father's change to out-of-town employment and the fact that he was facing serious criminal charges that could result in his incarceration, Maher J found it appropriate to grant the mother an interim order for custody, and directed the matter to proceed to pre-trial and ultimately to trial, if necessary.

On an application to vary a custody order pursuant to section 17(5) of the *Divorce Act*, the applicant must prove a material or pivotal change in the child's circumstances that requires variation of the order, having regard to the best interests of the child. Although common sense dictates that a child's parenting needs will change over the years from infancy to adulthood, the increased maturity of the child arising from the passage of time does not, of itself, constitute a material change as required by section 17(5) of the *Divorce Act*; nor is it sufficient that the non-custodial parent wishes to assume a more substantial role in the child's life. Common sense assumptions about the changing needs of children as they mature do not discharge the court's duty to consider whether the existing order should be varied because it no longer satisfies the child's parenting needs. In *Gray (Formerly Wiegers) v Wiegers*,[276] the Saskatchewan Court of Appeal held that the chambers judge had erred by ordering a substantial change in the parenting regime in the absence of evidence that the existing regime no longer served the child's best interests. The Saskatchewan Court of Appeal distinguished *Elliott v Loewen*,[277] wherein the Manitoba Court of Appeal held that the motions judge was entitled to

---

276 2008 SKCA 7; see also *Brown v Lloyd*, 2015 ONCA 46; *Fennig-Doll v Doll*, [2008] SJ No 177 (QB); *Mayne v Mayne*, 2009 SKQB 329; compare *Bromm v Bromm*, 2010 SKCA 149. See also *DME v RDE*, 2015 ABQB 47 (relevance of wishes of fourteen-year-old child).

277 (1993), 44 RFL (3d) 445 (Man CA).

take judicial notice of the fact that the needs of a three-year-old child in relation to his father are different from the needs of an eighteen-month-old child. The Saskatchewan Court of Appeal observed that, in *Elliott v Loewen*, limitations imposed on the father's access were specifically related to the child's very tender years when the order was made, which limitations were no longer appropriate and in the child's best interests as he emerged from infancy into early childhood. In contrast with *Elliott v Loewen*, the child in *Gray (Formerly Wiegers) v Wiegers* was just under four years of age when the parenting regime was established, and nine and one-half years old when the father brought his application for increased parenting time. The original order provided for joint custody, with the mother to have primary care of the child, and the father to have access midweek and on alternate weekends, in addition to equal time-sharing during school vacations and three weeks during the summer. These provisions, coupled with the fact that the parents had separated before the child was born and the mother had always been the primary caregiver, led the Saskatchewan Court of Appeal to conclude that there was no reason to assume that the order was contingent upon the child's tender years. Accordingly, the variation order of the chambers judge was set aside and the original order was reinstated, subject to a prior modification of midweek access to include overnight visits, which the parents had agreed to when the child was seven years old.

Ongoing and escalating conflict may constitute a change of circumstances that justifies variation of an existing custody order[278] but significant differences in parenting styles and philosophies may fall short of justifying variation of a shared parenting order.[279] A custodial parent's repeated intentional interference with the non-custodial parent's access privileges may constitute a material change of circumstances that justifies a change of custody, even though such a change will result in the child's extra-provincial relocation.[280]

A custodial parent's persistent attempts to alienate the children from the non-custodial parent may justify an order changing the custody of the children.[281] In granting such an order, it may be wise to structure the change in the children's primary residence in such a way as to promote a gradual transition and as little disruption as possible for the children. In *Rogerson*

---

278 *DLW v JJMV* (2005), 234 NSR (2d) 366 (CA); *MacKay v Murray*, [2006] NSJ No 270 (CA); *Yasinchuk v Farkas*, 2012 ONSC 2056; compare *Litman v Sherman*, 2008 ONCA 485.

279 *Stanners v Alexandre*, 2014 ABQB 253.

280 *Ross-Johnson v Johnson*, 2009 NSCA 128.

281 *NL v RL*, 2008 NBCA 79.

v Tessaro,[282] the Ontario Court of Appeal found the trial judge's remedy of granting custody to the father to be "dramatic" but justified by the mother's persistent, ingrained, and deep-rooted inability to support the children's relationship with their father. Since the appeal was primarily fact-driven and there was no manifest error of law, the mother's appeal was dismissed. Compare *Coyle v Danylkiw*,[283] wherein a father's appeal from a judgment awarding the mother sole custody of the child and permitting her to move with the child out of Ontario was allowed in part. The relocation provision was vacated by reason of the mother's return with the child to Ontario. The Court of Appeal dismissed the father's request for sole or joint custody based on his submissions that the trial judge had erred in failing to give adequate consideration to the maximum contact principle in section 16(10) of the *Divorce Act* by making an unreasonable finding that the mother would facilitate access, and in failing to accept the findings of a custody assessor. The Ontario Court of Appeal concluded that the trial judge's decisions on both these issues turned primarily on her findings of fact and her appraisal of the evidence, which should not be interfered with in the absence of a palpable and overriding error.

Less compelling evidence is required to vary access arrangements under a subsisting order, although the best interests of the child again constitute the determinative consideration.[284] The test to alter an order for access is that a material change in circumstance must have occurred that affects the best interests of the child.[285] However, this statutory requirement of a material change does not signify that an order, once made, calcifies and defies re-examination in the face of a child's changed needs. The cumulative effect of unrelenting stress on a child may constitute a material change that justifies termination of access.[286] As Helper JA, of the Manitoba Court of Appeal, has observed,

> The needs of a child in relation to each of his parents change frequently over the years from infancy to adulthood. No court order can be crafted to

282 [2006] OJ No 1825 (CA). See also *CMBE v DJE*, [2006] NBJ No 364 (CA); *CLJ v JMJ*, [2006] NSJ No 171 (SC). Compare *RPB v KDP*, [2006] AJ No 1192 (QB) (parental expert intervention ordered pursuant to *Family Law Practice Note No 7*).

283 [2006] OJ No 2061 (CA).

284 *Hamilton v Hamilton* (1992), 43 RFL (3d) 13 (Alta QB); *Magee v Magee* (1993), 111 Sask R 211 (QB).

285 *Cairns v Cairns* (1995), 10 RFL (4th) 234 (NBCA).

286 *M(BP) v M(BLDE)* (1992), 42 RFL (3d) 349 at 360 (Ont CA), Abella JA, with Tarnopolsky JA concurring; Finlayson JA dissenting (application under *Children's Law Reform Act*, RSO 1990, c C.12); leave to appeal to SCC refused (1993), 48 RFL (3d) 232 (SCC).

address those ever-changing needs and the concerns of separated parents as they relate to their child; thus, the need for variation.[287]

For the purposes of section 17(5.1) of the *Divorce Act*, a former spouse's terminal illness or critical condition shall be considered a change of circumstances of the child of the marriage, and the court shall make a variation order in respect of access that is in the best interests of the child.[288]

The wishes of the child may be taken into consideration when those wishes are free from interference or manipulation by either parent.[289] Discontinuance of access will only be ordered in exceptional circumstances. It may be reinstated where the custodial parent's objection to access is based on the child's fear of the non-custodial parent, which fear is attributable to the custodial parent's own improper influence,[290] although counselling may be necessary to avoid any threat to the child's emotional or psychological well-being. A *bona fide* change of residence by the custodial parent does not, of itself, warrant a change of custody, but may justify variation of the access arrangements so as to ensure that the child has as much contact with both parents as is consistent with the best interests of the child.[291]

Where an abusive relationship has left the custodial parent fearful of his or her former spouse and unwilling to continue to provide access, the trial judge may consider the possible adverse effects on the parent in continuing even limited access.[292] Allegations of sexual abuse that have surfaced since the making of the original order may require the variation of access arrangements.[293]

Access arrangements may be varied because of a child entering full-time attendance at school. The arrangements for a younger sibling may be varied to match these new arrangements, since it is appropriate that child-care arrangements should involve both children for the same periods of time.[294]

---

287   *Elliott v Loewen* (1993), 44 RFL (3d) 445 at 447 (Man CA).

288   Bill C-252, *An Act to Amend the Divorce Act*, 1st Sess, 39th Parl, 2006, s 1 (in force 31 May 2007). And see *Sandercock v Croll*, 2011 MBQB 138.

289   *Keyes v Gordon* (1989), 93 NSR (2d) 383 (Fam Ct). See also *NL v RL*, 2008 NBCA 79.

290   *Clothier v Ettinger* (1989), 91 NSR (2d) 428 (Fam Ct) (compare *M(BP) v M(BLDE)* (1992), 42 RFL (3d) 349 (Ont CA)); *Powley v Wagner* (1987), 11 RFL (3d) 136 (Sask QB).

291   *Matthews v Matthews* (1988), 72 Nfld & PEIR 217 (Nfld UFC); *Wainwright v Wainwright* (1987), 10 RFL (3d) 387 (NSTD), aff'd (1988), 15 RFL (3d) 174 (NSCA), leave to appeal to SCC refused (1989), 27 RFL (3d) xxxiii (note); *Sweeney v Hartnell* (1987), 81 NSR (2d) 203 (TD).

292   *Abdo v Abdo* (1993), 50 RFL (3d) 17 (NSCA) (application to terminate access under *Family Maintenance Act*, RSNS 1989, c 160).

293   *McIsaac v Stewart* (1993), 119 NSR (2d) 102 (Fam Ct).

294   *Peters v Karr* (1994), 93 Man R (2d) 222 (QB).

A judge may set out conditions in an original order, which, if followed by the access parent, may lead to a variation allowing increased access.[295]

Although the "best interests of the child" is the governing criterion in determining whether an access order should be varied pursuant to section 17(5) of the *Divorce Act*, this criterion is imprecise, vague, and difficult to define. While a wide variety of relevant factors should be taken into account, section 17(9) of the *Divorce Act* specifically endorses the guiding principle that a child should have maximum contact with his or her divorced parents to the extent that this is compatible with the child's best interests. The risk of harm to the child, while not the ultimate legal test, is also a factor to be considered.[296] There is a presumption that regular access to the non-custodial parent is in the best interests of a child. The right of the child to have contact with and maintain an attachment to the non-custodial parent is a fundamental right that should only be judicially withheld in the most extreme and unusual circumstances.[297] A parent who seeks to reduce normal access will usually be required to provide justification for taking such a position; the greater the restriction sought, the more important it becomes to justify that restriction.[298] Terminating access is without a doubt a measure of last resort reserved for those situations where access on the evidence offers no benefit to the child.[299] Relevant caselaw provides no standard criteria for terminating access orders, but in *VSG v LJG*,[300] Blishen J, of the Ontario Superior Court of Justice, identifies the following factors as those most frequently relied upon when courts terminate an access order or, alternatively, grant an order for supervised access:

1. Long-term harassment or harmful conduct towards the custodial parent that creates fear or stress for the child.
2. A history of violence; unpredictable, uncontrollable behaviour; alcohol or drug abuse that is witnessed by the child or presents a risk to the child's safety or well-being.[301]
3. Extreme parental alienation.

295 *Sparks v Sparks* (1994), 159 AR 187 (QB).
296 *Young v Young*, [1993] 4 SCR 3 at para 210.
297 See *VSG v LJG*, [2004] OJ No 2238 at para 128 (Sup Ct), citing *Jafari v Dadar*, [1996] NBJ No 387 (QB). See also *MH v JH*, 2013 NSSC 198; *Keown v Procee*, 2014 ONSC 7314.
298 *LaPalme v Hedden*, 2012 ONSC 6758.
299 *MJT v SAT*, 2010 NBQB 268; see also *Werner v Werner*, 2013 NSCA 6 (temporary denial of access pending court-ordered psychological assessment of father).
300 [2004] OJ No 2238 at para 135 (Sup Ct); see also *FK v MK*, 2010 BCSC 563; *WLC v PT*, 2014 NLTD(F) 4; *Abdo v Abdo* (1993), 50 RFL (3d) 17 (NSCA); *Miller v McMaster*, 2005 NSSC 259; *Young v Young*, 2013 ONSC 4423.
301 See *Doncaster v Field*, 2014 NSCA 39.

4. Persistent denigration of the other parent.
5. The absence of any relationship or attachment between the child and the non-custodial parent.[302]
6. Neglect or abuse of the child during access visits.
7. The wishes or preference of an older child to terminate access.

Justice Blishen further states that when terminating or restricting access, it is necessary for the court to weigh and balance numerous factors in the context of the child's best interests, including:

1. The maximum contact principle;
2. The right of a child to know and have a relationship with each parent;
3. A limitation of a consideration of parental conduct to that conduct which impacts on the child;
4. The risk of harm: emotional, physical and sexual;
5. The nature of the relationship between the parents and its impact on the child;
6. The nature of the relationship and attachment between the access parent and the child; and,
7. The commitment of the access parent to the child.[303]

She accepts that the judicial termination of access is a remedy of last resort that should be ordered only in the most exceptional circumstances. A court must carefully consider the option of supervision prior to termination.[304] A supervision order has the potential to protect a child from the risk of harm, to foster the parent-child relationship, to ensure counselling or treatment that will improve parenting ability, to create a bridge between no relationship and a normal parenting relationship, and to avoid or reduce parental conflict and its detrimental effect on the child. "Clinical issues" involving the access parent and reintroduction of children into the life of a parent after a significant absence are factors the courts have considered in ordering supervision.[305] Supervised access orders are normally granted for a limited time; they are seldom regarded as providing a long-term solution. There may, nevertheless, be situations in which medium- or longer-term supervised access is in the child's best interests.[306] In Blishen J's opinion, supervised access,

---

302 *Jirh v Jirh*, 2014 BCSC 1973.

303 *VSG v LJG*, [2004] OJ No 2238 (Sup Ct) at para 143; see also *Malone v Allar*, 2014 BCSC 1621. And see *LAMG v CS*, 2014 BCPC 172 at para 35 wherein Woods Prov Ct J lists 15 factors relevant to orders for supervised access.

304 See also *LAMG v CS*, 2014 BCPC 172 at para 36; *BC v JC*, 2014 NBQB 59 at para 7.

305 *MAG v PLM*, 2014 BCSC 126 at para 34, Fleming J.

306 See *KME v DMZ*, [1996] BCJ No 464 (SC); *LES v MJS*, 2014 NSSC 34; *WLC v PT*, 2014 NLTD(F) 4; *Kroupa v Stoneham*, 2011 ONSC 5824; *TLMM v CAM*, 2011 SKQB 326; see also

whether of short, medium, or long duration, should always be examined as an alternative to a complete termination of the parent-child relationship, unless the viability of supervised access has been negated by past experience or by the unwillingness of the non-custodial parent to abide by court-imposed conditions relating to treatment or counselling. The burden of proof falls on the parent requesting supervised access to demonstrate that restrictions are in the best interests of the children.[307]

Concerns voiced by one of the parents about a proposed supervisor can and should be listened to as they may provide useful information to aid the court in its determination of the child's best interests, but they cannot be absolutely deferred to; no parent has a veto over choice of supervisor.[308]

M. PARENTAL CONFLICT RESOLUTION

Custody litigation is relatively rare; access litigation is more common.[309] It is generally acknowledged that litigation should be the last resort for resolving parenting disputes. It is costly, not only in terms of money, but also in terms of emotional wear and tear. Litigation is not a therapeutic catharsis for the resolution of custody and access disputes. Children pay a heavy price when their parents engage in embittered custody and access disputes that lead to warfare in the courts. If litigation can be avoided without damage to the psychological, physical, or moral well-being of the children, it should be avoided. There will be exceptional cases where allegations of psychological, physical, or sexual abuse necessitate judicial intervention. In the vast majority of cases, however, both parents are fit to continue to discharge their responsibilities to the children after marriage breakdown or divorce.

Roadblocks to shared parental responsibilities after separation or divorce are often attributable to a lack of knowledge and to the inability of parents to communicate and segregate their interpersonal hostility from their role as parents. It is for these reasons that the Law Reform Commission of Canada recommended that a mandatory family conference be held in cases involving dependent children. In its *Report on Family Law*, the Law Reform Commission of Canada recommended as follows:

Merkand v Merkand, [2006] OJ No 528 (CA); *LAMG v CS*, 2014 BCPC 172; *MAG v PLM*, 2014 BCSC 126; *Tuttle v Tuttle*, 2014 ONSC 5011; Section G(1), above in this chapter.

307 *Slawter v Bellefontaine*, 2012 NSCA 48.

308 *JPG v VSG*, 2012 BCSC 946 at paras 65–68, Maisonville J.

309 See Canada, Department of Justice, *Evaluation of the* Divorce Act, *Phase II: Monitoring and Evaluation* (May 1990) at 61 and 110–15. See also Bruce Ziff, "Recent Developments in Canadian Law: Marriage and Divorce" (1990) 22 Ottawa L Rev 139 at 211–13.

3. Whenever children over whom the court has jurisdiction in dissolu-
    tion proceedings are involved, the law should require that there be an
    immediate informal meeting of the parties — an "assessment confer-
    ence" — before the court, a court officer, a support staff person or a
    community-based service or facility designated by the court, for the
    following purposes:

    (a) to ascertain whether the spouses have made appropriate arrange-
         ments respecting the care, custody and upbringing of the children
         during the dissolution process, and if not, to ascertain whether
         such arrangements can be agreed to by the spouses;

    (b) to ascertain whether the appointment of legal representation for
         children is indicated;

    (c) to ascertain whether a formal investigative report by a public au-
         thority (e.g. an Official Guardian or Superintendent of Child Wel-
         fare) is indicated;

    (d) to ascertain whether a mandatory psychiatric or psychological as-
         sessment of the situation is indicated;

    (e) to acquaint the husband and wife with the availability of persons,
         services and facilities in the court or the community to assist
         them in negotiating temporary arrangements respecting children
         during the dissolution process as well as permanent arrange-
         ments applicable on dissolution;

    (f) to enable the court to ascertain the need for, and where necessary
         to order the further appearance of the husband and wife before
         the court or a person, service or facility designated by the court to
         engage in one or more sessions of mandatory negotiation respect-
         ing the children; and

    (g) generally to help the husband and wife, where possible, to avoid
         contested temporary or permanent custody proceedings through
         negotiation and agreement, and otherwise to avoid bringing mat-
         ters involving the children before the court for adjudication.[310]

Although these proposals are confined to divorce, they are equally adaptable to proceedings for custody and access under provincial and territorial
legislation. If we accept that children are entitled to enjoy the benefits and
contributions of both of their parents, notwithstanding separation or divorce, the accessibility of relevant information would appear to be a vital
first step on the road towards the sharing of continued parental privileges
and responsibilities after separation.

---

310 Law Reform Commission of Canada, *Report on Family Law* (Ottawa: Information
     Canada, 1976) at 64–65.

N. VOICE OF THE CHILD[311]

Statutes in several provinces stipulate that the wishes of a child are a relevant factor to be considered in determining the best interests of a child in contested custody or access proceedings. Although there is no explicit provision to this effect in the *Divorce Act*, judicial practice has long acknowledged the relevance of an older child's wishes in custody and access proceedings arising under that Act. The best interests of a child are not to be confused with the wishes of the child, but a child's views and preferences fall within the parameters of a child's best interests.[312] When children are under nine years of age, courts have not usually placed much, if any, reliance on their expressed preference.[313] The wishes of children aged ten to thirteen have commonly been treated as an important but not a decisive factor. The wishes of the children increase in significance as they grow older and courts have openly recognized the futility of ignoring the wishes of children over the age of fourteen years.[314] Possibly because of the impact of the *United Nations Convention on the Rights of the Child*, Canadian courts appear to be placing more emphasis on children having a voice in contested custody/access proceedings.[315] In some recent cases, the views and preferences of children under the age of nine have been sought but there is no indication that the weight to be given to such a young child's opinion is any greater than it has been hitherto.[316] In an era of self-represented litigants and costly expert input, using age cut-offs to signify the weight to be given to a child's preference is a rough and ready tool that reflects past judicial decisions; it does not, of course, foreclose the need to look beyond the child's age. Caselaw in Canada demonstrates

---

311 See Rachel Birnbaum, *The Voice of the Child in Separation/Divorce Mediation and Other Alternative Dispute Resolution Processes: A Literature Review* (Ottawa: Department of Justice, Canada, 2009). And see Chapter 12, Part E (3).

312 *New Brunswick (Minister of Social Development) v SMJA*, 2015 NBQB 49; *Bhardwaj v Kaur*, 2014 ONSC 1163; *Knudsen v Knudsen*, 2013 SKQB 216.

313 *New Brunswick (Minister of Social Development) v SMJA*, 2015 NBQB 49.

314 See, generally, *DME v RDE*, 2015 ABQB 47; *O'Connell v McIndoe* (1998), 56 BCLR (3d) 292 (CA); *McArthur v McArthur*, 2012 BCSC 717; *Druwe v Schilling*, 2010 MBQB 75; *ADE v MJM*, 2012 NBQB 260; *FFR v KF*, 2013 NLCA 8 (limited weight given to wishes of seven-year-old child); *Parent v MacDougall*, 2014 NSCA 3; *Kincl v Malkova*, 2008 ONCA 524; *Fraser v Logan*, 2013 ONCA 93 (access); *Bhardwaj v Kaur*, 2014 ONSC 1163; *Droit de la famille — 07832*, [2007] RDF 250 (Que CA); *Bromm v Bromm*, 2010 SKCA 149; compare *Sandercock v Croll*, 2011 MBQB 138; *CD v KD*, 2010 NBQB 22; *Salem v Kourany*, 2012 ONCA 102; *Demong v Demong*, 2014 SKQB 170, citing *McGinn v McGinn*, 2006 SKQB 105 at para 12; *GWC v YDC*, 2012 YKSC 8.

315 See *RM v JS*, 2013 ABCA 441; *BJE v DLG*, 2010 YKSC 33; *Bhajan v Bhajan and The Children's Lawyer*, 2010 ONCA 714.

316 See, for example, *FFR v KF*, 2013 NLCA 8; *Parent v MacDougall*, 2014 NSCA 3.

that the significance of a child's wishes will depend on a number of factors, including the child's age, intelligence, maturity, the ability of the child to articulate a view, and any improper influence of either parent.[317] The court must look to the child's capacity to understand and appreciate the relevant and significant issues involved in making a wise, informed, reasoned, and responsible choice.[318] In *Decaen v Decaen*, the Ontario Court of Appeal stated:

> In assessing the significance of a child's wishes, the following are relevant: (i) whether both parents are able to provide adequate care; (ii) how clear and unambivalent the wishes are; (iii) how informed the expression is; (iv) the age of the child; (v) the maturity level; (vi) the strength of the wish; (vii) the length of time the preference has been expressed for; (viii) practicalities; (ix) the influence of the parent(s) on the expressed wish or preference; (x) the overall context; and (xi) the circumstances of the preferences from the child's point of view: See Bala, Nicholas; Talwar, Victoria; Harris, Joanna, "The Voice of Children in Canadian Family Law Cases", (2005), 24 C.F.L.Q. 221.[319]

It is unusual for a court to grant any order for custody after a child reaches the age of sixteen years.[320] However, in accordance with the definition of "child of the marriage" in section 2(1) of the *Divorce Act*, a court has jurisdiction under section 16 of the *Divorce Act* to grant an order for custody of or access to an adult child who is mentally or physically disabled.[321]

Where the central factual issue to be determined in the contested custody and access proceeding is whether it is the adult child himself or his mother who is effectively preventing the father from visiting the child, the court may

---

317   *SLT v AKT*, 2009 ABQB 13; *LEG v AG*, [2002] BCJ No 2319 (SC); *PB v CJ*, 2008 NBQB 375; *Poole v Poole*, [2005] NSJ No 68 (QB); *Hill v Hill*, [2008] OJ No 4730 (Sup Ct); *Kittelson-Schurr v Schurr*, [2005] SJ No 111 (QB); *CLP v RT*, [2009] SJ No 346 (QB).

318   *RM v JS*, 2013 ABCA 441 at para 25, citing *MLE v JCE (No 2)*, 2005 ONCJ 89 at paras 12–13; *Perino v Perino*, 2012 ONSC 328 (child with cognitive impairment); *Klingler v Klingler*, [1994] SJ No 620 (QB).

319   2013 ONCA 218 at para 42. And see *Abbott v Meadus*, 2014 NBQB 18 at para 70. See also RJ Williams, "If Wishes Were Horses Then Beggars Would Ride" (Paper presented at the National Judicial Institute, Family Law Program, Halifax, February 1999); Elizabeth Jollimore and Linda Tippett-Leary, "Voice of the Child in Court Proceedings," online: www.justice.gc.ca/eng/fl-df/spousal-epoux/topic-theme/voi3.html.

320   *MacKinnon v Harrison*, 2011 ABCA 283; *O'Connell v McIndoe* (1998), 56 BCLR (3d) 292 (CA); *JS v AB*, 2010 NBQB 429; *Kincl v Malkova*, 2008 ONCA 524; *Gharabegian v McKinney*, [2008] OJ No 5307 (Sup Ct) (access); *McBride v McBride*, 2013 ONSC 938; *Feist v Feist*, [2007] SJ No 722 (QB). Compare *TM v DM*, 2014 NBQB 132 (order granted for joint custody of eighteen-year-old child, with day to day care to the father, so as to avoid any uncertainty over any possible tax credits); *SGB v SJL*, 2010 ONCA 578.

321   *Perino v Perino*, 2012 ONSC 328.

order a medical examination of the child under Rule 30 of the *British Colum-bia Rules of Court* or appoint an independent expert under Rule 32A to inquire into and report on the facts.[322] While caselaw generally supports placing a great deal of weight on the views and preferences of children over twelve, in cases of parental alienation where one parent has undermined the child's relationship with the other parent, the child's views may not be seen as his or her own.[323] In the most serious cases of parental alienation, however, remedial options become increasingly limited once the child becomes a teenager.[324] A distinction can be drawn between a custody order that runs counter to a child's wishes and an access order that does the same. Absent evidence of harm, or the potential for harm or risk to a child if access is ordered, there is no compelling reason for a court to simply default to a child's wishes and the potential difficulty involved in enforcing an order.[325]

Although the child is the focal point of all disputed custody and access proceedings, the question arises as to who speaks for the child.[326] Even though judges apply the "best interests of the child" as the determinative criterion of custody and access disputes, the role of independent arbiter precludes a trial judge from acting as an advocate for the child. How, then, can the child's interests be protected? In some provinces, courts have exercised a discretionary jurisdiction to appoint an independent lawyer to represent the child in contested custody proceedings.[327] However, such appointments are exceptional and children are rarely represented by independent lawyers in settlement negotiations, and their voices may go unheard if mediation[328] is used as a means of resolving parenting disputes. In contested proceedings,

322 *Ross v Ross*, [2004] BCJ No 446 (CA). Compare *Perino v Perino*, 2012 ONSC 328.

323 *Letourneau v Letourneau*, 2014 ABCA 156; *VMB v KRB*, 2014 ABCA 334; *IMMS v DJS*, 2010 BCSC 306; *LDK v MAK*, 2015 BCSC 226; *FFR v KF*, 2013 NLCA 8; *NS v CN*, 2013 ONSC 556; *Fiorito v Wiggins*, 2014 ONCA 603; compare *SGB v SJL*, 2010 ONCA 578; *Grindley v Grindley*, 2012 ONSC 4538.

324 *LG v RG*, 2012 BCSC 1365.

325 *Corey v Corey*, 2010 NBQB 112 at paras 38–39, Wooder J; see also *Zaidi v Qizilbash*, 2014 ONSC 201 at paras 156–159.

326 See Christine Davies, "Access to Justice for Children: The Voice of the Child in Custody and Access Disputes" (2004) 22 Can Fam LQ 153.

327 For examples of provincial legislation that expressly provide for independent representation of children, see, Quebec *Code of Civil Procedure*, RSQ c C-25, art 394.1 (appointment of attorney to represent child); *Children's Act*, RSY 1986, c 22, s 167 (Official Guardian has exclusive right to determine whether any child requires independent representation); see also *Kalaserk v Nelson*, [2005] NWTJ No 3 (SC); and see, generally, *Payne's Divorce and Family Law Digest* (Don Mills, ON: Richard De Boo, 1982–93) tab 22.39 "Legal Representation of Child; *Amicus Curiae*."

328 See Bob Simpson, "The *Children Act* (England) 1989 and the Voice of the Child in Family Conciliation" (1991) 29 Family and Conciliation Courts Review 385.

some judges will interview the children privately to ascertain their wishes; other judges are averse to this practice.[329]

In *NL v RL*,[330] the New Brunswick Court of Appeal held that the trial judge made no palpable and overriding error by gleaning the child's views and preferences from a social worker's report instead of directly interviewing the child. In its opinion, since the mother had succeeded in alienating the child from her father, no purpose would be served by interviewing the child who would, no doubt, favour the mother.

In *BJG v DLG*,[331] at a hearing to consider applications by the father and mother of a twelve-year-old child to vary existing custody and child support orders granted pursuant to the *Divorce Act*, Martinson J, of the Yukon Territory Supreme Court, observed that the evidence relating to the child's custody did not include any information about the child's views, and she requested submissions from counsel on the issue of whether the court should hear from the child. After hearing from counsel, she determined that federal, provincial, and territorial legislation relating to child custody should be interpreted to reflect the values and principles found in the United Nations *Convention on the Rights of the Child*,[332] which was ratified by Canada, with the support of the provinces and territories, in 1991. Looking to the "best interests of the child" test in section 16(8) of the *Divorce Act* and to section 30(1)(c) of the *Children's Law Act*,[333] which requires a court to consider the views and preferences of a child, if they can be reasonably ascertained, Martinson J concluded that these statutory provisions should be interpreted to reflect the Convention's key premise that hearing from children is in their best interests. She placed particular reliance on Article 12 of the Convention, which specifically provides as follows:

1. State Parties shall assure to the child who is capable of forming his or her own views the right to express those views freely in all matters affecting the child, the views of the child being given due weight in accordance with the age and maturity of the child.

2. For this purpose, the child shall in particular be provided the opportunity to be heard in any judicial and administrative proceedings affecting the child, either directly, or through a representative or an

---

329 See Chapter 12, Section E.

330 2008 NBCA 79.

331 2010 YKSC 33; see also *NJK v RWF*, 2011 BCSC 1666; *MAS v JSS*, 2012 NBQB 285; *Libke v Sunley*, 2013 SKQB 109. Compare the more conservative stance of the Ontario Court of Appeal in *Bhajan v Bhajan and The Children's Lawyer*, 2010 ONCA 714, discussed in Chapter 12, Section E(3)(d).

332 Can TS 1992 No 3.

333 RSY 2001, c 31.

appropriate body, in a manner consistent with the procedural rules of national law.

She observed that there is no ambiguity in the language of the Convention. Pursuant to its provisions, *all* children capable of forming their own views have the legal right to be heard, without discrimination. No exception is made for high-conflict cases that may involve domestic violence and/or parental alienation. Decision makers have no discretion to disregard the legal rights conferred by Article 12 of the Convention because of the particular circumstances of the case or because of the view the decision maker may hold about children's participation. Legitimate concerns about hearing from children, particularly in complex cases such as those involving high conflict, domestic violence, or parental alienation, can be accommodated within the flexible legal framework provided by the Convention. This flexibility is manifested in the following contexts:

1) Children have the legal right to express their views, but they are not under any legal obligation to do so. They can choose not to participate.

2) There must be a determination of whether the child is capable of forming his or her own views before the child has the legal right to express them. In some parental alienation cases, the alienating conduct of a parent may render the child incapable of forming his or her own views.

3) Decision makers can deal with all of the circumstances of the case in determining the weight to be given to the child's views.

4) The views of the child may cover a wide variety of issues as distinct from a stated preference for either parent.[334]

5) Last but not least, there are many different ways of obtaining the child's views, depending on the family circumstances and the age and maturity of the child.[335] The appropriate method does not have to be intrusive or insensitive to the child's needs. Evidence can be presented by the child in person, in writing, or by videotape. But see *Gagné v Gagné*,[336] wherein a sealed letter from a ten-year-old child was deemed inadmissible because it was not under oath and there was no cross-examination, and the trial judge was, therefore, unable "to explore testimonial factors regarding the letter and its contents: memory, perception and sincerity." Evidence can also be proffered by a parent, by a lawyer,[337] or by a representative of the child. A neutral third party may be appointed by the court to ascertain

---

334 *MAS v JSS*, 2012 NBQB 285.

335 *NJK v RWF*, 2011 BCSC 1666 at para 204.

336 2010 ABQB 711 at paras 23–26, WA Tilleman J.

337 *Hackett v Leung*, 2010 ONSC 6412 (children given an opportunity to voice their views through the Office of the Children's Lawyer).

the child's views, or the child may be interviewed by the judge in chambers.[338] Justice Martinson urges Canadian judges to avoid token recognition of the United Nations *Convention on the Rights of the Child*. She states:

47 More than just lip service must be paid to children's legal rights to be heard. Because of the importance of children's participation to the quality of the decision and to their short and long term best interests, the participation must be meaningful; children should:

1. be informed, at the beginning of the process, of their legal rights to be heard;

2. be given the opportunity to fully participate early and throughout the process, including being involved in judicial family case conferences, settlement conferences, and court hearings or trials;

3. have a say in the manner in which they participate so that they do so in a way that works effectively for them;

4. have their views considered in a substantive way; and

5. be informed of both the result reached and the way in which their views have been taken into account

As stated in her judgment, "[a]n inquiry should be made in each case, and at the start of the process, to determine whether the child is capable of forming his or her own views, and if so, whether the child wishes to participate. If the child does wish to participate then there must be a determination of the method by which the child will participate."[339]

Applying the aforementioned legal criteria to the facts of the case, Martinson J observed that the existing consent order for custody reflected the wishes of the twelve-year-old child for alternating weekly custody, and the child had not manifested any desire for a change and apparently wanted to avoid getting caught in the middle of what, in essence, was a dispute between the parents about the amount of child support to be paid. As Martinson J ultimately decided,[340] the father's application to vary the custody arrangement was motivated by financial considerations, rather than by a genuine concern for the child's best interests; he was simply following through on threats he had previously made to apply for custody, if the mother pursued her application for increased child support.

There is little doubt that the voice of the child in contested custody/access proceedings will be louder in the future than it has been in the past. This is

---

338   See, generally, Alfred A Mamo & Joanna ER Harris, "Children's Evidence" in Harold Niman & Anita Volikis, eds, *Evidence in Family Law*, loose-leaf (Aurora, ON: Canada Law Book, 2010–) c 4 at 4–16 (July 2010).

339   *BJG v DLG*, 2010 YKSC 44 at para 6.

340   See *BJG v DLG*, 2010 YKSC 33.

apparent from the judgment of the Supreme Court of Canada in *AC v Manitoba (Director of Child and Family Services)*,[341] which pertains to court orders for medical and surgical treatment, wherein Abella J stated:

> [92] …With our evolving understanding has come the recognition that the quality of decision making about a child is enhanced by input from that child. The extent to which that input affects the "best interests" assessment is as variable as the child's circumstances, but one thing that can be said with certainty is that the input becomes increasingly determinative as the child matures. This is true not only when considering the child's best interests in the placement context, but also when deciding whether to accede to a child's wishes in medical treatment situations.
>
> [93] Such a robust conception of the "best interests of the child" standard is also consistent with international instruments to which Canada is a signatory. The *Convention on the Rights of the Child*, Can. T.S. 1992 No. 3, which Canada signed on May 28, 1990 and ratified on December 13, 1991, describes "the best interests of the child" as a primary consideration in all actions concerning children (Article 3). It then sets out a framework under which the child's own input will inform the content of the "best interests" standard, with the weight accorded to these views increasing in relation to the child's developing maturity. Articles 5 and 14 of the Convention, for example, require State Parties to respect the responsibilities, rights and duties of parents to provide direction to the child in exercising his or her rights under the Convention, "in a manner consistent with the evolving capacities of the child". Similarly, Article 12 requires State Parties to "assure to the child who is capable of forming his or her own views the right to express those views freely in all matters affecting the child, the <u>views of the child being given due weight in accordance with the age and maturity of the child</u>" (see also the Council of Europe's *Convention for the Protection of Human Rights and Dignity of the Human Being with Regard to the Application of Biology and Medicine: Convention on Human Rights and Biomedicine*, Eur. T.S. No. 164, c II, art. 6: "The opinion of the minor shall be taken into consideration as an increasingly determining factor in proportion to his or her age and degree of maturity.")

However, some of the methods for ascertaining the views of a child in disputed custody and access cases, particularly court-ordered assessments and independent legal representation for the child, are costly. Since provincial/territorial governments are unlikely to approve new major financial expenditures, judicial interviews are likely to occupy a more prominent role

---

341 2009 SCC 30 [emphasis in original].

in the determination of a child's views and preferences in the future. But this will require additional funding to be allocated to judicial educational programs relating to child development and interviewing and, even with such programs, some judges may conclude that they lack the necessary skills to properly interview a child.[342]

O. PARENTING PLANS

When economic disputes arise on separation or divorce, lawyers and courts insist on full financial disclosure as a condition precedent to resolving issues relating to property division and spousal or child support. The need for access to all relevant and available information is no less compelling when custody and access disputes arise. All too easily, however, the interests of children can be overlooked in custody and access litigation as parents engage in forensic combat for the purpose of ventilating their personal hostilities. Although it is generally acknowledged that separation and divorce sever the marital bond but should not sever parent-child bonds, adversarial conflict on marriage breakdown can present major obstacles to a meaningful relationship being preserved between children and a non-custodial parent.

The difficulty faced by a court when embittered spouses engage in custody litigation was exposed in the dissenting judgment of Bayda JA, of the Saskatchewan Court of Appeal, in *Wakaluk v Wakaluk*.[343] He stated:

> From the standpoint of custody the hearing of the petition was, in my respectful view, quite unsatisfactory. Virtually no evidence was directed to this issue. The parties primarily concerned themselves with adducing evidence to show whether, on the basis of the many marital battles engaged in by them, one or the other of them should be favoured by the trial judge in his determination of the issue of cruelty.
>
> No one bothered to bring forward much information in respect of the two individuals who of all the persons likely to be affected by these

---

342 For relevant commentary on the United Nations *Convention on the Rights of the Child* in particular, and on the voice of the child generally, see the following articles which are published by the Department of Justice, Canada, online: www.justice.gc.ca/eng/fl-df/index.html: Jean-François Nöel (with comments by Elizabeth Jollimore, QC), "The *Convention on the Rights of the Child*"; Linda Tippett-Leary (with comments by Elizabeth Jollimore, QC), "The Voice of the Child in Court Proceedings"; and Public Health Agency of Canada, "A Child's Age and Stage of Development Make a Difference," extracted from *Because Life Goes On . . . Helping Children and Youth Live With Separation and Divorce* (Ottawa: Health Canada, 1994). See also *Schamber v Schamber*, 2011 ABQB 473 (judicial interview of seven-year-old child); *Zaidi v Qizilbash*, 2014 ONSC 201 at para 132.
343 (1977), 25 RFL 292 (Sask CA); see also *EZ v MJ*, 2013 ONSC 606 at para 66.

proceedings least deserve to be ignored — the children. We know their names, sex and ages, but little else. Of what intelligence are they? What are their likes? Dislikes? Do they have any special inclinations (for the arts, sports or the like) that should be nurtured? Any handicaps? Do they show signs of anxiety? What are their personalities? Characters? What is the health of each? (This list of questions is not intended as exhaustive or as one that is applicable to all contested cases but only as illustrative of those questions which may be relevant.) In short, no evidence was led to establish the intellectual, moral, emotional and physical needs of each child. Apart from the speculation that these children are "ordinary" (whatever that means) there is nothing on which to base a reasoned objective conclusion as to what must be done for this child and that child, as individuals and not as mere members of general class, in order that the welfare and happiness of each may be assured and enhanced.

Nor was any direct evidence led to show which of the parents, by reason of training, disposition, character, personality, experience, identification with a child's pursuits, ability to cope with any special requirements of a child's health, religious observance and such other pertinent factors (again the list is intended as only illustrative of matters which may be relevant), is best equipped to meet the needs of each individual child. The evidence presented on behalf of each side was principally, if not exclusively, geared to do one thing: show how badly one spouse treated the other. Such evidence is hardly a proper basis upon which to make a determination — a crucial one indeed from the standpoint of the children — as to which parent is best suited to meet the needs of the children and upon which to found an order for custody. How inconsiderate one spouse is of the other, or how one spouse reacts towards the other in a marital battle and the ability of a spouse to come out of a marital battle a winner, either actual or moral, are not high-ranking factors, if factors they be at all, in determining where a child's happiness and welfare lie, particularly whether such happiness and welfare are better assured by placement with one parent or the other.

. . .

The welfare of the children dictates that a new trial be held, restricted to the issue of custody, and I would direct an order accordingly.[344]

Although spousal misconduct may sometimes provide insight into parenting capacity, it may also be put forward for ulterior motives that have nothing to do with the welfare of the child. The threat of mudslinging litigation can usually be avoided, however, unless both counsel pursue such a

---

344 *Wakaluk v Wakaluk* (1977), 25 RFL 292 (Sask CA) at 299–300 and 306.

course of action. An astute counsel for either spouse may avoid allegations of blame and fault by focusing pleadings, evidence, and submissions on the past parent-child relationship and on future plans for the care and upbringing of the child. In the words of Boisvert J, of the New Brunswick Queen's Bench,

> Spousal censure, or condemnation, has no place in custody disputes, unless it is directly and unmistakably linked with the disablement of one parent to answer to the children's best interests. A cogent and positive proposal aimed at sound child management, will, in most instances, lay by the heels arguments founded mainly on blame and accusations.[345]

It is ironic that judicial proceedings between spouses that involve matrimonial property and spousal and child support require sworn financial statements to be filed, yet no requirement is imposed in custody proceedings for the disputants to file detailed information concerning the children whose future is at risk. We hardly serve our children well when we insist on mandatory financial statements in spousal economic disputes, but in custody disputes, require no specific information respecting the personality, character, and attributes of the child and the ability of the disputants to contribute to the child's growth and development.

What is needed on separation or divorce is a perspective based on past family history and prospective parenting plans that can accommodate the different contributions that each parent can make towards the upbringing of the child.[346] There is no reason why separated and divorced parents should not be required to submit a detailed plan concerning their past and future parenting privileges and responsibilities. Such parenting plans should also take account of the contribution to the child's growth and development that has been and may continue to be made by members of the extended families, and especially the maternal and paternal grandparents.

Parenting plans will not eliminate hostile negotiations and protracted litigation by parents who are intent on battling through lawyers and the courts. What they can do, however, is shift the focus of attention to the child.

---

345   *Pare v Pare* (1987), 78 NBR (2d) 10 (QB).

346   See Julien D Payne & Kenneth L Kallish, "The Welfare or Best Interests of the Child: Substantive Criteria to Be Applied in Custody Dispositions Made Pursuant to the *Divorce Act*, RSC 1970, c D-8" in *Payne's Divorce and Family Law Digest* (Don Mills, ON: R De Boo, 1982–93) 1983 tab at 83-1201/1253, especially 83-1239/1243, and Essays tab, E-177 at 184–85. See also Julien D Payne, "The Dichotomy between Family Law and Family Crises on Marriage Breakdown" (1989) 20 RGD 109 at 121. For details concerning the use of parenting plans in the state of Washington, see Canada, Department of Justice, *Parents Forever: Making the Concept a Reality for Divorcing Parents and Their Children* by Judith P Ryan (31 March 1989) at 44–95. Compare *Children's Law Reform Act*, RSO 1990, c C.12, s 21, as amended by *Family Statute Law Amendment Act*, SO 2009, c 11, s 6.

Although parenting plans are not required to be filed in custody litigation, there is nothing to prevent parents from formulating such plans regardless of whether litigation is contemplated. Parenting plans can serve a useful purpose in assisting both parents to make appropriate arrangements for the upbringing of their children. Such plans can specifically define the contributions to be made by each parent and by third parties in the day-to-day and long-term upbringing of the children.

In December 1998, a Special Joint Committee of the Senate and House of Commons published its report entitled "For the Sake of the Children," which proposed abandonment of the terminology of custody and access in favour of the concept of "shared parenting."[347] This recommendation constitutes one of forty-eight specific proposals for changes in the law and in the processes for resolving parenting disputes. Although a few Canadian courts have endorsed the abandonment of legal jargon,[348] most lawyers and judges still speak in terms of "custody" and "access" rather than in the everyday language of "shared parenting" in its various forms. It is interesting to observe, however, that legislative changes in England[349] have abandoned the terminology of "custody" and "access" and substituted the notion of "shared parental responsibilities" as well as minimal judicial intervention.[350]

P. THIRD PARTIES

In divorce proceedings between the parents of a child, leave to apply for custody under section 16(3) of the *Divorce Act* may be granted to non-parents whose claim is not frivolous or vexatious. The onus of proving that the claim is frivolous or vexatious falls on the party opposing the application. Maternal grandparents with whom the child had been living may be added as third parties to a divorce proceeding between the child's parents, both of whom were opposed to the leave application.[351]

---

347 See Rachel Birnbaum *et al*, "Shared Parenting Is the New Norm: Legal Professionals Agree on the Need for Reform" *The Family Way* – The CBA National Family Law Section Newsletter (October 2014).

348 See *Abbott v Taylor* (1986), 2 RFL (3d) 163 (Man CA); *Lennox v Frender* (1990), 27 RFL (3d) 181 at 185–87 (BCCA); *Harsant v Portnoi* (1990), 27 RFL (3d) 216 (Ont HCJ).

349 *Children Act 1989* (UK), 1989, c 41.

350 See Janet Walker, "From Rights to Responsibilities for Parents: Old Dilemmas, New Solutions" (1991) 29 Family and Conciliation Courts Review 361. See also Andrew Bainham, "The *Children Act 1989*: Welfare and Non-Interventionism" [1990] Fam Law 143. And see *Family Law Act*, SA 2003, c F-4.5; *Family Law Act*, SBC 2011, c 25.

351 *Boychuk v Boychuk*, [2001] AJ No 1578 (QB). See Chapter 12, Section E(6).

Q. PROCESS

The *Divorce Act* is primarily concerned with the substantive rights and obligations of divorcing and divorced spouses and parents. Matters relating to evidence and procedure are primarily regulated by provincial and territorial legislation and rules of court. Only a few aspects of the divorce process are regulated by the *Divorce Act*. They include the statutory duties of lawyers and the courts respecting reconciliation and the duties of lawyers to promote the use of negotiation and mediation in resolving custody and access disputes.[352]

The definition of "court" in subsection 2(1) of the *Divorce Act* signifies that divorce is a matter that must be adjudicated by courts presided over by federally appointed judges. Provincially appointed judges have no jurisdiction to deal with divorce, although they have power to enforce orders for support or custody that have been granted in divorce proceedings.

The *Divorce Act* does not require that a divorce petition be tried in open court. Many provinces and territories have introduced so-called "desktop" uncontested divorces where the spouses do not personally appear in court. Instead, the relevant evidence is presented by way of affidavits.

The current *Divorce Act* introduced the innovative procedure of joint petitions for divorce and joint applications for support, custody, and access.[353] Joint petitions are only appropriate when the spouses are in agreement and there are no hotly contested issues. As stated previously, third parties, such as grandparents or other relatives, may be permitted to intervene in divorce proceedings for the purpose of pursuing claims for custody of or access to the children of the marriage.

R. HIGH CONFLICT: PARENTAL ALIENATION

Legal and mental health professionals are in general agreement that high-conflict parenting disputes, especially those involving parental alienation, require constructive institutional responses to ensure early intervention and assessment, the management of ongoing disputes by a single judge, and the

---

352 See Chapter 6, Section D.

353 *Divorce Act*, RSC 1985 (2d Supp), c 3, s 8(1) (divorce), ss 15.1(1) and 15.2(1) (support), s 16(2) (custody and access), and s 17(1) (variation proceedings).

expedition of any trial.[354] The Alberta Court of Appeal in *VMB v KRB*[355] has stated that section 16(10) of the *Divorce Act* makes parental alienation a relevant consideration in high conflict custody disputes and "[t]here is no rule of law that a finding of alienation can only be made based on expert evidence." It must be recognized, however, that the adversarial litigation system provides a forum that is ill-equipped to ensure the counselling that is so frequently necessary to address the deep-rooted and ingrained levels of distrust and animosity that exists between the parents. As Germain J, of the Alberta Court of Queen's Bench, has observed, "[b]adly needed court resources are committed to proceedings where the opportunity to create meaningful, responsive, and useful solutions is very limited, as there is no ability on the part of the courts to collect and gather evidence, or order the expenditure of state resources to assist the family in chronic distress.[356]

A finding that a custodial parent is guilty of parental alienation does not predetermine any one particular judicial remedy.[357] The law provides a veritable arsenal of sanctions that can be imposed to deter custodial and non-custodial parents from engaging in parental alienation. They include injunctions to restrain vexatious litigants, imprisonment,[358] fines and financial penalties for civil contempt,[359] costs against recalcitrant parents, and, depending on which parent is at fault, orders for a change of custody or for supervised access. Each of these sanctions may be found wanting. Judicial restraints on vexatious litigants do not preclude ongoing parental warfare outside the courtroom. Imprisonment may deprive the children of their primary caregiving parent, although this deprivation may be mitigated in some cases by the strategic use of intermittent periods of imprisonment while the non-custodial parent exercises court-ordered access, including compensatory

---

354 See *AA v SNA*, 2009 BCSC 387; *TLLL v JJL*, 2009 MBQB 148; *CM v DJL*, 2012 NBQB 188; *AJD v EED*, 2009 NLUFC 17; *Baker-Warren v Denault*, 2009 NSSC 59; *NS v CN*, 2013 ONSC 556. See also ABA Centre on Children and the Law, *High-Conflict Custody Cases: Reforming the System for Children* (2001) 34:4 Fam LQ 589; Canada, Department of Justice, *High-Conflict Separation and Divorce: Options for Consideration*, background paper 2004-FCY-1E by Glenn A Gilmour, online: www.justice.gc.ca/eng/rp-pr/fl-lf/divorce/2004_1/index.html. And see the Family Courts Review, January 2010 wherein several relevant articles are published by American and Canadian authors.

355 2014 ABCA 334 at para 16.

356 See *PMEL v BJL*, 2013 ABQB 227 at paras 31–33.

357 *LG v RG*, 2012 BCSC 1365 at para 220.

358 See Carr-Carey v Carey, 2014 ONSC 6764 (order for conditional sentence to be served in the community).

359 For a useful review of relevant caselaw exemplifying the diverse sanctions available for the wilful disobedience of a custody or access order, see *Rogers v Rogers*, 2008 MBQB 131 at paras 110–14, Little J. As to the essential elements of civil contempt, see *Godin v Godin*, 2012 NSCA 54.

access to the children. Orders for fines, financial penalties, and costs may operate to the economic prejudice of the children. A change of custody may not reflect the best interests of the children.

Supervised access is more appropriate as a temporary measure, rather than a permanent solution, to ongoing parental conflict. The need for parental and child counselling is often beyond dispute. However, the jurisdiction of a court to order parents to undergo counselling is perhaps open to question,[360] although a parent's rejection of a judicial recommendation for counselling may warrant an adverse inference being drawn. Recognition of the limitations of the law in responding to high-conflict parental disputes, including parental alienation, invites therapeutic intervention, which may include attendance at a family reunification program.[361] A court cannot take judicial notice of parental alienation. It requires expert evidence to inform any decisions that it might make based on allegations of parental alienation; the court cannot merely consult articles proposed by one of the litigants, or, even less, articles that the court itself may find on the Internet or elsewhere.[362] An insightful review of the indicia of parental alienation and possible options available to the court and their short-term and long-term risks and benefits for the child is provided in the judgment of MacPherson J, of the Ontario Superior Court of Justice, in *WC v CE*,[363] wherein heavy reliance was placed on the testimony of Dr Barbara Jo Fidler, an expert in the field of parental alienation and reunification therapy. Justice MacPherson states:

> 169 As confirmed by Dr. Fidler, each case of alienation must be considered on its own particular facts. In determining the appropriate remedy there must be a balancing of both the short term and long term risks and benefits which take into consideration the needs of this particular child. It is also necessary to consider the specific and multiple factors that have contributed to the situation.

---

360 See *Kaplanis v Kaplanis*, [2005] OJ No 275 (CA); see also Section F, above in this chapter. Compare *Bruno v Keinick*, 2012 NSSC 336.

361 See *Stanners v Alexandre*, 2014 ABQB 253; *JCW v JKRW*, 2014 BCSC 488; *LDK v MAK*, 2015 BCSC 226; *NRG v GRG*, 2015 BCSC 1062; *Frescura v Castellani*, 2015 BCSC 1089; *JKL v NCS* (2008), 54 RFL (6th) 74 (Ont Sup Ct); *Huckerby v Paquet*, [2014] SJ No 791. Compare *PAR v MLR*, 2011 ABQB 246; *BSM v JIM*, 2009 BCSC 477. And see *Fiorito v Wiggins*, 2011 ONSC 1868, subsequent proceedings, *AF v JW*, 2013 ONSC 4272; *JDL v RJJL*, 2012 NBQB 378. See also Joan B Kelly, "Commentary on 'Family Bridges: Using Insights from Social Science to Reconnect Parents and Alienated Children'" (Warshak, 2010)" (2010) 48:1 Fam Ct Rev 81.

362 See *SLT v AKT*, 2009 ABQB 13, wherein several articles were cited but a bilateral assessment was deemed necessary. Compare *NDL v MSL*, 2010 NSSC 68; see also *LG v RG*, 2012 BCSC 1365.

363 2010 ONSC 3575; see also *LDW v KDM*, 2011 ABQB 384; *RQ v MBW*, 2014 NLTD(F) 29.

CHAPTER 11

Appeals

A. DEFINITION OF "APPELLATE COURT"

Section 2(1) of the *Divorce Act* provides that "'appellate court,' in respect of an appeal from a court, means the court exercising appellate jurisdiction with respect to that appeal." This definition is relevant to the operation of sections 21 and 25(3) of the Act. An examination of the aforementioned provisions indicates that the determination of the appropriate appellate court and the procedure applicable on appeals has been delegated to the provinces.[1] Although section 96 of the *Constitution Act, 1867* binds both the Parliament of Canada and the provincial legislatures and precludes any appellate jurisdiction in divorce proceedings being exercised by tribunals other than those presided over by federally appointed judges, some flexibility exists for the provinces to select the appropriate appellate court in exercising their legislative jurisdiction over the administration of justice. The composition of the appellate court could also vary according to whether the appeal is in respect of an interim order or a permanent order for corollary relief.

B. GENERAL OBSERVATIONS

Section 21(1) of the *Divorce Act* confers a general right to appeal from any judgment or order, whether final or interim, made pursuant to the Act. Sections 21(2), (3) and (4), however, impose restrictions on the right of appeal, which vary according to whether the appeal relates to the judgment *qua*

---

1   As to the provincial power of a trial judge to reserve or refer matters to an appellate court, see *Arnold v Arnold* (1965–69), 2 NSR 348 (CA); *Iantsis v Papatheodorou* (1971), 3 RFL 158 (Ont CA).

marital status or to interim or final corollary orders. A non-party is not entitled to appeal.

C. RESTRICTIONS ON STATUS APPEALS

Pursuant to sections 12(3), (4), (5), and 21(2) of the *Divorce Act*, no appeal lies from a judgment granting a divorce once the time fixed by law for instituting an appeal has expired, unless an extension of the time for appeal has been sought or granted *before* expiry of the normal period fixed by law for instituting an appeal.[2]

Although section 21(2) expressly denies any right of appeal from a judgment granting a divorce on or after the divorce takes effect pursuant to section 12, it does not preclude rescission of the divorce judgment for proper cause.[3]

D. RESTRICTIONS ON COROLLARY ORDER APPEALS

In British Columbia and Saskatchewan, it has been held that section 21 provides an automatic right to appeal corollary orders under the *Divorce Act* that prevails over any conflicting provincial legislation which requires leave to appeal.[4] In Nova Scotia, it has been held that a consent order for corollary support requires leave to appeal to the Court of Appeal pursuant to section 39 of the *Judicature Act*.[5] In Ontario, it has been held that interim corollary orders under the *Divorce Act* require leave to appeal to the Divisional Court pursuant to section 19(1)(b) of the *Courts of Justice Act*.[6] The Ontario Court of Appeal reasoned that section 21(1) of the *Divorce Act* establishes the right to appeal an interim order but it must be read in light of section 21(6) of the *Divorce Act*, which stipulates that "an appeal under this section shall be asserted, heard and decided according to the ordinary procedure governing appeals," and having regard also to section 25, which empowers the provinces "to make rules regulating practice and procedure." And in Ontario, the "ordin-

---

2   Compare *Massicotte v Boutin*, [1969] SCR 818; *Kumpas v Kumpas*, [1970] SCR 438; *Novic v Novic*, [1983] 1 SCR 700, applying s 18(2) of the *Divorce Act*, 1968; and see current *Divorce Act*, s 21(6).

3   See Julien D Payne, *Payne on Divorce*, 4th ed (Scarborough, ON: Carswell, 1996) c 6, "Divorce Judgments," part 1, "Effective Date of Divorce Judgment; Appeals; Rescission of Divorce Judgment."

4   *Haigh v Haigh* (1987), 15 BCLR (2d) 375 (CA); *DeFehr v DeFehr*, 2002 BCCA 577; *Kotelmach v Mattison* (1987), 11 RFL (3d) 56 (Sask CA); *Rimmer v Adshead*, 2003 SKCA 19.

5   RSNS 1989, c 240. See *Inkumsah-Cosper v Cosper* (1995), 14 RFL (4th) 152 (NSCA).

6   *Elgner v Elgner*, 2011 ONCA 483, leave to appeal to SCC refused, [2011] SCCA No 341.

ary procedure" for appealing an interlocutory order is governed by section 19(1) of the *Courts of Justice Act,* which provides that "[a]n appeal lies to the Divisional Court from . . . (b) an interlocutory order of a judge of the Superior Court of Justice, with leave as provided in the rules of court." Addressing the conjoint operation of section 21 of the *Divorce Act* and section 19(1) of the *Courts of Justice Act,* the Ontario Court of Appeal determined that the doctrine of paramountcy is not engaged because there is no operational incompatibility between the federal and provincial legislative provisions. Applying the test of incompatibility set out in *Canadian Western Bank v Alberta*[7] as to whether it is impossible to comply simultaneously with both laws or whether the operation of the provincial law would frustrate the purpose of the federal legislation, the Ontario Court of Appeal observed that due compliance with both statutes is accommodated by a party seeking leave to appeal pursuant to section 19(2)(b) of the *Courts of Justice Act.* Pursuant to the conjoint operation of subsections 21(1) and 21(6) of the *Divorce Act,* RSC 1985, c 3 (2nd Supp) and articles 29 and 511 of the *Code of Civil Procedure,* RSQ, c C-25, an appeal from an interlocutory judgment rendered in the context of a divorce proceeding in Quebec requires leave of the court, regardless of the subject matter and object of the interlocutory proceeding and whether it relates to the interpretation of a provision of the *Divorce Act.*[8] In reaching this conclusion, the Quebec Court of Appeal accepted the analysis of the Ontario Court of Appeal in *Elgner v Elgner.*[9] Subject to section 21(4) of the *Divorce Act,* section 21(3) prohibits any appeal from an interim or final order for corollary relief, unless the appeal is instituted within thirty days after the day on which the order was made. The statutory requirements are satisfied if the appeal is filed on the thirtieth day, but the hearing is fixed for a subsequent date.[10] The Manitoba Court of Appeal has held that the time fixed by section 21(3) for filing a notice of appeal with respect to a corollary issue in divorce proceedings runs from the date of entry, not from the date of pronouncement of the order. In matters relating to corollary relief orders, it makes more sense for time to run from the date of entry and not from the date of pronouncement of the judgment because a trial judge has the privilege of varying his decision until the moment of entry so that variations in the

---

7   [2007] 2 SCR 3.

8   *Droit de la famille — 121718,* 2012 QCCA 1229; *Droit de la famille — 123147,* 2012 QCCA 1966; *Droit de la famille — 142281,* 2014 QCCA 1692; compare *K(H) c S(D)* (1988), 18 RFL (3d) 66 (Que CA).

9   2011 ONCA 483.

10   *Novic v Novic,* [1983] 1 SCR 700.

order can and do sometimes occur at the last minute.[11] As Baird JA, of the Manitoba Court of Appeal, observed in *Singh v Pierpont*, "[i]t is important to note that the requirement that an order be "entered" in the court granting the order before a notice of appeal is filed, as referred to in *Baird*, has been replaced with a requirement that an order be signed and filed in the court granting the order before an appeal is filed."[12] Cases in New Brunswick, Newfoundland and Labrador, and Nova Scotia have proceeded on the basis that a corollary relief order is "made" when the written order is issued.[13] According to the Alberta Court of Appeal, however, the word "made" in section 21(3) refers to pronouncement, not entry.[14] The British Columbia Court of Appeal has also concluded that the time for appeal runs from the date of the oral judgment and not from the date when the reasons for judgment have been transcribed and approved.[15]

Section 21(4) of the *Divorce Act* empowers an appellate court or judge thereof to extend the time for instituting an appeal where special grounds are established and an application for such extension may be made before or after expiry of the time ordinarily applicable. It is incumbent upon an applicant for an extension of time to file a notice of appeal (a) to show a *bona fide* intention to appeal while the right to appeal existed and that the failure to appeal was by reason of some special circumstances which served to excuse or justify such failure; (b) to account for the delay and to show that the other side was not so seriously prejudiced thereby as to make it unjust, having regard to the position of both parties, to disturb the judgment; (c) to show that he has not taken the benefits of the judgment from which he is seeking to appeal; and (d) to show that he would have a reasonable chance of success if allowed to prosecute the appeal.[16] An order extending the time for appeal can only be granted on special grounds and must be refused in the absence of a

---

11   *Baird v Baird*, [1977] 5 WWR 72 (Man CA); *Harvey v Harvey* (1989), 23 RFL (3d) 53 (Man CA).

12   2015 MBCA 18 at paras 19–28.

13   *Grant v Grant*, 2011 NBCA 113; *Duffy v Duffy*, 2009 NLCA 11; *MacDonald v MacDonald*, 2010 NSCA 34.

14   *Levesque v Levesque* (1992), 41 RFL (3d) 96 (Alta CA) (extension of time for appeal granted where appeal not prejudicial to respondent and not frivolous or hopeless); *Dang v Bahramloian*, [2007] AJ No 451 (CA) (extension of time for custody appeal denied).

15   See *Psaila v Psaila* (1984), 40 RFL (2d) 458 at 459 (BCCA); see also *Levesque v Levesque* (1992), 41 RFL (3d) 96; compare *Harvey v Harvey* (1989), 23 RFL (3d) 53 (Man CA), and *Kotelmach v Mattison* (1987), 11 RFL (3d) 56 (Sask CA).

16   *Cairns v Cairns*, [1931] 3 WWR 335 (Alta CA); *Buckley v Buckley*, [2004] AJ No 1046 (CA); *Vey v Vey* (1984), 54 BCLR 270 (CA); *Fritschij v Bazan*, 2007 MBCA 11; *Power v Power* (1979), 24 NBR (2d) 617 (CA); *Fitzgerald v Foote*, 2003 NLCA 25; *Zenner v Zenner*, 2012 PECA 5. See also *Dixon v Cole*, 2014 NSCA 100.

satisfactory explanation of the applicant's delay.[17] "Special grounds" within
the meaning of section 21(4) of the *Divorce Act* presuppose some sufficiently compelling reason to grant an extension, such as something in the reasons why an appeal was not taken on time or something in the proceedings
or about the judgment that would cause injustice if an extension were not
granted. An extension may be deemed appropriate where

(i)   the applicant intended to appeal within the prescribed time limit, but
      failed to do so because of misunderstandings;
(ii) the applicant had an arguable case; and
(iii) no effective prejudice would befall the respondent except, perhaps,
      some difficulty in recovering the costs of the appeal if it failed.[18]

An application for an extension will not be granted where the applicant
changed his or her mind or made a belated decision to appeal the disposition
at trial.[19] Grounds for appellate intervention, at least in an arguable form,
constitute a condition precedent to the court granting an extension of time
within which to appeal.[20] A mistake of counsel concerning the period within
which the notice of appeal shall be filed may not constitute special grounds
for an extension of the time for appeal.[21] Similarly, an application for an order extending the time for appeal may not be favourably entertained where
the prospective appellant failed to consult newly appointed counsel until after expiry of the statutorily designated period.[22] Where a spouse has changed
lawyers and the new lawyer has deferred filing notice of appeal pending receipt of the reasons for judgment, an extension of the time for appeal has
been granted.[23] A spouse has also been granted an extension of the time for
appeal where he intended to appeal within the prescribed time but was late
in instructing his solicitors to do so because he was out of the province and
honestly believed that he had more time to file an appeal and it appeared at
least arguable that the support order sought to be appealed was so excessive

---

17   Compare *MacIsaac v Seffern*, [1969] RP 183 (Que CA), applying s 17(4) of the *Divorce Act*,
     1968; see also *Stewart v Stewart* (1990), 30 RFL (3d) 67 (Alta CA); *Andronyk v Cox* (1984),
     57 BCLR 69 (CA).
18   *Wood v Wood*, [2001] SJ No 2 (CA).
19   *Psaila v Psaila* (1984), 40 RFL (2d) 458 at 460 (BCCA).
20   *Power v Power* (1979), 24 NBR (2d) 617 (CA); *Fraser v Fraser* (1979), 30 NSR (2d) 289 (CA);
     Re Beliveau and Director, Legal Aid, Hamilton, Ontario (1972), 6 RFL 1 (Ont CA).
21   See *Labelle v Robitaille*, [1970] RP 144 (Que CA); compare *Levesque v Levesque* (1992), 41
     RFL (3d) 96 (Alta CA); *Vey v Vey* (1984), 54 BCLR 270 (CA); *Re Saskatchewan Registration
     No 76-07-017181* (1985), 47 RFL (2d) 334 (BCCA). Compare *Dixon v Cole*, 2014 NSCA 100.
22   See *Botsis v Mourelatos*, [1970] RP 191 (Que BR).
23   *Wur v Wur* (1975), 17 RFL 251 (Man CA).

as to warrant a reduction. An application to extend the time for appeal will be dismissed in the absence of effective material in support of the application.

The factors that should influence a court in deciding whether to exercise its discretion to extend the time for filing a notice of appeal are not applicable with the same force or in the same way in deciding whether the court should exercise the discretion to extend the time for filing a factum embodying a notice of cross-appeal. The time limit for giving notice of the cross-appeal is set by reference to the time of filing the appellant's factum. Extensions of time for filing factums are given on much more flexible principles than those applicable to extensions of time for filing notices of appeal.[24]

E. ROLE AND POWERS OF APPELLATE COURT

Section 21(5) of the *Divorce Act* expressly empowers an appellate court to (a) dismiss the appeal, or (b) allow the appeal and (i) render the appropriate judgment or corollary order that should have been made,[25] or (ii) order a new hearing where this is necessary to avoid a substantial wrong or miscarriage of justice or to bring forth additional information.[26] Where a refusal to grant child care expenses under section 7(1)(a) of the Guidelines is reversed on appeal, the appellate court may conclude that it is impractical to remit the issue of the amount to the trial judge because of the costs involved. In that event, the appellate court may leave it open to the parties to agree upon the appropriate amount in light of current financial information available to them, while ordering that a fixed monthly sum shall be paid in the absence of agreement.

Appellate courts should not overturn support orders, unless there is an error of principle, a significant misapprehension of the evidence, or the order is clearly wrong.[27] It is not for the appellate court to intervene by substituting

---

24 *Newson v Newson* (1980), 18 BCLR 203 (CA).

25 *Kubel v Kubel* (1995), 15 RFL (4th) 356 (Alta CA); *Jens v Jens*, 2008 BCCA 392; *Perfanick v Panciera*, [2001] MJ No 528 (CA); *Williams v Williams*, [1999] NJ No 254 (CA); *Wedsworth v Wedsworth*, [2000] NSJ No 306 (CA); *R v R*, [2002] OJ No 1095 (CA); *Wilson v Grassick* (1994), 2 RFL (4th) 291 (Sask CA).

26 *Brill v Brill* (1995), 10 RFL (4th) 372 (Alta CA); *Kits v Kits*, [2001] BCJ No 898 (CA) (terms of order under appeal to continue in force pending rehearing); *Cabot v Mikkelson*, [2004] MJ No 240 (CA); *Lister v Gould*, [2000] NBJ No 419 (CA); *King v King* (1994), 2 RFL (4th) 407 (Nfld CA); *Gorman v Gorman* (1994), 132 NSR (2d) 396 (CA); *Wunsche v Wunsche* (1994), 70 OAC 380 (CA); *Rist v Rist*, [2000] SJ No 637 (CA).

27 *Hickey v Hickey*, [1999] 2 SCR 518; *DBS v SRG; LJW v TAR; Henry v Henry; and Hiemstra v Hiemstra*, [2006] 2 SCR 231; *Fleury v Fleury*, 2009 ABCA 43; *Cornelissen v Cornelissen*, [2003] BCJ No 2714 (CA); *Hansen v Clark*, 2009 MBCA 69; *Trevors v Jenkins*, 2011 NBCA 61; *Slade v Slade*, [2001] NJ No 5 (CA); *Brooks v Brooks*, 2014 NBCA 29; *Pirner v Pirner*, [2005] OJ No 5093 (CA); *Hamel v Hamel*, [2001] SJ No 692 (CA).

its own evaluative judgment for that of the trial judge.[28] An appellate court is not precluded from identifying errors in the trial judge's findings of fact where those findings are sufficiently palpable and important and have a sufficiently decisive effect that they warrant appellate intervention and review.[29] It is not sufficient, however, to identify errors in the details of the findings of fact made by the judge of first instance, if the overall characterization of the effect of the facts is correct in law.[30] Insofar as the *Federal Child Support Guidelines* are mandatory and not permissive, an appellate court is required to intervene where the trial judge made an error of law in not addressing the issues according to the Guidelines.[31] The exercise of discretion by a Master on a question of fact should not be disturbed on appeal unless it was "clearly wrong," but a judge sitting on appeal on a point of law from a Master has a conventional appellate jurisdiction in which the legal issue may be argued and decided on the merits.[32]

While disapproving the procedure, an appellate court may find no reversible error in the trial judge's decision not to allow evidence on all issues in dispute.[33]

An appeal may be allowed in part where the evidence before the trial court was insufficiently clear with respect to expenses sought pursuant to section 7 of the Guidelines.[34]

Where the passage of time has been too great or the appellant seeks to demonstrate a change of circumstances subsequent to the making of the order, variation proceedings may be a more appropriate avenue of recourse than the appellate court.[35] An appellate court may take into account a change of circumstances since the making of an order where a failure to consider the

28 *Willick v Willick*, [1994] 3 SCR 670 at 692, Sopinka J; *Hill v Hill*, [2002] BCJ No 672 (CA); *Scott v Scott*, [2004] NBJ No 468 (CA); *Green v Green*, [2005] NJ No 165 (CA); *Wedsworth v Wedsworth*, [2000] NSJ No 306 (CA); *Lacosse v Lacosse*, [2005] OJ No 4720 (Sup Ct); *Hamel v Hamel*, [2001] SJ No 692 (CA).

29 *Blyth v Brooks*, [2008] AJ No 100 (CA); *Hawco v Myers*, [2005] NJ No 378 (CA).

30 *Marinangeli v Marinangeli*, [2003] OJ No 2819 (CA) (trial judge's misapprehension of certain facts found insufficient to warrant appellate intervention).

31 *Zuk v Zuk*, [1998] AJ No 1425 (CA).

32 *Maynard v Maynard*, [1999] BCJ No 325 (SC).

33 *Ryba v Schoenroth*, [1999] SJ No 201 (CA).

34 *Wesolowski v Wesolowski*, [1999] AJ No 183 (CA).

35 *Nash v Nash*, [1975] 2 SCR 507; *Berry v Murray* (1983), 30 RFL (2d) 310 (BCCA); *Milinkovic v Milinkovic* (1991), 37 RFL (3d) 97 (Ont CA); *Thompson v Thompson* (1988), 11 RFL (3d) 422 (Sask CA); See also *Grohmann v Grohmann* (1991), 37 RFL (3d) 71 (BCCA), wherein Southin JA observed that "the [appellate] court, generally, should only exercise original jurisdiction where it has been shown that the judgment below was erroneous. If that is not shown, then it does seem to me that subsequent events are for a fresh application below."

change would lead the appellate court to make an order which would inevitably be varied on a fresh application.[36]

The launching of an appeal does not preclude an application to vary a subsisting order on the basis of a change that has occurred since the granting of the order.[37]

F. INTERIM ORDERS

An appellate court will only interfere with an interim order for child support if wrong principles of law have been applied or the order under appeal results in a patent injustice.[38] An appeal from a Master's order in a purely interlocutory matter should not be entertained unless the order was clearly wrong.[39]

In Ontario, leave to appeal an interim order for child support lies to the Divisional Court, not the Court of Appeal. Rule 62.02(2) of the Ontario *Rules of Civil Procedure* provides a time limit of seven days for service of the notice of motion for leave. A self-represented litigant, like a legally represented litigant, is bound by the Ontario *Rules of Civil Procedure*, and will not be granted an extension of time where no satisfactory explanation for the delay is furnished.[40]

G. DENIAL OF APPEAL; MOTION TO DISMISS APPEAL; REINSTATEMENT OF APPEAL

A spouse, who is in default under a support order, may be denied an audience in the Court of Appeal while he or she remains in contempt.[41] It is the practice of the British Columbia Court of Appeal not to hear appeals unless a convincing explanation is given for non-compliance with a subsisting court order. An exception may be admitted where the interests of justice require the appellate court to make a ruling on an unsettled question in order to avoid the expense of further litigation.[42]

Where the effluxion of time before the appeal is heard renders it appropriate, the appellate court may remit the issues of spousal and child support

---

36 *LeBlanc v LeBlanc* (1993), 48 RFL (3d) 457 (Man CA).

37 *Re Seeman* (1977), 28 RFL 275 (Ont HCJ).

38 *Klain v Klain*, [1998] NSJ No 20 (CA); compare *Dram v Foster*, 2009 MBCA 125.

39 *Von Sturmer v Von Sturmer*, [1998] BCJ No 1646 (SC).

40 *Orser v Grant*, [2001] OJ No 24 (Div Ct).

41 *Cyr v Cassista* (1986), 50 RFL (2d) 33 (NBCA).

42 *Kowalewich v Kowalewich*, [2001] BCJ No 1406 (CA) (successful appellant denied costs by reason of his failure to pay money owing under court orders which produced a financial strain on the respondent's resources).

to the trial court for a new hearing on up-to-date evidence. Pending the resolution of the matter in the trial court, the appellate court may order interim periodic spousal and child support, but may also direct that the interim order is purely a stop-gap measure and that it should not be taken as a guide to the proper order for the trial judge to make.[43]

An appellant who complies with the Rules of Court can pursue an appeal notwithstanding delay and the alleged impracticality of the appeal. It is only when an appeal is clearly moot or hopeless that it will be summarily dismissed. The normal remedy for improbable appeals lies in costs.[44]

An order to restore an appeal struck from the list is discretionary. Where the appeal appears to have been struck through the inadvertence of counsel and the matter is dealt with fairly, quickly, and responsibly thereafter, an order may be granted restoring the appeal to the list, unless the appeal is found to lack merit and the onus of proving this falls on the party who opposes the restoration application.[45]

H. EFFECT OF APPEAL

When an appeal is successful, the decision of the appellate court stands in the place of the order or judgment appealed from and takes effect from the date of the original order or judgment.[46] Where the successful appeal involves the right to or amount of child support, the appellate court has jurisdiction under section 21 of the *Divorce Act* to direct that its judgment shall take effect only from the date of the decision, but such an exceptional course of action can only be justified where there are circumstances that render it unjust to do otherwise.[47]

I. STAY OF ORDER PENDING APPEAL

Orders for child support should not be stayed pending appeal unless the respondent would be unduly prejudiced and suffer irreparable harm if a stay were not granted.[48]

---

43   *Forbes v Forbes* (1994), 5 RFL (4th) 79 (BCCA).

44   *Starko v Starko* (1991), 33 RFL (3d) 277 (Alta CA) (custody).

45   *Kieser v Kieser*, [2003] AJ No 611 (CA).

46   *Dennis v Wilson*, [1998] OJ No 4854 (CA).

47   *Preweda v Preweda* (1993), 48 RFL (3d) 190 (Man CA); see also *Metzner v Metzner*, [2000] BCJ No 104 (CA); *King v King* (1994), 115 Nfld & PEIR 56 (Nfld CA).

48   *Armstrong v Armstrong* (1992), 40 RFL (3d) 438 (Ont CA); *Zenner v Zenner* (1991), 32 RFL (3d) 11 (PEICA); see also *Ciachurski v Ciachurski* (1994), 47 BCAC 208; *Brooks-Gualtieri v Gualtieri*, [1998] OJ No 5591 (Gen Div) (arrears of child support; stay refused). Compare

A fairly heavy burden falls on the applicant who seeks to prevent the other party from immediately realizing his or her entitlement under the order. A three-stage test will be applied. First, a preliminary assessment must be made of the merits of the case to ensure that there is an arguable issue raised on the appeal. Second, it must be determined whether the applicant would suffer irreparable harm if a stay is refused. Third, an assessment must be made as to which of the parties would suffer greater harm from the granting or refusal of a stay pending the outcome of the appeal.[49] If the applicant fails to meet these criteria, she must satisfy the court that there are exceptional circumstances that would make it fit and just that the stay be granted. A partial stay of the child support order may be deemed appropriate to the circumstances of the appeal.

A stay of execution of a child maintenance order is not automatic but such a stay may be granted in the exercise of judicial discretion under Rule 15 of the Saskatchewan *Court of Appeal Rules*. The principles underlying Rule 15 are to prevent injustice, avoid delay in resolving child support obligations, and to ensure that the result is fair and equitable. Rule 15 applies to an order for the instalment payment of child maintenance arrears, even if the children are no longer dependent. A father's application for a stay should be denied where the appeal is likely to proceed in timely fashion and even total success on appeal, which is somewhat unlikely, would not result in any great loss, given that the order provides for payment by monthly instalments.[50]

J. ABSENCE OR DELAY OF REASONS FOR JUDGMENT

An appeal is from the formal order, not the reasons, and if the formal order reaches a correct conclusion in light of the evidence and the law, the appeal must be dismissed.[51] While it is not an error, in itself, for a trial judge to give a judgment without indicating the findings of fact and without giving the reasons for a support award, it is highly desirable for a trial judge to give reasons in order to facilitate an appellate court's task of determining whether

---

Hoar v Hoar (1992), 39 RFL (3d) 125 (Ont CA) (application under *Family Law Act*, RSO 1990, c F.3).

49   *Armstrong v Armstrong*, [1998] BCJ No 2309 (CA); *Hendrickson v Hendrickson*, [2004] NSJ No 304 (CA); *Tauber v Tauber*, [1999] OJ No 713 (CA) (appropriate amount of child support pending appeal fixed at $11,000; differential between this amount and higher amount ordered by trial court to be deposited in interest-bearing trust account).

50   *Primeau v Primeau*, [2004] SJ No 655 (CA).

51   *Stricker v Stricker* (1994), 4 RFL (4th) 29 (Alta CA); *Razutis v Garrett*, [1999] BCJ No 1505 (CA).

the trial judge's conclusions are supported by the evidence or whether they disclose an error in principle.

The absence of reasons for judgment places the appellate court under a serious disability. If they are not volunteered, counsel proposing to appeal should request the judge to give reasons for judgment to facilitate the appeal.[52]

A litigant is entitled to adequate, albeit not perfect, reasons for decisions made by a motion judge, even though these judges frequently have heavy daily dockets that require them to quickly decide urgent issues in the face of conflicting and incomplete evidence. A motion judge must give reasons for her decision so that a party can give informed consideration to the advisability of an appeal and interested members of the public can satisfy themselves whether or not justice has been done. The need for reasons is based on the following three rationales:

(i)   public confidence in the administration of justice;

(ii) the right of the losing party to know the reasons for having lost; and

(iii) to make the right of appeal meaningful.

The adequacy of reasons must be determined by a functional approach that applies the aforementioned rationales. Where the table amount of child support is ordered for adult children pursuing post-secondary education, an explanation of the specific amount is not required. But where a judge exercises his discretion to fix support for the children under section 3(2)(b) of the *Federal Child Support Guidelines*, reasons for the amount ordered must be provided. The amount of support ordered pursuant to section 3(2)(b) cannot be determined without findings of fact relating to "the condition, means, needs and other circumstances of the child[ren] and the financial ability of each parent to contribute to the support of the child[ren]." Where a motion judge has neither articulated the law nor the evidence relied upon in fixing the amount of support ordered under section 3(2)(b) of the *Federal Child Support Guidelines* and the record does not enable an appellate court to make the requisite findings, the appellate court has no alternative except to remit the matter for a fresh hearing with an appropriately enhanced record.[53]

Justice may sometimes be better served by an announcement of the disposition of the issues as soon as the deliberation process is completed, but before full written reasons can be made available to the parties. The filing of a notice of appeal after the disposition has been announced does not

---

52   *Bacon v Stonehouse*, (1990), 25 RFL (3d) 71 (Ont Div Ct); compare *Voortman v Voortman* (1994), 4 RFL (4th) 250 (Ont CA).

53   *Bodnar v Blackman*, [2006] OJ No 3675 (CA).

preclude the appellate court from considering the reasons for judgment that are subsequently released.[54]

K. FRESH EVIDENCE[55]

The following principles govern the admission of fresh evidence before an appellate court:

(i)   the evidence should generally not be admitted if by due diligence it could have been adduced at trial;

(ii)   the evidence must be relevant in the sense that it bears upon a decisive or potentially decisive issue at the trial;

(iii) the evidence must be credible in the sense that it was reasonably capable of belief; and

(iv)   the evidence must be such that if believed, it could reasonably be expected to have affected the result at trial.

However, an appellate court may take account of a change of circumstances since the making of the order where a failure to do so would result in long-term injustice[56] or in an order that would necessitate variation on a fresh application.[57] Evidence of a loss of employment after the delivery of the trial judgment may be admitted on appeal and the amount of child support may be varied by the appellate court to reflect these changed circumstances.[58] In the absence of an application to admit new evidence by way of affidavit on an appeal, the submissions of counsel are insufficient to establish a material change of circumstances.[59]

The tender of computer-generated tables, which are merely mathematical tools enabling the court to undertake complicated calculations, does not offend the "fresh evidence" rule that customarily applies to appeals.[60]

A judge is not *functus officio* where a formal order reflecting her reasons for judgment has not been entered. Where the Crown seeks reconsideration of a prior judicial remission of arrears based on the finding that the husband was unaware of his wife's receipt of social assistance, the Crown is not ex-

---

54   *Crocker v Sipus* (1992), 41 RFL (3d) 19 at 24 (Ont CA).

55   See, generally, Julien D Payne, *Payne on Divorce*, 4th ed (Scarborough, ON: Carswell, 1996) at 495–97.

56   *Jens v Jens*, 2008 BCAC 392.

57   *LeBlanc v LeBlanc* (1993), 48 RFL (3d) 457 (Man CA); *Williams v Williams*, [1999] NJ No 254 (CA).

58   *Forbes v Forbes* (1997), 33 RFL (4th) 251 (BCCA).

59   *Giles v Villeneuve*, [1998] OJ No 4492 (Gen Div).

60   *Meuser v Meuser*, [1998] BCJ No 2808 (CA).

empted from meeting the requirements of the "fresh evidence rule" simply because the court could have unilaterally relied upon the Provincial Court order on file to which neither party made reference in the original application. The fresh evidence rule is not rendered inapplicable because previously untendered evidence was available on the court file.[61]

L. APPEALS TO THE SUPREME COURT OF CANADA

Section 18 of the *Divorce Act, 1968*[62] specifically provided for appeals to the Supreme Court of Canada. No similar provision is included in the current *Divorce Act*. Accordingly, appeals to the Supreme Court of Canada now fall subject to the relevant provisions of the *Supreme Court Act*.[63]

Leave to appeal to the Supreme Court of Canada may be granted by a provincial appellate court in those rare cases in which an issue is raised of such obvious and compelling importance that the litigation calls for the attention of the country's highest court without regard to competing demands for the court's attention.[64]

---

61   *Williams v Williams*, [2001] AJ No 1558 (QB).

62   SC 1967–68, c 24.

63   RSC 1985, c S-26. Compare *Pelech v Pelech*, [1987] 1 SCR 801.

64   *Chartier v Chartier*, [1997] MJ No 574 (CA), applying *Ashmead v British Columbia*, [1992] 6 WWR 763 (BCCA).

CHAPTER 12

Remedies Available under Provincial and Territorial Legislation

A. SPOUSAL SUPPORT

1) Diversity under Provincial and Territorial Statutes

Separated spouses may opt to seek spousal support under provincial or territorial legislation or by way of corollary relief in divorce proceedings. Unmarried cohabitants of the opposite sex or of the same sex may also be entitled to seek "spousal" support under provincial or territorial legislation. Provincial spousal support legislation that discriminates against couples living in a "common-law relationship"[1] or in a same-sex relationship[2] has been struck down as contravening equality rights under section 15 of the *Canadian Charter of Rights and Freedoms*.[3]

In most provinces and territories, both federally and provincially appointed judges may adjudicate spousal and child support claims that arise independently of divorce.

Provincial and territorial statutes differ widely from each other in their specific provisions respecting spousal support. They also differ substantially from the language of the federal *Divorce Act*, which regulates spousal support on or after divorce.

British Columbia[4] provides general statutory criteria for spousal support orders that correspond to the factors and objectives defined in the federal *Divorce Act*. Several provinces, including New Brunswick,[5] Newfoundland

---

1   *Taylor v Rossu* (1998), 39 RFL (4th) 242 (Alta CA).

2   *M v H*, [1999] 2 SCR 3.

3   *The Constitution Act, 1982*, being Schedule B to the *Canada Act 1982 (UK)*, 1982, c 11.

4   *Family Law Act*, SBC 2011, c 25, ss 160–62.

5   *Family Services Act*, SNB 1980, c F-2.2, s 115(6).

and Labrador,[6] Nova Scotia,[7] Ontario,[8] Prince Edward Island,[9] and the Northwest Territories[10] provide a detailed statutory list of factors that the courts should take into account in determining the right to, duration of, and amount of spousal support. The shortcomings of an unrefined list of designated factors, which lead to unbridled judicial discretion, have been tempered in Newfoundland and Labrador,[11] the Northwest Territories,[12] Ontario,[13] and Saskatchewan[14] by the articulation of specific objectives for support orders. These objectives are similar but not identical to those defined in the current *Divorce Act*.[15] Accordingly, they promote consistency between provincial and federal statutory criteria but fall short of providing a blueprint for uniformity.

Provincial statutory spousal support rights and obligations are no longer conditioned on proof of a matrimonial offence. Alberta,[16] British Columbia,[17] Manitoba,[18] New Brunswick,[19] Newfoundland and Labrador,[20] the Northwest Territories,[21] Ontario,[22] Prince Edward Island,[23] Quebec,[24] Saskatchewan,[25] and the Yukon Territory[26] have all abandoned the traditional offence concept in favour of economic criteria that largely focus on needs and ability to pay. In Newfoundland and Labrador,[27] the Northwest Territories,[28] and Ontario,[29] the spousal support obligation "exists without regard to the conduct of either spouse, but the court may in determining the amount of support have regard to a course of conduct that is so unconscionable as to constitute an obvious

---

6   *Family Law Act*, RSNL 1990, c F-2, s 39(9).

7   *Maintenance and Custody Act*, RSNS 1989, c 160, s 4.

8   *Family Law Act*, RSO 1990, c F.3, s 33(9).

9   *Family Law Act*, SPEI 1995, c 12, s 33(9).

10   *Family Law Act*, SNWT 1997, c 18, s 16.

11   *Family Law Act*, RSNL 1990, c F-2, s 39(8).

12   *Family Law Act*, SNWT 1997, c 18, ss 16(4), (5), (6), (7), (8), & (9).

13   *Family Law Act*, RSO 1990, c F.3, s 33(8).

14   *Family Maintenance Act*, SS 1997, c F-6.2, s 5.

15   RSC 1985 (2d Supp), c 3, ss 15.2(6) and 17(7); see Chapter 8, Section G.

16   *Family Law Act*, SA 2003, c F-4.5, ss 58–60.

17   *Family Law Act*, SBC 2011, c 25, ss 160–62.

18   *Family Maintenance Act*, CCSM c F20, ss 4 and 7.

19   *Family Services Act*, SNB 1980, c F-2.2, ss 112 and 115(6).

20   *Family Law Act*, RSNL 1990, c F-2, ss 36 and 39(9).

21   *Family Law Act*, SNWT 1997, c 18, ss 15 and 16(5), (6), (7), (8), & (9).

22   *Family Law Act*, RSO 1990, c F.3, ss 31 and 33(9).

23   *Family Law Act*, SPEI 1995, c 12, ss 30, 33(6), and 33(9).

24   *Civil Code of Québec*, SQ 1991, c 64, art. 493, 511, and 585–96.

25   *Family Maintenance Act*, SS 1997, c F-6.2, ss 5 and 7.

26   *Family Property and Support Act*, RSY 2002, c 83, ss 32 and 34(5).

27   *Family Law Act*, RSNL 1990, c F-2, s 39(9).

28   *Family Law Act*, SNWT 1997, c 18, s 16(10).

29   *Family Law Act*, RSO 1990, c F.3, s 33(10).

and gross repudiation of the [spousal] relationship."[30] Although there has been some inconsistency in the application of these statutory provisions, there has been strong judicial resistance to spouses engaging in mutual recriminations.[31] Manitoba, which originally applied a similar criterion of unconscionability, abandoned conduct as a relevant consideration altogether by amending legislation in 1983.[32] In Alberta and British Columbia, courts may take misconduct into account only where it arbitrarily or unreasonably precipitates, prolongs, or aggravates the need for support, or affects the ability of the obligor to provide support.[33] In New Brunswick[34] and Nova Scotia,[35] the relevant legislation expressly stipulates that courts may take conduct into account if it unreasonably prolongs the need for support. These statutory provisions are consistent with the statutory obligation on each spouse to strive for financial self-sufficiency. In the Yukon Territory,[36] a court is specifically empowered to deny support to a spouse who has remarried or is cohabiting with a third party in a relationship of some permanence.

2) Differences between Federal *Divorce Act* and Provincial and Territorial Legislation

Differences in provincial and territorial legislation and in the federal divorce legislation are primarily differences of form rather than of substance,[37] whether the courts are dealing with conduct or any other matter. If Mrs Jones is separated from her husband, a judge is unlikely to allow the right to, duration of, and amount of support to depend on whether she has invoked the provisions of the applicable provincial or territorial statute or the relevant provisions of the *Divorce Act*.

However, certain important differences remain between the provincial and territorial support regimes and the federal divorce regime. In particular, provincial and territorial legislation confers broader powers on the courts with respect to the types of order that can be granted in proceedings for

---

30 Compare *Maintenance and Custody Act*, RSNS 1989, c 160, s 6(2).

31 See Julien D Payne, "The Relevance of Conduct to the Assessment of Spousal Maintenance under the Ontario *Family Law Reform Act*, SO 1978, c 2" (1980) 3 Fam L Rev 103, reprinted in *Payne's Digest on Divorce in Canada, 1968–1980* (Don Mills, ON: R De Boo, 1982) at 419. Compare *Bruni v Bruni*, 2010 ONSC 6568 (parental alienation). See also *Menegaldo v Menegaldo*, 2012 ONSC 2940.

32 *Family Maintenance Act*, SM 1983, c 54, s 4, now CCSM c F20, s 4(2).

33 *Family Law Act*, SA 2003, c F-4.5, s 59; *Family Law Act*, SBC 2011, c 25, s 166.

34 *Family Services Act*, SNB 1980, c F-2.2, s 115(6)(t).

35 *Maintenance and Custody Act*, RSNS 1989, c 160, s 6(1).

36 *Family Property and Support Act*, RSY 2002, c 83, s 34(5).

37 *Snyder v Pictou*, 2008 NSCA 19; *Hrenyk v Berden*, 2011 SKQB 305.

spousal support. The federal *Divorce Act*[38] empowers a court to grant orders to pay and secure a lump sum or periodic sums for spousal support. It does not empower a court to order a transfer of property in lieu of support payments. Most provincial and territorial support statutes[39] expressly confer wide powers on the courts with respect to such relief as lump sum payments, periodic payments, transfers or settlements of property, exclusive possession of the matrimonial home, security for support payments, and designation of a spouse as a beneficiary under a life insurance policy or pension plan. For constitutional reasons, orders respecting property rights can only be made by courts presided over by federally appointed judges.

B. CHILD SUPPORT UNDER PROVINCIAL AND TERRITORIAL LEGISLATION

Provincial and territorial statutory support regimes in Canada generally stipulate that parents owe an obligation to support their children.[40] For example, section 31 of the Ontario *Family Law Act*[41] provides as follows:

Obligation of parent to support child

31. (1) Every parent has an obligation to provide support, in accordance with need, for his or her unmarried child who is a minor or is enrolled in a full-time program of education, to the extent that the parent is capable of doing so.

(2) The obligation under subsection (1) does not extend to a child who is sixteen years of age or older and has withdrawn from parental control.[42]

Provincial and territorial statutory support regimes usually provide broad definitions of "parent" or "child" for the purpose of defining the ambit

---

38 RSC 1985 (2d Supp), c 3, s 15(2).

39 See *Family Law Act*, SA 2003, c F-4.5, s 49; *Family Law* Act, SBC 2011, c 25, s.170; *Family Maintenance Act*, CCSM c F20, s 10(1); *Family Services Act*, SNB 1980, c F-2.2, s 116; *Family Law Act*, RSNL 1990, c F-2, s 40; *Maintenance and Custody Act*, RSNS 1989, c 160, ss 7, 33, and 36; *Family Law Act*, SNWT 1997, c 18, s 21; *Family Law Act*, RSO 1990, c F.3, s 34; *Family Law Act*, SPEI 1995, c 12, s 34; *Family Maintenance Act*, SS 1997, c F-6.2, s 9; *Family Property and Support Act*, RSY 2002, c 83, s 38.

40 *Family Law Act*, SBC 2011, c 25, s 147; *Family Maintenance Act*, CCSM c F20, s 36; *Family Services Act*, SNB 1980, c F-2.2, s 113; *Family Law Act*, RSNL 1990, c F-2, s 37; *Maintenance and Custody Act*, RSNS 1989, c 160, s 8; *Children's Law Act*, SNWT 1997, c 14, s 58; *Family Law Act*, RSO 1990, c F.3, s 31; *Family Law Act*, SPEI 1995, c 12, s 31; *Civil Code of Québec*, SQ 1991, c 64, s 585; *Family Maintenance Act*, SS 1997, c F-6.2, s 3; *Family Property and Support Act*, R.S.Y 2002, c 83, s 32.

41 RSO 1990, c F.3.

42 See *Ball v Broger*, 2010 ONCJ 557.

of child support rights and obligations. Although these definitions take a variety of forms, it is common for child support obligations to be statutorily imposed on persons other than the natural parents where they stand in the place of parents to the children.[43] In British Columbia and Manitoba, the legal obligations of natural parents and those of step-parents or persons standing in the place of parents are regulated by statute so as to place the primary responsibility on the natural parents.[44]

Provincial and territorial statutes usually empower their courts to order support for children over the age of majority in circumstances involving illness, disability, or post-secondary education.[45]

Most jurisdictions in Canada have adopted provincial or territorial Child Support Guidelines that mirror the *Federal Child Support Guidelines*.[46] Little or no attention was paid to the possibility of a child instituting proceedings for support against both parents. Such a claim cannot be maintained under the *Divorce Act* and the *Federal Child Support Guidelines* because a child of the marriage has no standing to bring such an application under the *Divorce Act*.[47] A similar bar to relief does not necessarily exist, however, under provincial and territorial legislation. In *JDF v HMF*,[48] Levy J, of the Nova Scotia Family Court, concluded that a child has standing to apply for support against both parents under the *Maintenance and Custody Act*. In such proceedings, the *Nova Scotia Child Maintenance Guidelines*[49] apply. Furthermore, there is nothing inherently inappropriate with a child recovering the full table amount of child support from each parent. Indeed, such concurrent orders may be

---

43 *Family Law Act*, SA 2003, c F-4.5, ss 47–49; *Family Law Act*, SBC 2011, c 25, s 147; *Family Maintenance Act*, CCSM c F20, s 1; *Family Services Act*, SNB 1980, c F-2.2, s 1; *Family Law Act*, RSNL 1990, c F-2, s 2; *Children's Law Act*, SNWT 1997, c 14, s 57; *Family Law Act*, RSO 1990, c F.3, s 1; *Family Law Act*, SPEI 1995, c 12, s 1; *Family Maintenance Act*, SS 1997, c F-6.2, s 2; *Family Property and Support Act*, RSY 2002, c 83, s 1. See, generally, Nicholas Bala, "Who Is a 'Parent'? 'Standing in the Place of a Parent' and Section 5 of the *Child Support Guidelines*" in The Law Society of Upper Canada, *Special Lectures 2006: Family Law* (Toronto: Irwin Law, 2007) at 71–118.

44 See *Family Maintenance Act*, CCSM c F20, s 36; see also *Family Law Act*, SBC 2011, c 25, ss 147 (4) & (5).

45 *Family Law Act*, SA 2003, c F-4.5, s 46; *Family Law Act*, SBC 2011, c 25, s 146; *Family Maintenance Act*, CCSM c F20, s 35.1; *Family Law Act*, RSNL 1990, c F-2, s 37(7); *Family Services Act*, SNB 1980, c F-2.2, s 115(6), as amended; *Maintenance and Custody Act*, RSNS 1989, c 160, s 2; *Children's Law Act*, SNWT 1997, c 14, s 57; *Family Law Act*, RSO 1990, c F.3, s 31(1) (full-time education); *Family Law Act*, SPEI 1995, c 12, s 31; *Family Maintenance Act*, SS 1997, c F-6.2, s 4.

46 SOR/97-175 (*Divorce Act*).

47 *Levesque v Levesque* (1994), 4 RFL (4th) 375 (Alta CA); *Tapson v Tapson* (1970), 2 RFL 305 (Ont CA).

48 [2001] NSJ No 456 (Fam Ct).

49 NS Reg 53/98 (*Maintenace and Custody Act*).

required in circumstances where the child is under the provincial age of majority. If the child had attained the age of majority, however, the court may apply section 3(2) of the *Child Maintenance Guidelines* and order each parent to pay such an amount as the court deems appropriate having regard to the condition, means, needs, and other circumstances of the child and the financial ability of each parent to contribute to the child's maintenance.

Effective 1 October 2005, Alberta implemented provincial *Child Support Guidelines*[50] to be applied where child support is sought pursuant to provincial statute. Prior to that date, Alberta courts applied the *Federal Child Support Guidelines* as a yardstick for determining the amount of child support to be paid, and no distinction was drawn between the children of non-cohabiting unmarried parents and the children of divorcing or divorced parents.[51] In *WRA (Next friend of) and GFA*,[52] Kenny J, of the Alberta Court of Queen's Bench, calculated the amount of child support arrears payable under a court order to the legal guardian of a child by retroactively applying the *Federal Child Support Guidelines*. In so doing, Kenny J resolved an issue that was previously unclear under Alberta law. She concluded that a person who voluntarily consents to and is appointed as the private guardian of a child under the *Child Welfare Act* (Alberta) has a legal obligation to financially contribute towards the needs of the child. Consequently, the legal guardian cannot look to the non-custodial father of the child to exclusively assume the burden of child support after the mother's death.

C. NEED FOR RATIONALIZATION OF INCOME SUPPORT SYSTEMS

Sooner or later, the state must take steps to rationalize the diverse systems of income security in Canada. If every dollar in spousal and child support is set off against public assistance benefits or earned income, custodial parents and their children are no further ahead. What is needed is a rationalization of the laws governing the relationship between diverse sources of income, be it earned income, support payments, state subsidies, or any combination of these.

Although today's family law problem may be one of spousal and child support, tomorrow's will be the problem of elderly and infirm family members. People are living longer. Canada's population is growing older. Today's children will have to carry the tax burden for tomorrow's elderly. One in six

---

50   Alta Reg 147/205 (*Family Law Act*).

51   *Cavanaugh v Ziegler*, [1998] AJ No 1423 (CA); *DBS v SRG*, [2005] AJ No 2 (CA).

52   [2001] AJ No 1472 (QB).

children in Canada is now living in poverty. How can these children be realistically expected to contribute towards the future costs generated by an aging population? The state must invest in these children today in order for dividends to be reaped tomorrow.

D. ENFORCEMENT OF SUPPORT

One of the problems that has plagued Canadian law over many years is the degree to which court orders for spousal and child support have fallen into default. The enforcement of support orders, even those granted in divorce, is regulated primarily by provincial and territorial legislation. Provincial and territorial automatic enforcement processes have been established whereby the enforcement of orders is no longer left to the spouses or parents to whom the money is payable. Orders for support are now registered with provincial or territorial agencies that monitor the payments and take any necessary steps to enforce orders that have fallen into default. Ontario and several other provinces have a system for automatic deduction of spousal and child support payments from an employee's pay cheque. Employers must make the necessary deduction and forward it to the appropriate regional enforcement office.[53]

E. CUSTODY OF AND ACCESS TO CHILDREN UNDER PROVINCIAL AND TERRITORIAL LEGISLATION

1) Welfare or Best Interests of Child

Custody or access disputes involving unmarried parents, third parties, or married parents who have separated without instituting divorce proceedings are regulated by provincial and territorial statutes. Provincial and territorial legislation also regulates wardship proceedings where child protection agencies seek to intervene in dysfunctional family situations that threaten the physical, emotional, or economic well-being of any child.

The "welfare" or "best interests" of the child has long been considered the paramount consideration in custody and access disputes between parents or between parents and third parties. Almost ninety years ago, a judge of the Alberta Court of Appeal defined the criteria to be applied in contested custody proceedings in the following words:

53   See Statistics Canada, "Maintenance Enforcement Survey: Child and Spousal Support" *The Daily* (3 March 2008); Statistics Canada, Canadian Centre for Judicial Statistics, *Child and Spousal Support: Maintenance Enforcement Survey Statistics, 2006/2007* (Ottawa: Statistics Canada, 2008).

The paramount consideration is the welfare of the children; subsidiary to this and as a means of arriving at the best answer to that question are the conduct of the respective parents, the wishes of the mother as well as of the father, the ages and sexes of the children, the proposals of each parent for the maintenance and education of the children; their station and aptitudes and prospects in life; the pecuniary circumstance of the father and the mother — not for the purpose of giving the custody to the parent in the better financial position to maintain and educate the children, but for the purpose of fixing the amount to be paid by one or both parents for the maintenance of the children. The religion in which the children are to be brought up is always a matter for consideration, even, I think, in a case like the present where both parties are of the same religion, for the probabilities as to the one or the other of the parents fulfilling their obligations in this respect ought to be taken into account. Then an order for the custody of some or all of the children having been given to one parent, the question of access by the other must be dealt with.[54]

Provincial and territorial statutes across Canada have endorsed "the welfare of the child" or more commonly "the best interests of the child" as the determinative criterion in custody and access disputes.[55] In Alberta, the terms

---

54   *O'Leary v O'Leary* (1923), 19 Alta LR 224 at 253 (CA), Beck JA. See also *Leboeuf v Leboeuf* (1928), 23 Alta LR 328 (CA), Beck JA.

55   *Family Law Act*, SA 2003, c F-4.5, s 18 (best interests of child is determinative with respect to "parenting" and "contact" orders; relevant factors listed); *RL v MP*, [2008] AJ No 182 (QB); *TS v AVT*, [2008] AJ No 293 (QB); *Family Law Act*, SBC 2011, c 25, s 37 (best interests of child is determinative with respect to guardianship, parenting arrangements, or contact with a child; relevant factors listed); *Family Maintenance Act*, CCSM c F20, s 2 (best interests of child are paramount; child's views to be considered), s 39(2.1) (specific factors designated as indicative of child's best interests), s 39(3) (conduct only relevant to parenting ability); *Watts v Fex*, 2010 MBQB 268; *Family Services Act*, SNB 1980, c F-2.2, s 1 (definition of "best interests of the child" by reference to specific factors), s 129(2) (custody orders to be based on best interests of child); s 129(3) (access to be determined on basis of best interests of child); *Children's Law Act*, RSNL 1990, c C-13, s 31 (custody and access to be determined on basis of best interests of child; specific factors designated as indicative of child's best interests; domestic violence to be taken into account but past conduct otherwise considered only when relevant to parenting ability), s 71 (child entitled to be heard); *Maintenance and Custody Act*, RSNS 1989, c 160, s 18(5) (welfare of child is paramount); *Children's Law Act*, SNWT 1997, c 14, s 17 (custody and access to be determined on basis of best interests of child; specific factors designated; domestic violence to be considered but past conduct otherwise considered only when relevant to parenting ability; economic circumstances are not relevant to parenting ability); *Children's Law Reform Act*, RSO 1990, c C.12, s 24 (custody and access to be determined having regard to best interests of child in light of designated factors; past conduct only relevant to parenting ability); *Custody Jurisdiction and Enforcement Act*, RSPEI 1988, c C-33, s 15 (custody and access to be determined on basis of best

custody and access orders have been displaced by new terminology, namely, "parenting" and "contact" orders.[56] And in British Columbia, the *Family Law Act* does not use the terms "custody" or "access" but rather refers to "guardianship," "parenting arrangements," "parental responsibilities," and "parenting time."[57] Several provinces and territories, including Alberta, British Columbia, New Brunswick, Manitoba, Newfoundland and Labrador, Ontario, Saskatchewan, and the Yukon Territory, have statutorily designated particular factors that the courts must take into account in determining the best interests of a child.[58] Most of the provincial and territorial statutes, like the *Divorce Act*, expressly stipulate that the conduct of the parties is only relevant insofar as it affects parenting ability.[59]

To exemplify the type of statutory provisions found in most provinces and territories, it is appropriate to set out section 24 of the Ontario *Children's Law Reform Act*,[60] which provides as follows:

Merits of application for custody or access

24. (1) The merits of an application under this Part in respect of custody of or access to a child shall be determined on the basis of the best interests of the child, in accordance with subsections (2), (3) and (4).

Best interests of child

(2) The court shall consider all the child's needs and circumstances, including,

(a) the love, affection and emotional ties between the child and,

    (i) each person entitled to or claiming custody of or access to the child,

    (ii) other members of the child's family who reside with the child, and

    (iii) persons involved in the child's care and upbringing;

(b) the child's views and preferences, if they can reasonably be ascertained;

---

interests of child); *Civil Code of Québec*, art 33; *C(G) v V-F(T)*, [1987] 2 SCR 244; *Children's Law Act*, SS 1997, c C-8.2, ss 8 & 9 (custody and access to be determined having regard only to best interests of child; specific factors identified as relevant); *Children's Act*, RSY 2002, c 31, s 1 (best interests of child are paramount and prevail over wishes of parent), s 30 (specific factors designated as indicative of child's best interests; past conduct not considered, unless relevant to parenting ability; no presumption based on age or sex of child; rebuttable presumption in favour of sole physical custody but joint legal custody).

56 *Family Law Act*, SA 2003, c F-4.5, ss 32 and 35.

57 See *NU v GSB*, 2015 BCSC 105 at para 68, Warren J.

58 See above note 55.

59 *Ibid.*

60 RSO 1990, c C.12, as amended; see *Slaunwhite v McLaughlin*, [2009] OJ No 6314 (Sup Ct).

(c) the length of time the child has lived in a stable home environment;

(d) the ability and willingness of each person applying for custody of the child to provide the child with guidance and education, the necessaries of life and any special needs of the child;

(e) the plan proposed by each person applying for custody of or access to the child for the child's care and upbringing;

(f) the permanence and stability of the family unit with which it is proposed that the child will live;

(g) the ability of each person applying for custody of or access to the child to act as a parent; and

(h) the relationship by blood or through an adoption order between the child and each person who is a party to the application.

Past conduct

(3) A person's past conduct shall be considered only,

(a) in accordance with subsection (4); or

(b) if the court is satisfied that the conduct is otherwise relevant to the person's ability to act as a parent.

Violence and abuse

(4) In assessing a person's ability to act as a parent, the court shall consider whether the person has at any time committed violence or abuse against,

(a) his or her spouse;

(b) a parent of the child to whom the application relates;

(c) a member of the person's household; or

(d) any child.[61]

Same

(5) For the purposes of subsection (4), anything done in self-defence or to protect another person shall not be considered violence or abuse.

Additional considerations include the physical, psychological, and emotional well-being and security of the child; fulfillment of religious, ethical, and moral upbringing of the child in accordance with community norms; and the long-term welfare of the child, including provision for healthy growth and development of a child that will enable the child to face problems of life as an adult.[62]

Section 21(1) of the Ontario *Children's Law Reform Act* further provides that a parent of a child or any other person may apply to a court for an order

---

61 See *Ganie v Ganie*, 2014 ONSC 7500.

62 *Vacaru v Vacaru*, 2010 ONSC 7020.

respecting custody of or access to the child or determining any aspect of the incidents of custody of the child. Pursuant to section 21(2), an application under subsection (1) for custody of or access to a child shall be accompanied by an affidavit, in the form prescribed for the purpose by the rules of court, of the person applying for custody or access, containing,

(a) the person's proposed plan for the child's care and upbringing;

(b) information respecting the person's current or previous involvement in any family proceedings, including proceedings under Part III of the *Child and Family Services Act* (child protection), or in any criminal proceedings; and

(c) any other information known to the person that is relevant to the factors to be considered by the court under subsections 24 (2), (3) and (4) in determining the best interests of the child.[63]

Section 21.1 requires every non-parent who applies under section 21 for custody of a child to file with the court the results of a recent police records check respecting the person in accordance with the rules of court. The results obtained, and any information, statement, or document derived from the information contained in the results, are admissible in evidence, if the court considers it to be relevant. Evidence that is determined by the court to be admissible under section 21.1 will be considered in determining the best interests of the child under section 24.

Section 21.2 requires every non-parent who applies for custody of a child to submit a request to every society or other body or person prescribed by the regulations, for a report as to,

(a) whether a society has records relating to the person applying for custody; and

(b) if there are records and the records indicate that one or more files relating to the person have been opened, the date on which each file was opened and, if the file was closed, the date on which the file was closed.

A copy of each request must be filed with the court. The society or other body or person shall provide the court in which the application was filed with a report, a copy of which is provided to every party and to counsel, if any, representing the child, unless the court determines that all or part of the report should be sealed in the court file and not disclosed because some or all of the information contained in the report is not relevant to the application or the application is withdrawn. A report that is filed under section 21.2, and any information, statement, or document derived from the information

---

63 See *CAGP and SDP v CJ and MA*, 2010 ONCJ 175; *LR v VV*, 2011 ONCJ 16 (exemption).

contained in the report, is admissible in evidence in the application, if the court considers it to be relevant. Evidence that is determined by the court to be admissible shall be considered in determining the best interests of the child under section 24.[64]

Pursuant to section 21.3, where an application for custody of a child is made by a person who is not a parent of the child, the clerk of the court shall provide to the court and to the parties and counsel, if any, representing the child, information in writing respecting any current or previous family proceedings involving the child, and any current or previous criminal or family proceedings concerning any person who is a party to the application and who is not a parent of the child. Written information that is provided to the court under section 21.3, and any information, statement, or document derived from that information, is admissible in evidence in the application, if the court considers it to be relevant. Evidence that is determined by the court to be admissible shall be considered in determining the best interests of the child under section 24.

2) Types of Order

Provincial and territorial legislation confers wide powers on the courts in the exercise of their discretionary jurisdiction over custody and access. For example, courts may grant:

- interim or temporary orders;
- review orders and consent orders;
- joint guardianship and custody orders;
- third-party custody and access orders;
- orders dividing the incidents of custody;
- non-molestation or restraining orders;
- supervision orders;
- conditional orders restricting mobility or providing for notice of any intended change of residence;
- orders for the tracing of missing children;
- orders for the apprehension of children to prevent parental abduction;
- orders for the return of a child from outside the province or territory;
- orders for the enforcement of custody and access arrangements; and
- orders for the variation and termination of custody and access.

In proceedings for interim custody, courts are loath to disturb existing parenting arrangements, being of the opinion that the best interests of children

---

64   *KRG v RKD*, 2013 ONSC 1162.

are ordinarily served by not disturbing the *status quo*.[65] Absent some compelling reason, courts are also hesitant to vary interim custody orders, which constitute temporary measures that are put in place until the parenting dispute can be resolved by agreement or a trial judgment.[66] Appeals of interim orders are discouraged and great deference is owed to the exercise of discretion by a motion judge.[67]

Review orders are unusual in custody and access cases because some degree of finality is usually desirable to promote stability in the lives of the children. However, a trial judge may find it appropriate to order an automatic review and to remain seized with jurisdiction, where he or she perceives a real prospect that his or her original order may not prove to be in the best interests of the children having regard to foreseeable future problems. The doctrines of *res judicata* and *functus officio* constitute no bar to the trial judge remaining seized with custody and access issues for the purpose of the review. Section 17(5) of the *Divorce Act* does not exclude the possibility of providing a fast-track review procedure under section 16(6) of the *Divorce Act*, which co-exists with the right of either parent to seek a variation order upon proof of a material change of circumstances. The triggering factor under section 16(6) may be the passage of time, the occurrence of some event, or the existence of some condition. In upholding the review provision in the current appeal, the Newfoundland and Labrador Court of Appeal in *JMM v KAM*[68] observed that the availability of the fast-track review procedure enabled the trial judge to grant an order for increased access to the children by the father on a five-day rotational basis, secure in the knowledge that this order could be expeditiously revisited if the father's previous conduct in seeking to alienate the children from their mother were resumed in the future.

3)   Wishes of Child;[69] Judicial Interviews; Legal Representation

With respect to custody and access proceedings, statutes in several provinces expressly acknowledge that the wishes of the child are a relevant factor to

---

65   *DLJ v DJL*, 2009 PECA 6.

66   *Koeckeritz v Secord*, [2008] SJ No 129 (QB).

67   *Kozub v Burgess*, 2013 MBCA 64; *Greve v Brighton*, 2011 ONSC 4996; *Graham v Tomlinson*, 2010 SKCA 101; *Pawar v Pawar*, 2010 SKCA 134.

68   [2005] NJ No 325 (CA). For additional insights on review orders in custody/access proceedings, see *Sappier v Francis* (2004), 276 NBR (2d) 183 (CA) and see the annotation in (2004) 8 RFL (6th) 218, which is cited in *JMM v KAM*, [2005] NJ No 325 (CA), above in this note at para 26.

69   See Chapter 10, Section N.

be considered in determining the "best interests of the child."[70] The wishes of children are not to be confused with what parenting arrangements are in their best interests. It is the duty of the court to decide what is in a child's best interests.

Courts can take various steps to prevent either parent from embroiling their children in a contested custody/access proceeding. The presiding judge may exclude the children from the court, notwithstanding a parent's wish to have them present. Furthermore, although the children may be competent to give evidence, either sworn or unsworn, the judge may refuse to admit such evidence in the exercise of his or her inherent *parens patriae* jurisdiction, given that other avenues, such as assessments and home studies, are available to obtain the views and preferences of the children. A trial judge has the discretion to interview the children in chambers but this should not be undertaken lightly, and a record must be kept of the interview. A judicial interview should not go beyond ascertaining the wishes of the children; otherwise they become private witnesses and there is no basis in law for a court to admit such testimony.[71] The court must decide, on a case-by-case basis, whether interviewing a child would be in the best interests of the particular child.[72]

Although a thirteen-year-old child may be competent to give evidence in a highly conflictual parenting dispute, the court has discretion to refuse to permit the child to testify. Relevant factors to be considered in the exercise of the judicial discretion include the child's age; the child's aversion to or fear of testifying; the trauma that the child would suffer from testifying, even if the trauma does not involve long-term damage; the significance and probable weight of the child's evidence; whether the evidence could be obtained from another source; and the overall best interests of the child. In *SEC v GP*,[73] the father sought to call his thirteen-year-old daughter to testify on his behalf in response to the mother's allegations that the father had engaged in violent and abusive conduct during their cohabitation. The father also sought to have his daughter testify as to her wishes respecting future contact with her father. On the mother's

---

70 *Family Law Act*, SA 2003, c F-4.5, s 18(2)(iv); *Family Law Act*, SBC 2011, c 25, s 37(2)(b); *Family Maintenance Act*, CCSM c F20, s 2; *Family Services Act*, SNB 1980, c F-2.2, s 1; *Children's Law Act*, RSNL 1990, c C-13, s 31(2)(b); *Children's Law Act*, SNWT 1997, c 14, s 17(2)(b); *Children's Law Reform Act*, RSO 1990, c C.12, s 24(2)(b); *Custody Jurisdiction and Enforcement Act*, RSPEI 1988, c C-33, s 8; *Civil Code of Québec*, SQ 1991, c 64, s 34; *Children's Law Act*, SS 1997, c C-8.2, s 8(a)(vii) (custody) and s 9(1)(iv) (access); *Children's Act*, RSY 1986, c 22, s 131(h).

71 *MES v DAS*, [2001] AJ No 1521 (QB); *Chovin v Dancer-Chovin*, [2003] SJ No 598 (QB); see also *Perino v Perino*, 2012 ONSC 328.

72 *ALM v NJO*, 2015 BCSC 70 at para 55, Greyell J.

73 [2003] OJ No 2744 (Sup Ct).

application, Perkins J set aside the father's summons of his daughter as a witness because her emotional well-being would not be served by requiring her to testify, her evidence would not carry great weight having regard to the already available evidence addressing the general climate in the home over the years, and the reliability of any evidence presented would be suspect because the child was attached to her father and did not want to displease him.

The three most common methods of ascertaining the views and preferences of a child are (1) judicial interview; (2) the appointment of an independent expert able to ascertain the child's views; and (3) the appointment of independent legal counsel for the child.[74] Most judges discourage parents and their lawyers from calling the children as witnesses in contested custody or access litigation.[75] Some judges will, however, interview the children privately in chambers, in the absence of the parents, but with counsel and/or a court reporter present.[76] Several provincial statutes specifically empower a judge to privately interview a child without imposing any requirement of parental consent. Judicial interviews of children without parental consent have also been endorsed by appellate courts in Manitoba and Saskatchewan.[77] In *A(LJ) v A(L)*,[78] the British Columbia Court of Appeal expressed concern about the danger of a trial judge deciding a case on evidence of which the parents had no knowledge and no opportunity for cross-examination. Faced with significant cutbacks to legal aid services and in the use of third-party neutrals to ascertain a child's wishes, parents and their children may be denied justice if the voice of the child is not heard. In addressing these and other concerns, Martinson J, of the Supreme Court of British Columbia, has formulated the following conclusions:

---

74 *Kalaserk v Nelson*, [2005] 8 WWR 638 (NWTSC), Vertes J, citing Christine Davies, "Access to Justice for Children: The Voice of the Child in Custody and Access Disputes" (2004) 22 Can Fam LQ 153; *Puszczak v Puszczak*, [2005] AJ No 1715 (CA). As to the role of independent counsel for the child, see *AM (Guardian ad litem of) v KAAM*, 2008 NLUFC 25; *John v John*, 2012 NSSC 324; *KSW v SW*, 2012 ONSC 4545. See also *Foote v LaSaga*, 2014 NLTD(G) 164, citing Nicholas Bala *et al*, "The Voice of Children in Canadian Family Law Cases" (2005) 24 Can Fam LQ 221.

75 *Stefureak v Chambers*, [2004] OJ No 4253 (Sup Ct); *Mohamed v Salad*, 2014 ONSC 1601.

76 Express statutory authority for judicial interviews, including the conditions applicable thereto, is found in several provinces: *Children's Law Act*, RSNL 1990, c C-13, s 70; *Children's Law Act*, SNWT 1997, c 14, s 83; *Children's Law Reform Act*, RSO 1990, c C.12, s 65; *Custody Jurisdiction and Enforcement Act*, RSPEI 1988, c C-33, s 8. See also David M Siegel & Suzanne Hurley, "The Role of the Child's Preference in Custody Proceedings" (1977) 11 Fam LQ 1; Nicholas Bala, Victoria Talwar, & Joanna Harris, "The Voice of Children in Canadian Family Law Cases" (2005) 24 Can Fam LQ 221.

77 See *Jandrisch v Jandrisch* (1980), 16 RFL (2d) 239 (Man CA); *Hamilton v Hamilton* (1989), 20 RFL (3d) 152 (Sask CA); see also *RAL v RDR*, [2006] AJ No 1474 (QB).

78 (2002), 25 RFL (5th) 8 (BCCA).

1. A judge, at a trial, has the jurisdiction to interview a child in private, even in the absence of the consent of one or both parents. The judge must, on a case by case basis, decide whether such an interview is in the best interests of the child in question.

2. In exercising this discretion, the judge can consider the general purposes of such an interview, and the general benefits of and concerns relating to the judge interview process. In addition, the judge can consider case specific factors by looking at:

   a. the relevance of the information that would be obtained to the issues that have to be decided,

   b. the reliability of the information that might be obtained, and

   c. the necessity of conducting the interview rather than obtaining the information in another way. Other options might include evidence presented:

      i. by the parties in the form of expert evidence or no expert evidence

      ii. by a neutral third party expert

      iii. by a lawyer, acting as a lawyer for the child, an *amicus curiae*, (friend of the court), or a family advocate.

3. While a parent cannot simply veto an interview, a parent's specific reasons for withholding consent may be important to a determination of relevance, reliability, and necessity.[79]

In cases involving parental alienation, it may be inappropriate for a judge to see the children privately with a view to having them articulate their wishes.[80]

In *Stefureak v Chambers*,[81] where it was concluded that the wishes of a seven-year-old child may be relevant, but are not decisive, on a mother's application to vary an order for shared parenting, Quinn J, of the Ontario Superior Court of Justice, reviewed the first five of the following methods whereby a court may ascertain the views and preferences of a child:

a) Hearsay Evidence

Since the judgments of the Supreme Court of Canada in *R v Khan*[82] and *R v Smith*,[83] hearsay evidence of out-of-court statements of a child are admissible

---

79 *LEG v AG*, [2002] BCJ No 2319 (SC); see also *DNL v CNS*, 2011 BCSC 1535; *Rupertus v Rupertus*, 2012 BCCA 426 at paras 13–15; *BJG v DLG*, 2010 YKSC 33.

80 *SLT v AKT*, 2009 ABQB 13.

81 [2004] OJ No 4253 (Sup Ct). See also *Law v Law*, 2011 ONSC 2140; *PRH v MEL*, 2009 NBCA 18.

82 [1990] 2 SCR 531.

83 [1992] 2 SCR 915.

for their truth, if they meet the tests of necessity and reliability.[84] The nature and extent of the inquiry on the issue of necessity will depend on the facts of the particular case. Relevant factors for consideration would include counsel's consent to the admission of the evidence, and the child's age, emotional fragility, and level of understanding. The out-of-court statements of a child will satisfy the "necessity" test where the direct evidence of the child would be inadmissible. The reliability test will vary with the particular child and the attendant circumstances. There are many relevant considerations, such as timing, demeanour, the personality of the child, the intelligence and understanding of the child, and the absence of any reason to expect fabrication in the statement. The reliability test is satisfied where there are sufficient guarantees that the statements made are trustworthy. There may be some merit in a submission that the requirements of necessity and threshold reliability should be relaxed in custody cases, as compared to child protection proceedings and criminal prosecutions, if the custody case does not involve allegations of abuse, but this should not be regarded as a rigid rule; the degree of relaxation will depend on all the circumstances. Threshold reliability may be established if the out-of-court statements under consideration are made to more than one person, but their ultimate reliability will be determined only after all the evidence in the case is known.

With respect to out-of-court statements that had already been included in the mother's testimony without objection from the father's counsel, Quinn J concluded that it was impractical and inappropriate to revisit that evidence for the purpose of conducting after-the-fact *voir dires*. Insofar as future testimony was concerned, he made a blanket ruling that the necessity criterion had been met because it would be inappropriate for the child to be called as a witness. On the reliability issue, he concluded that the best approach would be to conduct a *voir dire* for each statement, with the onus falling on the proponent of the hearsay evidence to establish threshold reliability.[85]

b) In-Court Testimony of Young Children

There are no age-based statutory limitations on the competence of a child to testify. Testimony has been received by Canadian courts from children as young as four, and, by the age of seven, "most children who are proposed as witnesses are ruled competent."[86] In the same article, the authors state that it is rare for children to suffer any long-term emotional disturbance

---

84   See *Ganie v Ganie*, 2014 ONSC 7500.

85   See also *Zaidi v Qizilbash*, 2014 ONSC 201.

86   See John Philippe Schuman, Nicholas Bala, & Kang Lee, "Developmentally Appropriate Questions for Child Witnesses" (1999) 25 Queen's LJ 251. See also *KRD v CKK*, 2013 NBQB 211 at paras 141–42.

from testifying in court. Indeed, giving such testimony may be cathartic. In the absence of some reasonably perceived psychological trauma to the child, there are two major obstacles to allowing a young child to testify in contested custody and access cases, namely,

1) the typical absence of a developmentally appropriate explanation to the child regarding the need for his or her testimony; and
2) the lack of training of the Bench and Bar in asking developmentally appropriate questions.

While conceding that it might not be too late to remove the first obstacle, Quinn J found it to be too late for the second obstacle to be removed.

c) Interviewing Child in Chambers

In responding to counsel's request for a judicial interview of the seven-year-old child in chambers, Quinn J referred to section 64 of the Ontario *Children's Law Reform Act*, which expressly permits such interviews in custody and access proceedings instituted pursuant to that Act. Section 64 does not impose any duty on the judge to conduct an interview, nor does it provide any criteria that must be met before an interview can take place. It is a matter of judicial discretion. The only requirement is that the interview be recorded. Customarily, the parents are not present, but counsel may be present at the discretion of the judge. Caselaw suggests that a judge should only interview a child in chambers when other methods of ascertaining the child's views and preferences are unavailable. This suggestion is premised on the assumption that judges are not trained to interview children and the formality of a judicial interview in chambers is an intimidating environment in which it is difficult for the child to speak freely. Ultimately, however, the discretion whether to interview the child in chambers rests with the judge, and it may be exercised over the objections of either or both of the parents and their counsel.[87]

If a judge decides to interview the child in chambers, caselaw clarifies the use that may be made of the interview. The primary concern is to ensure that the views and preferences of the child are not confused with the child's best interests, which must be determined in light of the evidence as a whole. Judges must, nevertheless, face practical realities. For example, the wishes of a teenage child may be compelling because of the futility of ignoring those wishes. On the other hand, the wishes of a very young child, even if ascertainable, may carry little weight in the judicial determination of the child's best

---

87 But see Nicholas Bala & Rachel Birnbaum, "Why Judges Should Meet Kids More Often" *The Lawyers Weekly* (2 July 2010).

interests. In the final analysis, the weight to be given to any child's wishes will depend on the facts, including the child's age, intelligence, degree of maturity, and his or her ability to articulate an opinion. While some judges seek to obtain the views and preferences of the child, other judges may conduct an interview in chambers for the purpose of better understanding the child for the purpose of determining his or her best interests. Save in the most exceptional circumstances, it is wrong for a judge to obtain the confidence of a child by promising not to disclose any information provided. The judge has a discretion to decide whether anything should be disclosed about the results of the interview. In exercising this discretion, the judge must consider the ability of counsel to present argument at trial or on appeal, fairness to the parties, and potential embarrassment to the child. When a trial is already in progress, a properly conducted interview of the child in chambers may be the quickest and most efficient way to ascertain the views and preferences of a child, rather than ordering a lengthy adjournment for an assessment under section 30 of the Ontario *Children's Law Reform Act* or an investigation pursuant to section 112 of the Ontario *Courts of Justice Act*.[88] Many judges are disinclined to interview a child in chambers, however, because of their lack of training in conducting such an interview.[89] In *Stefureak v Chambers*, Quinn J found that a chambers interview was not feasible because he had no training or known skill in interviewing children.[90]

d) Investigation by the Children's Lawyer

Section 112 of the *Courts of Justice Act* empowers the Children's Lawyer of Ontario to investigate, report, and make recommendations to the court on all matters concerning the custody of or access to a child that arise in proceedings under the *Divorce Act* or the Ontario *Children's Law Reform Act*. There is a significant difference between a report ordered pursuant to section 112 of the *Courts of Justice Act* and an assessment ordered under section 30 of the *Children's Law Reform Act*.[91] The former is more in the nature of a fact-finding mission whereas the latter is a more clinical exercise which is usually more comprehensive.[92] In *Novoa v Molero*,[93] the Ontario Court of Appeal held that the use of the word "may" in sections 89(3.1) and 112 of the *Courts of Justice Act* clearly confers a discretion on the Children's Lawyer of Ontario to decide whether to act as the legal representative of a minor (section 89(3.1))

---

88 SO 1994, c 12.

89 See *KRD v CKK*, 2013 NBQB 211.

90 See also *Law v Law*, 2011 ONSC 2140.

91 See Section E(3)(e), below in this chapter.

92 *Richardson v Gardner* (1995), 11 RFL (4th) 292 (Ont Prov Ct).

93 2007 ONCA 800.

or to undertake an investigation and make a report and recommendations to the court on matters concerning the custody of and access to a child (section 112). Furthermore, there is no statutory or common law obligation on the Children's Lawyer to give reasons for its decisions. If the Children's Lawyer of Ontario becomes involved in a case pursuant to section 112 of the *Courts of Justice Act*,[94] a judge may request, but cannot require, the Children's Lawyer to have a report prepared by someone other than the worker who prepared an earlier report in the case. Where such a course of action is favoured by the judge, the Children's Lawyer should be given the opportunity to hear the judge's concerns and offer a response. Ultimately, it is up to the Children's Lawyer to decide how to proceed.[95] In *Bhajan v Bhajan*,[96] the Office of the Children's Lawyer (OCL) appealed the orders of a judge of the Ontario Superior Court of Justice that required the OCL to investigate or represent children in six separate family law matters. The OCL argued that the judge erred by exceeding his jurisdiction and by invoking the *parens patriae* jurisdiction of the Superior Court. It contended that he ought to have requested legal representation pursuant to section 89(3.1) or a social work report under section 112 of the Act and, if such request were refused, should have asked the OCL to reconsider its refusal or to consider other alternatives. It further contended that the Superior Court judge could only invoke the court's *parens patriae* jurisdiction to fill a legislative gap, and no such gap existed in light of sections 89(3.1) and 112 of the *Courts of Justice Act*. The Ontario Court of Appeal focused its attention on whether it was appropriate for the Superior Court judge to invoke the *parens patriae* jurisdiction to require the OCL to represent the children or undertake an investigation, having regard to existing provincial legislation and caselaw and the impact of the United Nations *Convention on the Rights of the Child*,[97] which was signed by Canada in May 1990 and ratified in December 1991. Of particular significance in this latter context, Article 12 of the Convention provides that a child, who has the requisite capacity, has the right to freely express his or her own views on all matters affecting him or her, and the views of the child shall be given due weight in accordance with the age and maturity of the child. Article 12 further provides that the child shall be provided with the opportunity to be heard in any judicial proceedings affecting the child, either directly, or through a representative or an appropriate body, in a manner consistent with the procedural rules of national law. Addressing the Convention, the Ontario Court of Appeal

---

94   RSO 1990, c C.43.
95   *Dabirian v Dabirian*, [2004] OJ No 846 (CA).
96   2010 ONCA 714.
97   Can TS 1992 No 3.

observed that several appellate judgments in Canada, including judgments of the Supreme Court of Canada, have concluded that, while the Convention has not been specifically incorporated into domestic law and its provisions are not directly enforceable, its values can help to inform the contextual approach to statutory interpretation and judicial review in Ontario and elsewhere in Canada. After acknowledging judicial reliance on the Convention for interpretive purposes, the Ontario Court of Appeal referred to three of its previous judgments holding that both sections 89(3.1) and 112 of the *Courts of Justice Act* are permissive, not imperative, and accordingly, the OCL has the discretion to decide whether to provide legal representation for a child or to cause an investigation to be made in custody/access proceedings. While noting that these decisions did not specifically consider the UN *Convention on the Rights of the Child*, the Ontario Court of Appeal observed that the *Courts of Justice Act* is not the only legislative source that implements the values in the Convention. Additional legislative sources that reflect the values of the Convention include:

1) section 16(8) of the *Divorce Act*, whereby the best interests of the child are determinative in custody/access disputes arising under that Act;

2) sections 24(1)(a) and 24(2)(b) of the *Children's Law Reform Act*,[98] whereby the court must determine custody/access disputes under that Act having regard to the best interests of the child and, in doing so, the court must consider the child's views and preferences if they can be reasonably ascertained;

3) section 30 of the *Children's Law Reform Act*, which empowers the court to "appoint a person who has technical or professional skill to assess and report to the court on the needs of the child and the ability and willingness of the parties or any of them to satisfy the needs of the child"; and

4) Rule 4(7) of the *Family Law Rules*,[99] which provides that where a child is not a party to a proceeding, the court may authorize a lawyer to represent the child who will then have the rights of a party unless the court orders otherwise.

In the opinion of the Ontario Court of Appeal, when viewed as a whole, existing legislation and jurisprudence in Ontario reflects the values of the United Nations *Convention on the Rights of the Child*, and the existence of the aforementioned alternative avenues for children to be heard in proceedings affecting them reinforces the conclusion that the provisions in the *Courts of Justice Act* respecting the OCL are discretionary and the previous court

---

98   RSO 1990, c C.12.
99   O Reg 114/99.

rulings under sections 89(3.1) and 112 of that Act do not require reconsideration. Speaking to the exercise of the *parens patriae* jurisdiction, the appellate court stated:

> [24] Assuming, without deciding, that absent words clearly ousting the Superior Court's inherent *parens patriae* jurisdiction the Superior Court has the power to order the OCL to act outside the *CJA*, it is reasonable to assume that the legislature intended that judges would respect the legislative scheme and not create a parallel procedure. To *order* and not *request* the OCL to act ignores the discretion embodied in the wording of the *CJA* and the underlying reason for that discretion. The OCL has limited resources and it, not the court, is in the best position to decide when and how to utilize its limited resources. Failure to respect the legislative scheme by pre-empting the exercise of the OCL's discretion is an error in principle.
>
> *The parens patriae jurisdiction must be exercised in a principled manner; it should not be exercised when other effective alternative remedies exist; it should not be used to second guess or to pre-empt a decision within the mandate of the OCL.*[100]

Applying the aforementioned principles, the Ontario Court of Appeal allowed the OCL's appeals.

In Re K,[101] the Full Court of the Family Court of Australia set out the following non-exhaustive list of criteria for the appointment of a child representative:

(a) Cases involving allegations of child abuse, whether physical, sexual, or psychological.

(b) Cases where there is an apparently intractable conflict between the parents.

(c) Cases where the child is apparently alienated from one or both parents.

(d) Where there are real issues of cultural or religious difference affecting the child.

(e) Where the sexual preferences of either or both of the parents or some other person having significant contact with the child are likely to impinge upon the child's welfare.

(f) Where the conduct of either or both of the parents or some other person having significant contact with the child is alleged to be anti-social to the extent that it seriously impinges on the child's welfare.

---

100   2010 ONCA 714 [emphasis in original].

101   (1994), 17 Fam LR 537 at paras 93–107 (Aust Fam Ct).

(g) Where there are issues of significant medical, psychiatric, or psychological illness or personality disorder in relation to either party or a child or other persons having significant contact with the children.

(h) Any case in which, on the material filed by the parents, neither parent seems a suitable custodian.

(i) Any case in which a child of mature years is expressing strong views, the giving of effect to which would involve changing a longstanding custodial arrangement or a complete denial of access to one parent.

(j) Where one of the parties proposes that the child will either be permanently removed from the jurisdiction or permanently removed to such a place within the jurisdiction as to greatly restrict or for all practical purposes exclude the other party from the possibility of access to the child.

(k) Cases where it is proposed to separate siblings.

(l) Custody cases where none of the parties is legally represented.

(m) Applications in the court's welfare jurisdiction relating in particular to the medical treatment of children where the child's interests are not adequately represented by one of the parties.

In *Stefureak v Chambers*, Quinn J stated that paragraphs (a) to (c) and (f) to (h) might arguably apply to the case before him. While acknowledging that section 112 could be invoked mid-trial or even mid-appeal, Quinn J held that section 112 should only be resorted to when there is a clearly defined need that merits an investigation. Such a need did not exist in that case because the views and preferences of the seven-year-old child were unlikely to have a significant role in the final decision. Given the father's belated mid-trial request for an investigation under section 112 of the *Courts of Justice Act*, Quinn J harboured a strong suspicion that the father might be seeking to prop up a weak case by requesting the intervention of the Children's Lawyer.

In *Puszczak v Puszczak*,[102] the Alberta Court of Appeal also cited the aforementioned thirteen factors in *Re K* and further stated that the Full Court of the Family Court of Australia has observed in the later case of *B and R and the Special Representative*[103] that cases may fall within those guidelines that do not require the appointment of a separate legal representative for the child. Furthermore, before appointing counsel for the child, the court must be satisfied that the child has the capacity to instruct counsel and that an appointee is independent and not aligned with or partial to either parent.

---

102 [2005] AJ No 1715 (CA); see also *CEZ v WNZ*, 2015 ABCA 56; *SW v CM*, 2012 NWTSC 41; *PL v JA*, 2013 NWTSC 3.

103 (1995), FLC 92-636 (Aust Fam Ct).

e) Court-Ordered Independent Assessment[104]

Section 30(1) of the Ontario *Children's Law Reform Act* empowers a court to order an independent expert assessment of a child's needs and the ability and willingness of the parents to satisfy those needs. While conceding that section 30(1) might be invoked mid-trial to ascertain the views and preferences of a child, Quinn J observed that the subsection is permissive in nature and caselaw indicates that assessments should only be ordered when there are clinical issues to be determined. In the circumstances before him in *Stefureak v Chambers*, Quinn J concluded that a court-ordered independent assessment was inappropriate for the same reasons as those indicated in the context of section 112 of the *Courts of Justice Act*. However, as Jollimore J, of the Nova Scotia Supreme Court, observed in *John v John*,[105] an independent children's wishes report can satisfy the need for unbiased information about the children's preferences and at the same time provide otherwise unavailable unbiased information about what motivates those preferences and whether the children's views are uninfluenced.

f) Legal Representation

Where a lawyer is appointed to act on behalf of a child in high-conflict custody or access proceedings, the role of the lawyer is to act as an advocate for the child and to ensure that the child's voice is heard in the dispute. If the child is sufficiently mature to express a preference on the vital issue of parental custody or access, the child has the right to have his or her wishes put in evidence before the court. Counsel representing the child has a professional right and duty to advise the child as to the possible consequences of the child's preferences. Counsel may also advise the child of counsel's perception of the child's best interests. In the final analysis, however, a mature child with powers of discernment has the right to have his or her personal wishes heard and advanced by counsel in court. The role of counsel is to serve as an advocate for the child and to put forward the evidence and submissions required to support the wishes of the child so that the child's voice can be heard. Counsel for the child is not a witness and is not entitled to press his or her opinions on the court as to what he or she perceives as being in the child's best interests. Counsel appointed to represent a child in a custody or access dispute is not there to determine what is in the child's best interests. That is the function of the trial judge, who will determine the best interests of the child after hearing all the evidence, including the evidence as to the child's

---

104 See Section E(5), below in this chapter.

105 2012 NSSC 324 at para 20; see also *Smith v Smith*, 2014 BCSC 61 at para 12 (court-ordered assessment).

wishes and his or her relationship with each parent. If there has been any improper manipulation or alienation of the child, the judge will weigh the wishes of the child in light of any evidence of that manipulation. Counsel for a mature child has no right to make recommendations to the court that are contrary to the child's own wishes. If counsel finds himself or herself unable to advocate for the child's wishes, then a new appointment of counsel for the child may be necessary.[106]

4) Mediation and Reconciliation Attempts; Confidentiality of Process

In several provinces and territories, including British Columbia,[107] Manitoba,[108] Newfoundland and Labrador,[109] the Northwest Territories,[110] Ontario,[111] Quebec,[112] Saskatchewan,[113] and the Yukon Territory,[114] enactments regulate the confidentiality of reconciliation counselling and of the mediation process in economic and parenting disputes on marriage breakdown. Provincial and territorial statutes regulating reconciliation and mediation or conciliation processes differ substantially in content. They do, however, have one feature in common. With the exception of Saskatchewan,[115] the provincial and territorial legislation presupposes judicial control or intervention and, unlike section 9 of the federal *Divorce Act*,[116] does not impose specific duties on lawyers who represent clients in family disputes. In other particulars, there are wide

---

106 *MF c JL*, [2002] JQ no 480 (CA), leave to appeal to SCC refused, [2002] CSCR no 218. In this case, the appellant mother of the child sought the removal and replacement of counsel representing the child on the ground that counsel intended to rely on the expert opinion of a psychologist and seek increased contact between the child and his father as being in the best interests of the child, notwithstanding that the child was averse to this. The appeal was successful and an order was made for the replacement of the child's current lawyer. See also *Fiorito v Wiggins*, 2014 ONCA 603, citing *Strobridge v Strobridge* (1994), 4 RFL (4th) 169 (Ont CA).

107 *Family Law Act*, SBC 2011, c 25, s 13.

108 Compare *Family Maintenance Act*, CCSM c F20, ss 12 and 47 (reconciliation).

109 *Family Law Act*, RSNL 1990, c F-2, s 4 (mediation); *Children's Law Act*, RSNL 1990, c C-13, ss 37 (mediation) and 41 (access enforcement).

110 *Family Law Act*, SNWT 1997, c 18, s 58 (mediation); *Children's Law Act*, SNWT 1997, c 14, s 71 (mediation).

111 *Family Law Act*, RSO 1990, c F.3, s 3 (mediation); *Children's Law Reform Act*, RSO 1990, c C.12, s 31 (mediation).

112 Quebec *Code of Civil Procedure*, RSQ c C-25, ss 815.2–15.3 (reconciliation and mediation).

113 *Children's Law Act*, SS 1997, c C-8.2, ss 10 & 11 (mediation) and 26 (access enforcement); *Family Maintenance Act*, SS 1997, c F-6.2, ss 15 & 16 (mediation).

114 *Children's Act*, RSY 2002, c 31, s 42.

115 *Children's Law Act*, SS 1997, c C-8.2, s 11.

116 See Chapter 6, Section D(1).

variations. Some statutory provisions are confined to reconciliation;[117] others are confined to mediation;[118] still others apply to both reconciliation and mediation.[119] In addition, some statutes render evidence of statements made to a counsellor or mediator inadmissible except on consent of the parties,[120] while others specifically distinguish "open" or "closed" mediation.[121] This latter statutory approach originated in Ontario with the enactment of section 31 of the *Children's Law Reform Act*,[122] which regulates the potential confidentiality of the mediation process with respect to parenting disputes. Court-ordered mediation on consent of the parties under section 31 requires the parties to decide whether the mediator will file a full report of the mediation or a report that simply stipulates the outcome of the mediation process. If parties elect the latter, evidence of any admission or communication made in the course of the mediation is inadmissible in any legal proceeding, except on consent of all parties to the proceeding.[123] Even in the absence of statutory provisions, however, judge-made law has accorded a common law privilege to communications made in an attempt to settle disputes.[124]

5) Court-Ordered Investigations, Assessments, and Reports

In *Young v Young*,[125] the Supreme Court of Canada confirmed that, although expert evidence may be helpful in some cases, it is not routinely required to establish the best interests of a child. That determination is normally possible from the evidence of the parties themselves and, in some cases, the testimony of the children involved. Under ordinary circumstances, a more

---

117   *Family Maintenance Act*, CCSM c F20, s 12 (duty of court to promote reconciliation).

118   *Family Services Act*, SNB 1980, c F-2.2, s 131 (court-ordered conciliation); *Family Law Act*, RSNL 1990, c C-13, s 4; *Children's Law Act*, RSNL 1990, c C-13, s 37; *Children's Law Act*, SNWT 1997, c 14, s 71; *Family Law Act*, SNWT 1997, c 18, s 58; *Children's Law Reform Act*, RSO 1990, c C.12, s 31; *Family Law Act*, RSO 1990, c F.3, s 3; *Children's Law Act*, SS 1997, c C-8.2, ss 10 & 11; *Family Maintenance Act*, SS 1997, c F-6.2, ss 15 & 16; *Children's Act*, RSY 2002, c 31, s 42.

119   Quebec *Code of Civil Procedure*, RSQ c C-25.

120   *Family Law* Act, SBC 2011, c 25, s 13; Quebec *Code of Civil Procedure*, RSQ c C-25, s 815.3; *Children's Law Act*, SS 1997, c C-8.2, s 10; *Family Maintenance Act*, SS 1997, c F-6.2, s 15.

121   See *Children's Law Act*, RSNL 1990, c C-13, s 37; *Family Law Act*, RSNL 1990, c C-13, s 4; *Children's Law Act*, SNWT 1997, c 14, s 71; *Family Law Act*, SNWT 1997, c 18, s 58; *Children's Law Reform Act*, RSO 1990, c C.12, s 31; *Family Law Act*, RSO 1990, c F.3, s 3; *Children's Act*, RSY 2002, c 31, s 42.

122   RSO 1990, c C.12.

123   *Ibid*, s 31(7).

124   *Sinclair v Roy* (1985), 47 RFL (2d) 15 (BCSC); *Porter v Porter* (1983), 32 RFL (2d) 413 (Ont UFC).

125   [1993] 4 SCR 3; see also *RKC v GSA*, 2012 ABQB 614.

limited role is appropriate for expert evidence, given the expense of such evidence, the time consumed in its preparation and presentation, and the often inconclusive results it generates.

Several provinces and territories have enacted statutory provisions whereby their courts may order investigations, assessments, and reports to be undertaken by independent experts in custody and access proceedings.[126] Some statutes confer this discretionary authority on the courts in very general terms; others provide more detailed statutory provisions to regulate the judicial discretion. By way of example, Ontario falls into the latter category. In that province, the power of the court to order an "assessment" of the child's needs and the ability of the parties to meet those needs is defined in section 30 of the Ontario *Children's Law Reform Act*.[127] This power is exercisable as soon as an application for custody or access is brought. An assessment may be ordered before or during the hearing of the application.[128] The court may order an assessment on the request of any party to the application or on its own initiative.[129] Where possible, the court will appoint an assessor chosen by the parties, but their failure to agree does not preclude the court from appointing an assessor who is willing to undertake the assessment and report to the court within the period of time designated by the court. The court may direct the parties to the application, the child, and other persons (for example, a "common-law spouse") to submit to an assessment, and any refusal to do so entitles the court to draw adverse inferences against a non-consenting adult respecting his or her ability or willingness to meet the needs of the child. The report of the assessor is filed with the court and copies are provided to the parties and to counsel, if any, for the child. The assessor may be required to attend as a witness at any subsequent hearing of the application for custody or access. The costs of the assessment are to be borne by the parties in such proportions as the court directs,[130] but the court may relieve a party from all or any of his or her financial responsibilities

---

126 *Family Law Act*, SBC 2011, c 25, s 211; *The Family Maintenance Act*, CCSM c F20, s 3; *The Court of Queen's Bench Act*, CCSM c C280, ss 49(1) and (2); see *Kopp v Burke*, 2014 MBQB 247; *Children's Law Act*, RSNL 1990, c C-13, s 36; *Children's Law Act*, SNWT 1997, c 14, s 29; *Maintenance and Custody Act*, RSNS 1989, c 160, s 19; *Children's Law Reform Act*, RSO 1990, c C.12, s 30; *Queen's Bench Act*, RSS 1978, c Q-1, s 23.5 as amended by SS 1994, c 27, s 6; *Children's Act*, RSY 2002, c 31, s 43.

127 RSO 1990, c C.12. For an excellent review of relevant caselaw interpreting and applying section 30 of the Ontario *Children's Law Reform Act*, see the judgment of Pazaratz J in *Baillie v Middleton*, 2012 ONSC 3728. See also *Ganie v Ganie*, 2014 ONSC 7500.

128 *Stefureak v Chambers*, [2004] OJ No 4253 (Sup Ct).

129 *Czegledy-Nagy v Seirli*, 2011 ONSC 6488.

130 *Durban v Medina*, 2012 ONSC 640 (fees under $6,000 apportioned to reflect respective parental incomes).

where serious pecuniary hardship would otherwise ensue. A court-ordered assessment does not preclude the parties or counsel representing the child from submitting other expert evidence respecting the needs of the child and the ability or willingness of the parties or any of them to satisfy those needs.

The role of an independent assessor, who is usually a psychiatrist, psychologist, or social worker, is to assist the court in its search for a custody or access disposition that reflects the best interests of the child. Opinions differ on whether assessors should include recommendations on appropriate parenting dispositions in their reports to the court.[131] The court must always be vigilant in ensuring that the opinion evidence elicited from an expert falls within the umbrella of the qualification afforded the witness by the court. Even when within the expert's qualification, the court is under no obligation to accept an expert's testimony.[132] Although the assessor is entitled but not compelled to recommend a specific disposition or course of action, the decision-making authority remains vested in the trial judge.[133] Assessment is not an exact science, and the assessor's report and recommendation must be reviewed by the trial judge in light of all the evidence that has been adduced.[134] In the words of Douglas ACJ, of the Manitoba Court of Queen's Bench,

> [r]ecommendations made in an assessment are only statements of opinion. Some may be accepted by the trier of fact and some may be rejected, all in the context of the totality of the other evidence. Assessments and recommendations must not usurp the duty and responsibility of the Court to make necessary decisions in a child's best interests.[135]

The party seeking a custody assessment must satisfy the court that it will likely provide evidence relating to the best interests of the child that would be otherwise unavailable. Court-ordered custody assessments are intrusive, costly, and may cause unwarranted delay. They should not be routinely ordered as a vehicle to promote settlement and should be limited to cases where there are behavioural or psychological issues, complex interpersonal dynamics, or other clinical issues that can only be appreciated by those with

---

131   *DLG v GDR*, 2012 NBQB 177 at para 257; see also *MAS v JSS*, 2012 NBQB 285.

132   *N v S*, 2008 NBQB 9; *MAS v JSS*, 2012 NBQB 285; *FFR v KF*, 2013 NLCA 8; see also *New Brunswick (Minister of Social Development) v NS*, 2013 NBCA 8 (psychologists deemed competent to give opinion evidence on mental health matters).

133   *Faber v Gallicano*, 2012 ONSC 764.

134   *Gauci v Malone*, [2009] OJ No 2627 (Sup Ct); *Ward v Ward*, [1995] SJ No 139 (QB); *CLP v RT*, [2009] SJ No 346 (QB).

135   *Burke v Moore*, 2010 MBQB 124 at para 18, Douglas ACJ; see also *Leis v Leis*, 2011 MBCA 99; *JDL v RJJL*, 2012 NBQB 378.

a particular expertise and about which the court would need assistance in understanding.[136]

In *PRH v MEL*,[137] Larlee JA, of the New Brunswick Court of Appeal, explained the role of assessors in the following terms:

> [15] There is no statutory authority under the *Divorce Act* to order an assessment by a child care professional who reports to the court and to counsel. If one is to be ordered, it would have to be done on one of the following possible bases: *parens patriae* jurisdiction of the trial judge or the inherent power of the court to control its own process. In Ontario, it appears that assessment reports are often given less weight in relocation matters than in other types of child-related cases; in fact they have more often than not been ignored. The jurisprudence stresses that an assessment is not necessary where there is no clinical issue requiring expert evidence raised on the facts and no real dispute between the parties with respect to how the children reacted to the family breakdown. A court should not order an assessment simply to obtain an apparently impartial third party's opinion on what is in a child's best interests: see *Stefureak v. Chambers*, [2004] O.J. No. 4253 (S.C.J.) (QL), where the court held that identifying the wishes of a seven year old did not justify an assessment where there were no clinical issues. A judge should only order an assessment, which involves expert opinion evidence, where there is some particular problem or issue that requires expert input (see *Sheikh v. Sheikh*, [2004] O.J. No. 4384 (S.C.J.) (QL)).
>
> [16] Furthermore a court should not delegate its duty to determine what parenting arrangement is in a child's best interests to an assessor: *Johnson v. Cleroux* (2002), 156 O.A.C. 197, [2002] O.J. No. 964 (QL); additional reasons at [2003] O.J. No. 981 (C.A.)(QL). See also *Snoddon v. Snoddon*, [2004] O.J. No. 1987 (QL), 2004 ONCJ 39 (C.J.). However, courts typically will give substantial weight to the recommendations of an assessor, but these must be only one factor to consider in the determination. A court may

---

136   *Linton v Clarke* (1994), 10 RFL (4th) 92 (Ont Div Ct); *Ursic v Ursic*, [2006] OJ No 2178 (CA); see also *Baillie v Middleton*, 2012 ONSC 3728 at paras 15–46, Pazaratz J; and compare *Glick v Cale*, 2013 ONSC 893 at paras 40–48, Kiteley J; and see *LEG v AG*, 2001 BCSC 649; *Blais v Blais*, 2008 BCSC 1785; *Kopp v Burke*, 2014 MBQB 247; *Moore v Moore*, 2013 NSSC 252; *JD v CCC*, 2013 ONSC 5678. Compare *Tucker v Tucker*, 1998 ABCA 281; *Smith v Smith*, 2014 BCSC 61 at para 12. See also *Hollis v Sachs*, 2014 ONSC 466 (unsuccessful application by grandparent for referral to Office of the Children's Lawyer for social work assessment). For relevant commentary, see Nicholas Bala & Annelise Saunders, "Understanding the Family Context: Why the Law of Expert Evidence is Different in Family Law Cases" (2003) 20 Can Fam LQ 277.

137   2009 NBCA 18; see also *AFG v DAB*, 2011 NBCA 100; *DHP v PLP*, 2012 NBQB 345 at paras 266–68. As to the mandate, parameters, and contents of a voice of the child report, see the instructive judgment of Walsh J in *MAS v JSS*, 2012 NBQB 285.

also choose to ignore the recommendations of an assessor, as in *Steeves v. Robinson* (2005), 278 N.B.R. (2d) 38, [2005] N.B.J. No. 52 (QL), 2005 NBQB 46. In the present case the lawyer for the appellant put it like this: "psychologists do not decide custody issues, judges do". I agree.

In the more recent case of *ADE v MJM*,[138] Tuck J, of the New Brunswick Court of Queen's Bench (Family Division), after noting that section 23 of the *Divorce Act* provides for provincial laws of evidence to apply in divorce proceedings, stated:

> I do not believe in the circumstance that *P.R.H., Appellant, and M.E.L., Respondent* [2009] N.B.J. No. 85 stands for the proposition that the court cannot order an assessment upon terms that mirror section 11.4 of the *Judicature Act* or section 8 of the *Family Services Act*. Further, to the extent the provisions of section 11.4 i.e. 11.4(3) (4) (5) (6) are considered laws of evidence of the Province, they could be utilized.

To properly evaluate an assessor's conclusions, a parent must have access to everything that played a role in the formation of those conclusions.[139]

Regarding the weight to be given to custody and access assessments, in *VSG v LJG*,[140] Blishen J, of the Ontario Superior Court of Justice, observed that the court must consider the following:

1. the expertise of the assessors,
2. the methodology used,
3. the reliability of the factual underpinnings for opinions provided,
4. bias, and
5. whether the opinion evidence is based on solidly grounded scientific knowledge.

Justice Blishen further observed that she was unaware of any standardized protocol for conducting assessments, although good assessments use a variety of methods to ensure the reliability of information obtained respecting a child and parents, including the following:

1. interviews with each parent and anyone living with the person seeking custody or access (e.g. new partners);
2. interviews with the child and observation of interaction between parents and children;

---

138 2012 NBQB 260 at para 249; but compare *JDL v RJJL*, 2012 NBQB 378 at paras 89–90.
139 *Samson v Simard*, 2008 NSSC 87.
140 [2004] OJ No 2238 (Sup Ct).

3. contact with others who have had significant involvement such as teachers or family doctors, as well as relatives who have a significant role in the lives of the children, such as grandparents;
4. a review of significant records or reports about the children or their parents; and,
5. psychological tests on parents and perhaps children, if a registered psychologist is involved.

The use and abuse of expert opinion evidence in guardianship, custody, and access disputes has in the past attracted critical attention.[141] It is generally conceded, however, that independent investigations, assessments, and reports can be of substantial assistance to courts and often produce parental settlements without recourse to protracted litigation. In Alberta, *Family Law Practice Note 7* currently confers jurisdiction on the Alberta Court of Queen's Bench to authorize two kinds of procedure, namely, interventions and assessments. An intervention signifies a short- or long-term therapeutic involvement by a parenting expert that is resolution-oriented to assist families to overcome conflict. The intervention is intended to support the family in a collaborative, child-centred manner. The types of intervention may include counselling/therapy; educational sessions; assisting parents to develop and implement a parenting plan or parallel parenting plans; evaluation; remedial facilitated access; and formulating recommendations to the court for longer-term counselling, mediation, arbitration, or other forms of intervention. An assessment is an objective, neutral evaluation carried out by a parenting expert as an aid to litigation. An assessment may address only one home or parent or child. Assessments may include psychological testing. An assessment may also explore individual issues such as the educational needs of a child, the mental health of an individual, and anything else that the litigants identify and the court orders. Assessments include bilateral custody assessments. The parenting expert submits an assessment report to the court with copies to the parties or their counsel. A parenting expert may be required to give

---

141 Saul V Levine, "The Role of the Mental Health Expert Witness in Family Law Disputes" in Rosalie S Abella & Claire L'Heureux-Dubé, eds, *Family Law: Dimensions of Justice* (Markham, ON: Butterworths, 1983) at 129; R Parry, *Custody Disputes: Evaluation and Intervention* (Toronto: Lexington Books, 1986); Gwynn Davis, *Partisans and Mediators: The Resolution of Divorce Disputes* (New York: Oxford University Press, 1988); Richard A Gardner, "My Involvement in Custody Litigation: Past, Present and Future" (1989) 27 Family and Conciliation Courts Review 1; Faith K Kaplan, Barbara L Landau, & Robert L McWhinney, "Custody/Access Assessment Guidelines: Report of the Interdisciplinary Committee for Custody/Access Assessments" (1989) 27 Family and Conciliation Courts Review 61; Paula J Caplan & Jeffery Wilson, "Assessing the Child Custody Assessors" (1990) 27 RFL (3d) 121.

viva voce evidence and is subject to cross-examination by the parties in any proceedings wherein the best interests of the child are in issue.[142]

In *DMM v DPL*,[143] Nash J, of the Alberta Court of Queen's Bench, endorsed the following principles respecting court-ordered assessments. The court has a discretion to order a custody/access assessment where it appears that one would be materially helpful. There must be some evidence upon which to base the exercise of discretion. The party seeking an assessment has the onus of justifying the request. The assessment process is time-consuming, expensive, and intrusive, and should not be ordered automatically. A custody/access assessment is to be considered together with all of the evidence in determining what parenting arrangements serve the child's best interests. In *Tucker v Tucker*,[144] Conrad JA, of the Alberta Court of Appeal, concluded that an assessment should not be routinely ordered nor should it permit a fishing expedition, but if a judge is satisfied that an assessment is necessary to protect or determine the best interests of the child, he or she has an obligation to obtain or receive the evidence. She rejected counsel's suggestion that an assessment cannot be ordered on an application to vary a custody order until a determination is made of a material change in circumstances, holding that this suggestion might remove from the judge the most objective method of determining whether a material change in the child's condition, means, needs, or other circumstances had occurred.

In *Goudie v Goudie*,[145] Parrett J, of the Supreme Court of British Columbia, explained the value and purpose of an investigation and report ordered pursuant to section 15 of the *Family Relations Act* (BC), now section 211 of the *Family Law Act*, in the following words:

> In family law cases generally, and in custody and access cases in particular, the issues are often obscured by the emotional overtones of such proceedings. In such circumstances, the court's power to order an investigation by an independent person with specialized training is an invaluable tool. The procedure anticipated by s 15 is one in which the investigator interviews the people involved, observes the relationship and the interaction between the spouses and the children and reports those observations, facts and impressions to the court. In the truest sense these individuals act as the court's eyes and ears in what are all too frequently highly emotional areas

---

142 See *RPB v KDP*, [2006] AJ No 1192 (QB); *Gordon v Towell*, 2010 ABQB 396; *Matty v Rammasoot*, 2011 ABCA 339; *Schoepp v Schoepp*, 2012 ABQB 88.

143 1999 ABQB 37; see also *Gordon v Towell*, 2010 ABQB 396.

144 1998 ABCA 281.

145 [1993] BCJ No 1049 at para 33 (SC); see also *McArthur v McArthur*, 2012 BCSC 717; *Shier v Shier*, 2014 BCSC 998.

of conflict. The safeguards built into the process include the early delivery of investigation reports, the opportunity to call the investigator to the witness stand and the opportunity to respond to the report generally by other evidence.

With respect to the transition from section 15 of the *Family Relations Act* to section 211 of the *Family Law Act*, Master Keighley in *TN v JCN* stated that "the general principles upon which the court might consider such an order remain unchanged" and "the evidentiary threshold remains a relatively low one."[146] Courts rely upon the investigator to ensure that the children are heard and/or that their support networks on both sides of the mother and father are heard and recommendations are made. The investigator must ensure that all information is fairly and accurately presented in a clear and unbiased manner.[147] Because the right to cross-examine a court-appointed investigator is an important safeguard integral to the custody and access process, and particularly to the ability of the court to rely on hearsay evidence, the court-appointed expert must attend any trial to explain or defend his report if requested to do so by a party or the judge.[148] While a trial judge should rarely preclude the cross-examination of the author of a report by a parent, either directly or by refusing an adjournment, the right to cross-examine is not absolute. It must always give way to the best interests of the children.[149]

The admissibility of a report ordered pursuant to section 211 of the *Family Law Act* (British Columbia) is not governed by the same evidentiary rules that apply when an expert's report is commissioned by one of the parties. Such a report may be admitted despite its inclusion of hearsay evidence and its reference to documents that will not be in evidence at the trial. The weight to be given to the opinions and recommendations of the assessor are to be determined in light of the evidence given at the trial relating to the facts and assumptions underlying the assessor's opinions.[150] A court may impose limitations on the scope of a section 211 assessment.[151] The preparation and reception of a court-ordered report has built-in safeguards that are an inherent part of a process designed to place important and sensitive information before the court. Jurisdiction is vested in the court to approve the person to be appointed to carry out the investigation, and the person

---

146   2013 BCSC 1870 at paras 13–14; see also *Smith v Smith*, 2014 BCSC 61 at para 12.
147   *PWC v ESC*, 2012 BCPC 77. As to updating of report, see *AEO v TKO*, 2011 BCCA 517.
148   *KMW v LJW*, 2010 BCCA 572, citing *LEG v AG*, 2003 BCSC 412 at paras 20 and 26.
149   *KMW v LJW*, 2010 BCCA 572.
150   *Wu v Sun*, 2006 BCSC 1891, [2006] BCJ No 3276.
151   *HDF v LMF*, 2013 BCSC 1301.

so appointed reports to the court. Copies of the investigator's report are provided to the parties before it is placed before the court, and any party is at liberty to compel the author's attendance for cross-examination and may lead evidence as to factual matters contained in the report. Given these various safeguards, the proper approach is to consider the factual aspects of the report to be *prima facie* evidence as to the truth of those facts. Where neither party challenges the report or requires the attendance of its author, the report should be considered a part of the evidence as a whole placed before the court. Faced with inaccurate and unreliable evidence on the part of both parents in *PAB v TKB*,[152] Parrett J placed substantial weight on the report of the court-appointed expert in concluding that a joint custody regime was precluded by acrimony and bitterness that prevented the parents from maintaining the level of communication necessary to make such a regime workable. Consequently, sole custody was granted to the mother, with the father being entitled to reasonable and generous access to the children. The opinions and recommendations of a court-appointed psychologist may be judicially discounted where the evidence as a whole leads the judge to assess the situation differently and parts of the report stray beyond the kind of investigation contemplated by the statute.

In *Leontowicz v Jacobsen*, the "recommendations" addressed a number of matters that the court was better qualified to evaluate, such as the significance of adherence to court orders, and some went directly to ultimate issues by applying the assessor's perception of the applicable legal criteria.[153] Evidence need not be called to cover all matters referred to in the report; if it were otherwise, the report would be superfluous. The court may accept or reject the opinions and recommendations in the report, in whole or in part. If the expert, in forming his or her opinion, relies on facts that are contradicted by evidence presented at the trial, the court will have to decide which of the conflicting versions, if either, should be accepted.[154] A court may order that the costs of a court-ordered report shall be shared by the parents in proportion to their respective incomes.[155]

A parental-capacity assessment sought pursuant to section 32F(1) of the *Judicature Act*[156] is appropriate where relevant clinical information would not otherwise be available to the court. Assessments are intrusive and involve additional costs and delay in the adjudicative process. They should not be

---

152 [2004] BCJ No 86 (SC); see also *KMW v LJW*, 2010 BCCA 572; *SEB v TJB*, 2009 BCSC 1650; *SMM v JPH*, 2011 BCSC 1084.

153 *Leontowicz v Jacobsen*, [2003] BCJ No 2723 (SC).

154 *Neault v Neault*, 2011 BCSC 1111 at para 69.

155 *Allen v Allen*, 2013 BCSC 1934; compare *Vlek v Graff*, 2013 BCSC 1906.

156 RSNS 1989, c 240. See also *Doncaster v Field*, 2014 NSSC 234.

ordered as a matter of course, nor should they be used as a fishing expedition.[157] The mere fact that an assessment would benefit or assist the court is not enough. The information or opinion sought must not be otherwise available than from an expert.[158] In *Lewis v Lewis*,[159] an interim application for a parental-capacity assessment was denied because the applicant failed to show that it was necessary and in the best interests of the children, and the court had grave concerns that the proposed assessment would be used as an attempt to put forward highly prejudicial sexual abuse allegations that would not otherwise be admissible as evidence. A trial judge is not obliged to accept an assessor's recommendation.[160]

An expert's opinion should be judicially dismissed where the evidence as a whole does not support significant factual assumptions made by the expert with respect to the parenting capabilities of the parties.[161]

An independent custody assessment report ordered pursuant to section 30 of the Ontario *Children's Law Reform Act* is admissible as expert evidence. Consequently, when asked to order an assessment, the court should consider the legal requirements relating to the admissibility of expert evidence. In *R v Mohan*,[162] the Supreme Court of Canada states that the admission of expert evidence depends on the application of the following criteria:

- relevance;
- necessity in assisting the trier of fact;
- the absence of any exclusionary rule; and
- a properly qualified expert.

Even when these criteria are met, the trial judge exercises a gatekeeper function by exercising judicial discretion in determining and weighing competing considerations to decide whether, on balance, they favour the admissibility of the evidence.[163] In *R v Abbey*,[164] the Ontario Court of Appeal observed that there is no closed list of the factors relevant to the reliability of an expert's opinion. However, the following questions may be relevant to the reliability inquiry:

---

157 *MacLean v Boylan*, 2011 NSSC 314, citing *Farmakoulas v McInnis*, 1996 CanLII 5447 (NSSC); *Doncaster v Field*, 2014 NSSC 234.

158 *Bignell v Martin*, 2012 NSSC 112 at para 6, O'Neil ACJSC(FD).

159 [2005] NSJ No 368 (SC).

160 *Ross-Johnson v Johnson*, 2009 NSCA 128; see also *Jarvis v Landry*, 2011 NSSC 116.

161 *Cade v Rotstein*, [2004] OJ No 286 (CA).

162 [1994] 2 SCR 9 at paras 17 and 22; see also *White Burgess Langille Inman v Abbott and Haliburton Co*, 2015 SCC 23; *AJU v GSU*, 2015 ABQB 6; *Wakeley v Wakeley*, 2015 ONSC 3561.

163 *White Burgess Langille Inman v Abbott and Haliburton Co*, above note 162; *Hayes v Goodfellow*, 2011 ONSC 1270.

164 [2009] OJ No 3534 (CA).

- To what extent is the field in which the opinion is offered a recognized discipline, profession, or area of specialized training?
- To what extent is the work within that field subject to quality assurance measures and appropriate independent review by others in the field?
- What are the particular expert's qualifications within that discipline, profession, or area of specialized training?
- To the extent that the opinion rests on data accumulated through various means such as interviews, is the data accurately recorded, stored, and available?
- To what extent are the reasoning processes underlying the opinion and the methods used to gather the relevant information clearly explained by the witness and susceptible to critical examination by a jury?
- To what extent has the expert arrived at his or her opinion using methodologies accepted by those working in the particular field in which the opinion is advanced?
- To what extent do the accepted methodologies promote and enhance the reliability of the information gathered and relied on by the expert?
- To what extent has the witness, in advancing the opinion, honoured the boundaries and limits of the discipline from which his or her expertise arises?
- To what extent is the proffered opinion based on data and other information gathered independently of the specific case or, more broadly, the litigation process?

The fact that expert evidence might be helpful is insufficient to satisfy the necessity requirement. Although necessity is not to be determined by too strict a standard, the expert's opinion must be necessary in the sense that it will provide information that is likely to be outside the experience and knowledge of the court. In *Linton v Clarke*,[165] the Ontario Divisional Court ruled that assessments should not be routinely ordered in custody and access disputes but should be limited to cases in which clinical issues must be determined. Although the necessity requirement may well be met in some cases by the presence of clinical issues, there are also cases in which clinical issues exist but the court considers that an independent assessment under section 30 of the Ontario *Children's Law Reform Act* is unnecessary. Courts in Alberta, British Columbia, and Manitoba do not appear to insist on the existence of a clinical issue.[166]

---

165   (1994), 21 OR (3d) 568 (Div Ct). But see text below in this section.
166   See *Tucker v Tucker*, 1998 ABCA 281; *LEG v AG*, 2001 BCSC 649; *Blais v Blais*, 2008 BCSC 1785; *CMH v TTH*, 2014 MBQB 65 at para 51.

Expert critiques of independent custody assessments have frequently been introduced without any consideration of the question of their admissibility. The rule for admissibility of expert evidence in family law cases is the same as that applicable in other cases: the four-part test as originally set out in *R v Mohan*, above, and refined in subsequent cases is applicable. In many cases relating to the evidence of a proposed expert, the critical question relates to necessity. Expert evidence will be necessary when it can provide a ready-made inference, which the judge, due to the technical nature of the facts, is unable to formulate; expert evidence is not necessary to address matters that fall within the scope of common sense. In most cases, it is neither necessary nor appropriate to introduce the evidence of a collateral critique of an independent custody assessment. Such a critique may be undertaken to assist counsel in formulating questions for cross-examination of the assessor or to assist counsel in developing an argument concerning the weight to be assigned to an assessment report, but it will not ordinarily be "necessary" to introduce the critique as original evidence or to call the expert who undertook the critique to give testimony.[167]

Courts should be extremely cautious about relying on untested professional reports at a motion pending trial, or implementing even some of an assessor's recommendations on a temporary basis.[168] In *Genovesi v Genovesi*,[169] Granger J, of the Ontario General Division, held that an independent custody assessment is usually ordered for use at a trial and it is only in rare cases that the information obtained by the assessor might require immediate scrutiny on an interim application to determine whether there should be some variation of the existing parenting arrangement. But, as Mitrov J, of the Ontario Superior Court of Justice, observed in *Bos v Bos*,[170] "although the general principle enunciated in *Genovesi* continues to be well founded, it is not so rigid and inflexible as to prevent a court on a motion to give some consideration to the content of an assessment report where that assessment report provides some additional probative evidence to assist the court, particularly where the court is making an order which is not a substantive departure from an

---

167 *Mayfield v Mayfield*, [2001] OJ No 2212 (Sup Ct); see also *Hejzlar v Mitchell-Hejzlar*, 2010 BCSC 1139; *Sordi v Sordi*, 2011 ONCA 665.

168 *Marcy v Belmore*, 2012 ONSC 4696; *Batsinda v Batsinda*, 2013 ONSC 7869 at para 32.

169 (1992), 41 RFL (3d) 27 (Ont Gen Div); see also *Stuyt v Stuyt*, [2006] OJ No 4890 (Sup Ct); *Kirkham v Kirkham*, [2008] OJ No 2459 (Sup Ct); *Winn v Winn*, [2008] OJ No 4854 (Sup Ct); *Caparelli v Caparelli*, [2009] OJ No 5640 (Sup Ct) (access); *Jegasothy v Jayaraj*, 2010 ONSC 4263 (Div Ct); compare *Kerr v Hauer*, 2010 ONSC 1995; compare also *Horvat v Cross*, 2010 BCSC 1472.

170 2012 ONSC 3425 at para 23; see also *Kirwan v Kirwan*, 2014 ONSC 3308; compare *Marcy v Belmore*, 2012 ONSC 4696.

existing order or status quo. In such circumstances, the court may consider some of the evidence contained in an assessment report without having to conclude that there are 'exceptional circumstances' as set out in *Genovesi*."[171] A court may draw an adverse inference against a parent who refuses to participate in a court-ordered assessment. Such a refusal may be judicially perceived as indicative of that parent's reluctance to co-operate in parenting, giving priority to his or her personal needs over the best interests of the child, or being preoccupied with control.[172]

An assessment in a mobility case is necessarily speculative and uncertain and is, therefore, of limited utility because the assessor is comparing two situations which presently do not exist rather than comparing two present situations and determining where the best interests of the child lie.[173]

While high conflict cases can be difficult, they do not necessarily present issues that the court is ill equipped to resolve without the assistance of an assessor.[174]

Where the children in a contested custody/access proceeding have independent legal counsel and an experienced social worker assigned by the Office of the Children's Lawyer, reports are available from a psychologist and from the children's family doctor, and direct evidence will also be provided by two Children's Aid Societies, the court may dismiss a parent's application for a court-ordered assessment under section 30 of the Ontario *Children's Law Reform Act* because the trial judge will be able to determine the issues raised in the case without the need for such an assessment. Any deficiencies identified by the applicant parent with respect to the work of the social worker appointed to assist the children's legal counsel may be dealt with by cross-examination and by direct evidence, and they do not, in themselves, justify a court-ordered section 30 assessment. The fact that both parents had previously agreed to such an assessment does not circumscribe the court's discretion under section 30 of the Ontario *Children's Law Reform Act*, and the agreement will carry little weight when it preceded the appointment of the lawyer and social worker by the Office of the Children's Lawyer.[175] If the Children's Lawyer of Ontario becomes involved in a case pursuant to section 112 of the *Courts of Justice Act*, a judge may request, but cannot require, the Children's Lawyer to have a report prepared by someone other than the worker who prepared an earlier report in the case. Where such a course of action is

---

171 See also *PLM v SYB*, 2014 NBQB 222. For more detailed guidelines, see *Ruddock v Williams*, 2013 ONCJ 225, citing *Bos v Bos*, 2012 ONSC 3425 and *SV v HC*, 2009 ONCJ 136.

172 *Rockell v Kent*, 2011 ONSC 4034, citing *Gregoire v Mogane*, [2001] OJ No 4076 (Sup Ct).

173 *Cozzi v Smith*, 2013 ONSC 3190.

174 *Kenny v Ratcliffe*, 2013 ONSC 4741 at para 41, Mesbur J.

175 *JJB v GGB*, [2003] OJ No 4073 (Sup Ct).

favoured by the judge, the Children's Lawyer should be given the opportunity to hear the judge's concerns and offer a response. Ultimately, it is up to the Children's Lawyer to decide how to proceed.[176]

In Saskatchewan, custody/access assessments take a variety of forms, including full custody/access assessments, access assessments only, focused assessments that concentrate on a specific aspect of the parenting arrangement and/or the welfare of the child(ren), and "voices of the children" reports, which set out the wishes and/or concerns of the children. This list is not exhaustive. Such reports may be ordered by a judge at any stage of a proceeding and the reasons for ordering such reports differ widely. Given the wide variety of assessments in Saskatchewan, when they may be ordered, and the different purposes for which they are ordered, it is not prudent to endorse hard and fast rules with respect to their use. There are a number of factors a court should consider in determining whether it is proper to take into account an assessor's report. These circumstances include, but are not limited to, the following:

1) the nature of the application (i.e., whether it is an interim application or an application for variation);

2) the nature of the relief sought (i.e., custody, access, a change from supervised to unsupervised visitations, etc.);

3) the purpose of the assessment (i.e., whether it is for use by the chambers judge and/or at trial);

4) the scope of the assessment (i.e., whether it is a full custody/access assessment, a focused assessment, a voices of the children report, etc.);

5) whether the assessment raises some immediate concern relating to the health and/or safety of the children;

6) whether the parties agree to the use of the assessment;

7) whether an evidentiary basis has been established for the opinions expressed in the assessment; and

8) whether the assessor can be subjected to cross-examination before the report is used.

In *Burka v Burka*,[177] applying these criteria to a full custody/access assessment that had been ordered at a pre-trial conference and was obviously intended for use by the trial judge, Ryan-Froslie J, (as she then was) of the Saskatchewan Court of Queen's Bench, endorsed Granger J's approach in *Genovesi v Genovesi* and refused to consider the assessment report on

---

176   *Dabirian v Dabirian*, [2004] OJ No 846 (CA).

177   [2003] SJ No 609 (QB); see also *Koeckeritz v Secord*, [2008] SJ No 129 (QB); *Gallant v Gallant*, [2009] SJ No 586 (QB); *Thogersen v Thogersen*, 2010 SKQB 287.

cross-applications by the parents to vary an interim order for joint custody by changing the child's primary residence so as to facilitate her attendance at a single kindergarten. Justice Ryan-Froslie, nevertheless, concluded that the existing interim order should be varied so that the child would ordinarily reside with the mother during the school week because it was not in the child's best interests to attend two different kindergartens in the separate communities in which the two parents lived. Two distinctions between an expert retained by one of the parents and an expert appointed by the court pursuant to section 97 of the *Queen's Bench Act* (Saskatchewan)[178] are found in subsections 97(2) and (3) of the Act, namely, (1) when a report is ordered for the assistance of the court, the expert may be called as a witness by the court and is subject to cross-examination by any party; and (2) a court-appointed expert is statutorily immune from civil liability for anything done or omitted to be done in good faith. Section 97 of the *Queen's Bench Act* does not preclude a parent from calling as his or her own witness an expert who is qualified to make observations and proffer opinions on the custody, access, and welfare of children. The admissibility of expert-opinion evidence in this area is subject to the same set of criteria that govern opinion evidence in other areas of expertise. The evidence must be necessary, relevant, and provide information likely to be outside the experience of the trier of fact. The evidence must not offend any other exclusionary rule, and the person offering the evidence must be suitably qualified. In *Johnston v Kurz*,[179] a section 97 assessment was not ordered, but the parents agreed that the father would retain and pay for his own assessor and the mother would co-operate in the assessment. The evidence of the assessor was deemed admissible. After reviewing the best interests of the children in light of all the evidence, and the criteria defined in sections 6(1), (5), (7), and (8) of the *Children's Law Act* (Saskatchewan), and in *Gordon v Goertz*,[180] M-E Wright J concluded that the mother, who had been the child's primary caregiver, should be granted permission to relocate with the child from Saskatchewan to New Brunswick to marry her fiancé and pursue available career opportunities there. The mother's wish to relocate under these circumstances was found to outweigh the consequential disruption of the child's close relationship with the father and paternal grandparents, which could be ameliorated to some degree by arrangements for frequent visits and contact by means of letters, telephone calls, emails, and webcam. Where an assessment report is ordered pursuant to section 97 of the *Queen's Bench Act* (Saskatchewan), there can be no doubt

---

178   SS 1998, c Q-1.1.
179   [2005] SJ No 558 (QB).
180   [1996] 2 SCR 27.

that the report is for the assistance of the court and both parents are afforded the liberty of full cross-examination. As *Larre v Cross*[181] demonstrates, where parents have jointly retained an assessor without recourse to section 97, one parent or the other is required to take "ownership" of the witness based on the assessor's subjective assessment of which of them came off better in the assessment. Because assessments are frequently critical of both parents and they may recommend joint custody for parents who are each seeking sole custody, *Larre v Cross* may result in the unintended consequence that neither parent calls the assessor, thus denying valuable evidence to the court. Such a result is contrary to the long-standing principle, which is acknowledged in *Redshaw v Redshaw*,[182] that all evidence that bears on the seminal question of a child's best interests should be made available to the court.

Trial judges should not abdicate their responsibilities as triers of fact and arbiters, by deferring to assessors.[183] A court cannot delegate its duty to determine what parenting arrangement is in a child's best interests to an assessor,[184] but the results of an assessment will be considered very carefully by the court. This does not mean that courts will simply "rubber stamp" the assessor's report.[185] A direction by a trial judge that access privileges shall be determined by an appropriate professional will be deemed to have been made in excess of jurisdiction, and constitutes a reversible error on appeal.[186] Where parties choose not to seek alternative methods of dispute resolution but rely on the adversarial process instead, the court has an obligation to render a judgment and not simply provide advice or instruct the parties as to how they may resolve their difficulties.[187]

6) Grandparents and Other Third Parties; Multiple Parents

Provincial and territorial legislation in Canada establishes that in custody and access disputes between parents and third parties, the best interests

---

181 [1998] SJ No 851 (QB).

182 (1985), 47 RFL (2d) 104 (Sask CA).

183 *MP v ADA*, 2011 NBQB 351.

184 *Mai v Schumann*, 2013 BCCA 365.

185 *Nagy v Bright*, 2012 ONSC 986.

186 *Stewart v Stewart* (1990), 30 RFL (3d) 67 (Alta CA); *Lake v Lake* (1988), 11 RFL (3d) 234 (NSCA); *Jarvis v Landry*, 2011 NSSC 116; *Strobridge v Strobridge* (1994), 4 RFL (4th) 169 (Ont CA); *CAM v DM*, [2003] OJ No 3707 (CA); *Azimi v Mirzaei*, [2008] OJ No 1208 (Sup Ct); *Hill v Hill*, [2008] OJ No 4730 (Sup Ct); compare *Kerr v Hauer*, 2010 ONSC 1995. And see Chapter 6, Section J.

187 *Jarrett v Jarrett* (1994), 10 RFL (4th) 24 (Ont Gen Div). But see *Family Law Act*, SBC 2011, Part 2, Division 3; *Rashtian v Baraghoush*, 2013 BCSC 994.

of the child are determinative, but parents and grandparents are not on an equal footing in a contested custody proceeding.[188] Unless there are grave reasons for concern about a child's well-being, a child should be placed in the custody of his or her parent.[189] Although there is no presumption in law favouring biological parents, there is a common-sense approach to custody disputes that, all things being equal, a parent should be entitled to raise his or her child.[190] Grandparents may be granted an order for custody in preference to a parent if the child has virtually spent her entire life being parented by the grandparents.[191]

Orders for grandparental access may be granted, but the right of separated parents to raise their children will not be lightly interfered with by an order for grandparental access that conflicts with the wishes of the parents and children. In the words of Abella JA, of the Ontario Court of Appeal, as she then was, in *Chapman v Chapman*,

> [I]n the absence of any evidence that the parents are behaving in a way which demonstrates an inability to act in accordance with the best interests of their children, their right to make decisions and judgments on the children's behalf should be respected, including decisions about whom they see, how often and under what circumstances they see them.[192]

As Abella JA further observes, however, each case turns on its own facts and must be determined in light of the children's best interests.[193] A grandparent has the onus of proving on a balance of probabilities that proposed access to

---

188 *Droit de la famille — 320*, [1987] 2 SCR 244; *JF v TE*, 2010 NBCA 14; *BM v KM*, 2013 NBQB 268; *Rai v Rai*, 2012 ONSC 4267; *Haygarth v Martel*, 2012 SKQB 439.

189 *JBE v FSL*, [2004] BCJ No 2438 (SC); *Fobert v Smith*, 2011 ONSC 1002. Compare *MS v GS*, 2013 BCSC 1744 at para 84; *SFR v JVH*, [2006] NJ No 202 (UFC), citing *Bailey v Flood*, [1988] NJ No 36 (TD); *Penney v Penney*, [2006] SJ No 175 (QB). See also *Hendricks v Swan*, [2007] SJ No 30 (QB); *BL v ML*, 2010 YKSC 41 (order for interim joint custody).

190 *Chera v Chera*, 2008 BCCA 374; see also *Redstar v Akachuk*, 2013 SKQB 223 at paras 53–54.

191 *JDM v ERD*, 2014 PESC 2.

192 [2001] OJ No 705 at para 21 (CA); see also *McLellan v Glidden* (1996), 177 NBR (2d) 38 (QB); *Hayes v Moyer*, 2011 SKCA 56; *Cust v Matthon*, 2013 SKQB 287; *GN v DN*, 2009 YKSC 75.

193 *Chapman v Chapman*, [2001] OJ No 705; see also *MEI v SMH*, 2011 BCSC 152; *GG v JW*, 2008 NBQB 338; *CB v MR*, [2007] NJ No 378 (UFC) (citing Martha Shaffer, "To Grandmother's House We Go? An Examination of Grandparental Access" (2003–2004) 21 Can Fam LQ 437 (wherein two approaches, namely, the "parental autonomy" and the "pro-contact" approaches were compared); *Campbell v Ramsden*, [2007] OJ No 1789 (Sup Ct); *Singh v Batoolall*, [2009] OJ No 1046 (Sup Ct); *Ekvall v Cooper*, [2007] SJ No 640 (QB); compare *GMK v CLH*, [2006] SJ No 399 (QB) (considering Dan L Goldberg, "Background Paper, Grandparent-Grandchild Access: A Legal Analysis," online: www.justice.gc.ca/eng/rp-pr/fl-lf/famil/2003_15/pdf/2003_15.pdf. And see *Scott v Walter*, [2006] MJ No 447 (QB) (access denied to former wife of biological father).

a grandchild is in the best interests of that child.[194] It is only upon evidence that the custodial parent is acting against the child's best interests by being unreasonable that the court should specify access.[195]

The following expansive list of relevant considerations is set out by Master Nitikman, of the British Columbia Supreme Court, in *Parmar v Parmar*:

1. Grandparents may be granted legal standing to apply for custody of or access to their grandchildren, but they have no legal right to custody or access corresponding to that of the parents.

2. If grandparents make a successful application for access, their entitlement is different from that of a non-custodial parent.

3. The best interests of the child are the paramount concern.

4. The love, affection, and ties between the child and the grandparents are factors expressly recognized as relevant to a determination of the child's best interests under section 24(1) of the *Family Relations Act* (British Columbia).[196]

5. In normal circumstances, the best interests of children are served by contact with their grandparents and other members of the extended family.

6. Considerable weight should be given to the wishes of the custodial parent and care should be taken to ensure that the court does not interfere unduly with the inherent right of the parent to determine the child's upbringing.

7. Grandparents are ordinarily expected to accommodate themselves to the parent's decision regarding the amount and type of access.

8. The child's wishes should be noted and accorded appropriate weight based on the child's age.

9. When the court finds grandparental access appropriate, the amount of time allotted is quite limited.[197]

Section 35(5) of the Alberta *Family Law Act* provides that before the court makes a contact order, the court shall satisfy itself that

---

194 *RC v CRS*, 2009 ABQB 376; *F(N) v S(HL)* (1999), 127 BCAC 66; *CT v JT*, [2007] BCJ No 937 (Prov Ct); *Chapman v Chapman*, [1993] BCJ No 316 (SC); *Goldstrand v Goldstrand*, 2009 MBQB 40; *Sochackey v Sochackey*, [2007] OJ No 1857 (Sup Ct); *Boyle v Gale*, [2007] OJ No 1873 (Sup Ct).

195 *BL v ML*, 2010 YKSC 41, citing *GN v DN*, 2009 YKSC 75. See also *Hayes v Moyer*, 2011 SKCA 56.

196 See now *Family Law Act*, SBC 2011, c 25, s.37(1)(c).

197 [1997] BCJ No 2094 at paras 11–19 (SC); see also *Lukyn v Baynes*, [2008] BCJ No 3 (SC); *SW v CM*, 2011 NWTSC 21; *Mitchell v Mitchell*, 2005 SKQB 458 at para 28; *GN v DN*, 2009 YKSC 75. As to contested proceedings between maternal and paternal grandparents, see *DPN v TJT*, 2013 ABQB 445 at paras 162–64.

(a) contact between the child and the applicant is in the best interests of the child;

(b) the child's physical, psychological, or emotional health may be jeopardized if contact between the child and the applicant is denied; and

(c) the guardians' denial of contact between the child and the applicant is unreasonable.[198]

In Newfoundland and Labrador, the special role of grandparents in a child's life is expressly recognized in the *Children's Law Act*[199] and the burden of proving that the grandparents should not have access falls on the parent who opposes such access.[200]

Access orders are not confined to genetic parents or blood relatives, but there is no presumption that maximizing contact to such an outside third party is in a child's best interests. The burden on a third-party applicant is demanding. Significant weight should be given to the view of the person having custody of the child. Consideration must be given to the confusion, turmoil, and disruption that could result to the child should access be granted.[201] In *GES v DLC*,[202] the appellant mother had given birth to twins by means of *in vitro* fertilization. The respondent had declined the mother's request that he be the sperm donor but had been supportive both financially and otherwise of the mother's recourse to bio-technological childbirth, having attended prenatal classes with the mother, being present at the birth of the twins, and having provided daily care for the twins after their birth. The mother's relationship with the respondent subsequently deteriorated and she no longer wished him to have any relationship with the twins. The trial judge found that the respondent had standing to apply for access to the twins as a person having a "sufficient interest" within the meaning of section 6(1) of the *Children's Law Act, 1997* (Saskatchewan), notwithstanding that he fell outside the traditional categories of third parties who seek access orders, namely, grandparents, other family relatives, and step-parents. In reaching this conclusion, the trial judge observed that the "primary focus must surely be on an assessment of what is in the true best interests of the child." While sharing the trial judge's finding that the respondent had a "sufficient interest" to bring an application for access to the twins, the Saskatchewan Court of Appeal concluded

---

198 See *RC v CRS*, 2009 ABQB 376 (grandparental contact order precluded by conflict with parents); see also *HB v AB*, 2010 ABQB 279; *Brown v Chipchura*, 2013 ABPC 315.

199 RSNL 1990, c C-13.

200 *Hemeon v Byrne*, 2013 NLTD(F) 14, citing *Sparkes v Brewer* (2001), 203 Nfld & PEIR 259 at paras 36–37 (Nfld UFC).

201 *Lake v Brown*, 2012 NLCA 39.

202 2006 SKCA 79.

that the trial judge had erred in applying the best interests of the child in the context of section 6(1) of the *Children's Law Act, 1997*. The Saskatchewan Court of Appeal observed that the Act contemplates two separate stages of analysis where a non-parent seeks an access order under that Act. First, the court must apply section 6(1), which imposes the threshold requirement that the applicant be either a "parent" or "other person having, in the opinion of the court, a sufficient interest." Second, only if this threshold requirement is satisfied will the court proceed to apply section 9 of the Act, which provides that the substantive merits of an application for an access order are to be considered by reference to the best interests of the child. In the opinion of the Saskatchewan Court of Appeal, the trial judge blurred these two separate steps by focusing on the best interests of the child when considering the threshold requirement of sufficient interest. With respect to the first step, the Saskatchewan Court of Appeal formulated the following guidelines to the application of section 6(1) of *the Children's Law Act, 1997*:

> [47] The proper focus of an inquiry in relation to the "sufficient interest" question, in my view, is the nature of the relationship between the applicant and the child. The question of the child's best interests does not enter the analysis at that point. In determining whether a non-family applicant is a person with a sufficient interest, the court should consider a variety of factors including, but not necessarily limited to: (a) the extent or degree of the applicant's involvement in the child's life, (b) the duration of that involvement, (c) the level of intimacy and the quality of the relationship between the applicant and the child, (d) how the relationship between the applicant and the child was represented to the world, and (e) whether the applicant provided financially for the child. Further, at least in relation to situations such as the one at issue in the appeal where there is no traditional family or blood relationship between the applicant and the child, it is necessary to consider whether the applicant can show a settled commitment to the child and an intention to be a continuing and meaningful presence in the life of the child. Overall, in the kinds of circumstances involved here, s 6 generally should be applied to screen out applicants who do not have both a significant relationship with the child and a demonstrated and settled ongoing commitment to the child.[203]

Although the record was characterized by conflicting evidence, the Saskatchewan Court of Appeal found it capable of sustaining the trial judge's conclusion that the unique relationship between the parties, as reflected in the

---

203 Compare *CH v LK*, 2013 SKQB 448 (successful access application by committed grandparents who had been denied access by an intransigent mother).

respondent's involvement in the pregnancy, birth, and care of the children, gave him a sufficient interest to bring the access application. In addressing the trial judge's further conclusion that access was in the best interests of the children, the Saskatchewan Court of Appeal stated that the trial judge appeared to have proceeded on the basis that, because the respondent had a "sufficient interest" and a positive relationship with the twins, access would be in their best interests. However, his approach and conclusion was held to be inconsistent with the overall trend of the law in cases involving an applicant who is not a parent, step-parent, or blood relative. In such cases, current caselaw in Saskatchewan and elsewhere confirms that the existence of an emotional bond between the applicant and the children is insufficient to justify an access order.[204] Thus, the court should not proceed on the assumption that ongoing contact is warranted, as would be the case in a dispute between parents in respect of whom the "maximum contact" principle applies. Where the application for access is brought by a person other than a parent, blood relative, or step-parent, it falls on the applicant to clearly and convincingly demonstrate that access is in the best interests of the child(ren). While caselaw does not always set out the rationale for this approach, it clearly stems from a deep social and legal norm that presumes fit parents generally act in their children's best interests. Consequently, a fit parent's assessment of a child's best interests should not be lightly interfered with. This does not signify that the court must completely defer to the parent's opinion that access is inappropriate; it means only that the views of the custodial parent should be given very substantial weight in determining the best interests of the children. In *GES v DLC*, the evidence established that the mother was an excellent parent, the twins were happy, well-adjusted, and well cared for, and there was no suggestion that they would lack anything in their lives or suffer in any way in the absence of access to the respondent. Given the mother's opposition to such access based on the respondent's past conduct and her legitimate concerns about his ongoing preparedness to make the sacrifices necessary to sustain an enduring relationship with the twins, the Saskatchewan Court of Appeal concluded that the respondent had failed to demonstrate in a clear and convincing way that access would be in the best interests of the children, and the trial judge had erred by failing to place any weight on the mother's objections to access and the reasons for her objections. The mother's appeal was accordingly allowed on the basis that the trial judge had

---

204 See *Lindstrom v Pearce*, 1999 SKQB 165; *Adams v Martin*, 1992 CarswellOnt 1679 (Prov Ct); *Re Lapp and Dupuis* (1985), 17 DLR (4th) 347 (Man CA); *Cyrenne v Moar* (1986), 41 Man R (2d) 108 (CA); *SAL v ST*, 2009 MBQB 150; *Elliott v Mumford* (2004), 1 RFL (6th) 193 (NSCA). Compare *Goldstrand v Goldstrand*, 2009 MBQB 40; *Ekvall v Cooper*, [2007] SJ No 640 (QB).

committed material errors in the course of granting the respondent access to the twins.

It is interesting to compare the judgment of the Saskatchewan Court of Appeal in *GES v DLC*, above, with the judgment of the Alberta Court of Appeal in *DWH v DJR*.[205] This latter appeal raised the question whether the chambers judge erred in failing to determine that the appellant stood in the place of a parent to a three-and-a-half-year-old child and in concluding that he should be denied a contact order by virtue of section 35(5) of the *Family Law Act* (Alberta). The appellant lived with the male respondent in a same-sex relationship for approximately six and one-half years. They became friends of a female couple living in a same-sex relationship and it was decided that the female respondent would attempt to birth children, one for each couple, using assisted conception with the male respondent donating the sperm in each case. The parties agreed that the first child born would be raised in the home of the appellant and the male respondent. The female respondent would remain involved in the child's life and would reside with the appellant and the male respondent for the first two-and-a-half months of the child's life. These plans became a reality and the child lived with the appellant and the male respondent from May 2003 until their separation in June 2006. The female respondent played an active role in the child's life and enjoyed frequent contact. After the separation, the male and female respondents refused to allow the appellant to have contact with the child. The appellant sought a contact order under section 35 of the *Family Law Act* (Alberta). It was denied by the chambers judge, who determined that the male and female respondents' wishes as guardians were entitled to considerable weight and the appellant had not shown how contact with the child would contribute to her best interests when her biological parents had decided otherwise. On appeal to the Alberta Court of Appeal, it was held that the chambers judge made a reversible error by failing to consider whether the appellant stood in the place of a parent to the child and in failing to assess the desirability of contact between the appellant and the child with that relationship in mind. Section 35(5) of the *Family Law Act* (Alberta) expressly provides that

> [b]efore a court makes a contact order, the court shall satisfy itself that contact between the child and the applicant is in the best interests of the child, including whether
> (a) the child's physical, psychological or emotional health may be jeopardized if contact between the child and the applicant is denied, and
> (b) the guardians' denial of contact between the child and the applicant is unreasonable.

---

205 2007 ABCA 57.

While acknowledging that section 35(5) does not draw any distinction between parents or persons standing in the place of parents and other persons seeking a contact order, the Alberta Court of Appeal concluded that a *de facto* parent-child relationship remains an important consideration. Indeed, there is a presumption in favour of post-separation contact that is rooted in a recognition that the unique relationship between such persons ought not to be easily or readily abandoned or displaced. The fact that section 35(2) of the *Family Law Act* (Alberta) makes it clear that a person standing in the place of a parent is not required to seek leave to bring a contact application underlines that the legal nature of the relationship is an important consideration in determining whether contact is in the best interests of the child and in considering whether the requirements of section 35(5) have been met. Given the uncontested evidence that the appellant stood in the place of a parent to the child for most of the child's life, being known to the child as "Papa," the Alberta Court of Appeal rejected the reasons offered by the respondents for the denial of contact. Their assertions that the appellant was HIV positive, had made poor choices in his love life, and was irrational for a short time following the separation were deemed an inadequate foundation for refusing a contact order in the circumstances of this case. Furthermore, their assertion that the child would suffer confusion and instability as a result of a contact order was not made out on the record. Indeed, their reasons failed to take into account the benefit that the child would derive from the affection of the appellant who had been directly involved in her parenting; they also ignored the potential for emotional harm occasioned by the sudden withdrawal of the appellant from the child's life. Accordingly, the Alberta Court of Appeal found that the respondents failed to provide any compelling reason to displace the presumption in favour of ongoing contact between the child and the appellant. The appeal was, therefore, allowed and the appellant was granted reasonable access as requested. It is noteworthy that, for the purpose of this interim application, the Alberta Court of Appeal found it unnecessary to determine whether it is possible to have more than one father or mother under the *Family Law Act* (Alberta) or whether the respondents satisfied the definitions of parent or guardian under the Act and what might flow as a result.

In a landmark decision in *AA v BB*,[206] the Ontario Court of Appeal held that a five-year-old child had three parents, namely, his biological father and mother and the long-time lesbian partner of the biological mother. On this partner's uncontested application for a declaration of parentage, the trial judge, Aston J, held that section 4 of the *Children's Law Reform Act* (Ontario)

---

206 2007 ONCA 2; see also *AWM v TNS*, 2014 ONSC 5420.

"contemplates a single mother and a single father" and "does not afford authority for the court to grant this application."[207] Addressing the applicant's alternative submission that the court could grant the application by exercising its *parens patriae* jurisdiction to fill a legislative gap, Aston J observed that, while a court may exercise such jurisdiction, it should not ignore the possibility that the gap may have been deliberate, in which case it is not a function of the court to exercise its *parens patriae* jurisdiction to rewrite legislation and social policy. While acknowledging that the granting of the application would serve the best interests of this particular child, whose primary care was being jointly provided by the biological mother and her lesbian partner and who had a meaningful relationship with the father through frequent visits, Aston J held that this was insufficient reason to resort to the exercise of the court's *parens patriae* jurisdiction. He observed that the court must also have regard to the best interests of other children, and the granting of the application in the present case would open the door to step-parents, extended family members, and others claiming parental status in less harmonious circumstances, and had the potential to generate or exacerbate custody or access litigation. The appellant's attempt to introduce a *Charter* challenge at the appellate level was rejected by the Ontario Court of Appeal on the basis that the appellant had not advanced any satisfactory explanation for not raising the *Charter* issues at first instance and had failed to discharge the onus of proving the absence of tactical reasons for deferring the *Charter* challenge.[208] The Ontario Court of Appeal found no fault with Aston J's conclusion that the language of the *Children's Law Reform Act*, and especially section 4, contemplates a single mother and father. It rejected the conclusion of Aston J, however, respecting the exercise of the *parens patriae* jurisdiction. In the opinion of the Ontario Court of Appeal, the radical changes that have occurred in legal and social responses to same-sex relationships and the advent of reproductive technology were outside the contemplation of the Ontario legislature when it enacted the *Children's Law Reform Act* in 1978. Accordingly, the present case manifested a legislative gap that was not deliberate, and the exercise of the *parens patriae* jurisdiction would conform to the purpose of the *Children's Law Reform Act*, which is to promote the equality of children born inside and outside of marriage. By way of clarifying the importance of the declaration of parentage that was designed to give the lesbian partner of the biological mother all the legal rights of a custodial parent, which include guardianship rights over the child under the *Children's Law Reform Act* (Ontario), Rosenberg JA listed the following results:

---

207 *AA v BB*, [2003] OJ No 1215 (Sup Ct).

208 See *R v Brown* (1993), 83 CCC (3d) 129 (SCC).

- the declaration of parentage is a lifelong immutable declaration of status;
- it allows the parent to fully participate in the child's life;
- the declared parent has to consent to any future adoption;
- the declaration determines lineage;
- the declaration ensures that the child will inherit on intestacy;
- the declared parent may obtain an OHIP card, a social insurance number, airline tickets, and passports for the child;
- the child of a Canadian citizen is a Canadian citizen, even if born outside of Canada (*Citizenship Act*, R.S.C. 1985, c C-29, s 3(1)(b));
- the declared parent may register the child in school; and
- the declared parent may assert her rights under various laws such as the *Health Care Consent Act*, 1996, S.O. 1996, c 2, Sched. A., s. 20(1)5.[209]

It is noteworthy that in 1999, the Ontario legislature enacted the *Amendments Because of the Supreme Court of Canada Decision in M v H Act*, which amended numerous Ontario statutes, including the *Children's Law Reform Act*,[210] but saw no reason to amend section 4 of that Act to accommodate same-sex relationships and the science of reproductive technology. Consequently, it is open to question whether the Ontario Court of Appeal was correct in concluding that a legislative gap justified the exercise of the *parens patriae* jurisdiction in *AA v BB*.

7) Provincial Parenting Programs

Provincial legislation may require divorcing or divorced parents to attend parenting education programs before seeking substantive relief under the *Divorce Act*. Such provincial legislation is procedural rather than substantive in nature, and therefore falls within the constitutional authority of the provincial legislature in the absence of any functional conflict with the *Divorce Act*.[211]

8) Enforcement of Access Orders[212]

Wilful contravention of an access order may trigger contempt proceedings wherein a variety of sanctions can be imposed. The sanctions will often be

---

209 *AA v BB*, [2007] OJ No 2 at para 14 (CA).

210 See SO 1999, c 6, s 7 (amending ss 24 and 78(2) of the *Children's Law Reform Act*).

211 *Flockhart v Flockhart*, [2002] SJ No 94 (QB).

212 See *Rogers v Rogers*, [2008] MJ No 178 (QB), especially paras 109–14; *Dephoure v Dephoure*, 2011 ONSC 7727. For a practitioner's perspective on the diverse civil sanctions that may appropriately be imposed for breach of an access order, see Brent D Barilla, "The Enforcement

multi-faceted and may include financial penalties, costs, make-up visits, attendance at parenting courses or for counselling, fines or imprisonment suspended on conditions, or changes of custody or care and control of the child.[213] In contempt proceedings, any order alleged to have been breached must be clear and precise in its directions.[214] A non-custodial parent may be found in contempt of court if he or she fails to return the child to the custodial parent at the end of an access visit.[215]

Where a parent persistently and adamantly refuses to comply with an order granting access privileges to the non-custodial parent, the court may impose a fine or imprisonment[216] or require the custodial parent to enter into a recognizance to keep the peace and be of good behaviour towards the non-custodial parent.[217] The court also has the option of taking custody away from the defaulting party and granting custody to the other parent.[218] Additional access privileges may be ordered to compensate for a prior loss of such privileges arising from the custodial parent's contempt of a subsisting order.[219] An access order may include a direction that the child and parents attend counselling.[220] Judicial opinion remains divided on the question whether a court-ordered reduction or suspension of child support is permissible as a sanction for a custodial parent's wilful refusal to allow the non-custodial

---

of Arrears" (September 2002) 2:3 The Saskatchewan Advocate. For an academic lawyer's perspective, see Martha Bailey, "Enforcement of Access Orders" (on Quicklaw, Commentary, Syrtash Collection of Family Law Articles, SFLRP/1998-008). As to the possibility of abduction charges under s 282 of the *Criminal Code*, RSC 1985, c C-46, s 282, see *R v Petropoulos* (1990), 29 RFL (3d) 289 (BCCA); *R v Wright* (1985), 10 RFL (4th) 236 (Alta CA).

213   *Rogers v Rogers*, 2008 MBQB 131, citing *Paton v Shymkiw*, [1996] MJ No 569 (QB); see also *Bruno v Keinick*, 2012 NSSC 140; *Stokes v Stokes*, 2014 ONSC 1311.

214   *Gurtins v Panton-Goyert*, 2008 BCCA 196; *Odgers v Odgers*, 2014 BCSC 717; *Stokes v Stokes*, 2014 ONSC 1311; *Vigneault v Massey*, 2014 ONCA 244.

215   *McIntyre v McIntyre* (1994), 5 RFL (4th) 86 (NBQB), aff'd (1995), 13 RFL (4th) 280 (NBCA).

216   *O'Byrne v Koresec* (1986), 2 RFL (3d) 104 (BCSC); see also *Salloum v Salloum* (1994), 154 AR 65 (QB) (application under *Children's Law Reform Act*, RSO 1990, c C.12; denial of request to declare custodial parent in contempt); *Kingwell v Kingwell* (1993), 45 RFL (3d) 242 (Ont CA) (contravention of order restraining removal of children from jurisdiction); *Rawlinson v Rawlinson* (1986), 5 RFL (3d) 166 (Sask QB) (violation of restraining order by non-custodial parent).

217   *Amaral v Myke* (1992), 42 RFL (3d) 322 (Ont UFC) (custodial parent also restrained from changing the child's name under *Vital Statistics Act*, RSO 1990, c V.4); *Wood v Miller* (1993), 45 RFL (3d) 244 (Ont UFC); see also *Boudreau v Boudreau* (1994), 143 NBR (2d) 321 (QB).

218   See *Tremblay v Tremblay* (1987), 10 RFL (3d) 166 (Alta QB); *Rose v Rose* (1989), 22 RFL (3d) 72 (Alta QB); *MacKenzie v MacKenzie* (1987), 9 RFL (3d) 1 (Man CA).

219   *Yunyk v Judd* (1986), 5 RFL (3d) 206 (Man QB); *Amaral v Myke* (1992), 42 RFL (3d) 322 (Ont UFC).

220   *Rector v Hamilton* (1989), 94 NSR (2d) 284 (Fam Ct); *JKL v NCS*, [2008] OJ No 2115 (Sup Ct); see also *LM v TM*, 2012 NBQB 238 (custody).

parent reasonable access to the child. Some courts have asserted that a custodial parent's misconduct is not a valid reason for reducing or suspending an order for child support.[221] Other courts have asserted that child support payments can be reduced or suspended as a last resort to compel due compliance with a prior access order.[222] As Ryan-Froslie J, (as she then was) of the Saskatchewan Court of Queen's Bench, concludes in *DAL(F) v DAL*,[223] "whichever approach is adopted, the best interests of the child must be the overriding consideration."

---

221 See, for example, *Lee v Lee* (1990), 29 RFL (3d) 417 (BCCA); *Gaulton v Hynes*, [2003] NJ No 44 (SC); *King v King*, [2008] NJ No 60 (SC).

222 See, for example, *Nielsen v Nielsen*, [2000] BCJ No 879 (CA); *Paynter v Reynolds* (1997), 34 RFL (4th) 272 (PEICA); *Fernquist v Garland*, [2000] SJ No 204 (CA); see also *Fernquist v Garland*, [2004] SJ No 584 (CA); *Fernquist v Garland*, [2005] SJ No 36 (QB).

223 [2003] SJ No 213 (QB).

CHAPTER 13

Matrimonial Property Rights

A. PROVINCIAL AND TERRITORIAL LEGISLATIVE DIVERSITY

Over thirty years ago, the Supreme Court of Canada in *Murdoch v Murdoch*[1] concluded that a wife who had worked alongside her husband in the fields was not entitled to any interest in the ranch that had been originally purchased with his money. Her homemaking role and hard physical labour on the farm counted for nothing. Several years later, the Supreme Court of Canada saw the error of its ways and invoked the doctrine of unjust enrichment to enable wives[2] and unmarried cohabitants[3] to share in property acquired or preserved by their partners during cohabitation. In the meantime, provincial legislatures introduced statutory reforms to ameliorate the harshness of the *Murdoch v Murdoch* decision so far as married couples are concerned.

Every province and territory in Canada has enacted legislation to establish property-sharing rights between spouses on marriage breakdown or divorce and, in some provinces, on death.[4]

---

1 (1973), 13 RFL 185 (SCC).

2 *Rathwell v Rathwell* (1978), 1 RFL (2d) 1 (SCC).

3 *Pettkus v Becker*, [1980] 2 SCR 834, 19 RFL (2d) 165; *Sorochan v Sorochan*, [1986] 2 SCR 38. And see Chapter 3, Section E.

4 See *Matrimonial Property Act*, RSA 2000, c M-8; *Family Law Act*, SBC 2011, c 25, Part 5; *Marital Property Act*, CCSM c M45; *Marital Property Act*, SNB 1980, c M-1.1; *Family Law Act*, RSNL 1990, c F-2, Part I (Matrimonial Home), Part II (Matrimonial Assets), Part IV (Domestic Contracts); *Matrimonial Property Act*, RSNS 1989, c 275; *Family Law Act*, SNWT 1997, c 18, Part I (Domestic Contracts), Part III (Family Property), Part IV (Family Home); *Family Law Act*, RSO 1990, c F.3, Part I (Family Property), Part II (Matrimonial Home), Part IV (Domestic Contracts); *Family Law Act*, SPEI 1995, c 12, Part I (Family Property), Part II (Family Home), Part IV (Domestic Contracts), *Civil Code of Québec*,

Three fundamental questions require consideration in any attempt to divide property between spouses on the termination of their relationship. They are as follows:

1) What kind of property falls subject to division?
2) How is the property to be valued? and
3) How will the sharing of property be achieved?

In some provinces and territories, a wide judicial discretion exists and distinctions are drawn between "family assets" that both spouses use and "business" or "commercial" assets that are associated with only one of the spouses. In others, no such distinctions exist. In most provinces and territories, the courts are empowered to divide specific assets. In Ontario, it is the value of property, as distinct from the property itself, that is shared; all assets must be valued and each spouse is presumptively entitled to an equal share in the value of the assets acquired by either or both of them.

Provincial and territorial matrimonial property statutes usually exclude premarital assets from division and also certain postmarital assets, such as third-party gifts or inheritances and damages or monetary compensation received by a spouse from a third party as a result of personal injuries.

Statutory property-sharing regimes are not dependent on which spouse owned or acquired the assets. Prior to marriage breakdown, however, the control and management of an asset is legally vested in the owner. Provincial and territorial statutes, nevertheless, prohibit a title-holding spouse from disposing of or encumbering the matrimonial home without the consent of his or her spouse.

Because the relevant provincial and territorial statutes differ markedly in content and approach, it is impossible to provide a comprehensive analysis of the diverse provincial matrimonial property regimes in the following pages. The authors will consequently focus on the Ontario statute, which represents the most comprehensive provincial legislation on matrimonial property rights in Canada.

SQ 1991, c 64, Book 2; *Matrimonial Property Act, 1997*, SS 1997, c M-6.11; *Family Property and Support Act*, RSY 1986, c 63, Part I (Family Assets), Part 2 (Family Home), Part 4, ss 1 and 58–65 (Domestic Contracts). Many of the aforementioned statutes have been amended from time to time. As to First Nation communities choosing to create their own matrimonial real property laws, see *Family Homes on Reserves and Matrimonial Interests or Rights Act*, SC 2013, c 20.

1) Introduction

In 1978, the province of Ontario enacted the *Family Law Reform Act*[5] to ameliorate the hardship and injustice arising under the doctrine of separation of property, whereby each spouse retained his or her own property on the breakdown or dissolution of marriage. Section 4 of the *Family Law Reform Act, 1978* empowered a court to order a division of "family assets" and, in exceptional circumstances, a division of non-family assets on marriage breakdown, regardless of which spouse was the owner of the assets. Generally speaking, a non-owning spouse would be granted an equal share of the family assets, which included the matrimonial home and other assets ordinarily used or enjoyed by the family, but no interest in business assets would be granted to the non-owning spouse.

As of 1 March 1986, Part I of the *Family Law Act*[6] eliminated the former distinction between "family assets" and "non-family assets" by providing for an equalization of the *value* of all assets accumulated by either spouse during the marriage in the event of marriage breakdown or death.

2) Objectives of *Family Law Act*

In general terms, the fundamental objective of Part I of the *Family Law Act* is to ensure that on marriage breakdown or death each spouse will receive a fair share, which will usually be an equal share, of the value of assets accumulated during the course of matrimonial cohabitation. Thus, subsection 5(7) of the *Family Law Act* provides as follows:

> (7) The purpose of this section is to recognize that child care, household management and financial provision are the joint responsibilities of the spouses and that inherent in the marital relationship there is equal contribution, whether financial or otherwise, by the spouses to the assumption of these responsibilities, entitling each spouse to the equalization of the net family properties, subject only to the equitable considerations set out in subsection (6).

This provision does not empower a court to deviate from the norm of equal division in the absence of circumstances that justify a finding of unconscionability

---

5   SO 1978, c 2.

6   RSO 1990, c F.3. For proposed changes, see Ontario Law Reform Commission, *Report on Family Property Law* (including Executive Summary) (Toronto: Ontario Law Reform Commission, 1993); see also Ontario Law Reform Commission, *The Rights and Responsibilities of Cohabitants under the* Family Law Act (including Executive Summary) (Toronto: Ontario Law Reform Commission, 1993).

within the meaning of subsection 5(6) of the *Family Law Act*.[7] As Hughes J, of the Ontario Superior Court of Justice, observed in *Janjua v Khan*, "[i]t is quite common for spouses to make unequal contributions of money and assets to their marriage. It is quite uncommon, however, for it to justify an unequal division of matrimonial property on the breakdown of their marriage."[8]

3) Definition of "Spouse"

For the purpose of Part I of the *Family Law Act*, subsection 1(1) specifically defines "spouse" as meaning a man and woman who are married to each other or who have entered into a void or voidable marriage, provided that in either of the latter circumstances, the person asserting a right under the Act acted in good faith.[9] "Good faith" within the meaning of section 1(1) of the Act signifies an intention to comply with the *Marriage Act*.[10] Same-sex relationships and "common-law relationships" fall outside the ambit of Part I of the *Family Law Act*.

Pursuant to section 7(1) of the Ontario *Family Law Act*, a former spouse may seek equalization of the spousal net family properties under section 5 of the Act. After a valid foreign divorce has been granted, the Ontario Superior Court of Justice has no jurisdiction to hear and determine an application for spousal support under the *Divorce Act* or under the *Family Law Act*, but the foreign divorce does not preclude the Ontario Superior Court of Justice from adjudicating an application for the equalization of the spousal net family properties under the *Family Law Act*.[11]

4) Foreign Immovable Property

Canadian courts lack jurisdiction to order the sale of foreign immovable property, although the value of such property may be taken into account in ordering an equalization of the net spousal properties under Part I of the Ontario *Family Law Act*.[12]

---

7   *Brett v Brett* (1999), 46 RFL (4th) 433 (Ont CA); *Fielding v Fielding*, 2014 ONSC 2272. See, generally, Section A(10)(a), below in this chapter.

8   2013 ONSC 44 at para 64.

9   See *Guptill v Wilfred*, 2009 NSSC 44.

10 *Debora v Debora*, [1999] OJ No 2 (CA); *Janjua v Khan*, 2013 ONSC 44.

11 *Okmyansky v Okmyansky*, 2007 ONCA 427.

12 *Bennett v Bennett*, [2001] OJ No 224 (Sup Ct); *Aning v Aning*, [2002] OJ No 2469 (Sup Ct); *Johnston v Adam*, 2011 ONSC 3808; see also *Duke v Andler*, [1932] SCR 734; *Teczan v Teczan* (1987), 11 RFL (3d) 113 (BCCA); *Catania v Giannattasio*, [1999] OJ No 1197 (CA); *Cork v Cork*, 2014 ONSC 2488; *Hunter v Hunter*, 2005 SKQB 93 at paras 25–27; *Aboo v Mota*, 2010 SKQB 368; see, generally, James G. McLeod, *The Conflict of Laws* (Calgary:

5) Domestic Contracts[13]

Subsection 2(10) of the *Family Law Act* provides that "[a] domestic contract dealing with a matter that is also dealt with in this Act prevails unless this Act provides otherwise."[14] A high threshold must be met before an Ontario court will find that an out-of-jurisdiction domestic contract prevails over the equalization provisions of the *Family Law Act*.[15]

6) Applications Respecting Ownership and Possession of Property

a) General

Section 10 of the *Family Law Act* empowers a spouse or former spouse to apply to the court for the determination of any question relating to the possession or ownership of property. It offers no direct guidelines to the court concerning the principles to be applied in determining questions of ownership and possession. The parties to such an application are entitled to invoke established principles of the common law and equity, including the doctrines of resulting and constructive trust. The right to assert the existence of a resulting or constructive trust in an application under section 10 of the *Family Law Act* is not precluded by an equalization of the net family properties under section 5 of the Act and may, indeed, be a prerequisite to calculating the net family property of each spouse for the purposes of any equalization claim.[16] In the vast majority of cases, however, the principles of unjust enrichment that were set out by the Supreme Court of Canada in *Kerr v Baranow* and *Vanasse v Seguin*[17] will have very limited significance for married couples because any unjust enrichment that arises as the result of a marriage will usually be fully addressed through the operation of the equalization provisions under the

---

Carswell, 1983); Stephen GA Pitel & Nicholas S Rafferty, *Conflict of Laws* (Toronto: Irwin Law, 2010) c 17.

13   See, generally, Chapter 4.

14   For special provisions respecting the division of pensions, see *Family Law Act*, RSO 1990, c F.3, s 56.1, added by *Family Statute Law Amendment Act*, SO 2009, c 11, s 37. As to the validity and efficacy of a waiver of spousal property and equalization rights under a contract that predates the *Family Law Act*, see *Lay v Lay* (2000), 4 RFL (5th) 264 (Ont CA), distinguishing *Bosch v Bosch* (1991), 6 OR (3d) 168 (CA) and applying s 70(3) of the *Family Law Act*.

15   *Webster v Webster Estate*, [2006] OJ No 2749 (Sup Ct).

16   *Rawluk v Rawluk*, [1990] 1 SCR 70; see also *Rarie v Rarie* (1997), 32 RFL (4th) 232 (Ont CA) and Professor James G McLeod's extremely lucid and informative annotation at 233–37. And see *McNamee v McNamee*, 2011 ONCA 533; *Cork v Cork*, 2014 ONSC 2488.

17   2011 SCC 10. For a summary of those principles, see Chapter 3, Section E.

Family Law Act.[18] A spouse may assert a beneficial ownership interest in property held in the other spouse's name where the value of that property has significantly increased between the date of the spousal separation and the date of trial.[19]

Section 10 of the *Family Law Act* cannot be invoked by third parties.[20] Where an application is brought by a spouse or former spouse, however, a third party may be added in accordance with the Ontario *Rules of Civil Procedure.*[21]

The assertion of ownership rights under subsection 10(1) of the *Family Law Act* is not conditioned on marriage breakdown. Such an application may be pursued even though the spouses are still cohabiting in a viable marriage. An application under subsection 10(1) may also be made or continued against the estate of a deceased spouse.[22]

b) Presumptions

At common law, when a husband purchased property in the name of his wife or transferred property to her, a presumption of advancement applied whereby he was presumed to have made a gift of the property to her. Where, however, the wife purchased property in her husband's name or transferred property to him, he would be presumed to hold the property on a resulting trust for his wife as the beneficial owner. The abolition of the presumption of advancement as between spouses, which was effectuated by paragraph 1(3)(d) of the *Family Law Reform Act, 1975* and continued under section 14 of the *Family Law Act*, establishes equality between the sexes in that, where either spouse purchases property in the name of the other spouse or transfers property to the other spouse, the purchase or transfer gives rise to a presumption of resulting trust, whereby the transferee holds the property for the benefit of the transferor. The presumption of advancement arising from a parent's gratuitous transfer of assets to his or her child under the age of majority, and the presumption of resulting trust that arises when the child is an adult, are unaffected by the statutory abrogation of the presumption of advancement as between spouses.[23] However, a spouse cannot claim that property

---

18   See *Martin v Sansome*, 2014 ONCA 14; *Fielding v Fielding*, 2014 ONSC 2272.

19   *Rawluk v Rawluk*, [1990] 1 SCR 70; *Parsalidis v Parsalidis*, 2012 ONSC 2963.

20   See *Chalmers v Copfer* (1978), 7 RFL (2d) 393 (Ont Co Ct).

21   RRO 1990, Reg. 194 (*Courts of Justice Act*). See *Bray v Bray* (1979), 9 CPC 241 (Ont HCJ).

22   *Family Law Act*, RSO 1990, c F.3, s 10(2); compare s 5(2) of the Act, whereby an application for an equalization of net family properties can only be brought by a surviving spouse whose net family property is less than that of the deceased spouse.

23   See *Pecore v Pecore*, [2007] SCJ No 17; *Madsen Estate v Saylor*, [2007] SCJ No 18; *Simcoff v Simcoff*, 2009 MBCA 80; *Farjad-Tehrani v Karimpour*, [2008] OJ No 5235 (Sup Ct); *Harrington v Harrington*, 2009 ONCA 39; *Klimm v Klimm*, 2010 ONSC 1479.

was received from a parent as a gift so as to be excluded from equalization of the spousal net family properties on marriage breakdown or death while asserting that the transfer was not a gift for tax purposes.[24]

Section 14 of the *Family Law Act* is confined in its application to questions of ownership or possession. It has no direct application to claims for an equalization of net family properties under section 5 of the Act.

The presumption arising under section 14 is a provisional presumption and not a conclusive presumption. It may be rebutted by cogent evidence that a gift was intended.[25]

The presumption of resulting trust has no application where property is held in the name of the spouses as joint tenants, and money on deposit in the name of both spouses is deemed to be held under joint tenancy. In either of these two circumstances, the beneficial interests of the spouses are governed by established principles of property law and they will be presumed to share equal beneficial interests.[26] The presumption may be rebutted by evidence to the contrary.[27]

A discussion of the significance of ownership to the resolution of an equalization claim under the *Family Law Act* appears later in this chapter.[28]

7) Triggering Events for Equalization of Net Family Properties

The *Family Law Act* preserves the doctrine of separation of property during matrimonial cohabitation. Subject to the provisions of section 21 of the Act, which ordinarily require spousal consent before the matrimonial home is disposed of or encumbered, each spouse has the freedom to acquire or dispose of property during matrimonial cohabitation.[29]

The doctrine of separation of property may cease to apply, however, in the event of marriage breakdown or death. Pursuant to subsections 5(1), (2), and (3) of the *Family Law Act*, a system of deferred property sharing is activated by the occurrence of any of the following triggering events:

---

24   *Karakatsanis v Georgiou* (1991), 33 RFL (3d) 263 (Ont Gen Div). And see Section A(9)(n), below in this chapter.

25   See *Meszaros v Meszaros* (1978), 22 OR (2d) 695 (Sup Ct); *DeBora v DeBora*, [2004] OJ No 4826 (Sup Ct), aff'd [2006] OJ 4826 (CA).

26   See *Ling v Ling* (1980), 17 RFL (2d) 62 at 66–67 (Ont CA); *Berdette v Berdette* (1991), 33 RFL (3d) 113 (Ont CA); *Murray v Murray*, 2010 ONSC 4278; *Zheng v Jiang*, 2012 ONSC 6043.

27   *Kosterewa v Kosterewa*, [2008] OJ No 3950 (Sup Ct); *Galla v Galla*, 2014 ONSC 37.

28   See Section A(9)(b), below in this chapter. As to the effect of bankruptcy on equalization claims, see *Green v Green*, 2013 ONSC 7265; see also Robert A Klotz, "Bankruptcy Problems in Family Law" in The Law Society of Upper Canada, *Special Lectures, 1993: Family Law: Roles, Fairness and Equality* (Scarborough, ON: Carswell, 1994).

29   See *Yasmin v Tariq*, 2015 ONSC 1248.

1) when a divorce is granted;
2) when a marriage is declared a nullity;
3) when the spouses are separated without any reasonable prospect of resuming cohabitation;
4) when a spouse dies, if the net family property of the deceased spouse exceeds that of the surviving spouse; or
5) when, during cohabitation, there is a serious danger that one spouse may improvidently deplete his or her net family property.

a) Separation as a Triggering Event

Where spousal separation is relied upon as the triggering event under subsection 5(1) of the *Family Law Act*, the court must be satisfied that there is no reasonable prospect that they will resume cohabitation. A reasonable prospect of reconciliation must be more than wishful thinking on the part of either party.[30] The court must find that there is no reasonable prospect that the spouses will resume cohabitation where either spouse is adamantly opposed to reconciliation.[31] The following factors have been identified as relevant to determining when spouses are living separate and apart:

1) There must be a physical separation.
2) There must be a withdrawal by one or both spouses from the matrimonial obligation with the intent of destroying the matrimonial consortium.
3) The absence of sexual relations is not conclusive but is a factor to be considered.
4) Other matters to be considered are the discussion of family problems and communication between the spouses, presence or absence of joint social activities, and the meal pattern.
5) Although the performance of household tasks is also a factor, help may be hired for these tasks, and greater weight should be given to those matters that are peculiar to the husband and wife relationship outlined above.[32]

Spouses may be "separated" within the meaning of subsection 5(1), notwithstanding that they remain under the same roof, provided that they are living

---

30 *Torosantucci v Torosantucci* (1991), 32 RFL (3d) 202 (Ont UFC); *Cramer v Cramer*, 2013 ONSC 4182; see also *Rosseter v Rosseter*, 2013 ONSC 7779.

31 See *Challoner v Challoner* (1973), 12 RFL 311 (NSCA); compare *Sheriff v Sheriff* (1982), 31 RFL (2d) 434 at 436 (Ont HCJ). See also *Vranich v Vranich*, [2008] OJ No 3765 (Sup Ct).

32 *Oswell v Oswell*, [1990] OJ No 1117 (HCJ), aff'd (1992), 12 OR (3d) 1995 (CA); *Joanis v Bourque*, 2014 ONSC 6183.

independent lives while sharing common accommodation.[33] The fact that the spouses have been living under different roofs does not signify that they are separated until it is accompanied by an intention to treat the marriage as over.[34] Only one of the spouses needs to form the intention to separate in order for a valuation date to be established.[35]

b) Death as a Triggering Event[36]

The death of a spouse constitutes a triggering event for an equalization of net family properties but only where the net family property of the deceased spouse exceeds the net family property of the surviving spouse.[37]

The death of a spouse did not constitute a triggering event for the purpose of a court-ordered property division under section 4 of the *Family Law Reform Act, 1978*.[38] Consequently, widows or widowers sometimes found themselves in a substantially inferior position to that enjoyed by separated spouses. This injustice has been eliminated by subsection 5(2) of the *Family Law Act*.

c) Improvident Depletion of Net Family Property

Pursuant to subsection 5(3) of the *Family Law Act*, if there is a serious danger that one spouse may improvidently deplete his or her net family property, the other spouse, though still cohabiting, may apply to have the net family properties divided as though the spouses were separated and had no reasonable prospect of resuming cohabitation.

If an order for division is made by reason of the triggering event of an apprehended improvident depletion of net family property, neither spouse can thereafter pursue any further application based on some other triggering event. This is so even if the spouses continue to cohabit after the court-ordered division, unless a domestic contract provides otherwise.[39]

A serious danger that a spouse may improvidently deplete his or her net family property could be attributable to factors beyond the control of the spouse responsible for its management. Physical or mental disability may render a spouse incompetent to manage the property and thus give rise to a

---

33   *Oswell v Oswell*, [1990] OJ No 1117; *De Acetis v De Acetis* (1991), 33 RFL (3d) 372 (Ont Gen Div), aff'd (1992), 39 RFL (3d) 327 (Ont CA); *Cramer v Cramer*, 2013 ONSC 4182. See also *Andrade v Andrade*, 2012 ONSC 2777, citing *Molodowich v Penttinen*, [1980] OJ No 1904 (Dist Ct).

34   *Tesfatsion v Berhane*, 2013 ONSC 75. See also *Brash v Brash Estate*, 2013 ONSC 2800.

35   *Ibid.*

36   See Section A(11), below in this chapter.

37   *Family Law Act*, RSO 1990, c F.3, ss 5(2) and 5(6).

38   SO 1978, c 2; see *Palachik v Kiss* (1983), 33 RFL (2d) 225 (SCC).

39   *Family Law Act*, RSO 1990, c F.3, ss 5(4) & 5(5).

reasonable apprehension of improvident depletion. Alternatively, an improvident depletion may be apprehended in consequence of prospective intentional or negligent misconduct on the part of the title-holding spouse. In circumstances involving a disability, the threatened spouse may be wiser to apply for a guardianship order respecting the estate of the disabled spouse, because a successful application made pursuant to subsection 5(3) of the *Family Law Act* bars any subsequent application by reason of the express provisions of subsection 5(4) of the Act.

d) Alternative Triggering Events

Notwithstanding the special provisions of subsection 5(4) of the *Family Law Act*,[40] it is submitted that any successful application for division by reason of one of the several alternative triggering events under subsection 5(1) or (2) will bar a subsequent application based on some other triggering event, assuming that the parties do not remarry each other.[41]

8) Limitation Periods

Subsection 7(3) of the *Family Law Act*[42] provides that an application for equalization of spousal net family properties on marriage breakdown or death shall not be brought after the earliest of (a) two years after the day the marriage is terminated by divorce or judgment of nullity; (b) six years after the day the spouses separate and there is no reasonable prospect that they will resume cohabitation; or (c) six months after the first spouse's death.

The court may extend a limitation period arising under subsection 7(3) of the *Family Law Act* pursuant to the provisions of subsection 2(8) of the Act. Subsection 2(8) provides that the court may, on motion, extend a time prescribed by this Act if it is satisfied that (a) there are *prima facie* grounds for relief; (b) relief is unavailable because of delay that has been incurred in good faith; and (c) no person will suffer substantial prejudice by reason of the delay.[43]

In *Johnsen v Johnsen*,[44] a husband's application to divide the wife's pension under the *Canadian Forces Superannuation Act (Canada)* was dismissed on the grounds that the limitation period respecting the equalization of the

---

40 *Ibid.*

41 Compare *Blomberg v Blomberg*, 367 NW 2d 643 (Minn Ct App 1985) (pension benefits earned during first marriage excluded from division on dissolution of remarriage).

42 RSO 1990, c F.3.

43 *Shafer v Shafer* (1998), 37 RFL (4th) 104 (Ont CA); *El Feky v Tohamy*, 2010 ONCA 647; *Horner v Horner*, 2014 ONSC 6320.

44 2012 ONSC 3079.

spousal net family properties under the *Family Law Act* had long since expired and the *Canadian Forces Superannuation Act* does not operate as standalone legislation; it simply provides a mechanism for the division of pension credits at source.

9) Equalization of Net Family Properties

a) General Observations

Pursuant to section 15 of the *Family Law Act*, the property rights of spouses arising out of the marital relationship are governed by the internal law of the place where both spouses had their last common habitual residence or, if there is no place where they had a common habitual residence, by the law of Ontario. The last common habitual residence of the spouses is the place where they last lived together as husband and wife and participated in everyday family life.[45]

Upon the occurrence of one of the triggering events specified in subsections 5(1), (2), and (3) of the *Family Law Act*, a spouse whose net family property is the lesser of the two net family properties is entitled to one-half of the difference between them, subject to the court's discretionary power to reapportion the sharing if an equalization of the net family properties would be unconscionable having regard to the specific factors enumerated in paragraphs (a) to (h) of subsection 5(6) of the Act.[46]

The concept of "net family property" is specifically defined in subsection 4(1) of the Act,[47] which provides as follows:

"net family property" means the value of all the property, except property described in subsection (2), that a spouse owns on the valuation date, after deducting,

(a) the spouse's debts and other liabilities, including, for greater certainty, any contingent tax liabilities in respect of the property, and

(b) the value of property, other than a matrimonial home, that the spouse owned on the date of the marriage, after deducting the spouse's debts and other liabilities, other than debts or liabilities related directly to the acquisition or significant improvement of a matrimonial home, calculated as of the date of the marriage.

---

45 See, generally, *Pershadsingh v Pershadsingh* (1987), 9 RFL (3d) 359 (Ont HCJ); *Vien v Vien Estate* (1988), 12 RFL 94 (Ont CA); *Nicholas v Nicholas* (1996), 24 RFL (4th) 358 (Ont CA); *Adam v Adam* (1994), 7 RFL (4th) 63 (Ont Gen Div), aff'd (1996), 25 RFL (4th) 50 (Ont CA); *Stefanou v Stefanou*, 2012 ONSC 7265.

46 See Section A(10), below in this chapter.

47 RSO 1990, c F.3, as amended by SO 2009, c 11, ss 22(1) & (2).

The terms "property" and "valuation date" are also specifically defined in subsection 4(1) of the *Family Law Act*.[48] The current definitions read as follows:

"property" means any interest, present or future, vested or contingent, in real or personal property and includes:

(a) property over which a spouse has, alone or in conjunction with another person, a power of appointment exercisable in favour of himself or herself,

(b) property disposed of by a spouse but over which the spouse has, alone or in conjunction with another person, a power to revoke the disposition or a power to consume or dispose of the property, and

(c) in the case of a spouse's rights under a pension plan, the imputed value, for family law purposes, of the spouse's interest in the plan, as determined in accordance with section 10.1, for the period beginning with the date of the marriage and ending on the valuation date.[49]

"valuation date" means the earliest of the following dates:

1. The date the spouses separate and there is no reasonable prospect that they will resume cohabitation.[50]

2. The date a divorce is granted.

3. The date the marriage is declared a nullity.

4. The date one of the spouses commences an application based on subsection 5(3) (improvement depletion) that is subsequently granted.

5. The date before the date on which one of the spouses dies leaving the other spouse surviving.

A spouse owes no duty to disclose extramarital affairs to his or her marital partner, and non-disclosure does not entitle a court to deviate from the statutorily defined "valuation date" in determining an application for equalization of spousal net family properties under Part I of the Ontario *Family Law Act*.[51]

In calculating a value as of a given date, the calculation shall be made as of the close of business on that date.[52]

Pursuant to the amended subsection 4(2) of the *Family Law Act*, the value of the following property that either spouse owns on the valuation date is excluded from the net family property:

---

48   RSO 1990, c F.3, as amended by SO 2009, c 11, s 22(4).

49   See *Family Law Statute Amendment Act*, SO 2009, c 11, ss 22(4) and 53(2).

50   *Tesfatsion v Berhane*, 2013 ONSC 75.

51   *Fleming v Fleming*, [2001] OJ No 1052 (Sup Ct).

52   RSO 1990, c F.3, s 4(4).

1. Property, other than a matrimonial home, that was acquired by gift or inheritance from a third person after the date of the marriage.

2. Income from property referred to in paragraph 1, if the donor or testator has expressly stated that it is to be excluded from the spouse's net family property.

3. Damages or a right to damages for personal injuries; nervous shock; mental distress; loss of guidance, care, and companionship; or the part of a settlement that represents those damages.

4. Proceeds or a right to proceeds of a life insurance policy, as defined in the *Insurance Act*,[53] that are payable on the death of the life insured.

5. Property, other than a matrimonial home, into which property referred to in paragraphs 1 to 4 can be traced.

6. Property that the spouses have agreed by a domestic contract is not to be included in the spouse's net family property.

7. Unadjusted pensionable earnings under the Canada Pension Plan.[54]

The onus of proving a "deduction" under the definition of "net family property" in subsection 4(1) of the Act and of proving an "exclusion" under subsection 4(2) of the *Family Law Act* falls on the person claiming the deduction or exclusion.[55] The Ontario Court of Appeal made it clear in *Homsi v Zaya*[56] that the party asserting the value of an asset must provide credible evidence as to its value. This requirement obliges the party to provide not just a guess but a realistic value based on credible evidence. At times, documentary evidence or expert valuations may be required and it may be necessary to obtain information in the possession of a third party.[57] Spouses should, therefore, prepare an inventory of their assets at the date of their marriage and maintain ongoing records respecting these assets and any other assets that fall within the ambit of subsection 4(2) of the *Family Law Act*. However, it is not always necessary to call expert evidence to prove values for minor assets and a court is entitled to ascribe a global value to ordinary household contents.[58]

The *Family Law Act* provides for the equalization of net family properties but does not necessarily involve the equalization of spousal debts or liabilities, although this may occur in certain circumstances.[59] There is no authority

---

53   RSO 1990, c I.8.
54   See Section A(9)(m), below in this chapter.
55   *Family Law Act*, RSO 1990, c F.3, s 4(3); *Pulitano v Pulitano*, 2010 ONCA 64; *Henderson v Casson*, 2014 ONSC 720; *Rebiere v Rebiere*, 2015 ONSC 1324.
56   2009 ONCA 457.
57   *Bakshi v Bakshi*, 2011 ONSC 3557; *Jacobs v Jacobs*, 2011 ONSC 2699.
58   *Rebiere v Rebiere*, 2015 ONSC 1324 at paras 14–15, Minnema J.
59   *Hutton v Hutton* (1985), 48 RFL (2d) 451 (Ont Co Ct).

under the *Family Law Act* to indemnify a spouse for a debt when there is no net family property.[60] Subsection 4(5) of the Act provides that the net family property of a spouse cannot be less than zero. If a spouse's net family property is less than zero, it is deemed to be equal to zero.

The overall significance of the aforementioned statutory provisions may be summarized in the following five steps:

1) Each spouse shall value his or her property, other than property excluded under subsection 4(2) of the Act, as of the date of the triggering event.

2) Each spouse shall calculate his or her debts and liabilities, apparently as of the date of the triggering event.

3) Each spouse shall calculate the value of property, other than a matrimonial home owned by that spouse on the date of the marriage,[61] and deduct from this value all debts and liabilities existing at the date of the marriage. The status of a matrimonial home is not immutable and a residence that was formerly occupied by the spouses, but is no longer so occupied prior to the cessation of matrimonial cohabitation, may entitle the owner spouse to a deduction of its premarital value under subsection 4(1) of the *Family Law Act*.[62]

4) The net family property of each spouse is then determined by subtracting the amounts calculated under paragraphs 2 and 3, above, from the amount calculated under paragraph 1, above. A spouse's net family property will be treated as having a zero value if the above calculations result in a deficit.

5) When the net family property of each spouse has been calculated, the spouse whose net family property is the lesser of the two is prima facie entitled to one-half of the difference between them.

In *Oliva v Oliva*,[63] the trial judge, McDermid LJSC, identified the following ten steps to be followed for the purpose of determining an equalization claim under Part I of the *Family Law Act*:

1. List and determine the value of all of the property owned by each spouse on the valuation date in this case the date of separation.

---

60 *Leppek v Leppek* (1991), 33 RFL (3d) 66 (Ont Gen Div); see also *Powers v Naston-Powers* (1990), 28 RFL (3d) 69 (Ont HCJ).

61 See *Nahatchewitz v Nahatchewitz* (1999), 1 RFL (5th) 395 (Ont CA); *Yeates v Yeates*, [2007] OJ No 1376 (Sup Ct); compare *Kukolj v Kukolj* (1986), 3 RFL (3d) 359 (Ont UFC); *Michalofsky v Michalofsky* (1989), 25 RFL (3d) 316 (Ont Div Ct), aff'd (1992), 39 RFL (3d) 356 (Ont CA); *Bosch v Bosch* (1991), 36 RFL (3d) 302 at 324 (Ont CA), Arbour JA.

62 *Folga v Folga* (1986), 2 RFL (3d) 358 (Ont HCJ); *Zabiegalowski v Zabiegalowski* (1992), 40 RFL (3d) 321 (Ont UFC).

63 (1986), 2 RFL (3d) 188 at 190–91 (Ont HCJ), var'd (1988), 12 RFL (3d) 334 (Ont CA).

2. List and determine the amount of each spouse's debts and other liabilities as of the valuation date.

3. Deduct the total obtained in para 2 from the total obtained in para 1 for each spouse.

4. List and determine the value of all the property, other than an interest in a matrimonial home, owned by each spouse on the date of the marriage.

5. List and determine the amount of each spouse's debts and other liabilities calculated as of the date of the marriage.

6. Deduct the total obtained in para 5 from the total obtained in para 4 for each spouse.

7. Deduct the total obtained in para 6 from the total obtained in para 3 for each spouse.

8. From the total obtained in para 7 deduct the value of the exclusions, if any, to which each spouse is entitled under s 4(2) of the Act.

9. Determine the amount which is 50 percent of the difference between the higher and lower values obtained for each spouse in para 8.

10. Having regard to the factors contained in s 5(6), decide whether the amount of the equalization payment is "unconscionable" and, if so, determine the proper amount which should be paid.

As Simmons JA, of the Ontario Court of Appeal, observed in *Townshend v Townshend*,[64]

> unlike the case with excluded property, the fact that property owned by a spouse on the date of marriage may have been distributed or invested jointly following the date of marriage is irrelevant. The claiming spouse is entitled to a deduction for the net value of property other than a matrimonial home owned on the date of marriage.

And as she later observed, "excluded property deposited into a joint account loses its exclusionary character to the extent of the one-half interest that is presumed to be gifted to the spouse."[65]

b) Significance of Ownership to Equalization Scheme

Sections 4 and 5 of the *Family Law Act* presuppose that the net family property of each spouse is distinct and separate. A determination of the net family property of each spouse may raise preliminary questions as to the

---

64 2012 ONCA 868 at para 12.

65 *Ibid* at para 28, citing *Goodyer v Goodyer*, [1999] OJ No 29 at para 76 (Gen Div); *Cartier v Cartier*, [2007] OJ No 4732 at footnote 4 (Sup Ct); and Ilana I Zylberman & Brian J Burke, "Tracing Exclusions in Family Law" (2006) 25 Can Fam LQ 67.

ownership of particular assets. For example, where property, such as a bank account, is held in the joint names of the spouses, the beneficial interest(s) in the property may or may not be reflected by the legal title. The presumption of joint beneficial interests arising under section 14 of the *Family Law Act* is provisional and not conclusive. It may be rebutted by cogent evidence pointing to a contrary intention. Even where property is held in the name of only one spouse, the doctrines of resulting and constructive trusts may have an impact on the beneficial ownership of such property. A determination of the beneficial ownership rights of each spouse is a condition precedent to any equalization of the net family properties of the spouses.[66] The need for such a determination becomes more apparent if one spouse has debts exceeding his or her assets at the valuation date.

Consider, for example, the following circumstances. A husband and wife have a joint bank account at the time of separation with a value of $100,000. The spouses have no other assets and the husband owes his creditors $100,000. If the joint bank account were purely one of convenience and all deposits had been made by the husband, his net family property would be valued at zero and there would be nothing to divide between the spouses. If, however, the circumstances revealed that the wife owned the account of convenience, she being the sole depositor, her net family property would be valued at $100,000 and her husband's at zero. The husband would accordingly be entitled to a presumptive equalization right of $50,000. If the joint bank account were beneficially owned in equal shares by both spouses, the husband's net family property would be zero and the wife's $50,000. The husband would accordingly be entitled to pursue an equalization claim in the amount of $25,000.

A monetary judgment based on the doctrine of unjust enrichment is unavailable as a remedy with respect to a premarital financial contribution towards the renovation of the matrimonial home where the contribution is adequately reflected in the subsequent transfer of title to the home into the names of both spouses as joint tenants.[67]

c) Definition of "Property"

The definition of "property" in subsection 4(1) of the *Family Law Act* is extremely broad. It includes the following:

- leasehold interests;
- life tenancies;[68]

---

66 *Rawluk v Rawluk*, [1990] 1 SCR 70.

67 *Roseneck v Gowling*, [2002] OJ No 4939 (CA).

68 See *Martin v Martin* (1986), 2 RFL (3d) 14 (Ont Dist Ct); *Crutchfield v Crutchfield* (1987), 10 RFL (3d) 247 (Ont HCJ); *Knapp v Knapp* (1992), 40 RFL (3d) 262 (Ont Gen Div).

- beneficial interests under wills or trusts;[69]
- financial planners' ongoing commissions from pre-existing life insurance policies;[70]
- pensions;[71]
- the cash surrender value of life insurance policies;[72]
- severance pay entitlements;[73]
- accumulated vacation pay;[74]
- accumulated sick leave;[75]
- workers' compensation benefits;[76]
- option rights;[77]
- partnership interests, business or professional goodwill;[78]
- accounts receivable;[79]
- shareholder loans;[80]
- book of business;[81] and
- accrued real estate commissions.[82]

Assigning value to unexercised options is more easily attainable in situations involving longer-standing stable companies, where there is a known market value for the options, where there is some level of certainty that real value will be derived from the options, in relation to companies whose stocks

---

69   See *Brinkos v Brinkos* (1989), 20 RFL (3d) 445 (Ont CA); *Black v Black* (1989), 18 RFL (3d) 303 (Ont HCJ); compare *Dunning v Dunning* (1987), 8 RFL (3d) 289 (Ont HCJ).

70   *Dunham v Dunham*, 2012 ONSC 2338.

71   See Section A(9)(d), below in this chapter.

72   *Blais v Blais* (1992), 38 RFL (3d) 256 (Gen Div).

73   *Marsham v Marsham* (1987), 7 RFL (3d) 1 (Ont HCJ); *Miller v Miller* (1987), 8 RFL (3d) 113 (Ont Dist Ct); *Emond v Emond* (1987), 10 RFL (3d) 107 (Ont CA); *Klein v Klein* (1987), 59 OR (2d) 781 (Dist Ct); *Butt v Butt* (1989), 22 RFL (3d) 415 (Ont HCJ); *Melanson v Melanson* (1991), 34 RFL (3d) 323 (Ont Gen Div); compare *Leckie v Leckie*, [2004] OJ No 1550 (CA) (post-separation severance package excluded from equalization): and see *Dembeck v Wright*, 2012 ONCA 852.

74   *Hodgins v Hodgins* (1989), 23 RFL (3d) 302 (Ont HCJ); *Duan v Li*, 2010 ONSC 1702.

75   *Hilderley v Hilderley* (1989), 21 RFL (3d) 383 (Ont HCJ); *Alger v Alger* (1989), 21 RFL (3d) 211 (Ont HCJ); *Cliche v Cliche* (1991), 36 RFL (3d) 297 (Ont CA); compare *Rickett v Rickett* (1989), 25 RFL (3d) 188 (Ont HCJ).

76   *Kelly v Kelly* (1987), 8 RFL (3d) 212 (Ont HCJ); *Buske v Buske* (1988), 12 RFL (3d) 388 (Ont Dist Ct).

77   *Ross v Ross*, [2006] OJ No 4916 (CA).

78   *Corless v Corless* (1987), 5 RFL (3d) 256 (Ont UFC); *Crutchfield v Crutchfield* (1987), 10 RFL (3d) 247 (Ont HCJ); *Christian v Christian* (1991), 37 RFL (3d) 26 (Ont Gen Div).

79   *Corless v Corless* (1987), 5 RFL (3d) 256 (Ont UFC); compare *Armstrong v Armstrong* (1986), 39 ACWS (2d) 162 (Ont Dist Ct).

80   *AB v LB*, 2014 ONSC 216.

81   *Mavis v Mavis* (2005), 15 RFL (6th) 369 at para 102 (Ont Sup Ct).

82   *Cosentino v Cosentino*, 2015 ONSC 271.

are publicly traded, or where an option is surrendered for something with a specified value that can be assigned to the options.[83] In determining the wife's entitlement to an equalization of the spousal net family properties under Part I of the Ontario *Family Law Act* in *Ross v Ross*,[84] a majority of the Ontario Court of Appeal (Rouleau JA, with O'Connor ACJO concurring, Borins JA dissenting) upheld the trial judge's ruling that employee stock options "earned" by the husband prior to the spousal separation but received three-and-one-half months thereafter constituted property owned by him on the valuation date (i.e., the date of the spousal separation) and, therefore, had to be included in the calculation of his net family property. All three judges agreed, however, that the trial judge had erred by using an "if-and-when" approach to divide the husband's stock options instead of valuing them in accordance with the Black-Scholes method, which is an accepted model for valuing stock options where the underlying security is publicly traded. Application of this model resulted in a huge reduction of the wife's equalization entitlement. Unlike the situation in other provinces, Ontario courts have no jurisdiction to bypass the valuation of property by ordering a division *in specie*. And, as noted by Aitken J in *Buttrum v Buttrum*,[85] the "if-and-when" approach "is not a valuation technique but a method of dividing property."[86]

University degrees and professional licences, and future income resulting therefrom, are not "property" for the purposes of subsection 4(1) of the *Family Law Act*.[87]

The definition of "property" under section 4(1) of the *Family Law Act* includes a future income stream payable pursuant to a non-competition agreement executed on the sale of an interest in a private company. Rights under such a contract fall within the definition of "property" under section 4(1) of the Act, where the right to the future income stream is not dependent on personal service. The non-taxability of such an income stream does not affect its characterization as "property" under section 4(1) of the *Family Law Act*, but does preclude any discounting of its value in light of notional future tax liabilities. An inability to transfer the contractual right to a future income stream does not affect its characterization as "property" under the *Family*

---

83   *Chowdhury v Chowdhury*, 2010 ONSC 781 at paras 42–44, Allen J, citing *Buttrum v Buttrum* (2001), 15 RFL (5th) 250 (Ont Sup Ct); *De Zen v De Zen*, 20 RFL (5th) 326 (Ont Sup Ct); *Ross v Ross* (2006), 34 RFL (6th) 229 (Ont CA).

84   [2006] OJ No 4916 (CA).

85   (2001), 15 RFL (5th) 250 (Ont Sup Ct).

86   See *Ross v Ross* (2006), 34 RFL (6th) 229 at paras 35–37 (Ont CA), overruling *Reid v Reid* (2003), 50 RFL (5th) 170 (Ont Sup Ct).

87   *Caratun v Caratun* (1992), 42 RFL (3d) 113 (Ont CA), leave to appeal to SCC refused (1993), 46 RFL (3d) 314 (SCC). And see Section A(9)(e), below in this chapter.

Law Act.[88] A spouse's right to future income from a trust established during the marriage has been held to fall within the definition of "property" in subsection 4(1) of the *Family Law Act*.[89] In *Da Costa v Da Costa*,[90] a spouse's future interest in the capital of a deceased's estate, dependent as it was upon the spouse surviving the deceased's grandchildren, was characterized as a contingent interest and thus property within the meaning of section 4(1), but it was discounted in value to reflect the possibility that he might predecease the grandchildren. But a mere expectation of inheritance under a third-party will does not confer a vested or contingent interest until the death of the testator and does not, therefore, constitute "property" within the meaning of section 4(1) of the *Family Law Act*.[91]

d) Pensions

Paragraph (c) of the definition of "property" in subsection 4(1) of the *Family Law Act* was legislatively amended in 2009 to read as follows:

> (c)   in the case of a spouse's rights under a pension plan, the imputed value, for family law purposes, of the spouse's interest in the plan, as determined in accordance with section 10.1, for the period beginning with the date of the marriage and ending on the valuation date.[92]

Section 10.1 provides as follows:

> Interest in a pension plan
>
> *Imputed value for family law purposes*
>
> 10.1 (1) The imputed value, for family law purposes, of a spouse's interest in a pension plan to which the *Pension Benefits Act* applies is determined in accordance with section 67.2 of that Act.[93]
>
> (2) The imputed value, for family law purposes, of a spouse's interest in any other pension plan is determined, where reasonably possible, in accordance with section 67.2 of the *Pension Benefits Act* with necessary modifications.

---

88   *Clegg v Clegg*, [2000] OJ No 2479 (Sup Ct).

89   *Brinkos v Brinkos*, (1989), 20 RFL (3d) 445 (Ont CA); compare *Jordan v Jordan* (1988), 13 RFL (3d) 402 (Ont CA).

90   *Da Costa v Da Costa* (1992), 40 RFL (3d) 216 (Ont CA).

91   *Dunning v Dunning* (1987), 8 RFL (3d) 289 (Ont HCJ).

92   See *Family Law Statute Amendment Act*, SO 2009, c 11, ss 22(4), 26, 37, 39, and 53.2. See also Guy Martel & Barbara Thompson, "New Regime in Town: Pension Update" (presented at the County of Carleton Law Association, 21st Annual Family Law Institute, Ottawa, 13 April 2012).

93   See *Heringer v Heringer*, 2014 ONSC 7291.

Order for immediate transfer of a lump sum

(3) An order made under section 9 or 10 may provide for the immediate transfer of a lump sum out of a pension plan but, except as permitted under subsection (5), not for any other division of a spouse's interest in the plan.

(4) In determining whether to order the immediate transfer of a lump sum out of a pension plan and in determining the amount to be transferred, the court may consider the following matters and such other matters as the court considers appropriate:

1. The nature of the assets available to each spouse at the time of the hearing.

2. The proportion of a spouse's net family property that consists of the imputed value, for family law purposes, of his or her interest in the pension plan.

3. The liquidity of the lump sum in the hands of the spouse to whom it would be transferred.

4. Any contingent tax liabilities in respect of the lump sum that would be transferred.

5. The resources available to each spouse to meet his or her needs in retirement and the desirability of maintaining those resources.

Order for division of pension payments

(5) If payment of the first instalment of a spouse's pension under a pension plan is due on or before the valuation date, an order made under section 9 or 10 may provide for the division of pension payments but not for any other division of the spouse's interest in the plan.[94]

(6) Subsections 9 (2) and (4) do not apply with respect to an order made under section 9 or 10 that provides for the division of pension payments.

Restrictions re certain pension plans

(7) If the *Pension Benefits Act* applies to the pension plan, the restrictions under sections 67.3 and 67.4 of that Act apply with respect to the division of the spouse's interest in the plan by an order under section 9 or 10.

Transition, valuation date

(8) This section applies whether the valuation date is before, on or after the date on which this section comes into force.

---

94   *Jovanovic v Jovanovic*, 2013 ONSC 7132.

Transition, previous orders

(9) This section does not apply to an order made before the date on which this section comes into force that requires one spouse to pay to the other spouse the amount to which that spouse is entitled under section 5.[95]

No presumption exists favouring transfers from a pension plan as contemplated by the new section 10.1 of the *Family Law Act* and section 26 of Ont Reg 287/11 implementing the changes to the *Pension Benefits Act*, RSO 1990 c P.8, as amended. Nor is there a statutory onus on a spouse entitled to an equalization payment to show that the new pension division mechanism brought into force by the *Family Law Statute Amendment Act, 2009*, SO 2009, c 11, s 26 should not be called into play in favour of immediate payment.[96]

e) Professional Licences and Practices; Goodwill

The definition of "property" in subsection 4(1) of the *Family Law Act* is sufficiently broad to include an interest in a business or professional partnership. In valuing a professional practice, "goodwill" is a factor to be considered.[97] It has been held inappropriate to value the goodwill of a professional practice by capitalizing excess earnings, where the spouse is a sole practitioner and there is no continuum of returning patients[98] or where the practice has no value on the open market.[99] It has also been held that an anaesthetist employed by a hospital has no "practice" that constitutes divisible property and that his future income should not be regarded as a divisible asset.[100] Similarly, a spouse's professional degree or licence, with its consequential enhanced earning capacity, has been excluded from division. In *Brinkos v Brinkos*,[101] Carthy JA, of the Ontario Court of Appeal, presented the following opinion by way of *obiter dicta*:

> I cannot accept that the entitlement to earn income as a judge, or under a licence, is a contingent interest in the pool of money which may be earned in the future. There is no identifiable property, except perhaps the licence itself. If it is property, and if it has a value (and no opinion is here expressed), that value cannot be a capitalization of the future income stream. The licence will earn nothing without the services of the licensee and the earnings are

---

95 A useful collection of articles on the pension amendments can be found online.
96 *Tupholme v Tupholme*, 2013 ONSC 4268 at paras 15–16, Vogelsang J; see also *VanderWal v VanderWal*, 2015 ONSC 384.
97 *Criton v Criton* (1986), 50 RFL (2d) 44 (Sask CA).
98 *Nassar v Nassar*, [1984] 6 WWR 634 (Man QB).
99 *Smith v Mackie* (1986), 48 RFL (2d) 232 (BCSC).
100 *Barley v Barley* (1984), 43 RFL (2d) 100 (BCSC).
101 (1989), 20 RFL (3d) 445 at 450 (Ont CA).

based upon the value of the services provided, not upon the mere existence of a licence to perform. . . .

In the case of a professional practising under a licence, it cannot be said that there is a contingent entitlement to income in the future within the legal meaning of those words where personal service and effort, rather than an external event, are required to produce that income.

In *Caratun v Caratun*,[102] the Ontario Court of Appeal specifically resolved the question whether a professional licence constitutes "property" under subsection 4(1) of the *Family Law Act*. In view of the fact that a professional licence is non-transferable and its value depends on the future labours of the licensee, the court concluded that a professional licence is not "property" within the meaning of subsection 4 of the *Family Law Act*, nor can it be subject to any proprietary interest in the form of a constructive trust. It was, nevertheless, concluded that the wife was entitled to compensatory spousal support under subsection 11(1) of the *Divorce Act, 1968*[103] in the amount of $30,000 for the sacrifice of her personal career advancement and for her substantial contribution to her husband's career aspirations.

f) Value

Although the notion of "value" is central to the application of Part I of the *Family Law Act*, there is no definition of "value" in the Act. Courts have employed a variety of approaches to meet the circumstances before them. The goal of the legislation is to arrive at the fairest and most equitable solution for the parties. Value must, therefore, be determined on the particular facts and circumstances of each case.[104] Where practicable, the courts will apply the concept of fair market value, which signifies "the highest price available in an open and unrestricted market between informed and prudent parties acting at arms length and under no compulsion to transact."[105]

g) Valuation of Business; Private Companies

In the words of Cameron J, of the Newfoundland Unified Family Court, in *Hart v Hart (No 3)*,

Generally there are four basic approaches to valuation of a business:

---

102 (1992), 42 RFL (3d) 113 (Ont CA).

103 SC 1967–68, c 24.

104 *Chowdhury v Chowdhury*, 2010 ONSC 781, Allen J.

105 *Christian v Christian* (1991), 37 RFL (3d) 26 (Ont Gen Div); see also *Montague v Montague* (1996), 23 RFL (4th) 62 (Ont CA) (costs of pollution cleanup taken into account in determining fair market value of husband's business).

1. Market price (in the case of public company);
2. Assets approach;
3. Earnings or investment value approach; and
4. A combination of the above . . . .

The assets approach is generally used where the hypothetical purchaser is really looking to the company's underlying assets and not to the shares *per se*. This method may also be appropriate where the business being valued is a going concern, but not earning an adequate return on its invested capital. A determination of a liquidation value is an asset approach.

. . .

The earnings or investment value approach is appropriate when the business is earning a reasonable return on its capital. In this approach the hypothetical purchaser wishes to acquire the future earnings of the business.

. . .

In the combined approach, as the name implies, the appraiser uses the different approaches referred to above and weights the resulting values in light of particular factors to determine a final valuation.[106]

Factors to be considered in valuing the shares of a private company include the following:

- the nature and history of the enterprise;
- the economic outlook;
- the book value and financial condition;
- the earning capacity;
- the dividend-paying capacity;
- the goodwill or other intangible values;
- the size of the block to be valued; and
- the market price of stock of similar corporations.

The valuation of the stock of a private company presents a unique factual situation that is not within the ambit of any exact science, and the reasonableness of any valuation thus depends upon the judgment and experience of the appraiser and the completeness of the information relied upon to support the opinions presented.[107] The evidence of experts may yield to experience

---

106   (1986), 60 Nfld & PEIR 287 (Nfld UFC); see also *Kuderewko v Kuderewko*, [2006] SJ No 726 (QB).

107   *Indig v Indig* (15 August 1986), Doc Windsor 14,252/84 (Ont SC), Carter LJSC; *Kuderewko v Kuderewko*, [2006] SJ No 726 (QB).

in light of a prior recorded sale of shares.[108] In determining the value of a business, the evidence of a person engaged in the "real world" of marketing such businesses may be preferred to that of a chartered accountant.[109]

Valuation is an art, not a science. In *Black v Black*,[110] three expert opinions were submitted on the value of the husband's shares in privately held companies. The lowest estimate, submitted by one of two experts on behalf of the husband, produced a figure of $8,950,310. The husband's second expert suggested a figure of $14,707,000, which was subsequently revised to $13,261,000. The wife's expert valued the shares at $34,801,000. The lowest and highest estimates were consequently in excess of $25 million apart. The trial judge accepted the value of $14,707,000. The experience in *Black v Black* suggests that there may be some advantage in spouses entering into a marriage contract to determine in advance the value of designated assets or, at least, a precise method for calculating value.

h) Valuation Date

The definitions of "net family property" and "valuation date" in subsection 4(1) of the *Family Law Act* imply that the court is unconcerned with changes in the value of property that occur between the valuation date and the date of the adjudication of an equalization claim.[111] In the absence of a resulting trust or constructive trust, any appreciation or depreciation in the value of property after the valuation date is irrelevant to a determination of the value of the net family property of each spouse, regardless of whether the change in value is attributable to extrinsic economic forces or to the conduct of a spouse.[112] The provisions of subsection 5(6) of the *Family Law Act* and particularly paragraphs (b), (d), (f), and (h) may enable the court to achieve equity between the spouses in the aforementioned circumstances by invoking its discretion to reapportion the entitlements of each spouse on the basis that an equalization of the net family properties as of the date of the triggering event would be unconscionable. The dissenting judgment of McLachlin J in the Supreme Court of Canada decision of *Rawluk v Rawluk*[113] concludes

---

108 *Sheehan v Sheehan* (31 March 1986) (Ont Sup Ct), citing *Remus v Remus* (1987), 5 RFL (3d) 304 (Ont HCJ); see also *Duff v Duff* (1988), 12 RFL (3d) 435 (Ont HCJ).

109 *Sheehan v Sheehan* (31 March 1986) (Ont Sup Ct); compare *Duff v Duff* (1988), 12 RFL (3d) 435 (Ont HCJ).

110 (1989), 18 RFL (3d) 303 (Ont HCJ).

111 But see *Rawluk v Rawluk*, [1990] 1 SCR 70. See also Sections A(6) and A(9)(b), above in this chapter.

112 *Kelly v Kelly* (1986), 50 RFL (2d) 360 (Ont HCJ); *Arndt v Arndt* (1991), 37 RFL (3d) 423 (Ont Gen Div), aff'd (1993), 48 RFL 353 (Ont CA), leave to appeal to SCC refused (1994), 1 RFL (4th) 63 (SCC).

113 [1990] 1 SCR 70.

that subsection 5(6) of the Act may be used to address any unconscionability that might arise as a result of equalization of the parties' net family properties when the property has significantly appreciated in value by the date of trial.[114] Alternatively, a "reverse constructive trust" could perhaps be invoked by a title-holding spouse when property has depreciated in value between the valuation date and the date of trial.[115]

i) Income Tax and Other Prospective Liabilities

Courts have allowed deductions for the present value of a future debt or liability.[116] The current definition of "net family property" in subsection 4(1) of the *Family Law Act*[117] explicitly provides for the deduction of "the spouse's debts and other liabilities, including, for greater certainty, any contingent tax liabilities in respect of the property" from the value of all non-excluded property owned by the spouse on the valuation date.

In calculating the "net family property" of either spouse for the purposes of an equalization claim under section 5 of the *Family Law Act*, prospective tax liabilities may be taken into consideration[118] in the absence of a spousal rollover.[119] In the words of Finlayson JA, of the Ontario Court of Appeal, in *McPherson v McPherson*,

> An allowance should be made in the case where there is evidence that the disposition will involve a sale or transfer of property that attracts tax consequences, and it should not be made in the case where it is not clear when, if ever, a sale or transfer of property will be made and thus the tax consequences of such an occurrence are so speculative that they can safely be ignored.[120]

---

114 See, generally, Section A(10)(a), below in this chapter.

115 See *McDonald v McDonald* (1988), 11 RFL (3d) 321 (Ont HCJ), Forestell LJSC, and James G McLeod, "Annotation," *ibid* at 322–23; see also *Arndt v Arndt* (1991), 37 RFL (3d) 423 (Ont Gen Div), aff'd (1993), 48 RFL 353 (Ont CA), leave to appeal to SCC refused (1994), 1 RFL (4th) 63 (SCC); *Socan v Socan*, [2005] OJ No 3992 (Sup Ct).

116 *Greenglass v Greenglass*, 2010 ONCA 675. Compare , *Zavarella v Zavarella*, 2013 ONCA 720. See also *Yar v Yar*, 2015 ONSC 151.

117 RSO 1990, c F.3, s 4(1), as amended by SO 2009, c 11, s 22(1).

118 *Savonarota v Savonarota*, 2011 ONSC 4842; *Reisman v Reisman*, 2012 ONSC 3148. As to the allocation of notional tax costs respecting an RRSP, which might be the subject of a tax-free rollover, see *Appleyard v Appleyard* (1998), 41 RFL (4th) 199 (Ont CA) and see James G McLeod, "Annotation," *ibid* at 199–201. See also *Heard v Heard*, 2014 ONCA 196.

119 *Billingsley v Billingsley*, 2010 ONSC 3381; see also *Buttar v Buttar*, 2013 ONCA 517.

120 (1988), 13 RFL (3d) 1 at 9 (Ont CA); see also *Livermore v Livermore* (1992), 43 RFL (3d) 163 (Ont Gen Div).

Although this opinion was formulated in the context of the *Family Law Reform Act, 1978*, it is equally applicable to its successor, the *Family Law Act*.[121] In the later appellate decision in *Sengmueller v Sengmueller*, McKinlay JA, delivering the opinion of the Ontario Court of Appeal, stated:

> From the *McPherson* case I glean three rules to apply in all cases:
>
> (1) Apply the overriding principle of fairness, *i.e.*, that costs of disposition as well as benefits should be shared equally;
>
> (2) Deal with each case on its own facts, considering the nature of the assets involved, evidence as to the probable timing of their disposition, and the probable tax and other costs of disposition at that time, discounted as of valuation day; and
>
> (3) Deduct disposition costs before arriving at the equalization payment, except in the situation where "it is not clear when, if ever" there will be a realization of the property.
>
> Under the *Family Law Act* it does not matter whether the third rule is applied as part of the valuation of the asset involved, or whether the deduction is made as an inevitable liability which exists on valuation day, although it is not payable until some time in the future.[122]

The Court of Appeal rejected the submission of counsel for the appellant that disposition costs should only be allowed if it were necessary to dispose of the asset in order to satisfy the equalization entitlement.

In addition to taking prospective taxes into account, consideration may also be given to real estate and legal fees likely to be incurred in consequence of any court-ordered equalization entitlement.[123]

j) Expert Evidence: "Splitting the Difference"

Valuation is not an exact science and expert opinions may differ on the value of specific assets and even on the appropriate method for effectuating a valuation. For example, the valuation of a spouse's shares in an active company could be based on a future earnings approach or on a liquidation approach, and the formula selected may radically affect the determination of their value.[124]

---

121 *Starkman v Starkman* (1990), 28 RFL (3d) 208 (Ont CA).

122 (1994), 2 RFL (4th) 232 at 241 (Ont CA); see also *Buttar v Buttar*, 2013 ONCA 517; *Fielding v Fielding*, 2014 ONSC 2272; *Mowers v Acland*, 2015 ONSC 1313.

123 *Kelly v Kelly* (1986), 2 RFL (3d) 1 (Ont HCJ); *Sullivan v Sullivan* (1986), 5 RFL (3d) 28 at 35 (Ont UFC); but see *contra, Folga v Folga* (1986), 2 RFL (3d) 358 at 363 (Ont HCJ).

124 See *Nurnberger v Nurnberger* (1983), 25 Sask R 241 at 246–47 (QB).

Where a court is faced with conflicting expert evidence respecting the value of specific assets, the court may find it appropriate to split the difference by averaging the appraisals submitted on behalf of the respective spouses. This practice cannot be universally applied, however, because it may lead to unjust and absurd results and would constitute an abrogation of the court's responsibility.[125]

In determining fair market value as of the "valuation date," which is usually the date on which the spouses separated, the court cannot invoke the benefit of hindsight.[126] While hindsight information cannot be used as part of the process of establishing the value of a private company on the valuation date, hindsight information relating to the actual results achieved after the valuation date may be compared against the projected or forecasted corporate results reached by the valuator and used to test the reasonableness of his or her assumptions.[127] Hindsight evidence can also be used to assist in determining which of the experts' evidence has greater validity where there are conflicting opinions as to value based on differing assumptions or forecasts.[128]

An order directing the transfer of property is unavailable under the *Family Law Act*[129] as a means of avoiding difficulties in valuation. Dispositive orders under section 9 of the *Family Law Act* presuppose that the equalization entitlement has already been established in light of the value of all relevant assets.[130]

k) Deduction of Debts and Liabilities

In undertaking the statutory calculations for the purpose of determining the "net family property" of each spouse, the definition of "net family property" in subsection 4(1) of the *Family Law Act*[131] explicitly provides for the deduction of "the spouse's debts and other liabilities, including, for greater certainty, any contingent tax liabilities in respect of the property" from the value of all non-excluded property owned by the spouse on the valuation

---

125 *Danecker v Danecker*, 2014 ONCA 239; *Budd v Budd*, 2015 ONSC 346; see also *Duff v Duff* (1983), 43 Nfld & PEIR 151 (Nfld CA).

126 *Best v Best*, [1999] 2 SCR 868 (pension); *Ruster v Ruster*, [2003] OJ No 3710 (CA) (premarital deduction); *Filiatrault-MacDonald v MacDonald*, 2014 ONSC 4972 (motion for financial disclosure), citing *Buttrum v Buttrum* [2001] OJ No 1390 at para 17 (Sup Ct).

127 *Debora v Debora*, [2006] OJ No 4826 (CA); see also *Jackson v Jackson*, [2009] OJ No 3391 (Sup Ct).

128 *Brown v Silvera*, 2011 ABCA 109.

129 RSO 1990, c F.3.

130 See *Marsham v Marsham* (1987), 7 RFL (3d) 1 (Ont HCJ); Section A(9)(d), above in this chapter; *Henry v Cymbalisty* (1986), 55 OR (2d) 51 at 54–55 (UFC); *Humphreys v Humphreys* (1987), 7 RFL (3d) 113 (Ont HCJ); *Cotter v Cotter* (1988), 12 RFL (3d) 209 (Ont HCJ).

131 RSO 1990, c F.3, s 4(1), as amended by SO 2009, c 11, s 22(1).

date.[132] Contingent liabilities are to be taken into account as long as they are reasonably foreseeable.[133] In determining the present value of a contingent liability, courts have looked at what was reasonably foreseeable on the valuation date.[134]

Paragraph (a) of the definition of "net family property" envisages the deduction of debts and other liabilities existing as of the "valuation date." It is immaterial whether the debts or liabilities were incurred for the benefit of the family as a whole or for the personal benefit of the spouse who incurred them. In calculating the equalization payment under Part I of the *Family Law Act*, the value of loans from the husband's parents may be substantially discounted where the debts are old and no demand was made for any repayment until after the spouses separated. In upholding the trial judge's finding in *Cade v Rotstein*[135] that the debts should be discounted to 5 percent of their face value, the Court of Appeal observed that the husband's father had testified that he would not have looked for the money or taken any action against his son to collect the debts. The Court of Appeal concluded that the trial judge had properly followed the approach in *Poole v Poole*[136] and *Salamon v Salamon*,[137] and expressly agreed with the following statement of Heeney J in *Poole v Poole*:

> Even though debt may have a specified face value, if the evidence indicates that it is unlikely that the promissor will ever be called upon to pay the debt, the value of the debt should be discounted to reflect that reality.[138]

Any debt that a spouse will not be required to pay due to his bankruptcy should be excluded from the calculation of the spouses's net family property.[139]

---

132 See Section A(9)(i), above in this chapter.

133 *Leslie v Leslie* (1987), 9 RFL (3d) 82 (Ont HCJ); *Nicol v Nicol* (1989), 21 RFL (3d) 236 (Ont HCJ); *Crutchfield v Crutchfield* (1987), 10 RFL (3d) 247 (Ont HCJ); *Drysdale v Drysdale* (1994), 9 RFL (4th) 20 (Ont UFC); *Greenglass v Greenglass*, 2010 ONCA 675. Compare *Cosentino v Cosentino*, 2015 ONSC 271 (post-valuation date income tax reassessment).

134 *Johnston v Johnston*, [1998] OJ No 5495 at para 59 (Gen Div), aff'd on other grounds 2000 CanLII 14718 (Ont CA), leave to appeal to SCC refused, [2000] SCCA No 234; *Greenglass v Greenglass*, 2010 ONCA 675.

135 [2004] OJ No 286 (CA); see also *Moorse v Moorse*, 2010 ONSC 663; *Stetler v Stetler*, 2012 ONSC 4466.

136 [2001] OJ No 2154 (Sup Ct).

137 [1997] OJ No 852 (Gen Div).

138 [2004] OJ No 286 at para 8 (CA); see also *MB v DT*, 2012 ONSC 840; *Zavarella v Zavarella*, 2013 ONCA 720.

139 *Radlo v Radlo*, 2013 ONSC 7329.

In *Pecore v Pecore*,[140] the Supreme Court of Canada held that the presumption of advancement, whereby a transfer between a parent and a child under the age of majority is presumed to be a gift, is inapplicable to adult independent children. In the event of such a transfer, there is a rebuttable presumption that the adult independent child is holding the property under a resulting trust for the parent. Evidence of intention is vital to ascertain whether a transfer was a loan or a gift. In *Locke v Locke*,[141] the British Columbia Supreme Court identified the following factors as relevant to the determination of the intention behind a transfer:

1. whether there were any contemporaneous documents evidencing a loan;

2. whether the manner for repayment is specified;

3. whether there is security held for the loan;

4. whether there are advances to one child and not others, or advances of unequal amounts to various children;

5. whether there has been any demand for payment before the separation of the parties;

6. whether there has been any partial repayment; and

7. whether there was any expectation, or likelihood, of repayment.

l) Valuation of Premarital Property

In calculating the value of property, the definition of "net family property" in subsection 4(1) of the *Family Law Act* requires the deduction of "(b) the value of property, other than a matrimonial home, that the spouse owned on the date of the marriage, after deducting the spouse's debts and other liabilities, other than debts or liabilities related directly to the acquisition or significant improvement of a matrimonial home, calculated as of the date of the marriage."[142] In *Houston v Houston*,[143] the husband owned residential property at the time of the marriage, which subsequently became the matrimonial home. As of the date of the marriage, there was a collateral mortgage on the property that secured a line of credit with a balance of $114,996.91. Of this amount, only $25,000 was related to the maintenance, preservation, or improvement of the home. In calculating the husband's net family property, it was determined that he was entitled to deduct $89,966.91 from the value of the pre-marital assets, other than the matrimonial home, that he owned.

---

140 [2007] 1 SCR 795; see also *Madsen Estate v Saylor*, [2007] 1 SCR 838; *Chung v La*, 2011 BCSC 1547; *Zivic v Zivic*, 2014 ONSC 7262; *SL v CB*, 2013 SKQB 333.

141 2000 BCSC 1300 at para 20; see also *Kim v Kim*, 2014 ONSC 4773; *JB v DM*, 2014 ONSC 7410.

142 RSO 1990, c F.3, s 4(1), as amended by SO 2009, c 11, s 22(2).

143 2011 ONSC 5610 (Div Ct); see also *Martin v Martin*, 2014 ONSC 7530.

If a spouse's premarital debts and liabilities exceed the value of his or her premarital assets, the deficit amount should be added to the net value of that spouse's assets at the valuation date for the purpose of determining the appropriate equalization payment to be ordered. Although judicial opinions have differed on this issue, the preponderance of authority asserts that debts that one spouse brings into a marriage and that are discharged during the marriage should be taken into account in calculating the appropriate equalization entitlement. This interpretation is endorsed in the reasons for judgment in *Jackson v Jackson*[144] and in *McDonald v McDonald*[145] and is exemplified by the calculation of the equalization payment in *Nahatchewitz v Nahatchewitz.*[146] These judgments reflect the objective of the *Family Law Act*, which is to equalize the value of property or wealth accumulated during the marriage, and this includes the reduction or elimination of a spouse's premarital debts.[147]

A spouse seeking to claim a deduction for a premarital asset bears the onus of proving its existence as of the date of marriage; the testimony of the spouse seeking the deduction may be insufficient without corroborating documentation.[148]

In determining the value of premarital property, paragraph (b) requires that the value be calculated as of the date of the marriage.[149] The value of this exemption cannot be indexed to any depreciation in the purchasing power of the dollar between the date of marriage and the "valuation date" as defined in subsection 4(1) of the Act.[150] Notional disposition costs are also ignored in valuing the premarital property deduction for the purpose of determining an equalization entitlement under Part I of the Ontario *Family Law Act*.[151]

Any appreciation in the value of premarital property will be shared equally by the spouses on the valuation date, unless the court finds that this would be unconscionable having regard to subsection 5(6) of the Act, and particularly paragraph (h) thereof. Where the appreciation in value during matrimonial cohabitation is attributable to extrinsic considerations, such as inflation or market conditions, subsection 5(6) of the Act presumably has

144 (1995), 5 RFL (3d) 8 at 12 (Ont HCJ), Kent J. See also *Menage v Hedges* (1987), 8 RFL (3d) 225 (Ont UFC).

145 (1995), 17 RFL (4th) 258 at 260 (Ont Gen Div), Rutherford J.

146 (1999), 178 DLR (4th) 496 (Ont CA).

147 See *McAndrew v Rooney-McAndrew*, [2003] PEIJ No 95 (CA).

148 *Wasylyshyn v Wasylyshyn* (1987), 8 RFL (3d) 337 (Ont Dist Ct); *Francis v Francis* (1987), 8 RFL (3d) 460 (Ont SC); *Birce v Birce*, [2001] OJ No 3910 (CA); *Torrone v Torrone*, 2010 ONSC 661; *Chowdhury v Chowdhury*, 2010 ONSC 781.

149 See *Oliva v Oliva* (1986), 2 RFL (3d) 188 (Ont HCJ), var'd (1988), 12 RFL (3d) 334 (Ont CA).

150 See *Burgmaier v Burgmaier* (1985), 47 RFL (2d) 251 (Sask QB).

151 *Pocs v Pocs*, [2001] OJ No 2808 (Sup Ct).

no application because an equal sharing of the increased value between the spouses would not appear to be unconscionable. In the converse situation, where premarital property has depreciated in value between the date of the marriage and the valuation date by reason of extrinsic economic conditions, the title-holding spouse is presumably entitled to a full deduction of the pre-marital value under paragraph (b) of the definition of "net family property" in subsection 4(1) of the Act, although paragraph 5(6)(h) of the Act may apply in these circumstances.[152]

Pursuant to the provisions of paragraph (b), above, and paragraphs 4(2)(1) and 4(2)(5) of the *Family Law Act*, the value of a matrimonial home is included in the determination of the "net family property" of each spouse.[153] It is immaterial under paragraph (b) that the home was owned by a spouse prior to the marriage, provided that the residence was ordinarily occupied by the spouses as a family residence on the date of their separation.[154] Similarly, it is immaterial under paragraphs 4(2)1 and 4(2)5 of the Act[155] that the matrimonial home was acquired by one of the spouses as a gift or inheritance from a third party after the date of the marriage or with the proceeds of such a gift or inheritance.[156] The regular usage of cottage property during the marriage renders it a matrimonial home within the meaning of section 18 of the *Family Law Act*, thereby precluding its exclusion from a spouse's net family property.[157] In *DeBora v DeBora*,[158] a cottage had been purchased before the husband's marriage as an investment by a numbered company in which the husband was the sole shareholder. During the marriage, the cottage was ordinarily occupied by the spouses as an all-season recreational residence. The trial judge held that the cottage constituted a "matrimonial home" within the meaning of section 18(1) of the *Family Law Act*, which provides that "[e]very property in which a person has an interest[159] and that is (or, if the spouses have separated, was) at the time of separation ordinarily occupied by the person and his or her spouse as their family residence, is their

---

152   See Section A(10)(i), below in this chapter.

153   *Shaver v Shaver* (1991), 37 RFL (3d) 117 (Ont UFC); *Durakovic v Durakovic*, [2008] OJ No 3537 (Sup Ct); see also Section A(9)(a), above in this chapter.

154   *Folga v Folga* (1986), 2 RFL (3d) 358 (Ont HCJ); see also *Michalofsky v Michalofsky* (1989), 25 RFL (3d) 316 (Ont Div Ct), aff'd (1992), 39 RFL (3d) 356 (Ont CA); *Bosch v Bosch* (1991), 36 RFL (3d) 302 (Ont CA); *Nahatchewitz v Nahatchewitz* (1999), 1 RFL (5th) 395 (Ont CA); *Janjua v Khan*, 2013 ONSC 44.

155   See Sections A(9)(m) and A(9)(r), below in this chapter.

156   *Harris v Harris* (1986), 39 ACWS (2d) 68 (Ont Dist Ct).

157   *Martin v Martin*, 2014 ONSC 7530, citing *Ethier v Cyr*, 2011 ONCA 387.

158   [2006] OJ No 4826 (CA). For further judicial insight on piercing the corporate veil, see *Wildman v Wildman*, [2006] OJ No 3966 (CA); *Lynch v Segal*, [2006] OJ No 5014 (CA).

159   As to the implications of a trust, see *Spencer v Riesberry*, 2012 ONCA 418.

matrimonial home."[160] Consequently, the husband could claim no deduction with respect to the premarital value of the cottage in light of the definition of "net family property" in section 4(1) of the *Family Law Act*. On appeal, the husband contended that he had no "interest" in the cottage within the meaning of section 18(1) of the Act because a shareholder does not own the assets of a corporation. Accordingly, he sought to deduct the value of his shares at the date of the marriage from their increased value on the date of the spousal separation as reflected in the market value of the cottage at these two dates. In addressing his contention, the Ontario Court of Appeal was called upon to examine section 18(2) of the *Family Law Act*, which provides that "[t]he ownership of a share or shares, or an interest in a share or shares, of a corporation entitling the owner to occupy a housing unit owned by a corporation shall be deemed to be an interest in the unit for the purposes of subsection (1)." In dismissing the husband's submission that section 18(2) primarily applies to a situation where a matrimonial home is a condominium or co-operative apartment or where the purpose of putting the home in the name of the corporation is to defeat the *Family Law Act*, the Ontario Court of Appeal stated:

> I disagree with this interpretation. The plain wording of the subsection does not limit a spouse's interest to a condominium or co-operative apartment and I can think of no reason to so limit it in this manner. The simple device of holding a house in the name of a personally owned corporation prior to the date of marriage would deprive the other spouse of the rights associated with the matrimonial home: an equal right to possession; the requirement that the consent of the other spouse to alienate or encumber the home be obtained; and the full value of the home being included in the calculation of a spouse's net family property on separation. Such an interpretation would defeat the desired effect of the *FLA*, which regards the matrimonial home as a unique asset and gives it special treatment.[161]

While acknowledging that there is no single all-encompassing rule as to when a court will pierce the corporate veil and that a contextual approach is required that respects the interests of innocent third parties, the Ontario Court of Appeal concluded that the circumstances in *Debora v Debora* warranted a finding that the corporation was the alter ego of the husband and was being used by him to defeat his wife's legitimate claim and he ought not to be allowed to hide behind the corporate veil.

---

160 See *Stevens v Stevens*, 2012 ONSC 706.
161 [2006] OJ No 4826 at para 18 (CA).

If property that includes a matrimonial home is normally used for a purpose other than residential, the matrimonial home is only the part of the property that may reasonably be regarded as necessary to the use and enjoyment of the residence.[162]

Where the matrimonial home represents only part of a multiple dwelling brought into the marriage, it will be necessary for the court to segregate the premarital value of the matrimonial home from the overall premarital value of the remainder of the property in order to determine the owner spouse's net family property.[163]

m) Excluded Property

Subsections 4(2) and 4(3) of the *Family Law Act*[164] provide as follows:

Excluded property

4. (2) The value of the following property that a spouse owns on the valuation date does not form part of the spouse's net family property:

1. Property, other than a matrimonial home, that was acquired by gift or inheritance from a third person after the date of the marriage.

2. Income from property referred to in paragraph 1, if the donor or testator has expressly stated that it is to be excluded from the spouse's net family property.

3. Damages or a right to damages for personal injuries, nervous shock, mental distress or loss of guidance, care and companionship, or the part of a settlement that represents those damages.

4. Proceeds or a right to proceeds of a policy of life insurance, as defined in the *Insurance Act*, [RSO 1980, c 218], that are payable on the death of the life insured.

5. Property, other than a matrimonial home, into which property referred to in paragraphs 1 to 4 can be traced.

6. Property that the spouses have agreed by a domestic contract is not to be included in the spouse's net family property.

7. Unadjusted pensionable earnings under the *Canada Pension Plan*.

(3) The onus of proving a deduction under the definition of "net family property" or an exclusion under subsection (2) is on the person claiming it.[165]

---

162   *Family Law Act*, RSO 1990, c F.3, s 18(3); *Williams v Williams*, [2006] OJ No 4986 (Sup Ct).
163   *Kraft v Kraft*, [1999] OJ No 1995 (CA).
164   SO 1986, c 4, as amended by SO 1986, c 35, now RSO 1990, c F.3.
165   *Qaraan v Qaraan*, 2014 ONCA 401.

There are no exclusions other than those listed in subsection 4(2). There is no deduction or exclusion from the net family property of a spouse for such things as children's furniture in the possession of that spouse.[166]

For the purposes of subsection 4(2) of the *Family Law Act*, the value of debt-encumbered property is the equity in the property.[167]

n) Property Acquired by Gift or Inheritance

The value of property that is acquired by one of the spouses by way of a gift[168] or inheritance from a third party after the marriage is excluded from the determination of that spouse's net family property, except insofar as any portion thereof has been invested in the matrimonial home.[169] The value of such property is to be determined as of the valuation date rather than the date of acquisition. This means that the whole value, including any non-income-based appreciation after the date of the gift or inheritance, is excluded.[170]

Third-party gifts or inheritances that are no longer owned or traceable by the recipient on the "valuation date" do not fall within the category of excluded property under paragraph 4(2)1 of the *Family Law Act*.[171] The provisions of paragraph 4(1)1 of the Act do not encompass interspousal gifts.[172]

Paragraph 4(2)5 of the *Family Law Act* makes it abundantly clear that the exclusion under paragraph 4(2)1 has no application to third-party postmarital gifts or inheritances to the extent that they have been invested in a matrimonial home.[173]

If an inheritance received during the marriage is placed by the recipient in a joint spousal bank account, a rebuttable presumption arises pursuant to section 14 of the *Family Law Act* that the spouses own the account as joint tenants and accordingly they share a joint beneficial interest in the account. If this presumption is not rebutted by evidence of a contrary intention,[174] it is open to question whether the entire inheritance will be included in the

---

166 *Davies v Davies* (1988), 13 RFL (3d) 103 (Ont HCJ).

167 *Reeson v Kowalik* (1991), 36 RFL (3d) 396 (Ont Gen Div).

168 For a useful analysis of the characteristics of a gift in the context of a corporate estate freeze, see *McNamee v McNamee*, 2011 ONCA 533.

169 *Family Law Act*, RSO 1990, c F.3, s 4(2)1; see *Theberge v Theberge* (1995), 17 RFL (4th) 196 (Ont CA); *Spikula v Spikula*, [2008] OJ No 3931 (Sup Ct).

170 See *Oliva v Oliva* (1988), 12 RFL (3d) 334 (Ont CA).

171 *Vogel v Vogel* (1989), 18 RFL (3d) 445 (Ont HCJ); *Sanders v Sanders* (1992), 42 RFL (3d) 198 (Ont Gen Div).

172 *Berta v Berta*, 2014 ONSC 3919. Compare *Family Law Act*, RSO 1990, c F.3, s 5(6)(c) and Section A(10)(d), below in this chapter.

173 *Lefevre v Lefevre* (1992), 40 RFL (3d) 372 (Ont Gen Div). For the statutory definition of "matrimonial home," see s 18 of the *Family Law Act*, RSO 1990, c F.3.

174 See *Galla v Galla*, 2014 ONSC 37.

calculation of the spousal net family properties for the purposes of the equalization process or whether the retained interest of the donor spouse remains exempt.[175]

o) Income from Third-Party Postmarital Gift or Inheritance

Subject to the express contrary intention of the donor or testator, the income generated by third-party postmarital gifts or inheritances is subject to inclusion in the determination of the net family property of the recipient spouse, provided that such income has not been spent on untraceable assets.[176] If the gift or inheritance is retained *in specie* and it is not a matrimonial home, its value will not form part of the spouse's net family property, and a similar exclusion presumably applies under paragraph 4(2)5 to any substituted property, other than a matrimonial home, that is traceable to the gift or inheritance.

Although the word "income" in paragraph 4(2)2 does not apparently include any appreciation in the capital value of the property received by gift or inheritance from the date of acquisition to the valuation date, any income from the property that is used to pay or reduce the interest or principal of a mortgage or is used in any other way to increase the equity or value of the property is included.[177]

The right of the donor or testator to expressly stipulate that income from the gift or inheritance shall be excluded from the recipient's net family property is specifically recognized by paragraph 4(2)2 of the Act and will have a significant impact on the drafting of relevant documents or wills.

p) Damages and Disability Benefits

Paragraph 4(2)3 of the Act could be construed to exclude from a spouse's net family property any damages awarded for injury to the person, including that portion of the damages that represents compensation for a future loss of income." In *de Champlain v de Champlain*,[178] Montgomery J, of the Ontario High Court of Justice, stated:

---

175 See *Belgiorgio v Belgiorgio*, [2000] OJ No 3246 (Sup Ct); *Cartier v Cartier*, [2007] OJ No 4732 (SCJ); *Townshend v Townshend* (2012), 113 OR (3d) 321 (CA). See also *Weeks v Weeks*, [2005] PEIJ No 10 (CA) (no exclusion under *Family Law Act* (PEI)); see *contra: Harrower v Harrower*, [1989] AJ No 629 (CA), wherein Stevenson JA observed that "a gift to a spouse of a joint interest removes that joint interest from the category of exempt property [but the] interest held by the donor spouse remains exempt in accordance with and to the extent recognized by the [*Matrimonial Property*] *Act* [Alberta]."

176 *Family Law Act*, RSO 1990, c F.3, ss 4(2)2 and 4(2)5.

177 *Oliva v Oliva* (1988), 12 RFL (3d) 334 (Ont CA), var'g (1986), 2 RFL (3d) 188 (Ont HCJ).

178 (1986), 2 RFL (3d) 22 at 23 (Ont HCJ).

This act is remedial in nature. It should therefore be broadly interpreted. In my opinion, "damages" in s 4(2)(3) includes both special and general damages; it includes past and future loss of income, future care cost, general damages for pain, suffering and loss of amenities of life. It encompasses all heads of damages that might be awarded by a court and those heads of damages for which settlement is negotiated in personal injury cases.[179]

In *Shaver v Shaver*,[180] however, a narrower interpretation of the meaning of section 4(2)3 was adopted by Mendes da Costa UFCJ, who concluded that "damages for lost wages and disability benefits do not satisfy the statutory test, and the value that qualified for exclusion was the general damage award of $25,000, which I understand, was compensation for pain and suffering." The latter exclusion was lost, however, pursuant to paragraph 4(2)5 of the *Family Law Act* because it formed part of the payment of an outstanding mortgage debt on the matrimonial home.[181] However, the judgment of the Ontario Court of Appeal in *Lowe v Lowe*[182] suggests a contrary conclusion. *Lowe v Lowe* proceeded by way of an application under Rule 21.01(a) of the Ontario *Rules of Civil Procedure* to determine, as a point of law, whether the disabled husband's entitlement to a future income stream derived from Workplace Safety and Insurance Board (WSIB) benefits must be capitalized and included in his net family property for the purpose of determining spousal equalization rights and obligations under the *Family Law Act*. After pointing to a lack of consistency in previous trial judgments dealing with this subject, the Ontario Court of Appeal applied the modern purposive and contextual approach to statutory interpretation in concluding that, while the definition of "property" in section 4(1) of the *Family Law Act* is extremely broad, it does not include any and every interest, even those bearing no relationship to the marriage partnership, merely because the interest is not specifically excluded. The Ontario Court of Appeal accepted Aitken J's analysis in *Hamilton v Hamilton*,[183] wherein she concluded that CPP and private insurance disability pensions should not be considered family property for equalization purposes. The Ontario Court of Appeal agreed with Aitken J's statement[184] that "the purpose of the disability payments is to replace in whole or in part the

---

179 For a valuable commentary on divergent judicial opinions in the United States, see Kathy P Holder, "In Sickness and in Health? Disability Benefits As Marital Property" (1985–86) 24 J Fam L 657.

180 (1991), 37 RFL (3d) 117 at 131 (Ont UFC); see also *Khanis [Khamis] v Noormohamed*, 2011 ONCA 127; *Cook v Cook*, 2011 ONSC 5920.

181 *Shaver v Shaver* (1991), 37 RFL (3d) 117 at 131–32.

182 [2006] OJ No 132 (CA).

183 [2005] OJ No 3050 (Sup Ct).

184 *Hamilton v Hamilton*, [2005] OJ No 3050 at para 113 (Sup Ct).

income that the person would have earned had he or she been able to work in the normal course." Thus, disability payments are "more comparable to a future income stream based on personal service" than to a retirement pension plan or a future stream of income from a trust,[185] both of which constitute "property" that falls subject to the equalization process. While conceding that disability benefits might be properly categorized as property when they are "part and parcel of an overall employee pension plan totally funded by the company,"[186] the Ontario Court of Appeal concluded that, ordinarily, disability payments replace income during the working life of the employee and, therefore, are appropriately treated as income, not property, in the context of property equalization and spousal support claims. The Ontario Court of Appeal acknowledged that it might be argued that the husband's permanent disability pension, which was payable for life, should be included as property because it was a fixed entitlement. However, it rejected that argument, being of the opinion that it is preferable, from the perspective of clarity and predictability, to treat all disability benefits in the same way, whether they are calculated to reflect lost income or as compensation for impairment of earning capacity. Consequently, the Ontario Court of Appeal set aside the decision of the application judge and amended her order to provide that the respondent husband's WSIB pensions are not included property under Part I of the Ontario *Family Law Act*.

In *Maphangoh v Maphangoh*,[187] the Ontario Court of Appeal found it necessary to distinguish between a retirement pension and disability benefits because a retirement pension constitutes "property," whereas disability payments do not constitute "property," for the purposes of an equalization of the spousal net family properties under Part I of the *Family Law Act*. In *Maphangoh v Maphangoh*, the husband had worked for the federal government prior to his resignation in 1991. Six years later, at the age of fifty-six, he became disabled. Pursuant to his federal government pension plan, he became immediately entitled to a disability pension. This pension was characterized by the Ontario Court of Appeal as, in essence, an entitlement to take early retirement without penalty. But for his disability, the husband would have had to attain the age of sixty before being entitled to an unreduced pension. For the purpose of determining the wife's entitlement to an equalization of the spousal net family properties under Part I of the *Family Law Act*, the trial judge excluded the value of the disability benefits to which the husband was entitled until age sixty but included the value of the pension thereafter. The

---

185   See *Brinkos v Brinkos* (1989), 69 OR (2d) 225 (CA).
186   See *McTaggart v McTaggart* (1993), 50 RFL (3d) 110 at para 19 (Ont Gen Div).
187   2007 ONCA 449.

Ontario Court of Appeal held that the trial judge had adopted the correct approach on the record before him, which included information describing how the *Pension Benefits Division Act*[188] provided for the division of the husband's pension without regard to the disability benefits received prior to his attainment of the age of sixty.

Damages for breach of contract clearly fall outside section 4(2)3 of the *Family Law Act*.[189]

q)   Life Insurance Policies

Pursuant to section 4(2)4 of the *Family Law Act*, proceeds or a right to proceeds of a policy of life insurance, as defined under the *Insurance Act*, that are payable on the death of the life insured, are excluded from the equalization of the spousal net family properties. The provisions of paragraph 4(2)4 should be examined in the context of section 6, and particularly, subsections 6(4), 6(6), and 6(6a) of the *Family Law Act*.[190] Subsection 4(2)4, unlike subsections 6(6) and 6(7), is of general application in that it is not confined to a life insurance policy taken out on the life of the deceased spouse and owned by the deceased spouse or taken out on the lives of a group of which he or she was a member.

Although the proceeds or a right to the proceeds of a life insurance policy are excluded from the net family property of either spouse, the court has the authority under paragraph 34(1)(i) of the *Family Law Act*, in support proceedings, to make an *inter vivos* interim or final order requiring a spouse with a life insurance policy to designate the other spouse or a child as the irrevocable beneficiary under that policy.

r)   Traceable Property

Where the value of property is excluded from the determination of a spouse's net family property under paragraphs 4(2)1 to 4 of the Act, a similar exclusion applies under paragraph 4(2)5 to any traceable substituted property. Paragraph 4(2)5 operates in relation to property "other than the matrimonial home" into which the "property referred to in paragraphs 1 to 4 can be traced." Consequently, an exclusion will be lost where the excluded property is traceable to the matrimonial home.[191] The technical rules of tracing, which

---

188   SC 1992, c 46, Sch II.

189   *Docherty v Docherty* (1994), 8 RFL (4th) 155 (Ont CA), aff'g (1992), 42 RFL (3d) 87 (Ont Gen Div).

190   See Section A(11)(b), below in this chapter.

191   *Shaver v Shaver* (1991), 37 RFL (3d) 117 (Ont UFC), discussed in Section A(9)(p), above in this chapter. For general analysis of the doctrine of tracing, see DWM Waters, *The Law of Trusts in Canada*, 2d ed (Toronto: Carswell, 1984).

evolved to protect beneficiaries of trust funds that are improperly commingled with other assets by the trustees, ought not to be applied in the context of section 4(2)5 of the Ontario *Family Law Act* where equity demands that a portion of the exclusion claimed should be allowed.[192]

s) Property Excluded by Domestic Contract

Pursuant to paragraph 4(2)6 of the *Family Law Act*, spouses may exclude any property from their "net family property" by the terms of a domestic contract, as defined in section 51 of the Act. Paragraph 4(2)6 co-exists with subsection 2(10) of the Act, which provides that "[a] domestic contract dealing with a matter that is also dealt with in this Act prevails unless this Act provides otherwise."[193]

Not all spousal agreements constitute "domestic contracts" as defined and regulated by Part IV of the *Family Law Act*.[194]

Where a domestic contract takes the form of a separation agreement, spousal reconciliation terminates the agreement unless it is clear from the circumstances that the parties intended the separation agreement, or specific terms thereof, to survive the resumption of cohabitation.[195] A specific release of all rights to a particular property can be viewed as evidence that the parties considered the disposition of that property final and binding, notwithstanding the subsequent spousal reconciliation.[196]

t) Domestic Contracts: *Canada Pension Plan*

Pursuant to section 4(2)7 of the *Family Law Act*, unadjusted pensionable earnings under the *Canada Pension Plan* are excluded property. They are not included in the calculation of the spousal net family properties because the federal legislation regulating such benefits itself provides for the splitting of credits between former spouses.[197] It is not possible in Ontario to contract out of the splitting of credits under the *Canada Pension Plan*.[198]

---

192 *Henderson v Casson*, 2014 ONSC 720.

193 *Armstrong v Armstrong*, [2006] OJ No 3823 (CA).

194 See, for example, *Miller v Miller* (1984), 41 RFL (2d) 273 (SCC), aff'g (1983), 29 RFL (2d) 395 (Ont CA).

195 *Bebenek v Bebenek* (1979), 11 RFL (2d) 137 (Ont CA); *Bailey v Bailey* (1982), 26 RFL (2d) 209 (Ont CA); *Livermore v Livermore* (1992), 43 RFL (3d) 163 (Ont Gen Div); compare *Avery v Avery* (1991), 33 RFL (3d) 288 (Ont Gen Div). See also *Evans v Evans*, 2014 NLTD(F) 26.

196 *Sydor v Sydor* (2003), 44 RFL (5th) 445 (Ont CA); *Emery v Emery*, [2008] OJ No 844 (Sup Ct).

197 See *Payne v Payne* (1988), 16 RFL (3d) 8 (Ont HCJ); see also *MacDonnell v MacDonnell* (1991), 33 RFL (3d) 52 (NSSC); *Czemeres v Czemeres* (1991), 32 RFL (3d) 243 (Sask QB).

198 See *Albrecht v Albrecht* (1989), 23 RFL (3d) 8 (Ont Dist Ct), rev'd (1991), 31 RFL (3d) 325 (Ont CA). And see *An Act to Amend the Canada Pension Plan and the Federal Court Act*, RSC 1985 (2d Supp), c 30. For statutory amendments protecting the interests of divorced

10) **Unequal Division of Net Family Properties**

a) Judicial Discretion Based on Unconscionability

Section 5(6) of the *Family Law Act* provides as follows:

> The court may award a spouse an amount that is more or less than half the difference between the net family properties if the court is of the opinion that equalizing the net family properties would be unconscionable, having regard to,
>
> (a) a spouse's failure to disclose to the other spouse debts or other liabilities existing at the date of the marriage;
>
> (b) the fact that debts or other liabilities claimed in reduction of a spouse's net family property were incurred recklessly or in bad faith;
>
> (c) the part of a spouse's net family property that consists of gifts made by the other spouse;
>
> (d) a spouse's intentional or reckless depletion of his or her net family property;
>
> (e) the fact that the amount a spouse would otherwise receive under subsection (1), (2) or (3) is disproportionately large in relation to a period of cohabitation that is less than five years;
>
> (f) the fact that one spouse has incurred a disproportionately larger amount of debts or other liabilities than the other spouse for the support of the family;
>
> (g) a written agreement between the spouses that is not a domestic contract; or
>
> (h) any other circumstances relating to the acquisition, disposition, preservation, maintenance or improvement of property.

Subsection 5(6) of the *Family Law Act* allows the court to award a spouse more or less than half the difference between the net family properties. A court is permitted to award an amount up to the whole of an offending spouse's net family property to compensate for unconscionable conduct.[199]

The court is empowered to deviate from the norm of equalization of the net family properties of the spouses only where equalization would be unconscionable and such unconscionability arises by reason of one or more of

---

spouses who had waived their *Canada Pension Plan* entitlements by way of a general release in an agreement executed before 4 June 1986, see *An Act to Amend the Canada Pension Plan (Spousal Agreement)*, SC 1991, c 14, which received Royal Assent on 1 February 1991. Compare *Leippi v Derbyshire*, 2008 SKQB 209. See also *Giesbrecht v Giesbrecht*, 2013 SKQB 16.

199 *Von Czieslik v Ayuso*, [2007] OJ No 1513 (CA); see also *Urquhart v Urquhart*, 2012 ONSC 5570.

the factors specifically identified in paragraphs (a) to (h) of subsection 5(6) of the *Family Law Act*.[200] The cumulative effect of the factors may result in unconscionability even though no single factor considered in isolation would give rise to unconscionability.[201]

An unequal contribution to child care is not included in the enumerated grounds in section 5(6) and does not justify an unequal division of the spousal net family properties.[202]

The onus of proving unconscionability within the meaning of subsection 5(6) of the *Family Law Act* falls on the party asserting it and the term "unconscionable" will be given a strict, not a liberal, interpretation.[203] The use of the word "unconscionable" should not be diluted so as to substitute the word "inequitable." The term "unconscionable" signifies a threshold that precludes resort to subsection 5(6) unless the imbalance to be addressed is "harsh and shocking to the conscience," "patently unfair," or "inordinately inequitable," and "one that simply cannot be left as it is."[204]

A spouse who has been denied specific deductions or exclusions based on the proper application of the statutory scheme cannot argue that such a result is "unconscionable" within the meaning of paragraph 5(6) of the *Family Law Act*. In the words of Mendes da Costa UFCJ, "the equalization regime cannot be challenged where the circumstances relied upon as unconscionable have arisen merely from the application of the statutory scheme.[205] Nor can it be argued that an unequal division is warranted based on alleged unconscionability that arises from property having been excluded by a valid domestic contract.[206]

b) Undisclosed Premarital Debts or Liabilities

Pursuant to the definition of "net family property" in paragraph 4(1)(b) of the *Family Law Act*, premarital debts or other liabilities that are still outstanding on the "valuation date" are deducted from the value of the divisible property of the obligated spouse.[207] Where such debts or other liabilities were not disclosed to the other spouse prior to their marriage, injustice could obviously

---

200 *Smith v Smith*, 2012 ONSC 1116; *Cosentino v Cosentino*, 2015 ONSC 271.

201 *Heal v Heal*, [1998] OJ No 4828 (Gen Div).

202 *Dhanesar v Dhanesar*, [2009] OJ No 4888 (Sup Ct).

203 *Roseneck v Gowling* (2002), 35 RFL (5th) 177 (Ont CA); *Janjua v Khan*, 2013 ONSC 44.

204 *Arndt v Arndt* (1991), 37 RFL (3d) 423 (Ont Gen Div), aff'd (1993), 48 RFL (3d) 353 (Ont CA), leave to appeal to SCC refused (1994), 1 RFL (4th) 63 (SCC); *Serra v Serra*, 2009 ONCA 105; *Ward v Ward*, 2012 ONCA 462; *Fielding v Fielding*, 2014 ONSC 2272.

205 *Shaver v Shaver* (1991), 37 RFL (3d) 117 (Ont UFC).

206 *Avery v Avery* (1991), 33 RFL (3d) 288 (Ont Gen Div).

207 See Section A(9)(l), above in this chapter.

result from an equalization of their net family properties. Paragraph 5(6)(a) of the *Family Law Act* provides a means whereby such injustice may be averted by a court order for an unequal apportionment of the difference between the net family property of each spouse.[208] Such unequal apportionment must satisfy the general criterion of unconscionability set out in subsection 5(6).

c)   Debts or Other Liabilities Incurred Recklessly or in Bad Faith

The right to deduct spousal debts and other liabilities from the value of the property owned on the valuation date is expressly recognized by the definition of "net family property" in subsection 4(1) of the *Family Law Act*. To offset the unconscionability that could result from an equalization of the net family property of each spouse, where debts or other liabilities were incurred recklessly or in bad faith, paragraph 5(6)(b) empowers the court to order an unequal apportionment between the spouses of their respective net family properties. Paragraph 5(6)(b) can only be invoked where the debts or other liabilities of the obligated spouse were incurred either recklessly or in bad faith. Financial mismanagement, even if negligent, falls outside the ambit of paragraph 5(6)(b).[209]

d)   Interspousal Gifts

Interspousal gifts form part of a spouse's net family property. Only gifts from third parties are excluded from a spouse's net family property under paragraph 4(2)1 of the *Family Law Act*.[210] Pursuant to paragraph 5(6)(c) of the Act, the court may order an unequal apportionment of the difference between the net family property of each spouse if unconscionable results would ensue from an equalization of their net family properties, having regard to the nature or value of any interspousal gifts.[211] In *Duff v Duff*,[212] Hoilett LJSC ordered an unequal division of the net family properties because the wife had received jewellery and a car as gifts from the husband during their relatively short marriage. In *Braaksma v Braaksma*,[213] an unequal division was ordered because the mentally-ill husband, in a period of lucidity one year prior to separation, had transferred the ownership of their only asset, the

---

208 See, for example, *Duff v Duff* (1988), 12 RFL (3d) 435 (Ont HCJ).

209 See *Moore v Moore* (1987), 7 RFL (3d) 390 (Ont HCJ); *Cowan v Cowan* (1987), 9 RFL (3d) 401 (Ont HCJ); see also *Crawford v Crawford* (1997), 33 RFL (4th) 381 (Ont CA); *Laing v Mahmoud*, 2011 ONSC 4047; *Smith v Smith*, 2012 ONSC 1116; *Honorat v Jean-Paul*, 2014 ONSC 6895.

210 See Section A(9)(m), above in this chapter.

211 *Ward v Ward*, 2012 ONCA 462.

212 (1988), 12 RFL (3d) 435 (Ont HCJ).

213 (1992), 41 RFL (3d) 304 (Ont UFC), aff'd (1996), 25 RFL (4th) 307 (Ont CA).

matrimonial home, into the wife's name, and any court-ordered equalization of the spousal net family properties would undermine the wife's ability to take care of two disabled children of the marriage.

e) Depletion of Net Family Property

Pursuant to paragraph 5(6)(d) of the *Family Law Act*, the court may deviate from the norm of equalization of the net family properties of each spouse, where it would produce unconscionable results by reason of a spouse's intentional or reckless depletion of his or her net family property.[214] With respect to section 5(6)(d), it has been held that reasonably undertaking a business investment that does not meet a party's financial expectations does not necessarily amount to reckless depletion of funds justifying a variation of the equalization payment.[215]

f) Duration of Cohabitation

Pursuant to paragraph 5(6)(e) of the *Family Law Act*, the court may order an unequal apportionment of the difference between the net family property of each spouse where equalization would produce unconscionable results by yielding a disproportionately large allocation to a spouse, having regard to the circumstance that cohabitation continued for less than five years. The misconduct of a spouse in bringing the marriage to an end is irrelevant in determining whether an unequal division is justified by reason of the relatively short period of matrimonial cohabitation.[216]

"Cohabitation" within the meaning of paragraph 5(6)(e) refers not only to matrimonial cohabitation but also to any period of premarital cohabitation.[217]

In the majority of cases of a short marriage under five years, the courts have followed the statutory scheme and have not found the result to be unconscionable. There are a handful of cases where courts have ordered an unequal division of assets based on a short marriage, but these are generally

---

214 *Lamantia v Solarino*, 2010 ONSC 2927; see also *Khanis [Khamis] v Noormohamed*, 2011 ONCA 127; *Gibson v Gibson*, 2011 ONSC 4406; *Dunn v Gordon*, 2015 ONSC 959.

215 *Smith v Smith*, 2012 ONSC 1116, citing *Fraser v Fraser*, 2004 CarswellOnt 3343 (Sup Ct); *Meade v Meade*, 2002 CarswellOnt 2670 (Sup Ct).

216 *Futia v Futia* (1990), 27 RFL (3d) 81 at 83–85 (Ont HCJ), West LJSC; *Reeson v Kowalik* (1991), 36 RFL (3d) 396 at 410 (Ont Gen Div); *Pope v Pope* (1999), 42 OR (3d) 514 (CA); *Mancuso v Mancuso*, [2004] OJ No 4824 (CA); *Stergiopoulos v Von Biehler*, 2014 ONSC 6391; see also *Burden v Burden*, 2014 ONSC 6319 at para 15 wherein Desotti J devised a formula based on the duration of the marriage.

217 *MacNeill v Pope* (1998), 43 RFL (4th) 209 (Ont CA); *Williams v Williams*, [2006] OJ No 4986 (Sup Ct); *Linov v Williams*, [2007] OJ No 907 (Sup Ct); *Murray v Murray*, 2010 ONSC 4278.

cases where the marriage has lasted for only one to two years.[218] Where the marriage has lasted close to five years, courts have tended either to not vary the share or to award a proportionate share based on the period of co-habitation.[219]

g) Debts and Other Liabilities Incurred for Support of Family

An unequal judicial apportionment of the difference between the value of the spousal net family properties may be ordered, pursuant to paragraph 5(6)(f) of the *Family Law Act*, if equalization would be unconscionable having regard to the fact that one spouse has incurred a disproportionately larger amount of debts or other liabilities than the other spouse for the support of the family.[220]

h) Written Agreement

Pursuant to paragraph 5(6)(g) of the *Family Law Act*, an unequal judicial apportionment of the difference between the net family property of each spouse may be ordered where equalization would be unconscionable in light of a written agreement between the spouses that does not constitute a do-mestic contract.[221] An improperly constituted "domestic contract" that fails to comply with the formal requirements of section 55 of the *Family Law Act* may satisfy the requirements of paragraph 5(6)(g) of the Act.[222] Indeed, the words "written agreement" are sufficiently broad to encompass any mutual arrangements that have been reduced to writing by the spouses, regardless of whether these arrangements constitute a legally binding contract under established principles of the law of contracts.

i) Any Other Circumstance Relating to the Acquisition, Disposition, or Management of Property

An unequal judicial apportionment of the difference between the net family property of each spouse may be ordered under paragraph 5(6)(h) of the *Family Law Act* where equalization would be unconscionable having regard to "any other circumstance relating to the acquisition, disposition, preservation,

---

218 *Murray v Murray, ibid*; compare *Karkulowski v Karkulowski*, 2015 ONSC 1057.

219 *Linov v Williams*, [2007] OJ No 907 (Sup Ct).

220 *Li v Zhao*, 2012 ONSC 2121; *Holden v Gagne*, 2013 ONSC 1423.

221 *Braaksma v Braaksma* (1992), 41 RFL (3d) 304 (Ont UFC), aff'd (1996), 25 RFL (4th) 307 (Ont CA) (transfer of matrimonial home by deed); see also *Crawford v Crawford* (1997), 33 RFL (4th) 381 (Ont CA).

222 Compare *Burton v Burton* (1981), 24 RFL (2d) 238 (Ont CA).

maintenance or improvement of property."[223] Paragraph 5(6)(h) may be read in light of subsection 5(7) of the Act, which provides as follows:

> The purpose of this section is to recognize that child care, household management and financial provision are the joint responsibilities of the spouses and that inherent in the marital relationship there is equal contribution, whether financial or otherwise, by the spouses to the assumption of these responsibilities, entitling each spouse to the equalization of the net family properties, subject only to the equitable considerations set out in subsection (6).

Paragraph 5(6)(h) of the *Family Law Act* cannot be invoked to justify an unequal apportionment of the difference between the net family property of each spouse merely by reason of a traditional division of functions between spouses whereby one spouse discharges the responsibilities of a homemaker and the other spouse those of a breadwinner. If both spouses have pulled their weight in the marriage according to their respective abilities, talents, and mutual or agreed perceptions of their roles within the marriage, equalization is a fair result.[224] An unequal apportionment of the difference between the net family property of each spouse may be justified, however, where a spouse, without just cause, fails to discharge his or her marital responsibilities as defined in subsection 5(7) of the *Family Law Act*.[225]

Post-separation events may be taken into account in determining whether an equal division of the spousal net family properties is unconscionable within the meaning of section 5(6) of the Ontario *Family Law Act*.[226]

---

223 See *Jordan v Jordan* (1988), 13 RFL (3d) 402 (Ont CA); *De Mornay v De Mornay* (1991), 34 RFL (3d) 101 (Ont Gen Div); *Braaksma v Braaksma* (1992), 41 RFL (3d) 304 (Ont UFC); *Ward v Ward*, 2012 ONCA 462.

224 *Reeson v Kowalik* (1991), 36 RFL (3d) 396 at 409 (Ont Gen Div).

225 *Klein v Klein* (1987), 59 OR (2d) 781 (Ont Dist Ct); *Henderson v Henderson* (1987), 10 RFL (3d) 150 (Ont Dist Ct); compare *Robinson v Robinson* (1982), 28 RFL (2d) 342 at 346–47 (Sask QB); *Bray v Bray* (1979), 16 RFL (2d) 78 (Ont Co Ct); *Grime v Grime* (1980), 16 RFL (2d) 365 (Ont HCJ); *Fenn v Fenn* (1987), 10 RFL (3d) 408 (Ont HCJ); see also *McCutcheon v McCutcheon* (1982) 29 RFL (2d) 11 (NBQB); *Sullivan v Sullivan* (1986), 5 RFL (3d) 28 (Ont UFC); *Moniz v Moniz*, [1986] OJ No 1183 (HCJ); *Wasylyshyn v Wasylyshyn* (1987), 8 RFL (3d) 337 (Ont Dist Ct), discussed above in this chapter.

226 *Merklinger v Merklinger* (1996), 26 RFL (4th) 7 (Ont CA); *Scherer v Scherer*, [2002] OJ No 1661 (CA); *Serra v Serra*, 2009 ONCA 105; *Kean v Clausi*, 2010 ONSC 2583; *Laing v Mahmoud*, 2011 ONSC 4047; *Borutski v Borutski*, 2011 ONSC 7099. See also dissenting judgment of McLachlin J, as she then was, in *Rawluk v Rawluk* (1990), 23 RFL (3d) 337 (SCC). Compare *Heard v Heard*, 2014 ONCA 196.

11) Entitlement on Death

a) Death as a Triggering Event

The death of a spouse constitutes a triggering event for an equalization of the net family property of each spouse, but only where the net family property of the deceased spouse exceeds that of the surviving spouse.[227] The right to an equalization of the net family property of each spouse on death is expressly confined to the surviving spouse and cannot be sought by the personal representative of a deceased spouse.

Public policy precludes a surviving spouse from pursuing an equalization claim where the survivor murdered the deceased spouse.[228]

b) Election by Surviving Spouse

The right of a surviving spouse to pursue an equalization claim under section 5 of the *Family Law Act* is subject to the exercise of an election under section 6 of the Act. A surviving spouse must make an election to assert his or her testate or intestate succession rights *or* to pursue an equalization claim under section 5 of the Act. The right of election is a personal right exercisable by the surviving spouse. Where no election has been exercised prior to the death of the surviving spouse, his or her personal representative is not entitled to file an election.[229]

Subsection 6(10) requires the election to be filed in the office of the Estate Registrar for Ontario within six months of the death.[230] This is subject to any extension of time permitted by the court under subsection 2(8) of the *Family Law Act*.[231] Where no election has been filed within the prescribed time limit, the surviving spouse is deemed to have elected to take under the will or intestacy, unless a court orders otherwise.[232]

Subsection 6(4) of the Act provides that a surviving spouse who elects to take under the will or to receive the entitlement under Part II of the *Succession Law Reform Act*,[233] or both in the case of a partial intestacy, shall also receive the other property to which he or she is entitled because of the first spouse's death. Such "other property" would include benefits under any life insurance policy taken out on the life of the deceased spouse or under a

---

227   *Family Law Act*, RSO 1990, c F.3, s 5(2).

228   *Maljkovich v Maljkovich Estate* (1995), 20 RFL (4th) 222 (Ont Gen Div), aff'd (1997), 33 RFL (4th) 24 (Ont CA).

229   *Rondberg Estate v Rondberg Estate* (1989), 22 RFL (3d) 27 (Ont CA); compare *Anderson v Anderson Estate* (1990), 74 OR (2d) 58 at 63–64 (HCJ).

230   See *Varga Estate v Varga* (1987), 26 ETR 172 (Ont HCJ).

231   *Laframboise v Laframboise*, 2012 ONSC 4508; *Mischuk v Mischuk*, 2013 ONSC 4128.

232   Section 6(11); see *Webster v Webster Estate*, [2006] OJ No 2749 (Sup Ct).

233   RSO 1990, c S.26.

pension plan that provides death benefits to the surviving spouse, or property received by the right of survivorship that vests in a joint tenant on the death of his or her co-owning spouse.

Subsection 6(4) of the Act may be contrasted with subsections 6(6) and 6(7),[234] which apply to a spouse who elects to pursue an equalization claim. Pursuant to subsection 6(6), such a spouse may assert rights (a) as a beneficiary under a life insurance policy taken out on the life of the deceased spouse and owned by the deceased spouse or taken out on the lives of a group of which he or she was a member, or (b) as a beneficiary under a pension or similar plan that provides for lump sum death benefits to the surviving spouse, or (c) as the recipient of property or a portion of property to which the surviving spouse becomes entitled by right of survivorship or otherwise on the death of the deceased spouse. However, the following rules apply under subsection 6(7) in the circumstances set out in subsection 6(6):

1. The amount of every payment and the value of every property or portion of property described in that subsection, less any contingent tax liability in respect of the payment, property or portion of property, shall be credited against the surviving spouse's entitlement under section 5.

2. If the total amount of the credit under paragraph 1 exceeds the entitlement under section 5, the deceased spouse's personal representative may recover the excess amount from the surviving spouse.

3. Paragraphs 1 and 2 do not apply in respect of a payment, property or portion of property if,
   i. the deceased spouse provided in a written designation, will or other written instrument, as the case may be, that the surviving spouse shall receive the payment, property or portion of property in addition to the entitlement under section 5, or
   ii. in the case of property or a portion of property referred to in clause (6)(c), if the surviving spouse's entitlement to the property or portion of property was established by or on behalf of a third person, either the deceased spouse or the third person provided in a will or other written instrument that the surviving spouse shall receive the property or portion of property in addition to the entitlement under section 5.

Pursuant to section 6(6) of the *Family Law Act*, the surviving spouse must identify those assets that flow to her as a designated beneficiary, including

---

234 RSO 1990, c F.3, as amended by SO 2009, c 11, s 23. See also *Ranking v Ranking Estate*, 2010 ONCA 315, aff'g [2009] OJ No 4628 (Sup Ct). Compare *Weatherdon-Oliver v Oliver Estate*, 2010 ONSC 5031.

pension benefits, retirement savings plans, and designated life insurance proceeds, and those amounts will be credited against any equalization entitlement.[235]

Pursuant to subsection 6(5) of the *Family Law Act*, a testator may expressly provide in his or her will that testamentary gifts shall be in addition to the surviving spouse's equalization entitlement under section 5. In the absence of any such express provision, testamentary gifts to a surviving spouse who elects to receive his or her entitlement under section 5 are revoked and the will is to be interpreted as though the surviving spouse had predeceased the testator.[236]

A spouse who elects to receive the entitlement under section 5 is deemed to have disclaimed any intestate succession rights that would otherwise arise under Part II of the *Succession Law Reform Act*.[237] There are conflicting authorities as to whether an election under section 6(1) of the *Family Law Act* is irrevocable or the court has a residual discretion to set aside the election to avoid an injustice.[238] Section 6 of the *Family Law Act* does not address "multiple" wills and only applies where there is a single will that is uncontested. Accordingly, a husband who would have received substantial benefits under his wife's former will, but who is excluded under her later will, may file an election under subsection 6(10) of the *Family Law Act* to preserve his rights under section 5, in the event that the later will is upheld. Under these circumstances, the election applies only with respect to the second will. Should the husband's challenge of that will prove successful, his election does not prevent or restrict his entitlement under the first will. Form 1 in Ontario Regulation 368 under the *Family Law Act*, which is technically deficient in that it is mandatory and does not permit a conditional election, should not be permitted to defeat the remedial nature of the Act, which was designed to enlarge rather than restrict the rights of spouses. In *Re Van der Wyngaard Estate*, the judge further observed that "an alternative suggestion, for future reference, might be to apply for an extension of time within which to file an election pursuant to section 6(10) of the [*Family Law*] *Act* until the issue as to the validity of the second will has been disposed of."[239]

Pursuant to subsections 6(12) and 6(13) of the Act, a spouse's equalization entitlement under section 5 has priority over third-party testamentary

---

235   *Laframboise v Laframboise*, 2012 ONSC 4508.

236   RSO 1990, c F.3, as amended by SO 2009, c 11, s 6(8); *Cimetta v Topler* (1989), 20 RFL (3d) 102 (Ont HCJ).

237   RSO 1990, c S.26; *Family Law Act, ibid*, s 6(9).

238   *Re Bolfan Estate* (1992), 38 RFL (3d) 250 (Ont Gen Div); compare *Iasenza v Iasenza Estate*, [2007] OJ No 2475 (Sup Ct).

239   *Re Van der Wyngaard Estate* (1987), 7 RFL (3d) 81 (Ont Surr Ct), McDermid Dist Ct J.

gifts, excepting those made pursuant to a contract entered into by the deceased in good faith and for valuable consideration and insofar as the value of the gift does not exceed the consideration. The spousal entitlement under section 5 also takes priority over a third person's right of intestate succession and any order made against the deceased spouse's estate for the support of family dependants under Part V of the *Succession Law Reform Act*, except an order in favour of a "child" of the deceased spouse as defined under paragraph 57(a) of the *Succession Law Reform Act*.

The personal representative of the deceased spouse is prohibited from distributing all or any of the deceased spouse's estate within six months of the death or after receiving notice of an application by the surviving spouse under section 5 of the Act, unless the surviving spouse gives written consent to the distribution or the court authorizes the distribution.[240] Contravention of these prohibitions renders the personal representative of the deceased spouse accountable for any improper distribution to the extent that it undermines or injuriously affects the surviving spouse's entitlement under section 5.[241]

Pursuant to subsection 16(20) of the Act, a surviving spouse may bring a motion for an order to suspend the administration of the deceased spouse's estate for such time and to such extent as the court may determine.

The test to justify an advance equalization payment where one spouse is deceased is the same test as that which applies where both spouses are alive.[242] That test is set out by Karakatsanis J (as she then was) in *Laamanen v Laamanen*, and establishes that (1) there is a reasonable requirement for the funds; (2) there is little doubt that the person making the request will receive an equalization payment of at least that amount; and (3) it is just in the circumstances.[243]

12) Property and Financial Statements[244]

Section 8 of the *Family Law Act* provides as follows:

> 8. In an application under section 7, each party shall serve on the other and file with the court, in the manner and form prescribed by the rules of the court, a statement verified by oath or statutory declaration disclosing particulars of,
> (a) the party's property and debts and other liabilities,

---

240 *Family Law Act*, s 6(14).
241 *Ibid*, s 6(19).
242 *Skrobacky (Attorneys for) v Frymer*, 2012 ONSC 4277.
243 (2006), 25 RFL (6th) 441 (Ont Sup Ct); *King v King*, 2012 ONSC 5614.
244 See Gerald P Sadvari & James A Debresser, "Reliability of Financial Statements in Matrimonial Litigation" (2007) 26 Fam LQ 279.

>   (i)   as of the date of the marriage,
>
>   (ii) as of the valuation date, and
>
>   (iii) as of the date of the statement;
>
> (b) the deductions that the party claims under the definition of "net family property";
>
> (c) the exclusions that the party claims under subsection 4(2); and
>
> (d) all property that the party disposed of during the two years immediately preceding the making of the statement, or during the marriage, whichever period is shorter.[245]

For the purpose of filing a financial statement, the ownership of property will be determined by reference to the title in which the property is registered.[246] Where property is jointly owned by the spouses, half of the value should be reported in the respective financial statements of each spouse.[247]

The objective of property and financial statements is to provide complete, up-to-date, and meaningful information to the parties and the court. The valuation of property by reference to its book value or depreciated cost value does not satisfy the requirements of section 8 of the *Family Law Act*. What is required is the estimated market value or actual worth of the property at the relevant time.[248] The onus is on the party asserting the value of an asset that he or she controls to provide credible evidence as to its value.[249] Where a party has filed a statement that is less than frank and complete, the court may draw unfavourable inferences against the party.[250] The court may also order costs against a party whose failure to comply with the letter and spirit of section 8 has resulted in unnecessary prolonging of the proceedings.[251]

---

245 See also Ontario *Family Law Rules*, Rule 13: Financial Statements. As to the sealing of files and publication bans, see *WS v RS*, 2010 ONSC 6981; *MEH v Williams*, 2012 ONCA 35.

246 *Schaefer v Schaefer* (1986), 38 ACWS (2d) 142 (Ont CA).

247 *Ibid.* See also *Skrlj v Skrlj* (1986), 2 RFL (3d) 305 at 310 (Ont HCJ).

248 *Silverstein v Silverstein* (1978), 1 RFL (2d) 239 at 241–42 (Ont HCJ), Galligan J; see Section A(9)(f), above in this chapter.

249 *Misner v Misner*, 2010 ONSC 2284, citing *Conway v Conway*, [2005] OJ No 1698 at para 14 (Ont Sup Ct) and *Homsi v Zaya* (2009), 65 RFL (6th) 17 (Ont CA); *Murray v Murray*, 2010 ONSC 4278.

250 *Silverstein v Silverstein* (1978), 1 RFL (2d) 239 (Ont HCJ); see also *Murray v Murray*, 2010 ONSC 4278; *Cunha v da Cunha* (1994), 99 BCLR (2d) 93 (SC); *Laxton v Coglon*, 2008 BCSC 42 and 2008 BCSC 955.

251 *Silverstein v Silverstein* (1978), 1 RFL (2d) 239 (Ont HCJ); *Payne v Payne* (1983), 31 RFL (2d) 211 at 217 (Ont UFC); *Skrlj v Skrlj* (1986), 2 RFL (3d) 305 (Ont HCJ).

13) Powers of Court

a)   General Observations

Section 9 of the *Family Law Act* provides as follows:

Powers of Court

9. (1) In an application under section 7, the court may order,

(a)   that one spouse pay to the other spouse the amount to which the court finds that spouse to be entitled under this Part;

(b)   that security, including a charge on property, be given for the performance of an obligation imposed by the order;

(c)   that, if necessary to avoid hardship, an amount referred to in paragraph (a) be paid in instalments during a period not exceeding ten years or that payment of all or part of the amount be delayed for a period not exceeding ten years; and

(d)   that, if appropriate to satisfy an obligation imposed by the order,

(i)   property be transferred to or in trust for or vested in a spouse, whether absolutely, for life or for a term of years, or

(ii)   any property be partitioned or sold.

Financial information, inspections

(2) The court may, at the time of making an order for instalment or delayed payments or on motion at a later time, order that the spouse who has the obligation to make payments shall,

(a)   furnish the other spouse with specified financial information, which may include periodic financial statements; and

(b)   permit inspections of specified property of the spouse by or on behalf of the other spouse, as the court directs.

Variation

(3) If the court is satisfied that there has been a material change in the circumstances of the spouse who has the obligation to make instalment or delayed payments, the court may, on motion, vary the order, but shall not vary the amount to which the court found the spouse to be entitled under this Part.

Ten year period

(4) Subsections (3) and 2(8) (extension of times) do not permit the postponement of payment beyond the ten year period mentioned in paragraph (1)(c).

Section 5 of the *Family Law Act*, which constitutes the basis of the statutory property-sharing regime on marriage breakdown or death, is premised on a sharing of the value of property, and not on a division of property *in specie*.[252] It endorses an accounting procedure that will ordinarily result in a money judgment that leaves the title to property undisturbed. Section 9 of the *Family Law Act*, nevertheless, provides a variety of means whereby a successful equalization claim may be satisfied. The court may select a combination of the various remedies provided by section 9 so that a fair and reasonable solution may be attained.[253]

Section 9 of the Act is expressly confined to equalization claims. It does not extend to applications under section 10 of the Act, which involve questions of ownership. Although section 10 confers certain powers on the court similar to those defined in section 9, they are by no means identical; see, however, section 11, which applies to orders made under both sections 9 and 10.[254]

b) Order for Payment

Paragraph 9(1)(a) of the *Family Law Act* empowers the court to order one spouse to pay to the other spouse a lump sum in satisfaction of the equalization entitlement under section 5 of the Act.[255]

The Ontario Superior Court of Justice has inherent jurisdiction to grant an interim order for an advance payment to be made against the recipient's entitlement to equalization of the spousal net family properties under Part I of the Ontario *Family Law Act*.[256]

c) Order for Security

Paragraph 9(1)(b) of the *Family Law Act* empowers the court to order that security be given for the performance of any obligation imposed by any order of the court made pursuant to subsection 9(1). The security may include a charge on property or on the proceeds of sale of designated property,[257] and such a charge may presumably be made on "excluded property" within the meaning of subsection 4(2) of the *Family Law Act*. An order for security lies in the discretion of the court and is not available as of right. The court may

---

252 *Henry v Cymbalisty* (1986), 55 OR (2d) 51 at 55 (UFC); *Skrlj v Skrlj* (1986), 2 RFL (3d) 305 at 309 (Ont HCJ). As to the effect of bankruptcy, see *Schreyer v Schreyer*, 2011 SCC 35; *Baker v Csori*, 2012 ONSC 231 at paras 14–19; *O'Halloran v O'Halloran*, 2013 ONSC 6282; *Ross v Ross*, 2014 ONSC 1828.

253 *Kukolj v Kukolj* (1986), 3 RFL (3d) 359 (Ont UFC); see also *Marsham v Marsham* (1987), 7 RFL (3d) 1 (Ont HCJ).

254 See Section A(13)(h), below in this chapter.

255 See *Leslie v Leslie* (1987), 9 RFL (3d) 82 (Ont HCJ); *Forster v Forster* (1987), 11 RFL (3d) 121 (Ont HCJ).

256 *Firestone v Pfaff*, 2012 ONSC 4909; see also *Stork v Stork*, 2015 ONSC 312.

257 *Jackson v Jackson* (1987), 5 RFL (3d) 8 (Ont HCJ); *Duff v Duff* (1988), 12 RFL (3d) 435 (Ont HCJ); *Van Dusen v Van Dusen*, 2010 ONSC 220.

impose such an order where the conduct of one spouse indicates that there may be difficulty collecting a lump sum equalization payment.[258] Where payment of the amount due is deferred or involves instalments pursuant to an order under paragraph 9(1)(c) of the Act, an order for security is appropriate,[259] particularly where assets are located in a foreign jurisdiction.[260] An order for security may be varied or discharged pursuant to section 13 of the Act.[261]

d) Deferred or Instalment Payments

Where there is evidence that an order for immediate payment would create hardship, the court has a discretionary jurisdiction under paragraph 9(1)(c) of the Act to order that the due amount be paid in instalments over a maximum period of ten years or that all or any part of the due amount be deferred for a period not exceeding ten years.[262] The terms of any such order may be subsequently varied under section 9(3) of the Act, but the court is expressly precluded from varying the amount or from extending the ten-year period for payment by the express provisions of subsections 9(3) and 9(4) of the Act.

e) Transfers of Property; Partition and Sale

Paragraph 9(1)(d) of the *Family Law Act* empowers the court to order that a spousal equalization entitlement shall be satisfied by property being transferred to, or in trust for, or vested in a spouse, whether absolutely, for life, or for a term of years.[263] The court may alternatively order the partition and sale of *any* property.[264] Courts have routinely ordered that the matrimonial home be transferred to and vested absolutely in the name of the payee in

---

258 *Verboom v Verboom* (1991), 34 RFL (3d) 312 (Ont Gen Div).

259 *Best v Best* (1992), 41 RFL (3d) 383 (Ont CA); *Kukolj v Kukolj* (1986), 3 RFL (3d) 359 (Ont UFC); and *Benke v Benke*, [1986] OJ No 2073 (Dist Ct) discussed at Section A(13)(d), below in this chapter.

260 *Da Costa v Da Costa* (1992), 40 RFL (3d) 216 (Ont CA).

261 See Section A(15), below in this chapter.

262 *Oliva v Oliva* (1986), 2 RFL (3d) 188 (Ont HCJ), var'd (1988), 12 RFL (3d) 334 (Ont CA); *Messier v Messier* (1986), 5 RFL (3d) 251 (Ont Dist Ct); *Marsham v Marsham* (1987), 7 RFL (3d) 1 (Ont HCJ); *Leslie v Leslie* (1987), 9 RFL (3d) 82 (Ont HCJ); *Randolf v Randolf* (1991), 34 RFL (3d) 444 (Ont Gen Div); *Roach v Roach* (1997), 33 RFL (4th) 157 (Ont CA); *Arndt v Arndt* (1991), 37 RFL (3d) 423 (Ont Gen Div), aff'd (1993), 48 RFL (3d) 353 (Ont CA), leave to appeal to SCC refused (1994), 1 RFL (4th) 63 (SCC).

263 See *Oliva v Oliva* (1986), 2 RFL (3d) 188 (Ont HCJ); *Schaarschmidt v Schaarschmidt*, [2008] OJ No 4186 (Sup Ct); *Morrison v Barclay-Morrison*, [2008] OJ No 4663 (Sup Ct); *Van Dusen v Van Dusen*, 2010 ONSC 220; *Verch v Verch*, 2012 ONSC 2621.

264 See *Leslie v Leslie* (1987), 9 RFL (3d) 82 (Ont HCJ); see also *McLean v McLean*, 2014 ONSC 2837.

order to satisfy in whole or in part the equalization payment to be made by the payor.[265]

A vesting order under section 9(1)(d)(i) of the *Family Law Act* should ordinarily be made only where there is a concern whether the court's order respecting net family property equalization will be carried out by the payor.[266]

Paragraph 9(1)(d) does not empower the court to order a division of specific property in lieu of undertaking the calculations necessary to determine a spouse's equalization entitlement, although such a division could be achieved by a valid domestic contract.[267] In *Humphreys v Humphreys*,[268] Galligan J categorically stated that the court has no power "to rearrange assets between the parties and compensate for any difference in value by way of an equalizing payment."[269]

f)   Financial Information and Inspections

The power of the court to order financial disclosure or inspections of property pursuant to subsection 9(2) of the Act is confined to circumstances where the court makes an order for instalments or deferred payments under paragraph 9(1)(c) or on a motion to vary such an order brought pursuant to subsection 9(3) of the Act.

g)   Variation of Order for Instalment or Deferred Payments

Subsection 9(3) of the *Family Law Act* empowers the court to vary an order made pursuant to paragraph 9(1)(c) for instalment or deferred payments in the event of a material change in the circumstances of the spouse obligated by such order. No corresponding statutory jurisdiction is vested in the court to accommodate material changes in the circumstances of the entitled spouse; for example, the death of this spouse. The powers of variation are expressly restricted under subsection 9(3) in that the court cannot vary the amount to which a spouse is entitled. Furthermore, subsection 9(4) of the Act precludes the court from postponing any payment beyond the ten-year period specified in paragraph 9(1)(c) of the Act.

---

265   *Jacobs v Jacobs*, 2011 ONSC 2699 at para 67.

266   *Caracciolo v Ruberto*, [2010] OJ No 247 (Sup Ct), Perkins J, citing *Lynch v Segal*, [2006] OJ No 5014 (CA).

267   See *Wilson v Wilson* (1988), 14 RFL (3d) 98 (Ont HCJ).

268   (1987), 7 RFL (3d) 113 (Ont HCJ).

269   See also *Buttar v Buttar*, 2013 ONCA 517; *Danecker v Danecker*, 2014 ONCA 239; *Rebiere v Rebiere*, 2015 ONSC 1324.

h) Operating Business or Farm

In both interspousal ownership and equalization disputes, court orders must avoid the sale of an operating business or farm or the serious impairment of its operation, unless there is no reasonable alternative method of satisfying the claim.[270] An order requiring the disposition or impairment of an operating business or farm may be made where there are no practicable means of otherwise satisfying the award.[271]

i) Interest

As a general principle, prejudgment interest is payable on an equalization payment. Exceptions have been admitted where the payor spouse cannot realize on the asset giving rise to the equalization payment until after the trial, does not have the use of it prior to trial, the asset generates no income, and the payor spouse has not delayed the case being brought to trial. Many of the exceptional cases involve the matrimonial home or a pension.[272] While prejudgment interest may be denied on an equalization payment because it is based largely on the payor's pension, postjudgment interest may be ordered.[273] Postjudgment interest is payable on an equalization payment, unless the court makes an order disallowing postjudgment interest.[274] Where equalization payments are made over a period of years, it should be the rule, rather than the exception, that the payments attract interest. To hold otherwise would effectively alter the amount of the equalization entitlement due to the time value of money.[275]

Trial judges have a wide discretion under section 130 of the Ontario *Courts of Justice Act* to allow prejudgment or postjudgment interest at a higher or lower rate than that prescribed.[276] In *Debora v Debora*,[277] the wife's appeal respecting the amount of prejudgment interest was dismissed. The trial judge had taken account of fluctuations in the applicable rates of interest during the lengthy litigation, and the rate selected was rationally connected to the interest rates that prevailed over the relevant period.

---

270 *Family Law Act*, RSO 1990, c F.3, s 11 see also *McLean v McLean*, 2014 ONSC 2837.

271 *Postma v Postma* (1987), 6 RFL (3d) 50 (Ont UFC); *Leslie v Leslie* (1987), 9 RFL (3d) 82 (Ont HCJ); see also *Godinek v Godinek* (1992), 40 RFL (3d) 78 (Ont Gen Div).

272 *McQuay v McQuay* (1992), 39 RFL (3d) 184 (Ont Div Ct); *Bigelow v Bigelow* (1995), 15 RFL (4th) 12 (Ont Div Ct); *Burgess v Burgess* (1995), 16 RFL (4th) 388 (Ont CA); *Purcell v Purcell* (1996), 26 RFL (4th) 267 (Ont CA); *Fielding v Fielding*, 2014 ONSC 2272.

273 *Kennedy v Kennedy* (1995), 19 RFL (4th) 454 (Ont CA).

274 *Bigelow v Bigelow* (1995), 15 RFL (4th) 12 (Ont Div Ct).

275 *LeVan v LeVan*, 2008 ONCA 388.

276 *MP v WP*, 2014 ONSC 6393.

277 [2006] OJ No 4826 (CA). See also *Henderson v Casson*, 2014 ONSC 720; *Qaraan v Qaraan*, 2014 ONSC 2191.

14) Restraining Orders and Preservation Orders

Section 12 of the *Family Law Act* empowers the court to make an interim or final order to restrain the depletion of a spouse's property, and for the possession, delivering up, safekeeping, and preservation of the property. The purpose of such an order is to ensure that there are sufficient assets available to satisfy any subsequent order for equalization of the spousal net family properties.[278] A court should decline to tie up all assets where this is unnecessary in light of the *prima facie* equalization entitlement of the party seeking a restraining order under section 12 of the *Family Law Act*.[279]

Interim preservation orders under section 12 of the Ontario *Family Law Act* are designed to prevent the dissipation of assets pending determination of an application for equalization of the spousal net family properties under Part I of the Act. In exercising its discretionary jurisdiction, the court should consider (1) the relative strength of the equalization claim; (2) the balance of convenience; and (3) the prospect of irreparable harm.[280]

An order granted pursuant to section 12 of the *Family Law Act* does not confer any property right on the successful applicant nor priority over third-party creditors of the spouse against whom the order is obtained.[281]

Section 12 of the *Family Law Act* is preventive rather than curative in nature. It cannot be invoked to set aside transactions that have already been completed. Relief, if any, in these circumstances, must be found elsewhere — as, for example, under the provisions of the *Fraudulent Conveyances Act*,[282] which has been successfully invoked to prevent a husband from frustrating his wife's right to seek an equalization of their net family properties by disposing of property to his adult children by *inter vivos* gifts.[283]

15) Variation and Realization of Security

An order for security or for the charging of property granted pursuant to paragraphs 9(1)(c) or 10(1)(d) of the *Family Law Act* may be varied or discharged under section 13 of the Act. In the alternative, the court may direct a sale of the property for the purpose of realizing the security, provided that

---

278 *Benvenuto v Whitman*, 2012 ONSC 2696; *Verch v Verch*, 2012 ONSC 2621; *Bos v Bos*, 2012 ONSC 3425.

279 *Ibid.*

280 *Bronfman v Bronfman*, [2000] OJ No 4591 (Sup Ct); *Chi v Wang*, 2010 ONSC 1366; *Kkabbazy v Esfahani*, 2012 ONSC 4591; see also *Gale v Gale*, 2008 MBCA 134.

281 *Nevarc Holdings Ltd v Orchid Communications Inc* (1990), 28 RFL (3d) 330 (Ont Gen Div); *Gaudet (Litigation Guardian of) v Young Estate* (1995), 11 RFL (4th) 284 (Ont Gen Div).

282 RSO 1990, c F.29.

283 *Stone v Stone*, [2001] OJ No 3282 (CA).

notice of the motion to vary is given to all persons with an interest in the property.

16) Retrospective Operation

Part I of the *Family Law Act* applies to property owned by spouses whether they were married before or after the date when the Act came into force, namely, 1 March 1986.[284] Part I of the *Family Law Act* also applies regardless of whether the property was acquired before or after the commencement of the Act.

17) Occupation Rent and Accountancy Claims

A spouse who remains in exclusive possession of the jointly owned matrimonial home after spousal separation may seek an accounting and contribution from the non-occupying spouse with respect to mortgage instalments, repairs, maintenance, or property taxes that have been paid by the occupying spouse. Where such an accounting is sought, the occupying spouse is subject to a counterclaim for occupation rent. In assessing an application for occupation rent, the court must exercise a certain amount of discretion in balancing the relevant factors in order to determine whether occupation rent is appropriate in the overall circumstances of the case. The following factors may be relevant in determining whether an order for occupation rent is appropriate:

- the conduct of the non-occupying spouse, including the failure to pay support;
- the conduct of the occupying spouse, including the failure to pay support;
- delay in making the claim;
- the extent to which the non-occupying spouse has been prevented from having access to his or her equity in the home;
- whether the non-occupying spouse moved for the sale of the home and, if not, why not;
- whether the occupying spouse paid the mortgage and other carrying charges of the home;
- whether the children resided with the occupying spouse and, if so, whether the non-occupying spouse paid, or was able to pay, child support;
- whether the occupying spouse has increased the selling value of the property; and
- ouster is not required, as once was thought in some early decisions.[285]

---

284 See *Vivier v Vivier* (1987), 5 RFL (3d) 450 (Ont Dist Ct).

285 *Higgins v Higgins*, [2001] OJ No 3011 (Sup Ct); *Meza v Lavie*, 2014 ONSC 2247; *LaFramboise v Laframboise*, 2015 ONSC 1752; *Ombac v George*, 2015 ONSC 1938. See also *Ross v Ross*, 2013 BCSC 1716; *Wiewiora v Wiewiora*, 2014 MBQB 218; *Casey v Casey*, 2013 SKCA 58.

The following factors have been identified by the Ontario Court of Appeal as consistently taken into account where occupation rent is sought:

- the timing of the claim for occupation rent;
- the duration of the occupancy;
- the inability of the non-occupying spouse to realize on his or her equity in the property;
- any reasonable credits to be set off against occupation rent; and
- any other competing claims in the litigation.[286]

The expenses of maintaining the matrimonial home are frequently presumed to offset any potential occupation rent.[287] Occupation rent is generally not awarded where the court has ordered exclusive possession.[288]

18) Disposition and Possession of the Matrimonial Home

a)   General Observations

Part II of the *Family Law Act* of Ontario includes special provisions concerning the disposition and possession of the matrimonial home.[289]

b)   Definition and Designation of "Matrimonial Home"

Section 18(1) of the *Family Law Act* defines the "matrimonial home" as every property in which either spouse has an interest that the spouses ordinarily occupy as their family residence or did so at the time of their separation.[290] Ontario caselaw holds that "ordinary occupation" within the meaning of section 18(1) of the *Family Law Act* usually signifies that a significant amount of time has been spent in and around the residence, and its occupation was not merely occasional or casual. Where usage is minimal or sporadic, the courts have focused on the intent of the parties at the time of separation; usage and intention post-separation is irrelevant.[291] Where the matrimonial home is on land that is normally used for a non-residential purpose, the matrimonial

---

286   *Griffiths v Zambosco* (2001), 54 OR (3d) 397 (CA); *Rebiere v Rebiere*, 2015 ONSC 1324.

287   *Morrison v Barclay-Morrison*, [2008] OJ No 4663 at para 43 (Sup Ct), citing *Malesh v Malesh*, [2008] OJ No 2207 (Sup Ct).

288   *JB v DM*, 2014 ONSC 7410 at para 151, Horkins J.

289   As to the special status accorded to the matrimonial home in the context of equalization claims under Part I of the *Family Law Act*, see Sections A(9)(l), A(9)(m), and A(9)(r), above in this chapter.

290   *Baudanza v Nicoletti*, 2011 ONSC 352; *Spencer v Riesberry*, 2012 ONCA 418 (property owned by trust); *Alcaniz v Willoughby*, 2011 ONSC 7045; *Oliver Estate v Oliver*, 2012 ONSC 718.

291   *Potter v Boston*, 2014 ONSC 2361 (Div Ct); *Farnsworth v Chang*, 2014 ONSC 1871.

home only extends to that part of the property that is reasonably necessary for the use and enjoyment of the residence.[292]

Section 18 of the *Family Law Act* clearly envisages that spouses may have more than one matrimonial home, as, for example, where they enjoy an urban residence as well as a cottage property.[293] However, section 20 of the *Family Law Act* permits the spouses to jointly designate and register one specific property as the matrimonial home, in which event any other non-designated property that would otherwise constitute a matrimonial home within the meaning of section 18 of the *Family Law Act* ceases to be a matrimonial home. A designation may be subsequently cancelled by the spouses, in which event other residences regain their status as matrimonial homes under section 18 of the Act.

c) Disposition of Matrimonial Home

Section 21 of the *Family Law Act* imposes a general prohibition against a spouse unilaterally disposing of or encumbering an interest in the matrimonial home. The need for spousal consent may be waived by the terms of a separation agreement. A court may also dispense with spousal consent to the disposition or encumbrance of the matrimonial home under section 23 of the *Family Law Act*. If a spouse unlawfully disposes of or encumbers an interest in the matrimonial home, the transaction may be set aside under section 23 of the *Family Law Act*, but the court's jurisdiction to set aside the transaction cannot be invoked against a *bona fide* purchaser for value without notice that the property was a matrimonial home.[294]

d) Possessory Rights in Matrimonial Home

Pursuant to subsection 19(1) of the *Family Law Act*, both spouses have an equal right to possession of the matrimonial home, regardless of whether title is vested in one or both spouses. The statutory right conferred by subsection 19(1) applies without regard to the conduct of the spouses or the state of their marital relationship. Pursuant to subsection 19(2) of the *Family Law Act*, this equal right of possession is a personal right as between the spouses[295] and expires when they cease to be spouses, unless a separation agreement

---

292 *Williams v Williams*, [2006] OJ No 4986 (Sup Ct).

293 *Reeson v Kowalik* (1991), 36 RFL (3d) 396 (Ont Gen Div); *Baudanza v Nicoletti*, 2011 ONSC 352; see also *Martin v Martin*, 2014 ONSC 7530.

294 *Pessotski v Toronto-Dominion Bank*, 2011 ONSC 2387; see also *Alcaniz v Willoughby*, 2011 ONSC 7045; *Yasmin v Tariq*, 2015 ONSC 1248.

295 *Royal Bank v King* (1994), 35 RFL (3d) 325 (Ont Gen Div); *Manufacturers Life Insurance Company v Riviera* (1998), 29 RFL (4th) 1 (Ont CA).

or court order provides otherwise.[296] Section 19 of the *Family Law Act* has no application to spouses who co-own the matrimonial home, because conjoint possessory rights in such a case derive from their ownership. During the existence of the marriage, either spouse may apply to a court for an exclusive possession order with respect to the matrimonial home, and such an application may be pursued regardless of the ownership or of the right of possession conferred by section 19 of the *Family Law Act*. However, section 24 of the Act is only available to a spouse as defined in section 1(1) of the *Family Law Act*; it cannot be invoked by a former spouse. If a divorced co-owning spouse wishes to pursue a possessory remedy, he or she must bring an application under section 2 of the *Partition Act*,[297] although Ontario courts have consistently acknowledged that where spouses co-own the matrimonial home under joint tenancy, there is a *prima facie* right to partition and sale that should not lightly be interfered with.[298] An interim order for sale of a matrimonial home pursuant to the *Partition Act* will normally not be made where it would prejudice the other spouse's right to assert a possessory interest in the home under the *Family Law Act*. The test is whether there is a genuine issue for trial regarding the possessory claim.[299] Where substantial rights in relation to jointly owned matrimonial property are likely to be jeopardized by an order for partition and sale, an application under the *Partition Act* should be deferred until the matter is decided under the *Family Law Act*. The bottom line is that an order for sale must not impair the resisting spouse's right to a trial of a substantial property issue.[300]

Subsection 24(3) of the *Family Law Act* identifies the following six factors that must be considered on an application to the court for exclusive possession of the matrimonial home:

(a)   the best interests of the children affected;

(b)   any existing orders under Part I of the *Family Law Act* and any existing support orders;

(c)   the financial position of both spouses;

296 *Miller v Miller* (1996), 20 RFL (4th) 191 (Ont CA); *Goldman v Kudeyla*, 2011 ONSC 2718.

297 RSO 1990, c P.4. See *Miller v Miller* (1996), 20 RFL (4th) 191 (Ont CA). As to proceeding for partition and sale under the *Partition Act*, RSO 1990. c P.4, see *Miller v Hawryn*, 2010 ONSC 6094, citing Mr Justice Perell, "A Partition Act Primer" (2005) 30 Adv Q 251.

298 See *Arlow v Arlow* (1990), 27 RFL (3d) 348 (Ont Div Ct), aff'd (1991), 33 RFL (3d) 44 (Ont CA); *Lauzon v Bentley*, 2011 ONSC 3232; *Mignella v Federico*, 2012 ONSC 5696; *Keyes v Keyes*, 2015 ONSC 1660.

299 *Lall v Lall*, 2012 ONSC 5166; *Afolabi v Fala*, 2014 ONSC 1713; see also *Keyes v Keyes*, 2015 ONSC 1660.

300 *Recoskie v Paton*, 2014 ONSC 4352 at para 16, Phillips J; *Shouldice v Shouldice*, 2015 ONSC 1948.

ıny written agreement between the parties;

the availability of other suitable and affordable accommodation; and

(f) any violence committed by a spouse against the other spouse or chil-dren.[301]

For the purposes of paragraph 24(3)(a) of the Act, subsection 24(4) re-quires the court to determine the best interests of a child having regard to

(a) the possible disruptive effects on the child of a move to other accom-modation; and

(b) the child's views and preferences, if they can reasonably be ascer-tained.[302]

The factors listed in subsection 24(4) of the *Family Law Act* are not necessarily exhaustive and do not exclude the court from considering other factors, such as the psychological stress to a child arising from persistent friction between the parents[303] or which party has the greater emotional attachment to the home.[304]

In *Caines v Caines*,[305] Fleury J listed the following relevant considerations:

(a) Any agreement, formal or informal, between the parties as to the fu-ture use of the home.

(b) The date when the property was acquired.

(c) The historical ties of any parties to the property in question.

(d) The extent to which the property may have been acquired by one of the spouses by gift or by special efforts.

(e) The number of children who would continue to reside in the home.

(f) The financial ability of the parties to continue to maintain the prop-erty as well as to continue to dwell under separate roofs.

(g) The special character of the neighbourhood including such considera-tions as the presence of friends, relatives, members of a specific ethnic community.

(h) The need of the respondent for immediate funds.

(i) The impact of a move on the children's ability to attend school or uni-versity or to continue extracurricular activities.

(j) The health of the children.

---

301 See *Keyes v Keyes*, 2015 ONSC 1660.

302 *Leckman v Ortaaslan*, 2013 ONSC 3324; *Sharma v Sharma*, 2014 ONSC 4801; *Recoskie v Paton*, 2014 ONSC 4352.

303 See *Pifer v Pifer* (1986), 3 RFL (3d) 167 (Ont Dist Ct).

304 *Hill v Hill* (1987), 10 RFL (3d) 225 (Ont Dist Ct). Compare *Gredig v Dennis*, 2012 ONSC 5223.

305 (1985), 42 RFL (2d) 1 (Ont Co Ct); see also *Bateman v Bateman*, 2013 BCSC 2026; *JM v LM*, 2013 NBQB 157; *Poitras v Poitras*, 2009 SKQB 196.

(k)   The reaction of the children to the marriage breakdown and their need for continued stability.

An order for exclusive possession of the matrimonial home is a drastic order in that it is likely to cause hardship to the dispossessed spouse, but this is to be balanced against the hardship that would be sustained by an unsuccessful applicant.[306] An order for exclusive possession should not be made on a motion where there is conflicting evidence that requires findings of credibility that are only available at trial.[307] Inconvenience is not enough to justify an exclusive possession order.[308] Where the children are healthy and well-adjusted and there is no difficulty in the custodial parent obtaining suitable accommodation in the same area, an application for an exclusive possession order should be dismissed.[309]

Orders for exclusive possession of the matrimonial home are difficult to obtain if there are no children. Even when there are children, long-term exclusive possession orders are relatively rare. It is not unusual, however, for courts to grant exclusive possession of the matrimonial home to a sole custodial parent and the children until the end of the children's school year. This avoids the upheaval of a change in schools at a time when the children are already encountering stress as a result of the breakdown of their parents' relationship.

The onus of proving that an order for exclusive possession of the matrimonial home is justified falls on the person seeking exclusive possession.[310] In determining whether there is other suitable and affordable accommodation within the meaning of paragraph 24(3)(e) of the *Family Law Act*, the following criteria apply:

1)   It need not match the present accommodation, but must be reasonably suitable for the needs required and relate to the standard of living previously enjoyed.

2)   If it provides reasonable amenities, the court will ignore the niceties of its physical layout.

---

306   *Bassett v Bassett*, [1975] 1 All ER 513 at 517 (Eng CA), Ormrod LJ; see also *Hughes v Erickson*, 2014 BCSC 1952, citing *Bateman v Bateman*, 2013 BCSC 2026 at para 44; *Re Ali* (1987), 5 RFL (3d) 228 (Ont HCJ).

307   *Menchella v Menchella*, 2012 ONSC 1861.

308   *Bassett v Bassett*, [1975] 1 All ER 513 at 521 (Eng CA), Cummings-Bruce J.

309   See *Allen v Allen* (1982), 24 RFL (2d) 152 (Ont Co Ct); see also *Koziarz v Koziarz* (1984), 39 RFL (2d) 417 (Ont HCJ); *Goldman v Kudeyla*, 2011 ONSC 2718; *Rofail v Naguib*, 2012 ONSC 931; compare *Jaremkow v Jaremkow* (1985), 48 RFL (2d) 206 (Ont Dist Ct).

310   See *Rondeau v Rondeau* (1979), 12 RFL (2d) 45 (Ont Co Ct); *Gies v Gies* (1983), 30 RFL (2d) 122 (Ont Co Ct).

3) The financial ability to secure and maintain such alternative accommodation should be considered.

In determining the best interests of the children with respect to alternative accommodation, the critical factors are the quality of the respective homes, their proximity to schools and other facilities, traffic hazards, and the effect of a change of environment on the children. Where the custodial parent's financial circumstances make the purchase or rental of alternative accommodation impossible and there is no pressing need for the non-custodial parent to realize the equity in the matrimonial home, an order for exclusive possession in favour of the custodial parent is justified.[311] In *Rosenthal v Rosenthal*,[312] McMahon LJSC concluded that the requirements of subsection 24(3) of the *Family Law Act* had not been satisfied where two of the three children were emancipated and the husband was contributing towards the college education of the third child. McMahon LJSC further concluded that an exclusive possession order was not justified by reason only of the emotional stress of the applicant resulting from the marriage breakdown and that an order should be denied where it is apparent that there are insufficient funds available to permit the continued occupation of the home by one of the spouses.

The provisions of a separation agreement take precedence over the statutory rights conferred by section 24 of the *Family Law Act*.[313] A provision in a marriage contract that purports to limit possession rights in the matrimonial home is unenforceable pursuant to subsection 52(2) of the *Family Law Act*. It does not follow that such a provision is to be ignored. A written agreement that does not satisfy the statutory definition of "domestic contract" may be relevant under paragraph 24(3)(d) of the *Family Law Act*.

Proof of any violence committed by one spouse against the other spouse or the children is expressly recognized by paragraph 24(3)(f) of the *Family Law Act, 1986* as of vital importance in determining whether an order for exclusive possession should be granted. In *Hill v Hill*,[314] Fitzgerald DCJ concluded that "violence" under subsection 24(f) includes "psychological assault upon the sensibilities of the other spouse to a degree that renders continued

---

311 *Gies v Gies* (1983), 30 RFL (2d) 122 (Ont Co Ct); *Francis v Francis* (1987), 8 RFL (3d) 460 (Ont SC); *Tward v Tward* (1982), 31 RFL (2d) 251 (Ont HCJ); *Jaremkow v Jaremkow* (1985), 48 RFL (2d) 206 (Ont Dist Ct).

312 (1986), 3 RFL (3d) 126 at 136–38 (Ont HCJ).

313 *Family Law Act*, RSO 1990, c F.3, ss 2(10) and 54.

314 (1987), 10 RFL (3d) 225 (Ont Dist Ct); see also *Menchella v Menchella*, 2013 ONSC 965; *Leckman v Ortaaslan*, 2013 ONSC 3324; compare *Gainer v Gainer*, [2006] OJ No 1631 (Sup Ct); *Akman v Burshtein*, [2009] OJ No 1499 (Sup Ct).

sharing of the matrimonial dwelling impractical." In *Perrier v Perrier*,[315] Kozak J found that confrontations between the spouses that involved some pushing and shoving by both of them could hardly be classified as acts of violence in the context of section 19(1) of the *Family Law Act*.

By virtue of section 28(1) of the *Family Law Act*, the authority of the court to grant exclusive possession of the matrimonial home or part of it to a spouse pursuant to s 24(1)(b) of the *Act* applies only to matrimonial homes that are in Ontario.[316]

e) Penalties for Contravention of Exclusive Possession Order

Subsection 24(5) of the *Family Law Act*[317] introduces significant penal sanctions that may be imposed for contravention of an order for exclusive possession. A person who is convicted of contravening an order for exclusive possession is liable in the case of a first offence to a fine not exceeding $5,000 and/or to imprisonment for a term not exceeding three months. In the event of a second or subsequent offence, the maximum penalty increases to $10,000 and/or imprisonment for two years.

Pursuant to subsection 24(6) of the Act, a police officer is expressly empowered to arrest without warrant a person the police officer believes on reasonable and probable grounds to have contravened an order for exclusive possession.

f) Variation of Possessory Orders

Orders respecting the exclusive possession of the matrimonial home are subject to judicial discharge, variation, or suspension in the event of a material change in circumstances. An application for this purpose may be brought by a person named in the order or by his or her personal representative.[318]

g) Severance of Third-Party Joint Tenancy in Matrimonial Home

Pursuant to subsection 26(1) of the *Family Law Act*, if a spouse dies owning an interest in the matrimonial home as a joint tenant with a person other than his or her spouse, the joint tenancy is deemed to be severed with a consequential loss of the right of survivorship immediately before the time of death. Subsection 26(1) is applicable regardless of whether a surviving spouse elects to take under the *Family Law Act* or the *Succession Law Reform Act*.[319] Consequently, the value of the deceased's interest as a tenant in common is

---

315   [1989] OJ No 826 (HCJ); see also *Harper v Harper*, 2010 ONSC 4845.

316   *Potter v Boston*, 2014 ONSC 2361 (Div Ct).

317   SO 1986, c 4, as amended by SO 1989, c 72, s 18, now RSO 1990, c F.3, s 24(5).

318   *Family Law Act*, RSO 1990, c F.3, s 25.

319   *Fulton v Fulton* (1994), 17 OR (3d) 641 (CA).

included in the calculation of his or her net family property for the purposes of an equalization claim brought against the deceased's estate pursuant to subsection 5(2) of the Act. Subsection 26(1) of the *Family Law Act* has no application to a joint tenant who died prior to the commencement of the Act, namely 1 March 1986.[320]

Pursuant to subsection 26(2) of the Act, a spouse who is occupying the matrimonial home without any proprietary interest therein at the time of the other spouse's death, is entitled to retain possession on a rent-free basis against the deceased spouse's estate for sixty days after the death. This right is exercisable notwithstanding the provisions of paragraphs 19(2)(a) and (b) of the Act and regardless of whether the possession right arose pursuant to an order for exclusive possession. The provisions of subsection 26(2) presumably override any order made pursuant to paragraph 24(1)(d) of the Act that required the spouse with exclusive possession to make periodic payments as occupation rent to the dispossessed spouse.

19) Registration of Orders against Land

Orders granted pursuant to Part II of the *Family Law Act* are registerable against land under the *Registry Act*[321] and the *Land Titles Act*.[322]

20) *Situs* of Matrimonial Home; Retrospective Operation of Part II of *Family Law Act*

The application of Part II of the *Family Law Act* is expressly confined to matrimonial homes that are situated in Ontario.[323] Pursuant to subsection 28(2) of the Act, Part II applies regardless of whether the spouses were married before or after 1 March 1986, and whether the matrimonial home was acquired before or after that date.

---

320 *Re Vaillancourt* (1986), 4 RFL (3d) 263 (Ont HCJ).
321 RSO 1990, c R20.
322 RSO 1990, c L.5.
323 *Family Law Act*, RSO 1990, c F.3, s 28(1); *Potter v Boston*, 2014 ONSC 2361 (Div Ct).

Table of Cases

Albrecht v Albrecht 690

Alcaniz v Willoughby (2010 Ont Sup
    Ct) 536

Alcaniz v Willoughby (2011 Ont Sup
    Ct) 176, 183, 709, 710

Alexander v Alexander 481

Alfaro v Alfaro 487

Alger v Alger 668

Algner v Algner 478

Ali v Ahmad 22, 30

Ali v Ali 20

Ali v Canada (Minister of Citizenship and
    Immigration) 21

Ali, Re 713

Alix v Irwin 534, 539

Allaire v Allaire 267, 277

Allaire v Lavergne 303

Allen v Allen (1982 Ont Co Ct) 713

Allen v Allen (2013 BCSC) 633

ALM v NJO 613

Almeida v Almeida 214

Alpugan v Baykan 296

Alspector v Alspector 23

ALY v LMY 435

AM (Guardian ad litem of) v KAAM 614

Amaral v Amaral 229, 499

Amaral v Myke 505, 650

AMD v AJP (sub nom Drygala v Pauli) 477

AMIH v JNM 544

AML v WLL 171

Amlani v Hirani 67

Amos v Fischer 410, 411

Amsterdam v Amsterdam 320

Anderson v Anderson (1972 Alta CA) 200,
    204

Anderson v Anderson (1973 SCC) 200, 204

Anderson v Anderson (1990 Man QB) 105

Anderson v Anderson (2002 Man CA) 279

Anderson v Anderson (2013 BCSC) 8

Anderson v Anderson (2014 NSSC) 309

Anderson v Anderson Estate 697

Anderson v Lambert 373, 375

Anderson v Luoma 42, 58

Anderson v Sansalone 321

Andrade v Andrade 76, 660

Andrade v Kennelly 520

Andrews v Andrews (1992 Sask CA) 373

Andrews v Andrews (1995 BCSC) 228

Andrews v Andrews (1999 Ont CA) 237,
    435, 436, 500

Andrews v Ross 25

Andries v Andries 465

Andronyk v Cox 591

Anema v Anema 184, 185

ANH v MKC 519

Aning v Aning 655

Anson v Anson 506, 507

Antemia v Divito 171

APGP v MSP 527

Appleyard v Appleyard 676

Arbou v Robichaud 324

ARJ v ZSJ 297

Arlow v Arlow 711

Arlt v Arlt (2003 Sask QB) 481

Arlt v Arlt (2014 Ont Sup Ct) 408

Armitage v Attorney General 189

Armoyan v Armoyan 179, 180, 181, 183

Armstrong v Armstrong (1986 Ont Dist
    Ct) 668

Armstrong v Armstrong (1992 Ont
    CA) 595

Armstrong v Armstrong (1998 BCCA) 596

Armstrong v Armstrong (2006 Ont
    CA) 690

Armstrong v Armstrong (2012 BCCA) 235,
    276

Arndt v Arndt 675, 676, 692, 704

Arnold v Arnold 587

Arsenault v Arsenault 179

AS v AS 26

Asghar v Doyle 189

Ashmead v British Columbia 599

Ashworth v Ashworth 194

ASK v MABK 558

Askin v Askin 520

Aspe v Aspe 235, 308, 321

Assinck v Assinck 489

Astle v Walton 175, 177

Attwood v Attwood 273

Aubé v Aubé 239, 321, 324, 332

Aucoin v Aucoin 104, 200, 209

Auigbelle v King 512

Austin v Austin (2007 Ont Sup Ct) 464,
    476

Austin v Austin (2008 Ont Sup Ct) 236

Austin v Goerz 45, 48

About the Authors

Julien D. Payne, CM, QC, LLD, LSM, FRSC, one of Canada's foremost family law specialists, has been called the architect of the Unified Family Court and No-Fault Divorce. He has taught family law at the Universities of Alberta, Western Ontario, Ottawa, and Saskatchewan and has written extensively about family law and family dispute resolution. His writings have been cited on hundreds of occasions by trial courts and appellate courts in Canada, including the Supreme Court of Canada. He was awarded the Law Society Medal by the Law Society of Upper Canada in 2002 and was made a member of the Order of Canada in 2004. Julien D. Payne is the co-author of *Child Support Guidelines in Canada, 2015*, published by Irwin Law.

Marilyn A. Payne is an experienced author and the founding editor of *Payne's Divorce and Family Law Digest*. She is the co-author of *Child Support Guidelines in Canada, 2015*, published by Irwin Law.